COSTS

Accounting, Analysis, and Control

Wiley/Hamilton Series in Accounting, and Information Systems
Consulting Editor John W. Buckley

Anderson and Raun
Information Analysis in Management Accounting

Buckley and Buckley
The Accounting Profession

Buckley, Nagaraj, Sharp, and Schenk
Management Problem-Solving with APL

DeCoster, Ramanathan, and Sundem
Accounting for Managerial Decision Making, 2nd

Estes
Accounting and Society

Estes
Corporate Social Accounting

Kircher and Mason
Introduction to Enterprise: A Systems Approach

Largay and Livingstone
Accounting for Changing Prices

Loeb
Ethics in the Accounting Profession

McCullers and Van Daniker
Introduction to Financial Accounting

McCullers and Van Daniker
Contemporary Business Environment: Readings in Financial Accounting

McCullerns and Schroeder
Accounting Theory: Text and Readings

Mock and Vasarhelyi
APL for Management

Patz and Rowe
Management Control and Decision Systems

Seidler
Social Accounting: Theory, Issues, and Cases

Seidler, Andrews, Epstein
The Equity Funding Papers: The Anatomy of a Fraud

Sethi
The Unstable Ground: Corporate Social Policy in a Dynamic Society

Vazsonyi
Finite Mathematics/Quantitative Analysis for Management

COSTS

Accounting, Analysis, and Control

A. Wayne Corcoran
University of Massachusetts

John Wiley & Sons
Santa Barbara New York Chichester Brisbane Toronto
A Wiley/Hamilton Publication

This book was set in 10 point
Times Roman by Syntax International.
The text was designed by Joe di Chiarro
and the cover by Bert Johnson.
Illustrations were prepared by
Jiro Creations and Kingsport Press
did the printing and binding
Chuck Pendergast supervised production.

Library of Congress Cataloging in Publication Data

Corcoran, A. Wayne.
Costs: accounting, analysis, and control.

(Wiley/Hamilton series in accounting and information systems)
"A Wiley/Hamilton publication."
1. Cost accounting. 2. Cost control. I. Title.
HF5686.C8C6818 657'.42 77-18798

ISBN 0-471-17251-0

Printed in the United States of America

10 9 8 7 6 5 4 3 2

To Sandy in fond recognition
of her cheerfulness and enthusiastic support

About the Author

A. Wayne Corcoran is a professor of accounting and management science at the University of Massachusetts. He previously taught full time at the University of Connecticut and The State University of New York at Buffalo. He has been a visiting professor of accounting at Rensselaer Polytechnic Institute and at Virginia Polytechnic Institute. He has taught part time for the United States Naval Postgraduate School, the University of Rochester, and the National Association of Accountants. He has taught a variety of courses in accounting, inventory theory, queuing theory, production management, applied mathematics, mathematical programming, and finance.

His undergraduate training took place at Cornell Univeristy. He earned his masters degree at The University of Rochester and his doctoral study was done at The State University of New York at Buffalo. He was awarded his CPA by the State of New York in 1960 and has a correspondence degree from the International Accountants Society.

Dr. Corcoran is the author of The Audit and the Punched Card, Mathematical Applications in Accounting, and Readings in the Methodology of Operations Research: An Accounting Emphasis, as well as numerous journal articles.

Preface

As much as anything, this is a book on philosophy. I think you will agree that, while there is a lot of "how" in the book, "why" dominates. There is examination of conflicting theories and frank expression of opinion. Where my opinions are too outrageous, too out of keeping with established thought, or too naive, I have asked a colleague who is a supporter of a more prevalent or a more informed view in the particular area to expound on the opposing theory, so that you may better understand the controversy and form your own opinion.

One of my aspirations in writing this textbook has been to encourage readers to think how they feel about one problem or another, rather than to parrot some series of edicts. This is not to say that logic should give way to feeling, or that, for instance, the book would sanction dividing by zero because that was what the reader felt like doing at the moment. There are, after all, immutable mathematical truths which are not subject to capricious manipulation. But which approach to take, which model to apply, what purposes are to be served, who desires the information, what is the decision maker's level of comprehension—these and many other questions are open to interpretation. They require thought—not an attitude of "Whenever situation A occurs, apply approach B."

I have tried to make the book self-contained from both accounting and mathematical perspectives. If you have not devoted a significant portion of your recent life to studying these subjects, you will find appendices on bookkeeping and mathematics that should help to fill in the gaps. Cost accounting does not, by and large, demand much knowledge of bookkeeping or make unrelenting use of it. There is some application of bookkeeping, however, since it is an excellent tool for tracing the flows of certain costs. There is, too, the preparation of profit and loss statements to summarize these flows and thereby facilitate control of costs through the interpretation of results.

The mathematical appendix assumes a command of ordinary algebra and delves into probability theory, matrix algebra, calculus, optimization, and transform theory. The more exotic and esoteric branches of mathematics do not really come into use until the second half of the text, when cost analysis becomes the primary focus. From a mathematical standpoint, the first half of the book rests solely on algebra and the rudiments of matrix algebra. Should you be unfamiliar with matrix algebra, a *half hour* spent with that appendix should suffice to make you "almost expert." For while serious study of matrix algebra might require several years and bring you in contact with many courses, the fundamentals of vector addition, matrix multiplication, and matrix inversion are quickly learned. A grasp of these opens a whole world of applications for exploration, including a vast variety of accounting allocations, regression analysis, linear programming, and Markov chains—to mention but a few of the more fascinating areas.

Computer programming is also incorporated into the chapters. This is partly because I don't believe in separating mathematics from computers, but rather in using one to supplement the other, and partly, it is because I am not interested in carrying out scads of arithmetic manually. And finally, it is because computers are becoming more ubiquitous every day. At this writing, for instance, a programmable hand calculator (TI 58) is available (for about $100) that will multiply and invert matrices, among many other things. And while inverting a 2×2 matrix manually is painless, 3×3 to 6×6 matrices take a little time, while larger matrices almost force the analyst to use a computer. Nevertheless, the nuisance (once you have inverted a few dozen matrices by hand, the thrill begins to wane) of inverting smaller, frequently encountered matrices is now virtually eliminated. Mathematical analysis, so expedited, cannot help but become more widespread.

I hasten to add that you should read only the output of the computer programs if programming is not one of your goals. The programs are written in the BASIC language on the grounds that this is probably the easiest scientific language to learn—should that be your goal. Rumor has it that at Dartmouth, where the language was first developed, admission to the computer programming course was contingent upon the student reading a 30-page pamphlet and showing up at the first class with the output of two programs. No output, no admission! The assignment, if rumor be true, took between three and five hours; the students had already taught themselves programming by the time they entered the programming class! Nonetheless, even though BASIC might better have been named SIMPLE, the language has variants from one computer installation to the next. The programs in this text were written over a period of four years at different universities and therefore necessarily using different compilers. Computers talk to computers no better than man talks to man; consequently, I would regard it as sheer luck if you were to reproduce some of these programs on your system and have them run without modification. The modifications should be minor, however. If you have done no computer programming, the programs are annotated, and by studying them carefully, you should be able to pick up the language.

The book treats all of the popular areas in cost accounting, such as direct costing, cost-volume-profit relationships, forecasting, job order and process costing systems, standard costs and variance analysis, joint-product costing, replacement costing, decisionmaking costs, project and period budgeting, responsibility accounting, and transfer pricing—along with several areas that are not yet in the "popular" category—such as sampling, inventory theory, queuing theory, and linear and nonlinear programming. If you only have time to cover the popular, then Chapters 1 through 11 are for you. If cost analysis is your focus, then you should concentrate on Chapter 3 and Chapters 12 through 20, skimming the remaining chapters quickly to see if they contain any "nuggets." In any event, do not fail to read Chapter 2 on human behavior, because mastery of all the accounting and mathematical techniques still leaves one with the problems of communication.

It would be arbitrary to say that this book is an accounting text; it could be used equally well in finance, production, economics, management science, and operations research courses. The dividing lines among these disciplines are mainly political; all are interested in cost, and that is what this book is about.

I have tried throughout to keep two of the goals of ancient Academe in mind:

(1) to provide a forum for the exchange of ideas, and
(2) to pursue excellence.

Excellence, of course, is elusive and one pursues it with whatever meager tools are at hand. I may have failed to achieve excellence—only you can be the judge of that—but you may rest assured that I pursued it with all the vigor at my command. I had help—lots of it—and I shall shortly acknowledge specific people who assisted me. If the text is good, they have had a significant role in making it so; if it is less than good, that will be no fault of theirs, but rather a reflection of my stubbornness and stupidity.

And now a few words for the teacher. To help you offer your course, I have prepared a very elaborate solutions manual that contains both detailed theoretical discussions and step-by-step solutions. You will find that much of the problem material is straightforward, but that a few problems are just plain tough. I acted on the notion that the student should at some time in his academic career encounter challenging depth and complexity. Therefore a few problems—such as problem 23 in the chapter on inventory theory—may well constitute a two-week homework assignment. I think I have cautioned the reader when such a problem occurs, but if my idea of what is difficult differs from yours, you should look at the solution manual before assigning problems.

The book has been class-tested. I used selected chapters in teaching different courses and I also tested the text as a whole in a class in which I handpicked the students. This class contained graduate mathematicians, two certified public accountants, an electrical engineer, an information systems major, and accounting majors. Four of the students were master's candidates, two were doctoral candidates, and the rest were undergraduates. The charge was to tear the book apart—to find fault in any and every way, to exchange misgivings and insights freely. What a course! Nothing was sacred and we all aged five years in one semester! Some perceptions of the challenge of the book to the student emerged clearly.

If you were to spend three semesters, you could do all the chapters and all the problems comfortably. Whatever else is possible depends on the motivation, ability, and maturity of your students. My select group unanimously agreed that one semester was barely enough to read the text, investigate one or two topics with care, and work only one or two of the softer problems in each chapter. All agreed that two semesters would be adequate if one course in cost accounting and another in cost analysis were offered and four or five problems of varying complexity were assigned in each chapter.

Where an undergraduate course in cost accounting is based on this text, I would advise you to cover the appendices on bookkeeping and matrix algebra and Chapters 1 through 11 with care, and to have the class skim read the end results of the models in the remaining chapters.

More than one type of course can be based on this text because as I discuss each subject, I provide a great deal of detail in developing solutions. If I had only provided setups and end solutions of problems, the text would have been considerably thinner, but the choice of type of course would have been limited. As the text stands, a course can focus on developing mathematical abilities as well as on studying the situations in which the techniques have been employed. Or if scope is the main objective, mathematical detail can be left to the student for self-study at his leisure. Time available ultimately determines what can be done. If time is limited, you may well decide to pass up detailed study in favor of scope. The text should accommodate all persuasions.

It will be apparent as you read that I use language that is today labelled sexist. Thus you will read sentences like, "The analyst first ascertains the limits of his study." I do not mean to exclude women from the ranks of analysts, or from the ranks of managers for that matter. I have long been an advocate of letting anyone become whatever he wishes—at equal pay and with equal prestige—provided the individual has the requisite talent. However, I dislike the intrusion of the feminist movement on the use of grammar.

I shall never be a chair*person* of anything, any more than I shall ever write the cumbersome symbology s/he, which, I suppose, becomes s/his in the possessive. I resent being told to use s/he or something like it as much as I would resent being told to abandon euphonious expression in favor of modern four-letter invective. If this labels me as an anachronism, so be it. My use of "man" and "he" is in a generic sense.

A. Wayne Corcoran
Amherst, Massachusetts

September 15, 1977

Acknowledgments

An army of people has assisted me in bringing this book to print. Some of their contributions have been indirect—but nonetheless significant—by way of encouragement and understanding. In this list I would put my wife, Sandy (although she helped directly as well), my sons (Matt, Mike, Tom, and Rob), my parents, and Dr. Howard L. Stoll, my father-in-law.

Others have helped to hone my ideas. Here some former students and colleagues come to mind: Dave Almond, Roy Ageloff, Rosanne Pane, Dave Lagone, Jack Hughes, Wayne Leininger, George Williams, Sangit Chatterjee, Gene Kaczka, Wynn Abranovic, Bill Lawler, and Don Stone.

Still others have taken an active role in writing the manuscript. Mr. William Burnham prepared the Poisson probability distribution and annuity tables. Messrs. Frederick Patrick, Gary Monroe, Bruce Hall, Brian Curtis, Richard Housman, William Pownall, and Raman Joneja and Professors Ronald Mannino, Bharath Ramachandran, Mawsen Liao, James Fremgen, Meyer W. Belovicz, Prabhakant Sinha, Anthony Butterfield, Roland Minch, and Andris Zoltners all either read the manuscript or portions thereof, or prepared problem material, or both.

Certain professors helped by not only reading sections of the manuscipt but also writing theoretical extensions thereto. They will be introduced in the course of the book but deserve special recognition here. Professor Gerald Zeisel (Boston University) read the entire manuscript, made many helpful suggestions, and wrote a section on transfer pricing theory. His assistance has been extensive, his excitement for the project contagious.

Professor William L. Ferrara (Pennsylvania State University) has fleshed out the discussion on responsibility accounting, an area in which he is a recognized expert.

Professor George Odiorne (University of Massachusetts), who is regarded by many as the father of Management by Objectives, graciously summarized how this theory applies in accounting.

Professor Edward L. Wallace (State University of New York at Buffalo) provided a perspective on decisionmaking costs that enriches the discussion of inventory costs.

I greatly appreciate the cooperation extended by Messrs. James Collier and James Bulloch of the National Association of Accountants for granting permission to use Certified Management Accounting examination questions.

I wish to thank Mr. William O. Doherty of the American Institute of Certified Public Accountants for allowing me to reprint selected questions from the Uniform CPA Examinations.

I am grateful to the Canadian Institute of Chartered Accountants for permitting me to borrow one of its examination questions.

Several executives from industrial concerns provided data on their company operations. Thus thanks are due to

Messrs. Richard M. Geisler (President), Robert G. Anderson (Controller), and Robert Youngs (Assistant to Controller) of the Spalding Division of Questor Corporation;

Messrs. William R. Haselton (President), John P. Berdolt (Controller), Walter D. Lauttenbach (Assistant Controller), Frank E. Higgins (Manager of Operations Accounting), and Philip H. Sharlach (Administrator of Cost Systems) of the St. Regis Paper Company; and

Messrs. Robert W. Roth (President) and Everett E. Cobb (Treasurer) of Jantzen, Inc.

Professor John W. Buckley (University of California at Los Angeles), who is the editor of this series of textbooks, not only expressed a great deal of enthusiasm for this project, but also read the entire manuscript in its various stages and offered excellent advice.

Various members of the Wiley/Hamilton organization have gone out of their way to be pleasant and sincerely helpful. I know that I must have been a trial on their patience and yet, in all the many letters I received and the telephone calls that were made, I never failed to read or hear: "If you have any further questions, please do not hesitate to get in touch with me." I cannot imagine a more courteous organization or a nicer group of professionals.

Lastly we come to a writer's best friends: his typists. Mathematical typing requires a high degree of skill, patience, and dedication. For the text chapters themselves I had the services of a most competent professional, Mrs. Vesta Powers. My wife, Sandy, typed chapter problems; having her take an active role in the production of the manuscript provided a great emotional lift. Mr. Glenn Stowell, one of my mathematically oriented accounting students, enthusiastically took up the typing of the solution manual. Their dedication was simply gratifying.

To one and all, my sincere thanks.

A. Wayne Corcoran
Amherst, Massachusetts

September 15, 1977

Contents

Introduction

1

Cost Accounting: What Is That?

Tradition has every book that discusses accounting begin with a definition of the subject. Unfortunately, once one becomes familiar with the philosophy of accounting, no definition of the subject seems to capture its essence. Well, our subject is cost accounting, and the appendage of the word "cost" in no way eases the burden of defining it. Why the difficulty?

Years ago a beginning student was considered to know what accounting was all about if he could say, "Accounting is the recording, classifying, summarizing, and interpreting of financial data." For the longest while, this nondefinition was held in the highest regard. Then someone remarked that categorizing or classifying was necessarily an integral part of recording (if you didn't have categories, you couldn't record usefully) and therefore the definition was redundant in part. Someone else expressed dissatisfaction with "summarizing" and suggested "reporting" in its stead. And many people observed that accountants did precious little interpreting of the statements they prepared. Furthermore, "financial data" was paradoxical—at once broad and narrow. All sorts of data not in dollar terms eventually cause dollar flows. But who said accounting was solely concerned with dollar flows? Another very significant group of accountants was dismayed that the definition of accounting did not emphasize helping management to make decisions. Still more recently those concerned about accounting's contributions to society have asked why accounting reports should be restricted only to stockholders, management, and the government.

All of which leads to the sticky question "Who should define accounting—the person who does it or the person who makes use of it, or both?" Each party has a different perspective; the practitioner, being human, could be expected to exaggerate scope and importance, while the consumer, being cursed with much the same condition, could be expected to limit scope to that with which he is familiar. Truth can be elusive.

Over time a great deal of confusion was generated by a lot of well-intentioned people. Eventually there occurred a schism or splitting of accounting into financial accounting and managerial accounting—a division that exists today. Nothing good seems to have come from this schism, for while there are many accountants who can participate in both financial and managerial accounting, the preponderance of accountants seems to disdain one for the other. "Managerial accounting is management, not accounting!" "Financial accounting is glorified bookkeeping; it misses the point of accounting entirely!" Sentiments like these characterize the antagonisms of the rival factions.

Other factions and schisms also exist. Thus there is governmental accounting, taxation accounting, cost accounting, mathematical accounting, national income accounting, nonprofit institutional accounting, fund accounting, and environmental (societal) accounting. Some of these could be forced into the managerial-financial categories, although their adherents might object. One might well ask, "If these are all different types of accounting, isn't there agreement on at least a few points?"

The philosophy of accounting cuts through artificial barriers and offers a basis for uniting all schisms into one discipline. Simply stated, that philosophy is: *Accounting seeks to help people plan and control by means of collecting and analyzing information and communicating the results.* This philosophy, however, is not the exclusive property of accounting. Management science, production management, finance, industrial engineering, and many other disciplines share much the same philosophy. It is a small world, indeed. But aren't these distinct disciplines?

There is a famous parable that may provide insight here. Three blind men were once asked to caress an elephant and then to describe it without being told what it was. One, who had hugged a leg, emphatically told the others that the object was a tree. Another, who had patted a side, convincingly declared the object to be a wall. The third blind man, who had grabbed the tail, jumped back in repulsion, swore violently, and insisted he had fondled a large snake. All three argued vehemently, not one of them swayed in the least by the protestations of the others. Viewed one way, all three were right; viewed another, all were wrong. Had they been able to trust one another and to exchange ideas, they might have arrived at the truth by determining what object possessed all three attributes.

So while many disciplines share a common philosophy, nevertheless, they pursue their separate courses. If they would exchange ideas, all would benefit. Some collect different information than others; some analyze their information using different techniques; still others view control differently. All have trouble when it comes to communication. Far too often, practitioners in any of these disciplines communicate mainly to other practitioners in that discipline. Thus the disciplines are esoteric—only the initiated seem to understand them.

It could be said that only the initiated *care* to understand them.

The intent of this book is to follow the philosophy stated above by integrating the most promising techniques of the various disciplines.

So much for the word "accounting." How about "cost"? Webster is a great help here; he offers:

> *Cost* 1: The amount of money, time, labor, etc. required to get a thing; price; expenditure
>
> 2: Loss; sacrifice; detriment

The problem is that accounting has a predeliction for restricting "cost" to dollar measurements. How this came about is not clear. Possibly it is a consequence of trying to make accounting an application of economics and of restricting economics to money conceptions. This, of course, is totally unfair to economics, which is generally defined as the study of how to allocate scarce resources among competing wants. There is no mention here of money.

When one talks about cost, he needs to know the situation involved, what assumptions are being made, and what purpose is to be served. By itself, "cost" is a very vague word.

And cost is certainly not restricted to money measurement. Much will be said about this later in the book, so we will not dwell on the idea now beyond offering a harmless but provocative illustration. Suppose a person really likes to eat. What is the cost of his doing so? The tempting response is "Whatever he spends for food." But a person who really likes to eat is quite apt to become fat. Unfortunately, a fat person is often unable to participate in many physical endeavors and may also be subject to ridicule. At this point the money purist might be seduced into declaring the cost of eating to be the sum of the expenditures for food and for following a diet-exercise regimen prescribed by his doctor. This answer, of course, fails to recognize the costs of embarrassment and of emotional disruption caused by abstaining during the diet from the food that he has got used to and has grown to love. It also fails to recognize (1) what the eater sacrificed because he spent his money—assumed to be a limited resource—on food and recovery from food instead of on other things, and (2) the pleasures forgone by the eater because he became physically incapable. And all of this is conjectural, because it is uncertain that a given eater will become a fatty—metabolism has something to do with the result.

Suffice it to say that although we may not know how to measure them, every benefit has its costs, not all of which may be measured in money.

We thus leave the field without a definition of cost accounting but with a firm conviction that cost accounting seeks to help people plan and control by means of collecting and analyzing information, not all of which is in money terms, and communicating the results.

Cost Determination

Perspective

The major responsibilities of cost accounting include the determination and control of costs. Just a little reflection on the scope and depth of this task will enable you to grasp its significance.

Suppose that, like many people, you spent a brief portion of your formative days selling lemonade. What did a glass of lemonade cost and was its price reasonable? Probably the cash cost to you was zero, because your mother provided the ingredients and did the mixing; hence, since you also had lots of time to waste, your price represented pure profit as far as you were concerned.

From your mother's viewpoint, matters were different. She saw two benefits from the activity: (1) she had a chance to develop her own little entrepreneur, and (2) you would be gainfully occupied for several hours and, therefore, rather less demanding of her attention. Her cash costs seemed slight: (1) the cost of a couple of lemons, (2) the cost of a cup of sugar, (3) the cost of a gallon of water, (4) the cost of an untold number of ice cubes, and (5) the cost of paper cups. She hoped that you would stay local and not require transportation to some construction site, although she had misgivings about that. She appreciated that a construction site would provide good business and encourage your entrepreneurial leanings, but she knew that once onto a good thing, you would keep her busy mixing and transporting all day and, consequently, never let her have a moment's peace. That would have been disastrous (that is, too costly), so she concocted a policy: "You must stay in the immediate neighborhood!" In her analysis, she intuitively recognized the probabilities of the outcomes of various actions, weighed *her* costs and benefits, made her decision, and let you think it was all your idea. Mothers are simply amazing!

Now let us complicate the situation by introducing choice and hence conflict. Suppose you had the additional option of going into the dog-walking business. If you sold lemonade, you couldn't walk dogs and vice versa. At this point you became aware that one of the costs of the lemonade business was the forgone profits of the dog exercising business. You had inadvertently discovered opportunity costs (that is, the profits sacrificed by not choosing the next best alternative); you learned that your time was worth something. Just how much it was worth you may not have known, because you were not sure about the demand for your services.

If the lemonade business represents zero on the scale of complexity, then something like predicting the cost of sending a manned rocket to the moon represents the other end of the scale. If viewed philosophically, the possible loss of astronaut lives might raise the cost to infinity (that is, the cost would exceed 50 trillion dollars). Of course, that would depend on whose philosophy was being considered. But ignoring this and other costs of failure, one (an army?) would still face an immense number of components that needed cost estimation. Furthermore, probably none of the opportunity costs would be measured in any but a subjective manner. This is largely because at present we do not technically know how to measure objectively such things as the social benefits involved in constraining pollution or poverty, which would be but two alternatives to the moon program. Nor, for that matter, do we know how to measure the benefits of being able to send men to the moon. Nevertheless, if we face a decision about what choice to make, we will want to reflect the opportunity costs in some way.

Let us put opportunity costs aside and take a more detailed look at how a cost accountant might prepare a Cost of Goods Manufactured Report that could be used as a supplement to a company's income statement.[1] Opportunity costs do not appear in this report because, if they did, the income reported would be incremental rather than total—incremental in the sense that the reported income, were opportunity costs reflected, would only be that which exceeded the income of the alternatives rejected.

Costs of Goods Manufactured

When you read a manufacturer's income statement, you encounter "cost of goods sold" listed as an *expense*. Let us now focus on the *asset* "cost of goods manufactured," which differs in amount from cost of goods sold only in that the cost of goods sold reflects the change in the finished goods inventory. In a merchandising business, every inventory is a "Finished Goods" inventory, because the goods merely await the customer's pleasure; generally nothing further need be done to finished goods to prepare them for sale. In a factory, however, two other main types of inventory exist: (1) Raw Materials Inventory, which reflects the historical costs of raw materials and purchased components, and (2) Work in Process Inventory, which reflects:

(a) the cost of raw materials requisitioned for production,
(b) the cost of direct labor on materials in production, and

[1] We are concerned here with the accountant's definition of income rather than the very appealing Hicksian definition (Hicks: Income is the maximum value which a man can consume during a week, and still expect to be as well off at the end of the week as he was at the beginning. See J. R. Hicks, *Value and Capital* [London: Oxford University Press, 1939], p. 172).

(c) the cost of "overhead" associated with the units being produced ("overhead" will be discussed shortly but in general it reflects costs not easily or directly traceable to specific products).

For control purposes, whenever work in process leaves one production department and enters another, the costs are transferred from the Work in Process account of the sending department to the Work in Process account of the receiving department. In this way the costs incurred by each department are attached to the product and accumulated until the production process is completed and the goods are transferred from the final department's Work in Process to the Finished Goods Inventory account. The idea is simply to trace the physical flow of the units in production and to build costs as the flow progresses.

Straightforward as the tracing idea is, nevertheless the question of how to accomplish the task entails enough choices to complicate matters before the goods are finally costed and sitting on the shelves awaiting sale.

Supplies of small parts like nails, screws, and glue are sometimes included in the raw materials inventory rather than in a separate supplies account. Though it would be possible, it would be impractical to charge the product directly for these items, because they have relatively small dollar cost. Customarily, supply items are referred to as "indirect materials" and are charged to the product as part of its overhead cost. An arbitrary decision is made as to what cost an item must have before it merits treatment as direct material. Given different companies of comparable size and making the same product, the same component item will be treated as a direct material by some and as indirect (overhead) by others. The resulting costs of the finished product will almost certainly differ for that reason.

What constitutes direct labor is another issue. When a mechanic is physically working on the product, that portion of his wage is clearly a component of direct labor. When the same man cleans up after a production run is over, that portion of his wage is apt to be considered indirect labor and be charged to the product as overhead. This seems to be a fine point: the wages "setting up" the machines prior to the run are often considered direct labor, while the wages "taking down" (cleaning up) the machines after the run are probably just as often treated as overhead. The custodial engineers (in former times, the janitors) and the factory supervisor are considered too far removed from physical production to merit treatment as direct labor; their wages and salaries attach to the product via an overhead charge.

The controversies associated with charging overhead costs to work in process are varied. Not only is there wide disparity in what items of cost are to be treated as overhead, but there are also differing viewpoints on what volume of activity—which activity is generally measured by direct-labor hours, or by units produced, or by standard machine hours—should be preselected to calculate a rate for allocating (or absorbing) overhead to the product. Another common difficulty is the question of whether fixed overhead costs should be treated as costs of the product or of the time period. For example, the factory supervisor's salary is fixed by contract. One view of his salary is to consider it overhead and assign it ratably to the units manufactured during the period. The opposing view observes that the decision to be in business for the period—to produce anything in the period—is tantamount to hiring the supervisor; hence, his salary is a cost of the period rather than a cost of the products. The first camp—that which charges fixed overhead to products—is referred to as advocating "full" or "absorption" costing. The second camp—that which charges fixed overhead as an operating expense of the period—is referred to as advocating "direct" or "variable" costing.

We have now discussed direct materials, direct labor, and overhead as well as the raw materials, work in process, and finished good inventories. How these accounts (with the exception of finished goods inventories) appear in a manufacturer's financial statement is demonstrated in Exhibit 1. Depicted there is the cost computed by the Aluminum Racket Company for manufacturing its tennis rackets during the month of October 1975.

Exhibit 1 Cost of Rackets Manufactured Statement
Aluminum Racket Company

For October 1975

Direct Materials:			
Raw Materials Inventory, 10/1/75	$152,000		
Purchases	683,000	$835,000	
Raw Materials Inventory, 10/31/75		(201,000)	
Raw materials used during October		$634,000	
Less indirect materials used		(38,000)	
Direct materials			$596,000
Direct Labor			802,000
Overhead Applied			471,000
Change in Work in Process:			
Work in Process Inventory, 10/1/75		$1,395,000	
Work in Process Inventory, 10/31/75		(1,200,000)	195,000
Cost of Rackets Manufactured			$2,064,000

Inspection of the statement reveals that the cost of rackets manufactured consists of costs for direct materials, direct labor, and applied overhead plus whatever change occurs in the cost of Work in Process.

Certain details of Exhibit 1 require emphasis:

1. The indirect materials of $38,000 are subtracted from the $634,000 of raw materials used because these indirect materials are included in the raw materials inventory and will be charged to production as part of applied overhead.

2. Applied overhead reflects the volume of production (however measured) during October multiplied by the overhead rate. The actual overhead costs—one of which is the $38,000 of indirect materials—probably differ in total from the $471,000 although probably nothing will formally be done about the difference until the end of the year. At the year's end, the difference between actual overhead and applied overhead will either be allocated to the year's cost of sales—if the difference is insignificant—or allocated proportionately to all the accounts (that is, Work in Process, Finished Goods, and Cost of Sales) that are in error—if the difference is significant. The monthly differences are not similarly treated because it is expected that they will largely offset one another in the course of the year. Monthly overhead rates could be calculated, of course, but if volume were small in one month, the resulting rate would be high; conversely, if volume were great one month, that month's overhead rate would be low. Furthermore, if certain costs occurred sporadically, as, for instance, in the case of a large repair or maintenance bill, the overhead rate for the month in which the bill was paid would be high even though the preceding months' activities created the need for repairs. The desirability of smoothing (normalizing) the monthly rates seems apparent; consequently, it is customary for a manufacturer both to use one overhead rate for an entire year and to dispose of the difference between actual overhead and applied overhead at the year's end.

Exhibit 1 might be used for control purposes by management just as it is, or it might be compared to similar statements for recent months as well as for the same month in previous years. As Exhibit 1 stands, we have no way of knowing if the results depicted are either reasonable or extraordinary in some respect. At most, we might feel curious about the magnitude of the changes in the inventories. Were such changes anticipated?

We have seen the end results of the bookkeeping process portrayed in Exhibit 1; now let us study the original data and see how they were treated to arrive at the Cost of Rackets Manufactured Statement.

The data for the Aluminum Racket Company for the month of October 1975 appear below.[2]

October 1 inventory balances:	
Raw Materials	$ 152,000
Work in Process	1,395,000
Finished Goods	622,000
Raw material purchases	683,000
Direct materials requisitioned for production	596,000
Indirect materials requisitioned for production	38,000
Direct labor	802,000
Indirect labor	198,000
Income taxes withheld	120,000
Social Security taxes withheld (6% of gross pay)	60,000
Other statutory withholdings	10,000
Depreciation	50,000
Repairs and maintenance	8,000
Heat, light, and power	23,000
Insurance	40,000
Payroll taxes and other employee benefits (14% of gross payroll)	140,000
Property taxes on factory	28,000
Miscellaneous production expenses	12,000

The budget for 1975 for overhead was $3,925,000 and was based on an anticipated volume of 500,00 rackets and the budget formula $y = \$2{,}500{,}000 + \$2.85x$, where x is volume.[3] Therefore, the overhead absorption rate was $7.85 per racket and consisted of allowances for fixed costs of $5 (that is, $2,500,000 ÷ 500,000) and for variable costs of $2.85.

The equivalent of 60,000 rackets was made in October, and the cost of rackets completed was $2,064,000.

The journal entries to record all these maneuvers appear below.

Raw Materials Inventory	683,000	
Vouchers payable		683,000
To record material purchases.		
Work in Process Inventory	596,000	
Overhead control-indirect materials	38,000	
Raw Materials Inventory		634,000
To record material requisitions.		
Work in Process Inventory	802,000	
Overhead control-indirect labor	198,000	
Payroll taxes payable		190,000
Vouchers payable		810,000
To record payroll and taxes withheld.		

[2] If your bookkeeping knowledge is not the magnificent thing it once was, a quick reading of Appendix B, which is a very condensed summary of journal entry construction, may help you to understand the journal entries that follow.

[3] Where such an overhead formula comes from will be examined in detail in Chapter 3.

Overhead control—depreciation	50,000	
—repairs and maintenance	8,000	
—heat, light, and power	23,000	
—insurance	40,000	
—payroll taxes	140,000	
—property taxes	28,000	
—miscellaneous	12,000	
Accumulated depreciation		50,000
Unexpired insurance		40,000
Prepaid property taxes		28,000
Vouchers payable		43,000
Payroll taxes payable		140,000
To record various overhead items.		
Work in Process Inventory	471,000	
Applied overhead		471,000
To absorb overhead (60,000 × $7.85).		
Finished Goods Inventory	2,064,000	
Work in Process Inventory		2,064,000
To record cost of sets completed.		

Note that the account "Overhead control" contains actual overhead charges, while "Applied overhead" contains the estimated, "smoothed" overhead charge. The two accounts could be treated as debits and credits of a single account, "Overhead," if preferred.

We shall see a great deal more of cost determination in later chapters when we study cost systems. Aluminum Rackets has provided us not only with some useful terminology but also with a preview of some of the topics—like overhead and direct costing—that will shortly occupy us at greater length. Let us next broaden our view of the cost accountant's role.

An Overview of Manufacturing Planning and Control

It is not uncommon to find business students who disdain technological learning in favor of "doing their own thing." When asked how they intend to operate in the managerial positions to which they aspire, these students conjure up legions of experts—one for every conceivable need—who will be at their instantaneous beck and call. One is reminded of the Biblical centurion who might be paraphrased: "I too am a man subject to authority, and have experts subject to me; and I say to my accountant, 'Budget,' and he budgets; and to my marketer, 'Advertise,' and he advertises; and to my mathematician, 'Model,' and he models."

Dismissing the absurdity of not having had to demonstrate your proficiency during some apprenticeship period, and assuming you have become nabob, almighty and exalted manager, how would you run a fair-sized manufacturing concern?

This is a formidable question even for someone who has already occupied such a position. Think of all it entails—demand for product must be generated; the work of hundreds of people must be focused and coordinated; funds must be available for payroll and other purchases as well as for such levies as federal, state, and local taxes; reputation must be maintained or enhanced; and profits must be adequate to permit an attractive choice in the future between continuing in business and cashing in. And many of these activities pose other tasks, such as seeking efficiency, undertaking product research and development, competing with other manufacturers, and investing in new facilities. Ready to become nabob?

How are these complicated tasks carried out in industry? Certain ideas seem relevant regardless of specific organization. The first is the humbling realization that in a fair-sized operation one man cannot cope directly with all the problems. Consequently, he must establish an organization and work through other people. This, of course, introduces very significant problems. A colleague of mine put it simply: "Wherever three or more people are gathered, politics will intrude with at least one person trying to gain ascendancy by forming alliances."[4] Depending on your persuasion, politics can be a welcome element because it creates excitement through intrigues, or it can be a cancer interfering with the work at hand. But there is no choice as to whether or not to have politics. As Brogan says, given at least three people, politics will exist.

Another people problem is how to motivate employees to pursue the goals of the company. This involves rapport, authority, communication, and diplomacy. The "centurion" who takes motivation for granted is easily replaced. A manager must identify and make known company goals, and he must motivate and coordinate his people.

Industry in general finds certain accounting reports useful—better, essential—in planning and controlling the efforts of employees. Foremost among these are the company balance sheet and income statement, which are really after-the-fact control devices that point to situations requiring attention in the future. The primary tool for internal planning and coordinating of future activities, however, is the budget, which comes in assorted time spans and detail. Thus there is the 5- or 10-year plan, which projects the major activities of the organization—as reliably as possible, given the uncertainties of the future—and the yearly and monthly budgets, which forecast the near future with greater accuracy and in more detail.

[4] I owe this insight into man's nature to Professor Howard Brogan, scholar and observer of man's inhumanity to man.

Yearly and monthly budgets are refined further to reflect the activities of individual departments and divisions. It is here that planning really becomes workable. The departmental and divisional budgets list expected sales, itemized expenses, and (sometimes) provisions for investments month by month. Where the departments and divisions are further subdivided, the monthly budgets become correspondingly further refined.

A great variety of studies and reports underlies the budgets at any level. Since most operations are dependent on sales volume, somewhere in the organization a study of demand must be undertaken that culminates in an estimate of sales activity.

One tool that works its way into the preliminary determination of sales volume is profit-volume analysis. It will make our discussion of planning more concrete if we spend a few moments looking at profit-volume analysis in some detail.

Profit-Volume Analysis

"What would sales volume have to be to realize profits of D dollars?" On the surface, this is an appealing question that is raised frequently during the planning phase of operations. Even more popular is the less ambitious query, "How much sales are needed to cover total expenses?" The second question is a variant of the first in which profits are zero. More commonly, the second question is referred to as determining the "breakeven sales." Breakeven points are interesting in that they represent zero on the profit scale.

Profit-volume analysis may be characterized as a "quick and dirty" approximating tool in that (1) it is buttressed by all sorts of rather heroic assumptions, (2) it avoids dealing with restrictions, and (3) it makes no attempt at estimating the best volume of operations. Yet for all its faults, it appears to be helpful in establishing policies. Recognizing restrictions, studying many combinations of variables, and searching for best solutions calls for a mathematical programming technique such as linear programming—and this necessitates a fair amount of time and patience. As opposed to these requirements, profit-volume analysis is virtually instantly available. In some ways the choice between approaches can be likened to that confronting a basketball coach who is torn between substituting a scrappy player with so-so scoring ability for a more deliberate player who waits for the perfect setup and is then almost certain to score. Sometimes the use of the deliberate player is a luxury; there just isn't enough time left.

In the simplest case, a company makes a single product in a perfectly competitive market; consequently, price stays constant regardless of the quantity produced. In this best of all worlds, company costs are expressed by a straight line. The equations are:

Revenue $= R = Px$ = price times quantity

Cost $= K = f + vx$ = fixed cost plus variable rate times quantity

Desired profit $= D$

Figure 1 depicts the breakeven point and its associated profit and loss regions.

continued to page 13

continued from page 12

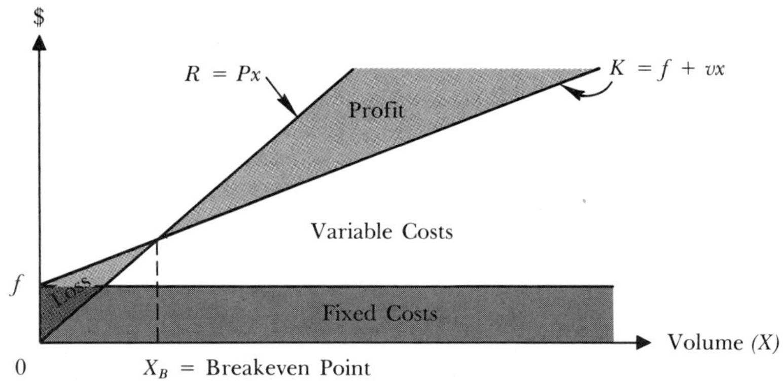

Figure 1

The breakeven point, x_B, is algebraically determined by solving for the intersection of the two equations:

$$\text{At } x_B, \quad R = K$$
$$Px_B = f + vx_B$$
$$x_B = f/(P - v)$$

The profit volume, x_D, that yields D dollars of profit is obtained by adding the desired profit to the fixed costs:

$$x_D = (f + D)/(P - v)$$

x_D would be greater than x_B by the amount $D/(P - v)$, which, in words, is the profit divided by the variable profit margin. The question for management is "Is it possible to generate sales of x_D?" Assuming that some value of x_D is ultimately chosen as practical, management would then set its sales and production programs accordingly.

If revenue and cost are represented by nonlinear equations, multiple breakeven points occur wherever the curves intersect (determined by setting the curves equal, as was done above).

If several products are made, as is usually the case, profit-volume analysis becomes more complicated. Facilitating assumptions are often made whereby an average proportion of products based on historical relationships of output (such as, say, $3x$ are made for every $2y$) is used to determine an average price. If costs are then adjusted similarly, the analysis can be carried out in the manner just developed. The results are, at best, as reliable as the calculated averages. If the proportion of products changes markedly, for example, all estimates are invalidated.

The difference between sales and production volumes is customarily assumed to be inapplicable to the purpose of profit-volume analysis. That is, it is assumed that whatever is produced is also sold.

Once sales volume has been estimated, policies about service level must be formulated. (Essentially, service level refers to how fast services and products are to be provided to customers.) These, in turn, may lead to studies of inventory and waiting lines, and to production schedules. Simultaneously, policies about quality are formulated from studies of the market and desired company image. These, in turn, lead to specific quality control plans. And in many companies, linear programming studies are performed to determine the best use of facilities, as, for example, in choosing the product line subject to capacity and demand constraints.

One way or another, if the findings of these studies are to be implemented, they should be reflected in budgets. And the budgets of the individual segments must then be aggregated to see (1) whether the company as a whole has sufficient resources to put them into effect, and (2) whether the timing is appropriate. If the five-year plan, for instance, says that it is too soon to try to penetrate some market to the extent recommended in a lower-level budget, then revisions in the lower-level budget must be made, assuming that the five-year plan is thought wise. If lower-level budgets call for substantial investment in equipment, these proposals must be subjected to further screening (referred to as *capital* budgeting procedures to distinguish them from *period* budgeting procedures, which study the flow of revenues and expenses for a designated period of time—the budgets we have been discussing for the last few paragraphs). Possibly capital budgeting screening will result in denying some departments their requested new equipment. If so, revisions in lower-level budgets must again be made. And every time a revision takes place, someone is told "No." So once again, as always, a human relations problem arises.

The chief motivating influence in adopting budgets is thought to lie in getting the people at every level to participate in setting the budget at their particular level. This is not entirely satisfactory. Gamesmanship, which is a form of political maneuvering, abounds in setting estimates; furthermore, people who have been denied their requests often feel less than compelled to abide with what is doled to them.

Let us shift emphasis from planning to control. This has always seemed an issue in semantics, for certainly control includes planning.[5] Nevertheless, we now assume budgets have been set and we turn our attention to seeing that they are kept, or better, if they are not kept, to discovering why and why they should have been set aside.

The seemingly easier issue to deal with is the setting aside of a budget. A budget is only an estimate that covers an arbitrarily chosen period of time. If an unforeseen opportunity arises, it seems obvious that supplementary

[5] This is a chicken-egg argument. Can one meaningfully control if he hasn't first planned? Conversely, can one meaningfully plan without providing for control?

funds should be raised, assuming benefits exceed costs. Partly the problem occurs because of the arbitrary choice of budget period. Those who don't supplement budgets apparently insist that all opportunities should arise on January 1—something simply could not be regarded as an opportunity if it occurred, for instance, on May 15 and had not been anticipated in that year's budget. Similarly, unexpected emergencies call for adjustment of budgets. To ignore the situation is somewhat akin to continuing the game plan when the other team is murdering you.

However, observe that granting a supplementary budget is not all that easy to do. First, the person who made the original budget estimates must admit to his superiors that he had not anticipated either the opportunity or the emergency. This may be tantamount to admitting incompetence unless the emergency comes under the category of Act of God (floods, earthquakes) or is due to highly unstable economic conditions (drastic inflation, widespread unemployment). Second, and probably more important because it is subtle, if supplementary budgets are commonplace, less care is apt to be taken in developing and abiding by the basic budgets. Thus allowing supplementary budgets in turn creates the need for supplementary budgets. Why stick to a tight budget if, by sulking, you can get it eased? To discourage this behavior, a company must carefully define what constitutes an opportunity and what an emergency.

Everywhere one turns, he finds human relations problems. That this is eminently so is amply evidenced by the behavior of people who have to explain why they have exceeded their allowed budget outlays. Deny responsibility, create fictitious causes, accuse other people and departments, plead unusual circumstances—every conceivable excuse is offered using every emotional appeal from tears to anger. The person who says, "Yes, it was a very bad month, but I am trying such-and-such and I believe this month will be better," reveals a maturity that is refreshing. Also welcome is the response "I've had a hard time this month, and I would like some advice and help." (After all, that is what higher levels of management are for.)

Budget variance reports and standard cost variance reports are the main accounting reports used in controlling spending.[6] These reports basically subtract actual results from planned (budget or standard) results. The manager ("controller") then tries to find explanations for the differences as guides for corrective action. Although he doesn't always do so, he should attempt to ascertain what could have been done under the circumstances that prevailed before passing judgment on whether the results were favorable or not.

[6] These should be referred to as "difference" reports rather than "variance" reports, since "difference" and "variance" have well-established mathematical-statistical meanings and these accounting reports only calculate differences. Variance is, however, the accepted accounting parlance, and it is used in the sense that some outcome is "at variance with" what was planned.

As budget comparisons are drawn between one level of the organization and the next, we enter the area known as responsibility accounting. Here it is common practice to "telescope" budget variance reports. Think (1) of a telescope that at first adjustment gives a broad view with few details and that with later adjustments homes in on a much narrower view while picking up a great deal of detail, and (2) of a hierarchy of managers with each level responsible for the level immediately below it. In responsibility accounting each manager is given a budget variance report that reflects only those activities for which he is thought responsible. At the lowest tier of management the detail is great; at the higher tiers of management the budget results of the tier below are summarized in the higher-level budget variance report, and detail diminishes. So scope gives way to depth as one contrasts the variance reports of top management with those of progressively lower rungs. And through it all runs the problem of getting people to accept responsibility.

This completes our overview of the planning and control processes—the *how*—of a manufacturer. It has also provided a rough sketch of how the ensuing chapters fit into the scheme of cost accounting and cost analysis. If you have gotten the notion that business is an amalgamation of *interrelated* activities, all of which are fraught with human relations problems, you have grasped the setting of cost accounting. *No* activity can take place that does not affect some other simultaneously; in one way or another, be it ever so indirect, all activities in a business are joint, all products are joint. All share common facilities during a common time span. Naturally, this complicates every step of planning, analysis, and control—but it also makes the cost accountant's work challenging and absorbing. The cost accountant does not just collect and publish facts in reports; when he does a thorough job, he has set the stage for action and has virtually done the manager's work for him.

Problems

1. **(a)** List all the ways you can imagine in which the reported profits of two manufacturers might differ, given that they make the same products, sell the same quantities of each, and otherwise have comparable facilities and resources.

(b) Comment on the accuracy of cost as found in financial statements.

(c) Is accounting an art or a science?

2. *Breakeven analysis.* A company can represent its revenues and costs by the following relationships:

$$\text{Revenue} = R = Px \quad = \$20x$$
$$\text{Cost} \quad = K = f + vx = \$75{,}000 + \$5x$$

(a) What is the breakeven point?

(b) If management would be pleased with profits of \$90,000, what minimum sales volume must be attained?

3. *Breakeven analysis: multiple points.* A company is in an oligopolistic market whereby each unit it sells reduces its selling price. In other words, price per unit is a function of quantity. The price (marginal revenue) and cost relationships are shown below.

$$\text{Selling price per unit} = P(x) = \$7{,}000 - \$.002x^2$$
$$\text{Total cost (for all units)} = K = \$2{,}000{,}000 + \$1{,}000x$$

(a) Graph the revenue and cost curves.

(b) Determine the breakeven points.

4. *Optimal profit determination.* For the data in problem 3, determine the sales volume that maximizes profit as well as the amount of anticipated profit at that volume.

5. *Multiproducts and profit-volume analysis.* A company makes two products, x and y, in the approximate proportion of $3x$ to $2y$. Prices for x and y are \$5 and \$20 respectively, while their variable costs per unit are \$2 and \$12 respectively. If company fixed costs are \$800,000, what total volume should the company produce to earn profits of \$200,000?

6. *Multiproducts and gross profit analysis.* The chapter did not go into the control report that is associated with profit-volume analysis. This area is referred to as *gross profit analysis,* and it involves calculating differences between forecasted and actual prices and forecasted and actual volumes, basically according to

$$(P + \Delta P)(Q + \Delta Q) = \underbrace{PQ}_{\text{Planned revenues}} + \underbrace{P\,\Delta Q}_{\text{Quantity variance}} + \underbrace{Q\,\Delta P}_{\text{Price variance}} + \underbrace{\Delta P\,\Delta Q}_{\text{Mixed variance}}$$

The same would be done for costs, and management would then have an explanation at hand of what went wrong with its forecasts. This could then be used to locate trouble sources and to improve the ensuing year's forecasts. Part (a) below injects yet another feature, change in purchasing power (inflation), while part (b) extends the analysis to two products.

(a) The books of ABC Manufacturing Company show the following:

Estimated sales at 1/1/83 = 400,000 units at \$10
Estimated costs = \$600,000 + \$6x
Actual sales through 12/31/83 = 500,000 units at \$10.80
Actual costs = \$600,000 + \$6x

The country suffered 5% inflation in 1983.

Determine:
1. Purchase-power variance
2. Profit-rate variance
3. Volume variance
4. Mix variance

Comment on the results.

(b)

	Products					
	A			B		
	Variable Cost	Price	Volume	Variable Cost	Price	Volume
Forecast	$3	$8	100,000	$15	$25	200,000
Actual	$2.50	$10	120,000	$18	$22	150,000

Analyze the causes of deviation from the desired gross profit.

7. *Direct costing.* The distinction between absorption and direct costing was stated in the chapter as resting on the treatment of fixed overhead costs (absorption costing considers these product costs, and direct costing takes them to be period costs). If there were no changes in inventory (in other words, if the sales and production volumes were identical), there would be no difference in reported profit. In the abbreviated statements below assume sales volume remains constant at 100 units over the three-year period; production volumes, however, for the three years are 120, 100, and 80 units respectively. Fixed overhead in each year is $60; all other period expenses likewise remain constant at $70.

	Year 1		Year 2		Year 3	
	Absorption	Direct	Absorption	Direct	Absorption	Direct
Sales	$400	$400	$400	$400	$400	$400
Cost of sales:						
Variable	$250	$250	$250	$250	$250	$250
Fixed overhead	50	—	58	—	72	—
Total	$300	$250	$308	$250	$322	$250
Gross profit	$100	$150	$ 92	$150	$ 78	$150
Expenses:						
Other	$ 70	$ 70	$ 70	$ 70	$ 70	$ 70
Fixed overhead	—	60	—	60	—	60
Total	$ 70	$130	$ 70	$130	$ 70	$130
Operating profit	$ 30	$ 20	$ 22	$ 20	$ 8	$ 20

The statements have been prepared on a FIFO (first units manufactured are considered the first sold = first in-first out) basis.

The president, whose background has been largely in marketing, is talking with his controller. They have before them the three years' statements prepared on an absorption costing basis.

President: These reports of yours are driving me up the wall! They show profits declining every year, even though sales have been stable throughout the period. We're down to $8 now and I hate to think what operating profit will be next year. I'm surprised we have any stockholders left now. After next year they'll have to paper their living rooms with their stock certificates! We can't be doing this badly.

Controller: Profits fluctuate with production: high production, high profits—low production, low profits.

President: That's ridiculous! You could produce until goods were piled up on the lawn, and if you didn't sell them, your business would fold. Profits ought to follow sales.

Controller: By reducing selling price, a business could achieve great sales revenue and still lose its shirt. Production is the key.

Required:

(a) Is a human relations problem brewing?

(b) Reconcile the argument.

(c) Show how direct costing might help.

(d) In year 2 fixed overhead is $58 under absorption costing. How did this figure arise?

(e) Could production increase while profits decline?

8. *Direct costing (prepared by Professor James M. Fremgen, U.S. Naval Postgraduate School).*
Let:

EA = net income before tax under absorption costing
ED = net income before tax under direct costing
S = actual number of units sold
O = actual number of units produced
B = budgeted number of units to be produced
p = selling price per unit
v = total variable cost per unit
R = actual variable overhead costs
T = actual fixed overhead costs
F = budgeted fixed overhead costs
N = actual fixed nonmanufacturing expenses
UV = underapplied variable overhead
UF = underapplied fixed overhead

Complete the right sides of the three equations below by using only symbols from the foregoing list. In the case of equation (c), reduce the right side to as few terms as possible.

(a) $EA =$

(b) $ED =$

(c) $EA - ED =$

9. *Direct costing.*

(a) Prepare an income statement on a direct-costing basis from the information given below.

Sales	$500,000
Material purchases	100,000
Direct labor	80,000
Overhead: Fixed	80,000
Variable	50,000
Operating expenses	190,000
Equivalent production during year	100,000 units
Ending inventory	5,000 units

What is the difference between net income reported this way and as it would be reported under a full-costing basis?

(c) Briefly discuss the advantages inherent in direct costing.

10. *Costs of goods manufactured.* Prepare a Cost of Goods Manufactured Statement from the data given below.

Direct labor	$220,000
Purchases of raw materials	780,000
Raw materials inventory 12/31/76	210,000
Raw materials inventory 1/31/77	300,000
Absorbed overhead	440,000
Work in process inventory 12/31/76	670,000
Work in process inventory 1/31/77	710,000

The sales on account were $4,800,000 for goods that cost $1,700,000. Write all journal entries.

11. *Cost of goods manufactured.* Write journal entries for the data below and prepare a Cost of Goods Manufactured Statement.

Beginning inventories:	
Raw Materials	$120,000
Work in Process	220,000
Finished Goods	450,000
Raw material purchases	215,000
Direct materials requisitioned	180,000
Indirect materials requisitioned	10,000
Direct labor (75,000 hours)	300,000
Indirect labor	40,000
Payroll taxes deducted	51,000
Actual overhead (other than indirect labor and materials)	168,000
Overhead absorption rate = $3 per direct-labor hour	
Cost of work completed	560,000

12. *Cost of goods manufactured.* Write journal entries and prepare a Cost of Goods Manufactured Statement for the data below.

1/1/70 Balances:	
Raw Materials	$200,000
Work in Process	250,000
Finished Goods	400,000
January Activities:	
Purchases of materials	380,000
Direct materials requisitioned	410,000
Indirect materials requisitioned	30,000
Direct labor	500,000
Income taxes withheld	80,000
Social Security taxes withheld (5%)	30,000
Other statutory withholdings	10,000
Depreciation	60,000
Repairs and maintenance	12,000
Heat, light and power	25,000
Insurance	20,000
Payroll taxes and benefits, 12% of gross payroll	72,000
Property taxes on factory	18,000
Miscellaneous production expenses	5,000
Indirect labor	100,000

The budget for the year for overhead was $y = \$2{,}000{,}000 + \$10x$ and the expected production was 200,000 units of product; hence the overhead absorption rate was $20 per unit. Assume 18,000 units were made in January (equivalent idea). The cost of the units completed was $1,000,000.

13. *Cost of sales.* Prepare a Cost of Sales Statement for the month of August 1980 from the data below and write all journal entries.

7/31/80 Balances:	
Raw materials	$200,000
Work in process	400,000
Finished goods	600,000
August activities:	
Purchase of materials	705,000
Direct materials requisitioned	810,000
Indirect materials requisitioned	62,000
Direct labor	928,000
Indirect labor	200,000
Income taxes withheld	150,000
Social Security taxes withheld	56,400
Other statutory withholdings	21,800
Depreciation	92,000
Repairs and maintenance	15,000
Heat, light, and power	18,300

Insurance	32,000
Company payroll taxes and benefits	115,000
Property taxes on factory	24,000
Miscellaneous production expenses	5,200

The overhead budget equation for the year is $y = \$3,600,000 + \$5x$ and the expected production for the year is 600,000 units. The equivalent of 48,000 units were made in August. The ending inventory of work in process was costed at $800,000, while ending finished goods amounted to $245,000. Determine the amount of the overhead spending variance.

14. *Multiple break-even points attributable to a step function (prepared by Professor Gary Monroe).* The Igloo Company is thinking of adding a new line of ice blocks to their currently existing line of ice blocks. This new line will require a fixed cost of $250,000 per month to manufacture 16,000 units. To manufacture between 16,000 and 60,000 units, the firm will have to spend an additional $100,000 in fixed costs per month. Anything above 60,000 units per month will require another $150,000 in fixed costs per month. Variable costs will also vary on a per unit basis similar to that of fixed costs. Variable costs will be $16.00 per unit for the first 16,000 units, $17.00 per unit for the next 44,000 units, and $20.00 per unit for anything produced in excess of 60,000 units per month. These cost behaviors are shown below.

Units	Total Fixed Costs	Variable Cost per Unit
0–16,000	$250,000	$16.00
16,000–60,000	350,000	17.00
60,000 and above	500,000	20.00

Selling price per unit $25.00.

The president of the company, I. M. Chilly, remembers break-even analysis from his undergraduate school years, but can't recall enough about break-even analysis to solve this problem. Therefore, he would like you to assist him.

Required: Compute the monthly break-even point(s) in units.

15. *Pizza, breakeven and profit volume analysis (adapted from Certificate in Management Accounting Examination, December 1973).* Mr. Calderone started a pizza restaurant in 1970. For this purpose a building was rented for $400 per month. Two ladies were hired to work full time at the restaurant and six college boys were hired to work 30 hours per week delivering pizza. An outside accountant was hired for tax and bookkeeping purposes. For this service, Mr. Calderone pays $300 per month. The necessary restaurant equipment and delivery cars were purchased with cash. Mr. Calderone has noticed that expenses for utilities and supplies have been rather constant.

Mr. Calderone increased his business between 1970 and 1973. Profits have more than doubled since 1970. Mr. Calderone does not understand why his profits have increased faster than his volume.

A projected Income Statement for 1974 has been prepared by the accountant and is shown below.

Calderone Company Projected Income Statement

For the Year Ended December 31, 1974

Sales		$95,000
Cost of Food Sold	$28,500	
Wages & Fringe Benefits of Restaurant Help	8,150	
Wages & Fringe Benefits of Delivery Boys	17,300	
Rent	4,800	
Accounting Services	3,600	
Depreciation of Delivery Equipment	5,000	
Depreciation of Restaurant Equipment	3,000	
Utilities	2,325	
Supplies (Soap, Floor Wax, etc.)	1,200	73,875
Net Income Before Taxes		$21,125
Income Taxes		6,338
Net Income		$14,787

Note: The average pizza sells for $2.50. Assume that Mr. Calderone pays out 30% of his income in income taxes.

Required:

(a) What is the breakeven point in number of pizzas that must be sold?

(b) What is the cash flow breakeven point in number of pizzas that must be sold?

(c) If Mr. Calderone withdraws $4,800 for personal use, how much cash will be left from the 1974 income-producing activities?

(d) Mr. Calderone would like an after-tax net income of $20,000. What volume must be reached in number of pizzas in order to obtain the desired income?

(e) Briefly explain to Mr. Calderone why his profits have increased at a faster rate than his sales.

(f) Briefly explain to Mr. Calderone why his cash flow for 1974 will exceed his profits.

Human Behavior

2

Chapter Overview

As we left the last chapter, one theme was predominating: People complicate the management of business. Hence the work of the cost accountant requires him to become people-conscious. He must secure the cooperation of those from whom he seeks information; he must perceive how they regard both him and his requests; he must understand what emotions are aroused by his reports; and he must realize that all these processes are ongoing events, with yesterday's report influencing today's request even though they pertain to different situations.

A popular position taken by legions of accountants is summarized in the declaration "I deal with information and just present the facts." Such pronouncements indicate lack of comprehension of communicative and human behavioral phenomena. There is no such thing as a report that has a *neutral* effect on the emotions of a reader with whom it has communicated. Communication is a two-way transactional process; if the accountant speaks but no one listens, there has been no communication. To be emotionally neutral, the mind of the reader would have to be elsewhere when perusing a report. Given mental alertness, a report reader will feel bored, excited, satisfied, dissatisfied, and/or any combination of these and other emotions; *he feels something.* What feelings does the cost accountant want to evoke?

To put it another way, the accountant either (1) fails outright (no audience) when he issues a report, or (2) fails to generate an appropriate emotional response, or (3) succeeds in producing a desired response. If he fails, he may cause more damage than if he had circulated a report containing erroneous data analysis. "Forgive and forget" is a doctrine that seems to ignore the nature of man; annoy a man in some way with one request or report, and you are apt to find him uncooperative thereafter.

In this chapter we shall review some of the fundamentals of human behavior, for it is not always wise to impute your feelings about something to other people. Just because you regard something in a particular way, it does not follow that others, who necessarily have different frames of reference (backgrounds), will feel the same way. Your feelings are a clue but they are not conclusive. We shall also examine the attitudes management hopes to instill in employees as well as two of the best-known schemes through which management proceeds. With these concepts in hand, we should be in better position to understand traditional accounting control systems and to search for improvements in them.

Attitudes

Let me but do my work from day to day
In field or forest, at the desk or loom,
In roaring market place or tranquil room.
Let me but find it in my heart to say,
When vagrant wishes beckon me astray,
"This is my work, my blessing, not my doom.
In all the world, I am the one by whom
This work can best be done, in the right way."

This excerpt from *The Three Best Things*, written by Henry van Dyke in the late nineteenth century, epitomizes attitudes that might strike today's managers as a mockery from a distant and oft-lamented past. The person in the poem is dedicated, eager to work, loyal, undemanding, and impervious to boredom; he obtains a high sense of achievement from his work; and he has feelings of pride and significance. One would have to search exhaustively to find employees today who exhibited such laudable attitudes.

Since these attitudes are not available in natural abundance, management seeks to manufacture them. What the accountant does can both help and hinder managerial efforts. The accountant, however, labors under the burden of tradition. Businesses have been run for decades using certain well-accepted accounting reports and methods of analysis. One has to be very cautious (and more than just a little courageous) in putting aside any of these time-tested tools. However, improving on old techniques, especially from a behavioral viewpoint, may be very possible. After all, the traditional techniques were developed in times when relatively little was known about human relations.

Keep in mind as we review behavioral fundamentals that cost accounting has to deal with all sorts of people, including those on the production line as well as those in various levels of management. Each group has its unique problems, but the fundamentals should shed light on every group.

Fundamentals of Human Behavior

Thorough study of human behavior would include books describing prehistoric man, the Bible, Machiavelli's *The Prince*, and a host of offerings in sociology, psychology, psychiatry, and management. The limitations of a single chapter are readily apparent. We can, however, identify the theories that seem to have attracted the greatest attention.

The starting point for what management regards as modern behavioral science is the research of Elton Mayo and his colleagues, which was conducted in the Hawthorne plant of the Western Electric Company in the late 1920s. Among other things, they found (1) that individual production employees would restrict their output rather than be ostracized by their groups, and (2) that productivity increased when employees felt that management cared about them.

The Hawthorne Study findings were followed about ten years later by the studies of social psychologist Kurt Lewin and his colleagues. They demonstrated that groups have their own personalities, which are reflected in the group's motivations, cohesiveness, goals, and values. They also showed that group beliefs replace group members' individual beliefs and that collectively the group has greater strength than the sum of the strengths of its individual members. Group behavior that you have observed undoubtedly supports these conclusions.[1]

After Lewin there came a flood of theories that began by emphasizing human relations and grew into today's behavioral science movement. Before looking into the work of a few of the renowned theorists, it would be well to recognize that behavioral science *does not* recommend emphasizing human relations to the point of ignoring productive efficiency and profits. The earlier human relations school paid no attention to efficiency and profit, but instead insisted on democratization and friendliness as the means to achieve high morale. The behavioralists, on the other hand, saw this as manipulative and insincere and observed that happy workers were not necessarily productive workers.

Magregor: Theory X Versus Theory Y

In his widely acclaimed book, *The Human Side of Management*, Douglas Magregor set the stage for today's behavioral science.[2] Magregor uses two sets of assumptions about worker attitudes, which he labels Theory X and Theory Y, to develop a philosophy of management that rests on proper

---

[1] I recall a drugstore gang that did some very obnoxious things when the group was fully assembled. As long as the drugstore housed only one or two members, however, things were very peaceful. As individuals the members were neither especially obnoxious nor courageous—they were typical insecure teenagers. But as a gang, they were simply formidable, a blight on mankind.

[2] Douglas Magregor, *The Human Side of Management* (New York: McGraw-Hill Book Co., 1960).

motivation of human resources. A manager who believes in Theory X assumes (1) that employees will avoid work because they naturally dislike it; (2) that, as a consequence, employees must be forced to work toward company goals; and (3) that the typical employee is ambitionless, shuns responsibility, wants to be told what to do, and seeks security above all. A manager who believes in Theory Y assumes (1) that work is as natural as play or rest; (2) that employees can learn to seek responsibility; (3) that external controls may be less effective in getting employees to pursue company goals than internal controls that are self-imposed because of a sense of commitment to company goals; (4) that commitment results from a perception of rewards; and (5) that most employees have innate creative ability and imagination to bring to the solution of company problems.

Magregor sees Theories X and Y as sets of assumptions and not as managerial strategies. He does not advocate either a hard approach (coercion, punishment) or a soft approach (satisfying employee demands, permissiveness)—because the hard approach often results in antagonism, sabotage, and restricted output, while the soft approach frequently leads to employee laziness and excessive demands in return for ever-diminishing output, and to managerial avoidance of responsibilities. Magregor advises that, where possible, management develop an atmosphere of mutual trust and respect. Once such an atmosphere is established, management should seek to *integrate* individual needs and company goals. Relying on the flexible, optimistic Theory Y assumptions, Magregor expects that the organization will then become more effective just by meeting employee needs. Set the atmosphere, show employees that their needs can be met by pursuing company goals, and reward employees by meeting their needs—this is Magregor's conception of informed management. However, he also recognizes that some adverse situations favor the adoption of a leadership style based on Theory X.

Magregor draws a distinction between consulting with employees and genuinely encouraging employee participation in the setting of goals. Consulting could be a placebo to delude employees and, besides being unethical, could destroy managerial efforts if employees come to realize the true state of affairs. So Magregor recommends that employee commitment to managerial objectives be sought by encouraging sincere participation in making significant decisions.

He sees traditional control mechanisms as extraneous, if not harmful, to the control of a *dedicated* employee. Instead of such controls he advises management to consider (1) how mature an employee is, (2) how absorbing is the work to be done, given the employee's maturity, (3) what rewards will arouse motivation, and (4) how the employee perceives his manager's method of operating and the significance of his own participation in the management process. If commitment cannot be obtained by acting on these considerations, Magregor would have management exercise its authority.

Maslow: The Hierarchy of Needs

The one researcher on whose efforts all subsequent theories seem to rest is Dr. Abraham Maslow. In his pioneering work, *Motivation and Personality*, Maslow observes that motivation comes from within an individual and cannot be imposed on him.[3] An individual seeks goals and *drives* himself to attain them. The actions he takes to carry out a drive give evidence of the individual's motivation. Hence goals create needs, which arouse motivation, which results in drive.

Maslow arranges needs in the following hierarchy (it is for this hierarchy that he is most famous):

(1) physiological needs (food, shelter, rest, sexual fulfillment);

(2) safety needs (emotional security, health);

(3) need for belongingness and love (need to be part of a group, to give and receive love);

(4) need for esteem (feelings of personal worth and competence, need for recognition and respect in others' eyes); and

need for self-actualization (realizing one's potential, becoming what one is capable of becoming).

Maslow makes the point that until one level of needs is fulfilled, behavior is not motivated by the next higher level of needs. When it is satisfied, a need ceases to be a motivator. However, the entire hierarchy of needs repeats itself over the course of a man's life. In other words, if a situation changes, the entire hierarchy may be reintroduced, starting with the primitive needs. Maslow cautions that because of immaturity, stunted growth, or neurosis, some people never get beyond the satisfaction of lower-level needs. People who are pursuing self-actualization needs involve themselves in gratifying, creative expressions that are self-perpetuating (new goals and means of expression are constantly formulated—self-actualization is an ongoing need).

Herzberg: Motivation-Hygiene Theory

Another famous theorist who has had a significant effect on management is Dr. Frederick Herzberg. Like Maslow, Herzberg is very concerned with motivation. His motivation-hygiene theory segregates two sets of factors that

[3] A. H. Maslow, *Motivation and Personality* (New York: Harper & Row, 1954).

describe attitudes toward jobs:

Motivation Factors (Satisfiers)	*Hygiene Factors (Dissatisfiers)*
Achievement	Company policy and administration
Recognition	Supervision
Work itself	Working conditions
Responsibility	Interpersonal relations
Advancement	Salary
Growth	Status
	Job security
	Personal life

The motivators all relate to job content, while the hygiene factors all relate to job context. Motivation results from the employee's commitment to accomplishing an interesting task and *not* from the context factors, according to Herzberg.

Herzberg is critical of industry's approach to motivating workers, which he feels focuses almost exclusively on job context factors. His research argues convincingly that hygiene (context) factors are dissatisfiers that operate only when they are regarded as inadequate or absent, and then negatively.[4] Herzberg, therefore, believes that management should concentrate on job content factors.

Herzberg favors job *enrichment*, which he is very careful to distinguish from job *enlargement*.[5] He views the latter as doing more of the same old thing, which may actually be demotivating. Job enrichment, on the other hand, adds challenge to a job, which should enhance feelings of accomplishment. Enrichment amounts to "loading a job vertically," for which Herzberg developed the following principles:

Principle	*Motivators Involved*
Removing some controls while retaining accountability	Responsibility and personal achievement
Increasing the individual's accountability for his own work	Responsibility and recognition
Giving a person a complete, natural unit of work (module, division, area, and so forth)	Responsibility, achievement, and recognition
Granting an employee additional authority in his activity; job freedom	Responsibility, achievement, and recognition

[4] See Herzberg, Mausner, and Snyderman, *The Motivation to Work* (New York: John Wiley & Sons, 1959) for the first presentation of Herzberg's theory.

[5] F. Herzberg, "One More Time: How Do You Motivate Employees?" *Harvard Business Review*, January–February 1968.

Principle	*Motivators Involved*
Making periodic reports directly available to the worker himself rather than to the supervisor	Internal recognition
Introducing new and more difficult tasks that the worker has not previously handled	Growth and learning
Assigning individuals specific or specialized tasks, enabling them to become experts	Responsibility, growth, and advancement

Argyris: Changing the Organization to Suit Employees

We next encounter another of the early precursors of behavioral science, Dr. Chris Argyris.[6] Argyris engenders controversy by blaming organizations for hindering employees from realizing their personal needs. As he sees it, the very structure of industrial organizations—by which he means things like the managerial ladder, formal roles, specialization, rigid lines of authority, accountability, sharply defined channels of communication, job descriptions, budgetary controls, production schedules, and salesmen's quotas—actually interferes with higher-level drives and makes employees submissive and dependent. He warns management that perceptive individuals, seeing that organizational objectives take precedence over their personal needs, may divert their energies to sabotaging organizational objectives and to promoting apathy, conflict, and tension.

Argyris writes:

> "Psychological success . . . means achieving challenging goals. Self-esteem is intimately related with responsibility to something or someone outside one's self. Why cannot the organization develop challenging goals for the members to strive to achieve? Is not the organization an excellent medium for experiencing responsibility? It is our hypothesis that organizations can be modified so that they offer increasingly meaningful challenges and opportunity for responsibility.[7]

How are these changes to be brought about? Argyris recommends developing an open climate and interpersonal competence and sincerity in

---

[6] Argyris has written many books that have attracted wide attention, including *Personality and Organization* (New York: Harper & Bros. 1957); *Interpersonal Competence and Organizational Effectiveness* (Homewood, Illinois: Richard D. Irwin, 1962); and *Integrating the Individual and the Organization* (New York: John Wiley & Sons, 1964).

[7] Argyris, *Integrating the Individual and the Organization*, p. 147.

relationships. He sees this as an effective means for dealing with personal differences that block communications and absorb energy uselessly; group cohesiveness should improve as a consequence.

When modifying the organization to suit the skills of its employees, Argyris would assign each employee a variety of tasks (as protection against boredom and apathy) and a wide scope of responsibility (to increase challenge and hence achievement). The employees would be given as much discretion as possible over pace, quality control, and choice of techniques. Then, as a further step in job enrichment, Argyris would rotate tasks among employees; it is to be hoped that in the process, group participation, interaction, and cohesiveness will improve.

Likert: Group Bestowing of Power

Dr. Rensis Likert, while stressing communication in organizations, departs from the individual conceptions of management we have been discussing and concentrates instead on groups and power generation.[8]

Likert encourages managers to develop open communication within their groups, mutual trust, consensus decision making, group definition of roles, and shared responsibility. He sees the payoff as including group accountability, enhanced group loyalty and cohesiveness, and the integration of individual and group objectives. A manager's authority, in turn, derives largely *from his group* and what it *allows* him to do. Hence authority flows upward in the organization as well as downward. Furthermore, the greater pull a manager enjoys with both his superior and his hierarchical peers, the more authority will be bestowed on him by his group.

The development of open communication offers the further advantage of encouraging supportive relationships within the group, which help to effect the identification of individual needs with group objectives. A supportive relationship exists in a group when a member feels that the others are genuinely concerned about him and communicate respect, recognition, and esteem through their actions. In such circumstances, individuals are apt to suppress personal differences in favor of the group objectives, thereby engendering harmony.

Perhaps you have heard of "Likert-type scales," which are devices for measuring feelings about something. Typically a statement is made and then a 5-point Likert scale asks whether you (a) strongly agree, (b) agree, (c) are uncertain, (d) disagree, or (e) strongly disagree. In *The Human Organization*

---

[8] The two books for which Likert is most famous are *New Patterns of Management* (New York: McGraw-Hill Book Co., 1961) and *The Human Organization* (New York: McGraw-Hill Book Co., 1967).

Table 1 Style of Management

Organizational Variable	Exploitive-Authoritative	Benevolent-Authoritative	Consultative	Participative-Group
Extent to which immediate superior in solving job problems generally tries to get subordinates' ideas and opinions and make constructive use of them	Seldom gets ideas and opinions of subordinates in solving job problems	Sometimes gets ideas and opinions of subordinates in solving job problems	Usually gets ideas and opinions and usually tries to make constructive use of them	Always gets ideas and opinions and always tries to make constructive use of them
Amount of responsibility felt by each member of organization for achieving organization's goals	High levels of management feel responsibility; lower levels feel less; rank and file feel little and often welcome opportunity to behave so as to defeat organization's goals	Managerial personnel usually feel responsibility; rank and file usually feel relatively little responsibility for achieving organization's goals	Substantial proportion of personnel, especially at high levels, feel responsibility and generally behave so as to achieve organization's goals	Personnel at all levels feel responsibility for organization's goals and behave so as to implement them
To what extent are subordinates involved in decisions related to their work?	Not at all	Never involved in decisions; occasionally consulted	Usually are consulted but ordinarily are not involved in decision making	Are involved fully in all decisions related to their work
Extent to which control data (e.g., accounting, productivity, cost, etc.) are used for self-guidance or group problem solving by managers and non-supervisory employees; or used by superiors in a punitive, policing manner	Used for policing and in punitive manner	Used for policing coupled with reward and punishment, sometimes punitively; used somewhat for guidance but in accord with orders	Largely used for policing with emphasis usually on reward but with some punishment; used for guidance in accord with orders; some use also for self-guidance	Used for self-guidance and for coordinated problem solving and guidance; not used punitively

Likert uses such a scale, expanded to 21 points, to examine four styles of management:

Exploitive-Authoritative
Benevolent-Authoritative
Consultative
Participative-Group

Some excerpts from the questionnaire used in the Likert study appear in Table 1.

A quick perusal of Table 1 (1) makes it plain that businesses can be rated at various points on the Likert scale, and (2) suggests that accounting cannot serve management well if it is inflexible and insists on a traditional approach to communications. Such an approach serves the authoritative organization well, but is apt to be a hindrance in the participative organization.

Likert also originated the idea of human-asset accounting in *The Human Organization.* He felt that if capable personnel leave an organization, the organization suffers as a consequence. Conversely, if capable people join a company, its assets increase. Likert felt that these events should be evaluated in the ledgers of the organization so that more attention would be paid to the investment in people. He outlined a theory of human-asset accounting that was designed to measure return on investment in employees. His ideas have excited a great deal of current, ongoing research in the accounting literature.

Other Theories

Let us expand our knowledge of behavioral fundamentals by extracting specific ideas from the theories of other researchers and scholars.

Drucker claims that the only standard that is motivating to a member of a group is the standard of the best performer in the group.[9] Nothing less motivates. Others, however, feel that all members must be equally capable for this to hold true; otherwise, less capable members will shun the comparison as being unrealistic—a natural defense mechanism.

McClelland and Winter observe that high achievers are absorbed by the thought of accomplishment for its own sake; for these people, money, status, and power are only secondary considerations.[10] High achievers (1) assume

[9] P. Drucker, *The Practice of Management* (Englewood Cliffs, N.J.: Prentice-Hall, 1956).

[10] D. C. McClelland and D. G. Winter, *Motivating Economic Achievement* (New York: Free Press, 1969).

responsibility for solving problems, (2) attempt to achieve moderate goals at calculated risks, and (3) prefer frequent feedback on results.

Many behavioral scientists espouse expectancy theory, according to which people exert greater effort when both the probability and magnitude of the reward are known in advance.[11]

Occupational-level theory takes issue with Herzberg by claiming that a person's occupational level determines whether content or context elements motivate him.[12]

The idea of participation leading to increased indentification and responsibility, and consequently to improved performance, has been reported in the findings of studies dealing with other nations.[13]

One man's meat is another man's poison. Du Brin observes:

> . . . Those individuals with strong needs and the capacity for creative expression will be motivated by an organizational climate or a superior that encourages creativity. In contrast, an individual with limited need or desire to make creative responses to his environment might display defensive or avoidant behavior in such an environment. This same individual would probably show high job satisfaction and high motivation in an environment that encouraged adherence to older modes of doing things.[14]

When motivators were being discussed, the role of money was not accorded special significance; in fact, Herzberg listed salary as a context factor—something that motivates only when inadequate. Du Brin observes that a bonus motivates only for a brief time, and that ". . . once the money is spent the motivational impact of the bonus is dissipated."[15] Gellerman observes that salary increases would have to be substantial enough to change

---

[11] See, for example,

V. H. Vroom, *Work and Motivation* (New York: John Wiley and Sons, 1964);

J. P. Campbell, M. D. Dunnette, E. E. Lawler, III, and K. E. Weick, Jr., *Managerial Behavior, Performance, and Effectiveness* (New York: McGraw-Hill Book Co., 1970);

G. Strauss and L. Sayles, *Personnel: The Human Problems of Management* (Englewood Cliffs, N.J.: Prentice-Hall, 1972).

[12] J. G. Darley and T. Hagenah, *Vocational Interest Measurement* (Minneapolis: University of Minnesota Press, 1955).

[13] See, for example, G. F. Farris and D. A. Butterfield, "Control Theory in Brazilian Organizations," *Administrative Science Quarterly*, December 1972, pp. 580–81.

[14] A. J. Du Brin, *Fundamentals of Organizational Behavior: An Applied Perspective* (New York: Pergamon Press, 1974), p. 55.

[15] Ibid., p. 58.

a person's life-style before money would be motivating.[16] On the other hand, money can be a demotivator. According to equity theory, an employee may become very hostile and demotivated if he perceives that he is getting less pay than another employee for the same work.[17] And no one will deny hearing or perhaps directly knowing about people who were paid so much that they got lazy and did *less* work.

Du Brin made a thought-provoking statement about money when discussing the research of P. F. Wernimount and S. Fitzpatrick:

> . . . Hard-core trainees attached the least importance to money of the groups studied. Complicating the findings further, it was noted that hospital sisters and college students view money as less important than do hard-core trainees. *One remote explanation here is that if you are deprived of money long enough, it begins to decrease in importance!* (Italics supplied)[18]

This would suggest that sustained deprivation causes substitute motivators to take prominence and, hence, that the inadequacy of a context factor may be transitory.

As long as we are talking about deprivation, let us go further and discuss penalties. Behavioral scientists look upon penalties with disfavor—mainly because they seem to alienate offenders; instead of improving performance, penalties turn offenders away from organizational objectives. Penalties and threats focus mainly on lower-level needs; furthermore, few people have learned to accept even criticism gracefully. Their natural reaction is to get their defense mechanisms churning, and if they feel bad enough, they may even retaliate with some sort of sabotage.

Even though your natural reaction to somebody who has goofed may be to blow up and penalize him heavily, you must ask yourself whether this is likely to achieve the results you want. The accountant's focus should be on achieving organizational objectives—not on controlling behavior for the pure satisfaction that may be had from it.

Your Author Speaks Out

Up to this point I have tried faithfully to summarize the theories of others—others who, I might add, are far more learned about behavior than I. But

[16] S. Gellerman, *Management by Motivation* (New York: American Management Association, 1968), pp. 203–18.

[17] C. S. Telly, W. L. French, and W. G. Scott, "The Relationship of Inequity to Turnover Among Hourly Workers," *Administrative Science Quarterly*, March 1971.

[18] Du Brin, *Organizational Behavior*, p. 64.

one cannot write about human relations very long before he feels like injecting his own opinion. So I shall seize this opportunity to display my ignorance.

Human relations considerations could become the paralysis of all action. The essence of good management lies not in analysis but in making decisions and then making those decisions work.[19]

Recognizing the needs of others does not, in my opinion, make or break a manager. I have worked for managers who seemed so concerned about my welfare that I perceived them as insincere and patronizing. I have also worked for a man who paid virtually no attention whatever to human relations but instead went about his work in an energetic, professional manner, issuing orders clearly and without fanfare; rarely did he even indicate approval. It was often enough. He expected high performance and he got it; furthermore, morale was spirited. This man was an aggressive leader whose style of management rested on establishing rapport and respect.

Now I am not calling for the abandonment of "need recognition" nor am I saying that authoritarians are necessarily good managers. I would merely like to suggest that for me, and perhaps for many others, sincerity, competence, and consistency are more important traits in a manager then pleasantness. For that matter, there is nothing wrong with pleasantness—provided it accompanies the more important traits.

As for analysis, and especially mathematical analysis, what I am observing is that if analysis consumes a great deal of time, if management is to be effective, it may have to make a decision before analysis can be completed. Suboptimal decisions are made all the time without disastrous results. Excellent managers stimulate and coordinate the efforts of others and *make* favorable outcomes occur. They go with whatever analysis time and talent has put at their disposal.

Although we never discussed it, I think my "aggressive leader" recognized a philosophy of letting the individual solve his own problems so that he could maintain his independence. Stated differently: *Any time you do something that makes someone dependent, you have done him a great disservice.* He is no longer in charge of his life; you (or your program) are. In the process you have diminished him to some degree—at a cost that cannot be measured in dollars!

Why should a company provide for the entire, ever-changing needs of its employees? What gives it the right? Is it ethical to try to seduce an employee by providing for his every need while he is on the job and then at the

[19] The world's foremost exponent of this credo must certainly be my wife, Sandy Corcoran. She takes in information over a brief period of time, makes a decision without waiting for further information and analysis, and then does whatever is necessary to back up the decision. She is most effective.

end of a day sending him home, where he must cope unaided with problems in a more natural setting? Is it moral to attempt to bring about the marriage of man and organization?

Are these not questions for the cost accountant to raise as he does his work? Certainly there is an ethical aspect to the cost accountant's work, although ethics is not widely discussed in the cost literature.

I would like to add support to Maslow's observation that some people never get beyond lower-level needs, and to Argyris' observations that in some situations, management should wisely adopt Theory X assumptions. Some years ago I was observing inventory counting during the audit of a manufacturer. Part of the product consisted of cylindrical steel tubes that were placed in bins after they were formed. I was told that each filled bin contained 720 tubes, but found, on checking, that some contained 960 tubes. When the tubes were arranged in neat echelons, there were indeed 720. When every other row was indented so that each tube in that given row fitted in the niche between the two tubes in the row above it, there were 960 tubes. (This was a practical instance of the mathematical puzzle known as the King's Chest.) The workers, who were paid on a piece rate basis, nearly staged a walkout when one of them overheard my musings! The company had been making this product for over 20 years, and during this period several hundred workers would have been exposed to the situation regularly. Were these thinking people, or had boredom rendered them automatons?

The existence of boredom on production lines was widely documented in newspaper and magazine accounts during 1972 and 1973. Any theory that relies on a thinking man is apt to be of little help in such cases. The question for accounting and management, however, is not how to motivate zombies, but rather how to prevent this condition from arising.

One of the main attacks on boredom comes through eliminating barriers to communication. Fortunately, improving his communicative abilities holds far greater significance for the accountant than helping to conquer employee boredom; improved communications will mean better financial reports and more effective analyses.

Just realizing what obstacles he faces should help an intelligent person to improve his communicative efforts. The main problems are

(1) poor sender skills (poorly organized, bad voice modulation, inability to write, impatient, unable to empathize with receiver or to deal with his frame of reference);

(2) poor receiver skills (inattentive reader, listener);

(3) stereotyping (categorizing an individual as a member of a group);

(4) selective perception (receiver shuts out threatening, undesirable material and cues in to positive material);

(5) halo effect (your generalized image of a person influences your judgment of a specific achievement);

(6) hostile receiver;

(7) poor timing;

(8) distractions of all sorts;

(9) distrust of sender;

(10) disinterest;

(11) disruptive atmosphere (treacherous, excessively formal or political);

(12) distrust of receiver;

(13) semantic difficulties (limited vocabulary, need to explain explanations);

(14) indirect channels (third-, fourth-hand information);

(15) inability to obtain or interpret prompt and accurate feedback; and

(16) message too complicated, contains too much information.

Space does not permit a discussion of these impediments. Behavioral research has indicated that fear-arousing information—like that contained in accounting reports—may elicit aggressive feelings, distorted recollection of report contents, aroused cautious reactions, rejection of arguments and conclusions, and denial of the personal relevance of the entire report.[20]

Politically Motivated Behavior

If employees were all equally well trained, confident, highly capable, and modest in their ambitions for advancement, organizations and their accountants would not have to worry much about politically motivated behavior. It is fantasy, of course, to think that an organization composed of such individuals ever existed.

What would constitute a personal political strategy in business? Some indications are offered by Bass, who contrasted political versus desirable social actions as follows:[21]

---

[20] One interesting report that also contains extensive references about this behavior is P. R. Robbins, "Level of Anxiety, Interference Proneness, and Defensive Reactions to Fear-arousing Information," *Journal of Personality*, June 1963.

[21] Bernard M. Bass, "How to Succeed in Business According to Business Students and Managers," *Journal of Applied Psychology*, June 1968, p. 258.

Political	*Social*
Withhold the release of information or time its release for when it will do the most good.	Level with others; be open, frank, and candid in their communications with others.
Act confidently when they are personally unsure about matters or when they lack relevant information.	Share in decision-making with their subordinates whenever possible.
Make political alliances with superiors and subordinates to foster and protect mutual interests.	Completely and openly commit themselves to a position or program.
Initiate actions which they are personally against but retard and delay carrying out the actions so that the actions are in progress but never completed.	Try to establish in advance mutual satisfactory objectives with others with whom they must work.
Maintain social distance; remain aloof, detached, uninvolved with others; always remain the boss when interacting with subordinates.	Foster mutual trust with others.
Openly compromise, yet privately divert or delay compromise plans so that their own aims will be pursued despite the stated compromise.	Arrange for their superiors and their subordinates to meet together to encourage group discussions among others above and below them in the organization with easy participation by all.

Undoubtedly you could add to the list if you took time to think about the lies, deceit, and ingratiating behavior that you have observed over the years.

Du Brin cites five causes of political maneuvering:

1. There is competition for power in organizations.
2. Employees distrust management's ability to measure the performance of its subordinates.
3. Managerial mobility is so great that there are insufficient gestation periods in which to assess performance on previous assignments.
4. The Peter Principle operates—that is, managers are promoted so rapidly that they wind up in positions that demand more ability than they possess.
5. Managers have trouble shifting from older, autocratic to newer, democratic styles.[22]

---

[22] Du Brin, *Organizational Behavior*, pp. 140–41. Chapter 5, on political maneuvering, is most illuminating.

Du Brin goes on to discuss strategies for career advancement and power acquisition such as maintaining mobility, ingratiating yourself with your boss, finding a sponsor who is highly placed in the organization, exhibiting and obtaining loyalty, discrediting others, empire building, securing unnecessarily large budgets, maintaining powerful alliances, embracing managers of merged associated organizations or dismissing them, dividing and ruling, manipulating classified information, making a quick showing on a minor problem collecting IOUs for past favors, avoiding decisive engagements, getting a toe in the door, creating crises, and avoiding subordinate participation in decisions.[23] When you stop to think that, as an accountant, you will probably *at least* be helping some manager to further his career on a political—as opposed to a competence—basis, you may well be annoyed—and possibly more interested in influencing others' behavior.

Procedural Schemes

Management by Exception

Modern corporations are so complicated and their transactions are so numerous that it is necessary to streamline all control systems. The manager simply cannot look at every transaction affecting his group, and this had led to wholesale adoption of the principle of management by exception. According to this principle, which lies at the heart of standard cost and budget variance analysis as well as that of production control procedures, management only investigates a performance that departs significantly from the accepted norm.

This seems to be a wise principle, but it has a subtle defect. Consider:

> Breathes there a man so intrepid
> Who ever to his wife has said,
> "Don't bore me with banalities;
> Just big events and crises, please."[24]

The husband who recognizes only the unusual is soon confronted by an indignant wife who feels he has taken her for granted. That is likewise the danger of management by exception as embodied in traditional accounting systems like standard cost variance analysis: performance at standard may

---

[23] Ibid., pp. 147–63.

[24] This poem was written by Mrs. Edwin A. Fessenden, a dear friend, who wrote it at my request when she was 89 years old.

simply be taken for granted. And this is to say nothing about the wisdom—from a behavioral viewpoint—of reprimanding employees because they have not achieved standard. Is this the best way to motivate human beings? Is not a new conception called for?

Management by Objectives

One scheme for managing people that has attracted many enthusiastic supporters is known as "management by objectives" or simply MBO. I could attempt to summarize the main tenets of MBO, especially as it might be applied in accounting, but its main proponent, Dr. George Odiorne, is a colleague and has graciously consented to speak for himself; George Odiorne:[25]

Management by Objectives

General Introduction

1. Management by objectives is a way of getting improved results in managerial action. It's not an addition to a manager's job, it's *a way of doing it.*

2. It's based on observations of what successful executives do in many companies and organizations (General Mills, General Motors, Minneapolis-Honeywell, IBM, and General Electric, to name a few).

3. It is especially pertinent in *managing managers*, and most applications have been limited to upper levels of management. It can extend down as far as first-line supervision, provided top management endorses and supports it through using it.

4. It relates to several key problems in managing an organization:
   (a) what is expected—in terms of *objectives;*
   (b) obtaining teamwork—by identifying common goals;
   (c) programming work—by setting *terminal dates* for tasks;
   (d) recognizing progress—through mutual agreement on goals and accomplishment against them;
   (e) administering salary—how would increases be allocated? and
   (f) assessing promotability—by identifying *potential* for it.

[25] Two of the many books Dr. Odiorne has written on MBO are *Management by Objectives: A System of Managerial Leadership* (New York: Pitman Publishers, 1965); and *Management and the Activity Trap*, (New York: Haper & Row, 1974).

5. In its briefest form, management by objectives can be described as a managerial method whereby the superior and the subordinate managers in an organization identify major areas of responsibility in which the man will work, set some standards for good—or bad—performance, and measure results against those standards.

6. The advantages of this kind of management are in better results, lower costs, improved performance, more promotable people, improved quality of service, more businesslike management of salaries, and the development of subordinates' best abilities.

How then does MBO serve as a motivator, and how does this bear upon accounting?

Accounting as a Motivational Influence

In the welter of information and theory from the behavioral sciences about motivation I can see three factors that produce or affect motivation. These are information, obstacle removal, and payoffs. Certainly accounting can have an influence in shaping the organization into a motivated body of people.

Information. Accounting affects motivation primarily by providing four kinds of information:

(1) what is expected in terms of budgets, profit plans, and the indicators by which success will be measured (ROI, earnings, return on gross assets and similar criteria);

(2) what resources will be available to achieve the objectives stated in the budgets and profit plans;

(3) what the results of actual—as compared with target—performance are; and

(4) what success and failure indicators are in accounting terms. Accounting should measure the financial consequences of behavior in the real world and should have an important effect on the amount and quality of that behavior through feedback.

It is known that feedback of success and failure are important influences in learning theory and motivation theory. One psychologist has stated that almost all motivation theory is rooted in feedback. While not all agree with this hard-nosed explanation, it has much to commend it.

Obstacle Removal. When results falter behind expectation, the accounting system can provide the motivational influence needed to remove obstacles. It can identify responsible persons. The whole field of responsibility accounting is rooted in psychological theory more than in accounting technique. It presumes that people who are committed to goals will feel obliged to seek them if they are responsible, know they are responsible, have made commitments to others whose opinion is important, and have some reason for doing so. The key question to be asked in the face of budget deviances or profit failures isn't always "Who is responsible and who's to blame?" but "What is wrong and what should be done to correct it?" Accounting that finds scapegoats rather than causes and cures can be countermotivational.

Payoffs. There are some chronic problems in managing people that accounting information helps solve.

1. Who is succeeding and who isn't?
2. Who should get a higher level of responsibility and who shouldn't?
3. What kind of training and coaching is needed to get things done better?
4. Are we doing the right things as well as doing things right?
5. How should we evaluate performance; against what criteria?
6. In the event of failure, can we refer back to the beginning of the period to assure ourselves that targets and goals were clear to the person failing? If not, should we withhold payoffs?

These are the three key areas of motivation from accounting. I would like to see accounting departments change their names to INFORMATION departments, to reflect what they *produce* rather than what they *do*.

Summary

This chapter has detailed some of the theories of famous behavioral researchers (and one amateur). The motivating idea was to provide background for the work ahead so that *you* might conceive ways to improve cost accounting systems, cost reports, and your overall relationships with your co-workers.

As an accountant, you must bear the burden of tradition and not seek to discard procedures that, however imperfect, have nonetheless contributed to the success of thousands of businesses. Improving procedures—as long as improvement is not" in the eye of the beholder"—is an admirable objective, but one that must be pursued cautiously. The possibilities for improvement may be blatantly obvious, but improvement involves change and may not be welcomed by all those it affects. Introducing a good idea at the wrong time and in the wrong way is not only frustrating but stupid. Besides, it does not do justice to the idea. Patience and perception—as well as creativity—are necessary if an idea is to be conceived and implemented successfully.

Problems

1. Describe how you would motivate an individual—in one sentence;—in one paragraph;—in a two-page essay.

2. How would you make use in cost accounting of some of the ideas of Magregor? Of Maslow? Of Herzberg? Of Argyris? Of Likert? Of Du Brin? Of Odiorne?

3. Elbert Green Hubbard, a popular American writer and philosopher who lived from 1856–1915, says:

> The typical auditor is a man past middle age, spare, wrinkled, intelligent, cold, passive, non-committal, with eyes like a codfish, polite in contact, but at the same time unresponsive, cold; calm and damnably composed as a concrete post or a plaster-of-paris cast; a human petrification with a heart of feldspar and without charm of the friendly germ, minus bowels, passion, or a sense of humor. Happily, they never reproduce and all of them finally go to Hell."

   If this is how people regard "the front-office cost accountant," how will it affect him and his work? Should he try to change his image? If so, how should he go about it?

4. Argyris has theorized that accountability, budgetary controls, production schedules, and quotas interfere with higher-level drives and make employees submissive and dependent. In describing MBO, Odiorne recommends that managers state their expectations in the form of budgets and other plans, compare results with targets, and use performance feedback to control behavior.

   (a) What are Argyris and Odiorne saying about the neutrality of reports?

   (b) Stage a debate in class with students arguing the opposing positions.

   (c) If both men are right, what does this say about the nature of people in business?

   (d) McClelland and Winters comment on high achievers. Where do their findings fit into the argument?

   (e) Would Du Brin clarify or complicate the discussion?

5. Reconcile Odiorne's position with the following statement in the text: "Behavioral research has indicated that fear-arousing information—like that contained in accounting reports—may elicit aggressive feelings, distorted recollection of report contents, aroused cautious reactions, rejection of arguments and conclusions, and denial of the personal relevance of the entire report."

6. Comment on Peter Drucker's position that the standard of the best performer is the only one that can motivate the work of others.

7. Wernimount and Fitzpatrick suggest that if one is deprived of money long enough, it may begin to decrease in importance. Tie this idea to Herzberg's motivation-hygiene theory, equity theory, and the danger of penalties.

8. Which theory best explains why you are reading this book? What needs of yours are being met?

9. What needs of yours are not being met?

10. In this chapter participation in goal setting has been treated almost like a panacea. Interestingly, were you to read Likert extensively, you would decide that he thinks all organizations would be better off using the Participative-Group style of management. Do you agree?

11. Does an employee have a right to be a loner? Must he leave his individuality and solitude outside the corporate door?

12. The "corporate ladder" is a well-known phenomenon. Criticize it from a behavioral standpoint.

13. How often does standard, good, and bad performance need recognition?

14. *Don't forget Machiavelli (prepared by Mr. William Pownall).* A new man is brought in as regional sales manager for a large college textbook publisher. In the past his region has been known as one in which it is so difficult to sell books that very little sustained effort has been made in that direction. His first actions are to fire several salesmen who have not made much effort to do their jobs properly for several years. He also institutes much tighter controls over quotas for individual salesmen, and makes sure they are met. He does this without promising his people anything except that they will be in trouble and may lose their jobs if they do not measure up.

(a) According to Magregor, he is using:
  (1) Theory X
  (2) Theory Y

(b) Is the act of firing improper for a manager?

As time goes by, however, the same manager does all he can to get large raises for his employees from the home office; furthermore, he helps them in their efforts to obtain bonuses and promotions for their sales efforts and special awards for excellence.

(c) According to the theories of Maslow, he is attending to which of the five basic needs of the individual?
(1) physiological
(2) safety
(3) belongingness
(4) esteem
(5) self-actualization
(6) needs 1, 2, 4, and 5
(7) all of these
(8) none of these

(d) The same company hires a new national sales manager. During the first national sales meeting he institutes a session (never attempted before on such a scale) in which the employees are encouraged to "brainstorm" ways in which the company and its procedures can be improved. He has tried a device described closely by which of the theorists described in this chapter?
(1) Magregor: X vs. Y Theory
(2) Maslow: the hierarchy of needs
(3) Herzberg: the motivation-hygiene theory
(4) Argyris: changing the organization to suit employees
(5) Likert: group bestowing power

(e) Whichever answer you chose, defend it in 100 words or less.

15. *Compensation plan and motivation (adapted from Certificate in Management Accounting Examination, December 1973).* The Parsons Co. compensates its field sales force on a commission and year-end bonus basis. The commission is 20% of standard gross margin (planned selling price less standard cost of goods sold on a full absorption basis) contingent upon collection of the account. Customer's credit is approved by the company's credit department. Price concessions are granted on occasion by the top sales management, but sales commissions are not reduced by the discount. A year end bonus of 15% of commissions earned is paid to salesmen who equal or exceed their annual sales target. The annual sales target is usually established by applying approximately a 5% increase to the prior year's sales.

Required

(a) What features of this compensation plan would seem to be effective in motivating the salesmen to accomplish company goals of higher profits and return on investment? Explain why.

(b) What features of this compensation plan would seem to be countereffective in motivating the salesmen to accomplish the company goals of higher profits and return on investment? Explain why.

Cost Behavior and Forecasting

3

Where Are We Going?

We just finished an extensive chapter on human behavior. It seems only fitting that we allow equal time for examining cost behavior.

Cost behavior is the study of how costs are affected when variables such as volume change. Some costs are not influenced in any way by volume; these are called "fixed" costs in accounting. Other costs change proportionally with volume changes; these are referred to as "variable" costs. In between these extremes are found costs that are known as "semifixed" or "semivariable" because they consist of portions that do not vary with volume changes coupled with portions that do vary.

Cost accountants are very concerned with cost behavior because, among other things, it is fundamental (1) to developing control—variable costs are considered controllable at the lowest levels of management, while fixed costs are often only controllable at the very highest levels; (2) to calculating overhead rates; (3) to preparing period budgets; and (4) to implementing responsibility accounting.

Sometimes cost behavior does not require much analysis, as for instance when electricity is billed to a company at a monthly charge of $500 plus $.01 per kilowatt hour (situation A in Figure 1) or when a secretary is hired for every three office professionals or fraction thereof and paid $8,000 per year (situation B in Figure 1).

The major tool for studying cost behavior in circumstances where relationships are not explicitly stated is regression analysis. Regression is used to estimate some underlying relation in the data, with straight lines—which are curves without any bends in them—being, by far, the most popular curve form. Essentially regression expresses past relationships in a formula that may then be used to forecast costs.

Regression, of course, is not the only way to accomplish forecasting. We shall also study exponential smoothing, another forecasting technique, in

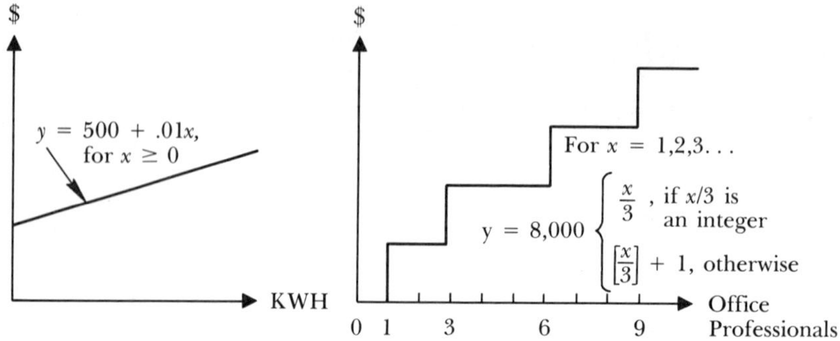

Situation A (Electric Bill)

Situation B (Secretarial Cost)

Note: In Situation B, brackets have been employed to designate the largest integer part of $x/3$ (e.g., $[8/3] = 2$).

Figure 1

this chapter. Later chapters will develop the use of probabilities and models as means of estimating costs, revenues, and profits.

We will begin discussion with the "high-low" method, which is a traditional technique in accounting that is used when time and/or cost do not permit a complete regression study. High-low is fast and uncomplicated, albeit a very weak substitute for regression. Listed in Table 1 are data that

Table 1

	Cost (000 omitted)	Volume (000 omitted)			← Variance Information →		
					Total	Explained	Unexplained
Year	y	x	x^2	xy	$(\bar{y} - y)^2$	$(\bar{y} - \hat{y})^2$	$(\hat{y} - y)^2$
1963		60	3,600	15,720	1,806.25	2,784.70	105.48
1964	230	55	3,025	12,650	5,550.25	4,761.99	30.17
1965	247	72	5,184	17,784	3,306.25	190.48	1,909.56
1966	258	62	3,844	15,996	2,162.25	2,141.41	.05
1967	240	58	3,364	13,920	4,160.25	3,512.34	27.41
1968	330	75	5,625	24,750	650.25	16.48	873.75
1969	314	74	5,476	23,236	90.25	53.39	282.46
1970	340	85	7,225	28,900	1,260.25	807.40	50.20
1971	348	88	7,744	30,624	1,892.25	1,455.95	28.55
1972	360	94	8,836	33,840	3,080.25	3,322.52	4.59
1973	350	92	8,464	32,200	2,070.25	2,615.97	31.88
1974	375	100	10,000	37,500	4,970.25	5,948.37	43.90
Totals ($\sum$)	$3,654	915	72,387	287,120	30,999.00	27,611.00	3,388.00

will be used in subsequent discussions in the chapter. Cost for each year is found in the column containing y values, while the corresponding volume appears under the column containing x values.
Thus,

$$y_i = \text{cost in year } i$$

$$x_i = \text{volume in year } i$$

The column labelled xy shows the product of the x_i and y_i readings and the x^2 column merely squares the x_i readings. A plot of the readings appears in Figure 2.

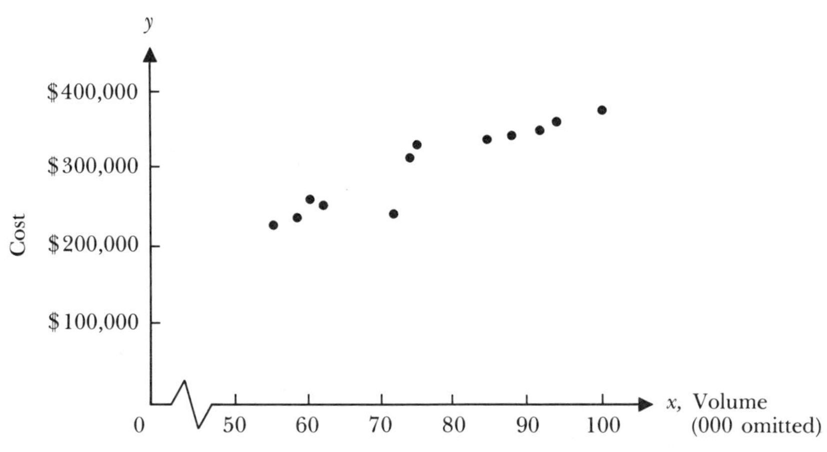

Figure 2

The High-Low Method

In the strict application of the high-low method, the highest and lowest points are used to fit a straight line, $y = a + bx$. In our case this would not seem to generate any appreciable error because, as you can see from the plot of the data, a straight line would apparently very nearly touch every data point. Were it otherwise—with the highest and lowest points resting at an angle to one another that was considerably different from the angle of the line that would appear to accommodate most of the other points—then use of the highest and lowest points would yield very unreliable results. In such a case it would usually be wiser to take two other points that were more representative.

	Year	y	x
Highest point:	1974	\$375,000	100,000
Lowest point:	1964	230,000	55,000
Δ (difference):		\$145,000	45,000

$$\text{The slope of the unknown line} = \Delta y/\Delta x = \$145{,}000/45{,}000 = \$3.22 = b$$

$$\text{The equation for the unknown line: } y = a + bx = a + \$3.22x$$

$$\text{When } x = 100{,}000, \text{ we obtain: } y = \$375{,}000 = a + \$3.22(100{,}000)$$
$$\therefore, \quad a = \$53{,}000$$

$$\text{The equation for costs becomes: } y = \$53{,}000 + \$3.22x = \text{fixed cost} + \text{variable cost}$$

What have we learned? We now know that y is a semi-variable cost, and we can use the equation to estimate (forecast) next year's cost provided we can first obtain some idea of volume. Say 1975 volume is estimated at 80,000; then the estimated 1975 cost is

$$y = \$53{,}000 + \$3.22(80{,}000) = \$310{,}600$$

We do not know, unfortunately, how well the forecasting equation fits the data. And this is a troublesome point. Had we used the data for 1963 and 1972, for instance, the line would then be

$$y = \$89{,}200 + \$2.88x$$

This equation is significantly different from the previous one. If we can learn one thing from this difference, it is that sometimes plots of points appear more linear than they are, owing to the scales chosen for the axes. Secondly, we have come upon an important caveat: A slight difference in slope (the variable rate) can cause a great difference in intercept (the fixed cost). In the present example, a 10.6% decrease in slope resulted in a 68.3% increase in intercept. Knowing that such variation is possible, the accountant may hesitate to rely on the high-low method.

If you do not have time to peruse the rest of this chapter carefully, you should at least skim it, skipping the details of proofs and noting the caveats inherent in fitting lines to data. If time is not a problem, you will be far better off if you understand the basic theory and mechanics of regression analysis, which is a vastly superior tool to the high-low method, as well as the technique of exponential smoothing, which is useful in forecasting when greater reliance is to be placed upon certain data. If you have never studied sampling theory before, you might want to read the Chapter 13 first. However, this is not necessary, since the regression material is fairly self-contained and, in fact, could be viewed as providing motivation for studying sampling.

Regression and Correlation Analysis

Background

When a statistician performs regression analysis, he "reasons" back from one variable to a set of one or more other variables to determine their association. If a cause-effect relationship exists, it is *brought* to the analysis, not *discovered* (*or created*) by it; all the regression analysis does is to state how variables are related (associated). Variables, unfortunately, can be related without the existence of causality. Thus an automobile manufacturer's sales may be *related* to the number of entering freshman coeds at a given university by the equation $S = 500C + 10{,}000$. The sales might even be *related* to the number of fleas on the hide of a particular all-American dog. However, it seems ridiculous to say that the sales were *caused* by the number of coeds or by the number of fleas. Of course the coeds (or their misguided fathers) do buy cars, and we would feel somewhat more confident in saying that the number of coeds caused the number of car sales than we would in saying that the sales were brought about by the fleas. The statistician, however, would avoid such causality arguments altogether unless the association was justifiable on other grounds. He might not feel bad saying that automobile sales were caused by the extent of personal disposable income in the economy, but even then he would prefer to recognize that several variables might collectively "cause" sales. He would be more willing to say that automobile sales were "strongly associated" with personal disposal income.

Usually the statistician would choose words other than "strongly associated." He would say something like, "Automobile sales exhibit a high, positive correlation with personal disposable income." By choosing this terminology, he indicates "strong" by "high," "association" by "correlation," and the direction of association by "positive" (that is, as one variable increases, so does the other one). Determining the degree of association is, then, the subject of correlation analysis.

As our discussion of regression and correlation unfolds, remember that what we are doing is measuring association and not establishing causality.

Suppose you had extensive data on a particular cost that exhibits fluctuation. What single estimate would you make of this cost for the coming year? Many people would answer this question by saying, "Just about the same amount as last year." This might be a fine answer, even though it ignores the fluctuation previously observed. Many other people might respond, "The average cost would seem to be as relevant as any other figure." This, too, might be a good answer; in the absence of any further information, the average incorporates all the fluctuating data and has the support of mathematical theory. However, there might well be other data obviously related to the cost that have to do with some level of activity in the organization and/or in the economy in which it resides. Knowing the level of activity may permit the use of regression to improve the estimate of the cost. In determining whether improvement has occurred, comparisons are drawn among regression estimates, the observed data, and the mean (average) of the past costs.

The Regression Line

Take the time to study Figure 3, which depicts (1) the observations; (2) the estimating equation that runs through the middle of the data (technically, the equation that makes the sum of the distances between it and the observations above and below equal to zero); (3) the fact that the estimating line passes through the point $(\bar{x}, \bar{y})$; and (4) the various differences between y_i, $\bar{y}$, and $\hat{y}_i$ (that is, the ith observation of cost, the average cost, and the ith regression estimate of cost). For the moment we shall ignore the fact that our observations are considered samples from a population, because *initially* our goal is to determine the estimating line and not to make probabilistic statements about the result.

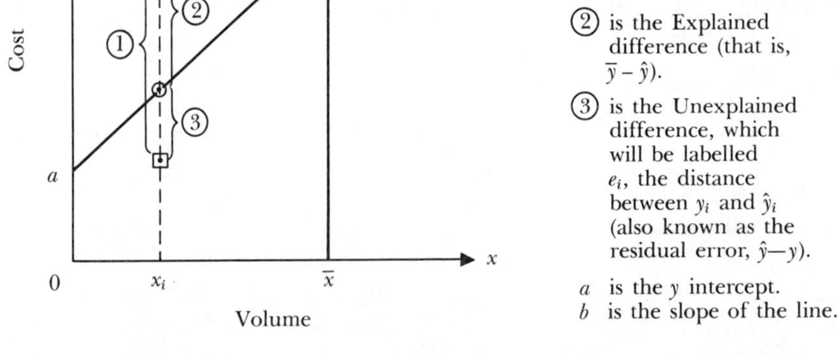

Figure 3

It has been observed that if the error terms were simply summed (i.e., $\sum(\hat{y}_i - y_i) = \sum e_i$), the result would be 0 and the totality of positive errors would simply offset the totality of negative errors. To prevent this and to give each error a weighting so that large errors are considered worse than small errors, each error term is squared. We sum the squares of the error (e_i) terms and minimize the sum S, keeping in mind that we are trying to estimate the unknowns in the regression equation, a and b (and not x and y, which are empirical data).

$$S = \sum e_i^2 = \sum(y_i - \hat{y}_i)^2 = \sum(y_i - a - bx_i)^2$$

We assume subscripts are understood to simplify notation and then take partial derivatives to determine the values of a and b that minimize the sum S:

$$\frac{\partial S}{\partial a} = -2\sum(y - a - bx) = 0, \quad \text{at the minimum}$$

$$\therefore, \quad \sum y = \sum(a + bx) = \sum a + \sum bx$$

Since $\sum a$ says that a appears in each of the n equations, we have $\sum a = na$.

Therefore, $$\sum y = na + b\sum x.$$

$$\frac{\partial S}{\partial b} = -2\sum x(y - a - bx) = 0$$

$$\therefore, \quad \sum xy = \sum x(a + bx)$$

$$\sum xy = a\sum x + b\sum x^2$$

Interestingly enough, we could have obtained these results more easily by taking the equation for a straight line, $y = a + bx$, and (1) summing both sides of the equation to obtain $\sum y = na + b\sum x$, and (2) multiplying both sides of the equation by x and then summing to obtain $\sum xy = a\sum x + b\sum x^2$.[1]

We now have what are known as the normal equations of the regression line:

$$na + b\sum x = \sum y$$

$$a\sum x + b\sum x^2 = \sum xy$$

[1] Using second-order partial derivatives to prove that a minimum has been reached with the values of a and b that result from solving these equations will be left to the reader as problem 5.

In matrices this system of equations becomes

$$\begin{bmatrix} n & \sum x \\ \sum x & \sum x^2 \end{bmatrix} \begin{bmatrix} a \\ b \end{bmatrix} = \begin{bmatrix} \sum y \\ \sum xy \end{bmatrix}$$

Relabelling the matrices in symbols we shall shortly explain and regularly use, we obtain

$$(X^T X)\, B = \qquad (X^T Y)$$

Solving:

$$\underbrace{(X^T X)^{-1}(X^T X)}_{I}\, B = (X^T X)^{-1}(X^T Y)$$

$$B = (X^T X)^{-1}(X^T Y)$$

$$B = (X^T X)^{-1}(X^T Y)$$

Here matrix X contains the observed x data as well as a column of ones to allow for an intercept.

B is a label for the regression coefficient estimates and provides for both a and b in the two-dimensional case. This formula is widely used in mathematical statistics for a number of reasons, one being that it remains unchanged (except for the number of columns in the X matrix) whether two, three, four, or more variables are used in the analysis. You will come to appreciate this more when we discuss multiple regression.

Let us see how all this looks in terms of matrix elements:

$$\overset{X^T}{\begin{bmatrix} 1 & 1 & \cdots & 1 \\ x_1 & x_2 & \cdots & x_n \end{bmatrix}} \overset{X}{\begin{bmatrix} 1 & x_1 \\ 1 & x_2 \\ \vdots & \vdots \\ 1 & x_n \end{bmatrix}} = \overset{X^T X}{\begin{bmatrix} n & \sum x \\ \sum x & \sum x^2 \end{bmatrix}},$$

the left-hand side matrix in equation (1)

$$\overset{X^T}{\begin{bmatrix} 1 & 1 & \cdots & 1 \\ x_1 & x_2 & \cdots & x_n \end{bmatrix}} \overset{Y}{\begin{bmatrix} y_1 \\ y_2 \\ \vdots \\ y_n \end{bmatrix}} = \overset{X^T Y}{\begin{bmatrix} \sum y \\ \sum xy \end{bmatrix}},$$

the right-hand side vector in equation (1)

$$\overset{B}{\begin{bmatrix} a \\ b \end{bmatrix}} = \overset{(X^T X)^{-1}}{\frac{\begin{bmatrix} \sum x^2 & -\sum x \\ -\sum x & n \end{bmatrix}}{n\sum x^2 - (\sum x)^2}} \overset{X^T Y}{\begin{bmatrix} \sum y \\ \sum xy \end{bmatrix}} = \frac{\begin{bmatrix} \sum x^2 \sum y - \sum x \sum xy \\ n\sum xy - \sum x \sum y \end{bmatrix}}{n\sum x^2 - (\sum x)^2}$$

Inserting the data for cost and volume shown in Table 1, we obtain

$$\overset{X^T}{\begin{bmatrix} 1 & 1 & \cdots & 1 \\ 60 & 55 & \cdots & 100 \end{bmatrix}} \overset{X}{\begin{bmatrix} 1 & 60 \\ 1 & 55 \\ \vdots & \vdots \\ 1 & 100 \end{bmatrix}} = \overset{X^TX}{\begin{bmatrix} 12 & 915 \\ 915 & 72{,}387 \end{bmatrix}}$$

$$\overset{X^T}{\begin{bmatrix} 1 & 1 & \cdots & 1 \\ 60 & 55 & \cdots & 100 \end{bmatrix}} \overset{Y}{\begin{bmatrix} 262 \\ 230 \\ \vdots \\ 375 \end{bmatrix}} = \overset{X^TY}{\begin{bmatrix} 3{,}654 \\ 287{,}120 \end{bmatrix}}$$

$$B = \quad (X^TX)^{-1} \quad X^TY$$

$$= \frac{\begin{bmatrix} 72{,}387 & -915 \\ -915 & 12 \end{bmatrix}}{12(72{,}387) - 915^2} \begin{bmatrix} 3{,}654 \\ 287{,}120 \end{bmatrix}$$

$$= \frac{\begin{bmatrix} 72{,}387 & -915 \\ -915 & 12 \end{bmatrix}}{31{,}419} \begin{bmatrix} 3{,}654 \\ 287{,}120 \end{bmatrix}$$

$$= \begin{bmatrix} 2.3039243 & -.0291225 \\ -.0291225 & .0003819 \end{bmatrix} \begin{bmatrix} 3{,}654 \\ 287{,}120 \end{bmatrix} = \begin{bmatrix} 56.8859 \\ 3.2472 \end{bmatrix}$$

The estimating equation is $\hat{y} = 56.8859 + 3.2474x$ and, upon restoration of the omitted 000, becomes

$$\hat{y} = \$56{,}885.90 + \$3.2474x$$
$$= \text{fixed cost} + \text{variable cost}$$

Goodness of fit. How good is this equation? For that matter, how does one measure "good"? Goodness of fit in regression is measured by the coefficient of determination (designated r^2), which is the ratio of explained variation divided by total variation, that is,

$$r^2 = \frac{\text{Explained variation}}{\text{Total variation}} = \frac{\sum(\bar{y} - \hat{y})^2}{\sum(\bar{y} - y)^2}$$

We shall investigate what is explained, unexplained, and total and prove that the total variation equals the sum of the explained variation plus the unexplained variation. The logic of this dichotomous separation of whole into parts seems apparent, but when it is viewed observation-by-observation, and when the squared differences are considered, what was obvious soon becomes doubtful (for example, $10 = 8 + 2$ but $10^2 \neq 8^2 + 2^2$).

We seek to prove that the total variation equals the sum of the explained and unexplained variations. By "explained" variation we mean the decrease in total variation that is brought about by the fact that we will estimate a value of the dependent variable based on the additional (associated) information we have about the independent variable—instead of just estimating the dependent variable to be equal to its own average. Refer to the numbers in Figure 3 and its key; we wish to prove:

①		②		③
Total Variation	=	Explained Variation	+	Unexplained Variation
$\sum(\bar{y} - y)^2$		$= \sum(\bar{y} - \hat{y})^2$		$+ \sum(\hat{y} - y)^2$

Substitutions:

$$\hat{y} = a + bx$$

From the normal equations which are in terms of actual observations:

$$\sum y = na + b\sum x = \sum(a + bx) = \sum \hat{y}$$

$$\sum xy = a\sum x + b\sum x^2$$

Also

$$\sum y\hat{y} = \sum y(a + bx) = a\sum y + b\sum xy$$

Proof:

$\sum(\bar{y} - \hat{y})^2 + \sum(\hat{y} - y)^2 =$ the sum of explained variation and unexplained variation

$$\begin{aligned} &= \sum(\bar{y}^2 - 2\bar{y}\hat{y} + \hat{y}^2) + \sum(\hat{y}^2 - 2y\hat{y} + y^2) \\ &= \sum\bar{y}^2 - 2\bar{y}\sum\hat{y} + 2\sum\hat{y}^2 - 2\sum y\hat{y} + \sum y^2 \\ &= \sum\bar{y}^2 - 2\bar{y}\sum y + 2\sum\hat{y}^2 - 2\sum y\hat{y} + \sum y^2 \end{aligned}$$

But

$$\begin{aligned} \sum y\hat{y} &= a\sum y + b\sum xy \\ &= a(na + b\sum x) + b(a\sum x + b\sum x^2) \\ &= na^2 + 2ab\sum x + b^2\sum x^2 \\ &= \sum(a^2 + 2abx + b^2x^2) \\ &= \sum(a + bx)^2 \\ &= \sum\hat{y}^2 \end{aligned}$$

$$= \sum \bar{y}^2 - 2\sum \bar{y}y + 2\sum \hat{y}^2 - 2\sum \hat{y}^2 + \sum y^2$$
$$= \sum (\bar{y}^2 - 2\bar{y}y + y^2)$$
$$= \sum (\bar{y} - y)^2 = \text{the total variation, as was to be shown}$$

We can now form the ratio and determine r^2 for our regression line:

$$\frac{\text{Explained variation}}{\text{Total variation}} = \frac{\sum(\bar{y} - \hat{y})^2}{\sum(\bar{y} - y)^2} = \frac{27{,}611}{30{,}999} = .89 = r^2$$

The figures above have been drawn from the appropriate column totals in Table 1. For the sake of concreteness let us compute the figures in the first row of Table 1 for each of the last three columns; the other rows would be similarly obtained.

$$\bar{y} = \sum y/n = 3{,}654/12 = 304.5$$
$$y = 262$$
$$\hat{y} = 56.8859 + 3.2474(60) = 251.73$$

Therefore,
$$(\bar{y} - y)^2 = (304.5 - 262)^2 = 1{,}806.25$$
$$(\bar{y} - \hat{y})^2 = (304.5 - 251.73)^2 = 2{,}784.70$$
$$(\hat{y} - y)^2 = (251.73 - 262)^2 = 105.47$$

We also note:

Explained variation	27,611
Unexplained variation	3,388
Total variation	30,999

Before leaving the coefficient of determination, let us examine its components to see that $r^2 = [\text{Cov}(x, y)]^2 \div V(x)V(y)$, a fact that will later be useful to know.

$$r^2 = \frac{\sum(\bar{y} - \hat{y})^2}{\sum(\bar{y} - y)^2} = \frac{\sum(\bar{y} - \hat{y})^2/n}{\sum(\bar{y} - y)^2/n} = \frac{\sum(\bar{y} - \hat{y})^2/n}{V(y)}$$

However,
$$\frac{1}{n}\sum(\bar{y} - \hat{y})^2 = \frac{1}{n}\sum(\hat{y} - \bar{y})^2 = \frac{1}{n}\sum(a + bx - \bar{y})^2$$
$$= \frac{1}{n}\sum(a + bx)^2 - \frac{2}{n}\sum(a + bx)\bar{y} + \frac{1}{n}\sum \bar{y}^2$$
$$= a^2 + 2ab\bar{x} + b^2(\textstyle\sum x^2/n) - 2a\bar{y} - 2b\bar{x}\bar{y} + \bar{y}^2$$
$$= (a - \bar{y})^2 + 2b\bar{x}(a - \bar{y}) + b^2\textstyle\sum x^2/n$$

continued to page 58

continued from page 57

Completing the square by adding and subtracting $b^2\bar{x}^2$ and grouping terms:

$$\frac{1}{n}\sum(\bar{y}-\hat{y})^2 = [(a-\bar{y})+b\bar{x}]^2 - b^2\bar{x}^2 + b^2\sum x^2/n$$

Using the first normal equation and dividing both sides by n, we see that $\bar{y} = a + b\bar{x}$; hence

$$\frac{1}{n}\sum(\bar{y}-\hat{y})^2 = 0 + b^2((\sum x^2/n) - \bar{x}^2)$$

$$= b^2 V(x)$$

But $$b = \frac{n\sum xy - \sum x \sum y}{n\sum x^2 - (\sum x)^2} = \frac{n^2\text{Cov}(x, y)}{n^2 V(x)} = \frac{\text{Cov}(x, y)}{V(x)}$$

So $$\frac{1}{n}\sum(\bar{y}-\hat{y})^2 = (\text{Cov}(x, y))^2/V(x)$$

$$\therefore, \quad r^2 = \frac{[\text{Cov}(x, y)]^2}{V(x)V(y)}$$

The square root of the coefficient of determination is known as the coefficient of correlation (that is, $r = \sqrt{r^2}$) and is another, albeit less accurate, measure of association. r is usually assigned the sign (+ or −) of b in $\hat{y} = a + bx$.

The Standard Error

At this point the high value obtained for r^2 suggests that regression has significantly improved our ability to estimate cost. There is room for improvement—we have explained only 89% of past variation, not 100%. However, we have appreciably reduced variation and can make more precise estimates. That this is so can best be shown by looking at the standard deviations before and after regression. This brings us to the *standard deviation of regression*, which is also popularly referred to by the somewhat misleading title of the *standard error of the estimate.* (Actually this latter title has led to a whole barrage of statistical puns along the lines that some statisticians' errors are so frequent that they have become standardized. Undoubtedly this sort of merriment accounts for the popularity of the title.)

The standard deviation of regression is designated by $s_{y \cdot x}$ and equals the square root of the *unexplained variance:*

$$s_{y \cdot x} = \sqrt{\frac{\sum(\hat{y}-y)^2}{n}} = \sqrt{\frac{3{,}388}{12}} = 16.80, \text{ in our problem}$$

Had we ignored the volume variable and considered only the random variable sales, we would have obtained the sample standard deviation, s_y, which is simply the square root of total sales variation:

$$s_y = \sqrt{\frac{\sum(\bar{y} - y)^2}{n}} = \sqrt{\frac{30{,}999}{12}} = 50.83, \text{ in our problem}$$

Good practice would have us adjust these estimates for the degrees of freedom lost. For s_y we lose one degree of freedom for having had to use our data to estimate $\bar{y}$; for $s_{y \cdot x}$ we lose two degrees of freedom for estimating the parameters a and b. The modified standard deviation estimates become

$$\hat{s}_y = s_y \sqrt{\frac{n}{n-1}} = 50.83 \sqrt{\frac{12}{11}} = 53.09$$

$$\hat{s}_{y \cdot x} = s_{y \cdot x} \sqrt{\frac{n}{n-2}} = 16.80 \sqrt{\frac{12}{10}} = 18.41$$

The standard error is used primarily to establish confidence limits around estimates in much the same way as a statistician prepares production control charts (a subject that will be addressed at length in Chapter 13), with the result that the estimate can be stated with a desired precision (tolerance) and reliability (confidence).

If we were willing to *assume* (or had reason to believe) that our y observations and consequently the error terms e_i were *normally distributed* (Table 6 in Appendix A), we could then say that had we taken 100 samples of data points, roughly 68 of them would yield lines that lie within plus and minus one standard deviation of regression (somewhat modified to reflect distance from $\bar{x}$, as we shall shortly see) from the line determined from our present sample data. Roughly 95 would lie within plus and minus two standard deviations of regression, and so forth. Unfortunately our sample size is small, and this compels us to use the t distribution (see Table 7 in Appendix A) and the following formula, which will shortly be derived, to obtain a desired *confidence band:*

$$\hat{y} \pm t_{n-2,\alpha/2}\hat{s}_{y \cdot x} \sqrt{\frac{1}{n} + \frac{(x - \bar{x})^2}{\sum(x - \bar{x})^2}}$$

Here, $t_{n-2,\alpha/2}$ is a reading from the t distribution (Table 7 in Appendix A).

Assuming it was desired to establish a 95% confidence band for our cost line, $t_{n-2,\alpha/2} = t_{10,.025} = 2.228$, and the formula becomes

$$(56{,}885.90 + 3.2474x) \pm 2.228(18.41) \sqrt{\frac{1}{12} + \frac{(x - 76.25)^2}{2618.25}}$$

A graph of the results appears in Figure 4.

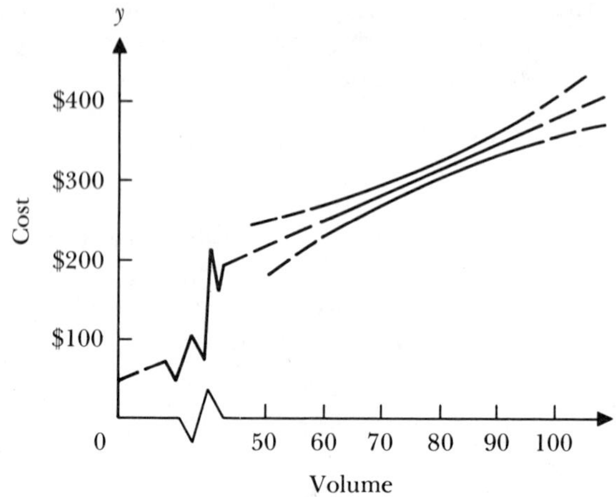

x	Upper	Lower
55	256	215
58	264	226
60	269	234
62	275	242
72	303	278
74	309	285
75	312	289
85	347	319
88	358	328
92	373	338
94	381	344
100	404	359

Figure 4

Note that the confidence band curves. This is due not to the deviation between the y and $\hat{y}$ figures as reflected in $\hat{s}_{y \cdot x}$, for—as inspection of the formula shows—$\hat{s}_{y \cdot x}$ is a constant (this is the assumption of *homoscedasticity*, which will soon be discussed). Rather, the curvature is due to the distance a given x value is from $\bar{x}$ (observe the $(x - \bar{x})^2$ in the formula).[2]

A Preliminary Review and Further Reflection on Regression Theory

Let us focus on some of the theoretical explanations. To begin with, regression analysis is a form of sampling that, like all sampling, has the goal of making inferences about the population based on the information provided by a sample. Many assumptions are made when performing linear regression analysis. Initially it is assumed that the relationship between x and y may be adequately described by a straight line. To ascertain this, a scattergram is often drawn as a preliminary step in the analysis. Secondly, the dependent variable y and the error term e are considered random variables, while the

---

[2] Since variance around an average is less than variance around individuals, the statistician computes a confidence interval for an individual y prediction:

$$\hat{y} \pm t_{n-2,\alpha/2}\hat{s}_{y \cdot x}\sqrt{1 + \frac{1}{n} + \frac{(x - \bar{x})^2}{\sum(x - \bar{x})^2}}.$$

The distinction is that the confidence band around $\hat{y}$ is claiming with 95% confidence that the true population regression line will fall in this band, while the band above gives the 95% confidence interval within which an individual y observation will fall given the corresponding x value.

independent variable x is selected by the experimenter and is not random. Of course if the experimenter wishes to make statements about causality, the variables chosen must implicitly have this relationship, since the analysis measures association and does not determine causality.

There are also a number of assumptions having to do with the fact that *each* value of X (where X indicates the entire population of x values) has an accompanying *set* of Y values (where Y designates a set of y values). Stated differently, each set of Y values is conditional to the chosen X value. Furthermore, the set of Y values is usually assumed to be normally distributed, with the consequence that the error terms are correspondingly normally distributed. Normality does not have to be assumed, however, to apply regression techniques, although if one wishes to make statements about the confidence limits that invoke either the F, t, or normal distributions, the y observations had better be distributed according to the t or normal curves. In any case the error term is assumed to be independent of the chosen x value and to have a mean of 0, that is, $E(e) = 0$, as well as an unknown variance, $V(e)$. When plotted, the *means* of these sets of Y values, which may be designated $E(Y|X)$, must form a straight line that is known as the population regression line. In symbols, $E(Y|X) = A + Bx$. A particular y value may then be expressed as $y = E(Y|X) + e$. Additionally, the variance of each subset of y values is assumed equal to the variance of the error term. This equal or constant variance condition is known as the *homoscedasiticity* assumption (nonconstant variance is called *heteroscedasticity*). Finally, it is assumed that these relationships pertain only over the observed range of x values; extrapolation of resulting relationships beyond that range is to be avoided.

In summary, in regression analysis it is usually assumed that the variation about the line holds for its entire length, and that at any given x value within the range of past observations there is a set of y values such that the point on the line is the expected value of the set and the standard deviation of regression is the standard deviation of the set. Since past observations of x may not include $x = 0$, taking $y = f(x = 0) = a$—which is often done—represents an extrapolation that should be looked upon with suspicion. Outside the observed range of x values, entirely different relationships may pertain—relationships that may even be curvilinear rather than linear. The statistician is not exactly thrilled by interpolation either (interpolation would be the assumption that the previously determined regression line pertains for some value of x that is within the range of past observations but which has not previously been specifically observed). However, interpolation is not as bad as extrapolation, since it is supported by evidence to its left and right, while extrapolation is, at best, supported on only one side. Actually, the statistician is only really content when you ask him to use the regression results to predict y for values of x near $\bar{x}$. His position is more readily comprehended if you think about the curved confidence band and the fact that it has a relatively narrow central section.

With all these assumptions supporting regression, it is perhaps easy to understand that something could go wrong in making inferences from the regression sample. One might not know, for instance, that he could rely on homoscedasticity being present. If heteroscedasticity prevails, then the quality of the regression coefficients is endangered. Unfortunately, to test for this condition, one must have a lot of data on hand from which the variance of each subset of y values (that is, the y values associated with each given x) may be calculated. Since having such a wealth of data available is apt to be a luxury, one frequently has to fit the line and hope for the best.

Troubles (via excessively large standard errors of the regression coefficients that interfere with precision and distort statistical testing) also arise if the error terms are not independent of one another. This particular complaint is referred to as *autocorrelation.* One oft-encountered autocorrelation situation is: Given a reading which is far from the regression prediction, it may well happen that the next reading also shows a similar large discrepancy because insufficient time has passed for corrective action to take effect. When this happens, the data on a scattergraph may appear to form waves, thereby indicating a seasonality phenomenon, when in fact the data are simply suffering from autocorrelation.

Perhaps the best-known test for autocorrelation is the Durbin-Watson statistic, d, which has the following formulation:

$$e_t = \text{residual error at time } t = \hat{y}_t - y_t, \text{ for } t = 1, 2, \ldots, m$$

$$d = \sum_{t=2}^{m} (e_t - e_{t-1})^2 \Big/ \sum_{t=1}^{m} e_t^2$$

An abridged D–W table appears as Table 2.

It should be noted that small sample sizes are not well suited to checking autocorrelation even though D–W tables may indicate applicability. For reliable results, the statistician prefers samples of at least size 50.
If there is dependence, the y readings, and hence the residuals, will be linearly related: $e_t = pe_{t-1} + \text{error}$, where $|p| < 1$. If $p = 0$, independence is present and autocorrelation is no problem. For testing the null hypothesis $H_o: p = 0$ against the alternative hypothesis $H_1: p > 0$, the table is consulted and these rules govern:

$$d \geq D_U; \text{ accept (better, "cannot reject") } H_o$$

$$d_L < d < D_U; \text{ the test is inconclusive}$$

$$d \leq D_L; \text{ reject } H_o$$

For testing $H_o: p = 0$ against $H_1: p < 0$, substitute $4 - d$ in the foregoing rules.

Autocorrelation may be treated by introducing additional variables or transforming the data. Sometimes dummy variables—such as a separate

Table 2 Durbin–Watson Table

		k = number of regressors (excluding intercept)									
		1		2		3		4		5	
Sample Size	One-Tail Probability	D_L	D_U	D_L	D_U	D_L	D_U	D_L	D_U	D_L	D_U
15	.01	.81	1.07	.70	1.25	.59	1.46	.49	1.70	.39	1.96
	.025	.95	1.23	.83	1.40	.71	1.61	.59	1.84	.48	2.09
	.05	1.08	1.36	.95	1.54	.82	1.75	.69	1.97	.56	2.21
20	.01	.95	1.15	.86	1.27	.77	1.41	.68	1.57	.60	1.74
	.025	1.08	1.28	.99	1.41	.89	1.55	.79	1.70	.70	1.87
	.05	1.20	1.41	1.10	1.54	1.00	1.68	.90	1.83	.79	1.99

variable each for summer, fall, winter, and spring with a reading of 1 if the season pertains and 0 otherwise—are employed for this purpose. (Actually, only three of the four seasons would be given separate variables; with all four separately recognized, dependency prevents the inversion of X^TX.)

Another hang-up occurs when the data are not homogeneous and include new effects. Measuring costs, for instance, may involve changes in technology or machine efficiency in one period that were not present in another. Dummy variables often help here also.

These and other problems occur regularly to muddy the waters of regression analysis. We shall go into further detail concerning some of these areas; however, the interested reader would do well to read a few good statistics books on the subject.[3]

Derivation of the Variance-Covariance Matrix and the Confidence Band Formula

For simplicity, we have been writing $B = (X^TX)^{-1}X^TY$ instead of the more appropriate $\hat{\beta} = (X^TX)^{-1}X^TY$. The difference is simply that the data constitute a sample drawn from a population. Had the volumes occurred in

[3] With the absolute certainty that I am neglecting to mention many excellent statistics books that address the subject of regression and its problems, I would suggest that the interested reader consult the appropriate chapters in at least the following offerings: A. M. Mood, *Introduction to the Theory of Statistics* (New York: McGraw-Hill Book Co., 1950); G. Snedecor, *Statistical Methods* (Ames, Iowa: Iowa State Press, 1956); J. Johnston, *Econometric Methods* (New York: McGraw-Hill Book Co., 1960); ———, *Statistical Cost Analysis* (New York: McGraw-Hill Book Co., 1960); J. E. Freund, *Mathematical Statistics* (Englewood Cliffs, N.J.: Prentice-Hall, 1962); A. S. Goldberger, *Econometric Theory* (New York: John Wiley & Sons, 1964); M. J. Moroney, *Facts from Figures* (Baltimore: Penguin Books, 1967); D. F. Morrison, *Multivariate Statistical Methods* (New York: McGraw-Hill Book Co., 1967); Y. Chou, *Statistical Analysis: With Business and Economic Applications* (New York: Holt, Rinehart & Winston, 1969); R. J. and T. H. Wonnacott, *Econometrics* (New York: John Wiley & Sons, 1970); R. Parsons, *Statistical Decision Analysis: A Decision-Making Approach* (New York: Harper & Row, 1974).

some other sequence, for instance, the costs would probably have been different. Even if the sequence remained the same, the costs would probably have changed if the company had had an opportunity for a second try at things, just because of the random nature of the process.

In classical regression, the population set of parameters is β and values of y may be obtained by $Y = X\beta + \varepsilon$, where ε is an error term. (Note that $X\beta$ was written and not βX, which would neither satisfy matrix multiplication nor produce a scalar.) This error term is related to, but unlike, the residual error discussed earlier. Given any reading of X (say $X = t$), it is assumed that there is a distribution of y_t values around the estimated y associated with that X (that is, $\hat{y}_t$) such that the error ($\varepsilon_t = y_t - \hat{y}_t$) is spread about according to the normal probability distribution with mean 0 and standard deviation σ. Consequently, the expected value of ε_t is $E(\varepsilon_t) = 0$. It is further assumed that the error term for some other value of X (say $X = s$ and ε_s is the new error term), has (1) the same standard deviation (σ); (2) an expected value of $E(\varepsilon_s) = 0$; and (3) no correlation (association) with any different error term—that is, $E(\varepsilon_t \varepsilon_s) = 0$ where $t \neq s$. (If $E(\varepsilon_t \varepsilon_s) \neq 0$, the condition of *autocorrelation* would be present.)

If you wished to express the variance of the error terms, the vector product could be used with the following result:

$$E(\varepsilon\varepsilon^T) = \sigma^2 I$$

This constant variance concept is known as *homoscedasticity;* regardless of the chosen X value, the variance of its error term is σ^2. The actual value of σ^2 is unknown; therefore the sampling variance—previously calculated as $\hat{s}^2_{y \cdot x}$—is used as a proxy for σ^2.

Let us see how $\hat{\beta}$ and β are related.

$$\begin{aligned}
\hat{\beta} &= (X^T X)^{-1} X^T Y \\
&= (X^T X)^{-1} X^T (X\beta + \varepsilon) \quad \textbf{(Recall: } Y = X\beta + \varepsilon\textbf{)} \\
&= (X^T X)^{-1} (X^T X)\beta + (X^T X)^{-1} X^T \varepsilon \\
&= \beta + (X^T X)^{-1} X^T \varepsilon
\end{aligned}$$

The variance becomes

$$\begin{aligned}
V(\hat{\beta}) &= E[(\beta - \hat{\beta})(\beta - \hat{\beta})^T] \\
&= E[(\beta - (\beta + (X^T X)^{-1} X^T \varepsilon)) \quad (\beta - (\beta + (X^T X)^{-1} X^T \varepsilon))^T] \\
&= E[((X^T X)^{-1} X^T \varepsilon)((X^T X)^{-1} X^T \varepsilon)^T] \\
&= E[(X^T X)^{-1} X^T \varepsilon\varepsilon^T X (X^T X)^{-1}]
\end{aligned}$$

The matrix rule that the transpose of the product of two or more matrices equals the product of their transposes in reverse order was applied above.

Additionally, because of the symmetry of X^TX, it was recognized that $[(X^TX)^{-1}]^T = (X^TX)^{-1}$. Now, observing that X is simply a matrix filled with known readings and can therefore be treated as a constant, we can factor $(X^TX)^{-1}X^T$ outside the expectation operator:

$$\begin{aligned} V(\hat{\beta}) &= (X^TX)^{-1}X^TE(\varepsilon\varepsilon^T)X(X^TX)^{-1} \\ &= (X^TX)^{-1}X^T\sigma^2IX(X^TX)^{-1} && \text{(Recall: } E(\varepsilon\varepsilon^T) = \sigma^2 I) \\ &= (X^TX)^{-1}(X^TX)\sigma^2(X^TX)^{-1} && \text{(Because } \sigma^2 \text{ is a scalar, it is free to commute—i.e., } \sigma^2X = X\sigma^2) \\ &= \sigma^2(X^TX)^{-1} \\ V(\hat{\beta}) &= \hat{s}^2_{y\cdot x}(X^TX)^{-1} && \text{(Recall: } \hat{s}^2_{y\cdot x} \text{ is a proxy for } \sigma^2.) \end{aligned}$$

This result is known as the *variance-covariance matrix*, which will hereafter be designated by V.

$$V = \hat{s}^2_{y\cdot x}(X^TX)^{-1} = \text{variance-covariance matrix}$$

To obtain a confidence band, we need to proceed from $V(\hat{\beta})$ to $V(\hat{y})$. The linkage is through recognizing that specific readings of $\hat{y}$ may be obtained by multiplying the corresponding specific row of X by the regression parameters in $\hat{\beta}$, that is, $\hat{y} = x_i\hat{\beta}$. We have

$$V(\hat{y}) = V(x_i\hat{\beta}) = x_iVx_i^T$$

This quadratic form may be restated as

$$V(\hat{y}) = \hat{s}^2_{y\cdot x}\left[\frac{1}{n} + \frac{(x-\bar{x})^2}{\sum(x-\bar{x})^2}\right],$$

the use of which has already been illustrated when drawing the confidence bands in Figure 4.

Using the Variance-Covariance Matrix

Let us return to our previous example and see how useful the variance-covariance matrix is. First we prepare the variance-covariance matrix from bits and pieces already developed:

$$V = \hat{s}^2_{y\cdot x}(X^TX)^{-1} = \begin{bmatrix} 780.569 & -9.8667 \\ -9.8667 & .129399 \end{bmatrix}$$

(Here v_{ii} is the variance of regression coefficient i, while v_{ij} is the covariance of coefficients i and j.) Next, if we designate a row vector of X by x_i, we can obtain the difficult part of the confidence band formula by

$$V(\hat{y}) = x_i V x_i^T$$

Using $x = 55$ for illustration: $(1, 55)V\left[\begin{smallmatrix}1\\55\end{smallmatrix}\right] = (86.66)$

The formula for the confidence band then becomes

$$\begin{aligned}\hat{y} \pm t_{n-2,\alpha/2}\sqrt{V(\hat{y})} &= 56.886 + 3.25(55) \pm 2.228\sqrt{86.66}\\ &= \{215; 256\}, \text{ to the nearest integer.}^4\end{aligned}$$

If you wanted to know the standard error of each of the beta coefficients, you could take the square root of each diagonal element of the variance-covariance matrix. Thus the standard error of fixed cost (the a or B_0 parameter is $\sqrt{780.567} = \$27.94$ (i.e., \$27,940 with 000 restored), while the standard error of the variable cost rate is $\sqrt{.129399} = \$.36$. The smaller the standard errors are in relation to their respective coefficients, the more reliable the latter are. If an analyst wished to talk about the marginal cost of a change in volume, he would take the first derivative of $\hat{y}: d\hat{y}/dx = b = 3.25$. If he wished to speak about the 95% confidence range of marginal cost, he would declare the range to be $3.25 \pm 2.228\ (.36) = \{2.45, 4.05\}$. Had the sample size been large (30 or more), the normal reading of 1.96 would replace the t reading of 2.228 in this calculation.

There are yet other uses for the variance-covariance matrix. Its elements are employed by the statistician for formal testing of regression results.[5] If regression *does not pertain in the population*, the *slope* of the *population* regression line $(E(Y|X) = A + BX)$ will be *zero* (in our notation, $B = 0$). The statistician formulates the null hypothesis $H_o: B = 0$ and the alternative hypothesis $H_1: B \neq 0$. Then, assuming a 95% confidence level, the t value for $n - 2 = 10$ degrees of freedom is ± 2.228, and the testing statistic becomes

$$t = \frac{b - B}{\sqrt{V(b) = v_{22}}} = \frac{3.2474 - 0}{.36} = 9.02$$

Since the value of t exceeds the critical value of 2.228, the statististician concludes that the alternative hypothesis cannot be rejected, and hence that the regression line should be retained.[6] The analyst may also test whether the

[4] The formula for an individual estimate of y is $\hat{y} \pm t_{n-2,\alpha/2}\sqrt{V(\hat{y}) + \hat{s}^2_{y \cdot x}}$. See footnote 2 for rationale.

[5] If you have had no formal exposure to hypothesis testing, you may wish to postpone reading the rest of this section until you have read Chapter 13.

[6] If the sample had been 30 or larger, we could have used the normal distribution and the statistic $Z = (b - B)/\sqrt{V(b)}$.

true population intercept is 0, using a similar approach:

$$t = \frac{a - A}{\sqrt{V(a) = v_{11}}} = \frac{56.8859 - 0}{27.94} = 2.04$$

This value is less than the critical value of 2.228, so the statistician concludes that the null hypothesis cannot be rejected and that the population intercept may pass through the origin. But this is unsatisfactory, for it seems to say that fixed costs may be zero even though intuition and the regression line say otherwise. What to do? Statisticians, generally, do not pay too much attention to the t test of the intercept, because usually the intercept lies outside the relevant independent variable range and hence represents an extrapolation. Once outside the range of previous independent variable observations, the same straight line may not pertain—it might even become a true curve. The assumption that the intercept, a, represents the fixed costs is really only that—an assumption! It is, however, an assumption supported by the linearly related data in the observed range, and the accountant may wish to base his estimate of fixed costs on this supporting evidence. But there are also times when he chooses to ignore the intercept as an estimate. For example:

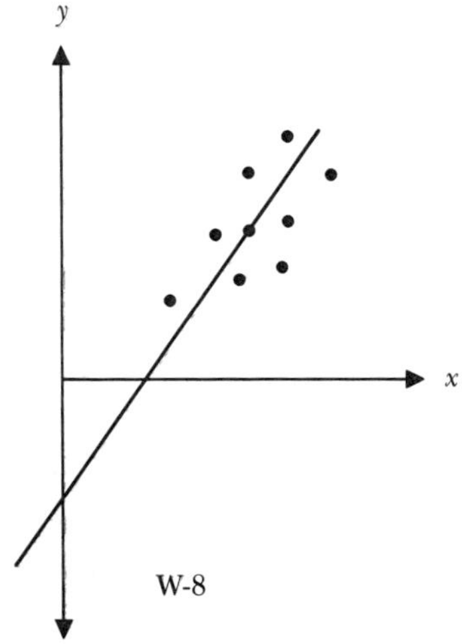

W-8

Here the intercept is negative and the regression line would simply be useful for predicting total costs over the relevant (observed) range. This situation suggests the advisability of segregating accounting data into separate fixed, variable, and semivariable accounts and then applying regression only to the variable and semivariable accounts.

Another use of the variance covariance matrix is to relate the standard error of a regression coefficient to the standard deviation of the associated variable. The formula is:

$$\sqrt{(n-1)v_{ii}} = \hat{s}_{y\cdot x}/\sqrt{\sum(x_i - \bar{x}_i)^2/(n-1)}$$

$$\text{Standard error of regression coefficient} = \frac{\text{Standard error of regression}}{\text{Standard deviation of regressor variable}}$$

Simplifying, $\sqrt{v_{ii}} = \hat{s}_{y\cdot x}/\sqrt{(n\sum x^2 - (\sum x)^2)/n}$

Inserting data, $\sqrt{.129399} = 18.41/\sqrt{31{,}419/12}$

$= .3597$

Analysis of Variance and the *F* Test

There are other tests the statistician may apply. The F test is one that appears at first glance to duplicate the t test on slope. In fact, however, F tests the whole estimating equation at once with all its beta coefficients reflected and not just one beta coefficient at a time.

If regression does not pertain in the population, there will be no slope; consequently, $E(b) = \beta_1 = 0$. However, if regression truly pertains, the explained variation will be relatively great while the unexplained variation will be relatively small. When these variations are divided by their respective degrees of freedom, the resulting variances become estimates of the population variance and are known as the "mean square" estimates. And when the respective mean square estimates are divided, the quotient is the F ratio, which (1) measures how many times greater the variance estimate based on the explained variation is than the variance estimate based on the unexplained variation, and (2) makes it possible to determine whether a ratio of this magnitude is likely to have arisen by chance.

To facilitate the F ratio calculations, an "analysis of variance" table is customarily prepared. Table 3 illustrates the standard notation.

Table 3 Analysis of Variance Table Anova

Source of Variation	Degrees of Freedom	Sum of Squares	Mean Squares
Regression (R)	m	$SSR = \Sigma(\bar{y} - \hat{y})^2$	$MSR = SSR/m$
Error (E)	$n - m - 1$	$SSE = \Sigma(\hat{y} - y)^2$	$MSE = SSE/(n - m - 1)$
Total (T)	$n - 1$	$SST = \Sigma(\bar{y} - y)^2$	$MST = SST/(n - 1)$

Key:

n = number of observations
m = number of independent variables
SSi = mean square estimate for variation i
i = R (regression), E (error or residual), T (total)

Table 4 contains the relevant figures for our illustration.

Table 4 Analysis of Variance Table (Anova)

Source of Variation	Degrees of Freedom	Sum of Squares	Mean Squares
Regression	1	27,611.00	27,611.00
Error	10	3,388.00	338.80
Total	11	30,999.00	2,818.09

We calculate F:

$$F = \frac{MSR}{MSE} = \frac{27{,}611}{338.8} = 81.50$$

Table 5 is an abridged table of critical F values at the 5% significance level.

Table 5

Degrees of Freedom:		Denominator ($n - m - 1$)											
		1	2	3	4	5	6	7	8	9	10	15	20
Numerator	1	161	18.51	10.13	7.71	6.61	5.99	5.59	5.32	5.12	4.96	4.54	4.35
(m)	2	200	19.00	9.55	6.94	5.79	5.14	4.74	4.46	4.26	4.10	3.68	3.49
	3	216	19.16	9.28	6.59	5.41	4.76	4.35	4.07	3.86	3.71	3.29	3.10
	4	225	19.25	9.12	6.39	5.19	4.53	4.12	3.84	3.63	3.48	3.06	2.87

The null hypothesis is $H_o: \beta_1 = 0$, while the alternative hypothesis is H_1: $\beta_1 \neq 0$. If a 5% rejection region is created, the critical F is $F_{1,10} = 4.96$. Since we exceed this figure, we reject H_o and hence conclude that our data could not have come from a population in which regression was not present.

It is the ability to make probabilistic statements—like "Volume was significant at the .05 level" or "There is 95% reliability (confidence) in the predicting equation"—that makes the F test superior to the coefficient of determination, which only measures the goodness of overall fit.

A Computer Program and Nonlinear Regression

Exhibit 1 contains an annotated computer program written in the BASIC language that carries out all the computations we have been discussing and a few others as well. The program offers the choice of fitting either a straight line or a power function using one or more independent variables. The same regression formula, $\hat{\beta} = (X^T X)^{-1} X^T Y$, applies once logarithms of the data are taken to bring the power function into linear form.

With suitable data modifications the matrix formula becomes applicable to a variety of curved functions. Study the listed functions below and note how the suggested modifications put things in linear form.

Function	*Data Modification*
1. $y = b_0 + b_1 x + b_2 x^2$ (quadratic)	Treat x and x^2 as if they were x_1 and x_2.
2. $y = ax^b$ (power function)	$\log y = \log a + b \log x$
3. $y = ae^{bx}$ (exponential function)	$\ln y = \ln a + bx$
4. $y = a + \frac{b}{x}$ (hyperbola)	$y = a + b\left(\frac{1}{x}\right)$
5. $y = \frac{1}{a + bx}$ (hyperbola)	$\left(\frac{1}{y}\right) = a + bx$

These and other functions may be brought into linear form by the manipulations shown above (that is, by substituting new variables, taking logs, and forming reciprocals). Perhaps you would enjoy adding some of these other options to the program in Exhibit 1.

Exhibit 1

```
100  DIM X(50,6),A(6,50),B(6,1),C(6,6),D(6,50),E(6,6),Y(50,1)
102  DIM Z(50,6),V(6,6),G(1,6),H(6,1),J(1,6),M(1,1),W(1,1),K(1,6)
110  REM X IS THE MATRIX WITH INDEPENDENT VARIABLE READINGS
112  REM Y IS THE VECTOR WITH THE DEPENDENT VARIABLE READINGS
114  REM Z IS THE MATRIX FROM WHICH THE X MATRIX IS FORMED
116  REM B IS THE VECTOR WITH THE BETA COEFFICIENTS
118  REM M1 = NUMBER OF OBSERVATIONS
120  REM M2 = NUMBER OF POSSIBLE INDEPENDENT VARIABLES + INTERCEPT
122  REM M3 = 0 IF STRAIGHT LINE IS DESIRED,1 IF POWER FUNCTION
124  REM M4 = APPROPRIATE T OR NORMAL VALUE NEEDED
126  REM        TO PRODUCE DESIRED CONFIDENCE LEVEL
150  READ M1,M2,M3
152  REM R1 TELLS HOW MANY COLUMNS THERE ARE IN THE X MATRIX
154  PRINT"HOW MANY INDEP. VARIABLES (COUNT INTERCEPT AS A VARIABLE)?"
156  INPUT R1
158  REM K IS A VECTOR WITH THE APPROPRIATE COLUMN SUBSCRIPTS FROM Z
160  PRINT"WHICH INDEPENDENT VARIABLES (INTERCEPT = 1 AND?)?"
162  MAT INPUT K(1,R1)
164  PRINT"WHAT T OR NORMAL VALUE IS NEEDED FOR YOUR"
166  PRINT"DESIRED CONFIDENCE BAND?"
```

Exhibit 1 (*cont.*)

```
168  INPUT M4
170  MAT A = ZER(R1,M1)
171  MAT B = ZER(R1,1)
172  MAT C = ZER(R1,R1)
173  MAT D = ZER(R1,M1)
174  MAT E = ZER(R1,R1)
175  MAT G = ZER(1,R1)
176  MAT H = ZER(R1,1)
177  MAT J  = ZER(1,R1)
178  MAT V  = ZER(R1,R1)
200  LET  P1  = 0
202  LET  P2  = 0
204  LET  P3  = 0
206  LET  P4  = 0
208  LET  G8 = 0
210  LET  N1 = M1 - 1
212  LET  N2 = R1 - 1
214  LET  N3 = N1 - N2
240  MAT READ Z(M1,M2)
242  MAT READ Y(M1,1)
246  IF M3 > 0 THEN 276
250  FOR I = 1 TO M1
252  LET P1 = P1 + Y(I,1)
254  NEXT I
256  GO TO 300
274  REM IF CURVE IS A POWER FUNCTION, DATA ARE LOGGED
276  FOR I = 1 TO M1
278  FOR I1 = 2 TO M2
280  LET Z(I,I1) = LOG(Z(I,I1))
282  NEXT I1
284  LET Y(I,1) = LOG(Y(I,1))
286  LET P1 = P1 + Y(I,1)
288  NEXT I
300  REM THE AVERAGE Y VALUE IS COMPUTED
302  LET Y1 = P1/M1
340  MAT X = ZER(M1,R1)
350  FOR I = 1 TO M1
352  FOR I1 = 1 TO R1
354  LET X(I,I1) = Z(I,K(1,I1))
356  NEXT I1
358  NEXT I
400  REM THE USUAL MULTIPLE REGRESSION FORMULA IS NOW IMPLEMENTED
402  MAT A = TRN(X)
404  MAT E = A*X
406  MAT C = INV(E)
408  PRINT"THE DETERMINANT IS";
410  PRINT DET
412  MAT D = C*A
414  MAT B = D*Y
436  REM NEXT:SQUARED DIFFERENCES & THE COEFFICIENT OF DETERMINATION
438  PRINT "           TOTAL           EXPLAINED         UNEXPLAINED"
440  PRINT "         VARIANCE          VARIANCE            VARIANCE"
442  FOR I = 1 TO M1
444  FOR I1 = 1 TO R1
446  LET G(1,I1) = X(I,I1)
448  NEXT I1
```

Exhibit 1 (*cont.*)

```
450 MAT W = G*B
452 LET G1 = (Y1 - W(1,1))**2
454 LET G2 = (Y1 - Y(I,1))**2
456 LET D1 = W(1,1) - Y(I,1)
458 LET G3 = (W(1,1) - Y(I,1))**2
460 LET P2  = P2 + G1
462 LET P3  = P3 + G2
464 LET P4  = P4 + G3
466 PRINT USING 468,G2,G1,G3
468 :    ###########.##     ###########.##     ###########.##
470 LET G4 = D1
472 IF I < 2 THEN 478
474 LET G7 = (G4 - G5)**2
476 LET G8 = G8 + G7
478 LET G5 = G4
480 LET G6 = (G5**2) + G6
482 NEXT I
484 PRINT "   ---------------   ---------------   ---------------"
486 PRINT USING 468,P3,P2,P4
488 PRINT "   ---------------   ---------------   ---------------"
490 LET R2 = P2/P3
492 PRINT"THE COEFFICIENT OF DETERMINATION IS:";R2
494 LET G9 = G8/G6
496 PRINT"THE DURBIN-WATSON STATISTIC IS:";G9
530 LET S1 = P2/N2
532 LET S2 = P4/N3
534 LET S3 = P3/N1
538 PRINT  "---------------------------------------------------------"
540 PRINT  "               ANALYSIS OF VARIANCE TABLE (ANOVA)         "
542 PRINT  "SOURCE OF     DEGREES OF     SUM OF       MEAN"
544 PRINT  "VARIATION      FREEDOM      SQUARES     SQUARES"
546 PRINT  "---------    ----------    ---------    --------"
548 PRINT USING 550,N2,P2,S1
550 :REGRESSION    ###     ###########.##     ###########.##
552 PRINT USING 554,N3,P4,S2
554 :ERROR         ###     ###########.##     ###########.##
556 PRINT USING 558,N1,P3,S3
558 :TOTAL         ###     ###########.##     ###########.##
560 PRINT  "---------------------------------------------------------"
562 LET F = S1/S2
564 PRINT "THE F RATIO IS:";F
570 PRINT "THE VARIANCE-COVARIANCE MATRIX:"
572 MAT V = (S2) * C
574 MAT PRINT V
575 PRINT "MATRIX E = X'X:"
580 MAT PRINT E
586 REM A CONFIDENCE BAND IS COMPUTED FOR THE ESTIMATING EQUATION
588 PRINT "CONFIDENCE BAND:        UPPER LIMIT        LOWER LIMIT"
590 FOR I = 1 TO M1
592 FOR I1 = 1 TO R1
594 LET G(1,I1) = X(I,I1)
596 LET H(I1,1) = G(1,I1)
598 NEXT I1
600 MAT J  = G*V
602 MAT M = J*H
604 MAT W = G*B
```

Exhibit 1 (*cont.*)

```
606 LET Y2 = M4 * (M(1,1)**(.5))
608 LET Y3 = W(1,1) + Y2
610 LET Y4 = W(1,1) - Y2
612 PRINT USING 614,Y3,Y4
614 :        ###########.##          ###########.##
616 NEXT I
640 PRINT "VECTOR B (CONTAINS THE BETA COEFFICIENTS):"
642 IF M3 < 1 THEN 660
644 REM WE OBTAIN THE ANTILOG OF THE FIRST BETA COEFFICIENT
646 LET B(1,1) = EXP(B(1,1))
660 MAT PRINT B
700 DATA 12,5,0
710 DATA 1,60,16,94.5,1
712 DATA 1,55,13,94.7,2
714 DATA 1,72,15,96.6,3
716 DATA 1,62,15,99.8,4
718 DATA 1,58,14,100.0,5
720 DATA 1,75,21,102.5,6
722 DATA 1,74,16,106.5,7
724 DATA 1,85,18,110.4,8
726 DATA 1,88,19,113.9,9
728 DATA 1,94,18,119.1,10
730 DATA 1,92,15,134.7,11
732 DATA 1,100,14,160.1,12
750 DATA 262,230,247,258,240,330,314,340,348,360,350,375
800 END
READY.

RNH

HOW MANY INDEP. VARIABLES (COUNT INTERCEPT AS A VARIABLE)?
? 2
WHICH INDEPENDENT VARIABLES (INTERCEPT = 1 AND?)?
? 1,2
WHAT T OR NORMAL VALUE IS NEEDED FOR YOUR
DESIRED CONFIDENCE BAND?
? 2.228
THE DETERMINANT IS 31419.

TOTAL          EXPLAINED      UNEXPLAINED
VARIANCE       VARIANCE       VARIANCE

 1806.25        2784.70          105.48
 5550.25        4761.99           30.17
 3306.25         190.48         1909.56
 2162.25        2141.41             .05
 4160.25        3512.34           27.41
  650.25          16.48          873.75
   90.25          53.39          282.46
 1260.25         807.40           50.20
 1892.25        1455.95           28.55
 3080.25        3322.52            4.59
 2070.25        2615.97           31.88
 4970.25        5948.37           43.90
 -----          -----            -----
30999.00       27611.00         3388.00
 =====          =====            =====
```

Exhibit 1 (*cont.*)

THE COEFFICIENT OF DETERMINAT IS .890706
THE DURBIN-WATSON STATISTIC IS 1.524

ANALYSIS OF VARIANCE TABLE (ANOVA)

SOURCE OF VARIATION	DEGREES OF FREEDOM	SUM OF SQUARES	MEAN SQUARES
REGRESSION	1	27611.00	27611.00
ERROR	10	3388.00	338.80
TOTAL	11	30999.00	2818.09

THE F RATIO IS 81.4965
THE VARIANCE-COVARIANCE MATRIX

780.569	−9.8667
−9.8667	.129399

MATRIX E = X′X

12	915
915	72387

CONFIDENCE BAND:	UPPER LIMIT	LOWER LIMIT
	269.33	234.13
	256.23	214.75
	303.02	278.38
	274.67	241.78
	264.05	226.42
	312.32	288.56
	309.17	285.22
	346.67	319.16
	357.78	327.53
	380.65	343.63
	372.95	338.34
	404.04	359.21

VECTOR B (CONTAINS THE BETA COEFFICIENTS)
56.8859

3.2474

The program allows you to select how many and which variables you would like to use. Thus all independent data are loaded in a matrix Z from which various variables can be drawn for inclusion in matrix X. The program then generates output for the selected independent variables. For example, I entered time as a variable (with 1963 set equal to 1, 1964 set equal to 2, . . .) and regressed with this instead of output. The coefficient of determination was then .84 with an F of 50.6. Since these statistics were lower than those in Exhibit 1, I retained volume as an independent variable. With both volume and time as variables, $r^2 = .9$, while $F = 40.8$ (which must be contrasted with $F_{2,9} = 4.26$). But this carries us into multiple regression and will therefore be postponed.

The additional data appearing in lines 710 through 732 will be explained when we discuss multiple regression.

Multiple Regression Analysis

Multiple regression extends the concepts of simple regression to the situation in which there are several independent variables. This complicates matters somewhat. First of all, if you are the type of person who likes to see graphs of his mathematical functions, you will be disappointed whenever there are three or more predicting variables. In fact, multiple regression is apt to cure you of "graphitis" once you are in the position of graphing four- or five-dimensional space and have to abandon rectangular coordinates! Secondly, when several independent variables are involved, the problem of their being closely correlated arises. (This is known as *multicollinearity*.) Indeed, many statisticians feel that regression analysis with more than three or four independent variables is pointless.[7] It is not too difficult to understand that after a few variables have been introduced, one may begin to correlate with another or with a subset of the other explanatory variables. In any case, the closer the correlation between two predictors is to ± 1, the less essential it is to include both variables in the analysis. Furthermore, multicollinearity causes the variance-covariance matrix of regression coefficients to have relatively large elements, thereby distorting standard errors and interfering with tests for significance (t tests).

On the bright side of things, you can still similarly apply the notions of total, explained, and residual variances, since y and $\bar{y}$ remain unchanged, and $\hat{y}$ can be calculated with estimating equation that results from the formula $\hat{\beta} = (X^T X)^{-1} X^T Y$. As before (as *always*), we may check the matrix formula by deriving the normal equations by summing the squares of the error terms and minimizing the resulting sum. In symbols:

$$\text{Minimize } E = \sum e_1{}^2 = \sum (y - \hat{y})^2 = \sum (y_i - b_0 - b_1 x_{i1} - b_2 x_{i2})^2$$

I shall illustrate using the example we have been working with as a vehicle. Let us call the volume of Table 1 "machine hours" and add "labor hours" and the Wholesale Price Index—All Commodities. These data appear in Table 6.

Including the Wholesale Price Index (WPI) as a separate variable is an attractive way of recognizing the effects of inflation. Alternatively, cost could be divided by WPI with the quotients used as the y values. Since it is easier to reflect inflation with WPI as a separate variable, this is the approach that

---

[7] One such prominent statistician is M. J. Moroney. See his *Facts from Figures* (Baltimore: Penguin Books, 1967), p. 304.

Table 6

Year	y Cost	x_1 Machine Hours	x_2 Labor Hours	x_3 Wholesale Price Index
1963	262	60	16	94.5
1964	230	55	13	94.7
1965	247	72	15	96.6
1966	258	62	15	99.8
1967	240	58	14	100.0
1968	330	75	21	102.5
1969	314	74	16	106.5
1970	340	85	18	110.4
1971	348	88	19	113.9
1972	360	94	18	119.1
1973	350	92	15	134.7
1974	375	100	14	160.1
	(000 omitted)			

Comment: A fourth independent variables, year number (1 = 1963, 2 = 1964, . . .), is here being ignored, although year number should always be given consideration in practice.

will be employed in this chapter. Nevertheless, the alternative approach—as well as the possibility of just using the difference between the index and 100 as a reading of WPI—should be investigated in practice.

When all three independent variables are used, the X matrix becomes

$$X = \begin{bmatrix} 1 & 60 & 16 & 94.5 \\ 1 & 55 & 13 & 94.7 \\ \vdots & \vdots & \vdots & \vdots \\ 1 & 100 & 14 & 160.1 \end{bmatrix}$$

The computer program of Exhibit 1 shows that the estimating equation is then $\hat{y} = -100.82 + 1.309x_1 + 9.570x_2 + 1.357x_3$, and it results in $r^2 = .964$ and $F = 71.5$. To two decimal places, the variance-covariance matrix is

$$V = \begin{bmatrix} 2{,}062.67 & 20.80 & -96.36 & -18.72 \\ 20.80 & .46 & -1.25 & -.32 \\ -96.36 & -1.25 & 5.68 & .90 \\ -18.72 & -.32 & .90 & .26 \end{bmatrix}$$

The r^2 and F statistics favor the retention of the equation but they do not preclude multicollinearity just because they are so favorable.

To test for multicollinearity, you might check the standard error of each regression coefficient, $\sqrt{v_{ii}}$, against the corresponding coefficient b_i. If the standard error is large—say equal to or greater than the coefficient—this would be indicative that the multicollinearity problem is present.

It is customary to check for multicollinearity by preparing a correlation coefficient matrix, which appears as follows for our problem:

	x_1	x_2	x_3		Machine hours x_1	Labor hours x_2	WPI x_3
x_1	1	r_{12}	r_{13}	x_1	1	.3422	.8419
x_2	r_{21}	1	r_{23}	$= x_2$	.3422	1	.0878
x_3	r_{31}	r_{32}	1	x_3	.8419	.0878	1

Each correlation coefficient is calculated as

$$r_{ij} = \frac{\text{Cov}(x_i, x_j)}{\sqrt{V(x_i)}\sqrt{V(x_j)}} = \frac{[n\sum x_i x_j - \sum x_i \sum x_j]/n^2}{\sqrt{(n\sum x_i^2 - (\sum x_i)^2)(n\sum x_j^2 - (\sum x_j)^2)}/n^2}$$

For example, consider the correlation of machine hours and the Wholesale Price Index.

Shown below is the $X^T X$ matrix (matrix E in Exhibit 1).

$$\begin{bmatrix} 12 & 915 & 194 & 1{,}332.8 \\ 915 & 72{,}387 & 14{,}930 & 104{,}394.8 \\ 194 & 14{,}930 & 3{,}198 & 21{,}502.6 \\ 1{,}332.8 & 104{,}394.8 & 21{,}502.6 & 152{,}160.72 \end{bmatrix}$$

If you were to label selected elements you would find

$$e_{12} = \sum x_1 = 915 \qquad e_{22} = \sum x_1^2 = 72{,}387$$

$$e_{14} = \sum x_3 = 1{,}332.8 \qquad e_{44} = \sum x_3^2 = 152{,}160.72$$

$$e_{24} = \sum x_1 x_3 = 104{,}394.8$$

Therefore,

$$r_{13} = \frac{12(104{,}394.8) - 915(1{,}332.8)}{\sqrt{(12(72{,}387) - 915^2)(12(152{,}160.72) - 1{,}332.8^2)}}$$

$$= .841889$$

Had you regressed machine hours on Wholesale Price Index, the square root of the coefficient of determination would be $r_{13} = .841889$.

The high value of r_{13} suggests that either machine hours or WPI should be dropped as a predictor.

So which equation should be used? If we were only interested in forecasting, we could ignore multicollinearity so long as we did not attempt to use values of the correlated variables that are far removed from their line or plane of collinearity. But if we wish to estimate marginal cost, multicollinearity interferes with the *ceteris paribus* assumptions of $\partial y/\partial x_i$. That is, with multicollinearity present, we cannot hold all other variables constant while changing x_i; a change in x_i also compels a change in some other variable or variables.

Assuming we were interested in marginal costs, the least multicollinearity—as shown by the correlation coefficient matrix—occurs with labor hours and WPI as predictors. We obtain the equation

$$\hat{y} = -160.56 + 13.148x_2 + 2.273x_3$$

$$r^2 = .947$$

$$F = 80.6$$

It is interesting to observe that neither variable explains the variation in cost very well by itself. The results from simple regressions were

$$y = 118.37 + 11.514x_2 \qquad y = 67.67 + 2.132x_3$$

$$r^2 = .264 \qquad r^2 = .606$$

$$F = 3.6 \qquad F = 15.4$$

A statistician always has one reservation about how representative—how homogeneous—the data are. Perhaps observations that diverge widely from the fitted equation should be disregarded, thereby changing the equation and its coefficient of determination.

It may be instructive to reconstitute the multiple regression formula and show how it would be used for forecasting 1975 costs:

$$\hat{y} = -\$160{,}560 + \$13{,}148x_2 + \$2{,}273x_3$$

If 1975 is expected to see 15,000 direct-labor hours and a WPI of 172, then the cost estimate is

$$\hat{y} = -\$160{,}560 + \$13{,}148(15) + \$2{,}273(172) = \$427{,}616$$

Exponential Smoothing

How should one make forecasts if he feels that all the data of the past should not be considered equally relevant? There are probably many answers to this question if we take personal preferences into account. We shall examine one popular, easily understood method that permits us to weight the most recent experience heavily or lightly, as desired.

Consider the formula for an average:

$$\bar{x}_n = \sum_{j=0}^{n-1} x_{n-j} \div n$$

Here each x_{n-j} is given a weight of $1/n$. Suppose equal weighting were put aside in favor of geometric weighting, using the factor $a^j/\sum a^j$. The result would be

$$\bar{x}_n = \sum_{j=0}^{n-1} a^j x_{n-j} \div \sum_{j=0}^{n-1} a^j$$

Now consider that a very large number (assume infinity) of x readings are available, and that we wish to compute the average for period i. We obtain

$$\bar{x}_i = \sum_{j=0}^{\infty} a^j x_{i-j} \div \left(\frac{1}{1-a}\right)$$

The sum of an infinite geometric series, where $0 < a < 1$, may be obtained by

$$\sum_{j=0}^{\infty} a^j = \Delta^{-1} a^j \Big]_0^{\infty} = \frac{a^j}{a-1}\Big]_0^{\infty} = \frac{a^{\infty} - a^0}{a-1} = \frac{0-1}{a-1} = \frac{1}{1-a}$$

This finite calculus approach to summing series is discussed in Appendix C.

$$\bar{x}_i = (1-a)\sum_{j=0}^{\infty} a^j x_{i-j}$$

$$= (1-a)\left[x_i + a x_{i-1} + a^2 x_{i-2} + \cdots\right]$$

Replace i by $i + 1$ throughout:

$$\bar{x}_{i+1} = (1-a)[x_{i+1} + a x_i + a^2 x_{i-1} + \cdots]$$

$$\bar{x}_{i+1} = (1-a)x_{i+1} + (1-a)a[x_i + a x_{i-1} + a^2 x_{i-2} + \cdots]$$

$$\bar{x}_{i+1} = (1-a)x_{i+1} + a\bar{x}_i$$

Let $\alpha = 1 - a$ and back the above equation down one period:

$$\bar{x}_i = \alpha x_i + (1 - \alpha)\bar{x}_{i-1}$$

This is the basic exponential smoothing formula: The average for period i equals α times the reading for period i plus $(1 - \alpha)$ times the previous period's average. α is known as the "smoothing constant" and lies in the range $0 < \alpha < 1$. The *estimate* for period $i + 1$ then becomes $\hat{x}_{i+1} = \bar{x}_i$.

Observe that if α were set equal to 1, the current average would degenerate to the current reading. Conversely, if α were set equal to 0, the current average would equal the previous average and would consequently remain constant.

Exponential smoothing is associated with moving averages. In fact, the number of terms of a moving average that generates similar results is related to α by the formula $n = (2 - \alpha) \div \alpha$ (for example: $n = 4, \alpha = 4; n = 19, \alpha = .1; n = 199, \alpha = .01$). Exponential smoothing, however, has the distinct advantage of requiring less data to be remembered.

Example: Inventory demand in period i is designated by x_i. Demand for the ensuing period is to be estimated by the formula

$$\hat{x}_{i+1} = \bar{x}_i = .2x_i + .8\bar{x}_{i-1}$$

To start things off, assume $\bar{x}_{1-1} = x_i$ for the initial period.

i	x_i	$.2x_i + .8\bar{x}_{i-1} = \bar{x}_i$	$\hat{x}_{i+1}$
1	30	.2(30) + .8(30) = 30	30
2	18	.2(18) + .8(30) = 27.6	27.6
3	35	.2(35) + .8(27.6) = 29	29
4	40	.2(40) + .8(29) = 31.2	31.2
5	24	.2(24) + .8(31.2) = 29.8	29.8
6	12	?	?

Challenges:

1. Answer the questions.

   How well is this system functioning?

3. What α value would you recommend?

If you computed $\bar{x}_6 = 26.2 = \hat{x}_7$, you understand the process. If you got some other figure, restudy the above calculations.

Some idea of the efficiency of the system can be obtained by assuming that a purchase order is placed for the rounded estimate of demand, comparing the result with the actual demand, and assuming that shortages cannot be made up, nor can overages be kept in inventory:

i	Ordered	Demanded (x_i)	Δ_i	(% Error) Δ_i/x_i
2	30	18	+12	+ .67
3	28	35	− 7	− .20
4	29	40	−11	− .28
5	31	24	+ 7	+ .29
6	30	12	+18	+1.50

The system seems to have significant forecasting error. There are not enough data to determine a pattern, or the presence of enduring randomness, or a probability distribution. The data appear to be jumping around in a random fashion, and this suggests choosing an α that weights the most recent experience more heavily. Let us try $\alpha = .3$:

i:	1	2	3	4	5	6
x_i:	30	18	35	40	24	12
$.3x_i + .7\bar{x}_{i-1} = \bar{x}_i$:	30	21.6	25.6	29.9	28.1	23.3
Ordered:	30	22	26	30	28	23
Δ_i:	—	+4	−9	−10	+4	+11
Δ_i/x_i:		+.22	−.26	−.25	+.17	+.92

This system functions better than the previous one, although there appears to be room for improvement. Did you find a better α? Probably a computer program is needed to find the best α, and perhaps some tolerable percentage of error should be specified.

There is more to exponential smoothing than is presented above. For instance, second-order smoothing—the averaging of averages—is used to track straight lines. Eventually one winds up with difference and differential equations and the use of Z and Laplace transforms to solve them. However, first-order smoothing has the virtue of simplicity and will be adequate for our purposes.

Summary

We have examined some of the basic ideas of both cost behavior—how costs respond to changes in independent variables—and forecasting in this chapter. In the process we have investigated the fundamentals of high-low, regression and correlation, and exponential smoothing.

The high-low method is fast but apt to be misleading if the high and low points chosen are not representative of the data. Additionally, (1) there is no measure of how well the resulting line fits the data, and (2) there is no way to incorporate reliability and precision in making estimates based on the line.

Regression is much more deliberate than high-low but it does (1) permit one to measure goodness of fit—via the coefficient of determination—and (2) provide measures of reliability and precision—via the use of the standard errors and appropriate t or normal probability table readings. A single formula, $B = (X^T X)^{-1} X^T Y$, may be used to fit straight lines or curves using one or more independent variables.

Regression provides the fit and correlation measures the degree of association. But neither is a panacea. Causality is brought to the analysis, not discovered by it. Extrapolations can be hazardous, as, for example, when b_o, the intercept, is interpreted as fixed costs. Attention must be paid to the problems of autocorrelation, nonhomogeneity of data, heteroscedasticity, and multicollinearity.

While regression treats all data similarly, exponential smoothing offers a means for giving more weight to certain data. This can be very useful. However, obtaining the smoothing constant that yields the best forecasts is not as simple as it would appear.

Now that we know what the tools are, we shall see how the accountant can put them to use.

Problems

1. *Fitting a quadratic.* Use multiple regression to fit a quadratic equation to the following data:

x:	2	3	7	5	6	9	4
y:	13	26	138	70	101	230	45

2. *Power function.* Fit a power function relating production time and the number of the unit being produced from the data given below.

Unit:	1	2	3	4	5	6	7	8
Time:	120	92	80	70	61	59	54	52

3. *Power function.* Given the chapter data on cost and labor hours, would a power function fit better than a straight line?

4. *Fitting a curve with a cross-product term.* Use the data shown below and the matrix formula to fit the curve $y = a + bx_1x_2 + cx_3$.

x_1	x_2	x_3	y
1	2	5	29
3	4	3	43
2	5	2	36

Hint:

Substitute $x_4 = x_1x_2$ and prepare matrix X from x_4 and x_3. Do not use logs. You should get $B^T = (10, 2, 3)$. Note that every point falls on this line.

5. Use partial derivatives on $\partial E/\partial a$ and $\partial E/\partial b$ to prove that the values of a and b that result from solving the normal equations do indeed minimize the sum E.

6. Prove that

$$\hat{y} \pm t_{n-2,\alpha/2}\hat{s}_{y \cdot x}\sqrt{\frac{1}{n} + \frac{(x-\bar{x})^2}{\sum(x-\bar{x})^2}} = \hat{y} \pm t_{n-2,\alpha/2}\sqrt{V(\hat{y})}$$

7. *Perfect multicollinearity.* Two variables x_1 and x_2 are perfectly correlated; therefore, $x_1 = ax_2$. Show that (X^TX) has no determinant, and consequently that perfect multicollinearity would lead to a variance-covariance matrix with infinite elements.

8. *Using WPI differences: theory.* When the Wholesale Price Index (WPI), was introduced, it was suggested that the differences between the index and 100 be used as variable readings instead. Why might this be an attractive idea?

9. *Using WPI differences: practice.* Regress chapter costs on labor hours and the differences between WPI and 100. Does this improve forecasting?

10. *Altering WPI.* Suppose a company were founded in 1965 and wished this year to be 100 on the WPI scale. How should the WPI readings be changed? What advantages and disadvantages face the company if it does this?

11. *Orthogonality.* If two variables are independent, they are said to be orthogonal and their covariance equals 0. When this is the case, the regression coefficients obtained from simple regressions will be the same as the corresponding multiple regression coefficients.

(a) Demonstrate the truth of this statement using the data shown below.

y	2	4	6	8
x_1	−1	−1	1	1
x_2	1	−1	1	−1

(b) Note how attractive the additivity of regression coefficients is when the variables are orthogonal. Discuss this attractiveness.

(c) Discuss the chapter regression of costs using labor hours and WPI from the standpoint of orthogonality.

12. *Marginal cost.* Given $\hat{y} = -\$160.56 + \$13.148x_2 + \$2.273x_3$ and the variance-covariance matrix

$$V = \begin{bmatrix} 1{,}455.07 & -51.64 & -5.45 \\ -51.64 & 2.97 & .03 \\ -5.45 & .03 & .04 \end{bmatrix},$$

where x_2 is labor hours and x_3 is WPI. Assuming the regression was based on 12 observations, what is the marginal cost of a labor hour given that a 95% confidence range is desired for the estimate?

13. *Dummy variables.* Regress electricity cost on machine hours, using whatever dummy variables you think appropriate:

		1968		1969	
Month	Season	Electricity Cost	Machine Hours	Electricity Cost	Machine Hours
J	winter	$3,200	12,000	$3,000	12,900
F	winter	3,300	12,700	3,300	13,200
M	winter	3,280	13,000	3,380	14,000
A	spring	2,850	14,500	2,960	14,000
M	spring	2,800	14,000	3,100	15,200
J	summer	2,870	11,000	2,700	10,700
J	summer	2,500	8,000	2,500	7,500
A	summer	2,660	8,200	2,410	7,000
S	fall	2,600	9,500	2,520	9,000
O	fall	2,700	10,800	2,930	12,200
N	winter	3,000	11,200	3,150	11,800
D	winter	2,920	11,100	3,000	11,000

14. *Counter-intuitive correlation.* Regress the repair costs below on the machine-hour readings of Problem 13 and interpret the result.

	1968	1969
J	$7,500	$7,400
F	7,480	7,300
M	7,350	7,210
A	7,200	7,240
M	7,300	7,000
J	7,900	7,800
J	8,400	8,500
A	8,300	8,700
S	8,220	8,100
O	7,910	7,600
N	7,700	7,630
D	7,750	7,800

15. *Using economic indicators.* In his book *Econometric Theory*, A. S. Goldberger regresses real gross national product, y, on labor input, x_1, real capital, x_2, and time, x_3. Determine the resulting regression plane given the data he used.

Year	y	x_1	x_2	x_3
1929	142	47	54	1
1930	127	43	59	2
1931	118	39	57	3
1932	98	34	48	4
1933	94	34	36	5
1934	102	36	24	6
1935	116	38	19	7
1936	128	41	18	8
1937	140	42	22	9
1938	131	37	24	10
1939	143	40	23	11
1940	157	42	27	12
1941	182	47	36	13
1946	209	51	9	18
1947	214	53	25	19
1948	225	53	39	20
1949	221	50	51	21
1950	243	52	62	22
1951	257	54	75	23
1952	265	54	94	24
1953	276	55	108	25
1954	271	52	118	26
1955	291	54	124	27

Key: y is recorded in billions of dollars.
x_1 is recorded in millions of man-years.
x_2 is recorded in billions of dollars.
x_3 lists the years 1929–1941 and 1946–1955.

16. *Data problems.* Read pp. 662–669 in G. J. Benston's "Multiple Regression Analysis of Cost Behavior," *The Accounting Review*, October 1966, to understand what causes of data nonhomogeneity and other regression problems prompt him to say, "If the data are simply taken from the ordinary cost-accounting records of the company, it is unlikely that the output of the regression model will be meaningful."

17. *Functional form of equation (based on a problem discussed by G. J. Benston—see Problem 16 above).* Given: C = costs of Shipping Department, T = percentage of pounds shipped by truck, P = pounds shipped, and A = average weight of a sale. Benston (p. 669):

> If the accountant believes that the change in cost due to a change of each explanatory variable is unaffected by the levels of the other explanatory variables, a linear form could be used, as follows:
>
> $$C = a + bP + cT + dA$$
>
> . . . However, if the marginal cost of each explanatory variable is thought to be a function of the levels of the other explanatory variables, the following form would be better:
>
> $$C = aP^bT^cA^d$$

(a) Under what conditions would the linear form shown above pertain given the stated assumptions? (Hint: Read question 11.)

(b) What is the effect of multicollinearity on both forms?

(c) How would you fit the curve of the second form?
(d) What are the marginal costs of each form?

18. *Exponential smoothing.* Using the data given below, determine a suitable smoothing constant to estimate sales via exponential smoothing.

Week:	1	2	3	4	5	6	7	8
Sales:	6,000	9,400	10,800	5,200	17,500	18,000	12,000	9,800

19. *Real-life experience.* Conduct your own experiment of a managerial situation using at least two predicting variables. Submit your *supported* and *interpreted* results in good form.

20. *Multicollinearity and its effects on standard deviations.* Assume cost, y, is related to x_1 (machine hours) and x_2 (labor hours) as follows:

y:	4	7	10	12	15	20
x_1:	1	2	3	4	5	6
x_2:	.7	2.1	3.3	3.8	4.5	6.6

Determine a linear equation for purposes of forecasting.

21. *Direct costing and high-low analysis.* The Crosby Corporation wishes to determine the change in its net profits that would result from the adoption of direct-costing techniques. Accordingly, the controller has amassed the data shown below.

Opening inventory	10,000 units	\$98,000
Estimated costs during period:		
Raw materials		300,000
Direct labor	75,000 units	200,000
Overhead		250,000
Estimated ending inventory	15,000 units	
Estimated sales		850,000
Estimated selling and administrative cost		120,000

The company uses the FIFO method of costing.

Past production data indicated that total overhead costs amounted to \$300,000 when volume reached 100,000 units and \$240,000 when volume was 70,000 units. Ignore any possible adjustments in opening inventory. Compute the net profit under the full-costing and the direct-costing approaches and show your work.

22. *Matrix proofs (prepared by Professor Gary Monroe, Duke University).* In deriving the normal equations, this chapter minimized the sum of the squared residuals (i.e., $S = \sum e_i^2$). In matrix notation, $S = \varepsilon^T \varepsilon$, where $\varepsilon = y - \hat{y} = (y - X\beta)$ in population line terms.

(a) Prove, using matrix notation, that $\hat{\beta} = (X^T X)^{-1} X^T Y$.

(b) Using the end result from part (a), prove that $\hat{\beta}$ is an unbiased estimator of β (i.e., prove that $E(\hat{\beta}) = \beta$).

(c) Prove that total variation equals the sum of explained and unexplained variation.

23. *Overhead expenses, standard error and standard deviation of coefficients, computing probabilities for estimates (prepared by Professor Mawsen Liao, University of Houston).* Assume that the following regression equation has been computed for your department's monthly overhead expense from the data observed in the past 10 months.

$$y = 120 + 23.5x_1 + 42x_2$$

Where x_1 = direct labor hours per month
x_2 = number of orders processed per month
standard error of estimate $(\hat{s}_{y,x}) = 60$
standard deviation of monthly direct labor hours = 8
standard deviation of monthly number of orders processed = 5

Required:

(1) Calculate the standard error of the regression coefficient for x_1 and x_2.

(2) Assess the probability that the true coefficient of x_1 is between 20 and 31.

(3) If the total variance of monthly overhead expense over the past ten months is \$100,000, calculate the coefficient of correlation, r.

(4) Estimate the probability that the overhead expense will be between \$300 and \$500 for a month where $x_1 = 4$ and $x_2 = 5$ if normality can be assumed.

(5) Test whether the presence of each independent variable contributes significantly toward explanation of the changes in the dependent variable (at 99% confidence level).

Period Budgeting and Responsibility Accounting

4

Chapter Overview and Some Caveats

We took a broad look at business planning and control procedures in Chapter 1. During the course of that discussion it became apparent that people constitute both a blessing and a curse on the operations of a business; hence Chapter 2 examined tenets of human behavior theory. Then, since this text deals with costs, Chapter 3 developed some of the major tools and theory for studying cost behavior and making forecasts. We stand now on the threshold of opportunity or the brink of disaster, depending on how one looks at it, for it is time to use the tools to put details into the broad canvas that is cost accounting.

Disaster awaits like Charybdis and Scylla: we could drown in the whirlpool of creativity or smash against the rock of tradition. Genuine improvement requires a cautious blending of exploration and preservation as well as consideration for all the people involved.

Mr. Herman C. Krannert provides eloquent advice for this delicate balancing of new and old:[1]

> I want to congratulate you on your achievement. Most of you have finished four years in an excellent engineering school, graduating in the upper third of your class; and now you have completed a year of what our faculty tells me is a very rigorous program in Industrial Administration. You will soon have your master's degree and you have reason to be proud of what you have done. If you keep on learning and, in addition, learn to use your knowledge, you will have a fine future.
>
> Despite these achievements, as I look forward to the problems you are going to face, I think I must say to you: *You aren't really ready to practice the*

[1] Space will only permit excerpting Krannert's speech, which I consider simply extraordinary. If you can beg, borrow, or ____ a copy, do so. Herman C. Krannert, "Commencement Address Before Graduate Students of the Krannert Graduate School of Industrial Administration" (Purdue University, July 27, 1967).

difficult art of management. Formal education is not enough. And today I want to talk to you about this additional preparation you are going to have to have. In fact, I have wondered whether we shouldn't withhold your diploma until you have combined your education with the ten years of experience you will need to be certified in this most difficult of all professions—the profession of management.

As it is, some company is going to subsidize each of you for the next five years because, as of now, you are not worth what you are going to be paid.

Another reason is this. It is important, for every future change you may wish to make, to understand how things run at the company today—and why they are that way. After all, this is a successful outfit you will be joining and you can't get very far by overlooking the wisdom that is already in it. Instead, you need to really understand it and the only way to do so is to participate in it, to be one of the boys. You may think some of the forms and practices are for the birds, but I urge you to go along with them until you know first-hand why they exist and how they work.

Let me give you some advice on this line that will be helpful during your initiation period. You may want, as a matter of pride, to be a little different from the other people with whom you're working. *But this is not the time to emphasize any differences.* Your first important task is to identify yourself with the group you join—and I don't think you will compromise yourself if you emphasize the similarities rather than the differences.

You may wonder why, with your fine education, you can't become a company president within the next five years. And I guess my answer to you is that you must learn first to deal with people, to command their imagination and their loyalty. And this takes much time—and lots of people—and a willingness to be immersed in the life of the organization.

I have been telling you that during the initiation and experience stages you will need to conform in order to learn how the organization functions. I have also told you that you should understand the wisdom that has made the organization you are in successful. And now I am going to reverse myself to tell you that in the end, to succeed as a leader, you will need to be a creative nonconformist. In other words, you're going to use a predictable organization to accomplish novelty. This capacity to use order to achieve change is a rare ability.

One should have a detailed understanding and appreciation of the reasons for an organization's success before he seeks to introduce change. Few organizations survive as a matter of pure good fortune; the very fact of survival indicates that clever people have been at the helm. It is something of a luxury to initiate a business and its cost systems. More often one faces a going concern, which is not unlike starting a novel at page 200. Nonetheless, you should never foresake pursuit of more promising methods—ultimately, better ways of doing things are the hallmark of a successful business.

Specifically, in this chapter we shall discuss how businesses plan for the periods ahead and formalize these plans in budgets. But planning is apt to be worthless if it does not include means for controlling performance. Controlling calls for acceptance of responsibility, feedback, and adjustment. The principal accounting reports used in these ongoing activities are the departmental budget, the cash budget, and the budget variance report. We shall look at these reports and others, although we shall postpone examining special studies that support budgetary estimates—like inventory, queuing, capital budgeting, and linear programming studies—until later in the text. This is a recurrent problem in cost accounting. With so many activities interrelated, where does one begin?

The Setting

There are two settings that need to be examined in the study of period budgeting:

(1) the traditional, sterile setting, in which focus is solely upon the theoretical tasks; and

(2) the behavioral setting, which, if the gamesmanship is not controlled, can wreck the theory of budgeting and render the process detrimental to the health of the organization.

According to theory, budgets are instruments for coordinating organizational activity, communicating organizational objectives, and achieving organizational efficiency. In practice, statements like "Spend now or have less later" and "Scrimp today and set the pattern for tomorrow" (the sentiment is that if one shows this year that he can do with less, he will thereafter be asked to do with less) characterize the attitudes of many—perhaps most—departmental managers who are subject to budgetary control. As a consequence, budgets tend to set a level of expenditures, even though less spending might be both possible and desirable.[2] Theory advocates the establishment of departments and divisions of approximately equal size to take advantage of competition among peers. In practice, budgets seem to be divisive and to encourage political maneuvering for personal and departmental advantage. Additionally, budgets give rise to a significant number of both idle promises and excuses for inadequate performance. Of course, promises and excuses also happen without budgets; after all, there is no way to suspend human nature.

[2] Note how the manager who spends unnecessarily to avoid having his future budget allotments cut resembles the production worker who restricts output for fear that an impressive showing today will result in tighter standards tomorrow.

Put yourself in the shoes of the chief executive officer. Do you want to budget for next year or not? Put another way: Will you take what comes, or will you assume command and make desirable things happen? Some executives I know choose wait-for-fate for two reasons: (1) fate might not be so unfavorable, and (2) they will probably be retired and pensioned before the axe falls. They admit they are not dynamic leaders.

The decision whether to budget is really based on the question "Are we opting to stay in business or to fold?" If the answer is "Fold," the next question is "How fast?" If folding is an easy matter quickly accomplished, then budgeting seems unnecessary. If winding down will take time, then budgeting will expedite an orderly retreat.

It probably goes without saying that budgets are an utter waste of time or worse if the upper echelons of management don't take them seriously. Can you imagine the lower levels taking a budget seriously if their superiors don't?

Having opted to stay in business, management should adopt some form of budgeting. And having chosen to budget, management reluctantly accepts the people problems involved. People who are being controlled say, in essence, "Minimize the bother, maximize my personal showing, and observe the fragility of my feelings." Sometimes their objections are easily put aside. "I am having troubles enough right now; why bother me about next year's budget?" is easily answered by "If I don't bother you now, the organization may not be synchronized enough next year to grant you the luxury of even being employed." If said with a smile, this sort of response disarms resistance.

Overt objections do not pose the subtle problems that eagerness and ambition do. There is probably no system that cannot be "beat." Perceiving this, certain managers scheme, cajole, and exhort their superiors to win favor. "*Beware the Mouth*" is good advice for top management, whether the subject is budgeting or not. The "Mouth" is not necessarily an obnoxious individual, but rather one who, because of his persuasive abilities, is very convincing albeit sometimes very wrong.

The ambitious are not necessarily young, but they are apt to be. They want power and they want their departments to grow, even if this is not in the overall interests of the organization. Yet ambition is a virtue when coupled with wisdom and should not be crushed. Hence, top management is sometimes faced with the task of denying an ambitious manager's budgetary requests while wondering whether he will leave if he is not encouraged. If the ambitious are also convincing, they are apt to obtain undue advantage, which, in turn, will make more taciturn people resent them. Encouraging yet controlling the ambitious is a delicate matter that requires patience and wisdom on the part of superiors.

Managing managers—or as Krannert calls it, "the difficult art of management"—reminds me of the pursuit of a beautiful woman. Relentless pursuit is apt to be unrewarded; instead, one must play her like an elusive fish, alternately luring her and ignoring her, and all in an unhurried fashion. Even though she is driving you to distraction, to win you must appear desirable but only obtainable with effort—for that which is easily caught is soon discarded. Or so I've been told.

Managing managers is not easy, no matter how the task is approached, and it involves saying "No." Some mothers are fascinating in this respect—when they deny their children's requests, they instantly suggest an attractive alternative, thereby encouraging them while showing concern and maintaining control.

These, then, are but a few of the real problems that require recognition in budgeting. To summarize:

1. Some coordinated plan for the forthcoming period is desirable.
2. Traditional budgetary procedures set the level of expenditures.
3. The ambitious want to advance, regardless.
4. Creativity and enthusiasm should be encouraged.
5. Some recommendations may be appealing only because of the way they are presented.
6. There is a tendency to pad budgetary estimates.
7. Competition can be overdone.

If we add to this list

(1) Maslow's observation that people engaged in self-actualization continuously formulate new goals and means of expression;

(2) Herzberg's dissatisfiers (hygiene factors), as well as his principles for loading a job vertically;

(3) the interfering structure of industrial organizations perceived by Argyris;

(4) the group bestowing of power described by Likert;

(5) Drucker's insistence on standards based on excellent performance;

(6) Du Brin's warning that individuals with limited creativity needs exhibit defensive or avoidant behavior in an environment that favors creativity;

(7) the behavoralists' belief that penalties avert offenders from organizational goals instead of improving their performance;

(8) the assertion by Maslow, Argyris, and others that some people ("Zombies") never get beyond the pursuit of lower-level needs;

(9) the emphasis by behavioral researchers that fear-arousing feedback may elicit aggressive feelings, distorted recollection of report contents, aroused cautious reactions, rejection of arguments, and denial of personal relevance of reports; and

(10) the need for management by objectives as described by Odiorne—

we should have a sense of the immensity of the accountant's tasks. Then reflect that employee and corporate needs are forever changing—that the lamb of today may become the tiger of tomorrow—and you will probably appreciate why accountants hesitate to alter any time-tested procedure.

Let us see what these procedures are and then challenge them.

Period Budgeting

Given that the decision to remain in business has been made, and a coordinated plan for the coming period's activities is to be developed, what is the next step in the budgetary process?[3] Top management must next decide what the objectives are for the coming year. Foremost among these objectives lies the decision to retrench, or to maintain industry position, or to expand. Often the option of retrenchment is ignored, although once it was accomplished, the smaller, more efficient operation might suit the owners and managers better. Perhaps retrenchment is ignored because the great preponderance of business literature concentrates on the "going concern," which even shortchanges maintaining present size in favor of growth. Growth is put forth as healthy, as a natural consequence of the economic multiplier and accelerator principles whereby an organization must run faster just to stay in the same place. However, "staying in the same place" may not really be what is wanted. There is nothing inherently bad about being smaller.

Retrenchment is difficult to achieve. People must be fired if retirements, resignations, and deaths are insufficient to reduce the work force to an acceptable level. Then too, seniority provisions in contracts and governmental minority regulations may prevent the company from firing selectively.

[3] Where a budget covers a period of more than a year, say three or five years, it is commonly referred to as a plan. Detail and certainty diminish with increasing time; however, the basic process remains constant. Unless otherwise specified, a year will be assumed for purposes of discussion.

If there is extensive firing, ill will may damage the company image. Along these same lines, any sizable reduction in operations may lead to false rumors of fiscal weakness which, in turn, could endanger the organization's credit standing. It is not easy to liquidate capital assets no longer required by reduced activities; nevertheless, such a reduction resembles labor force reduction in that not replacing equipment can be likened to not replacing employees who retire. On the positive side, if the process is not done hastily, retrenchment may be effected by subcontracting sales orders and discontinuing certain products and divisions. Consider an example: virtually no baseball gloves are manufactured in the United States. Declining productivity relative to labor costs and Taiwan's ability to provide gloves at a much more attractive cost simply led almost all American sporting goods manufacturers to drop production and concentrate on marketing. Profits increased while bother (fights with unions) decreased, furthermore, there was little equipment to get rid of or redirect to other production, since baseball glove manufacturing has many manual operations.

Once the question of organizational size is resolved, management determines (1) what should be measured, and (2) which restrictions should be observed. Deciding what to measure poses monumental problems. For instance, if the company is to retrench, profits might possibly decrease (although this is not a necessary consequence of retrenchment) along with the chaos. Some people would feel better, even though less profit was being generated. How would you measure this new satisfaction? Two things are apparent: dollar profits are insufficient measures of success, and there is no direct measure of "feeling better" in popular managerial use today. For that matter, it is not clear whose feelings count. The euphoria of the managers and surviving employees might be offset by the discontent of the owners and cashiered employees. Perhaps the owners could be mollified by some basically unprovable statement like "With a more efficient organization, profits will undoubtedly improve in the future." But little else can be done by way of measurement than calculating dollar profits and observing that a more compact and efficient organization has resulted. Still, it is worthwhile to supplement the dollar calculations with the organizational information—for this may both help explain the reason for retrenchment and ease the owners' worries about the future.

Too often measurement is restricted by inconvenience and the ready availability of the obvious. For example, legislators have been known to declare their state universities "great" because they boast a lot of magnificient buildings and pay their professors "princely" salaries. These characteristics may contribute to greatness, but other, more substantial attributes are vital. Socrates ran a great school that had neither magnificient buildings nor high pay scales. Indeed, Socrates was a poor man, financially speaking. Greatness today would call for inspired teachers, a significant record of meaningful research; enthusiastic, hardworking students, teachers, and staff; a challenging atmosphere of inquiry and exchange—as well as an outstanding computer, an excellent library, dedicated alumni, and suitable-equipment. There are probably no more than two dozen great universities in the world. Measuring buildings and pay scales is easy but almost irrelevant; measuring the meaningfulness of research, the inspiration of teachers, and the extent of challenge in the intellectual atmosphere is highly relevant but extremely arduous. Again we see that dollar measurements are insufficient.

What might be measured in business? This is a very broad question—one that depends heavily on the interests, skills, imagination, and wisdom of the person asking as well as on those of the person doing the measuring. Profit (in some conception of the word); flows of customers, cash, and units produced; service levels such as number of shortages, duration of waiting; time needed to produce or to sell, and time consumed in waiting for various events; attitudes such as enthusiasm, depression, and anxiety—these are some possible measures of success or lack thereof. Dollars, though they facilitate counting, are overrated as measures of value because (1) many important things do not have an established market price and (2) good yardsticks are characterized by stability. Dollars are just not an excellent common denominator any more—if indeed they ever were.

Let us turn briefly to restrictions that must be recognized at the beginning of (and throughout) budgeting. Prior-year results may point to various excessive expenditures that need to be curtailed. The economic environment may limit activities in certain geographical locations. Certain facilities (for example, delivery trucks) may no longer be available in the accustomed abundance. Competition may have rendered some action inadvisable. Standards, say of quality, and policies, say for services, may need to be changed. New laws may have been passed. These and many other things can lead to restrictions that should be recognized and announced. Additionally, policy should be drawn on supplementary budgets, which are really a special form of restriction. Since the subtleties of supplementary budgets were presented in Chapter 1, they will not be discussed again here. The need to formulate clear definitions of opportunities and emergencies—definitions that are well understood before the situations arise—is apparent. Then, since the possibility of supplementary budgets is apt to detract from the care devoted to the basic budget, it seems advisable (1) to prohibit supplementary budgets, and (2) to provide for a tight, presidentially administered opportunity-emergency fund available only in extraordinary circumstances. Some such fund must exist simply because budgets deal with forecasts and not with 20–20 hindsight.

Sales forecasting. The last of the important preliminaries to period budgeting is arriving at a reliable forecast of sales, for it is on the sales estimate that cash, production, and expense budgets are based. A sloppy job done on the sales forecast would destroy the usefulness of the resulting organizational budgets.

In large organizations the market research staff has primary responsibility for developing the sales forcast. Market research regresses sales on various economic indicators, such as Personal Disposable Income, Unemployment, and Housing Starts, as well as on advertising outlays in various media and other variables. Additionally, market research may study market share via a Markov chain. A Markov chain may be represented by a transition matrix containing elements that show the probability of moving from one state (here, brands A, B, C, . . .) to another given the passage of time.

Example: Two companies, A and B, share a market with A presently holding 35% and B 65%. Company A's research staff has determined by surveys that a customer who now buys A has a .7 probability of buying A next year, while a customer who now buys B has a probability of .8 of sticking with B next year. If next year's total market is estimated as $4,000,000, how much sales revenue will A enjoy?

Present Shares		Transition Matrix	Next Year's Shares
		To:	
$A \quad B$			$A \quad B$

$$(.35, .65) \quad \text{From:} \begin{array}{c} A \\ B \end{array} \begin{bmatrix} .7 & .3 \\ .2 & .8 \end{bmatrix} = (.375, .625)$$

Comments:

1. Note how the rows of the transition matrix sum to 1 because A and B form an exhaustive set of possible states (either A or B must happen).

2. Since A should have .375 of the market ($4,000,000), its sales revenue should amount to $1,500,000 next year.

Marketing Research may also—with the help of sales personnel—prepare demand curves for products that relate selling price to quantity demanded. Regression may be used to obtain such curves. Of course, if there are many suppliers, the going market price is set for all of them; conversely, if there are very few suppliers, each one has a significant effect on price and can make some use of its demand curve, although only the monopoly has free use of its curve.

Salesmen's opinions of the forthcoming sales activity are another source of information on which to base a sales forecast. It is good, however, to keep in mind (1) that salesmen, as a group, have a reputation for optimism, and

(2) that salesmen appear to have a vested interest in making enthusiastic estimates. Thus the salesman who says that his sales may drop next year is not showing the enthusiasm many companies want and may, by this admission, raise doubt about his competence in his manager's mind. Hence it is dangerous to rely heavily on such sales estimates. At the very least, the track record of salesmen's forecasts should be reviewed to see if adjustment in current estimates is advisable.

The sales forcast will also be influenced by answers to the following questions:

1. It the sales force to be expanded or reduced?
2. Have there been any recent advertising campaigns?
3. Will the extent or methods of advertising be changed this year?
4. What is competition doing?
5. Will we have a full product line?
6. Has the gestation period (time between introducing a product and its first generation of revenues) for some new product ended?
7. If any of our products are complementary to (or substitutes for) other products, what lies in store for these other products?
8. Have we induced sales for the present period at the expense of the coming period?
9. Are we going to change any of our credit and/or discount policies?
10. Will we offer any special inducements such as cash rebates on expensive items?[4]

The Cash Budget

I have done work for a hospital that was very sound financially and well managed but nevertheless did not at that time prepare a cash budget. The hospital is located in a climate where the summers are humid and people go away for vacations. As a result, the daily hospital census declines about 10%, causing the hospital to delay paying its bills (bills that would usually have

[4] Note that cash rebates were an instrument used to entice automobile buyers in the depressed times of 1974 and 1975, and that they could have an adverse effect on sales. If one week the rebate on a car is $200 and two weeks later it is $300, some customers might postpone purchasing a car in anticipation that the rebate will go even higher. Of course, the buyer who hesitates runs the risk of the rebate offer being withdrawn.

been paid in 30 days were then paid in 45) to accommodate its obligations to the reduced flow of cash receipts. This is a mild consequence of not doing cash budgeting, and one that the hospital planned to remedy.

A more serious result occurs if delaying payment causes one to lose cash discounts. Two percent off if paid in 10 days, balance due in 20 days, would amount to a loss of $(1 + .02)^{360/10} - 1 = 104\%$ of principal if theoretically compounded every 10 days for one year (here, 360 days) or $36(2\%) = 72\%$ if simple interest only is considered. Either way the cost of lost discounts is formidable; few investments earn so much.

The history of bankruptcies gives ominous testimony to the result of failure to prepare a cash budget. Needs and desires arise that lead to excessive spending (known as "deficit spending" when done by governments) relative to cash receipts. Eventually cash reserves disappear and emergency measures must be taken. If these are inadequate, bankruptcy follows. The need to prepare a cash budget at the company level transcends considerations that the process may inhibit self-actualization on the part of individual managers.

The cash budget, therefore, is a most important tool. It is used to forecast receipts and disbursements to ensure that sufficient cash funds are available to the organization at all times.[5] Stripped to the bare essentials, a cash budget looks like this:

Opening balance
+Receipts
–Disbursements

Ending balance

Naturally, the ending balance of the preceding month becomes the opening balance of the present month. In aggregated form, an example of a three-month budget would look like this:

	January	February	March
Opening cash	\$ 200,000	\$ 130,000	\$ 300,000
+Receipts	1,450,000	1,580,000	1,120,000
–Disbursements	(1,520,000)	(1,410,000)	(1,380,000)
Ending cash	\$ 130,000	\$ 300,000	\$ 40,000

Observe how the ending cash balance fluctuates in the illustration shown above. If the company can make do with \$40,000 one month, why should other months be higher? There may be good reasons, but nonetheless the

[5] Many inventory models—especially those dealing with hoarding—attack the same problem as the cash budget. Cash, after all, is but one type of inventory.

question should be asked. Then again, shouldn't extra ending cash be invested in short-term obligations to earn interest?

It is another aim of cash budgeting to point out the need for investment of idle cash. But what constitutes "idle"? Viewed from a different perspective, why does one (a business) carry cash? Economists say that cash is carried

(1) As a provision for ordinary transactions,

(2) as a precaution against possible emergencies, and

(3) as a ready source of funds for speculative purposes.

Psychologists would add that cash is carried because it is emotionally satisfying to do so. —why? For all of the foregoing reasons, and also perhaps because a person simply likes the looks and feel of cash or wants to be able to impress others. Whatever the reasons, management should establish a range (example, $\$30,000 \leq \text{balance} \leq \$50,000$) for the ending cash balance, keeping in mind that many of the monthly cash receipts and disbursements are just estimates that are subject to error. Cash in excess of the upper range limit should be considered idle and available for investment; cash that is short of the range indicates the need for fund raising.

Let us look into a more detailed example.

Example: Ross Fabricators, Inc. has assembled the following information prepatory to completing a cash budget for the first three months of the year:

	January	February	March
Sales (all on credit)	$400,000	$500,000	$700,000
Purchases (cash)	200,000	380,000	150,000
Operating expenses (cash)	230,000	210,000	150,000

Sales in the preceding October, November, and December were $450,000, $700,000, and $600,000 respectively.

Cash collections are estimated according to the formula

$y_i = .7x_{i-1} + .2x_{i-2} + .05x_{i-3}$, where, y_i are collections and x_i are sales in month i

Dividends of $150,000 must be paid January 25th.

The yearly mortgage payment is due March 15th (the mortgage was a 10-year, 8% contract originally for $2,013,030).

Short-term borrowings may be made and repaid in multiples of $10,000 at 1% per month interest; principal and interest are payable in the ensuing month.

The cash balance at December 31st will be \$87,000 and no short-term loans will be outstanding.

The cash balance must fall in the range \$70,000 $\leq$ balance $\leq$ \$100,000.

The cash budget appears in Exhibit 1 along with comments about how certain figures were obtained and what interpretations might be given the budget results. Comment 3 deals with the calculation of the mortgage payment; if you have not previously had experience with discounting money flows, just use Table 4 in Appendix A as directed for the present. When you get to Chapter 9, compounding and discounting processes will be explained in detail. You should also note comments 4 and 5, which point to possible financial difficulties for Ross Fabricators, Inc.

Exhibit 1 Cash Budget for January, February, and March Ross Fabricators, Inc.

	January	February	March
Opening balance	\$ 87,000	\$ 89,500	\$ 74,500
Receipts: Accounts receivable	582,500	435,000	460,000
Short-term bank loan	–0–	140,000	280,000
Total	\$669,500	\$664,500	\$814,500
Disbursements: Purchases	\$200,000	\$380,000	\$150,000
Operating expenses	230,000	210,000	150,000
Dividends	150,000	–0–	–0–
Mortgage	–0–	–0–	300,000
Short-term bank loan	–0–	–0–	140,000
Interest on above loan	–0–	–0–	1,400
Total	\$580,000	\$590,000	\$741,400
Ending balance	\$ 89,500	\$ 74,500	\$ 73,100

Comments:

1. Cash collections for January $= y_J = .7x_D + .2x_N + .05x_O = .7(600{,}000) + .2(700{,}000) + .05(450{,}000) = 582{,}500$.

2. The amount of the short-term loan in February was determined by adding the February disbursements and the minimum desired cash balance, subtracting the sum of opening balance and receipts (from accounts receivable), and rounding the remainder to the next highest multiple of \$10,000.

3. The uniform mortgage payment was determined by dividing the original amount of the mortgage (\$2,013,030) by the 10-year, 8% factor—B(10, 8)—found in Table 4, Appendix A.

4. Management might well be alarmed by the large increase in short-term bank loans that has taken place after only three months.

5. Management should ascertain when short-term financing will no longer be necessary by calling for cash budgets for the ensuing months (April, May, . . .). If this is not attended to, any refusal by the bank to continue the line of credit might precipitate emergency actions (like selling capital assets or trying to sell bonds or stocks on short notice) or even bankruptcy if other actions fail.

Markov Chains and Estimating Collections

Possibly the formula for cash collections from accounts receivable struck you as convenient. Regression analysis might provide such a formula, but a more interesting approach that may yield better estimates of collections lies in applying a Markov chain to aged accounts receivable totals.[6]

The type of Markov chain that will now be used differs from the ordinary chain used earlier to predict market shares. We shall use an "absorbing" Markov chain that contains the transient (nonabsorbing) states 0, 1, 2, 3, 4 (where 0 indicates a current account, 1 indicates an account that is one month past due, and so forth) and the absorbing (trapping) states P and B (which stand for paid and bad, respectively) to study how the states change in one month's time. What is changing (transiting) is the dollars in each account, not the accounts themselves. Predictions will be improved if accounts are first grouped according to size and a transition matrix for each group is then calculated. Otherwise, if there are very large accounts mixed in with lots of small accounts, any time a large account makes a payment, the transition probabilities will be drastically affected. Once the dollars in an account are paid or declared doubtful of payment (bad), they have been "absorbed" and cannot thereafter be resurrected to bounce around again (that is, transit) among the nonabsorbing states. In canonical form, the transition matrix looks like this:

$$\begin{array}{c} \\ P \\ B \\ 0 \\ 1 \\ 2 \\ \vdots \\ n \end{array} \begin{array}{c} P\ \ B\ \ 0\ \ 1\ \ 2 \ldots n \\ \left[\begin{array}{c|c} I & \varnothing \\ \hline R & Q \end{array}\right] \end{array}$$

I = the identity matrix for the trapping states; once in a trapping state, the probability of remaining there is 1

$\varnothing$ = the null matrix that reflects the impossibility of leaving the trapping states

R = the settlement matrix showing the probability of absorption

Q = the matrix of nonabsorbing (transient) states

Shown below are aged accounts receivable data provided by a cooperating manufacturer. Each account has had its balance distributed among the aging categories depending on when the separate charges comprising it arose; what appear below are the totals of the individual charges in each category.

---

[6] The application of Markov chains to accounts receivable was first suggested in R. M. Cyert, H. J. Davidson, and G. L. Thompson, "Estimation of the Allowance for Doubtful Accounts by Markov Chains," *Management Science*, August 1962, pp. 287–303. The approach that is developed in this chapter differs considerably from the approach in this pioneering article. The approach in this chapter (1) uses partial-balance aging of accounts receivable, (2) provides for updating of the transition matrix via exponential smoothing, and (3) ignores steady-state results as not being germane to the problem of estimating flows in ordinary circumstance.

Because steady-state analysis may be employed in other ways, and because the Cyert, *et al* study is so theoretically interesting in itself, it is summarized in the appendix to this chapter.

Month	Total	0	1	2	3	4
M	13,691,904	7,295,147	4,335,869	801,665	294,535	964,688
J	11,842,230	5,854,814	2,612,295	2,165,863	404,018	805,240
J	10,845,787	5,546,897	2,028,221	1,234,956	1,239,993	795,720
A	9,995,614	5,047,815	2,125,711	886,125	583,364	1,352,599
S	12,330,014	7,496,454	2,132,382	1,043,350	506,721	1,151,107

Since the data in state 4 in month i exceed the data in state 3 in month $i - 1$; it is clear that accounts are carried on the ledger that are, in fact, more than 120 days past due. Bad debts are only recognized in state 4 because, although bad customers usually have no intention of paying even at time of purchase, it takes a while to discover who is good and who is bad.

The amount of bad debts recognized in each of the above months was

Month	Bad Debts
M	76,817
J	58,649
J	12,698
A	48,483
S	74,596

We shall form the Markov chain transition matrix for each month from the above data. Observe that there is considerable variation in both the monthly balances and their agings. To track this variation, exponential smoothing will be introduced, using the matrix formula $\hat{A}_{i+1} = \bar{A}_i = .8T_i + .2\bar{A}_{i-1}$, where $\bar{A}$ is the exponentially smoothed matrix and T is the transition matrix. The smoothing constant, .8, was determined to be best by trial-and-error use of a computer program incorporating over three years of data. Another result of the computer program was the average matrix for May, $\bar{A}_M$:

	P	B	0	1	2	3	4
P	1	0	0	0	0	0	0
B	0	1	0	0	0	0	0
0	.64817	0	0	.35183	0	0	0
1	.62677	0	0	0	.37323	0	0
2	.53756	0	0	0	0	.46244	0
3	.40000	0	0	0	0	0	.60000
4	.40206	.05265	0	0	0	0	.54528

Here elements a_{PP} and a_{BB} both equal 1 to indicate that once a dollar has been paid or declared bad, it has been absorbed.

Note that the a_{3P} element equals .40000. This reflects the apparently tenable assumption that probability of payment declines as accounts get older. Whatever error in estimating cash is made (by assuming that three-month-old accounts have only a .4 probability of paying in the fourth month) will be corrected when introducing the bad debt data to calculate a_{4P} and a_{4B}.

Here is how the transition matrix for June (that is, T_J) is calculated:

The general scheme is to note how many dollars go from state j in month i to state $j + 1$ in month $i + 1$ with the difference being considered paid. We start with May as month i; hence June is $i + 1$.

i, j		$i+1, j+1$		Paid	Probability of Paid
7,295,147	−	2,612,295	=	4,682,852	4,682,852/7,295,147 = .64191
4,335,869	−	2,165,863	=	2,170,006	2,170,006/4,335,869 = .50048
801,665	−	404,018	=	397,647	397,647/801,665 = .49603
294,535	−	176,721	=	117,814	117,814/294,535 = .40000
*(964,688 + 176,721)	−	(805,240 + 58,649)	=	277,520	277,520/964,688 = .28768
					Probability of Bad
					58,649/964,688 = .06080

* Note: Sixty percent of $t_{i,3}$ is assumed to get one month older and enter $t_{i+1,4}$. Therefore, .6(294,535) = 176,721. Also recall that the July bad debts = 58,649.

The transition matrix, T_{JUNE}, is prepared from these probabilities and the fact that the rows in a stochastic matrix sum to 1:

	P	B	0	1	2	3	4
P	1	0	0	0	0	0	0
B	0	1	0	0	0	0	0
0	.64191	0	0	.35809	0	0	0
1	.50048	0	0	0	.49952	0	0
2	.49603	0	0	0	0	.50397	0
3	.40000	0	0	0	0	0	.60000
4	.28768	.06080	0	0	0	0	.65152

Observe that in one month's time an account that was current (state 0) can either be paid (P) or become one month old (1). With partial balance aging, it is not possible for it to remain current.

With the transition matrix for June at hand, it becomes a simple matter to calculate the average (or exponentially smoothed) matrix for June and to use the result as an estimate of the July average matrix. In symbols:

$$\hat{A}_{\text{JULY}} = \bar{A}_{\text{JUNE}} = .8T_{\text{JUNE}} + .2\bar{A}_{\text{MAY}}$$

	P	B	0	1	2	3	4
P	1	0	0	0	0	0	0
$= B$	0	1	0	0	0	0	0
0	.64316	0	0	.35684	0	0	0
1	.52574	0	0	0	.47426	0	0
2	.50433	0	0	0	0	.49567	
3	.40000	0	0	0	0	0	.60000
4	.31055	.05917	0	0	0	0	.63028

The last matrix may now be multiplied by the June aging vector, J_A, to obtain an estimate of the July collections, bad debts, and aging:

$$\text{June}_A \qquad\qquad \hat{A}_{\text{JULY}} = \text{July}_E$$

$$(0;\ 0;\ 5{,}854{,}814;\ 2{,}612{,}295;\ 2{,}165{,}863;\ 404{,}018;\ 805{,}240)\hat{A}_{\text{j}} = (6{,}642{,}954;\ 47{,}646;\ 0;\ 2{,}089{,}232;\ 1{,}238{,}907;\ 1{,}073{,}553;\ 749{,}938)$$

Note: The June$_A$ vector above comes from the aging data previously presented. The leading zeros are for states P and B so that dimensional rules of multiplication may be observed.

Comment: The sum of the June aging vector equals the sum of the July aging vector.

As long as we attempt to predict only one month in advance, we will not need to estimate current sales. The present process can be repeated without change. The arithmetic involved in doing so, of course, borders on the unbearable; consequently, it is advisable to resort to the computer. My program yielded these results:

$$\text{August}_E = (5{,}964{,}006;\ 19{,}454;\ 0;\ 1{,}933{,}108;\ 959{,}452;\ 688{,}052;\ 1{,}281{,}715)$$
$$\text{September}_E = (5{,}285{,}528;\ 72{,}545;\ 0;\ 1{,}899{,}395;\ 944{,}088;\ 433{,}608;\ 1{,}360{,}450)$$
$$\text{October}_E = (6{,}541{,}765;\ 63{,}135;\ 0;\ 3{,}097{,}576;\ 1{,}026{,}710;\ 579{,}411;\ 1{,}021{,}417)$$

The most demanding test of this approach is to contrast actual results with the above estimates:

Month	Actual Paid	Estimated Paid	Actual − Estimated	Percent Error
July	6,530,642	6,642,954	−112,312	−1.72%
August	5,849,505	5,964,006	−114,501	−1.96%
September	5,087,458	5,285,528	−198,070	−3.89%
October	7,097,561	6,541,765	555,796	7.83%

The actual payments can be calculated by using the aging vectors and bad debts data for months i and $i + 1$.[7]

The manufacturer for whom this study was conducted wanted to forecast cash flow for four months ahead and to update the four-month forecast each month. The procedures just described did a considerably better job (much

[7] Other tests could be devised. It would be more common practice to ignore exponential smoothing, to develop the average of many month's transition matrices, and to assume it representative of every month. (The smoothed average could be so used, of course.) Using the average matrix, the fundamental matrix of the system could be developed, and from it a variance could be calculated. Then, by invoking the central limit theorem, the analyst could say, for instance, that the expected collections plus and minus two standard deviations represented the range in which actual collections would fall about 95% of the time. Such a procedure, however, is not a test in the sense that would appeal to most businessmen. Rather, it is a means of announcing the uncertainty of the estimate. It helps to hedge on the estimate; the analyst can look at actual payments, for instance, and say, "Well, that falls in the tolerance range." The exponentially smoothed approach could also operate in this way by getting the manager to express some acceptable percentage of error. The test against actual is the acid test as far as businessmen are concerned.

less error) of updating than his ordinary approach, which relied on arithmetic and educated guesswork.

To move ahead four months at a time (or longer, if desired), regression analysis was introduced to forecast sales. Scattergraphs of sales over a three-year period generated curves like those in Figure 1.

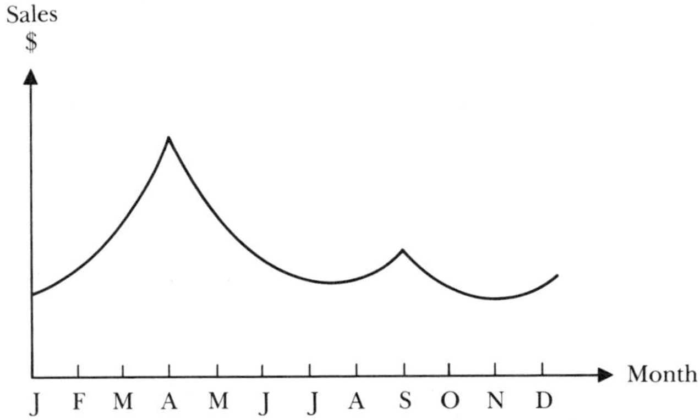

Figure 1

A series of three quadratic equations was obtained:

$S = \$7{,}425{,}950 - \$6{,}517{,}580X + \$2{,}073{,}360X^2$, where $X = 1, 2, 3$, or 4 (January, February, March, April) and the coefficient of determination (r^2) was .951

$S = \$19{,}149{,}400 - \$3{,}267{,}800X + \$189{,}262X^2$, where $X = 5, 6, 7$, or 8 (May, June, July, August) and the coefficient of determination was .903

$S = \$105{,}692{,}000 - \$18{,}432{,}700X + \$837{,}093X^2$, where $X = 9, 10, 11$, or 12 (September, October, November, December) and the coefficient of determination was .904

Using these equations, the monthly sales estimates became

(J, F, M, A) = (2,981,730; 2,684,230; 6,533,450; 14,529,390)
(M, J, J, A) = (7,541,950; 6,356,032; 5,548,638; 5,119,768)
(S, O, N, D) = (7,597,859; 5,068,900; 4,214,019; 5,033,216)

Incorporating sales estimates into the computer program, and having it use actual aging when updating the first of the four months in the sub-period and introducing sales estimates and prior-month aging forecasts to go ahead for the additional three months, resulted in a number of branching decisions. A flowchart illustrating the process is shown in Figure 2.

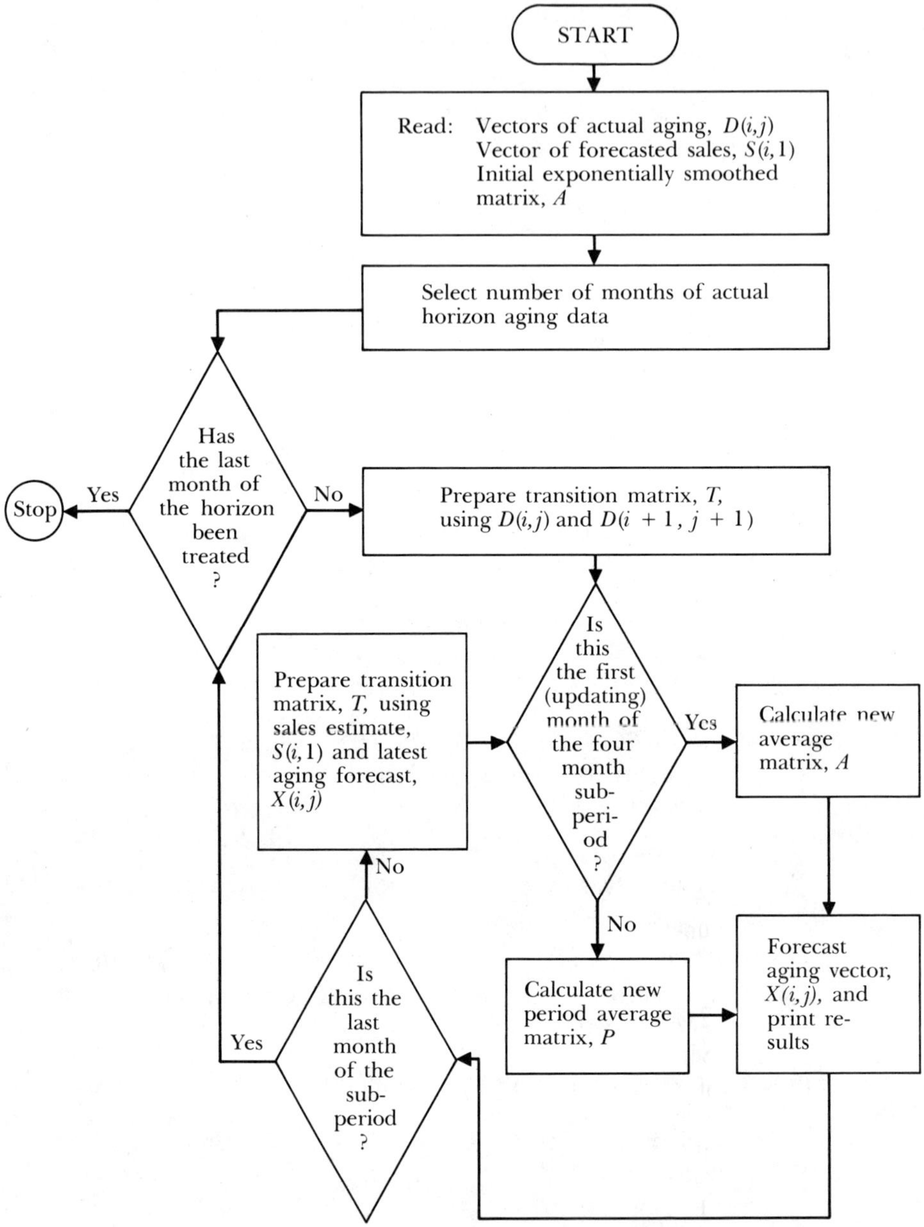

Comment: Although the logic of this flowchart is sound and should be easy to follow, the chart itself could be simplified, since it can be shown that the sub-period transition matrices duplicate the updated average matrix, A.

Figure 2

In this scheme, it is possible to read in many months of actual aging data to cover any desired horizon and then to see how the estimates would have gone for each four-month subperiod. This makes it possible to experiment with the smoothing constant to determine what value best reflects the change in customer paying habits. Eventually, of course, the horizon becomes the current month and the program forecasts results for the coming four months.

Given the goal of updating July and forecasting the ensuing three months based on estimated sales, the program generated the cash flows shown below.

Month	Actual Paid	Estimated Paid	Actual − Estimated	Percent Error
July	6,530,642	6,642,982	−112,340	−1.72%
August	5,849,505	5,954,200	−104,695	−1.79%
September	5,087,458	5,425,958	−338,500	−6.65%
October	7,097,561	6,850,199	247,362	3.49%

Naturally, as one attempts to estimate further and further into the future, he gets the increasingly uncomfortable feeling of being out on a limb of a very skinny tree. He expects forecasts to be less reliable as the estimation period is extended. Nevertheless, there is little difference between the error percentages shown above and those calculated previously when forecasting only one month in advance.

The manufacturer found these cash estimates highly acceptable. Furthermore, the forecasted aging vectors were useful for the purpose of anticipating a large inventory of older charges that required control. When the monthly transition matrix changed appreciably, the manager of accounts receivable sought the reason why.

Does everything go as smoothly as the above analysis would indicate? Most certainly not. In this study, about one month in five the error exceeds 10% and may go as high as 30%. But alarming as this may seem, it is to be expected when the size of customer balances varies significantly and the pattern of payment fluctuates. The focus should not be so much on the remaining high error, but rather on the results of the methods presently in use by the business. In general, my limited investigations seem to show that once cash-flow estimates have been prepared for the budget, no business checks thereafter to see what error is generated by the methods it used. So in subjecting the Markovian approach to the acid test of actual payments, we have unnecessarily exposed in to scrutiny and ridicule.

It is necessary to maintain the computer programs involved. The regressions may need changing as time goes on and new smoothing constants must be investigated. In time, if the paying habits (as distinguished from the buying habits reflected in sales) of customers formed a pattern, cyclical Markovian analysis might be appropriate.

It is also comforting to keep in mind that (1) errors that vary in sign (positive in one month and negative in the next) offset one another; and (2) some errors are easier to live with than others—it is a pleasant surprise to find you have underestimated cash flow and something else in the case of overestimation. Another way of viewing offsetting errors is that the cash budget for the quarter or for the half year may be very accurate even though individual months missed the mark.

The company whose data was just presented felt it important to influence customers to pay faster. With inflation running nearly 1% per month, purchasing power of payments received was eroding at the same rate; consequently, the company introduced campaigns offering discounts for early payment. This, of course, interfered with the transition matrices, which could only reflect changes in paying patterns (via the smoothing constant) after the fact. The exponentially smoothed matrix, however, was still considered useful for two reasons:

1. The Markovian estimates were used as the base for estimating changes (for example, "cash collections should be 10% higher than the Markovian estimate for month i and 10% lower in $i + 1$") that resulted from the campaign.
2. The Markovian estimates were assumed to measure what would have happened had there been no campaign. Therefore, by subtracting the estimates from the actual results, a measure of the effectiveness of the campaign was obtained for comparison with the cost of the campaign. This revealed that some campaigns were unjustified financially—in other words, the benefits of obtaining receipts sooner were less than the cost of obtaining them.

Where the customers' paying habits form no recognizable pattern (not the case in this example, but decidedly the case in another example dealing with the accounts receivable of a medium-sized hospital), exponential smoothing *may* be dropped in favor of simple averaging of many months' transition matrices. This is like using a probability distribution and its expected value. The differences between estimates and actuals become greater—perhaps significantly so. But even in this situation, the Markovian estimates appear to be at least as good as those obtained by guesswork.

Responsibility Accounting

We have technically developed the sales estimate and the cash budget with some of the flows it reflects. Now let us extend period budgeting into the area of responsibility accounting and in the process accomplish the marriage of planning and control. As a vehicle for our discussions we shall use the financial operating statements of the Lumber & Plywood Division of the St. Regis Paper Company for June 1975.[8]

St. Regis is one of the largest integrated forest products companies in the world; its Lumber & Plywood Division is headquartered in Tacoma, Washington. Exhibit 2 shows various processing stages of the Tacoma sawmill and studmill. Actually there are five departments in the Tacoma operations: Sawmill (dimension lumber 2 inches thick, timbers at least 4 inches by 4 inches thick); Studmill (2″ × 4″ × 8′ studs, nominal measurements); Sawmill Chipper (whole-log chipping for particleboard); Studmill Chipper (whole-log chipping for particleboard); and Logging (forest maintenance, receipt and storage of logs cut from forests). The accounting of the Sawmill, for example, is organized around service and production responsibility centers, which consist of one or more major pieces of equipment or labor operations. The production responsibility centers are: Log Handling, Sawmilling, Drying, Surfacing, and Shipping.

---

[8] Forest industries will be used for several illustrations in this textbook because I feel people should know more about them. Consider:

1. Lumber is basically the only renewable energy resource.
2. Lumber products are extremely diversified and often essential.
3. Lumber products are biodegradable and hence are not a source of pollution in the sense that glass, plastic, and metal products are.
4. Forests contain many forms of wildlife whose safety and continued existence mandate cautious managerial practices.
5. Forests provide recreational facilities as well as watersheds that must also be managed if social costs are to be tolerable.
6. Forests are scenic wonders that serve to restore one's spirits.

To help you appreciate the costs involved—what would your life be like if you were deprived of forests and all they offer? While contemplating the list above, you might like to include the fact that, unlike animals, which consume oxygen and give off carbon dioxide, growing trees consume carbon dioxide and produce oxygen. Mature trees, however (1) yield little oxygen, (2) are a hazard to other trees, (3) do very little growing in their cambium layers, and (4) are a waste of timber if not harvested.

It does not take much reflection to appreciate the vast importance of forests in one's life. It is not difficult to become disturbed when you learn that commercial forests (of the 500 million acres of such forests in the United States, the federal government owns 22%, private individuals 59%, industry 13%, and state and local governments 6%) under federal govermental control grow at about half the rate of industrially owned forests because of (a) insufficient funds for management, (b) less desirable tracts, and (c) legal restrictions; offer for sale about three-fourths of the harvest they could provide on a sustained yield basis with existing stands; and can be used as a fiscal tool to regulate inflation and housing costs (by limiting supply and thereby raising price). Furthermore, it is likely that preservationists (as distinguished from conservationists) will use the Wilderness Act of 1964 to remove millions of acres of National Forests from the harvestable category and put them into the Wilderness System along with deserts, barren promontories, and rocky canyons. In the Wilderness System lack of management causes these forests to become eyesores while increasing the hazards of fire and disease infestation; furthermore, the wilderness is a worse habitat for wildlife than the managed forest.

When one realizes that companies like St. Regis, Weyerhaeuser, Georgia Pacific, U.S. Plywood, and International Paper maintain healthy "oxygen factories" and permit use of their lands for public recreation, in addition to providing watersheds and forest products, he may even come to feel a sense of indebtedness.

Exhibit 2

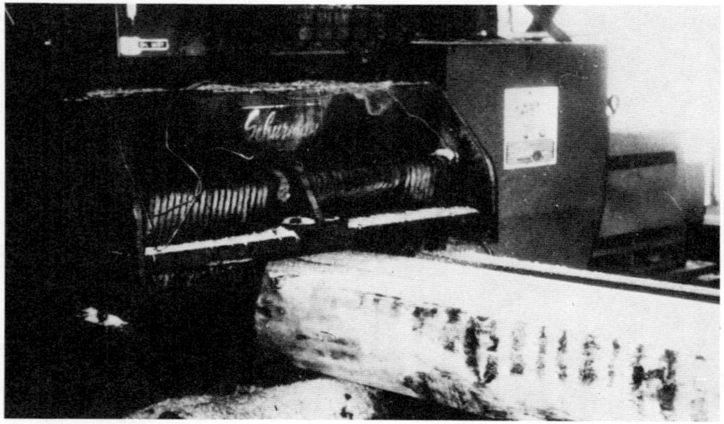

Double Arbor Edger

Rough Trim Saw

Log Deck

Ring Debarker

Exhibit 2 (*cont.*)

Log Yard

Hauling Logs

Logs Going to Scaling

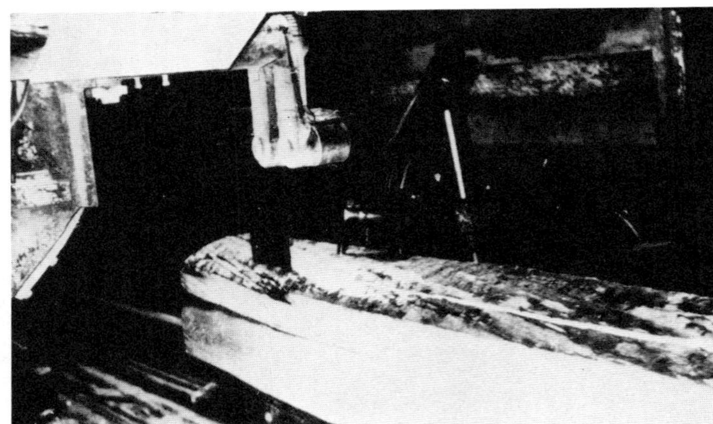

Headrig

Exhibit 3 (Line Management) Tacoma Sawmill Summary of Net Results for June 1975

Current Month

Volume	Sales	Production
Actual	5,973,593 ft.	6,309,365 ft.
Budget	6,960,000 ft.	6,960,000 ft.
Variance	(986,407) ft.	(650,635) ft.

	Lumber Scale	Log Scale	Overrun	%
Fir	3,178,707	2,256,465	922,242	40.87
Hemlock	3,130,658	2,013,345	1,117,313	55.50
Total	6,309,365	4,269,810	2,039,555	47.77

Sales:	Actual Volume	Total Amount	Average Per M	Budget Per M	Variance Per M
Gross Trade Sales-Lumber	2,567,617	$341,575.69	$133.03	$ 95.88	$ 37.15
Less: Cash Discounts		(6,828.79)	(2.66)	(1.92)	(.74)
Net Trade Sales-Lumber	2,567,617	$334,746.89	$130.37	$ 93.96	$ 36.41
Interdivisional Sales—D/Y	3,287,566	411,418.55	125.14	109.85	15.29
Interdivisional Sales—Other	97,536	14,363.20	147.26	—	147.26
Intramill Sales	9,153	1,391.94	152.07	210.00	(57.93)
Plant Usage	11,721	1,477.37	126.04	109.86	16.18
Subtotal—Net Sales-Lumber	5,973,593	$763,397.95	127.79	106.40	21.39
Net Sales-Chips (bone dry tons)	3,647.87	184,840.85	50.67	62.48	(11.81)
Net Sales-Bark Mulch (Cu. Yds.)	2,060.00	2,884.00	1.40	1.40	—
Net Sales-Other By-Products	—	2,145.74	—	—	—
Total Net Sales	5,973,593	$953,268.54	$159.58	$137.61	$ 21.97

Cost of Lumber Sales:

No. of Op. Hrs.	Rough Green Lumber Costs	Actual Volume	Total Amount	Average Per M	Budget Per M	Variance Per M
	Logs Used-Log Scale	4,269,810				
	Over-run %	47.77				
	Logs Used-Lumber Scale	6,309,365	$532,636.42	$ 84.42	$ 78.00	$ (6.42)
282	Log Handling	”	14,565.90	2.31	1.01	(1.30)
282	3% Property, Fire, Safety	”	1,229.56	.19	.15	(0.4)
	Subtotal: Log Costs	6,309,365	$548,431.88	$ 86.92	$ 79.16	$ (7.76)

Year-To-Date

The same arrangement as "Current Month"—with cumulative data

	Sawmilling Costs					
4135	Sawing	6,309,365	$195,907.25	$ 31.05	$ 24.29	$ (6.76)
702	Sorting	5,969,637	18,274.13	3.06	4.03	1.00
279	Unit Stacker	"	8,864.30	1.48	1.46	(.02)
421	Timber Deck	339,728	8,162.45	24.03	29.21	5.18
449	Yarding	6,309,365	14,867.72	2.36	.83	(1.53)
1029	Clean-Up	"	17,331.74	2.75	1.98	(.77)
7015	60% of Property, Fire, Safety	"	24,591.17	3.89	2.92	(.97)
	Subtotal: Sawmilling Costs	"	$287,998.76	45.65	36.59	(9.06)
	Cost of Rough Green Lumber Produced	6,309,365	$836,430,64	$132.57	$115.75	$ (16.82)
	Drying Costs					
109	Dry Kiln "C"	2,940,000	$ 15,717.50	$ 5.35	$ 5.64	$ .29
87	Dry Kiln "F"	1,498,000	14,404.36	9.62	7.36	(2.26)
⋮	⋮		⋮			
244	2% of Property, Fire, Safety	4,438,000	819.71	.18	.22	.04
	Total Drying Costs	4,438,000	$ 32,291.22	$ 7.28	$ 7.22	$ (.06)
	⋮		⋮			
	Total Surfacing Costs	6,400,605	$100,464.54	$ 15.70	$ 13.48	$ (2.22)
	⋮		⋮			
	Total Shipping Costs	5,973,228	$ 12,943.89	$ 2.17	$ 5.10	$ 2.93
	Total Cost of Lumber Produced	6,309,365	$982,130.29	$155.66	$138.99	$ (16.67)
	Beginning Inventory	3,630,962	$312,843.69	$ 86.16	$ 84.36	$ 1.80
	Ending Inventory	(3,966,734)	(341,773.80)	(86.16)	(84.36)	1.80
	Total Cost of Lumber Sales	5,973,593	$953,200.18	$159.57	$138.99	$ (20.58)
	Total Chipping Costs	3,647.87	33,687.70	9.24	9.89	.65
	Total Selling & Administrative Expense	5,973,593	33,317.95	5.58	4.62	(.96)
	Total Expenses	5,973,593	$1,020,205.83	170.79	148.43	22.36
	Net Operating Income (Loss)	5,973,593	$ (66,937.29)	$ (11.21)	$ (10.82)	$ (.39)

Exhibit 4 (Middle Management) Tacoma Sawmill Earnings Report for June 1975

Net Sales:	Actual Volume	Actual Amount ($)	Actual Unit ($)	Budget Volume	Budget Amount ($)	Budget Unit ($)	Over (Under) Budget Volume	Over (Under) Budget Amount ($)	Over (Under) Budget Unit ($)
Lumber: Trade	2,567,617	334,747	130.37	3,622,000	340,336	93.96	(1,054,383)	(5,579)	36.41
Intercompany	3,405,976	428,651	125.85	3,338,000	400,230	119.90	67,976	28,421	5.95
Total	5,973,593	763,398	127.80	6,960,000	740,556	106.40	(986,407)	22,842)	21.40
Chips: Trade									
Intercompany	3,648	184,841	50.67	3,397	212,253	62.48	251	(27,412)	(11.81)
Total	3,648	184,841	50.67	3,397	212,253	62.48	251	(27,412)	(11.81)
Bark/Other: Trade		2,973			4,237			(1,264)	
Intercompany		2,057			720			1,337	
Total		5,030			4,957			73	
Total Net Sales	5,973,593	953,269	159.58	6,960,000	957,766	137.61	(986,407)	(4,497)	21.97
Cost of Sales									
Lumber:									
Logs-Fir	3,178,707	304,746	95.87	2,038,000	185.651	88.91	1,090,707	119,095	6.96
Hemlock	3,130,658	227,890	72.79	4,872,000	357,229	73.32	(1,741,342)	(129,339)	(.53)
Subtotal	6,309,365	532,636	84.42	6,960,000	542,880	78.00	(650,635)	(10,244)	6.42
Log Handling									
—Labor (L)	"	9,272	1.46	"	6,948	1.00	"	2,324	.46
—Other (O)	"	5,294	.84	"	26	—	"	5,268	.84
Sawmilling—L	"	163,830	25.97	"	158,848	22.82	"	4,982	3.15
—O	"	99,578	15.78	"	75,507	10.85	"	24,071	4.93
Drying —L	4,438,000	7,834	1.77	4,872,000	12,411	2.55	(434,000)	(4,577)	(.78)
—O	"	23,638	5.33	"	21,652	4.44	"	1,986	.89
Surfacing —L	6,400,605	74,076	11.57	6,756,000	72,058	10.67	(355,395)	2,018	.90
—O	"	13,273	2.07	"	7,406	1.10	"	5,867	.97
Shipping —L	5,973,228	6,579	1.10	6,960,000	16,656	2.39	(986,772)	(10,077)	(1.29)
—O	"	5,136	.86	"	16,637	2.39	"	(11,501)	(1.53)
Property Expense	6,309,365	37,002	5.86	6,960,000	31,002	4.45	(650,635)	6,000	1.41
Fire Protection	"	2,509	.40	"	3,804	.55	"	(1,295)	(.15)
Safety	"	1,474	.23	"	1,523	.22	"	(49)	.01
Manufacturing Cost	6,309,365	982,131	155.66	6,960,000	967,358	138.99	(650,635)	14,773	16.67
Inventory Change	(335,772)	(28,930)			—		(335,772)	(28,930)	
Cost of Sales —Lumber	5,973,593	953,201	159.57	6,960,000	967,358	138.99	(986,407)	(14,157)	20.58

Chips:									
Debarker —L	3,648	9,996	2.74	3,397	6,657	1.96	251	3,339	.78
—O	"	7,998	2.19	"	12,946	3.81	"	(4,948)	(1.62)
Chipping —L	"	5,489	1.50	"	5,818	1.72	"	(329)	(.22)
—O	"	3,261	.89	"	2,288	.67	"	973	.22
Bark Mulch—L	"	75	.02	"	133	.04	"	(58)	(.02)
—O	"	109	.03	"	360	.11	"	(251)	(.08)
Property Expense	"	5,252	1.45	"	3,922	1.15	"	1,330	.30
Cost of Sales —Chips	3,648	32,180	8.82	3,397	32,132	9.46	251	48	(.64)
Selling Expense	5,973,593	4,131	.69	6,960,000	4,439	.64	(986,407)	(308)	.05
Administrative Expense	"	13,674	2.29	"	13,674	1.96	"	—	.33
Local Administrative Expense	"	17,020	2.85	"	15,511	2.23	"	1,509	.62
Total	5,973,593	34,825	5.83	6,960,000	33,624	4.83	(986,407)	1,201	1.00
Net Income (Loss)	5,973,593	(66,937)	(11.21)	6,960,000	(75,348)	(10.82)	(986,407)	8,411	(.39)

Exhibit 5 (Top Management) Lumber & Plywood Division Earnings Report for June 1975

	Actual			Budget			Over (Under) Budget		
Net Sales:	Volume	Amount ($)	Unit ($)	Volume	Amount ($)	Unit ($)	Volume	Amount ($)	Unit ($)
Sawmill	5,973,593	763,398	127.80	6,960,000	740,556	106.40	(986,407)	22,842	21.40
Studmill	4,663,301	588,667	126.23	2,640,000	243,408	92.20	2,023,301	345,259	34.03
Chip:									
Sawmill (residual)	3,648	184,841	50.67	3,397	212,253	62.48	251	(27,412)	(11.81)
Studmill (residual)	4,721	231,374	49.01	2,526	146,114	57.84	2,195	85,260	(8.83)
Sawmill (whole log)	6,640	413,253	62.24	19,615	975,876	49.75	(12,975)	(562,623)	12.49
Studmill (whole log)	3,876	189,155	48.80	3,952	172,198	43.57	(76)	16,957	5.23
Logging	19,223,709	2,851,438	148.33	3,484,300	4,366,060	125.31	(15,619,291)	(1,514,622)	23.02
Bark and Other:									
Sawmill		5,030			4,957			73	
Studmill		62,320			25,526			36,794	
Sawmill-Chipper		1,267			3,364			(2,097)	
Total Revenues		5,290,743			6,890,312			1,599,569	
Cost of Sales:									
Sawmill		985,381			999,490			(14,109)	
Studmill		656,887			360,193			296,694	
Sawmill Chipper		409,448			974,930			(565,482)	
Studmill Chipper		188,717			171,151			17,566	
Logging		2,405,845			4,073,960			(1,668,115)	
Total		4,646,278			6,579,724			(1,933,446)	
Operating Expenses:									
Selling Expense		9,395			9,204			191	
Administrative Expense		37,346			37,346			–0–	
Local Administrative Expense		86,887			77,397			9,490	
Total		133,628			123,947			9,681	
Total Expense		4,779,906			6,703,671			(1,923,765)	
Net Income		510,837			186,641			324,196	
Sawmill		(66,937)			(75,348)			8,411	
Studmill		199,397			30,556			168,841	
Sawmill Chipper		–0–			–0–			–0–	
Studmill		–0–			–0–			–0–	
Logging		378,377			231,433			146,944	
Net Income (as above)		510,837			186,641			324,196	

You will see the costs for June 1975 for some of these processes and responsibility centers in Exhibits 3, 4, and 5. In the Sawmill, Log Handling sees to forklifting and debarking of logs, which are then fed via conveyors to Sawmilling. Sawmilling includes sawing (which, in turn, includes the head-rig, edger, and trimmer), sorting (which includes marking and automatic sorting), unit stacker (stacks prepared for drying), timber deck, yarding (generally: hauling and truckloading), and cleanup. Once sawn, the lumber may be sold green or it may be passed on to Drying. Drying includes two types of kilns and storage. Customers may ask for rough lumber or smooth lumber. If they ask for smooth, the lumber goes to Surfacing, where it is planed. Finally, Shipping wraps lumber stacks in steel bands (and plastic wraps if the customer wishes) and loads them on trucks and railroad cars.

Shading has been used in Exhibits 3, 4, and 5 to indicate how detail is summed to appear as a single figure (or two figures) on the report that goes to the next higher level of management. Thus you will see the following examples of "telescoping":

From Exhibit 3		From Exhibit 4	
Sawmilling Costs			
Sawing	$195,907.25	Sawmilling—L	$163,830
Sorting	18,274.13	—O	99,578
Unit Stacker	8,864.30		
Timber Deck	8,162.45		
Yarding	14,867.72		
Cleanup	17,331.74		
	$263,407.59		$263,408
Drying Costs			
Dry Kiln "C"	$ 15,717.50	Drying—L	$ 7,834
Dry Kiln "F"	14,404.36	—O	23,638
Unstacking	1,399.46		
Cleanup	(49.81)		
	$ 31,471.51		$ 31,472

Notice that Exhibit 3 has allocated Property, Fire, and Safety expenses that total $40,985 (that is, 37,002 + 2,509 + 1,474), to the various production responsibility centers (Log Handling, Sawmilling, Drying, Surfacing, and Shipping). Exhibit 4 shows these as separate expenses.

Comments:

1. There is yet another level of even greater detail that is available as support for The Summary of Net Results (Exhibit 3). This is a

computer printing of the charges to the individual *cost centers*, such as Sawing in the Sawmilling *responsibility center*. Here are listed the amounts spent on such items as hourly wages, overtime, supervision, payroll taxes, payroll benefits, saws, supplies, water, lubricants, miscellaneous overhead expenses and allocations from various *service* responsibility centers (such as Steam, Power, and Repairs and Maintenance).

2. Note that budget information is arrayed alongside actual costs and revenues, and that differences (variances) are calculated. Exhibit 4 shows how the period budget ultimately appears that we were discussing earlier in this chapter. The variances are used for control on a management-by-exception basis. Attention is directed, by the managers who have responsibility for the centers, only to those variances which are thought significant.

3. The extensive use of unit costs in the Tacoma reports is bothersome to a person who is not familiar with them. By comparing the unit costs of one month with those of another, the managers can exercise control. Unit costs, however, can also be misleading. For example, when the two types of lumber—fir and hemlock—are added together in Exhibit 4 to calculate cost of logs used, the unit cost of $84.42 per thousand board feet is obtained and transferred to Exhibit 3. Of what use is this unit cost? Suppose the corresponding unit cost is $90 in the next month. Is this bad? Should line management (Exhibit 3) get excited? Or does it indicate that there was a greater proportion of fir used that month? At best the change in unit costs signals the need for investigation. Why was more fir used? Often the explanations would turn out to be obvious, with the result that the time spent in investigating them was wasted. Possibly a better way to prepare these reports could be found. Undoubtedly, however, experience helps the manager to decide what differences and variances are significant enough to require examination.

The basic procedure of using (1) budgets to formalize plans and (2) responsibility centers to carry out control is found in many businesses. There are, as one might suspect, variations from one organization to the next. Some companies would prepare Exhibit 4 by showing total costs for each responsibility center instead of dividing total costs into labor and "all other" portions. This would appear simpler and could well be done for Tacoma; however, the interests of middle management dictate the present breakdown.

Generally the accountant tries to provide information in the most useful form, "useful" being left for the managers to define. When existing managers leave their positions, the accountant should ask their successors to redefine "useful." If this is not done, the accountant's reports are apt to become worthless with the passage of time and the turnover of managers.

It is very common in responsibility accounting systems to divide costs into controllable and noncontrollable classifications—based mainly on whether the given costs are variable or fixed. The idea is straightforward; its variations are what cause confusion. The manager should be willing to accept responsibility for those costs he can control. But what is meant by "control"?

In an illuminating article Professor William Ferrara writes, "Implicit in the concepts of responsibility accounting and cost control is the idea that it is appropriate to charge to an area of responsibility only those costs which are subject to the control of the person in charge of each area of responsibility. The costs which are not controllable by one individual or group are always controllable by another individual or group. There is no place in the framework of responsibility accounting for the idea of a noncontrollable cost. All costs are controllable at some point in time by some person or group."[9]

To attack the sticky issue: how direct must a manager's control over a cost be before he can reasonably be assigned responsibility for its incurrence? Many years ago, accounting theory held that a manager should be charged not only with costs his department directly incurred and costs he could influence indirectly (depending on policies adopted for service departments), but also with costs for which he was not responsible. Ferrara argued convincingly, "Obviously, the cost report to a foreman should include the costs he is responsible for. If the costs he is not responsible for are included in the report, they must be separated from the costs he is responsible for. However, the reason for including costs the foreman is not responsible for must be understood in its proper light. Without the inclusion of these other costs in his report, the foreman will perhaps not realize the size and extent of the useful and necessary organization behind him which is costly to operate. It is this point which is the major argument for including (but distinguishing) costs a foreman is not responsible for in the report covering the foreman's cost responsibility."[10]

There is much to recommend in this approach; however, it does seem to have the obvious drawbacks of increasing pressure throughout the organization and of interfering with any given manager's autonomy—everyone minds his business! Realizing this, some businesses in recent years have limited responsibility to costs that are *directly incurred* and that are *controllable at the given manager's level.* Hence one often sees costs divided into fixed and variable portions and the responsibility centers charged with variable costs and with such fixed costs as are subject to their direct control.

---

[9] W. L. Ferrara, "Responsibility Accounting—A Basic Control Concept," *NAA Bulletin*, September 1964, p. 11.

[10] Ibid., p. 16.

Ferrara has attempted to accomplish a similar result by including only budgeted amounts for items not subject to the control of a particular manager. By excluding or eliminating the actual column for "noncontrollable" items, variances cannot be calculated. This means that variances will only be calculated for items subject to the control of the manager. See Exhibits 6 and 7 for illustrations of this approach. (Exhibits supplied by Professor Ferrara.)

Exhibit 6 Departmental Cost Report Covering All Departmental Costs and Including Cost Distinctions Necessary for Control (Thousands of Dollars)

	BUDGET		OVER OR (UNDER) BUDGET	
	CURRENT MONTH	YEAR TO DATE	CURRENT MONTH	YEAR TO DATE
DIRECT MATERIALS	322.9	1,411.0	(5.5)	(8.6)
DIRECT LABOR	153.6	693.8	8.1	5.4
FACTORY OVERHEAD				
Dept. Head's Responsibility				
Indirect labor	88.6	364.6	(5.3)	(5.2)
Idle time	19.6	79.4	(.8)	(1.1)
Fuel	16.7	71.6	3.3	1.9
Utilities	15.4	62.3	(1.1)	(.8)
Sundry supplies	61.4	210.6	(4.3)	(4.9)
Stationery	4.6	16.3	.2	.4
TOTAL—DEPT. HEAD'S RESPONSIBILITY	682.8	2,909.6	(5.4)	(12.9)
Other Responsibility				*
Salaries	2.1	8.4		
Payroll taxes	5.2	21.6		
insurances	1.1	3.7		
Depreciation	10.2	40.8		
Service department allocations	18.4	81.6		
TOTAL DEPARTMENT COSTS	719.8	3,065.7		

Other Data (Add 000)	CURRENT MONTH BUDGET	CURRENT MONTH ACTUAL
Units produced—Good	2,680.7	2,672.4
Units rejected	134.0	155.6
Lbs. material used	708.2	705.1
Direct labor hours	74.3	77.6
Machine hours	54.6	57.4
Overtime hours	1.5	2.5
No. of employees	370	365

* No data reported in order to avoid variance calculations which might be attributed to the department foreman.

Exhibit 7 XYZ Company
Report to Sales Manager—District A
District Net Profit Report Including Profit Concepts Applicable to Control
(All Figures in Thousands)
April, 19

	BUDGET		ACTUAL	
	$	%	$	%
SALES	2,128.1	100.0	2,378.5	100.0
STANDARD COST OF SALES	1,542.5	72.5	1,649.1	69.3
GROSS PROFIT	586.6	27.5	729.4	30.7
DISTRICT SELLING EXPENSES				
Sales Manager's Responsibility				
Bonus	1.1	.1	1.3	.1
Commissions	34.3	1.6	43.2	1.8
Travel—Salesmen	13.1	.6	10.1	.4
Travel—General	1.3	.1	1.1	.1
Stationery	.6	.0	.7	.0
Postage	.5	.0	.5	.0
Telephone	2.2	.1	1.6	.1
Total	53.1	2.5	58.5	2.5
SALES MANAGER'S PROFIT CONTRIBUTION	532.5	25.0	670.9	28.2
District Expenses—Other Responsibility			*	
Salaries	4.2	.2		
Employee benefit programs	1.3	.1		
Depreciation	5.6	.3		
Taxes	1.2	.1		
Insurance	.1	.0		
Advertising	10.5	.5		
Total	23.1	1.2		
DISTRICT PROFIT CONTRIBUTION	509.4	23.8		
Allocated Home Office Costs	106.4	5.0		
DISTRICT NET PROFIT BEFORE TAX	403.0	18.8		
Taxes (50%)	201.5	9.4		
DISTRICT NET PROFIT AFTER TAXES	201.5	9.4		

	BUDGET	ACTUAL
No. of customers	3,600	3,550
New customers added	100	75
Customers lost	50	100
No. of calls	750	763
No. of orders	400	410
Miles traveled	9,600	10,200
No. of man working days	84	84
No. of man-days on road	60	68

* No data reported in order to avoid variance calculations which might be attributed to district manager.

It has been observed that detail decreases while scope increases as reports are prepared for each higher level of management. Additionally, reports at higher levels will include costs that did not appear on any lower level report, because they were considered noncontrollable at lower levels.

Every dollar cost is controllable at some level of management. It may be difficult to control some cost. It may even require a good deal of time (for example, property taxes can be avoided by a presidential decision to close the plant or to move—yet even though the decision has been made, moving or closing takes time to accomplish and hence has little immediate effect on property taxes). Nevertheless, every cost is controllable at some managerial level, be it the president's or the board of trustees'.

Policies

We have been talking about responsibility and control, but there has been little mention of policies and how the latter relate to the former. Managerial policies can facilitate responsibility and control, but they can also be very troublesome because they (1) create the "system" that people try to beat, (2) provide one approach for controlling where often several are needed for different individuals and departments, (3) tend to be inflexible in application, and (4) acquire permanence rather quickly.

When developing a policy, it is advisable to imagine how it could be selfishly misused. Does one individual or department get stuck for performing while another enjoys the service free of charge and unburdened by responsibility?

Policies come in many kinds, but to make the discussion fairly general, let us focus on dollar cost *rates* as opposed to *flat amounts*. Suppose two governmental policies were being considered with respect to providing hospital care for patients. Under the first policy, people would be charged a fixed fee (a flat amount) each year regardless of how much they used hospitals. Under the second policy, patients would pay for every service they received (at whatever rates the hospitals charge). What behavior would logically result from each policy? The flat-amount policy would encourage anyone who had a hangnail to have it trimmed in the emergency room.[11] The second policy, on the other hand, would result in essentially vacant hospitals inhabited only by the desperately ill. Since neither outcome is attractive, officials should search for a more satisfactory policy—perhaps one that charges a basic flat amount plus enough extra for each visit to discourage minor annoyance cases.

[11] The social cost of the flat-amount policy would be exhorbitant. The hospital would be so crowded with minor annoyance cases that the truly ill might go virtually unattended.

The flat-amount idea reappears whenever a job is to be recompensed on a total-contract basis. Dollar cost rates, on the other hand, occur when this same job is paid for on a daily or hourly basis. But what behavior is motivated under each policy? Under the flat-amount scheme, workers might be tempted to work rapidly at the expense of quality. The sooner the job is done, the sooner new jobs can be started and bring in more money. Under the daily or hourly basis, the worker might be tempted to be lazy—that is, to increase his total pay by taking too much time. Both policies encourage waste, albeit in different ways. One policy introduces a quality problem; the other gives rise to a laziness problem. Both policies tend to reduce morale, which is very costly in its own right as well as in its contagious effects. Here again compromise policies might be sought if management thinks that educating workers (about the sense of accomplishment that attends quality work) would be futile.

Although we shall examine them later in greater detail, let us now briefly explore how policies affect transfer prices. First, what is a transfer price? A transfer price is a charge placed on the services or products produced by one department or division and consumed by another department or division in the same organization. This sounds innocuous, but in fact it is fraught with pitfalls. Should the transfer price allow the producer to make a profit? If so, how much profit? If not, should the price equal total cost or should it be something less? These questions in turn introduce other questions. How is performance to be measured in each department? By quantity? By quality? By some combination of the two? By return on investment? By cost? Furthermore, who is to be responsible and for what?

Suppose a business had a service department—like a typing pool, a computer center, or a duplicating facility—and wished to develop a policy for charging for its services. Now any of these services requires supplies (such as paper), time, personnel, equipment, and so forth; moreover, each service involves a number of irritations, such as rush jobs and congestion. Given that businesses generally want departments managed frugally and efficiently, what policies should be developed to ensure that this will happen? We can imagine the thoughts of the adversaries:

Provider	*Consumer*
1. I should be allowed to require lead time (time between receiving an order and filling it) to help me avoid congestion.	1. I should be allowed to use the service whenever I want.
2. I should be allowed to charge extra for rush jobs and for all overtime work.	2. I should not be charged for overtime, since I have no control over scheduling regular-time service.
3. It would be wise to charge for this service at outside company rates.	3. I should not be charged for this service at all.

Provider	*Consumer*
4. I should be allowed to decide whose work should be given priority.	4. My requests should be given priority.
5. I do not want any amateurs telling me when the quality of my work is unacceptable.	5. I should have the final say with regard to quality.
6. I should not be held responsible for inefficiencies caused by the irregular demands of my customers.	6. I am not responsible for the inefficiencies of that department.

Some of the irritations brought about by rush jobs and congestion may be alleviated by bizarre means. One example of a "possible but not very likely" means follows. The provider of, say, computer services issues weekly tickets entitling the possessor to computer time. White tickets are good for an hour of regular time, red tickets are good for an hour of rush time, and yellow tickets are used for slow time. (Each week when you pass GO, you collect new tickets.) If you need a rush job done but do not have any red tickets left, you may go to a neighboring department and barter for some of its red tickets. However, no red ticket, no rush job is the policy. Prizes could be awarded to the department having the most tickets remaining after a specified period of time. Bargaining for a bigger allotment of tickets could be formalized by presenting justifying arguments before the budgetary group. The tickets would go beyond the mere paper transfers of dollars, which are often regarded as "funny money." After all, the dollar exchanges are between members of the same company, which does not get richer merely because money is transferred between its left and right pants pockets. The tickets, on the other hand, could make the difference between getting computer work done this week or next. Ingratiating oneself with the computer center and all neighboring departments might also be beneficial to the company.

Now let us investigate some dollar policies that might be applicable to the transfer price situations. Let us assume a central typing service.

Policy 1: *Don't charge anything for service.* The consumer has no responsibility for costs and hence probably uses the service whether he should or not. The provider is burdened with all the costs—which are apt to be constantly increasing—and all the headaches. The consumer does not have his staff do typing but instead sends as much of it as possible to central typing. Soon typists in the consumer's department are "unable" to do certain types of work.

Policy 2: *Charge for service at full cost.* The consumer has responsibility for costs but may be stuck for periods with extensive idle time. Thus if the full costs of central typing are to be spread over fluctuating demands for each period, the full cost for the service may be inordinately high in a period of low demand. As a consequence, the consumer may seek some typing service outside the company because it is cheaper. The provider, recognizing the situation, attempts to drum up business for his typists. If his efforts are successful, his typing pool will have less cost per job than its outside-company competitors. After a while, this will lead to an inundation of work for his typists. The increased activity is apt to lead to such increased costs for overtime, repairs, extra staff, and so forth that in time the full-cost central typing charge may become unfavorable compared to that of the competition. And so the cycle would repeat itself, always ranging between feast and famine.

Policy 3: *Charge for service at a set rate per page.* The consumer isn't bothered about efficiency, since his cost remains the same for anything sent to central typing; however, he is responsible for creating the demand for the service and is concerned about the cost he incurs as a result. The provider is concerned about both his department's costs and its volume of activity. Given this transfer price, if he can make his staff type faster and more accurately, he stands to make a substantial "paper" profit.

Policy 4: *Charge for service at variable cost.* This policy favors the use of the in-house central typists over both departmental and outside typists. The outside typists must charge more than variable cost if they are to remain in business. Departmental typists can either be dismissed or assigned to other pressing work. The consumer snatches at the bargain; the provider must restrain demand if he is to control cost. If the variable rate is per hour, the consumer may attempt to speed up the central typists.

Policy 5: *Charge for service at standard cost.* Develop full costs for an extended period of time but spread them over some total anticipated volume for the same period, thereby smoothing out the effects of irregular costs and fluctuating demands. The consumer is responsible for costs and hence is not apt to incur them thoughtlessly. He will look for bargains in outside rates. The provider is concerned about efficiency and about estimating both costs and volume of activity. If his standard cost becomes unfavorable in comparison with that of outside typists, he will lose business. This is unlikely, however, since outside typists must generate profit to stay employed. If the standard cost is per hour, the consumer may urge central typists to work faster.

Policy 6: *Charge for service based on total consumer man-hours.* This policy would divide provider costs among the total man-hours (or some such measure) of all consumers. The consumer incurs a cost whether he uses the service or not, so he should use as much of it as he can. The provider is responsible for efficiency and seeks to limit demand. Some consumers object to the choice of man-hours as an allocation basis.

These and other policies might be considered. Each has advantages and disadvantages that have not been mentioned. For instance, it would be disadvantageous to become dependent on outside help that might not be available when needed. It would also be bad if outside help were called upon so infrequently that it was not forthcoming when needed. Additionally, community relations might suffer if local sources were not used sufficiently. On the favorable side, company providers should be given the opportunity to stay familiar with the situation (like a typist's ability to read a consumer's handwriting) and to improve with practice. The company providers have a long-run reliability that should also be reflected—even though an outside source can now provide a service more cheaply, it probably cannot be relied upon to do so forever.

All this leads one to form the opinion that a planning and control system should be judged by the strength and direction of the motivation it provides. These same issues lead Professor Ferrara to draw the following distinction between modern and historical versions of responsibility reporting.

Modern Version

The essence of responsibility reporting is the specification of decision centers within the firm in order to identify the decisionmaking powers of each person and group in the organization. Reports prepared for each and every organization level must recognize the specific decisionmaking powers delegated to each decision center in order to further goal congruence. Accordingly, the utility of responsibility reports (and those who design and prepare them) will be enlarged from mere appraisal devices to devices which recognize and utilize appropriate motivational factors that can and will affect performance before it takes place.

Historical Version

The essence of responsibility accounting is the accumulation of costs and revenues according to areas of responsibility in order that deviations from standard costs and budgets can be identified with the person or group responsible.
(*Both versions supplied through courtesy of Professor Ferrara.*)

In conclusion, it can be said that setting policies calls for the study, not only of costs, but of many subtleties as well. It is not a task for someone who is in a hurry.

Summary

In this chapter we have examined period budgeting and responsibility accounting and have offered a few caveats about these processes. The caveats about human behavior were intended to warn the reader that one must understand people before one attempts to influence their behavior or introduces change.

The problem of forecasting sales was discussed next. The resulting estimate rested on one or more of the following: (1) regression analysis, (2) Markovian analysis of brand shares, (3) demand schedules, and (4) salesmen's expectations. Estimating sales is crucial to preparing cash, production, and operating budgets.

The discussion then turned to the cash budget and the need to provide sufficient cash so that business can proceed smoothly. A Markovian approach for more accurately estimating cash flows from accounts receivable was examined. This approach not only provides cash estimates for budgetary purposes, but also aids in the control of accounts receivable balances while estimating the amount of monthly bad debts.

Notwithstanding Argyris's objections to the stifling effects of budgets on self-actualization, the need to provide for overall organizational continuity requires companywide cash budgets be prepared. Total cash flows must be synchronized if fiscal embarrassment is to be avoided.

The chapter then turned to responsibility accounting. Reports were presented that showed (1) how operating budgets and budget variances were used for control and (2) how data were aggregated as reports were prepared for the successive levels of management. Many companies use even greater data aggregation in their responsibility reporting than was illustrated in this chapter. In addition, recent years have seen greater reliance placed on the splitting of costs into variable and fixed portions. This expedites the assignment of responsibility and thereby enhances control.

Finally, the subtleties of policies and how they affect costs and responsibility accounting were examined. Selecting a fair policy is far from easy; what looks reasonable from the service consumer's viewpoint is apt to look punitive from the viewpoint of the service provider.

Appendix

Absorbing Markov Chains and Steady State

Footnote 6 lists some differences between the Cyert, Davidson, and Thompson (CDT) article and the approach developed in the chapter. CDT is simply ingenious from a theoretical perspective; moreover, it offers an excellent vehicle for the study of absorbing chains and steady-state analysis. Consequently the material below presents some of its main features, which will later be applied to other situations. Unfortunately, nothing that can be written in the few pages of this appendix does justice to the original manuscript. Read it!

The primary focus of the CDT study was predicting both steady-state collections and bad debts arising from accounts receivable. Aging was done by the total-balance method, according to which the entire balance of an account was considered to have the age of its oldest charge. For example,

	Customers						Aging		
Age of Charge	A	B	C	D	Total	Paid	0	1	2
$i = 0$	\$ 3,000	\$ 5,000	\$6,000	\$ 8,000					
$i - 1 = 1$	4,000	8,000	—	100					
$i - 2 = 2$	5,000	—		10					
Balance at i:	\$12,000	\$13,000	\$6,000	\$ 8,110	39,110		6,000	13,000	20,110
$i + 1$: Paid	(9,000)	(8,000)	(6,000)	(10)		23,010	6,000	8,000	9,010
Charged	2,000	6,000	4,000	5,000					
Balance at $i + 1$:	\$ 5,000	\$11,000	\$4,000	\$13,100	33,100		4,000	16,000	13,100

$$
\text{From:}\;
\begin{array}{c} \\ P \\ 0 \\ 1 \\ 2 \end{array}
\overset{\text{To:}}{\begin{array}{c|ccc} P & 0 & 1 & 2 \end{array}}
\left[\begin{array}{c|ccc}
1 & 0 & 0 & 0 \\ \hline
6{,}000 & 0 & 0 & 0 \\
8{,}000 & 0 & 5{,}000 & 0 \\
9{,}010 & 0 & 0 & 11{,}100
\end{array}\right]
\div
\begin{array}{c} \text{Row Sum} \\ 1 \\ 6{,}000 \\ 13{,}000 \\ 20{,}110 \end{array}
=
\begin{array}{c} P \\ 0 \\ 1 \\ 2 \end{array}
\overset{\text{Transition Matrix}}{\left[\begin{array}{c|ccc}
1 & 0 & 0 & 0 \\ \hline
1 & 0 & 0 & 0 \\
.615 & 0 & .385 & 0 \\
.448 & 0 & 0 & .552
\end{array}\right]}
$$

Comment: The calculations shown above have been altered somewhat from the CDT study, the better to recognize payment of part of an individual balance. Knowing about new charges is not necessary to perform the calculations shown above.

Note how this method of aging makes it possible for a month to pass and yet for an account to remain in the same state, or even become younger, going from state j to state $j - a$, where $a = 1, 2, \ldots, j - 1$. Note further that a current charge enters the system in the state of its account's oldest unpaid charge when aging. In general, the study relied on an absorbing Markov chain with two trapping states—Paid and Bad debts. For illustrative purposes, the matrix shown below was introduced.

$$
\begin{array}{c} \\ P \\ B \\ 0 \\ 1 \end{array}
\begin{array}{c}
\begin{array}{cccc} P & B & 0 & 1 \end{array} \\
\left[\begin{array}{cc|cc}
1 & 0 & 0 & 0 \\
0 & 1 & 0 & 0 \\
\hline
.3 & 0 & .5 & .2 \\
.5 & .1 & .3 & .1
\end{array}\right]
\end{array}
$$

Steady-state results rely on the fundamental matrix, N, of the absorbing chain, which is derived as follows (here I and $\varnothing$ have the dimensions of Q, and $Q^n \approx \varnothing$, for some value of n):

$$(I - Q)(I + Q + Q^2 + \cdots + Q^{n-1}) = I - Q^n = I - \varnothing = I$$

But $$(I - Q)(I - Q)^{-1} = I$$

Therefore, $$(I + Q + Q^2 + \cdots + Q^{n-1}) = (I - Q)^{-1} = N$$

Now suppose there is a vector w that shows the number of accounts in each age category at the end of the month just prior to the start of the steady (stabilized) arrival of new accounts. These new accounts will be reflected in vector x, which will show the number of new accounts entering in each age category; each and every month on into the future will experience the same entering vector x. Once things settle down, how many accounts would be on the ledgers in each age category? Let y_i = the vector showing the distribution of accounts in each state at the end of month i; then

$$y_1 = wQ + xI$$

$$y_2 = wQ^2 + xI + xQ$$

$$y_3 = wQ^3 + xI + xQ + xQ^2$$

$$\vdots$$

$$y_n = wQ^n + xI + xQ + \cdots + xQ^{n-1}$$

But $Q^n \approx \varnothing$, so

$$y_n = w\varnothing + x(I + Q + \cdots + Q^{n-1})$$

$$y_n = xN$$

Thereafter, we find

$$\begin{aligned} y_{n+1} = y_nQ + xI &= x(I + Q + \cdots + Q^{n-1})Q + xI \\ &= x(Q + Q^2 + \cdots + Q^n) + xI \\ &= xN, \text{ because } Q^n = \varnothing \end{aligned}$$

Hence we have arrived at the steady state and can write $y = xN$, which shows the number of accounts in each age category (state) at present and for each month into the foreseeable future. If xN were multiplied by a sum vector (all elements $= 1$)S, we would have xNS, which estimates the total accounts needing attention at any time. Having an estimate like this available theoretically allows management to determine the extent of resources (office personnel, machines, and files) needed to take care of all these accounts.

Dollars could be introduced by multiplying x by an average charge; however this would force the average to be the same for each category. To allow the averages to vary from state to state, let C be a vector containing the dollars that enter each category each month in the steady state. Exhibit 8 shows the main steady-state results. Much interesting information is now at hand, including

(1) the value of the asset, accounts receivable, which is $CNS = \$133.35$, where S is a sum vector;

(2) the number of months charges remain on the books (NS);

(3) the monthly collections, \$46.67, and bad debts, \$3.33 (CNR);

(4) the eventual settlement of a given month's balance (CN^2R);

(5) the probability of settlement, conditioned on the starting state (NR);

(6) an estimate of present value of receipts (CN_DR_1);

(7) an estimate of asset balance where sales are cyclical; and

(8) an estimate of the number and age of accounts needing care in the steady state (xN).

CDT goes into many extensions of these ideas, including obtaining variances to permit range predictions of estimates.

Exhibit 8

1. The fundamental matrix of the absorbing chain:

$$N = (I - Q)^{-1} = \left(\begin{bmatrix} 1 & 0 \\ 0 & 1 \end{bmatrix} - \begin{bmatrix} .5 & .2 \\ .3 & .1 \end{bmatrix}\right)^{-1} = \begin{bmatrix} 2.308 & .513 \\ .769 & 1.282 \end{bmatrix}$$

2. Average number of months before absorption, given start in states 0 and 1 respectively:

$$NS = N\begin{bmatrix} 1 \\ 1 \end{bmatrix} = \begin{bmatrix} 2.821 \\ 2.051 \end{bmatrix}$$

Exhibit 8 (*cont.*)

3. The probability of settlement in the steady state:

$$NR = \begin{array}{c} \\ 0 \\ 1 \end{array}\begin{array}{c} \quad P \quad\quad B \\ \begin{bmatrix} .949 & .051 \\ .872 & .128 \end{bmatrix} \end{array}$$

4. The dollar balance of accounts in the steady state—states 0, 1:

$$CN = (40, 10)N = (100.01, 33.34)$$

5. The monthly settlements—states P, B:

$$CNR = (100.01, 33.34)R = (46.67, 3.33)$$

6. The eventual settlements of any given month's balances:

$$CN(NR) = CN^2R = (123.98, 9.37)$$

7. Assuming that receipts are to be discounted at 3%, the present value of collections is

$$1/1.03 = .9709 = D$$

$$N_D = (I - DQ)^{-1} = \left(\begin{bmatrix} 1 & 0 \\ 0 & 1 \end{bmatrix} - \begin{bmatrix} .485 & .194 \\ .291 & .097 \end{bmatrix}\right)^{-1} = \begin{bmatrix} 2.210 & .475 \\ .712 & 1.260 \end{bmatrix}$$

$$CN_DR_1 = (40, 10)\begin{bmatrix} 2.210 & .475 \\ .712 & 1.260 \end{bmatrix}\begin{bmatrix} .3 \\ .5 \end{bmatrix} = (\$43.46)$$

8. The dollar balance of accounts in the steady state, assuming a repetitive two-month cycle and growth at 2% per two-month period:

$$C_i = (40, 10); \qquad C_{i-1} = (35, 15)$$

Growth and the two-month cycle lead to $C_i = 1.02^k C_{i-2k}$, for $k = 0, 1, 2, \ldots$

$$N_G = (I - 1.02Q^2)^{-1} = \begin{bmatrix} 1.516 & .199 \\ .300 & 1.116 \end{bmatrix}$$

$$\text{Balances} = (C_i + C_{i-1}Q)N_G = (99.54, 32.98)$$

9. Letting the steady-state new charges in each state be $x = (70, 30)$, the inventory of steady-state accounts is $xN = (184.63; 74.37)$, which sums to $xNS = (259)$ accounts.

Problems

1. *Markov chains and brand shares.* Two companies share a market. At present company A enjoys 70% of this market, but company B is coming on strong. If a customer is presently using A, there is an 80% probability that he will continue to do so; however, if the customer is presently using B, there is only a 10% probability that he will change.

A market research firm has presented a convincing case that it can change things so that a customer presently using B will have only a 60% probability of remaining with B. The fee for this service is $125,000.

Assuming the market is set at $10,000,000 and that

(a) A enjoys 15% of sales as a *gross* profit on sales; and

(b) A requires one period justification of the $125,000 outlay,

determine whether A should lay out the $125,000.

Also determine the steady-state share of A if it invests.

2. Describe the cash budgetary process; use list form.

3. *Cash budget.* Prepare a cash budget for January, February, March 1973 from the data given below.

(a) Cash balance should be in the range $10,000 to $30,000.

(b) December 31st cash balance was $28,000; no loans were then outstanding.

(c) Cash may be borrowed in multiples of $10,000 and repaid in multiples of $10,000. Interest must be paid the following month on the balance outstanding the previous month at the rate of 1% per month.

(d) Cash collections obey the lagged forecasting equation shown below.

$$C_i = .5S_i + .3S_{i-1} + .1S_{i-2},$$

where C_i = cash collected in month i

S_i = sales of month i

(e) Predicted sales:

November	$200,000
December	300,000
January	120,000
February	180,000
March	240,000

(f) Monthly cash payroll is $50,000.

(g) Accounts payable must be paid as follows:

January	$170,000
February	80,000
March	80,000

(h) In Mach 1971, a 15-year, 10% ordinary mortgage was signed to purchase a building costing $76,061. The 1973 payment must be remitted.

(i) Excess cash may be invested in securities.

4. *Cash budget (prepared by Professor James Fremgen, U.S. Naval Postgraduate School. Made available through courtesy of the Richard D. Irwin Publishing Co.).* The Romberg Steel Products Company's operating budget for 1973 includes the following revenues and expenses involving cash receipts and disbursements:

	First Quarter	Second Quarter	Third Quarter	Fourth Quarter
Sales on account	$2,000,000	$1,500,000	$1,800,000	$2,400,000
Purchases of materials on account	400,000	400,000	450,000	500,000
Payroll	700,000	700,000	800,000	900,000
Miscellaneous expenses	300,000	300,000	300,000	300,000

The company's experience indicates that 70% of accounts receivable are collected in the quarter in which the sales are made; 20% are collected in the following quarter; 6% are collected in the second following quarter; and 4% prove to be uncollectible. Sales in the third and fourth quarters of 1972 were $1,600,000 and $1,800,000, respectively.

Half of the materials purchased during a quarter are paid for in that quarter, and the other half are paid for in the following quarter. Purchases during the fourth quarter of 1972 totaled $420,000. Payrolls and miscellaneous expenses are paid for in the quarter in which they are incurred.

Nonoperating cash outlays call for dividend payments of $75,000 on the last day of each quarter. In addition, bond interest in the amount of $50,000 is payable on June 30; and $30,000 is payable on December 31. Further, serial bonds in the principal amount of $800,000 will mature on June 30, 1973, and must be paid from the regular cash account.

The cash balance at January 1, 1973, will be $120,000. The minimum cash balance considered necessary is $100,000.

Required:

Prepare a cash budget, by quarters, for 1973. If borrowing is necessary at any time during the year, include it in this budget. Assume that all borrowing will be for a period of one quarter (but may be renewed by new loans for additional periods of one quarter) and will bear interest at 8% per annum.

5. *Cash budget.* Prepare a cash budget for the months of January, February, and March from the following data:

(a) All sales are on a charge basis.

(b) The experience of the company indicates that 40% of the sales of a month are paid for by the customers by the end of that month, 50% are paid in the following month, and 8% in the third month.

(c) Sales:

	October	(actual)	$140,000
	November	(actual)	80,000
	December	(actual)	120,000
	January	(estimated)	40,000
	February	(estimated)	50,000
	March	(estimated)	56,000

(d) Payments:

Accounts Payable	January	$70,000
	February	40,000
	March	30,000
Dividends	February	20,000
Repayment of loan	January 31	15,000

(e) Purchase of machinery March 18,000

(f) Cash balance December 31st 8,000

(g) The company has a policy that the cash balance (x) at the end of a month must lie in the range $\$5{,}000 \leq x \leq \$15{,}000$

(h) Loans may be made in multiples of $10,000 but may be repaid in multiples of $1,000; principal and $\frac{1}{2}\%$ interest are to be paid in the ensuing month according to the established terms of the company's bank.

6. *Cash budget.* Prepare a cash budget for the months of April, May, and June.

(a) 3/31 balances: Cash $ 22,000
Accounts receivable 120,000 (March sales $300,000)

(b) Monthly sales, purchases, and cash operating expense estimates:

	Sales	Purchases	Operations
April	$410,000	$198,000	$162,000
May	460,000	204,000	166,000
June	535,000	240,000	175,000

Notes:

(1) 60% of sales are collected in month of sale, and 30% in the next month; remainder is never remitted.

(2) The company must pay for its purchases and expenses in the month.

(c) Loans may be taken out in even multiples of $1,000 and must be repaid with 1% interest by the end of the following month.

(d) $\$10{,}000 \leq$ cash balance $\leq \$50{,}000$ is policy.

(e) Two years ago the company signed a mortgage payable for $138,687, agreeing to pay 8% interest and six equal installments (due yearly on May 31—interest is part of the equal installment amount).

7. *Markov chain and the CDT study.* Given the accounts receivable transition matrix shown below, answer the questions that follow.

	Paid	Bad	0	1
Paid	1	0	0	0
Bad	0	1	0	0
0	.30	0	.20	.50
1	.20	.15	.40	.25

(a) How many accounts will be in each nonabsorbing category in the steady state if each month has (400; 200) new charges?

(b) How many accounts will be paid up and how many declared bad each month in the steady state?

(c) If the average balance is $1,000, how much money will be tied up in the asset "accounts receivable" in the steady state?

(d) What uses might be made of this sort of analysis?

8. *Markov chains and the CDT study.* Age movements according to the total-balance method.

From	To	
0	Paid	$25,000
0	0	10,000
0	1	15,000
		$50,000
1	Paid	$ 6,000
1	0	8,000
1	1	2,000
1	2	4,000
		$20,000
2	Paid	$ 2,000
2	Bad	3,000
2	0	1,000
2	1	3,000
2	2	1,000
		$10,000
	Total Balance	$80,000

Note: Comment on the managerial significance of every computation.

(a) Given the foregoing empirical distribution of accounts receivable, you are to compute for the steady state

(1) The transition matrix.

(2) The percentages of collections and renegs (bad debts) for each state.

(3) The number of months to settlement for each state.

(4) The ultimate settlement of the present inventory balance of (50,000; 20,000; 10,000).

(5) The amount to be reserved for bad debts, assuming the amount should equal the expected renegs plus two standard deviations. To calculate a standard deviation

[*a*] divide the aged vector in (4) by its total,
[*b*] multiply the result of [*a*] by NR,
[*c*] square the elements of the product of [*b*] and subtract them from [*b*],
[*d*] multiply the vector resulting from [*c*] by the total in [*a*], and
[*e*] take the square root of any element in [*d*].

(6) The present value of expected collections given a 1% per month rate of discount.

(b) Suppose that in the long run 1,000 charges will occur each month, and that 60%, 30%, and 10% will be the age distributions. Compute the total number of accounts (and their distribution) expected to be open in any given month. If each new account averages \$80, what *monthly* and *ultimate* collections and write-offs will be made?

(c) How can there be a movement from i to i, that is, say, from 1 to 1?

(d) How can a new charge be aged as, say, three months old?

9. *Cash budgeting via Markov chain.* Partial-balance aging is followed. The probabilities were determined by tracing what happened to the total-account balances in each age category each month. Assume that the transition matrix is multiplied by the smoothing constant $\alpha = 1$, and that 30% of the accounts in state 2 go bad.

The transition matrix is
0 = current
1 = 1 month old
2 = 2 months old

	Paid	Bad	0	1	2
Paid	1	0	0	0	0
Bad	0	1	0	0	0
0	.5	0	0	.5	0
1	.6	0	0	0	.4
2	.7	.3	0	0	0

The aging of accounts receivable at December 31 is reflected in the vector (\$600,000; \$300,000; \$100,000).

Other data for the forthcoming quarter follow.

	January	February	March
Sales (all charged)	$400,000	$500,000	$700,000
Purchases (cash)	$200,000	$380,000	$150,000
Operating expenses (cash)	$230,000	$210,000	$150,000

Dividends of $150,000 must be paid January 25th.
The cash balance, x, must fall in the range $\$70,000 \leq x \leq \$100,000$.
Borrowings may be made and repaid in multiples of $10,000 at 1% per month interest, payable in the ensuing month.
Beginning cash balance is $82,000.
Prepare a three-month cash budget, by months.

10. *Markov chain and partial-balance aging.* Shown below are aged accounts receivable data.

Month	Total	0	1	2	3	4
J	9,951,582	6,563,689	1,439,841	703,155	306,055	938,842
F	13,032,130	10,186,824	764,160	815,798	388,940	876,408
M	15,800,382	12,291,968	1,705,101	431,932	479,472	891,909
A	18,217,207	14,829,687	1,547,322	729,475	240,622	870,101
M	14,652,393	7,868,266	5,142,265	643,052	286,003	712,807
J	15,591,707	8,230,361	3,232,838	3,048,400	408,362	671,746
J	14,838,302	8,168,415	2,741,697	1,472,788	1,757,637	697,765

Assume that 50% of the balance in age 3 gets paid the following month, and that settlements from age 4 are split evenly between the paid and bad-debts categories. Use $\alpha = .9$ to weigh the current transition matrix in an exponential smoothing formula and obtain the current average matrix. Then use the resulting matrix to forecast the flows for the following month. Comment on the results.

11. A graduate school has regularly had the experience depicted by the absorbing Markov chain shown below, where $\{G, F, 1, 2\}$ stand for graduate, fail, first year, and second year respectively.

	G	F	1	2
G	1	0	0	0
F	0	1	0	0
1	.1	.2	.1	.6
2	.8	.1	0	.1

If 1,000 students are admitted every year to begin their first years, and transfer students are not accepted,

(a) What would the long-run number of students attending the institution be in any given year and what years would they be in?

(b) How many students would graduate each year in the long run and how many would fail?

(c) If there are now 1,200 first-year graduate students and 600 second-year students, how many students will graduate at the end of this coming year?

(d) How might this information be of use in budgetary calculations?

12. A certain graduate school of business has organized its program into three main areas of concentration—quantitative, behavioral, and systems—that are taken sequentially over a period of time. The school feels that students need a firm foundation in the quantitative area, and that command of both these tool areas is necessary before they can do anything worth doing in systems study. Students, unfortunately, do not always proceed smoothly through the system; hence a number drops out for one reason or another. It also happens that some students elect to take more time to complete the quantitative requirements. Accordingly, at any given period of time 10% of those then in quantitative continue in quantitative next period, while 60% go on to behavioral. Eighty percent of those in behavioral go on to systems, and 70% of those in systems graduate. The school plans to accept 400 new candidates into the program each period. What is the expected total enrollment in the steady state?

13. *Markov chains and Christmas trees.* The Stoll Nursery is in the business of planting and selling Christmas trees on a sustained-yield basis. If it plans to reforest at the rate of 1,000 one-year-old seedlings each year, and its experience with harvesting (sales), deaths (due to disease, failure to take root, failure to sell after eight years), and aging is depicted in the matrix below, determine the receipts expected on a regular basis.

Trees sell at $1 per foot and grow at the rate of one foot per year (starting with seedlings that are approximately one foot high). If receipts of $5,000 are desired each year, how many seedlings must be planted?

Key:

H = harvested
D = "died"

		To:									
		H	D	1	2	3	4	5	6	7	8
	H	1	0	0	0	0	0	0	0	0	0
	D	0	1	0	0	0	0	0	0	0	0
From:	1	0	.3	0	.7	0	0	0	0	0	0
	2	0	.2	0	0	.8	0	0	0	0	0
	3	0	.2	0	0	0	.8	0	0	0	0
	4	0	.1	0	0	0	0	.9	0	0	0
	5	.2	.1	0	0	0	0	0	.7	0	0
	6	.3	.1	0	0	0	0	0	0	.6	0
	7	.4	0	0	0	0	0	0	0	0	.6
	8	.9	.1	0	0	0	0	0	0	0	0

14. *Regression and the forecasting of cash flow from receivables.* This chapter described how to forecast cash flows using an equation like $y_i = .5x_i + .4x_{i-1} + .05x_{i-2}$. Use sales in months $i-1, i-2, i-3, i-4, i-5$ to determine an equation with which to predict collections in month i using the data below. Comment on the results.

Sales	Month	Collections
4,825,854	D	
3,471,735	J	
3,319,544	F	3,825,296
6,592,410	M	3,482,156
16,120,115	A	5,743,776
7,950,437	M	13,125,670
6,372,495	J	8,941,949
6,035,321	J	7,260,286
5,030,227	A	5,914,003
7,991,270	S	5,918,342
4,962,502	O	7,498,599
4,351,583	N	5,414,593
4,951,275	D	3,592,273
2,899,752	J	5,528,258
3,604,164	F	3,546,909
3,691,699	M	4,146,991
14,283,812	A	3,972,513
8,761,716	M	12,019,942
4,871,093	J	8,406,642
6,417,842	J	6,399,312

15. In this chapter I said, "... budgets will be an utter waste of time or worse if the upper echelons of management don't take them seriously." What was implied by "or worse"?

16. In footnote 2 output restriction for a production worker was contrasted with unnecessary spending by a manager to maintain the level of his budget. Relate these actions to the ideas of Maslow, Herzberg, and Argyris and suggest remedies for the problem.

17. What is the significance to responsibility accounting of apparent goal congruence?

18. Do you think responsibility centers should be established on the basis of equal size?

19. *Policy and pricing.*

(a) What motivation (and associated behavior) is apt to result from a selling price that is "cost plus a fixed fee"?

(b) What motivation is apt to result from "cost plus a fixed percentage of cost"?

20. One frequently encounters the term "common" costs. Does this bear any relationship to differential costs?

21. Comment on the remark "Production, expense, sales, and master budgets may be likened to preregistration in a university. Preregistration is a game with no penalties for not showing; there is little dedication and lots of participation. On balance, preregistration is a waste of time and paper!"

22. "Budgeting is gamesmanship." Do you agree?

23. Suppose you overheard the conversation below between a plant manager and a marketing manager. State what is happening from a behavioral viewpoint and relate the conversation to responsibility accounting and policies.

Plant Manager:	The feast-or-famine situation I confront is all your fault! If sales were increased, my plant would be uniformly busy.
Marketing Manager:	Nonsense! If your plant were efficient, we could get orders filled on time and therefore sell more.

24. *Preparing a departmental performance report (prepared by Professor William L. Ferrara, Pennsylvania State University).* During the month of February 19x6, the R. X. Company produced 60,000 units of a standard product in its forming department. Materials required per standard unit are 2 pounds of X and 4 pounds of Y. Standard material prices are $0.50 per pound of X and $0.40 per pound of Y. Actual material usage in the forming department was as follows:

Material	Weight in Pounds	Cost per Pound
X	126,000	$0.48
Y	235,000	0.41

Direct labor required for each unit formed is 0.75 hours at a standard rate of $2.00 per hour. Actual direct labor hours were 48,128, while actual direct labor costs were $97,148.

Budgeted activity for the month was 50,000 units based upon a two-shift, five-day work week. The actual production was produced with two shifts on a five-day work week, except for two weeks when both shifts worked six days.

Factory overhead costs are budgeted as follows:

Salaries—Monthly

Base budget:	Amount
One general foreman	$ 700
One shift foreman	600
One inspector	550
One production clerk	400
One time clerk	350
Total	$2,600

Add for each additional shift:

One shift foreman	$ 600
One inspector	550
One production clerk	400
One time clerk	350
Total	$1,900

Add for sixth-day operation: 5% of base salarv for each sixth day worked

	Fixed	Variable per Direct-Labor Hour
Indirect labor	$4,450	$0.40
Supplies	130	0.20
Maintenance material	80	0.18
Maintenance labor	680	0.25
Stationery	200	
Travel	100	
Depreciation of equipment	1,800	
Allocated service department costs	3,200	

Actual factory overhead costs for the forming department were as follows:

Salaries—general foreman	$ 770
Salaries—staff	4,180
Indirect labor	22,100
Supplies	9,400
Maintenance material	8,025
Maintenance labor	12,150
Stationery	210
Travel	80
Depreciation of equipment	1,950
Allocated service department costs	2,980

Required:

(a) Prepare a performance report for the forming department that is intended to cover the performance of the general foreman. Show budgeted costs, actual costs, and variances.

(b) Comment on the control implications of the performance report.

25. *Hospital laundry department, budget imposed (adapted from Certificate in Management Accounting Examination, December* 1974). The Argon County Hospital is located in the county seat. Argon County is a well-known summer resort area. The county population doubles during the vacation months (May-August), and hospital activity more than doubles during these months. The hospital is organized into several departments. Although it is a relatively small hospital, its pleasant surroundings have attracted a well-trained and competent medical staff.

An administrator was hired a year ago to improve the business activities of the hospital. Among the new ideas he has introduced is responsibility accounting. This program was announced along with quarterly cost reports supplied to department heads. Previously cost data were presented to department heads infrequently. Excerpts from the announcement and the report received by the laundry supervisor are presented below.

"The hospital has adopted a 'responsibility accounting system.' From now on, you will receive quarterly reports comparing the costs of operating your department with budgeted costs. The reports will highlight the differences (variations) so you can zero in on the departure from budgeted costs. (This is called 'management by exception.') Responsibility accounting means you are accountable for keeping the costs in your department within the budget. The variations from the budget will help you identify what costs are out of line, and the size of the variation will indicate which ones are the most important. Your first such report accompanies this announcement."

Argon County Hospital
Performance Report—Laundry Department
July–September 1973

	Budget	Actual	(Over) Under Budget	Percent (Over) Under Budget
Patient Days	9,500	11,900	(2,400)	(25)
Pounds Processed—Laundry	125,000	156,000	(31,000)	(25)
Costs				
Laundry Labor	$ 9,000	$ 12,500	$ (3,500)	(39)
Supplies	1,100	1,875	(775)	(70)
Water, Water Heating, and Softening	1,700	2,500	(800)	(47)
Maintenance	1,400	2,200	(800)	(57)
Supervisor's Salary	3,150	3,750	(600)	(19)
Allocated Administration Costs	4,000	5,000	(1,000)	(25)
Equipment Depreciation	1,200	1,250	(50)	(4)
	$ 21,550	$ 29,075	$ (7,525)	(35)

Administrator's Comments: Costs are significantly above budget for the quarter. Particular attention should be paid to labor, supplies, and maintenance.

The annual budget for 1973 was constructed by the new administrator. Quarterly budgets were computed as one-fourth of the annual budget. The administrator compiled the budget from analysis of the prior three years' costs. The analysis showed that all costs increased each year, with more rapid increases between the second and third year. He considered establishing the budget at an average of the prior three years' costs, hoping that the installation of the system would reduce costs to this level. However, in view of the rapidly increasing prices, he finally chose 1972 costs less 3 percent for the 1973 budget. The activity level measured by patient days and pounds of laundry processed was set at 1972 volume, which was approximately equal to the volume of each of the past three years.

Required:

(a) Comment on the method used to construct the budget.

(b) What information should be communicated by variations from budgets?

(c) Does the report effectively communicate the level of efficiency of this department? Give reasons for your answer.

26. *Cash budget (adapted from Certificate in Management Accounting Examination, December 1973).* The Jafa Corporation uses direct costing for managerial purposes. They prepared their December 31, 1973 balance sheet on a direct-costing basis as follows:

JAFA CORPORATION
BALANCE SHEET
As of December 31, 1973

Current Assets			
Cash		$ 10,000	
Marketable Securities		50,000	
Accounts Receivable		80,000	
Inventories			
Finished Goods	$ 67,500		
Work in Process	45,000		
Raw Materials	9,000	121,500	
Total Current Assets			$ 261,500
Long-Term Assets			
Equipment (factory)	$ 300,000		
Less: Accumulated Depreciation	72,000	$228,000	
Plant	$1,000,000		
Less: Accumulated Depreciation	180,000	820,000	
Property		200,000	
Total Long-Term Assets			1,248,000
Other Assets			
Intangibles (net)		$ 10,000	
Loan to Officer of Company		10,000	20,000
Total Assets			$1,529,500

JAFA CORPORATION
BALANCE SHEET
(cont'd)

Current Liabilities		
Accounts Payable	$ 25,680	
Other Payables	10,000	
Notes Payable (one month note due January 15, 1974)	50,000	
Current Portion of Long-term Debt (due March 31, 1974)	50,000	
Total Current Liabilities		$ 135,680
Long-term Debt (8%, 10 years, interest payable December 31, repayment of principal at rate of $50,000 per year begining in 1974)		450,000
Total Liabilities		$ 585,680
Owners' Equity		
Common Stock (issued and outstanding, 70,000 shares, $10 per share)	$700,000	
Retained Earnings	243,820	
Total Owners' Equity		943,820
Total Equities		$1,529,500

Some recent and forecast data are

	Actual		Forecast			
	Nov.	Dec.	Jan.	Feb.	Mar.	Apr.
Cash Sales (units)	1,200	1,200	1,000	1,000	1,000	2,000
Credit Sales (units)	10,000	10,000	8,000	8,000	8,000	20,000
Selling and Administrative Expenses	$20,000	$20,000	$20,000	$20,000	$20,000	$20,000
Fixed Manufacturing Expenses*	15,000	15,000	15,000	15,000	15,000	15,000

* excluding depreciation and amortization

The company manufactures an automobile safety seat for children, which it sells directly to a number of automobile dealers in its four-state region and to retail customers through its own outlet. The selling price through its own outlet is $30; to the dealers the price is $20.

Since all sales through its own outlet are on a cash basis, and sales to dealers, all on account, have been long established, bad debts are negligible. Terms of credit sales are net 30. Sixty percent of the credit sales are paid in the month of the sale, and the remaining 40% of the credit sales are paid in the month after the sale.

Raw materials cost $5 per unit. All purchases of raw materials are on account. Accounts payable are on terms of net 30 days. Forty percent are paid in the month of purchase, and 60% are paid in the following month. Direct-labor and variable manufacturing overhead costs are $10 per unit. Direct-labor and variable manufacturing overhead costs are incurred in direct proportion to the percentage of completion and paid in cash when incurred.

At the end of each month, desired inventory levels are as follows:
Raw materials: 20% of next month's requirements
Work in process: 50% of next month's requirements
Finished goods: 50% of next month's requirements
Work in process is assumed to be 50% completed at the end of the month. Raw materials are added at the beginning of production.

Depreciation on the equipment is $4,000 per month and depreciation on the plant is $5,000 per month. Amortization of intangibles is $500 per month.

Selling and administrative expenses are all fixed. Half are paid in the month incurred and the balance are paid in the following month.

Fixed manufacturing expenses that require cash payments are paid in the month incurred.

Long-term debt-principal is to be paid each March 31, starting in 1974, at a rate of $50,000 per year.

The loan to the officer was made on December 31, 1973 and is due March 31, 1974. The loan is to be repaid on March 31, 1974 plus interest at 6% per annum.

The firm requires a minimum cash balance of $10,000 at the end of each month. If the balance is less, marketable securities are sold in multiples of $5,000 at the end of the month. If necessary, cash is borrowed in multiples of $1,000 at the end of the month. Marketable securities earn 6% per annum and the interest is collected at the end of each month. The short-term interest rate on notes payable is 12% per annum and is paid at the time the note is repaid.

Taxes are to be ignored.

Required:

Prepare a statement forecasting the cash balance, including any necessary cash transactions to achieve company cash management objectives for January, 1974.

Overhead Rates

5

Overview

Has it ever occurred to you how incredible manufactured products really are? The products themselves strike me as extraordinary in that they so often offer little indication of the innumerable decisions that had to be made to bring them into existence. Manufacturing is not just using home facilities to make lemonade or a piece of furniture. First one must decide what business he is going to engage in; then he must select a business location and invest in equipment. Next he must hire help, provide for a line of credit, establish an accounting system, engage in a promotion program, compete with established companies—the whole works! In no way could this process be described as simple.

So far, our entrepreneur has not made any decisions about product features. Even with an uncomplicated product, there are many critical choices to be made. Let the product be tennis rackets. Figure 1 shows a drawing of a racket accompanied by a list of choices.

The brief list of questions raised in Figure 1 by no means exhausts all the possibilities. In particular, this chapter focuses on how a company loads (or "attaches") the overhead costs, for example, of its Personnel and Assembly Departments on each racket. In general, cost accountants make use of the fact that only the production departments physically work on products. They first allocate the service-department costs to the production departments and then calculate overhead absorption rates—based on estimated total activity for the period (usually a year) ahead—for allocating total overhead costs to products.

More specifically, the early stages in the loading procedure are referred to as primary and secondary overhead allocations, because the first step is to estimate overhead costs by individual accounts for every factory department (this is primary allocation) and the second step is to reallocate (secondary allocation) service department costs to production departments. Primary allocation is based on specific departmental cost identification as well as on such measures as meter readings, cubic (or square) footage in each department, value of machines and average inventory in each department, and departmental payroll. Secondary allocation is most often based on some

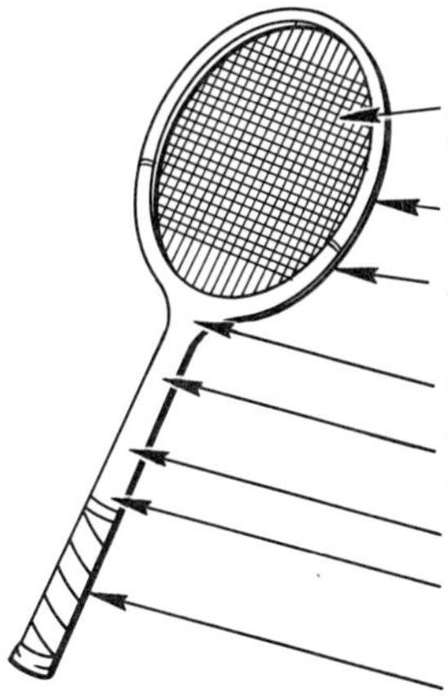

Figure 1

measure of service consumption, such as number of kilowatt hours where there is a Power (service) Department, or hours worked (effort) or number of machines (or both) where there is a Repairs and Maintenance (service) Department. Finally, individual production department overhead rates are calculated by dividing their total allocated costs by their respective estimates of departmental activity volumes for the coming period (year).

The idea behind absorption rates is to smooth overhead charges over an extended period of time. Were overhead not smoothed, the irregular occurrence of certain overhead charges—such as a major repair bill—and any pronounced fluctuations in monthly volume would result in monthly rates that varied widely. If price were based on cost, it would then be possible that a month with low volumes of activity would have high overhead rates, which could lead, in turn, to prices high enough to discourage customers. Thus a month of depressed activity would tend to generate further depression. Besides, there is a theoretical question of equity: Which month should be stuck with the repair bill? The months preceding necessitate the repairs; those following enjoy the benefits of the refurbished machine. The current month merely endures the misfortune of seeing to the payment of the bill. This kind of thinking is very prevalent in cost accounting. It leads to what might be termed the *Principle of Smoothing.*

There is another issue of equity in allocation. On what basis would you decide to allocate costs? How would allocating the greatest portion of a service department's overhead costs to the biggest production department appeal to you? This would be known as the "ability to bear" (or, more popularly, the "ability to pay") criterion and is considered unsatisfying by most theorists. Behaviorally speaking, the foreman of the production department may resent being charged with the lion's share—especially if his department doesn't consume such a high proportion of the service. To this foreman, the exhorbitant allocation is a penalty for bigness. Even though the big department may benefit from having the smaller production departments around, it would be an unusual foreman who would not balk at "carrying" his smaller neighbors' shares of the service department's costs.

A more appealing criterion of allocation is that of usage, which comes in two types: actual and potential. Where actual usage is involved, the allocation reflects past service and the accountant speaks of "services used" or "benefits received." Where potential usage is at issue, the allocation reflects "facilities provided" or the "ability to serve." The idea may be easier to comprehend if we focus on, say, a factory first-aid service department. Then, if all factory jobs are approximately equally hazardous and if no age group is considered more accident-prone than another, the department with the greatest number of employees might be fairly charged with a proportionately high share of the service. After all, the first-aid facilities were provided in anticipation of need, not after the fact. In theory, the fixed costs of a service department should be allocated based on potential usage, while the variable costs should be distributed based on actual usage. In practice, this refinement is not observed, because it is impractical.

The criterion of usage also applies in primary overhead allocation. Here the accountant speaks of "physical identification" or "traceability," but what he is concerned with is actual usage of machines, materials, personnel, and so forth by each factory department.

The Spalding Smasher

Let us put aside our imaginary tennis racket and investigate the cost build-up of a real one. Spalding, a division of Questor Corporation, has for many decades manufactured fine athletic equipment. One of the products made in its Chicopee, Massachusetts, plant is the aluminum Smasher tennis racket. A "make-or-buy" analysis revealed that aluminum extruding equipment was too costly and the volume of Smashers was too small to justify in-house manufacture of the frame. Therefore, Spalding purchases the frame from another company that extrudes aluminum tubing according to Spalding specifications, rivets an aluminum throat into place that is strategically

Exhibit 1

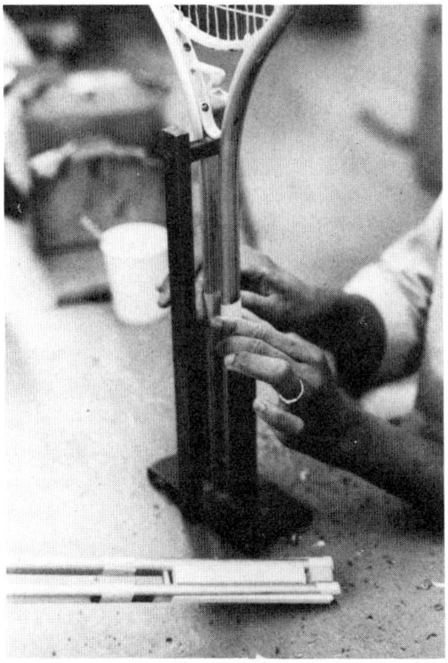

Apply balsa strips

Injection molding of polyurethane grip

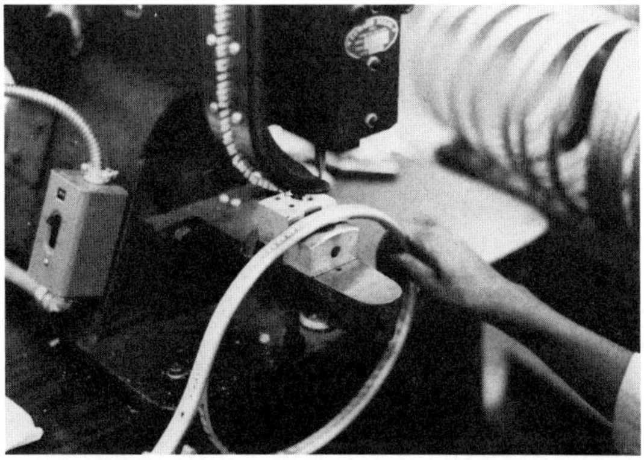

Insert eyelets

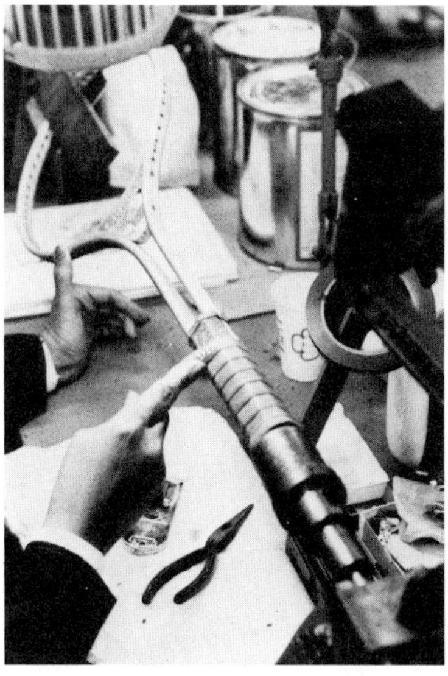

Grip winding

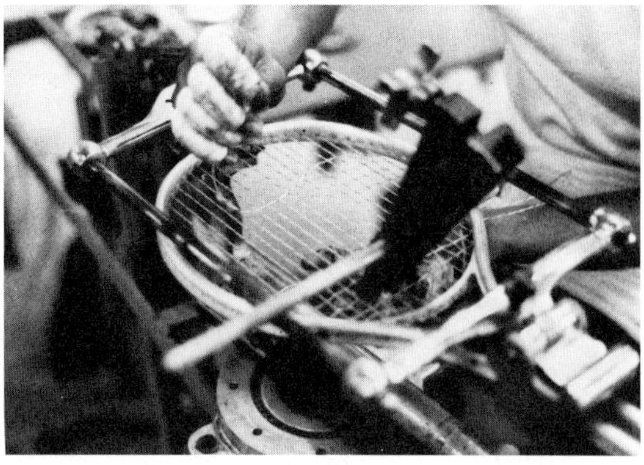

String racket

designed to reduce torque, and punches holes in the frame for holding grommets. The Spalding plant then places grommets in the string holes, molds a polyurethane grip over a balsa wood core, wraps leather around the molded grip, puts labels in appropriate places, strings the racket

Exhibit 1 (*cont.*) Terri Ann Keeler, Instructor, All American Sports Tennis Camp, Amherst College, Amherst, Massachusetts

(generally, but not always), inspects the end product, places the racket in a cover, and packs the covered rackets in cartons for shipment to dealers. All these steps are carried out in the Tennis Racket Department, which is organized as a single production responsibility center.

Exhibit 1 (*cont.*) Buddy Weiner, Instructor, All American Sports Tennis Camp, Amherst College, Amherst, Massachusetts

Pictures of various stages of production in the Tennis Racket Department are shown in Exhibit 1.

The standard cost sheet for making 100 Smashers—strung or unstrung—appears in Exhibit 2 in abridged form and with synthetic dollar amounts.

Exhibit 2 SMASHER: STANDARD COST SHEET

Description	Material	Labor	Total Overhead (125% Labor)	Cumulative Total	Fixed (.55) Overhead	Variable (.45) Overhead
Hollow frames	1,000.00			1,000.00		
Inspect frames		12.00	15.00	1,027.00	8.25	6.75
Grip labels	2.00			1,029.00		
Balso strips	10.50			1,039.50		
Urethane foam	12.40			1,051.90		
Mold grips		14.80	18.50	1,085.20	10.18	8.32
⋮	⋮	⋮	⋮	⋮	⋮	⋮
Grommets 87402B	22.00			1,175.40		
Insert grommets		10.20	12.75	1,198.35	7.01	5.74
Decals	1.10			1,199.45		
Place decals		1.25	1.56	1,202.26	.86	.70
Inspect		8.40	10.50	1,221.16	5.78	4.72
Weigh & check grips		5.20	6.50	1,232.86	3.58	2.92
Spray paint		6.00	7.50	1,246.36	4.13	3.37
Racket covers	90.00			1,336.36		
⋮	⋮	⋮	⋮	⋮	⋮	⋮
Inspect		4.00	5.00	1,481.00	2.75	2.25
Pack		5.25	6.56	1,492.81	3.61	2.95
SUBTOTALS: FRAME	1,194.25	132.69	165.87	1,492.81	91.23	74.64
Nylon strings	72.00			72.00		
String rackets		84.00	105.00	261.00	57.75	47.25
⋮	⋮	⋮	⋮	⋮	⋮	⋮
Inspect		8.00	10.00	328.40	5.50	4.50
SUBTOTALS: STRINGINGS	91.95	105.09	131.36	328.40	72.25	59.11
TOTALS	1,286.20	237.78	297.23	1,821.21	163.48	133.75

Note the material, labor, and overhead costs entered on the Standard Cost Sheet. The materials and labor are at standard levels that have been set by the purchasing agent, union contracts, and plant engineers. These are "should be" costs, which we shall study in detail in Chapter 8. For the present we are concerned with the overhead charges which, as shown in Exhibit 2, equal 125% of labor cost and wind up being split into 55% fixed and 45% variable portions. Where does the 125% come from, and why is the overhead split into fixed and variable portions?

The answer to the first question is found in Exhibit 3, which shows the forecasted operating budget for the Tennis Racket Department; again all figures are synthetic dollar amounts. Note how Exhibit 3 shows the division of overhead costs into fixed and variable portions and includes allocated service department costs among the fixed overhead items. These allocated

Exhibit 3 FORECASTED OPERATING BUDGET

Tennis Racket Department

Standard direct labor			$160,000
Overhead:			
Variable:	Labor—handling	$ 5,200	
	—machine setup	1,000	
	—maintenance	4,800	
	—shift premium	3,000	
	—overtime	9,000	
	—instruction time	1,500	
	—sick leave	800	
	—downtime	500	
	—rework	1,200	
	Scrap	500	
	Repairs and maintenance	8,400	
	Indirect materials	7,000	
	Payroll fringe benefits	47,100	$ 90,000
Fixed:	Labor—foreman	$16,400	
	—janitors	3,600	
	Payroll fringe benefits	3,800	
	Inventory-based charges	4,800	
	Depreciation	12,500	
	Other	6,000	
	Allocated services:		
	Plant	10,000	
	Power & boiler	6,000	
	Material handling	12,300	
	Quality control	18,500	
	Personnel	10,500	
	Technical services	5,600	110,000
	TOTAL OVERHEAD		$200,000

$$\text{Overhead rate} = \frac{\text{Total overhead costs}}{\text{Standard direct labor}} = \frac{\$200{,}000}{\$160{,}000} = 125\%$$

$$\text{Fixed portion} = \frac{\text{Fixed overhead}}{\text{Total overhead}} = \frac{\$110{,}000}{\$200{,}000} = .55$$

service department costs result from secondary allocation and can be traced to Exhibit 7, which will be presented in the next section. All other overhead costs in Exhibit 3 arise in primary allocation.

To answer the second question, Exhibit 4 has been prepared. The budget figures in Exhibit 4 come from dividing Exhibit 3 budget estimates by 12; the actual figures of Exhibit 4 are synthetic. We see responsibility accounting at work in Exhibit 4. Spalding has chosen to split costs into variable and fixed portions to expedite assignment of responsibility. This division, however, is not quite sufficient to distinguish controllable from uncontrollable

Exhibit 4 COMPARATIVE EXPENSE REPORT

Tennis Racket Department

May 1974

Expense Classification	Month Actual	Month Budget	Month Variance	Year-to-date
Direct labor	$18,100	$18,700	$ (600)	The same as "Month" with cumulative data.
Guarantee wages	1,400	–0–	1,400	
TOTAL DIRECT LABOR	$19,500	$18,700	$ 800	
Overhead-controllable:				
Foreman	$ 1,240	$ 1,367	$ (127)	
Janitor	320	300	20	
Fringe benefits-F	305	317	(12)	
Handling	450	433	17	
Setup	382	400	(18)	
⋮	⋮	⋮	⋮	
Overtime	675	750	(75)	
⋮	⋮	⋮	⋮	
Scrap	108	63	45	
Repairs & maintenance	610	700	(90)	
Indirect materials	842	583	259	
Fringe benefits-V	4,215	3,925	290	
TOTAL CONTROLLABLE	$ 9,900	$ 9,483	$ 417	
Overhead-uncontrollable:				
Insurance	$ 250	$ 250	$–0–	
Storage	150	150	–0–	
Depreciation	1,100	1,042	58	
Other	510	500	10	
Allocated services:				
Plant	833	833	–0–	
Power & boiler	500	500	–0–	
Material handling	1,025	1,025	–0–	
Quality control	1,541	1,541	–0–	
Personnel	875	875	–0–	
Technical	467	467	–0–	
TOTAL UNCONTROLLABLE	$ 7,251	$ 7,183	$ 68	
TOTAL OVERHEAD	$17,151	$16,666	$ 485	

costs. Observe that the foreman, janitor, and fringe benefits-F costs—which are considered fixed costs—are, nevertheless, treated as controllable costs at the departmental level. Not all companies would make this same decision; apparently it is useful for Spalding. Also note how the allocated services are charged to Tennis Rackets on a budgetary basis so as to cause no variance. The foreman is reminded that these service costs exist and that his department was partially responsible for their magnitude, but he does not have to cope with variances for them. If service costs became inordinately high, the Tennis Racket foreman might object that he could obtain these services outside the company at less cost. This introduces the policy discussions of Chapter 4. Some companies would prefer to charge service department variances as well to production departments, to make production managers more interested in service department efficiency. Spalding apparently feels that the production and service managers have enough to be concerned about in their own departments, and avoids introducing further peer pressures.

In summary, the exhibits have shown, among other things, (1) that overhead costs are allocated based on estimated actual usage to every factory department (primary allocation); (2) that service department overhead costs are then reallocated to production departments (secondary allocation); (3) that production department overhead totals are next related to some index of activity (direct-labor dollars in the Spalding factory); and (4) that overhead is attached to each product in proportion to its activity reading (the standard cost for overhead is charged to each Smasher at the rate of 125 percent of standard direct-labor cost).

Spalding Elite Centurion Golf Clubs

It is somewhat unusual for a complicated product to be manufactured in just one production department. Generally too many diverse operations must be performed to include all the equipment and all the labor skills in a single production department. We now take a more typical illustration—that of golf clubs—and see how Spalding builds golf club costs.

Exhibit 5 shows the stages of production in various golf club production departments along with sequence photographs that show the testing of the finished product. Exhibit 6 contains the abridged standard cost sheets (using synthetic amounts) for making 100 Elite Centurion woods and 100 Elite Centurion irons. Note how each of several departments adds its costs as the product passes through its process. If a club is irretrievably damaged in a process, the operation at which the loss occurred can be located on the standard cost sheet and the cost of the club (and hence the amount of loss) through that point can be immediately determined. (Journal entry: Debit *Department X Scrap; Credit Work in Process.*) In a similar way, the standard cost sheet can be used to evaluate ending inventory of work in process.

Total overhead is expressed as a percentage of departmental standard direct-labor cost in both Exhibits 2 and 6. Exhibit 7 shows just where these percentages originate, using synthetic dollar amounts. The top portion of this exhibit shows the percentage of usage *by* each service consumer *of* each service provided. These percentages are used for secondary allocation

Exhibit 5

Drilling holes—Wood Turning

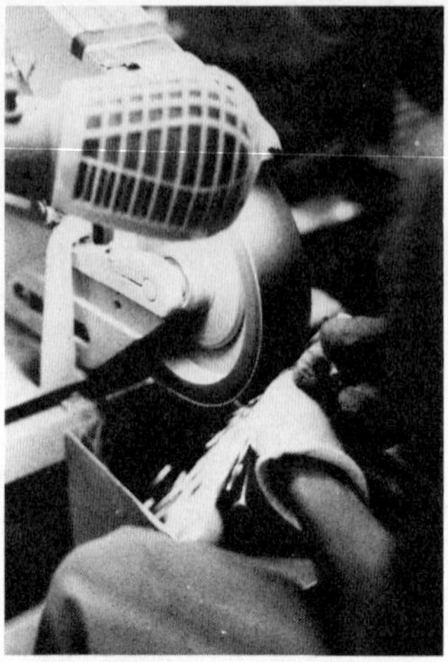

Grinding heads—Irons Finishing

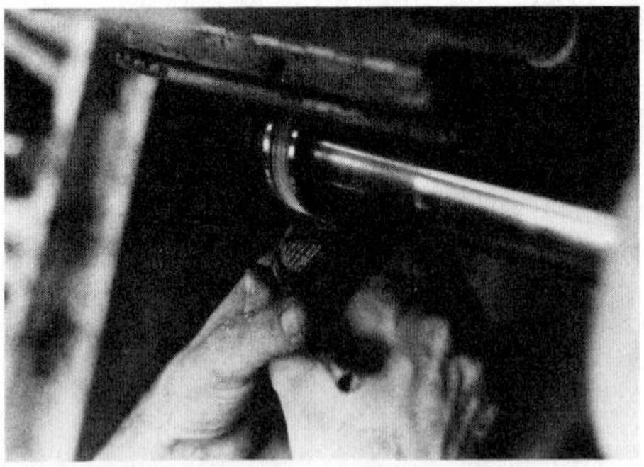

Cutting backspin grooves—Wood Finishing

Cutting shafts—Irons Assembly

Winding whipping—Woods Assembly

Aligning grip—Irons Assembly

Exhibit 5 (*cont.*)
Tom Toski, Professional,
Hickory Ridge Country Club,
South Amherst, Massachusetts

Exhibit 6 ELITE CENTURION GOLF CLUBS: STANDARD COST SHEET

Description	Material	Labor	Total Overhead	Cumulative Total	Fixed Overhead	Variable Overhead
Woods: Turning Dept.			550%		.80	.20
Laminated heads	120.00			120.00		
⋮	⋮			⋮		
Sand sole		2.00	11.00	171.50	8.80	2.20
⋮		⋮	⋮	⋮	⋮	⋮
Drill holes		1.50	8.25	214.40	6.60	1.65
Woods: Wood Head Finishing			180%		.62	.38
Brass backweights	25.00			239.40		
⋮	⋮			⋮		
Face inserts	16.20			587.20		
Assemble face inserts		12.00	21.60	620.80	13.39	8.21
Cement inserts to head		4.80	8.64	634.34	5.36	3.28
⋮		⋮	⋮	⋮	⋮	⋮
Apply soleplate		6.50	11.70	921.25	7.25	4.45
⋮		⋮	⋮	⋮	⋮	⋮
Buff backpiece & soleplate		7.00	12.60	1,086.00	7.81	4.79
⋮		⋮	⋮	⋮	⋮	⋮
Paint		16.80	30.24	1,143.80	18.75	11.49
Woods: Assembly			150%		.65	.35
Shafts	180.00			1,323.80		
⋮	⋮			⋮		
Rubber grips	52.00			1,490.75		
Apply slide collar		4.00	6.00	1,500.75	3.90	2.10
Apply & align grip		2.00	3.00	1,505.75	1.95	1.05
⋮		⋮	⋮	⋮	⋮	⋮
Wind whipping		5.25	7.88	1,551.20	5.12	2.76
⋮		⋮	⋮	⋮	⋮	⋮
Check swing weight		6.00	9.00	1,592.00	5.85	3.15
⋮		⋮	⋮	⋮	⋮	⋮
Quality control		5.00	7.50	1,628.55	4.88	2.62
Woods: Packing			160%		.60	.40
⋮		⋮	⋮	⋮	⋮	⋮
Final inspection		4.80	7.68	1,850.00	4.61	3.07
TOTALS	740.00	407.00	703.00	1,850.00	446.05	256.95

and the bases for allocation are

Department	*Allocation Basis*
S_1 = Power & boiler	Water, oil, gas, electricity—plant engineering study All other expenses—floor space occupancy
S_2 = Plant	Fringe benefits—departmental wages All other expenses—floor space
S_3 = Engineering	Effort
S_4 = Material handling	Effort
S_5 = Quality Control	Effort
S_6 = Personnel	Effort
S_7 = Technical services	Effort

Exhibit 6 (*cont.*)

Description	Material	Labor	Total Overhead	Cumulative Total	Fixed Overhead	Variable Overhead
Irons: Machine			480%		.58	.42
Castings	470.00			470.00		
Weigh and sort		2.80	13.44	486.24	7.80	5.64
Irons: Finishing			320%		.52	.48
Quality inspection		1.20	3.84	491.28	2.00	1.84
Tap hosel		4.50	14.40	510.18	7.49	6.91
Polish		8.20	26.24	544.62	13.64	12.60
⋮		⋮	⋮	⋮	⋮	⋮
Mask head		5.00	16.00	681.20	8.32	7.68
Vapor blast face		2.60	8.32	692.12	4.33	3.99
⋮		⋮	⋮	⋮	⋮	⋮
Paint		4.35	13.95	865.74	7.25	6.70
Make sets & sock heads		5.18	16.58	887.50	8.62	7.96
Irons: Assembly			150%		.65	.35
Weight heads		3.00	4.50	895.00	2.93	1.57
Shafts	156.00			1,051.00		
⋮	⋮			⋮	⋮	⋮
Rubber grips	52.00			1,111.10		
Apply & align grip		3.00	4.50	1,118.60	2.93	1.57
⋮		⋮	⋮	⋮	⋮	⋮
Allen set screw	4.20			1,130.00		
⋮		⋮	⋮	⋮	⋮	⋮
Swing weigh		5.20	7.80	1,160.00	5.07	2.73
⋮		⋮	⋮	⋮	⋮	⋮
Brass ferrule	4.80			1,182.10		
⋮		⋮	⋮	⋮	⋮	⋮
Quality control		7.20	10.80	1,209.45	7.02	3.78
Irons: Packing			160%		.60	.40
⋮		⋮	⋮	⋮	⋮	⋮
Final inspection		3.60	5.76	1,340.50	3.46	2.30
TOTALS	710.20	201.10	429.20	1,340.50	233.31	195.89

Consider Plant services, which are distributed using two bases—how does one percentage result? Suppose that \$94,000 of the total budgeted Plant primary costs (\$940,000 in Exhibit 7) is for fringe benefits, that total budgeted salaries and wages are \$4,000,000, and that Tennis Rackets occupies 2,681 square feet out of a total factory area of 500,000 square feet. Then the percentage of service provided by Plant and consumed by Tennis Rackets is

$$\frac{\text{Fringes}}{\text{Total primary}}\left(\frac{\text{Direct labor and indirect labor}}{\text{Total salaries and wages}}\right) + \left(1 - \frac{\text{Fringes}}{\text{Total primary}}\right)\left(\frac{\text{Departmental area}}{\text{Total factory area}}\right) = \%$$

$$\frac{\$94{,}000}{\$940{,}000}\left(\frac{\$160{,}000 + \$47{,}000}{\$4{,}000{,}000}\right) + \left(1 - \frac{\$94{,}000}{\$940{,}000}\right)\left(\frac{2{,}681}{500{,}000}\right) = .01$$

Exhibit 7 OVERHEAD ALLOCATION RATES

		S_1	S_2	S_3	S_4	S_5	S_6	S_7	Consumers: ← Woods → ... Turning	Woods Finishing	← Irons → Machine	Irons Finishing	Assembly	Packing ...	Tennis Racket
Providers:	S_1	—	.10	.02	.04	.02	.03	.01	.01	.06	.01	.07	.06	.02	.03
	S_2	.04	—	.05	.11	.01	.01	.01	.02	.03	.01	.04	.03	.01	.01
	S_3	.01	.02	—	.01	—	—	—	.04	.10	.02	.09	.06	.01	—
	S_4	—	—	—	—	—	—	—	.02	.09	.02	.05	.07	.02	.02
	S_5	—	—	—	—	—	—	—	.03	.03	—	.10	.01	—	.05
	S_6	.01	.03	.01	.02	.01	—	—	.01	.04	—	.07	.02	.01	.03
	S_7	—	—	—	—	—	—	—	.04	.01	.01	—	.02	.01	.02
Primary Costs:		200,000	940,000	237,000	494,000	356,000	306,000	268,000	87,900	654,750	398,900	531,750	345,650	76,400	137,100
Secondary:	S_1	(200,000)	20,000	4,000	8,000	4,000	6,000	2,000	2,000	12,000	2,000	14,000	12,000	4,000	6,000
	S_2	—	(960,000)	50,000	110,000	10,000	10,000	10,000	20,000	30,000	10,000	40,000	30,000	10,000	10,000
	S_3	—	—	(291,000)	3,000	—	—	—	12,000	30,000	6,000	27,000	18,000	3,000	—
	S_4	—	—	—	(615,000)	—	—	—	12,300	55,350	12,300	30,750	43,050	12,300	12,300
	S_5	—	—	—	—	(370,000)	—	—	11,100	11,100	—	37,000	3,700	—	18,500
	S_6	—	—	—	—	—	(322,000)	—	3,500	14,000	—	24,500	7,000	3,500	10,500
	S_7	—	—	—	—	—	—	(280,000)	11,200	2,800	2,800	—	5,600	2,800	5,600
TOTALS			–0–	–0–	–0–	–0–	–0–	–0–	160,000	810,000	432,000	704,000	465,000	112,000	200,000
Standard direct labor costs									30,000	450,000	90,000	220,000	310,000	70,000	160,000
Overhead percentages									550%	180%	480%	320%	150%	160%	125%

S_1 = Power & boiler
S_2 = Plant
S_3 = Engineering
S_4 = Material handling
S_5 = Quality control
S_6 = Personnel
S_7 = Technical services

Effort is the one basis of allocation that causes cost accountants the most aggravation, regardless of the type of business involved. When records of time spent working for each department are meticulously kept, the disadvantages of using this basis are minimized. Such records, however, are often not available and this leads to guesswork. At this point cost accountants all seem to get the same awful feeling that whatever departments were most recently served are apt to have been assigned a disproportionately high percentage of the service being allocated. They also worry about the influence of moods on the estimator's judgment—whether his wife was pleasant to him that morning, and so forth.[1] Their concern is understandable. The costs they determine appear in financial statements and *may* be used for many purposes, including setting prices and selecting the level and kinds of service. They want cost estimates to be reliable, to be able to withstand scrutiny. Many accountants would like to replace effort as an allocation basis with some combination of concrete measures, such as floor space and payroll. And if effort cannot be replaced as a basis, cost accountants try to insist that time records be carefully maintained. Their insistence, however, seems to fall on deaf ears, for service department managers commonly reply, "I have better things to do with my time than do bookkeeping for you." This response has led to the devising of elaborate policies—like those discussed in the preceding chapter—to make it worthwhile to the service manager to maintain records. It is not obvious that the overall company benefits as a result.

It is unfortunately true, owing to the jointness of operations—all products and all departments share the same corporate name, the same president, the same corporate goals, the same time span, and often the same buildings and equipment—that *any* allocation basis can be faulted. This is true even of the tangible bases. For example, consider the use of floor space as a basis. Even though square footage may be physically determined, some departments will enjoy higher ceilings than others (and hence may use overhead cranes and require greater heating). Other departments will enjoy better views (and perhaps have higher morale); nevertheless, other things being equal, others will be exposed to warming rays of sunshine (and need less heat and illumination) or to cooling breezes (and need less air conditioning). Certain sections of the factory will be in better repair than others and have more value as real estate (these sections would therefore be favored if a real-estate tax bill were apportioned on the basis of overall square footage). Certain sections of the factory will endure more traffic than others and may be

[1] Some students of mine were investigating secondary overhead allocation in a hospital. In particular, they were interested in checking the costs allocated to the Mental Health Department. Effort was the most frequent basis for allocating service department costs. When they interviewed one service department manager in the morning, he said 3% of his department's work was done for Mental Health. Two hours later in a conversation with another service department manager at which the students were present, the "guesstimate" became 10%.

similarly favored if they are charged for plant costs based on square footage.

Or consider payroll as a basis. It often happens that a company pays two managers—one the successor to the other—different salaries. Perhaps the higher paid manager is so favored because he is resourceful and self-sufficient and therefore has less use for particular service departments whose costs might be allocated based on payroll. Other things being equal, the higher paid man uses less service but is charged more because his salary is greater. Then too, why should a production manager's salary be specifically identified with a particular department when he devotes a significant portion of his time, say, to improving corporate image and to levelling feast-and-famine production activity?

If I make x and you make y and we both work in the same company, will sales of x not influence—one way or another—sales of y? After all, perfect market segmentation is virtually impossible to achieve. Or won't x interfere with the production efficiency of y? If there is a limit to facilities, won't the fact that x gets a new machine or additional space mean that y will be deprived, at least temporarily?

Any allocation basis can be discredited. Professor W. J. Vatter put it succinctly:

> Every cause has a number of effects; every event arises from many causes; all incidents and observations are bound together by many ties. All costs are more or less interwoven in a complex fabric; in large measure, costs are joint as to their incurrence, as well as to their associations with various costing units.[2]

Nevertheless, if for no other purpose than product costing, the well-entrenched conception of accounting income requires primary and secondary allocations. The cost accountant strives to be reasonable when making these allocations; he knows he can never precisely divide the indivisible. When the cost analyst engages in decision making, however, he avoids all arbitrary allocations and deals with totals wherever possible.

Return now to Exhibit 7. Primary costs are shown in total; in detail they would appear similar to the costs listed in Exhibit 3 above "Allocated services." The secondary allocation in the lower part of Exhibit 7 is accomplished by what is known as the "step allocation" method. In step allocation, service providers—in an arbitrary sequence—have their costs allocated to service consumers, and reciprocal services are ignored if the costs of a service

[2] William J. Vatter, "Limitations of Overhead Allocation," *Accounting Review*, 20, no. 2, pp. 164–65.

provider have already been distributed. Sometimes companies allocate the provider that serves the most consumers first; at other times, companies allocate the providers in the order of their magnitudes of primary costs, with the greatest cost being distributed first. The sequence in Exhibit 7 is arbitrary; it is not that used by Spalding.

Let us use Plant Services, S_2, to illustrate how reciprocal services are ignored where providers have already been allocated. S_1, the Power and Boiler Department, has already been distributed; consequently, even though it consumed 4% of S_2 services, S_1 will not be charged for these services. S_2 costs will therefore be allocated using .96 as a denominator and each consuming department's percentage as its numerator. For Irons Finishing:

S_2 primary costs	$940,000
S_2 share of S_1 costs	20,000
S_2 total costs	$960,000

$$\text{Irons Finishing share} = \frac{.04}{.96}(\$960{,}000) = \$40{,}000$$

All the amounts in secondary allocation are calculated in a similar way.

Exhibit 7 relates overhead costs to standard direct-labor costs. Depending on how markedly wage rates change, the use of labor costs may be a nuisance. In periods of rapid inflation, many companies would prefer to use labor hours as a base instead. These too could lead to instability where learning curves (to be discussed in Chapter 8) were in effect. Least subject to change would be machine hours, although learning curves also affect machine times, albeit not as much. As was stated earlier, labor intensive departments should probably use labor hours, while capital intensive departments should probably use machine hours. A combination of the two also makes sense, provided labor and machine hours are not highly correlated (in which case, using both variables would amount to an unnecessary complication).

Different levels of activity are used to estimate whatever base is chosen to calculate overhead rates. The normal level of yearly activity should be chosen if the year ahead is anticipated to be normal. If not, the level of expected activity (which equals the normal level in a normal year) should be chosen.[3] A final alternative, one that has fallen into disfavor, is to use the ideal level of activity which equals the engineering capacity of machines reduced by some allowance for machine downtime caused by the need for

[3] "Should" is used in a normative sense. In depressed times a company might decide to retain its former overhead rates to avoid setting cost-based prices that were discouragingly high. This would be another example of *smoothing* and could be wise policy.

repairs and the existence of vacations. At one time this ideal level was popular because it was the greatest activity level and resulted in lower overhead rates, which, in turn, caused unfavorable volume variances (to be discussed in Chapter 8). With such unfavorable variances at hand, it was thought that management could accuse the factory of laziness and thereby supposedly stimulate greater effort. Today, the use of expected volumes is favored because the artifice of tight rates is no longer regarded as useful for motivational purposes, and using normal volumes in an abnormal year causes difficulty in planning. Moreover, whatever level is chosen, if the overhead variances are significant, the underabsorbed or overabsorbed overhead will be distributed at year's end to ending inventories of Finished Goods and Work in Process and to Cost of Sales, thereby eliminating from the financial statements the obvious effects of estimating level incorrectly.

Before investigating another method of computing secondary allocations, let us take time to note that secondary allocation basically transfers costs from one set of departments to another. We shall encounter this phenomenon again in Chapter 17, when we examine transfer pricing—a most perplexing area in managerial accounting. Transfer pricing causes many disputes over behavior, largely because it is coupled with a performance measure called "return on investment (ROI)." In secondary allocation, the disputes have been essentially resolved by responsibility accounting. The production departments are usually not held responsible for costs of service departments beyond their control, unless some ill-considered policy—like some of those mentioned in Chapter 4—is in effect. Secondary allocation and responsibility accounting would seem to hold a message concerning transfer pricing.

Simultaneous Allocation

Step allocation has two shortcomings: 1. The sequence of distributing service department costs is arbitrary. 2. Some reciprocal services are ignored. There is another method that suffers from neither of these shortcomings and at the same time facilitates further analysis. This is the simultaneous allocation method. It gets its name from the fact that simultaneous equations are developed to relate all service and production departments. While we investigate the simultaneous method, let us also see how a hospital makes use of primary and secondary allocation and in the process form some notion of how hospital services are "manufactured."

Hospitals have both service and production departments—the latter are referred to as ancillary (revenue-billing) departments. Examples of service departments and their bases for secondary allocation appear on page 165.

Service Department	*Common Allocation Base*
Maintenance	Square feet
Housekeeping	Square feet
Plant operations	Square feet
Laundry	Poundage
Dietary	Patient days
Cafeteria	Number of employees
Medical records	Patient days, estimated effort
Admissions	Patient days
Administration	Estimated effort
Accounting	Estimated effort
Nursing	Payroll
Superintendence	Payroll, estimated effort
Purchasing	Estimated effort, square feet
Data Processing	Estimated effort

Note: "Estimated effort" refers to time spent in a particular department. It is a widely used basis for allocation—one that is subject to all the objections discussed earlier.

The ancillary departments include Inpatients, Radiology, Laboratory, Electrocardiograph (EKG), Electroencephalograph (EEG), Physical Therapy, Emergency Ambulance, Outpatient, and Mental Health. (Observe that some of these departments do not exist separately in some hospitals but instead are grouped in some way.)

Hospital production flows are like those of manufacturing companies in that hospital patients—who are theoretically, but rather inhumanly, the products—pass through the ancillary departments. It would be possible to continue the familiar process by lodging service department costs in the ancillary departments and then developing billing rates.

An additional use of primary and secondary allocations is to establish hospital reimbursement rates. The patient ultimately pays directly or indirectly through a third party such as Blue Cross, Medicare, Medicaid, or some commercial insurance company. The third party insurer pays the hospital using a predetermined reimbursement rate, which does not generally recognize all hospital costs. At the end of each year, a report that requires secondary allocation is prepared to help revise reimbursement rates. In some states—notably Michigan and Rhode Island—hospitals may use simultaneous allocation, but in the majority of states step allocation is mandatory.

Situation: A hospital has two service departments, S_1 and S_2, and three ancillary departments, A_1, A_2, and A_3. The cost and service consumption data are given below. Determine the secondary allocation under both the step and simultaneous methods.

Service Consumers:

		S_1	S_2	A_1	A_2	A_3
Service Providers:	S_1	0	.2	.3	.4	.1
	S_2	.4	0	.1	.1	.4
Primary Costs:		\$92,000	\$184,000	\$224,000	\$306,000	\$194,000

Solution:

STEP METHOD

		S_1	S_2	A_1	A_2	A_3
Primary:		\$92,000	\$184,000	\$224,000	\$306,000	\$194,000
Secondary:	S_1	(92,000)	18,400	27,600	36,800	9,200
	S_2		(202,400)	33,733	33,733	134,934
Totals:		\$0	\$0	\$285,333	\$376,533	\$338,134

Comments:

1. Row S_1 in secondary allocation was obtained by multiplying \$92,000, the S_1 direct cost, by 0, .2, .3, .4, and .1 respectively.
2. Row S_2 in secondary allocation was obtained by multiplying the sum of \$184,000 (S_2 primary costs) plus \$18,400 (S_2 share of S_1 primary costs) by 0, 0, .1/.6, .1/.6, and .4/.6 respectively.
3. Even though S_1 used .4 of the services of S_2, nothing was charged to S_1 in secondary allocation because its costs had already been distributed.

SIMULTANEOUS METHOD

	S_1	S_2	A_1	A_2	A_3
Primary:	\$92,000	\$184,000	\$224,000	\$306,000	\$194,000
Secondary:	(92,000)	(184,000)	76,000	94,000	106,000
Totals:	\$0	\$0	\$300,000	\$400,000	\$300,000

Comments:

1. The simultaneous equations that were solved to obtain the secondary allocation above are

$$S_1 = 92{,}000 + .4S_2 + 0A_1 + 0A_2 + 0A_3$$

$$S_2 = 184{,}000 + .2S_1 + 0A_1 + 0A_2 + 0A_3$$

$$A_1 = 224{,}000 + .3S_1 + .1S_2 + 0A_2 + 0A_3$$
$$A_2 = 306{,}000 + .4S_1 + .1S_2 + 0A_1 + 0A_3$$
$$A_3 = 194{,}000 + .1S_1 + .4S_2 + 0A_1 + 0A_2$$

The equations have been developed by reading down the columns of the percentages table. Note that the first two equations only involve the service departments. This makes it possible to treat the equations separately and to insert their solution in the last three equations to determine the amounts of total allocation. The simplified service equations are

$$S_1 - .4S_2 = 92{,}000$$
$$-.2S_1 + S_2 = 184{,}000$$

Proceeding in matrices and letting B be the matrix of coefficients and p the vector of primary service department costs, we obtain

$$\underset{B}{\begin{bmatrix} 1 & -.4 \\ -.2 & 1 \end{bmatrix}} \underset{S}{\begin{bmatrix} S_1 \\ S_2 \end{bmatrix}} = \underset{p}{\begin{bmatrix} 92{,}000 \\ 184{,}000 \end{bmatrix}}$$

Inverting, the solution is

$$\underset{S}{\begin{bmatrix} S_1 \\ S_2 \end{bmatrix}} = \underset{B^{-1}}{\frac{\begin{bmatrix} 1 & .4 \\ .2 & 1 \end{bmatrix}}{.92}} \underset{p}{\begin{bmatrix} 92{,}000 \\ 184{,}000 \end{bmatrix}} = \underset{S}{\begin{bmatrix} 180{,}000 \\ 220{,}000 \end{bmatrix}}$$

Transposing the ancillary percentages, placing them in matrix A, and multiplying S yields the secondary allocations, s:

$$\underset{A}{\begin{bmatrix} .3 & .1 \\ .4 & .1 \\ .1 & .4 \end{bmatrix}} \underset{S}{\begin{bmatrix} 180{,}000 \\ 220{,}000 \end{bmatrix}} = \underset{s}{\begin{bmatrix} 76{,}000 \\ 94{,}000 \\ 106{,}000 \end{bmatrix}}$$

2. Reciprocal services have been reflected under this method.

3. The differences in total costs in the ancillary departments are significant (about 5%, 6%, and 12% in the respective departments). This would not always be the case.

4. The simultaneous results are the correct results, which the step method should approximate.

Further analysis can be done using the matrix approach. First we simplify the allocation process:

$$\overset{A}{\begin{bmatrix} .3 & .1 \\ .4 & .1 \\ .1 & .4 \end{bmatrix}} \overset{B^{-1}}{\frac{\begin{bmatrix} 1 & .4 \\ .2 & 1 \end{bmatrix}}{.92}} = \frac{\begin{bmatrix} .32 & .22 \\ .42 & .26 \\ .18 & .44 \end{bmatrix}}{.92} = \overset{D}{\begin{bmatrix} .3478 & .2391 \\ .4565 & .2826 \\ .1957 & .4783 \end{bmatrix}}, \quad \text{to four decimal places}$$

Here, d_{ij} is the share of service department i consumed by ancillary department j. Using D as a mnemonic designation for "direct," we can obtain secondary allocation *directly* by $Dp = s$; hence the direct matrix times the primary service cost vector yields the secondary allocation vector. Now suppose, for some reason, that p changes to $\begin{bmatrix} 100{,}000 \\ 210{,}000 \end{bmatrix}$. Then

$$D \begin{bmatrix} 100{,}000 \\ 210{,}000 \end{bmatrix} = \overset{s}{\begin{bmatrix} 84{,}991 \\ 104{,}996 \\ 120{,}013 \end{bmatrix}} = \text{the new secondary allocation}$$

The direct matrix could be used in this manner as long as the original percentages matrix did not change.

When could the percentages matrix be expected to remain constant? The percentages might well remain constant when flexible budgeting was performed. Flexible budgeting essentially uses $y = a + bx$ to estimate overhead costs, y, given varying levels of volume, x, during the same year; Chapter 8 will have more to say on the subject. The point is that in flexible budgeting the amounts in primary allocation change, but this may not necessitate a corresponding change in the percentages.

The percentages need not necessarily change if a cost savings program is being studied. Thus the direct matrix might be used to examine the effects of a budget cut in a service department.

It might also be the case that the percentages matrix would remain unchanged from one year to the next.

Besides (1) dispensing with the selection of an arbitrary sequence for distributing primary costs, and (2) recognizing all reciprocal services, the direct matrix is easily programmed on a computer and, once programmed, can generate allocations in seconds. When you compare this time with the time it takes to do step allocations, which are usually done manually, you will instantly appreciate the mechanical advantages of matrix allocation.

In passing, it would seem advisable for hospitals to use the simultaneous approach for internal planning purposes, even if external reports to third parties require step allocation.

Summary and Concluding Comments

This chapter has examined the construction of overhead rates and described how they are used in product costing. The theory and difficulties of primary and secondary allocations were presented at length in the contexts of (1) an athletic equipment manufacture and (2) hospital reimbursement rates. It was observed that secondary allocation is really a form of transfer pricing and one that causes fewer behavioral problems.

Step allocation is the most popular means of accomplishing secondary allocation. It is, however, inferior to simultaneous allocation and has led to abuses in the areas of hospital cost reimbursement. It has not been uncommon for hospital controllers in the past to juggle the sequence of service department allocation to obtain a desired total cost in departments that are fully reimbursed. A Mental Health unit, for example, has difficulty in obtaining full cost reimbursement from third-party insurers. This is partly because mental health problems are obscure, compared to the obvious problems associated with, say, broken legs. A leg is either broken or it is not; it is tangible. An emotional problem, on the other hand, comes in different degrees, not all of which are considered sufficiently abnormal to require treatment. Third-party insurers are apparently reluctant to reimburse for an illness that may be feigned. The message for hospitals, then, is to load costs on the Broken-Leg department and to avoid charging the Mental Health unit. Juggling the sequence of allocation is one rather illegitimate way to accomplish this.

The simultaneous method can be reduced to matrices and further streamlined to expedite cost savings analysis and flexible budgeting. Additionally, as long as departmental usage percentages remain constant, the direct matrix can be used to calculate secondary allocations for ensuing years.

The enduring popularity of step allocation is due mainly to habit. When the simultaneous method required the solving of a dozen or more equations by hand, it was understandable that accountants should shun it. With computers so widely available to eliminate this drudgery, one would expect step allocation to be abandoned. Once entrenched, however, the habitual seems to govern the accounting discipline. It is unfortunate.

Problems

1. *Step allocation.* Prepare a step allocation schedule from the following information. Direct-labor hours are to be used as a base in arriving at rates for applying manufacturing expenses. Department A is to be distributed first.

Service Departments:	Area	Direct Labor Hrs.	Indirect Labor	Direct Labor Cost	Other Factory Expenses	Portion of Department A Costs
A	20,000		$ 60,000		$309,000	—
B	30,000		80,000		324,000	.1
Production Departments:						
C	60,000	100,000	$220,000	$400,000	$543,000	.4
D	40,000	20,000	100,000	100,000	286,000	.3
E	50,000	30,000	140,000	200,000	338,000	.2

Rent is estimated at $24,000 with $16\frac{2}{3}\%$ considered the selling and administrative offices' collective share. Payroll taxes (*all* treated as overhead) attributable to the factory are estimated at $156,000. C, D, and E consume the same proportions of B's services as they do of A's.

2. *Overhead rate and budget variance report.* Estimated monthly overhead costs and their behavior are shown below along with the actual costs when the department worked 100,000 hours.

	Estimated		
	Variable Rate per Hour	Fixed	Actual
Indirect materials	$.20	$ -0-	$22,000
Indirect labor	.50	6,000	54,000
Payroll expenses	.07	600	7,200
Depreciation	-0-	8,000	7,500
Utilities	.10	5,000	16,200
Repairs	.25	3,000	30,000
Rent	-0-	10,000	10,000
Miscellaneous	.10	2,500	10,000

(a) Determine a monthly absorption rate given that the expected production is 100,000 hours each month.

(b) Prepare an overhead expense report showing accounting budget variances.

3. *Primary and secondary overhead allocation.*
S_i = service department i
P_j = production department j
Service consumption matrix:

		Consumers:			
		S_1	S_2	P_1	P_2
Renderers:	S_1	0	.2	.7	.1
	S_2	.1	0	.4	.5
Primary Overhead Costs:		$49,000	$147,000	$325,000	$153,500
Normal Machine Hours:				15,000	6,000

Required:

(a) Compute overhead absorption rates using matrices.

(b) List five components of primary overhead and discuss how they might be allocated.

4. *Primary and secondary overhead allocation.*
S_i = service department i
P_j = production department j
Service consumption matrix:

		Consumers:			
		S_1	S_2	P_1	P_2
Renderers:	S_1	0	.3	.4	.3
	S_2	.2	0	.2	.6
Primary Costs:		$94,000	$141,000	$312,000	$403,000
Secondary Costs:					
Σ					
Normal Machine Hours:				40,000	25,000
OH Rates:					

Required:

(a) Compute overhead absorption rates using matrices.

(b) List five components of primary overhead and discuss how they might be allocated.

(c) How might the percentages in the service consumption matrix be determined?

(d) Compute a "direct" matrix and use it to calculate the overhead rates that would result if the primary costs for S_1 and S_2 were $100,000 and $180,000 respectively.

5. *Flexible budgets.* What are they? How are they formed? What benefits? What variances could be developed from flexible budgets and how could these variances be useful?

6. What is the idea behind overhead rates?

7. If you had to explain the process of developing overhead rates to an interested (but somewhat detached, not ready for too many details) person, what would you say?

8. The primary allocation schedule for a firm that manufactures golf clubs is shown below. If expected volumes of output for the production departments are 6,000,000 clubs, and 500,000 sets respectively, determine departmental overhead rates given that secondary allocation is based on usage of services as follows:

Consuming Departments:		Repairs	Power	Heading	Shafting	Gripping
Rendering Departments:	Repairs	0	40%	10%	30%	20%
	Power	25%	0	45%	20%	10%

PRIMARY OVERHEAD ALLOCATION

		Departments				
		Service		Production		
Cost	Allocation Basis	Repairs	Power	Heading	Shafting	Gripping
Indirect materials	Specific	$ 24,000	$ 6,000	$1,200,000	$ 918,000	$ 720,000
Indirect labor	Specific	216,000	72,000	2,400,000	1,728,000	600,000
Depreciation	Specific	16,800	144,000	227,940	116,560	74,920
Water	Meters	2,400	192,000	7,200	9,600	4,800
Property taxes	Cubic footage	12,000	24,000	24,000	17,280	14,400
Insurance	Value of machines & average inventory	9,600	30,000	24,000	24,000	9,600
Payroll taxes	Payroll	21,600	7,200	240,000	192,000	60,000
Misc.	Specific	6,900	15,600	21,600	31,200	12,000
		$309,300	$490,800	$4,144,740	$3,019,440	$1,495,720

9. *Regression [overhead = f (labor)], (adapted from Certificate in Management Accounting Examination, December 1974).* The Raman Co. manufactures a wide range of products at several different plant locations. The Franklin Plant, which manufactures electrical components, has been experiencing some difficulties with fluctuating monthly overhead costs. The fluctuations have made it difficult to estimate the level of overhead that will be incurred for any one month.

Management wants to be able to estimate overhead costs accurately in order to plan its operation and financial needs better. A trade association publication to which Ramon Co. subscribes indicates that, for companies manufacturing electrical components, overhead tends to vary with direct-labor hours.

One member of the accounting staff has proposed that the cost behavior pattern of the overhead costs be determined. Then overhead costs could be predicted from the budgeted direct-labor hours.

Another member of the accounting staff has suggested that a good starting place for determining the cost behavior pattern of overhead costs would be an analysis of historical data. The historical cost behavior pattern would provide a basis for estimating future overhead costs. The methods proposed for determining the cost behavior pattern include the high-low method, the scattergraph method, simple linear regression, multiple regression, and exponential smoothing. Of these methods, Ramon Co. has decided to employ the high-low method, the scattergraph method, and simple linear regression. Data on direct-labor hours and the respective overhead costs incurred have been collected for the past two years. The raw data are as follows:

1973	Direct-Labor Hours	Overhead Costs
January	20,000	$84,000
February	25,000	99,000
March	22,000	89,500
April	23,000	90,000
May	20,000	81,500
June	19,000	75,500
July	14,000	70,500
August	10,000	64,500
September	12,000	69,000
October	17,000	75,000
November	16,000	71,500
December	19,000	78,000
1974		
January	21,000	86,000
February	24,000	93,000
March	23,000	93,000
April	22,000	87,000
May	20,000	80,000
June	18,000	76,500
July	12,000	67,500
August	13,000	71,000
September	15,000	73,500
October	17,000	72,500
November	15,000	71,000
December	18,000	75,000

Using linear regression, the following data have been obtained:

Coefficient of determination	.9109
Coefficient of correlation	.9544
Coefficients of regression equation	
Constant	39,859
Independent variable	2.1549
Standard error of the estimate	2.840
Standard error of the regression coefficient for the independent variable	.1437
True t-statistic for a 95% confidence Interval (22 degrees of freedom)	2.074

Required:

(a) Prepare a scattergraph and derive the regression results.

(b) Using the high-low method, determine the cost behavior pattern of the overhead costs for the Franklin Plant.

(c) Using the results of the regression analysis, calculate the estimate of overhead costs for 22,500 direct-labor hours.

Of the three proposed methods (high-low, scattergraph, linear regression), which one should Ramon Co. employ to determine the historical cost behavior pattern of Franklin Plant's overhead costs? Explain your answer completely, indicating the reasons why the other methods should not be used.

10. *Flexible budget, budget variance report (adapted from Certificate in Management Accounting Examination, December 1973).* The Melcher Co. produces farm equipment at several plants. The business is seasonal and cyclical in nature. The company has attempted to use budgeting for planning and controlling activities, but the variable nature of the business has caused some company officials to be skeptical about the usefulness of budgeting to the company. The accountant for the Adrian plant has been using a system he calls "flexible budgeting" to help his plant management control operations. The company president asks him to explain what the term means, how he applies the system at the Adrian plant, and how it can be applied to the company as a whole. The accountant presents the following data as part of his explanation:

Budget data for 1973	
Normal monthly capacity of the plant in direct-labor hours	10,000 hours
Material costs 6 lbs. @ $1.50	$9.00 unit
Labor costs 2 hours @ $3.00	$6.00 unit
Overhead estimate at normal monthly capacity	
Variable (controllable):	
Indirect labor	$6,650
Indirect materials	600
Repairs	750
Total variable	$8,000
Fixed (noncontrollable):	
Depreciation	$3,250
Supervision	3,000
Total Fixed	$6,250
Total Fixed and Variable	$14,250
Planned units for January 1973	4,000
Planned units for February 1973	6,000

Actual data for January 1973	
Hours worked	8,400
Units produced	3,800
Costs incurred:	
Material (24,000 lbs.)	$36,000
Direct labor	25,200
Indirect labor	6,000
Indirect materials	600
Repairs	1,800
Depreciation	3,250
Supervision	3,000
Total	$75,850

Required:

(a) Prepare a budget for January.

(b) Prepare a report for January comparing actual and budgeted costs for the actual activity for the month.

(c) Can flexible budgeting be applied to the nonmanufacturing activities of the company? Explain your answer.

Job Order (Batch) Costing

6

Costing Systems Overview

Chapter 1 spoke of a factory as if it consisted of a single cost center. As subsequent chapters have suggested, such an arrangement would be most unusual, because there are just too many men and machines whose efforts must be coordinated. Instead, what happens is that the factory is divided into many cost centers, each of which has its own responsibilities and specialties. There are Maintenance Departments, Stores Departments, Cutting Departments, Grinding Departments, Polishing Departments, Assembling Departments, and Painting Departments—to mention but a few. Costs are incurred by each cost center and are charged to and accumulated by the products as each center performs its function.

When products are of regular design and are made continuously, a process-costing system is in effect; when they are made sporadically in batches and are of varying design (variety is customary but not mandatory), a job order or batch costing system is in effect. Large quantity, although not definitive, also helps to distinguish a process costing system—certainly, if only a few units are made, a job order system clearly exists. Hence, process costing deals with continuous systems while job order costing deals with discrete systems. Superimposed on either system one may find a system of standards ("should be") costs. In practice one sees job order and process systems that are maintained in actual costs, job order and standard systems that are maintained in standard costs, and job order and process systems that are some odd blend of actual and standard costs. In this chapter we shall focus on job order costing.

Job Order Costing

The essentials of a job order costing system may be depicted for any given time period as shown on the next page.

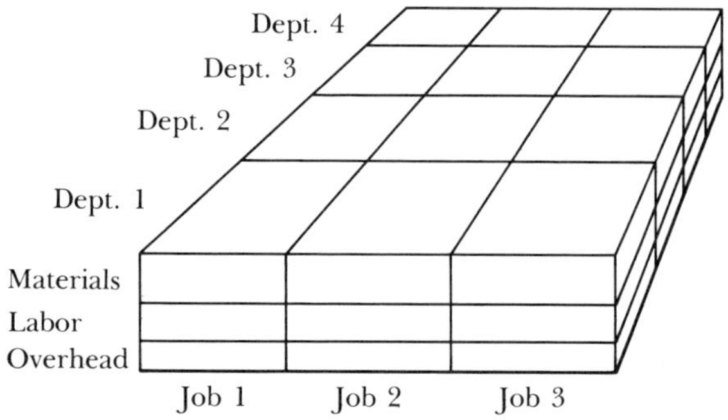

The total cost, T, of work in process is simply the sum of all elements:

$T = \sum_{h,i,j,k} C_{hijk}$, where C_{hijk} is the cost for month h of type i ($i = 1$ materials, 2 labor, 3 overhead) charged to job j ($j = 1, 2, \ldots, m$) by department k ($k = 1, 2, \ldots, n$) and $\sum_{h,i,j,k}$ merely adds all the cost elements

By taking a cross section through any dimension of the diagram—which would be the same as selecting one subscript to remain constant while summing over the other two subscripts—any subtotal can be obtained for information and control purposes. For example, the costs of any department can be found by adding the material, labor and overhead costs that have been charged by that department to each of the jobs in process. In a system that is maintained manually, this is a simple matter of consulting the job cost sheets for each job and adding the costs thereon designated by the code number of the department in question.

Since a variety of products is usually made under a job order system, the quantity produced of each—an *output* measure—is not apt to be suitable for determining overhead rates. Instead, the number of either direct-labor or standard-machine hours is customarily employed, because this measure of *input* is common to all products. With such activity measures, any uneveness in product complexity or size automatically results in the allocation of higher or lower charges—whichever is appropriate—to the products.

Example:

Log Builders, Inc. specializes in the design and construction of log homes. Besides the aesthetic appeal of their frontier appearance, these homes are sold on the bases of durability and economy (the logs themselves provide interior and exterior finishes as well as highly efficient insulation; furthermore, logs need no framing, no interior panelling, and no painting).

Log Builders occasionally buys lots and constructs demonstration homes on them, but the company's usual mode of operation is to build homes on customers' lots to each customer's specifications. Figure 1 indicates the basic log structure common to every home the company erects.

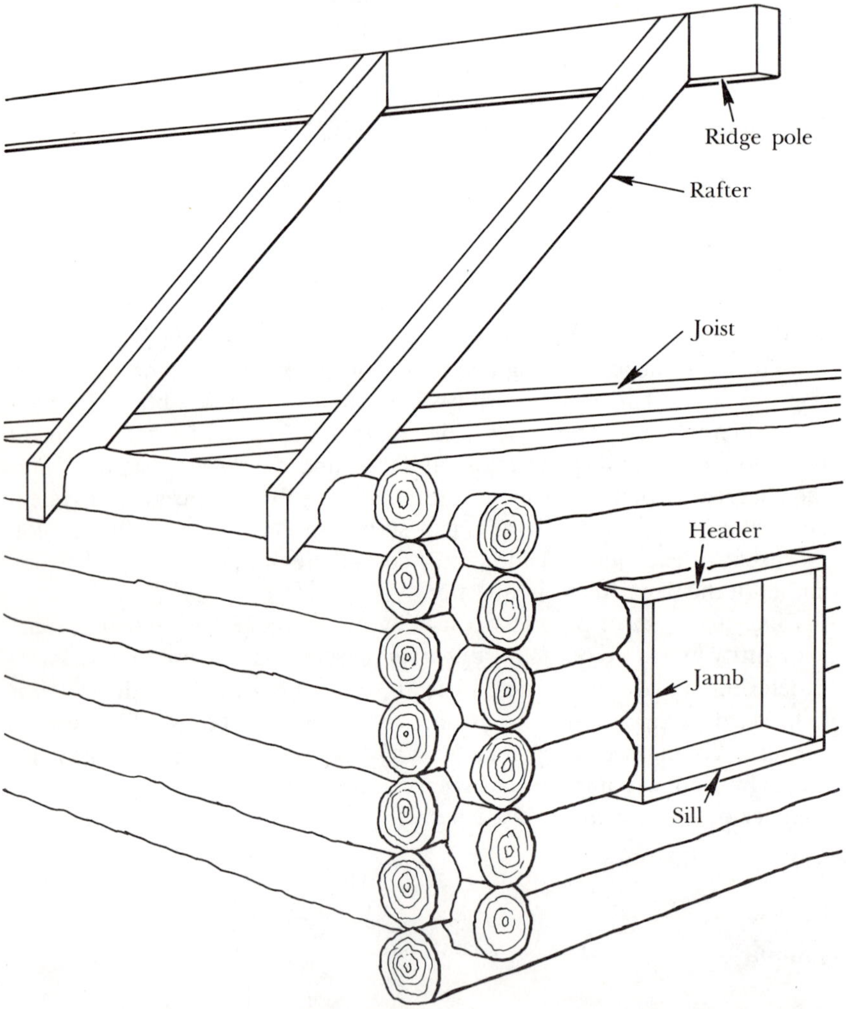

Figure 1

As materials are sent to a site, they are charged to the job number associated with that site. As carpenters, masons, plumbers, and electricians employed by Log Builders use their skills, they charge their time to the appropriate job numbers. The work of the carpenters and masons is identified with the Construction Department, while the plumbers and electricians constitute the Fixtures Department. Overhead is apportioned based on labor hours. In this way costs are matched against selling prices to determine income. If income on each job does not meet expectations, costs and price are reviewed to determine why.

Data:

Opening Inventory (5/31/74):	Raw Materials	$42,500
	Work in Process*	43,860
	Finished Homes—#21	22,000
	#25	18,000
	#26	27,600

* See detail in Exhibit 1

Transactions during June:

a) Logs, lumber, roofing, and nail purchases $124,200

	Construction	Fixtures
b) Materials requisitioned—#23	$ 2,400	$ 600
#24	2,800	1,400
#27	6,800	1,700
#28	1,800	6,200
#29	14,000	7,000
#30	12,000	4,000
Indirect materials and supplies	1,800	400

c) Labor (based on time tickets)

	Hours		Cost	
	Construction	Fixtures	Construction	Fixtures
#23	72	24	$ 576	$ 240
#24	48	16	384	160
#27	64	16	512	160
#28	200	56	1,600	560
#29	160	64	1,280	640
#30	120	40	960	400

Payroll taxes withheld (both departments) $1,494

d) Indirect labor	$2,200		$ 900
Payroll taxes withheld		$1,000	

e) Payroll benefits incurred by company (15%, of gross payroll to nearest dollar)

		Construction	Fixtures
f) Overhead expenses	—Utilities	$ 400	$100
	—Insurance	300	100
	—Property taxes	440	110
	—Depreciation	1,200	300
	—Repairs and maintenance	480	140
	—Miscellaneous	200	78

g) Administrative and selling expenses $6,740

h) The overhead absorption rates per direct-labor hour are $12 and $10, respectively.

i) Production for #24, #28, and #29 was completed during the month.

j) Homes #25, #26, and #29 were sold for $25,200, $40,000, and $41,000, respectively; 10% down payments were received.

k) Income taxes should be estimated at 60% of operating income.

Required:
1. Job Cost Summary
2. Journal entries to record all transactions
3. Income Statement with a detailed Cost of Goods Sold section
4. Comment on the Income Statement

Solution: Since it provides a framework for the solution, the first step in analyzing this problem is to prepare the Job Cost Summary. Although there are many forms, the Job Cost Summary typically provides separate columns for each job and allows row space for each type of cost for each department working on the products. Since the construction period may include more than one cost reporting period (in our example reports are prepared monthly), there is a four-way classification present: input cost type, output (job) designation, production department, and time. Getting all four classifications segregated in one report can lead to confusion. It is better to hold one classification constant in a preliminary summary, detail the other three in relation to it, and then sum the preliminary summaries to obtain the overall job cost summary. It is a matter of indifference which classification is held constant as far as the ending summary is concerned. The question reduces to deciding what preliminary summary would be most useful. For that matter, nothing precludes preparing different preliminary summaries for different purposes. Thus the accountant can achieve the following effects:

Classification Held Constant	*Emphasis Achieved*
1. Time	Costs for the current month are isolated to facilitate journal entry and statement preparation.
2. Department	Segregation of departmental costs for departmental control purposes.
3. Job	Cumulative comparison against job cost and profit estimates.
4. Cost input	Cumulative total spent on each input.

Of the four choices, the least appealing would seem to be the last. We shall use the first; the results appear in Exhibit 1.

Exhibit 1 Preliminary Summary—Work in Process 5/31/74

	Jobs:	23	24	27	28	29	30	Σ
Construction:	M	12,000	16,800					28,800
	L	768	1,440					2,208
	O	1,152	2,160					3,312
Subtotals		13,920	20,400					34,320
Fixtures:	M	3,000	5,000					8,000
	L	320	450					770
	O	320	450					770
Subtotals		3,640	5,900					9,540
Totals		17,560	26,300					43,860

Preliminary Summary—Costs for June

	Jobs:	23	24	27	28	29	30	Σ
Construction:	M	2,400	2,800	6,800	18,000	14,000	12,000	56,000
	L	576	384	512	1,600	1,280	960	5,312
	O	864	576	768	2,400	1,920	1,440	7,968
Subtotals		3,840	3,760	8,080	22,000	17,200	14,400	69,280
Fixtures:	M	600	1,400	1,700	6,200	7,000	4,000	20,900
	L	240	160	160	560	640	400	2,160
	O	240	160	160	560	640	400	2,160
Subtotals		1,080	1,720	2,020	7,320	8,280	4,800	25,220
Totals		4,920	5,480	10,100	29,320	25,480	19,200	94,500

Job Cost Summary—6/30/74

	Jobs:	23	24	27	28	29	30	Σ
Construction:	M	14,400	19,600	6,800	18,000	14,000	12,000	84,800
	L	1,344	2,024	512	1,600	1,280	960	7,520
	O	2,016	2,736	768	2,400	1,920	1,440	11,280
Subtotals		17,760	24,160	8,080	22,000	17,200	14,400	103,600
Fixtures:	M	3,600	6,400	1,700	6,200	7,000	4,000	28,900
	L	560	610	160	560	640	400	2,930
	O	560	610	160	560	640	400	2,930
Subtotals		4,720	7,620	2,020	7,320	8,280	4,800	34,760
Totals		22,480	31,780	10,100	29,320	25,480	19,200	138,360
			Complete		Complete	Complete		

The journal entries may be prepared from the given data and the appropriate totals in the job cost summary:

	Debit	Credit
a) Raw Materials	124,200	
Vouchers Payable		124,200
To record log, lumber, and supply purchases.		
b) Work In Process	76,900	
Overhead—Construction	1,800	
Overhead—Fixtures	400	
Raw Materials		79,100
To record requisitions for June.		
c) Work In Process	7,472	
Payroll Taxes Payable		1,494
Vouchers Payable		5,978
To record direct labor.		
d) Overhead—Construction	2,200	
Overhead—Fixtures	900	
Payroll Taxes Payable		1,000
Vouchers Payable		2,100
To record indirect labor.		
e) Overhead—Construction	1,127	
Overhead—Fixtures	459	
Accrued Payroll Benefits		1,586
To estimate payroll benefit costs.		
f) Overhead—Construction	3,020	
Overhead—Fixtures	828	
Prepaid Expenses		950
Accumulated Depreciation		1,500
Vouchers Payable		1,398
To record various overhead expenses.		
g) Administrative & Selling Expenses	6,740	
Various		6,740
To record various A & S expenses.		
h) Work In Process	10,128	
Absorbed Overhead—Construction		7,968
Absorbed Overhead—Fixtures		2,160
To apply overhead to jobs at $12 and $10, respectively, per direct-labor hour.		
i) Finished Homes	86,580	
Work In Process		86,580
To record the completion of jobs.		
j) Cash	10,620	
Accounts Receivable	95,580	
Sales		106,200
Cost of Homes Sold	71,080	
Finished Goods		71,080
To record the selling price and cost of sale for homes #25, #26, and #29; 10% downpayment was received.		
k) Income Tax Expense	17,028	
Accrued Income Taxes		17,028
To estimate income taxes at 60% of income.		

To help you keep track of the activity in the overhead accounts, the T-accounts shown below have been prepared.

	Construction Overhead		Fixtures Overhead	
	Actual	Absorbed	Actual	Absorbed
Indirect materials	1,800	7,968	400	2,160
Indirect labor	2,200		900	
Payroll benefits	1,127		459	
Utilities	400		100	
Insurance	300		100	
Property taxes	440		110	
Depreciation	1,200		300	
Repairs	480		140	
Miscellaneous	200		78	
Total	8,147	7,968	2,587	2,160
Absorbed	7,968		2,160	
Underabsorbed	179		427	

Comments: Fixtures has a 16.5% underabsorbed net variance that should be investigated.

T-accounts for the other accounts or a worksheet could be prepared to expedite the development of the income statement; however, such extra work is rarely necessary. By using the Job Cost Summary, the given data, and the journal entries, an income statement may easily be completed. The result, with comments thereon, is shown in Exhibit 2.

Before leaving this example, it would be wise to note that costs may exhibit undesirable fluctuation under such an actual cost system. Thus if the efficiency of employees varies with experience, age, or time of year, costs for the same type of dwelling might vary considerably. Similarly, if production runs in a feast-or-famine fashion, fixed overhead costs will be spread over different volumes. As a result overhead may be significantly under- or over-absorbed, thereby necessitating reallocation of differences at year end. If prices are set based on fluctuating costs, they are apt to discourage sales in periods of famine and encourage sales in periods of feast. For these reasons, many businesses advocate the development of standard costs and attempt to smooth the effects of irregular events.

Unanswered Question Not Previously Asked

Suppose a product manufactured on a job order basis is subject to spoilage for some reason. Given an order for x units of this product, how many

Exhibit 2

LOG BUILDERS, INC.
INCOME STATEMENT
JUNE 1974

Sales			$106,200
Cost of Homes Sold:			
Materials: Inventory, 5/31/74	$ 42,500		
Purchases	124,200		
Indirect Materials	(2,200)		
Inventory, 6/30/74	(87,600)	$76,900	
Direct Labor		7,472	
Absorbed Overhead		10,128	
Change in Work In Process:			
Inventory, 5/31/74	$ 43,860		
Inventory, 6/30/74	(51,780)	(7,920)	
Cost of Homes Completed		$86,580	
Change in Finished Homes:			
Inventory, 5/31/74	$ 67,600		
Inventory, 6/30/74	(83,100)	(15,500)	
Cost of Homes Sold			71,080
Gross Margin			$ 35,120
Selling and Administrative Expenses			6,740
Operating Income			$ 28,380
Estimated Income Taxes			17,028
Net Income After Taxes			$ 11,352

Comments:

1. If this statement were recast to detail individual profit per home, the gross margin rates would show 28.6%, 31%, and 37.9% respectively for #25, #26, and #29. Perhaps this would lead the managers to question the reasons for the variation and to adopt different pricing policies. If so, the altered form of the income statement would probably be preferable to the form illustrated above.
2. All inventories seem to be increasing substantially. This may not be advisable, since it ties up cash. In any case, the situation should be investigated—perhaps sales inducements should be offered. On the other hand, if costs of input resources are expected to increase, "hoarding" in anticipation of the increase is apt to be wise policy.

units should be started in production to obtain the desired amount? This causes yield variances and is known as the production overrun problem. In its simplest form, yield equations may be used to estimate the needed starting quantity. Thus, if there is a 5% yield loss and a customer's order specifies receipt of 475 units, the number to start is x, where

$$.95x = 475$$

$$x = 500$$

This is apt to be an oversimplified approach to a significant problem that involves probability theory and limited time in which to fill contracts. We shall delay further study of the production overrun problem until Chapter 19. For the present, accept the fact that it is a challenging and interesting problem for the cost accountant. The production overrun problem would seem to be a necessary part of any study of job costing.

Problems

1. What is going on in job order costing? How would you determine the cost of a completed job? Of ending inventory?

2. What are your feelings about using direct materials as a basis for allocating overhead costs?

3. Prepare an income statement (supported by job cost sheets) from the data given below. Also give journal entries for all transactions during the month.

Opening inventory:	JOBS		
	372	375	373
Work in process	$20,000		$32,500
Finished goods		$80,000	

Monthly transactions:

	JOBS	
Raw material requisitioned:	372	$12,000
	373	18,000
	378	21,000

Direct labor: JOBS	Dept. A Hours		Dept. B Hours	
372	600	$1,800	400	$1,600
373	500	$1,600	700	$2,500
378	1,000	$3,500	600	$2,300

Overhead absorption rates:

Dept. A—$5 per direct-labor hour
Dept. B—$8 per direct-labor hour

Job 372 was completed and sold for $60,000.
Job 375 was sold for $125,000.
Job 373 was completed; 400 of the 1,000 units made were sold for $45,000 each.
Selling and administrative expenses were $52,000.

4. A manufacturer uses batch processing in two departments, A and B. Opening inventory data:

Materials	$201,000
Work in process	–0–
Finished goods	$ 72,000
Finished goods consists of Job 0	

Transactions during month:

(a) Materials were purchased on account, $80,000.

(b) Department A requisitioned materials for Jobs 1, 2, and 3 in the amounts of $10,000, $15,000, and $28,000 respectively. Department B made similar requisitions in the amounts of $42,000, $27,000, and $23,000.

(c) The payroll amounted to $100,000 with direct labor of $82,500 and indirect labor for the difference; employee taxes and fringe benefits were deducted in the amount of $22,000. The hourly rate of pay is $5 in A and $8 in B. Department A charged Jobs, 1, 2, and 3 for 4,000, 2,500, and 6,000 hours respectively. Department B charged 500, 1,200, and 800 hours. The indirect labor is divided evenly between A and B.

(d) The overhead absorption rates are $2 and $6 per direct-labor hour for A and B respectively.

(e) Actual overhead expenses:

Depreciation	$12,000
Repairs	1,000
Insurance	1,000
Property taxes	3,000
Payroll benefits	10,000

One-fifth of these expenses goes to A; the balance to B.

(f) Selling and administrative expenses amounted to $42,000.

(g) Jobs 1 and 2 were completed.

(h) Job 0 sold for $110,000; Job 2 sold for $125,000. Sales were for cash.

Required:

(1) Prepare journal entries for all transactions.

(2) Prepare a Job Cost Summary.

(3) Prepare an income statement with detailed cost of goods sold section.

5. A manufacturer uses a job order costing system. You are

(a) to prepare journal entries for all transactions during October;

(b) to construct a Job Cost Summary;

(d) to prepare and critique an income statement with a detailed cost of goods sold section.

9/30 inventories:	Raw materials	$230,000
	Work in process	–0–
	Finished goods (consisting of Job 10)	140,000

October transactions:

(1) Materials were purchased on account, $340,000.

(2) Departments A and B requisitioned materials for Jobs 11, 12, 13 as follows:

A: $60,000, $30,000, and $70,000 respectively
B: $40,000, $20,000, and $5,000 respectively

(3) Direct labor was paid and charged to jobs 10, 11, and 12 as follows:

A: $10,000, $12,000, and $14,000 respectively
B: $8,000, $12,000, and $4,000 respectively

Indirect labor was $5,000 for A and $6,000 for B. Payroll deductions for the total departmental salaries and wages were $9,800.

(4) The overhead absorption rates for A and B were $.50 and $.80 per dollar of direct-labor cost.

(5) Other actual overhead expenses were

	A	B
Depreciation	$8,000	$5,000
Repairs	6,000	500
Insurance	4,000	3,000
Property taxes on the factory	2,800	2,400
Payroll benefits	6,200	3,100

(6) Selling and administrative expenses were $38,000.

(7) Jobs 11 and 13 were completed.

(8) Jobs 10 and 13 were sold for cash for $185,000 and $157,200 respectively.

6. *Sensuous Swimwear Company.* Sensuous Swimwear manufactures stylish women's bathing suits in a variety of colors, designs, fabrics, and sizes. There are three major lines; Seduction (for the daring sophisticate who wishes to appear alluring in diaphanous, revealing creations), Deception (for the woman who wishes to be devastating but must overcome some figure proportion problem), and Immersion (for the woman who actually intends to swim). Every swimsuit passes through two departments. Department A does cutting and structuring; Department B does the sewing, filling, trimming, and packaging. Swimsuits are made in batches by style numbers; varying sizes are manufactured simultaneously under a given style number.

Data:

Opening inventory (12/31/81) data:

Raw materials		$98,000
Work in process		–0–
Finished suits:		
Style #681		$22,000
	192	$115,000
	806	$65,000

Transactions during January 1982:

(a) Fabrics, filler, and trim purchases $78,000

(b) Direct material (fabric, filler) requisitioned for production:

		A	B
Seduction	#920	$15,000	$ 3,000
Deception	#190	36,000	45,000
Immersion	#515	20,000	10,000

(c) Indirect materials (trim) requisitioned (A, B) = ($0; $3,000)

(d) Direct labor (A, B): #920 (1,000, 1,200)
#190 (800, 1,200) hours, ($6/hour; $8/hour)
#515 (400, 100)

(e) Indirect labor ($6,300; $4,600)

(f) Payroll taxes withheld from employees $4,000

(g) Employee benefits paid by company (10% of gross payroll)

(h) Factory expenses $(A, B):

Depreciation	$(2,300; 1,800)
Utilities	$(800; 600)
Insurance	$(600; 600)
Property taxes	$(1,200; 1,000)
Repairs and maintenance	$(200; 300)
Miscellaneous	$(100; 200)

(i) Administrative and selling expenses $125,000

(j) Overhead absorption rates per direct-labor hour ($7.00; $4.00)

(k) Production for #920 and #515 was completed during the month, and 500 dozen and 2,000 dozen suits respectively were obtained.

(l) During the month all of styles 192 and 681 were sold to a department store chain for $70,800 and $200,000 respectively. In addition, 300 dozen of #920 and 800 dozen of #515 were sold for $200 and $60 per dozen respectively.

(m) Income taxes should be estimated at 60% of operating income.

Required:

(a) Journal entries to record all transactions.

(b) Job Cost Summary

(c) Income statement with detailed cost of goods sold and cost of goods manufactured sections.

(d) Comment on analysis and other data that might improve control.

Process Costing

7

Distinguishing Process from Batch Costing

Process costing deals with products that are regular in specification and made continuously. Such products would be found, for example, in the basic steel, aluminum, plastic, lumber, cement, flour, and petroleum industries. The fundamental idea, as with job order (batch) costing, is to allocate costs of material, labor, and overhead inputs to the output designations of the system. Unlike job order costing, however, process costing uses as output designations not jobs, but rather units lost, units in ending inventory (still being worked on), and units transferred (completed as far as the present department is concerned) to the next department in the series. A typical series of departments looks like this:

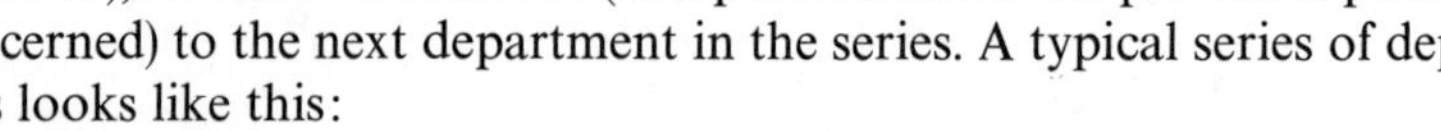

Department B in this series has as an additional input the costs transferred to it by department A. Similarly, department C has the costs transferred to it by B. It may also happen that C is an assembling department (connected in parallel to A and B instead of in series); when this is the case, the diagram looks like this:

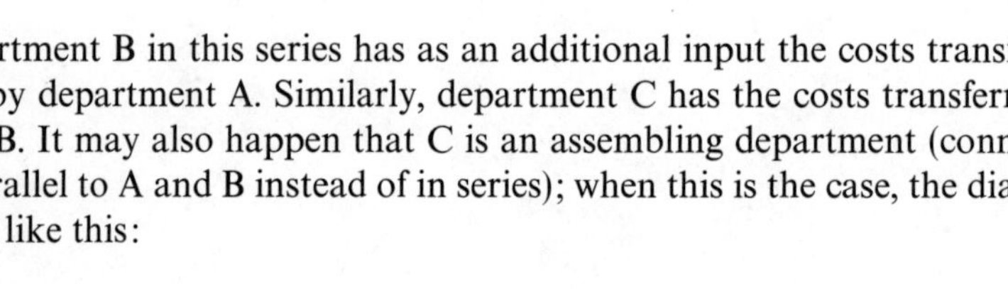

It improves understanding to realize that the output designations are all-inclusive; output of a department must show up in one of the lost, ending, or transferred categories. Nothing else is possible. The lost category is the catchall category; it might be used to isolate the costs of such things as by-products, or to segregate the costs of units that have been irretrievably damaged in some way.

Equivalent Production

Suppose you wanted to measure the amount of work done in a department and you found 6,000 units that were about two-thirds of the way through the processes of the department. If you were restricted to measuring work by a single number, what number would you choose? Would it seem plausible to say that 6,000 units of work were done? I hope that answer bothers you because it overstates the actual work done. What is needed is a work equivalent or substitution concept. The idea developed by accounting reasons somewhat simplistically that 4,000 completed units are the same as 6,000 units that are two-thirds completed. In other words, if the production manager had only started 4,000 units instead of 6,000, work on them in the department would have been completed. This type of substitution is used to calculate a measure known as equivalent production. Unfortunately, since materials are often added to a process at the beginning of processing, while labor and overhead (the costs of which are referred to as conversion costs) are added gradually throughout processing, it is customary to compute separate equivalent production measures for each type of input cost.

Accountants disagree over whether to include work done on lost units in the measurement of equivalent production. Many accountants prefer to include only work done on "good" units (those transferred and in ending inventory), reasoning that the costs will eventually have to be borne by those units. It is, however, mechanically easier to treat all output categories alike; furthermore, this latter procedure permits easy isolation of the cost of lost units for purposes of control.

Even assuming agreement on the inclusion of lost units in measuring equivalent production, there are still two basic ways for measuring—the average method and the FIFO method. The two methods are related as follows:

Units transferred out (total)
+ Units in ending inventory (to extent done *this* month)
+ Units lost (to extent done this month)

Average Equivalent Production

− Units in opening inventory (to extent done last month)

FIFO Equivalent Production

Note that the two methods only differ by the extent of work done in the preceding month on the opening inventory (that is, on the ending inventory of the preceding month). The better measure of work actually done is the FIFO measure; however, equivalent production itself is seldom used for any purpose other than costing, and hence the average method may be just as effectively employed in cost allocations as the FIFO method.

Example:

Opening inventory	3,000 units,	$\frac{2}{3}$ done last month as to conversion
Transferred out	50,000 units,	complete
Ending inventory	4,000 units,	$\frac{1}{4}$ done as to conversion
Lost units	1,000 units,	$\frac{1}{2}$ done as to conversion

Equivalent production of conversion computation:

Transferred	=	50,000
Ending	=	1,000
Lost	=	500
Average Production	=	51,500
Opening	=	− 2,000
FIFO Production	=	49,500

Comment: Sometimes FIFO equivalent production is described as viewing (Transferred minus Opening) instead as (Units started and completed this period plus work done to complete Opening). This alternate computation follows.

Started and completed (50,000 − 3,000)	=	47,000
Opening (work done this month)	=	1,000
Ending	=	1,000
Lost	=	500
FIFO Production (as above)	=	49,500

The same figure for equivalent production is obtained regardless of the approach adopted.

Once equivalent production has been calculated, it is possible to use it both to determine a cost per equivalent unit and to allocate the pertinent unit input cost among the transferred, ending, and lost output categories in proportion to the number of equivalent units in each category.

Lost Units

Once equivalent production is understood, the only remaining point that is apt to cause difficulty in ordinary process costing is the treatment of lost units. Conceptually, lost units may be broadly defined to include damaged units that need to be reworked, by-products, units that evaporate, and units that are totally ruined. There are two main viewpoints: (1) lost units provide practice that benefits all units worked on thereafter, and (2) some units must be lost if a certain amount of good production is to be achieved.

Where it is practical to estimate the lost-unit cost, accountants make provision for it in the overhead rate; hence every unit produced is charged for a share of the lost-unit cost as overhead is applied to it. When the overhead rate contains such a provision, the actual cost of lost units for the period is removed from work in process and charged to the departmental overhead account. If this were not done, "good" (units transferred and in ending inventory) production would bear a double charge for lost units—once by way of the overhead rate, and again when the actual lost cost was reallocated at month's end.

When lost-unit cost cannot be readily estimated and treated as a portion of overhead, the accountant reallocates it to units transferred and in ending inventory. He customarily tries to determine which good units have been responsible for the loss, and therefore which good units have immediately benefitted. If loss takes place at the very end of processing, only the units that have passed that point, that is, transferred units, are considered to have benefitted. If loss occurs at the very start of processing or while the units are awaiting processing (as in the case of an evaporation loss), all good units put into production are considered to have benefitted. If loss happens during processing, the units that benefit are those that have passed the point of loss. Here it is the practice to use an average fraction of completion to determine how many units have passed this point. This is an expedient but inaccurate procedure, because such an average would only coincidentally equal the number of units that had actually passed the critical point. Of course, not every circumstance is clearly resolvable by considering the point of loss detection. For instance, a lost unit might be discovered in the middle of production that was caused by defective materials or defective production received from a preceding department; in such a case the point of detection is not the point of loss. In practice, however, it would undoubtedly be too expensive to ascertain cause of loss just to accommodate some refinement in reallocating lost-unit costs. An averaging approach is thought adequate.

The following rules for reallocating lost-unit costs evolve from the above reasoning:

Stage of Loss	*Procedure for Reallocating*
Beginning of processing	Use "good" equivalent production of materials for the first production department in sequence; for subsequent departments use "good" equivalent production of units received from preceding department (assuming that the

Stage of Loss	*Procedure for Reallocating*
	present department puts these units into processing at the very beginning of its operations). Note that if units received from preceding department are mixed with departmental materials at the start of processing, their equivalent productions will be the same.
During processing	Use "good" equivalent production of conversion.
End of processing	Distribute lost cost entirely to units transferred.

If loss is not treated using an average fraction of completion, it would be consistent with the above procedures to determine which units had passed the point of loss and apportion the loss to them—again assuming no provision for loss in the overhead rate.

It is theoretically desirable—from a smoothing standpoint—to charge production for some average rate of loss. Any average, of course, implies dispersion and in production this leads to control charts. The control chart has a mean and upper and lower control limits that are typically determined according to the normal probability distribution. Thus, if production is measured by the equivalent production of conversion and the mean rate of spoilage is 10% with a standard deviation of 1%, 95% reliability (tolerance) limits would be $10\% \pm 2(1\%)$ (that is, the lower and upper control limits would be 8% and 12% respectively). Production would be charged with 10% regardless, with the difference—to the limits of the tolerance region—going to a Spoilage Random Fluctuation overhead account and any amount beyond the control limits being charged to an expense account such as Loss From Abnormal Spoilage. In time, the Spoilage Random Fluctuation account should reduce to approximately zero; hence the 10% normal rate will have the effect of smoothing minor monthly fluctuations in spoilage rates. The Abnormal Loss account calls management's attention to production that is apparently out of control. If spoiled units have a salvage value, this should be used to reduce loss by a journal entry setting up the recoverable value (Debit: Accounts Receivable (or Cash); Credit: Work in Process—Present Department).

Example

Let us see how these concepts are carried out in a complete situation where we are dealing with a middle production department that adds materials gradually to the base product it receives from a preceding department.

Prepare an equivalent production schedule and a cost report from the following data. Use (1) the average method and (2) the FIFO method.

	Units
Opening inventory (75% done last month as far as departmental materials are concerned, 40% as far as conversion is concerned)	20,000
Received from preceding department (converted to units of this department)	400,000
Additional materials put into process	180,000
	600,000
Transferred to finished goods	530,000
Ending inventory ($66\frac{2}{3}$% done this month for departmental materials; 40% for conversion)	60,000
Lost units (lost gradually during processing; 60% departmental materials, 50% conversion; no provision in overhead rate; .006 of good equivalent production of conversion is normal with a tolerance range of .004 to .008; $3.00 per converted equivalent unit is taken as the value of a lost unit)	10,000
	600,000

Note: the process is such that the materials from the preceding department are the base to which departmental materials are added.

Cost Data		
	Opening inventory:	
	Materials from preceding department	$ 20,000
	Departmental materials	12,400
	Departmental conversion costs	5,000
	Cost of materials received from preceding department during the month	580,000
	Departmental costs during month:	
	Materials	448,400
	Conversion costs	330,400

Solution: Average Method

Exhibit 1 develops the equivalent production schedule and the cost report under the average method. The exhibit has three main sections: (1) the equivalent production section, (2) the unit cost section, and (3) the cost report section. The first two sections culminate in the third section. Equivalent production is computed using the average costing method for each type of input cost. The columns contain units in the transferred, ending, and lost categories, and when the equivalent units in each category are added across, the sum equals the equivalent production for the type of cost reflected in the row. The unit cost section adds the cost in opening inventory to the cost during the month for each type of cost and then divides the sum by the appropriate equivalent production previously determined. Here is where the name "average costing" takes meaning since the total of the opening inventory and during-month costs are averaged over the equivalent production of the month to obtain a unit cost. The cost report section is then obtained by multiplying the equivalent productions of section 1 by the unit costs of

Exhibit 1 Average Method

EQUIVALENT PRODUCTION

Cost Type	Transferred	Ending	Lost	Total (*EP*)
Preceding department costs	530,000	60,000	10,000	600,000
Departmental material costs	530,000	40,000	6,000	576,000
Departmental conversion costs	530,000	24,000	5,000	559,000

UNIT COSTS

	Opening Inventory	Cost During Month	Total	Unit Cost (Total/*EP*)
Preceding department costs	$20,000	$ 580,000	$ 600,000	$1.00
Departmental material costs	12,400	448,400	460,800	.80
Departmental conversion costs	5,000	330,400	335,400	.60
	$37,400	$1,358,800	$1,396,200	

COST REPORT

	Transferred	Ending	Lost	Total Cost to be Accounted For
Preceding department costs	$ 530,000	$ 60,000	$10,000	$ 600,000
Departmental material costs	424,000	32,000	4,800	460,800
Departmental conversion costs	318,000	14,400	3,000	335,400
Totals	$1,272,000	$106,400	$17,800	$1,396,200
Lost cost*—abnormal	–0–	–0–	(1,704)	(1,704)
—random	–0–	–0–	(3,324)	(3,324)
—normal	9,540	432	(9,972)	–0–
Total Cost Accounted For	$1,281,540	$106,832	$ 2,800	$1,391,172

* When only the "good" outputs (that is, transferred and ending) are considered, the equivalent production of conversion becomes 554,000 units. Hence, since the normal loss rate is .006 and the upper control limit is .008,

Normal loss	= [.006(554,000) = 3324]	\$3 = \$ 9,972
Random loss	= [.002(554,000) = 1108]	\$3 = \$ 3,324
Abnormal loss	= [5,000 – 3,324 – 1,108 = 568]	\$3 = \$ 1,704
Residual lost-unit cost (due to inaccuracy of provision of \$3)		= \$ 2,800
		\$17,800

Normal lost cost is reallocated according to equivalent production of conversion because the units were lost gradually during processing. Since 530,000 units were transferred and 24,000 units were in ending inventory, the normal lost cost of $9,972 is apportioned 530/554 to transferred and 24/554 to ending or $9,540 and $432, respectively. The residual lost cost would generally be insignificant in relation to total costs and could therefore be treated as an addition to Cost of Goods Sold.

section 2 and summing the rows and columns. It then remains only to reallocate the lost-unit cost (the method is described in the footnote to Exhibit 1) because there is no provision in the overhead rate for lost units.

Observe that if all inputs are synchronized, it is never necessary to worry about input units where all the output units are known. Equivalent production is calculated based on the output and costs are allocated according to equivalent production. Thus if the input of the preceding department is synchronized with the present department (which would be known as a "balanced line" in production terminology) and is in pounds while the work of the present department is in gallons, the nuisance of converting pounds to gallons can be avoided entirely if all output gallons are given.

Comment

There is a fine point in process costing that can be a real nuisance. It has to do with the word "normal" as in "normal loss." In Exhibit 1, normal has been used in a control chart sense implying a probability distribution of loss—and, perhaps, the normal distribution. The control chart would have to be kept in percentages because production would undoubtedly vary from period to period, thereby making number of units inapplicable. If there were a provision for loss in the overhead rate, it would be, say \$$a$ per unit produced. The actual loss would then be charged to overhead using \$$b$ per unit—apportioned among normal, random and abnormal units. Because these designations have been chosen by percentages, \$$b$ exceeds \$$a$. If p is the expected loss percentage, $a = pb$. In other words, a is a cost assessed on every unit processed, while b is a cost associated with actual lost units. In Exhibit 1, \$$b$ = \$3 and is very high relative to current costs. Had cost estimation been more accurate, it is likely that \$$b$ would more closely approximate current unit costs.

The other use of the word "normal" is in the sense of "ordinary" or "not unexpected." This is a much less precise usage and the procedures for treating the loss allocation are much simpler. Loss *has occurred* and, noticing it, the production supervisor says it is "normal," "expected," or "ordinary." The cost of the loss that has occurred is then allocated proportionally in keeping with the rules presented earlier. No price per unit (\$$b$) need be introduced.

Basically, the difference between the two meanings lies in whether there is a formal provision for loss in overhead or not. If there is such a provision, a standard for loss is set; if there is not, whatever losses occur are apportioned proportionally as they occur with no effort at smoothing such costs. There are hybrid systems, of course, but if there is a provision in overhead, there should be some unit cost b; apportioning actual loss is inconsistent with

Exhibit 2 FIFO Method

EQUIVALENT PRODUCTION

Cost Type	O.I.	Transferred S & C	Ending	Lost	Total (EP)
Preceding department costs	0	510,000	60,000	10,000	580,000
Departmental material costs	5,000	510,000	40,000	6,000	561,000
Departmental conversion costs	12,000	510,000	24,000	5,000	551,000

UNIT COSTS

	Costs During Month	÷ EP_i	= C_i
Preceding department costs	$ 580,000	580,000	$1.00000
Departmental material costs	448,400	561,000	.79929
Departmental conversion costs	330,400	551,000	.59964
	$1,358,800		

COST REPORT

	Transferred	Ending	Lost	Total Cost to be Accounted For
Preceding department costs	$ 510,000	$ 60,000	$10,000	$ 580,000
Departmental material costs	411,634	31,972	4,794	448,400
Departmental conversion costs	313,012	14,391	2,997	330,400
Opening inventory cost	37,400		0	37,400
Totals	$1,272,046	$106,363	$17,791	$1,396,200
Lost Cost*—abnormal	-0-	-0-	(1,896)	(1,896)
—random	-0-		(3,276)	(3,276)
—normal	9,396	432	(9,828)	-0-
Total Costs Accounted For	$1,281,442	$106,795	$ 2,791	$1,391,028

*Normal loss = [.006(546,000) = 3276] $3 = $ 9,828
Random loss = [.002(546,000) = 1092] $3 = $ 3,276
Abnormal loss = [5,000 − 3,276 − 1,092 = 632] $3 = $ 1,896
Residual lost-unit cost = $ 2,791

$17,791

Normal lost cost, $9, 828, is reallocated according to the "good" equivalent production of conversion:

$$\$9{,}828\left[\frac{12+510}{(12+510)+24}, \frac{24}{(12+510)+24}\right] = (\$9{,}396;\ \$432)$$

the smoothing concept underlying the overhead provision. Problem 14 should help you understand why.

Solution: FIFO Method

Exhibit 2 details the solution of this problem according to the FIFO method. Note that equivalent production for units transferred is now computed in terms of work done *this period* on opening inventory and units started (this period) and completed, instead of simply taking the total units transferred. The costs during the month (*only*) are then divided by their respective equivalent productions to obtain unit costs. The unit costs are next multiplied by the equivalent productions in each output designation to obtain the major part of the cost report. Then, by adding opening inventory costs to costs allocated to transferred (because the opening inventory units are the first-in units that are assumed to be the first-out [transferred] units in the FIFO method), and by reallocating lost-unit costs as described in the footnote to Exhibit 2, the allocation process may be completed.

When the two exhibits are compared, the resulting allocations suggest that the distinction between average and FIFO is a big fuss over nothing. However, the differences could be significant if the proportion of opening inventory to total production were large. Average is simpler, but FIFO offers a more precise measure of equivalent production.

Let us use Exhibit 2 to illustrate appropriate journal entries:

Work in Process—Present Department	580,000	
Work in Process—Preceding Department		580,000
To record the transfer of 50,000 units of Preceding output (= 400,000 units in terms of Present output) to Present.		
Work in Process—Present Department	448,400	
Raw Materials		448,400
To record direct material requisitions.		
Work in Process—Present Department	330,400	
Accrued Payroll Absorbed Overhead—Present Department }		330,400
To record direct labor and to absorb overhead (based on direct labor).		
Work in Process—Next Department	1,281,442	
Loss from Abnormal Spoilage	1,896	
Residual Lost-Unit Cost	2,791	
Present Department Overhead-Spoilage Random Fluctuations	3,276	
Work in Process—Present Department		1,289,405
To record (1) the transfer of 530,000 units from the Present to the Next Department and (2) the random, abnormal, and residual lost-unit costs. It is assumed that spoiled units have no salvage value.		

Exhibit 3 Matrix Approach—Average Method

Key: T = transferred, E = ending inventory, L = lost,
P = preceding, M = departmental materials, C = departmental conversion

EQUIVALENT PRODUCTION (EP):

$$\begin{array}{c} \\ P \\ M \\ C \end{array}\begin{array}{c} \begin{array}{ccc} T & E & L \end{array} \\ \begin{bmatrix} 1 & 1 & 1 \\ 1 & 2/3 & 3/5 \\ 1 & 2/5 & 1/2 \end{bmatrix} \end{array} \begin{array}{c} T \\ E \\ L \end{array} \begin{bmatrix} 530{,}000 \\ 60{,}000 \\ 10{,}000 \end{bmatrix} = \left[\overset{T}{\begin{bmatrix} 530{,}000 \\ 530{,}000 \\ 530{,}000 \end{bmatrix}} + \overset{E}{\begin{bmatrix} 60{,}000 \\ 40{,}000 \\ 24{,}000 \end{bmatrix}} + \overset{L}{\begin{bmatrix} 10{,}000 \\ 6{,}000 \\ 5{,}000 \end{bmatrix}} \right] = \overset{EP}{\begin{bmatrix} 600{,}000 \\ 576{,}000 \\ 559{,}000 \end{bmatrix}}$$

UNIT COSTS (C_i):

Opening inventory$_i$	+ Cost during month$_i$	= Total$_i$	C_i = Total$_i$ ÷ EP_i
P: \$20,000	+ \$580,000	= \$600,000	C_P = \$1.00
M: \$12,400	+ \$448,400	= \$460,800	C_M = \$ .80
C: \$ 5,000	+ \$330,400	= \$335,400	C_C = \$ .60

COST REPORT:

$$\begin{array}{c} C_P \\ C_M \\ C_C \end{array} \begin{bmatrix} 1.00 & 0 & 0 \\ 0 & .80 & 0 \\ 0 & 0 & .60 \end{bmatrix} \left[\overset{T}{\begin{bmatrix} 530{,}000 \\ 530{,}000 \\ 530{,}000 \end{bmatrix}} + \overset{E}{\begin{bmatrix} 60{,}000 \\ 40{,}000 \\ 24{,}000 \end{bmatrix}} + \overset{L}{\begin{bmatrix} 10{,}000 \\ 6{,}000 \\ 5{,}000 \end{bmatrix}} \right] = \text{Cost Report}$$

COST REPORT:

	Transferred	Ending	Lost	Totals
Preceding department costs	\$ 530,000	\$ 60,000	\$10,000	\$ 600,000
Departmental material costs	424,000	32,000	4,800	460,800
Departmental conversion costs	318,000	14,400	3,000	335,400
Totals	\$1,272,000	\$106,400	\$17,800	\$1,396,200
Lost cost—abnormal	–0–	–0–	(1,704)	(1,704)
—random	–0–	–0–	(3,324)	(3,324)
—normal	9,396	432	(9,972)	–0–
Totals	\$1,281,442	\$106,795	\$ 2,800	\$1,391,172

Comments:

1. Lost-cost reallocation was carried out as described in Exhibit 1.
2. Since little purpose is served by the details of the cost report, the totals can be obtained directly by

   $$(1.00, .80, .60)[[T] + [E] + [L]] = ((1{,}272{,}000) + (106{,}400) + (17{,}800)) = (1{,}396{,}200)$$

   The diagonalized matrix was used only to demonstrate how the report in Exhibit 1 would be generated.
3. Where several previous departments feed a production department, as might be the case if it were an assembly department, or where there were several types of materials or classes or labor, new rows would be added to the above matrices for each new input.

The Matrix Approach

As you readily understand, what was accomplished in Exhibit 2 was simply allocation of input costs (preceding, materials, and conversion) to output categories (transferred, ending, and lost). Matrix algebra is well suited to carrying out such allocations. Many accountants have found that when process cost problems are recast in matrices, a certain structure becomes available that enables them to prepare cost reports in half the time or less. Let us consider the average method first.

The one matrix that requires concentration nonetheless rests on a very simple question: On average, what fraction of each input appears in each output? Thus the fraction is 1 (this is a fraction in approximately the same sense that a straight line is a curve with no bend in it) for each input appearing in each unit transferred. The remaining fractions depend on how far along—for each input—the units in ending inventory and lost have gotten. Now take the fractions matrix and multiply it by a column vector partitioned as to total units transferred, in ending inventory, and lost to obtain both an equivalent productions matrix detailed by inputs and outputs and a total equivalent productions vector.[1] Simple!

Once the total equivalent productions are known, they can be used to calculate unit costs by dividing them into the respective total input costs—just as was done in Exhibit 1. Finally, by entering the unit costs in a diagonalized matrix and multiplying it by the detailed equivalent productions matrix, the cost report is obtained. All these calculations are carried out in Exhibit 3. In addition, the comments in Exhibit 3 describe how the matrix approach can eliminate unnecessary detail from the cost report (comment 2) as well as how it can be adapted to cope with more complex problems (comment 3).

Just why is certain detail unnecessary? The cost report is used to account for total costs and thereby support the journal entry for costs transferred out. While it may be interesting to know how much of each input cost appears in each output designation, it does not seem to be particularly useful information. Using a vector to premultiply the detailed equivalent production matrix yields totals directly; that is,

$$(C_P, C_M, C_C)[[T] + [E] + [L]] = ((1{,}272{,}000) + (106{,}400) + (17{,}800))$$

Since providing extraneous information tends to glut an information system and thereby create noise instead of signal, it would seem advisable to streamline the cost report.

In a more complex situation, a department might simultaneously receive inputs from several preceding departments and also have several materials

[1] Partitioned matrix multiplication is discussed in Appendix C.

and different types of labor of its own. The problem is then apt to become one of lack of synchronization, with different inputs being incorporated at different stages of processing. Thus some of the Preceding inputs and Present departmental materials might be added at start of processing, while others

---

Exhibit 4 Matrix Approach—FIFO Method

Key: O = opening inventory, S & C = started and completed,
T = transferred, E = ending inventory, L = lost,
P = preceding, M = departmental materials, C = departmental conversion

EQUIVALENT PRODUCTION (EP):

$$\begin{array}{c} \\ P \\ M \\ C \end{array} \begin{array}{c} \begin{array}{cccc} O & S\&C & E & L \end{array} \\ \left[\begin{array}{cc|c|c} 0 & 1 & 1 & 1 \\ 1/4 & 1 & 2/3 & 3/5 \\ 3/5 & 1 & 2/5 & 1/2 \end{array}\right] \end{array} \begin{array}{c} O \\ S\&C \\ E \\ L \end{array} \left[\begin{array}{c} 20{,}000 \\ 510{,}000 \\ 60{,}000 \\ 10{,}000 \end{array}\right] = \left[\overset{T}{\left[\begin{array}{c} 510{,}000 \\ 515{,}000 \\ 522{,}000 \end{array}\right]} + \overset{E}{\left[\begin{array}{c} 60{,}000 \\ 40{,}000 \\ 24{,}000 \end{array}\right]} + \overset{L}{\left[\begin{array}{c} 10{,}000 \\ 6{,}000 \\ 5{,}000 \end{array}\right]} \right] = \overset{EP}{\left[\begin{array}{c} 580{,}000 \\ 561{,}000 \\ 551{,}000 \end{array}\right]}$$

UNIT COSTS (C_i):

Cost during month$_i$ $\div$ EP_i $= C_i$
P: \$580,000 $\div$ 580,000 = \$1.00
M: \$448,400 $\div$ 561,000 = \$ .79929
C: \$330,400 $\div$ 551,000 = \$ .59964

COST REPORT:

$$\begin{array}{c} C_P \\ C_M \\ C_C \end{array} \left[\begin{array}{ccc} 1.00000 & 0 & 0 \\ 0 & .79929 & 0 \\ 0 & 0 & .59964 \end{array}\right] \left[\overset{T}{\left[\begin{array}{c} 510{,}000 \\ 515{,}000 \\ 522{,}000 \end{array}\right]} + \overset{E}{\left[\begin{array}{c} 60{,}000 \\ 40{,}000 \\ 24{,}000 \end{array}\right]} + \overset{L}{\left[\begin{array}{c} 10{,}000 \\ 6{,}000 \\ 5{,}000 \end{array}\right]} \right] = \text{Cost Report}$$

COST REPORT

	Transferred		Ending		Lost		Totals
Preceding department costs	\$ 510,000		\$ 60,000		\$10,000		\$ 580,000
Departmental materials costs	411,634	+	31,972	+	4,794	=	448,400
Departmental conversion costs	313,012		14,391		2,997		330,400
Opening inventory cost	37,400		0		0		37,400
Totals	\$1,272,046		\$106,363		\$17,791		\$1,396,200
Lost cost—abnormal	-0-		-0-		(1,896)		(1,896)
—random	-0-		-0-		(3,276)		(3,276)
—normal	9,396		432		(9,828)		-0-
Totals	\$1,281,442		\$106,795		\$ 2,791		\$1,391,028

Comments:
1. Lost-cost reallocation was carried out as described in Exhibit 2.
2. The cost report can be streamlined to show totals only by

$$(C_P, C_M, C_C)[[T] + [E] + [L]] + [[37{,}400] + [0] + [0]] =$$
$$[(1{,}272{,}046) + (106{,}363) + (17{,}791)] = (1{,}396{,}200)$$

might be added during processing and still others at the end. Furthermore, there is no reason to believe that the Preceding departments will give the Present separtment the exact quantities it needs to complete the units it is working on—that would amount to extraordinary interdepartmental synchronization. Thus there are "intra" synchronization and "inter" synchronization problems in such an assembly department. The matrix approach, however, easily deals with these problems by the addition of separate rows in the fractions matrix for each input. This automatically provides for intra-synchronization; inter-synchronization may be dealt with by having fractions of ending inventory that are greater than 1. Thus if ending inventory had 10,000 units but some Preceding department provided enough of its output to make 35,000 units, the element in the fractions matrix would be 3.5. This would have the effect of increasing equivalent production for that input and temporarily lodging the cost of the excess units in ending inventory.

Suitable adaptations to make the matrix approach track FIFO cost flows are shown in Exhibit 4.

So far, all our calculations have centered on tracing flows for income statement purposes. But what about control? Equivalent production *may* be useful for control purposes depending on whether encouraging increased equivalent production is wise—more will be said about this in the next section. Use of unit costs for control purposes is unwise if unit costs fluctuate because of varying material costs and changing labor efficiency and labor wage rates. If these fluctuations are not present, then unit costs would be suitable for control; however, stability seems unlikely. To get around these drawbacks, accountants usually superimpose standards on their process costing systems. They also do this—for similar reasons—to job costing systems.

Joint Products and By-Products

Process costing gives rise to yet another kind of problem, which is more or less unique to it (that is, the problem occurs *far more often* in process costing than in job costing). It often happens that in manufacturing one product, several others are obtained simultaneously. Assuming that each product has significant sales value, the products are collectively known as joint products because they share the common operation. Thus when petroleum is processed, several derivative products are obtained from the crude oil. Up to the point of *separation*, there is only one joint product, but past this point separate products are developed from the common base (joint) product.

In the lumber industry, as logs are debarked, bark (useful for mulch) and logs are obtained. As the headrig cuts into the log, cants (thick, rectangular lengths of wood that are later broken down into dimension lumber and timber, slabs (rounded lengths that are later put through the chipper), and sawdust are obtained. The sawdust and bark are usually considered by-products, which brings us to a definition: *A by-product is a joint product that has relatively little value.* Value, of course, changes from one locality to the next; some sawmills consider both chips and sawdust by-products. When the cants are processed through edger (or sashgang saw) and trimmer, they are still a mixture of lumber grades and hence are joint products. It is only at the sorting table that grades are finally designated; this is the point of separation.

For decisionmaking purposes, one should avoid allocating joint costs; essentially this amounts to dividing the indivisible. If a man buys a cow, how much has he paid for its tenderloin and round steaks? How much for its bones? It does not matter that the local butcher can declare a selling price for each part of the cow. The decision was to invest in the cow; presumably the buyer envisioned that the investment would earn a return by way of later sales of its components. Nevertheless, the decision was to buy a whole cow, not a compilation of its parts.

For income determination purposes, however, it is customary to allocate the cost of the cow to its various parts. Any allocation scheme chosen must be arbitrary, but some schemes are less atrocious than others. For instance, apportioning the cost of the cow according to the weight of each part would be unreasonable. Apportioning by weight would attribute equal value to a chuck steak, a knuckle, and a tenderloin steak—assuming all three were of equal weight. For similar reasons, apportionment based on volume would probably be rejected. The most attractive scheme, assuming that one insists on allocation, would be allocating cost based on relative sales value of the respective parts. Probably relative sales value was the buyer's main consideration when he originally acquired the cow. He purchased it with the idea of profiting from each part in proportion to that part's relative sales value.

The accountant favors relative sales value for allocating joint costs if it can be determined at point of separation. If there is no sales value at the separation point, then he uses ultimate market values reduced by "separable" production costs for each product. "Separable" production costs are those costs incurred after the separation point to develop each specific product.

Example: A process simultaneously generates 300 units of A, 200 units of B, and 400 units of C at a cost of $1,800. The A and C units can be sold at the separation point for $6 and $2 respectively, while the B units must undergo further processing at a cost of $100 before they can be sold for $1 each.

1. How would the joint cost be allocated using units produced?

2. How would the joint cost be allocated using relative sales value?

3. Is the separable cost of B justifiable?

Solution:

	Units	Sales Value	Separable Costs	Net Sales Values	← Allocation by → Units	Net Sales
A	300	$1,800	$ 0	$1,800	$ 600	$1,200
B	200	200	100	100	400	67
C	400	800	0	800	800	533
	900			$2,700	$1,800	$1,800

The $600 assigned to A on the basis of units equals (300/900) × $1,800 (the joint cost). The $67 assigned to B on the basis of net sales value equals ($100/$2,700) × $1,800. Can the separable cost of B be justified?

Wrong but seductive approaches:		Units Basis		Net Sales Basis
Sales		$200		$200
Costs—Separable	$100		$100	
—Allocated	400	500	67	167
Profit (loss)		($300)		$ 33

Correct approach:

Additional revenue	$200
Additional cost	100
Opportunity gain	$100

Decision: There is a $100 opportunity gain to be made from paying the separable cost; hence, it should be incurred. The profits and losses resulting after reflecting allocated joint costs are absolutely irrelevant to the decision. If the separable costs are incurred, $100 gain will be made; if the separable costs are not incurred, the $100 gain will be forgone. The $1,800 joint cost will not be affected by the decision.

Comment: For calculating income, however, the net sales value allocations would be useful. In this way, if 100 units of, say, A are sold this year, a profit can be declared. Without such an allocation, no profit would be recognized until all units of A, B, and C were sold.

By convention, the accountant favors reducing production costs by the sales proceeds of by-products. Because of their minor sales value, it would be somewhat unusual to incur separable costs on by-products, although separable costs should be incurred if they are exceeded by sales proceeds and selling the by-products is the best way to make use of them.

Example: Costs are to be allocated using the FIFO method in two production departments of a sawmill. The Log Handling Department moves logs from storage and debarks them. The Sawing and Chipping (S & C) Department contains the headrig, sashgang, trimmer, and chipper. Two joint products (lumber and chips) and one by-product (sawdust) are recognized in the S & C Department. Not until the lumber leaves S & C and goes to Sorting are the joint products (lumber grades and timber) contained in the lumber separated.

By-product proceeds are credited against production costs. Bark is sold as mulch for \$2.50 per cubic yard, while sawdust is used as a fuel by the sawmill. One BDT (bone dry ton) of sawdust is the equivalent of 114 gallons of fuel oil, which has a market value of \$.36 per gallon; therefore one BDT has a value of \$.36 × 114 = \$41.04.

In general, trees are measured in the forest in terms of some log scale, which, however, does not reflect the board feet of bark. Although the species of tree would introduce variation, bark usually amounts to an additional 10% of the log scale measure. This modified log scale is used in the Log Handling Department.

The S & C Department changes from log scale to lumber scale, which is considerably higher (1) because log scale is a rough measure and (2) because dimension lumber has nominal measurements (a 2″ × 4″ stud, for instance, measures about $1\frac{5}{8}''$ × $3\frac{5}{8}''$). Debarked logs are expected to yield 55%, 35%, and 10% respectively for lumber, chips, and sawdust. The conversion formula for hemlock is:

$$\text{lumber scale} = 2.82725 \times \text{log scale}$$

Observation: Control could be exercised by checking actual lumber production against .55(2.82725) = 1.555 of log scale.

Rough green lumber, which requires several operations past S & C, sells for \$125 per MBF (i.e., 1,000 board feet), while chips sell for \$50 per BDT. The production cost for the operations subsequent to S & C is \$15 per MBF, while the cost of collecting chips and loading them in trucks is \$2 per BDT. One cubic foot of dry, uncompacted chips weighs 10 pounds; one cubic foot of dry, uncompacted sawdust weighs 6 pounds.

Log Handling data for hemlock:
(Figures in parentheses are material (log) and conversion fractions for work done in the current month.)

	Log Scale Units	Costs
Opening inventory (0, 1/3)	66 MBF	$ 7,414
Requisitions	2,200 MBF	246,400
Total	2,266	
Transferred	1,974 MBF	
Ending inventory (1, 1/2)	72 MBF	
Bark	220 MBF	
Total	2,266	
Conversion costs for the month		8,744
Total		$262,558

There is no provision in the overhead rate for the cost of bark.
Sawing and Chipping data for hemlock:

Opening inventory—lumber (0, 1/2)	100 MBF	$ 9,309
—chips (0, 1/3)	63 MBF	1,007
Received from Log Handling	? MBF	?
Total	?	
Transferred —lumber	3,050 MBF	
—chips	1,946 MBF	
Ending inventory—lumber (1, 2/3)	120 MBF	
—chips (1, 9/10)	70 MBF	
Sawdust	? MBF	
Total	?	
Conversion costs for the month		97,784
Total		?

There is no provision in the overhead rate for the cost of sawdust.

Solution: This is a very elaborate problem. It would be even more so if similar data for other species of lumber that go through the mill were also included. The treatment of these other species would parallel that given the hemlock data, with the result that cost allocations for each department would merely sum the individual allocations for each specie. Exhibits 5 and 6 detail the solution. Exhibit 6 may appear especially formidable at first glance; unfortunately, the complexity of the problem compels a complicated solution, so read slowly.

Comments:

1. As shown in Exhibit 5, 1974 MBF were transferred out of Log Handling at a cost of \$252,216.

Exhibit 5 LOG HANDLING

Hemlock

EQUIVALENT PRODUCTION:

$$\begin{matrix} M \\ C \end{matrix} \overset{\begin{matrix} O & S\&C & E & \text{Bark} \end{matrix}}{\begin{bmatrix} 0 & 1 & 1 & 1 \\ 1/3 & 1 & 1/2 & 1 \end{bmatrix}} \begin{bmatrix} 66 \\ 1{,}908 \\ 72 \\ 220 \end{bmatrix} = \left[\overset{T}{\begin{bmatrix} 1{,}908 \\ 1{,}930 \end{bmatrix}} + \overset{E}{\begin{bmatrix} 72 \\ 36 \end{bmatrix}} + \overset{\text{Bark}}{\begin{bmatrix} 220 \\ 220 \end{bmatrix}} \right] = \overset{EP}{\begin{bmatrix} 2{,}200 \\ 2{,}186 \end{bmatrix}}$$

UNIT COSTS:

M: \$246,400 ÷ 2,200 = \$112
C: \$ 8,744 ÷ 2,186 = \$ 4

COST REPORT:

$$(112, 4) \left[\overset{T}{\begin{bmatrix} 1{,}908 \\ 1{,}930 \end{bmatrix}} + \overset{E}{\begin{bmatrix} 72 \\ 36 \end{bmatrix}} + \overset{\text{Bark}}{\begin{bmatrix} 220 \\ 220 \end{bmatrix}} \right] = [(221{,}416) + (8{,}208) + (25{,}520)]$$

	T	*E*	Bark	Σ
Costs during month	\$221,416	\$8,208	\$25,520	\$255,144
Opening inventory	7,414	–0–	–0–	7,414
Bark: Cost reallocation	25,053	467	(25,520)	–0–
Proceeds	(1,667)	(31)	–0–	(1,698)
Totals	\$252,216	\$8,644	\$ –0–	\$260,860

Comments:
1. Bark proceeds:

220,000 bd. ft. ÷ (12 × 27) = 679 cu. yds

679 × \$2.50 = \$1,698

2. Bark is a by-product and the proceeds from its sale as mulch have been credited to good production using equivalent production of conversion.
3. Production is measured in MBF, log scale (that is, 1,000 board feet, log scale).

2. S & C works in lumber scale; consequently the units received from Log Handling, which are in log scale, must be converted as follows: 2.82725(1,974 MBF) = 5,581 MBF, lumber scale. Conversion would not have been necessary, of course, if the given data had been complete from the output side. The board feet of sawdust, however, must be calculated:

Opening inventory—L	100	Transferred —L	3,050
—C	63	—C	1,946
Received	5,581	Ending inventory—L	120
		—C	70
		Subtotal	5,186
		Sawdust	558
	5,744		5,744

3. The journal entry to record bark proceeds is

Accounts Receivable	1,698	
Work in Process—Log Handling		1,698
To record bark sales.		

4. Exhibit 6 departs from the usual cost allocation procedures of process costing because these lead to equal unit costs being assigned to every unit of output, thereby ignoring relative sales values of the joint products.

Exhibit 6 SAWING & CHIPPING

Hemlock

EQUIVALENT PRODUCTION:

← Lumber → ← Chips →

$$\begin{array}{c} \\ P \\ C \end{array}\begin{array}{c} \begin{array}{ccc|ccc|c} O & S\&C & E & O & S\&C & E & \text{Sawdust} \end{array} \\ \begin{bmatrix} 0 & 1 & 1 & 0 & 1 & 1 & 1 \\ 1/2 & 1 & 2/3 & 1/3 & 1 & 9/10 & 1 \end{bmatrix} \end{array} \begin{bmatrix} 100 \\ 2{,}950 \\ 120 \\ 63 \\ 1{,}883 \\ 70 \\ 558 \end{bmatrix} = EP$$

$$EP = \left[\overset{\text{Lumber}}{\left[\overset{T}{\begin{bmatrix} 2{,}950 \\ 3{,}000 \end{bmatrix}} + \overset{E}{\begin{bmatrix} 120 \\ 80 \end{bmatrix}} \right]} + \overset{\text{Chips}}{\left[\overset{T}{\begin{bmatrix} 1{,}883 \\ 1{,}904 \end{bmatrix}} + \overset{E}{\begin{bmatrix} 70 \\ 63 \end{bmatrix}} \right]} + \overset{\text{Sawdust}}{\begin{bmatrix} 558 \\ 558 \end{bmatrix}} \right]$$

Equivalent production—excluding the by-product—expressed as a linear combination of preceding and conversion costs = EP':

Preceding department costs	$252,216	=	72.06%
Departmental conversion costs	97,784	=	27.94%
Total Monthly Costs	$350,000	=	100.00%

Exhibit 6 (*cont.*)

$$EP' = (.7206, .2794)\left[\left[\begin{bmatrix}2{,}950\\3{,}000\end{bmatrix} + \begin{bmatrix}120\\80\end{bmatrix}\right] + \left[\begin{bmatrix}1{,}883\\1{,}904\end{bmatrix} + \begin{bmatrix}70\\63\end{bmatrix}\right]\right]$$

$$\begin{array}{lcccc} & \multicolumn{2}{c}{\text{Lumber}} & \multicolumn{2}{c}{\text{Chips}} \\ & T & E & T & E \\ = (((2{,}964) & + & (108)) + ((1{,}889) & + (68))) \\ = \;((3{,}072) & + (1{,}957)) \end{array}$$

Price of rough green lumber per MBF	\$125
Cost for sorting, stacking, yarding, timber deck, cleaning up per MBF	15
Net price at separation point per MBF	\$110
Price of chips per BDT	\$ 50
Cost for loading per BDT	2
Net price at separation point per BDT	\$ 48

Conversion of BDT to MBF:

1 cubic foot of dry, uncompacted chips		= 10 pounds	
1 board foot		= 5/6 pounds	
1957 MBF		= 1,630,833 pounds	
1,630,833 pounds ÷ 2,000		= 815.4 BDT	
Market value of lumber and timber	= \$110(3072)	= \$337,920 =	89.62%
Market value of chips	= \$ 48(815.4) =	39,139 =	10.38%
Total market value at separation point		\$377,059 =	100.00%

Cost allocation:

Preceding department costs	\$252,216 = .7206 (\$350,000)
Department conversion costs	97,784 = .2794 (\$350,000)
Proceeds from sawdust (see below)*	(5,725)
Net Monthly Costs	\$344,275

*Sawdust proceeds
558,000 bd. ft. ÷ 12 = 46,500 ft.^{3}
46,500 (6 pounds per ft.^{3}, when dry) = 279,000 pounds
279,000 ÷ 2,000 = 139.5 BDT
139.5 (\$41.04) = \$5,725

$$\$344{,}275\left[\left\{\overset{\text{Lumber}}{\left[\overset{T}{.8962\left(\frac{2{,}964}{3{,}072}\right)}\right] + \left[\overset{E}{.8962\left(\frac{108}{3{,}072}\right)}\right]}\right\} + \left\{\overset{\text{Chips}}{\left[\overset{T}{.1038\left(\frac{1{,}889}{1{,}957}\right)}\right] + \left[\overset{E}{1038\left(\frac{68}{1{,}957}\right)}\right]}\right\}\right] = \textit{Allocation}$$

COST REPORT

	Lumber		Chips		
	T	*E*	*T*	*E*	Σ
Allocation of net monthly costs	\$297,671	\$10,848	\$34,493	\$1,243	\$344,275
Opening inventory costs	9,309	0	1,007	0	10,316
Totals	\$307,000	\$10,848	\$35,500	\$1,243	\$354,591

The determining of relative sales values per unit at separation point simply involves subtraction of additional processing costs from known market values. Thereafter it is a matter of converting MBF to BDT to obtain total market values. This is not as easy as it sounds, for the accountant must decide what units should be used to multiply net relative sales prices per unit. Should the total units transferred be used? If so, what about the units in the ending inventories of the joint products? And if including the units in ending inventory sounds attractive, why not use equivalent units? If this idea has appeal, which equivalent units—Preceding or Conversion? We are dividing the indivisible and anything we choose will be arbitrary; nevertheless, we would prefer to be reasonable. If equivalent production of conversion were used, departmental effort would be emphasized; however, departmental conversion costs are apt to be only a fraction of the input costs responsible for obtaining salable output. This leads to the scheme of weighting each type of equivalent production by the percentage its associated cost bears to total monthly costs.

5. Once total proceeds from sawdust are calculated by converting MBF to BDT and multiplying by the savings in heating costs per BDT, it is possible to calculate net monthly costs requiring allocation. The journal entry for sawdust proceeds is

Overhead—Boiler Department	5,725	
Work in Process—S & C Department		5,725
To record value of 558 MBF of sawdust in terms of equivalent heating cost.		

6. The total market values at separation point are expressed as percentages to be distributed first to lumber and chips and then to transferred and ending inventory (in proportion to respective weighted equivalent productions) within these joint product categories. Opening inventory costs are then apportioned to transferred costs of lumber and chips to preserve FIFO costing flows.

7. The journal enttry transferring costs becomes

Work in Process—Sorting Department	307,000	
Work in Process—Shipping Department	35,500	
Work in Process—S & C Department		342,500

To record lumber and chip costs transferred out of S & C.

Control. With product costing completed, let us consider the use of equivalent production as a control measure. In particular, if management were informed that a department had equivalent production of x units, why would this be useful?

Argument in favor of equivalent production

1. If an estimate of equivalent production that should have been obtained is available, and x differs considerably from it, then investigation is indicated.

Arguments against equivalent production

1. Equivalent production can be increased simply by inputting longer, wider, and better-quality logs and cutting longer, wider, and thicker stock. Thus 12" wide dimension is three times as wide as 4" wide dimension and counts the same in board feet as three 4" boards; however, cutting one 12" board requires far less labor.
2. If number of cuts is used for control, the message is to cut furiously.
3. Quantity emphasis may be obtained at the expense of quality; the message is to do the fastest thing possible with each log.
4. If a measure emphasizes quality, the results achieved largely reflect the input log quality, which is not generally controllable by the departmental foremen. Garbage in, garbage out.
5. Equivalent production, by itself, does not reflect the grades and quantities desired for marketing.
6. In the kiln operation doing whatever comes along in FIFO order is not efficient; wise kiln management sorts lumber first to take advantage of uniform drying times.
7. What should have been done, given the circumstances that prevailed, is the only desirable criterion on which to base measurement. Traditionally, this leads to the development of standard costs. It would be even more appealing to set the standards based on linear programming (or some other form of mathematical programming).

We shall discuss joint product control at greater length after we discuss linear programming.

Summary

Process costing is the costing system that deals with continuous production flows. This system depends on equivalent production to measure the amount of each input that appears in each output.

If the average method is used, the costs of the opening inventory for an input are added to its costs during the month. The total is divided by an equivalent production that reflects units in the opening inventory (all units—regardless of period of origination) coupled with units that were started and completed, in ending inventory, and lost. In short, all the costs are divided by all the units. The resultant unit costs are then multiplied by the equivalent units found in each output designation to complete the basic allocation.

If the FIFO method is used, the cost for a given input during a month is divided by its equivalent production for the present month (only) to obtain a unit cost. The unit cost is then distributed to the output designations according to the equivalent units each contains. To complete the basic allocation, the cost of opening inventory is added to the cost already apportioned to transferred.

If the unit costs from month to month did not change, there would be no difference in the ultimate cost allocations rendered under the average and FIFO methods.

Since unit costs are apt to change from month to month, and since costs of units received from the preceding department are spread over these units uniformly, the distinction between preceding opening inventory and during-month costs disappears. Hence FIFO is not pure FIFO as viewed from the entire factory; it is first-in, first-out only for the individual departments.

Lost units, in whatever form they occur, cause control problems. The cost accountant tries to control these costs and—where the factory maintains control charts—buttresses the factory's control efforts by reporting extraordinary (out of control) losses under a Loss From Abnormal Spoilage expense caption. Any salvage value associated with lost units is simultaneously set up in the ledger as an asset and as a reduction of Work in Process. In this way the lost units are established as an official entity and not just left lying around the shop encouraging pilferage.

When joint products and by-products occur in process costing, matters become complicated because allocation can then be done only on an arbitrary basis. Joint products are obtained simultaneously from a process and have significant value; by-products are also obtained simultaneously but have trivial value. By accounting convention, by-product proceeds are usually subtracted from main product production costs. Other treatments, such as considering these proceeds as other revenue, are also encountered in practice.

The favored treatment of joint products is to split production costs according to the relative sales values of process outputs. Weighted equivalent production is useful in determining relative total market values.

Problems

1. (a) What is the criterion governing the reallocation of lost-unit costs where loss occurs gradually during production?

(b) How is the criterion applied when there is an inspection station and all units in ending inventory are past this point?

2. What is the major conceptual difference between job order and process costing systems?

3. *Process costing: FIFO basis, one production department.*

	Units
Opening inventory (complete as to materials; .75 complete as to labor & overhead)	12,000
Put into process during period	90,000
	102,000
Completed & transferred to Finished Goods	82,000
Ending inventory (.4 complete as to materials, labor, & overhead)	20,000
	102,000

Cost data:

Opening inventory of work in process	$ 75,900
Costs during period:	
Materials	390,000
Labor	162,000
Overhead	202,500

Required: Prepare a cost report on the FIFO basis and all journal entries. Also write entries for sales, assuming that there is no opening inventory of finished goods and that 60,000 units were sold at $15 each.

4. *Process costing: average basis, one production department.*

	Units
Opening inventory (.5 complete as to materials, .25 complete as to labor and overhead)	8,000
Put into process during period	62,000
	70,000
Transferred to finished goods	60,000
Ending inventory (complete as to materials, .6 complete as to labor and overhead)	10,000
	70,000

Cost data:	Opening Inventory	During Period
Materials	$32,000	$598,000
Labor	12,000	463,200
Overhead	8,000	308,800

Required: Prepare a cost report on the weighted average basis and all journal entries. Also write entries for sales, assuming that there was no opening inventory of finished goods and that 50,000 units were sold at a price of $40 per unit.

5. *Problem illustrating that there is no difference in results between FIFO and average costing bases given constant unit costs.*

Quantity report:	Units
Opening inventory (complete as to materials, .5 complete as to conversion)	10,000
Put into process during period	200,000
	210,000
Transferred	180,000
Ending inventory (complete as to materials, $.\overline{3}$ complete as to conversion)	30,000
	210,000

Cost data:	Opening Inventory	During Period
Materials	\$100,000	\$2,000,000
Conversion	75,000	2,775,000

Required: Prepare cost reports under both the FIFO and average bases and comment on the results.

6. *Average costing, preceding department, conversion of units, lost units.* From the following data, prepare a cost report on an average costing basis. There is no provision for lost units in overhead.

(P, M, C) = portion of production done during present month for P (goods received from preceding department), M (departmental materials), C (departmental conversion costs).

Effervesce, Inc. produces a chemical. When the poundage of chemicals from the preceding department is received, it is dumped in a vat containing the present department's liquid materials. This happens at the very start of processing and no work is involved for the present department, since the preceding department does the dumping. Instantly upon contact there is a violent bubbling that causes evaporation loss.

Quantity data:

Opening inventory (0, 0, 2/3)	30,000 gallons
Received from preceding	1,680,000 pounds
Departmental materials	410,000 gallons
Transferred out	600,000 gallons
Ending inventory (1, 1, 1/2)	40,000 gallons

Note: 8 pounds of preceding chemicals add 1 gallon to the output of present.

Cost data:	Opening Inventory	During Month
Preceding department's cost	\$90,000	\$1,860,000
Present material costs	30,000	620,000
Present conversion costs	5,000	305,000

7. *Normal loss, average costing, preceding department.* Use matrices, the average method of costing, and the data below to prepare a cost report and an appropriate journal entry. There is no provision for lost units in overhead. Department B uses

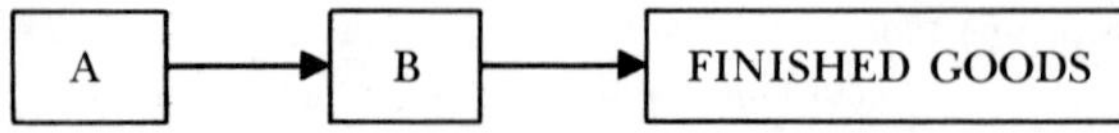

the material received from department A as a base and then adds, at the end of processing, its own materials.

Costs for department B:	Opening Inventory	During Month
Costs from department A	$182,000	$378,000
Departmental material	35,000	135,000
Departmental conversion	40,000	128,000

Unit data:	
Transferred	17,000
Ending inventory (1/3 converted)	9,000
Lost (1/2 converted)	2,000

Comments: Loss is normally in the 2% to 6% range of "good" equivalent production of conversion and occurs gradually throughout processing. The value of a lost unit is taken to be $35.

8. *FIFO basis, profit and loss statement, one production department.*

A company operates with only one production department, which utilizes the first-in, first-out (FIFO) assumption in distributing its production costs. The processing is such that units are never lost.

Required:

From the data below you are to prepare

(a) A schedule of equivalent production

(b) A cost report

(c) A profit and loss statement

(d) Comments on the profit and loss statement

Quantity Data:	Units
Opening inventory of work in process (3/5 completed as to materials, 1/4 completed as to labor and overhead)	40,000
Put into process during period	260,000
Ending inventory of work in process (2/3 completed as to materials, 1/2 completed as to labor and overhead)	60,000

Financial Data:

Inventories:	Opening	Ending
Raw materials	$ 85,000	$119,000
Work in Process	$140,000	?
Finished Goods	$328,000	$450,000
Purchase of raw materials (net)		$802,000
Direct labor		$650,000
Overhead absorbed		$845,000
Operating expenses		$1,111,500
Sales		$3,600,000

9. *Joint cost distribution.* Two products are produced simultaneously at a cost of $100,000. 1,000 units of product A are produced; these can be sold for $80.00 each. 4,000 units of product B are produced; these can be sold for $20.00 each. What is the gross profit per unit sold for each product?

10. *Difference Between Joint Products and By-Products.*

 (a) Explain the basic difference between the method of accounting for joint products and that for by-products.

 (b) State the conditions under which an item should be treated as a by-product rather than as a joint product.

 (c) Explain the two principal methods of assigning joint costs to the joint products, and state the circumstances under which each would be appropriate.

11. *Average costing, preceding department, conversion of input, lost units.* Prepare a cost report on the average costing basis from the data below.

 Key: (P, M, C) = portion of production done during present month for P (goods received from preceding department), M (departmental materials), C (departmental conversion costs).

 Quantity data:

Opening inventory (0, 1/4, 1/2)	40,000
Received from preceding department during period*	1,440,000
Units added by present department	100,000
Ending Inventory (1, 2/3, 1/2)	150,000
Lost units (normal loss occurring gradually during processing; no provision in overhead rate: 1, 2/5, 1/3)	30,000

 * Note: These are quarts. Preceding department measures its output in quarts; present department measures its output in gallons.

Cost data:	Opening Inventory	During Month
Preceding department's costs	$120,000	$1,380,000
Departmental material costs	60,000	804,000
Departmental conversion costs	60,160	1,187,240

12. *Average basis, lost units, two departments (Certified Public Accountancy Examination, May 1964*).* The Mantis Manufacturing Company manufactures a single product that passes through two departments: Extruding and Finishing-Packing. The product is shipped at the end of the day on which it is packed. The production in the Extruding and Finishing-Packing Departments does not increase the number of units started.

* Material from the Uniform CPA Examinations, copyright © (May 1964) by the American Institute of Certified Public Accountants, Inc., is adapted with permission.

The cost and production data for the month of January are as follows:

Cost Data:	Extruding Department	Finishing-Packing Department
Work in process, January 1:		
Cost from preceding department	—	$60,200
Materials	$ 5,900	—
Labor	1,900	1,500
Overhead	1,400	2,000
Costs added during January:		
Materials	20,100	4,400
Labor	10,700	7,720
Overhead	8,680	11,830
Percentage of completion of work in process:		
January 1:		
Materials	70%	0%
Labor	50	30
Overhead	50	30
January 31:		
Materials	50	0
Labor	40	35
Overhead	40	35
January Production Statistics		
Units in process, January 1	10,000	29,000
Units in process, January 31	8,000	6,000
Units started or received from preceding department	20,000	22,000
Units completed and transferred or shipped	22,000	44,000

In the Extruding Department, materials are added at various phases of the process. All lost units occur at the end of the process, when the inspection operation takes place.

In the Finishing-Packing Department, the materials added consist only of packing supplies. These materials are added at the midpoint of the process, when the packing operation begins. Cost studies have disclosed that one-half the labor and overhead costs apply to the finishing operation and one-half to the packing operation. All lost units occur at the end of the finishing operation, when the product is inspected. All the work in process in this department at January 1 and 31 was in the finishing-operation phase of the manufacturing process. (The company uses the average costing method in its accounting system.)

Required:

(a) Compute the units lost, if any, for each department during January.

(b) Compute the equivalent units for the calculation of unit costs for each department by January.

(c) Prepare a cost of production report for both departments for January. The report should disclose the departmental total cost and cost per unit (for materials, labor, and overhead) of the units (a) transferred to the Finishing-Packing Department and (b) shipped. Assume that January production and costs were normal. (Submit all supporting computations in good form.)

13. *Weighted average, preceding department, abnormal spoilage* (*Canadian Governmental Accounting Association Examination**). The H Co. Ltd. manufactures a single product that is processed in three departments. The process costing procedure in use bases inventory values on the weighted average cost method. The following cost and production data are available for Department 2 for the month of April:

Opening work in process inventory—1,500 units:	
Cost from preceding department	$12,000
Dept. 2 material (added at the beginning of the process)	2,041
Dept. 2 labor and applied overhead (These units were 40% complete as to conversion costs.)	4,168
Transferred in during April from Dept 1: 6,000 units	46,800
Department 2 costs for April:	
Materials	8,459
Labor and applied overhead	41,727

Production Data:

5,900 units were completed and transferred to Dept. 3; 1,000 units were still in process (20% complete) at the end of April; the balance were spoiled units, detected at the end of the Dept. 2 processing. One-half the spoilage is abnormal in nature and is to be charged to an abnormal spoilage loss account.

Required:

Prepare a cost of production report for April.

14. *The pitfalls of expediency.* Recall the problem in Exhibit 1 in this chapter, which dealt with normal, random, and abnormal lost units. In that problem no provision was made for lost unit cost in the overhead rate. The cost of lost units was segregated into portions for normal, random, and abnormal loss. The random portion was charged to overhead, the abnormal portion went to an expense account, and the normal portion was distributed to Transferred and Ending Inventory. The statement of a $3 value for each converted equivalent unit lost may have seemed unnecessary. It may have seemed more expedient to divide the $17,800 lost-unit cost in the percentage each loss (normal, random, abnormal) bore to the total units lost; moreover, this would have dispensed with the annoyance of treating the residual lost-unit cost. Consider what would happen if no units were lost (you need not make calculations) and comment on the acceptability of the expedient alternative procedure.

* Reprinted with permission from The Canadian Institute of Chartered Accountants, Toronto, Canada.

15. *Regression and the calculation of yield.* An accountant wishes to estimate yield from production. He defines yield as 1 – (percentage that lost units bear to total output). He has these data available from the last six months:

Total Production	Lost Units
600,000 units	15,000 units
550,000 units	18,000 units
400,000 units	9,000 units
800,000 units	25,000 units
400,000 units	10,000 units
500,000 units	14,000 units

He thinks regression analysis might help, although he is not sure.

(a) What should he declare as the yield percentage?

(b) How might knowledge of yield be useful in process costing?

16. *Average costing, provision for loss in overhead rate, preceding department, tie-in to standard costing.* Vulture Sporting Goods, Inc. manufactures golf clubs continuously in its Golf Club Division. The production departments and their tasks are

Department	Task
Forging	Forge iron club heads
Wood heads	Laminate and shape wood heads
Scoring	Cut and insert striated club faces
Boring	Drill the hosel in iron heads
Stamping	Emboss iron numbers and trademarks
Classifying	Sort heads according to weights
Polishing	Vibrate and buff iron heads
Painting	Paint brand names on irons and paint the entire wood heads
Shafting	Insert shafts in clubheads
Gripping	Place grips on the shafts
Testing	Subject the clubs to machine and hand trials
Packing	Inspect the clubs and arrange them in sets.

The Shafting Department receives iron and wood club heads from the Painting Department and performs three operations on each club: (1) inserting a shaft, (2) driving a rivet through the club head and the shaft to prevent slippage when the club is swing, and (3) shearing the excess shaft. During the riveting operation, some clubs are damaged irretrievably by rivet holes that are punched off center, a condition that eventually leads to checking (splitting) in wood club necks, to expansion of the hole in iron club necks, and to cracking of shafts. Once so damaged, the club can only be sold as scrap. The scrap price received approximately equals the cost of gathering these lost units and taking them to the scrap dealer. When Shafting completes its work, the clubs are passed on to the Gripping Department, which places a rubberized sheath over the shaft.

The average method of costing is used by the Shafting Department. The following data pertain for the month of October:

Key: (P, M, C) = portion of production done during October for P (preceding department's costs), M (Shafting Department materials), and C (Shafting Department conversion costs).

		Clubs
Quantity data:	Opening inventory (0, 0, 2/3)	90,000
	Transferred in (from Painting)	510,000
		600,000
	Transferred out to (Gripping)	474,000
	Ending inventory (1, 3/4, 1/2)	120,000
	Lost clubs (1, 1, 9/10)	6,000
		600,000
Cost data:	Opening inventory costs:	
	Preceding department's costs	$ 90,000
	Shafting material costs	36,450
	Shafting conversion costs	35,550
	Costs during October:	
	Preceding department's costs	510,000
	Shafting material costs	191,550
	Shafting conversion costs	611,730
	Total Costs to be Accounted for	$1,475,280

Prepare a cost report assuming the number of lost clubs, L, is expected to be normally distributed in the range $2\% \leq L \leq 4\%$ of total equivalent production of conversion. There is a provision of $.072 per club—based on equivalent production of conversion—for loss in the overhead rate.

17. *Average costing, synchronization, preceding departments.* Department C assembles subassemblies it receives from departments A and B. Prepare a cost report on the average costing basis from the data below.*

Key = (A, B, materials, conversion) = the fractions of inputs pertaining to work done this period.

Quantity data:	Units
Opening inventory (0, .4, .4, .5)	20,000
Received from A	300,000
Received from B in B's units	70,000
Ending inventory *being worked on* (1, .3, .3, .1)	40,000
Lost (at end of processing)	10,000

* Notes:
1. Units of A form the base of the product assembled by C.
2. C's product requires .1 unit from B, which is added in mid-process.
3. Neither C's materials nor B's subassembly increases the number of units of C's output.
4. Assume opening inventory contains no other inputs than those indicated (that is, assume [1, .6, .6, .5] were last month's inputs).
5. No provision for lost units is contained in overhead.

Cost data:	Opening Inventory	During Month
A	$200,000	$3,000,000
B	6,000	350,000
C materials	12,000	280,000
C conversion	20,000	548,000

18. *Markov chains, joint costs, and process costing.* A department produces three chemicals in a three-stage process, each stage of which takes one day to complete. All products have a common beginning in stage 1, where chemicals are mixed thoroughly with those received from a preceding department. In the course of a day, the chemicals are distilled and the three products—A, B, and C—result along with a useless residue. The next day, products B and C proceed to stages 2 and 3 respectively, where they are completed and suffer evaporation. At this point they may be judged unacceptable and be returned for rework—B to the start of stage 2 and C to stage 1. A is marketable as it comes from stage 1, assuming it does not need rework. No materials are added in stages 2 and 3.

> Note: The problem is being structured to allow every unit (here, a gallon) the same opportunity for processing in a given period (here, a day). If processing were done on a FIFO basis and each unit did not have equal opportunity for processing, a Markov chain should not be used, because in this case the probabilities would not pertain to each and every unit, but rather to selected units only. Physical mixing of beginning inventory and units started this period would, however, restore equal opportunity to the system regardless of how costing was carried out.

(a) In one day, 10% of the units in stage 1 became residue and a like amount required rework; 40% became A; 30% went on to stage 2; and 10% went on to stage 3. B units that were begun at the start of the day went to stage 2, where 20% evaporated, 10% were returned to the start of stage 2 for reprocessing, and the remainder were completed. C units begun at the start of the day went to stage 3, where 20% were returned for rework (to stage 1), 20% were lost, and the remainder were completed. A, B, and C sell for $1, $2.50, and $2, respectively.

	← Gallons			→	← $			→
	A	B	C	Σ	A	B	C	Σ
Opening inventory: regular	—	2,700	1,000	3,700	—	810	260	1,070
rework	1,000	300	200	1,500	200	285	100	585
Preceding department				5,000				1,145
Present department								
Materials				1,800				75
Conversion: 1								320
2								1,155
3								240
				12,000				$4,590

Prepare a Markov chain by treating the percentages as representative of the transition probabilities. Then prepare a cost report using whatever allocation scheme seems appropriate.

(b) If 10,000 gallons are to be processed (starting in stage 1) each day for the foreseeable future, and if the transition matrix developed in part (a) is considered representative of a typical day, what outputs can be expected on a daily basis? Of what use is such knowledge?

(c) Is this a process costing or a job costing system?

(d) Criticize the whole approach. What do you think of it?

Standard Costs

8

Overview

We encountered standard costs when we were illustrating the development of overhead rates with data from Spalding. As a result, you probably suspect (1) that standard costs include material, labor, and overhead costs that are loaded on a product as it gradually takes shape; and (2) that these costs are predetermined. Standard costs are spoken of as "should be" costs and in this chapter we shall see why.

Standard costing is not an additional cost accounting system, although many industrial accountants speak of it as if it were. Rather, standard costs are superimposed on job order costing where production is in batches and on process costing where production is continuous. If the factory is very busy, one batch directly follows the next and physical distinctions may be harder to draw.

Standard costing is exceedingly popular in the United States—far more popular in medium-sized and larger businesses than ordinary job order and process costing. The main appeal of standard costing lies in the fact that it has a built-in cost control system. The cost control feature relies on (1) the principle of management by exception, and (2) the calculation of cost variances. According to this scheme, management only investigates those cost variance that are significant. As I mentioned in Chapter 2, management-by-exception has one potential shortcoming: people who perform at standard are apt to be ignored, to be taken for granted.

To be theoretically sound, standard costs must reflect "should be" costs and this favors regular updating. This also poses something of a paradox, for if costs change often, the instability suggests that no standard exists. People who are bothered by this paradox have a static conception of a standard. The dynamic conception seems better to fit the theory that standard costs represent a measure of what should be done under the circumstances that prevail. On the other hand, in the extreme case, cost changes could be so frequent that the standard costs in effect become actual costs. At this point the Principle of Smoothing intrudes.

Smoothing was presented in Chapter 5 when, with regard to distributing a major repair bill, I observed, "The months preceding necessitate the repairs; those following enjoy the benefits of the refurbished machine. The current month merely endures the misfortune of seeing to the payment of the bill." Smoothing occurs in other ways. For example, accountants avoid penalizing a product with specific overtime costs just because its production takes place when regular time is unavailable. Instead, as you saw in Exhibit 3 in Chapter 5, overtime is estimated in advance and becomes part of the overhead charge that is borne by all products made in the specific department. For yet another example, not all machines (or all workers) in a department are equally efficient. In standard costing, the accountant uses the same production times and cost rates for every machine or worker that is performing the same production tasks. In this way, the products that are made by the best people on the best machines are not accorded a fortuitous advantage.[1]

Where costs are constantly changing, many companies decide to leave their standard costs alone as long as the change is within, say, 5%. Other companies require that cost changes persist for an extended period of time before reflecting them in their standard costs. Where changes are all in one direction—where costs are inflating, say—it would be possible to keep standards abreast of inflation by introducing a growth factor. Thus, $S' = Se^{rt}$, would serve to update the standard cost, S', by multiplying the original standard cost, S, by the growth factor e^{rt}, where r is the estimated monthly inflation rate and t is the number of months since the original standard was adopted.

Example: The standard cost for a material is now \$30 but the supplier plans to pass on the effects of inflation in the form of regular price increases. If inflation is estimated at 1% per month, what will the new standard cost be three months hence?

$$S' = \$30e^{.01(3)} = \$30(1.0305) = \$30.92$$

Table 5 in Appendix A contains values for e^x. (This sort of updating would make sense in period budgeting, too.)

Allied to the concept of updating costs is the theoretical desirability of using replacement costs instead of historical costs. This is especially pertinent when standard costs are used in setting prices. The theory is reflected in J. R. Hicks's attractive definition of income: "Income . . . is the maximum value he [a man] can consume during a week, and still expect to be as well off at the end of the week as he was at the beginning."[2] An example may help.

---

[1] Perhaps a better name for the smoothing principle would be the "timing" principle. The timing of cost flows is what causes the problem, while smoothing is the action taken to cope with it.

[2] J. R. Hicks, *Value and Capital* (London: Oxford University Press, 1939), p. 172.

Example: A store sells for $2.50 an item for which it paid $1.00. What is its income if the cost to replace the unit sold is $2.00?

	Historical Basis	Replacement Basis
Sales price	$2.50	$2.50
Cost	1.00	2.00
Profit	$1.50	$ .50

Unless the store used replacement costs, it would wind up declaring a profit of $1.50 and pay tax on that amount (although they have been approved by the Security and Exchange Commission, replacement costs are not now sanctioned by the Internal Revenue Service. If it paid a 50% tax, it would now have $1.75 (i.e., $2.50 – $.75) with which to replenish its inventory; hence it would be obliged to dip into its capital to do so. Why is it necessary to invade capital if a profit had been made? Hicks would say, "Preserve capital first; the residue is profit." The same line of argument applies to equipment. The cost of using a piece of equipment is equal to the cost of securing its replacement. It is an illusion to charge depreciation to production based on some past investment outlay and to think that this measures the cost of using the equipment. Nevertheless, regulations prevent the adoption of replacement costs in reports used for external purposes, and few companies are ready to maintain a second set of books for use in setting prices. This is most disappointing, and it is undoubtedly a significant factor in bankruptcies.

This chapter will focus on how standards are set, how variances are calculated and interpreted, and how learning curves can help you to measure what could be done under the circumstances that prevail. In the process of discussing learning curves an interesting "make-or-buy" question will be examined. The use of linear programming as an extension of standard costing theory will be deferred until a later chapter.

Standard Costing Fundamentals

The fundamentals of standard costing are easier to understand if they are related to a specific product. Let us create a mythical company, The Harmless Ski Company, and endow it with an equally mythical product that is untried and, if produced, would undoubtedly be unsuited for its purpose. Shown below is the standard cost for a particular model of Harmless ski.

Direct materials:	
Steel (7 feet @ \$.15 per foot)	\$ 1.05
Fiberglass (7 feet @ \$.35 per foot)	2.45
Plastic (7 feet @ \$.10 per foot)	.70
Wood (7 feet @ \$.05 per foot)	.35
Direct labor (2 hours @ \$5.00 per hour)	10.00
Overhead (2 hours @ \$5.00 per hour)	10.00
	\$24.55

Where did all the measurements and unit costs come from? The material measurements result from engineering designs for the ski, while the material costs usually come from the company's purchasing agent, who refers to price lists from suppliers as well as industry prices quoted in trade publications. The labor hours and rate come from engineering studies and factory pay schedules respectively. The overhead cost has merely been related to the direct-labor hours. As you might expect, there are refinements to these notions, but for the present let us stick with the basics of standard costing.

In standard costing, all transactions in the Work in Process and Finished Goods inventory accounts are recorded at standard costs; any differences between actual and standard costs are analyzed to determine the probable cause and segregated in separate "variance" accounts. Rather unfortunately, the word "variance" is not used here in a mathematical or statistical sense, but rather as a synonym for "difference," which, incidentally, would be a precise mathematical term for what goes on. Nevertheless, standard costing isolates "variances" for control purposes. The variances for materials and labor all have different names in accounting literature, but these reduce generically to price, quantity, and mixed (or price-quantity) variances. With respect to overhead, the names depend on how many variances are isolated; we shall focus on the three-variance method, which isolates spending, efficiency, and volume variances.

Material and Labor Variances

A few symbols help with variance analysis. Let P stand for the standard purchased price of a material (or labor). Let Q stand for the standard quantity of the material (or labor). Then PQ is the standard cost of the material (or labor). If we then introduce ΔP and ΔQ to represent any differences between standard and actual price and quantity, respectively, $(P + \Delta P)(Q + \Delta Q)$

yields actual cost of the material. It also yields standard cost and all the variances as well:

Actual price	Actual quantity		Standard Cost		Quantity Variance		Price Variance		Mixed or "Price-Quantity" Variance
$(P + \Delta P)$	$(Q + \Delta Q)$	=	PQ	+	$P\,\Delta Q$	+	$Q\,\Delta P$	+	$\Delta P\,\Delta Q$

Comment: $P\Delta Q$ = Quantity Variance = change in quantity times standard price.

Suppose Harmless made a ski for which direct labor actually took 2.5 hours at a cost of $4.50 per hour instead of the 2 hours and $5 in the standard. Then the above equation would take on these values:

$$(P + \Delta P)(Q + \Delta Q) = PQ + P\,\Delta Q + Q\,\Delta P + \Delta P\,\Delta Q$$

$$(\$5 - \$.50)(2 + .5) = \$10 + \$2.50 + (-\$1.00) + (-\$.25)$$

$$\$4.50(2.5) = \$11.25$$

The same sort of calculation could be done for each of the materials. Here a minus sign would be interpreted as being favorable (and a plus sign as unfavorable) in *relation to the standard.*

Alternative approach to material variances:
The previous approach assumed that variances would be isolated *after* materials were put into ("requisitioned for") production. This is one way the matter of material variances is treated in practice. Another way is to segregate material variances *at the time of purchase.* Thus if 80,000 feet of fiberglass were acquired at a cost of $.40 per foot, the material price variance recognized upon purchase would be

$$80{,}000(\$.40 - \$.35) = \$4{,}000 \text{ (unfavorable)}$$

Since usage is not known at time of purchase, the material quantity variance is not recognized until usage of materials has taken place. If, for instance, 10,000 skis were made and 72,000 feet of fiberglass were used in the process, instead of the 70,000 feet called for by the standard, the fiber glass quantity variance would be

$$\$.35(72{,}000 - 7(10{,}000)) = \$700 \text{ (unfavorable)}$$

There is no mixed variance under this scheme. Because this is so, accountants using the requisition method often tack the mixed variance on to the price variance thereby eliminating the mixed variance as a separate entity.

The alternative approach can only be used for materials. Because of their nature, materials can be stockpiled in actual known amounts. Labor quantity, on the other hand, cannot be precisely known in advance.

The variances are useful for control purposes because they help identify significant differences. However, they neither reveal anything conclusive about their causes nor enable the analyst to describe them as *absolutely* favorable or unfavorable. All the analyst can say in this respect is that a particular type of variance is favorable or unfavorable *relative* to the standard. Until he knows how good—how realistic—the standard is, he can say nothing more definite. Thus the labor quantity variance (determined above) served to increase the standard cost by $2.50 and was unfavorable relative to the standard. But suppose that same ski were made by an inexperienced worker. For him to miss the standard by $2.50 might, in fact, represent a very favorable, even commendable, performance in view of the performance usually forthcoming from beginners. Furthermore, the real cause of the quantity variance might have nothing to do with quantity. It might lie in a union pay contract that raised the wages of experienced employees so high that the company could no longer afford to use anybody but a beginner for the work.

This indirect cause of an otherwise named variance occurs frequently. A sudden shortage of a material may compel the production foreman to have the purchasing agent place a rush order at a higher price than usual. The difference would show up as a price variance that would look at first like the purchasing agent's responsibility, even though the foreman might have caused the quantity shortage. A significantly unfavorable quantity variance, on the other hand, might be caused by defective materials, which might even have been purchased at a bargain price that resulted in a favorable price variance. Of course, price variances are often caused by the purchasing agent's haggling, just as quantity variances are often due to the foreman's managerial efforts (or lack thereof—poor morale, for instance, could cause quantity variances).

The mixed variance once prompted a renowned theorist to devise an analogy: "You ask me whose responsibility the mixed variance is—the foreman's or the purchasing agent's? I cannot tell you. It is as if a glass falls to the floor and breaks. What is responsible—the fragility of the glass or the hardness of the floor?" Since the mixed variance does not exist if price variances are isolated at time of purchase, most theorists tack the mixed variance to the price variance when investigating causes. The analyst can name variances, but he cannot state their causes until he has investigated.

It is not uncommon to find companies that have preprinted laundry lists of causes of labor variances. Such lists contain explanations (excuses?) like "Defective materials," "New employee," "Broken tool," "Broken machine," "New machine," "Delay in receiving product from previous department," "No previous experience with product," "Product from previous department faulty," and so forth. The idea behind such lists is to pinpoint trouble (or opportunities) and thereby expedite control. The temptation to prevent investigation by higher levels of management through "divide and conquer" tactics may be enough to invalidate the use of laundry lists. A department with a single significant inefficiency problem, for example, could spread the inefficiency over so many causes that none of them appeared serious by itself. Wherever there are people, there will be behavioral problems.

Overhead Variances

Overhead variances, like material and labor variances, help in controlling costs. In a standard cost system, Work in Process is charged with *absorbed* overhead costs equal to the volume of output *obtained* multiplied by the standard overhead rate. But there are several other overhead figures floating around, including actual overhead costs and different budgeted overhead costs. Undoubtedly you are no longer confused about actual and estimated ("budgeted") overhead costs, now that you have perused the Spalding Comparative Expense Report, Tennis Racket Department (Exhibit 4, Chapter 5). But now we need to consider how *different* budgeted overhead costs arise.

A factory can be set to run at different levels of activity; when this happens, there is a different budget, for example, if the level of activity is 80,000 or 90,000 or 100,000. These budgets are expressed in fixed and variable costs and have a linear form $y = a + bx$, where y is total overhead cost, a is fixed cost, and bx is variable cost related to activity level x. In fact, the equation might change with each of the above levels, but there will be ranges of activity level where one equation pertains, as well as ranges where other equations apply. The business may not have used regression analysis and it may not even have formalized the equation; nevertheless, businesses segregate their accounts into fixed and variable portions, and these may be expressed in linear[3] form, $y = a + bx$. By using one or more of these equations, the business can formulate *flexible budgets*, which simply estimate budget allowances for overhead costs at *any* level of activity. The same procedures for overhead variance analysis are used whether one budget equation or several have been developed; for simplicity, however, we shall speak as if there were only one such equation for the relevant range. We shall use this equation to estimate budgeted overhead costs at an input level—the number of hours actually worked—*and* at an output level—the number of hours needed to obtain the output according to the standard.

Example: A firm has actual overhead costs of \$189,000. Its flexible budget equation is $y = \$60{,}000 + \$3x$, where x designates the number of direct-labor hours. The standard overhead absorption rate is \$4.50 and is based

[3] Disaster would not strike, for that matter, if the form were nonlinear. Accounting, though, has a predilection for straight lines.

on an expected volume of 40,000 direct-labor hours (and hence a \$1.50 allowance for fixed overhead and a \$3.00 allowance for variable overhead). Forty-two thousand direct-labor hours were worked (input), while the output achieved calls for 39,000 direct-labor hours.

Analysis:

	Overhead costs			
+13,500, Net	Actual		= 189,000	
				+ 3,000, Spending
	Budget at input	= 60,000 + 3(42,000)	= 186,000	
				+ 9,000, Efficiency
	Budget at output	= 60,000 + 3(39,000)	= 177,000	
				+ 1,500, Volume
	Absorbed	= 39,000(4.50)	= 175,500	

Comments:

1. Subtract the number at the bottom of an arrow from the number at its top.

2. A − sign indicates favorable (and a + sign indicates unfavorable).

3. The Spending Variance represents the difference between the actual overhead costs and the costs that are budgeted at the actual (input) volume. The totals could be itemized into component accounts to see which accounts were significantly out of line.

4. The Efficiency Variance represents the variable overhead rate allowance multiplied by the difference between input and output volumes. In this case, the inefficient use of labor cost an additional \$9,000 in variable overhead costs.

5. When only two variances are isolated, the Spending and Efficiency Variances are combined into the "Budget" Variance, which was illustrated in Exhibit 4, Chapter 5. The second variance in the two-variance system is the Volume Variance.

6. The Volume Variance represents the fixed-cost allowance in the standard overhead rate (that is, \$1.50) multiplied by the difference between the expected and output volumes (that is, 40,000–39,000). It may be instructive to see how the volume variance appears when graphed. Figure 1 shows the absorbed and budgeted-at-output equations and identifies the amount of the volume variance as favorable or unfavorable depending on whether output volume exceeds, or is exceeded by, expected volume.

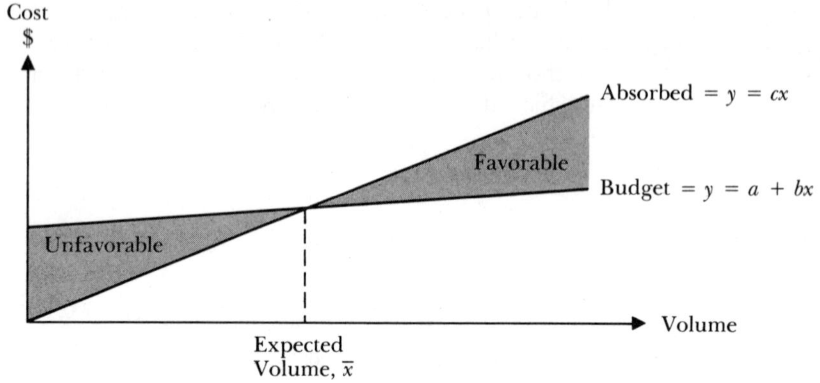

Figure 1 Volume Variance

The expected volume occurs at the intersection of the two lines. At this point the absorbed and budgeted overheads are equal; therefore, expected volume, $\bar{x}$, may be expressed as

$$c\bar{x} = a + b\bar{x}$$

$$\bar{x} = a/(c - b)$$

Hence, expected volume equals fixed costs divided by the fixed-cost provision in the overhead rate (c is the total overhead rate, while b is its variable cost provision). Were management to set expected volume higher, the value of c would decrease, thereby reducing the slope of the absorbed line, forcing the intersection to shift to the right, and increasing the range of unfavorable variance.

Since management is free to declare what expected volume is, the volume variance is within its control, although the efforts of (1) the Sales Department in getting orders and (2) the factory in scheduling and filling these orders do affect output volume. One school of behavior says that output will increase if the production foreman is kept slightly discouraged; therefore, some companies set expected volume somewhat high. There is a limit to such manipulations, however, since they interfere with planning efforts; besides, standard costs appear on the financial statements in the Inventory and Cost of Goods Sold accounts. Scrutiny by external auditors, financial analysts, and stockholders encourages the use of reasonable expected volumes.

As I mentioned in Chapter 5, expected volume would equal normal volume only in a normal year. It would be consistent with the Principle of Smoothing to use normal volume even though expected volume was less if it were also anticipated that ensuing years would have expected volumes higher than normal, and it was thought wise to smooth (or average) volumes.

This might be appropriate, for example, if selling price were based on cost and using the lower expected volumes would lead to higher prices that would further depress activity. *After all, the selection of a year for setting overhead rates is a convenient but arbitrary choice.* Given that a year has been chosen, the expected level of activity seems most appropriate. Choosing a markedly different normal volume would seriously alter the overhead rate. To be consistent, since he recognizes significant changes in material and labor costs, the cost accountant would then want to drop normal volume in favor of expected volume.

Let us summarize these concepts and illustrate the typical journal entries of a standard cost system by continuing the example of the Harmless Ski Company.

Additional Data: There was no work in process on April 30, 1970. During May 1970 the factory requisitioned 287,000 feet each of the steel, fibreglass, plastic, and wood components. Eighty-three thousand direct-labor hours were worked and 37,000 skis were manufactured in May. The last batch of 3,000 skis was still in process at the end of May with about one-third of the work remaining to be done; all materials for these skis, however, had been requisitioned. The material components cost \$.20, \$.30, \$.11, and \$.08 respectively, and the labor wage amounted to \$5.25 per hour. Actual overhead costs were \$342,000; the budget for monthly overhead costs was $y = \$216{,}000 + \$2x$ (where x stands for direct-labor hours) and expected monthly volume was 72,000 direct-labor hours.

As a first step in the analysis, let us calculate all the price, quantity, and mixed variances for the various materials and labor. The price and quantity standards were stated at the beginning of this section. Next it is necessary to determine the output standard equivalent of units manufactured. Skis are probably a batch operation, but if the factory is busy, one batch will follow on the heels of another so as to give the appearance of a continuous (process) operation. The job numbers may be for various styles, but the styles may require almost exactly the same production steps; consequently, one could forget the job numbers and treat production flows by process costing techniques. Indeed, it makes no difference whether we use job order or process costing (FIFO method) in tracking costs when standard costs are superimposed. Observe:

Process Costing:

$$\begin{matrix} \\ M \\ C \end{matrix}\overset{\begin{matrix} O & S\,\&\,C & E \end{matrix}}{\left[\begin{array}{cc|c} 0 & 1 & 1 \\ 0 & 1 & 2/3 \end{array}\right]}\left[\begin{array}{c} 0 \\ 37{,}000 \\ \hdashline 3{,}000 \end{array}\right] = \left[\overset{T}{\begin{bmatrix} 37{,}000 \\ 37{,}000 \end{bmatrix}} + \overset{E}{\begin{bmatrix} 3{,}000 \\ 2{,}000 \end{bmatrix}}\right] = \overset{\text{Equivalent Production}}{\begin{bmatrix} 40{,}000 \\ 39{,}000 \end{bmatrix}}$$

Job Order Costing:

$$\begin{aligned}\text{Materials} &= 37{,}000 + 3{,}000 = 40{,}000 \text{ standard units}\\ \text{Labor} &= 37{,}000 + 2{,}000 = 39{,}000 \text{ standard units}\end{aligned}$$

The differences in prices and quantities may now be determined from the given data and the standard output equivalents.

Item	Actual Price	Actual Quantity	Standard Cost	Quantity Variance	Price Variance	Mixed Variance	Totals
	$(P + \Delta P)$	$(Q + \Delta Q)$	$= PQ$	$+ P\,\Delta Q$	$+ Q\,\Delta P$	$+ \Delta P\,\Delta Q$	
Steel	(.15 + .05)	(280,000 + 7,000)	= \$ 42,000	+ \$ 1,050	+ \$14,000	+ \$ 350	= \$ 57,400
Fiberglass	(.35 − .05)	(280,000 + 7,000)	= \$ 98,000	+ \$ 2,450	− \$14,000	− \$ 350	= \$ 86,100
Plastic	(.10 + .01)	(280,000 + 7,000)	= \$ 28,000	+ \$ 700	+ \$ 2,800	+ \$ 70	= \$ 31,570
Wood	(.05 + .03)	(280,000 + 7,000)	= \$ 14,000	+ \$ 350	+ \$ 8,400	+ \$ 210	= \$ 22,960
		TOTALS	\$182,000	+ \$ 4,550	+ \$11,200	+ \$ 280	= \$198,030
Labor	(5 + .25)	(78,000 + 5,000)	= \$390,000	+ \$25,000	+ \$19,500	+ \$1,250	= \$435,750

Partitioned matrices can be used to organize these calculations more efficiently:

$$\begin{matrix} P \\ \Delta P \end{matrix}\left[\begin{array}{c|c|c|c||c} .15 & .35 & .10 & .05 & 5.00 \\ .05 & -.05 & .01 & .03 & .25 \end{array}\right] \begin{matrix} Q \quad\quad \Delta Q \\ \left[\begin{array}{cc} 280{,}000 & 7{,}000 \\ \hline 280{,}000 & 7{,}000 \\ \hline 280{,}000 & 7{,}000 \\ \hline 280{,}000 & 7{,}000 \\ \hline\hline 78{,}000 & 5.000 \end{array}\right] \end{matrix}$$

$$= \left[\begin{array}{c|c|c|c||c} P_1 & P_2 & P_3 & P_4 & P_5 \end{array}\right] \left[\begin{array}{c} Q_1 \\ \hline Q_2 \\ \hline Q_3 \\ \hline Q_4 \\ \hline\hline Q_5 \end{array}\right] = \left[[P_1Q_1 + P_2Q_2 + P_3Q_3 + P_4Q_4] + P_5Q_5\right]$$

$$= \left[\left[\underset{\text{Steel}}{\begin{bmatrix} 42{,}000 & 1{,}050 \\ 14{,}000 & 350 \end{bmatrix}} + \underset{\text{Fiberglass}}{\begin{bmatrix} 98{,}000 & 2{,}450 \\ -14{,}000 & -350 \end{bmatrix}} + \underset{\text{Plastic}}{\begin{bmatrix} 28{,}000 & 700 \\ 2{,}800 & 70 \end{bmatrix}} + \underset{\text{Wood}}{\begin{bmatrix} 14{,}000 & 350 \\ 8{,}400 & 210 \end{bmatrix}}\right] + \underset{\text{Labor}}{\begin{bmatrix} 390{,}000 & 25{,}000 \\ 19{,}500 & 1{,}250 \end{bmatrix}}\right]$$

$$= \left[\begin{matrix} \text{Materials} \\ \text{Standard}\quad\text{Quantity} \\ \begin{bmatrix} 182{,}000 & 4{,}550 \\ 11{,}200 & 280 \end{bmatrix} \\ \text{Price}\quad\text{Mixed} \end{matrix} + \begin{matrix} \text{Labor} \\ \text{Standard}\quad\text{Quantity} \\ \begin{bmatrix} 390{,}000 & 25{,}000 \\ 19{,}500 & 1{,}250 \end{bmatrix} \\ \text{Price}\quad\text{Mixed} \end{matrix}\right]$$

Comments:

1. Separate standard and variance amounts have been computed for each cost component.
2. Double partitioning permitted summarization into a materials matrix and a labor matrix.
3. With P arrayed above ΔP, it is easy to calculate $\%_P = \Delta P/P$ and to select those components for investigation that show a significant percentage change. Similarly, $\%_Q = \Delta Q/Q$ can be calculated and investigated if it is significant.

As the next step in the analysis, let us calculate the overhead variances:

Net		Computation	Amount	Variance
−48,000, Net	Actual		= 342,000	
				− 40,000, Spending
	Budget at input	= 216,000 + 2(83,000)	= 382,000	
				+ 10,000, Efficiency
	Budget at output	= 216,000 + 2(78,000)	= 372,000	
				18,000, Volume
	Absorbed	= 5(78,000)	= 390,000	

Comments:

1. The standard overhead rate was computed by dividing the budget equation for overhead costs by the expected volume, that is,

$$\frac{\$216{,}000 + \$2(72{,}000)}{72{,}000} = \$5 = \$3 \text{ fixed} + \$2 \text{ variable}$$

2. Actual spending is so low relative to the budget and absorbed figures that the accountant's suspicions would be aroused. Was something omitted from Actual, such as a missing depreciation entry? Was some major bill for repairs incurred but not received from the vendor? Is the flexible budget equation unrepresentative of overhead costs?
3. The Volume Variance prompts the questions: Should the overhead rate be challenged? Is expected monthly volume too low?
4. The Net Variance equals the difference between the two ledger accounts "Actual Overhead" and "Absorbed Overhead" (or the net difference of the single account "Overhead," if only one overhead account is maintained with debits for actual and credits for absorbed).
5. Many manufacturers would choose not to recognize monthly overhead variances in the general ledger. Rather, they would prepare a variance report as an aid to monthly control efforts, letting the monthly overhead amounts accumulate and offset one another in the ledger over the course of the year. Where this is the procedure, the usual absorption entry (Debit Work in Process, Credit Absorbed Overhead) is written. We, however, shall isolate the overhead variances in the general ledger. To avoid some bother, the accountant may credit Overhead Control directly, thereby dispensing with the Absorbed Overhead account.

The journal entries to record these transactions follow.

Account	Debit	Credit
Overhead Control	342,000	
Raw Materials (or Supplies) Payroll Payable Payroll Taxes Payable Prepaid Insurance Prepaid Property Taxes Accumulated Depreciation Vouchers Payable		342,000

To record the actual overhead costs.

Work in Process	182,000	
Materials Price Variance	11,200	
Materials Quantity Variance	4,550	
Materials Mixed Variance	280	
Raw Materials		198,030

To record direct-materials and material variances.

Work in Process	390,000	
Labor Price Variance	19,500	
Labor Quantity Variance	25,000	
Labor Mixed Variance	1,250	
Payroll Payable		435,750

To record direct-labor and labor variances.

Work in Process	390,000	
Overhead Efficiency Variance	10,000	
Overhead Spending Variance		40,000
Overhead Volume Variance		18,000
Overhead Control		342,000

To absorb overhead and to recognize overhead variances.

Finished Goods	908,350	
Work in Process		908,350

To recognize the cost of skis manufactured ($24.55 × 37,000).

If, at the end of a year, the variance accounts are insignificant in amount, their total would be added to Cost of Goods Sold on the income statement and so become an additional expense for the year. If the variances are significant, they should be added to the ending inventories of both Work in Process and Finished Goods and to Cost of Goods Sold in proportion to the types of cost (those corresponding to the types of variance) appearing in these accounts at the year's end. Thereafter the costs of the inventories must be reviewed to see that they comply with lower-of-cost-or-market inventory evaluation rules. If the inventories were too high, for instance, the excess would be treated as an expense (Cost of Goods Sold or Loss from Inventory Devaluation).

Perhaps one point deserves more emphasis. When standard costs are superimposed, it makes no difference whether job order or process costing techniques are followed *provided* equivalent production is computed on a *FIFO basis*. Why? In either case, only standard quantities and standard prices are charged to Work in Process. If process costing were computed on the *average basis*, the work done on opening inventory would be double counted—once as part of the equivalent units included in the previous period's ending inventory and again as part of the equivalent units transferred this period. Such double counting would interfere with standard quantities.

So far nothing has been said about bills of materials and how to incorporate refinements into standards. To understand these things, and to gain a further appreciation of standard costs and their relation to prices, we turn to Jantzen, Inc. and the fashion industry.

Jantzen's Cool Ice and Free Style

Jantzen, Inc. is perhaps the best-known manufacturer of fine sportswear in the world. Headquartered in Portland, Oregon, Jantzen has been considered the fashion leader of its industry since it was founded in 1910. Jantzen, by its name alone, projects the image of high fashion and outstanding quality in the minds of American women.

For fifty years Jantzen has employed standard costs in the determination of price and income and the control of costs. Commenting on price, Mr. Everett E. Cobb, the Jantzen Treasurer, has said:

> The price set by the Merchandiser is probably most influenced by cost factors. However, those responsible for pricing the lines must always keep the ultimate consumer in mind and not price the garments out of the market.

Let us investigate the Jantzen standard cost system and some of the decisions that are related to it. Of necessity we enter in the middle of the scene, when decisions about styles, quantities, and sizes have already been made.

Jantzen buys some fabrics and knits others; all fabrics are processed further in its Fabrics Department. Three other production departments work with the finished fabrics in the Portland factory: Cutting, Sewing, and Final Assembly. We shall trace the cost buildup of swimsuit styles 1L208 (Cool Ice one-piece) and 1L257 and 1L265 (Free Style halter and bikini respectively) as they pass through these departments. Exhibit 1 shows photographs of various stages of production and of the finished products.

Exhibit 2 shows the Style Cost Cards for Cool Ice and Free Style. All dollar amounts are synthetic. A great deal of information is summarized in Jantzen's Style Cost Cards. In the rightmost column you will find retail price per unit and cost and profit per dozen; multiplying unit retail price by 12 and subtracting net wholesale price gives retailer gross margin. The leftmost column ("Costing Base") contains standard direct labor (SDL) time allowances (in minutes) per suit for each of the production departments (all departments have the same pay rate). The column adjacent to this ("Costing") shows the standard direct labor *rate* ($3.00 per hour) and the cost per minute per dozen for each department. The rates are next multiplied by the time allowances to arrive at the labor costs for a dozen and for a unit, following which the labor costs are summed.

Beneath labor in the "Costing" column, you will find the burden (another popular name for overhead) absorption rates, which are based on total direct-labor cost. Note how separate provision has been made for controllable

Exhibit 1

Electronic Knitting Machine

Electric Scissors

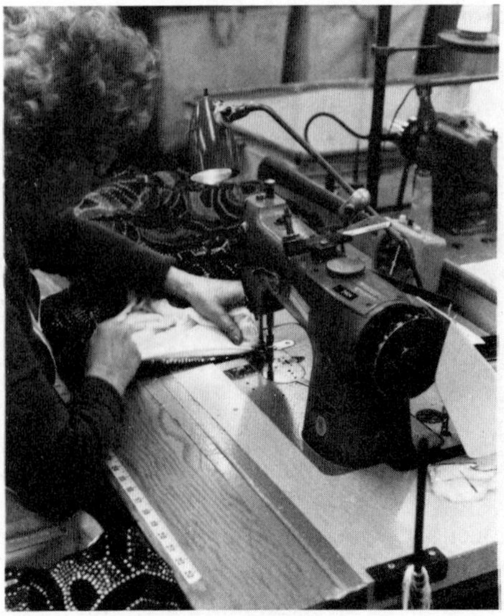

Sewing Machine

Final Assembly

burden as opposed to uncontrollable burden. This distinction has been drawn—generally based on segregation of fixed and variable portions of overhead costs—to expedite Jantzen's analysis of burden variances and so advance cost control efforts in its responsibility accounting system. Controllable costs include items like salaries and maintenance. Fixed costs beyond the influence of departmental foremen, such as plant insurance, property taxes, building rent, and equipment depreciation, comprise the uncontrollable burden costs.

Exhibit 1 (*cont.*)

Models 1, 2   Model 2 wears Cool Ice Mio   1L 208

Models 1, 2, 3   Model 2 wears   Free Style Halter 1L 257   Free Style Bikini 1L 265   Models 4, 5

Exhibit 2 STYLE COST CARD

Style: 1L208	Season: '75 Spr/Summer	Estimated Dozen:	Cost Card Dates Estimated Original 8/20/74 Revision 1 2 3
Category: Misses Swims	Group:	Factory: Portland	
Description: Cool Ice Mio			

Costing Base S D L Minutes/Unit	Costing	Dozen	Units	Dozen	Units
Cut Base Min 3.24 −8% Allow Total 3.00	Rate: 3.00 .60 Labor Cut	1.80	.15		
Sew Base Min 38.16 −6% Allow Total 36.00	Rate: 3.00 .60 Labor Sew	21.60	1.80		
Final Base Min 4.00 −% Allow Total 4.00	Rate: 3.00 .60 Labor Final	2.40	.20		
Total Base Min 45.40 Allow Total 43.00	Total Labor	25.80	2.15		
	Rate: 140% Controllable Burden	36.12	3.01		
	Rate: 25% Uncontrollable Burden	6.45	.54		
	Total Labor & Burden	68.37	5.70		
	Cost Fabric	53.68	4.47		
	Cost Sundry	18.20	1.52		
	Total Factory Cost	140.25	11.69		
	Cost Packaging	2.40	.20		

Profit Recap	Target	Actual
Retail	$	$ 36.00
Net Wholesale	$	$203.79
Total Shelf Cost	$	$142.65
Gross Profit	$	$ 61.14
Gross Margin	%	30.0

Style: 1L208

Style: 1L257	Season: '75 Spr/Summer	Estimated Dozen:
Category: Misses Swims	Group:	Factory: Vancouver
Description: Free Halter		

Cost Card Dates

Estimated
Original 8/20/74
Revision 1
2
3

Costing Base S D L Minutes/Unit	Costing	Dozen	Units	Dozen	Units
Cut Base Min 3.68 6% Allow Total 3.90	Rate: 3.00 .60 Labor Cut	2.40	.20		
Sew Base Min 14.57 5% Allow Total 15.30	Rate: 3.00 .60 Labor Sew	9.24	.77		
Final Base Min 3.06 8% Allow Total 3.30	Rate: 3.00 .60 Labor Final	2.04	.17		
Total Base Min 21.31 Allow Total 22.50	Total Labor	13.68	1.14		
	Rate: 140% Controllable Burden	19.15	1.60		
	Rate: 25% Uncontrollable Burden	3.42	.29		
	Total Labor & Burden	36.25	3.03		
	Cost Fabric	28.60	2.38		
	Cost Sundry	5.00	.42		
	Total Factory Cost	69.85	5.83		
	Cost Packaging	1.40	.12		
	Total Shelf Cost	71.25	5.95		

Profit Recap

	Target	Actual
Retail	$	$ 20.00
Net Wholesale	$	$118.75
Total Shelf Cost	$	$ 71.25
Gross Profit	$	$ 47.50
Gross Margin	%	40.0

Style: 1L257

Exhibit 2 STYLE COST CARD (*cont.*)

Style: 1L265	Season: '75 Spr/Summer	Estimated Dozen:	Cost Card Dates Estimated Original 8/20/74 Revision 1 2 3
Category: Misses Swims	Group:	Factory: Vancouver	
Description: Free Style Bikini-Trunk only			

Costing Base S D L Minutes/Unit	Costing	Dozen	Units	Dozen	Units
Cut Base Min 1.89 6% Allow Total 2.00	Rate: 3.00 .60 Labor Cut	1.20	.10		
Sew Base Min 7.14 5% Allow Total 7.50	Rate: 3.00 .60 Labor Sew	4.56	.38		
Final Base Min 1.67 8% Allow Total 1.80	Rate: 3.00 .60 Labor Final	1.08	.09		
Total Base Min 10.70 Allow Total 11.30	Total Labor	6.84	.57		
	Rate: 140% Controllable Burden	9.58	.80		
	Rate: 25% Uncontrollable Burden	1.71	.14		
	Total Labor & Burden	18.13	1.51		
	Cost Fabric	22.20	1.85		
	Cost Sundry	5.10	.43		
	Total Factory Cost	45.43	3.79		
	Cost Packaging	1.40	.12		

Profit Recap	Target	Actual
Retail	$	$ 13.00
Net Wholesale	7.00×.9 $ × 12	$ 80.74
Total Shelf Cost	$	$ 46.83
Gross Profit	$	
Gross Margin	%	42.0

Style: 1L265

Jantzen treats the entire factory as one department when applying overhead to products. Hence there is only one absorption rate, which is applied based on standard direct-labor hours in each production department. Costs in all factory departments are controlled by contrasting actual expenditures against departmental budgetary allowances.

Following the burden costs, you will see various material standard costs. These material costs are supported in detail by the Bills of Materials that appear in Exhibit 3. Trace the totals in the rightmost column of each of the Bills of Materials to their respective Style Cost Cards. Note that although the fabric and packaging costs occasionally disagree with their standard cost allowances, the differences were not considered sufficiently great to require an updating of standard costs. If updating were thought necessary, a new Style Cost Card would be completed.

The vacant set of columns in the Style Cost Card would be used if a garment were made partly in one factory and partly in another.

Now that we have finished tracing the basic cost buildup, there are a number of fascinating questions we can address:

1. *How much do actual costs have to change before standard costs are recomputed?*

Once the line of merchandise is costed and turned over to Marketing, the costs are not changed. Swimsuits are stylish items and have limited life. If a suit enjoys a second season, new current prices would be obtained. Generally, fabric commitments for price and volume are made before the start of the season and remain firm during the season.

2. *Locate the Cool Ice standard direct-labor allowance in the Sewing Department and observe that the base of 38.16 minutes per suit has been reduced by 6% to 36.00 minutes. What is the reason for this reduction?*

The base allowance, 38.16 minutes, is for the standard one-piece suit. Cool Ice has been determined by engineers to be less elaborate than the standard, and this is the reason for the 6% reduction. The Free Style suit, on the other hand, is fancier than the basic bikini and additional time has been allotted to it. Although Jantzen doesn't do it this way, the percentage reduction could be used to reflect learning curve allowances (a subject that will be discussed in the next section).

3. *Observe the models demonstrating the finished products in Exhibit 1. How would you estimate costs, prices, and margins for both products? Try to make some estimates before checking with Exhibits 2 and 3. Now check your estimates with the exhibits. Do you find any puzzling or unexplained differences?*

Exhibit 3

Dates: Original 4/11/74 Revision 10/10/74

Supplier	Use	Min Width	Description	Qty/Doz.	$ Per	If Pro-Rated Ext	%	Weighted $/Doz Supplied by Jantzen	Contract	
Henry Glass	Outer	45	645L/4017	8.6 yd						
S/C Grain-tie			Cut: 3/16″ Fin	.2 yd						Cost card
			Total Fabric	8.8 yd	5.25			46.20		53.68
Jantzen	Lining	38″ diag. Jantzen 109		4.4 yd	1.80			7.92		Combined
						Total =		54.12		54.12
Jantzen	S/C Grain		Labor & burden cost	.2 yd	.10			.02		
Spring Mills		44/45″	Three Cheers	.15 yd	.70			.11		
Fastner Supply	Grommet	AA	W/Washer	4.0 dz	.20			.80		
Metric	Bra		M-700 CD/74	1.0 dz	8.20			8.20		
⋮			⋮					⋮		
Rhode Island	Bra-legs	3/8″	4502 Elastic	65.0 yd	.06			3.90		
Coats & Clark	Sewing	0/3	6000 yd cn	.6 cn	4.00			2.40		Combined
						Total =		18.20		18.20

	Label	L118C		1.0 dz	.20			.20		
	Tab	Care & Size J-4 Gold, Sz: 8-16		1.0 dz	.10			.10		
	Tag	Soabar	'75 Special	1.0 dz	.30			.30		
	Hanger	P-4000		1.0 dz	.60			.60		
	Bag	15 × 36		1.0 dz	.50			.50		
	Shapeboard	Shape Retainer		1.0 dz	.70			.70		Combined
						Total =		2.40		2.40

Jantzen, Inc.—BILL OF MATERIALS Mfgr, Portland	Cleaning Code 4	Content 85% Antron 15% Lycra	Style 1L208	

Dates: Original 5/6/74 Revision 6/11/74						If Pro-Rated		Weighted $/Doz Supplied by		
Supplier	Use	Min Width	Description	Qty/Doz.	$ Per	Ext	%	Jantzen	Contract	
Gilbert Frank	Bra	58/60	10354L/Erotica	3.50 yd						
S/C Grain	Spag. tie	15.25	Lin Yd: 1″ Cut. 1/4″ Fin	.40 yd						
S/C Grain: Ext.	9.91 Lin yd: $1\frac{3}{4}$″ Cut. 3/4″ Fin.			.50 yd						
			Total Fabric	4.40 yd	6.50			28.60		Combined
						Total =		28.60		28.60

Exhibit 3 (*cont.*)

Jantzen	S/C Grain		Labor & burden cost	.65 yd	.10			.07		
MCS	Back bra	3/4″	Non adjustable	1.0 dz	.45			.45		
Ansley	Filter cord		40 Cord	16.0 yd	.03			.48		
Rhode Island	Bra	3/8″	4502 Elastic	5.0 yd	.06			.30		
Plymouth	Bra Sds	1/4″	Rubber Elastic D-176	20.0 yd	.05			1.00		
⋮			⋮					⋮		
Coats & Clark	Sewing	0/3	6000 yd cn	.6 cn	4.00			2.40		Combined
							Total =	5.00		5.00
	Label		L118C	1.0 dz	.20			.20		
	Tab	Care & Size (J-4 Gold)B-C-D		1.0 dz	.10			.10		
	Tag	Soabar		1.0 dz	.30			.30		
	Hanger		P-4000	1.0 dz	.60			.60		
	Bag		15 × 17	1.0 dz	.20			.20		
										Combined
							Total =	1.40		1.40
Jantzen, Inc.—BILL OF MATERIALS Mfgr, Vancouver			Cleaning Code 4	Content 85% Antron 15% Lycra			Style 1L257			

Supplier	Use	Min Width	Description	Qty/Doz.	$ Per	If Pro-Rated Ext	%	Weighted $/Doz Supplied by Jantzen	Contract	
Gilbert Frank	Trunk	58/60	10354L/on Erotica	2.8 yd						
S/C Grain	Tab	5.23	Lin Yd $1\frac{3}{4}''$ Cut	.2 yd						
			Total Fabric	3.0 yd	6.50			19.50		
Jantzen	Lining	38″ diag Jantzen 109		1.5 yd	1.80			2.70		Combined
						Total =		22.20		22.20
Jantzen	S/C Grain		Labor & burden cost	.15 yd	.10			.02		
Superior Bias	Tab lining	$1\frac{1}{8}''$	S/C Stay cloth	6.0 yd	.04			.24		
Rochester	Button	19/2	Como Button	2.0 dz	.05			.10		
Rhode Island	Wst-legs	3/8″	4502 Elastic	25.0 yd	.06			1.50		
⋮			⋮					⋮		
Coats & Clark	Sewing	0/3	6000 yd cn	.6 cn	4.00			2.40		
										Combined
						Total =		5.10		5.10
	Label		L118C	1.0 dz	.20			.20		
	Tab	Care & Size (J-4 Gold)Sz: S-M-L		1.0 dz	.10			.10		Cost card
	Tag	Kimbal & Separate Tent		1.0 dz	.30			.30		1.40
	Hanger		No. 55	1.0 dz	.75			.75		
	Bag		15 × 17	1.0 dz	.20			.20		
										Combined
						Total =		1.55		1.55

Jantzen, Inc.—BILL OF MATERIALS Mfgr, Vancouver	Cleaning Code 4	Content 85% Antron 15% Lycra	Style 1L265

I had expected (1) Cool Ice to have more, and more expensive, fabric as well as a greater gross profit. I had expected (2) Free Style to require more labor, hence more overhead. As the Bills of Materials show, Cool Ice has more but less expensive fabric. The Style Cost Cards show that Cool Ice requires more labor than Free Style. So I was wrong on two counts; designers would not make such errors. The point is that many decisions had to be made about design, fabric, suppliers, quality, and price before even a simple product like the bikini came into existence. Cost estimation is demanding, complicated work.

4. *How many of each garment is made?*

Any given style goes through the factory in 24- or 100-dozen lots, with smaller bundles of 1 or 2 dozen at a time passing from one worker to the next. The quantity to make—by sizes—is determined by the Production Planning Department, which uses historical data and current booking patterns as guides.

5. *Why does the gross margin percentage vary from one garment to the next?*

The percentage varies from one suit to another, and from the bikini to the halter in the same suit, because of market considerations. Ultimately, as was mentioned earlier, the consumer sets the limits to price.

6. *What is the "Target" column in the profit recapitulation section used for?*

Note the entry in the "Target" column on the Style Cost Card for 1L265. Shown here is the previous year's unit price, $7, and the goal of 90% for this year's wholesale price. This target is an added control feature. Even though the target of $75.60 was exceeded, nonetheless the present net wholesale price represents a significant reduction over the $84 previously charged. Such a target tends to encourage production efficiency and the attainment of the desired gross margin.

Learning Curves

Basic Concepts

One refinement in standard costing that has received an enormous amount of attention has to do with the effect of learning (or progress) curves on standards. Under the usual conception of standards, as has just been discussed, the accountant determines total standard labor time by multiplying the number of units made by a constant number of labor hours—2 hours per ski in the Harmless Ski Company example. However, people learn from regular, repeated experience and will continuously improve on their performance if they are encouraged and instructed how to do so. If the first unit takes 50 hours to make, the second may take 40 hours, the third 32 hours, the fourth 26 hours, and so forth. The graph below portrays what happens in such a learning situation. Just this sort of improvement was first recognized in the aircraft industry during World War II. It was so frequently encountered in aircraft component production that the phenomenon became known variously as the "80% learning curve" and the "airframe curve." Researchers soon found that learning curves applied to many other industries as well.

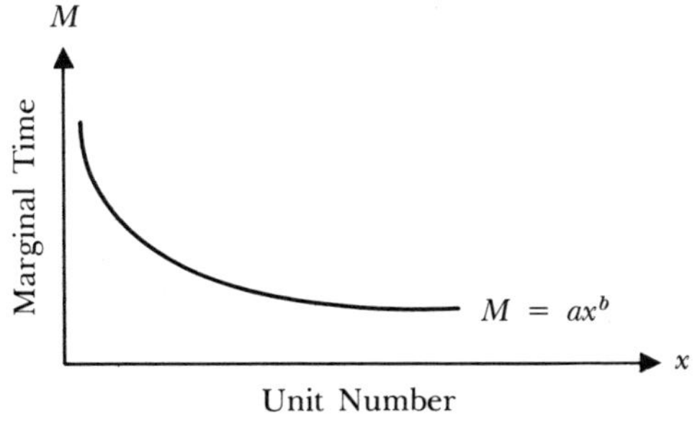

Learning curves can be used not only to set standards, but also to establish prices, to set production schedules, and to decide whether a component should be manufactured in-house or purchased outside, ("make or buy").

A company obtains a learning curve (1) from assuming the experience of its industry or (2) from its own previous experience with similar products or (3) from fitting a regression line to observed pilot study results.[4]

Although there are a great many other learning curves, let us concern ourselves for the present with the 80% learning curve. We initiate the discussion by designating a unit as a group of one or more of an item (for example, a unit might consist of 10 of a particular commodity with the result that unit 1 consisted of items 1 to 10, unit 2 consisted of items 11 to 20, and so forth). We can then estimate the marginal time needed to make unit x by solving:

$$M(x) = ax^b = 50x^{-.322}$$

Here the coefficient 50 is the approximate time needed to make the first unit of some commodity. The exponent $-.322$ is used to adjust time so that the

[4] One form of the learning curve is $y = ax^b$, which by taking logs of the x and y readings may be brought into linear form, $\log y = \log a + b \log x$. After $B = (X^TX)^{-1}X^Ty$ is applied, b_0 must be antilogged to return to the real-world curve.

time for unit x is 80% of that needed to make unit $x/2$. Thus,

$$\begin{aligned} &\text{Unit 1:} && = 50 \text{ hours} \\ &\text{Unit 2: } .8(50) && = 40 \text{ hours} \\ &\text{Unit 4: } .8(40) && = 32 \text{ hours} \\ &\text{Unit 8: } .8(32) && = 25.6 \text{ hours} \end{aligned}$$

Note that time for unit 4 could also be calculated as $.8(.8)\,50 = .8^2(50)$, while time for unit 8 could be calculated as $.8(.8).8(50) = .8^3(50)$. This relationship holds generally, and therefore it is possible to relate the doubling and 80% notions as follows:

$50(.8^i) = 50(2^i)^b$, where i shows how many doublings (1, 2, 4, 8, . . .) are involved and b is that number which will make the equation true

But the law of exponents allows $(2^i)^b$ to be written as $(2^b)^i$; hence

$$50(.8^i) = 50(2^b)^i$$

From this we see $.8 = 2^b$ and we may use logarithms to solve for b:

$$\log .8 = b \log 2$$

or

$$b = \frac{\log .8}{\log 2} = \frac{.9031 - 1}{0.3010} = \frac{-.0969}{0.3010} = -.322$$

This doubling—80% effect occurs throughout the curve and not just at the doubling points mentioned. For example,

Unit 3	Unit 6
$M(3) = 50(3)^{-.322}$	$M(6) = 50(6)^{-.322}$
$-.322 \log 3 = -.322(0.4771)$ $= -.1536$ antilog $-.1536 =$ antilog $.8464 - 1$ $= .7021$	$-.322 \log 6 = -.322(0.7782)$ $= -.2506$ antilog $-.2506 =$ antilog$(.7494 - 1)$ $= .5615$
$M(3) = 50(.7021) = 35.105$ hours	$M(6) = 50(.5615) = 28.075$ hours

Observe that $.8(35.1) = 28.08$, and hence the time for unit 6 is 80% of that for unit 3.

Just how would learning curves be used in standard costing? Suppose a manufacturer has made 500 units of the product we have been discussing and wishes to make an additional 200 units. We could estimate the total time needed—designated below by $T(m + n|n)$—by[5]

$$T(m + n|n) = \frac{a}{b+1}[\text{antilog}((b + 1)\log(m + n)) - \text{antilog}((b + 1)\log n)]$$

For our example, $a = 50$, $b + 1 = -.322 + 1.000 = .678$, $m = 200$, $n = 500$.

$$\begin{aligned} T(700|500) &= \frac{50}{.678}[\text{antilog}(.678 \log 700) - \text{antilog}(.678 \log 500)] \\ &= 73.746[\text{antilog}(.678(2.8451)) - \text{antilog}(.678(2.6990))] \\ &= 73.746[\text{antilog } 1.9290 - \text{antilog } 1.8299] \\ &= 73.746(84.92 - 67.60) \\ &= 1{,}277 \text{ hours} \end{aligned}$$

It should take approximately 1,277 hours to make the next 200 units. Had learning been ignored, and had the 50 hours for the first unit been considered applicable to all subsequent units, the estimate would have been 200(50) = 10,000 hours.

If the learning curve was used in the factory, the 1,277 hours could now be multiplied by the wage rate and overhead rate (the overhead rate would still be determined by dividing total overhead costs by the expected yearly volume of direct-labor hours) to arrive at standard labor and overhead costs. For pricing purposes, it would be consistent with the Smoothing Principle to avoid favoring units manufactured late in the year by estimating an average time for the year (by calculating total time for the year and dividing this by total units manufactured).

The problem we encounter in trying to apply learning curves in present-day circumstances lies chiefly in the unions' restriction of output. Where restrictions are imposed by one's peers, one lacks the encouragement one needs to allow learning curve effects to occur. Some industries, pointing to the American workers' declining productivity relative to their wages, have turned over production responsibilities to foreign countries and concentrated entirely on distributing the finished products. The unions in these industries have, in effect, restricted their members out of jobs—which was not wise management on the part of the union officials. "Don't be a pacesetter; let us take care of the wage incentives by bargaining collectively for a general wage increase" can be very shortsighted and expensive advice.

Even if union activity proves an insurmountable obstacle to the introduction of learning curves, management can use the curves to estimate the

[5] These results follow from

$$T(m + n|n) = \int_n^{m+n} ax^b\,dx = \left.\frac{ax^{b+1}}{b+1}\right]_n^{m+n}$$

costs that should be, and, by subtracting these costs from those actually incurred, arrive at the loss in earnings caused by output restrictions. "Loss Caused by Output Restriction" would make an interesting caption on an income statement.

Alternate Forms

Instead of calculating marginal time in the manner described above, many analysts use cumulative average time. Study the example shown below to understand the difference in the marginal times under the two methods.

		Labor Time (Hours)		
Units Made	Cumulative Units	Average	Total	Marginal
1	1	50	(1 × 50) = 50	(1 unit) 50
1	2	(.8 × 50) = 40	(2 × 40) = 80	(1 unit) 30
2	4	(.8 × 40) = 32	(4 × 32) = 128	(2 units) 48
4	8	(.8 × 32) = 25.6	(8 × 25.6) = 204.8	(4 units) 76.8

The cumulative units are multiplied by the average time to obtain total time, and marginal time is now calculated as the differences in successive total times. These are different conceptions of the learning curve form. The choice between them would depend on the behavior of the system being studied—one form may fit the observed behavior better than the other. The form originally presented is usually preferable, because it is simpler.

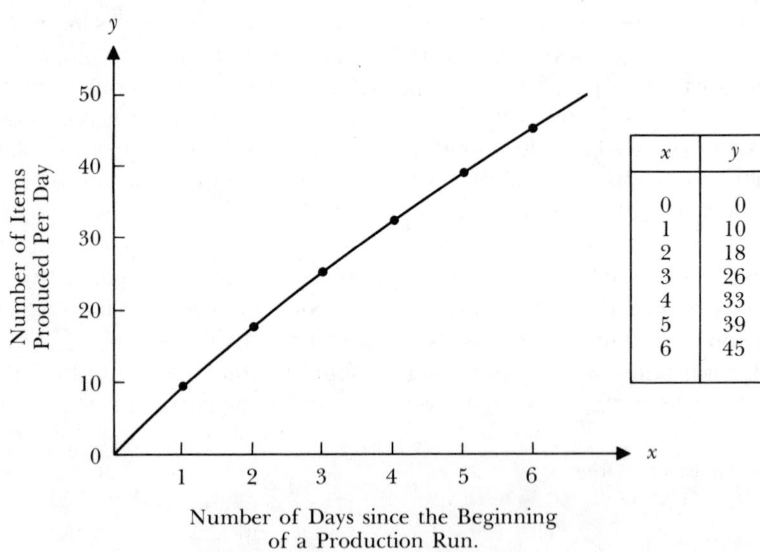

Yet another form of learning curve is popular in management literature for relating outcomes such as production to time and sales to advertising. In production this curve starts at zero and gradually climbs to steady-state performance; the graph appears on page 252.

Example: In a factory, daily production, y, is a function of the number of days, x, since the start of the production run, and is given by

$$y = 100(1 - e^{-.1x}) \qquad \text{(See graph above)}$$

How long will the run last if 400 units are to be made?

Solution: There are several approaches to determining the length of the production run. Because there will be relatively few days in this particular example, each day's output could easily be summed (manually or on a computer). A more classical approach involves solving for n in the following equation:

$$400 = \sum_{x=0}^{n} 100(1 - e^{-.1x}) = 100 \sum_{x=0}^{n} (1 - .9048^x), \text{ where}$$

$$e^{-.1} = .9048$$

Employing finite calculus, we find

$$400 = 100\Delta^{-1}(1 - .9048^x)\Big]_0^{n+1}$$

$$4 = \Delta^{-1}(1x^{(0)} - .9048^x)\Big]_0^{n+1}$$

$$= x^{(1)} - \frac{.9048^x}{.9048 - 1}\Bigg]_0^{n+1}$$

$$= \left[(n+1) + \frac{.9048^{n+1}}{.0952}\right] - \left[0 + \frac{1}{.0952}\right]$$

$$4(.0952) = (n+1).0952 + .9048^{n+1} - 1$$

$$1.2856 = .0952n + .9048^{n+1} = .0952n + e^{-.1(n+1)}.$$

By solving for n (that is, by finding the root of $f(n) = .0952n + e^{-.1(n+1)} - 1.2856$), the number of days in the run may be determined. This may be done by using the Newton-Raphson formula:

$$n_{i+1} = n_i - f(n_i)/f'(n_i),$$

where i designates the iteration, and

$$f'(n) = .0952 - .1e^{-.1(n+1)}$$

For example, taking $n_i = 9$ yields

$$n_{i+1} = 9 - \left[\frac{.0952(9) + e^{-1} - 1.2856}{.0952 - .1e^{-1}}\right] = 10.0428$$

$$\text{Iterating, } n_{i+2} = 10.0428 - (f(10.0428)/f'(10.0428)) = 10.0106$$

$$n_{i+3} = 10.0106 - (f(10.0106)/f'(10.0106)) = 10.0122$$

$$n_{i+4} = 10.0122 - (f(10.0122)/f'(10.0122)) = 10.0117$$

$$n_{i+5} = 10.0117 - (f(10.0117)/f'(10.0117)) = 10.0117,$$

the same.

Had calculations been carried to six or eight decimal places, the root determined would undoubtedly be somewhat different from 10.0117 days. At any rate, in approximately ten days the run will be complete. Here

> Many analysts prefer to approximate the finite results by using integration:
>
> $$400 = \int_0^n 100(1 - e^{-.1x})\,dx = 100(x + 10e^{-.1x})\Big]_0^n$$
>
> $$= 100(n + 10e^{-.1n} - 10)$$
>
> $f(n)$ then becomes
>
> $$f(n) = n + 10e^{-.1n} - 14, \text{ with } f'(n) = 1 - e^{-.1n}$$
>
> The Newton-Raphson formula would now be applied as before.

we have seen an interesting employment of a standard—in formula form—to determine the production time needed to fill an order. It will help in scheduling production and in telling the customer when he can expect delivery. In addition, the formula gives new meaning to input and output times in flexible budgets, standards, and overhead variance analysis.

Make or Buy?

Manufacturers must constantly decide whether to make a product (or portion of a product) themselves or to buy it from an outside supplier. Fundamental to such decisions is the fact that volume of production may or may not justify either acquisition of the necessary equipment or deployment of presently owned equipment to the specific product. If an extended period of time is involved in production, then the analysis requires the use of discount factors to recognize the time value of money. This comes under the heading of capital budgeting and will be postponed until Chapter 11. On the other hand, if the production period is short, discounting may safely be ignored.

Example: A production manager is choosing whether to make or buy a particular item. It has been estimated that it will take 80 hours to make the first unit, and that marginal time to produce unit x will be 70% of the time necessary for unit $x/2$. The pertinent factory costs are

Materials	\$320 per unit
Labor	\$ 5 per hour
Labor related costs:	
—"Out-of-pocket" overhead	\$ 2 per hour
—Profits forgone by diverting factory resources from production of next most profitable item that must be discontinued or at least delayed.	\$ 1 per hour

If the item may be purchased for \$440 per unit, approximately how many units must be manufactured before the total accumulated costs under both alternatives would be equal?

Solution: We first solve for the learning exponent:

$$2^b = .7$$

$$b = \frac{\log .7}{\log 2} = \frac{-.1549}{.3010} = -.5146$$

At unit n, total purchased cost equals total manufactured cost; therefore,

$$\$440n = \$320n + \$8 \int_0^n 80x^{-.5146}\,dx$$

$$120n = \frac{640(n^{.4854})}{.4854}$$

$$\frac{n}{n^{.4854}} = \frac{640}{120(.4854)} = 10.9875$$

$$n^{.5146} = 10.9875$$

$$.5146 \log n = \log 10.9875 = 1.0410$$

$$\log n = 1.0410/.5146 = 2.0229$$

$$n = 105.4$$

Comments:

1. If the company plans to make at least 106 units, it would probably be better off to make this product.

2. It is difficult to estimate the profits forgone by diverting resources from the next most profitable item that must be discontinued or delayed. If the present item is bought, production capacity is increased by this subcontracting; hence the discontinued item can be produced. If it is produced, it too may enjoy the advantages of a learning curve. How would this be reflected by a constant \$1?

3. If the company decides to buy, it becomes subject to the vagaries of the supplier, who may (1) change his price, (2) decrease his quality, or (3) even go out of business. To resume production at a later date is to forgo valuable practice in the interim, thereby losing the benefits of learning.

Summary

We have studied many aspects of standard costing in this chapter. If one idea predominated, it was that standard costs should reflect those costs which should be incurred in the circumstances that prevail. Sometimes updating can consist simply of multiplying a cost by a compounding factor (e^{it}). At other times, learning curves must be reflected because input efficiency changes.

Variance analysis provides a means for controlling costs using the management-by-exception principle. However, no variance can be declared absolutely favorable or unfavorable until the circumstances have been investigated.

Where standard costs are superimposed on either a job order or a process costing system, the same costs will be obtained under both methods, provided equivalent production is determined by the FIFO method.

It was observed that the frequency of updating is limited by the desirability of smoothing costs. Even a span of good years and bad years shares corporate facilities and reputation. It might easily be argued that costs in a good year are favorable because the corporation managed to live through bad years. Smoothing is an art, not a science.

Linear programming can further extend the theory of standard costing. We shall see how in a later chapter. Suffice it to say now (1) that LP can provide data for calculating variances in terms of profits lost rather than in terms of costs that have not been accurately absorbed; and (2) that standards for individual products do not exist where joint products are manufactured;

instead what is needed is a standard for the package of products, and LP is an attractive means of obtaining it.

Problems

1. Discuss standard costs and variance analysis. Include in your discussion illustrations of overhead rate determination; cost estimation for 100 units of a product subject to the learning curve TIME $= 200x^{-.2}$; material, labor, and overhead (total, spending, efficiency, and capacity) variances.

2. Compute labor variances using matrices for the data shown below. Discuss resulting variances and comment on pros and cons of variance analysis.

	Standard		Actual	
Labor Type	Wage/Hour	Hours	Wage/Hour	Hours
A	\$3.00	1,000	\$2.80	800
B	2.50	1,500	2.75	1,600
C	4.25	200	4.00	250

3. Compute total, spending, efficiency, and volume variances and discuss both the results and the conception of overhead variance analysis.

   Overhead budget line $= y = 200{,}000 + 6x$
   Actual overhead cost was \$780,000.
   Normal volume for the period was 100,000 hours.
   It took 98,000 hours to make what should have required only 92,000 hours according to the standard.

4. *The standard costing-variance analysis approach related to gross profit analysis.* Shown below are two years' data for a company. Take year 1 as the standard and find the purchasing power, profit rate, volume, and mixed variances.

	Year 1	Year 2
Sales	(325,000 @ \$5.75)	(550,000 @ \$5.25)
Cost of sales	(325,000 @ \$4.50)	(550,000 @ \$4.75)
Average price index for year	115	105

5. *Standard costs and process costing.* The Genuine Antiques Company manufactures Colonial furniture. It achieves a certain beat-up patina in its line by striking items with chains and burning them with a torch—all very carefully. The standard cost card for Dry Sink-Style A, which is the sole product of the Dry Sink Department, shows:

   Materials: 90 board feet, yellow pine @ \$.40/bd. ft.
   Labor: 3 hours @ \$4.50/hour
   Hinges, glue, and stain are treated as overhead, which is applied at 150% of direct labor.

During June, 40,000 board feet of yellow pine were purchased for \$17,000 and 35,000 board feet were requisitioned for Dry Sink-Style A production. Eleven hundred hours of labor at an hourly wage of \$4.75 were paid. By the end of the month 380 sinks were completed and another 10 were in process, complete as to materials and about half done as to conversion. At the end of May, 20 sinks had been in process, complete as to materials and one quarter along in processing; the inventory records carried these sinks at material, labor, and overhead costs of \$720, \$67.50, and \$101.25 respectively.

Required:

Prepare journal entries and a materials and labor variance analysis. Assume price variances are recognized at time of purchase. Also assume FIFO costing.

6.

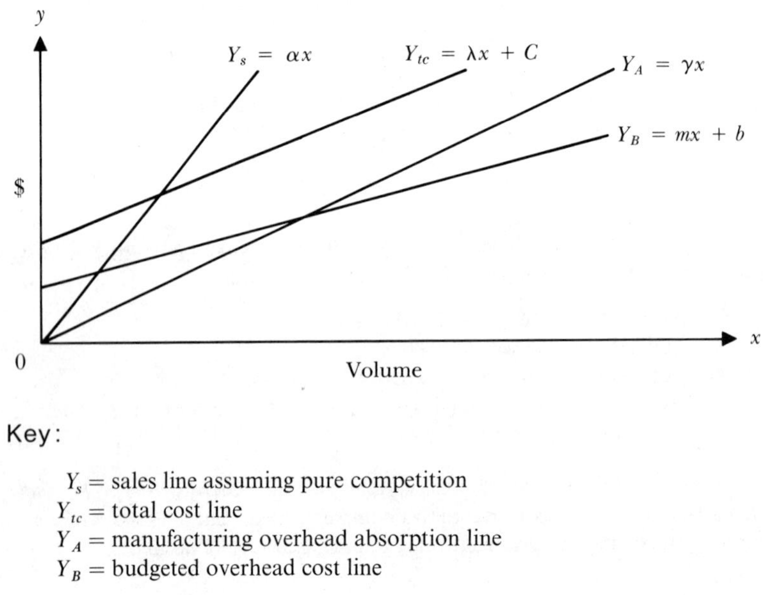

Key:

Y_s = sales line assuming pure competition
Y_{tc} = total cost line
Y_A = manufacturing overhead absorption line
Y_B = budgeted overhead cost line

If

$x \quad y$

$a = (13{,}000, \$74{,}000)$ (actual overhead)
$m = \$4$
$\gamma = \$6$
$\alpha = \$8$
$b = \$20{,}000$
$\lambda = \$7$
$C = \$70{,}000$, determine the normal volume, the break-even point, and the overhead variances (i.e., net, spending, and volume variances).

Discuss these variances from the standpoint of their significance and possible causes. If the variances are significant, suggest what remedial action might be taken.

7. (a) Compute the net, spending, efficiency, and volume variances from the data shown below.

Actual overhead:	\$325,000
Budget line:	$y = \$20x + \$150{,}000$
Input—	10,000 standard machine hours (SMH)
Output—	11,000 SMH
Standard overhead rate:	\$30 per SMH

(b) State in words what these variances measure.

(c) What is the normal or standard volume?

8. *"Roll your own" overhead variance analysis and responsibility accounting.*

Key:

x_i = volume at i for $i = I$ (input), O (output), N (normal)
V = variable portion of the overhead rate
F = fixed portion of the overhead rate
α = actual variable overhead rate
β = actual fixed costs

Using this key, for example,

$$\text{Actual} = A = \alpha x_I + \beta = \alpha x_I + F x_N \text{ because } \beta \approx F x_N \text{, usually}$$
$$\text{Budget at input} = B_I = V x_I + F x_N$$

It is then true that $B_N = (V + F)x_N = A_N$, absorbed at normal

Required:

Six variances are mentioned in the literature:

Net:	difference between actual and absorbed
Spending:	difference between actual and budget allowance at input
Efficiency:	difference between input and output volumes extended at variable overhead rate
Effectiveness:	overhead cost of misused facilities measured by the difference between input and output volumes extended at fixed overhead rate
Idle Capacity:	overhead cost of unused facilities measured by the difference between normal and input volumes extended at fixed overhead rate
Volume:	difference between input and output volumes extended at the fixed overhead rate

(a) Express all variances symbolically.

(b) Comment on which variances, if any, make any sense, keeping human behavior and responsibility accounting foremost in mind.

9. *Overhead variance analysis and the "idle capacity" and "efficiency and effectiveness" variances.* Read question 8 and proceed with the data shown below.

Actual OH cost:	\$175,000
Budget formula:	$Y_b = 65x + 45{,}000$, where x = direct-labor hours
Absorbed Formula:	$Y_a = 85x$
Volume (DLH):	Input 1900 DLH
	Output 1800 DLH

How are the following variances measured? (Show figures)

(a) Volume variance

(b) Idle capacity variance

(c) Efficiency and effectiveness variance

Given a net unfavorable variance of \$22,000, compute efficiency and effectiveness, idle capacity, and spending variances.

10. *Two-variance analysis.* Though all costs are controllable at some level in a company, nevertheless it is a common oversimplification to treat fixed costs as noncontrollable at the level of the production department. Some responsibility systems therefore isolate only two explanatory variances.

During the month of September the Crosby Company incurred \$60,000 of overhead costs and produced an output of 2,000 units. If budgeted fixed costs were \$37,000, the controllable variance was \$5,000 favorable, and the net (overall) variance was \$2,000 unfavorable, what is the normal volume? Criticize this system.

11. Lindquist and Nordean Company manufacture L & N golf clubs, the latest and snazziest equipment a deprived golfer could possibly own. Walter Faddis, the controller, notes that the standard cost of a set of irons consists of

Materials:	Shafts (9 @ \$1)	\$9.00
	Iron (special alloy, 5 lbs. @ \$.50)	2.50
	Leather (2 sq. ft. @ \$.90)	1.80
		\$13.30
Labor:	($\frac{1}{2}$ hour @ \$8)	4.00
Overhead:	(? per labor hour)	
		\$

The monthly overhead budget for the Irons Department follows the flexible budgeting equation $y = \$88{,}000 + \$6x$, where x is measured in direct-labor hours. Twenty-two thousand hours is considered the normal monthly volume.

November activities:

(a) Actual overhead costs were \$235,000.

(b) Two hundred sixty thousand shafts were purchsed for \$1.10 each. Raw materials inventory is kept at actual cost.

(c) Twenty-one thousand direct-labor hours were worked at a cost of $189,000. The equivalent of 40,000 sets of irons was accomplished.

(d) Three hundred eighty thousand shafts, 95 tons of iron, and 82,000 sq. ft. of leather were used at a cost of $.90 per shaft, $1,100 per ton, and $1 per square foot.

(e) Thirty six-thousand sets were completed.

Required:

(a) Compute variance of all sorts.

(b) Write all journal entries.

(c) List possible causes of each variance.

(d) Is the variance analysis of any use to Mr. Faddis? How so?

12. Ganz & Lagone, Inc. manufactures steel tennis rackets for various clients, such as Spazinger, Tilson, and Marcia. Each order is for a different quantity and a different model, but there is no difference in the cost to manufacture any given model—each racket has a steel frame, varying somewhat in shape, and a plastic handle covered with cowhide. The company does not do stringing. Occasionally a racket frame warps or snaps or has holes drilled improperly, all of which lead to discarded units. There are five producing departments: Bending, Drilling, Extruding, Assembly, and Packaging. Steel grommets, screws, and packaging materials are all treated as indirect materials. The standard cost per racket with all departments treated collectively, is

Materials:	Steel (1 pound @ $.50/pound)	$ .50
	Plastic (1 set @ $.30/set)	.30
	Leather ($1\frac{1}{2}$ feet @ $.20/foot)	.30
		$1.10
Labor:	(10 minutes @ $9.00/hour)	$1.50
Overhead:	(? per labor hour)	
	Total	$

The monthly flexible overhead budget equation for the factory is $y = \$180{,}000 + \$12x$, where x is measured in direct-labor hours. The established standard monthly volume is 10,000 hours.

February activities:

(a) Forty-five thousand rackets were completed and 10,000 rackets were still being worked on. (All were completed through drilling, 2,000 had plastic handles in place, and 500 had leather set aside but not wrapped. Half of the conversion process is involved with drilling, a quarter is involved in extruding, and the remaining work is in assembling and packaging.) Five hundred frames were spoiled. There was no opening inventory of work in process.

(b) Actual overhead costs were \$324,000.

(c) Steel tubing was purchased (50 tons @ \$1,050 per ton). Raw materials inventory is kept at actual cost.

(d) Nine thousand direct-labor hours were worked at a cost of \$7.50 per hour.

(e) Actual requisitions of materials were 56,000 pounds of steel tubing: \$33,600; 53,000 sets of plastic handles: \$14,840; 67,000 feet of cowhide: \$16,750.

Required:

(a) Compute variances.

(b) Write all journal entries.

13. *Learning curves and "make or buy."* A manufacturer has been approached by a supplier who offers to sell him a component for \$245 each for the next 400 units. The manufacturer has already made 600 units of this component subject to a production time learning curve of $M(x) = 20x^{-.2}$. Materials cost him \$200, labor runs \$5 per hour, and out-of-pocket overhead is \$3 per hour. Should the manufacturer accept the offer based on the data presented? What other factors should he consider? How would the learning curve be determined? Be technologically specific.

14. *Learning curves and regression.* Fit a learning curve to the unit numbers and time data shown below. Be sure to calculate the coefficient of determination.

Unit Number	Production Time
1	120
2	110
3	82
4	66
5	61
6	58
7	54
8	52

15. A firm produces machines subject to the learning curve. $MT(x) = 60x^{-.28}$

(a) How much time do you expect will be required to produce the next 200 units if the firm has already produced a total of 700 units?

(b) Of what use is a knowledge of learning curves to accountants?

(c) How can such curves be determined? Be specific.

16. A company has just completed manufacturing three units of a new product and is now considering an offer by an outside company willing to supply the completed product at a cost of \$500 per unit. Units 1, 2, and 3 took 76.5, 65.0, and 59.1 hours, respectively, to manufacture. Materials for the product cost \$200. Labor and variable overhead amount to \$3.15 and \$2.00 per hour respectively.

In view of the improvements in production time that the company has already experienced, management believes that a learning curve is at work. Given this assumption, management wishes to know

(a) the actual learning curve apparently in effect;

(b) what percentage learning curve this is;

(c) how much time it would take, including the time already spent, to produce the first 20 units; and

(d) the approximate number of units that would have to be manufactured before the total variable production costs, including the cost of the first three units, would equal the total theoretical cost of purchasing (that is, the cost had all units been purchased).

Find the answers to these questions. Based on all this information, what should management decide?

17. *Learning Theory.*

(a) How much time would you schedule for production of the next 200 units of an item given that 500 units have already been made and the marginal time, MT, to produce a unit follows the curve $MT = 102x^{-.32}$?

(b) Learning curves are also expressed using exponential functions. Determine the production time needed to manufacture the next 200 units given that 300 have already been made and the marginal time obeys $MT = 100e^{-.002x}$

(c) If there is little manual work in the production process, how does this affect the use of learning curves?

18. *Cumulative average learning curve.* A manufacturer has recently introduced an amazing product, "Listlesscorks." Forty units have already been made, and, for purposes of analysis, these have been segregated into groups of 10, 10, and 20 units. The first 10 units took 400 hours to produce, the next 10 required 160 hours, and the last 20 units took 224 hours. Materials cost \$24 per unit, while labor and out-of-pocket overhead cost \$15 per hour. The policy has been established that selling price will include a 40% markup (based on selling price) over these product costs. An order for 280 Listlesscorks has been received.

(a) What price will be quoted?

(b) What percentage learning curve is at work?

19. *Production scheduling, startup, standards, and regression.* The Pownall Forge Works experiences a "warmup" period in its production of a particular casting. Daily output has been measured and the three readings* shown below were obtained.

---

* Only three readings have been given and they will fall exactly on the curve to permit you to check variable shifting and scaling in doing the regression analysis. In practice many readings should be used in fitting the curve, and of course they would not usually be measured to the nearest hundredth unit.

Day	Output
1	18.13
2	32.97
3	45.12

Required:

(a) Fit a learning curve of the form $y = a(1 - e^{bx})$ to the data.

(b) Determine how much time will be needed to complete an order for 10,000 units.

(c) Discuss how you would use the curve to set production and cost standards.

Moving Money Through Time

9

Introduction

Astonishing as it may seem, there are those who do not appreciate that time influences the value of money apart from whatever influence it may have in changing the purchasing power of the dollar. Forgetting about inflated and deflated dollars temporarily, concentrate on the dollar's interest-earning power. Simply stated, the dollar invested today is worth more tomorrow and conversely, the dollar to be obtained tomorrow is worth less if it could be received today.

In this chapter we shall discuss how to move dollars around in time so that when the urge arises to add payments for this year to payments for next year and for the year thereafter, we shall not be adding apples to grapefruit and calling the result apples (which, incidentally, is also the problem involved with purchasing power of money).

To perform the "moving" procedures, it will be necessary to compute numbers like $(a + b)^n$. To do this, you could multiply $a + b$ by itself n times or, more easily, you could use the binomial expansion

$$(a + b)^n = \sum_{i=0}^{n} \binom{n}{i} b^i a^{n-i}$$

In our applications, a, b, and n will all be simple numbers. $\binom{n}{i}$ is a compressed way of writing $\frac{n!}{i!(n-i)!}$ $\left(\text{for example, } \binom{5}{3} = \frac{5!}{3!(5-3)!} = \frac{5 \times 4 \times 3 \times 2 \times 1}{(3 \times 2 \times 1)(2 \times 1)} = \frac{120}{6(2)} = 10\right)$.

For a numerical example of the binomial expansion, let us assume we have an investment opportunity calling for an initial outlay of \$5,000 that will earn interest at the rate of 4% every six months and will return the accumulated balance at the end of 2.5 years. We wish to know what sum of money we will then have. It will help us to understand the calculation if we draw a diagram known as a continuum:

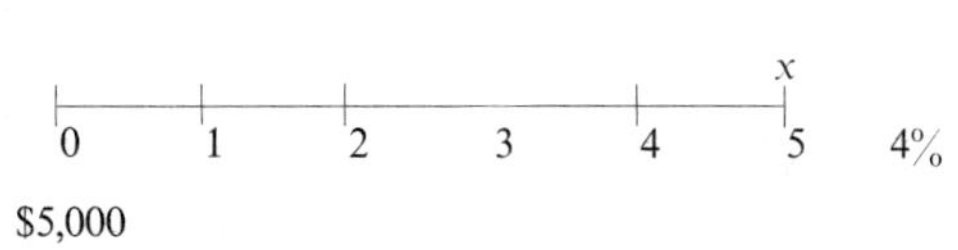

Before using the binomial theorem (which, incidentally, would not be used in this kind of problem because it is too cumbersome), let us put together an accumulation table by computing 4% interest on the balance of the investment at the beginning of each period.

Accumulation Table

Period	Beginning Balance	Interest at 4%	Ending Balance
1	\$5,000.00	.04(5,000.00) = \$200.00	\$5,200.00
2	5,200.00	.04(5,200.00) = 208.00	5,408.00
3	5,408.00	.04(5,408.00) = 216.32	5,624.32
4	5,624.32	.04(5,624.32) = 224.97	5,849.29
5	5,849.29	.04(5,849.29) = 233.97	6,083.26 = x

We see that after five six-month periods, the balance, x, will equal \$6,083.26 because \$1,083.26 of interest will have been earned.

Here is how the binomial theorem could be used to calculate x, the balance of the investment after 2.5 years:

$$x = \$5{,}000(1 + .04)^5$$

$$= \$5{,}000 \sum_{i=0}^{5} \binom{5}{i} 1^i (.04)^{5-i}$$

$$= \$5{,}000 \left[\binom{5}{0} 1^0(.04)^5 + \binom{5}{1} 1^1(.04)^4 + \binom{5}{2} 1^2(.04)^3 + \binom{5}{3} 1^3(.04)^2 + \binom{5}{4} 1^4(.04)^1 + \binom{5}{5} 1^5(.04)^0 \right]$$

Since $1^i = 1$, we may drop this factor from each term.

$$= \$5{,}000 \frac{5!}{0!5!}(.04)^5 + \frac{5!}{1!4!}(.04)^4 + \frac{5!}{2!3!}(.04)^3 + \frac{5!}{3!2!}(.04)^2 + \frac{5!}{4!1!}(.04)^1 + \frac{5!}{5!0!}(.04)^0$$

$$= \$5{,}000[(.04)^5 + 5(.04)^4 + 10(.04)^3 + 10(.04)^2 + 5(.04)^1 + 1(.04)^0]$$

$$= \$5{,}000[.0000001024 + 5(.00000256) + 10(.000064) + 10(.0016) + 5(.04) + 1]$$

$$= \$5{,}000(1.2166529024)$$

$$= \$6{,}083.26$$

Fortunately, there are tables in Appendix A that perform these calculations for the analyst. Our task now is to see how they may be used.

Discrete Compounding and Discounting

Consider again the continuum previously presented and the accompanying accumulation table. What was being done? An initial sum of money was brought forward in time, accumulating interest as it went along. Let us use the notation below to develop the accumulating process.

$f(i, r)$, where: f indicates the forward direction.
i indicates that i periods have passed, where $i = 0, 1, 2, \ldots, n$.
r indicates the rate of interest.

Suppose we have \$1 (or 1 monetary unit regardless of national designation) and wish to determine its value after one period has passed and $r\%$ interest has been earned. We would have

$$f(1, r) = 1 + r(1) = (1 + r)$$

Now assume we wish to know the value of our original \$1 after two periods have passed and interest has been earned (compounded) on the interest at the end of the first period as well as on the original principal (in other words, interest has been earned on the balance at the end of the first period). We would have

$$\begin{array}{rcccc} & \text{Original dollar} & \text{First period's interest} & \text{Second period's interest} \\ f(2, r) = & 1 & + \; r & + \; r(1 + r) \\ = & \multicolumn{3}{l}{1 + 2r + r^2 = (1 + r)^2} \end{array}$$

After three periods we have

$$\begin{array}{rccccc} & \text{Original dollar} & \text{First period's interest} & \text{Second period's interest} & \text{Third period's interest} \\ f(3, r) = & 1 & + \; r & + \; r(1 + r) & + \; r(1 + r)^2 \\ = & \multicolumn{4}{l}{1 + r + r + r^2 + r + 2r^2 + r^3} \\ = & \multicolumn{4}{l}{1 + 3r + 3r^2 + r^3} \\ = & \multicolumn{4}{l}{(1 + r)^3, \textit{according to the binomial theorem}} \end{array}$$

Similarly, after i periods, we obtain

$$f(i, r) = (1 + r)^i \tag{1}$$

This is the formula for Table 1 in Appendix A.

Let us use (1) to solve our previous problem. The continuum is repeated on page 268.

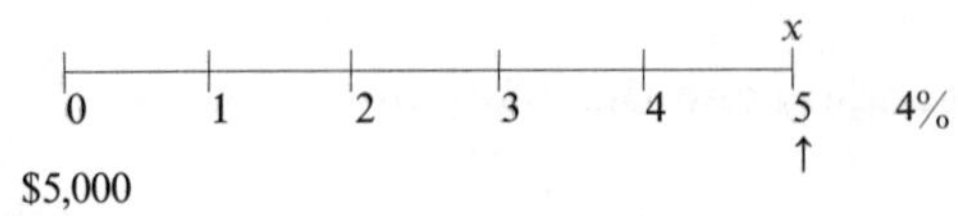

We wish to bring the \$5,000 forward (in relation to the arrow) 5 periods:

$$x = \$5{,}000(1.04)^5 = \$5{,}000f(5, 4)$$
$$= \$5{,}000(1.2167)$$
$$= \$6{,}083.50$$

Note that $(1.04)^5$ is $(1 + .04)^5$ or a particular example of $(1 + r)^i$.

(The \$.24 difference between our answer using the binomial expansion, \$6,083.26, and the answer obtained using Table 1, \$6,083.50, is due to the fact that Table 1 is only a four-place table; with six- or eight-place tables, the difference would vanish. For most applications, four-place accuracy is quite adequate.)

In cost analysis applications, it is much more customary to consider the reverse or discounting process. In these cases, estimates of future sums of money must be brought backward in time. The formula for discounting could be developed in much the same way as the formula for compounding. The result would be

Key:

$b(i, r)$, where: b indicates the backward direction.
i indicates that i periods have passed, where $i = 0, 1, 2, \ldots, n$.
r indicates the rate of interest.

$$b(i, r) = \left(\frac{1}{1 + r}\right)^i \qquad \textbf{(2)}$$

This is the formula for Table 2 in Appendix A.

Formula (2) would be used to solve the problem diagrammed in the continuum below.

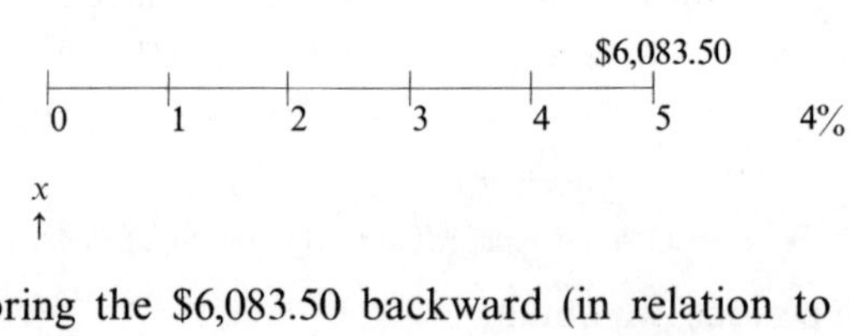

We wish to bring the \$6,083.50 backward (in relation to the arrow) five periods:

$$x = \$6{,}083.50\left(\frac{1}{1.04}\right)^5 = \$6{,}083.50b(5, 4)$$
$$= \$6{,}083.50(.8219)$$
$$= \$5{,}000.03$$

(This would be an even \$5,000 if we had six- or eight-place tables and had used \$6,083.26.) Observe that discounting has here undone the results of our former compounding process in symbols,

$$f(i, r)b(i, r) = (1 + r)^i \left(\frac{1}{1 + r}\right)^i = 1.$$

So far we have discussed moving only single amounts forward or backward through time. What would we do if there were adjacent repetitions of these amounts? Such adjacent repetitions are called annuities. We can see what it is all about by considering two cases.

Case 1:

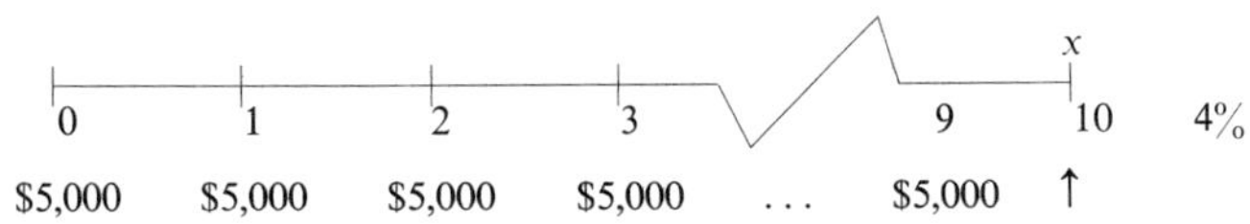

A man agrees to invest \$5,000 each period, starting immediately and continuing until 10 such investments have been made. He will receive his total investment back in ten periods with interest compounded at 4%. How much will he receive?

We shall bring all the \$5,000 investments forward in relation to the arrow:

$$\begin{array}{lllll} & \text{Investment at 0} & & \text{Investment at 1} & & \text{Investment at 9} \\ x = & \$5{,}000f(10, 4) & + & \$5{,}000f(9, 4) & + \cdots + & \$5{,}000f(1, 4) \end{array}$$

$$= \$5{,}000 \sum_{i=1}^{10} f(i, 4)$$

It would be convenient to have a table that did this summation for us. And so we have—Table 3 in Appendix A. The formula for Table 3 is[1]

$$F(n, r) = \sum_{i=1}^{n} (1 + r)^i = \sum_{i=1}^{n} f(i, r)$$

$$\begin{aligned} x &= \$5{,}000F(10, 4) \\ &= \$5{,}000(12.4864) \\ &= \$62{,}432.00 \end{aligned}$$

[1] The reader can perhaps convince himself that this relationship is true as follows:

$$\begin{aligned} f(1, 4) &= 1.0400 \\ f(2, 4) &= 1.0816 \\ f(3, 4) &= 1.1249 \\ F(3, 4) &= \underline{\underline{3.2465}} \end{aligned}$$

Case 2:

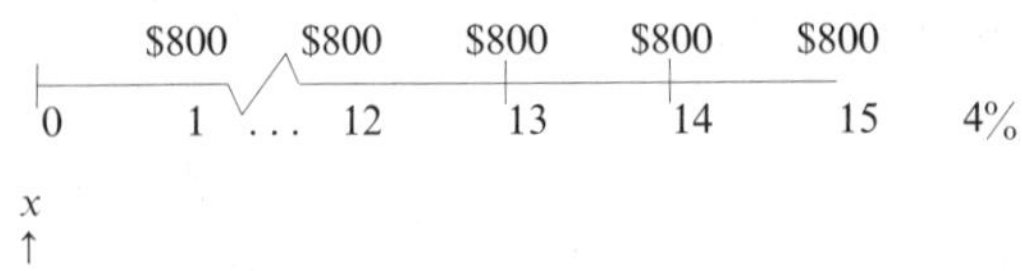

An investment promises to return \$800 each period, beginning at the end of the present period and continuing until the end of period 15. If 4% interest can be earned each period, what is the maximum amount that should be invested today?

We shall bring all the \$800 payoffs backward in relation to the arrow:

Payoff at 1	Payoff at 2		Payoff at 14	Payoff at 15

$$x = \$800b(1, 4) + \$800b(2, 4) + \cdots + \$800b(14, 4) + \$800b(15, 4)$$

$$x = \$800 \sum_{i=1}^{15} b(i, 4)$$

Table 4 in Appendix A conveniently performs this summation for us. The formula for Table 4 is[2]

$$B(n, r) = \sum_{i=1}^{n} \left(\frac{1}{1+r}\right)^{i} = \sum_{i=1}^{n} b(i, r)$$

$$\begin{aligned} x &= \$800B(15, 4) \\ &= \$800(11.1184) \\ &= \$8{,}894.72 \end{aligned}$$

This is the maximum amount we should invest, because if we invest anything more than this, we shall not get a 4% return. Conversely, if we invest less than \$8,894.72, we shall get a return in excess of 4%.

[2] The reader can check this relationship as follows:

$$\begin{aligned} b(1, 4) &= .9615 \\ b(2, 4) &= .9246 \\ b(3, 4) &= .8890 \\ B(3, 4) &= \underline{\underline{2.7751}} \end{aligned}$$

Preliminary Summary

Direction in Relation to Equating Point (Arrow)	Single Figure	Adjacent Repeated Amounts
Forward	$f(n, r)$	$F(n, r)$
Backward	$b(n, r)$	$B(n, r)$

With just a few more wrinkles we shall have a real grasp of moving money through time. Consider this problem:

A father wishes to provide his son with a small, varying annual income, beginning when the son is 27 and ending when he is 50. To provide this income, the father has agreed to make four equal annual deposits into a fund, beginning when the son is 20. The fund earns varying rates of interest during the term of the contract. The schedule of withdrawals and the applicable rates are

Birthdays	Yearly Withdrawal
27 through 29	\$6,000
30	\$8,000
31 through 50	\$9,000

Birthdays	Rate
20 to 29	6%
29 to 30	8%
30 through 50	10%

How much is each of the four payments made by the father?

As with all these problems, it is *highly advisable* to draw the continuum before attempting an algebraic model of the situation.

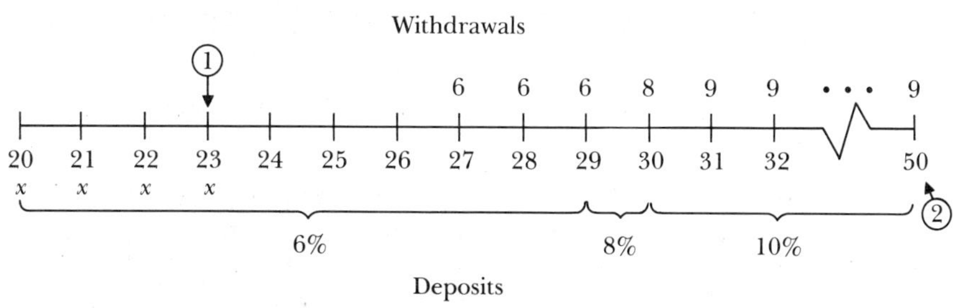

We are now faced with choice as to the point where we will equate the input (deposit) and output (withdrawal) cash flows. *Any of the* 31 *points above will yield the same answer*, although the algebra becomes more complicated at certain points. "Good" (in the sense of "easy") points are 20, 23, 24, 25, 26, 27, 29, 30, 31, and 50. Let us use age 23 (arrow 1) first.

$$\text{Deposits} = \text{Withdrawals}$$

$$\begin{aligned} x[F(3, 6) + 1.0000] &= \$9{,}000B(20, 10)b(1, 8)b(6, 6) \\ &\quad + \$8{,}000b(1, 8)b(6, 6) \\ &\quad + \$6{,}000B(3, 6)b(3, 6) \end{aligned}$$

$$\begin{aligned} x(3.3746 + 1.0000) &= \$9{,}000(8.5136)(.9259)(.7050) \\ &\quad + \$8{,}000(.9259)(.7050) \\ &\quad + \$6{,}000(2.6730)(.8396) \end{aligned}$$

$$x = \frac{\$68{,}703.58}{4.3746} = \$15{,}705.11$$

Comments:

1. Consider the input stream. To age 23 there are four payments of x and only three periods. $F(3, 6)$ brings payments at 20, 21, and 22 forward to 23. The payment at 23 does not require either compounding or discounting; hence we add 1.0000. Perhaps it will help to ponder the following equation:

$$x[F(3, 6) + 1.0000] = x \sum_{i=1}^{3} (1.06)^i + x = x \sum_{i=0}^{3} 1.06^i$$

2. The output streams are interrupted by breaks in the interest rates, which *must be honored*. Consequently, we first bring the 9,000 stream back to year 30 by $9{,}000B(20, 10)$. Since we have multiplied by $B(20, 10)$, we now have a single sum [$9,000(8.5136) = $76,622.40] sitting at 30. Using 8%, we bring this single sum back to the next interest break (at 29) by $b(1, 8)$. Our new single sum [$76,622.40(.9259) = $70,944.68] at 29 is then brought back at 6% for six periods to age 23 by $b(6, 6)$.

3. The $8,000 single figure is brought back (toward the arrow at age 23) in steps that *recognize the interest breaks.*

4. The three $6,000 withdrawals are first brought back three periods to age 26 by $B(3, 6)$. This makes them into a single figure [$6,000(2.6730) = $16,038], which is then brought back to our equating point at age 23 by $b(3, 6)$. It may help to contemplate the following equation:

$$\$6{,}000B(3, 6)b(3, 6) = \$6{,}000 \sum_{i=1}^{3} \left(\frac{1}{1.06}\right)^{i} \left(\frac{1}{1.06}\right)^{3}$$
$$= \$6{,}000 \sum_{i=1}^{3} \left(\frac{1}{1.06}\right)^{i+3}$$
$$= \$6{,}000 \sum_{i=4}^{6} \left(\frac{1}{1.06}\right)^{i}$$

This suggests an easier way (known as a "deferred annuity") to accomplish our purpose where the *interest rate does not change from the point of interest to the end of a particular series of payments.*

$$\$6{,}000 \sum_{i=4}^{6} b(i, 6) = \$6{,}000[B(6, 6) - B(3, 6)]$$
$$= \$6{,}000(4.9173 - 2.6730)$$
$$= \$13{,}465.80$$

Essentially we say that there are six payments of \$6,000 and then subtract the three nonexistent payments. Observe that this simple subtraction has replaced the complicated multiplication that follows:

$$\$6{,}000B(3, 6)b(3, 6) = \$6{,}000(2.6730)(.8396)$$
$$= \$13{,}465.50$$

The slight difference is due to the use of four-place tables.

For our second illustrative equating point we should probably use year 20, since most of the capital budgeting applications that we shall later study talk about "present values." However, I will select year 50 instead, since it will be more instructive. I strongly urge you to try year 20 for practice; you should get an answer very close to $x = \$15{,}705.11$.

Let us equate deposit and withdrawal streams at age 50:

$$xF(4, 6)f(5, 6)f(1, 8)f(20, 10) = \$6{,}000[F(2, 6) + 1.0000]f(1, 8)f(20, 10)$$
$$+ \$8{,}000f(20, 10)$$
$$+ \$9{,}000[F(19, 10) + 1.0000]$$

$$x(4.6371)(1.3382)(1.0800)(6.7275) = \$6{,}000(2.1826 + 1.0000)(1.0800)(6.7275)$$
$$+ \$8{,}000(6.7275)$$
$$+ \$9{,}000(56.2750 + 1.0000)$$

$$45.086337x = \$708{,}081.50$$

$$x = \frac{\$708{,}081.50}{45.086337} = \$15{,}705.01$$

Comments:

1. The input stream was first brought forward by $F(4, 6)$ to age 24, since that point represents four payments and four periods. The single amount ($xF(4, 6)$ = some single, but unknown, amount) was then brought forward from age 24 to the interest break at 29 using $f(5, 6)$. If we restate this process in summation notation, we will see an easier way to perform the calculation:

$$xF(4,6)f(5,6) = x \sum_{i=1}^{4} (1.06)^i (1.06)^5$$

$$= x \sum_{i=1}^{4} (1.06)^{i+5}$$

$$= x \sum_{i=6}^{9} (1.06)^i$$

$$= [F(9,6) - F(5,6)]$$

Here we essentially say that there are nine payments of x and then subtract the nonexistent five payments pertaining to years 24, 25, 26, 27, and 28. We can do this because *the interest rate has not changed over this range.*

$$xF(4,6)f(5,6) = x(4.6371)(1.3386) = 6.205367x$$

$$x[F(9,6) - F(5,6)] = x[12.1808 - 5.9753] = 6.2055x$$

(Six- or eight-place tables would eliminate the small difference.) The resulting single sum is now brought forward from 29 to the next interest break at 30 by $f(1, 8)$. Finally, the new single sum is brought forward to the point of equation, age 50, by $f(20, 10)$.

2. In the \$6,000 withdrawal series we must bring the amount forward initially to year 29. Since the \$6,000 at 29 needs no compounding to reach 29, we use

$$\$6{,}000[F(2,6) + 1.000] = \$6{,}000\left[\sum_{i=1}^{2} (1.06)^i + 1.0000\right]$$

$$= \$6{,}000 \sum_{i=1}^{2} 1.06^i + \$6{,}000$$

The resulting single figure [\$6,000(3.1836) = \$19,101.60] is then brought forward to year 50 in two stages to recognize the interest breaks.

3. The single figure of \$8,000 may be brought forward directly to year 50 by $f(20, 10)$.

4. The \$9,000 series includes 20 payments but only 19 interest periods; consequently, we use $F(19, 10)$ to compound 19 of the payments (years 31 through 49) and the term 1.0000 for the \$9,000 at year 50, which does not require compounding.

   We have

$$\$9{,}000[F(19, 10) + 1.0000] = \$9{,}000 \sum_{i=1}^{19} (1.10)^i + \$9{,}000.$$

$$= \$9{,}000 \sum_{i=0}^{19} (1.10)^i$$

Summary

1.

Direction in Relation to Chosen Equating Point (Arrow)	Single Figure	Adjacent Repeated Amount
Forward	$f(n, r)$	$F(n, r)$
Backward	$b(n, r)$	$B(n, r)$

2. Draw a continuum before attempting an algebraic solution.

3. If, in bringing an amount forward or backward, you encounter an interest break, determine an interest factor to that point (thereby obtaining a single sum). Then continue on to the next interest break or your point of equation, whichever comes first.

4. If you have adjacent repetition of an amount (an annuity), and the number of payments does not equal the number of periods,
   (a) you may have to add 1 to the interest factor to account for the *extra* payment; or
   (b) you may wish to consider using a deferred annuity technique to account for the *missing* payment or payments. This technique simplifies the arithmetic, but it is only available where the interest rate has not changed over the pertinent range.

5. You can solve money flow problems at any point on their continuums, but be careful not to make more algebraic work for yourself than necessary by choosing a "bad" (in the sense of "difficult") point.

Continuous Discounting

In our previous discussions of compounding and discounting, we limited ourselves to money flows that occurred at the beginning or end of a long period, such as a year. In many cases the assumption that a cash inflow happens at a particular instant is unrealistic indeed. To say that yearly earnings or yearly maintenance costs of a machine take place all at once on December 31 is somewhat unsettling. Rather, such earnings and costs occur at various recognizable times, in smaller amounts, during the entire year. How can we treat the discounting of such money flows? Well, one way to proceed would be to come up with a discounting rate for, say, a day and then go through 365 discountings each year $\left(\text{that is, } \left[1\Big/\left(1+\frac{r}{365}\right)\right]^{365}\right)$. However, it would soon dawn on us that a day, too, was arbitrary, and that precision would improve if the rate was for a second, or a microsecond. In the limit, we would abandon discrete intervals altogether and turn to continuous discounting.

But what does "continuous" mean symbolically? By continuous compounding at $r\%$, we mean use of the following compounding factor:

$$\lim_{n\to\infty}\left(1+\frac{r\%}{n}\right)^n = e^{r\%}$$

The corresponding discounting factor would be $e^{-r\%}$.

Consider next what is meant by nominal, as opposed to effective, interest.

Example: 4% compounded twice a year equals a "nominal" interest rate of 8% a year but yields, in fact, an "effective" rate of 8.16%, since $(1.04)^2 - 1 = 8.16\%$.

If we had an annual effective rate of $a\%$ and wished to compound n times a year, we would use a nominal rate, $r\%$ where $r < a$, as follows:

$$1 + a\% = \left(1+\frac{r\%}{n}\right)^n$$

In the limit, as $n \to \infty$, we would have

$$1 + a\% = \lim_{n\to\infty}\left(1+\frac{r\%}{n}\right)^n = e^{r\%}$$

The value $r\%$ may be obtained as follows:

$$1 + a\% = e^{r\%}$$

$$\ln(1 + a\%) = r\%$$

Reminder:
By definition, $n = 10^{\log n}$
Therefore, $\ln n = \log n \ln 10$
$= 2.30259 \log n$

If $a = 10\%$, $2.30259 \log(1.1) = r\%$
$2.30259(.0414) = .0953$

$$\begin{aligned} \text{Check: } \quad e^{.1} &= 1.1052 \\ -(e^{.09} &= 1.0942) \\ & \underline{\underline{.0110}} \times .53 = .0058 \end{aligned}$$

$\therefore$, $e^{.0953} = 1.0942 + .0058 = 1.1$ and $a\% = .1$, as expected.

In applied work, an analyst must be careful to distinguish which rate is called for. If the annual rate is *nominal*, continuous compounding at this annual rate may be performed. Furthermore, if the year is subdivided into, say, months, the annual money flows and the nominal annual rate are both divided by 12. For example,

$$\int_0^3 \$6{,}000e^{-.1t}\,dt = \int_0^{36} \$500e^{-.008\bar{3}t}\,dt$$

$$\frac{\$6{,}000}{-.1}(e^{-.3} - 1) = \frac{\$500}{-.008\bar{3}}(e^{-.3} - 1)$$

$$-60{,}000(.7408 - 1) = -60{,}000(.7408 - 1)$$

$$15{,}552 = 15{,}552$$

Note that e^{-r} is actually $e^{-r(1)}$ and is the continuous discounting factor for one period, whereas e^{-rt} is the factor for exactly t periods. The integration is used to smooth the dollar flows evenly over the period. It is easier to understand just why this results if you think about receiving a series of equal payments at n regularly spaced times during, say, one year ($T = 1$) and then sum the discounted series, that is:

$$\sum_{t=1}^{Tn} \frac{\$1}{n} e^{-tr(n)}.$$

Now increase the number of payments, n, and reduce the rate, $r(n)$, accordingly to see what the new summed series equals. Continue to do this, and as n gets very large, you will readily agree that the smoothing is reflected by $\int_0^T \$1e^{-rt}\,dt$.

Example: A building contractor is trying to decide whether to purchase a fleet of six trucks. He wishes to have approximately a 15% annual return on his investment and needs to know what minimum amount of monthly revenues is necessary to generate this return. A truck costs \$20,000 and should have a useful life of four years, at the end of which time it may be sold for \$3,000. Monthly costs for maintenance, repairs, gas, oil, licenses, road taxes, and so forth have been estimated to average \$600 per month per truck.

Solution: Key: M = monthly revenue

$$\frac{15\%}{12} = .0125$$

$$\overbrace{\int_0^{48} (M - \$600)e^{-.0125t}\,dt}^{\text{Earnings}} + \overbrace{\$3{,}000e^{-.6}}^{\text{Salvage}} = \overbrace{\$20{,}000}^{\text{Cost}}$$

$$\frac{(M - \$600)}{-.0125}(e^{-.6} - 1) + \$3{,}000e^{-.6} = \$20{,}000$$

$$80(\$600 - M)(.5488 - 1) + \$3{,}000(.5488) = \$20{,}000$$

$$\$600 - M = \frac{18353.6}{80(-.4512)} = \$-508.47$$

$$M = \$1{,}108.47$$

Consequently, if the contractor can expect normalized monthly revenues for each truck of (\$1,108.47) or \$53,206.56 in total, he will achieve a 15% effective annual return on his investment.

Problems

1. Dick Wargo purchased a Chrysler for \$6,000. He was granted a trade-in allowance of \$1,352.44 for his old car and agreed to repay the balance in 12 equal monthly payments at $\frac{1}{2}\%$ per month interest (this is equivalent to a nominal annual rate of 6%). Assuming the first payment is due one month from the date of purchase, determine the amount of the monthly payments.

2. An enthusiast purchased a set of skis costing \$200 by paying \$36.02 down and signing an installment contract that called for 18 equal monthly payments beginning one month hence with interest at 1% per month. How much were his monthly payments?

3. Mrs. Strong purchased a family airplane for $132,434. She signed a contract calling for a 25% down payment and equal annual payments for the next four years, each payment to be made at the end of the year with interest at 8%. How much were Mrs. Strong's annual payments? Prepare a mortgage amortization table in support of your answer.

4. *Semiannual interest calculation, deposits received annually.* Solve for x:

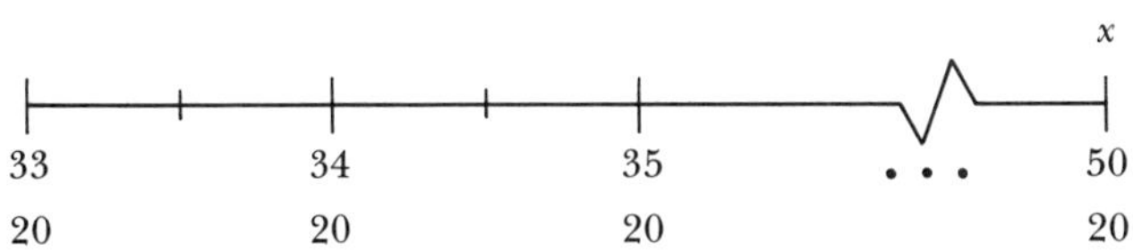

Nominal 10% per year, compounded semiannually

Comment: Since interest is compounded semiannually at 5%, more than 10% per year is *effectively* received. Once this rate is found, the deposits can be treated as consecutive instead of alternating.

5. Suppose interest were compounded monthly. State how you would treat this change in problem 4.

6. Mr. R. Comerford squirrels away $1,000 on January 1 of each year in a bank that pays him 6% annual interest compounded semiannually. He has been doing this since he was 20 and wishes to know how much he will have when he makes his annual deposit at age 40.

7. Roy Thompson wishes to provide for his retirement in style. He wants to know how much he would have 10 years from now if he deposits $20,000 immediately and a like sum each year thereafter including the 10th anniversary of the plan. He will receive 8% annual interest, but it will be computed semiannually. How much will these deposits amount to?

8. Wayne Corcoran devoutly wishes to establish a retirement (otherwise strangely known as a "sinking") fund to provide for him in his dotage when he attains the age of 45. Assuming that he is now 38, and that he feels $500,000 should suffice, what annual sum should he invest now and each year hereafter to and including year 45, at 8% interest compounded quarterly, to achieve his goal? Suppose he will settle for $100,000 when he is 39, all other facts remaining constant. Prepare an accumulation table to verify the new amount he must deposit to have $100,000 at age 39.

9. A company wishes to establish a *sinking fund* for the redemption of a bond issue 10 years hence. The fund will accumulate interest at 6% and the first of the equal payments into the fund will be made immediately, while the last payment will occur on the day of redemption. To redeem the issue, $200,000 will be needed. How much will each payment be?

10. A family is planning a vacation to the Bahamas, which will require \$12,304. There are five months to go until the day the family is to leave, and there is a financial institution available that will pay a nominal 6% interest per year, compounded monthly. What amount should be deposited immediately (March 1st) and each month thereafter to and including the day of departure to finance this little sojourn?

11. Population in a city is now 200,000, but it is growing geometrically at a rate of 5% per year. What will the population be 10 years hence?

12. A project is estimated to generate \$2,000 earnings for each of its first five years of life and \$1,000 for each of its remaining three years. If the required rate of return is 10%, what is the most that could be considered as an acceptable investment now? Assume that the forecasted cash earnings commence one year from now.

13. Solve for x at age 31:

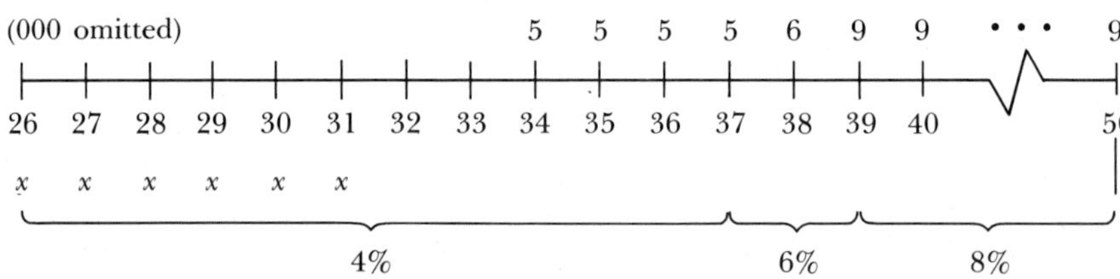

State your answer in sigma notation first, then in terms of f, F, b, B as needed, and finally numerically. Also, what answer do you obtain if you solve at age 37? (Answer: \$10.972)

14. Solve for x at age 18.

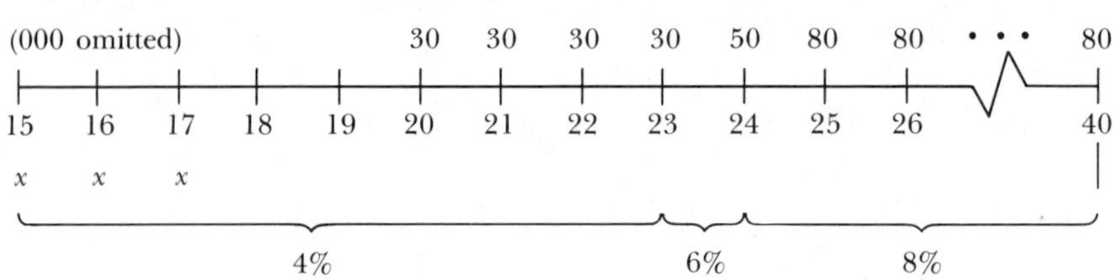

State your answer in sigma notation first, then in terms of f, F, b, B as needed, and finally numerically. Also, what answer do you obtain if you solve at age 24? (Answer: \$213,317.17)

15. A father wishes to provide his son with a small, varying annual income beginning when the son is 27 and ending when he is 50. To provide this income, the father has agreed to make four annual deposits into a fund, beginning when the son is 20. The fund established earns varying rates of interest during the term of the contract. The schedule of withdrawals and the rates applicable are as follows:

Birthdays	Yearly Withdrawal
27th to and including 29th	\$6,000
30th	\$8,000
31st to and including 50th	\$9,000

Interest rate schedule: Birthdays	Rate
From 20th to and including 29th	6%
From 29th to and including 30th	8%
From 30th to and including 50th	10%

Determine the amount of each deposit.

Note: Streams are to be equated at age 24.

16. Study the continuum shown below.

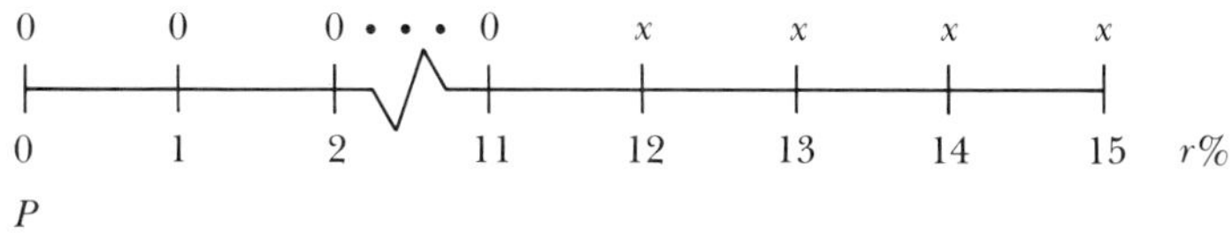

Other than taking each amount x back to time 0 separately, two approaches for obtaining the value P were discussed in the chapter. What are these approaches? Prove they are equal.

17. *Derivation of* $\int_0^T \$1e^{-rt}\,dt$. When discussing continuous discounting, instructions were given to derive

$$\lim_{n\to\infty} \sum_{t=1}^{Tn} \frac{\$1}{n} e^{-tr(n)} = \int_0^T \$1\, e^{-rt}\, dt$$

Either follow those instructions and obtain an intuitive feeling for how the integration smooths cash flows over a period, or determine a proof of the relationship shown above by the use of calculus. If you do the latter, you should keep the Maclaurin expansion for e^{ax} in mind, that is,

$$e^{ax} = \sum_{i=0}^{\infty} (ax)^i/i!$$

Bond prices: Problems 18 to 20 deal with the setting of bond prices. In its basic form, a bond is a contract that—in return for an invested amount—provides for the payment of a maturity value m years in the future as well as for a "coupon" interest payment each year (or half year) equal to a stipulated rate (the "coupon" rate) multiplied by the maturity value. The bond price (the invested amount) reflects a "yield" rate, which is greater than the coupon rate if the price is less than the maturity value and is less than the coupon rate if the bond price is greater than the maturity value. Bonds are "floated" (sold) at a "discount" when price is less than maturity value and at a "premium" when price exceeds maturity value.

18. A \$100,000, 3% coupon bond with a 10-year maturity is to be sold to yield 4%. Compute the proceeds from the sale of the issue.

19. A three-year bond with a 6% coupon and a maturity value of \$1,000,000 is to be sold at a discount to yield 10%. Prepare an accumulation table.

20. A company wishes to float a 5% coupon, \$100,000 bond issue that has a 10-year maturity. If the issue is to yield 4%, and interest is to be paid semiannually, how much can the company expect as proceeds from the sale? How much interest expense will show on the company's books for the first year, assuming the issue is floated January 1st?

Cost and installment sales: Most sales in the United States are facilitated by allowing customers to pay for their acquisitions in a series of equal installments extended over a period of time. These contracts are mortgages and at one time led to some interesting journal entries wherein the profits on the sales were not recognized until cash payments were recived. This seemed reasonable and objective; however, the procedure did give rise to an anomalous and provocative caption on the balance sheet called "Deferred Gross Profits from Sales." Apparently the embarrassment or the nuisance created by this caption, along with the desire to recognize the results of this year's sales this year, led the Accounting Principles Board in its Opinion 10 to outlaw the installment treatment. In its stead they substituted the requirements that (1) installment sales be treated as ordinary sales, and (2) provision for bad debts expense be made if doubt exists as to collections. The effect was to increase profits (because of instantaneous sales recognition) along with taxes. Furthermore, tax money was expended before collections sufficient to cover costs and taxes had been received, thereby depleting assets. In the installment characterization of the procedure, the sale of a product was encouraged (if not actually made possible) if it was essentially "sold a little at a time." Hence recognizing profit a little at a time had logic in its favor. Although the argument is subject to rebuttal, it could be said that the cost of nuisance and embarassment caused the overthrow of logic. *Note that there are no dollar measurements associated with nuisance and embarrassment, and yet they represent detriment and sacrifice.* How do you feel about these arguments concerning the treatment of installment sales?

Problems 21 to 22 ask you to compute payments and to formulate journal entries on an installment basis. Use your common sense and imagination as guides in writing the entries if you have never seen such entries before.

21. During 1973 \$600,000 of merchandise was sold on an installment basis with terms of \$100,000 down, 10% interest, and three equal annual payments for the balance. The merchandise cost \$400,000 and payments were received according to schedule—with no defaults. Prepare an amortization table and write journal entries for 1973 and 1974.

22. In days of yore, the Curtis-Burnham Company sold stage-coaches on an installment contract basis. During 1832, the company sold 10 coaches, which cost \$150,000, for \$225,000. The company received \$26,274 as down payment, and 8%, four-year contracts were written for the balance. In 1833 the company received \$55,000 from nine customers; the tenth never remitted because his coach was attacked by Indians and he, along with his business, was terminated. No recoveries of any sort were possible. Record journal entries for 1833 and 1834 and prepare an amortization table.

23. *Tax-sheltered annuities: boon or boondoggle? (prepared by Professors A. W. Corcoran and Gary Munroe).* Tax-sheltered annuities (TSA) were being sold (circa 1970) on the basis that the buyer could deposit money with an insurance company and postpone having it taxed until he retired, when, it was assumed, he would be in a lower tax bracket. The company would pay interest on the deposited money, charging a fee, of course, for the service. Postponing taxes is attractive; in reality, it may amount to eliminating them if present value of future tax payments is considered. On the other hand, dollars received many years from now may have low or zero present value, especially if the purchasing power of money is allowed for. Should a TSA have been considered a boon or a fraud given the assumed data below?

Yearly deposit: \$600	Tax rate until year 20: 35%
Yearly service fee: \$50	Tax rate in year 20 and after: 25%
Years to retirement: 20	Inflation: 5% per year
Private earnings rate: 8%	Company interest rate: 5%

Note:

For ease of computation, (1) ignore the mortality (probability of living to age x) distribution, which would render computations more challenging, and (2) assume that the policyholder would receive his accumulated fund upon retirement in year 20.

24. A company has amassed the following data on a particular machine, with the purpose of deciding both whether to buy the machine and when to replace it if it is purchased:

Immediate investment $\quad$ \$24,000
Salvage value $\quad$ $\$24{,}000e^{-.2T}$, where T is in terms of years

Annual earnings net of operating costs $\quad$ $\$10{,}000 - \$800T$

Required rate of return: 10%
Use continuous discounting.

Hint:

Determine the optimal replacement period (the "economic life") first and then use this result to decide whether the machine is acceptable.

Solving for n, the optimal replacement period, will require either

(1) trial-and-error employment of a table of logarithms or a table of values of e^{-x},

(2) use of the Newton Formula for finding roots: $x_{i+1} = x_i - f(x_i)/f'(x_i)$, or

(3) a computer program for finding roots.

25. *Economic life and Leibnitz's rule.* Find the economic life, t, for the model below, where economic life is defined as that value of t which maximizes V.

$$V = \int_0^t [R(T) - E(T)]e^{-iT}\,dT + S(t)e^{-it} - K$$

Key:

V = net present value of the investment
$R(T)$ = revenues expressed as a function of life, T
$E(T)$ = expenses expressed as a function of life, T
$S(T)$ = salvage value expressed as a function of life, T
K = original installed cost of the investment
i = annual rate of interest

26. *The multiplier.* The multiplier is a famous concept in economics. According to this concept, if the marginal propensity to consume is m, then each seller of goods in turn spends $m\%$ of what he receives, with the ultimate effect that the original investment, I, leads to total sales that are a scalar multiple of I.

Situation:

A homeowner hires a carpenter to build an addition for \$5,000. The carpenter spends 75% of this money on materials. His suppliers likewise spend 75% of what they receive. Seventy-five percent is, in fact, the society's marginal propensity to consume. Calculate (1) total sales resulting from the original investment, and (2) the associated multiplier.

Decisionmaking Costs

10

Every benefit has its costs, some of which may even be measurable in dollars

Corcoran

Introduction

The subject of cost accounting is far from exhausted once the discussion of cost systems and period budgeting is ended. Planning and controlling—or more simply, managing, since this broader term encompasses both—becomes the center of attention. Where are we going? How should we get there? These are the central questions that open a treasure chest full of complex and fascinating problems and techniques.

While it is possible for an adroit person to interpret past results so that they appear to favor his schemes, this in no way enables him to alter what has already happened. To talk down the effects of a catastrophe, and to appear unsurprised at any outcome—favorable or unfavorable—is certainly part of managing. But any effort to control an outcome must perforce precede the outcome itself. Since managing in this latter sense compels the manager to study the future, the costs and revenues that are relevant to the analysis are all estimates. Past costs are only pertinent insofar as they represent best estimates of future costs.

Relevant Costs and Revenues

In decisionmaking, the relevant costs and revenues are referred to broadly as incremental (or differential) costs and revenues. Differential costs are those future costs which will be incurred if a proposal is implemented, but which will not be incurred otherwise. Differential costs include the changes in future cost outlays brought about by a proposal, as well as opportunity costs and imputed costs. Such cost analysis requires the use of an active imagination; it cannot be done by calling upon memorized techniques. What costs—whether identified in records or not, whether quantified at present or not, whether in dollar terms or not—are likely to be affected by the proposals being analyzed?

Exhibit 1 summarizes the interrelationships among, and relevancies of, many types of cost.[1] Let us look more closely at some of them.

Opportunity Costs

The most difficult of the cost concepts presented in Exhibit 1 is that of opportunity costs. Opportunity costs, as traditionally defined in economics

Exhibit 1 Relationship of Future Differential Costs to Commonly Used Concepts for Planning Purposes

Name of the Specific Concept	Definition[1]	Relationship to Future Differential Costs
1. Variable cost	Costs that change in total with changes in the rate of output.	A reasonable approximation of future differential costs where factors other than volume exert no significant effect upon the behavior of total future costs and either the concept of value in alternate use is inapplicable or current recorded costs of variable services on hand are roughly equal to their anticipated future replacement costs.
2. Fixed cost	Costs that do not change in total as the rate of output of a concern or process varies.	Services may have future differential cost if they possess value in alternate use; otherwise inapplicable to planning.
3. Opportunity cost	Measurable advantage forgone as a result of rejecting alternate uses of resources.	Synonymous with future differential costs, except that the measure of advantage forgone from other alternatives is excluded from the cost calculation and reintroduced in the form of comparative margins.
4. Outlay cost	Financial expenditures recorded in the books of account.[2]	An element of future differential cost representative of future outlays. Does not take account of value in alternate use of services on hand or residual.

[1] Source: Edward L. Wallace, "Some Comments on the Statement of Planning Costs," *The Accounting Review*, July 1957, p. 458.

Exhibit 1 (Cont.)

Name of the Specific Concept	Definition[1]	Relationship to Future Differential Costs
5. Out of pocket	Costs that, with respect to a given decision of management, give rise to cash expenditures.	Same as future outlay costs.
6. Imputed cost	Costs that do not at any time involve actual cash outlay and which do not, as a consequence, appear in the financial records; nevertheless, such costs involve a forgoing on the part of the persons whose costs are being calculated.	Future differential cost.
7. Discretionary cost	Costs not essential to accomplishment of a managerial objective.	If to be incurred on a project, they are future differential costs subject to the same limitations as future outlay costs.
8. Postponable cost	Costs that may be shifted to the future with little or no effect on the efficiency of current operations.	Same as discretionary costs.
9. Differential cost	Increases or decreases in total costs; or changes in specific elements of cost, that result from any variation in operations.	Synonymous with future differential costs if not based upon recorded costs. Otherwise a good approximation where value in alternate use is inapplicable or where current recorded cost of differential services on hand is roughly equal to anticipated future replacement cost.
10. Unavoidable cost	Costs that cannot be avoided by contraction of operations.[3]	Services may have future differential cost if they possess value in alternate use; otherwise not a planning cost.
11. Avoidable cost	Costs that can be avoided by a contraction of operations.[4]	Same as recorded differential costs
12. Sunk cost	Historical costs that are irrecoverable in a given situation.	Not a future differential cost; inapplicable to planning.

[1] Except where otherwise noted the definitions set forth have been taken from the "Report of the Committee on Cost Concepts and Standards" *Accounting Review*, April, 1952.

[2] Joel Dean, *Managerial Economics* (Englewood Cliffs, N.J.: Prentice-Hall, 1951), pp. 259–66.

[3] Ibid.

[4] Ibid.

under the assumption of full employment of resources, represent a forgoing of advantage that the firm would have enjoyed had the item being valued been employed in its next best alternative use. Full employment of resources may be taken to mean that resources are not idle and substitute services are not available. These costs are very important for planning purposes. Where a decision must be made to continue the production of a product, to determine a minimally acceptable selling price, or to select one investment proposal instead of another, opportunity costs must be considered. For example, in decision making the cost of using idle capacity in a factory is zero unless usage causes earlier asset retirement, or unless the production facilities may be leased to an outside party or used to produce something else. If it is the greatest amount, the forgone rental income is the opportunity cost of using the facilities for some proposed activity.

Assume that inputs (resources) have greater value in alternative use as replacements than they have in terms of net proceeds from disposal (that is, selling prices of resources less their costs to dispose). Under this condition, income forgone in the next best alternative is the measure of opportunity costs only where no substitutes are known to be available. Where substitutes are known to be available, the measurement becomes not that of income forgone, but rather that of determination of the theoretical cost of obtaining such substitute or replacement services for the alternative project as would enable it to be implemented. Thus where no substitute input is available, the use of even the smallest, seemingly insignificant input in the chosen employment results in an opportunity cost equal to the entire forgone income of the next best alternative proposal. On the other hand, if the input employed in one alternative has ready substitutes, the opportunity cost of so using it is measured in terms of replacement costs. Wallace has commented on this point:

> Services may have utility on other projects being planned for execution concurrent with the project in question, or following it. If this is the case, these services have an alternate use value on other projects and it should be measured, adjusted for time differences and interim costs, and compared with net proceeds [of disposal]. Cash equivalent, under these conditions, is the higher of net proceeds or adjusted replacement costs.[2]

Example: A machine that generates profits at a rate of $200 per hour has a unique part. The acquisition of another machine that needs this part is being contemplated; however, if the part is removed, the first machine stops.

[2] Ibid., p. 453.

Exhibit 2 Examples of Opportunity Costs

When value in alternative use is considered, variable costs may not be a cost for planning purposes while fixed costs may. For example, end of season style merchandise may have no value in alternate use except as special sale merchandise. For planning purposes there is no alternative; therefore, the merchandise has no cost. Nevertheless, these merchandise costs will appear as variable costs. On the other hand, a warehouse now owned by the company may, at least insofar as recorded depreciation is concerned, be considered a fixed cost not applicable to planning. If it could be rented, however, it has a cost for planning purposes equal to the rent foregone by its use in operations.[1]

. . . In a cloth mill that spins its own yarn, for example, the cost of yarn is really the price at which the yarn could be sold if it were not woven into cloth. For the problem of measuring the profitability of the weaving operations in order to decide whether to expand them or abandon them, it is this opportunity cost—the foregone revenue from not selling the yarn—that is relevant. In periods of boom demand, the use of a versatile bottleneck factor, such as scarce steel or scarce loom capacity, for making one product, involves the opportunity cost of not using it to make some other product that can also produce profits. The opportunity cost of producing heating oil in a modern, flexible refinery, for example, is the value of the gasoline that might otherwise have been made. For this reason, "gasoline equivalent" costing has considerable acceptance in this industry.[2]

For example, construction of a new building may exhaust available capacity of the central steam heating plant. Immediate expansion of the steam plant is unnecessary, but because the new building will be built expansion will be necessary before another can be constructed. One point of view might be that no differential cost attaches to the present building, but future construction will be charged with the whole of the cost of expanding the heating plant. Taken in another context, however, it might be presumed that management has considered alternate uses of the steam plant, including its use in the future for other buildings, and has decided to employ the present excess capacity for the projected building. This is to say management is willing to employ the capacity rather than withhold it for use in lieu of a future replacement, and that the cash equivalent of the heating plant input for the projected building is a proportionate share of expected future costs of expanding the heating plant after the project period has ended, adjusted for the time differences.[3]

[1] Edward L. Wallace, "Some Comments on the Statement of Planning Costs," *The Accounting Review*, July 1957, p. 449.

[2] Joel Dean, *Managerial Economics* (New York: Prentice-Hall, 1951), p. 259.

[3] Wallace, "Statement of Planning Costs," p. 453.

If the part could be readily replaced at a cost of $.10, then the cost of using the part for the proposal would be $.10.

Alternatively, if it takes a long time to acquire a replacement, even though the replacement only costs $.10, the cost to use the part on the proposal would be $200 per hour for every hour of leadtime discounted to the time of decision. At the expiration of the leadtime, when the part arrives, its $.10 cost would also be discounted.

If no replacement can ever be fashioned, the cost of using the part on the proposal is $200 per hour, discounted, for the life of the proposal (which would be limited either by the market life of the product, or by the life of the business, or by the life of the part, whichever was smallest).

Exhibit 2 contains further examples of opportunity costs. Note that the name "opportunity cost" indicates what these costs are; one must have an "opportunity" (in the sense of an alternative) before one can determine magnitude of the "cost." It is essential to keep in mind Dean's admonition:

> ... In business problems the message of opportunity costs is that it is dangerous to confine cost knowledge to what the firm is doing. What the firm is not doing but could do is frequently the critical cost consideration which it is perilous but easy to ignore.[3]

Imputed Costs

Another type of cost that causes some confusion is imputed cost. Imputed costs are those decisionmaking costs which do not at any time involve cash outlays but which, nevertheless, represent a sacrifice. The typical example of an imputed cost is the calculation of an interest charge on the capital committed to a project. There seem to be two popular ways of viewing the matter. Either the cost analyst uses the firm's cost of capital rate of return and views this as a measure of the benefit forgone by employing capital in the project, or he uses the borrowing rate of interest under the assumption that this reflects the cost that would have been incurred had funds actually been borrowed. In the first case, imputed interest is the same as opportunity cost in that the charge is for forgone revenue. In the second case, the analyst is approximating the cost of borrowing money. Since this latter situation ignores the pool concept of funds (which will be described in the next chapter), this book takes the position that interest should be imputed—where applicable—at the cost of capital.

[3] Joel Dean, *Managerial Economics* (New York: Prentice-Hall, 1951), p. 260.

Sunk Costs

A third type of cost that merits further consideration is sunk cost. Sunk costs are past cost outlays. Such costs are of no concern in planning. As an example, consider a machine that is obsolete and can never, in any way, be used again. Suppose further that the scrap value of the machine is equal to the costs of dismantling it, that the machine has a book value (original cost minus accumulated depreciation charges) of \$10,000, and that there is a 60% tax rate in effect. Then the sunk cost of the machine may be computed as follows:

Sunk cost = book value:	\$10,000
Opportunity value of machine when "employed" as disinvested capital (disposal) = tax savings recovered through write-off of the machine:	\$ 6,000

Oversights

Undoubtedly the preceding discussion aroused in you an appreciation of the complexity of the challenge of calculating decisionmaking costs. Yet the capriciousness of these costs has barely been exposed. Moreover, the presentation has focused solely on dollar measurements; it has made no mention of the effects that people and their attitudes have on the analysis and its implementation. Decisionmaking costs are elusive apparitions—they exist in alternatives, many of which go unrecognized.

How does one measure the forgoance in those alternatives which have been recognized? More precisely, how does one achieve acceptance of his measurements? Numbers can be assigned to anything. For instance, I can look at a building and say, "That is a 29." My problem is to convince you that I have not succumbed to idiocy. And if I get by you, how many others must I then confront? The economist would probably stop me sooner or later with some caustic remark to the effect that my measure could never be considered a common denominator like dollars. And he would be right; dollars are objective in the sense of being generally recognized as a common denominator. If objectivity is a prerequisite to respectability in measurement, the analyst would have to restrict measurement to popular yardsticks. To do so, however, would be to restrict his usefulness in the decisionmaking process. It may make sense to use "29" if the scale is understood by the decision maker irrespective of whether the rest of the world comprehends. After all, this sort of thing is done all the time in questionnaires that ask the reader to rate something on a scale of, say, 1 to 10. Subjectivity is, therefore, condoned in measurement.

The economist, when the truth is known, is not always pleased with subjective measurements. Years ago, two renowned men—one a mathematician, the other an economist—developed a construct known as utility theory that attempted to recognize that decision makers felt worse, for example, about losing $5,000 than they felt good about gaining $5,000. Through a series of questions they developed a utility function that reflected dollars and feelings for those dollars—however inspired. Yet, attractive as utility theory is theoretically, it has never achieved its deserved popularity practically. Among the reasons for its failure were the assertions that (1) once the function was determined, it could not be relied upon to exhibit stability from one day to the next—the decisionmaker's feelings changed from day to day; (2) the decisionmaker often turned out to be a group rather than an individual, and the group lacked unanimity; and (3) determining the function was time consuming and a nuisance to everyone involved. We shall develop utility concepts later.

There are practical measures of utility, fortunately, although they are not generally recognized as such. More will be said about these when we present inventory and queuing theory. These measures have to do largely with service level (probability of shortage or time spent waiting, for example) in a system.

Perhaps the wisest measurement of nondollar costs is simply to state what projects will be abandoned—at least temporarily—if some present proposal is implemented. For example, let us say that $6,000,000 will serve to construct a new library, or to extend a highway, or to expand some social program. *The cost to build the library is not just the $6,000,000 but also whatever* net benefits (*benefits net of* $6,000,000) *would have been forthcoming had the road been extended or the social program undertaken, and which must be forgone because they cannot now be funded. Alternatively, we can say that the cost to build the library is simply the forgone* benefits *of the road or the social program.* The sacrifice is diminished, of course, if these programs can be undertaken in the future. It is pedantic to ask whether the roads or the social program's benefits are the measure of the sacrifice, because this in turn calls for measures not now nor ever likely to be available. (If they became available, it would mean that everyone agreed on a common denominator, which would require Herculean persuasive effort or incredible legislation.)

It may help you visualize the immensity of the measurement requirements if you focus on the social program. Say that the program should result in the saving of a single life. What is the value of that single life? If the person were an Einstein, you might agree that the life had an infinite value. If the person were a derelict, you might agree his life had a zero value, but even then you might want to conjecture that he would do something of great value if he were saved. Of course, the person might also be saved only to do some great evil. The problem is eased somewhat if many people are saved because you could then enjoy the safety of numbers—given enough saving, someone worth the effort should be included. This is reminiscent of an argument made by John Maurice Clark in 1923:

> It only takes one bullet to kill a man, if it hits him, but "it takes a ton of lead," counting the bullets that miss. And the bullets that miss are just as necessary as those that hit, because no one can tell, when the ammunition is served out, which will find a mark . . . . In selling, the bullets that hit must pay for those that miss, and in many kinds of selling effort the hits are a small percentage, so that most of the expense must be allotted.[4]

Similar arguments about the saving of lives might be raised for the proposal to extend roads. And with either alternative, other measures than lives arise—"conveniences" of one sort or another are also among the benefits.

For emphasis, I will state again my personal conclusion that the wisest thing the analyst can do is to measure the dollar costs and to list what projects will be forsaken if a proposal is chosen.

Measuring the dollar costs and listing the forsaken projects may be very adequate for the decisionmaker's needs. It would certainly be more informative than just measuring dollar costs. To return to our previous example, a mayor interested in reelection might decide that building the roads would win him the most votes. He could defend his choice on the grounds that he had helped the greatest number of people given the limited resources at his disposal. The humanists would criticize him for not helping those in the greatest need (the program), and the intellectuals would find fault with him for not providing means to develop great minds (the library). (We have now come full circle to the parable of the three blind men and the elephant with which this book opened.)

We have also arrived at the effect people and their attitudes have on costs. The unwritten assumption underlying all our discussions has been that our analyst was omniscient, persevering, unselfish, and working for a decision maker who wished to know the truth. The absurdity of this kind of assumption drew the following comment in 1923:

> One source of confusion lies in the fact that the economist . . . tends to give terms the meaning they would have to an omniscient observer, forgetting that if such beings exist they have no need of his analyses.[5]

---

[4] John Maurice Clark, *Studies in the Economics of Overhead Costs* (Chicago: The University of Chicago Press, 1923), p. 61.

[5] Ibid., p. 44.

Most people assess nondollar costs all the time. In their conversations, for instance, they constantly decide whether saying all that is on their minds is worth the cost. The tendency, indeed the advisability, of adapting comments to the listener occurs in written analysis as well as in speech.

If we are not to delude ourselves, we must be ever aware that costs are estimated for some people by some other people, and that every man who ever lived did whatever he did because he sought his own happiness either immediately or in the future. The philanthropist is merely one who has had

Exhibit 3 Attitudinal Determinants of Cost

What we really have to deal with here is a minimum cost rather than a constant cost, although "shutdown cost" would be even more descriptive. This minimum is itself somewhat indefinite, because the question how much expense it is worthwhile to incur in tiding over a shutdown depends entirely on how long the winter of discontent is likely to be and how warm a summer may be expected afterward. If the manager is confident of a quick and complete resumption, he may keep his foremen and his best laborers on the payroll, while if there are no very definite prospects of improvement he will merely try to keep the plant from serious deterioration with as little expense as possible.[1]

"External" costs are those costs of a decision or program that fall beyond the boundaries of the decisionmaker's organization or beyond the scope of interest of the cost analyst's customer. Obviously, whether a given cost is external or internal depends upon how high up in the decisionmaking hierarchy the decisionmaker happens to be or how comprehensive his concern . . . . As a matter of practicality and of choice, therefore, the cost analyst must determine the effective boundaries of his concern—and these boundaries will be less than worldwide and everlasting.[2]

As we mentioned earlier, cost depends not only upon the decisionmaking level but also upon the imagination and ingenuity of the decisionmaker. Every time Colonel Smith, for instance, discovers a new and better alternative use for his airmen, the cost of using them to repair a runway increases. Similarly, of course, every time he thinks of some more ingenious new way to repair the runway, the cost of repairing it decreases. But what level of imagination should the cost analyst assume?[3]

Dollars are not all alike. It matters a good deal whether the dollars spent for a given program come from your pocket or someone else's. It also matters whether the dollars saved by a department are available to that department or whether they will revert back to the (company) treasury.[4]

[1] John Maurice Clark, *Studies in the Economics of Overhead Costs* (Chicago: The University of Chicago Press, 1923), p. 54.

[2] R.E. Bickner, "Concepts of Economic Costs," in *Cost Considerations in System Analysis*, ed. Gene H. Fisher (New York: American Elsevier Publishing Co., 1971), pp. 37–38.

[3] Ibid., p. 46.

[4] Ibid., p. 50.

the good fortune to achieve public acclaim when pursuing his happiness; nevertheless, he remains as selfish as you and I.[6]

Cost calculations are influenced by optimism, pessimism, imagination, ingenuity, the decisionmaker's level in the organization, scope of interest, concern over who pays the cost and who enjoys the benefits, and appreciation of what must be sacrificed because resources are limited. Exhibit 3 gives some further insights into the effects of human behavior and attitudes.

Alexander Dumas is Alive and Well

To illustrate the calculation of incremental costs, and to further appreciation of how attitudes and personalities influence the costs that are calculated, it seems appropriate to contrive a plausible story in which costs are manipulated to suit the designs of a conspirator. So, with apologies to Alexander Dumas, we commence our tale:

Caribou Snow Equipment Company

Characters: Hagar l'Horrible, president of Caribou Snow Equipment Company
Catherine de'Medici, vice-president of the Ski Division
Edmund Dantes, controller of the Ski Division

Scene I

Setting: The Caribou Snow Equipment Company is situated in Caribou, Maine. The time is October 1974. Caribou manufactures a variety of winter sports equipment and accordingly has separate divisions for sleds, toboggans, skis, snowshoes, skates, and flying saucers. The president is a blustery, energetic person, blundering but well liked,

---

[6] This comes under the doctrine of hedonism, which declares pleasure to be the principal good that should be the aim of all action. Usually hedonism reduces to arguments between egoism and utilitarianism. Egoism seeks self-happiness first. Utilitarianism seeks the greatest happiness of the greatest number first, and self-happiness second. Intention would appear to be the issue, with the egoist having ever at hand the irrefutable argument that even in the extreme one may do distasteful things because this makes him happier than if he did otherwise. For further discussion read John Stuart Mills' *Utilitarianism*, or the Encyclopedia of Philosophy.

although only occasionally given to attacks of cleverness. The vice-president of the ski division, on the other hand, is diabolically clever, Machiavellian in nature, and constantly involved in intrigue. The controller is a pleasant and capable young man but one who is easily duped. The president and vice-president are speaking in the former's office.

Hagar: Great morning, Kate. A bit brisk but just look at that sun shine! Care for a cigar? Oh, uhh. . . sorry.

Catherine: That's all right. I've tried cigars but most brands have seemed harsh. I have a friend, Monsieur Remy, who makes very aromatic cigars especially for me. I'll ask him to make a box for you sometime soon. I often give them as gifts to friends who like to smoke.

Hagar: I think I have been around some of those before. Very nice. Didn't your son Charlie smoke them fairly regularly? Too bad he passed away. The company had great expectations for Charlie, but of course we have been very pleased that you were able to take his place.

Catherine: I miss Charlie, too. He was considerate and imaginative and often sought my advice. But I'd rather not talk about him—it is still too recent. . . . I like your description of the brisk morning. Did you know that it was 23° below at 6 A.M.? I was rather hoping that you wanted to send me to Florida to look into the water ski business.

Hagar: No way. In fact, on the contrary. Your division shows a substantial estimated net loss for this year, and I think Caribou should perhaps get out of the ski business.

Catherine: I was aware of the loss but I thought that some of the other divisions—Flying Saucers comes to mind—had done worse.

Hagar: No, Kate, your division was the only one to suffer a loss. Snowshoes seems to be doing well, and so are Sleds, Toboggans, and Skates. Flying Saucers are slowing but still generating profit. The saucer fad is undoubtedly over but the residual sales seem to be substantial enough to justify keeping saucers in the product line. No, Skis is the problem.

Catherine: Well the results may not have been favorable, but surely the future is not as bleak as you seem to think. You must remember that I inherited a lot of problems.

Hagar: Like what?

Catherine: My predecessor had very poor organization and even less grasp of the pulse of ski market clientele. Not only was the flow of work poorly arranged, but his scheduling encouraged feast-or-famine production. As a result, morale was low and the factory spent too much time and money hiring and training personnel. Add to this the fact that the winter weather in 1974 was mild and virtually snowless and you will understand some of the problems I had to face.

Hagar: I had no idea Charlie was so disorganized.

Catherine: Oh yes! But his lack of understanding of the market was by far the worst cause of difficulties.

Hagar: How so?

Catherine: He just did not realize the philosophy of our times. He did not see that parents today feel compelled to give their children at least as much as other kids their age have. I don't think he knew that psychologists tell parents they cannot raise their children much differently from their peers without creating social misfits. The message comes insistent and ubiquitous: To deprive your child of things his friends enjoy is to risk wounding his psyche—to create an outcast.

Hagar: Is that so? I guess I recognized this but always resented the kids as a bunch of pampered freeloaders.

Catherine: Well you were certainly perceptive. Furthermore, have you noticed how the kids act collectively on individual parents?

Hagar: What do you mean?

Catherine: Typically a kid approaches his parent with "The gang is all going to the dance. Can I go? I'll be home by 1:30." Or with "Jim Smith has a 10-speed bike. So do Susan Jones and Mike Jacobs. Several of the other kids have said their parents were going to buy them one. Will you get me a 10-speed?" To say "No" seems heartless and tantamount to admitting failure; moreover, biking is healthy and good fun.

Hagar: Oh, sure. That's the old "Together we conquer; divided, we fall" ploy. Those kids may be pampered, but they're not dumb! You mean to say Charlie didn't understand all this?

Catherine: If it ever did cross his mind, he never appreciated how the pattern could be used to Caribou's advantage.

Hagar: He must have been dumb or blind. Uhh. . . . how would you make use of the pattern?

Catherine: The "collective-individual, deprived" pattern is open to many strategies. If you went to a leading ski resort and observed the skiers, you would see that the greatest proportion of the crowd was under twenty, dressed in flashy parkas and deluxe buckle boots, and riding on shiny, new expensive skis with elaborate bindings—all while carrying a $25 set of poles. Simple wood skis are passé; their owners are either impoverished or adults (or both). Even adults—though few in number—mostly have complete regalia. It is status to them, as much as anything.

Hagar: I went skiing twice last year and found myself part of an immense crowd just like you describe. On the first outing I was forever being shoved back in lift lines by kids with fancy new skis who pushed in front of me. About the fourth time it happened, I drove my pole into one of the kid's new skis and raked a scratch ten inches long. That made me feel some better. Later I was almost run over by a teenager who was skiing as fast as he could down the fall line. Was I mad! Not ten minutes afterwards, the same thing happened with a different kid. I could have killed him! On the second outing, however, I came equipped with a can of mace. Unfortunately, I missed on my first two tries because I had not allowed for the speed of closure. I nailed the third guy, though, and you never saw such a wreck!! Snapped a pole, released a ski and dragged it while he bounced fifty yards all the while clutching his eyes. It was beautiful! I tell you that irresponsible bum learned one hell of a lesson that day.

Catherine: What an aggressive leader you are! It is a pleasure to work with someone so courageous and inventive.

Hagar: Well it was little enough to do. Someone has to teach manners if the parents fail to do so. But I have digressed and distracted you from saying how you would use the "collective-deprived" pattern.

Catherine: I believe it would be an easy matter to identify the athletic leaders in grade schools and high schools. Then, having isolated the most admired athletes, I would give them Caribou skis. This would not fail to draw the attention of the other kids, who would then set the pattern to work.

Hagar: Amazing!

Catherine: Then I would raise price and put Caribou in the luxury class. We can outproduce competitors and the quality of the Caribou ski is unquestioned. I think we could segment the market, putting our present ski at the top of the price list, and then utilizing our remaining productive capacity to make lower quality skis for beginners.

Hagar: Right on, Kate—we haven't been thinking big enough. I would need some data, though, to convince the board of trustees.

Catherine: I'll look into that. Dantes should be able to provide appropriate breakdowns with my help.

Scene II

Setting: Ms. de'Medici's office, one hour later. Mr. Dantes has just entered.

Dantes: I just received word that you wished to see me, Ms. de'Medici.

Catherine: Yes, Edmund, we have a special study to do for Mr. l'Horrible. He was disturbed about Skis' estimated $90,000 loss for this year and is considering dropping us from the product line. We have to convince him that Skis has vitality.

Dantes: Just what do you have in mind?

Catherine: Well, as Hagar observes, Caribou is not running a charity. If it can get greater return by depositing the money tied up in Skis in a bank account, then that is what should be done.

Dantes: That is an awful cold position to take, what with all the dismissals it would entail. Yet it may be wise management, nevertheless. On balance, though, I don't see how he can be thinking of dropping Skis. Caribou sells sleds, skates, and other things because Skis has made the name known and recognized for quality. Stop producing skis and Caribou will go out of business in two or three years.

Catherine: That may or may not be true, Edmund, but nevertheless we should maintain that perspective when preparing our analyses. If we can't show that Skis can expect good profits in 1975, I fear you and I and the whole division will be looking for new work in the near future. Partly, the troubles of 1974 can be attributed to the lack of snowfall. Fortunately, early predictions for this winter are that it will be favorably cold. I also think we can raise prices while offering beginners' and masters' models. On the negative side, however, skis might be regarded as a postponable luxury commodity in the 1975 recession-depression period. Then, too, if there is another fuel shortage, the ski slopes may beckon to our customers in vain. In any case, whatever sales we estimate must be able to withstand the brunt of inquiry.

Dantes: Actually, the ordinary income statement is misleading in the type of study needed here. Certain expenses are apportioned to Skis that would continue whether Skis existed or not. What we need to know is, first, whether Skis is contributing to profits, and second, if it is, whether Skis consumes scarce resources efficiently with relation to the rest of Caribou.

Catherine: Edmund, I don't want you to concern yourself about the rest of Caribou—at least not just now. Our task is to stay alive in Skis. A year from now or possibly sooner, if Skis shows marked improvement, we may be promoted.

Dantes: But if you were to be promoted, the only position you could occupy would be president. I had not heard that Mr. l'Horrible was planning to retire.

Catherine: Well stranger things have often happened. Certainly the board cannot be overjoyed with Caribou's recent progress, and then, too, Hagar is no longer a young man.

Dantes: But assuredly you would do nothing to suggest Hagar's diminishing competence to the board?

Catherine: I doubt that it would be necessary. One thing I am sure of, though, is that your loyalty and diligence will be rewarded if I become president.

Dantes: You are most geneous, Madame.

Catherine: (looking intently at Dantes and speaking gravely) To my friends, my generosity is a sacred obligation; to my enemies, my vengeance is irresistible.

Dantes: (repressing an involuntary shudder) A logical beginning for our study is to determine Skis' income on a differential basis for 1974. Our regular income statement neither itemizes overhead nor indicates cost behavior for either the overhead or the selling and administration items. I shall have to prepare this data first and when I have done so, I'll show you the report. After that I shall need to determine alternative uses of Skis' resources—within the limitations you have so clearly stipulated—so that we may calculate the incremental costs of the Ski Division.

Catherine: Fine. You will be discreet of course.
Dantes: You may count on it, Madame.
Catherine: Do what you must and have your report ready by tomorrow afternoon at four.

Scene III

Setting: Ms. de' Medici is alone in her office. Five minutes have passed since the departure of Edmund Dantes. She has furtively pressed a mechanism on her desk that reveals a small black book in a hidden drawer. Pensively, she has located a name and has dialed the associated number.
Catherine: Bonjour, Monsieur Remy. It is I.
Remy: Your servant, Madame.
Catherine: I shall have need of a box of your special cigars, Monsieur Remy. I shall have two thousand dollars for you if you have them ready by the day after tomorrow.
Remy: Consider it done, Madame. I'll await your arrival at ten p.m.
Catherine: I shall be there. Adieu.
Catherine: (musing to herself) Now who is the trustee most susceptible to suggestion? Timing will be all-important. Not only must Hagar develop an indisposition, but the seeds of dissatisfaction must be sown before he does so and I must have made my competence known. . .

Scene IV

Setting: Ms. de'Medici's office at four the following afternoon. Dantes is presenting his preliminary report (see Exhibit 4).
Dantes: I used a computer regression program to obtain a breakdown of the costs and expenses for 1974. Does it suggest anything to you?
Catherine: As I understand it, Edmund, your next step will not be to develop strategic changes for 1975 at this time, but rather an analysis of the costs that should have been charged in 1974 to Skis on an incremental basis.
Dantes: That is true, but it would help in the work ahead if I knew where we were heading. It won't be easy going to the other divisions to find out whether or not they have alternative uses for Ski facilities, especially when I can't divulge our purposes. To have to return a second time to ask more questions would only arouse suspicions.

Exhibit 4 SKI DIVISION ESTIMATED INCOME STATEMENT*
for 1974

	Fixed	Variable		
Sales				
Cost of Sales in Terms of its Components:				$850,000
Raw materials consumed			$300,000	
Direct Labor			200,000	
Burden Charges:	Fixed	Variable		
Indirect wages	$ 10,000	$ 60,000		
Payroll taxes	1,000	6,000		
Repairs & maintenance	20,000	30,000		
Rent	20,000			
Utilities	8,000	20,000		
Depreciation:				
Factory equipment	40,000			
Cost accounting equipment	1,000			
Insurance on inventory		4,000		
	$100,000	$120,000	$220,000	$720,000
Gross Profit				$130,000
Selling and Administrative Expenses:				
	Fixed	Variable		
Salaries	$30,000	$ 40,000		
Payroll taxes	3,000	4,000		
Salesmen's commissions		10,000		
Advertising	20,000	20,000		
Depreciation	5,000			
Interest:				
On equipment notes	2,000			
On investment in working capital and equipment		13,440		
Other prorated expenses	29,000	44,000		
	$89,000	$131,440		$220,440
Estimated Net Loss				($ 90,440)

* All data reflect nine months' actual experience and three months' pro forma.

Catherine: Very shrewd. I'll tell you what my plans are shortly, but first tell me how you intend to approach the other divisions.

Dantes: I believe the crucial thing is to convince them that we are studying ways to retrench, to reduce the scale of our operations. If I need to, I can dangle our $90,000 loss in front of them. Besides, some of the questions I'll have to ask may make them believe that their divisions can obtain additional equipment or space for nothing. I doubt if it will occur to anyone that retrenchment may be one way to turn losses into profits and regain competitive advantage. Most managers are conditioned to believing that profits increase only if growth in volume and facilities occurs first.

Catherine: You won't have to deceive our colleagues; stupidity and greed will take care of that. As for our new program, I see three major steps. First, we must increase our sales price and volume. Second, we must reduce all maintenance efforts and eliminate all avoidable repairs. And finally, we must increase our promotion efforts.

Dantes: Is putting aside our repairs and maintenance advisable? If we don't maintain it regularly, our equipment will fall apart within two or three years.

Catherine: You are forgetting that our primary goal is to survive this next year. One year from now, you and I shall either have been promoted or we shall be working for other employers. I want to see your next report three days from now.

Dantes: I think three days will be sufficient.

Catherine: Timing is very important to our success. Three days is all you have.

Scene V

Setting: Dantes has worked frantically for three days. He has diplomatically exercised his commission, being careful not to betray the scheme outlined by Catherine and ever focusing on the dire condition of Skis. He has not lied, and yet he has contrived to deceive the other divisions by allowing them to misconstrue his remarks. Ever an apt pupil, he has learned from Catherine to prod his listeners at certain times and then to remain quiet while their obtuseness and cupidity carry them to false conclusions. As a consequence, the other divisions have been sympathetic and cooperative in the hope of obtaining equipment idled by the supposedly retrenching Ski Division. Haggard from these wearisome negotiations, and sepulchral of countenance from going without sleep, Dantes collapses into a chair in Catherine's office.

Catherine: My God, man! What has happened?

Dantes: Nothing fatigues me like dissimulation and nothing makes the strain worthwhile like seeing avaricious men exercise their stupidity. Truly I have learned more about men in these past few hours than in the twenty-odd years that preceded them. I shall be fine once I have had rest and something to drink.

Catherine: (engaging the intercom to her secretary) Betty, coffee on the double!

Betty: It is on its way.

Catherine: (receiving coffee from Betty and handing it to the exhausted Dantes) You look better already. What do you have to tell me?

Dantes: Here is a copy (Exhibit 5) of the differential income statement. As I shall show you, all the figures are sup-

Exhibit 5 SKI DIVISION DIFFERENTIAL INCOME STATEMENT for 1974

Sales			$850,000
Cost of Sales:			
Raw materials		$300,000	
Direct labor		200,000	
Burden:			
Indirect wages	$70,000		
Payroll taxes	7,000		
Repairs and maintenance	50,000		
Rent	–0–		
Utilities	20,000		
Depreciation—Factory	30,000		
—Cost accounting	2,000		
Insurance	4,000	183,000	683,000
			$167,000
Selling and Administrative Expenses:			
Salaries		$ 50,000	
Payroll taxes		5,000	
Salesmen's commissions		10,000	
Advertising		40,000	
Depreciation		–0–	
Interest—equipment notes		–0–	
—investment in working capital		3,000	
Other prorated expenses		–0–	108,000
Differential Income			$ 59,000

portable either from Ski accounting records or from the information I recorded after each interview. Following your instructions, I have not concerned myself about the efficient utilization of Caribou resources and that, I believe, is the only ground on which these estimates might be vulnerable. And three facts augur against this vulnerability being discovered. First and foremost, in all my recent conversations with our colleagues I did not meet a single man clever enough to raise the issue. Second, even if there were such a person, the undertaking would be enormously complicated, for it would involve the whole company; hence we should be able to rely on both the unwillingness and the natural indolence of even such a clever person. Third, we can offer enough detail and supporting argument to camouflage the study from all but the most penetrating and persistent scrutiny. In other words, with so much detail and logic, attention will be rivetted to the portion of the question we have chosen to present. He who makes the rules has no excuse for not winning the game.

Catherine: Really, Edmund, though I have known you to be alert and capable, it is only now that I appreciate your true depth.

Dantes then Described in Great Detail how Exhibit 5 was Prepared. The Substance of His Presentation Follows.

The single most important point to note is that instead of a net loss of $90,440, Skis now shows a differential income of $59,000. Here is the rationale behind this striking metamorphosis. The decision to continue the Ski Division is obviously a matter of the future, not of the past. Underlying this analysis is the prediction that next year's figures will all be identical to the current year's as shown in the estimated income statement (Exhibit 4). However, in the ultimate report, the best estimates available for 1975 would be employed, no matter how different the figures were from those of 1974. Furthermore, observe that whether an expense is fixed or not makes little difference in differential cost analysis; the notion of fixity is merely a matter of convenience for describing short-run business phenomena for a going concern. In differential (incremental) cost analysis, we are no longer burdened with assuming that things must continue. Rather, we consider bringing an abrupt halt to operations, and in the process many costs lose their rigidity.

Prorated Expenses

Prorated expenses are those expenses incurred for the overall administration of a business which are allocated to its various divisions on some arbitrary basis such as floor space or sales volume. Before a division is charged incrementally with a portion of such expenses, the effect on the total of the expenses if the division were hypothetically discontinued must be determined. If with discontinuance the total administrative expenses would decrease, say, \$20,000, then the division should be charged \$20,000. In the case of the Ski Division, rent, salaries, payroll taxes thereon, and other prorated expenses were all subjected to the "discontinuance test" before any portion was included under differential costs.

Rent. The analysis assumes (1) that the total rent bill would remain the same even if the Ski Division were vacated, (2) that no other division could use the space, and (3) that it would not be possible to sublet the space. Hence, its facilities cost Skis nothing (the cost of using such idle facilities is zero if usage does not cause earlier retirement). If contrary assumptions were made, the highest of either the decrease in rent or the loss of rent from subletting, or the expense to another division of renting equal space elsewhere or the cost of earlier retirement would be an opportunity cost of Skis.

Salaries and Payroll Taxes. The "discontinuance test" showed that only \$20,000 of salaries would remain; therefore, the differential cost to Skis is \$50,000 (= \$70,000 − \$20,000) and the payroll taxes thereon.

Other Prorated Expenses. The "discontinuance test" further revealed that the total of these expenses would remain unchanged. Therefore no charge for these expenses has been included under differential costs.

Avoidable Costs

Avoidable costs are those costs which stop automatically if it is decided to discontinue operations. Skis contains several avoidable costs: raw materials, direct labor, repairs, indirect wages and payroll taxes thereon, advertising, the variable portions of utilities expense, insurance on inventory, and salesmen's commissions. It does not matter, for instance, that \$10,000 of the indirect wages (supervisory salaries) are considered fixed for income determination purposes; if the salaries would disappear (as reflected in Exhibit 5) with the discontinuance of Skis, then they are an incremental cost of manufacturing. The fixed portion of utility expense is not a differential cost, since that portion of the expense is unavoidable whether Skis is continued or not.

This position is easily defended when it is recalled that buildings subject to weather as cold as the weather in Caribou must be heated nearly yearlong to prevent the water lines from bursting.

Depreciation Charges

Determining a charge for depreciation (or more precisely, for use of fixed assets) for inclusion in differential costs is very different from calculating depreciation for a profit and loss statement.

If a piece of equipment is so specialized that it cannot be used by any other cost center, and if proceeds from its disposal are approximately equal to its dismantling costs, and if use does not precipitate either earlier retirement or need for complementary facilities (as described in the third paragraph of Exhibit 2), then it can be said that there is no differential cost in using the equipment. If there is any value in alternative use, then there is an opportunity cost, which must be included in a differential analysis.

Let us first consider depreciation on factory equipment. Two alternative uses for this equipment existed at the start of 1974:

1. The manager of Toboggans said that if he owned Skis' machines, he would have saved rental fees and would have had cash earnings of $30,000.
2. The equipment could have been sold for its book value ($87,000 at the end of 1973 and $75,000 at the end of 1974). Furthermore, there was an investment opportunity available to Caribou that required $87,000 and promised a 15% rate of return over its one-year life.

Three situations must be studied:

	Start	End
What happened in Skis:	$87,000	$ 75,000
Toboggans:	$87,000	$ 30,000 $ 75,000
Investment:	$87,000	$100,050

Keep in mind that interest on capital is to be imputed at the required return of 12%. In keeping with the opportunity cost concept, however, if one of the above alternatives generates a greater return, then imputation on the $87,000 would not be appropriate. Automatically, therefore, the 15% on the investment cancels imputation. Whether the Toboggans or the investment alternative is the measure of forgoance remains to be considered. It is clear that Toboggans returns more ($105,000), than investment ($100,050) and represents the greater sacrifice. But what is the measure of the cost?

One view is that there has been erosion in the value of the asset to the extent of $12,000 ($87,000 – $75,000) and a sacrifice of Toboggan's earnings of $30,000 for a total cost of $42,000.

Another view is that Toboggans would have started the period with $87,000 and would have ended it with $105,000 for a gain of $18,000. This, too, seems attractive as a measure of foregoance.

So what is the cost? Is it neither $42,000 nor $18,000 but rather $30,000, which is the gain Toboggans would have shown on its continuum had it owned the machine, plus the $12,000 erosion in asset value?

The cost measure is $30,000 and it represents Skis' sacrifice of the $18,000 gain enjoyed by Toboggans plus the $12,000 decline in asset value.

This doesn't seem to consider Investment adequately, but it does. Think about the $100,050 received at the end of the period from Investment as consisting of $75,000 with which to buy equipment and $25,050 of earnings on the $87,000; comparisons then become easier to draw.

Next let us examine depreciation on cost accounting equipment. Another division said that it could have used the equipment and thereby saved rental charges of $2,000. The equipment had no market value at the start of the year. Therefore, the differential cost is $2,000.

This leaves depreciation—administration. The "discontinuance test" revealed that no disposals of administrative furnishings, fixtures, and equipment would take place; therefore, there is no differential cost to Skis.

Imputed Interest Charges

Imputed interest is that interest which is estimated and charged to a division to recognize the fact that money is tied up in some way (in inventory and equipment) in the division, and that the money so invested could instead be earning a return in some other employment. In keeping with the principle of best alternative use, the percentage return should be that of the next best investment opportunity; however, where such an alternative cannot be readily identified, Caribou's required rate of return (12%) is used instead. Since the production equipment has a greater return in alternative use that was considered earlier, the only remaining investment in Skis was its working capital. The imputed cost was \$13,440 (Exhibit 4). When the interest on the equipment (\$87,000 × .12 = \$10,440) is subtracted, the remainder is \$3,000. Observe that interest on equipment notes has not been included under differential costs. To include it there would be to ignore the pooling concept of funds.[7]

Upon Completion of Dantes' Presentation, the Meeting Ended

Catherine: This is excellent, Edmund. You have done well. Now go sleep and come to see me at 10 tomorrow morning.

Scene VI

Setting: The scene is Ms. de'Medici's home, which is situated on two hundred rolling, wooded acres in a secluded area ten miles north of Caribou. She is talking with Edmund, who appears much restored, having slept for fourteen hours.

Catherine: The differential income analysis coupled with your explanations will suffice nicely for my dealings with Hagar. He will need time to cogitate on your explanations and perhaps to check into some of the alternatives you have unearthed. It will not occur to him that we have included no increases in sales until he has become familiar with the report. When he comes to this realization, I shall say that I merely wished to show him a conservative view of Skis in 1975—one in which sales volume and prices remained as in 1974. I can then stall for time by saying that figures for the new program were still being prepared, that such estimates required careful review of the market and the economy if they were not to be misleading.

Dantes But I could have reasonably reliable estimates by the middle of next week. Why must we delay?

Catherine: Prepare your estimates for Wednesday, Edmund—sooner, if possible.

---

[7] The pooling concept of funds will be discussed at length in the next chapter. It is a theoretical construct for recognizing the jointness of the various sources of funds available to an organization and for dealing with the timing of investments so that earlier proposals are not favored at the expense of later proposals.

Dantes: It is done. But again, why must we delay showing Hagar a finalized estimate for this year? Did you not say that our primary goal was to survive and that time was of the essence? Have I been killing myself for nought?

Catherine: Events are transpiring, Edmund, of which you have no knowledge. Hagar will not fail to be confused by them, the more so the longer he confronts the problems unaided. Not all his blustering nor yet his energy will serve to shield his blundering from the eyes of the trustees. And from this labyrinth of confusion and mediocre performance you and I shall emerge as the beacon of hope. I shall become president and you, Edmund, shall be my minister of efficiency, second only to myself.

Dantes: I am overcome.

Catherine: I will meet soon with Baron Danglars and Monsieur Fernand Mondego, two of the trustees. The affair is one that requires finesse and delicacy, but I shall contrive an introduction at the propitious moment. I shall draw from them an admission of disappointment with Caribou's recent fiscal results and I shall lay before them plans to enhance performance—on a company level but with emphasis on Skis. I shall not fail to focus their attention on the need for reform and a new controlling voice. They will investigate and, seeing Hagar's confused state, they will turn to me to put our plans into execution.

Dantes: How wonderful it all sounds. To have the power to seek efficiency would be a seductive challenge indeed.

Catherine: Not "would be," Edmund, "will be"! It is now that I wish you to beome concerned with efficient use of company resources. It is today that we must decide how best to enhance sales. What is our strategy?

Dantes: Your notion to segment the ski market into a high-priced masters line and a lower priced novice line seems promising. And I think we might use installment sales contracts to make the prices more palatable in the recession period.

Catherine: Excellent! We could price a set of skis for $150 and allow the purchaser to pay for it monthly over a one-year period with a provision for interest at, say, 12%. What would that make the monthly payment, Edmund?

Dantes: (after manipulating a slide rule) $13.33 per month, assuming the first payment occurs one month from date of purchase.

Catherine: Splendid! Scarcely more that the price of a weekend tow ticket. Of course there would be some bother—cost of contracts, repossessions—but considering that our top price is now $80 and we could, if necessary, permit weekly payments or even stretch payments over a longer time, we could withstand a lot of grief and still show marked improvement. We should also buttress the price change by an extensive promotion campaign. From the cost standpoint, this might simply have the effect of transferring dollars from the repairs to the advertising category.—Excuse me, Edmund, while I answer that ringing telephone. . . .Hello.

Hagar: Good morning, Kate. I just thought I would let you know how much I am enjoying those cigars you dropped off. Sorry I wasn't here to receive them.

Catherine: I am happy you like them.

Hagar: Oh, I have had several already. Their odor reminds me of campfires in the woods—you know, sort of a mixture of a grove of pines, burning coals, and fresh mountain air. And they're so soothing!

Catherine: You sound very happy and relaxed.

Hagar: I am. Oh, there was another reason for calling. Now let me see, what was it? . . .Trees? Err, . . .uhh, no. Fires? Uhh. . . , no. Mountains? No, no! Oh, yes. Do you think you could have some figures on Skis to discuss, say, toward the end of next week?

Catherine: How would Thursday afternoon be?

Hagar: Great. And thanks again for the cigars, Kate.

Dantes: (after Catherine has hung up) Was that one of the trustees?

Catherine: No. That was Hagar and things are progressing even faster than I had supposed. I think a chance meeting with Danglars and Mondego should be arranged for Friday. That means you must prepare our final report at once and begin a review of company operations with augmenting both efficiency and sustained profit in mind. Again you must be discreet. In two weeks, however, we shall be in charge and then you will find accurate information difficult to obtain, since the divisions will exaggerate to gain advantage. Now is the time to make true assessments; later we shall deal with the organizational problem. Close cooperation and dedication to our new goals will be assured if first we dismiss a few vice-presidents and controllers. So in your investigations this week try to determine who is most dangerous to our succession. For I assure you, as we stand here, their futures hang by a thread which we shall soon sever.

Dantes: You shall have the finished report by Monday. What should we do about delaying shipments and getting the new prices into effect?

Catherine: There is not much we can do until we have the reins. As you suggest, however, we might delay shipments by telling the packaging people that we are studying a new box to key in with our advertisements. Possibly the skis that are now being manufactured can become the new novice line and be packaged accordingly. Then the masters line can be marketed by adding some inexpensive furbelow to the ski to differentiate it.

Dantes: That should be very adequate. I'll see to it.

Scene VII

Setting: It is Monday afternoon. Dantes is seated in Ms. de' Medici's office and has just handed her the forecasted differential income statement (see Exhibit 6).

Dantes: I have taken a few liberties in preparing this statement but I believe you will not find them objectionable. The most striking result is the $700,000 increase in differential income, which in turn rests on the vast increase in sales. In 1974 Skis sold approximately 11,000 sets. I believe we can sell 20,000 sets in 1975 by increasing sales price by introducing installment sales contracts, tripling our advertising, and raising salesmen's commissions to 1.5%. I think half our business will be in the masters line at $150 per set and the remainder in the novice line at $80 per set. I estimate that $1,000,000 of our sales will be on the installment basis, and that we shall probably experience 5% costs in writing and administering contracts and recovering from those who renege on payments. All other costs have followed the notions of last year's differential income statement, with two exceptions. Variable costs have been adjusted to reflect the new volume of activity. And inflation of costs has generally been recognized in keeping with the economy.

Exhibit 6 SKI DIVISION FORECASTED DIFFERENTIAL INCOME STATEMENT
for 1975

Sales (see Note)			$2,300,000
Cost of Sales:			
Raw materials		$600,000	
Direct labor		480,000	
Burden:			
Indirect wages	$70,000		
Payroll taxes	7,000		
Repairs and maintenance	30,000		
Rent	-0-		
Utilities	45,000		
Depreciation—Factory	30,000		
—Cost accounting	2,000		
Insurance	8,000	192,000	1,272,000
			$1,028,000
Selling and Administrative Expenses:			
Salaries		$ 50,000	
Payroll taxes		5,000	
Salesmen's commissions (1.5%)		34,500	
Advertising		125,000	
Depreciation		-0-	
Interest—equipment notes		-0-	
—investment in working capital		5,000	
Other prorated expenses		-0-	
Installment contract costs		50,000	269,500
1975 Forecasted Differential Income			$ 758,500

Note: Cash flow will be less than $2,300,000 because sales will be on an installment basis. How much less will depend on the terms of the installment contracts.

Catherine: Excellent! I see you even have an explanation in advance of why cash position at year's end will not be as favorable as indicated by the sales estimate. This will not fail to excite Danglars and Mondego. Have you anything further to discuss?

Dantes: Well, my investigations are still in the early stages, but I think a new $60,000 edging machine for Skis could be justified and would further enhance the forecasted income. As long as our goal had been the survival of Skis, the purchase seemed postponable; however, given our present plans for efficiency and expansion, I think the edger should be acquired.

Catherine: If you feel it can be justified, then prepare a preliminary analysis. Anything else?

Dantes: Not beyond my original notion of checking the efficiency of the Caribou product line composition via linear programming. As I have said before, this study will take time; unfortunately, the best I can do by Thursday is to sketch a simple model that will show the type of information we will get once real parameters and constraints are available. Beyond this, in the next two days I also hope to unearth some of the problems confronting the other divisions and to identify their talented and vocal managers, some of whom we may wish to dismiss while others we may wish to elevate to fill vacancies.

Catherine: I shall see you first thing Thursday morning, Edmund, unless you need my help or have something specific to report in the interim. I will leave the morning open so that you may familiarize me with your findings. In the afternoon, I shall confer with Hagar and on Friday with the trustees. They shall see him as he is, forgetting any past good he has done—for as Shakespeare remarked, "The evil that men do lives after them. The good is oft interred with their bones."

Finis

Problems

1. Paul A. Samuelson, the Nobel Prize-winning economist, once said, "First, let's suppose you are interested in giving people what they want, not in telling them what they ought to want." Relate his comment to the calculation of differential costs.

2. *Differential Costs.*

   (a) What are they? Define and discuss.

   (b) Are fixed costs relevant to differential cost analysis?

   (c) How would you apply the "discontinuance" test?

   (d) Are directly identifiable costs relevant? Consider from the standpoint of (1) specific interest paid on a machine used in the process under consideration, (2) imputed interest, and (3) specific depreciation on this above machine.

3. *Dropping a product line.* A company in Iceland presently produces and markets several products, one of which, X, seems to be incurring a substantial net loss each

year. The company wishes to determine whether or not it should drop this product from its line. One wing of the factory is devoted entirely to product X. Other alternatives, such as subcontracting production or adopting a different marketing arrangement, may be ruled out because of exorbitant costs. In other words, the two alternatives under consideration are either to continue with product X or to drop it completely.

PRODUCT X
PROFIT AND LOSS STATEMENT

	Fixed	Variable		
Sales				$800,000
Cost of Sales in Terms of its Components:				
Direct materials			$300,000	
Direct labor			200,000	
Overhead:	Fixed	Variable		
Indirect wages	$10,000	$ 60,000		
Payroll taxes	1,000	26,000		
(A) Rent	20,000			
Heat, light, and power	8,000	20,000		
Depreciation	40,000			
Insurance-inventory		5,000		
	$79,000	$111,000	190,000	690,000
Gross Profit				$110,000
lling and Administrative Expenses:				
(B) Salaries			$ 70,000	
Commissions			40,000	
Advertising			50,000	
(B) Other expenses			30,000	190,000
Net Loss				$(80,000)

(A) Prorated
(B) One-half Prorated

4. *Pricing.* The Wee Gypsum Company is faced with a special sale pricing decision for one of its products, Z. Another firm, not one of the Gypsum's regular customers, has offered to buy a significant quantity (1,200) units of Z for distribution to the warden of a penitentiary as part of a rehabilitation program for the inmates. Z has never before been marketed to such consumers, and it is believed highly unlikely that a repeat sale will ever take place. The purchase price is yet to be negotiated, but Mr. Wee, the president, intends that the selling price shall be such as to yield *at least* a 20% contribution margin. Mr. Gypsum, the vice-president in charge of finance, has accordingly undertaken to determine the minimum price that could be set. Mr. Gypsum has ascertained the following facts:

(a) It would take three years to produce this additional quantity of Z.

(b) The customary cost of one unit of Z is regularly computed as shown below.

Materials	$100
Direct labor	80
Manufacturing overhead:	
Fixed portion at normal yearly volume (500 units)	60
Variable portion	40
Selling and administrative costs:	
Fixed portion at normal volume	50
Variable portion	20
Unit Cost	$350

(c) If the extra Z is made, then Y cannot be produced and $60,000 of net cash receipts must be forgone. The facilities in question could be otherwise employed, but Y is the best alternative employment. Dropping Y would have no significant effect on the product line.

(d) The production of the extra Z would require the use of a machine that is essential to the manufacture of X; fortunately, a substitute machine could be acquired for X at a cost of $8,000. It could be disposed of after X is completed (estimated time to complete X is two years) for $2,000, net of dismantling costs. The manufacture of X is not expected to take place until one year after work on Z is begun. The machine now on hand has a book value of $5,700 and a disposal value of $4,000. In three years its economic life will have ended and the cost to dismantle it will be approximately equal to the proceeds obtainable from selling it at that time.

(e) Material costs are expected to increase 10% on the average over the next three-year period; wages, according to union contract, are to increase an average of 25% over this period.

(f) If this special order for Z is not taken, one foreman whose salary is $12,000 a year will be cashiered; other nonvariable overhead costs will be unaffected.

(g) Eight thousand dollars of Mr. Wee's and Mr. Gypsum's salaries has been included in the fixed portion of selling and administrative costs charged to Z; of the remaining fixed portion, 50% could be saved by not producing any Z whatsoever.

(h) The variable portions of manufacturing overhead and selling and administrative costs are not expected to change significantly during the next three years.

(i) The production of the additional order is expected to be continuous (but unaffected by any learning curve) in lots of 60. Deliveries will be made uniformly so that a simple average inventory will be carried. It may be assumed that the customer will pay on a C.O.D. basis.

(j) Cost of capital is 8%. (Consider this as a rate for discounting future cash flows; the next chapter will discuss cost of capital at length.)

5. "*Make or buy,*" (*Certified Public Accountancy Examination, November 1968**). Southwest Company, your audit client, requested your assistance in deciding whether the company should continue to manufacture or should purchase mansers, a component of their major product. The annual requirement for mansers is 10,000 units and the part is available from an outside supplier in any quantity at $5 per unit. The following information is available:

(a) The Machining Department starts and substantially completes mansers, and minor finishing is completed by the use of direct labor in the Finishing Department. The Assembly Department places mansers in the finished product.

(b) Machinery used to produce mansers could be sold for its book value of $15,000 and the proceeds invested at 6% per year if the mansers were purchased. Property taxes and insurance would decrease $300 per year if the machinery were sold. The machinery has a remaining life of 10 years with no estimated value.

(c) The Machining Department is devoted about 25% to the production of mansers, but labor and some other costs for mansers in this department could be reduced without affecting other operations. The Finishing Department's costs include direct labor totaling $800 devoted to mansers. If mansers were not manufactured, one-half of the resulting available direct labor would be used as indirect labor and the remaining one half would result in paid idle time of employees.

(d) In 1967 when 10,000 mansers were produced, pertinent Machining Department costs were

	Total Costs	Costs Allocated to Mansers
Materials	$95,000	$24,200
Direct labor	39,400	12,200
Indirect labor	20,600	7,800
Heat and light	12,000	3,000
Depreciation	6,000	1,500
Property taxes and insurance	15,000	3,750
Production supplies	4,000	800

(e) In addition the Machining Department total costs included $18,300 payroll taxes and other benefits.

(f) Overhead allocated on the basis of 200% of direct labor cost was $40,000 for the Finishing Department and $20,000 for the Assembly Department in 1967. Overhead in these department is 25% fixed, and 75% variable.

(g) If mansers are purchased, Southwest will incur added costs of $.45 per unit for freight and $3,000 per year for receiving, handling and inspection of the product.

Required:

(a) Prepare a schedule comparing Southwest's total annual cost of mansers if manufactured with their annual cost if purchased. (Ignore income taxes.)

(b) Without regard to your solution to part (a) assume the total annual cost of mansers if manufactured and if purchased were both $60,000. Compute the annual net cash outflow (1) if mansers are manufactured and (2) if mansers are purchased. (Ignore income taxes.)

(c) Southwest's management must consider working capital requirements in deciding whether to manufacture or to purchase mansers. Explain the working capital requirements which should be considered.

6. *Product line analysis* (*Certified Public Accountancy Examination, May 1970**). Vernon Enterprises designs and manufactures toys. Past experience indicates that the product life cycle of a toy is three years. Promotional advertising produces large sales in the early years, but there is a substantial sales decline in the final year of a toy's life.

Consumer demand for new toys placed on the market tends to fall into three classes. About 30% of the new toys sell well above expectations, 60% sell as anticipated and 10% have poor consumer acceptance.

A new toy has been developed. The following sales projections were made by carefully evaluating consumer demand for the new toy:

Consumer Demand for New Toy	Chance of Occurring	Estimated Sales in Year 1	Year 2	Year 3
Above average	30%	$1,200,000	$2,500,000	$600,000
Average	60	700,000	1,700,000	400,000
Below average	10	200,000	900,000	150,000

Variable costs are estimated at 30 percent of the selling price. Special machinery must be purchased at a cost of $860,000 and will be installed in an unused portion of the factory which Vernon has unsuccessfully been trying to rent to someone for several years at $50,000 per year and has no prospect for future utilization. Fixed expenses (excluding depreciation) of a cash-flow nature are estimated at $50,000 per year on the new toy. The new machinery will be depreciated by the sum-of-the years'-digits method with an estimated salvage value of $110,000 and will be sold at the beginning of the fourth year. Advertising and promotional expenses will be incurred uniformly and will total $100,000 the first year, $150,000 the second year, and $50,000 the third year. These expenses will be deducted as incurred for income tax reporting.

Vernon believes that state and federal income taxes will total 60% of income in the foreseeable future and may be assumed to be paid uniformly over the year income is earned.

---

* Material from the Uniform CPA Examinations, copyright © (May 1970) by the American Institute of Certified Public Accountants, Inc., is adapted with permission.

Required:

(a) Prepare a schedule computing the probable sales of this new toy in each of the three years, taking into account the probability of above-average, average, and below average sales occurring.

(b) Assume that the probable sales computed in (a) are $900,000 in the first year, $1,800,000 in the second year, and $410,000 in the third year. Prepare a schedule computing the probable net income for the new toy in each of the three years of its life.

(c) Prepare a schedule of net cash flows from sales of the new toy for each of the years involved and from disposition of the machinery purchased. Use the sales data given in part (b).

(d) Assuming a minimum desired rate of return of 10%, prepare a schedule of the present value of the net cash flows calculated in (c). The following data are relevant:

Year	Present Value of $1.00 Due at the End of Each Year Discounted at 10%	Present Value of $1.00 Earned Uniformly Throughout the Year Discounted at 10%
1	.91	.95
2	.83	.86
3	.75	.78

7. *The last of the wooly ones.* In the early days of the West there was a furtive figure who wore a white mask and rode a great black stallion called Charcoal that could travel with the speed of light. This man, known as Big Jim Wolfe, was not a champion of justice; no indeed, he was a gunrunner doing business with hostile Indian tribes. His was a hazardous but thriving undertaking. His profit and loss statement, which seldom varied significantly from year to year, showed the figures given below.

Sales		$100,000
Purchases		40,000
		$ 60,000
Operating expenses:		
Salary Speedy	$ 5,000	
Red-eye	12,000	
Traveling	13,000	
Depreciation	6,000	
Prorated expenses	14,000	50,000
Net Income		$ 10,000
Rake-off at 30%		3,000
Net Income after rake-off		$ 7,000

Big Jim purchased guns from a manufacturer in a small town in Nebraska (the town was also the headquarters for several of his other enterprises). Several times a year Jim would load a shipment of rifles onto a wagon and he and his sidekick, Speedy Huff, would commence another journey into hostile territory. They would stop in towns along the way to pick up news about local uprisings and to purchase copious quantities of red-eye to spur sales on—sort of an advertising expense, as it were. When they left a town they were continuously on the lookout for their customers, who might well be lurking behind trees and boulders. When they accosted a potential customer they said, "Take us to your chief." The chiefs usually agreed to Big Jim's terms, which were a bottle of red-eye per warrior and a proportionate share for the chief—based on tribal sales—of 30% of the annual net income of the business.

The depreciation charge shown on the profit and loss statement was based on the following figures:

	Cost	Useful Life	Depreciation
Charcoal	$28,000	7 years	$4,000
Wagon	14,000	7 years	2,000

At December 31, 1821, the horse had a book value of $20,000 and the wagon had a book value of $10,000. The cost of the horses used to pull the wagon was included in the prorated expenses in an amount of $4,000 per year. The balance of prorated expenses is based on 10% of sales and represents administrative costs common to the several enterprises.

Toward the end of 1821, Big Jim and Speedy had had a couple of rather close encounters—one with a few of their customers and the other with a tall man wearing a black mask and riding a big white horse called Silver. As a result, Big Jim was considering employing his assets in other ways. Speedy, on the other hand, seemed relatively unimpressed by these events, for he was aptly named. Whenever danger was imminent, Speedy would simply dismount and run like h____. For short distances he was even faster than the great horse, Charcoal.

Jim was certain that Speedy could carry on without him but that sales and certain expenses would undoubtedly drop in half. He found that he could buy out the business that supplied him with the guns if he could lay his hands on $60,000. The annual profits of this manufacturing business, which envisioned full capacity operations for another 10 years regardless of what happened to Big Jim's gunrunning business, amounted to $9,000 after deduction for depreciation of $1,000.

A horse-loving acquaintance of Big Jim's, Lilly Miller (the Boston Lilly), had recently expressed her admiration for Charcoal and offered to buy him from Jim for $50,000. Jim believed that with each additional year of hard treatment the offer for Charcoal would drop by $10,000. The wagon couldn't be used for anything else, nor could it be sold—it was just too big and heavy. He reasoned that the Dry Gulch Bank would be willing to loan him as much as $25,000 at 4% interest if he offered security for the loan.

Back at headquarters Big Jim pondered what he should do. He recognized that all business involved some sort of gambling and that the Lone Ranger and the hostile Indians were really just another gamble. He determined not to let them interfere with his decision, which he intended to base on rate of return analysis.*

Did Jim retire and begin a life of tranquility, or did he continue to lead the carefree, adventurous existence that had already established him as one of the legends of the West?

*Note:

Rate of return analysis basically amounts to finding that discount rate which will make future cash earnings equal present cash investment. Use a trial-and-error approach in the discounting tables to find this rate.

8. *Caribou Snow.* If time permits and you believe in the need to be able to speak effectively, assign roles to selected friends and have them act out the Caribou Snow play.

9. *Caribou Snow and accounting ethics.* In the Caribou Snow play, Edmund Dantes was what some might term the "ultimate" accountant. He was very capable; he did exactly as his superior asked. Yet he knew the purposes of the analysis he was preparing and took no corrective steps. Did he act in an ethical manner? If not, how should he have acted? What are the implications of your answers for accounting in general?

10. *Allocation, subcontracting (prepared by Professor Ronald Mannino).* The Acme Machine Shop operates a plant with two service departments and two producing departments.

The company anticipates the following overhead budgets for the year 1974:

	Overhead Budget by Department Before Allocation
Repair	$ 1,040
Power	4,000
Machining	50,000
Assembly	40,000
	$95,040

The Machining Department allocates overhead to production on the basis of machine hours; 10,000 machine hours are expected to be worked during 1974. The Assembly Department allocates overhead to production on the basis of direct-labor hours worked; 20,000 direct-labor hours are expected to be worked during 1974. The service departments, Repair and Power, deliver their service as follows:

	Hours of Service Received by				
Source	Repair	Power	Machining	Assembly	Total Service Hours Worked
Repair Shop	0	600	1,000	400	2,000
Power Plant	400	0	400	200	1,000

Required:

(a) Using the linear algebra method, allocate service costs to the Machining and Assembly Departments.

(b) Using the direct method, allocate service costs to the Machining and Assembly Departments.

(c) The Acme Machine Shop has been considering closing down its Repair Shop and subcontracting the work to an outside firm. An investigation of costs within Acme indicates that all of the costs in the Repair Shop and Power Shop are totally variable. The subcontractor will provide all of Acme's repair needs for $2,900 a year. Using cost considerations only, should Acme buy from outside subcontractors? Show cost comparisons.

11. *Differential costing, income projection (adapted from Certificate in Management Accounting Examination, December 1974).* The *Metropolitan News*, a daily newspaper, services a community of 100,000. The paper has a circulation of 40,000 with 32,000 copies delivered directly to subscribers. The rate schedule for the paper is

	Daily	Sunday
Single-issue price	$0.15	$0.30
Weekly subscription (includes Daily and Sunday)	$1.00	

The paper has experienced profitable operations as can be seen from the Income Statement for the Year Ended September 30, 1974 (000 omitted):

Revenue		
Newspaper Sales	$2,200	
Advertising Sales	1,800	$4,000
Costs and expenses		
Personnel costs		
Commissions		
Carriers	$ 292	
Sales	73	
Advertising	48	
Salaries		
Administration	250	
Advertising	100	
Equipment Operators	500	
Newsroom	400	
Employee Benefits	195	$1,858
Newsprint		834
Other supplies		417
Repairs		25
Depreciation		180
Property taxes		120
Building rental		80
Automobile leases		10
Other		90
Total costs and expenses		$3,614
Income before income taxes		$ 386
Income taxes		154
Net income		$ 232

The Sunday edition usually has twice as many pages as the daily editions. Analysis of direct edition variable costs for 1973–1974 is shown in the schedule given below.

	Cost per Issue	
	Daily	Sunday
Paper	$0.050	$0.100
Other supplies	0.025	0.050
Carrier and sales commissions	0.025	0.025
	$0.100	$0.175

Several changes in operations are scheduled for the next year, in addition to the need to recognize increasing costs.

(a) The building lease expired on September 30, 1974 and has been renewed with a change in the rental fee provisions from a straight fee to a fixed fee of $60,000 plus 1% of newspaper sales.

(b) The Advertising Department will eliminate the payment of a 4% advertising commision on contracts sold by its employees. An average of two-thirds of the advertising has been sold on a contract basis in the past. The salaries of the four who solicited advertising will be raised from $7,500 each to $14,000 each.

(c) Automobiles will no longer be leased. Employees whose jobs require automobiles will use their own and be reimbursed at $0.15 per mile. The leased cars were driven 80,000 miles in 1973–1974, and it is estimated that the employees will drive some 84,000 miles next year on company business.

(d) Cost increases estimated for next year:

(1) Newsprint $0.01 per daily issue and $0.02 for the Sunday paper.

(2) Salaries:

Equipment operators	8%
Other employees	6%

(3) Employee benefits (from 15% of personnel costs excluding carrier and sales commissions to 20%)

(e) Circulation increases of 5% in newstand and home delivery are anticipated.

(f) Advertising revenue is estimated at $1,890,000 with $1,260,000 from employee solicited contracts.

Required:

(a) Prepare a projected income statement for the *Metropolitan News* for the 1974–75 fiscal year using a format that shows the total variable costs and total fixed costs for the newspaper (round calculations to the nearest thousand dollars).

(b) The management of the *Metropolitan News* is contemplating one additional proposal for the 1974–75 fiscal year—raising the rates for its newspaper to the following amounts:

	Daily		Sunday
Single-issue price	$0.20		$0.40
Weekly subscription (includes Daily and Sunday)		$1.25	

It is estimated that the newspaper's circulation would decline to 90% of the currently anticipated 1974–75 level for both newsstand and home delivery sales if this change is initiated. Calculate the effect on the projected 1974–75 income if this proposed rate change is implemented.

12. *Full costs, sunk costs, opportunity costs,* (*adapted from Certificate in Management Accounting Examination, December 1972*). George Jackson operates a small machine shop. He manufactures one standard product available from many other similar businesses, and he also manufactures products to customer order. His accountant prepared the annual income statement shown below:

	Custom Sales	Standard Sales	Total
Sales	$50,000	$25,000	$75,000
Material	$10,000	$ 8,000	$18,000
Labor	20,000	9,000	29,000
Depreciation	6,300	3,600	9,900
Power	700	400	1,100
Rent	6,000	1,000	7,000
Heat and light	600	100	700
Other	400	900	1,300
	$44,000	$23,000	$67,000
	$ 6,000	$ 2,000	$ 8,000

The depreciation charges are for machines used in the respective product lines. The power charge is apportioned on the estimate of power consumed. The rent is for the building space which has been leased for 10 years at $7,000 per year. The rent, and heat and light are apportioned to the product lines based on amount of floor space occupied. All other costs are current expenses identified with the product line causing them.

A valued custom parts customer has asked Mr. Jackson if he would manufacture 5,000 special units for him. Mr. Jackson is working at capacity and would have to give up some other business in order to take this business. He can't renege on custom orders already agreed to, but he could reduce the output of his standard product by about one-half for one year while producing the specially requested custom part. The customer is willing to pay $7.00 for each part. The material cost will be about $2.00 per unit and the labor will be $3.60 per unit. Mr. Jackson will have to spend $2,000 for a special device that will be discarded when the job is done.

Required:

(a) Calculate and present the following costs related to the 5,000-unit custom order:

(1) the incremental cost of the order,

(2) the full cost of the order,

(3) the opportunity cost of taking the order, and

(4) the sunk costs related to the order.

(b) Should Mr. Jackson take the order? Explain your answer.

13. *Common costs, standard costs, adding a department (adapted from Certificate in Management Accounting Examination, December 1973).* The management of Bay Company is considering a proposal to install a third production department within its existing factory building. With the company's present production setup, raw material is passed through department I to produce materials A and B in equal proportions. Material A is then passed through Department II to yield product C. Material B is presently being sold "as is" at a price of $20.25 per pound. Product C has a selling price of $100.00 per pound. The per pound standard costs currently being used by the Bay Company are as follows:

	Department I (Materials A & B)	Department II (Product C)	Material B
Prior department costs	$ —	$53.03	$13.47
Direct material	20.00	—	—
Direct labor	7.00	12.00	—
Variable overhead:	3.00	5.00	—
Fixed overhead:			
Attributable	2.25	2.25	—
Allocated (2/3, 1/3)	1.00	1.00	—
	$33.25	$73.28	$13.47

These standard costs were developed by using an estimated production volume of 200,000 pounds of raw material as the standard volume. The company assigns Department I costs to materials A and B in proportion to their net sales values at the point of separation, computed by deducting subsequent standard production costs from sales prices. The $300,000 of common fixed overhead costs are allocated to the two producing departments on the basis of the space used by the departments.

The proposed Department III would be used to process material B into product D. It is expected that any quantity of product D can be sold for $30.00 per pound. Standard costs per pound under this proposal were developed by using 200,000 pounds of raw material as the standard volume and are as follows:

	Department I (Materials A & B)	Department II (Product C)	Department III (Product D)
Prior department costs	—	$52.80	$13.20
Direct material	$20.00	—	—
Direct labor	7.00	12.00	5.50
Variable overhead	3.00	5.00	2.00
Fixed overhead:			
Attributable	2.25	2.25	1.75
Allocated (1/2, 1/4, 1/4)	.75	.75	.75
	$33.00	$72.80	$23.20

Required:

(a) If (1) sales and production levels are expected to remain constant in the foreseeable future, and (2) there are no foreseeable alternative uses for the available factory space, should the Bay Company install Department III and thereby produce product D? Show calculations to support your answer.

(b) Instead of constant sales and production levels, suppose that under the present production setup $1,000,000 additions to the factory building must be made every 10 years to accommodate growth. Suppose also that proper maintenance gives these factory additions an infinite life and that all such maintenance costs are included in the standard costs that are set forth in the text of the problem. How would the analysis that you performed in part (a) be changed if the installation of Department III shortened the interval at which the $1,000,000 factory additions are made from 10 years to 6 years? Be as specific as possible in your answer.

14. "*Make or buy*" *a new product*, (*adapted from Certificate in Management Accounting Examination, December, 1972*). The Vernom Corporation, which produces and sells to wholesalers a highly successful line of summer lotions and insect repellents, has decided to diversify in order to stabilize sales throughout the year. A natural area for the company to consider is the production of winter lotions and creams to prevent dry and chapped skin.

After considerable research, a winter products line has been developed. However, because of the conservative nature of the company management, Vernom's president has decided to introduce only one of the new products for this coming winter. If the product is a success, further expansion in future years will be initiated.

The product selected (called Chap-off) is a lip balm that will be sold in a lipstick type tube. The product will be sold to wholesalers in boxes of 24 tubes for $8.00 per box. Because of available capacity, no additional fixed charges will be incurred to produce the product. However, a $100,000 fixed charge will be absorbed by the product to allocate a fair share of the company's present fixed costs to the new product.

Using the estimated sales and production of 100,000 boxes of Chap-off as the standard volume, the accounting department has developed the following costs:

Direct labor	\$2.00/box
Direct materials	\$3.00/box
Total overhead	\$1.50/box
Total	\$6.50/box

Vernom has approached a cosmetics manufacturer to discuss the possibility of purchasing the tubes for Chap-off. The purchase price of the empty tubes from the cosmetics manufacturer would be \$.90 per 24 tubes. If the Vernom Corporation accepts the purchase proposal, it is estimated that direct labor and variable overhead costs would be reduced by 10% and direct material costs would be reduced by 20%.

Required:

(a) Should the Vernom Corporation make or buy the tubes? Show calculations to support your answer.

(b) What would be the maximum purchase price acceptable to the Vernom Corporation for the tubes? Support your answer with an appropriate explanation.

(c) Instead of sales of 100,000 boxes, revised estimates show sales volume at 125,000 boxes. At this new volume additional equipment, at an annual rental of \$10,000, must be acquired to manufacture the tubes. However, this incremental cost would be the only additional fixed cost required even if sales increased to 300,000 boxes. (The 300,000 level is the goal for the third year of production.) Under these circumstances should the Vernom Corporation make or buy the tubes? Show calculations to support your answer.

(d) The company has the option of making and buying at the same time. What would be your answer to part (c) if this alternative was considered? Show calculations to support your answer.

(e) What nonquantifiable factors should the Vernom Corporation consider in determining whether they should make or buy the lipstick tubes?

15. *Contribution margins and dropping a product (adapted from Certificate in Management Accounting Examination, December 1972).* The Justa Corporation produces and sells three products. The three products, A, B, and C, are sold in a local market and in a regional market. At the end of the first quarter of the current year, the following income statement has been prepared:

	Total	Local	Regional
Sales	\$1,300,000	\$1,000,000	\$300,000
Cost of goods sold	1,010,000	775,000	235,000
Gross margin	\$ 290,000	\$ 225,000	\$ 65,000
Selling expenses	\$ 105,000	\$ 60,000	\$ 45,000
Administrative expenses	52,000	40,000	12,000
	\$ 157,000	\$ 100,000	\$ 57,000
Net income	\$ 133,000	\$ 125,000	\$ 8,000

Management has expressed special concern with the regional market because of the extremely poor return on sales. This market was entered a year ago because of excess capacity. It was originally believed that the return on sales would improve with time, but after a year no noticeable improvement can be seen from the results as reported in the above quarterly statement.

In attempting to decide whether to eliminate the regional market, the following information has been gathered:

	Products		
	A	B	C
Sales	$500,000	$400,000	$400,000
Variable manufacturing expenses as a percentage of sales	60%	70%	60%
Variable selling expenses as a percentage of sales	3%	2%	2%

	Sales by Markets	
Product	Local	Regional
A	$400,000	$100,000
B	300,000	100,000
C	300,000	100,000

All administrative expenses and fixed manufacturing expenses are common to the three products and the two markets and are fixed for the period. Remaining selling expenses are fixed for the period and separable by market. All fixed expenses are based upon a prorated yearly amount.

Required:

(a) Prepare the quarterly income statement showing contribution margins by markets.

(b) Assuming there are no alternative uses for the Justa Corporation's present capacity, would you recommend dropping the regional market? Why or why not?

(c) Prepare the quarterly income statement showing contribution margins by products.

(d) It is believed that a new product can be ready for sale next year if the Justa Corporation decides to go ahead with continued research. The new product can be produced by simply converting equipment presently used in producing Product C. This conversion will increase fixed costs by $10,000 per quarter. What must be the minimum contribution margin per quarter for the new product to make the changeover financially feasible?

16. *Contribution margins and pricing: boats (adapted from Certificate in Management Accounting Examination, December 1973).* E. Berg and Sons build custom-made pleasure boats, which range in price from $10,000 to $250,000. For the past 30 years, Mr. Berg, Sr. has determined the selling price of each boat by estimating the costs of material, labor and a prorated portion of overhead, and adding 20% to these estimated costs.

For example, a recent price quotation was determined as follows:

Direct Materials	$ 5,000
Direct Labor	8,000
Overhead	2,000
	$15,000
Plus 20%	3,000
Selling Price	$18,000

The overhead figure was determined by estimating total overhead costs for the year and allocating them at 25% of direct labor. If a customer rejected the price and business was slack, Mr. Berg, Sr. would often be willing to reduce the markup to as little as 5% over estimated costs. Thus average markup for the year is estimated at 15%.

Mr. Ed Berg, Jr. has just completed a course on pricing and believes the firm could use some of the techniques discussed in the course. The course emphasized the contribution margin approach to pricing, and Mr. Berg, Jr. feels such an approach would be helpful in determining the selling prices of their custom-made pleasure boats.

Total overhead which includes selling and administrative expenses for the year, has been estimated at $150,000 of which $90,000 is fixed and the remainder is variable in direct proportion to direct labor.

Required:

(a) Assume the customer in the example rejected the $18,000 quotation and also rejected a $15,750 quotation (5% markup) during a slack period. The customer countered with a $15,000 offer.

(1) What is the difference in net income for the year between accepting or rejecting the customer's offer?

(2) What is the minimum selling price Mr. Berg, Jr. could have quoted without reducing or increasing net income?

(b) What advantages does the contribution margin approach to pricing have over the approach used by Mr. Berg, Sr.?

(c) What pitfalls are there, if any, to contribution margin pricing?

Capital Budgeting

11

Introduction

Perhaps the most fascinating area in the field of cost analysis is capital (or project) budgeting. It seems as if nearly everyone has something relevant to say about this subject, including managers, accountants, financial analysts, management scientists, industrial engineers, economists, and psychologists. Capital budgeting is a simply limitless topic—just when you think you have cleverly incorporated some elaborate technique to reflect realism, you can turn to the literature in some other discipline and find that you have overlooked huge gaps or have naively taken something for granted. The area is at once humbling and enormously seductive—it abounds with challenges.

Capital budgeting is the allocation of limited resources to investment alternatives in such a way as to maximize return (profit) on the resources. There are usually many more investment alternatives than can be undertaken with the available resources. Deciding which proposals (alternatives) to implement and which to reject is the crucial task. As it is most often conceived, capital budgeting involves the use of interest rates to equate—at the time of decision—a proposal's incoming and outgoing streams of cash and cash equivalents. Since the cash flows necessarily take place in the future, the costs and revenues that are relevant to the analysis are all estimates; past costs are only pertinent insofar as they represent best estimates of future costs. This is reminiscent of our discussion of differential costs; however, as we shall see, dollar cost measurements are not always satisfactory. "Return" and "profit" in the definition of capital budgeting do not necessarily connote spendable money.

Let us begin our study by investigating the interest rates used for moving money through time.

Discounting Rates

Cost of Capital

Cost of capital is that rate of return which serves as a benchmark in capital budgeting If a proposal can earn a rate of return equal to or greater than the cost of capital, then the company's earnings position will either be preserved or improved by investing in the proposal.

The sources of capital are not independent of one another; they are linked together like a chain. If a company floats a bond issue one time, then this source of exogenous capital is unavailable for a while. If more exogenous capital is needed during the interim, more capital stock must be sold. But the terms on which the capital stock can be sold will depend in part on the extent of the bonded indebtedness. In time the amount of bonds that may be floated will depend in part on how much capital stock is outstanding. How much endogenous capital can be raised depends in part on how much capital stock and bonds are issued and on dividend and interest charges. Hence the various sources of funds are best viewed as entering a pool. Then, when an investment is made, the exact source of the funds can no longer be identified. Diagrammatically, we have

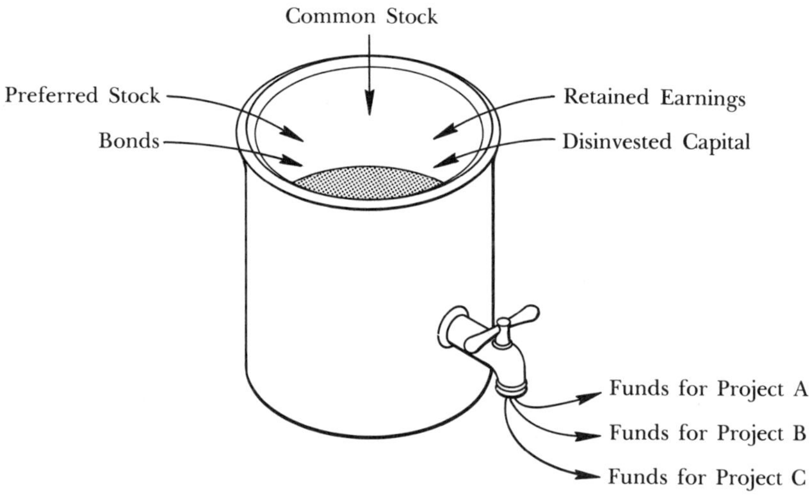

Bond dollars, stock dollars, earnings dollars, and sale-of-asset dollars all enter the pool, where they become indistinguishable as to source; they are now simply money available for investment.

Although there may be variations, cost of capital is basically computed as follows:

$$i = \frac{\Sigma c_j a_j}{\Sigma c_j}$$

Key:

i = cost of capital

c_j = amount of capital expected to be raised over, say, a three-to-five-year interval from source j ($j = B$ [bonds], P [preferred stock], C [common stock], R [retained earnings], D [disinvested capital])

a_j = the after-tax cost of source j

Management computes the values for c_j by estimating the firm's capital structure (that is, the amounts of bonds, stocks, retained earnings, and so forth, for say, three to five years hence). Then the amounts constituting the present capital structure are subtracted and the differences are the c_j values. The calculation of the a_j costs is discussed below.

a_B: The after-tax cost of bonds is equal to the effective interest rate multiplied by the complement of the tax rate—in symbols, $a_B = b\,(1 - t)$. The idea is that the interest charges are a deduction for tax purposes and therefore they offset an equal amount of revenue. The taxes on this revenue are effectively cancelled. Consequently, the actual net out-of-pocket cost of interest equals the effective interest paid less the savings from not having to pay so much taxes.

a_p: The after-tax cost of preferred stock is the stipulated dividend rate for the shares. Since dividends are not a tax deduction, the rate is the same before or after taxes.

a_C: The after-tax cost of common stock is the same as the before-tax cost, since dividends are not tax deductible. The cost is estimated as follows:

$$a_C = \bar{E}_f \div M_p$$

Key:

$\bar{E}_f$ = future after-tax average earnings per share assuming no new investments are made

M_p = present market value

The objective here is to measure the shareholders' present position, assuming (1) that market value is stable and representative of existing worth of stock, and (2) that only the presently owned facilities will generate earnings. An alternative view focuses on the cash receipts expected by the shareholder, according to which $a_C = (\bar{D}_f/M_P) + g$. Here $\bar{D}_f$ is the dividend expectation and g is the expected growth rate in dividends. The viewpoint here seems to be that the shareholder is not an owner, but rather some sort of temporary creditor who must be paid off. This may be a more realistic view of his status.

a_R: The after-tax cost of retained earnings is equal to the cost of common stock multiplied by the complement of the shareholders' assumed, collective personal tax rate—in symbols, $a_R = a_C(1 - p)$. It is assumed that all retained earnings would be hypothetically distributed as dividends, and that the shareholders would reinvest such dividends in the company's stock. However, the dividends would first be subjected to the tax imposed on the stockholders' personal earnings. Hence, the corporation would not receive all the dividends it had hypothetically distributed. If the stockholders' tax rate is not known, it is customary to assume 30% to 40%. Retained earnings is first adjusted for noncash expenses and revenues (like depreciation and gains on disposals).

a_D: Same after-tax cost as a_R for proceeds of asset disposals.

Note: Many theorists prefer to reduce M_p by the costs of selling stock when computing a_C but leave M_p intact when computing a_R. The thought is that in one case an actual sale of stock would have to take place while in the other, no sale is necessary and market price represents the value of an existing shareholder's investment per share.

A numerical example of these cost-of-capital computations is shown below.

j	Source	c_j Capital Expected To Be Raised Over Next Three Years (000 omitted)	a_j After-Tax Cost	$c_j a_j$
B	Bonds	\$ 200	.025	\$ 5
P	Preferred Stock	300	.06	18
C	Common Stock	400	.10	40
R	Retained Earnings	500	.07	35
D	Disinvested Capital	100	.07	7
		$\Sigma c_j =$ \$1,500		$\Sigma c_j a_j =$ \$105

$$i = \frac{\Sigma c_j a_j}{\Sigma c_j} = \frac{\$105}{\$1{,}500} = 7\%$$

Additional computations:

$$a_C = \bar{E}_f \div M_p = \$10 \div \$100 = .10$$

$$a_R = a_D = a_C(1 - p) = .10(1 - .30) = .07$$

Cost of capital is not without its deprecators. Many theoreticians argue against it on the following grounds:

1. The computation of cost of capital involves too many estimates; hence it is more like a butcher's meat axe than a surgeon's scalpel.
2. In the computation, management places a limit on the amount of money that can be raised over a given period of time. In practice, however, it is felt by many managers that if a proposal is sufficiently promising, somehow money will be raised to implement it.

3. In computing after-tax cost of common stock, market price is assumed to be relatively stable. In many instances such as assumption is untenable.
4. The computation of after-tax costs of retained earnings and disinvested capital assumes that the only leakage of hypothetically distributed dividends would be income taxes. Other leakages (new golf clubs, new?) would also take place.

However vulnerable to criticism the cost-of-capital computations are, the concept enjoys three unquestioned theoretical advantages: (1) indistinguishability of funding sources, (2) elimination of proposal timing advantages, and (3) stability over the planning horizon. I discussed indistinguishability when I illustrated the jointness of fund sources. And stability is fairly obvious—without it, new rates would be constantly recalculated. Now let us examine proposal timing.

Suppose that a new building is to be constructed with the proceeds of a bond issue. Would you say that the bond interest charges constituted the "true" financial costs of the building? Or do you feel that earlier events set the stage for the favorable sale of bonds, and consequently that the bond interest charges should be augmented by the financing costs of those events? Again, don't you feel that the building should also bear some share of the ensuing higher financing costs brought about by the less favorable debt-equity ratio that exists once the bonds are issued? In this example, the building gets to the cheap money before, say, equipment and thus would be favored with low interest charges in the absence of pooling and the cost-of-capital concept. On the other hand, the equipment would then be saddled with higher financing charges. If an analyst were to use these separate rates in justifying the investments, the building might pass inspection while the equipment fails. But building and equipment jointly share available funds, if one visualizes funds within a three-to-five year span, rather than seeing them as unrelated in time—as differing magnitudes that happen to be available at particular instants. With cost of capital, the varying rates are smoothed into one, and it doesn't matter which proposal happens to arise first.

Required Rate of Return

Another objection to the use of cost of capital as a benchmark in selecting acceptable proposals is that it makes no provision for uncertainty.[1] To

[1] A distinction should be drawn between risk and uncertainty. Risk implies that the probability of a future event may be predicted according to a known probability distribution. Hence risk may be objectively determined. Uncertainty, however, refers to a situation in which the probability distribution is unknown. Hence uncertainty can only be subjectively assessed. Theoretically, then required rates of return can be set to deal with uncertainty. Risk should be dealt with directly in determing differential cost and revenues, as will be shown in the next chapter.

remedy this deficiency theorists advocate that the decisionmaker select some required rates of return for use in capital budgeting.[2] "Rates" was used in the previous sentence to indicate that different proposals might be subjected to different required rates because of differing degrees of uncertainty. Presumably, a required rate is at least as high as cost of capital would be if it were calculated.

As might be suspected, there is dispute over how the required rates are to be selected as well as over a number of other things—including the fact that the rates innocently incorporate a risk aversion attitude that would not suit risk seekers.[3] More will be said later about risk attitudes.

Constraints

The extent of investment that can be undertaken during any given period is constrained by:

(1) the requirement that proposals individually earn at least a cost-of-capital or required return;

(2) the amount of capital that is available;

(3) the physical capacities of men, plant, and machines;

(4) the existence of superior proposals that are expected to arise in the future, but which will not be implemented unless the firm abstains from making some present investments;

(5) the policies of management; and

(6) the attitudes of management towards risk.

Thus proposals that have a higher "internal" rate of return than the cost of capital may not be accepted because funds are not available. Conversely, funds may be available, but the proposals under consideration may have internal rates of return that are lower than the cost of capital.

---

[2] The use of required rates has been advocated by Committee on Cost Concepts and Standards, "Tentative Statement of Cost Concepts Underlying Reports for Management Purposes," *The Accounting Review*, April 1956;

Edward L. Wallace, "Some Comments on the Statement of Planning Costs," *The Accounting Review*, July 1957, p. 460.

Charles T. Horngren, *Cost Accounting: A Managerial Emphasis* Englewood Cliffs, N.J.: Prentice-Hall, 1962), Chapter 21.

[3] For negative commentary on required rates, read A. A. Robichek and S. C. Myers, *Optimal Financial Decisions* (Englewood Cliffs, N.J.: Prentice-Hall, 1965).

Actually many theorists do not accept available capital as a legitimate constraint for two reasons. First, they feel that capital can somehow be raised to implement any truly promising alternative. Secondly, the amount of capital available in any given period is partly a function of the cash generated by the implemented proposals themselves. This involves a circular argument; if more proposals are implemented, more capital is made available for investment, and if more capital is available, more proposals can be implemented. Ultimately, the process halts because some other constraint, interferes—perhaps a managerial policy against excessive expansion, or a lack of really promising alternatives, or the promise of very attractive future proposals, which makes present forbearance advisable.

It is very easy to overlook the fact that adding proposals may strain existing facilities. It is clear that added activity generally leads to increased needs for working capital; however, the effects on other facilities and resources may be more subtle. For instance, the addition of a machine may exhaust floor space or supervisory time, or even render inadequate the capacity of the employees' parking lot. Such capacity restrictions suggest that capital budgeting should be approached almost exclusively with mathematical programming techniques.

Physical capacities also influence the selection of proposals in another way. If the department requesting funds for investment has idle capacity, then there is little to be gained by adding to that capacity. Bottleneck departments should have priority.

A managerial policy that deserves special consideration has to do with the desire for flexibility. In a way, this desire reflects management's preference for liquidity. At any rate, in these times of phenomenally rapid technological advances, it is important for businesses to be able to adopt changes quickly. If capital is mostly frozen in long-term proposals, immobility may result. Hence it may be wise to structure capital budgeting to include a significant proportion of short-term proposals. Although the rate of return on such proposals may be less than on some available long-term proposals, nevertheless the short-term proposals liquidate faster, thereby providing more capital and with it more flexibility. Such a structured capital policy implicitly recognizes the opportunity costs of inflexibility. Furthermore, this need for flexibility (liquidity) increases the importance of adopting proposals with short payback periods (that is, the length of time it takes for the earnings of a proposal to offset the amount of investment in the proposal).

Ranking and Screening

Candidate proposals should be screened (are they acceptable?) and (what is the order of desirability of the acceptable proposals?). But what traits may be considered desirable? Three criteria come to mind: need, liquidity, and profitability. If an absolutely essential piece of equipment falls apart, desperate need for a replacement exists. Therefore, desperation proposals have priority. Other proposals, however, must stand or fall on their liquidity and profitability rankings.

Many procedures have been devised for screening and ranking a series of investment proposals; the most popular of these are described below.

1. *Payback period.* Payback period equals investment divided by average annual earnings. Payback period is a measure not of profitability but of liquidity; for this reason it is an inferior tool of analysis. If liquidity were of prime concern, there would be no point in making the investment, since merely by refraining from investing, the existing liquidity position would be retained.

2. *Simple rate of return.* Simple rate of return is the reciprocal of the payback period. Simple rate of return does measure profitability; however, it ignores the time value of money and must therefore be classified as an inferior technique.

3. *Time adjusted rate of return.* The time adjusted rate of return (TAR), also referred to as the internal rate of return (IRR), is a profitability measure. It determines a proposal's internal rate of return and then contrasts it to either the firm's cost-of-capital rate or its required rate. If the internal rate of return is greater, the proposal is acceptable.

4. *Net present value.* Net present value (NPV), also known as discounted cash flow, is also a profitability measure. Under this method inflows are discounted to a present value using either the firm's cost-of-capital rate or its required rates. If the present value of inflows exceeds that of outflows, the proposal is acceptable.

5. *Profitability index method.* Under the profitability index method, the present value of inflows is divided by the present value of the investment to obtain an index of profitability. Some analysts refer to this index as the "benefit-cost ratio."

6. *Normalized cash-flow method.* The normalized cash-flow method uses discounting to substitute a theoretical annuity of equal cash flows for real, uneven, and irregular cash flows that have equivalent present value. By contrasting the normalized cash flows of competing, mutually exclusive proposals, acceptability can be determined.

7. *Discounted payback.* To reflect profitability to some degree, the payback period is determined using discounted cash flows.

8. *Incremental analysis.* Incremental analysis compares the discounted differences in earnings of two proposals to the differences in their investments with the objective of deciding whether the former merit the latter. Either NPV or TAR can be used.

Some ranking methods have more appeal than others. Thus the notion of an internal rate of return is easy to understand, as is the "net gain" idea of NPV. NPV, however, could be criticized for focusing on quantity while virtually ignoring quality (although quality has been attended to somewhat when the analyst used the appropriate discount rate). Profitability index remedies this by comparing present value of benefits (the numerator) to the present value of investment (the denominator). Thus profitability index, like TAR, concentrates on quality by comparing output to input. But quality, too, can be misleading in the absence of quantity. If project A has an index of 2 while B has an index of 1.5, it would still be important to know that A came from \$4,000/\$2,000 while B came from \$300,000/\$200,000. Obviously, knowing that NPV_A is \$2,000 while NPV_B is \$100,000 changes your perspective somewhat.

Illustration 1. A proposal promises net cash earnings (or cash throw-offs) of \$8,000 each year for five years. If the investment presently required is \$24,000, what is the proposal's internal rate of return (or time-adjusted rate of return, TAR)? If the required rate is 15%, how should the proposal be classified?

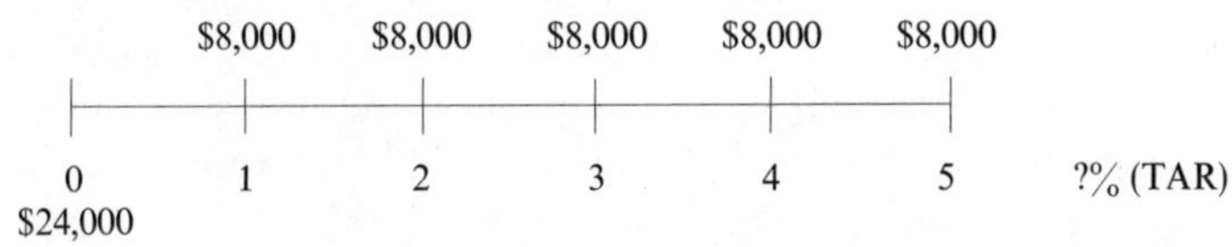

To find TAR, the investment may be divided by the annual earnings to obtain a factor to look for on row 5 (there are five years of life for this proposal) of Table 4 in Appendix A. When the factor is located, TAR is the percentage associated with the column in which the factor is found. Sometimes interpolation is required in this process. The calculations are as follows:

$$\text{Payback period} = \frac{\text{Investment}}{\text{Annual earnings}} = \frac{I}{E} = \frac{\$24{,}000}{\$8{,}000} = 3.000$$

In Table 4, 18% corresponds to a factor of 3.127 and 20% corresponds to a factor of 2.991. Most analysts would say that 2.991 is close enough to 3.000, especially where there is a difference of .136 (that is, 3.127 – 2.991); hence, they would say that TAR = 20%.

The significant difference between time adjusted rate of return (TAR) and simple rate of return (which ignores the time value of money) is:

$$\text{TAR} = 20\%$$

$$\text{Simple rate of return} = \frac{\$8,000}{\$24,000} = 33\tfrac{1}{3}\%$$

Now to classify the proposal. Since 20% exceeds the 15% required rate of return, the proposal is "acceptable." Note that it is not "accepted," however, until it competes successfully against all other candidate proposals. (Had the TAR been less than 15%, it would have been rejected.)

Illustration 2. The data for two mutually exclusive proposals are shown below.[4]

	Proposal A	Proposal B
Net cash earnings:		
e_1	\$ 8,000	\$ 6,000
e_2	8,000	6,000
e_3	6,000	6,000
e_4	4,000	8,000
Totals	\$26,000	\$26,000
Investment:	\$19,600	\$17,900
Cost of capital: 10%		

Required:

1. Compute the net present value (NPV) for each proposal.
2. Compute the TAR for each proposal.
3. Decide which proposal should be accepted.
4. Describe alternate ways of arriving at the same decision.

Comment: It should be observed that this is a far from easy decision. For while both proposals yield the same total earnings over their durations, A generates cash much faster than B and has a shorter payback period. On the other hand, A requires a larger investment than B.

[4] Two investments are said to be mutually exclusive when the acceptance of one necessitates the rejection of the other. If either or both alternatives may be accepted simultaneously, the proposals would be described as being independent of one another. And if the acceptance of one proposal depended upon the acceptance of a prior proposal, the proposals would be described as being contingent.

The solution to each part follows:

First we compute the discounted cash outflows from the project:

1. $DCF_A = \$8{,}000B(2, 10) + \$6{,}000b(3, 10) + \$4{,}000b(4, 10) = \$21{,}124$

   $DCF_B = \$6{,}000B(3, 10) + \$8{,}000b(4, 10) = \$20{,}385$

   Next we subtract the discounted cash inflows (the investments):

$$NPV = DCF - I$$
$$NPV_A = \$21{,}124 - \$19{,}600 = \$1{,}524$$
$$NPV_B = \$20{,}385 - \$17{,}900 = \$2{,}485$$

   Obviously, B is preferable.

2. Since the annual earnings are not equal, the computation of TAR is more complicated than it was in Illustration 1. One procedure is to test different rates of return until one is found that equates the present value of the earnings to the investment, that is: $I = \Sigma e_i b(i, r)$

   After a trial-and-error approach using several different rates, the TAR for each proposal was found to be:

   A: $\$19{,}600 = \$8{,}000B(2, 14) + \$6{,}000b(3, 14) + \$4{,}000b(4, 14)$

   B: $\$17{,}900 = \$6{,}000B(3, 16) + \$8{,}000b(4, 16)$

   Consequently, on the basis of time adjusted rate of return, proposal B is preferable, since it earns 16% while A only earns 14%.

   An alternative approach to searching the discount tables is to employ a root-searching routine. This will be illustrated shortly.

3. Since both NPV and TAR favor B, this appears to be the better proposal. Nonetheless, as we shall see, investments always come in packages, largely because existing asset investments should be constantly reviewed using updated earnings estimates and current investment values (determined on either a replacement cost or opportunity basis). In the present case, no package containing A could be better than one containing B; however, in general, if the worse proposal requires a lower investment, the worse proposal might still be selected because its package can make better use of the incremental investment (that is, of $I_B - I_A$).

4. *Profitability index.* By dividing the DCF of each proposal by the present value of its investment, the profitability index for the proposal is obtained.

$$\text{A:}\quad \frac{\$21{,}124}{\$19{,}600} = 1.078 \qquad \text{B:}\quad \frac{\$20{,}385}{\$17{,}900} = 1.139$$

   Once again B is preferable to A.

   Differential approach. Obtain the differential cash flows of each proposal and see whether the proposal with the greater investment is justified by having a sufficiently higher discounted revenue stream:

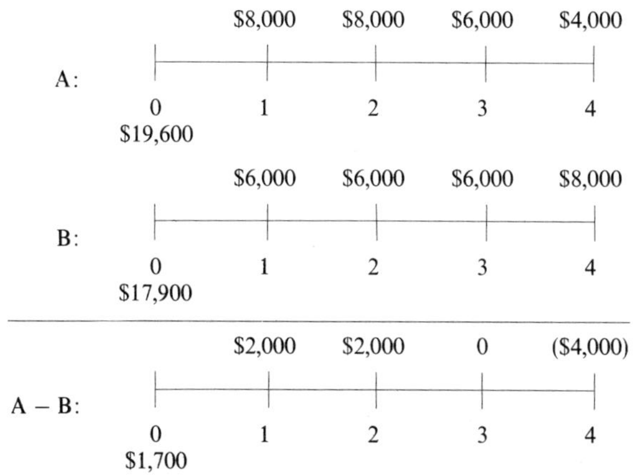

$$\$1,700 \overset{?}{\leqq} \$2,000B(2, 10) - \$4,000b(4, 10)$$
$$\$1,700 > \$739$$

Therefore, select B, since the additional investment in A is not merited. An important thing to remember when comparing two alternatives in this manner is to be sure that the "standard" proposal (B above) is acceptable on its individual merits. Whenever comparisons are made, it is necessary to know how good the standard is before it can be said whether the thing being compared to standard is good or not. For if the standard is poor (unacceptable), something can be better than standard without actually being good (acceptable) itself. It is a question of relatives and absolutes—one thing may be *relatively* better than another without being *absolutely* good.

Before leaving this problem, let us calculate the discounted paybacks of these proposals:

	A	B
e_1:	$8,000$b(1, 10)$ = $ 7,273	$6,000$b(2, 10)$ = $ 5,455
e_2:	$8,000$b(2, 10)$ = $ 6,611	$6,000$b(2, 10)$ = $ 4,958
e_3:	$6,000$b(3, 10)$ = $ 4,508	$6,000$b(3, 10)$ = $ 4,508
	$18,392	$14,921
e_4:	$4,000$b(4, 10)$ = $ 2,732	$8,000$b(4, 10)$ = $ 5,464
	$21,124	$20,385

Observe that A will require about one-half of its fourth-year earnings to recoup its $19,600 investment. B, on the other hand, will need a little over one-half of its fourth year earnings before its $17,900 will be recouped. The difference is too slight to be significant; nevertheless, discounted payback favors A. Finally, a caveat: Do not expect that all the screening methods will agree on the same signal. For ranking purposes, theorists prefer net present value for reasons that will soon be explained. Nevertheless, TAR and payback have their uses; profitability index and incremental analysis are really just different ways of looking at NPV.

Illustration 3. Let us turn to a problem that deals with both unequal lives of proposals and the effects of income tax regulations.

Problem: A company is considering replacing a machine. The presently owned machine (the defendant) will last physically for another two years. At present it has a book value of $10,000 and generates net cash earnings of $7,000 per year. It can be traded in for $3,000 or sold for $2,000. At the end of two more years, the machine will be worthless (scrap value will equal cost of carting it to a junk dealer). The replacement machine (the claimant) is expected to have a five-year economic life. It costs $50,000 on the market and will require an additional $9,000 to install. It is estimated that the resale value of the claimant will decline exponentially at the rate of 50% per year. The expected annual cash earnings of the claimant are $25,000. The tax rate in effect is 60% and the company requires earnings after taxes of 10%. What decision should the company make?

Let us start by computing the cost of the claimant:

Market price	$50,000
Less trade-in	3,000
Net cost	$47,000
Installation	9,000
Cost before investment credit	$56,000
Investment credit[5]	1,300
Net cost	$54,700

[5] Although there are limitations and buildings don't qualify (note that this favors non-building type investments), investments (at the time this problem was composed) give rise to tax credits according to the following schedule:

Life (t) in Years	Net Credit Percentages
$4 \leq t < 6$	$7\% (\frac{1}{3}) = .0233$
$6 \leq t < 8$	$7\% (\frac{2}{3}) = .0467$
$t \geq 8$	$7\% (1) = .07$

$\$56{,}000\ (.0233) \approx \$1{,}300$

There is a ceiling on the amount of credit that can be taken in any year; however, unused credit can be carried over to ensuing years.

The federal adjusted basis for depreciation may be computed as follows: The computations for taxes are shown below.

Defendant:	Net cash earnings	\$ 7,000	
	Depreciation (straight line)	5,000	
		\$ 2,000	
	Tax rate	60%	
	Taxes	\$ 1,200	
Claimant:	Net cash earnings	\$25,000	\$25,000
	Depreciation (see below)	21,967	15,973
		\$ 3,033	\$ 9,027
	Tax rate	60%	60%
	Taxes—year 1, 2	\$ 1,820	\$ 5,416

Depreciation (Sum-of-the-Years' Digits Method)[6]:
Salvage is exponential at the rate of 50% per year:

$S = Me^{-.5t}$, where M is the market price uninstalled and t represents years

$S = \$50{,}000e^{-.5(5)} = \$50{,}000(.082) = \$4{,}100$

Depreciation special allowance (see Note): limit \$2,000

Depreciation = (Basis − salvage − special allowance) rate:

$D_1 = (\$66{,}000 - \$4{,}100 - \$2{,}000)\ 5/15 = \$19{,}967$

$D_2 = (\$66{,}000 - \$4{,}100 - \$2{,}000)\ 4/15 = \$15{,}973$

Total for first year = \$2,000 + \$19,967 = \$21,967

Note: At time of writing, federal tax laws allowed a first-year extra allowance of 20% or up to \$2,000 per year. This should be considered where limitations are not effective and one wishes to maximize return on investment. Because discounting reduces cash flows of later years more than it does those of earlier years, it is wise to use extra allowance and accelerated depreciation techniques to obtain the lowest tax cash flows. *Where many proposals are available in a given year and the \$2,000 limitation will be collectively exceeded, it should be ignored in computation, since allocating it arbitrarily favors some proposals.*

---

[6] Yearly depreciation under the sum-of-the years' digits method follows the formula

$$D_i = (C - S)\left[\frac{N - i + 1}{N(N+1) \div 2}\right],$$ where i = the year, N = the asset life, C = cost, S = salvage.

C may be further reduced by first-year extra depreciation allowance, as in the present example.

The problem could generally be diagrammed as follows:

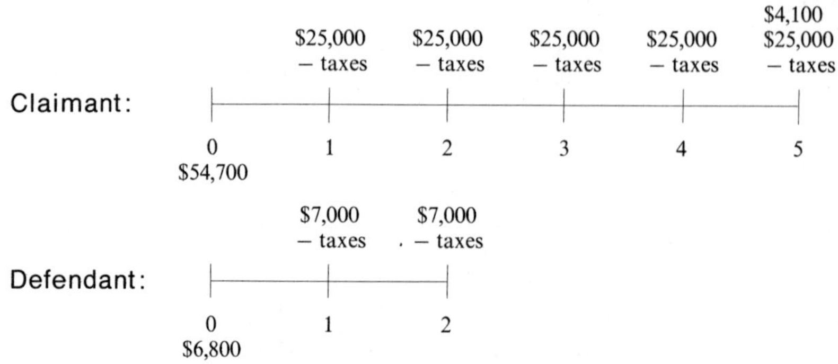

Several things require study at this point. First, we must ask ourselves what the investment in dollars will be if the claimant is chosen. This has already been computed to be \$54,700. Second, we must decide what the investment in the defendant is at this time. If we sold the defendant, we would get \$2,000 plus the tax savings on the loss, that is, 60% (\$10,000 book value–\$2,000 proceeds) or \$4,800. So \$6,800 is the cash equivalent of our investment in the defendant.[7] *Taxes, however, are computed using the remaining book value of the defendant, since these taxes are the actual cash outlays involved.* Finally, we note the disparity in lives of the two investments. There are two popular approaches to treating this disparity:

1. Assume a replacement machine must be bought at the end of two years if the defendant is kept now. The defendant's financial data are assumed to hold for the replacement unless the defendant type of machine will no longer be available. At the end of five years, the present claimant must be replaced. Such replacements may be assumed either in perpetuity or for a period of, say, 30 years. After 30 years the discounting factors are so small that further assumed replacements have no effect on the decision. This procedure is cumbersome at best and rests on many assumptions that become less tenable with the passage of time.

2. Compute a salvage value for the claimant at the end of the defendant's life. This is very easy to do. In this case, our salvage value formula yields

$$S = f(x) = f(2) = \$50{,}000e^{-.5(2)} = \$50{,}000(.368) = \$18{,}400$$

(We see now why taxes were computed for only two years.)

[7] Some authors reduce the investment in the claimant by the \$6,800, thereby implicitly asserting that there is no investment in the defendant. This, of course, is fallacious.

Note that *it would not be proper* to discount the cash inflows for years 3, 4, and 5 at the required rate to obtain some sort of residual value of the claimant at the end of year 2. This is improper because the residual value would then be discounted to the time of decision. In effect we would not have recognized that the comparison is over a two-year period—the life of the defendant. We would have obtained the present value of the inflows of all five years. In effect we would have $B(3, 10)b(2, 10)$, and this is merely the present value of an annuity deferred two periods.

The problem may now be solved by first noting whether the defendant proposal is acceptable on its own merits and then doing an incremental analysis. (The defendant is the standard in the incremental analysis.)

Defendant:

$$\$6{,}800 \overset{?}{\leq} \$(7{,}000 - 1{,}200)B(2, 10)$$
$$\$6{,}800 < \$(5{,}800)(1.736) = \$10{,}068.80$$

Defendant is, therefore, acceptable.

Incremental Analysis:

Claimant:

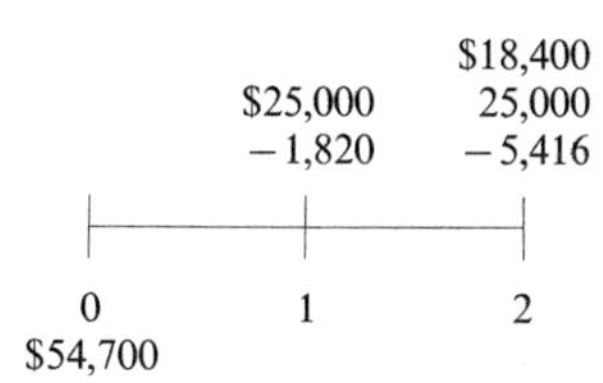

Defendant:

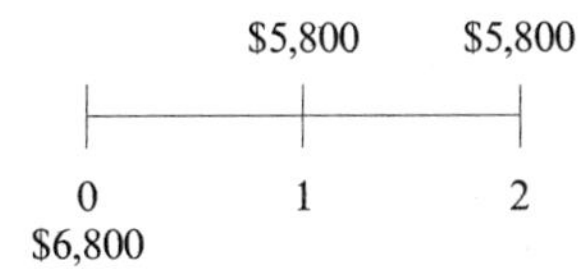

Claimant minus Defendant:

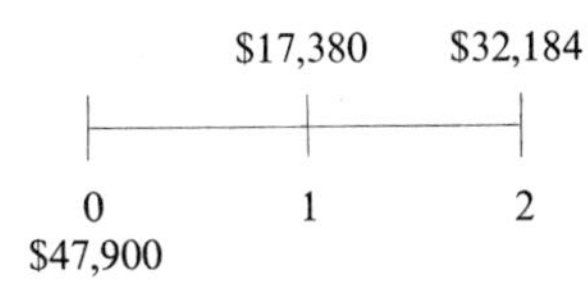

$$\$47{,}900 \overset{?}{\leq} \$17{,}380b(1, 10) + \$32{,}184b(2,10)$$
$$\$47{,}900 > \$17{,}380(.909) + \$32{,}184(.826) = \$42{,}382$$

Consequently, the extra earnings of the claimant do not merit the extra investment. The decision would be made to retain the defendant.

Comments:

1. It would be impossible to illustrate how every wrinkle in the tax laws affects capital budgeting analysis mainly because the laws change constantly as one pressure group or another succeeds in bending them to its advantage.

2. Whether investment credit and additional first-year depreciation allowance should be reflected depends entirely on whether some proposal will be favored arbitrarily. The carryover provision of the investment credit tends to prevent troubles from arising there, but the $2,000 limitation on first-year extra depreciation allowance would cause difficulties if more than one depreciable asset of substantial cost were acquired in a given year. Recall the timing argument from the cost of capital discussion and you will realize that one goal of capital budgeting is to eliminate advantages occasioned by arbitrary timing. A company happens to get machine A earlier in the year than machine B. Is this a race, with the winner getting the extra allowance? And again, who says we couldn't give B the allowance instead of A? Certainly not the Internal Revenue Service.

Illustration 4. Let us see how normalized cash flow could be used to choose between two proposals with both uneven lives and investments but no explicit revenue data.

Problem: A company must choose between two machines. The machine it needs is one of several used in a production process. Calculating revenue generated is thought unnecessary because the same substantial, though unmeasured, revenues will be earned regardless of which machine is acquired. A 20% return before taxes is required and cash expenses have been estimated as follows:

		A	B
Investment		$74,000	$130,000
Yearly costs:	c_1	$15,000	$ 12,000
	c_2	18,000	12,000
	c_3		15,000
	c_4		15,000
	c_5		15,000

Suppose A's cycle were repeated (that is, a second A machine were purchased at the start of year 3).

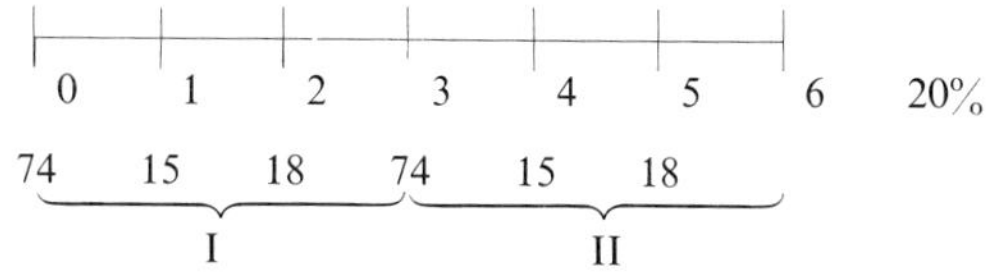

$$PV_1 = \text{present value of cycle I} = \$74{,}000 + \$15{,}000b(1, 20) + \$18{,}000b(2, 20) = \$\ 98{,}998.70$$
$$PV_2 = \text{present value of cycle II} = \$98{,}998.70b(3, 20) = 57{,}290.55$$
$$\Sigma PV_i = \text{present value of both cycles} \quad \$156{,}289.25$$

If costs were normalized, x dollars would be paid each year. For two cycles the continuum would look like this:

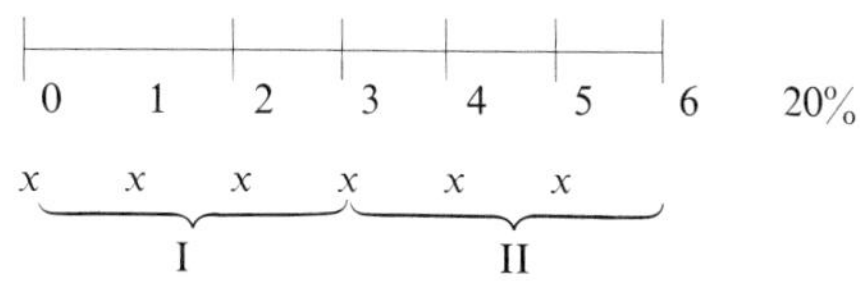

Assuming it makes no difference to the company what the pattern of costs is so long as the same present value results, we can determine the normalized cost for cycle I as follows:

$$PV_1 = \$98{,}998.70 = x \sum_{i=0}^{2} \left(\frac{1}{1.2}\right)^i = x(B(2, 20) + 1.0000) = 2.5278x$$

$$x = \frac{\$98{,}998.70}{2.5278} = \$39{,}163.98$$

The normalized cost for both cycles is

$$PV_i = \$156{,}289.25 = x \sum_{i=0}^{5} \left(\frac{1}{1.2}\right)^i = x(B(5, 20) + 1.0000) = 3.9906x$$

$$x = \frac{\$156{,}289.25}{3.9906} = \$39{,}164.35$$

The difference in the two values of x is entirely due to using only four-place tables; were six- or eight-place tables used, there would be no difference.

What does this tell us? It simply says that the normalized cost is the same whether one cycle, or two cycles, or n cycles are considered; therefore, calculate normalized cost for only one cycle.

The normalized cost for B is

$$\$130{,}000 + \$12{,}000B(2, 20) + \$15{,}000B(3, 20)b(2, 20) = x(B(5, 20) + 1.0000)$$
$$\$170{,}275.60 = 3.9906x$$
$$x = \$42{,}669.17$$

Decision: Since the normalized cost for B exceeds that for A, choose A.

Critique:

1. Should the company be indifferent between the estimated investment and its cost pattern, and the normalized pattern? If $x < I$, as is likely, $I - x$ (= \$74,000 − \$39,164, in the case of A) is *theoretically* available for investment. The normalization has reflected the required return, but what if there is a project available that can use $I - x$ dollars at a return that is greater than the required rate? In this theoretical plane, the pooling concept comes to our aid—why should this particular machine investment be penalized by the burden of bearing excessive interest? And when all investments are considered over the planning horizon, the analysis returns to the required rate.

2. When repeating cycles, shouldn't allowance be made for differences in the purchasing power of money? R. E. Bickner answers this question succinctly:

> If [the cost analyst] is estimating future costs of a program he is probably assuming, for purposes of his cost estimates, that prices will remain at current levels. In other words, he does not have to take price changes out of his estimates because he has not put any such changes into his estimates. His unadjusted cost estimates represent an estimate in 'constant dollars'—that is, in dollars that are all equivalent in purchasing power. Only if he wants to estimate actual dollar expenditures for financial planning purposes, will he need to become concerned about general price changes. If he wants to compare real costs of alternative programs, general price level changes due to monetary phenomena may be ignored.[8]

Illustration 5. How do combinations affect choice of investments? When you consider that every asset presently owned should be rechallenged regularly to see whether it merits its present (as opposed to "historical") investment, you may better appreciate the complexity of this question. In the real world, there are so many projects (assets) that the use of mathematical programming is the only humane way to choose the best combination. Nevertheless, some feeling for the subtleties involved can be obtained from investigating a small problem especially trumped-up for the purpose.

---

[8] R. E. Bickner, "Concepts of Economic Costs," in *Cost Considerations in Systems Analysis*, ed. Gene H. Fisher (New York: American Elsevier Publishing Co., 1971), p. 52.

Suppose a company has amassed the data shown below. Assume that projects A and A′ are mutually exclusive with both NPV and TAR indicating that A is preferable. Further assume that D represents all the existing, already implemented projects (assets), and that the company can borrow at most \$500,000 this year. Required return is 20%.

Data:

Project	Life (Years)	Annual Earnings	DCF	I	NPV	TAR
A	3	\$158,261.23	\$ 333,337	\$ 300,000	\$ 33,377	27%
A′	1	124,000.00	103,329	100,000	3,329	24%
B	12	322,129.00	1,430,039	1,200,000	230,039	25%
C	6	83,850.41	278,845	200,000	78,845	35%
D	5	303,593.79	907,928	800,000	107,928	26%

	Package 1				Package 2		
Decision:	TAR	I	NPV		TAR	I	NPV
A′	24%	\$ 100,000	\$ 3,329	A	27%	\$ 300,000	\$ 33,377
B	25%	1,200,000	230,039	C	35%	200,000	78,845
				D	26%	800,000	107,928
		Σ \$1,300,000	\$233,368			Σ \$1,300,000	\$220,150

Package 1 is preferable.

Comments:

1. Ignoring the relationship between A and A′, first note the different rankings:

	NPV	TAR
A	4	2
A′	5	5
B	1	4
C	3	1
D	2	3

As far as the screening for acceptability of an individual project is concerned, it makes no difference whether NPV or TAR is used, for if TAR $\geq r$, then NPV ≥ 0, and if TAR $< r$, NPV < 0. However, when a group of projects is ranked, the rankings by NPV need not agree with those by TAR.

2. Note that the time adjusted returns appear vastly better for package 2, and yet package 1 is clearly preferable because it yields a \$233,368 NPV (as opposed to a \$220,150 NPV for package 2). *Even though*

TAR and NPV give the same signal for individual project acceptability, when combinations are considered, NPV, which maximizes wealth, is the ranking method to use in the absence of more explicit information about risk and uncertainty.

Since it seems reasonable to choose proposals with the greatest time adjusted returns, the choice of package 1 is something of a surprise. What is the rationale behind this choice? Note that both packages include proposals with varying lives. *TAR assumes that funds generated by shorter-term proposals are reinvested at their first-cycle rates, while NPV assumes that funds generated by proposals can only earn a required return (and therefore add 0 to NPV).* The more heroic assumption—that of repeated cycle rates—is more easily discarded. For similar reasons NPV is preferable to profitability index for ranking purposes as well.

It may soothe your intuitions to view the situation as follows: having chosen A′ instead of A, the company has available \$200,000 in package 1 to invest in B, which earns 25% for its whole life of 12 years. If the company had chosen A in package 2, it would earn 27% on the extra \$200,000 for three years and only 20% for the time (12 − 3 = 9 years) thereafter.

Illustration 6. Proposals requiring investment in subsequent years (and calculations of internal rates for incremental analyses where net inflows and outflows alternate somewhat) give rise to multiple internal rates of returns. Suppose two mutually exclusive projects may be diagrammed as shown below. Determine the TAR for the incremental flows.

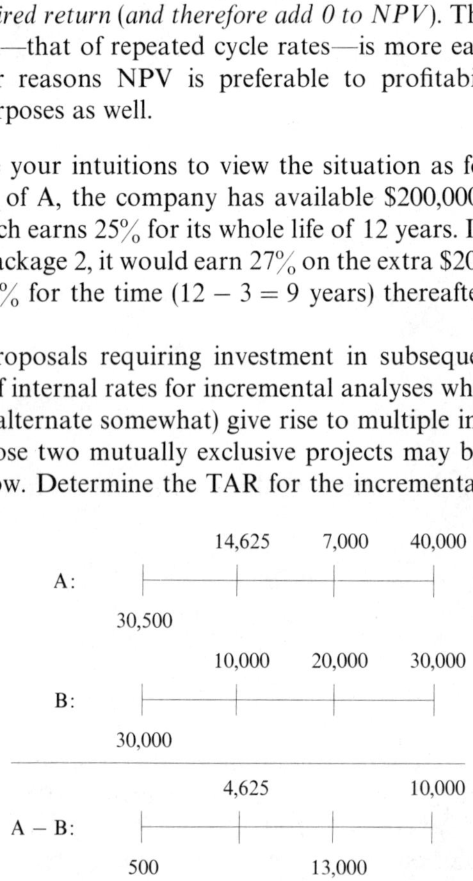

$$500 = 4{,}625\left(\frac{1}{1+r}\right) - 13{,}000\left(\frac{1}{1+r}\right)^2 + 10{,}000\left(\frac{1}{1+r}\right)^3$$

If we let $x = 1/(1 + r)$, we may state this equation as a function: $f(x) = 4{,}625x - 13{,}000x^2 + 10{,}000x^3 - 500$. We may now search for the roots of

$f(x)$, using the Newton-Raphson formula:[9] $x_{i+1} = x_i - [f(x_i)/f'(x_i)]$. Since $f(x)$ is a polynomial, the Birge-Vieta method for implementing the Newton-Raphson formula is especially pertinent. We try first to find a range over which the function crosses the axis (determined by a change in sign of the function) at least once. $f(x = 0) = -500$ and $f(x = 1) = 1{,}125$; therefore, there is at least one root between $0 \leq x \leq 1$. For a starting guess, try $x = .9$.

Birge-Vieta method: $f(x) = 10{,}000x^3 - 13{,}000x^2 + 4{,}625x - 500$

Iteration 1

	x^3	x^2	x^1	x^0		
	10,000	−13,000	4,625	−500	.9	$x_{i+1} = .9 - (f(.9)/f'(.9))$
Start →	+0	+.9(10,000)	+.9(−4,000)	+.9(1,025)		$= .9 - (422.5/5{,}525)$
	10,000	−4,000	1,025	(422.5) = $f(.9)$		$= .9 - .0765 = .8235$
	+0	+.9(10,000)	+.9(5,000)			
	10,000	5,000	(5,525)	= $f'(.9)$		

Iteration 2

10,000	−13,000	4,625	−500	.8235	$x_{i+1} = .8235 - (77.27/3{,}558.5)$
0	8,235	−3,924	577.27		$= .8235 - .0217 = .8018$
10,000	−4,765	701	(77.27) = $f(.8235)$		
0	8,235	2,857.5			
10,000	3,470	(3,558.5)	= $f'(.8235)$		

Iteration 3

10,000	−13,000	4,625	−500	.8018	$x_{i+1} = .8018 - (5.45/3{,}064.7)$
0	8,018	−3,994.6	505.45		$= .8018 - .0018 = .8$
10,000	−4,982	630.4	(5.45)		
0	8,018	2,434.3			
10,000	3,036	(3,064.7)			

Iteration 4

10,000	−13,000	4,625	−500	.8	Since $f(.8) = 0$, $x = .8$ is a root. We have
0	8,000	−4,000	500		
10,000	−5,000	625	0		$f(x) = (x - .8)(10{,}000x^2 - 5{,}000x + 625)$

continued to page 352

[9] Developed from the first two terms of the Taylor series in Appendix C.

continued from page 351

The remaining roots may be found by applying the quadratic formula

$$\frac{-b \pm \sqrt{b^2 - 4ac}}{2a} = \frac{5{,}000 \pm \sqrt{5{,}000^2 - 4(10{,}000)625}}{2(10{,}000)} = .25 \pm 0$$

Keeping in mind that the quadratic equation is always set equal to 0 so that a constant may be factored, we find

$$f(x) = (x - .8)(x - .25)^2 10{,}000 = 10{,}000x^3 - 13{,}000x^2 + 4{,}625x - 500$$

Thus $x = \{.8, .25, .25\}$ are the roots

Hence,

$$x = \frac{1}{1+r} = .8 \qquad x = \frac{1}{1+r} = .25$$

$$1 = .8 + .8r \qquad 1 = .25 + .25r$$

$$.25 = r \qquad 3 = r$$

Conclusion: There are two unique internal rates of return; TAR = 25% and 300%

You need not really know how to do the Birge-Vieta method if you have access to a computer that has a root-searching software routine in its library.

How do you feel about multiple rates of return? Would you accept the incremental investment in A if the required return (or cost of capital) were, say, 30%? The most popular way to resolve the quandary is to see if the incremental investment has a positive NPV at 30%. If it has, then project A is superior and acceptable.[10] Once again, NPV charges to the rescue!

Illustration 7. The problem that we now address concerns the determination of the life of an investment and the subsequent decision concerning its acceptability.

Available Facts: Investment in machine = $8,000

Salvage value = S = $\$8{,}000e^{-.4t}$

Estimated annual earnings of investment net of cash operating costs:

$E = \$6{,}000 - \$500t$, where t represents the number of years the investment is kept

Required rate = 10%

$$\text{Net present value} = \text{NPV} = \int_0^n (6{,}000 - 500t)e^{-.1t}\,dt + 8{,}000e^{-.4n}e^{-.1n} - 8{,}000$$

[10] Another way of resolving the multiple rate of return issue is discussed in Ezra Solomon, "The Arithmetic of Capital Budgeting Decisions," *Journal of Business*, April 1956.

Since an optimal life (n) is to be determined, the derivative of NPV with respect to n must be obtained and set equal to zero.

$$\frac{d(\text{NPV})}{dn} = (6{,}000 - 500n)e^{-.1n} - 4{,}000e^{-.5n} = 0$$

$$6{,}000 - 500n = \frac{4{,}000e^{-.5n}}{e^{-.1n}} = 4{,}000e^{-.4n}$$

$$n = 12 - 8e^{-.4n}$$

By trial-and-error use of a table of exponentials or use of the Newton-Raphson formula, n may be computed to be approximately 12. Is the proposal acceptable?

$$\begin{aligned}\text{NPV} &= \int_0^{12} (6{,}000 - 500t)e^{-.1t}\,dt + 8{,}000e^{-.5(12)} - 8{,}000 \\ &= (6{,}000 - 500t)(-10e^{-.1t}) + 50{,}000e^{-.1t}]_0^{12} + 8{,}000(.0025) - \$8{,}000 \\ &= [0 + 50{,}000e^{-1.2}] - [(6{,}000 - 0)(-10e^0) + 50{,}000e^0] + 20 - 8{,}000 \\ &= \$15{,}059.50 + \$10{,}000 + \$20 - \$8{,}000 = \$17{,}079.50\end{aligned}$$

Consequently, the proposal is acceptable.

Sensitivity Analysis

It has probably struck you as strange that we have treated all the cash flows in the preceding examples as if they were amounts guaranteed in contracts. Whenever it has been necessary to forecast cash flows, the figures used were simply estimates—expected values of variables. (Modes or medians could be used, but they are not as tractable mathematically and hence are not in vogue.) Thus the figures could fluctuate in value, and, given sufficient unfavorable fluctuation, the screening measures would fall below acceptable levels. A logical question to ask is "How much unfavorable fluctuation can this proposal withstand?" Questions like this fall under the heading of sensitivity analysis.

In the simplest form of sensitivity analysis, one simply resorts to break-even concepts as illustrated below.

Given:

$$\begin{aligned} I &= \$41{,}925 \\ n &= 10 \text{ years} \\ E &= \$10{,}000 \text{ per year} \\ r &= 15\% \\ \text{TAR} &= 20\% \end{aligned}$$

What reduction in earnings could occur and still leave the proposal acceptable?

$$\text{NPV} = 0 = E'B(10, 15) - \$41{,}925$$

$$= 5.0188E' \quad - \$41{,}925$$

$$E' = \$8{,}353.59$$

Therefore, earnings can drop by \$1,646.41($E - E'$) per year. What would the breakeven life be?

$$\text{NPV} = 0 = \$10{,}000B(?, 15) - \$41{,}925$$

$$B(?, 15) = 4.1925$$

So the critical life is about seven years—$B(7, 15) = 4.1604$—and estimated life can be off by about three years.

Next let us see how the normal probability distribution might be introduced to do this sort of work.[11] The safety margins are calculated as follows:

1. Decide on the normal curve mean and standard deviation values for each of the investment parameters.
2. Calculate the value of the parameter that would just render the proposal acceptable.
3. Decide the probability of being in error by the difference; if this probability is less than a predetermined value, the proposal's parameter has a sufficient safety margin.

Example:

I = immediate investment in a proposal = \$50,000
E = expected value of annual cash earnings = \$15,000
E' = critical earnings
n = expected life of proposal = 6 years
r = required rate of return = 8%

Let us first test the sensitivity of E. The minimal earnings that would just render the proposal acceptable would be

$$I = E'B(6, 8)$$

$$\$50{,}000 = E'(4.6229)$$

$$\$10{,}816 = E'$$

[11] The technical assumption being made here is that of perfect correlation of yearly earnings distributions. This will be explained in the next chapter.

We now ask the decisionmaker to estimate (1) the amount of deviation in earnings he expects, and (2) the safety margin he requires. Suppose he responds that he thinks the earnings estimate has an even change (50-50) of being off by \$2,000, and that if there is a 20% probability of losing money on the proposal, he will reject it. We have the situation portrayed below.

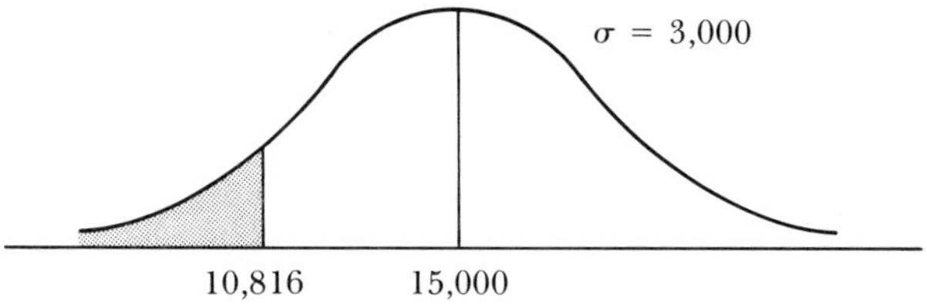

The standard deviation may be calculated as follows (observe that $2/3\sigma \approx 25\%$, which corresponds to the 50-50 chance):

$$\$2{,}000 = 2/3\sigma$$

$$\$3{,}000 = \sigma$$

The probability of the earnings being \$10,816 (the critical value, E') or worse is the shaded area and may be determined as follows:

Probability of \$15,000 or less minus probability of the earnings between \$10,816 and \$15,000.	
Probability of \$15,000 or less:	.5000
Probability of between \$10,816 and \$15,000:	−.4184
$Z = \dfrac{x - \bar{x}}{\sigma} = \dfrac{10{,}816 - 15{,}000}{3{,}000} = -1.395$	
From Table 8, $P(-1.395) \approx .4184$	
	.0816

Hence there is approximately an 8% chance of loss, and consequently a 12% safety margin (20% − 8%).

Now let us test n. The minimum life that would just render the proposal acceptable would be

$$I = EB(?, 8)$$

$$\$50{,}000 = \$15{,}000B(?, 8)$$

$$3.3333 = B(?, 8)$$

By consulting the table for B, we see that $B(4, 8) = 3.3121$; therefore, the critical life is approximately four years.

Suppose the decisionmaker decides that, owing to technological change and induced obsolescene, the estimate of life has a 30% probability of being high by three years. Furthermore, he feels as before that if there is a 20% probability of losing money on the proposal, it should be rejected. The normal curve presentation of the situation is shown below.

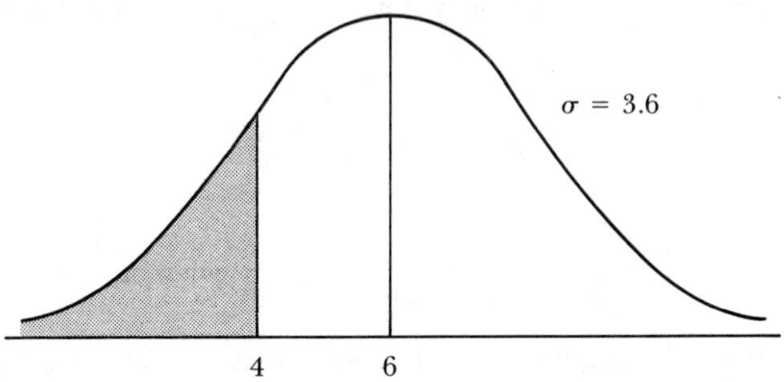

The standard deviation corresponding to 30% probability is $.84\sigma$. Therefore

$$3 = .84\sigma$$

$$3.6 \approx \sigma$$

The probability of the life being four years (the critical value) or less is the shaded area.

Probability of six years or less:	.5000
Probability of between four and six years:	−.2105

$$Z = \frac{x - \bar{x}}{\sigma} = \frac{4 - 6}{3.6} = -.555$$

From Table 8, $P(-.555) \approx .2105$

	.2895

Because there is approximately a 29% probability of loss, the proposal should be rejected on the basis of this test. However, it should be recognized (1) that the two tests are not mutually independent (that is, the test for *E* assumes *n*, while the test for *n* assumes *E*), and (2) that the proposal comfortably passed the sensitivity test for *E*. The decisionmaker may therefore want to take a second look at his estimates. He should also consider other techniques for expressing his risk preferences (next chapter).

A Parting Comment

Long and elaborate as this chapter has been, it has barely introduced the subject of capital budgeting. The next chapter incorporates risk and attitudes towards risk, and ensuing chapters will advance the subject a little at a time in the discussions of various models. While our last example introduced probability theory, the work ahead will rely much more heavily on probability theory.

Problems

1. *Oil field exploitation.* A company has been asked to invest in an oil field exploitation contract. The investment is to be on an equal installment basis with the forecasted cash earnings shown below. Given the specified returns, determine the amount of the investment installment that will just generate the returns. Set up the solution only, equating flows at year 73.

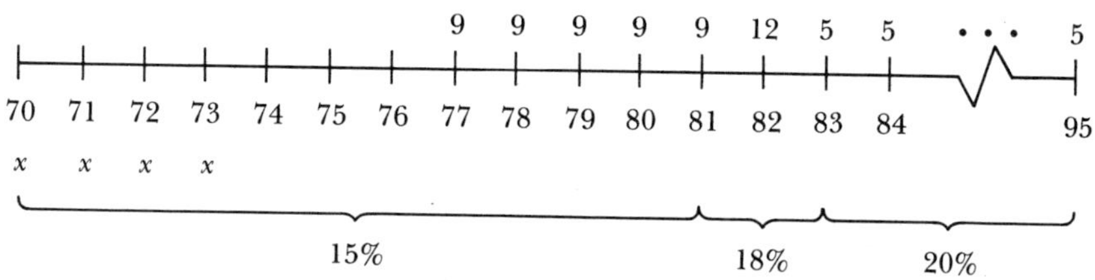

2. *Provision for differential treatment of distant flows, profitability index.* The cost benefit analysis of a proposal is depicted in the continuum shown below. Investment takes place now and at the end of the next two years, while cash inflows are delayed for five years. The company's policy is to discount estimated cash flows that occur seven years or more into the future at a heavier rate, to compensate for the uncertainty of these estimates. Compute a profitability index and state whether or not it indicates acceptability.

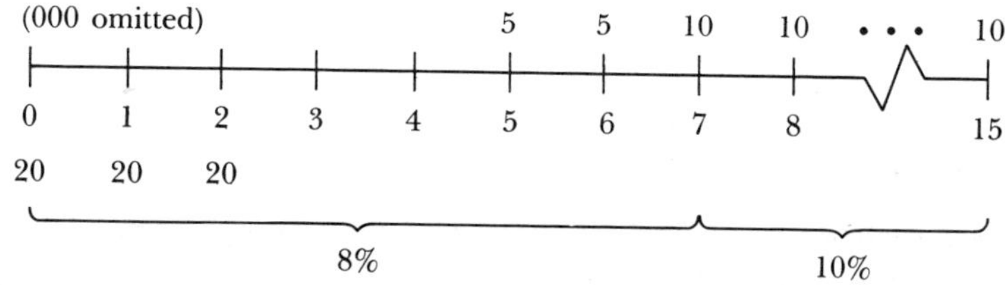

3. *Basics, TAR, profitability index.*

(a) A business has estimated that the annual cash earnings of a project will be \$80,000, and that this amount will be forthcoming each year for 14 years. If the project requires an initial investment of \$480,168, what is its internal rate of return?

(b) A project is expected to yield \$800,000 cash earnings in each of its first three years of life, \$600,000 in the fourth year, and \$300,000 in each of its remaining four years of life. If an initial investment of \$2,600,000 is required and cost of capital is 16%, what is the project's profitability index? Is this project acceptable?

4. *Discounted payback.* Although it is a very popular capital budgeting ranking technique, payback has often been criticized because it measures only liquidity. If liquidity is your primary concern, as I observed earlier, then don't bother to invest and liquidity will remain intact. However, if the cash flows are first discounted and payback is then applied, the resulting technique reflects both liquidity and profitability.

   Given: Investment at t_0 = \$15,000
   Net cash earnings—t_1 = \$10,000
   —t_2 = \$ 8,000
   —t_3 = \$ 7,000
   —t_4 through t_8 = \$ 6,000
   Required return = 20%

   Required:

   Determine the payback period on a discounted basis.

5. Given: The labelled continuums shown below.

A:	Investment \$40,000	\$21,000	\$18,000	\$15,000	Cash earnings
B:	Investment \$19,520	\$10,000	\$10,000	\$10,000	Cash earnings

A − B:	\$20,480	\$11,000	\$ 8,000	\$ 5,000	Required return = 20%

   Required:

   Determine net present values, time adjusted returns, and profitability indices for each project and then perform an incremental analysis. Assuming these are mutually exclusive proposals, what conclusion would you reach?

6. *Normalized stream, uneven lives, uneven investments.* Two machines can fill the same function. Their costs and lives vary as shown below.

	Costs	
Period	A	B
0	\$6,000	\$8,000
1	1,000	600
2	2,000	900
3		2,000

   Required return before taxes: 20%.
   Use the normalized stream approach to choose between the machines.

7. *Basics, even lives, even total returns, uneven investments.*

Net cash earnings:	Proposal A	Proposal B
t_1	$ 6,000	$ 8,000
t_2	6,000	8,000
t_3	6,000	8,000
t_4	7,000	5,000
t_5	5,000	5,000
t_6	5,000	5,000
t_7	5,000	5,000
t_8	5,000	1,000
Totals	$45,000	$45,000
Investment:	$26,700	$30,000
Cost of capital: 10%		

Required:

(a) Compute the amount of discounted cash inflow for each proposal.

(b) Compute the internal rate of return for each proposal.

(c) Which proposal should be accepted? Why?

(d) Name two ways other than the one you used in your answer to (c) that would enable you to reach the same decision.

8. *Basics, uneven earnings and investments.* The data for two mutually exclusive proposals are

Net cash earnings:	A	B
t_1	$20,480	$ 5,500
t_2	15,360	5,500
t_3	7,840	5,500
t_4	12,520	13,150
Investment:	$40,000	$18,000
Required return: 10%		

Compute (a) net present values, (b) time adjusted returns, (c) profitability indices, and (d) the incremental approach. What decision should be made?

Hint:

Think about the decision from the standpoint of what would be done with an incremental investment given no specific additional information about other proposals.

9. *Incremental analysis.* Use incremental analysis to determine the better of the following alternatives:

(a) The present machine generates net cash receipts of $2, $3, and $2 for the next three years respectively and has a present investment of $4.

(b) The replacement machine can generate net cash receipts of \$7, \$5, and \$4 for the next three years respectively and can be bought for \$10.

The required return is 20% before taxes and all cash estimates given above are on that basis (before taxes).

10. What is capital budgeting all about? Be brief, but be sure to discuss time adjusted rate of return, net present value, and incremental analysis along the way.

11. *Uneven lives, earnings, and investments.* Decide between A and B, assuming revenues are obviously acceptable and maintenance costs—which put things in shape for the ensuing year—are as follows:

Net cash costs:	A	B
t_0 (investment)	\$10,000	\$4,000
t_1	1,000	2,000
t_2	2,000	
t_3	3,000	
t_4	4,000	
Required return: 15%		

12. *Proof with regard to normalized stream simplification.* Using generalized notation, prove that the normalized stream of a single cycle equals the normalized stream where two cycles are computed, making computation of the latter redundant.

13. *Cost of capital (adapted from Certified Management Accounting Examination, December 1972).* The Conner Company has the following capital structure:

Mortgage Bonds (6%)	\$ 20,000,000
Common Stock (one million shares)	25,000,000
Retained Earnings	55,000,000
	\$100,000,000

(a) Mortgage bonds of similar quality could be sold at a net of 95 to yield $6\frac{1}{2}$%.

(b) The common stock has been selling for \$100 per share. The company has paid 50% of earnings in dividends for several years and intends to continue the policy. The current dividend is \$4 per share. Earnings are growing at 5% per year.

(c) If the company sold a new equity issue, it would expect to net \$94 per share after all costs.

(d) The marginal tax rate is 50%.

Conner wants to determine a cost of capital to use in capital budgeting. Additional projects would be financed to maintain the same relationship between debt and equity. Additional debt would consist of mortgage bonds and additional equity would consist of retained earnings.

Required:

(a) Calculate the firm's weighted average cost of capital.

(b) Explain why you used the weighting system you used.

14. How would you suggest dealing with inflation when setting a cost-of-capital rate?

15. *Basics, taxes.* A project has forecasted cash earnings of $90,000 for each of the next 10 years. It requires an investment of $200,000 in machinery, which will have no salvage value after 10 years. Assuming straight-line depreciation, taxes of 60% of net income, and an after-tax cost of capital of 16%, should this project be accepted? Why? Are there any circumstances under which you might not accept, other than those implied by the cost-of-capital criterion?

16. *Lease vs. buy.* A company has a choice of two plans for acquiring equipment. It can buy the equipment for $2,200,000 now, or it can lease it for the same figure over a six-year period—rent due in advance. If the equipment is leased, the first of six equal annual payments—with interest at 12%—will be due immediately. If the equipment is bought, a residual value of $100,000 will be recognized at the end of its six-year life and sum of the years' digits depreciation will be employed. The tax rate is 60% and is paid at the end of each year. A 5% return after taxes is required. Which plan should be chosen? Why? Support your answer.

17. *Lease vs. buy.* A company must decide whether to lease or purchase new equipment. If the equipment is leased yearly, rental payments of $40,000 must be paid at the beginning of each year. If the equipment is purchased, $108,000 must be paid immediately.

The firm has existing equipment with a book value of $30,000 that can be sold for $10,000. Although the present equipment should last physically for another 6 years, it is very inefficient. Management has decided to sell it.

The new equipment is expected to have an economic life of 12 years with no salvage value. Estimated operating savings from use of the new equipment, exclusive of depreciation or rent, are $60,000 per year.

Assuming a tax rate of 60% and a cost of capital of 15%, and ignoring the effects of leasing on the company's cost of capital, which alternative should be adopted? Why?

18. *Profitability index, accelerated depreciation, and taxes.* Compute the profitability index for a machine that costs $60,000, has a five-year life, and can be sold at the end of five years for $15,000. The earnings before taxes and depreciation are estimated as $35,000, $32,000, $29,000, $26,000, and $23,000 for the respective years. Depreciation is calculated by the sum-of-the-years' digits method. The tax rate is 60% and the required return is 10%.

19. *Challenger-defender, taxes (like kind exchange).* A company has a machine that will last 5 more years and will then be worth $2,000 as scrap. The machine originally cost $32,000 and was thought to have a life of 15 years. Depreciation has been taken on a straight-line basis for the past 10 years using the $2,000 residual value. The machine could presently be sold for $8,000. The cash costs for operating amount to $18,000 per year.

The company could buy a new machine for $40,000 that would last 5 years and then be worth $10,000. If it does so, cash operating costs will be reduced to $7,000 per year.

Income taxes amount to 60%, and this would be considered a like kind exchange, meaning that any difference between book value and sale price of the old machine would have to be added to the cost of the new machine for tax purposes. Required return is 10% after taxes.

Required:

Do an incremental analysis to determine which machine to employ.

20. *Continuous discounting, net present value, economic life, generalized notation.* Given the symbols below, (a) prepare a formula for NPV using integration and continuous discounting, and (b) determine the economic life where this is the life that maximizes profits in the formula for NPV.

Key:

NPV = net present value of the investment
$R(T)$ = revenues expressed as a function of time, T
$E(T)$ = expenses expressed as a function of time, T
$S(T)$ = salvage value at time, T
K = cost of investment
i = required rate of return per unit of time

21. *Continuous discounting, economic life, optimal net present value.* A factory manager is trying to make a case for replacing equipment earlier than the controller's office allows. The controller believes the 10-year life advocated by the Internal Revenue Code is suitable.

The manager estimates that cash earnings from this type of equipment will be $4,000 per year, while operating costs will increase linearly with time at the rate of $600 per year (hence net yearly earnings will be $4,000 – 600T$). The purchase price of the equipment is $12,000, while its salvage value is expected to decay in time according to the formula $12{,}000e^{-.1T}$.

The required before-tax rate of return on this sort of investment is 20% and continuous discounting is used. Has the manager a chance of modernizing more regularly? *About* how often? What is the optimal net present value?

22. *Multiple internal rates.* A used machine can be acquired for $720 and can be used for one year to generate cash earnings of $2,780. In its second year, the machine can earn $2,170 but will require a major overhaul costing $5,000. Another overhaul, costing $1,200, will be necessary in the third year, when the machine should earn $1,000. In the fourth year, the machine can earn $800 and can be sold for $200 without further maintenance.

Required:

(a) Determine the internal rates of return before taxes.

(b) Graph the function using rate of return as the independent variable.

(c) If the required return is 30%, should this machine be acquired? What if required return were 20%?

23. *Alternative economic lives.* A company invests $8,000 in a machine that promises earnings of $E(i) = \$4{,}000 - \$600i$, where i designates age in years. The salvage value of the machine will be $5,000 regardless of when it is removed from service. The required return before taxes is 20%, compounded discretely.

Required:

(a) Determine the alternative economic lives of the machine.

(b) Determine the net present value using economic life.

24. *Investment combinations and intuitions.* In comment 2 to Illustration 5, I said that NPV assumes that funds generated by proposals can earn only a required return. Assuming the opportunity rate in the company is the required return (or cost of capital—it doesn't matter here), determine the future value of the sum generated over 12 years by both investment packages under the NPV assumption. Comment on the results.

25. *The family's cost of capital.* A family buys a new car for $5,000 with money that it has received in a bequest. Because no monthly payments need be made, the father says that he has no interest costs. Discuss.

26. *Sensitivity.* Mr. Deming owns a construction company and has asked your advice about the advisability of acquiring a large power shovel. The "mole" model that he is considering has a cost of $300,000 and a salvage value of $40,000 regardless of when the used shovel is removed from production. Unfortunately, Mr. Deming is uncertain about both the cost savings and the life of the new shovel. He believes that savings will be normally distributed with mean $100,000 and a 25% probability of being off in either direction by $30,000. He also thinks that life will be normally distributed with a mean of six years and a 70% probability of being no lower than three years. If there is a 20% probability of losing money on the deal, he will reject it; he also has a required return of 14%. What would you advise?

27. *Cost of capital (adapted from Certificate in Management Accounting Examination, December 1974).* The treasurer of a new venture, Start-up Scientific, Inc., is trying to determine how to raise $6,000,000 of long-term capital. His investment adviser has devised the alternative capital structures shown below.

Alternative A	
$2,000,000	9% Debt
$4,000,000	Equity

If this alternative is chosen, the firm would sell 200,000 shares of common stock to net $20 per share. Stockholders would expect an initial dividend of $1.00 per share and a dividend growth rate of 7%.

Alternative B	
$4,000,000	12% Debt
$2,000,000	Equity

Under this alternative, the firm would sell 100,000 shares of common stock to net $20 per share. The expected initial dividend would be $0.90 per share, and the anticipated dividend growth rate is 12 percent.

Assume that the firm earns a profit under either capital structure and that the effective tax rate is 50%.

Required:

(a) What is the cost of capital to the firm under each of the suggested capital structures? Explain your result.

(b) Explain the logic of the anticipated higher interest rate on debt associated with alternative B.

(c) Is it logical for shareholders to expect a higher dividend growth rate under alternative B? Explain your answer.

28. *Capital budgeting* (*Certified Public Accountancy Examination, May 1967**). Niebuhr Corporation is beginning its first capital budgeting program and has retained you to assist the budget committee in the evaluation of a project to expand operations designated as Proposed Expansion Project #12 (PEP #12).

(a) The following capital expenditures are under consideration:

Fire sprinkler system	$ 300,000
Landscaping	100,000
Replacement of old machines	600,000
Projects to expand operations (including PEP #12)	800,000
Total	$1,800,000

(b) The corporation requires no minimum return on the sprinkler system or the landscaping. However, it expects a minimum return of 6% on all investments to replace old machinery. It also expects investments in expansion projects to yield a return that will exceed the average cost of the capital required to finance the sprinkler system and the landscaping in addition to the expansion projects.

(c) Under Proposed Expansion Project #12 (PEP #12) a cash investment of $75,000 will be made one year before operations begin. The investment will be

* Material from the Uniform CPA Examinations, copyright © (May 1967) by the American Institute of Certified Public Accountants, Inc., is adapted with permission.

depreciated by the sum-of-the-years' digits method over a three-year period and is expected to have a salvage value of \$15,000. Additional financial data for PEP #12 follow.

Time Period	Revenue	Variable Costs	Maintenance, Property Taxes, and Insurance
0–1	\$80,000	\$35,000	\$ 8,000
1–2	95,000	41,000	11,000
2–3	60,000	25,000	12,000

The amount of the investment recovered during each of the three years can be reinvested immediately at a rate of return approximating 15%. Each year's recovery of investment, then, will have been reinvested at 15% for an average of six months at the end of the year.

(d) The capital structure of Niebuhr Corporation follows.

	Amount	Percentage
Short-term notes at 5% interest	\$ 3,500,000	10%
Four percent cumulative preferred stock, \$100 par	1,750,000	5
Common stock	12,250,000	35
Retained earnings	17,500,000	50
	\$35,000,000	100%

(e) Additional data available to you are summarized below.

	Current Market Price	Expected Earnings per Share	Expected Dividends per Share
Preferred stock, noncallable	\$120	—	\$4.00
Common stock	50	\$3.20	1.60

The average marginal tax rate for Niebuhr stockholders is estimated to be 25%.

(f) Assume that the corporate income tax rate is 50%.

(g) The present value of \$1.00 due at the end of each year and discounted at 15% is

End of Year	Present Value
Two years before 0	\$1.32
One year before 0	1.15
0	1.00
One year after 0	.87
Two years after 0	.76
Three years after 0	.66

(h) The present values of $1.00 earned uniformly throughout the year and discounted at 15% follow.

Year	Present Value
0–1	$ .93
1–2	.80
2–3	.69

Required:

(a) Assume that the cutoff rate for considering expansion projects is 15%. Prepare a schedule calculating

(1) The annual cash flows from operations for PEP #12

(2) The present value of the net cash flows for PEP #12

(b) The budget committee has asked you to check the reasonableness of the cutoff rate. You realize that one of the factors to be considered is an estimate of the average cost of capital to this firm. Prepare a schedule, supported by computations in good form, to compute the average cost of capital weighted by the percentage of the capital structure which each element represents.

(c) (1) Assume that the average cost of capital computed in (b) is 9%. Prepare a schedule to compute the minimum return (in dollars) required on expansion projects to cover the average cost of capital for financing the sprinkler system and the landscaping in addition to expansion projects. Assume that it is necessary to replace the old machines.

(2) Assume that the minimum return computed in (1) above is $150,000. Calculate the cutoff rate on expansion projects.

29. "*Make or buy*" (*prepared by Professor Edward L. Wallace, SUNY at Buffalo*). The Curtis Machine Company has been having certain operations on a part used in its product performed by a neighboring company at a cost of 50 cents per part. The annual production of this part is expected to average 6,000 pieces. The Curtis Machine Company can perform this operation itself by bringing into operation two machines, a spare lathe, which has a net book value of $2,000, and a new machine, which can be purchased for $7,000. The new machine is expected to last seven years. The old machine has a remaining life of ten years. The final salvage value of both machines is considered negligible. In performing the operation itself, the Curtis Company will incur out-of-pocket costs for direct labor, power, supplies, and so forth of 20 cents per part.

Prepare an analysis (including explanatory comments) that would help to determine whether it is profitable for the Curtis Company to perform these operations itself. The company normally expects to earn a rate of return before taxes of about 15% on its invested capital. Determine how much of an increase (or decrease) in annual production would be necessary to switch the decision.

30. *Challenger-defender, no sales information (prepared by Professor Edward L. Wallace, SUNY at Buffalo).* The Patrick Cotton Company is currently considering the installation of weaving equipment with a total cost, including freight and installation, of $40,000. It would replace equipment that three years before cost $50,000 and is still in good running order, but that, due to the greater efficiency of the new equipment, now has resale value of only $5,000. The cost of removing the old equipment and revamping the machine service facilities will be $15,000, of which $5,000 is considered a part of the installation cost and is included in the $40,000 to be capitalized, while the remaining $10,000 is to be charged to expense. The manufacturing cost tabulation shows a substantial reduction in labor cost and total cost, as follows:

	Present	After New Installation
Annual expenses:		
Labor	$ 12,500	$ 3,000
Supplies, repairs, and power	4,000	3,400
Taxes, insurance, and miscellaneous	900	1,000
Depreciation (10% of cost)	5,000	4,000
Total	$ 22,400	$ 11,400
Annual Production—units	400,000	500,000

If a 10% return on investment after taxes is required, if losses on disposal of assets can be treated for tax purposes as additions to depreciation in the year of disposal, and if there is no contemplated use of the additional capacity, would you recommend the expenditure? Assume a tax rate of 60%.

31. *How can I compute taxes if I don't know original costs for calculating depreciation? What a dumb problem!* R.P.I. Company is analyzing a proposal to replace an existing piece of equipment with a more technologically advanced model. The present machine has a book value of $80,000 but could be sold today for only $30,000. If kept, this machine would be sold at the end of the forecasted market life of the product made on the machine—that is, in three years—for $5,000. In the meantime, cash earnings would be $50,000, $40,000, and $30,000 respectively in each of the ensuing years. The replacement machine will require an investment of $140,000, will be worth $40,000 in three years, and in the meantime will enjoy cash earnings of $90,000 in each of the respective years. Required return after taxes of 40% is 10%. Assume that the tax law is such that the gain or loss on the disposal of the present machine must be declared immediately and treated just like ordinary depreciation. Use the sum-of-the-years' digits depreciation method.

Required:

(a) Compute the following ranking statistics:

(1) TAR,

(2) NPV,

(3) profitability index,

(4) discounted payback, and

(5) incremental analysis.

(b) Comment on the results of (a) and make a decision.

32. *Project analysis (adapted from Certified Management Accounting Examination, December 1972).* The Baxter Company manufactures toys and other short-lived fad items. The research and development department came up with an item that would make a good promotional gift for office equipment dealers. Aggressive and effective effort by Baxter's sales personnel has resulted in almost firm commitments for this product for the next three years. It is expected that the product's value will be exhausted by that time.

In order to produce the quantity demanded, Baxter will need to buy additional machinery and rent some additional space. It appears that about 25,000 square feet will be needed; 12,500 square feet of presently unused, but leased, space is available now. (Baxter's present lease, with 10 years to run, costs $3.00 a foot.) There is another 12,500 square feet adjoining the Baxter facility, which Baxter will rent for 3 years at $4.00 per square foot per year if it decides to make this product.

The equipment will be purchased for about $900,000. It will require $30,000 in modifications, $60,000 for installation, and $90,000 for testing; all of these activities will be done by a firm of engineers hired by Baxter. All of the expenditures will be paid for on January 1, 1973.

The equipment should have a salvage value of about $180,000 at the end of the third year. No additional general overhead costs are expected to be incurred.

The following estimates of revenues and expenses for this product for the three years have been developed:

	1973	1974	1975
Sales	$1,000,000	$1,600,000	$800,000
Material, labor and incurred overhead	400,000	750,000	350,000
Assigned general overhead	40,000	75,000	35,000
Rent	87,500	87,500	87,500
Depreciation	450,000	300,000	150,000
	$ 977,500	$1,212,500	$622,500
Income before tax	$ 22,500	$ 387,500	$177,500
Income tax (40%)	9,000	155,000	71,000
	$ 13,500	$ 232,500	$106,500

Required:

(a) Prepare a schedule which shows the incremental, after-tax, cash flows for this project.

(b) If the company requires a two-year payback period for its investment, would it undertake this project? Show your supporting calculations clearly.

(c) Calculate the after-tax accounting rate of return for the project.

(d) A newly hired business school graduate recommends that the company consider the use of net present value analysis to study this project. If the company sets a required rate of return of 20% after taxes, will this project be accepted? Show your supporting calculations clearly. (Assume all operating revenues and expenses occur at the end of the year.)

Capital Budgeting: Some Extensions

12

The future is known
to God alone, and right
now He and I are not in touch.

How To Obtain Probability Distributions

Control in a firm's future is largely a function of investments made in its past. Ideally, management does the most with what it has, but what it has often results from decisions made many years earlier. Of necessity, the cost analyst must study the future through clouded spectacles. Most of his estimates are random variables with associated probability distributions, and one of his biggest problems is obtaining those distributions.

In the happiest of circumstances, an expert might provide the distribution. For example, an engineer might assign probabilities to the number of barrels of oil a new well will deliver as follows:

Barrels x	Probability $P(x)$	$xP(x)$	$[x - E(x)]^2 P(x)$
1,000	.05	50	450,000
2,000	.10	200	400,000
3,000	.20	600	200,000
4,000	.30	1,200	–0–
5,000	.20	1,000	200,000
6,000	.10	600	400,000
7,000	.05	350	450,000
		$E(x) = \Sigma xP(x) = 4{,}000$	$V(x) = \Sigma[x - E(x)]^2 P(x) = 2{,}100{,}000$

The estimates shown above have been symmetrically distributed around an average daily quantity, $E(x)$, or 4,000 barrels. Apparently, the well is sure to deliver at least 1,000 barrels, but will never deliver more than 7,000 barrels. Now this distribution is excellent as it is; however, an analyst might like both to take advantage of its symmetry and to obtain probabilities for, say, 3,329 barrels. If one does not insist on mathematical rigor, the estimates and their probabilities could now be translated to normal curve (Table 8 in Appendix A) terminology by observing that $E(x) \pm 3\sigma$ covers essentially the whole range of possibilities. Then, by substituting figures, σ may be determined:

$$E(x) + 3\sigma = 4{,}000 + 3\sigma = 7{,}000$$

$$\sigma = 1{,}000$$

Alternatively, more precision can be obtained by using the "method of moments," in which the moments of an observed distribution are set equal to the moments of some desired theoretical distribution. Since the normal distribution requires a mean and standard deviation, 4,000 barrels $= E(x)$ and $\sqrt{V(x)} \approx 1{,}450$ barrels $= \sigma$ would be taken from the engineer's distribution. In addition, the analyst should correct for truncation (the normal curve is for $-\infty < x < \infty$, and barrels only go $1{,}000 \leq x \leq 7{,}000$), often by finding the area under the curve between 1,000 and 7,000 and dividing the result into the tabled probabilities:[1]

$$\int_{1,000}^{7,000} N(x\!:\!\mu = 4{,}000; \sigma = 1{,}450)\, dx = .961, \quad \text{where } N(x\!:\!\mu, \sigma) \text{ designates the normal density}$$

The probability of 6,000 barrels can be taken as all barrels between 5,500 and 6,500 and calculated as follows:

$$P(5{,}500 < x < 6{,}500) = \frac{1}{.961} \int_{5,500}^{6,500} N(x\!:\!4{,}000; 1{,}450)\, dx = \frac{.1082}{.961} = .1126$$

The Z transformation, $Z = (x - 4{,}000)/1{,}450$, yields

$$\begin{aligned} P(0 < Z < [6{,}500 - 4{,}000)/1{,}450] = 1.724) &= .4577 \\ -P(0 < Z < [5{,}500 - 4{,}000)/1{,}450] = 1.0344) &= -.3495 \\ & \ \ \underline{\underline{.1082}}, \text{ as above} \end{aligned}$$

The result, .1126, is reasonably close to the engineer's .10, and the analyst now not only has probabilities that can be looked up in a readily available table, but also can assign a probability to any outcome between 1,000 and 7,000 not just the previously listed outcomes.

Temporarily putting aside the niceties of the method of moments, let us see how else the engineer might have expressed himself. He might assume a normal distribution of the number of barrels delivered and be willing to

[1] The truncation correction restores the "sum-to-unity" probability axiom (that is, $1 = .961/.961$).

estimate the mean within a certain range. He might decide, for example, that the mean has a 50% probability of being in the range of 3,000 to 5,000 barrels. Because of the symmetry of the normal curve, the engineer's estimate may be restated as: the mean is 4,000 barrels with a 25% probability of being greater or lesser by 1,000 barrels. Now $(2/3)\sigma$ yields a probability of approximately 25%; therefore we can determine σ as follows:

$$2/3 = \frac{x - E(x)}{\sigma} = \frac{5{,}000 - 4{,}000}{\sigma}$$

$$(2/3)\sigma = 1{,}000$$

$$\sigma = 1{,}500$$

Notice that this mode of estimating does not require the degree of skill (and patience) that the first method did.

Keep in mind that many decisions are first-time decisions. In the classical sense of probability, where there is no experience there is no distribution. Consequently, the analyst is often seeking subjective estimates of the distribution based on the decisionmaker's feelings. The decisionmaker mentally weighs outcomes in terms of his intuitions. If the analyst can get him to express these intuitions, the modelling can more explicitly recognize what is going on inside the decisionmaker's head. Then, once a decision has been made and implemented, the original distribution can be modified.[2]

If there is a similar or pilot operation on which to base estimates of an operation presently being contemplated, the estimates have objective support and become educated guesses. But what if there is no pilot operation and the decisionmaker is inexperienced? How then could one obtain a probability distribution?

If direct assessment of probabilities is not forthcoming, and if the decision maker is unwilling to assume normality and specify the probability of obtaining some central range of outcomes, then the analyst can ask him to choose a shape that represents how he feels by showing him a catalogue of graphs of various theoretical distributions like those in Exhibit 1.

It is usually possible in existing systems to take empirical observations of time or demand or whatever the random variable is. One must be careful, though, that unrepresentative data are not included, as for instance when time to perform some act is clocked during a slow activity period but the study deals only with peak activity periods. Similarly the analyst must be aware of incomplete data, as for instance when he wishes to determine a distribution of demand and data have not been kept for those instances when items were demanded but the business was out of inventory.

---

[2] The use of subjective probabilities and their revision comes under the heading of Bayesian statistics and will be discussed in Chapter 13.

Exhibit 1

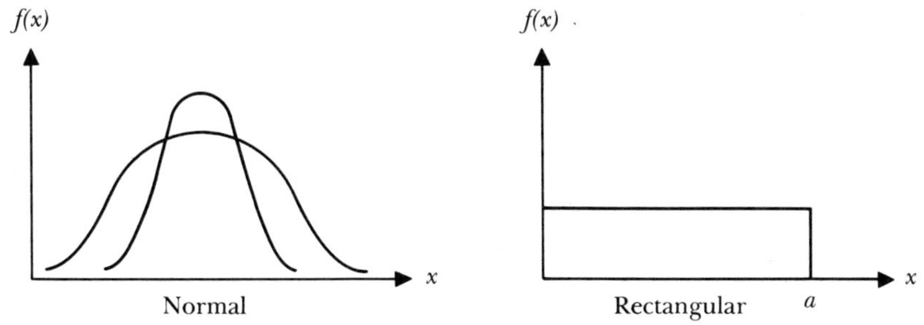

$$f(x) = \frac{1}{\sigma\sqrt{2\pi}} e^{-\frac{1}{2}\left(\frac{x-\mu}{\sigma}\right)^2} \qquad f(x) = 1/a$$

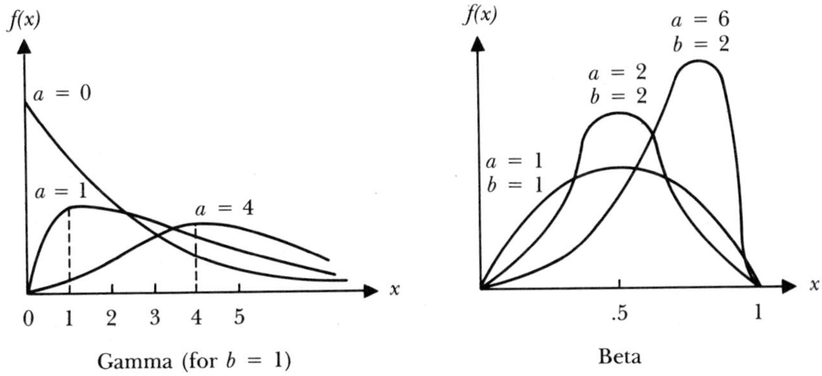

$$f(x) = \frac{b^{a+1} x^a e^{-bx}}{\Gamma(a+1)} \qquad f(x) = \frac{(a+b+1)!}{a!\,b!} x^a (1-x)^b$$

How To Obtain Utility Functions

Preliminary notions about utility theory were presented in Chapter 10. Most people are risk averse—they feel worse about losing, say, \$10,000 than they feel good about winning \$10,000. On the other hand, there are people who are risk seekers, who are willing to fly in the face of the odds in the slim chance of winning a very attractive stake. People go to Reno and Las Vegas knowing that beating the house is a relatively rare occurrence, but drawn nevertheless by the hope of striking it rich. Finally, there are people who are risk neutral. These are people who feel no better about gaining than they do about losing any equal sum of money in a wide range of amounts. The width of this range is what distinguishes the risk neutral individual from the risk averter or risk seeker, both of whom are apt to be neutral for smaller sums of money. Over the range of neutrality, decisions may appropriately be based on expected values; however, if any sum of money falls outside the range, utilities of all individual gains and losses, weighted by their respective probabilities, should govern.

Figure 1 shows typical graphs for risk attitudes.

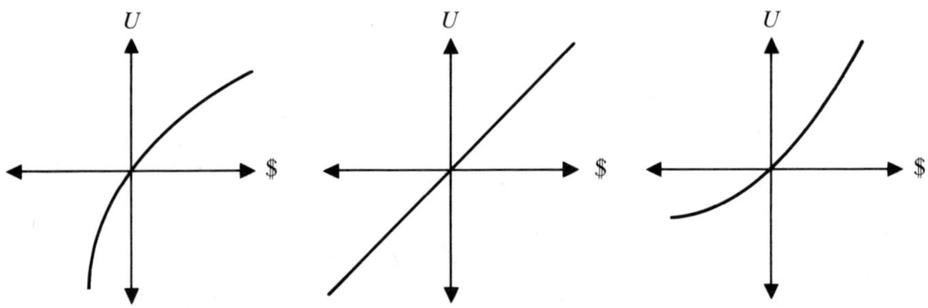

Risk Averse   Risk Neutral   Risk Seeker

Figure 1

If the decisionmaker is confronted with these typical curves, he may be able to choose the one that reflects his attitude. Note how rapidly negative utility for losses mounts in the risk averse graph.

Alternatively, a utility function may be determined by the standard-gamble method.

1. Start with two extreme rewards, x_0 and x_n, and assign them utility measures of, say, 0 and 1.

2. Take any reward x (where $x_0 < x < x_n$), assign it a probability of 1 (certainty), and set it equal to the expected value of alternative extreme rewards.

3. Assign probability of P to one extreme reward and $(1 - P)$ to the other extreme. Vary P until the decisionmaker is indifferent.

4. Substitute utilities of 0 and 1 for the extreme rewards and solve for the utility of reward x.

5. Repeat the process for a new x, but this time substitute the previous reward x for the reward x_0.

The utilities obtained are also referred to as "utiles."

Example:

$$x_0 = \$0 \qquad \text{(utility } (U) = 0)$$
$$x_n = \$50{,}000 \qquad \text{(utility} = 1)$$

Find the respective utilities of \$10,000; \$30,000; \$60,000. Assume the decision maker becomes indifferent at the probabilities shown below.

$$U(\$10{,}000) = (1/3)U(\$50{,}000) + (2/3)U(\$0) = (1/3)(1) + (2/3)(0) = 1/3$$

$$U(\$20{,}000) = (1/4)U(\$50{,}000) + (3/4)U(\$10{,}000) = (1/4)(1) + (3/4)(1/3) = 1/2$$

$$U(\$20{,}000) = (4/5)U(\$10{,}000) + (1/5)U(\$60{,}000);$$

$$1/2 = (4/5)(1/3) + (1/5)U(\$60{,}000); \qquad U(\$60{,}000) = 7/6$$

The process can be varied to break up the monotony. For example, while performing step 2, the decisionmaker might be asked, "What reward would you take cash in hand in lieu of these other rewards and their probabilities?" To establish negative utilities (disutilities) the question could be reversed to "What would you pay for insurance against the indicated losses and their probabilities?" In this manner, utility measures for any set of points may be established.

The consistency of the measures can be checked by varying the rewards and their probabilities. Consistency, you will recall, is one of the grounds on which utility theory is critized; however, some analysts have noted remarkable consistency and believe that even if the decisionmaker's wealth changes, if his old curve began to bend at 10% of his former wealth, his new curve will likewise bend at 10% of his new wealth.

Regardless of whether utility theory is popular in practice, it remains most attractive theoretically. In blending dollars and attitudes toward those dollars, utility theory removes decisionmaking from the arena of dollars and places it in the broader sphere of attitudes that reflect both dollar and nondollar costs.

How is a utility curve put to work?

Example:

	Project A		Project B		Project C	
Outcomes:	x	$P(x)$	x	$P(x)$	x	$P(x)$
	\$ – 50,000	.50	\$ – 10,000	.25	\$ – 40,000	.60
	100,000	.25	100,000	.40	200,000	.20
	300,000	.15	200,000	.35	400,000	.09
	700,000	.10			600,000	.06
					800,000	.05
$E(x) =$	\$115,000		\$107,500		\$128,000	

Utility curve = $.75x - .04x^2$, where x is measured in terms of $100,000. In terms of expected utilities, we obtain

Project A			Project B			Project C		
U	$P(U)$	$UP(U)$	U	$P(U)$	$UP(U)$	U	$P(U)$	$UP(U)$
−.3850	.50	−.19	−.0754	.25	−.02	−.3064	.60	−.18
.7100	.25	.18	.7100	.40	.28	1.3400	.20	.27
2.8900	.15	.43	1.3400	.35	.47	2.3600	.09	.21
3.2900	.10	.33				3.0600	.06	.18
						3.4400	.05	.17
$\sum UP(U) =$		.75			.73			.65

On the basis of expected return, the rankings are C, A, B in descending order of desirability. Because the decisionmaker is risk averse, however, rankings by expected utility are A, B, C in descending order. C had too great a chance of loss and too little chance of great reward to be really attractive to the decisionmaker. Indeed, the most conservative project, B, is almost as appealing to him as A, which has sufficient promise of great reward to overcome its great chance of loss. With the costs of embarassment and the joys of reward reflected subjectively along with objectively measured costs and rewards, the decisionmaker has changed his rankings.

Markovian Replacement

We first encountered Markov chains in Chapter 4, where we used an absorbing Markovian matrix to estimate cash flow from accounts receivable for period budgeting purposes. Let us now employ an ordinary (nonabsorbing) Markov chain to study the group replacement versus individual replacement problem.

The best-known setting of this problem is the relamping situation. Possibly you have seen men go through a plant (or even throughout a city) unscrewing light bulbs that you knew were still working perfectly well. Perhaps you even hazarded some charitable remark like, "Hasn't that idiot got anything better to do than waste time and money?" If you did say something to this effect, I hope to convince you in the next few pages that the pot should refrain from calling the kettle black!

We shall not work with light bulbs, for this connotes dollar insignificance. But light bulbs are an excellent vehicle for helping you to appreciate the subtlety of the group replace vs. the individual replace problem. How would one recognize that a light bulb replacement problem existed? Rooms are well lit, morale is as usual, there is no inconvenience beyond replacing a blown bulb occasionally. Perhaps someone notices that the lighting appears dimmer (bulbs grow less efficient with age), but he is likely to blame this on his advancing myopia. Nothing is wrong. Where is the problem? The subtle, unrecognized problem can be very significant; it falls in a category that should be labelled "creeping extravagance." Problems in this category do not involve deprivation of service; they just amount to doing the service in an unnecessarily expensive way and being oblivious of the fact.

For our vehicle we shall use typewriters. Company cars would do as well, as would anything that has a limited life of varying duration and is subject to substantial savings if acquired in bulk (the quantity discount concept). Actually anything that can be done more cheaply if it is done all at once as opposed to a little at a time might benefit from the scrutiny of our present model. Signing equipment maintenance contracts at the time the machines are acquired instead of waiting until they need maintenance would be an example. Such maintenance contracts involve far from trifling amounts, and managers seem to sign them almost automatically, without thought or perhaps with the single thought that it is the usual thing to do.

We shall need not only a discounting rate but also a unit cost, C_G, for purchasing typewriters in a group and a unit cost, C_S, for acquiring them individually as specific machine replacements. Then let us assume some total number of typewriters, N, in the entire business at one or all of its locations. Finally let us assume the typewriter mortality distribution is known and thought to be stable: 25% of the machines fail after one year, 45% fail in their second year, and 30% fail in the third year. Furthermore, assume salvage value is reflected in C_S and C_G. We have

t	$P(t)$
1	.25
2	.45
3	.30
	1.00

$$r = 20\% \text{ (before taxes)}$$

$$C_G = \$400$$

$$C_S = \$600$$

$$N = 1{,}000$$

Failures must be replaced as they occur; otherwise, a secretary may be idle. These replacements in turn, may fail and require replacement. Although we shall find that a Markov chain vastly simplifies the calculations, nevertheless you should understand what is taking place; therefore let us temporarily dissect our analysis.

Our problem calls for determining the probabilities of first, second, third, etc. failures at a specific time, where each layer of replacements reintroduces the original probability distribution, thereby leading to a folding action.

Example: Find the probability of a second failure $[f_2(t)]$ at the end of the third year.

$$f_2(t) = \sum_{x=1}^{t-1} P(x)P(t-x)$$

$$f_2(3) = \sum_{x=1}^{2} P(x)P(3-x) = P(1)P(2) + P(2)P(1)$$

Reasoning:

1. To have a failure, it takes at least one year; hence years(x) start at 1.
2. To have a second failure, there must have been a first failure that took at least one year; hence the top limit cannot be t, since that would preclude a second failure at time t—we would be dealing only with first failure.
3. Second failures contribute nothing to $f_2(t)$ in year 1 and beyond year 6, since it is impossible to have a second failure at the end of year 1 and it would require at least a third failure to have a failure at the end of year 7.
4. A replacement that occurs in year 1 may itself be replaced one, two, or three years later. We are interested here only in year 3. One way to have a second failure in year 3 is to have a first failure in year 1 followed by failure of the replacements two years later. Since these events are independent, we multiply their probabilities and obtain $P(1)P(2) = .25(.45)$. Another way to have a second failure in year 3 is to have a first failure in year 2 followed by failure of the replacements one year later. This yields $P(2)P(1) = .45(.25)$. Then, because the two ways are mutually exclusive, we add their probabilities to obtain

$$f_2(3) = .25(.45) + .45(.25) = .225$$

If you will define $P(0) = P(4) = P(5) = \cdots = 0$ and let N stand for the total population, a general formula for expected yearly failures—and consequently for expected yearly replacements—may be stated as follows:

$$f(t) = N\left[P(t) + \sum_{x=1}^{t-1} P(x)P(t-x) + \sum_{y=2}^{t-1}\sum_{x=1}^{y-1} P(x)P(y-x)P(t-y) + \cdots\right]$$

Matrices offer an easy way to calculate these probabilities as shown in Exhibit 2. The calculations have been performed only for the first three years because now we are ready to see how a Markov chain can further simplify the analysis.

Exhibit 2 Folded Probability Calculations

Place the mortality distribution in column and row vectors and multiply:

$$\begin{bmatrix} .25 \\ .45 \\ .30 \end{bmatrix} [.25, .45, .30] = \begin{bmatrix} .0625 & .1125 & .0750 \\ .1125 & .2025 & .1350 \\ .0750 & .1350 & .0900 \end{bmatrix}$$

Add elements cross-diagonally to obtain the 2-fold distribution (two failures, i.e., a failure followed by a replacement that fails):

t	2	3	4	5	6
$P^{\{2\}}(t)$	.0625	.2250	.3525	.2700	.0900

$$\begin{bmatrix} .25 \\ .45 \\ .30 \end{bmatrix} [.0625, .2250, .3525, .2700, .0900]$$

$$= \begin{bmatrix} .015625 & .056250 & .088125 & .067500 & .022500 \\ .028125 & .101250 & .158625 & .121500 & .040500 \\ .018750 & .067500 & .105750 & .081000 & .027000 \end{bmatrix}$$

Add cross-diagonally to obtain the 3-fold distribution:

t	3	4	5	6	7	8	9
$P^{\{3\}}(t)$	.015625	.084375	.208125	.293625	.249750	.121500	.027000

Results:
$f(1) = 1{,}000(.25) = 250$
$f(2) = 1{,}000[.45 + .0625] = 513$
$f(3) = 1{,}000[.30 + .2250 + .015625] = 541$

Before formulating the transition matrix, let us focus on the vectors that will premultiply it. We have three states in our typewriter problem, and if we multiply the probability vector by N, the resulting vector will show the distribution of the N machines according to age; we have (a_1, a_2, a_3) or $(a_1, a_2, N - a_1 - a_2)$. This vector actually forces a certain structure on the transition matrix; the probability row vectors of the transition matrix, T, must pertain to machines that are one, two and three years old respectively. In other words, row one of T pertains to the a_1 machines, row two of T pertains to the a_2 machines, and row three of T pertains to the a_3 machines. This means that each row of T must reflect probabilities for the particular age involved; therefore,

$$T = \text{From:}\begin{matrix} \\ 1 \\ 2 \\ 3 \end{matrix} \overset{\begin{matrix} & \text{To:} & \\ 1 & 2 & 3 \end{matrix}}{\begin{bmatrix} .25 & .75 & 0 \\ .60 & 0 & .40 \\ 1.00 & 0 & 0 \end{bmatrix}}$$

Reasoning:

$T_{11} = .25$ because if the machines begin the stage in period 1 there is a .25 probability that they will fail by the end of period 1. This automatically leads to their replacement, thereby returning them to period 1 at the beginning of the next stage.

$T_{12} = .75$ because there is a .75 probability that the machines that start the stage in period 1 will survive to period 2.

$T_{21} = .6$ because machines that are two periods old to begin with would have a .45 probability of failing—and therefore of being replaced and returned to period 1—at the end of the current period and a .3 probability of surviving to the next period. Hence we are dealing with conditional probabilities and, to adjust for the reduced sample space, we divide by .75 to obtain $.45/.75 = .6$ and $.3/.75 = .4$.

$T_{23} = .4$ (for the reason just presented.)

$T_{22} = 0$ because it is impossible for a machine to return to period 2 given that it started in period 2.

$T_{31} = 1$ because a machine that begins the stage in period 3 is sure to fail and be replaced when the stage is ended.

Now we are ready to put T to work. Keep in mind that element a_1 expresses the total failure-replacements for each stage (a_1 was previously designated $f(t)$). Let us start business afresh with 1,000 new typewriters; we then have

$$(1{,}000;\,0;\,0)T = (250;\,750;\,0)$$

$$(250;\,750;\,0)T = (513;\,187;\,300)$$

$$(513;\,187;\,300)T = (540;\,385;\,75)$$

$$(540;\,385;\,75)T = (441;\,405;\,154)$$

$$(441;\,405;\,154)T = (507;\,331;\,162)$$

We could continue in this way indefinitely, but enough has been done to establish the fact that the Markov chain approach is generating not only the same yearly failures as the approach shown in Exhibit 2 (that is, 250, 513, 540 [off by 1 due to rounding], 441, 507 in that order) but also gives information about the age of the equipment in use. This additional information may be useful in determining quality of service rendered by the typewriters.

If the replacement of replacements policy went on indefinitely, we would eventually arrive at the steady-state replacement situation. The steady-state calculations follow:

$$(a_1, a_2, a_3)\begin{bmatrix} .25 & .75 & 0 \\ .60 & 0 & .40 \\ 1.00 & 0 & 0 \end{bmatrix} = (a_1, a_2, a_3)$$

$$.25a_1 + .60a_2 + a_3 = a_1 \qquad \textbf{(1)}$$

$$.75a_1 = a_2 \qquad \textbf{(2)}$$

$$.40a_2 = a_3 \qquad \textbf{(3)}$$

and

$$a_1 + a_2 + a_3 = 1{,}000 \qquad \textbf{(4)}$$

Simplifying equations (2) and (3) and using the results together with equation (4) yields

$$\begin{bmatrix} .75 & -1.00 & 0 \\ 0 & .40 & -1.00 \\ 1 & 1 & 1 \end{bmatrix}\begin{bmatrix} a_1 \\ a_2 \\ a_3 \end{bmatrix} = \begin{bmatrix} 0 \\ 0 \\ 1{,}000 \end{bmatrix} \qquad \textbf{(5)}$$

$$\begin{bmatrix} a_1 \\ a_2 \\ a_3 \end{bmatrix} = \frac{\begin{bmatrix} 28 & 20 & 20 \\ -20 & 15 & 15 \\ -8 & -36 & 6 \end{bmatrix}}{41}\begin{bmatrix} 0 \\ 0 \\ 1{,}000 \end{bmatrix} = \begin{bmatrix} 488 \\ 366 \\ 146 \end{bmatrix}$$

Consequently, in the steady state 488 machines will fail each year, while 366 will enjoy a second year of service and 146 will hold up long enough to provide a third year of service.

Interestingly enough, we could have determined the steady-state results by dividing the total number of typewriters by the expected life of a typewriter—that is, $N/\Sigma tP(t)$:

$$488 = \frac{1{,}000}{1(.25) + 2(.45) + 3(.30)}$$

Actually the steady-state results are of only academic interest. They show what would probably happen in a company that was unaware that a policy of replacing only as needed might be extravagant. Let us see what an optimal policy would be.

Recall the "normalized" stream approach wherein an analyst first finds the present value of a given varying stream of payments and then calculates that single sum of money which, if received (or disbursed) regularly, would yield the same present value. We should be willing to select that cycle which has the smallest normalized cost. Our expected cost for a cycle lasting t years, where $t = 2, 3, 4, \ldots, n$ is

$$E[K(t)] = \left[NC_G + C_S \sum_{i=1}^{t-1} f(i)b(i, r) \right] \div \sum_{i=0}^{t-1} \left(\frac{1}{1+r} \right)^i \qquad \textbf{(6)}$$

Let us use the policy of group replacing every three years to illustrate.

$$E[K(3)] = \left[1{,}000(400) + 600 \sum_{i=1}^{2} f(i)b(i, 20) \right] \div \sum_{i=0}^{2} \left(\frac{1}{1.2} \right)^i$$

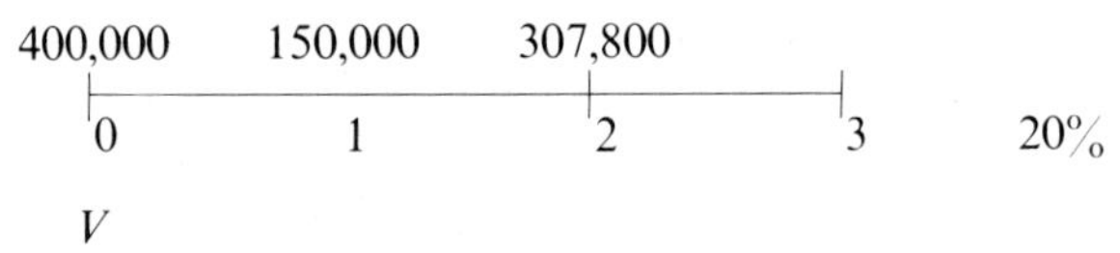

The present value of one cycle is

$$V = \$400{,}000(1) + \$150{,}000(.8333) + \$307{,}800(.6944) = \$738{,}732$$

$$V = \$738{,}732 = x \sum_{i=0}^{2} 1.2^{-i} = x[B(2, 20) + 1.000] = 2.5278x$$

$$\therefore, \quad x = \$292{,}243 = E[K(3)]$$

If you proceeded in this fashion you would find the respective normalized costs for $t = 1, 2, \ldots, 5$ were \$400,000, \$286,367, \$292,243, \$298,159, \$293,657. The vacillation of these amounts is somewhat disturbing and makes one hesitate to declare two years the least costly, and hence the best, cycle. One could resolve the problem by taking the first difference of (6) (that is, $\Delta E[K(t)]$) and locating the optimal value of t. In lieu of this, the analyst could write a computer program like that in Exhibit 3.

Examination of the output of Exhibit 3 shows slight differences from the results reported above. This is solely because the discounting factors are calculated to far greater accuracy in the computer program. The program shows that the best cycle indeed lasts two years. It also shows that the normalized cost is stabilizing at about \$293,939, which may be thought of as the steady-state result of forever replacing replacements. Since many companies ignore group replacement, they would find themselves in this steady state. Then, since they should group replace every two years at a normalized cost of \$286,364, these companies would incur an unnecessary yearly expenditure of about \$7,575. And that is "creeping extravagance."

Exhibit 3

```
050  REM A  = VECTOR SHOWING ORIGINAL INVENTORY OF MACHINES BY AGE
055  REM T  = MARKOVIAN TRANSITION MATRIX
060  REM H  = VECTOR SHOWING LATEST INVENTORY OF MACHINES BY AGE
065  REM C1 = GROUP REPLACEMENT COST PER MACHINE
070  REM C2 = INDIVIDUAL REPLACEMENT COST PER MACHINE
075  REM M  = TOTAL YEARS OF LIFE
080  REM R  = DISCOUNT RATE
085  REM X  = TOTAL INVENTORY OF MACHINES
100  DIM A(1,20),T(20,20),H(1,20),I(20,20)
105  READ C1,C2,M,R,X
110  MAT READ T (M,M)
115  MAT READ A (1,M)
116  MAT I  = IDN(M,M)
118  LET G  = 1 / (1 + R)
119  LET Z  = 1 / (1 - G)
120  LET C  = 0
125  FOR L  = 1 TO 15
130  REM THE DISCOUNTING FACTOR, P, FOR YEAR L IS COMPUTED
135  LET P  = G ↑ L
140  REM THE NORMALIZING DISCOUNT FACTOR, F, IS CALCULATED
145  LET F  = Z * (1 - P)
150  REM THE PRESENT VALUE OF INITIAL GROUP REPLACEMENT AND
151  REM SUBSEQUENT REPLACEMENTS IS V
155  LET  V = (C1 * X) + C
160  REM REPLACEMENTS FOR THE YEAR ARE CALCULATED AND COST IS UPDATED
165  MAT H = A*T
166  MAT A = H*I
170  LET  C = (C2 * A(1,1) * P) * C
175  REM COST IS NORMALIZED
180  LET  N = V/F
190  PRINT
195  PRINT "NORMALIZED COST FOR A CYCLE LASTING";L;"YEARS IS $";N
197  PRINT "THE AGE VECTOR IS:",A(1,1),A(1,2),A(1,3)
200  NEXT L
202  DATA 400,600,3,.2,1000
205  DATA .25,.75,0
210  DATA .60,0,.40
215  DATA 1.00,0,0
220  DATA 1000,0,0
225  END
```

```
RUN

NORMALIZED COST FOR A CYCLE LASTING 1 YEARS IS $ 400000
THE AGE VECTOR IS:              250             750             0
NORMALIZED COST FOR A CYCLE LASTING 2 YEARS IS $ 286363.636
THE AGE VECTOR IS:              512.5           187.5           300
NORMALIZED COST FOR A CYCLE LASTING 3 YEARS IS $ 292170.33
THE AGE VECTOR IS:              540.625         384.375         75
NORMALIZED COST FOR A CYCLE LASTING 4 YEARS IS $ 298169.709
THE AGE VECTOR IS:              440.78125       405.46875       153.75
NORMALIZED COST FOR A CYCLE LASTING 5 YEARS IS $ 293640.984
THE AGE VECTOR IS:              507.226563      330.585937      162.1875
```

Exhibit 3 (*cont.*)

NORMALIZED COST FOR A CYCLE LASTING 6 YEARS IS $ 294718.028
THE AGE VECTOR IS: 487.345703 380.419922 132.234375
NORMALIZED COST FOR A CYCLE LASTING 7 YEARS IS $ 294539.131
THE AGE VECTOR IS: 482.322754 365.509277 152.167969
NORMALIZED COST FOR A CYCLE LASTING 8 YEARS IS $ 294227.267
THE AGE VECTOR IS: 492.054224 361.742065 146.203711
NORMALIZED COST FOR A CYCLE LASTING 9 YEARS IS $ 294275.6
THE AGE VECTOR IS: 486.262506 369.040667 144.696826
NORMALIZED COST FOR A CYCLE LASTING 10 YEARS IS $ 294178.596
THE AGE VECTOR IS: 487.686853 364.696879 147.616267
NORMALIZED COST FOR A CYCLE LASTING 11 YEARS IS $ 294129.872
THE AGE VECTOR IS: 488.356108 365.76514 145.878752
NORMALIZED COST FOR A CYCLE LASTING 12 YEARS IS $ 294101.671
THE AGE VECTOR IS: 487.426862 366.267081 146.306056
NORMALIZED COST FOR A CYCLE LASTING 13 YEARS IS $ 294067.74
THE AGE VECTOR IS: 487.92302 365.570147 146.506832
NORMALIZED COST FOR A CYCLE LASTING 14 YEARS IS $ 294045.544
THE AGE VECTOR IS: 487.829676 365.942265 146.228059
NORMALIZED COST FOR A CYCLE LASTING 15 YEARS IS $ 294026.834
THE AGE VECTOR IS: 487.750837 365.872257 146.376906

Reflecting Risk Preference in Probability Distributions

Many theorists feel that use of expected net present values does not give the decisionmaker explicit enough information about the individual losses and gains involved. Still others feel that the decisionmaker, because of his risk preferences, should know what the distribution looks like. In Figure 2 we see two distributions having about the same mean and variance. Curve *A* has a higher modal value but some probability of very poor performance, while curve *B* has a lower modal value with some probability of very good per-

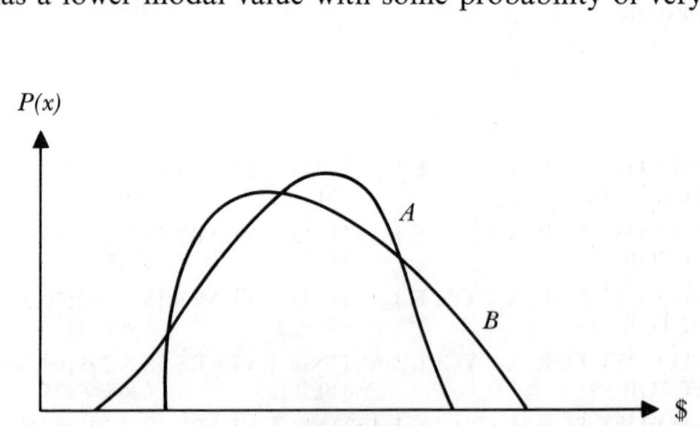

Figure 2

formance. It is not clear that one investment should be universally preferred to the other.

Since capital budgeting investments cover spans of several years, and the dollar flows need to be discounted, we need to know how to obtain a probability distribution for the summed discounted flows of several years. This brings us to the subject of convolutions.

Convolutions

A convoluted probability distribution is one that sums the distributions of two or more independent random variables. To be concrete, obtaining a convoluted distribution would be helpful

(1) if demand for inventory were known for one month, say, and one wished to study a situation (for example, leadtime) involving several months' demand;

(2) if the distribution for net earnings for, say, one year were known and one wished to sum several years' net earnings to calculate net present value; and

(3) if the distribution for a customer's service time in a waiting line system were known and one wished to have a distribution for several customers' time.

There are other situations in which it is necessary to obtain a convoluted probability distribution. We shall first briefly discuss convolution procedures and then discuss all three cases described above. In particular, this chapter will study the second situation.

Suppose an analyst knows a demand distribution for one day and wishes to calculate the distribution for the total of two days' demand (we could say n days, but that would unnecessarily complicate the discussion without introducing any new procedures). Thus we seek the distribution of $x = D_1 + D_2$, where D_i is the quantity demanded on day i. D_1 and D_2 need not have the same distribution, although that simplifies matters somewhat, but they must be independent of one another.

$$\text{By definition, } F(x) = \sum_{D_1=0}^{x} P_1(D_1)P_2(x - D_1)$$

Observe that a folding action has been specified; a total of x is needed, and D_2 (which equals $x - D_1$) takes up wherever D_1 leaves off.

Example:

D_1	$P_1(D_1)$	D_2	$P_2(D_2)$
0	.2	1	.4
1	.3	2	.3
2	.5	3	.2
		4	.1

> Recall that the probability of an impossible event = 0. Therefore, for example, even though they are not listed, $P_1(D_1 = 3) = P_1(D_1 = 4) = \ldots = P_1(D_1 = n) = 0$

To illustrate the definition, assume we wish to compute $F(x = 3)$.

$$F(x=3) = \sum_{D_1=0}^{3} P_1(D_1)P_2(3-D_1) = P_1(0)P_2(3) + P_1(1)P_2(2) + P_1(2)P_2(1) + P_1(3)P_2(0)$$

$$= .2(.2) + .3(.3) + .5(.4) + 0(0)$$

$$= .33$$

It is easier, however, to use matrices as shown in Exhibit 2:

$$\begin{bmatrix} .2 \\ .3 \\ .5 \end{bmatrix} [.4, .3, .2, .1] = \begin{bmatrix} .08 & .06 & .04 & .02 \\ .12 & .09 & .06 & .03 \\ .20 & .15 & .10 & .05 \end{bmatrix}$$

Add elements cross-diagonally to obtain

x	$F(x)$	
1	.08	
2	.18	
3	.33	← $F(x = 3)$, as obtained above by applying the definition
4	.23	
5	.13	
6	.05	
	1.00	

In this way, any empirical probability distribution may be convoluted. If the same distribution is applicable to both days, the definition becomes

$$P^{\{2\}}(x) = \sum_{D=0}^{x} P(D)P(x-D)$$

If n days are involved in summation, a recursive definition (that is, the *nth* fold in terms of the $n - 1$st fold) applies:

$$P^{\{n\}}(x) = \sum_{D=0}^{x} P(D)P^{\{n-1\}}(x-D)$$

Certain theoretical distributions fold very neatly. One of these is the Poisson, which has the following probability mass function:

$$P(D) = \lambda^D e^{-\lambda}/D!,$$

where $\lambda =$ the mean of the distribution.

By definition,

$$P^{\{2\}}(x) = \sum_{D=0}^{x} \left(\frac{\lambda^D e^{-\lambda}}{D!}\right)\left(\frac{\lambda^{x-D} e^{-\lambda}}{(x-D)!}\right)$$

$$= e^{-2\lambda}\lambda^x \sum_{0}^{x} \frac{1}{D!(x-D)!} \qquad \text{(Law of exponents)}$$

$$= \frac{e^{-2\lambda}\lambda^x}{x!} \sum_{0}^{x} \frac{x!}{D!(x-D)!} \qquad \text{(Multiplication by 1 in the form } x!/x!\text{)}$$

$$= \frac{e^{-2\lambda}\lambda^x}{x!} \sum_{0}^{x} \frac{x!}{D!(x-D)!} 1^D 1^{x-D} \qquad \text{(More multiplication by 1)}$$

Recall the binomial expansion:

$$(a+b)^n = \sum_{i=0}^{n} \frac{n!}{i!(n-i)!} a^i b^{n-i} = \sum_{i=0}^{n} \binom{n}{i} a^i b^{n-i}$$

$$= \frac{e^{-2\lambda}\lambda^x}{x!}(1+1)^x$$

$$= \frac{e^{-2\lambda}\lambda^x 2^x}{x!}$$

$$= \frac{e^{-2\lambda}(2\lambda)^x}{x!}$$

Hence, the 2-fold Poisson simply doubles the 1-fold mean and can be read from Table 9 in Appendix A just as easily as a 1-fold.

x	0	1	2	3	4	5	6	7	8
$P(x: \lambda = 1)$	.368	.368	.184	.061	.015	.003	.001	0	0
$P(x: 2\lambda = 2)$	.135	.271	.271	.180	.090	.036	.012	.004	.001

You might enjoy checking the 2-fold results shown above by treating the 1-fold as an empirical distribution and using matrices.

Usually it is easier to use Z-transforms when obtaining convolutions of discrete distributions. For the Poisson, we first find the closed form of a transformed 1-fold:

$$T\{P(D)\} \equiv \sum_{D=0}^{\infty} P(D)Z^D = \sum_{D=0}^{\infty} \frac{(e^{-\lambda}\lambda^D)}{D!} Z^D = e^{-\lambda} \sum_{D=0}^{\infty} \frac{(\lambda Z)^D}{D!}$$

> Recall (see Appendix C) that the Maclaurin expansion of
>
> $$f(x) = e^{ax} = \sum_{i=0}^{\infty} (ax)^i/i!$$

$$= e^{-\lambda}e^{\lambda Z} = e^{-\lambda(1-Z)}$$

Then, since the distributions are independent, we may multiply their transforms (as in joint probabilities):

$$P^{\{2\}}(Z) = e^{-\lambda(1-Z)}e^{-\lambda(1-Z)} = e^{-2\lambda(1-Z)},$$

which just doubles the mean of a 1-fold transformed Poisson; hence the inverse transform

$$T^{-1}\{e^{-2\lambda(1-Z)}\} = e^{-2\lambda}(2\lambda)^x/x!,$$

which agrees with our previous result obtained by definition. This procedure is perfectly general; therefore the n-fold Poisson simply multiplies the mean by n. Do not expect all theoretical distributions to behave so nicely, however.

Because a great deal of our work will utilize the normal distribution, let us see how it may be convolved. With continuous distributions the definition becomes

$$g(x) = \int_0^x f_1(D_1)f_2(x - D_1)\, dD_1$$

It will be swifter, however, if we go directly to transforms. In this instance, we use the S-transform

$$f(S) \equiv \int_{-\infty}^{\infty} f(D)e^{-SD}\, dD = \int_{-\infty}^{\infty} \frac{e^{-SD}e^{-\frac{1}{2}\left(\frac{D-\mu}{\sigma}\right)^2}}{\sigma\sqrt{2\pi}}\, dD$$

$$= \frac{1}{\sigma\sqrt{2\pi}} \int_{-\infty}^{\infty} e^{-SD} e^{-\frac{1}{2}\left(\frac{D^2 - 2\mu D + \mu^2}{\sigma^2}\right)}\, dD$$

$$= \frac{1}{\sigma\sqrt{2\pi}} \int_{-\infty}^{\infty} e^{-\frac{1}{2}\left(\frac{D^2 + 2(\sigma^2 S - \mu)D + \mu^2}{\sigma^2}\right)}\, dD$$

So far we have just expanded $(D - \mu)^2$ and inserted $-SD = -2\sigma^2 SD/2\sigma^2$.

Now (1) we recognize that $e^{-\frac{1}{2}\left(\frac{\mu}{\sigma}\right)^2}$ is just a constant and may be factored out, and (2) we complete the square in the exponent. To have a complete square, we need something of the form

$$(D + a)^2 = D^2 + 2aD + a^2$$

We have $D^2 + 2(\sigma^2 S - \mu)D$, so, comparing the middle terms, we see

$$a = \sigma^2 S - \mu$$

and we therefore add 0 in the form $+a^2 - a^2 = +(\sigma^2 S - \mu)^2 - (\sigma^2 S - \mu)^2$

$$= \frac{e^{-\frac{1}{2}\left(\frac{\mu}{\sigma}\right)^2} e^{\frac{1}{2}\left(\frac{\sigma^2 S - \mu}{\sigma}\right)^2}}{\sigma\sqrt{2\pi}} \int_{-\infty}^{\infty} e^{-\frac{1}{2\sigma^2}(D^2 + 2(\sigma^2 S - \mu)D + (\sigma^2 S - \mu)^2)}\, dD$$

$$= \frac{e^{\frac{\sigma^2 S^2 - 2\mu S}{2}}}{\sigma\sqrt{2\pi}} \int_{-\infty}^{\infty} e^{-\frac{1}{2\sigma^2}(D + (\sigma^2 S - \mu))^2}\, dD$$

Substitution of variable:

$$Z = \frac{D + \sigma^2 S - \mu}{\sigma} \qquad Z_{\text{upper}} \doteq \infty$$

$$\frac{dZ}{dD} = \frac{1}{\sigma}, \quad \text{so } dD = \sigma\, dZ \qquad Z_{\text{lower}} \doteq -\infty$$

$$= \frac{e^{\frac{\sigma^2 S^2 - 2\mu S}{2}}}{\sigma\sqrt{2\pi}} \int_{-\infty}^{\infty} e^{-Z^2/2} \sigma\, dZ$$

$$= e^{\frac{\sigma^2 S^2 - 2\mu S}{2}} \int_{-\infty}^{\infty} \frac{e^{-Z^2/2}}{\sqrt{2\pi}}\, dZ$$

But the integral is the standardized normal distribution (Table 8 in Appendix A) and equals 1; therefore,

$$f(S) = e^{\frac{\sigma^2 S^2 - 2\mu S}{2}}$$

If we had two independent normal distributions with different means and variances, we could multiply their transforms:

$$f_1(S)*f_2(S) = e^{\frac{\sigma^2 S^2 - 2\mu_1 S}{2}} e^{\frac{\sigma_2{}^2 S^2 - 2\mu_2 S}{2}}$$

$$= e^{\frac{(\sigma_1{}^2 + \sigma_2{}^2)S^2 - 2(\mu_1 + \mu_2)S}{2}}$$

This shows that the convoluted distribution has the same form as the 1-fold transformed normal, except that the separate variances and means are added. Consequently, the inverse transform would be

$$T^{-1}\left\{e^{\frac{(\sigma_1{}^2 + \sigma_2{}^2)S^2 - 2(\mu_1 + \mu_2)S}{2}}\right\} = N(x:\mu_1 + \mu_2; \sqrt{\sigma_1{}^2 + \sigma_2{}^2})$$

—which, of course, is our previous notation for the normal density.

If both days have the same mean and standard deviation,

$$f^{\{2\}}(S) = e^{\frac{2\sigma^2 S^2 - 4\mu S}{2}} = e^{2\left(\frac{\sigma^2 S^2 - 2\mu S}{2}\right)}$$

—which just doubles the parameters of the 1-fold transformed normal; hence

$$T^{-1}\left\{e^{2\left(\frac{\sigma^2 S^2 - 2\mu S}{2}\right)}\right\} = N\{x:2\mu; \sqrt{2}\sigma\}, \quad \text{where } \sqrt{\sigma^2 + \sigma^2} = \sqrt{2}\sigma$$

This is perfectly general; therefore, $f^{\{n\}}(x) = N\{x:n\mu; \sqrt{n}\sigma\}$. Our conclusion is that an n-fold normal can be read from a standardized normal table simply by multiplying the mean by n and the standard deviation by $\sqrt{n}$.—Which, obviously, is very pleasant.

Variances and Covariances

Now that we have convolution theory at our disposal and all is going smoothly, it is time to introduce some snags. It is one thing to sum random variables, $X_i/(1 + r)^i$, where X_i is the net earnings in year i. At first blush, this would appear to be a special case of using $\mu_i \neq \mu_j \neq \cdots \neq \mu_k$, and under the proper conditions it is. Unfortunately, the world is not always so co-operative.[3]

[3] What will be presented here in greater detail but in narrower scope is the gist of F. S. Hillier's pathbreaking article, "The Derivation of Probabilistic Information for the Evaluation of Risky Investments," *Management Science*, 9, no. 3 (April 1963): pp. 443–57). I strongly recommend that you read this article.

First of all, we should recognize that if the number of years, n, is large, the Central Limit Theorem asserts that even if the X_i are not normally distributed themselves, their sum will be. In the event of small n, what we shall develop will hold true regardless of the basic distributions. If those distributions were not normal, we could not say that the summed distribution was itself normal. However, since the normal distribution has its mode (the most probable outcome) equal to its mean, and because of the Central Limit Theorem, it often makes sense to assume that the X_i are normally distributed; consequently, so is their sum.

There are only three cases that need examination: (1) the X_i are independent, (2) the X_i are perfectly positively correlated, and (3) the X_i are a mixture of (1) and (2). Where more than two years are concerned, the X_i could not be perfectly negatively correlated, because the transitivity relation will fail (that is, if X_1 is perfectly negatively correlated with X_2, and X_3 is perfectly negatively correlated with X_2, then X_3 would be perfectly *positively* correlated with X_1).

Fortunately, certain ideas pertain regardless of how the X_i are related. Every $X_i = \mu_i + Z\sigma_i$ where μ_i and σ_i are the expected value and standard deviation respectively, and Z is some number of standard deviations. If we let W—itself a random variable—stand for the present worth of the sum, we will always get

$$W = \sum_{i=0}^{n} \mu_i/(1+r)^i = \sum_{i=0}^{n} A_i, \quad \text{for convenience}$$

From probability theory we will also always have

$$\begin{aligned} V(W) &= V(A_0 + A_1 + \cdots + A_n) = E[\textstyle\sum A_i - E(\sum A_i)]^2 \\ &= V(A_0) + V(A_1) + \cdots + V(A_n) + 2 \sum_{\substack{i,j \\ i<j}} \text{Cov}(A_i, A_j) \end{aligned}$$

Independence

If two variables, A_i and A_j, are independent, their covariances are zero ($\text{Cov}(A_i, A_j) = 0$). Hence the variance for each is

$$V(A_i) = \sum_{k=1}^{m} \left[\frac{x_{ik} - \mu_i}{(1+r)^i}\right]^2 P(x_{ik}) = \left(\frac{1}{1+r}\right)^{2i} \sigma_i^2,$$

and for their sum, the variance is $V(A_i + A_j) = V(A_i) + V(A_j)$

More generally, $$\begin{aligned} V(W) &= V(A_0) + V(A_1) + \cdots + V(A_n) \\ &= \sigma_0^2 + \frac{\sigma_1^2}{(1+r)^{2(1)}} + \cdots + \frac{\sigma_n^2}{(1+r)^{2(n)}} \\ &= \sum_{i=0}^{n} \left[\frac{\sigma_i}{(1+r)^i}\right]^2 \end{aligned}$$

Perfectly Correlated

If X_i and X_j are perfectly correlated, their readings fall on a straight line and

$$\frac{\text{Cov}(X_i, X_j)}{\sigma_i \sigma_j} = 1, \quad \text{or } \text{Cov}(X_i, X_j) = \sigma_i \sigma_j$$

> Recall, from Chapter 3, that $B = (X^T X)^{-1} X^T Y$ where the slope in 2-space is designated by B_1.
>
> $$B_1 = \frac{n\sum xy - \sum x \sum y}{n\sum x^2 - (\sum x)^2} = \frac{\frac{\sum xy}{n} - \bar{x}\,\bar{y}}{\frac{\sum x^2}{n} - \bar{x}^2} = \frac{\text{Cov}(x, y)}{V(x)}$$
>
> —which, if x and y are perfectly correlated,
>
> $$= \frac{\sigma_x \sigma_y}{\sigma_x{}^2} = \frac{\sigma_y}{\sigma_x}$$
>
> Hence $$y = \frac{\sigma_y}{\sigma_x} x + B_0$$

Since the readings fall on a straight line,

$$X_i = \frac{\sigma_i}{\sigma_j} X_j + B_0 \quad \text{and, inversely,} \quad X_j = \frac{\sigma_j}{\sigma_i} X_i - \frac{\sigma_j}{\sigma_i} B_0$$

Now suppose that year i precedes j, and that, as originally stated, $X_i = \mu_i + Z\sigma_i$, where Z is a specific number of standard deviations. Let us see what must happen to X_j because of perfect correlation.

$$X_j = \frac{\sigma_j}{\sigma_i} X_i - \frac{\sigma_j}{\sigma_i} B_0 = \frac{\sigma_j}{\sigma_i}(\mu_i + Z\sigma_i) - \frac{\sigma_j}{\sigma_i} B_0$$

$$= \left(\frac{\sigma_j}{\sigma_i}\mu_i - \frac{\sigma_j}{\sigma_i} B_0\right) + Z\sigma_j$$

> Consider the expectation of X_j:
>
> $$E(X_j) = E\left(\frac{\sigma_j}{\sigma_i} X_i - \frac{\sigma_j}{\sigma_i} B_0\right) = \frac{\sigma_j}{\sigma_i} E(X_i) - \frac{\sigma_j}{\sigma_i} E(B_0)$$
>
> But the expected value of a variable is its mean, while the expected value of a constant is the constant. Hence
>
> $$E(X_j) = \mu_j = \frac{\sigma_j}{\sigma_i}\mu_i - \frac{\sigma_j}{\sigma_i} B_0, \quad \text{as above.}$$

$$= \mu_j + Z\sigma_j$$

We see that as a consequence of there being Z standard deviations in year i, there will also be Z standard deviations in year j, because of the perfect correlation. Thus if perfect positive correlation were assumed in the yearly flows of an investment, the analyst would be saying that whatever number of standard deviations from its mean the first year experienced, the ensuing years would be off their means by exactly the same number of standard deviations. In perfect positive correlation, if the first year's estimates prove low, then all ensuing years' estimates will also be low.

Let us see how this affects the variance of the sum.

$$\begin{aligned} V(W) &= V(A_0 + A_1 + \cdots + A_n) \\ &= V(A_0) + V(A_1) + \cdots + V(A_n) + 2\sum_{\substack{i,j \\ i<j}} \operatorname{Cov}(A_i, A_j) \\ &= \frac{\sigma_0^{\,2}}{(1+r)^{0(2)}} + \frac{\sigma_1^{\,2}}{(1+r)^{1(2)}} + \cdots + \frac{\sigma_n^{\,2}}{(1+r)^{n(2)}} + 2\sum_{\substack{i,j \\ i<j}} \frac{\sigma_i \sigma_j}{(1+r)^{i+j}} \end{aligned}$$

$$V(W) = \left[\sum_{i=0}^{n} \frac{\sigma_i}{(1+r)^i}\right]^2$$

We have now arrived at a curious result:

$$V(W) = \begin{cases} \sum[\sigma_i/(1+r)^i]^2, & \text{if } X_i \text{ are independent} \\ [\sum \sigma_i/(1+r)^i]^2, & \text{if } X_i \text{ are perfectly correlated} \end{cases}$$

The truly curious thing is that the standard deviation in the perfect correlation case is

$$\sigma(w) = \sqrt{V(w)} = \sum \sigma_i/(1+r)^i$$

Some analysts, seeing that standard deviations have been added, feel that the result must be wrong. The usual thing is to add variances not standard deviations; however, perfect correlation is the exception.

Mixture

It seems reasonable to assume that the majority of investment flows are neither independent nor perfectly correlated, but a little of each. In Hillier's classical illustration, he has a revolutionary new product hitting the market while facing the uncertainty caused by varying component reliability, lack of production experience on the product, and rumors of competitors with similar products on the drawing board.[4] The dollar estimates are accordingly

[4] Ibid., p. 451.

divided into (1) a portion for sales revenue minus costs of promotion; this portion reflects the assumption that, should reception exceed expectations in the first year, it will continue to do so; and (2) a portion for production expenses that reflects deviations due to random fluctuations in irregular items of production cost.

If we break X_i into two portions, we have $X_i = X_i' + X_i''$, where X_i' is the portion that varies independently and X_i'' is the portion that is perfectly correlated. The present worth of the sum is

$$W = \sum_{i=0}^{n} (\mu_i' + \mu_i'')/(1+r)^i$$

$$V(W) = \sum_{i=0}^{n} [\sigma_i'/(1+r)^i]^2 + \left[\sum_{i=0}^{n} \sigma_i''/(1+r)^i\right]^2$$

The σ_i'' may, in turn, consist of several portions that are perfectly correlated with corresponding (subscript k) portions in other years. Where this is the case, the variance formula becomes

$$V(W) = \sum_{i=0}^{n} [\sigma_i'/(1+r)^i]^2 + \sum_{k=1}^{m} \left[\sum_{i=0}^{n} \sqrt{V(X_{ik}'')}/(1+r)^i\right]^2$$

Example: An investment requires exactly \$500,000.

Required rate of return before taxes is 20%.

Production costs have been estimated to obey normal distributions with the means and standard deviations shown in Table 1. The production process faces random fluctuations in costs; hence, the distributions are considered independent of one another.

Salvage value is expected to be independently normally distributed as shown in Table 1.

Marketing revenues net of promotion costs are normally distributed as shown in Table 1; however, the early reception of the product should dictate its acceptance in later years as well. Hence the net marketing revenue distributions are considered perfectly correlated.

Table 1 Investment: Cash Flows

	Production Costs		Salvage Value		Net Marketing Revenues		Net
Year	μ_i'	σ_i'	μ_i'	σ_i'	μ_i''	σ_i''	μ_i
1	\$80,000	\$15,000			\$200,000	\$30,000	\$120,000
2	50,000	10,000			400,000	50,000	350,000
3	50,000	10,000			300,000	50,000	250,000
4	50,000	10,000			200,000	40,000	150,000
5	40,000	4,000	\$100,000	\$3,000	100,000	20,000	160,000

Required:

1. Find the summed distribution for the net cash flows for the five years.
2. Find the probability of loss, $P(L)$.
3. Find the expected gain, $E(G)$, and expected loss, $E(L)$.

Solution: Since production cost and salvage value are independent, and since one is an outflow while the other is an inflow, we can obtain the standard deviation for year 5 by square rooting:

$$\begin{aligned} V(A-B) &= E([A-B]^2) - [E(A-B)]^2 \\ &= E(A^2) - 2E(AB) + E(B^2) - [E(A) - E(B)]^2 \\ &= [E(A^2) - (E(A))^2] + [E(B^2) - (E(B))^2] - 2[E(AB) - E(A)E(B)] \\ &= V(A) + V(B) - 2\,\mathrm{Cov}(A, B) \\ &= V(A) + V(B), \quad \text{since } A \text{ and } B \text{ are independent} \end{aligned}$$

$$5000^2 = 3{,}000^2 + 4{,}000^2$$

We shall choose not to include investment in the calculation of the summed distribution, although that is what has been contemplated in our discussions. This will make no difference in our answer (had investment a normal distribution, including it would be the better approach), and it will permit us to investigate more clearly a particularly popular type of integral so that it need not be reillustrated in later chapters.

$$\begin{aligned} W &= 120{,}000b(1, 20) + 350{,}000b(2, 20) + 250{,}000b(3, 20) \\ &\quad + 150{,}000b(4, 20) + 160{,}000b(5, 20) \\ &= 624{,}364 \end{aligned}$$

i	$b(i, 20)$	σ'	$\sigma' b$	$(\sigma' b)^2$	σ''	$\sigma'' b$
1	.8333	15,000	12,500	156,250,000	30,000	25,000
2	.6944	10,000	6,944	48,219,136	50,000	34,720
3	.5787	10,000	5,787	33,489,369	50,000	28,935
4	.4823	10,000	4,823	23,261,329	40,000	19,292
5	.4019	5,000	2,009.5	4,038.090	20,000	8,038
				265,257,924		115,985

$$V(W) = 265{,}257{,}924 + 115{,}985^2 = 13{,}717{,}778{,}149$$

$$\sigma_W = \sqrt{V(W)} = 117{,}123$$

The answer to the first requirement is that the summed distribution, *with investment reflected, is*

$$N(x{:}\mu = 124{,}364;\ \sigma = 117{,}123)$$

The probability of loss is $P(L) = .5 - P\left(0 < Z < \dfrac{124{,}364}{117{,}123}\right)$

$$P(L) = .5 - .3558$$

$$P(L) = .1442$$

If we diagram the *investment as separate* from the other cash flows, we see

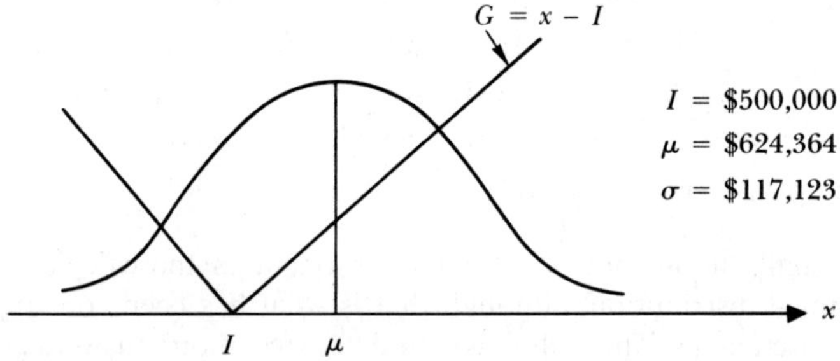

For expected gain we weight each dollar in excess of I by the probability that cash flow, x, will get as large as x.

$$E(G) = \int_{500{,}000}^{\infty} \frac{(x - 500{,}000)e^{-\frac{1}{2}\left(\frac{x-624{,}364}{117{,}123}\right)^2}}{117{,}123\sqrt{2\pi}}\,dx = \int_I^{\infty} \frac{(x - I)e^{-\frac{1}{2}\left(\frac{x-\mu}{\sigma}\right)^2}}{\sigma\sqrt{2\pi}}\,dx$$

$$= \frac{1}{\sqrt{2\pi}} \int_I^{\infty} \left(\frac{x-\mu}{\sigma}\right) e^{-\frac{1}{2}\left(\frac{x-\mu}{\sigma}\right)^2} dx + \frac{(\mu - I)}{\sigma} \int_I^{\infty} \frac{e^{-\frac{1}{2}\left(\frac{x-\mu}{\sigma}\right)^2}}{\sqrt{2\pi}}\,dx$$

Substitution of variables:

$$Z = (x - \mu)/\sigma;\quad dZ/dx = 1/\sigma,\ \therefore,\quad \sigma\,dZ = dx$$

$$Z_{\text{upper}} \to \infty;\qquad Z_{\text{lower}} = (I - \mu)/\sigma = -z$$

Taking $1/\sqrt{2\pi} = 1/\sqrt{44/7} = .4$,

$$E(G) = .4 \int_{-z}^{\infty} Ze^{-Z^2/2}(\sigma\,dZ) + (\mu - I)\int_{-z}^{\infty} \frac{e^{-Z^2/2}\,dZ}{\sqrt{2\pi}}$$

The first integral is now in $\left[\int f'(x)e^{f(x)}\,dx\right]$ form, while the second integral is the integral for the standardized normal.

$$E(G) = -.4\sigma e^{-Z^2/2}\Big]_{-z}^{\infty} + (\mu - I)[.5000 + P(-z < Z < 0)]$$

$$E(G) = .4\sigma e^{-z^2/2} + (\mu - I)[.5000 + P(-z < Z < 0)]$$

Inserting given values for z, μ, and I:

$$\begin{aligned} E(G) &= .4(117{,}123)e^{-(-1.062)^2/2} + (624{,}364 - 500{,}000)[.5000 + .3558] \\ &= 46{,}849.2(.5690) + 106{,}431 \\ &= 133{,}088 \end{aligned}$$

Since
$$E(NPV) = E(G) - E(L)$$

$$124{,}364 = 133{,}088 - E(L)$$

$$\therefore, \quad E(L) = 8{,}724$$

Conclusion: We are now able to give the decisionmaker considerably more information than he had when he was focusing solely on NPV. He now has some idea what to expect by way of separate gains and losses. He also knows the parameters and shape of the underlying probability distribution and hence the probabilities of losing or gaining any amount. Important information about uncertainty is no longer submerged in a single expected value figure.

Notes on Treating Truncation

Truncation is a problem in probability modelling in which a distribution cannot be used for outcomes above or below some value. For example, the normal distribution is essentially totally contained between $\mu \pm 3\sigma$. If for some reason the random variable, x, can only take on values in the range $\mu - 2\sigma < x < \mu + 3\sigma$, the cumulative area is $.4772 + .4987 = .9759$ and not 1. Truncation has therefore occurred.

How should an analyst treat truncation? Assume the random variable is normally distributed except that $\int N(\mu;\sigma) < 1$. If $\int N(\mu;\sigma) > .95$, practice seems to ignore the truncation problem as being insignificant. If $\int N(\mu;\sigma)$ is significantly less than 1, two approaches make sense:

1. Restore the sum-to-unity axiom by dividing the probability distribution by its sum. This procedure treats the probabilities as conditional, as if they were outcomes occurring in a subset of the original sample space. The effect is that the normal distribution is scaled and cut off—that is, raised off the axis and prohibited from

continued to page 398

continued from page 397

tailing off to negative and/or positive infinity (depending on the imposed limitation or limitations). The result is no longer a strictly normal distribution.

2. Recognize a cumulative probability at the imposed limit or limits. The result is no longer a normal distribution but rather a normal with a "blip" or two in place of one or both tails. Essentially this approach splits the probability distribution into two (three if both tails are cut off) portions: the probability at the end point and the remaining normal-curve probabilities.

Example: Sales are distributed normally with mean 4,000 and standard deviation 3,000. Determine expected shortage if 5,000 units are in stock. Observe that negative sales make no sense; consequently, the lower limit is 0 and the setup, which recognizes that demand exceeds supply, is

$$E(\text{Shortage}) = \int_{5000}^{\infty} (x - 5{,}000)N(\mu = 4{,}000;\ \sigma = 3{,}000)$$

$$= 766 \text{ units,} \quad \text{using the procedures illustrated above}$$

Scaling

$$\int_{0}^{\infty} N(\mu;\ \sigma) = \int_{-1.\overline{3}}^{\infty} N(\mu = 0;\ \sigma = 1) = .5000 + .4088$$

where

$$Z = (x - 4{,}000)/3{,}000$$

$$Z_U \to \infty$$

$$Z_L = (0 - 4{,}000)/3{,}000 = -1.\overline{3}$$

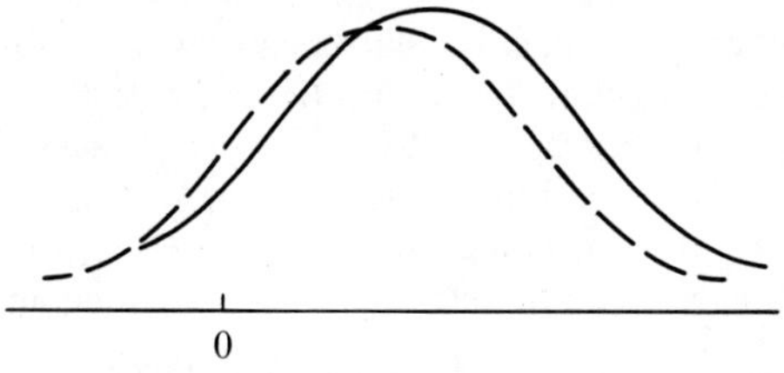

Total area is therefore only .9088. If scaling is used, the setup would become what it is now divided by .9088, or 766/.9088 = 843 units.

Blip

The probability of 0 sales is the probability that sales are less than or equal to .5 units (up to .499999, rounding to the nearest integer would yield 0 units):

continued to page 399

continued from page 398

$$P(x < .5) = \int_{-\infty}^{.5} N(\mu; \sigma)$$

Let $Z = (x - 4{,}000)/3{,}000$, so $Z_U = (.5 - 4{,}000)/3{,}000 = -1.3331\bar{6}$

$$P(x < .5) = \int_{-\infty}^{-1.13331\bar{6}} N(\mu, \sigma) = (.5 - .4087)$$

$$= .0913$$

$$P(x > .5) = \qquad .9087$$

$$1.0000$$

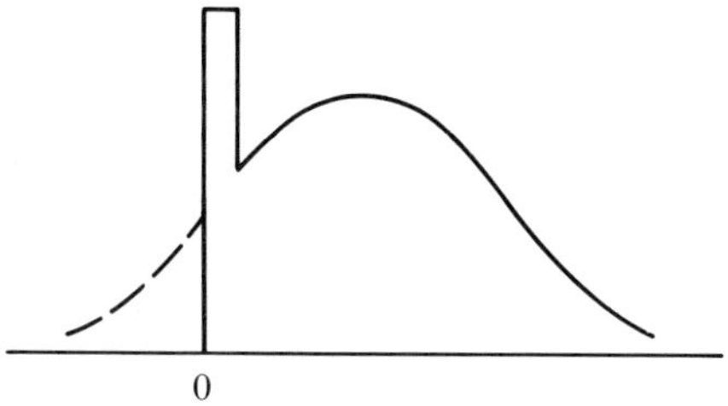

Since the range of expected shortage does not include $x < .5$, the initial calculation holds: $E(\text{Shortage}) = 766$ units. Which treatment for truncation is better? It is a matter more of art than of science. I often prefer the blip approach because (1) scaling can lead to some strange results as, for instance, if an initial probability of, say, .4 becomes .5 after adjustment and it is clear that the event really has less than an even chance of occurring (see problem 21), and (2) I feel that the blip view frequently does the least damage to what is intended by assuming normality. There are other times, however, when the conditional or scaling approach is not only easier to use but more in keeping with the facts.

Method of Moments and Goodness of Fit

The hour groweth long—and so does this chapter. Let us bring our present affairs to a swift completion with a brief discussion of the question "Can a well-known distribution be substituted for an empirical distribution?" "Is there any point in making such a substitution, assuming that it is feasible?"

We frequently substitute a well-defined distribution for an empirical distribution to avail ourselves of the properties of the well-defined distribution. When this is done, it is customary to determine how well the overall shape of the theoretical distribution fits the actual data by employing a chi-square test. In other words, we test for goodness of fit. We shall use an example that relies on the uniform (all outcomes equally likely) distribution to learn how such a test is conducted.

Example: A six-sided die, assumed to be fair, has been rolled 300 times. The expected frequency for each face would be 50, since one face is as likely to show up on a fair die as any other and (1/6)300 = 50. The observed frequencies are summarized in Table 2.

Table 2 Chi-Square Test: Dice

	1	2	3	4	5	6
Observed (O_i)	55	71	45	48	40	41
Expected (E_i)	50	50	50	50	50	50

$$\chi^2 = \sum_{i=1}^{n} \frac{(O_i - E_i)^2}{E_i}, \quad \text{where } n \text{ is the number of categories}$$

$$= \frac{(55-50)^2}{50} + \frac{(71-50)^2}{50} + \frac{(45-50)^2}{50} + \frac{(48-50)^2}{50} + \frac{(40-50)^2}{50} + \frac{(41-50)^2}{50}$$

$$= 686/50 = 13.7$$

To use the χ^2 table (Table 7 in Appendix A) and our statistic 13.7, we must first determine the "degrees of freedom." The number of degrees of freedom of a statistic is designated by the letter v, which is determined according to the formula $v = n - 1 - p$ (here p is the number of population parameters that must be estimated from the sample). Now p is subtracted *only* if the parameters need to be estimated. For instance, if we were going to estimate λ, the mean of the Poisson, from the observed frequencies, we would have $v = n - 1 - 1$. However, if we had already determined λ from a previous sample and had assumed it was the population mean, and if we now wished to decide whether a more recent sample permitted us to retain our former estimate of λ, we would have $v = n - 1$.

We subtract 1 from n in determining the degrees of freedom because we know the total frequencies, N, and once the frequencies for $n - 1$ categories have been specified, the nth category is forced to take the residual number of frequencies that result in the total N. In other words, $n - 1$ categories are "free" to take whatever frequency values they wish, but the nth category is constrained.

We next establish a *confidence interval*, that is, the level of probability we require to accept the *hypothesis* that the die is fair. Here it is wise to re-

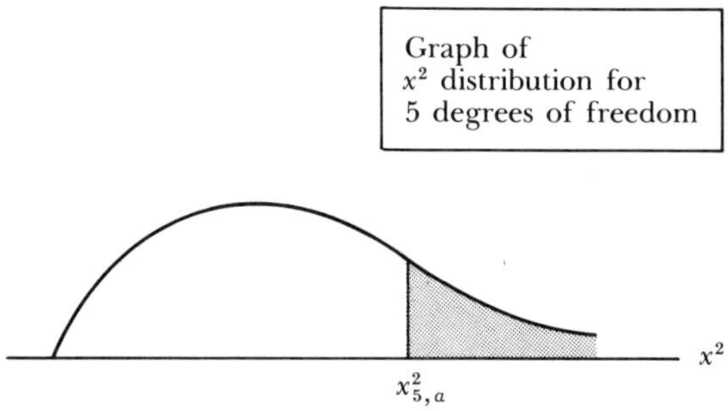

member that the chi-square distribution may be lopsided (skewed) as shown above.

Typically, a 95% confidence interval is chosen and a one-tailed test is administered.[5] Consequently $\chi^2_{5,\alpha}$ is $\chi^2_{5,.95}$ in the diagram shown above and 5% of the distribution's area lies in the shaded tail. Since we do not need to estimate any parameters for a fair die, our number of degrees of freedom is

$$v = n - 1 = 6 - 1 = 5$$

Reading from Table 7 in Appendix A, we see χ^2 for 5 degrees of freedom has a value 11.1. Since 13.7 > 11.1, we reject the hypothesis that the die is fair.

Understanding the χ^2 Table

Say $v = 4$, while the rejection probability $\alpha = .05$. Then the crucial χ^2 statistic is determined by solving for ? in

$$.05 = \int_?^\infty \frac{1}{2^2\Gamma(2)} (\chi^2)^{\frac{4-2}{2}} e^{-\chi^2/2} \, d(\chi^2)$$

For simplicity, let $y = \chi^2$. Then, since $\Gamma(2) = 1$, we have

$$.05 = .25 \int_?^\infty ye^{-y/2}\, dy = .25 \left[\frac{ye^{-y/2}}{(-1/2)} - \frac{e^{-y/2}}{(-1/2)^2} \right]_?^\infty$$

$$.05 = .25 \left[\frac{?e^{-.5?}}{.5} + \frac{e^{-.5?}}{.25} \right]$$

$$.1 = e^{-.5?}(? + 2)$$

[5] Formerly statisticians preferred a two-tailed test, but the thinking has changed in recent years in favor of a one-tailed test. The outstanding reference on the subject is M. G. Kendall and A. Stuart, *The Advanced Theory of Statistics* New York: Hofner Publishing Co., 1967), 2: Chapter 30 (see especially p. 422).

continued from page 401

Now we could trial-and-error our way to determining ?, the critical statistic (note that $? = \chi^2_{4,\alpha}$), or get a computer to help us. However, the purpose of going through the integration shown above was to demonstrate where the χ^2 table figures came from and what they mean. Were you to look up the $\alpha = .05$ with 4 degrees of freedom entry in the χ^2 table in Appendix A, you would find 9.488. When we insert 9.488 for ? in our last equation, we obtain

$$.1 = e^{-.5(9.488)}(9.488 + 2) = e^{-4.744}(11.488) = .008704(11.488) = .1$$

Conclusion: The entries in the χ^2 table are the readings of the statistic such that the area under the curve to the right of the statistic equals the rejection probability.

We shall look at another example shortly, but first I would like to emphasize in your thinking that χ^2 deals directly with frequencies and not probabilities. There is also an adjustment that should be made if the expected frequency in a given category is less than 5. In such a situation those categories with less than 5 are grouped with as many adjacent categories as are needed to achieve an aggregated frequency at least equal to 5 (and the greater the better, especially when fewer than five categories exist). Some analysts insist on a minimum of 10.

Method of Moments

When trying to replace an empirical distribution by a theoretical one, it is common practice to employ the Method of Moments. The reasoning is that a good substitution would have the same moments (mean, variance) in both the empirical and the theoretical distribution. The first step in applying the method is to calculate as many moments from the empirical distribution as there are needed parameters in the specification of the theoretical probability function. The number of moments needed, therefore, varies with the distribution; for example: Poisson requires one—the mean; normal requires two—the mean and standard deviation; and gamma requires two—the mean and variance. The second step is to set the moments equal. For example, the gamma density is $f(x) = b^{a+1}x^a e^{-bx}/a!$ for $x > 0$ and $a = 0, 1, 2, 3, \ldots$; its mean is $(a + 1)/b$ and its variance is $(a + 1)/b^2$. Assume the empirical mean is 2 and its variance is 1. Then the Method of Moments proceeds as follows:

$$(a + 1)/b = 2$$

$$(a + 1)/b^2 = 1$$

Hence $2/b = 1$ and $b = 2$ while $a = 3$. The gamma, which has a flexible, and therefore very useful, shape, becomes $f(x) = 2^4 x^3 e^{-2x}/3!$

Example: A business observes that demand for a particular item has been distributed over a 100-day period as follows:

D	Frequency	$P(D)$
0	62	.62
1	28	.28
2	7	.07
3	2	.02
4	1	.01
	100	1.00

The accountant decides to fit a Poisson curve to these data. To do so, he calculates the mean as follows:

$$E(D) = \lambda = 0(.62) + 1(.28) + 2(.07) + 3(.02) + 4(.01) = .42$$

To simplify computations, he decides to set $\lambda = .4$. Can the business accept this proxy at a 95% confidence level? This question can be restated as the null hypothesis (H_o) as follows:

H_o: The observed and expected frequencies are generated by the same distribution.

Solution:

Table 3 Chi-Square Test: Poisson Distribution

	Original					Aggregated		
	0	1	2	3	4	0	1	2, 3, 4
Observed	62	28	7	2	1	62	28	10
Expected ($\lambda = .4$)	67	26.8	5.4	.7	.1	67	26.8	6.2

$$\chi^2 = \frac{(62-67)^2}{67} + \frac{(28-26.8)^2}{26.8} + \frac{(10-6.2)^2}{6.2} = 2.756$$

Because λ had to be estimated from the frequency data, the number of degrees of freedom is 1 (that is, $v = 3 - 1 - 1$). Consequently, the control limit for $\chi^2_{1,.05}$ is 3.84. Since $2.756 < 3.84$, it can be said that the hypothesis that the observed and expected frequencies come from the same distribution cannot be rejected at the 95% level. Had our statistic fallen near 0 or 3.84, our suspicions would have been aroused, and to allay them we would have had to take further observations.

Parting Comments

In this chapter we have come a very long way beyond our initial discussions in Chapter 11. But much remains to be said. Ensuing chapters will discuss inventory and queuing theory and their relationship to the broad area of cost analysis, which includes capital budgeting as a subset. In Chapter 14 we shall investigate a very attractive extension of capital budgeting known as the Markowitz portfolio model. In Chapter 16 we shall address something in capital budgeting known as the Lorie-Savage problem.

One thing seems clear from this sort of study of cost analysis: the cost accountant who does not embrace mathematics, statistics, and the computer runs the risk of doing a disservice to his decisionmakers by forcing them either to make mental adjustments for risk and uncertainty or to ignore the phenomena altogether. If he then insists on using dollar measures only, he completes the damage.

Problems

1. *Utility theory.* Given the data below, rank the projects by expected values and by expected utilities and comment on any differences.

Project x		Project y		Project z	
x	$P(x)$	y	$Q(y)$	z	$R(z)$
\$–60,000	.20	\$–100,000	.35	\$–20,000	.10
200,000	.30	200,000	.25	120,000	.20
120,000	.50	200,000	.25	90,000	.30
		200,000	.15	80,000	.25
				40,000	.15

The utility curve $= .6i - .15i^2$, where i is in units of \$100,000, and $i = x, y, z$.

2. *Markovian replacement analysis.* A furniture manufacturer has 2,000 ultra high-wattage lamps that are used in both a wood-drying process and a gluing operation. These lamps have varying lives; 20% fail after six months of use, 40% fail after one year of use, and the remaining 40% fail after eighteen months of use. If all 2,000 units are replaced simultaneously, the planned interruption of the production processes and the available quantity discount limit the cost of replacement to \$10 per lamp. However, if fixtures are replaced as they fail, the cost is \$20 per unit. The firm has a required rate of return of 20% per year before taxes. What replacement policy should the business follow?

3. *Markov chains and fleet investment.* A company has a fleet of 100 cars, most of which are used by salesmen. The life of a car follows the distribution

Age	Probability
1	.1
2	.6
3	.3

Thus because it occasionally buys a lemon and because some cars are driven longer and harder, the company finds that 10% of new cars must be retired after one year of driving. Because company policy is based largely on feelings about public image, any three-year-old cars are retired at the end of their third years.

If the whole fleet is replaced at once, the company can deal directly with Detroit and pay \$2,000 per car. If cars are individually replaced, the company buys from local dealers at an average cost of \$3,000 per car. Cars also cost (\$200 × age) per year to maintain whether they are turned in or not. Treat maintenance cost as occurring at year end. Consider that a car that has been "retired" has salvage value that is reflected in the purchase prices.

Use a Markov chain to determine the optimal replacement policy. The required rate of return before taxes is 20%.

Discuss the significance of this sort of modelling for financial accounting.

4. *Markovian estimates of discounted flow and reforestation.* The Stoll Nursery has reflected the history of aging, "departing," and harvesting in its Christmas tree farm in the Markovian matrix shown below. If trees sell for \$1 per foot and height in feet is approximately equal to age, what is the maximum amount—considering only dollar costs to the firm—that the firm can invest in annual reforestation costs (planting seedlings one foot high, pruning, etc.) given the additional data shown below.

Key: H = harvested
D = "departed"

To:

From:	*H*	*D*	1	2	3	4	5	6	7	8
H	1	0	0	0	0	0	0	0	0	0
D	0	1	0	0	0	0	0	0	0	0
1	0	.3	0	.7	0	0	0	0	0	0
2	0	.2	0	0	8	0	0	0	0	0
3	0	.2	0	0	0	8	0	0	0	0
4	0	.1	0	0	0	0	.9	0	0	0
5	.2	.1	0	0	0	0	0	.7	0	0
6	.3	.1	0	0	0	0	0	0	.6	0
7	.4	0	0	0	0	0	0	0	0	.6
8	.9	.1	0	0	0	0	0	0	0	0

Additional data:
(a) Required return before taxes = 20%

(b) Planned steady-state number of seedlings to be planted each year = 1,000

Suppose that Stoll planted trees for lumber purposes and that it took 50 years for the trees to attain harvestable size. Comment on the reforestation investment that could be justified financially if the 20% return before taxes remained a requirement.

Hint: Professor Yuji Ijiri is credited with introducing discounting into the financial use of Markov chains in the article summarized in the appendix to Chapter 4. The problem here is an application of the methodology discussed there.

5. *Buying land for lumber production.* It takes an average of 40 years before a tree is mature and ready to be harvested. To facilitate study of such a long rotation period, we shall assume that the Stoll Lumber Company does its analyses in terms of five-year periods—after all, the use of a year for preparing financial reports is merely a popular convention (a year is as arbitrary as any other time span). Stoll has the opportunity to buy acreage for $15,000. Its forester has examined the land and has estimated the number of trees in each age category i, where $i = 1$ (age 0–5), 2 (age 5–10), . . . , 8(age 25–40), as shown in vector v.

$v = (600, 800, 800, 400, 500, 500, 300, 200)$, (4,100 trees in all)

By making a study of similar stands, Stoll has reflected the harvesting-mortality pattern of trees in the transition matrix T.

	Harvest	Die	1	2	3	4	5	6	7	8
H	1	0	0	0	0	0	0	0	0	0
D	0	1	0	0	0	0	0	0	0	0
1	0	.4	0	.6	0	0	0	0	0	0
2	0	.3	0	0	.7	0	0	0	0	0
$T =$ 3	0	.2	0	0	0	.8	0	0	0	0
4	0	.1	0	0	0	0	.9	0	0	0
5	0	0	0	0	0	0	0	1	0	0
6	.1	0	0	0	0	0	0	0	.9	0
7	.5	.1	0	0	0	0	0	0	0	.4
8	.9	.1	0	0	0	0	0	0	0	0

Trees in categories 6, 7, and 8 have a value of $60, $75, and $100 respectively. The land clear-cut of trees would be worth $10,000. If Stoll buys this tract, it will postpone harvesting until the end of the first period because the trees in the inventory are generally at the start of each age category and Stoll's present supply of timber is ample. It will commence a reforestation program of 500 trees per period beginning five years from now and continuing in perpetuity. It costs $1 per tree to reforest and $1 per tree annual maintenance for every tree in the tract. (Assume this is all variable cost—as in contract maintenance—with no fixed cost. For simplicity, assume $5 per tree maintenance is paid at the end of each period based on the number of trees in the inventory at the start of the period, and that reforestation costs are also incurred at the end of the period.) It costs $5 to harvest a tree and take it to the mill (assume that harvesting occurs at the end of each period). Stoll's required return is 10% per year before taxes.

Required: What will the sustained yield (steady state) be? Should Stoll make this investment? Comment on your solution.

6. *Expected shortage.* Sales of a particular product follow the probability distribution $f(x) = .001e^{-.001x}$, where x is the random variable for sales and has the domain $0 < x < \infty$. If 1,200 units are manufactured, determine the expected number of units short (that is, units that are demanded but not available). Of what use is it to know the expected shortage?

7. *Method of moments and goodness of fit.* A baker has amassed the following data on daily demand for a particularly intricate cake:

Demand	0	1	2	3	4	5	6
Frequency	15	25	24	20	8	5	3

The baker wishes to know if he can use a Poisson distribution with mean of 2.1 in lieu of the empirical distribution. He will be satisfied with a 95% confidence level.

8. *Method of moments and goodness of fit.* In performing an analysis of a queuing system, a mathematician determined the following empirical probabilities of arrivals:

Units	0	1	2	3	4	5
Probability	.420	.372	.130	.039	.027	.012

The analyst feels that a Poisson curve with $\lambda = .8$ yields an acceptable approximation. Determine by a chi-square test whether the analyst is right. If he is wrong, use sample results to determine an appropriate λ and test this.

9. *Method of Moments: fitting a gamma.* Given observations that have wide range and no negative readings, a gamma distribution avoids truncation problems: furthermore, because of its pliable shape, gamma provides a good fit in such circumstances. Use the Method of Moments to fit a gamma to the data below. These were collected by a department store on its sales of a particular commodity.

Sales (Units)	Number of Weeks
0– 99	2
100–199	5
200–299	7
300–399	15
400–499	18
500–599	20
600–699	13
700–799	8
800–899	7
900–999	5
	100

What are the expected sales and their variance? Round the parameter estimates obtained and use a chi-square test to see if this is acceptable. Graph the empirical and gamma probability functions that result and comment on the fit. If 750 units are on the shelves now, what will be the expected ending inventory?

10. *Convolutions: empirical distribution.* A company has heretofore enjoyed a one-week leadtime period (time between placing an order and receiving it). Recently, however, its supplier announced that deliveries would now require two weeks, because he planned to decrease the level of inventories he carried. The distribution of demand for one week was

D	$P(D)$
0	.1
1	.3
2	.4
3	.2

What is the distribution for demand now that leadtime is two weeks? What would it be if leadtime became three weeks? What if half the time it was two weeks and half the time three?

11. *Convolutions: the binomial.* The probability mass function for the binomial distribution if $P(x) = \binom{n}{x} p^x q^{n-x}$, for $x = 0, 1, \ldots, n$ and $p + q = 1$. Find the Z transform of the binomial function and use it to determine the 2-fold convolution. Comment on the result.

12. *Convolutions: the Bernoulli.* The Bernoulli distribution is the simplest probability distribution for dichotomies (on-off, black-white, good-bad). The probability mass function is

x	$P(x)$
0	q
1	p

and $\sum_{x=0}^{1} P(x) = 1 = q + p$

Find the Z transform of the Bernoulli function and then determine what other distribution is the n-fold convolution of the Bernoulli.

13. *Convolutions: the exponential.* The probability density function for the exponential function is

$$f(x) = ae^{-ax}, \quad \text{for } x > 0$$

Find the Laplace transform (definition: $F(S) = \int_{\infty}^{0} f(x)e^{-Sx}\,dx$, where S is treated as a constant) of the exponential function and then determine what other distribution is the n-fold convolution of the exponential (by consulting Table 10 in Appendix A).

14. *Z transforms and moment generation.* Moments (like the mean and variance) may be generated by use of a *Z*-transformed function (which is then referred to as a "moment-generating function"). Thus

$$\text{Mean} = E(x) = D_Z F(Z)|_{Z=1} \quad \text{(Take the derivative with respect to Z and then set } Z = 1.)$$

$$E(x^2) - E(x) = D_Z{}^2 F(Z)|_{Z=1} \quad \text{(Second derivative evaluated at } Z = 1.)$$

From this, variance may be calculated by $V(x) = E(x^2) - [E(x)]^2$. Compute the mean and variance for the Poisson and binomial distributions using their *Z*-transformed functions.

15. *Laplace transforms and moment generation.* Moments may also be generated with Laplace transforms; the resulting formulas are termed "moment-generating functions." These moments are around the origin and are obtained as follows:

$$E(x) = -D_S F(S)|_{S=0} \quad \text{(Take the derivative with respect to } S \text{ and then set } S = 0.)$$

$$E(x^2) = D_S{}^2 F(S)|_{S=0}$$

From this, $V(x) = E(x^2) - [E(x)]^2$

Compute the mean and variance for the exponential distribution $[f(x) = ae^{-ax}$, for $x > 0]$, the normal, and the gamma via their transformed functions.

16. *Self-insurance and convolutions.* Of the premiums charged by an insurance company, 30% to 50% goes toward its administrative costs. Realizing this, the Pane Company is studying whether it would be wiser to become a self-insurer for certain hazards. Pane is well enough off that it can absorb moderate losses under $100,000 without seriously impairing operations. Pane has 30 buildings that are unattached. They are protected by sprinkler systems and custodial watchmen at night, and by employees during the day. They are all reasonably near fire hydrants and fire departments. Consequently, the company feels not only that the probability of a fire is small, but also that, should a fire occur, the damage would not be extensive. The controller has decided that the randomness and independence of an event like a fire would suggest a Poisson distribution. After consulting a Poisson table, he has decided that a mean of .1 would provide a suitable distribution of yearly loss for each site, as shown below.

x(loss)	$0	$1,000	$2,000	$3,000	$4,000
$P(x\|\lambda = .1)$	.9048	.0905	.0045	.0002	0

Company cost of capital is 10%; corporate tax rate is 60%.

Required:

(a) If an insurance company has bid a premium of $4,500 per year, should Pane accept or self-insure?

(b) If the insurance company offered a three-year policy for \$11,250, should Pane accept?

(c) Comment on how self-insuring affects Pane's capital budgeting routine.

17. Prove that $\mathrm{Cov}(x, y) = E(x, y) - E(x)E(y)$

18. Prove that if x and y are perfectly correlated, then $\mathrm{Cov}(x, y)/\sigma_x\sigma_y = 1$

19. *Expected gain.* Compute expected gain for the diagram shown below.

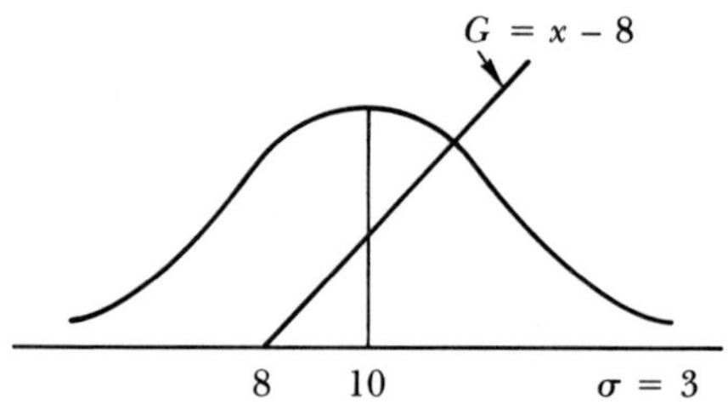

20. *Linear loss and normal probabilities.* A businessman has an \$80,000 investment at stake. He makes \$160 on every unit sold, and he believes that sales are normally distributed with a .4 probability of being between 545 and 755 units. Compute his expected opportunity loss. What else should you know to make the analysis more meaningful?

21. *Indigency and other vicissitudes.* A young college man wishes to determine his expected shortage of funds if he writes a letter to his parents when his cash balance drops to \$120, and if his need for money for the time between mailing the petition letter and receiving the replenishing funds is normally distributed with a probability of .6 of falling in the range $\$16 < D < \$184$. Also determine his probability of being short.

22. *Generalizing the expected linear loss function.* Develop a closed-form expression (one without an operator such as an integral sign) for a linear loss function that is weighted by normal probabilities (that is, 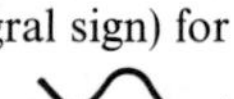). What could be done with the resulting equation?

23. *Throughput and interruptions.* In production, the output of a process is often referred to as "throughput." It is desirable to estimate this volume, if for no other reason than to set production schedules. Complications always arise via interruptions of one sort or another—machine breakdown, material shortage, coffee breaks, restroom calls, and so forth. The longer the run between interruptions, the better—as we have seen from prior discussion of learning curves. Throughput, x, is dependent on time, t, and is represented by the conditional probability function $f(x|t)$, while interruptions are a function of time $g(t)$. The goal is to obtain $f(x)$ by forming the joint probability distribution $f(x, t)$ and integrating over the range of t (thereby obtaining the desired marginal function).

The output of a process is Poisson distributed with a mean of five units per hour. Machine breakdowns occur in Poisson fashion at the rate of two in each eight-hour shift. Determine the expected number of units produced between breakdowns.

Caution: The *occurrence* of breakdowns is Poisson; consequently, the *time* between breakdowns is exponential at the same mean rate.

24. *Staging a new opera production.* An internationally acclaimed opera house is studying whether to mount a new production of Verdi's *Il Trovatore.* Management has a great deal of information about box office appeal, casts, sets, preparation time, and so forth. Certain costs are not relevant to the decision—for example, salaries of house choristers, dancers, and musicians are fixed by union contracts and the company already owns the theatre. Payments to extra singers, dancers, and musicians, for overtime, for unscheduled rehearsals, for stars (not just anyone can sing the roles of Manrico and Leonora), and for covers (if Tebaldi or Corelli cannot perform, you need a Price or Pavarotti to fill in) constitute the differential production costs. These costs are an independent random variable that is thought to be normally distributed with mean \$100,000 and standard deviation \$15,000 for each of the five years considered to be the life of the investment.

The investment amounts to \$400,000 for costumes and sets. After five years of wear, they should be worth a value that is independently normally distributed with mean \$80,000 and standard deviation \$20,000.

The yearly box office receipts (net of promotion costs) will depend a great deal on how the new production is initially received. These receipts are estimated to be normally distributed with mean \$450,000 and standard deviation \$120,000.

The required return is 15%. Determine (a) the probability of loss, and (b) all the dollar expectations.

Statistical Sampling

13

If at first you don't
succeed, try, try again.

Wilbur Edward Hickson

Introduction

Perhaps you have heard the fable of the Neanderthal man who introduced commerce in the Paleolithic age. It seems that history has not recorded the actual date of his birth, although a description of the man and tales of his exploits have been preserved through the years. His name was, quite naturally, Bus and it was in his honor that society coined the word "business." Bus, unlike his hairy contemporaries, was slow of foot, frail, and emaciated. Partly his condition resulted from his being an inept hunter and therefore going hungry a lot of the time. Gifted with a keener mind than his fellows and prodded by his empty stomach, Bus sought another means of survival. He discovered clay and soon found that by pummeling and kneading the material he could fashion pots for holding substances like water.

Realizing the significance of his discovery, Bus decided to barter pots for dinosaur steaks. He had, however, one trouble. His "customers," as he began to call them because of their mode of speech, were hunters who usually carried big stone clubs, which they used to beat in the heads of their prey. Quite by habit they would determine the quality of Bus's pots by winding up and delivering a skull-shattering blow to each pot. As with skulls, so with the pots. Bus, clever Neanderthal that he was, instantly recognized the problem. It was multifaceted: not only must he be able to assure his customers of the quality of his pots, but he must also (1) teach those dumb ______ that pots didn't require great strength to carry things, and (2) devise some test that most of his pots could withstand. He did not want to acquire the reputation for "selling" fragile pots though, and consequently he wanted the test to be fair.

His predicament led him to experiment with smaller stone clubs. But these too shattered the pots—including pots that he felt were pretty good. Temporarily he was in a dilemma—he knew that by temperament and habit his customers could not resist giving his pots full-blooded clouts, and yet he knew that the pots were good even though they broke under such treatment. And he was getting hungrier and hungrier. What to do?

In the midst of his deliberations, Bus found himself in a swarm of flies. Instinctively he reached for a long-stemmed, rubber plant leaf he kept for the purpose (you see he had already invented the flyswatter). Inspiration overcame him: Why not let his customers swat his pots with such a long-stemmed, stiff leaf? They could give the task their best efforts without damaging the pots. He, on the other hand, could tap the pots gently beforehand with a stone club and remove any really fragile ones. That these procedures were indeed successful is attested to by the popularity of pots today. And we owe it all to Bus, who grew fat in his old age.

These (or something similar) were the origins of torture testing and quality control and of sampling in general. But whereas Bus tested each and every pot, it became apparent where great quantities were involved that a representative portion of the population could be examined and inferences drawn about the whole based on the part.

Increasingly accounting has come to accept such sampling concepts and procedures. Often it is simply a matter of convenience—of practicality; but more and more it is appreciation of quality in estimates that leads an accountant to adopt some sampling procedure. For example, auditors are concerned about the rate of errors in files. Prior to about 1960, if an auditor encountered many errors, he had to decide whether the errors were material enough to require a disclaimer of opinion, whether to make adjustments, whether to extend his sample, and whether to require his client to rework entire records. In no case, however, was he able to make a statement about the quality of his sample. He *could* say that he had followed standard auditing procedure and had looked at every large item (over, say, $10,000) and about 10% of the remaining items. Unfortunately, he *could not* say that, had he taken 100 similar samples, 90 of them would have included the true average rate of error in the ranges determined by, say, $\pm 2\%$ of the average calculated from each sample. Without statistical sampling the auditor could say simply nothing about *precision* (the $\pm 2\%$ leeway) or *reliability* (the .9 probability)—which are the measures of quality in sampling.[1]

Permutations, Combinations, and Hypergeometric Sampling

If there is anyone still reading this book who is suffering from any psychological impediment to learning mathematics, the title of this section has undoubtedly intensified his anxieties. Onward. . .

[1] Reliability is often also referred to as "confidence."

A little reflection on precision and reliability is in order. If I did not know better, I would certainly think extraordinary a claim like "$b\%$ of the samples would include the population statistic within their average $\pm a\%$ ranges." It sounds like the overconfidence of a braggart. But it isn't. It is the magic of statistical inference. Note that the claim is not that the population statistic would fall in the precision range of any one sample. After all, a particular sample might be unusual and simply not representative of the population.

The support for the precision-reliability statement comes from probability theory itself. Any time one cares (1) to count the number of possible ways a *given* outcome can occur when a sample is drawn randomly without being replaced (turned back into the population before any ensuing random sample is drawn)—and where both the proportion of "successes" (any characteristic of interest—for instance, errors) and the size of the population are known or assumed; and (2) to divide the number of ways the *given* outcome can occur by the number of ways *all* outcomes can occur, one will find the probability of the given outcome obeys the hypergeometric probability distribution. In other words: known population size, known proportion of successes, and random sampling without replacement are characteristics that call uniquely for hypergeometric probabilities. Let us see why.

Suppose you have the letters A, B, C, D, and E and wish to know in how many ways you can select three letters from the five without replacing a drawn letter and without distinguishing the sequence in which the three letters are drawn. That is, ABC and CBA are different sequences (or "permutations"), but they form the same combination.[2] There are 10 possible combinations:

ABC	ABD	ABE	ACD	ACE
ADE	BCD	BCE	BDE	CDE

Had there been 100 objects from which to draw sets of 3, we would have had to list 161,700 combinations! Clearly you can appreciate the need for an easy way to count combinations. Combinatorial notation provides the easy way:

$$\binom{n}{x} = \frac{n!}{x!(n-x)!} = \frac{n(n-1)\cdots(n-(x-1))(n-x)!}{(x(x-1)\cdots 1)(n-x)!}$$

$$= \frac{n(n-1)\cdots(n-x+1)}{x(x-1)\cdots 1}$$

[2] While permutations offer another way of deriving the hypergeometric distribution and are of interest in other mathematical applications, we shall not need them. For the interested reader, however, the number of permutations $= P_x^n = x!\binom{n}{x} = n^{(x)}$

Specifically, if three letters are picked out of five,

$$\binom{5}{3} = \frac{5!}{3!(5-3)!} = \frac{5 \times 4 \times 3 \times 2 \times 1}{(3 \times 2 \times 1)(2 \times 1)} = \frac{5 \times 4 \times 3 \times 2!}{3 \times 2 \times 1 \times 2!} = \frac{5 \times 4 \times 3}{3 \times 2 \times 1} = 10, \quad \text{as above}$$

So much for permutations and combinations; now for hypergeometric probabilities.

Example: It is believed that a production process yields 10% defectives. Batches of 200 units are usually produced and to test whether a given batch is acceptable, samples of 10 are drawn at random and without replacement. If management decides to reject any batch where the sample has two or more defectives, how many batches will be rejected in the long run, assuming there is no change in the percentage defective?

Solution: It will be easier to calculate the probability of accepting a batch first and then obtain the probability of rejection as the complement of acceptance. A batch will be accepted if either *no* defects are found or *one* defect is found. If no defects are found, the sample will contain 10 good units. Since there are thought to be 10% (200 units) = 20 defective (D) units and 180 good (G) units in each batch, there are $\binom{20}{0}$ ways to obtain $O\ D$ and $\binom{180}{10}$ ways to obtain $10G$. Similarly, there are $\binom{20}{1}$ ways to obtain $1D$ and $\binom{180}{9}$ ways to obtain $9G$. If we let $W(D, G)$ = the number of ways to obtain a combination of D defects and G good units, we see that the number of ways acceptance can occur is

$$W(0, 10) = \binom{20}{0}\binom{180}{10} = 1\left(\frac{180}{10} \cdot \frac{179}{9} \cdot \frac{178}{8} \cdots \frac{171}{1}\right)$$

$$W(1, 9) = \binom{20}{1}\binom{180}{9} = 20\left(\frac{180}{9} \cdot \frac{179}{8} \cdot \frac{178}{7} \cdots \frac{172}{1}\right)$$

$$\text{Total Number of Ways Acceptance can Occur} = W(0, 10) + W(1, 9)$$

The total number of *all* possible combinations of 200 units taken 10 at a time is $\binom{200}{10} = \frac{200}{10} \cdot \frac{199}{9} \cdot \frac{198}{8} \cdots \frac{191}{1}$. (Note how nonreplacement reduces the number of combinations—with replacement, for example, 200^{10} would be the total number of possible combinations.) Consequently, the probability of acceptance is $P(D \leq 1)$, which is calculated by dividing the number of ways acceptance can occur by the total number of possible outcome combinations:

$$P(D \leq 1) = [W(0, 10) + W(1, 9)] \div \binom{200}{10} = .7368$$

Hence, the probability of rejection is

$$P(D \geq 2) = 1 - P(D \leq 1) = 1 - .7368 = .2632$$

In the long run, approximately 26% of the batches will be rejected under the chosen sampling plan. If this is unacceptable, a less strict plan, such as rejecting when there are three or more defectives, might prove satisfactory. Of course, management would hope the population defect rate could be improved, too.

Instead of counting the ways success occurs and dividing by the total number of ways all outcomes occur, it is more direct to employ the hypergeometric probability distribution (which is obtained by the same process) to compute probabilities of success:

$$P(x) = \binom{Np}{x}\binom{N - Np}{n - x} \div \binom{N}{n}$$

Key:

N = population size
p = proportion of "successes" in the population
n = sample size
x = number of "successes" obtained in the sample

Returning to the example, we find

$$P(D = 0) = \binom{20}{0}\binom{180}{10} \div \binom{200}{10} = .3396$$

$$P(D = 1) = \binom{20}{1}\binom{180}{9} \div \binom{200}{10} = .3972$$

$$P(D \leq 1) = .7368, \text{ as above}$$

Now that we know where the hypergeometric distribution comes from, what it looks like, and what it does, we need to know what its expected value (mean) and variance are, for these are the bases on which precision and reliability estimates are made.

The expected value, E(x), of the hypergeometric:

$$E(x) = \sum_{x=0}^{n} x\binom{Np}{x}\binom{N - Np}{n - x} \div \binom{N}{n}$$

continued to page 417

continued from page 416

But when $x = 0$, the summand equals 0; therefore, $x = 0$ can be omitted.

$$E(x) = \sum_{x=1}^{n} x \frac{(Np)!}{x!(Np-x)!} \frac{\binom{N-Np}{n-x}}{\binom{N}{n}} = Np \sum_{x=1}^{n} \frac{(Np-1)!}{(x-1)!(Np-x)!} \frac{\binom{N-Np}{n-x}}{\binom{N}{n}}$$

Substitution of variables: $y = x - 1$; $M = Np - 1$

$$= Np \sum_{y=0}^{n-1} \frac{M!}{y!(M-y)!} \frac{\binom{N-(M+1)}{n-(y+1)}}{\binom{N}{n}}$$

But $\binom{N}{n} = \frac{N}{n}\binom{N-1}{n-1}$

Substitution of variables: $m = n - 1$; $Z = N - 1$

$$= \frac{Np}{N/n}\left[\sum_{y=0}^{m} \binom{M}{y}\binom{Z-M}{m-y} \div \binom{Z}{m}\right],$$ where the quantity in brackets is the cumulative hypergeometric distribution

$$= np[1]$$

$$E(x) = np$$

The variance, $V(x)$, of the hypergeometric:

$$V(x) = E(x^2) - [E(x)]^2$$

$$= \sum_{x=0}^{n} x^2 \binom{Np}{x}\binom{N-Np}{n-x} \div \binom{N}{n} - (np)^2$$

But $x^2 = x(x-1) + x$, so

$$V(x) = \sum_{x=2}^{n} x(x-1)\binom{Np}{x}\binom{N-Np}{n-x} \div \binom{N}{n} + \left[\sum_{x=0}^{n} x\binom{Np}{x}\binom{N-np}{n-x} \div \binom{N}{n}\right] - (np)^2$$

$$= Np(Np-1) \sum_{x=2}^{n} \frac{(Np-2)!}{(x-2)!(Np-x)!} \frac{\binom{N-Np}{n-x}}{\binom{N}{n}} + [np] - (np)^2$$

Substitution of variables: $y = x - 2$; $M = Np - 2$

$$= Np(Np-1) \sum_{y=0}^{n-2} \binom{M}{y} \frac{\binom{N-(M+2)}{n-(y+2)}}{\frac{N(N-1)}{n(n-1)}\binom{N-2}{n-2}} + np - (np)^2$$

continued to page 418

continued from page 417

Substitution of variables: $m = n - 2; Z = N - 2$

$$= \frac{Np(Np-1)}{N(N-1)/(n(n-1)}\left[\sum_{y=0}^{m}\binom{M}{y}\binom{Z-M}{m-y} \div \binom{Z}{m}\right] + np - (np)^2$$

$$= \frac{n(n-1)p(Np-1)}{N-1}[1] + np - (np)^2$$

$$= \frac{(n^2-n)(Np^2-p) + (nPN - np) - (n^2p^2N - n^2p^2)}{N-1}$$

$$= (n^2p^2N - n^2p - nNp^2 + np + npN - np - n^2p^2N + n^2p^2) \div (N-1)$$

$$= np(1-p)(N-n) \div (N-1)$$

Let $q = 1 - p$, then

$$V(x) = npq\left[\frac{N-n}{N-1}\right]$$

We now know that the expected value and variance of the hypergeometric are respectively

$$E(x) = np$$

$$V(x) = npq[(N-n) \div (N-1)]$$

If instead of *number* of errors we wanted to know about *rate* of errors, we would divide number of errors by sample size and obtain

$$E(x/n) = \sum_{x=0}^{n}\frac{x}{n}\binom{NP}{x}\binom{N-Np}{n-x} \div \binom{N}{n} = p$$

$$V(x/n) = \sum_{x=0}^{n}\left(\frac{x}{n}\right)^2\binom{Np}{x}\binom{N-Np}{n-x} \div \binom{N}{n} - p^2 = \frac{pq}{n}[(N-n) \div (N-1)]$$

Take note of the $(N - n) \div (N - 1)$ factor in the variance expressions, for it has been given the special name "finite population correction factor" in sampling. Often the denominator is changed and the factor becomes $(N - n)/N$, which is somewhat easier to use; as long as N is not very small (say, under 20), the results are very close to those obtained from $(N - n) \div (N - 1)$.

How is the hypergeometric used in terms of precision and reliability? Exhibit 1 shows hypergeometric output for the case where a file contains a population of 1,000 items which is thought to have a 5% error rate and from which a random sample of 200 is drawn. Since there are no lowercase letters in computer programming, our previous notation has to be changed somewhat. Population size, rate of successes, and sample size are N, P, and M respectively in the program. The number of errors found, x, the probability

Exhibit 1 Hypergeometric Distribution

```
100  DIM P(200),L(200),R(200)
110  INPUT N,P,M
120  PRINT USING 125
125  FIELD (9X,"X",11X,"P(X)",12X,"X/M"10X,"XP(X)",6X,"(X/M)P(X)")
150  LET Q = 1 – P
160  LET P(0) = 1
170  FOR X = 0 TO M–1
180  LET F = ((N*Q) – X)/(N – X)
190  IF F < .001 THEN 250
200  LET P(0) = F * P(0)
210  NEXT X
220  PRINT USING 230,0,P(0),0,0,0
230  FIELD (F10.0,4F15.4)
250  FOR G = 1 TO M
260  LET A = (N*P) – G + 1
270  LET B = M + 1 – G
280  LET C = (N*Q) – M + G
290  LET D = (A*B)/(C*G)
300  LET P(G) = D * P(G–1)
400  IF P(G) < .00001 THEN 525
410  LET H = G/M
420  LET L(G) = G * P(G)
430  LET R(G) = H * P(G)
500  PRINT USING 510,G,P(G),H,L(G),R(G)
510  FIELD (F10.0,4F15.4)
520  NEXT G
525  LET U,V = 0
530  FOR J = 0 TO G
535  LET U = U + L(J)
540  LET V = V + R(J)
545  NEXT J
550  PRINT USING 555
555  FIELD (49X,"––––",9X,"––––")
560  PRINT USING 565,U,V
565  FIELD (1X,"THE EXPECTED VALUE, RATE,RESPECTIVELY =",2F15.4)
570  PRINT USING 575
575  FIELD (49X,"====",9X,"====")
600  FOR K = 1 TO 2
605  LET Z = K * .01 * M
610  LET Z1 = M * P
615  LET Z2 = Z1 – Z
620  LET Z3 = Z1 + Z
625  LET W = 0
630  FOR L = Z2 TO Z3
635  LET W = P(L) + W
640  NEXT L
650  PRINT "        ––––(+–)PRECISION––––","CORRESPONDING RELIABILITY"
655  PRINT USING 660,Z,K,W
660  FIELD (3X,F10.0,1X,"UNITS",5X,F4.2,1X,"%",15X,F10.4)
665  NEXT K
700  END

RUN

?
1000,.05,200
```

Exhibit 1 (*cont.*)

	X		P(X)	X/M	XP(X)	(X/M)P(X)
	0		.0000	0	0	0
	1		.0001	.0050	.0001	.0000
	2		.0009	.0100	.0018	.0000
	3		.0038	.0150	.0113	.0001
	4		.0116	.0200	.0463	.0002
	5		.0277	.0250	.1383	.0007
	6		.0535	.0300	.3210	.0016
	7		.0862	.0350	.6032	.0030
	8		.1179	.0400	.9434	.0047
	9		.1392	.0450	1.2529	.0063
MEAN →	10	.9 {	.1434	.0500	1.4345	.0072
	11		.1302	.0550	1.4326	.0072
	12		.1050	.0600	1.2598	.0063
	13		.0756	.0650	.9830	.0049
	14		.0489	.0700	.6848	.0034
	15		.0285	.0750	.4281	.0021
	16		.0151	.0800	.2413	.0012
	17		.0072	.0850	.1230	.0006
	18		.0032	.0900	.0569	.0003
	19		.0013	.0950	.0239	.0001
	20		.0005	.1000	.0092	.0000
	21		.0002	.1050	.0032	.0000
	22		.0000	.1100	.0010	.0000
	23		.0000	.1150	.0003	.0000
THE EXPECTED VALUE, RATE, RESPECTIVELY =					9.9999	.0500

(The bracket labelled .9 spans X = 6 through 14.)

----(+ −)PRECISION----		CORRESPONDING RELIABILITY
2. UNITS	1.00 %	.6358
----(+ −)PRECISION----		CORRESPONDING RELIABILITY
4. UNITS	2.00 %	.9000

of finding this number of errors, $P(x)$, the rate of errors found, x/M, the weighted product of exactly that number of errors, $xP(x)$, and the weighted product of exactly that rate of errors, $(x/M)P(x)$, are the respective columns of Exhibit 1. Beneath the columns are shown the expected number of errors, $E(x)$, and the expected error rate, $E(x/M)$. The exhibit concludes by listing precision—both for the number of errors and their rate—and the corresponding reliability.

It might be instructive to dwell further on precision and reliability as shown in the illustration in Exhibit 1. By the formulas previously developed, $E(x) = np = 200(.05) = 10$ and $E(x/n) = p = .05$. If we allowed $E(x)$ to be in error by $\pm 2\%$ of the sample size, we would be saying that the average or mean number of errors would fall in the range $10 \pm .02(200)$. This would be the same as saying that the expected rate of errors falls in the range of $.05 \pm .02$. If we add the probabilities for this range (that is, $\sum_{x=6}^{14} P(x) = .0535 + .0862 + \cdots + .0489$), we find that the sum is .9. This is the reliability of our estimate. If we take one random sample of 200 from a population of 1,000 that has an error rate of 5%, we might get any number of errors between

$0 \leq x \leq .05(1{,}000) = 50$. If we take 100 such samples, however, 90 of them should show errors in the range $6 \leq x \leq 14$.

More formally, the statistician would state a "null" hypothesis and an "alternative" hypothesis:

"Null" $H_0 : E(x|n) = p = .05$ (or $H_0 : E(x) = nP = 10$, which is the same thing)

"Alternative" $H_1 : E(x|n) = p \neq .05$ (or $H_1 : E(x) = np \neq 10$)

The alternative here implies a "two-tailed" test, although with errors in files a "one-tailed" test would usually be more appropriate because errors on the low side are generally not of concern. Before the null hypothesis can be tested, however, a decision rule for accepting or rejecting the results must be formulated. It is here that precision and reliability enter. If, say, $\pm .02$ is agreeable for precision, it remains only to specify the desired reliability. In our example, where $N = 1{,}000$, we have seen that a .9 reliability calls for a sample size of $n = 200$. Had we specified some other reliability, a different sample size would be required. If we stated the alternative hypothesis as $H_1 : p > .05$, we would have specified a one-tailed test $(+.02)$ and would enjoy .9441 reliability from drawing a sample of 200 (this is $\sum_{x=0}^{14} P(x)$ in Exhibit 1).

Given our hypotheses and our decision rule to accept the null hypothesis if errors fall in the range $6 \leq x \leq 14$, how would our sampling proceed? If we took the sample and found nine errors, we would accept the null hypothesis that the population mean was $p = .05$. Of course, we could be wrong. The true rate might be something else. In that case, by accepting the null hypothesis when it is false, we commit what is known as a Type II (or "beta") error.

If there is a Type II error, one might conjecture that there must a Type I error. And so there is. If we took a sample and found 20 errors, we would reject the null hypothesis. Nonetheless, p might still equal .05. In that case, by rejecting the null hypothesis when it is true, we commit a Type I (or "alpha") error.

Measuring an alpha error is simple—it is just the complement of reliability: $1 - .9 = .1$, in our example. Measuring a beta error is another matter. Suppose the auditor feels that a rate of errors as high as .1 would be intolerable and he wishes to know what the probability is (the beta error) of not detecting such a rate given the present decision policy. Recall that under the present policy any number of errors outside the range $6 \leq x \leq 14$ will lead both to rejection of the null hypothesis and to further investigation, which, it may be assumed, would uncover the changed rate. If, assuming $p = .1$, the number of errors fell in the $6 \leq x \leq 14$ range, the change would not be detected, because the null hypothesis would be accepted and no further investigation would take place. The beta error is therefore $P(6 \leq x \leq 14)$ given $N, p, n = 1{,}000, .1{,}200$.

Undoubtedly our earlier calculations of hypergeometric probabilities struck you as cumbersome—hardly the sort of thing you would want to do manually. The introduction of the computer program in Exhibit 1 provides relief only if you have ready access to a time-sharing terminal. That failing, you might find relief in Table 1. This is an abbreviated hypergeometric table that may be used in either of two ways:

1. Decide on the desired precision and reliability for the given population and proportion of sucesses, and then search the table for the associated sample size.

2. Select a comfortable sample size for the given population and proportion of successes, search the table for the associated precision and reliability, and then decide whether these are satisfactory.

Table 1 Hypergeometric Probability Table

Size of Population	Rate of Successes	Sample Size	±1% Precision (Units, Reliability)	±2% Precision (Units, Reliability)
1,000	.02	100	(1, .7501)	(2, .9585)
1,000	.02	200	(2, .8482)	(4, .9907)
1,000	.02	300	(3, .9196)	(6, .9989)
1,000	.05	100	(1, .5313)	(2, .7778)
1,000	.05	200	(2, .6358)	(4, .9000)
1,000	.05	300	(3, .7327)	(6, .9618)
1,000	.10	100	(1, .4011)	(2, .6207)
1,000	.10	200	(2, .4897)	(4, .7650)
1,000	.10	300	(3, .5791)	(6, .8657)
5,000	.02	200	(2, .8107)	(4, .9821)
5,000	.05	200	(2, .5927)	(4, .8673)
5,000	.10	200	(2, .4522)	(4, .7218)
10,000	.02	200	(2, .8064)	(4, .9810)
10,000	.05	200	(2, .5879)	(4, .8634)
10,000	.10	200	(2, .4481)	(4, .7169)
15,000	.02	200	(2, .8049)	(4, .9806)
15,000	.05	200	(2, .5863)	(4, .8621)
15,000	.10	200	(2, .4467)	(4, .7153)
20,000	.02	200	(2, .8042)	(4, .9084)
20,000	.05	200	(2, .5855)	(4, .8615)

Binomial Sampling

Another distribution that deals with dichotomies (black-white, good-bad) and hence enjoys great popularity is the binomial probability distribution. Unlike the hypergeometric, however, the binomial theoretically requires that the random sampling be done *with* replacement. Thus as soon as an observation is made on a sample item, the item is returned to the population before another sample item is drawn. Consequently, it would be possible to draw the same item over and over again—which, of course, would provide no new information about the population. For this reason one would suspect that binomial sampling was not as efficient as hypergeometric sampling, that binomial samples would have to be larger to obtain the same amount of information as can be derived from the hypergeometric. This is the case. If it were not that the rules are relaxed in drawing samples, its ability to deal with dichotomies might not save the binomial from the ignominious oblivion suffered by discarded probability distributions. The "with replacement" rule is suspended whenever the population is so large that the taking of a sample has essentially no effect on the probability of a success.

Where does the binomial come from?[3] Suppose that the probability of a success is p for every sample item drawn (this stability of p is what "with replacement" is intended to preserve). Further suppose that a total sample of n items is drawn, and that you wish to know the probability that exactly x successes are included in the total sample. We therefore want a total sample that consists of x sucesses and $n - x$ nonsuccesses.

Example: The same situation that was used to illustrate the hypergeometric discussion: we will assume batches of 200 units, 10% of which are defective; a sample of 10 is drawn *with* replacement, and if two or more defectives are included, the batch is rejected.

Solution: Acceptance of a batch occurs if $D \leq 1$, as before.

$$W(D, G) = \text{number of ways to get } D \text{ defects and } G \text{ good}$$

$$W(0, 10) = (20^0)(180^{10})$$

$$W(1, 9) = (20^1)(180^9)$$

The total number of ways of drawing anything $= 200^{10}$. But there are $\binom{10}{0}$ ways to draw $W(0, 10)$ and $\binom{10}{1}$ ways to draw $W(1, 9)$.

Therefore,

$$P(D \leq 1) = \frac{\binom{10}{0}(20^0)(180^{10}) + \binom{10}{1}(20^1)(180^9)}{(200^{10})} = .7361$$

Hence the probability of rejection is

$$P(D \geq 2) = 1 - P(D \leq 1) = 1 - .7361 = .2639$$

[3] The binomial can be motivated in other ways than the one you are about to study—for example, by forming an n-fold convolution of the Bernoulli distribution, which is the "on-off" distribution: $P(x = 0,1) = (1 - p,p)$.

The procedures described above may be used to derive the binomial distribution, which can be used more directly in calculations:

$$P(x) = \binom{n}{x} p^x q^{n-x}, \quad \text{with all symbols defined as before}$$

$$P(0) = \binom{10}{0} .1^0\ .9^{10} = .3487$$

$$P(1) = \binom{10}{1} .1^1\ .9^9 \quad = \underline{.3874}$$

$$P(D \leq 1) = \underline{\underline{.7361}}, \quad \text{as above}$$

The expected value and the variance of the binomial may be determined in the same way as was illustrated for the hypergeometric with the following results:

Number of Errors	Rate of Errors
$E(x) = np$	$E(x/n) = p$
$V(x) = npq$	$V(x/n) = \dfrac{pq}{n}$

The similarities to the hypergeometric results are readily apparent—the same means are obtained in either case and the variances only differ by the finite population correction factor. When the binomial is used to analyze rate of errors, it is often referred to as the "sampling distribution of the proportion." There seems to be no corresponding name when the hypergeometric is used to analyze rates.

Poisson Sampling

When the population to be sampled is very large and the rate of occurrence is relatively very small, the statistician turns to the Poisson distribution. Poisson events are characterized by randomness and independence or, in less technical terms, by events that are confronted by an immense number of opportunities in which to occur but that are bashful and pass up the vast majority of opportunities; furthermore, once an opportunity is chosen, this in no way precludes the ensuing opportunity from being similarly chosen nor does it establish any recognizable pattern. Were the Poisson event human, it might be described as arrogant, stubborn, and forgetful. However, the mathematician puts these labels aside and substitutes the less colorful "random" and "independent."

The Poisson probability distribution has the formula

$$P(x) = e^{-np}(np)^x/x!$$

where $e = 2.7183$, n is the sample size, and p is the rate of occurrence. The expected value of the Poisson is $E(x) = np$, while its variance is $V(x) = np$; hence the Poisson mean and variance have the same value and its standard deviation is $\sigma = \sqrt{np}$.

Example: An auditor is conducting a voucher test. He has defined an error as a missing approval, missing documentation such as purchase orders or receiving slips, or a mistake in arithmetic. The population consists of 20,000 vouchers which, judging from prior year's working papers and client representations, is thought by the auditor to be in error 2% of the time. Assuming that the desired precision could be as high as 1%, (the upper control limit is therefore .03), and that desired reliability is .95, the usual hard-decision rule is to accept the sample only if no errors are discovered. What size sample should be drawn? How should sample results be interpreted?

Solution: The sample size is determined from the complement of reliability $(1 - .95 = .05)$ and the probability of finding no errors:

$$.05 = e^{-.03n}(.03n)^x/x!$$

which, since $x = 0$, becomes

$$.05 = e^{-.03n}$$

Using logs:

$$\ln .05 = -.03n \ln e$$

$$-2.99573 = -.03n(1)$$

$$n = \frac{2.99573}{.03} = 100$$

Further suppose that two errors were detected; what happens then? Assuming reliability is to remain at .95, the auditor would

(1) reject the null hypothesis that the error rate is .03, and

(2) find the rate that says that in a sample of 100, two or fewer errors found 5% of the time: $.05 = \sum_{x=0}^{2} P(x)$, and this is approximately true when $np = 100(.0625)$.

Hence the auditor has 95% confidence that if errors had occurred at a rate greater than .0625, he would have found more than two of them. His sample results support an estimate of $2/100 = .02$ as the population error rate, if precision and reliability are put aside.

The Normal Distribution

The binomial, hypergeometric, and Poisson distributions deal with "attribute sampling." In attribute sampling there is no measurement of large magnitudes but instead there is measurement of the number of occurrences of whatever attributes—good, bad, large, small—are of interest. "Variables sampling" measures large magnitudes and is treated by the normal and t distributions.

In Chapter 12 we saw the normal at work in measuring expected gains and losses. Its PDF (probability density function) is

$$f(x) = e^{-\frac{1}{2}\left(\frac{x-\mu}{\sigma}\right)^2} \div \sigma\sqrt{2\pi}, \quad \text{for } x - \infty < x < \infty$$

Here μ is the population mean and σ is the standard deviation. To use Table 8 in Appendix A, which is in standard form with $\mu = 0$ and $\sigma = 1$, the transformation of variables $Z = (x - \mu)/\sigma$ is employed.

Let us commence study of the normal's use in sampling by seeing how it helps in the selection of sample size.

The classical approach to sample size rests on the relationship between the variance of sample means and the population variance according to which ${\sigma_{\bar{x}}}^2 = \sigma^2/n$. It is usually necessary in practical situations to estimate the population variance and to specify both an acceptable level of risk and the desired precision with regard to the variance of sample means.[4]

The central limit theorem states that the distribution of sample means will tend to be normal; furthermore, this tendency improves as the sample size gets larger. Hence, when samples are drawn, it is customary, though not mandatory, both to draw fairly large samples ($n \geq 30$) and to invoke the normal distribution. Then, if one is interested in variables sampling, $Z = (\bar{x} - \mu)/\sigma_{\bar{x}}$ while, if one is interested in proportions (percentages, probabilities) $Z = (\overline{x/n} - p)/\sigma_{\overline{x/n}}$ (as before, $\overline{x/n}$ is the sample proportion).

---

[4] Again, if the population being sampled were small, the finite population correction factor would be introduced and the relationship between the variances would become

$${\sigma_{\bar{x}}}^2 = \frac{\sigma^2}{n}\left(\frac{N-n}{N-1}\right).$$

Observe that for a given value of n, the correction factor, which is a fraction, simply reduces the resulting sample variance. Hence, by specifying any given number of standard deviations, the width of the resulting confidence interval would be less with the correction factor than without it. If the correction factor were *ignored*, a claim, for example, that the population mean was within $\pm 1.96\sigma_x$ from the sample mean would have *at least* a .95 probability of being true. There would be a built-in safety factor.

What happens in the case of sampling for means is

$$Z = \frac{\bar{x} - \mu}{\sigma_{\bar{x}}} = \frac{\bar{x} - \mu}{\sigma/\sqrt{n}} \approx \frac{\bar{x} - \mu}{s/\sqrt{n}}$$

Since the population standard deviation, σ, is not known, it is common practice to take a preliminary sample of about 30 and to use the resulting sample standard deviation, s, as a proxy for σ. If we refer to the difference $\bar{x} - \mu$ as the allowable error (E) or desired precision, we may write

$$Z = \frac{\bar{x} - \mu}{s/\sqrt{n}} = \frac{E}{s/\sqrt{n}}$$

Solving for n, the sample size, yields

$$n = \left(\frac{Zs}{E}\right)^2, \quad \text{where } s \text{ is a proxy for } \sigma.$$

Example: A research team found the following times between arrivals at a time-sharing terminals room (in minutes):

5.2	4.2	2.1	12.0	5.3	2.7
8.3	4.0	7.1	12.5	5.0	3.0
2.1	.0	5.0	1.0	5.6	4.9
.6	3.7	3.0	1.6	9.2	8.0
7.0	12.3	11.3	6.0	8.3	7.0

Here,

$$\bar{x} = \sum x/n = 168/30 = 5.6$$

$$s = \sqrt{\sum(x - \bar{x})^2/(n-1)} = \sqrt{355.12/29} = 3.5$$

The team wishes to know what additional samples should be drawn to be 95% confident (in other words, they are willing to risk drawing an incorrect conclusion with .05 probability) that the error in the population mean arrival time is no greater than .5. Table 8 in Appendix A provides a reading of $Z = 1.96$, which corresponds to a probability of $.95/2 = .475$.

$$n = \left(\frac{1.96(3.5)}{.5}\right)^2 = 188$$

Since 30 sample items have already been drawn, only 158 more need be recorded.

If proportions are of concern, it will help if you recall that division of the binomial mean and standard deviation (that is, np and $\sqrt{npq}$) by n accomplishes the necessary scaling to obtain the proportion parameters. Sampling is done to determine these population parameters and the sample proportion, x/n, is used both as a proxy for p and in calculating the sample standard deviation, s. Thus

$$Z = \frac{\overline{x/n} - p}{\sigma_{\overline{x/n}}} = \frac{\overline{x/n} - p}{\sigma/\sqrt{n}} \approx \frac{\overline{x/n} - p}{s/\sqrt{n}}$$

where $s = \sqrt{\left(\frac{x}{n}\left(1 - \frac{x}{n}\right)\right)/(n-1)}$ and is the preliminary sample standard deviation which is used as a proxy for σ. If we refer to the difference $\overline{x/n} - p$ as the allowable error (E) or desired precision, we may write

$$Z = \frac{\overline{x/n} - p}{s/\sqrt{n}} = \frac{E}{s/\sqrt{n}}$$

Solving for n, the sample size, yields

$$n = \left(\frac{Zs}{E}\right)^2, \quad \text{as before, but now with different formulas for } s \text{ and } E$$

Example: An accountant randomly selected 30 invoices from a file containing hundreds of thousands of invoices. He inspected each invoice carefully and found that one invoice contained a significant mistake. How many more invoices should he select to be 95% confident that the error in the population mistake proportion is no greater than .01?

$$s = \sqrt{\frac{1}{30}\left(1 - \frac{1}{30}\right)/29} = .0333$$

$$n = \left(\frac{1.96(.0333)}{.01}\right)^2 = 43$$

Since 30 samples have already been taken, he need only take 13 more.

Comments: After drawing the preliminary sample, the task here is tantamount (1) to formulating the hypotheses $H_0: \sigma = s$ and $H_1: \sigma \neq s$ and (2) to performing a two-tailed test while keeping the same level of risk (.05). Note that keeping the same level of risk means that .025 of the area (and *not* .05) lies in the right-hand tail. Hence, $Z = 1.96$ and *not* 1.645. If the analyst were willing to increase his risk to .10, he would use $Z = 1.645$ and consequently draw a smaller sample.

Instead of using basic distributions like the hypergeometric and binomial directly, it is practice to invoke the normal distribution. This is done because normal tables are readily available and easy to use, and because there were virtually no computers—especially time-sharing computers—prior to about 1950. *But easy as it is to use normal*

continued to page 429

continued from page 428

tables, doing so has its cost. In Exhibit 1 the expected rate or errors is 5% in a population of 1,000 and a sample of 200 shows that there is a .9 probability that the expected rate will fall between 3% and 7%. The normal distribution would be introduced based on the central limit theorem; accordingly, the calculation for sample size for .9 reliability and 2% precision is

$$E = Z\sqrt{\left(\frac{N-n}{N-1}\right)\frac{pq}{n}},$$ where the quantity under the radical is the hypergeometric variance and Z is the number of standard normal deviations corresponding to the desired reliability

$$.02 = 1.645\sqrt{\left(\frac{1{,}000-n}{1{,}000-1}\right)\frac{.05(.95)}{n}}$$

$$.0004 = 1.645^2\left[\left(\frac{1{,}000-n}{999}\right)\frac{.0475}{n}\right]$$

$$.3996n = 2.706025(47.5 - .0475n)$$

$$n = 243$$

Hence, sample size increases by 43—or 21.5%—when the proxy is substituted for the theoretically correct hypergeometric distribution. The increase in sample size varies with each sampling situation.

Had extensive tables of the basic distribution been readily available, it is doubtful that the normal would have been so freely invoked, especially since the method of sampling and the structure of the population calls for the hypergeometric.

The *t* Distribution

If small samples (under 30) are to be drawn, the normal distribution gives way to the t distribution, which is also symmetrical. Table 12 in Appendix A is a t table. A popular notation for critical t values taken from the table for a one-tailed test is $t_{v,\alpha}$; for a two-tailed test the notation becomes $t_{v,\alpha/2}$. v is the number of degrees of freedom and equals sample size minus the number of parameters estimated. Thus for the single variable case, $v = n - 1$. α is the level of risk to be tolerated and equals 1 minus the chosen reliability level.

The statistic t is similar to the statistic Z:

$$Z = \frac{\bar{x}-\mu}{\sigma_{\bar{x}}} = \frac{\bar{x}-\mu}{\sigma/\sqrt{n}} \approx \frac{\bar{x}-\mu}{s/\sqrt{n}}; \quad t = \frac{\bar{x}-\mu}{s/\sqrt{n}}$$

Comments: It may help to remember that the denominator always corresponds to the numerator. If you are confronted with sampling means, the denominator is the standard deviation of sampling means. If you are working with an individual value of x, then the standard deviation of the population, σ, appears in the denominator.

The formulas appear identical but the size of the preliminary sample in t sampling is smaller—under 30 and perhaps even under 10. If the calculated t value is less than the critical t, H_o prevails.

Control Charts

One of the most important applications of inferential sampling occurs when control charts are constructed. One can think of the basic control chart as merely being a normal curve standing on tiptoe and explicitly stating the mean, μ, upper control limit (UCL), and lower control limit (LCL).

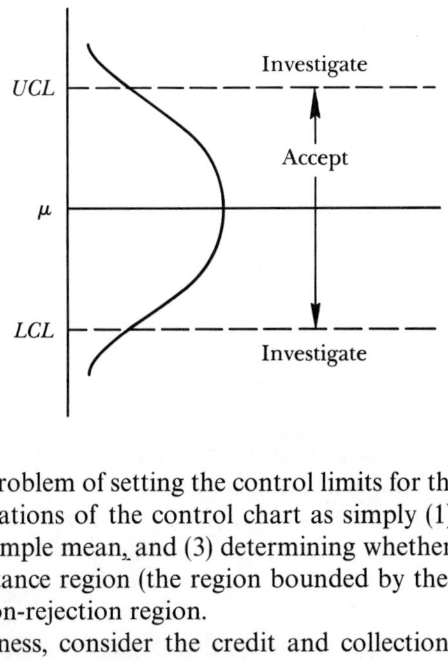

If we ignore the problem of setting the control limits for the moment, we can describe the operations of the control chart as simply (1) taking a sample, (2) plotting the sample mean, and (3) determining whether the sample mean falls in the acceptance region (the region bounded by the control limits) or in the investigation-rejection region.

For concreteness, consider the credit and collection policy of Hypothetical Company. Hypothetical determines the effectiveness of the credit and collection procedures of each of its branches by taking random samples of 64 customer receivable cards from each branch and seeing whether the sample average balance falls between \$1,000 ± \$400, that is, between \$600 and \$1,400. The management feels that beyond \$1,400 the credit and collection activities are too lax, while below \$600 the activities are too restrictive.

Hypothetical, therefore, has a control chart with $\mu = 1{,}000$, $UCL = 1{,}400$ and $LCL = 600$. But where did these control limits come from? Control limits come from (1) selecting a rejection (or critical) region probability, α; (2)

determining the mean and standard deviation of the variable to be controlled, and (3) observing how many standard deviations from the mean result in a probability area of $1 - \alpha$. Alternatively, the control limits may be set at desired levels and the value of α that corresponds to those levels is thereby implicitly determined. For our purposes let us say that the sampling standard deviation is \$200. The associated value of α may then be calcluated by means of the familiar Z formula:

$$Z = \frac{\bar{x} - \mu}{\sigma_{\bar{x}}} = \frac{1{,}400 - 1{,}000}{200} = 2$$

$P(0 < Z < 2) = .4772$, from Table 8 in Appendix A. Since this is only the right-hand side of the normal curve, the probability of acceptance—that is, of having an observed mean fall between \$600 and \$1,400—is 2(.4772) or .9544. The probability of rejection, α, is $1 - .9544 = .0456$, which consists of a probability of .0228 in each of the two tails of the distribution.

But what is the interpretation of α? α is the probability of rejecting a branch as being out of control when in fact it is in control. Since an error in judgment has been made, the α probability is usually referred to as the Type I error; we have blown the whistle unnecessarily. We have really just randomly selected a rare day on which to sample a particular branch's accounts.[5]

Suspicion would also arise if *several* of the sample means fell on one of the control limits. In such a case, the samples have not fallen in the rejection area, but the fact that several of them were on the verge of doing so constitutes a warning that results may have been rigged by some dishonest employee.

As I remarked earlier, there is another error that varies inversely with the Type I error—as one increases, the other decreases. This is the Type II error—the probability (usually designated by β) that given a shift in the process mean, the shift will not be detected. To illustrate, suppose the Hypothetical management wished to know the probability of not detecting a shift in the average accounts receivable balance from \$1,000 to \$1,100. It is first assumed that the standard deviation remains unchanged at \$200. Pictorially, we may envision the β probability as the shaded region on page 432.

---

[5] Because it is both wasteful and costly to investigate needlessly a well-functioning process, many statisticians operate under a "double-sampling" plan. Under such a plan a second sample is taken if the first sample falls in the rejection region. Then if this sample, which is independent of the first if the process is functioning properly, is also rejected, the statistician knows that there is a probability of approximately $\frac{\alpha}{2}\left(\frac{\alpha}{2}\right) = \frac{\alpha^2}{4}$ of such rejection happening with a "healthy" process. Since this probability is so low (perhaps on the order of .0006), he concludes that the unacceptable performance is really due to an "ailing" process that ought to be investigated.

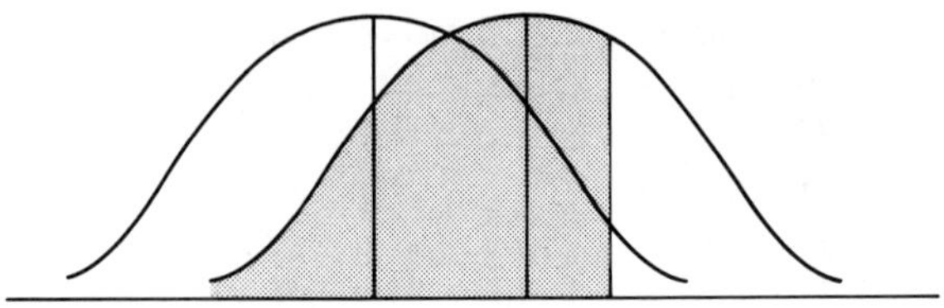

With the old mean we had an upper control limit of 1,400, and anything greater than 1,400 would have been questioned. Now we *assume* that the *shift* to the new mean, 1,100, *has taken place*, and we ask what the probability is—under the old control limits—of a sample mean being accepted. This is the Type II error. Consequently, there is approximately a 93% chance of

$$\beta = P[(600 < \bar{x} < 1{,}400)|(\mu = 1{,}100; \sigma = 200)]$$

$$P[(1{,}100 < \bar{x} < 1{,}400)|(\mu; \sigma)] = P\left(0 < Z < \left(\frac{1{,}400 - 1{,}100}{200}\right)\right) = .4332$$

$$P[(600 < \bar{x} < 1{,}100)|(\mu; \sigma)] = P\left(0 < Z < \left(\frac{600 - 1{,}100}{200}\right)\right) = \underline{.4938}$$

$$\underline{\underline{.9270}}$$

not discovering an increase in the average balance of \$100. This circumstance may be wholly unsatisfactory to management, but if the Type II error is to be lowered, the Type I error will have to be raised.

Now let us see how the t distribution might be used instead of the normal. Assume management (1) has selected a population mean of \$1,000, (2) has no knowledge of the population standard deviation, and (3) has just chosen 10 accounts that show $\bar{x} = \$1{,}384$ and $s = \sqrt{\sum(x - \bar{x})^2/(n - 1)} = \$632$. Can management have 95% confidence that the chosen population mean is reasonable? In other words, management is in the process of setting up its policy and wants to check its reasonableness using a preliminary small sample.

$$t = \frac{1{,}384 - 1{,}000}{632/\sqrt{10}} = \frac{384}{200} = 1.92$$

To state the hypotheses as a two-tailed test,

$$H_0: \mu = 1{,}000 \qquad H_1: \mu \neq 1{,}000$$

From Table 12 in Appendix A, $t_{9,\,.05/2} = 2.26$, and since $t = 1.92$ is less than this critical value, the statistician cannot reject the null hypothesis. H_0 might be wrong, but this sample does not support such a conclusion.

Management could now set new control limits that would call for samples of size 10:

$$1{,}000 \pm 2.26(632/\sqrt{10}) = \{548; 1{,}452\}$$

These limits are looser than the prior limits obtained from the normal curve; furthermore, the present t control chart has more risk. Given the same reliability of .95, $Z = 1.96$ while $t_{9,.05/2} = 2.26$. Then, if $\sigma_{\bar{x}}$ is also the same, the price of taking smaller samples (the t situation) is loss of precision.

Bayesian Sampling

As a Bayesian sees it. The analyst with a Bayesian bent adds a few *a priori* and *a posteriori* wrinkles to his decision making.

A REVIEW OF BAYESIAN FUNDAMENTALS

There are three types of probabilities:

1. *Axiomatic* probabilities are based on such things as the toss of a fair coin or the roll of a fair die.
2. *Empirical* probabilities are based on historical evidence.
3. *Subjective* probabilities are based on feelings.

Empirical probabilities are derived from the assumption that if a great number of experiments were conducted, the resulting probability measures would be very nearly the same as those probabilities determined from the evidence already at hand. This is the classical or sampling approach to arriving at probabilities. Suppose, however, you have to make "first-time" decisions, that is, the only evidence you have concerning the decision outcomes is your feelings. Certainly your impressions are better than nothing! The Bayesian approach starts with your impressions and continually blends in evidence as it comes along until, given enough evidence, your original hunches may have scarcely any effect. Were one to insist on using a classical approach with such a first-time decision, one would insist in vain. No help would be forthcoming from the classical approach until the decision had been made repeatedly and a history of outcomes could be compiled.

What is now known as Bayesian analysis actually began with a subtlety attributed to the Reverend Thomas Bayes who (a few years back—circa 1750) noticed that

Key: E_i = event i

Since $$P(E_1|E_2) = P(E_1 \cap E_2) \div P(E_2),$$

$$P(E_2|E_1) = P(E_2 \cap E_1) \div P(E_1),$$

and $$P(E_1 \cap E_2) = P(E_2 \cap E_1) \quad \text{(because set intersection is commutative)},$$

then $$P(E_1|E_2)P(E_2) = P(E_1 \cap E_2) = P(E_2|E_1)P(E_1).$$

continued to page 434

continued from page 433

This is Bayes' Theorem, and it says that you can determine $P(E_1|E_2)$ by considering its reverse $P(E_2|E_1)$.

The theorem can be made even more useful by applying a few of the laws of the algebra of sets:

$$\begin{aligned}(E_2 \cap E_1)\cup(E_2 \cap E_1^c) &= E_2 \cap (E_1 \cup E_1^c) && \text{(Distributive law)}\\ &= E_2 \cap U && \text{(Complement law)}\\ &= E_2 && \text{(Identity law)}\end{aligned}$$

Hence one can obtain a set by summing (the union operation, $\cup$) the subsets that it intersects (designated by $\cap$). We apply these results to Bayes' theorem:

We start with the statement given above:

$$P(E_1|E_2)P(E_2) = P(E_1 \cap E_2) = P(E_2|E_1)P(E_1)$$

Dividing through by $P(E_2)$, we obtain

$$P(E_1|E_2) = \frac{P(E_1 \cap E_2)}{P(E_2)} = \frac{P(E_2|E_1)P(E_1)}{P(E_2)}$$

Since (1) $\quad P(E_2|E_1)P(E_1) = P(E_1 \cap E_2),$

and (2) $\quad P(E_2) = \sum_{i=E_1,E_1^c} P(E_2 \cap i)$

(as just proven using the laws of the algebra of sets), we may rewrite Bayes' theorem in either of the following forms (which have been labelled with their Bayesian names):

Posterior Probability		Joint Probability		Conditional Probability	Prior Probability

$$P(E_1|E_2) = \frac{P(E_2 \cap E_1)}{\sum_{i=E_1,E_1^c} P(E_2 \cap i)} = \frac{P(E_2|E_1) \quad P(E_1)}{\sum_{i=E_1,E_1^c} P(E_2|i)P(i)}$$

Note: $\Sigma P(E_2 \cap i) = P(E_2)$ which is referred to as the marginal probability.

It is often worthwhile to prepare a joint probability table to implement Bayes' theorem. Table 2 illustrates the appropriate form.

Table 2 Joint Probability Table

	E_2	E_2^c	Marginal Probabilities
E_1	$P(E_1 \cap E_2)$	$P(E_1 \cap E_2^c)$	$P(E_1)$
E_1^c	$P(E_1^c \cap E_2)$	$P(E_1^c \cap E_2^c)$	$P(E_1^c)$
Marginal Probabilities	$P(E_2)$	$P(E_2^c)$	1

To illustrate how a Bayesian approaches process control through sampling, assume we are observing a production system in which defective units are reworked at a cost of \$10 each. The automatic machine that produces 200 units of this item each day has a history of generating defectives at the rates of 5%, 10%, and 15% with an a priori probability distribution for these rates of .6, .2, .2. Now it is a bother (and costs \$58) to monitor the setting of the machine, but if this is done defectives can be kept down to the rate of 5%.

To reduce the quantity of numbers floating around, let us refer to the 5%, 10%, and 15% settings as good, bad, and disastrous. If the machine has the good setting, the expected number of defectives is *np* (there is a binomial distribution at work) or 200(.05) = 10. Expected costs are therefore a minimum of 10(\$10) = \$100. If the setting is bad, expected defects equal 20 with an expected rework cost of 20(\$10) = \$200. However, we could reduce this cost to \$58 + 10(\$10) = \$158 by monitoring. Similarly, if the setting is disastrous, there would be 30 defective units, an acceptance cost of 30(\$10) = \$300, and a monitoring cost of \$158, as before. These data are summarized below.

	← Costs →		← Probability →	
Setting (I)	Proceed	Monitor	Prior $P(I)$	Reject (p_I)
Good (G)	\$100	\$158	.6	.05
Bad (B)	\$200	\$158	.2	.10
Disastrous (D)	\$300	\$158	.2	.15

If we *proceed* now, the expected cost would be \$160—that is, .6(100) + .2(200) + .2(300); on the other hand, *if* we *monitor* now, the cost would be \$158. It would seem to be less costly to monitor. However, the estimates of the prior probabilities might be in error. With this in mind, a Bayesian statistician might sample production to determine what to do. But he needs a sampling plan.

A true Bayesian never forgets that sampling costs money! He would be severely embarrassed if he paid more for sampling than the improvement in the decision was worth. (Such thinking is perhaps better referred to as "cost benefit" thinking.) The best he could do if he had perfect knowledge (an absurd but useful assumption) would be to proceed when the setting was G and to monitor when the setting was either B or D. Assuming the priors are correct, the expected cost with such perfect information would be \$123.20—that is, .6(\$100) + .2(\$158) + .2(\$158). At present we would monitor and incur a cost of \$158; consequently, sampling had better not cost more than \$34.80 (that is, \$158.00 − \$123.20). This \$34.80 is known as "the expected value of perfect information." If each sample costs \$1.75 then the maximum sample size the Bayesian would consider would be 19. (Doesn't this approach appeal to you—pragmatically speaking?)

Temporarily putting aside any questions we might have about where it came from, suppose the decision rule with regard to sampling is to draw a sample of three and to monitor if 2 or more rejects are found. By placing the prior probabilities in a diagonalized matrix and multiplying this by a matrix showing the binomial probabilities for number of rejects given the respective settings, we obtain a joint probability table for rejects and settings (Table 3).

$$\overset{P(I)}{\begin{bmatrix} .6 & 0 & 0 \\ 0 & .2 & 0 \\ 0 & 0 & .2 \end{bmatrix}} \overset{\displaystyle P(R|I)}{\overset{\begin{matrix} \quad 0 & \quad\; 1 & \quad\; 2 & \quad\; 3 \end{matrix}}{\begin{bmatrix} .8574 & .1354 & .0071 & .0001 \\ .7290 & .2430 & .0270 & .0010 \\ .6141 & .3251 & .0574 & .0034 \end{bmatrix}}} = P(R \cap I)$$

Table 3 $P(R \cap I)$ Joint Probability Table

		Rejects (R)				
		0	1	2	3	$P(I)$
	G	.51444	.08124	.00426	.00006	.60000
Setting (I)	B	.14580	.04860	.00540	.00020	.20000
	D	.12282	.06502	.01148	.00068	.20000
	$P(R)$	.78306	.19486	.02114	.00094	1.00000

We have sufficient information at our disposal now to determine an expected cost for this decision rule.

Key:

$n =$ sample size
$c =$ critical number of rejects; monitoring is done if $R \geq c$
$E[K(n, c)] =$ expected cost of the decision rule
$C(I|c) =$ cost of setting I given the critical number of rejects, c

$$E[K(n, c)] = \sum_R \sum_I P(R \cap I)C(I|c) + \$1.75n$$

For our decision policy we reject, and therefore monitor, whenever $R \geq 2$; so

$$\begin{aligned} E[K(3, 2)] &= .51444(\$100) + .08124(\$100) + .00426(\$158) + .00006(\$158) \\ &\quad + .14580(\$200) + .04860(\$200) + .00540(\$158) + .00020(\$158) \\ &\quad + .12282(\$300) + .06502(\$300) + .01148(\$158) + .00068(\$158) \\ &\quad + 3(\$1.75) \\ &= \$163.54 \end{aligned}$$

If we computed $E[K(n, c)]$ for every combination (n, c), we could decide on the least expensive decision rule. A computer program that does these calculations for us is contained in Exhibit 2. We see that the least expensive decision rule is $(n, c) = (3, 1)$.[6] A decision tree may help you to understand what the objective of these procedures is.

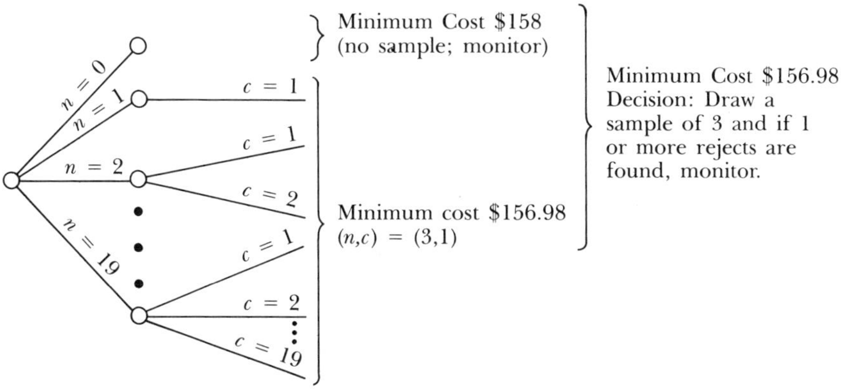

We next take a sample of size 3. Assuming we discover two rejects in the sample, we decide to monitor. In addition, to a Bayesian statistician, this is evidence that should be blended in with the previous prior estimates to obtain the new priors. The new priors will, in turn, equal the present posteriors. Using column $R=2$ in the joint probability table, we determine the new priors:

I	$P(2 \cap I)$	$P(R = 2)$	$P(I \mid 2)$	
G	.00426		.20151	These present posteriors become the new priors.
B	.00540	÷ .02114 =	.25544	
D	.01148		.54305	
	.02114		1.00000	

These new priors would be used to decide on the optimal sampling rule for the next day. Thus the sample size as well as the critical number of rejects might change from day to day.

[6] Exhibit 1 restricts sample size, n, to range from 1 to 6 to keep the exhibit at a reasonable length. If you inspect the output, you will see that a minimum had already been attained at (3,1); the cost of taking the sample simply makes larger samples too expensive. With different values for the settings (for example, "catastrophic" with a probability of a defect equalling, say, .6) the optimal sampling decision rule could yield critical rejects, c, greater than one.

Exhibit 2

```
100  DIM  P(1,10),K(1,10),Q(10,10),S(1,10),B(10,20),T(20,1),J(10,20)
105  DIM  Z(10,20),U(1,20),V(1,1)
130  REM P  IS A VECTOR WITH PROBABILITY OF REJECTS FOR EACH SETTING
135  REM K  IS A VECTOR WITH COSTS FOR EACH SETTING AND FOR MONITORING
140  REM Q  IS A DIAGONAL MATRIX CONTAINING PRIORS
145  REM S  IS A SUM VECTOR
150  REM T  IS A SUM VECTOR
155  REM B  IS THE CONDITIONAL PROBABILITIES MATRIX
160  REM J  IS THE JOINT PROBABILITIES MATRIX
165  REM MAT Z IS THE EXPECTED COSTS MATRIX
170  REM C  IS THE CRITICAL NUMBER OF REJECTS
175  REM N  IS THE SAMPLE
200  MAT READ P(1,3)
205  MAT READ K(1,4)
210  MAT READ Q(3,3)
215  MAT READ S(1,3)
250  FOR  N  = 1 TO 6
25:  REM SINCE THE BINOMIAL TAKES ON N+1 VALUES,AUGMENTATION IS NEEDED
255  LET  M = N + 1
260  MAT B  = ZER(3,M)
267  MAT T  = ZER(M,1)
270  MAT Z  = ZER(3,M)
300  FOR  J  = 1 TO M
305  LET  T(J,1) = 1
310  NEXT J
399  REM THE PROGRAM NOW GENERATES BINOMIAL PROBABILITIES RECURSIVELY
400  FOR  I  = 1 TO 3
405  LET  B(I,1) = (1 - P(1,I))↑N
410  LET  F  = P(1,I)/(1 - P(1,I))
450  FOR  J  = 2 TO M
452  LET  K  = J - 1
455  LET  B(I,J) = (N - K + 1)*F*B(I,K)/K
460  NEXT J
480  NEXT I
499  REM THE JOINT PROBABILITY TABLE IS NOW CALCULATED
500  MAT J  = Q * B
598  REM COSTS OF PROCEEDING AND MONITORING ARE INTRODUCED; SINCE
599  REM COSTS DEPEND ON THE CRITICAL NUMBER OF REJECTS, C IS VARIED
600  FOR  C  = 2 TO M
605  FOR  I  = 1 TO 3
610  FOR  L  = 1 TO C - 1
615  LET  Z(I,L) = K(1,I) * J(I,L)
620  NEXT L
625  FOR  R  = C TO M
630  LET  Z(I,R) = K(1,4) * J(I,R)
635  NEXT R
640  NEXT I
650  MAT U  = S * Z
655  MAT V  = U*T
705  LET  W1 = V(1,1)
710  LET  W2 = W1 * (1.75 * N)
715  PRINT "E[K(";N;",";C - 1;")] = ";W2
750  NEXT C
800  NEXT N
900  DATA .05,.10,.15
```

Exhibit 2 (*cont.*)

```
902  DATA 100,200,300,158
904  DATA .6,0,0
905  DATA 0,.2,0
906  DATA 0,0,.2
908  DATA 1,1,1
950  END

RUN

E[K( 1 , 1 )] = 158.39
E[K( 2 , 1 )] = 157.416
E[K( 2 , 2 )] = 162.864
E[K( 3 , 1 )] = 156.9781
E[K( 3 , 2 )] = 163.5418
E[K( 3 , 3 )] = 165.1501
E[K( 4 , 1 )] = 156.9914
E[K( 4 , 2 )] = 163.9382
E[K( 4 , 3 )] = 166.6454
E[K( 4 , 4 )] = 166.985
E[K( 5 , 1 )] = 157.38377
E[K( 5 , 2 )] = 164.171919
E[K( 5 , 3 )] = 167.962621
E[K( 5 , 4 )] = 168.683919
E[K( 5 , 5 )] = 168.74777
E[K( 6 , 1 )] = 158.093952
E[K( 6 , 2 )] = 164.332857
E[K( 6 , 3 )] = 169.100042
E[K( 6 , 4 )] = 170.3252
E[K( 6 , 5 )] = 170.488278
E[K( 6 , 6 )] = 170.499668
```

Although it is not necessary, because the manner in which we calculated the optimal decision rule reflects these costs, we could verify the propriety of our decision to monitor by using the new priors to compute conditional expected costs as follows:

				Conditional Expected Costs	
Setting	Priors	Proceed	Monitor	Proceed	Monitor
G	.20151	$100	$158	$20.15	
B	.25544	$200	$158	51.09	
D	.54305	$300	$158	162.92	
				$234.16	$158

We see that since there were two rejects in our sample of three, there would be a higher expected cost if we decided to proceed than if we decided to monitor.

continued to page 440

continued from page 439

Had we sampled and found no rejects, we would use column $R=0$ in the joint probability table to determine the new priors. The conditional expected costs would then be

				Conditional Expected Costs	
Setting	Priors	Proceed	Monitor	Proceed	Monitor
G	.65696	$100	$158	$65.70	
B	.18619	$200	$158	37.24	
D	.15685	$300	$158	47.06	
				$150.00	$158.00

Having found no rejects, we would proceed. This verifies our chosen decision rule.

It might fix ideas in your mind if we considered what would happen with other data. Let us say that the cost to monitor reduces to $150, that the cost to sample increases to $3.75, and that the priors on a given day are .45, .30, and .25 respectively. Then the expected cost of proceeding would be $180—that is, .45(100) + .30(200) + .25(300). The results of using the computer program show that the least costly decision rule, if we decide to sample, is again $(n, c) = (3, 1)$—at a cost of $175.92. The best action with perfect information would be $127.50—that is, .45(100) + .30(150) + .25(150). Since monitoring costs $150, the expected value of perfect information would be $22.50, and this would allow a maximum sample of six (that is, $22.50 ÷ $3.75). In such circumstances, the best sampling plan is not to sample at all but to monitor directly. Reasoning:

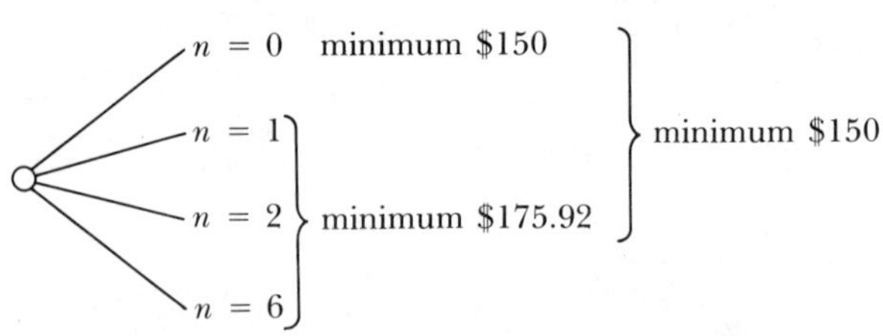

Now suppose that the priors on a given day are such that proceeding has a lower cost than either monitoring or sampling. No sample is drawn because the cost does not justify it, and hence the priors remain fixed. Is the question of proceeding and monitoring settled for all time? Definitely not! The Bayesian would still be maintaining records of the daily frequency of the *G*, *B*, and D settings. After consulting these records, he might again challenge the "fixed" set of priors by hypothesizing some other set of priors and thereby reintroducing the proceed-monitor question.

Bayesian Sampling and the Preposterior Distribution

Let us extend our discussion of Bayesian sampling by studying how the normal distribution may be used to calculate opportunity costs and to determine sample size. Three distributions are involved: the prior, the posterior, and the preposterior. As before, the prior is the distribution before any sampling is done, and the posterior is the distribution after a sample has been taken. The preposterior sounds like an inconsistency (something that is both pre- and post-), but it is not. In the preposterior the statistician is trying to determine parameters of a posterior distribution prior to taking a sample. The result is especially helpful in determining sample size; however, some estimate of the posterior variance must first be available from some new source.

We shall be choosing between two actions A_1 and A_2 that have costs $C_1 = m_1\mu + d_1$ and $C_2 = m_2\mu + d_2$ respectively, and where, say, $0 \le m_2 \le m_1$ and $0 \le d_1 \le d_2$. Therefore, the breakeven point, μ_b, is

$$
\begin{aligned}
C_1 &= m_1\mu + d_1 \\
-C_2 &= -(m_2\mu + d_2) \\
\hline
0 &= \mu_b(m_1 - m_2) + (d_1 - d_2) \\
\mu_b &= -(d_1 - d_2)/(m_1 - m_2)
\end{aligned}
$$

Hence $\mu_b > 0$, and since $d_1 \le d_2$ and $m_2 \le m_1$, action A_1 is less costly when $\mu < \mu_b$. Let us assume $\mu_b > E(\mu) = \mu_0$, the prior mean. Then Figure 1 portrays the situation:

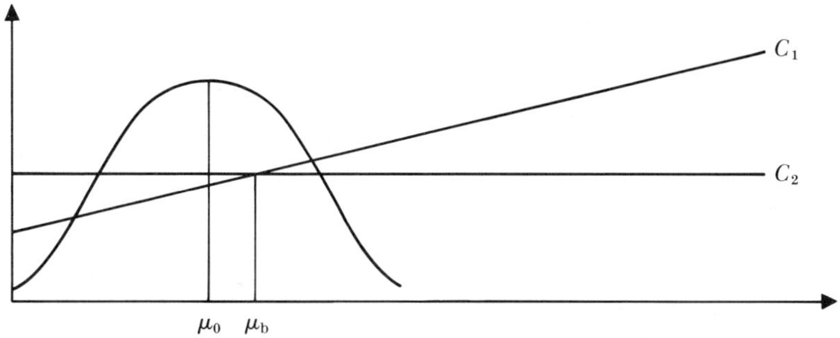

Figure 1

As long as $\mu < \mu_b$, A_1 is the better action; but once $\mu > \mu_b$, A_2 is less costly, and having chosen A_1, we experience regret (opportunity cost) in the amount $C_1 - C_2$. Had we been able to switch strategies, taking A_1 up to μ_b and A_2 thereafter, we would experience no loss in the light of this perfect behavior. The opportunity cost of A_1 is known as the expected value of perfect information, EVPI, and it is calculated using the prior distribution $N(\mu:\mu_0;\sigma_0)$ as follows:

$$\text{EVPI} = \int_{\mu_b}^{\infty} (C_1 - C_2)N(\mu:\mu_0;\sigma_0)\,d\mu$$

$$C_1 - C_2 = (m_1\mu + d_1) - (m_2\mu + d_2) = (m_1 - m_2)\mu + (d_1 - d_2)$$

$$\text{But } \mu_b = -(d_1 - d_2)/(m_1 - m_2);\text{ hence, } \mu_b(m_1 - m_2) = -(d_1 - d_2)$$

$$\text{So, } C_1 - C_2 = (m_1 - m_2)\mu - (m_1 - m_2)\mu_b$$

$$\text{EVPI} = \int_{\mu_b}^{\infty} \frac{(m_1 - m_2)(\mu - \mu_b)e^{-\frac{1}{2}\left(\frac{\mu-\mu_0}{\sigma_0}\right)^2}}{\sigma_0\sqrt{2\pi}}\,d\mu$$

$$\text{EVPI} = \sigma_0(m_1 - m_2)\left[\frac{e^{-z_b^2/2}}{\sqrt{2\pi}} - z_bP(z > z_b)\right]$$

Comments:

1. The integration is done as shown on page 396.
2. Here, $z_b = (\mu_b - \mu_0)/\sigma_0$
3. $P(z > z_b) = .5 - N(z_b)$
4. Had μ_0 been greater than μ_b, symmetry of the normal and the loss function would lead to the same value of EVPI, but the values of μ being less than μ_b would lead to a minus sign. This could be remedied by changing the integrand to $\mu_b - \mu$, but it is equally acceptable to use absolute values:

$$\text{EVPI} = \sigma_0|m_1 - m_2|\left|\frac{e^{-z_b^2/2}}{\sqrt{2\pi}} - z_bP(z > z_b)\right|$$

Let us next focus on the posterior distribution. Assume that we have a random variable, X, that is normally distributed with mean μ and variance σ^2. μ has a prior probability distribution with mean μ_0 and variance $\sigma_0{}^2$. A sample of size n is drawn, and the resulting distribution of the sample mean $\bar{X}$ is normal with mean μ and variance $\sigma_{\bar{x}}{}^2 = \sigma^2/n$. The posterior distribution of μ is then the conditional distribution of μ given $\bar{x}$. The scheme follows these lines:

Posterior	Joint		Prior Conditional (Sampling)
$h(\mu\mid\bar{x})$	$= \dfrac{f(\mu, \bar{x})}{h(\bar{x})}$		$= \dfrac{g(\mu)g(\bar{x}\mid\mu)}{h(\bar{x})}$
	Marginal		Marginal

Steps:

1. Form the joint from the prior and sampling distributions:

$$f(\mu, \bar{x}) = g(\mu)g(\bar{x}\mid\mu)$$

$$f(\mu, \bar{x}) = [N(\mu\!:\mu_0;\, \sigma_0)][N(\bar{x}\!:\mu;\, \sigma_{\bar{x}})]$$

$$f(\mu, \bar{x}) = e^{-\frac{1}{2}\left[\left(\frac{\mu-\mu_0}{\sigma_0}\right)^2 + \left(\frac{\bar{x}-\mu}{\sigma_{\bar{x}}}\right)^2\right]} \Big/ 2\pi\sigma_0\sigma_{\bar{x}}$$

2. Obtain the marginal by integrating $f(\mu, \bar{x})$ over the range of μ. How this is done is described in Exhibit 3; the result is

$$h(\bar{x}) = e^{-\frac{(\bar{x}-\mu_0)^2}{2(\sigma_0^2+\sigma_x^2)}} \Big/ \left(\sqrt{2\pi}\sqrt{\sigma_0^2 + \sigma_{\bar{x}}^2}\right)$$

3. Derive the posterior by

$$h(\mu\mid\bar{x}) = \frac{f(\mu, \bar{x})}{h(\bar{x})} = \frac{\sqrt{\sigma_{\bar{x}}^2 + \sigma_0^2}}{\sqrt{2\pi}\sigma_0\sigma_{\bar{x}}}\, e^{-\frac{(\sigma_{\bar{x}}^2+\sigma_0^2)}{2(\sigma_0\sigma_{\bar{x}})^2}\left[\mu - \frac{\sigma_{\bar{x}}^2\mu_0 + \sigma_0^2\bar{x}}{\sigma_{\bar{x}}^2+\sigma_0^2}\right]^2}$$

In conclusion, we see from its exponent that the posterior distribution is normal with mean

$$\mu_1 = \frac{\sigma_{\bar{x}}^2\mu_0 + \sigma_0^2\bar{x}}{\sigma_{\bar{x}}^2 + \sigma_0^2}$$

and variance

$$\sigma_1^2 = \frac{\sigma_0^2\sigma_{\bar{x}}^2}{\sigma_{\bar{x}}^2 + \sigma_0^2}$$

Exhibit 3 The Marginal Distribution

Key: $a = \mu, \quad b = \mu_0, \quad c = \sigma_0^2, \quad d = \sigma_{\bar{x}}^2, \quad e = \bar{x}$

$$h(\bar{x}) = \int_{-\infty}^{\infty} f(\mu, \bar{x})\, d\mu = h(e) = \int_{-\infty}^{\infty} \frac{e^{-\frac{1}{2}\left[\frac{(a-b)^2}{c} + \frac{(e-a)^2}{d}\right]}}{2\pi\sigma_0\sigma_{\bar{x}}}\, da$$

Exhibit 3 (*cont.*)

But $$-\frac{1}{2}\left[\frac{(a-b)^2}{c}+\frac{(e-a)^2}{d}\right]=\frac{-1}{2cd}\left[d(a^2-2ab+b^2)+c(e^2-2ea+a^2)\right]$$

$$=-\frac{1}{2cd}\left[(d+c)a^2-2a(db+ce)+(db^2+ce^2)\right]$$

$$=-\frac{(d+c)}{2cd}\left[a^2-2a\left(\frac{db+ce}{d+c}\right)+\left(\frac{db^2+ce^2}{d+c}\right)\right]$$

Complete the square in a:

$$=-\frac{(d+c)}{2cd}\left[a^2-2a\left(\frac{db+ce}{d+c}\right)\pm\left(\frac{db+ce}{d+c}\right)^2+\left(\frac{db^2+ce^2}{d+c}\right)\right]$$

$$=\underbrace{-\frac{(d+c)}{2cd}\left[a-\left(\frac{db+ce}{d+c}\right)\right]^2}-\frac{(d+c)}{2cd}\left[-\left(\frac{db+ce}{d+c}\right)^2+\left(\frac{db^2+ce^2}{d+c}\right)\right]$$

$$=\qquad\text{same}\qquad-\frac{1}{2cd}\left[-\frac{(db+ce)^2}{d+c}+(db^2+ce^2)\right]$$

$$=\text{same}-\frac{\left[-d^2b^2-2bcde-c^2e^2+d^2b^2+cde^2+cab^2+c^2e^2\right]}{2cd(d+c)}$$

$$=-\frac{(d+c)}{2cd}\left[a-\left(\frac{db+ce}{d+c}\right)\right]^2-\frac{(e-b)^2}{2(d+c)}$$

Therefore,

$$h(e)=\int_{-\infty}^{\infty}\frac{e^{-\frac{(d+c)}{2cd}\left[a-\left(\frac{db+ce}{d+c}\right)\right]^2-\frac{(e-b)^2}{2(d+c)}}\,da}{2\pi\sqrt{cd}}$$

$$=\frac{e^{\frac{-(e-b)^2}{2(d+c)}}}{\sqrt{2\pi cd}}\int_{-\infty}^{\infty}\frac{e^{-\frac{(d+c)}{2cd}\left[a-\left(\frac{db+ce}{d+c}\right)\right]^2}\,da}{\sqrt{2\pi}}$$

Let $Z=\left[a-\left(\frac{db+ce}{d+c}\right)\right]\sqrt{\frac{d+c}{cd}}$; $\quad\frac{dZ}{da}=\sqrt{\frac{d+c}{cd}}$

$$=\frac{e^{\frac{-(e-b)^2}{2(d+c)}}}{\sqrt{2\pi cd}}\sqrt{\frac{cd}{d+c}}\int_{-\infty}^{\infty}\frac{e^{-Z^2/2}\,dZ}{\sqrt{2\pi}}$$

Restoring original notation:

$$h(\bar{x})=e^{-(\bar{x}-\mu_0)^2/2(\sigma_0{}^2+\sigma_{\bar{x}}{}^2)}/(\sqrt{2\pi}\sqrt{\sigma_0{}^2+\sigma_{\bar{x}}{}^2})$$

What parameters would the posterior have if, instead of taking a sample, we could obtain information from a pilot study (or some other source—be it intuitions or even a preliminary small sample)? All that is needed is an estimate of $\sigma_{\bar{x}}^2$; with this the preposterior distribution may be developed. Again we assume that the prior distribution is $N(\mu : \mu_0, \sigma_0)$, and that $f(\mu, \bar{x})$ is as developed previously. We want to consider the mean of the posterior before taking a sample, and hence we compute $f(\mu, \mu_1)$ by using the formula for μ_1 (just derived) to transform variables:

$$\mu_1 = (\sigma_{\bar{x}}^2 \mu_0 + \sigma_0^2 \bar{x})/(\sigma_{\bar{x}}^2 + \sigma_0^2)$$

$$\bar{x} = \frac{\mu_1(\sigma_{\bar{x}}^2 + \sigma_0^2)}{\sigma_0^2} - \frac{\sigma_{\bar{x}}^2 \mu_0}{\sigma_0^2}$$

$$\frac{d\bar{x}}{d\mu_1} = \frac{\sigma_{\bar{x}}^2 + \sigma_0^2}{\sigma_0^2}$$

With this transformation reflected, we obtain

$$f(\mu, \mu_1) = \frac{(\sigma_0^2 + \sigma_{\bar{x}}^2)}{2\pi\sigma_0^3\sigma_{\bar{x}}} e^{-\frac{1}{2}\frac{(\sigma_0^2 + \sigma_{\bar{x}}^2)}{(\sigma_0\sigma_{\bar{x}})^2}\left[(\mu - \mu_1)^2 + \frac{\sigma_{\bar{x}}^2}{\sigma_0^2}(\mu_1 - \mu_0)^2\right]}$$

How the exponent was brought into the above form is shown in Exhibit 4.

Exhibit 4 The Joint Distribution

Key: $\quad a = \mu, \quad b = \mu_0, \quad c = \sigma_0^2, \quad d = \sigma_{\bar{x}}^2, \quad e = \bar{x}, \quad i = \mu_1$

$$f(\mu, \bar{x}) = e^{-\frac{1}{2}\left[\left(\frac{\mu - \mu_0}{\sigma_0}\right)^2 + \left(\frac{\bar{x} - \mu}{\sigma_{\bar{x}}}\right)^2\right]} \Big/ 2\mu\sigma_0\sigma_{\bar{x}}$$

Transforming $\bar{x}$ to μ_1:

$$f(\mu, \mu_1) = \frac{e^{-\frac{1}{2}\left[\left(\frac{\mu - \mu_0}{\sigma_0}\right)^2 + \left[\left[\left(\frac{\mu_1(\sigma_{\bar{x}}^2 + \sigma_0^2)}{\sigma_0^2} - \frac{\sigma_{\bar{x}}^2}{\sigma_0^2}\mu_0\right) - \mu\right]^2 \Big/ \sigma_{\bar{x}}^2\right]\right]}}{2\pi\sigma_0\sigma_{\bar{x}}} \left(\frac{\sigma_{\bar{x}}^2 + \sigma_0^2}{\sigma_0^2}\right)$$

$$f(a, i) = e^{-\alpha/2}(d + c)/2\pi c^{3/2} d^{1/2},$$

where
$$\alpha = \left[\frac{(a - b)^2}{c} + \left[\left[\left(\frac{i(d + c)}{c} - \frac{d}{c}b\right) - a\right]^2 \Big/ d\right]\right]$$

$$= \left[\frac{d(a - b)^2}{dc} + \frac{1}{c^2 d}[(d + c)i - db - ca]^2\right]$$

$$= [dc(a - b)^2 + [c(i - a) + d(i - b)]^2]/dc^2$$

$$= [dc(a - b)^2 + c^2(i - a)^2 + 2cd(i - a)(i - b) + d^2(i - b)^2]/dc^2$$

$$= [dc(a^2 - 2ab + b^2 + 2i^2 - 2ib - 2ia + 2ab) + c^2(i - a)^2 + d^2(i - b)^2]/dc^2$$

Exhibit 4 (*cont.*)

Cancelling where possible and splitting the remaining doubled terms:

$$= [dc[(a^2 + i^2 - 2ia) + (b^2 + i^2 - 2ib)] + c^2(i - a)^2 + d^2(i - b)^2]/dc^2$$
$$= [dc[(a - i)^2 + (b - i)^2)] + c^2(i - a)^2 + d^2(i - b)^2]/dc^2$$
$$= [(a - i)^2(dc + c^2) + (b - i)^2(dc + d^2)]/dc^2$$
$$= [c(a - i)^2(d + c) + d(b - i)^2(d + c)]/dc^2$$
$$= \frac{(d + c)}{dc}\left[(a - i)^2 + \frac{d(b - i)^2}{c}\right]$$

Restoring original notation:

$$f(\mu, \mu_1) = \frac{(\sigma_0{}^2 + \sigma_{\bar{x}}{}^2)}{2\pi\sigma_0{}^3\sigma_{\bar{x}}} e^{-\frac{1}{2}\frac{(\sigma_0{}^2 + \sigma_{\bar{x}}{}^2)}{(\sigma_0\sigma_{\bar{x}})^2}\left[(\mu - \mu_1)^2 + \frac{\sigma_{\bar{x}}{}^2}{\sigma_0{}^2}(\mu_0 - \mu_1)^2\right]}$$

The marginal, $h(\mu_1)$, may be determined by summing over the variable μ:

$$h(\mu_1) = \int_{-\infty}^{\infty} f(\mu, \mu_1)\, d\mu = \sqrt{\frac{\sigma_0{}^2 + \sigma_{\bar{x}}{}^2}{2\pi\sigma_0{}^4}}\, e^{-\frac{1}{2}\frac{(\sigma_0{}^2 + \sigma_{\bar{x}}{}^2)(\mu_1 - \mu_0)^2}{\sigma_0{}^4}}$$

We see that $h(\mu_1)$ is normally distributed with mean $E(\mu_1) = \mu_0$ and variance $V(\sigma_1) = \sigma_0{}^4/(\sigma_0{}^2 + \sigma_x{}^2)$. $h(\mu_1)$ is the preposterior distribution and would be used in determining the expected value of sample information (EVSI) in the same way that the prior was used to calculate EVPI:

$$\text{EVSI} = \sigma_1 |m_1 - m_2| \left| \frac{e^{-z_b{}^2/2}}{\sqrt{2\pi}} - z_b P(z > z_b) \right|$$

As the name suggests, EVSI would be useful for determining sample size.

Example: A company is considering automating an operation. The machine requires an immediate investment of \$80,000 and will save \$10 per hour in labor costs. Preliminary studies suggest that the average number of hours saved, μ, will be normally distributed with $P(12{,}480 < \mu < 17{,}520) = .6$. Subsequent information obtained from a survey of 12 companies indicates that the standard deviation is 3,300 hours. If the required discounting rate before taxes is 20% per year, and if there are 2,000 working hours in a year, determine the opportunity loss from not automating (EVPI) and the expected value of sample information (EVSI).

Solution: Since this problem involves a significant number of hours, the labor savings extend well into the future and should be discounted;

this forces a modification in the previous modelling. The discounting rate per hour is $r = .2/2{,}000 = .0001$, and the break-even point, μ_b, is

$$\$80{,}000 = \int_0^{\mu_b} \$10e^{-.0001\mu}\, d\mu$$

$$8{,}000 = \frac{-e^{-.0001\mu}]_0^{\mu_b}}{.0001}$$

$$.8 = 1 - e^{-.0001\mu_b}$$

$$\mu_b = \ln .2/-.0001 = 16{,}094$$

The formula for the opportunity cost, EVPI, becomes

$$\text{EVPI} = \int_{\mu_b}^{\infty} \frac{(m_1 - m_2)e^{-r\mu}(\mu - \mu_b)e^{-\frac{1}{2}\left(\frac{\mu-\mu_0}{\sigma_0}\right)^2}}{\sigma_0\sqrt{2\pi}}\, d\mu$$

After completing the square in μ and integrating, we get

$$\text{EVPI} = (m_1 - m_2)e^{-\frac{r}{2}(2\mu_0 - r\sigma_0{}^2)}\left[\frac{\sigma_0 e^{-z_L{}^2/2}}{\sqrt{2\pi}} + [(\mu_0 - r\sigma_0{}^2) - \mu_b]P(z > z_L)\right],$$

where $$z_L = [\mu_b - (\mu_0 - r\sigma_0{}^2)]/\sigma_0$$

Prior parameters: $$\mu_0 = (12{,}480 + 17{,}520)/2 = 15{,}000$$

$$.84\sigma_0 = 17{,}520 - 15{,}000$$

$$\sigma_0 = 3{,}000$$

Sampling variance: $$\sigma_{\bar{x}}{}^2 = 3{,}300^2$$

$$z_L = [16{,}094 - (15{,}000 - .0001(3{,}000^2))]/3{,}000 = 1{,}994/3{,}000 = .66\overline{46}$$

$$\text{EVPI} = (10 - 0)e^{-\frac{.0001}{2}(2(15{,}000) - .0001(3{,}000^2))} \cdot \left[\frac{3{,}000e^{-\frac{.66\overline{46}^2}{2}}}{\sqrt{2\pi}} - 1{,}994(.2469)\right]$$

$$\text{EVPI} = \$1{,}142$$

To obtain the expected value of sample information, the variance of the preposterior must first be calculated:

$$V(\sigma_1) = \sigma_0{}^4/(\sigma_0{}^2 + \sigma_{\bar{x}}{}^2) = 3{,}000^4/(3{,}000^2 + 3{,}300^2) = 2{,}018^2$$

Consequently, $$z_L = [\mu_b - (\mu_0 - rV(\sigma_1))]/\sqrt{V(\sigma_1)} = 1{,}501/2{,}018 = .7438$$

$$\text{EVSI} = (10 - 0)e^{-\frac{.0001}{2}(2(15{,}000) - .0001(2{,}018^2))}\left[\frac{2{,}018e^{-\frac{.7438^2}{2}}}{\sqrt{2\pi}} - 1{,}501(.2715)\right]$$

$$\text{EVSI} = \$466$$

Comments: The \$466 indicates that there is little to be gained from further sampling. Had the EVSI been promising, sampling (at a cost no greater than EVSI) would be advisable, and this would have led to the calculation of the posterior distribution.

Example: An auditor wishes to validate the amount of accounts receivable shown on company ledgers. The ledgers put the balance at \$500,000. From other testing he has done, the auditor believes that there is a .95 probability that the balance is not off by more than \$5,000 in either direction. There are approximately 10,000 customers who collectively make up this balance, and the standard deviation of individual accounts is \$10 according to statistics kept in the accounts receivable department. As a measure of his distress if he is wrong in accepting the book balance, the auditor feels that \$.0004 · (difference between actual and ledger balance)^2 is appropriate because his distress increases rapidly as the difference grows (mathematically this is equivalent to saying that cost of being wrong is proportional to the square of the error). The cost of sampling is \$1 per account. What sample size should he take?

Solution: The auditor's feelings may be taken as the prior distribution; hence, if normality is assumed,

$$\mu_0 = \$500{,}000$$

$$\sigma_0 = \$5{,}000/2 = \$2{,}500 \text{ (2 standard deviations yields .95)}$$

$$\sigma_{\bar{x}} = \sigma/\sqrt{n} = \$10(10{,}000)/\sqrt{n}$$

The preposterior variance is then

$$V(\sigma_1) = \sigma_0{}^4/(\sigma_0{}^2 + (\sigma^2/n)) = 2{,}500^2(n/(n + 40^2))$$

Symmetry around μ_0 permits doubling in calculating EVSI:

$$\text{EVSI} = 2\int_{\mu_0}^{\infty} \frac{.0004(\mu - \mu_0)^2}{\sqrt{V(\sigma_1)}\sqrt{2\pi}} e^{-\frac{1}{2}\left(\frac{\mu - \mu_0}{\sqrt{V(\sigma_1)}}\right)^2} d\mu = .0004V(\sigma_1)$$

$$\text{EVSI} = .0004(2{,}500^2)(n/(n + 40^2)) = 2{,}500(n/(n + 40^2))$$

The expected net gain in sampling (ENGS) is

$$\text{ENGS} = \text{EVSI} - (a + bn), \quad \text{where } a + bn \text{ is sampling cost}$$

$$\text{ENGS} = \frac{2{,}500n}{n + 40^2} - (0 + \$1n)$$

The optimal sample size is

$$\frac{d(\text{ENGS})}{dn} = \frac{(n + 40^2)2{,}500 - 2{,}500n}{(n + 40^2)^2} - 1 = 0$$

$$\hat{n} = 400$$

Comments:

1. It is possible that the optimal sample size called for by $d(\text{ENGS})/dn$ will exceed population size. In such a case the optimum occurs at the end point—the total population—and the distress at making an error is vast.

2. Bayesian sampling also regularly makes use of linear error functions. These are easier to work with, but intuitively distress with larger errors and virtual indifference about small errors favors nonlinearity.

3. For comparison purposes, the sample size under the classical approach would be

$$n = \left(\frac{Z\sigma}{E}\right)^2 = \left[\frac{2(100{,}000)}{5{,}000}\right]^2 = 1{,}600$$

The incorporation of the prior and the costs of distress and of sampling have therefore reduced the sample to 25% of that called for by the classical approach. Such significant efficiency does not hold true generally, however. Had the cost of distress been \$.25 instead of \$.0004, for instance, the Bayesian approach would call for a sample size equal to the entire population, while the classical approach would still have $n = 1{,}600$.

Stratified Sampling

Another common sampling technique divides a population into "strata" according to some attribute and then samples each stratum, treating it initially as a separate population. In the process information about the various strata is developed that helps in controlling them individually, making it possible, for instance, to avoid stating an overall policy that restricts some strata while liberating others. In addition, if the strata are internally homogeneous, their standard deviations will be relatively small, thereby enabling smaller samples to generate as precise estimates as larger samples would were the strata treated as a single population and reliability held constant. Sometimes things like geographic barriers make stratified sampling the only practical method.

For the total population, the estimated standard deviation is

$$s = \sqrt{\sum_{j=1}^{n} \frac{(x_j - \bar{x})^2}{n-1}}$$

For each stratum, the estimated standard deviation is

$$s_i = \sqrt{\sum_{k=1}^{n} \frac{(x_{ik} - \bar{x}_i)^2}{n_i - 1}}$$

The total sample $= n = \sum_{i=1}^{M} n_i$, where n_i is the sample in the ith stratum and there are M strata.

Weighting each standard deviation by the proportion its strata size bears to the total population, introducing the finite population correction factor, dividing by sample size, squaring, and summing yields the formula for the variance of the estimate of the population mean obtained from the strata:

$$V(\bar{x}_{st}) = \sum_{i=1}^{M} \left(\frac{N_i - n_i}{N_i}\right)\left(\frac{N_i}{N}\right)^2 \frac{s_i^2}{n_i}$$

Here N is total population, N_i is the population of the ith stratum, and we have estimated the variance of the *population mean.* If we wish to estimate the variance of the *total population,* we need $V(N\bar{x}_{st}) = N^2 V(\bar{x}_{st})$. For example, if the problem is to estimate, say, the variance of the average invoice value, $V(\bar{x}_{st})$ is of interest; however, if the problem is to estimate the variance of the total value of all invoices, $N^2 V(\bar{x}_{st})$ is pertinent.

As yet there has been no mention of how to allocate the total sample among the strata. One very popular method allocates in proportion to strata size; thus $N_i/N = n_i/n$ and $n_i = n(N_i/N)$. The optimal method, assuming the cost of sampling is $C = a + \sum c_i n_i$, uses weighted strata standard deviations and is obtained by minimizing the variance, $V(\bar{x}_{st})$, subject to the constraint on budgeted cost. This process involves Lagrangean optimization (see Appendix C) as follows:

$$T = \sum_{i=1}^{M} \left(\frac{N_i - n_i}{N_i}\right)\left(\frac{N_i}{N}\right)^2 \frac{s_i^2}{n_i} - \lambda\left(C - a - \sum c_i n_i\right)$$

$$\frac{\partial T}{\partial n_i} = \left(\frac{N_i}{N}\right)^2 s_i^2 \left[\frac{N_i n_i(-1) - (N_i - n_i)N_i}{(N_i n_i)^2}\right] + \lambda c_i = 0$$

$$n_i\sqrt{\lambda} = N_i s_i/(N\sqrt{c_i})$$

The expression for the total sample, n, may be obtained by summing:

$$\sum n_1\sqrt{\lambda} = n\sqrt{\lambda} = \sum[N_i s_i/(N\sqrt{c_i})]$$

The proportion of n_i to n is then

$$\frac{n_i}{n} = \frac{N_i s_i/\sqrt{c_i}}{\sum N_i s_i/\sqrt{c_i}}$$

Hence the optimal allocation has

$$n_i = n\left[\frac{N_i s_i/\sqrt{c_i}}{\sum N_i s_i/\sqrt{c_i}}\right]$$

If the variable cost of sampling per unit is the same for each stratum, $\sqrt{c_i} = \sqrt{c}$, which then factors, leaving

$$n_i = n\left[\frac{N_i s_i}{\sum N_i s_i}\right]$$

Therefore, optimal allocation relies on a weighting of strata standard deviations.[7]

Choosing the sample size depends on whether it is necessary to stratify and on whether one has prior knowledge of standard deviations—perhaps from a preliminary study. If it is neither necessary nor particularly desirable to stratify, it may be less expensive to use aggregate population data. If normality is assumed, the precision-reliability-standard error equation shown below is used. $E = Zs_e$, where s_e is the standard error and

$$s_e = \begin{cases} (N^w\sigma/\sqrt{n})\sqrt{(N-n)/N}, & \text{if the aggregate population is sampled and } w = 0 \\ & \text{(if error in total is sought), 1 (if error in mean is sought)} \\ \dfrac{1}{N^w}\sqrt{\displaystyle\sum_{i=1}^{M}\left(\frac{N_i - n_i}{N_i}\right)\frac{N_i^2 s_i^2}{n_i}}, & \text{if strata are sampled} \end{cases}$$

Key:

E = allowed error or precision
Z = number of standard normal deviations corresponding to desired reliability
σ = aggregate population standard deviation

Situation: A manufacturer is installing an ABC inventory control system that will direct differentiated attention to the items in the three categories. A items, although few in number, account for the preponderance of inventory investment and will be carefully modelled. C items, which

[7] Stratified sampling goes far beyond what will be presented in this chapter. A definitive work on sampling is W. G. Cochran, *Sampling Techniques* (New York: John Wiley & Sons, 1963). Stratified sampling is the subject of Chapter 5, pp. 87–114.

are vast in number, nevertheless account for only a small portion of inventory investment and will receive minimal attention. B items fall between these extremes and will receive moderate attention. In this way control efforts can be directed to the most significant areas, instead of spreading managerial effort so thin that little real control actually results.[8]

Four preliminary samples of size 30 were taken, one from the unstratified inventory and one each from the ABC categories. The goal at this stage is to devise a way of estimating total inventory value (assuming the normal distribution) with .95 reliability and $20,000 precision. The variable cost of sampling will be the same for any item. Available data:

			←——Preliminary Results——→	
		N_i	$\bar{x}_i = \sum x/n_i$	$s_i = [\sum(x_{ik} - \bar{x}_i)^2/(n_i - 1)]^{1/2}$
Strata:	A	150	\$5,200	\$100
	B	300	\$ 600	\$ 50
	C	1,050	\$ 225	\$200
Unstratified:		$N =$ 1,500	\$ 875	\$400

Samples are to be drawn optimally from strata.

Solution: *Stratified sampling*

$$n_i = nN_is_i/\sum N_is_i$$

$$n_1 = 150(100)n/(150[100] + 300[50] + 1{,}050[200]) = .0625n$$

$$n_2 = \qquad .0625n$$

$$n_3 = \qquad .8750n$$

The precision of the total estimate is to be $20,000; therefore, since 95% reliability calls for 1.96 standard deviations,

$$20{,}000 = 1.96\sqrt{\sum\left(\frac{N_i - n_i}{N_i}\right)\frac{(N_is_i)^2}{n_i}}$$

$$= 1.96\sqrt{\frac{57{,}600{,}000{,}000}{n} - 64{,}500{,}000}$$

$$n = 341.6$$

[8] One hears about management "always putting out brush fires" rather than really planning and controlling. Often this condition of being constantly busy and making little headway may be attributed to treating everything equally instead of discriminating among tasks and dealing with important ones first. The ABC system attempts to put managers in control.

Allocation:

$$n_1 = .0625(341.6) = 21$$
$$n_2 = \qquad 21$$
$$n_3 = \qquad 299$$
$$\underline{\underline{341}}$$

Comments:

1. It would be customary to add 5% or 10% to the sample size in each stratum to be sure that the resulting standard deviations yielded at least the chosen reliability.

2. The samples might be drawn in some other way—perhaps proportionally, or by drawing, say, 100% of A and the balance in B and C. In this case and assuming optimal allocation of samples to strata, the model shown above would be resolved with N being replaced by $N - N_A = 1{,}350$ and stratum A omitted from summation.

3. Some n_i might exceed N_i. If so, use N_i and re-solve the model with the remaining categories.

4. The variance of the stratified estimate of the population mean under optimal allocation is $V(\bar{x}_{st}) = (20{,}000/1.96)^2$; however, this will undoubtedly change, since more than the optimal strata sample sizes for n_1 and n_2 have already been drawn on the preliminary sampling.

Nonstratified sampling

The precision of the total is \$20,000, and $w = 1$ in the aggregate population (nonstratified) formula:

$$20{,}000 = 1.96 \frac{(1{,}500)400}{\sqrt{n}} \sqrt{\frac{1{,}500 - n}{1{,}500}}$$

$$n = 1{,}046$$

Comments:

1. It helps to remember that 100% sampling theoretically yields 100% precision; hence any degree of precision can be achieved with any desired reliability provided the sample is large enough.

2. The stratified sample is only one-third as great as the nonstratified sample. Some such efficiency is expected if the strata are internally homogeneous. If they are not entirely so, luck of the draw might lead to unrepresentative estimates of strata standard deviations, thereby causing strata samples to exceed a nonstratified sample in size.

Perhaps the most interesting thing about the nonstratified sample is that it uses $N\sigma$, not $\sqrt{N}\sigma$. Recall the discussion of independent and perfectly correlated variables in Chapter 12. There we discussed

Independent variables: $V = \sum\sigma^2$; hence, $\sqrt{V} = \sqrt{N}\sigma$

Perfectly correlated variables: $V = (\sum\sigma)^2$; hence, $\sqrt{V} = N\sigma$

Intuitively, it seems reasonable to think about the various inventory items as going above and below some average value at random; these are the assumptions of independence. And if this reasoning has appeal, the assumption that all deviations will be above some average value—which is the assumption of perfect correlation—will be unpalatable. Intuitively, you would assume independence, seek the sum $x = x_1 + x_2 + \cdots + x_N$, and invoke the convoluted normal, $N(x{:}N\bar{x};\sqrt{N}\sigma)$. Yet such intuitions are misleading!

There is no doubt that the inventory items would actually exhibit independence; however, only one sample average and standard deviation are employed in estimating the statistics for the total population. $\bar{x}$ is being used to estimate the value of x_1 and of x_2 and of all x_i. All covariances equal one, not zero (as in independence); the correlation is perfect. Therefore, $N\sigma$ is correct.

Note how this contrasts with the situation in which yearly earnings were *assumed independent* and distributed normally using the same parameters for each year. When sampling and using the results for each and every item in the population, it is not possible to assume independence, because the sampling process simply creates perfect correlation.

Summary

The accountant who is engaged in cost analysis invariably calls upon sampling, because his models need data and probability distributions. But there is a great deal of choice about how to go about sampling, and this creates problems.

How one samples involves cost. In fact, this consideration has governed the selection of the techniques that appear in this chapter. (What would be more appropriate for a book on cost analysis?) Too often sampling is approached using the normal distribution as a proxy for other theoretically preferable distributions. Excessive sample sizes are apt to be the price of this approach. Stratified sampling can also reduce sampling costs (1) if the strata reflect internal homogeneity, and (2) provided the sample that would otherwise be drawn from the unstratified population is not extraordinary—reflecting little variance where great variance exists. And, depending on costs of distress and sampling and on the prior distribution, Bayesian sampling may further reduce sample size. Bayesian sampling, however, minimizes costs in every case, while classical sampling procedures—other than stratified sampling—do not *explicitly* recognize cost at all.

One additional side benefit of this chapter has been the insight it has provided into the relationship between Bayesian sampling and capital budgeting. One chapter, of course, cannot replace the study of good books entirely devoted to the subject. A few of these are listed below.

Suggested References

Chou, Y. *Statistical Analysis with Business and Economic Applications.* New York: Holt, Rinehart & Winston, 1969.

Clelland, R. C., deCani, J. S., and Brown, F. E. *Basic Statistics with Business Applications.* New York: John Wiley & Sons, 1973.

Cochran, W. G. *Sampling Techniques.* New York: John Wiley & Sons, 1963.

Schlaifer, R. *Introduction to Statistics for Business Decisions.* New York: McGraw-Hill Book Co., 1961.

Problems

1. *Inventory.* Consider that special type of inventory known as cash. For present purposes, cash will be restricted to checks received from customers, and there will be good and bad inventory in the sense that there are good checks as well as those distinguishable by their elasticity. Of the checks received, 95% are good. If 10 checks are in the inventory, what is the probability that at least 2 of them are bad?

2. *Defective bulbs.* It is known that five defective bulbs were produced in a lot of twenty-five. If four bulbs are chosen at random, find the probability that no more than one is defective.

3. *Dice.* A pair of fair dice is thrown. Given that the first die is a 5, what is the probability of obtaining a sum of at least 9?

4. *Machine output.* Machines A, B, and C produce, respectively, 50%, 20%, and 30% of the output of a factory. The percentages of defective output of these machines are 8%, 6%, and 10% respectively. An item is found to be defective. What is the probability that it came from machine B?

5. *Variants on style (prepared by Professor M. W. Belovicz, Wake Forest University).* A woman owns 100 pairs of gloves. Sixty are white and 40 are blue. She keeps all the right-handed gloves in one drawer and all the left-handed gloves in another drawer. Whenever she wants to wear gloves she picks one glove out of each drawer *without looking in the drawer.*

   (a) What is the probability the gloves will match?

   (b) During the last month she has worn gloves 20 times. What is the probability that they matched on exactly 10 of those days?

(c) What is the probability that they matched on 2 or fewer of those 20 days?

(d) Redo (a) through (c) above assuming that 99 pairs were white and one blue.

(e) What is wrong with this lady?

6. *Defectives, sampling without replacement.* It is known that a production process yields 5% defectives. Batches of 100 are usually produced and to test whether a given batch is acceptable, samples of 5 will be drawn without replacement. If management decides to reject any batch where the sample has 2 or more defectives, how many batches will be rejected in the long run, assuming there is no change in the percentage defective? Is this a job order or a process costing system?

7. *All is not gold that glitters (prepared by Professor M. W. Belovicz, Wake Forest University).* A coast-to-coast station-to-station call costs $1.35 during the day. A person-to-person call during the same hours costs $3.55.

(a) Is it true that you save $2.20 by calling station-to-station? Explain.

(b) If the probability of your party being available is less than 1, below what probability would you call person-to-person? Support your answer with appropriate computations.

(c) How would your answer to (b) be affected if the utility (or value) associated with a successful call was nonlinear?

8. *Inventory and Bayesian estimation.* There is a special kind of inventory known as accounts receivable in which shortages are known as bad debts. This problem studies an aspect of this type of inventory.

The management of a certain business estimates that the probability of a customer being a bandit is .1 (Note: All customers charge their purchases; none carries a gun; and this is bad, since it makes it harder to detect bandits.) An enterprising new employee who has recently completed an MBA decides to keep track of down payments. Based on his empirical research, he estimates that the probability of receiving a large down payment from a bandit is .3 and from a good customer, .5.

(a) Find the probability of a customer being a bandit given that he makes a large down payment.

(b) Find the probability of a customer being good given that he makes a large down payment.

(c) Assuming the MBA is a Bayesian, what suggestion should he make about estimating the probability of bandits? How should he present his case verbally?

9. *Chi-square testing.* The Credit and Collection Department of a retail store feels that its accounts receivable are 70% current, 25% old-but-good, and 5% old-but-doubtful. An internal auditor has been assigned the task of sampling the accounts to determine whether this statement of the distribution of accounts may be relied on. The accounts have been divided into four groups, each containing over 100,000 accounts. The auditor has taken a sample of 100 from each of the groups with the following results:

Group	Current	Old-but-Good	Old-but-Doubtful
A	75	18	7
B	67	25	8
C	60	35	5
D	73	18	9
	275	96	29

Can the stated distribution be relied on?

10. *Sample size.* A manufacturer wishes to be 90% certain that he produces fuses with no more than 5% defectives. If quality is to be checked by drawing samples of size n, and rejecting the hypothesis that the process is in control if two or more defective fuses are found, what is the size of the sample that should be drawn if defectives are now running at 3%?

11. *Voucher test.* An auditor wishes to perform a voucher test. His prior working papers indicate that the rate of error is .02, where error is defined to include (a) mistakes in invoice extensions, (b) neglect of available discounts, (c) omission of receiving reports, and (d) improper payment authorization. (Note: Errors in typing of company names, for instance, do not count as defects.)

(a) What size sample should the auditor draw, assuming that (1) he wishes 95% confidence, and (2) he has adopted the customary decision rule that no errors should be found in an acceptable sample?

(b) Assuming that he finds three errors and that he wishes to retain 95% confidence, what error rate is indicated by his results?

(c) Disregarding confidence, what error rate is indicated by his results?

12. *Computer center check.* An auditor is checking the accuracy of the punching operation in a computer center and comes across a drawer-file with 300,000 cards in it. He is told that only 1 card in 1,000 has an error punched on it. He wishes to verify the claim and is willing to risk erroneous rejection with a probability of .01. What size sample should he take? What size sample should he take if he is willing to risk erroneous agreement with a probability of .4?

13. *Small sample.* A manufacturer claims that his rope has an expected breaking strength of 9,000 pounds. To test this assertion, a sample of nine ropes was taken. The sample resulted in a mean breaking strength of 7,800 pounds and a standard deviation of 240 pounds. Can the claim be supported, and if so, at what level?

14. *Change in testing procedures.* A manufacturer supplies a retailer with a made-to-order type of cable that is to have a breaking strength of 3,000 pounds. The manufacturer customarily produces this cable with a mean of 3,200 pounds and a standard deviation of 100 pounds to be 97.5% sure of meeting the retailer's rigid standard.

Heretofore, the customer has tested lengths of cable from each lot of cable delivered. The manufacturer has recently ascertained that this procedure is to change: the customer will now average the results of four such tests. Assuming the manufacturer will change his policy (but not his confidence requirement) with any change in the customer's standards, what should his new policy be?

15. *Receivables aging verification.* Auditors verify the aging of accounts receivable whenever the receivables balance is a significant portion of balance sheet assets. The client does the aging and the auditor checks it. The partial balance method of aging is invariably followed. In this method each invoice comprising an individual account's balance is assigned to the age category to which the invoice pertains. Error occurs when an invoice is assigned to a wrong category. More generally, however, the auditor would count the number of accounts that were aged improperly without noting whether one invoice or several within a given account were incorrectly categorized. It appears to be the practice to require the client to redo the entire aging whenever some critical percentage of total accounts is in error. (It is debatable whether dollar value of the erroneous accounts should be weighed when selecting the critical number of accounts. Ten incorrect accounts with an aggregate balance of \$1,000 might or might not pose the grievous problem that three accounts with an aggregate balance of \$100,000 do. It is a question of judgment whether frequency of error or amount of dollars is more important in determining unacceptability.)

An auditor confronts a file of 200,000 accounts in a department store. He feels that a rate of one error in 1,000 accounts is acceptable and wants to calculate sample size. He wants .95 reliability and will reject the aging if he finds more than two erroneously aged accounts. How many accounts should he check (assuming, of course, that the accounts are selected randomly—with the aid of a table of random numbers).

If he finds four errors, (a) what error rate best explains the result, and (b) what error rate best explains the result keeping the .95 reliability level?

16. *Accounts receivable valuation.* An auditor wishes to estimate the value of accounts receivable in one stratum consisting of 200 accounts. He takes a preliminary sample of 30 and finds

$$\sum_{i=1}^{30} \frac{x_i}{30} = \$4{,}500; \quad \sqrt{\sum \frac{(x - 4.500)^2}{29}} = \$500$$

He wishes 95% reliability and a precision of $\pm\$100$. What should his eventual sample size be, assuming 10% additional samples will be drawn for safety? After drawing this total sample, n, he finds

$$\sum x/n = \$4{,}620; \quad [\sum(x - 4{,}620)^2/(n - 1)]^{.5} = \$400$$

What estimate should he make for the value of accounts receivable in that stratum?

17. *Book value of inventory.* (*Certified Public Accountancy Examination, November 1973*). You desire to evaluate the reasonableness of the book value of the inventory of your client, Draper, Inc. You have already satisfied yourself as to inventory quantities. During the examination of the pricing and extension of the inventory, the following data were gathered, using appropriate unrestricted random sampling with replacement procedures:

Total items in the inventory (N):	12,700
Total items in the sample (n):	400
Total audited value of items in the sample:	\$38,400
$\sum_{j=1}^{400} (x_j - \bar{x})^2$	312,816

Formula for estimated population standard deviation:

$$\sqrt{\frac{\sum_{j=1}^{j=n} (x_j - \bar{x})^2}{n-1}}$$

Formula for estimated standard error of the mean:

$$SE = \frac{S_{X_j}}{\sqrt{n}}$$

Confidence level coefficient of the standard error of the mean at a 95% confidence (reliability) level: ± 1.96

Required:

(a) Based on the sample results, what is the estimate of the total value of the inventory? Show computations in good form where appropriate.

(b) What statistical conclusion can be reached regarding the estimated total inventory value calculated in (a) above at the confidence level of 95%? Present computations in good form where appropriate.

(c) Independent of your answers to (a) and (b), assume that the book value of Draper's inventory is \$1,700,000, and that, based on the sample results, the estimated total value of the inventory is \$1,690,000. The auditor desires a confidence (reliability) level of 95%. Discuss the audit and statistical considerations the auditor must evaluate before deciding whether the sampling results support acceptance of the book value as a fair presentation of Draper's inventory.

18. *Inventory supply, testing distribution parameters, beta error.* In your audit of a baking company, you find that the company models its production of pies—which have a one-day shelf life before being declared stale—as follows:

$$E[K(S)] = C_h \int_0^S (S - D)f(D)\, dD + C_s \int_S^\infty (D - S)f(D)\, dD + C_0$$

$$\frac{dE[K(S)]}{dS} = C_h \int_0^S f(D)\, dD - C_s \int_S^\infty f(D)\, dD = 0$$

$$C_h \int_0^S f(D)\, dD - C_s\left[1 - \int_0^S f(D)\, dD\right] = 0$$

$$\int_0^S f(D)\, dD = \frac{C_s}{C_s + C_h}$$

The company has determined that the distribution of demand is normal with mean 1,000 pies and standard deviation of 200 pies; consequently,

$$f(D) = \frac{e^{-\frac{1}{2}\left(\frac{D - 1{,}000}{200}\right)^2}}{200\sqrt{2\pi}}$$

Having satisfied yourself with the model setup and the use of Leibnitz' Rule in its solution, you review costs and prices and find that selling price is \$2.25 and production cost is \$.75 per pie. You also find that the bakers make 1,200 such pies each day, and that the company policy calls for discarding unsold pies, so as to protect its reputation for quality.

Required:

(a) The company controller says, "No CPA firm I ever heard of and no AICPA auditing standard or procedure I've seen calls for the external auditor to do the checking you propose. How do you justify it? I admit I think it's a waste of good money." Respond.

(b) Are the bakers producing the optimal number of pies?

(c) How would you test the parameters of the normal distribution? You may assume (1) satisfaction with 10% precision and 95% reliability, and (2) that a preliminary sample of 30 days showed a mean of 1,100 pies and a standard deviation of 300.

(d) Given that the final sample in (c) verified $N(1{,}100;\ 300)$, what beta error is implicit if the true mean shifts to 1,500? Does this beta error seem acceptable?

19. *Beta error.* An illustrious business school wishes to graduate students who are no more than 5% defective, quantitatively speaking. The dean checks quality by occasionally drawing a sample of 20. If 2 or fewer defectives are found, he decides that affairs are progressing satisfactorily; otherwise, there is a curriculum review. If defects are running at the rate of 20%, what is the probability that the dean will fail to detect the catastrophe? You may assume a large population.

20. *The errant records (prepared by Professor M. W. Belovicz, Wake Forest University).* The Middleville Police Department receives about 6,000 calls each month. Each one is recorded and classified by the "beat"—a geographical area under the responsibility of one officer. There are 60 beats. Lieutenant Smith is in charge of 6 beats, which have received an average of 100 calls per month per beat. Today he received a report from the Research Department that listed 625 calls for last month. A detailed analysis indicated that of those 625 calls, 35 were misclassified, 30 were from a three-block area in another part of the city and 5 seemed to be from other areas in the city. In addition, 6 calls his men answered were not listed. He called the Planning Department and was told that the errors were either due to keypunching (they have a card system) or the computer program. The man in charge of Keypunching blamed the program. The Data Processing Department (responsible for programming) blamed Keypunching.

Required:

Resolve the argument as best you can, indicating the direction the investigation should take in order to rectify the problem. (Hint: Relevant concepts and distributions are hypothesis testing, Type I error, Type II error, and binomial.)

21. *Truth or consequences (prepared by Professor M. W. Belovicz, Wake Forest University).* This year an auditing procedure for a certain company randomly selects five out of twenty junior accountants. For each person chosen, eight of his entries are selected at random for intense scrutiny. Unknown to the auditors or the company, Mr. Spencer, one of the twenty, has been embezzling funds in collaboration with Mr. Kash in the financial office. One percent of Mr. Spencer's entries have been used in the embezzlement. Since he was not very careful in his coverup, he is almost certain to be detected if any of these entries is selected for study.

(a) Spencer is one of the five people chosen for study, what is the probability that his embezzlement will be detected?

(b) What is the probability that it will not be detected?

(c) Redo (a) assuming you do not know whether Spencer was chosen.

(d) Redo (b) assuming you do not know whether Spencer was chosen.

22. *Normal mean and variance.* Use expectation definitions—and not the S transform—to obtain the mean and variance of the normal probability distribution.

Poisson mean and variance. Use expectation definitions—and not Z transforms—to obtain the mean and variance of the Poisson probability distribution.

24. *Recursion and probability distributions.* Recursion is a mathematical procedure that develops the present reading in terms of the preceding reading. In probability distributions this would appear $P(x) = \alpha P(x - 1)$, and the problem is to calculate α. The method of finding α is straightforward: find expressions for $P(x)$ and $P(x - 1)$ and then divide the first by the second. Thus, $P(x)/P(x - 1) = \alpha$. Use recursion to develop (a) binomial and (b) Poisson probabilities.

25. *Food for cars (prepared by Professor M. W. Belovicz, Wake Forest University).* The Super Luxury Deluxe (SLD) car is advertised as being a high gas mileage car. An independent test was made with five production line SLDs on a drive from Atlanta to Washington. The five SLDs were driven by three nonprofessional drivers and two professional drivers at speeds not exceeding the posted limits. Test results were as follows:

Driver	MPG
Professional Driver #1	20.3
Professional Driver #2	16.4
Nonprofessional Driver #1	20.2
Nonprofessional Driver #2	16.3
Nonprofessional Driver #3	19.7

Average test results reveal 18.8 mpg.

(a) An estimate of the standard deviation of mileage was made by dividing the range of MPG by 4. What is that estimate? Is that a reasonable procedure? Justify your answer.

(b) Based upon the estimate in (a) above, determine a 90% confidence interval for mileage for all test drivers. A 95% interval for all drivers. A 90% interval for nonprofessional drivers.

(c) Suppose you had estimated the standard deviation of the mileage by dividing by 6. What would the estimate be? Is that a better, equally good, or worse procedure than the one used in (a) above? Why?

(d) Redo question (b) using your estimate from question (c).

(e) Redo question (b) assuming the estimate by the standard deviation from (a) was acceptable, but that there were 8 professional and 12 nonprofessional drivers. Assume the same averages as for the original sample.

26. *Statistical quality control techniques and budgeting.* A company wishes to establish upper and lower control limits for its overhead budget. In this way management hopes that the number of needless investigations into insignificant variations from budget will be curtailed. The following costs have been incurred in the past when the budget has been set at the pertinent production level:

$102,000
96,000
108,400
106,700
99,400
100,000
98,000
94,000
109,200
101,800

Management believes a 90% acceptance region should be established. If this is done, 5%, on average, of the variances in either direction will be needlessly investigated.

Required:

(a) What control limits should be set if a normal distribution is assumed?

(b) Management would like to know the magnitude of the β error should the population mean shift to $106,000.

27. *Quality control (prepared by Professor M. W. Belovicz, Wake Forest University).* No-Defect Manufacturing Co. manufactures widgets in lots of 10. For quality control they select a random sample of 5. After testing, they accept the lot if one or no defects are found in the samples.

(a) Construct a table computing the probability of acceptance assuming alternate levels of actual quality (i.e., assume zero defective, one defective, etc.), when the decision rule is to accept when X (defects in sample) ≤ 1.

(b) What is the probability of a Type 1 error if the acceptable quality level is 20% defective?

(c) If the acceptable quality level is 40%, what is the probability of a Type II error?

28. *Control charts for crime statistics—a quality control extension (prepared by Professor M. W. Belovicz, Wake Forest University).* The chief of Police of Middleville is considering several new crime reduction proposals. A very promising one deals with burglaries. The staff is enthusiastic. They are all ready to accept this proposal when a lieutenant asks the impertinent question "How will we know whether or not it worked?" The staff has the following data available. The program is implemented on May 1.

Month	Burglaries	Month	Burglaries
1 (Jan. 1974)	118	15	150
2	103	16	100
3	110	17	120
4	101	18	124
5	115	19	120
6	112	20	121
7	113	21	125
8	114	22	169
9	160	23	155
10	145	24	150
11	152	25 (Jan. 1976)	118
12	140	26	76
13 (Jan. 1975)	165	27	101
14	142	28	130

(a) Determine the mean and standard deviation. Plot the data with one and two standard deviation control limits.

(b) Is it reasonable to analyze data of this type as in question (a)? Why?

(c) In November 1976 the staff is given the following data:

Month	Burglaries
May	120
June	130
July	135
August	100
September	125
October	130

What conclusions would you draw regarding the program? Why? Show any supporting computations.

(d) In November 1976 there are 160 burglaries. What does this mean? Why?

29. *Control charting for process costing.* An accountant is interested in establishing normal and abnormal loss percentages to facilitate the writing of process cost journal entries. After ascertaining that nothing unusual happended in the last 10 runs, he obtained the data shown below. X stands for the number of defective (lost) units.

Run Size	x	x^2
250	30	900
250	23	529
⋮	⋮	⋮
250	18	324
2,500	220	5,280

Required:

(a) Prepare a percentage defective control chart assuming reliability of 68% is desired and precision $\pm 0.5\%$. Determine sample size.

(b) However you prepared your answer to (a) (that is, using a proper probability distribution or a normal approximation), develop the other approach and comment on the differences.

30. *Bayesian revision of priors, comparision of hypergeometric and binomial results.* A business has a high incidence of overdue accounts because the economy is in a recession. Management feels that good public relations require understanding and accepting the circumstances. Nevertheless, it samples the accounts regularly to see whether conditions are improving or deteriorating. Significant improvement would be a signal favoring certain plans, while significant deterioration might suggest tightening of credit, intensified collection efforts, and certain other retrenchment strategies.

Last week the probabilities of an account being overdue, p_i, and the probabilities of that incidence of "overdueness", $P(p_i)$, were as follows:

p_i	.8	.85	.90	.95
$P(p_i)$	.30	.35	.25	.10

This week 30 accounts were drawn without replacement and 25 were found to be overdue.

Find the posterior probabilities using the hypergeometric distribution (you will need a computer program). Then assume the sample was drawn with replacement and determine what the binomial distribution would show. Compare the two results. Should the retrenchment plan go into effect?

31. *Derivation of posterior.* Assuming that $f(\mu, \bar{x})$ and $h(\bar{x})$ are at hand, derive $h(\mu|\bar{x})$.

32. *Derivation of the preposterior distribution.* Marginal distributions may be obtained by summing joint distributions over the other variable or variables. Derive the preposterior distribution from $h(\mu_1) = \int_{-\infty}^{\infty} f(\mu, \mu_1)\, d\mu$, assuming the joint distribution is available.

33. *Proof of discounted EVPI formula.* In the example having to do with hours saved by automating an operation, continuous discounting was introduced to calculate expected value of perfect information. Derive the formula for EVPI and discuss other applications of the formula.

34. *Proofs of EVSI and optimal sample size given quadratic loss function.* In the example that dealt with the accounts receivable balance, EVSI and optimal sample size were calculated for the given data. Develop general formulas assuming a quadratic loss function.

35. *Bayesian analysis and births.* The history of arrivals in a queuing system suggests that 70% of the time they are Poisson at a mean rate of four per hour, while 30% of the time they are Poisson at a mean rate of seven per hour. A sample is drawn that shows five arrivals in the hour. Management wishes to determine an average arrival rate for use in its queuing formulas.

36. *Capital budgeting and Bayesian analysis.* An investment requiring \$100,000 promises to save \$12 per hour in labor costs. The average number of hours saved, μ, will be normally distributed with $P(8{,}710 < \mu < 15{,}290) = .90$. A survey of six other companies indicates that the standard deviation is 1,800 hours. The required rate of return (discount rate) is 15% and there are 2,000 working hours in a year. Determine the opportunity loss from not investing and the expected value of sample information.

37. *Stratified sampling.* A company operates a sales office six days a week. Sales for Friday and Saturday are three times as great as for the other days. Sales average \$25 on Friday and Saturday and \$18 on the other days with standard deviations of \$7.50 and \$5.75 respectively. Overall, sales number 10,000 and average \$20 with a standard deviation of \$6. The management wishes to determine the sample size necessary to determine average invoice value with a precision of $\pm$\$1.68 and 95% reliability. Samples will be drawn without replacement. What sampling plan should be adopted?

38. *Estimating accounts receivable via stratified sampling.* A manufacturer wants to estimate the amount of his accounts receivable. The data below are available; the probability distribution has been prepared from the historical split of number of accounts among the dollar strata (N_i/N).

Stratum	Dollar Range	N_i/N	Variance of \$ in Preliminary Sample
1	0–200	.2	400
2	200–400	.4	10,000
3	400–600	.3	25,600
4	>600	.1	78,400

The manufacturer wants to estimate to within \$300,000 of the amount of accounts receivable with .95 reliability. The total population consists of 50,000 accounts. What size sample should be taken and how should it be drawn? What estimate of the balance would be made if the additional sampling does not change variance estimates on hand?

39. *Producer and consumer risks, selection of sample size, and critical number of defectives.* Production quality control has its own jargon, which includes the following definitions:

AQL = acceptable quality level that indicates the performance of the production process; it is the average number of defective units remaining after inspection divided by lot size.
α = producer's risk of a Type I error; it is the probability of rejecting lots of AQL.
LTPD = lot tolerance percent defective; it is a very poor quality level.
β = consumer's risk of a Type II error; it is the probability of accepting lots from a LTPD level.
D = number of defective units
C = critical number of defective units; reject lots with $D > C$.
n = sample size

The scheme is to have management express its desires in terms of α and β risks (*note how a concept of service is being substituted for dollar outlays*—this idea will be developed in Chapter 14) and then to work out the C and n values that correspond. Assuming a healthy sample size, the Poisson curve comes into play. The probability of accepting a lot of AQL is

$$P(D \leq C|\text{AQL}) = \sum_{D=0}^{C} [n(\text{AQL})]^D e^{-n(\text{AQL})}/D! = 1 - \alpha$$

Similarly, the probability of accepting an LTPD lot is

$$P(D \leq C|\text{LTPD}) = \sum_{D=0}^{C} [n(\text{LTPD})]^D e^{-n(\text{LTPD})}/D! = \beta$$

Computational difficulties arise, however, because the Poisson uses discrete values of n and D (hence, C) and these may not exactly correspond to the selected α and β probabilities. Therefore, management will undoubtedly have to decide how much deviation in its specifications is acceptable. In the meantime, it is necessary to home in on values for n and C. This is not difficult if an extensive Poisson table is at hand, or if the accountant has ready access to a computer. These options failing, he may resort to recognizing the normal approximation to the binomial (since the basic split is between good and bad) and using the normal transformation $Z = (C - np)/\sqrt{npq}$, where p is first AQL and then LTPD. This results in two equations,

$$Z_{1-\alpha} = \frac{C - n(\text{AQL})}{\sqrt{\text{AQL}(1 - \text{AQL})n}} \quad \text{and} \quad Z_\beta = \frac{C - n(\text{LTPD})}{\sqrt{\text{LTPD}(1 - \text{LTPD})n}},$$

which are in the two unknowns, C and n. Letting $A = AQL$, $\bar{A} = 1 - AQL$, $L = LTPD$, and $\bar{L} = 1 - LTPD$ and solving simultaneously leads to

$$\hat{n} = [(Z_\beta(L\bar{L})^{.5} - Z_{1-\alpha}(A\bar{A})^{.5})/(A - L)]^2$$

$$\hat{C} = Z_{1-\alpha}[A\bar{A}\hat{n}]^{.5} + A\hat{n}$$

The rounded (up and down) values of $\hat{n}$ and $\hat{C}$ may then be inserted in the Poisson formulas to determine the values for α and β from which management should choose.

Required:

(a) Given that management has preliminarily selected AQL = .02, LTPD = .06, $\alpha = .05$, and $\beta = .10$, calculate the ultimate α and β values.

(b) Derive the formulas for $\hat{n}$ and $\hat{C}$.

(c) Discuss the substitution of service level quality measures for dollar costs.

40. *Simulation of an office queue.* One popular use of sampling is to simulate experience by drawing random numbers, converting these to probabilities and outcomes, and arriving at expectations. In the following problem the given random numbers are taken from a table of random normal numbers. These pertain to the normal distribution with $\mu = 0$ and $\sigma = 1$ and are the *number* of standard deviations that should be multiplied by the *amount* of a standard deviation and either added or subtracted to the mean as indicated by the sign in the given values. In this way demand and production for each hour may be estimated and used (a) to determine excess of demand over production given different staff sizes, and (b) to provide for the excess either by letting it accumulate until a day when production exceeds demand, or by paying overtime to eliminate the excess on the day it occurs.

A company has a "demand" (normally distributed) of 50 letters per hour with a standard deviation of 10 letters per hour. It has also been estimated that a secretary can normally type 10 letters per hour with a standard deviation of 2 letters per hour. Secretaries have regular-time pay of $105 for a 35-hour week and overtime pay at time-and-a-half. Delay in typing letters is considered to cost the company $1 per letter per day. Space restrictions do not permit the hiring of more than six secretaries. In any event, the week must end with no work hanging over to the following Monday.

How many secretaries should be in the pool? For the sake of simplicity, you may simulate five days' experience as representative of a typical week. Use the random normal numbers given below.

"Demand"	"Supply"
−.508	− .513
−.992	−1.055
.969	− .488
.983	1.556
2.731	.621

Note:

Assume the results for the first hour each day are repeated for the remaining hours of that day. (This is the assumption of perfect correlation.)

41. *Bayesian control of golf ball production.* In golf ball manufacturing grade is typically designated by dropping balls from a tube suspended 20 feet above a tilted steel plate. The bounce of the balls determines the bins in which they fall—the lower the height of the bin, the lower the grade.

The Witless Company produces two grades of ball: Out of Sight and Stop on a Dime. 5,000 balls are produced each day—unless the production process is being monitored, in which case output is reduced by 10%. Out of Sight sells to professionals for \$.75 each and retails to golfers for \$1.50, while Stop on a Dime sells to professionals for \$.50 each and retails for \$1.20. The cost per ball is the same regardless of grade. Witless sells to professionals only.

The process has three performance levels, which are believed to have the prior probabilities shown below.

Level	Prior	Distribution
Excellent	.6	(.7, .3)
Mediocre	.1	(.4, .6)
Calamitous	.3	(.3, .7)

The fractions shown under "Distribution" reveal the proportions of output for each grade.

The statistician is paid a salary of \$30,000 a year for an expected 2,000 hours of service. To draw a ball, test it, record results, and so forth takes five minutes per ball on average.

Required:

(a) Manually determine dollar results if a sample of five is drawn and it is decided to check and monitor the whole process if two or more SODs are found.

(b) Calculate the posteriors if three SODs are found in (a).

(c) Use a computer program to calculate the best sampling plan.

Inventory Theory and Cost Control

14

Overview

Inventories are not just items being manufactured or awaiting sale; rather, they are stockpiles—of anything. Coins in one's pocket, students in a classroom, cash in the bank, accounts receivable, number of typewriters in an office, number of company cars, time available, everything you see—all may be conceived of as inventories. Inventory models for items manufactured or awaiting sale should be studied as prototypes of many other kinds of inventories that may not even be generally recognized as such.

Because inventory is so broad a subject, there is an immense number of models that could be examined. Indeed, we have already discussed several inventory models in earlier chapters. The length of a chapter necessarily restricts the scope of coverage, and hence we confront the question "Which inventory models should be selected?" The models in this chapter have been chosen for one or more of the following reasons:

1. The model is in widespread use, although its popularity seems undeserved.
2. The model deals with a realistic situation frequently encountered.
3. The model emphasizes a decision based on nondollar measures.
4. The model advances study of applied mathematics and, therefore helps to develop a mental framework for applying these tools in the analysis of other phenomena.

In the process of discussing inventory costs, we shall obtain further insights into incremental costs.

Economic Order Quantity Models and a Few Caveats

In 1915 F. W. Harris developed what came to be known variously as the "Economic Order Quantity (EOQ)" model or "*The* Inventory Model."[1] EOQ is the world's most popular inventory model and the great majority of institutions practicing "scientific inventory management" employ it in some form. The model is associated with two graphs:

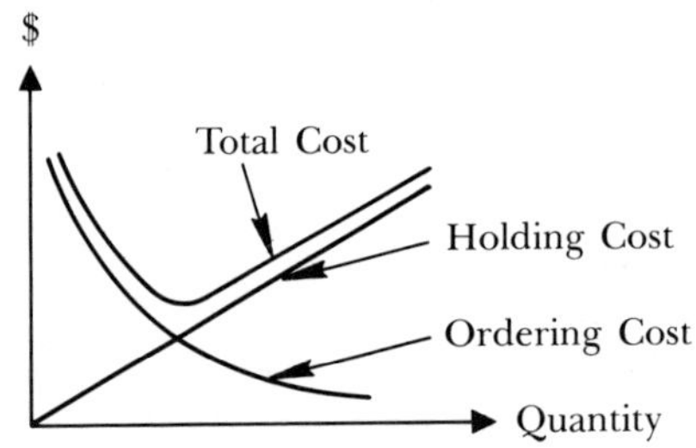

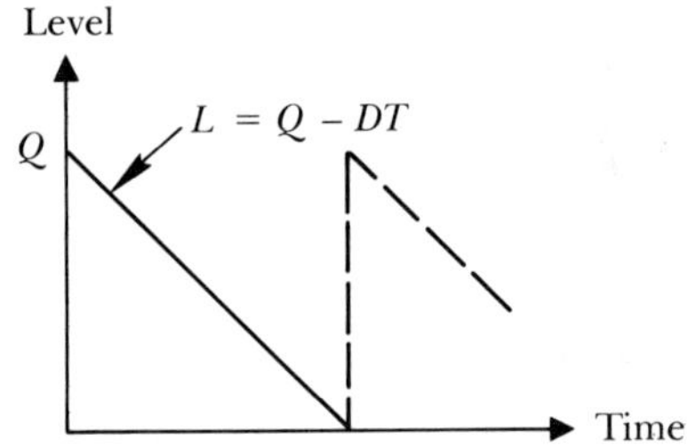

Key for all EOQ models:

- K = cost, say, per day
- L = inventory level in units
- Q = quantity at the start of a cycle; a reading of L
- D = units demanded per day
- P = units produced per day
- T = time period variable, here, days
- t = number of days in an inventory cycle; a reading of T
- C_o = cost of placing an order
- C_h = cost of holding a unit for a day
- C_s = cost of being short per unit per day
- C_u = purchase price per unit

Total cost per day = ordering cost per day + holding cost per day
The model is[2] $K = (C_o/t) + (C_hQ/2)$
However, since $Q = Dt$ when $L = 0$, the model becomes

$$K = (C_oD/Q) + (C_hQ/2)$$

$$\frac{dK}{dQ} = -\frac{C_oD}{Q^2} + \frac{C_h}{2} = 0$$

[1] F. W. Harris, *Operations and Cost*, Factory Management Series, (Chicago: A. W. Shaw Co., 1915).

[2] It would not be wrong—although it would be unnecessary, and therefore it is not done in practice—to include purchased cost of inventory per day. In optimizing the function, this term would disappear because it is a constant (that is, $QC_u/t = QC_u(D/Q) = C_uD$).

The best quantity to order is then $\hat{Q}$:

$$\hat{Q} = \sqrt{2C_oD/C_h}, \quad \text{which is a minimum because } d^2K/dQ^2 = 2C_oDQ^{-3}, \text{ which is positive}$$

A *dimensional analysis* establishes the agreement among the terms of the model:

$$K = (C_o/t) + (C_hQ/2) \text{ (The 2 is considered “dimensionless.”)}$$

$$K = \$/\text{day}$$

$$C_o/t = \$/\text{day}$$

$$C_hQ/2 = (\$/\text{unit/day}) \text{ units} = [\$/(\text{unit(day)})] \text{ units} = \$/\text{day}, \text{ where the dimensions of } C_h \text{ have been rewritten}$$

$$(\$/\text{unit})/\text{day} = (\$/\text{unit})x(1/\text{day}) = \$/[\text{unit (day)}]$$

Exhibit 1 shows other models that are related to EOQ. These introduce, among them, the concepts of shortage and delayed replenishment.

Exhibit 1

Shortage model:

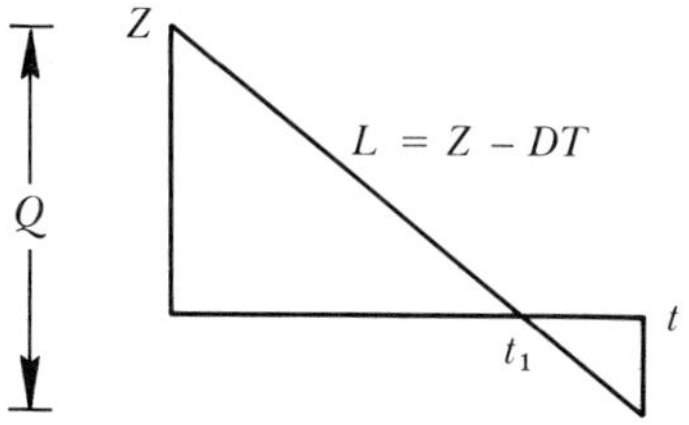

$$K = \frac{C_o}{t} + \frac{C_hZ}{2}\left(\frac{t_1}{t}\right) + \frac{C_s(Q-Z)}{2}\left(\frac{t-t_1}{t}\right)$$

$$\hat{Q} = \left[\frac{2C_oD}{C_h}\left(\frac{C_h + C_s}{C_h}\right)\right]^{1/2}$$

Delayed replenishment:

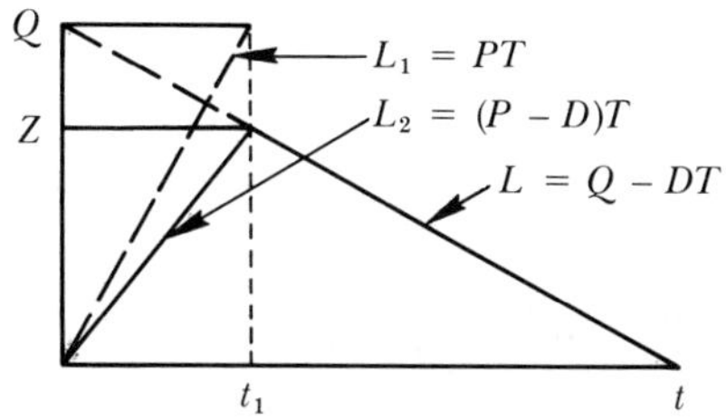

$$K = \frac{C_o}{t} + \frac{C_hZ}{2}$$

$$\hat{Q} = \left[\frac{2C_oD}{C_h}\left(\frac{P}{P-D}\right)\right]^{1/2}$$

Combination of delayed and shortage:

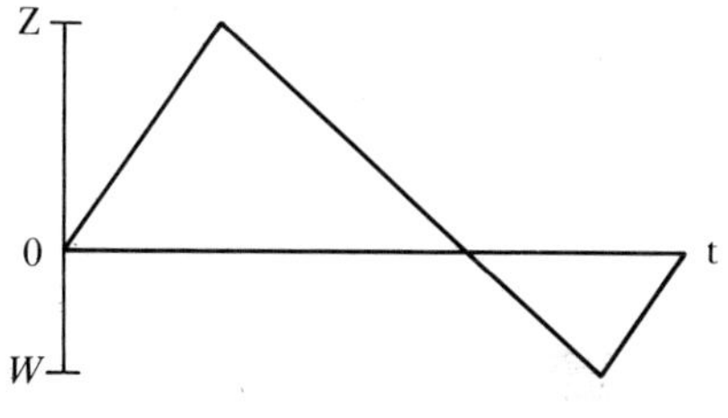

$$K = \frac{C_o}{t} + \frac{C_hZ^2P}{2Q(P-D)} + \frac{C_s(QP - ZP - DQ)^2}{2QP(P-D)}$$

$$\hat{Q} = \left[\frac{2C_oDP(C_h + C_s)}{C_sC_h(P-D)}\right]^{1/2}$$

Exhibit 1 ***(cont.)***

Comments:

1. When shortage occurs, partial derivatives are needed to determine $\hat{Q}$, the economic order quantity.

2. In each of these models it is helpful to use the laws of similar triangles to reduce the number of variables in the model via substitution. Using the shortage model as an illustration:

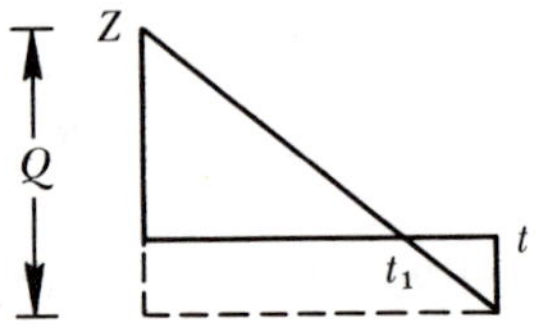

$$\frac{Z}{Q} = \frac{t_1}{t} \quad \text{and} \quad \frac{Q-Z}{Q} = \frac{t-t_1}{t}$$

The model becomes

$$K = \frac{C_o}{t} + \frac{C_h Z}{2}\left(\frac{Z}{Q}\right) + \frac{C_s(Q-Z)}{2}\left(\frac{Q-Z}{Q}\right)$$

3. In each of the models the cycle lasts t days and demand is D units per day; hence $t = Q/D$.

The basic EOQ model has three inherent drawbacks.

1. It assumes demand is a constant D units per time period.
2. It assumes instantaneous replenishment when supply is exhausted.
3. It assumes the cost of each unit short is infinity.

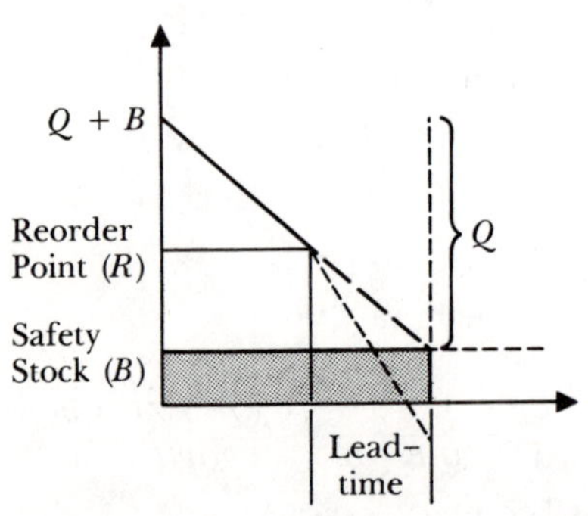

Reorder Point = inventory level at which a replenishment order is placed.

Leadtime = time between placing and receiving a replenishment order.

Safety Stock = units of inventory held as protection against an increase in the demand rate. Also referred to as "buffer stock."

Figure 1

Despite the fact that these assumptions are largely untenable (demand usually fluctuates, replenishment takes time, and shortage is rarely disastrous), EOQ has not been discarded. Instead, its deficiences have been remedied (to some degree) by the curious inconsistency of assuming demand is both constant *and* varying in the same model. This leads to Figure 1, which introduces some useful ideas and terminology.

Figure 1 contains definitions of "reorder point," "leadtime," and "safety (buffer) stock" and shows pictorially how these are related. Let R, L, and B stand for reorder point, leadtime, and buffer stock respectively. Then

$R = \bar{D}\bar{L} + B$ The reorder point equals expected leadtime demand plus the buffer stock.

$B = (\bar{D} + b\sigma_D)L_m$ Buffer stock equals the average demand rate plus b standard deviations of that rate, all times the maximum leadtime length. (Some systems employ average leadtime instead of maximum leadtime. Still other systems employ maximum demand and maximum leadtime.) If D is assumed normally distributed and if b is 1.645, there is only a .05 probability that the assumed demand rate will be exceeded.

Note that demand is treated as a constant prior to the reorder point and as a random variable thereafter. If things go well, demand will be constant (customarily, $D = \bar{D}$) and the safety stock will not be needed. On the other hand, if demand varies, the cycle will not be exactly t time periods and the system will not begin each cycle with $Q + B$ units. If demand varies, Q will not equal Dt.

Granted that a model is an abstraction of reality, nevertheless, attempting to rescue EOQ in this manner seems highly inappropriate. If demand is a random variable—as it so often is—then it should be treated as such throughout, using a suitable probabilistic model. Again, carrying buffer stock involves holding and shortage costs and should be analyzed using what is known as a "newsboy" model or one of the models in the newsboy family. What is implicit in all the previously given formulas for B is that "service level" only should govern the decision.

What is "service level"? There are several definitions but in an inventory system they essentially amount to allowed frequency of stockouts or quantity of shortage. "In any given inventory cycle, we should have no more than a 5%frequency of shortage" would be an example of a service level policy. *Implicit* in this policy is recognition of competition, efficiency, courtesy, *and* dollar effectiveness. Choosing a policy based on service level analysis is akin to using utility theory concepts—with the additional advantage that service level is more practically measured. If the decisionmaker is astute, service level is a superior approach to one that just emphasizes dollars. It minimizes the "tyranny of analytical detail" whereby a decisionmaker must be courageous to set aside a finely detailed dollar cost analysis in favor of his intuitive feelings. On the other hand, if reliable cost estimates are available, it seems wise to reflect them along with the service analysis.

This is a big "if," especially where ordering costs are concerned.

Inventory Costs

As a guiding rule, incremental costs are needed in inventory modelling. If a cost does not change because of the decision at hand, it is of no interest as far as the model is concerned. The converse, however, is not always true; an incremental cost may not be properly includable in the model, as we shall see. Let us first generally review the ideas behind C_o, C_h, and C_s.

C_o: order or setup costs. If the inventory item concerned is being purchased, the costs of placing and receiving an order are involved. If the inventory item is being manufactured, the costs of preparing the machinery are involved. In either case, the cost is fixed for each batch, and cost control lies in deciding how large each batch should be and, consequently, how often the order costs should be incurred. Order costs include clerical expenses for placing and handling the order, receiving, checking quality, and storing it. Setup costs include payments to the employees for preparing the machines, costs associated with machine downtime (such as lost production), costs of spoilage attendant to checking machine settings, and costs of takedown and cleanup.

C_h: holding (carrying) costs. Holding costs, or "carrying costs" as they are often called, include costs associated with deterioration, obsolescence, storage, handling, interest, insurance, and taxes. What it costs to store inventory, for example, may well be what the space could be rented for to an outside party. The interest charge, for another example, equals the earnings that could have been generated by investing an equal amount of funds at the discounting rate used by the company.

C_s: shortage (stockout) costs. Shortage or "stockout" costs are those costs associated with failing to meet demand. Such failure may occur from either (1) the consumer's viewpoint, when a product cannot be delivered or can be delivered only after a delay; or (2) the producer's viewpoint, when machine or plant shutdown occurs because of lack of materials. Shortage costs also include the costs of any preventive measures, such as the cost of carrying safety stocks. Sometimes shortage cost amounts to the forgone profits on units demanded but not available; however, if a customer harbors bad feelings because of a stockout, he may not only sever relations for all future time but also spread the contagion of his discontent to other potential customers. Then accurately measuring shortage cost becomes truly arduous.

Let us examine the complications that arise in measuring one of these cost parameters so that we may appreciate the difficulty of the task in measuring all of them. Cost parameters for inventory models are often assumed by theorists to be available as if by magic; no assumption in modelling could be more wrong. Sophisticated models with erroneous cost parameters are apt to be worthless—if not worse! No amount of elaborate manipulation will in any way alter this fact.

Focus on the numerator of $\hat{Q}$ in the basic EOQ model and think what the magnitude of C_o is under the operating conditions that pertain probably 90% of the time when inventory is purchased. The secretary in the purchasing department types an order, which is then mailed to the regular supplier. In time he fills the order and sends it to his customer's plant, where it is received by a warehouseman. The secretary and the warehouseman get paid salaries whether this order exists or not; the incremental outlay considered in C_o amounts to the cost of the piece of paper on which the order was typed, the envelope, and the stamp—a grand total of perhaps \$.20. To all intents and purposes, this is zero in relation to the kind of money ordinarily assumed for C_o (the range appears to be about $\$20 \leq C_o \leq \$500$). In essence, then, both C_o and $\hat{Q}$ are zero and the EOQ model doesn't apply for the purchasing situation.

"But surely there must be times when C_o becomes significant," someone says. This is so if a search for a supplier must be conducted. However, where the regular supplier is involved, the answer is simply "None that could not be considered either debatable or bizarre." It would be bizarre if the supplier charged a set amount in addition to the cost of the item ordered—a set fee for the intrusion on his time and facilities, as it were. It would be debatable to add to order cost the freight paid to get the order from the supplier's plant to the receiving dock. One view of the freight charge is that it makes the goods available for sale, which is, after all, what the paper, envelope, and stamp helped to achieve. Another view is that the freight charge is the addition to product cost (C_u) that achieves position utility. Thus a product that is owned but which resides in the supplier's plant has little utility from a sales perspective. It is not until it is placed on the receiving dock that the product attains its full utility. The freight bill is as integral a part of the product as the materials from which it is made.

Let us look at one of the more usual situations that might tempt one to think C_o had a significant value.

Suppose a company was considering paying a secretary to come in after regular hours to type a particular order. Shouldn't the overtime pay be added to C_o? It seems to be an incremental cost and it is—but of which order? The present order might have been placed earlier—in regular time—had some preceding order not been prepared when it was, thereby causing the present order to be delayed. And what caused the preceding order to be placed when it was? There are two possibilities:

1. The order before the preceding one caused its delay.

2. The need for the preceding order suddenly arose when the secretary was free. Either way one thing is apparent: the incremental cost is not solely attributable to the present order but is rather the result of two or more orders.

Suppose, instead, that overtime is scheduled in lieu of delaying other work (orders or whatever) the next day. This is again an incremental cost, and again we must ask which order should be charged. One view is that the present order should be charged for the delay it causes, and that the opportunity cost of delay is either the replacement cost of the scarce resource (secretarial time) or the profit forgone because of an irreplaceable resource. Another view is that the ensuing order compels the present haste. Once more we see the jointness of orders at work.

This jointness suggests that several items share a common order cost. In the simplest case, where the items can be ordered simultaneously from one supplier, the EOQ model becomes

$$K = \frac{C_o}{t} + \sum_i \frac{C_{hi} D_i t}{2}$$

Key:

$t =$ the optimal cycle length (found by $dK/dt = 0$)
$D_i t = Q_i$, the optimal quantity of the ith item

By probing a little deeper, we shall come to question even this aggregated formulation for the purchasing situation.

Let us escalate our discussion of jointness to the level where a new secretary is hired to provide for many future orders. Should these future items share the added salary as a major component of C_o? Two approaches to this question seem relevant. The first observes the direct costing argument: when a company decides to be in business, certain costs result from that decision and become costs of the period (year, usually) rather than costs of the product. Thus deciding to do business implies the existence of a Purchasing Department and the salaries of its personnel.

The second approach makes the analyst confront a fascinating conflict of two theories: the pooling concept and the opportunity costing concept. One important concern of the pooling concept of capital budgeting is: Given a time horizon during which (1) many projects and activities share common facilities, and (2) the amount of cheap money (one example, bonds) depends on the amount of expensive money (one example, preferred stock) in the capital structure and vice versa, one project should not be given preferential treatment merely because it arises at a time when it can be financed with cheap money. Pooling states that timing should not result in preferential treatment; all proposals of equal risk should face the same discounting rate. The opportunity costing concept, however, calls for explicit recognition of alternatives as they exist at the time of decision. In short, pooling eliminates timing advantages, while opportunity costing recognizes them.

How do these conflicting concepts relate to order costs? Under pooling the question arises "Why should the present order (or the next group of orders) be penalized for occurring when it did instead of earlier when regular facilities could provide for it?" This is again the jointness issue—all orders are responsible for the overtime (or for the hiring of the new secretary).

Under opportunity costing the question becomes "What costs would be incurred if the order (or the next group of orders) were placed at this time and what costs could be avoided if it were not?" Not only the cash outlays but also costs of delay would be considered.

Which theory prevails? Jointness exists no matter how one tries to separate actions. Products share common facilities, time, reputation, resources in general. If A is ordered, B is delayed—be it ever so little—and if B is delayed, this affects C. If C cannot be delivered promptly, then reputation declines and A and B suffer; conversely, if C is well received, this enhances the market for A and B. Though not thoroughly incapacitating, jointness is a stumbling block for opportunity costing and the reason for the existence of pooling. It is pooling that should prevail.

Back in 1915 the model might have made sense from a parameter standpoint. Possibly then the secretary was paid on a piecework basis. If so, every time the person typed, the wage would have been like the order form, envelope, and stamp from a cost perspective. The difference between piecework pay and overtime pay has to do with the regular employment of the secretary's time. They appear similar only at first glance. When do you think secretaries (and warehousemen) in the United States will return to a piecework pay basis? When that day comes, pull EOQ out of the mothballs for purchasing situations, if you can live with its mathematical assumptions. Speaking of which, one of my students in an inventory theory course made the astute observation that, if the assumptions of the EOQ model were accurate, a company need place only one order for all foreseeable time, with the supplier automatically delivering a set quantity at regular intervals.

Notice that *factory* employees are usually paid hourly wages and that cost of setup C_o would then include a wage charge. If a factory employee does not work, he customarily receives no pay. On the other hand, if he were paid whether he worked or not, then his wage would be a salary and should not be charged to C_o.

Those who favor EOQ models might argue that they are used extensively in the real world and have an enviable record of cost reduction. The answer is that the reduction resulted from systematizing the ordering function, not from EOQ per se. Had good models been used, the cost reductions would have been even better, perhaps staggering!

The views on inventory costs just espoused would be regarded as highly controversial by most theorists and practitioners alike. Acting on the belief that good theory should survive under attack, I sought the reactions of a scholar whose work has previously been excerpted (in Chapter 10) to the material you have just been reading. Professor Edward L. Wallace (SUNY, Buffalo) replied:

> I reviewed the material on inventory costs sent me.
>
> There are only one or two comments I would like to make. First, the only meaningful way to estimate order costs is to look at them in the aggregate and to estimate increases in their total as total orders increase. Second, since processing orders is only one of many functions such people are involved in, a reasonable assumption appears to be that if these people were not producing orders they could be doing other equally productive work and not sitting around idle. Under the above assumptions, the average increment in ordering cost per order as order volume increases appears to be a reasonable estimate for most situations. Of course, one can always think of a number of situations where this is not true, but in general we build theory on the usual, not the special, case.

Professor Wallace's argument appears to be pragmatical. He does not specifically reject my argument that the decision to be in business calls for a purchasing department in any fair-sized organization, and that salary and other departmental costs are therefore costs of a "nonordering" decision. Nor does he reject my argument that the decision to add service facilities later in the year is not chargeable to orders that use those facilities because of the jointness of all orders and the consequent inability to attribute individual responsibility either to orders that use up regular facilities or to orders that employ the "extra" facilities. Professor Wallace apparently feels that the jointness of activities and the commonness of their costs require that total departmental costs be smoothed on the basis of departmental activity, and the recognition that, if the services of the purchasing staff were not available, they would require the hiring of substitute services.

Both viewpoints recognize jointness—on this point there is no quarrel. They disagree as to which decision the costs are related to. Are the costs period expenses of electing to be in business, or are they costs of procuring inventory? One observation may clarify the issue. Additional facilities acquired late in the year could easily have been contemplated earlier even though acquisition was delayed. Thus the additional facilities acquire the same status as the original facilities and may be considered period costs. Furthermore, salaries that would be paid regardless of the amount of service performed cannot be construed as an *incremental* cost. Finally, as mentioned earlier, additional facilities might be regarded as incremental costs—but of which orders? How do you tell a regular order from an incremental one? As to the matter of delaying other activities by filling out the present order, it would not always be the case that there would be a cost of delay. There might be no pressing hurry to do these other things. In which case, the EOQ model would be imposing a charge for a non-existent cost of delay.

The difference between period and "product" cost remains the issue and it is a difficult one; it appears to be a matter of how one perceives expenditures. Fortunately, another input helps to resolve the quandary; this input is the complications caused by human behavior.

Outwitting People: Policy Considerations

The discussion has been conducted as if people were not involved and everything was done harmoniously in the best interests of the overall business. Many chapters ago, when we were discussing behavior and policies, I observed that a free service is apt to induce great demand. The Purchasing Department is a service department for the rest of the company whether the business is retailing or manufacturing. For concreteness, let us talk in terms of manufacturing. In a business that manufactures a product, Purchasing is doing a service the charge for which is being embodied in the Production inventory models. It does not follow the more customary practice, in which a manager mentally weighs costs before deciding either to use the service or to seek some other means of accomplishing the task. Consider what message is conveyed to Production if the cost charged by Purchasing to place an order is zero. On that basis, Purchasing ought to be frantically busy placing orders. In the EOQ model, as we have seen, inventory would be ordered only when needed, and then only in the amount immediately called for.

Similar observations might be made when discussing the costs of a Quality Control Department that was performing its service. If there were no charge, much more analysis might be called for, although in this situation extensive physical interference with manufacturing might be regarded as a nuisance and therefore operate to limit demand.

So where does this leave us? It brings us to the recognition of an art form—to the delicate setting of a transfer price and to the creation of policy. If an inappropriate cost is chosen, the service will suffer from either feast or famine. If the fee is set too low, the plethora of orders that is apt to result will cause unnecessary expansion of Purchasing facilities; conversely, if famine occurs because of high fees, the advantages of central purchasing will be lost as Production attends to its own ordering. A reasonable fee should therefore be set, and this is more in the realm of art than of science. What motivates today may deter tomorrow.

On the other hand, if the costs of motivation may be ignored because everyone in the company is striving harmoniously for the common good, then I would prefer the "jointness, period cost" approach presented initially.

Nonlinear Programming

An Inventory Investment-Storage Problem

Putting aside whatever misgivings we may have about EOQ, let us investigate its use in a classical constrained optimization setting. The discussion will involve Lagrangean methodology, the theory behind which is presented in Appendix C. The situation calls for the minimization of the collective cost of several items subject to budgeting and storage capacity restrictions. The notation will be the same as before except that we shall need subscripts i and j to denote basis ($i = R$ [restricted], N [nonrestricted]) and item type ($j = 1, 2, \ldots, n$), and C_h will now be replaced by rC_{uj} (that is, cost of holding is now a percentage, r, times unit purchase price for item j). Otherwise,

B = budgetary limitation on investment in average inventory
W = warehouse capacity restriction in cubic feet
V_j = volume (cubic feet) required to store item j
f_k = fraction needed to convert total inventory investment ($k = B$) or total inventory cubic footage ($k = W$) to the magnitudes dictated by B and W

The daily cost for the nonrestricted problem may be stated as the sum of n individual models:

$$K_N = \sum\left(\frac{C_{oj}D_j}{Q_j} + \frac{C_{uj}rQ_j}{2}\right)$$

$$\frac{\partial K_N}{\partial Q_j} = -\frac{C_{oj}D_j}{Q_j^2} + \frac{C_{uj}r}{2} = 0$$

The optimal value of Q_j on basis N is $\hat{Q}_{Nj}$:

$$\hat{Q}_{Nj} = (2C_{oj}D_j/C_{uj}r)^{1/2} \tag{1}$$

$$K_N = \sum\left(\frac{C_{oj}D_j}{(2C_{oj}D_j/C_{uj}r)^{1/2}} + \frac{C_{uj}r}{2}\left(\frac{2C_{oj}D_j}{C_{uj}r}\right)^{1/2}\right)$$

$$K_N = \sum(2C_{oj}C_{uj}D_jr)^{1/2} \tag{2}$$

The daily cost for the restricted problem is the Lagrangean function

$$K_R = \sum\left(\frac{C_{oj}D_j}{Q_j} + \frac{C_{uj}rQ_j}{2}\right) - \lambda_1(B - f_B\sum C_{uj}Q_j) - \lambda_2(W - f_W\sum V_jQ_j), \qquad \textbf{(3)}$$

where $f_B\sum C_{uj}Q_j \leq B$ and $f_W\sum V_J Q_J \leq W$ and respectively state the budgetary and spacial limitations

To find the optimum of this function, it would be customary to employ the Newton root-searching routine (see Appendix C) whereby $x_{i+1} = x_i - H^{-1}\nabla$, H is the Hessian of (3), and ∇ is its gradient. The gradient vector containing the first-order partial derivatives is labelled below.

$$\nabla = \begin{array}{r} \partial K_R/\partial\lambda_1 \rightarrow \\ \partial K_R/\partial\lambda_2 \rightarrow \\ \partial K_R/\partial Q_1 \rightarrow \\ \partial K_R/\partial Q_2 \rightarrow \\ \partial K_R/\partial Q_3 \rightarrow \end{array} \begin{bmatrix} -(B - f_B\sum C_{uj}Q_j) \\ -(W - f_W\sum V_jQ_j) \\ \dfrac{-C_{o1}D_1}{Q_1^2} + \dfrac{C_{u1}r}{2} + f_B\lambda_1 C_{u1} + f_W\lambda_2 V_1 \\ \dfrac{-C_{o2}D_2}{Q_2^2} + \dfrac{C_{u2}r}{2} + f_B\lambda_1 C_{u2} + f_W\lambda_2 V_2 \\ \dfrac{-C_{o3}D_3}{Q_3^2} + \dfrac{C_{u3}r}{2} + f_B\lambda_1 C_{u3} + f_W\lambda_2 V_3 \end{bmatrix}$$

The numerical value of the gradient changes, of course, with each new point x (the coordinates of which are readings of λ_1, λ_2, Q_1, Q_2, and Q_3) encountered in the iterative process. The Hessian (or, more precisely, the bordered Hessian) matrix containing the second order partial derivatives appears as follows:

$$H = \begin{array}{c} \\ \lambda_1 \\ \lambda_2 \\ Q_1 \\ Q_2 \\ Q_3 \end{array} \begin{array}{c} \begin{array}{ccccc} \lambda_1 & \lambda_2 & Q_1 & Q_2 & Q_3 \end{array} \\ \begin{bmatrix} 0 & 0 & f_B C_{u1} & f_B C_{u2} & f_B C_{u3} \\ 0 & 0 & f_W V_1 & f_W V_2 & f_W V_3 \\ f_B C_{u1} & f_W V_1 & \dfrac{2C_{o1}D_1}{Q_1^3} & 0 & 0 \\ f_B C_{u2} & f_W V_2 & 0 & \dfrac{2C_{o2}D_2}{Q_2^3} & 0 \\ f_B C_{u3} & f_W V_3 & 0 & 0 & \dfrac{2C_{o3}D_3}{Q_3^3} \end{bmatrix} \end{array}$$

An Illustration

The following data will be used to illustrate these formulas:

j	D_j	C_{oj}	C_{uj}	V_j
1	100	\$50	\$ 20	20
2	640	\$50	\$ 50	10
3	50	\$50	\$250	50

$r = .2$ (assume volatile products that require expensive storage)
$f_B = \frac{1}{2}$ (because inventory for each item goes from Q to 0; consequently the average inventory investment $= \frac{1}{2}\sum C_{uj}Q_j$)
$f_W = 1$ (because inventory replenishment occurs all at once and, by assumption, simultaneously for all n items; consequently the storage space required is simply $\sum V_jQ_j$. (If replenishment were not simultaneous for all items, f_W would be some positive fraction less than 1.)
$B = \$3{,}000$
$W = 5{,}000$ cubic feet

Inserting these data into equations (1) and (2) yields the following results for the unrestricted problem:

$$\hat{Q}_{N1} = (2C_{oj}D_j/C_{uj}r)^{1/2} = (2(50)100/20(.2))^{1/2} = 50$$

$$\hat{Q}_{N2} = 80$$

$$\hat{Q}_{N3} = 10$$

$$K_N = \sum(2C_{oj}C_{uj}D_jr)^{1/2} = \$1{,}500$$

The average investment required is

$$\sum \hat{Q}_{Nj}C_{uj}/2 = (50(20) + 80(50) + 10(250))/2 = \$3{,}750$$

The space requirements are

$$\sum \hat{Q}_{Nj}V_j = 50(20) + 80(10) + 10(50) = 2{,}300 \text{ ft}^3$$

Since the budget is \$3,000 and capacity is 5,000 cubic feet, we see that the only pertinent constraint is the budgetary limitation. Hence the restricted problem would be formulated with the single budgetary constraint.

But let us pause a moment to see what would have happened had we gone directly to the solution of the restricted problem and used both, constraints.

In Exhibit 2 you will see a computer program that finds the optimal values. The condition that signifies the arrival at these optimal values is the appearance of a null (or approximately null) gradient vector at some iteration. Unfortunately, we would still not know whether this optimum was a maximum or a minimum. The program, however, provides for the printing of

Exhibit 2

```
LIST
100  DIM  A(10,10),G(10,1),H(10,10),X(10,1),Y(10,1),Z(10,1),I(10,10)
101  DIM  T(10,10)
105  READ N,Fl,F2,D1,D2,D3,O1,O2,O3,U1,U2,U3,V1,V2,V3,B,W,R
110  MAT A = ZER(N,N)
115  MAT G = ZER(N,1)
120  MAT I = IDN(N,N)
125  MAT READ X(N,1)
130  FOR J  = 1 TO 20
131  LET  A(1,1) = 0
132  LET  A(1,2) = 0
133  LET  A(1,3) = F1*U1
134  LET  A(1,4) = F1*U2
135  LET  A(1,5) = F1*U3
136  LET  A(2,1) = 0
137  LET  A(2,2) = 0
138  LET  A(2,3) = F2*V1
139  LET  A(2,4) = F2*V2
140  LET  A(2,5) = F2*V3
141  LET  A(3,1) = A(1,3)
142  LET  A(3,2) = A(2,3)
143  LET  A(3,3) = (2*O1*D1)/X(3,1)↑3
144  LET  A(3,4) = 0
145  LET  A(3,5) = 0
146  LET  A(4,1) = A(1,4)
147  LET  A(4,2) = A(2,4)
148  LET  A(4,3) = 0
149  LET  A(4,4) = (2*O2*D2)/X(4,1)↑3
150  LET  A(4,5) = 0
151  LET  A(5,1) = A(1,5)
152  LET  A(5,2) = A(2,5)
153  LET  A(5,3) = 0
154  LET  A(5,4) = 0
155  LET  A(5,5) = (2*O3*D3)/X(5,1)↑3
156  IF J < > 1 THEN 169
157  FOR  K = 1 TO N
158  MAT T = ZER(K,K)
159  FOR M = 1 TO K
160  FOR L  = 1 TO K
161  LET  T(M,L) = A(M,L)
162  NEXT L
163  NEXT M
165  MAT D = INV(T)
166  PRINT "THE PRINCIPAL MINOR, D(";K;"), IS:"
167  PRINT DET
168  NEXT K
169  PRINT "   H   "
170  MAT PRINT A
171  MAT H = INV(A)
185  PRINT
190  LET  G(1,1) = -(B-F1*(U1*X(3,1)+U2*X(4,1)+U3*X(5,1)))
191  LET  G(2,1) = -(W-F2*(V1*X(3,1)+V2*X(4,1)+V3*X(5,1)))
192  LET  G(3,1) =(-O1*D1/X(3,1)↑2)+U1*((R/2)+F1*X(1,1))+F2*X(2,1)*V1
193  LET  G(4,1) =(-O2*D2/X(4,1)↑2)+U2*((R/2)+F1*X(1,1))+F2*X(2,1)*V2
194  LET  G(5,1) =(-O3*D3/X(5,1)↑2)+U3*((R/2)+F1*X(1,1))+F2*X(2,1)*V3
```

Exhibit 2 (*cont.*)

```
195 PRINT "  THE GRADIENT VECTOR IS:  "
200 MAT PRINT G
201 PRINT
205 MAT Z = H*G
210 MAT Y = X-Z
215 PRINT "  THE POSITION VECTOR AFTER ITERATION";J;"IS:  "
220 MAT PRINT Y
225 MAT A = ZER(N,N)
230 MAT X = I*Y
235 NEXT J
240 DATA 5,.5,1,100,640,50,50,50,50,20,50,250,20,10,50,3000,5000,.2
245 DATA 10,10,50,80,10
250 END

RUN

THE PRINCIPAL MINOR, D( 1 ), IS:
  0
THE PRINCIPAL MINOR, D( 2 ), IS:
  0
THE PRINCIPAL MINOR, D( 3 ), IS:
  0
THE PRINCIPAL MINOR, D( 4 ), IS:
  160000
THE PRINCIPAL MINOR, D( 5 ), IS:
  1300000
    H
0       0       10      25      125
0       0       20      10      50
10      20      8E-2    0       0
25      10      0       .125    0
125     50      0       0       5

    THE GRADIENT VECTOR IS:
  750
-2700
  300
  350
  1750

    THE POSITION VECTOR AFTER ITERATION 1 IS:
  .778846154
-1.13942307
237.5
  15.3846154
  1.92307692
    H
0       0       10                25              125
0       0       20                10              50
10      20      7.46464499E-4      0              0
25      10      0                 17.5759998      0
125     50      0                 0               703.040003

    THE GRADIENT VECTOR IS:
  5.96046447E-7
  2.38418579E-7
-13.0886426
-122.123076
-610.615386
```

Exhibit 2 (*cont.*)

```
   THE POSITION VECTOR AFTER ITERATION 2 IS:
 6.55778393
-3.37445983
 237.5
 15.3846153
 1.92307692
   H
 0        0        10                25         125
 0        0        20                10         50
 10       20       7.46464499E-4     0          0
 25       10       0                 17.576     0
 125      50       0                 0          703.04

   THE GRADIENT VECTOR IS:
 0
 0
 0
-5.58793544E-9
 2.6077032E-8

   THE POSITION VECTOR AFTER ITERATION 3 IS:
 6.55778393
-3.37445983
 237.5
 15.3846153
 1.92307692
```

the principal minors (discussed in Appendix C); see statements 157 through 168.

The program puts each new position vector in vector x and takes the unconstrained problem's optimal values for Q_i along with a value of 10 for each of the unknown λ values as the starting point. The formulas (second-order partials) for each element of the Hessian matrix (designated as matrix A) have been written as arithmetic statements in statements 131 through 155. The gradient vector (vector G) has been similarly entered in statements 190 through 194.

As shown by Exhibit 2, $(\hat{Q}_{R1}, \hat{Q}_{R2}, \hat{Q}_{R3}, \lambda_1, \lambda_2) = (237.5, 15.4, 1.9, 6.6, -3.4)$. Since there is a minus sign accompanying λ_2, we would know from Lagrangean optimization theory that the capacity restriction was inactive and that none of the figures was worth keeping.

The restricted problem may be reformulated with just the budgetary constraint as follows:

$$K_R = \left(\frac{C_{oj}D_j}{Q_j} + \frac{C_{uj}rQ_j}{2}\right) - \lambda(B - f\sum C_{uj}Q_j) \tag{4}$$

$$\frac{\partial K_R}{\partial Q_j} = -\frac{C_{oj}D_j}{Q_j^2} + \frac{C_{uj}r}{2} + \lambda f C_{uj} = 0$$

Therefore, $\hat{Q}_{Rj} = (2C_{oj}D_j/(C_{uj}(r + 2f\lambda)))^{1/2}$ **(5)**

$$\frac{\partial K_R}{\partial \lambda} = -(B - f\sum C_{uj}Q_j) = 0$$

Inserting (5) we obtain

$$f\sum C_{uj}\left(\frac{2C_{oj}D_j}{C_{uj}(r + 2f\lambda)}\right)^{1/2} = B$$

Multiplying both sides by $r^{1/2}$ and factoring the constant $(r + 2f\lambda)^{1/2}$ yields

$$\sum(2C_{oj}C_{uj}D_jr)^{1/2} = \frac{B(r + 2f\lambda)^{1/2}r^{1/2}}{f}$$

Now the left-hand side is K_N (see equation (2)); therefore,

$$K_N = B(r + 2f\lambda)^{1/2}r^{1/2}/f$$

$$K_N{}^2 = B^2(r + 2f\lambda)r/f^2$$

$$(r + 2f\lambda) = \frac{f^2K_N{}^2}{rB^2}$$

$$\lambda = \frac{fK_N{}^2}{2rB^2} - \frac{r}{2f} \quad \textbf{(6)}$$

Our shadow price λ measures the incremental return promised by investing additional budgetary funds in inventory. λ is a return beyond the charge for using capital that is part of the holding cost percentage r. However, a single value of λ does not pertain for each dollar added to the budget. λ is a marginal return and would change with every increment in the budget, because with each budgetary change we would need to solve a new problem that would be stated as follows:

$$K_R = \sum\left(\frac{C_{oj}D_j}{Q_j} + \frac{C_{uj}rQ_j}{2}\right) - \lambda(B + \Delta B - f\sum C_{uj}Q_j)$$

This causes an indirect change in the formula (equation 5) for $\hat{Q}_{Rj}$ and a corresponding change in (6) to

$$\lambda = \frac{fK_N{}^2}{2(B + \Delta B)^2r} - \frac{r}{2f} \quad \textbf{(7)}$$

Hence, the new λ would be smaller assuming ΔB is positive.

What use can be made of λ? Management might be willing, when faced with the question, to specify some critical value of λ, say λ_c, below which increased investment would not be approved. Given λ_c, the maximum additional budgetary allotment may be determined from equation (7) as follows:

$$\lambda_c = \frac{fK_N^2}{2(B+\Delta B)^2 r} - \frac{r}{2f}$$

$$\frac{2f\lambda_c + r}{2f} = \frac{fK_N^2}{2(B+\Delta B)^2 r}$$

$$\frac{(B+\Delta B)^2 r}{fK_N^2} = \frac{f}{2f\lambda_c + r}$$

$$\Delta B = \left[\frac{f^2 K_N^2}{r(2f\lambda_c + r)}\right]^{1/2} - B \tag{8}$$

Now that the main arguments have been completed, we may test for second-order conditions without interrupting our thought processes. From (4) we developed

$$\frac{\partial K_R}{\partial Q_j} = -\frac{C_{oj}D_j}{Q_j^2} + \frac{C_{uj}r}{2} + \lambda f C_{uj}$$

$$\frac{\partial K_R}{\partial \lambda} = -(B - f\sum C_{uj}Q_j)$$

Therefore, $\dfrac{\partial^2 K_R}{\partial Q_j \partial \lambda} = fC_{uj} = \dfrac{\partial^2 K_R}{\partial \lambda \partial Q_j}; \quad \dfrac{\partial^2 K_R}{\partial Q_j \partial Q_i} = 0; \quad \dfrac{\partial^2 K_R}{\partial Q_j^2} = \dfrac{2C_{oj}D_j}{Q_j^3}; \quad \dfrac{\partial^2 K_R}{\partial \lambda^2} = 0$

$$H = \begin{array}{c} \\ \lambda \\ Q_1 \\ Q_2 \\ Q_3 \end{array} \begin{array}{c} \begin{array}{cccc} \lambda & Q_1 & Q_2 & Q_3 \end{array} \\ \left[\begin{array}{cccc} 0 & fC_{u1} & fC_{u2} & fC_{u3} \\ fC_{u1} & 2C_{o1}D_1/Q_1^3 & 0 & 0 \\ fC_{u2} & 0 & 2C_{o2}D_2/Q_2^3 & 0 \\ fC_{u3} & 0 & 0 & 2C_{o3}D_3/Q_3^3 \end{array}\right] \end{array}$$

Expanding by the top row yields the following principal minors:

$$\Delta_4 = -4f^2\left[C_{u3}^2\left(\frac{C_{o1}D_1}{Q_1^3}\right)\left(\frac{C_{o2}D_2}{Q_2^3}\right) + C_{u2}^2\left(\frac{C_{o1}D_1}{Q_1^3}\right)\left(\frac{C_{o3}D_3}{Q_3^3}\right) + C_{u1}^2\left(\frac{C_{o2}D_2}{Q_2^3}\right)\left(\frac{C_{o3}D_3}{Q_3^3}\right)\right]$$

$$\Delta_3 = -2f^2\left[C_{u1}^2\left(\frac{C_{o2}D_2}{Q_2^3}\right) + C_{u2}^2\left(\frac{C_{o1}D_1}{Q_1^3}\right)\right]$$

Since both principal minors are less than zero, a minimum has been attained.

The numerical answers resulting from the one-constraint problem stated and solved in equations (4), (5), and (6) are

$$K_R = \$1{,}537.50$$
$$\hat{Q}_{R1} = 40$$
$$\hat{Q}_{R2} = 64$$
$$\hat{Q}_{R3} = 8$$
$$\lambda = .1125$$

Now let us assume that management is willing to add more budgetary funds as long as $\lambda \geq .03$, that is, as long as the return in excess of the ordinary charge for invested capital (reflected in r) is 3% or better. From equation (8) the supplemental budgetary allotment may be determined to be

$$\Delta B = \left[\frac{(.5)^2(1{,}500)^2}{.2(2(.5)(.03) + .2)}\right]^{1/2} - 3{,}000 = 497$$

(For comparison purposes, if management insisted on $\lambda \geq .1125$, no supplemental allotment would be forthcoming.) A graph of λ and B appears below.

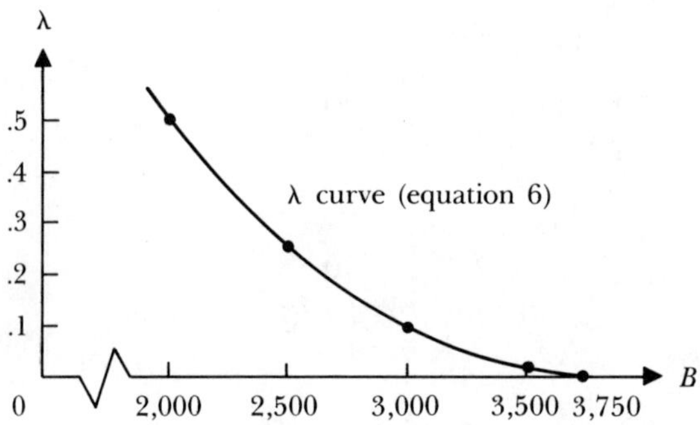

B	λ
$ 100	281.0500
500	11.0500
1,000	2.6125
1,500	1.0500
2,000	.5031
2,500	.2500
3,000	.1125
3,500	.0296
3,600	.0170
3,700	.0054
3,710	.0043
3,725	.0027
3,750	.0000

Although we know the space limitation can never be binding—5,000 cubic feet is far in excess of the quantity required by the optimal unrestricted solution—the situation could occur in which the limitation constant of a pertinent constraint is increased sufficiently to render that constraint subsequently redundant and some previously redundant constraint subsequently pertinent. Hence, once an increase in a limitation constant occurs, the problem should be re-solved with all constraints reflected.

The shadow price, λ, together with r and f may be used to relate K_R and K_N and therefore to show the effect of the constraint on cost as follows: Kuhn-Tucker condition III, $\lambda g(x, y) = 0$, allows us to write (4) as

$$K_R = \sum\left(\frac{C_{oj}D_j}{Q_j} + \frac{C_{uj}rQ_j}{2}\right)$$

Inserting (5) yields

$$K_R = \sum (2C_{oj}C_{uj}D_j)^{1/2}(r + f\lambda)/(r + 2f\lambda)^{1/2}$$

If we then multiply by 1 in the form $r^{1/2}/r^{1/2}$,

$$K_R = \sum (2C_{oj}C_{uj}D_j r)^{1/2}(r + f\lambda)/(r^2 + 2rf\lambda)^{1/2}$$

Therefore,

$$K_R = \frac{K_N(r + f\lambda)}{(r^2 + 2rf\lambda)^{1/2}}$$

Comments:

1. It is common in Lagrangean problems to have more then one positive λ_i value.
2. If management changes capacities, it is common to re-solve the new problem.

The Markowitz Model

The Markowitz model attempts to select a portfolio of investments that minimizes risk—as measured by the investment portfolio variances—while yielding a rate of return that is at least acceptable. Here risk is measured by the variances and covariances of the different investments. Stating that yield must be at least a minimum figure is only one of many possible constraints. Other constraints, of course, may be introduced, such as requiring the optimal portfolio to consist of at least or, perhaps, at most a stipulated percentage in a designated investment.

What the investor hopes to do is depicted in Figure 2.

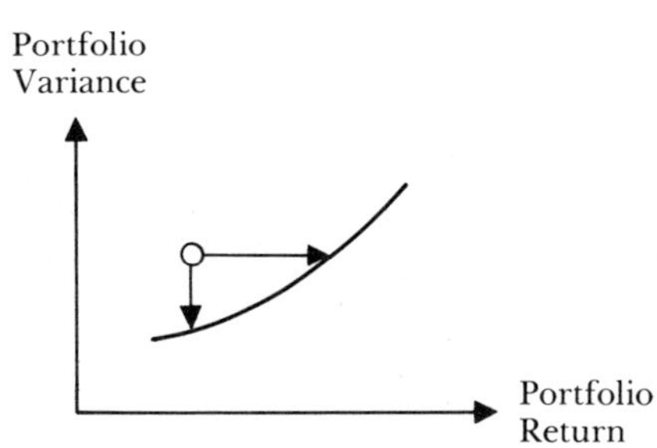

Figure 2

If the investor is in the position designated by the circle in the diagram, he can choose to move down to the curve and thereby reduce the portfolio variance or to move to the right and increase the portfolio return. Only a position on the curve is rational.

We may as well talk in terms of an example; however, instead of presenting the data all at once, allow me to introduce information as it is convenient to do so. Assume there are three competing investments: Risky, Dependable, and Savings. These investments will be designated by the subscript j, where $j = 1$ (Risky), 2 (Dependable), 3 (Savings). Risky and Dependable are stocks while Savings is simply a savings account. We will be concerned with the performance of each investment in year i, where $i = 1, 2, \ldots, 10$. Performance will be denoted by p_{ij}, which is a percentage reflecting dividends, capital appreciation, and interest for investment j in year i. Knowing the performance of each investment, we could talk about the overall portfolio yield in any year if we knew the fraction, f_j, of our investable funds that had been assigned to investment j. Hypothetical data, of course, could be substituted for genuine experiences. Yield is a crucial point; permit me to illustrate it. Suppose we had the following data for year i:

j	p_{ij}	f_j
1	.20	.5
2	.10	.4
3	.05	.1

If we had \$10,000 to invest, \$5,000 (= .5 × \$10,000) would be in Risky ($j = 1$), \$4,000 in Dependable, and \$1,000 in Savings. The yields, $\bar{p}_i$, would be:

$$\bar{p}_i = \frac{.2(5{,}000) + .1(4{,}000) + .05(1{,}000)}{10{,}000}$$

$$= \frac{1{,}450}{10{,}000} = \sum_{j=1}^{3} p_{ij} f_j = .2(.5) + .1(.4) + .05(.1)$$

Actual portfolio yield in year i:

$$\bar{p}_i = \sum_{j=1}^{3} p_{ij} f_j \tag{1}$$

We now have the yield per year and we seek to determine the average yield, $\bar{p}$, over the 10-year period.

$$\bar{p} = \frac{1}{10} \sum_{i=1}^{10} \bar{p}_i = \frac{1}{10} \sum_{i=1}^{10} \sum_{j=1}^{3} p_{ij} f_j \qquad \text{(by substituting (1))}$$

$$= \sum_{j=1}^{3} \left(\frac{\sum_{i=1}^{10} p_{ij}}{10} \right) f_j$$

$$\bar{p} = \sum_{j=1}^{3} \bar{p}_j f_j \tag{2}$$

Note that $\bar{p}_j$ is the average performance for investment j.

Next we develop an expression for the variance of the annual yield:

$$\sigma^2 = \frac{1}{9} \sum_{i=1}^{10} (\bar{p}_i - \bar{p})^2$$

Substituting (1) and (2) for $\bar{p}_i$ and $\bar{p}$ results in

$$\begin{aligned}
\sigma^2 &= \frac{1}{9} \sum_{i=1}^{10} \left[\sum_{j=1}^{3} p_{ij} f_j - \sum_{j=1}^{3} \bar{p}_j f_j \right]^2 \\
&= \frac{1}{9} \sum_{i=1}^{10} \left[\sum_{j=1}^{3} (p_{ij} - \bar{p}_j) f_j \right]^2 \\
&= \frac{1}{9} \sum_{i=1}^{10} \left[\sum_{j=1}^{3} d_{ij} f_j \right]^2 \qquad (3)
\end{aligned}$$

In (3) the symbol d_{ij} has been substituted for the difference between the yearly performance of investment j and its 10-year average performance. Make a point of remembering this substitution. Expanding (3), we obtain

$$\sigma^2 = \frac{1}{9} \sum_{i=1}^{10} \begin{bmatrix} d_{i1}{}^2 f_1{}^2 + 2d_{i1} f_1 d_{i2} f_2 + 2d_{i1} f_1 d_{i3} f_3 \\ + 2d_{i2} f_2 d_{i3} f_3 + d_{i2}{}^2 f_2{}^2 + d_{i3}{}^2 f_3{}^2 \end{bmatrix} \qquad (4)$$

We now break up the doubled terms, sum each separate term, and arrive at weighted variances and covariances for each fund. Let us designate these variances by v_{kj}, where

$$v_{kj} = \frac{1}{9} \sum_{i=1}^{10} d_{ki} d_{ij} \qquad (5)$$

With (5) available, we may easily express the variance of the annual yield in the quadratic form:

$$\sigma^2 = \sum_{k=1}^{3} \sum_{j=1}^{3} f_k v_{kj} f_j = f^T V f \qquad (6)$$

Equation (6) will become the objective function for our quadratic programming problem; we will seek to minimize investment portfolio risk by minimizing the sum of the variances and covariances of the portfolio. This idea has great intuitive appeal because the smaller the positive covariances and the greater the negative covariances, the greater the economic diversification of the portfolio. (Reasoning: if two investments vary together—are highly positively correlated—whatever happens to one investment will presumably happen to the other. The result will be no diversification and hence little protection against risk. Conversely, if they are highly negatively correlated, their performances are opposite and risk is reduced.)

Equation (5) is the key to formulating the variance-covariance matrix. The general scheme is: (1) to come up with a vector for year i, d_i, whose elements, d_{ij}, show the difference between year i performance for j and the 10-year average for j; (2) to transpose this vector; (3) to form the product $d_i d_i^T$ to obtain V_i; (4) to repeat the process for each of the 10 years; (5) to sum the

V_i and divide by the scalar 9 to obtain V, the variance-covariance matrix—that is, $V = \frac{1}{9}(V_1 + V_2 + \cdots + V_{10})$. Assume the following performance data for the three investments:

i	Risky	Dependable	Savings
1	20%	16%	3%
2	27%	14%	3%
⋮	⋮	⋮	⋮
10	31%	15%	6%
$\sum_i p_{ij}/10$	25%	15%	5%

Thus,

$$\begin{aligned} d_1 &= (20 - 25, 16 - 15, 3 - 5) = (-5, 1, -2) \\ d_2 &= (27 - 25, 14 - 15, 3 - 5) = (2, -1, -2) \\ &\vdots \\ d_{10} &= (31 - 25, 15 - 15, 6 - 5) = (6, \ 0, \ 1) \end{aligned}$$

Hence,

$$V_1 = \begin{bmatrix} -5 \\ 1 \\ -2 \end{bmatrix} [-5, 1, -2] = \begin{bmatrix} 25 & -5 & 10 \\ -5 & 1 & -2 \\ 10 & -2 & 4 \end{bmatrix}$$

Continuing in this way, summing, and dividing by 9 yields the variance matrix

$$V = \begin{bmatrix} 50 & 1 & -10 \\ 1 & 1 & 0 \\ -10 & 0 & 10 \end{bmatrix}$$

I used the following BASIC program to obtain V:

```
100  DIM  A(10,10),D(1,10),T(10,1),B(10,10),S(10,10)
105  READ N,M
110  MAT A = ZER(N,N)
115  FOR  K = 1 TO  M
120  MAT READ  D(1,N)
125  MAT T  = TRN(D)
130  MAT B  = T*D
135  MAT PRINT B
140  PRINT
150  PRINT
155  MAT S  = (1)*A
160  MAT A = B+S
165  NEXT K
170  MAT X = (1/9)*A
172  PRINT "  THE VARIANCE-COVARIANCE MATRIX  "
175  MAT PRINT X
200  DATA 3,10
       :
     DATA
250  END
```

Hence the objective function is

Minimize $\sigma^2 = f^T V f = 50f_1^2 + 2f_1 f_2 - 20f_1 f_3 + f_2^2 + 10f_3^2$

Check for convexity:

$$V = \begin{bmatrix} 50 & 1 & -10 \\ 1 & 1 & 0 \\ -10 & 0 & 10 \end{bmatrix}$$

$\Delta_1 = 50$; $\Delta_2 = 49$; $\Delta_3 = 390$

Since all principal minors are positive, the matrix is positive definite; therefore the function is convex, and a local minimum occurs.

Let us formulate some reasonable constraints. We begin by assuming that the 10-year average performance for each investment is a useful measure of present performance, although the anticipated return for the coming year could also be used. If we then insist on at least a 10% yield from the portfolio, our first constraint becomes

$$25f_1 + 15f_2 + 5f_3 \geq 1{,}000$$

As you can see, percents have been multiplied by 100, as have the fractions. Since any spare pocket change can be thrown into Savings, we have

$$f_1 + f_2 + f_3 = 100$$

Assume further that we have some interest in liquidity; accordingly, we require, say, that the portfolio consist of at least 10% Savings:

$$f_3 \geq 10$$

Finally, we observe $\qquad f_1, f_2 \geq 0$

A "less than" inequality can be converted into an equality by adding a slack variable to provide for a reading of the residual resource should the optimal solution not entirely consume it. A "greater than" inequality can be converted into an equality by subtracting a surplus variable that shows the amount by which a stipulated goal is exceeded. Thus $\sum a_i x_i \geq b$ becomes $\sum a_i x_i - s = b$, where s is a surplus variable.

Two surplus variables are called for—one in the first constraint and one in the third. This yields the optimum directly. Unfortunately, this would not illustrate the usefulness of the signs of the Lagrangean multipliers. Therefore, we shall omit one surplus variable and see what happens.

The Lagrangean restatement of the problem with one surplus variable included, which variable serves both to illustrate the method and to cure a negative reading of another variable that otherwise occurs, is

$$L = 50f_1^{\,2} + 2f_1f_2 - 20f_1f_3 + f_2^{\,2} + 10f_3^{\,2} - \lambda_1(-1000 + 25f_1 + 15f_2 + 5f_3 - S_1) - \lambda_2(100 - f_1 - f_2 - f_3) - \lambda_3(-10 + f_3)$$

Comments:

1. Recognizing f_1, $f_2 \geq 0$ explicitly will not be necessary.
2. S_1 will show how much return beyond the required 10% is achieved.
3. If a surplus variable were introduced for the third constraint, the fact that f_3 is in the unconstrained objective function might lead to f_3 going to zero and the surplus variable becoming overactive in the constraint. Hence no surplus will be created for this constraint.

The usual partial derivatives are

$$\begin{aligned}
\partial L/\partial\lambda_1 &= -(-1000 + 25f_1 + 15f_2 + 5f_3 - S_1) = 0\\
\partial L/\partial\lambda_2 &= -(100 - f_1 - f_2 - f_3) = 0\\
\partial L/\partial\lambda_3 &= -(-10 + f_3) = 0\\
\partial L/\partial f_1 &= 100f_1 + 2f_2 - 20f_3 - 25\lambda_1 + \lambda_2 = 0\\
\partial L/\partial f_2 &= 2f_1 + 2f_2 - 15\lambda_1 + \lambda_2 = 0\\
\partial L/\partial f_3 &= -20f_1 + 20f_3 - 5\lambda_1 + \lambda_2 - \lambda_3 = 0\\
\partial L/\partial S_1 &= \lambda_1 = 0
\end{aligned}$$

Two approaches are attractive for obtaining an optimal solution:

1. The system could be converted to matrices and solved as is. Unfortunately, this would yield no indication of whether a maximum or minimum had been attained. Either points nearby would need to be examined to see if they were greater or lesser in value than the critical point, or, alternatively, principal minors of the unconstrained objective can be studied as in the earlier check for convexity using V. This is possible because the constraints are linear and therefore neutral (both convex and concave) as far as affecting convexity is concerned.

2. The first-order partials can be placed in a gradient vector and second-order partials can be entered in a Hessian matrix to invoke the Newton root-searching formula. The Hessian is

$$H = \begin{array}{c} \lambda_1 \\ \lambda_2 \\ \lambda_3 \\ f_1 \\ f_2 \\ f_3 \\ S_1 \end{array} \overset{\begin{array}{ccccccc} \lambda_1 & \lambda_2 & \lambda_3 & f_1 & f_2 & f_3 & S_1 \end{array}}{\begin{bmatrix} 0 & 0 & 0 & -25 & -15 & -5 & 1 \\ 0 & 0 & 0 & 1 & 1 & 1 & 0 \\ 0 & 0 & 0 & 0 & 0 & -1 & 0 \\ -25 & 1 & 0 & 100 & 2 & -20 & 0 \\ -15 & 1 & 0 & 2 & 2 & 0 & 0 \\ -5 & 1 & -1 & -20 & 0 & 20 & 0 \\ 1 & 0 & 0 & 0 & 0 & 0 & 0 \end{bmatrix}}$$

When the gradient and Hessian are entered in the program in Exhibit 2 along with an initial estimate for the x vector of

$$(\lambda_1, \lambda_2, \lambda_3, f_1, f_2, f_3, S_1)^T = (0, 0, 0, 5, 80, 15, 400)^T,$$

the answer after several interations is

$$\begin{bmatrix} \lambda_1 \\ \lambda_2 \\ \lambda_3 \\ f_1 \\ f_2 \\ f_3 \\ S_1 \end{bmatrix} = \begin{bmatrix} 0 \\ -180 \\ -20.82 \\ 2.0408 \\ 87.9592 \\ 10 \\ 420.408 \end{bmatrix}$$

Since the gradient vector at this iteration is essentially zero, these are the critical values of the variables. λ_2 has a negative value, which indicates that the objective function could be further minimized if we did not insist on investing 100% of our money. As mentioned in Appendix C, equality constraints have no restrictions as to the sign of their multipliers, although a negative sign means that abandoning insistence on strict equality will both improve the objective function *and* use fewer resources in the process—if abandoning is possible.

If the $\sum f_i = 100\%$ constraint is discarded (because $\lambda_2 < 0$) and the problem is re-solved, the risk decreases along with the return; furthermore, only 71.4% of the funds available are invested. Returning to the original solution, note that $S_1 = 420.408$, which means that the total yield from the optimal program is 14.2% and not just the minimum 10%. $L = 8895.9$.

Also note that the inclusion of a slack or surplus variable in the Hessian may serve to cure dependency among the rows or columns. Judicious use of slack and surplus variables should always be considered as a means for budging a seemingly intractable problem. Sometimes such variables are useful for curing dependency, and at other times they are convenient for displaying excesses and shortages; on the other hand, there are times when these variables only complicate analysis.

The fact that $\lambda_3 < 0$ indicates that the objective function can be improved if the last constraint is dropped. For variety, the reduced system can be set up in matrices simply as

$$\begin{bmatrix} 0 & 0 & 25 & 15 & 5 & -1 \\ 0 & 0 & 1 & 1 & 1 & 0 \\ -25 & 1 & 100 & 2 & -20 & 0 \\ -15 & 1 & 2 & 2 & 0 & 0 \\ -5 & 1 & -20 & 0 & 20 & 0 \\ 1 & 0 & 0 & 0 & 0 & 0 \end{bmatrix} \begin{bmatrix} \lambda_1 \\ \lambda_2 \\ f_1 \\ f_2 \\ f_3 \\ S_1 \end{bmatrix} = \begin{bmatrix} 1000 \\ 100 \\ 0 \\ 0 \\ 0 \\ 0 \end{bmatrix}$$

This yields

$$\begin{bmatrix} \lambda_1 \\ \lambda_2 \\ f_1 \\ f_2 \\ f_3 \\ S_1 \end{bmatrix} = \begin{bmatrix} 0 \\ -177.6770 \\ 2.2779 \\ 86.5604 \\ 11.1617 \\ 411.1620 \end{bmatrix}$$

L is now minimum at 8,883.8, but the return drops from 14.2% to 14.1%. This is the optimal solution. It is now apparent that a viable simplification would have been to ignore all single variable constraints initially and to introduce them subsequently had they been needed (that is, if the simplified initial solution had violated a single variable constraint—which would not be the case in the present problem).

Probabilistic Inventory Models

Instantaneous Demand

The recognition that demand fluctuates introduces the need for reflecting probability distributions in our models. Perhaps the most famous probabilistic inventory model is known as the newsboy model. The newsboy deals with a product that obsolesces rapidly and he wishes to know the best quantity of newspapers to supply to maximize his profit, which in this case is the same thing as minimizing his opportunity costs. He knows selling price, acquisition cost, salvage value, and probability distribution for demand.

The newsboy model is characterized by the need to reflect instantaneous demand—in any basic cycle there is only a brief portion during which sales are made. If the basic cycle is a week, the cost of holding a unit for a week is calculated and multiplied by the remaining inventory to arrive at the associated holding cost for the week. The same is true for calculating shortage cost. Since many levels of demand are possible, many levels of holding and shortage result, each of which is weighted by the probability of its occurring. Diagrammatically, we have

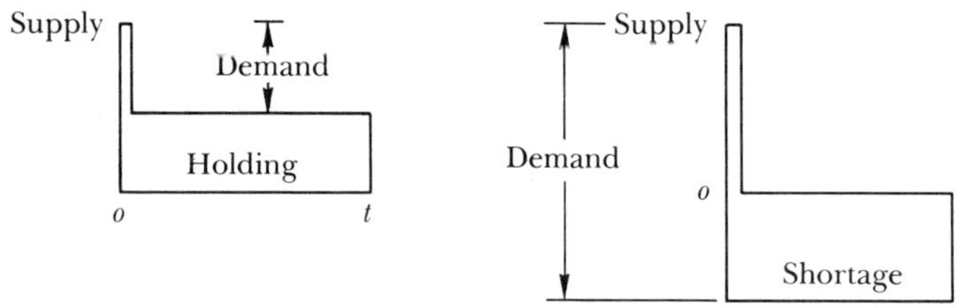

In brief, the instantaneous-demand situation develops expected holding and expected shortage, and the newsboy model minimizes their combined costs. The dimension of each expectation is unit-periods, as can be seen from the diagrams. The area of the holding rectangle, for instance, is $(S - D)t$; however, since t is usually taken as one day or one week or one month, area becomes $(S - D)1 = S - D$.

If the product suffers *rapid* obsolescence or staleness, or perishability in general, the incremental cost of holding a unit equals acquisition cost minus salvage value. If the product is long-lived, holding cost includes costs of storage, insurance, taxes, and forgone earnings. Cost of shortage for the perishable product is the forgone profit from not supplying enough to meet demand and, in practice, equals selling price minus acquisition cost. In theory, cost of shortage includes loss of future business as well, which involves estimating forgone profits from disenchanted customers and from all those they convince to buy papers elsewhere. For the long-lived product, cost of shortage may be the same or, if customers agree to being placed on a waiting list (backorder list), it may simply amount to the cost of delaying them.

Some examples of short-lived products are newspapers, weekly magazines, fresh cake, bread, and pie, as well as meats, fruit, and vegetables that cannot be frozen. Many fashionable items, such as stylish, exclusive gowns, also become obsolete quickly.

The newsboy model is sometimes inappropriately applied. For example, the inventory literature unwisely recommends its application in controlling "insurance spares." The classical example is the acquisition, at time of construction, of extra boiler systems for ships. It is reasoned that it will be cheaper to construct these extras now than to do so many years from now, when they are needed. Not only is discounting necessary here, but so are distributions for demand and time of demand. It is stretching simplicity far too thin to model this inventory situation as a newsboy problem.

If demand is for large quantities, the newsboy problem is modelled using continuous probability distributions. If demand is for small quantities, discrete distributions are employed; this is the classical setting, for it was never assumed that the newsboy was a Hercules who could lift thousands of newspapers.

Key:

$$\begin{aligned} E[K(S)] &= \text{expected cost of stocking } S \text{ units} \\ C_h &= \text{cost of holding per unit per basic time period} \\ C_s &= \text{cost of shortage per unit per basic time period} \\ S &= \text{supply} \\ D &= \text{demand} \\ P(D) &= \text{probability of demand} \end{aligned}$$

Model: $E[K(S)] = \text{expected holding cost} + \text{expected shortage cost}$

$$E[K(S)] = C_h \sum_{D=0}^{S} (S - D)P(D) + C_s \sum_{D=S+1}^{S} (D - S)P(D)$$

Comments:

1. For expected holding, $(S - D)$ is the number of papers remaining and this happens with a probability $P(D)$. There are many possible values of $S - D$, for once S is chosen, D may vary. After each holding outcome, $S - D$, is weighted by its respective probability, $P(D)$, the results are summed over all possible holding outcomes to obtain the expected number of papers held, each of which costs C_h.
2. Expected shortage cost is reasoned similarly.
3. The model setup could include C_o but it would disappear in optimization.

Solution: We obtain the forward difference, $\Delta E[K(S)]$:

$$\Delta E[K(S)] = E[K(S+1)] - E[K(S)]$$

$E[K(S+1)]$ calls for replacing S in $E[K(S)]$, wherever S appears, by $S + 1$:

$$\begin{aligned} \Delta E[K(S)] = &\left[C_h \sum_{0}^{S+1} ((S+1) - D)P(D) + C_s \sum_{S+2}^{\infty} (D - (S+1))P(D) \right] \\ &- \left[C_h \sum_{0}^{S} (S - D)P(D) + C_s \sum_{S+1}^{\infty} (D - S)P(D) \right] \\ &= C_h \left[\sum_{0}^{S+1} (S + 1 - D)P(D) - \sum_{0}^{S} (S - D)P(D) \right] \\ &+ C_s \left[\sum_{S+2}^{\infty} (D - S - 1)P(D) - \sum_{S+1}^{\infty} (D - S)P(D) \right] \end{aligned}$$

Since each term in the summand may be summed separately—for example, $\sum(S+1-D)P(D) = \sum SP(D) + \sum 1P(D) - \sum DP(D)$—we may gather terms conveniently:

$$\begin{aligned}
\Delta E[K(S)] &= C_h\left[\sum_0^{S+1} 1P(D) + \left(\sum_0^{S+1}(S-D)P(D) - \sum_0^{S}(S-D)P(D)\right)\right] \\
&\quad + C_s\left[\sum_{S+2}^{\infty}(-1)P(D) + \left(\sum_{S+2}^{\infty}(D-S)P(D) - \sum_{S+1}^{\infty}(D-S)P(D)\right)\right] \\
&= C_h\left[\sum_0^{S+1} P(D) + (S-(S+1))P(S+1)\right] \\
&\quad + C_s\left[-\sum_{S+2}^{\infty} P(D) - ((S+1)-S)P(S+1)\right] \\
&= C_h\left[\sum_0^{S+1} P(D) - P(S+1)\right] - C_s\left[\sum_{S+2}^{\infty} P(D) + P(S+1)\right] \\
&= C_h\sum_0^{S} P(D) - C_s\sum_{S+1}^{\infty} P(D)
\end{aligned}$$

Now recalling that $1 = \sum_0^\infty P(D) = \sum_0^S P(D) + \sum_{S+1}^\infty P(D)$, we may substitute its cumulative complement for $\sum_{S+1}^\infty P(D)$:

$$\Delta E[K(S)] = C_h\sum_0^S P(D) - C_s\left(1 - \sum_0^S P(D)\right)$$

$$\Delta E[K(S)] = (C_h + C_s)\sum_{D=0}^{S} P(D) - C_s$$

Similarly, the backward difference, $\nabla E[K(S)] = E[K(S)] - E[K(S-1)]$, could be obtained with the following results:

$$E[K(S)] = (C_h + C_s)\sum_{D=0}^{S-1} P(D) - C_s$$

If $E[K(S)]$ is the minimum cost, then both $E[K(S+1)]$ and $E[K(S-1)]$ are the same or higher; therefore, $\Delta E[K(S)] \geq 0$ and $\nabla E[K(S)] \leq 0$. This leads to

$$(C_h + C_s)\sum_{D=0}^{S} P(D) - C_s \geq 0$$

$$(C_h + C_s)\sum_{D=0}^{S-1} P(D) - C_s \leq 0$$

Hence,

$$\sum_{D=0}^{S-1} P(D) \leq \frac{C_s}{C_s + C_h} \leq \sum_{D=0}^{S} P(D)$$

We seek the value of S that makes this expression hold, for this is the amount of supply that will minimize expected cost, $E[K(S)]$.

Comments: If $\sum_0^S P(D) = C_s/(C_s + C_h)$, then more than one value of S will yield the same minimum cost. Having more than one way to generate the same optimal value is referred to as having *alternative optima*.

Example: A newsboy sells papers for \$.15 each and buys them for \$.09 each. Any unsold papers may be turned in for \$.05 per paper. From records he has diligently kept, he has prepared the distribution of demand shown below.

D	25	26	27	28	29	30	31	32
$P(D)$	.10	.12	.17	.18	.15	.11	.10	.07

What quantity of papers should he stock to minimize his regret (opportunity cost)?

Solution: C_h = acquisition cost − salvage value = \$.09 − \$.05 = \$.04
C_s = sales price − acquisition cost = \$.15 − \$.09 = \$.06
$C_s/(C_s + C_h) = .06/(.06 + .04) = .6$
By adding the probabilities, we find $P(S \leq 28)$ is .57 and $P(S \leq 29) = .72$; therefore, the optimal supply is $S = 29$, because it is the supply that has the cumulative probability that first exceeds .6.

Gradual Demand

The newsboy model is characterized by items with very brief periods of demand. We turn now to products that are sold gradually during the whole cycle. As with the instantaneous-demand model, it is necessary in the gradual-demand model to weight holdings and shortages by the proportion of the cycle during which these conditions persist. In the instantaneous model, residual inventory (positive or negative) is weighted by the whole period; but in the gradual model, average inventory is weighted by the corresponding portion of the cycle.

The gradual-demand model starts each cycle with S units in stock and proceeds to recognize a holding period. If demand is less than supply, holding occurs for the whole cycle; conversely, if demand exceeds supply, there is an initial period of holding followed by a period of shortage.

Model: $E[K(S)]$ = expected cost when $S \geq D$ + expected cost when $D > S$

$$E[K(S)] = C_h \sum_{D=0}^{S} \left(S - \frac{D}{2}\right) P(D) + \left[C_h \sum_{D=S+1}^{\infty} \frac{S^2}{2D} P(D) + C_s \sum_{D=S+1}^{\infty} \frac{(D-S)^2}{2D} P(D)\right]$$

Comments:

1. The setup of the model should include C_o but this would disappear in optimization.

2. To understand the setup, consider the diagrams shown below and let A = average inventory.

$S \geq D$:

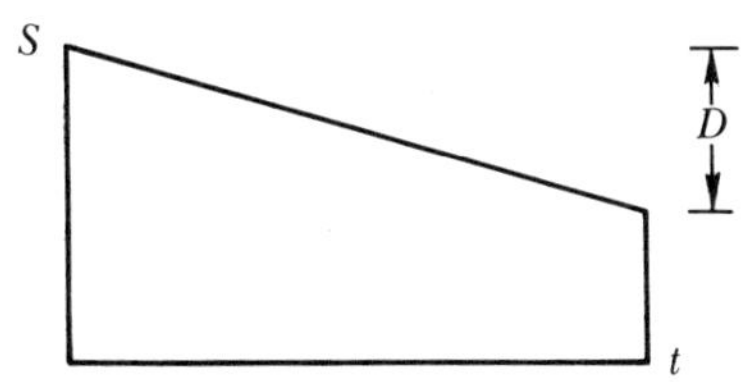

$$A = \frac{S + (S - D)}{2}$$

$$A = S - (D/2)$$

A pertains for the whole cycle, therefore it is weighted by $t/t = 1$.

$D > S$:

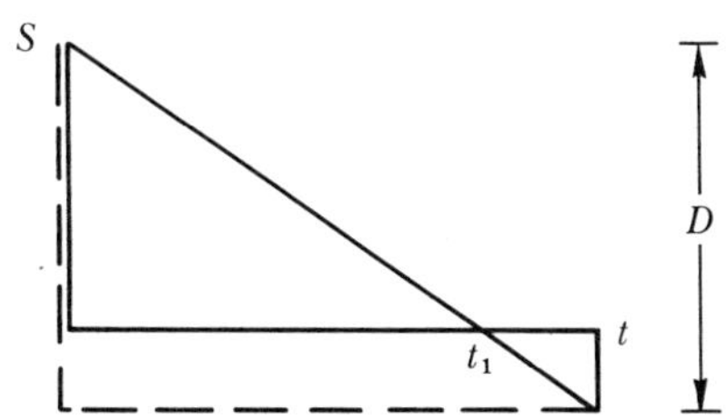

$$A_h = S/2$$

$$A_s = (S - D)/2$$

Each average is weighted for the portion of the cycle during which it persists:

$$\text{holding} = \frac{S}{2}\left(\frac{t_1}{t}\right)$$

$$\text{shortage} = \frac{(S - D)}{2}\left(\frac{t - t_1}{t}\right)$$

By the law of similar triangles, sides may be compared to the dashed triangle:

$$\frac{S}{D} = \frac{t_1}{t} \quad \text{and} \quad \frac{(S - D)}{D} = \frac{t - t_1}{t}$$

Therefore,

$$\text{holding} = \frac{S}{2}\left(\frac{S}{D}\right) = \frac{S^2}{2D}$$

$$\text{shortage} = \frac{(S - D)}{2}\left(\frac{S - D}{D}\right) = \frac{(S - D)^2}{2D}$$

There are, of course, many possible average holdings and shortages and their corresponding durations. Each is weighted by the probability of demand getting D units high. The results are then summed and multiplied by C_h or C_s as the case may be to obtain expected holding and shortage costs. It is necessary to split the probability distribution into $S \geq D$ and $D > S$ portions, and to recognize that even though $D > S$, there is an initial holding period that ends only when beginning supply is exhausted.

Solution:

$$\sum_{D=0}^{S-1} P(D) + (2S-1)\sum_{D=S}^{\infty}\frac{P(D)}{2D} \le \frac{C_s}{C_s + C_h} \le \sum_{D=0}^{S} P(D) + (2S+1)\sum_{D=S+1}^{\infty}\frac{P(D)}{2D}$$

Comment: This answer is obtained using the detailed methods that were presented in the solution of the newsboy model.

Example: A manufacturer finds it convenient to make runs of a particular product either once a month or once every two months and wishes to determine which of these plans is better. He also wants to know how many units to produce each time and how much the annual cost of the better plan is expected to be. Demand is gradual, the product enjoys longevity, and backorders are permitted.

$$C_h = \$240 \text{ per unit per month}$$

$$C_s = \$960 \text{ per unit per month}$$

$$C_o = \$2{,}000 \text{ per batch}$$

Monthly demand, D	1	2	3
$P(D)$	.3	.5	.2

Solution: *One month*: $C_s/(C_s + C_h) = 960/(960 + 240) = .8$

$$\sum_{D=1}^{1} P(D) + (2(2)-1)\sum_{D=2}^{3}\frac{P(D)}{2D} \le .8 \le \sum_{D=1}^{2} P(D) + (2(2)+1)\sum_{D=3}^{3}\frac{P(D)}{2D}$$

$$.3 + \frac{3}{2}\left(\frac{.5}{2} + \frac{.2}{3}\right) = .775 \le .8 \le .3 + .5 + \frac{5}{2}\left(\frac{.2}{3}\right) = .967$$

Consequently, if one month is chosen, enough units should be produced so that two units will be in stock at the beginning of each month. The expected monthly cost of this policy will be

$$E[K(2)] = 240\left[\frac{3}{2}(.3) + 1(.5) + \frac{2}{3}(.2)\right] + 960\left[\frac{1}{6}(.2)\right] + 2{,}000 = \$2{,}292$$

In a year, this policy costs 12($2,292) = $27,504.
Two months:
The convoluted distribution (see page 386) is

$D = D_1 + D_2$	2	3	4	5	6
$P(D)$	.09	.30	.37	.20	.04

Holding and shortage costs double; therefore

$$C_s/(C_s + C_h) = 1{,}920/(1{,}920 + 480) = .8$$

$$\sum_{D=2}^{2} P(D) + (2(3) - 1) \sum_{D=3}^{6} \frac{P(D)}{2D} \leq .8 \leq \sum_{D=2}^{3} P(D) + (2(3) + 1) \sum_{D=4}^{6} \frac{P(D)}{2D}$$

$$.688 \leq .8 \leq .877$$

Consequently, if the two-month policy is chosen, enough units should be produced so that three units will be in stock at the start of every other month. The expected cost for two months is

$$E[K(3)] = 480\left[2(.09) + 1.5(.3) + \frac{9}{2}\left(\frac{.37}{4} + \frac{.20}{5} + \frac{.04}{6}\right)\right]$$

$$+ 1{,}920\left[\frac{1}{8}(.37) + \frac{2}{5}(.20) + \frac{3}{4}(.04)\right] + 2{,}000 = \$2{,}600.60$$

In a year, this policy costs 6($2,600.60) = $15,603.60
This is a considerably less expensive policy.

Comment:

1. It is helpful to do a dimensional analysis on some term:

$$\frac{C_h t S^2}{2D} \rightarrow \frac{\$}{\text{Unit day}} \frac{\text{Days units}^2}{\text{Units}} = \$,$$

where the denominator 2 is dimensionless, as is the omitted probability distribution; both are weightings.

2. If shortage cost were such that backorders were permitted, then the same dimension, $, would result. Furthermore, if shortage results in lost business as, for instance, if a car dealer loses sales because he does not have particular models immediately available, the gradual demand model becomes a hybrid and includes a $C_s(D - S)$ portion, which has dimension $\$ = \frac{\$}{\text{Unit}}$ Units (note the change in C_s).

3. The analysis could be continued for three months or four months or whatever number of months results in the minimal cost. At some point, time might become sufficiently significant to make discounting advisable. Unfortunately, the model is not well suited to discounting. Any simple approach requires unsuitable assumptions such as presuming that costs occur at the middle of the cycle or at its end. The latter is particularly unsatisfactory because shortage occurs only toward the end of the cycle, while holding occurs right away, ceasing

at t_1 (at the earliest). The most satisfactory approach to discounting this model, in my view, might be termed the "decomposition" approach, a sketch of which follows:

a. Find the transform of the monthly distribution and "decompose" this to a daily distribution by raising the transformed function to the $1/30th$ power and then finding the inverse transform. The scheme is to so reduce the basic time period that averaging units over the period is unnecessary—the ending inventory of the day can be assumed to represent the whole day (as in the newsboy problem). If a day is unsatisfactory, then decomposing to an hour (or less) may be necessary.
b. In convolutions,

$$D = x_1 + x_2 + \cdots + x_n \quad \text{and} \quad E(D) = \sum_{i=1}^{n} E(x_i) = n\bar{x},$$

since the x_i are independent, identically distributed random variables for daily demand.
c. Therefore, where holding occurs, the inventory balance after T days is $S - T\bar{x}$. The amount of shortage for T periods is $T\bar{x}$. The base model then becomes

$$E[K(S)] = C_0 + C_h \sum_{T=1}^{t_1} (S - T\bar{x})b(T, r) + C_s \sum_{T=t_1+1}^{30} T\bar{x}b(T, r)$$

Here $t_1 = S/\bar{x}$ and r is interest for a day.

Isolating the Cost of Shortage

In practice it is often difficult to obtain an estimate of C_s; however, if the demand probability distribution and cost of holding are known, and if management has already chosen a stocking level, S, it is an easy matter to calculate an implicit range for C_s. To illustrate, assume $C_h = \$100$,

$$P(D \le S - 1) = .75, \qquad P(D \le S) = .8; \text{ then}$$

$$.75 \le \frac{C_s}{C_s + 100} \le .8$$

$$.75(C_s + 100) = C_s; \quad \therefore, \quad C_s = 300$$

$$.8(C_s + 100) = C_s; \quad \therefore, \quad C_s = 400$$

Consequently, *if* the chosen level of S is indeed the optimal level, the cost of shortage falls in the range $\$300 \le C_s \le \$400$. If the decisionmaker believes C_s is less than \$300 and can now specify the proper amount, the model should be re-solved with the given value of C_s to determine the proper amount to stock.

Incidentally, once the optimal level of S is found, this approach may be used to see how much change in C_s or in C_h may be tolerated before seeking a new optimum.

Cost: A Broad Interpretation

Thus far, this chapter has illustrated decisions based on dollar values and has only mentioned that service level is desirable because it reflects many things. Which approach should be used? How is service level measured? How can both approaches be presented simultaneously? These are some of the questions this section addresses.

Someone who has been trained to think of costs in terms of dollars and who prefers objective measurement would undoubtedly choose the dollar approach. But dollars can be very limiting and to insist on them exclusively can render analysis narrow. Businesses worry about meeting competition, being courteous and friendly to customers, seeing to customer comfort in general, and creating goodwill with employees as well as with competitors, the public, and the government. It is difficult to measure these things in dollar terms and it is often unnecessary. Knowing the probability of shortage or the expected shortage of an inventory item is one way of assessing the associated service level, and yet the focus is on units, not on dollars. Selecting the service level implicitly recognizes competition, comfort, and courtesy as well as dollar cost, albeit indirectly. Service level is akin to the economist's utility measurement except that service level is more practically measured.

In defense of the dollar approach, one need only observe how objective it is. It is not nearly as abstract as are many of the things that are implicitly recognized by the units approach. And dollars have some stability as a measure that is not possible when one attempts to ascertain how one person in a business feels about, say, the importance of courtesy as opposed to how some other decisionmaker in the same organization feels.

Fortunately, we are in a false dilemma, for as I mentioned earlier, nothing prohibits us from using both approaches. The manager, for instance, might not care for the service level associated with a "minimum" cost solution and could decide that raising service level is worth the difference in dollar costs. Put differently, in his judgment the costs not recognized in the dollar approach would, if they could be measured, raise the optimal solution to the value that reflects an acceptable service level.

Let us now focus on measures of service level and at the same time see how to treat leadtime in probabilistic modelling.

The Discrete Leadtime, Order Level Model

What is needed is a model that recognizes: (1) variability of demand and leadtime, (2) duration and magnitude of holdings and shortages, and (3) fluctuating levels of beginning and ending inventory. The model is complex simply because the situation is complicated. In a typical operating period any of three situations could occur:

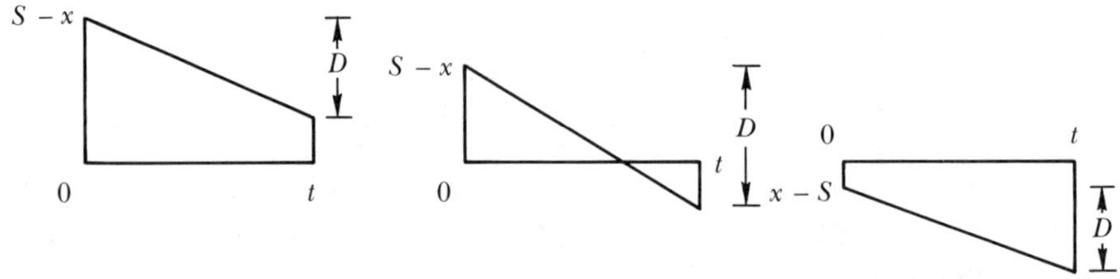

Demand during leadtime leaves a positive beginning inventory. Demand during the operating period leaves ending inventory at either a positive or a zero level.

Demand during leadtime leaves a positive beginning inventory but operating demand results in a shortage as an ending inventory.

Demand during leadtime causes a shortage as a beginning inventory which is intensified by operating demand.

Note: x is the random variable for leadtime demand and is a convolution of D, the random variable for operating demand.

The aim is to determine the target or order level, S, that minimizes the costs of the typical operating period. The expected cost of having any order level is expressed as follows:

$$E[K(S)] = \left\{ \begin{aligned} & C_o + tC_h\left[\sum_{x=0}^{S}\sum_{D=0}^{S-X}\left(S - x - \frac{D}{2}\right)P(D)L(x)\right. \\ & \left. + \sum_{x=0}^{S}\sum_{D=S-x+1}^{\infty}\frac{(S-x)^2}{2D}P(D)L(x)\right] \\ & + tC_s\left[\sum_{x=0}^{S}\sum_{D=S-x+1}^{\infty}\frac{(D+x-S)^2}{2D}P(D)L(x)\right. \\ & \left. + \sum_{x=S+1}^{\infty}\sum_{D=0}^{\infty}\left(x + \frac{D}{2} - S\right)P(D)L(x)\right] \end{aligned} \right\}$$

Explanation of Model:

1. C_h and C_s are multiplied by t, the duration of the operating period, to adjust them from, say, a daily basis to costs per unit for the operating period.

2. Beginning inventory is always equal to the target level minus the demand that occurred during leadtime. Stated differently, beginning inventory reflects ending inventory plus whatever replenishment order has just then

arrived. Ending inventory, on the other hand, is always equal to beginning inventory minus current operating demand. These relationships may be seen in the diagram shown below, which has a two-week leadtime and a one-week operating period. Dashed lines indicate stock on order.

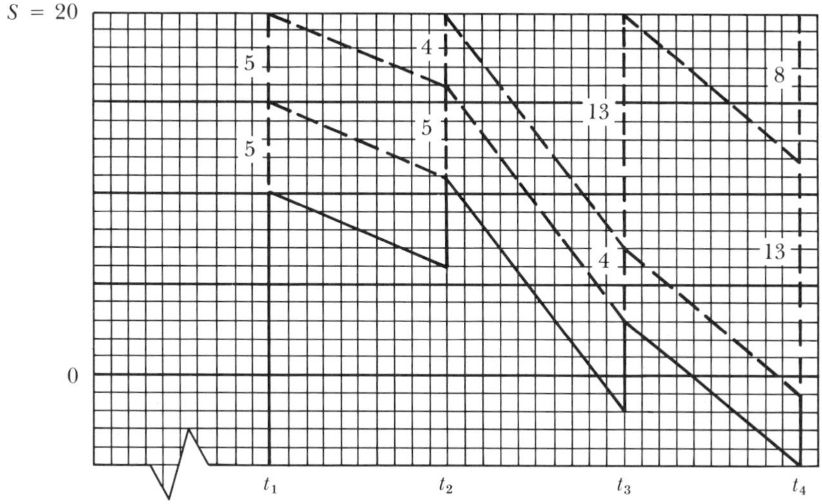

For example, demand of 4 occurs in the period from t_1 to t_2 and results in an ending inventory of 6 at t_2. Five replenishment units ordered two weeks earlier arrive at t_2 bringing opening inventory at t_2 to 11. An order is then placed for $20 - (6 + 5 + 5) = 4$ units. It therefore takes a week to register a demand, which amount is ordered at the end of that week to be received two weeks later (thus 4 units are ordered at t_2 and were received at t_4). In general, orders, P_k, follow the equation

$$P_k = S - \left(E.I. + \sum_{i=k-L}^{k-1} P_i \right)$$

3. The leadtime and the length of the operating period must be compatible. For example, incompatibility would occur if the operating period were two weeks while leadtime were either one, two, or three weeks according to some probability distribution. In such circumstances, the one- and three-week leadtimes would result in replenishments being received in the middle of the operating period. Leadtimes of two, four, six, etc. would, however, be compatible with a two-week operating period. In other words, compatibility requires leadtimes to be integer multiples of the length of the operating period.

Exhibit 3 contains an annotated computer program, written in the BASIC language, that solves this model. With this program leadtimes of

Exhibit 3

```
100  REM X( ) = ONE PERIOD DEMAND DISTRIBUTION
105  REM T( ) = LEADTIME DISTRIBUTION
110  REM --CAUTION--IF LEADTIME HAS A POSITIVE PROBABILITY OF
111  REM                    BEING 0, DO NOT READ IN T(0); THAT IS, OMIT T(0).
115  REM V( ) = THE PREVIOUS CONVOLUTED FOLD OF DEMAND
117  REM U( ) = DEMAND DURING OPERATING PERIOD DISTRIBUTION
120  REM W( ) = AN ACCUMULATING ARRAY FOR TEMPORARY SUMMING
125  REM P( ) = DEMAND DURING LEADTIME DISTRIBUTION
130  REM N    = MAXIMUM LEADTIME
135  REM M    = MAXIMUM AMOUNT DEMANDED IN ONE PERIOD
140  REM Z    = MINIMUM AMOUNT DEMANDED IN ONE PERIOD
145  REM E    = CHOSEN LENGTH OF OPERATING PERIOD
200  DIM  X(200),T(200),V(200),W(200),P(200)
205  READ M,N,Z,E,C1,C2,C3
210  LET  G = (N+E) * M
211  IF N < E THEN 214
212  LET  M = N
213  GO TO 215
214  LET  H = E
215  FOR  I  = 0 TO G
220  LET  X(I) = 0
225  LET  V(I) = 0
230  LET  W(I) = 0
235  LET  P(I) = 0
240  NEXT I
260  FOR  I = Z TO M
265  READ X(I)
270  NEXT I
280  FOR  J = 1 TO M
285  READ T(J)
290  NEXT J
300  FOR  K = 1 TO N
310  FOR  D = 0 TO G
320  IF K > = 2 THEN 350
330  LET  V(D) = X(D)
335  LET  P(D) = (V(D) *T(1)) + P(D)
340  GO TO 385
350  FOR  I = 0 TO D
360  LET  W(D) = (X(I) * V(D - I)) + W(D)
370  NEXT I
380  LET  P(D) = (W(D) * T(K)) + P(D)
385  NEXT D
390  IF K = 1 THEN 412
395  FOR J = 0 TO D
400  LET  V(J) = W(J)
405  LET  W(J) = 0
410  NEXT J
412  FOR  I = 0 TO G
413  IF K < > E THEN 425
414  LET U(I) = V(I)
418  PRINT USING 420,I,U(I)
420  FIELD ("U(",F3.0,") = ",F6.4)
425  NEXT I
426  PRINT
450  FOR D = 0 TO G
455  IF K<>N THEN 468
```

Exhibit 3 (*cont.*)

```
460  PRINT USING 465,D,P(D)
465  FIELD ("P(",F3.0,") = ",F6.4)
468  NEXT D
470  NEXT K
472  PRINT
473  PRINT
480  FOR S = 0 TO G
481  LET A,A1,A2,A3 = 0
482  FOR D = S+1 TO G
484  FOR X = 0 TO G
486  LET A = P(D) * U(X)
488  LET A1 = A1 + A
490  LET A2 = (A*(D-S+(X/2))) + A2
492  NEXT X
494  NEXT D
500  FOR D = 0 TO S
502  FOR X = S-D+1 TO G
504  LET A = P(D) * U(X)
506  LET A1 = A1 + A
508  LET A2 = (A*((D + X - S)↑2)/(2*X)) + A2
509  LET A3 = (A*((S-D)↑2)/(2*X)) + A3
510  NEXT X
512  NEXT D
514  FOR D = 0 TO S
516  FOR X = 0 TO S-D
518  LET A  = P(D)*U(X)
520  LET A3 = (A*(S-D-(X/2))) + A3
522  NEXT X
524  NEXT D
526  LET A4 = E*C2*A2
528  LET A5 = E*C1*A3
530  LET A6 = C3 + A4 + A5
540  PRINT "PROBABILITY OF SHORTAGE, GIVEN S = ";S;",IS";A1
542  PRINT "EXPECTED SHORTAGE, GIVEN S = ";S;",IS";A2;"UNITS"
544  PRINT "EXPECTED COST OF TARGET LEVEL";S,",IS";A6;"DOLLARS"
546  PRINT
550  NEXT S
600  DATA 2,3,0,1,5,25,50
610  DATA .2,.5,.3
620  DATA .3,.4,.3
700  END

RUN

U(  0) = .2000
U(  1) = .5000
U(  2) = .3000
U(  3) =     0
U(  4) =     0
U(  5) =     0
U(  6) =     0
U(  7) =     0
U(  8) =     0

P(  0) = .0784
P(  1) = .2480
P(  2) = .2938
```

Exhibit 3 (*cont.*)

```
P(  3) = .2115
P(  4) = .1197
P(  5) = .0405
P(  6) = .0081
P(  7) =     0
P(  8) =     0

PROBABILITY OF SHORTAGE, GIVEN S= 0,IS .98432
EXPECTED SHORTAGE, GIVEN S= 0,IS 2.75 UNITS
EXPECTED COST OF TARGET LEVEL 0 IS 118.75 DOLLARS

PROBABILITY OF SHORTAGE, GIVEN S= 1,IS .89552
EXPECTED SHORTAGE, GIVEN S= 1,IS 1.79116 UNITS
EXPECTED COST OF TARGET LEVEL 1 IS 94.9848 DOLLARS

PROBABILITY OF SHORTAGE, GIVEN S= 2,IS .68924
EXPECTED SHORTAGE, GIVEN S= 2,IS .99388 UNITS
EXPECTED COST OF TARGET LEVEL 2 IS 76.0664 DOLLARS

PROBABILITY OF SHORTAGE, GIVEN S= 3,IS .42564
EXPECTED SHORTAGE, GIVEN S= 3,IS .455925 UNITS
EXPECTED COST OF TARGET LEVEL 3 IS 64.92775 DOLLARS

PROBABILITY OF SHORTAGE, GIVEN S= 4,IS .20781
EXPECTED SHORTAGE, GIVEN S= 4,IS .1651275 UNITS
EXPECTED COST OF TARGET LEVEL 4 IS 61.203825 DOLLARS

PROBABILITY OF SHORTAGE, GIVEN S= 5,IS 7.641E-2
EXPECTED SHORTAGE, GIVEN S= 5,IS 4.38075E-2 UNITS
EXPECTED COST OF TARGET LEVEL 5 IS 62.564225 DOLLARS

PROBABILITY OF SHORTAGE, GIVEN S= 6,IS 1.863E-2
EXPECTED SHORTAGE, GIVEN S= 6,IS 7.4925E-3 UNITS
EXPECTED COST OF TARGET LEVEL 6 IS 66.474775 DOLLARS

PROBABILITY OF SHORTAGE, GIVEN S= 7,IS 2.43E-3
EXPECTED SHORTAGE, GIVEN S= 7,IS 6.075E-4 UNITS
EXPECTED COST OF TARGET LEVEL 7 IS 71.268225 DOLLARS

PROBABILITY OF SHORTAGE, GIVEN S= 8,IS 0
EXPECTED SHORTAGE, GIVEN S= 8,IS 0 UNITS
EXPECTED COST OF TARGET LEVEL 8 IS 76.25 DOLLARS
```

varying lengths can be accommodated and operating period duration can be varied to permit the lowest cost arrangement to be identified—provided leadtimes are compatible with the chosen length of the operating period. For purposes of illustration, the exhibit uses $C_h = \$5$; $C_s = \$25$; $C_o = \$50$; probability of weekly demand of zero, one, or two being .2, .5, and .3 respectively; and probability of leadtime of one, two, or three weeks being .3, .4, and .3 respectively.[3] These data are entered on lines 600, 610, and 620. The output of the program shows the probability distributions for operating period and leadtime (properly weighted by the probabilities that leadtime will last one, two, or three weeks), probability of shortage, expected shortage, and expected cost of the selected target level.

---

[3] Also, for simplicity, it is assumed that replenishment orders are placed on the same source of supply and are, therefore, received in their original sequence.

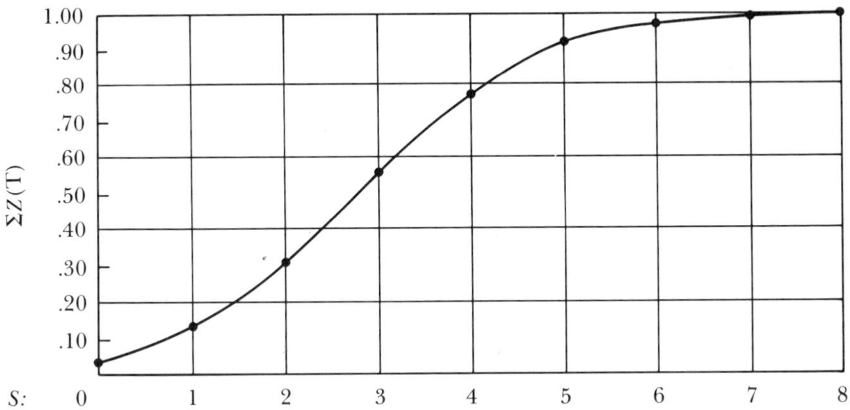

S:	0	1	2	3	4	5	6	7	8
E(shortage):	2.750	1.791	.994	.456	.165	.044	.007	.001	0
P(shortage):	.984	.896	.689	.426	.208	.076	.019	.002	0
$\$(E[K(S)])$:	118.75	94.98	76.07	64.93	61.20	62.56	66.47	71.27	76.25
$\$(\Delta E[K(S)])$:	118.75	−23.77	−18.91	−11.14	−3.73	+1.36	+3.91	+4.80	+4.98

Key: $Z(T)$ = the probability distribution of total demand reflects both leadtime and operating demand. $Z(T) = P(D) * L(x)$

$\$(E[K(S)])$ = The expected cost of target level *S*.

$\$(\Delta E[K(S)])$ = The incremental cost of target level *S*.

Figure 3

Figure 3 reflects all the data from Exhibit 3 plus a plot of the cumulative distribution of the convolution of the leadtime and operating demand distributions. This is perhaps the most significant figure in this text, for it relates dollar costs and service level, whether measured in probability of shortage or expected shortage. (Expected shortage could be measured in units only or, as in Exhibit 3, in units weighted by time.) If the company now has a target level of three units, this is an irrational policy, because *both* dollar cost and service level can be improved by setting the target at four, which has associated with it the lowest expected cost of \$61.20. However, for an additional \$1.36 per week, the probability of shortage can be reduced from .208 to .076 by going to a target level of five units. The decisionmaker must decide if the improvement in service is worth the incremental dollar cost.

This model, which is referred to as an (S, t) model in the literature, assumes that items have long life and that backorders are possible. If backorders are impossible, shortage results in lost business. This would change the formula for $E[K(S)]$.

The Continuous Leadtime, Order Level Model.

The (S, t) model just presented has its continuous probabilistic formulation, which will provide a challenging way of concluding this chapter. Let us apply the model to an unusual inventory and deal with another way of estimating C_h and C_s.

Example: A university plans to "modernize" its undergraduate curriculum, to develop new graduate courses at the master's level, and to offer new doctoral programs in many disciplines. It contemplates continuous improvement and enhancement of these offerings. Of course, the existing tried and proven curriculum will be offered simultaneously. The main obstacle to these plans is the absence of unlimited funds; the university wants quality but must generate it within tight budgetary confines.

Because of this budgetary stringency and the large number of professors needed, the strategy is to hire younger men with enthusiasm and potential and to give them a two-year period in which to develop their teaching techniques, assess the ability of the student body, determine standards, and so forth. Following this two-year gestation period, the "trainees" will be expected to launch the new courses and programs. This is to be a continuing pattern of operation.

Now professors are a noble lot with understanding wives and great dedication to academe. They are willing to overlook personal economic disadvantage in the interests of acquiring and communicating knowledge. They love committee work and willingly volunteer for further assignments. They are impervious to the temptations of both competing educational institutions and industry. Unlike other men, professors never conceive that the grass might be greener elsewhere. Climate never enters into their thinking. To them salary is always adequate, intellectual environment is always stimulating, and solitude is always obtainable. They crave to spend endless hours counseling students, assuaging their fears, and smoothing their paths. They yearn to be active in community activities of a political or social or whatever nature. In short, professors are selfless individuals.

Bull!

Professors are human beings and cursed with "blind-man-elephantitis" like everybody else; they do get annoyed by all kinds of things and they do get enticed by competing offers. They leave for greener pastures. Leakages occur.

When professors decamp, they must be replaced by more experienced professors if the new courses and programs are to proceed on schedule.

These more experienced professors, who require little or no gestation period, are always considerably more costly and must be pirated from other institutions. Or if professors from the tried and proven courses are asked to "double up" their teaching work load, costly concessions and very costly morale problems arise. If the new programs do not materialize, disappointment sets in, the calendar is set back, reputation is jeopardized, and the top students go elsewhere. Consequently, there are definite costs of shortage. On the other hand, if too many professors are hired, their salaries must still be paid, since direct firing is both a humanly difficult task and injurious to reputation, and "phasing people out" takes a while. In the meantime, the surplus professors are apt to duplicate one another's work, bringing about a particular (costly) academic problem known as course or subject "overlap." Therefore, there are definite costs of holding.

Measuring the holding and shortage costs precisely could be extremely troublesome. It is, however, considerably easier to estimate how many times greater the shortage cost is than the holding cost, and this is perfectly adequate for the cost model. It would not seem unreasonable for this problem to say that shortage cost was perhaps five times as great as holding cost. (It would be interesting to see what salaries professors would hold out for if they could ascertain that shortage cost was assumed to be five times as great as holding cost.)

We assume that requirements are reviewed once a year. (This is the set operating period—a year has been chosen but in practice any unit of length—say, a month—would do as well.) "Orders" are placed at that time to bring the professorial inventory to a level S at the beginning of the next year.

The situation confronting the university in a given operating period could be any of the cases A, B, or C. The cost model can therefore be constructed as follows, using y as the variable indicating shrinkage (demand) in staff during the two-year training period (leadtime) preceding the start of an operating period, and x as the variable for shrinkage during the operating period.

$$E[K(S)] = K = K_A + K_B + K_C + C_o$$

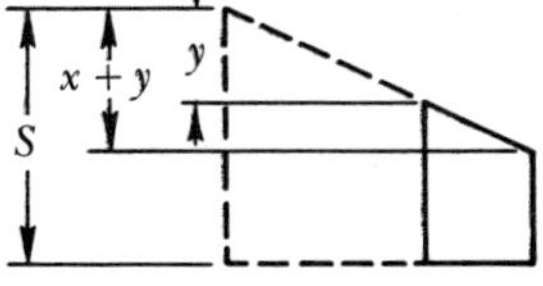

Case A:

$$0 < y < S$$
$$0 < x < S - y$$

$$\frac{(S-y)+(S-y-x)}{2} = S - y - \frac{x}{2}$$

$$K_A = C_h \int_0^S \int_0^{S-y} \left(S - y - \frac{x}{2}\right) f(x)\,dx\,g(y)\,dy$$

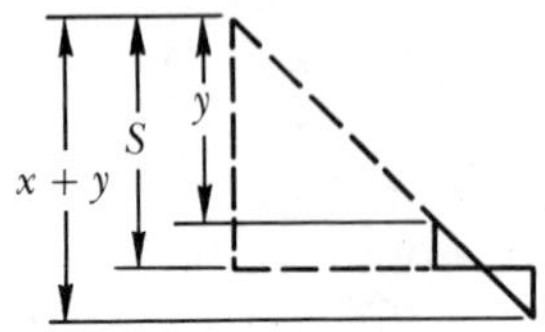

Case B:

$$0 < y < S$$
$$S - y < x < \infty$$

$\frac{((S-y)+0)}{2}\frac{t_1}{t};\quad \frac{((x+y-S)+0)}{2}\frac{(t-t_1)}{t}$ But by similar triangles $\frac{S-y}{x} = \frac{t_1}{t}$ and $\frac{(x+y-S)}{x} = \frac{(t-t_1)}{t}$ Therefore: $\frac{(S-y)^2}{2x};\quad \frac{(x+y-S)^2}{2x}$

$$K_B = \int_0^S \int_{S-y}^{\infty} \left[C_h \frac{(S-y)^2}{2x} + C_s \frac{(x+y-S)^2}{2x} \right] f(x)\, dx\, g(y)\, dy$$

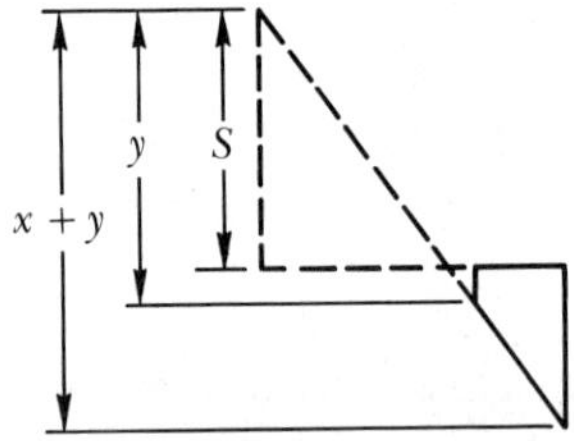

Case C:

$$S < y < \infty$$
$$0 < x < \infty$$

$\frac{(y-S)+(x+y-S)}{2} = \frac{x}{2} + y - S$

$$K_C = C_s \int_S^{\infty} \int_0^{\infty} \left(\frac{x}{2} + y - S \right) f(x)\, dx\, g(y)\, dy$$

A few words of caution:

1. When taking the derivative of an integral, *do not forget* that $f(x)$—or $g(y)$—is part of the integrand.
2. When taking the derivative of an integral, *do not forget* that the original integrands must be evaluated using the upper and lower limits (and *not* using the derivative of the original integrand).
3. If a limit is a constant (or in some cases ∞), the derivative of the limit will be zero and you need not bother to evaluate the integrand at that limit.
4. Go slow.

$$K_A = \int_0^S \int_0^{S-y} C_h \left(S - y - \frac{x}{2} \right) f(x)\, dx\, g(y)\, dy$$

Let $$I_A(S, y) = \int_0^{S-y} C_h \left(S - y - \frac{x}{2} \right) f(x)\, dx$$

continued to page 515

continued from page 514

Therefore, $$K_A = \int_0^S I_A(S, y)g(y)\,dy$$

$$\frac{dK_A}{dS} = \int_0^S \frac{\partial I_A(S, y)g(y)}{\partial S}\,dy + I_A(S, S)g(S)(1) - 0$$

$$= C_h \int_0^S \left[\int_0^{S-y} f(x)\,dx + \left(\frac{S-y}{2}\right) f(S-y)(1) - 0\right] g(y)\,dy$$

$$+ C_h \int_0^{S-S} \left(S - S - \frac{x}{2}\right) g(S) f(x)\,dx$$

$$= C_h \int_0^S \left[\int_0^{S-y} f(x)\,dx + \frac{(S-y)}{2} f(S-y)\right] g(y)\,dy$$

Proceeding in this fashion, we obtain

$$\frac{dK_B}{dS} = \int_0^S \left[\begin{array}{l} \displaystyle\int_{S-y}^{\infty} \left[C_h \frac{(S-y)}{x} - C_s \frac{(x+y-S)}{x}\right] f(x)\,dx \\ \displaystyle - \frac{C_h(S-y)f(S-y)(1)}{2} \end{array}\right] g(y)\,dy$$

$$+ C_s g(S) \int_0^{\infty} \frac{x}{2} f(x)\,dx$$

$$\frac{dK_C}{dS} = \int_S^{\infty} \int_0^{\infty} - C_s f(x)\,dx\, g(y)\,dy - C_s g(S) \int_0^{\infty} \frac{x}{2} f(x)\,dx$$

Next all the separate sections are put together to obtain dK/dS, which is then set equal to zero to determine the optimal value of S. To expedite your reading, let us abbreviate the notation. From this point on, $f(x)\,dx$ will be written as f and $g(y)\,dy$ will be written as g. $f(S-y)$ and $g(S)$ will remain the same notationally. The results are shown in Exhibit 4.

Data: The operating demand distribution for professorial departures is $f(x) = .008^2 x e^{-.008x}$

Its Laplace transform is $L(S) = \int_{\infty}^{0} f(x)e^{-Sx}\,dx = [.008/(.008 + S)]^2$

The leadtime demand distribution is the 2-fold convolution

$$g(y) = L^{-1}\{[.008/(.008 + S)]^4\} = .008^4 y^3 e^{-.008y}/3!$$

Inserting $f(x)$ and $g(y)$ into the results obtained in Exhibit 4 and letting $\alpha = .008$,

$$\int_0^S \left[\int_0^{S-y} \alpha^2 x e^{-\alpha x}\,dx + \int_{S-y}^{\infty} \frac{(S-y)}{x} \alpha^2 x e^{-\alpha x}\,dx\right] \frac{\alpha^4 y^3 e^{-\alpha y}}{3!} = \frac{C_s}{C_s + C_h} = 5/6$$

Exhibit 4

We begin by collecting terms having the same outside integral:

$$\frac{dK}{dS} = \int_0^S \left[\int_0^{S-y} C_h f + C_h \frac{(S-y)}{2} f(S-y) \right.$$

$$+ \int_{S-y}^{\infty} \left[C_h \frac{(S-y)}{x} - C_s \frac{(x+y-S)}{x} \right] f - C_h \frac{(S-y)}{2} f(S-y) \Bigg] g$$

$$+ C_s g(S) \int_0^{\infty} \frac{x}{2} f - \int_S^{\infty} \int_0^{\infty} C_s f g - C_s g(S) \int_0^{\infty} \frac{x}{2} f = 0$$

Split up the integrand containing the numerator $C_s(x + y - S)$:

$$\int_0^S \left[\int_0^{S-y} C_h f + \int_{S-y}^{\infty} C_h \frac{(S-y)}{x} f - \int_{S-y}^{\infty} C_s f + \int_{S-y}^{\infty} C_s \frac{(S-y)}{x} f \right] g - \int_S^{\infty} \int_0^{\infty} C_s f g = 0$$

If we set as a goal the obtaining of $C_s/(C_h + C_s)$ as a right-hand side expression, we will want to be able to factor out $(C_h + C_s)$ and to generate $-C_s$ from the left-hand side of this equation. To do so, we add zero as follows:

$$\int_0^S \left[\int_0^{S-y} C_h f + \int_{S-y}^{\infty} C_h \frac{(S-y)}{x} f - \int_{S-y}^{\infty} C_s f \pm \int_0^{S-y} C_s f \right.$$

$$+ \int_{S-y}^{\infty} C_s \frac{(S-y)}{x} f \Bigg] g - \int_S^{\infty} \int_0^{\infty} C_s f g = 0$$

After collecting terms, this equation reduces to

$$(C_h + C_s) \int_0^S \left[\int_0^{S-y} f + \int_{S-y}^{\infty} \frac{(S-y)}{x} f \right] g - \int_0^S \int_0^{\infty} C_s f g - \int_S^{\infty} \int_0^{\infty} C_s f g = 0$$

Once the abbreviations f and g are restored to their full glory, and it is recognized that the last two integrals on the left-hand side together sum *all* the joint probabilities to produce $-C_s$, this equation reduces to

$$\int_0^S \left[\int_0^{S-y} f(x)\,dx + \int_{S-y}^{\infty} \frac{(S-y)}{x} f(x)\,dx \right] g(y)\,dy = C_s/(C_h + C_s)$$

Using deluxe integration by parts (see Appendix C):

$$\frac{\alpha^6}{3!} \int_0^S \left(\left[\frac{xe^{-\alpha x}}{-\alpha} - \frac{e^{-\alpha x}}{(-\alpha)^2} \right]_0^{S-y} + (S-y) \left[\frac{e^{-\alpha x}}{-\alpha} \right]_{S-y}^{\infty} \right) y^3 e^{-\alpha y}\,dy = 5/6$$

$$\frac{\alpha^4}{3!} \int_0^S (y^3 e^{-\alpha y} - y^3 e^{-\alpha S})\,dy = 5/6$$

$$\frac{\alpha^4}{3!} \left[\frac{y^3 e^{-\alpha y}}{-\alpha} - \frac{3y^2 e^{-\alpha y}}{(-\alpha)^2} + \frac{6ye^{-\alpha y}}{(-\alpha)^3} - \frac{6e^{-\alpha y}}{(-\alpha)^4} - \frac{y^4 e^{-\alpha S}}{4} \right]_0^S = 5/6$$

$$-\frac{\alpha^4}{3!} e^{-\alpha S} \left[\frac{S^3}{\alpha} + \frac{3S^2}{\alpha^2} + \frac{6S}{\alpha^3} + \frac{6}{\alpha^4} + \frac{S^4}{4} \right] + \frac{\alpha^4}{3!} \frac{6}{\alpha^4} = 5/6$$

Collecting terms after distributing the $\alpha^4/3!$ coefficient leads to

$$\sum_{i=0}^{4} \frac{(\alpha S)^i e^{-\alpha S}}{i!} = \sum_{i=0}^{4} \frac{(.008S)^i e^{-.008S}}{i!} = 1/6$$

This is the cumulative Poisson distribution with the mean $\lambda = .008S$. Consulting a Poisson table, we find $P(i \le 4|\lambda = 7.1) = .166$. Therefore,

$$\begin{aligned} .008S &= 7.1 \\ S &= 888 \text{ faculty members} \end{aligned}$$

Comments: Note how we started with an exponential distribution, $f(x) = \alpha^2 x e^{-\alpha x}$, convoluted it to obtain a gamma distribution, $g(y) = \alpha^4 y^3 e^{-\alpha y}/3!$, and then integrated the gamma to obtain a Poisson $P(i) = (\alpha S)^i e^{-\alpha S}/i!$

Summary and Concluding Remarks

The focus in this chapter has really been on the use of costs in applied mathematics. Inventory models have been the vehicle because they apply in so many situations. But the broader objective—that of pursuing the philosophy of accounting—remains the guideline. Inventory models require the gathering and analysis of data to help people make decisions.

We began with the famous EOQ model and examined some of its imperfections and how these are remedied in practice. One imperfection, the cost of ordering, seems beyond remedy in the typical purchasing situation; fortunately, the cost of setup in the production case does not pose a similar problem.

Proceeding to nonlinear programming, we first studied how constraints affect costs and how Lagrange multipliers may be used in allocating additional capital outlays. The discussion then applied the Lagrange technique to the selection of an inventory of securities. Here risk was measured by variances and covariances and we minimized risk subject to a variety of constraints. I hope that minimizing variances suggests other applications of this model to you. *Note that variance itself was treated as a broader measure of cost.*

The discussion then took a more realistic turn by emphasizing probability theory. The newsboy model deals with instantaneous demand situations, whereas the gradual-demand model treats those situations in which demand is spread out over the entire cycle. Holdings and shortages are weighted by their durations when determining expectations in these models. The weightings are incorporated to adjust to cost period dimensions; expected units *only* would require no weighting by time, and in appearance would resemble the linear ($S - D$ and $D - S$) portions of the newsboy model. For these models, replenishment should require insignificant time.

It was noted that decisions about optimal supply (or target level) *may* not change with changes in cost parameters. In other words, the models may not be highly cost sensitive; a cost parameter may vary—within limits—and not cause a change in the optimal supply.

The gradual-demand model was used to study how often production runs should be made to minimize dollar costs while satisfying demand.

It should be a point of interest for accountants who are primarily concerned with assets on balance sheets that both the instantaneous- and gradual-demand models—as well as those which conclude the chapter—deal realistically with the optimal level (S in all models) of assets. Since financial accountants are careful to distinguish other assets from current assets, the use of inventory models seems particularly promising in helping choose categories—perhaps quantities in excess of S should be treated as other assets.

The chapter concluded with a study of the leadtime, order level model and the measuring of service level as an extension of cost theory to nondollar measures. The leadtime, order level model has much to recommend it for practical situations because it recognizes that replenishment often takes time, and it sets a regular period for the placing of a replenishment order. How to incorporate *both* dollar and nondollar approaches was illustrated in Figure 3. The cost parameters in the final illustration introduced scalar multiple, measurement of cost. Almost everyone favors cardinal measurement because it appears to be accurate and objective; however, subjectively estimating how much greater C_s is than C_h is perfectly acceptable for making decisions. Undoubtedly in times of retrenchment C_s and C_h approach equality or even $C_h > C_s$, for some inventories.

Space does not permit going into many other worthwhile inventory models and systems. There is the ABC system, in which, say, 10% of the inventory items account for, say, 70% of the dollar volume of inventory activity, 30% of the items for 20% of the volume, and 60% for 10% of the volume. The scheme is to model and closely control the high-volume items, give somewhat less attention to the middle-volume items, and perhaps give the low-volume items scarcely any attention at all. Another useful inventory model popularly employed in industry is the "two bin" system, in which replenishment orders are placed when the first bin becomes empty. Quantity discount models and price increase anticipation models each address interesting problems. Finally, the use of Z and Laplace transforms to study the effects of changes in multistage inventory systems offers a means of assessing the efficiency of these systems. Some of these promising models will be treated in the problems at the end of this chapter.

One branch of inventory modelling will receive attention in the next chapter. This is queuing (or waiting line) theory. If everything you see may be construed as an inventory, it is equally true to say that everything and everybody waits—all the time and usually for many events simultaneously.

We will couple probability theory and constrained optimization in Chapter 19.

Selected References

Eliezer Naddor, *Inventory Systems* (New York: John Wiley & Sons, 1966).

J. Buchan and K. Koenigsberg, *Scientific Inventory Management* (Englewood Cliffs, N.J.: Prentice-Hall, Inc., 1963).

G. Hadley and T. M. Whitin, *Analysis of Inventory Systems* (Englewood Cliffs, N.J.: Prentice-Hall, Inc., 1963).

Problems

1. Inventory rules are common—like "Have three months' supply of X on hand at all times." Can you justify such a rule in the light of inventory theory?

2. Set up, but do not solve, the basic inventory shortage model under both deterministic and stochastic assumptions. Then discuss the differences and advantages of each model and what information must be gathered to employ each one.

3. *Exponential smoothing.* A bakery is trying to develop a forecasting model for a particular cake. The most recent 10 days demand experience has been 15, 29, 10, 12, 16, 22, 18, 27, 25, and 13, in that order. While carrying figures to the nearest whole number, try to develop an exponential smoothing model that seems adequate. Your solution should show three or four attempts to determine an appropriate smoothing constant, graphs of your results, and a description of how you would attempt to refine your chosen model.

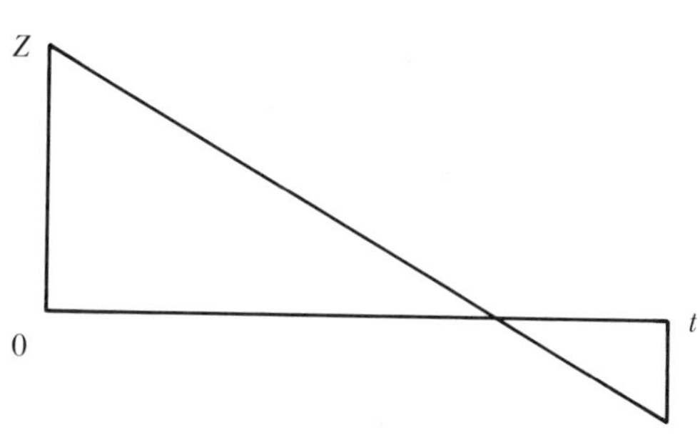

4. *EOQ shortage model derivation.* Derive the optimal order quantity and optimal cost per day for the model sketched above.

   Relate the optimal cost, $\hat{K}$, of this model to $\hat{K}_{\text{EOQ}}$, the basic EOQ model cost.

5. *Common supplier.* When C_o was discussed in this chapter, reference was made to an aggregative EOQ model where several items could be ordered simultaneously from the same supplier. The model was

$$K = \frac{C_o}{t} + \sum \frac{C_{hi} D_i t}{2}$$

   Determine the optimal quantities to order for each item and express the minimum value of K in closed form.

6. *Lot size, rapid demand.* Determine economic lot size for the situation graphed below:

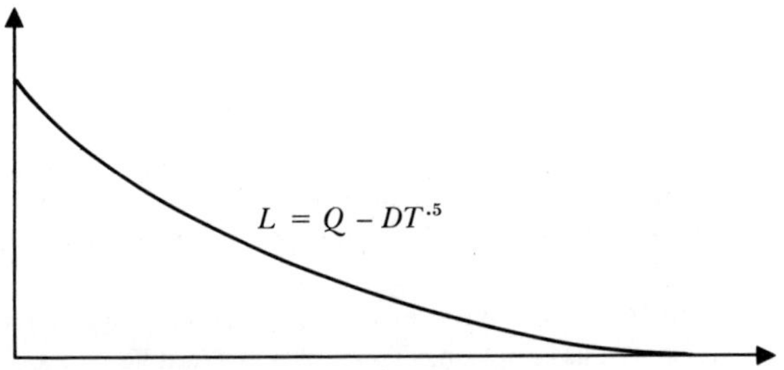

   What situation is depicted by the level equation?

7. *Regression, slow start-up, optimal order quantity, dimensioning.* The Curtis Steel Mill wishes to control its investment in one of its main, expensive products. It has regularly regressed inventory level against cycle length (which has varied because there have been different starting quantities) and arrived at $L = Q - DT^2$ with D invariant. Use the data given below to determine D.

T	L
0	1,000
1	990
2	960
3	910
4	840
5	750
6	640
7	510
8	360
9	190
10	0

The model to be developed is based on the diagram shown below.

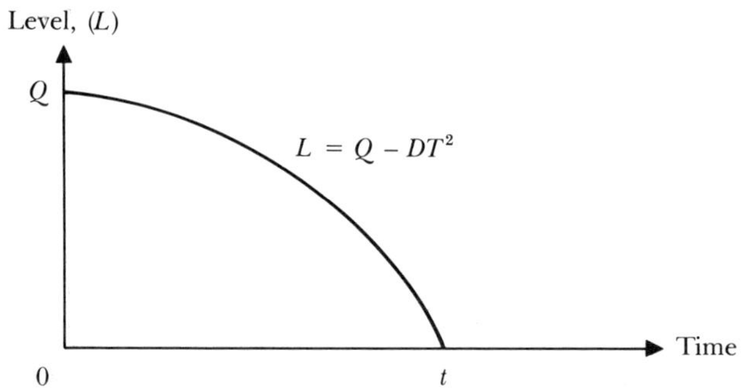

Key:
Q = Quantity ordered
D = Rate of demand per day
t = Length of cycle in days (a reading of T)
C_o = Setup costs = \$4,608
C_h = Holding costs per unit per day = \$.20

Determine the optimal order quantity. It would be advisable to consider what the units of area under the curve are, and to complete a dimensional analysis prior to optimizing the cost function.

8. *Optimal lot size and learning curves.* In Chapter 8 the learning curve $Y = 100(1 - e^{-.1T})$, where T is the number of days and Y is daily production, was presented. The curve reflected the fact that people become more efficient as they get practice. Of course, this means that the level of raw material inventory drops slowly at first and then picks up speed—as depicted in the diagram below:

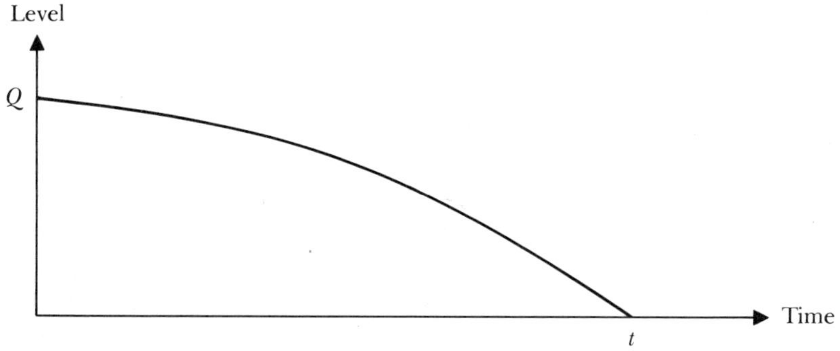

If cost to set up a production run is \$4,400, and if holding costs \$.10 per unit per day, and if management will not countenance shortage and a work stoppage, what is the optimal order size?

Caution:

Time is apt to be measured in a small number of days. Consequently, it would be advisable to use finite calculus in optimization rather than to employ infinitesimal calculus in the hope that it will yield a good approximation. (It might—but why not use the appropriate tool and be sure?)

9. *Step functions and price break modelling.* An EOQ model with a purchase price break may be graphed as shown below:

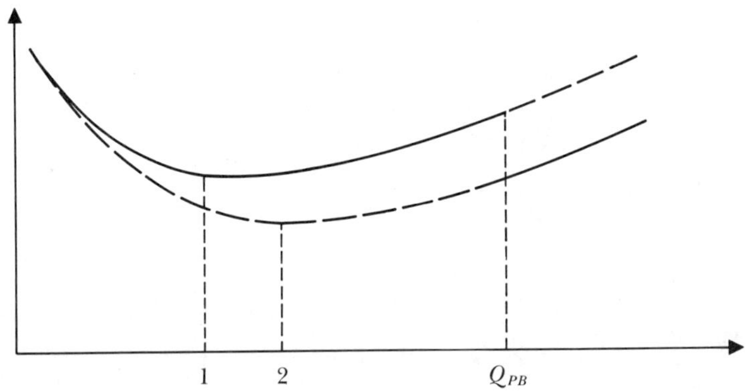

These are total-cost curves. They are drawn solid over the range pertinent to their purchase prices, C_u, and dashed when they go past the price break quantity, Q_{PB}. Thus, for $0 < Q < Q_{PB}$, C_{u1} is the purchase price in force, while for $Q_{PB} \leq Q < \infty$, C_{u2} is the pertinent purchase price, where $C_{u2} < C_{u1}$. This is the familiar "quantity discount" situation. The key to introducing purchase price into the ordinary EOQ model is to express holding cost not as C_h, but rather as rC_{ui}, where r is some rate that generates holding cost when multiplied by purchase price.

Required:

(a) Express cost per day, $K(Q)$, in terms of parameters.

(b) Decide what is the best quantity to order assuming that this graph is merely illustrative and could change shape.

(c) Comment on how you feel about expressing holding cost in this manner and therefore automatically decreasing holding cost per unit when a favorable price break occurs.

10. *Hoarding.* If a supplier has announced a price increase commencing some time in the near future, it makes sense to consider anticipating this price increase by hoarding (placing a large order for immediate delivery). Study the diagram that follows.

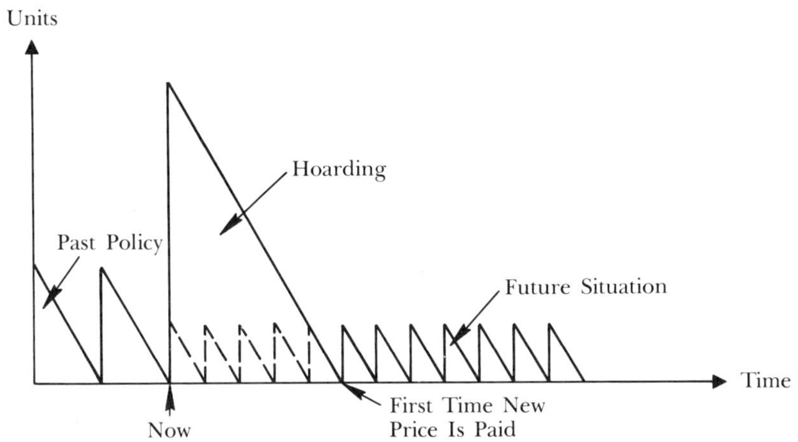

Note that the rate of demand (indicated by slope) remains constant throughout. If space to store is freely available, then cost of holding per unit should also stay constant. Cost of ordering might be expected to increase with the hoarding order, but in general hoarding should save on order costs that would otherwise have been necessary as well as on purchase cost. Essentially hoarding replaces the costs of many of the new and shorter cycles. Develop a generalized model (and optimize it) that maximizes the savings. Use primes on the ordinary parameters and variables to designate the hoarding portion of the model.

11. *Lagrangean optimization.* Management wishes to limit its investment in the inventory of a certain class of items to \$4,000. The EOQ model is in use for these items, which have the daily demands, order costs, and purchase prices shown below.

j	D_j	C_{rj}	C_{uj}
1	225	\$30	\$ 40
2	810	\$20	\$ 50
3	100	\$40	\$200

The holding cost percentage (based on C_u) is $r = 2\%$ per unit per day. For the purposes of satisfying the budgetary restriction, management will consider average quantity in inventory.

(a) Compute an optimal ordering policy, showing all mathematical manipulations.

(b) Comment on what sort of costs would apt to be reflected in rC_u.

(c) Develop a formula for λ_c and determine the additional investment (budgetary allotment) that would be forthcoming if management insisted on a critical return of 10%.

12. *Select a season's program of operas (prepared by Professors A. Wayne Corcoran and Frederick Patrick).* A well-known opera house faces the problem of selecting the works for its coming season's program. Operas are categorized under three headings: artistic (e.g., *Werther, Le Cid, Eugen Onegin*), popular (e.g., *La Traviata, Carmen, Cavalleria Rusticana, Lucia di Lammermoor*), and new (written by some contemporary composer). The management has kept careful records over the last dozen years concerning box office performance in terms of the percentage of full-house seats sold:

Year	Artistic	Popular	New
1965	78%	89%	62%
1966	82	94	72
1967	60	92	75
1968	70	88	74
1969	86	90	71
1970	92	95	67
1971	85	93	72
1972	83	88	75
1973	78	96	76
1974	91	90	72
1975	80	87	73
1976	75	90	75

Certain facts have been determined:

(a) If 80% of full house is achieved, enough contributions can be raised from a fund drive and performing arts sponsors to enable operating expenses to be met from combined receipts.

(b) At least 5% of the operas presented should be new works to encourage modern composers.

(c) The director of the opera company believes that its reputation will be enhanced if its program consists of at least 40% of new and artistic works.

Required:

(a) What mix should the house adopt for its coming season? What "house count" can be expected with this mix?

(b) Because the economy is in a recession, contributions have fallen off somewhat. It now appears that at least 85% of a full house is necessary to stay in the black. What changes, if any, must be made to achieve this new requirement?

(c) Criticize the model that you used and the program it selected.

(d) The director feels that the primary goal of the house is to minimize the risk of an unpopular season because a bad season has long run unfavorable consequences. It is assumed that how well one opera is received is related to how well other operas have done.

13. *Inventory systems theory*. You are engaged by a client to set up an inventory system. Discuss

(a) Problems you might anticipate and how you would solve them.

(b) Model parameters you might need to measure and how you would measure them.

(c) Policies you might suggest for management's consideration.

(d) System implementation problems that might confront management.

Direct the *bulk* of your answers to probabilistic systems.

14. *Cakes.* A reputable and exclusive bakery wishes to determine how many cakes of a particularly elaborate sort to bake each day. The ingredients cost $6.00 per cake and the selling price is $9.00. Any cake remaining unsold at the end of the day is sold as stale merchandise for $3.00 to a bakery several miles away. The distribution of demand in the past has been

X	$P(X)$
20	.10
21	.15
22	.18
23	.17
24	.25
25	.15

(a) Develop the solution in detail and comment on it. Specify other circumstances that would lead you to consider other costs.

(b) What characteristics of this problem made you model it in the way you did?

(c) What other items might be gainfully studied in this way?

15. *Stewardesses (difficult problem requiring careful reasoning and artistic modelling).* An airline has 15 flights leaving a given base each day, each with one stewardess. The airline has a policy of keeping three reserve stewardesses on call to replace stewardesses scheduled for flights who become sick. The probability distribution for the daily number of sick stewardesses is as follows:

S	$P(S)$
0	.1353
1	.2707
2	.2707
3	.1804
4	.0902
5	.0361
6	.0120
7	.0034
8	.0009
9	.0002
10	.0001
	1.0000

Records show that any time a flight is cancelled, the airline loses \$1,078.52, on average, which is the net of revenues and variable costs. If a stewardess's pay averages \$60 a day (she must be paid a weekly five-day salary of \$300), and she can only serve one flight each day, do you agree with the policy of having only three reserves? Support your answer with logic; be cautious! (You may want to study the empirical distribution—it is Poisson.)
Would you include pilot salaries in the variable costs? What other approaches might you consider before you set policy?
Note: There are very few extended illnesses; almost all are limited to one day's duration.

16. *Determining deductibles in insurance policies.* In theory, insurance is taken to guard against catastrophic loss. Accordingly, policies are written with deductible features whereby the insured pays for any losses under the deductible amount and the insurer pays for any losses in excess of that amount. If collision insurance costs \$5 per \$100 of valuation, and if yearly loss in units of \$100 is distributed according to the Poisson curve with mean of 10 (that is, 10 \$100 units), determine the best deductible amount.

17. *Continuous newsboy.* The daily demand for a particular cake in a large bakery is normally distributed as $N(x\!:\!500;\,100)$. The selling price of the cake is \$2.50 and it costs \$1.10 to make. If stales (leftover cake) can be marketed for \$.50, how many cakes should be baked daily? What is the probability of shortage given the optimal baking program? How could the program be termed "optimal" without simultaneously considering service level and effect on reputation?

18. *Gradual-demand model proof.* The gradual-demand model is set up as follows:

$$E[K(S)] = C_h \sum_{D=0}^{S} \left(S - \frac{D}{2}\right) P(D) + C_h \sum_{D=S+1}^{\infty} \frac{S^2}{2D} P(D) + C_s \sum_{D=S+1}^{\infty} \frac{(D-S)^2}{2D} P(D) + C_o$$

(a) Use finite calculus to determine the optimal quantity to supply.

(b) Recast the model in continuous terms and find its optimal supply using infinitesimal calculus.

(c) If you wanted to apply the results for two periods, what modifications would you introduce?

(d) Using the results of part (b), find $\hat{S}$ given $C_h = \$5$, $C_s = \$95$ and demand is distributed exponentially:

$$f(D) = De^{-D}, \quad \text{for } 0 < D < \infty$$

19. *Optimal supply.* Every week a company manufactures a product that obsolesces just as rapidly—that is, within one week. The product sells for \$10,000 and costs \$3,029.50. Units not sold within a week may be sold as obsolete for \$2,255. The president wishes to manufacture that weekly quantity which will minimize his regrets. The distribution of weekly demand follows:

D	$P(D)$
10	.12
11	.12
12	.13
13	.14
14	.12
15	.12
16	.06
17	.05
18	.05
19	.05
20	.04

20. *Estimating shortage cost.* Assume that a discrete gradual demand model is in use along with the following distribution:

D	30	31	32	33	34	35
$P(D)$	.10	.18	.24	.24	.15	.09

Holding cost is \$240, but cost of shortage is unknown. If the supply level is 34, what is the implicit range for C_s? How would an analyst use this information?

21. *Newsboy, computer program, and regret matrix.* In presenting an analysis to management, most accountants agree that (a) communications will improve if there are no mathematical symbols in sight, and (b) confidence in the analysis will increase if the model is reduced to a computer program. With these notions in mind, prepare a computer solution to the newsboy problem. Show the separate costs of holding and of shortage—weighted by their respective probabilities—in a "regret" matrix (a matrix showing opportunity costs of individual strategies and their possible outcomes) and sum the costs associated with each strategy (possible supply level) to permit easy selection of the strategy having the minimal regret.

Demand	60	61	62	63	64	65	66	67
Probability of demand	.04	.06	.10	.20	.25	.18	.12	.05

Cost of holding = \$15
Cost of shortage = \$10
Comment on the solution and explain what causes any unusual features of the optimal supply level.

22. *Computer program, gradual demand, cycle length.* Write a computer program to determine cycle length for the gradual-demand model. Use the data given on page 528.

Data: Demand is Poisson distributed with mean $\lambda = 1$ for one period.

$C_h = \$1$
$C_s = \$97$
$C_o = \$300$

23. *How often should runs be made? (gradual demand, continuous units).* The Hall Distillery wishes to decide how often runs of a particular product should be made, given that only three possibilities are practical: once a month, once every two months, or once every three months. Fortunately, the product enjoys longevity. Monthly demand for the product, which is measured in gallons, follows the distribution

$$f(D) = .0001^2 De^{-.0001D}, \quad \text{for } D > 0$$

and the cost data are as follows:

$C_h = \$.10$ per gallon per month
$C_s = \$.90$ per gallon per month
$C_o = \$2{,}000$ per batch

Discounting rate = 20%, if usable.
Demand for one month is independent of demand for another. What significance does your answer hold for accounting theory?

Caution:

This is a very difficult problem, conceptually as well as mathematically. If, additionally, you seek a generalized solution, the problem poses a severe challenge. Should you accept that challenge, go very slowly and be painstakingly careful.

24. *Calculating and using a leadtime distribution.* Two distributions, one for daily demand and one for length of leadtime, are shown below. Assume demand for one day is independent of demand for the next day. Then determine (a) expected shortage if the reorder point is set at four units, and (b) what reorder point should be set if probability of shortage is to be .10 or less.

D	$P(D)$	L(Days)	$M(L)$
1	.3	1	.5
2	.4	2	.4
3	.3	3	.1

25. *Convoluting the leadtime distribution, given Poisson.* In inventory problems the length of leadtime is often variable. If the distribution for daily demand is known and the distribution for the length of leadtime is available, convolution theory provides a means for arriving at a distribution for total demand during leadtime. Given the Poisson distribution for demand shown below and the accompanying empirical distribution of leadtimes, determine the probability that total demand during leadtime is two units.

Demand		Leadtime	
D	$P(D)$	t	$P(t)$
0	.670	1	.2
1	.268	2	.5
2	.054	3	.3
3	.007		
4	.001		

26. *Leadtime distribution, convolutions, and the normal curve.* Demand for a single period is distributed according to $N(D{:}1000;\ 300)$ and leadtime obeys the following distribution:

T	$P(T)$
1	.4
2	.3
3	.3

Complete the portion of the distribution of x, demand during leadtime, shown below in table form.

x	$P(x)$
1,000–1,500	
1,500–2,000	
2,000–2,500	

27. *Service level, truncation, probability distribution critique.* Mr. Bill Burnham runs the hot dog concession for a football stadium. Old B.B. has adopted the policy of ordering 10,000 dogs on a game day. (There is no chance of ordering more, should they be needed, and having them arrive in time to do any good.) He judges that the number of customers is normally distributed with $P(2{,}960 < C < 7{,}040) = .39$

(a) Determine B.B.'s expected shortage (treat truncation as a scaling adjustment).

(b) At what level should the order be set to have probability of shortage $= .05$?

(c) Criticize B.B.'s probability distribution.

(d) Would the newsboy model be appropriate?

28. *Synonyms and recognizing inventory situations.* List as many synonyms for inventory terms (e.g., shortage = overdraft) as you can. State how you would apply an inventory model (be specific) to the control of some other stockpile not usually considered an inventory (e.g., accounts receivable).

29. *The continuous lead time, order level model.* The university faculty problem was sectionalized as $E[K(S)] = K_A + K_B + K_C + C_o$ and the development of dK_A/dS was demonstrated. Find dK_B/dS and dK_C/dS and check your results with those given in the chapter. If time permits, redo the entire problem.

30. *The (S, t) model.* Assume that the optimal solution to an (S, t) model is given:

$$\int_0^S \left[\int_0^{S-y} f(x)\,dx + \int_{S-y}^{\infty} \frac{(S-y)}{x} f(x)\,dx \right] g(y)\,dy = C_s/(C_s + C_h)$$

and that one period demand is distributed $f(x) = xe^{-x}$. If lead time is two periods long and if $C_s = 9C_h$, compute $\hat{S}$.

31. *Convoluted leadtime and the instantaneous demand model.* When leadtime is significant and demand is not only probabilistic but also essentially instantaneous, the diagrams shown below pertain.

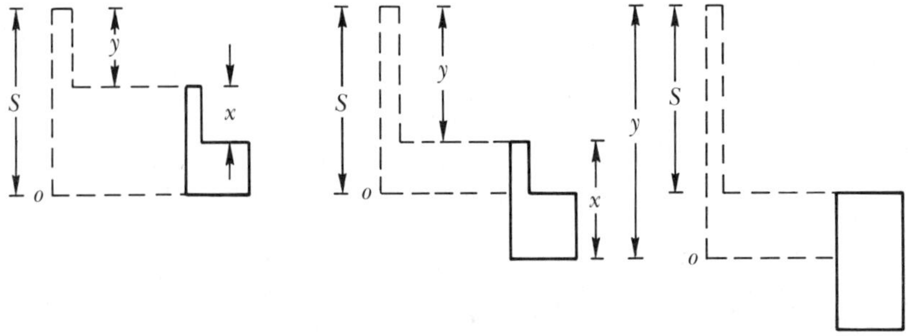

(a) Set up a continuous probability model and explain the setup. Be sure to comment on what is here meant by convoluted leadtime demand (i.e., since daily demand is instantaneous, and if leadtime were, say, two days, does the convoluted demand mean that the two days' demand took place all at once?).

(b) Develop a solution for the optimal value of S.

(c) Given $f(x) = xe^{-x}$ for $x > 0$, leadtime lasts three periods (say, days), and $C_s = 19C_h$, determine target level S.

32. *Further insight into models embodying convolutions.* These three diagrams reflect the three possible circumstances that confront the analyst in the time scheduling period for which he wishes to compute costs. A represents the case where no shortages occur; B represents the case where some shortage occurs, and C represents the case where there are no holdings. The question is: How does a problem reach the condition depicted by C? Most inventory systems start out with a quantity on hand (Q or S in our previous models), and this necessarily means that there is some original holding. How then do we arrive at case C?

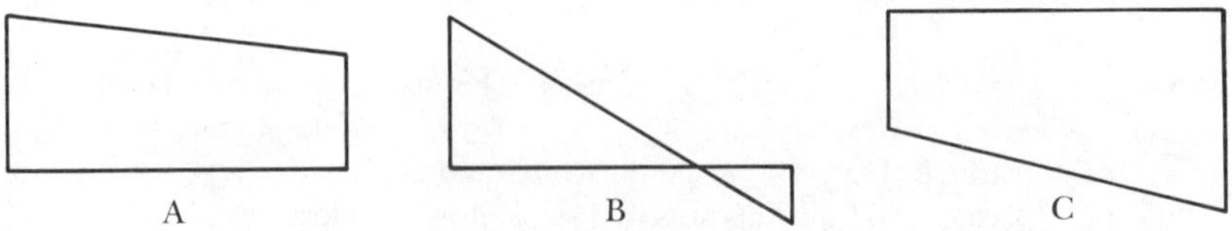

The chapter demonstrated the use of convolutions to extend the gradual-demand (newsboy family) model to the analysis of two or more periods. Contrast this gradual-demand model, which has only situations A and B, with the (S, t) leadtime model, which has situations A, B, and C. Discuss how the gradual model could be structured as an (S, t) model.

33. *Z transform proof*. Develop the closed form for the Z transform of $P(n) = \sum_{i=0}^{n} P(i)$, where $P(n)$ is the cumulative production through period n. This is an application of Z transform number 11 in Table 11 in Appendix A.

34. Z transforms and multiple-stage inventory systems. The previous problem asked you to prove Z transform number 11 to refresh your knowledge of this tool. We now put that transform to work.

(a) Key:

$D(n)$ = change in demand *during* period n
$P(n)$ = change in production *during* period n
$S(n)$ = inventory shortage or surplus at the *end* of period n, relative to the changes in demand and production from their expected levels. (Note that we can speak of an inventory shortage even though there are many units still on our shelves; it is a relative shortage rather than an absolute shortage—relative, that is, to the normal level.)

The inventory shortage is simply the difference between the cumulative demand changes and cumulative production changes:

$$S(n) = \sum_{i=0}^{n} (D(i) - P(i))$$

If, then, the policy is to make the production change for the next period a percentage of the inventory shortage for the period just ended, we obtain

$$P(n+1) = aS(n) = a\left[\sum_{0}^{n} (D(i) - P(i))\right]$$

Therefore,

$$P(n+1) + a\sum_{0}^{n} P(i) = a\sum_{0}^{n} D(i)$$

Required:

Use Z transforms—as demonstrated in Appendix C—to develop a transfer function for the system. Then test the system by subjecting it to (1) unit impulse, (2) unit step, and (3) unit ramp driving functions. Discuss system response in each case.

(b) Assume that the factory consists of two stages, that the output of the first stage is the input of the second stage, and that both stages follow the policy for $P(n+1)$ mentioned above. (Hint: the driving function of stage $2 = D_2(Z) = P_1(Z)$, the production function of stage 1.)

Required:

Find the effect of a unit impulse in demand (the driving function) in stage 1 on the inventory condition ($S_2(n)$) of stage 2.

Waiting Lines and Cost Control

15

Overview

Queuing or waiting-line theory is another method of cost analysis that permits insight into both dollar costs and service level. There are also definite connections between queuing and capital budgeting. Queuing employs rates of arrival and service, measures expected numbers and times, and can be used to minimize the sum of costs of waiting and costs of providing service.

Service Level and Waiting Lines

Some years ago, I began a talk on costs to a group of executives with these words:

> Does cost benefit analysis impede your decisionmaking? Perhaps the question should be rephrased: Are you surrounded by well-intentioned analysts who besiege you with inquiries about your estimates of this or that cost or of the revenues you anticipate from undertaking some proposal? And then, having provided the estimates, do you feel that the analysis you receive in return is coercing your decision along lines that somehow seem irrelevant? Well if this is your circumstance, what you are probably looking for is a substitute for the monetary criterion. Quite possibly you would find a service level criterion more suitable.

Let us approach our study of queuing theory through the avenue of service level.

Service policies affect many aspects of business. In inventory situations, order levels are often set so that either the probability or the frequency of stockout is held to some acceptable figure. Thus, management might establish a service policy like "The probability of shortage shall be no greater than .02" and to implement this policy, an order level of, say, 2,000 units might be determined. There would be a certain dollar cost associated with this 2,000-unit policy, but the decision might be based not on the cost, but rather on the .02 probability of shortage. The decisionmaker reflects his feeling for the costs by observing that a policy of no shortages might be as prohibitively costly as a policy in which stockouts occurred more frequently and endangered customer loyalty.

Perhaps less well known than inventory service policies, but equally important nevertheless, are waiting-line service policies. The executive who says, "I don't want our customers waiting for attention any longer than five minutes on average" has specified such a service level policy. Summed up in that policy are his feelings about the company's obligations to its customers, his notions about courtesy, and his knowledge of competitors' service capabilities. Also implicit in the policy is the assumption that whatever the cost of implementing the chosen service level is, it is reasonable. Given the policy, there is no need to fuss over costs, some of which are so difficult to measure that they can only be charitably categorized as fiction. Where costs become so figmentized, one could become cynical and begin to doubt the aphorism "A best guess is better than nothing."

Figmentized cost (or revenue) estimates exist whether the subject is inventory or waiting-line (queuing) analysis. Indeed, it is difficult to distinguish between inventory and waiting-line problems, since flows into and out of an inventory may be better studied as the flows of a queue.

When costs are considered in queuing theory, they come under two headings: the costs of having units wait and the costs of providing the facilities. When inanimate objects do the waiting, the cost of waiting is somewhat easier to calculate. But what is the cost of waiting when customers are in the line? How would you measure this cost? The cost of waiting is easily defined as the forgone profits caused by dissatisfied customers. But which profits? Only those of the present transactions? Or are we concerned about the profits on the customers' trade for all time to come? Wouldn't we also wish to include the forgone profits of those other customers to whom the malcontents speak? When one contemplates the contagious effects of customer dissatisfaction, one becomes attracted to the notion of awarding cash (or other) consolation prizes to regular customers who have to wait more than a specified time. Such a prize would serve as an apology and should mitigate irritations.

Consider next the cost of providing service facilities. To make the discussion more concrete, suppose we are concerned about bank tellers to whom we give an adding machine and a change-making machine. Is this the extent of the investment in the facilities? Certainly not. We also have the investment in each teller's salary and the concomitant increase in working capital that customarily arises when operations are expanded. In the teller's case, the working capital is the basic fund we give him to carry on daily transactions. Have we now an exhaustive listing of component investment costs? Again, no. There is still the cost of counters, drawers, and windows—not to mention the cost of space. But if the space (or the counter) already exists, is there a cost to using it? Theory tells us there is no cost if the space has no other use and if using it now does not hasten its replacement.

One can only wonder how realistic and practical the measurement of all these cost components is. It seems unlikely that the analyst could ever be sure that he has not overlooked something. It appears debatable that the decisionmaker acts properly if he focuses exclusively on dollar flows. Service level could indeed be more crucial than dollars.

Let us pause to reflect on the counterargument. Simply stated, if reliable cost estimates are available, management may well decide to minimize expected costs rather than to select a suitable service level policy. If estimating forgone profits in order to introduce them as an opportunity cost—of customer waiting in queuing (or of stock shortage in inventory)—is practical, and if other component costs are readily identifiable and measurable, then the decisionmaker may wisely stress costs, although he ought not explicitly ignore service. If the minimum-cost solution has unacceptable service performance, something is wrong!

Illustrations of Queuing Situations: Theoretical Analysis

Queuing theory relies on rates of arrival and of service to accomplish its predictions. The classical approach to the subject emphasizes that demands on the system (arrivals) should obey the Poisson probability distribution, while the system itself should require negative exponentially distributed time to furnish supplies (services). These probability distributions are stated below. How the analyst determines whether they govern the system being studied is discussed and illustrated in Appendix A to this chapter.

Poisson distribution: $P(x) = e^{-\lambda t}(\lambda t)^x/x!$, for $x = 0, 1, 2, \ldots$

Exponential distribution: $f(t) = \mu e^{-\mu t}$, for $t > 0$

Key:

$P(x)$ = probability of x arrivals
$f(t)$ = probability density function for time
λ = rate of arrivals
μ = rate of service

Many other probability distributions are used in queuing analysis. The Erlangian distribution, which is a convolution of the exponential distribution, receives special attention. Nevertheless, the fundamentals of the theory are developed around the Poisson and exponential distributions, and a fair amount of applied work can be accomplished using just them.

Situation: A single facility, very large population needing service. An analyst was asked to study the adequacy of the services offered by a Xerox machine.

Analysis: The analyst first determined the arrival and service rates and how they were distributed. Appendix A to this chapter details how this stage of the analysis was conducted. He found that customers arrived in Poisson fashion at the rate of .12 customers per minute, and that the facility service time was distributed exponentially at a rate of .2 customers per minute. Hence the arrival and service rates were $\lambda = .12$ and $\mu = .2$ respectively.

The analyst next determined the system expectations, that is, the expected number in the queue, $E(Q)$; the expected number being served, $E(s)$; the expected number in the entire system (in queue plus being served), $E(n)$; the expected time waiting in the queue, $E(w)$; the expected time in service, $E(t_s)$; and the expected time in the system, $E(t)$. The appropriate formulas and his calculations follow. See Appendix B to this chapter for derivation.

$$E(n) = \lambda/(\mu - \lambda) = .12/(.2 - .12) = 1.5 \text{ customers}$$
$$E(Q) = \lambda^2/[\mu(\mu - \lambda)] = .12^2/[.2(.2 - .12)] = .9 \text{ customers}$$
$$E(s) = \lambda/\mu = .12/.2 = .6 \text{ customers}$$
$$E(t) = 1/(\mu - \lambda) = 1/(.2 - .12) = 12.5 \text{ minutes}$$
$$E(w) = \lambda/[\mu(\mu - \lambda)] = .12/[.2(.2 - .12)] = 7.5 \text{ minutes}$$
$$E(t_s) = 1/\mu = 1/.2 = 5 \text{ minutes}$$

Armed with this information, the analyst approached management to ascertain whether these expectations were reasonable insofar as desired customer service was concerned. More specifically, he asked whether the average customer should have to wait 7.5 minutes for service and whether the operator should take as long as 5 minutes to complete the average service. Having observed that enough space had been provided to accommodate 10 waiting customers, he questioned whether the extra space might be converted to some other use.

Situation: Multichannel facilities, limited population needing service. The prototype problem we now address calls for determining *how many* service renderers (say, mechanics) are needed to care for a designated number of service consumers (say, machines). The model requires that each service consumer arrive in a Poisson fashion at an average rate of, say, λ per hour, and that the service renderers can each attend to μ units per hour, with the time between each service completion being distributed exponentially. There are M (for maximum) units that require service from time to time.

Analysis: The analyst would first need to locate formulas for calculating the probability that n machines were down requiring service.[1] He would find the following results, which recognize that there are k servers (channels) available:

$$P_n = \begin{cases} \dfrac{M^{(n)}}{n!}\left(\dfrac{\lambda}{\mu}\right)^n P_0, & \text{for } n = 0, 1, \ldots, k \\ \dfrac{M^{(n)}}{k!k^{n-k}}\left(\dfrac{\lambda}{n}\right)^n P_0, & \text{for } n > k \end{cases} \tag{1}$$

(Comment: $M^{(n)} = (M - 0)(M - 1)(M - 2)\cdots(M - (n - 1))$, where there are n factors.)
Since the sum of an exhaustive set of probabilities is unity:

$$1 = \sum_{n=0}^{M} P_n, \tag{2}$$

factoring permits definition of P_0:

$$P_0 = 1 \div \left[\sum_{n=0}^{k} \frac{M^{(n)}}{n!}\left(\frac{\lambda}{\mu}\right)^n + \sum_{n=k+1}^{M} \frac{M^{(n)}}{k!k^{n-k}}\left(\frac{\lambda}{\mu}\right)^n\right] \tag{3}$$

Equations (1) and (3) define the steady-state probabilities for n units down in a system that has k servers. The distribution could now be used to determine the expected number of units down per time period according to

$$E(n) = \sum_{n=0}^{M} nP_n \tag{4}$$

Once the expected number of units in the system has been determined, costs of downtime, C_D, and costs for each of the servers, C_S, can be used to determine the expected cost of the system with k servers, $E[C(k)]$

$$E[C(k)] = C_D E(n) + C_S k$$

Dimensional analysis:

$$\frac{\$}{\text{Period}} = \frac{\$}{(\text{Unit period})}\text{Unit} + \frac{\$}{(\text{Server period})}\text{Server}$$

[1] Appendix B to this chapter develops these formulas for the reader who is curious about how they originate.

The other system expectations are calculated as follows:

$$E(Q) = \sum_{n=k}^{M} (n - k)P_n \tag{6}$$

$$E(R) = M - E(n), \quad \text{where } R \text{ designates the machines that are running} \tag{7}$$

$$E(s) = E(n) - E(Q) \tag{8}$$

$$E(w) = E(Q) \div \{\mu[E(s)]\} \tag{9}$$

$$E(t) = E(w) + (1/\mu) \tag{10}$$

Unfortunately, solving for the system expectations calls for much cumbersome arithmetic. Typically, an analyst would either look up answers in Peck and Hazlewood, *Finite Queuing Tables* (New York: John Wiley & Sons, 1958) or write a computer program, thereby creating "software" for later use. Therefore, computer software is one practical way to study finite population queues.

Exhibit 1 contains an annotated computer program written in the BASIC language that computes the probabilities and the expected cost, provided one is willing to input data about

	In Exhibit 1
M, the number of units in the population	20
K, the number of servers	Variable
A, the rate of arrivals per hour	1.875
U, the rate of service per hour	7.5
C_1, the cost per hour for a mechanic	\$10
C_2, the cost per hour for a machine that is down	\$ 5

As shown in Exhibit 1, the minimum expected hourly cost in \$68.43 and occurs when there are four servers. It is important, however, to observe that the computer program permits the analyst to perform sensitivity study easily by varying his one line of input data. Thus the effect of changing the number of servers is made apparent, as would be the effect of changing waiting and facility costs.

It is also very possible that management might not approve of, say, the expected time in the queue that is associated with the minimum-cost model. Here, when there are four mechanics, .0785 (60 minutes) = 4.7 minutes is the expected time each machine spends just waiting for attention. When there are three mechanics, 14.3 minutes per machine are so wasted. Similarly, when there are five mechanics, the average machine spends only 1.5 minutes in queue. Management might well contrast these results and select five mechanics, for instance, because the 1.5 wasted minutes seem more relevant than minimizing expected costs. Of course, this amounts to an implicit disapproval of the cost estimates. The important point is that the decision might

Exhibit 1

```
100  DIM  F(50),P(50)
105  REM M = THE SIZE OF THE CALLING POPULATION
110  REM K  = THE NUMBER OF SERVERS
115  REM A  = THE RATE OF ARRIVALS
120  REM U  = THE SERVICE RATE
125  REM C1 = THE COST PER HOUR PER SERVER
130  REM C2 = THE COST PER UNIT DOWN PER HOUR
135  PRINT "WHAT ARE THE VALUES OF:M,K,A,U,C1,C2";
140  INPUT M,K,A,U,C1,C2
145  REM COMPUTE UTILIZATION FACTOR
150  LET  L=A/U
155  REM INITIALIZE VARIABLES
160  LET  N=0
165  LET  X=0
170  LET  G=1
175  LET  F1=1
180  LET  F2=1
200  REM COMPUTE K
205  FOR  Y = 1 TO K
210  LET  F2=F2*Y
215  NEXT Y
220  REM DETERMINE "BASES" FOR PROBABILITY DISTRIBUTION
225  FOR  Z=0 TO M
230  IF Z>0 THEN 245
235  F(Z)=1
240  GO TO 800
245  LET  B=1
250  REM COMPUTE N
255  LET  F1=Z*F1
260  REM COMPUTE M/(M-N) AS M↑[N]
265  LET  G = (M-Z+1)*G
270  REM RECOGNIZE THE SPLIT IN THE DISTRIBUTION
275  IF Z > =K THEN 700
280  LET F(Z) = G*(1/F1)*(L↑Z)
285  GO TO 800
700  LET F(Z) = G * (1/F2) * ((1/K)↑(Z - K)  *(L↑Z)
750  REM OBTAIN A TOTAL OF "BASES" ,I.E., THE INVERSE OF P(O)
800  LET  X=X+F(Z)
850  NEXT Z
880  REM COMPUTE PROBABILITIES
900  FOR I=0 TO M
905  LET  P(I)=F(I)/X
906  PRINT "   P(";I;")   =   ";P(I)
910  NEXT I
912  REM COMPUTE EXPECTED NUMBER IN SYSTEM
913  FOR I=0 TO M
914  LET  N=I*P(I)+N
915  NEXT I
918  REM COMPUTE EXPECTED NUMBER IN QUEUE
920  FOR  I=K TO M
921  LET  Q=(I-K)*P(I)+Q
922  NEXT I
930  LET  S=N-Q
935  LET  R=M-N
940  LET  W=Q/(U*S)
```

Exhibit 1 (*cont.*)

```
945  LET  T = W + (1/U)
949  REM COMPUTE EXPECTED POLICY COST
950  LET  D=(K*C1)+(N*C2)
955  PRINT"THE EXPECTED NUMBER IN THE SYSTEM IS";N
957  PRINT"THE EXPECTED NUMBER IN THE QUEUE IS";Q
959  PRINT"THE EXPECTED NUMBER FUNCTIONING PROPERLY IS";R
961  PRINT"THE EXPECTED TIME IN THE QUEUE IS";W
963  PRINT"THE EXPECTED DOWNTIME IS";T
965  PRINT"THE EXPECTED HOURLY COST FOR";K;" SERVERS IS";D
970  END

RUN

WHAT ARE THE VALUES OF:M,K,A,U,C1,C2?
20,3,1.875,7.5,10,5
     P( 0 ) = 2.20561598E-3
     P( 1 ) = 1.10280799E-2
     P( 2 ) = 2.61916898E-2
     P( 3 ) = 3.92875347E-2
     P( 4 ) = 5.56573408E-2
     P( 5 ) = 7.42097878E-2
     P( 6 ) = 9.27622347E-2
     P( 7 ) = .108222607
     P( 8 ) = .117241157
     P( 9 ) = .117241157
     P( 10 ) = .107471061
     P( 11 ) = 8.95592178E-2
     P( 12 ) = 6.71694133E-2
     P( 13 ) = 4.47796089E-2
     P( 14 ) = 2.61214385E-2
     P( 15 ) = 1.30607192E-2
     P( 16 ) = 5.44196636E-3
     P( 17 ) = 1.81398878E-3
     P( 18 ) = 4.53497196E-4
     P( 19 ) = 7.55828661E-5
     P( 20 ) = 6.29857217E-6
THE EXPECTED NUMBER IN THE SYSTEM IS 8.21945879
THE EXPECTED NUMBER IN THE QUEUE IS 5.27432348
THE EXPECTED NUMBER FUNCTIONING PROPERLY IS 11.7805412
THE EXPECTED TIME IN THE QUEUE IS .238781264
THE EXPECTED DOWNTIME IS .372114597
THE EXPECTED HOURLY COST FOR 3 SERVERS IS 71.0972939

RUN

WHAT ARE THE VALUES OF:M,K,A,U,C1,C2?
20,4,1.875,7.5,10,5
     P( 0 ) = 6.96160461E-3
     P( 1 ) = 3.4808023E-2
     P( 2 ) = 8.26690548E-2
     P( 3 ) = .124003582
     P( 4 ) = .131753806
     P( 5 ) = .131753806
     P( 6 ) = .123519193
     P( 7 ) = .108079294
     P( 8 ) = 8.78144264E-2
     P( 9 ) = 6.58608198E-2
     P( 10 ) = 4.52793136E-2
```

Exhibit 1 (*cont.*)

```
    P( 11 ) = 2.8299571E-2
    P( 12 ) = 1.59185087E-2
    P( 13 ) = 7.95925435E-3
    P( 14 ) = 3.48217377E-3
    P( 15 ) = 1.30581516E-3
    P( 16 ) = 4.08067239E-4
    P( 17 ) = 1.02016809E-4
    P( 18 ) = 1.91281518E-5
    P( 19 ) = 2.39101898E-6
    P( 20 ) = 1.49438686E-7
THE EXPECTED NUMBER IN THE SYSTEM IS 5.68644871
THE EXPECTED NUMBER IN THE QUEUE IS 2.10806089
THE EXPECTED NUMBER FUNCTIONING PROPERLY IS 14.3135512
THE EXPECTED TIME IN THE QUEUE IS 7.85478826E-2
THE EXPECTED DOWNTIME IS .211881215
THE EXPECTED HOURLY COST FOR 4 SERVERS IS 68.4322435

RUN

WHAT ARE THE VALUES OF:M,K,A,U,C1,C2?
20,5,1.875,7.5,10,5
    P( 0 ) = 9.95080419E-3
    P( 1 ) = 4.97540209E-2
    P( 2 ) = .118165799
    P( 3 ) = .177248699
    P( 4 ) = .188326743
    P( 5 ) = .150661394
    P( 6 ) = .112996046
    P( 7 ) = 7.90972322E-2
    P( 8 ) = 5.14132009E-2
    P( 9 ) = 3.08479205E-2
    P( 10 ) = 1.69663563E-2
    P( 11 ) = 8.48317815E-3
    P( 12 ) = 3.81743017E-3
    P( 13 ) = 1.52697206E-3
    P( 14 ) = 5.34440223E-4
    P( 15 ) = 1.60332067E-4
    P( 16 ) = 4.00830167E-5
    P( 17 ) = 8.01660335E-6
    P( 18 ) = 1.2024905E-6
    P( 19 ) = 1.2024905E-7
    P( 20 ) = 6.01245251E-9
THE EXPECTED NUMBER IN THE SYSTEM IS 4.58436658
THE EXPECTED NUMBER IN THE QUEUE IS .730458235
THE EXPECTED NUMBER FUNCTIONING PROPERLY IS 15.4156334
THE EXPECTED TIME IN THE QUEUE IS 2.52716002E-2
THE EXPECTED DOWNTIME IS .158604933
THE EXPECTED HOURLY COST FOR 5 SERVERS IS 72.9218329
```

justifiably be based on system performance disregarding facility and waiting costs.

The computer program in Exhibit 1 would not only enable management to select a better service policy, it would also permit easy calculation of the concomitant increase in recognized expected costs. Thus with four mechanics, 4.7 minutes are spent in queue and the expected cost is \$68.43. With five mechanics, 1.5 minutes are spent in queue and the expected cost is \$72.92. Hence to reduce queue time by 3.2 minutes will cost \$4.49 per hour.

There is yet another way in which Exhibit 1 generates investment related information. The number of units in queue indicates the extent of facilities needed to accommodate units awaiting service in those circumstances where the machines are brought to the mechanics. Thus when there are four mechanics, two machines are waiting for attention, and if a machine is roughly 12 cubic feet in size, waiting facilities of roughly 24 cubic feet should be adequate.

When the cost for a server, C_S, must reflect not only his wages but also the cost of equipping him, it is convenient to normalize the equipment cost via present-value techniques (this is the capital recovery concept). To illustrate, assume each mechanic must be provided with \$3,000 worth of equipment, which will last two years and then be worth \$400. Also assume that the company has a required return before taxes of 20% per year, and that there are 2,000 working hours per year. The normalized hourly cost of the equipment, x, is

$$x \sum_{i=0}^{3,999} \left(\frac{1}{1.0001}\right)^i = 3{,}000 - 400\left(\frac{1}{1.0001}\right)^{4,000}$$

$$\frac{x[.9999^i]_0^{4,000}}{-.0001} = 3{,}000 - 400(.9999)^{4,000}$$

using logs:

$$1{,}000x(1 - .69183) = 3{,}000 - 400(.69183)$$
$$x = \$.88$$

With this hourly equipment cost added to the previous C_S (that is, C_1 in Exhibit 1), the expected hourly costs for three, four, and five servers become \$73.74, \$71.95, and \$77.32 respectively.

When the demanding population is very large (infinite), the multichannel queuing formulas become

For $n \leq k$: $$P_n = (\lambda/\mu)^n P_0/n! \quad \textbf{(11)}$$

For $n \geq k$: $$P_n = (\lambda/\mu)^n P_0/(k!k^{n-k}) \quad \textbf{(12)}$$

$$P_0 = 1 \div \left[\sum_{n=0}^{k-1} \frac{(\lambda/\mu)^n}{n!} + \frac{(\lambda/\mu)^k k\mu}{k!(k\mu - \lambda)}\right] \quad \textbf{(13)}$$

$$E(Q) = \frac{\lambda\mu(\lambda/\mu)^k}{(k-1)!(k\mu - \lambda)^2} P_0 \quad \textbf{(14)}$$

$$E(w) = \frac{E(Q)}{\lambda} = \frac{\mu(\lambda/\mu)^k}{(k-1)!(k\mu - \lambda)^2} P_0 \quad \textbf{(15)}$$

$$E(t) = E(w) + \frac{1}{\mu} = \frac{\mu(\lambda/\mu)^k}{(k-1)!(k\mu - \lambda)^2} P_0 + \frac{1}{\mu} \quad \textbf{(16)}$$

$$E(n) = \lambda E(t) = \lambda\left[E(w) + \frac{1}{\mu}\right] = E(Q) + \frac{\lambda}{\mu} = \frac{\lambda\mu(\lambda/\mu)^k}{(k-1)!(k\mu-\lambda)^2}P_0 + \frac{\lambda}{\mu} \tag{17}$$

These formulas could also be obtained as shown in Appendix B to this chapter (that is, by using a Markov chain matrix and performing extensive algebra on the expectation calculations). The program in Exhibit 1 computes these statistics when it is told that the population is considered infinite, which is done by feeding the program a number, M, that is in excess of the greatest factorial value the computer can calculate. (For example, the computer at hand could compute 160! but nothing higher; therefore, I could obtain infinite population analysis by entering $M = 161$.)

There is one basic difference between the finite-population and infinite-population models that is subtle and apt to lead to error. Both populations use λ; however, for the finite population, λ is a rate for each individual member of the population, while for the infinite population, λ is a collective rate that applies to the total population.

Poisson Arrivals, Erlangian Service

It might be said, "To add a little spice to your queuing consider an Erlangian distribution." You can form some notion of the variety thereby made possible by reflecting on Morse's comment:

> These distributions, called Erlang distributions, provide a family of service-time distributions which range all the way from the "pure random" exponential type to the completely regular, constant service-time situation. They will not fit all possible service-time distributions, but they will fit many (and perhaps most) of the ones encountered in practice.[2]

We shall discuss some of these observations within the context of an infinite-population, single-channel, Poisson arrivals system.

Under the Erlangian scheme, a service channel is divided into k phases, each of which has an exponential service time distribution with parameter $k\mu$ (that is, $E(t_i) = k\mu e^{-k\mu t_i}$). It is not necessary that these separate phases physically exist. They may be assumed to exist in order that the actual single-channel service time distribution, which is not exponential (had it been exponential, the model that introduced the chapter would apply), may be

[2] P. M. Morse, *Queues, Inventories and Maintenance* (New York: John Wiley & Sons, 1958), p. 41. Morse goes on to develop Erlangian arrivals as well, which we shall not study here. If you are interested in reading further on Erlangian arrivals, read T. L. Saaty, *Elements of Queueing Theory* (New York: McGraw-Hill Book Co., 1961), pp. 166–70.

simulated by the Erlangian distribution. The Erlangian is constructed from its exponential phases using a Laplace transform as follows:

$$L\{E(t_i) = k\mu e^{-k\mu t_i}\} = E_i(S) = k\mu/(k\mu + S)$$

Since the phases follow one another sequentially (that is, they are arranged in series), the total time to complete all k phases is $t = \sum_{i=1}^{k} t_i$. Then, assuming the time to complete one phase is independent of the time to complete any other phase, we obtain the convoluted distribution for total time in the usual way:

$$E(S) = \prod_{i=1}^{k} E_i(S) = [k\mu/(k\mu + S)]^k$$

$$L^{-1}\{[k\mu/(k\mu + S)]^k\} = E_k = (k\mu)^k t^{k-1} e^{-k\mu t}/(k-1)!$$

Inspection of E_k, a common symbolism for the Erlangian distribution, shows that if $k = 1$, the ordinary exponential distribution results. What is not so obvious is that the constant service time "distribution" (note the quotation marks—if service time is constant, it has a distribution in about the same sense that a straight line is a curve without any bend in it) results when k approaches infinity. The expected value of any Erlangian distribution is $1/\mu$,[3] while its variance is $1/(k\mu^2)$. Hence, if $k \to \infty$, the variance disappears, leaving a constant service time. A constant-time facility can serve exactly μ units per time period and it will take exactly $1/\mu$ time periods to serve each unit.

Developing the Erlangian formulas calls for complicated work with iterated transforms that will not be detailed in this text. The results are

$$E(n) = \frac{2k\rho - k\rho^2 + \rho^2}{2k(1-\rho)} = \left(\frac{k+1}{2k}\right)\frac{\lambda^2}{\mu(\mu-\lambda)} + \frac{\lambda}{\mu}$$

This is $E(n) = E(Q) + E(s)$. By dividing $E(n)$ by λ, we obtain $E(t) = E(w) + E(t_s)$. In summary,

$$E(Q) = \left(\frac{k+1}{2k}\right)\frac{\lambda^2}{\mu(\mu-\lambda)}$$

$$E(w) = \left(\frac{k+1}{2k}\right)\frac{\lambda}{\mu(\mu-\lambda)}$$

$$E(n) = \left(\frac{k+1}{2k}\right)\frac{\lambda^2}{\mu(\mu-\lambda)} + \frac{\lambda}{\mu}$$

$$E(t) = \left(\frac{k+1}{2k}\right)\frac{\lambda}{\mu(\mu-\lambda)} + \frac{1}{\mu}$$

[3] This result has intuitive appeal if you remember that only one facility is involved—in spite of its k phases, which may be either real or imagined. In fact, the service time distribution for each phase uses parameter $k\mu$ just to bring about the $1/\mu$ expected time for the aggregate operation.

(Observe that if phasing is discarded, $k = 1$ and the expectations shown above become the same as those for a single-server, infinite-population queue.) If service time is constant, we find $\lim_{k\to\infty} \frac{k+1}{2k} = \frac{1}{2}$.

Example: In a leading sporting goods factory, the next-to-last step in the tennis racket manufacturing process is the wrapping on of a leather grip. This takes one man exactly two minutes to complete. If rackets arrive at his area in a Poisson fashion at a rate of 29 per hour, and if 10 rackets require three cubic feet of space, determine an appropriate size for the bin used to store his incoming work.

Solution: This is an instance of constant service time; we need to know the expected queue size. $\lambda = 29$, $\mu = 30$

$$E(Q) = \frac{\lambda^2}{2\mu(\mu - \lambda)} = \frac{29^2}{2(30)(30 - 29)} = 14 \text{ rackets}$$

$$\text{Bin size} = \frac{14}{10}(3) = 4.2 \text{ cubic feet}$$

Example: A welfare clinic has a dentist who treats incoming patients as they appear. There are three stages to his work:

Stage 1: Novocain and chat while mouth gets numb. Some patients forgo Novocain (!!!); hence it may take zero time to complete this stage.

State 2: Drill and pick and scrape decayed teeth. In a checkup, this stage is sometimes unnecessary.

Stage 3: Sterilize, dress, and fill all gaping holes. No holes, no stage.

The time to complete each stage is exponentially distributed with mean time of six minutes.
Patients arrive randomly in a Poisson fashion at an average rate of three per hour.
How long can an arriving patient expect to spend in the dental clinic?

Solution: We need to calculate the expected time in the system.

$$\lambda = 3, \quad \mu = \frac{60}{3(6)} = 3.333$$

$$E(t) = \left(\frac{k+1}{2k}\right)\frac{\lambda}{\mu(\mu - \lambda)} + \frac{1}{\mu} = \left(\frac{3+1}{2(3)}\right)\left(\frac{3}{3.333(.333)}\right) + \frac{1}{3.333} = 2.1 \text{ hours}$$

(Does this help you to appreciate the notion of making appointments to reduce randomness?)

If you wish to *assume* an Erlangian service time distribution, you may use the Method of Moments to estimate a value for k. For example, if the observed mean time is, .4 and the corresponding variance is .04, then setting the moments of the Erlang equal to the observed moments yields

$$\frac{1}{\mu} = .4 \quad \text{and} \quad \frac{1}{k\mu^2} = \frac{1}{k}(.4)^2 = .04; \quad \therefore, \quad k = 4$$

The Interface of Queuing with Capital Budgeting and Cost Analysis

Now the forgoing discussions could easily be faulted for omissions by any serious student of waiting-line theory. The only service discipline employed was that of first-in, first-out (FIFO). There was no calculation of business lost because of line truncation. There was no discussion of servers arranged in multistage sequence. No delays in server setup or takedown time were explicitly recognized in the models. And so on.[4] Enough queuing theory was demonstrated, however, to show that queuing addresses investment related questions. What remains is to relate queuing to capital budgeting and cost analysis.

The benefits of doing this are twofold. First, it is probable that executives presented with detailed capital budgeting or cost analyses are influenced to accept the results because they are supported by finely detailed argument. Even though the person who has done the analysis says that the executive may wish to consider "other things" before deciding, he is apt merely to mention these "other things" when he submits the detailed cost or capital budgeting analysis. The executive is put into the position of accepting the results or departing from the "cold, hard facts." Second, there is much to be gained from realizing the limitations of capital budgeting and cost analysis.

In the previous illustrations the effects of varying policies were reflected in associated changes in costs. This is the essence of sensitivity studies in cost analysis. Hence queuing can be considered a tool for cost analysis.

Philosophically speaking, the queuing illustrations conceptually extend cost analysis into that purer state in which dollars may be ignored.

Must everything done by a business be legitimized by dollar considerations rooted in economic theory? Might not some things better be rooted in psychology?

It seems naive to require all measurements to be reflected eventually in dollars when they are conducting financial analysis. Decisionmakers'

[4] Interestingly, many of these nuances can be treated by simulation.

feelings are based on their experience and judgment. If we require them to justify their feelings in terms of dollar advantages, we risk stifling their imaginations and inhibiting their creative search for alternatives.

Let us turn our attention to capital budgeting. Earlier, when present values were used to calculate normalized facility investment costs, a connection was made with capital budgeting theory. It is possible to link queuing and capital budgeting more directly. Suppose the company that had 20 machines to be cared for had only three mechanics and wished to add a fourth. Further assume (1) that \$3,000 worth of equipment that will last two years and then be worth \$400 must be provided for this fourth mechanic; (2) that there are 2,000 working hours in a year; and (3) that the company requires a 20% annual rate of return before taxes. The cost savings without reflecting normalized equipment charges would be as shown in Exhibit 1 and would equal \$71.10 – \$68.43 or \$2.67 per hour. The profitability index for this proposal would be

Profitability index = discounted cash flow ÷ Present value of investment

$$= \frac{\sum_{i=1}^{4,000} 2.67\left(\frac{1}{1.0001}\right)^{i} + 400\left(\frac{1}{1.0001}\right)^{4,000}}{3,000}$$

$$= \frac{8,227.34 + 276.73}{3,000} = 2.83$$

Since profitability indices are one of the popular ranking techniques of capital budgeting, and since some other ranking technique might just as easily have been chosen, queuing can be considered a tool for capital budgeting.

Conclusion

The decisionmaker is not interested in either cost analysis or capital budgeting per se. He is interested in decision modelling, which encompasses cost analysis and capital budgeting, among other things, and does not blindly insist on adherence to dollar measurements.

It would be artificial for a decisionmaker to select facilities based on activity flows and thereafter, having estimated monetary benefits, to stick the project in the pile for capital budgeting scrutiny. If the decisionmaker must have the facilities, he can easily render the scrutiny superfluous by manipulating cost and revenue estimates. Or he may be more forthright and simply declare the facilities strategic to the operations of the business, thereby obviating further screening.

An executive must be about his work. If he does not think entirely in terms of dollars, to confine him to dollars is to impede him. The analyst who insists on dollar recognition is inflicting his myopia on the executive.

Another major thrust of this chapter has been to suggest that queuing theory is a neglected but practical means for analyzing commonly encountered situations. The elaborate situations should be left for specialists who are highly trained in the requisite mathematics. The ordinary situations, however, can be treated effectively by analysts who understand the essentials of sampling theory (how to calculate arrival and service rates and how to judge whether they are Poisson exponential) and who could employ the program just presented.

To avoid conveying an oversimplified picture of queuing theory, allow me to close on a caveat. It is important to keep in mind that the extent of facilities is likely to influence the demand made on them. For instance, if a room contains only one computer terminal, it may go relatively unused because people think there will be a great deal of waiting for only one machine. On the other hand, if there are five terminals, they may all be kept busy because people think it won't take long to obtain a terminal. All of which introduces the annoying question "How can I tell *in advance* what rate of arrivals and their distribution will be?" If a similar pilot operation is being conducted elsewhere, this may be a clue to the answer. If not, assessing the number of users by questionnaire or personal consultation may provide the needed evidence. And if neither of these avenues seems practical, then resort to management for a best guess as to rates may be all that is left. Assuming a Poisson-exponential system, is commonly done since so many phenomena have been observed to fit that pattern.

Appendix A

Empirically Determining Poisson and Exponential Distributions

This appendix describes the initial procedures actually followed in conducting the study of the Xerox machine situation. The analyst wished to determine both the rate of customer arrivals and how these arrivals were distributed. He arbitrarily chose to keep track of events in terms of five minute intervals and took the following preliminary sample:

	Arrivals		Arrivals		Arrivals
8:30–8:35	1	9:20– 9:25	0	10:10–10:15	0
8:35–8:40	0	9:25– 9:30	0	10:15–10:20	0
8:40–8:45	0	9:30– 9:35	2	10:20–10:25	1
8:45–8:50	0	9:35– 9:40	0	10:25–10:30	0
8:50–8:55	1	9:40– 9:45	0	10:30–10:35	1
8:55–9:00	1	9:45– 9:50	1	10:35–10:40	0
9:00–9:05	0	9:50– 9:55	2	10:40–10:45	0
9:05–9:10	0	9:55–10:00	1	10:45–10:50	0
9:10–9:15	0	10:00–10:05	3	10:50–10:55	1
9:15–9:20	0	10:05–10:10	1	10:55–11:00	2

Summary:

x	Frequency	$P(x)$
0	17	.567
1	9	.300
2	3	.100
3	1	.033
	30	1.000

The expected number of customers in a five-minute period $= E(x)$

$$E(x) = \sum xP(x) = .6$$

The variance of this average $= V(x)$

$$V(x) = \frac{n}{n-1}\sum(x - E(x))^2 P(x) = .66$$

With this estimate of the arrival population variance at hand, the analyst used classical sampling theory to estimate the total sample size:

$$Z = \frac{\overline{x} - \mu}{\sigma_{\overline{x}}} = \frac{\overline{x} - \mu}{\sigma/\sqrt{n}} \approx \frac{\overline{x} - \mu}{s/\sqrt{n}} = \frac{E}{s/\sqrt{n}}$$

Hence, $n = (Zs/E)^2$

Where:

Z represents the number of standard deviations that correspond to a selected risk level.

E represents the allowable error between the sample mean, $\bar{x}$, and the population mean, μ.

s represents the preliminary sample proxy for the population standard deviation (here, $s = \sqrt{V(x)}$).

n represents the appropriate total sample size. The analyst was willing to risk being wrong about the population arrival rate, $E(x)$, 10% (this is 5% on both the high and low sides) of the time. He was satisfied with an error equal to 25% of the mean (in practice, a 25% error would not seem sufficiently precise—5% or 10% would be better). Therefore, he calculated a total sample size of 79 as follows:

$$n = \left(\frac{Zs}{E}\right)^2 = \left(\frac{1.645\sqrt{.66}}{.25(.6)}\right)^2 = 79$$

He then proceeded to draw 49 more samples of five-minute intervals with the following final results:[1]

x	Frequency	$P(x)$	
0	45	.570	$E(x) = .581$
1	24	.304	$V(x) = .603$
2	8	.101	
3	2	.025	
	79	1.000	

Next he conducted a chi-square test to see whether his sample results would permit the use of the Poisson distribution. To facilitate calculations, he decided to round $E(x)$ to .6, which then became λt in the Poisson formula:

$$P(x) = (\lambda t)^x e^{-\lambda t}/x! = .6^x e^{-.6}/x!$$

Using $P(x)$ as the theoretical distribution, he prepared the table shown below.

x	Observed Frequency	Theoretical $P(x)$	Theoretical Frequency $(79P(x))$	$(O_i - T_i)^2/T_i$
0	45	.549	43.4	.059
1	24	.329	26.0	.154
2	8	.099	7.8 }	.016
3	2	.020	1.6 }	
4	0	.003	.2 }	
		1.000		.229

[1] Often, as a safety measure, analysts will draw 5% or 10% more samples than those strictly called for in the calculation for n.

(Note that the last three values of x were grouped to comply with the chi-square sanction of at least a frequency of 5 in any theoretical category.) Since there are only three categories, 2 degrees of freedom are present, and the critical χ^2 value is $\chi^2_{2,.05} = 5.991$

Because $.229 < 5.991$, the analyst concluded that his sample results justified the assumption of Poisson arrivals at a rate of .6 customers per five-minute interval or, equivalently, at a rate of .12 customers per minute.

The analyst next timed to the nearest minute (an arbitrary but useful time interval) how long it took the operator to complete each job. Again he took a preliminary sample to determine a proxy for the population standard deviation and specified risk and desired precision so that he could determine an appropriate total sample size. This turned out to be 120. He then prepared the table shown below.

	← Frequencies	→	
Minutes	Observed (O)	Theoretical (T)	$(O - T)^2/T$
1	34	31	.290
2	15	16	.063
3	13	13	0
4	15	11	1.455
5	7	8	.125
6	7	7	0
7	7	6	.167
8	0	5 }	1.000
9	6	4 }	
≥10	16	19	.474
	120	120	3.574

Comment:

By recognizing that total time divided by total frequencies yields average time, and that average time with the exponential distribution is

$$E(t) = \int_0^\infty t\mu e^{-\mu t}\, dt = 1/\mu,$$

some preliminary estimate of μ, the service rate, may be made. Here, multiplying minutes by observed frequencies (and taking ≥ 10 minutes as 10 minutes) and summing the individual products yields an approximation for total time of 503 minutes.

Therefore, $$\frac{\text{total time}}{\text{total frequencies}} = \frac{503}{120} = \frac{1}{\mu} \text{ and } \mu = .24$$

But the catchall category of ≥ 10 minutes, if detailed, would yield a higher total time; consequently, the estimate of μ should be adjusted downward. A convenient rounded figure is $\mu = .2$, and this was used to prepare the table shown above.

2. The probability of completing a service, for instance, in three minutes is

$$\int_{2.5}^{3.5} .2e^{-.2t}\,dt = -e^{-.2t}\Big]_{2.5}^{3.5} = -e^{-.7} + e^{-.5} = .1099$$

Since there were 120 completions, 120(.1099) = 13, the theoretical number of completions.

There are nine categories (after grouping), hence eight degrees of freedom. The critical χ^2 value is $\chi^2_{8,\,.05} = 15.507$. Because $3.574 < 15.507$, the analyst accepted the hypothesis that service time is distributed exponentially at a rate of $\mu = .2$ services per minute.

Appendix B

Mathematical Foundations

The Single-Channel, Infinite-Population Model

The classical queuing model calls for a single channel, an infinite population, arrivals occurring in a Poisson manner at a rate λ, and services occurring in exponential fashion at a rate μ. The first step is to determine a probability distribution for the number in the entire system (service plus queue).

Key:

$$
\begin{aligned}
P_n(t) &= \text{probability of } n \text{ units in system at time } t \\
\lambda\,\Delta t &= \text{probability of an arrival during } \Delta t \\
\mu\,\Delta t &= \text{probability of a service (departure) during } \Delta t \\
1 - \lambda\,\Delta t &= \text{probability of no arrivals during } \Delta t \\
1 - \mu\,\Delta t &= \text{probability of no services during } \Delta t
\end{aligned}
$$

We could wind up with n in the system if we started with n and there were no arrivals or service completions in the interval. We could also wind up with n if we started with $n + 1$ and experienced no arrivals but completed one service. All told, there are four paths to winding up with n; these are shown in equation (1) below.

$$
\begin{aligned}
P_n(t + \Delta t) = {} & P_n(t)(1 - \lambda\,\Delta t)(1 - \mu\,\Delta t) + P_{n-1}(t)\lambda\,\Delta t(1 - \mu\,\Delta t) \\
& + P_{n+1}(t)(1 - \lambda\,\Delta t)\mu\,\Delta t + P_n(t)\lambda\,\Delta t\mu\,\Delta t
\end{aligned} \tag{1}
$$

Expanding this equation:

$$
\begin{aligned}
P_n(t + \Delta t) = {} & P_n(t) - P_n(t)\,\Delta t(\lambda + \mu) + P_n(t)\lambda\mu(\Delta t)^2 + P_{n-1}(t)\lambda\,\Delta t - P_{n-1}(t)\lambda\mu(\Delta t)^2 \\
& + P_{n+1}(t)\mu\,\Delta t - P_{n+1}(t)\mu\lambda(\Delta t)^2 + P_n(t)\mu\lambda(\Delta t)^2
\end{aligned}
$$

Now take $P_n(t)$ across, factor Δt, and group terms having a Δt remaining in them:

$$
\begin{aligned}
\frac{P_n(t + \Delta t) - P_n(t)}{\Delta t} = {} & -P_n(t)(\lambda + \mu) + P_{n-1}(t)\lambda + P_{n+1}(t)\mu + (\Delta t)\lambda\mu \cdot \\
& \cdot [2P_n(t) - P_{n-1}(t) - P_{n+1}(t)]
\end{aligned}
$$

Take the limit (let $\Delta t \to 0$) on both sides of the equation:

$$
\frac{dP_n(t)}{dt} = -P_n(t)(\lambda + \mu) + P_{n-1}(t)\lambda + P_{n+1}(t)\mu + 0 \tag{2}
$$

If we now concern ourselves with the steady state, the probabilities will no longer depend on t—which is the same as saying that the probability, $P_n(t)$, is a constant; then $\frac{dP_n(t)}{dt} = \frac{dP_n}{dt} = 0$. Consequently,

$$0 = -P_n(\lambda + \mu) + P_{n-1}\lambda + P_{n+1}\mu$$

$$P_n = \frac{\lambda}{\lambda + \mu} P_{n-1} + \frac{\mu}{\lambda + \mu} P_{n+1} \tag{3}$$

Now think about $n = 0$, that is, no units in the system. We note that $P_0 \equiv P_0$ and that P_{-1} is impossible, and therefore has a probability of 0. Returning then to (2), we may reduce it to

$$\frac{dP_0}{dt} = 0 = -P_0(\lambda + \mu) + 0(\lambda) + P_1\mu \tag{4}$$

However, there can be no departures if there are 0 in the system; hence, $P_0\mu = 0$ and we have

$$P_0\lambda = P_1\mu$$

$$P_1 = \frac{\lambda}{\mu} P_0$$

With experimentation you would find that an inductive process yields a simpler formula for P_n, that is,

$$P_n = \left(\frac{\lambda}{\mu}\right)^n P_0 \tag{5}$$

For example, we might determine P_3 from (3) as follows:

$$P_1 = \frac{\lambda}{\lambda + \mu} P_0 + \frac{\mu}{\lambda + \mu} P_2$$

Substituting for P_2:

$$P_1 = \frac{\lambda}{\lambda + \mu} P_0 + \frac{\mu}{\lambda + \mu}\left[\frac{\lambda}{\lambda + \mu} P_1 + \frac{\mu}{\lambda + \mu} P_3\right]$$

$$P_1 = \frac{\lambda}{\lambda + \mu} P_0 + \frac{\mu\lambda}{(\lambda + \mu)^2} P_1 + \left(\frac{\mu}{\lambda + \mu}\right)^2 P_3$$

$$P_3 = \left[\left(1 - \frac{\mu\lambda}{(\lambda + \mu)^2}\right) P_1 - \frac{\lambda}{\lambda + \mu} P_0\right]\left(\frac{\lambda + \mu}{\mu}\right)^2$$

$$P_3 = \frac{(\lambda^2 + \mu\lambda + \mu^2)}{\mu^2} P_1 - \frac{\lambda(\lambda + \mu)}{\mu^2} P_0$$

Substituting for P_1:

$$P_3 = \frac{(\lambda^2 + \mu\lambda + \mu^2)\,\lambda}{\mu^2}\,\frac{}{u}\,P_0 - \frac{(\lambda^2 + \lambda\mu)}{\mu^2}\,P_0$$

$$P_3 = \frac{(\lambda^3 + \mu\lambda^2 + \mu^2\lambda - \mu\lambda^2 - \lambda\mu^2)}{\mu^3}\,P_0 = \left(\frac{\lambda}{\mu}\right)^3 P_0$$

Since the sum of all probabilities = 1, we have

$$1 = \sum P_i = P_0 \sum_{i=0}^{\infty} \left(\frac{\lambda}{\mu}\right)^i = P_0 \sum_{i=0}^{\infty} \rho^i \qquad \textbf{(6)}$$

In waiting-line jargon, λ/μ is called the "traffic intensity ratio," or the "utilization factor,"or the "clearing ratio." I apologize for the use of ρ (rho) as a substitute symbol for λ/μ, but ρ, like λ and μ, is standard notation in the queuing literature. We may find a closed-form expression for (6) by using finite calculus and *requiring* $0 < \rho < 1$; the calculations follow:

$$1 = \lim_{n\to\infty} P_0 \sum_{i=0}^{n} \rho^i = P_0 \lim_{n\to\infty} \Delta^{-1}\rho^i \Big]_0^{n+1}$$

$$= P_0 \lim_{n\to\infty} \left[\frac{\rho^{n+1} - 1}{\rho - 1}\right] = P_0\left(\frac{1}{1-\rho}\right) \qquad \textbf{(7)}$$

Consequently, $P_0 = 1 - \rho = 1 - (\lambda/\mu)$

With equations (5) and (7) available, all the formulas presented in the first situation can be developed by recognizing

$$E(n) = \sum_{n=0}^{\infty} nP_n = \lambda/(\mu - \lambda)$$

$$E(Q) = \sum_{n=1}^{\infty} (n-1)P_n = \lambda^2/[\mu(\mu - \lambda)]$$

$$E(s) = E(n) - E(Q) = \lambda/\mu$$

$$E(t) = E(n)/\lambda = 1/(\mu - \lambda)$$

$$E(t_s) = \int_0^{\infty} \mu T e^{-\mu T}\, dT = 1/\mu$$

$$E(w) = E(t) - E(t_s) = \lambda/[\mu(\mu - \lambda)]$$

The least satisfying of these is $E(t)$ because, as is shown above, it relies entirely on intuitions. It will be instructive to provide a firmer base for these intuitions. To do so, we turn to transform theory:

The Laplace transform of the exponential is

$$L\{\mu e^{-\mu T}\} = \int_0^{\infty} \mu e^{-\mu T} e^{-ST}\, dT = \mu/(\mu + S)$$

The n-fold convolution of the exponential is the gamma:

$$L\{[\mu/(\mu + S)]^n\} = \mu^n T^{n-1} e^{-\mu T}/(n-1)! = g_n(T)$$

Since there might be 0 units in the system, n could equal 0; therefore, upon an arrival, there would be at least $n + 1$ units in the system. We really need to work with the $n + 1$st convolution of the exponential to seek the probability that the arriving unit must wait at least t units of time:

$$g_{n+1}(T \geq t) = \int_t^\infty [\mu^{n+1} T^n e^{-\mu T}/n!]\, dT$$

Using deluxe integration by parts:

$$= \frac{\mu^{n+1}}{n!}\left[\frac{T^n e^{-\mu T}}{-\mu} \frac{-nT^{n-1}e^{-\mu T}}{(-\mu)^2} + \cdots + \frac{(-1)^n n! e^{-\mu T}}{(-\mu)^{n+1}}\right]_t^\infty$$

$$= \sum_{i=0}^{n} (\mu t)^i e^{-\mu t}/i!, \quad \text{the cumulative Poisson.}$$

It now remains to weight each fold of the convolution—each having been incorporated to recognize that it reintroduced the exponential distribution that commenced at the time the service on the preceding unit was completed—by the probability that n units are in the system to obtain the cumulative probability for time in the system:

$$F(T > t) = \sum P_n g_{n+1}(T > t)$$

$$= (1 - \rho) \sum_{n=0}^{\infty} \rho^n \sum_{i=0}^{n} (\mu t)^i e^{-\mu t}/i!$$

Expanding the summations yields

$$= (1 - \rho)[1 + \rho(1 + \mu t) + \rho^2(1 + \mu t + (\mu t)^2/2!)\ldots]e^{-\mu t}$$

$$= e^{-\mu t}\begin{bmatrix} 1 + \rho(1 + \mu t) + \rho^2(1 + \mu t + (\mu t)^2/2!) + \ldots \\ -\rho \qquad\qquad - \rho^2(1 + \mu t) \qquad\qquad - \ldots \end{bmatrix}$$

$$= e^{-\mu t}[1 + \rho\mu t + (\rho\mu t)^2/2! + \ldots]$$

$$= e^{-\mu t} \sum_{i=0}^{\infty} (\rho\mu t)^i/i!$$

But the summation is a Maclaurin expansion for $e^{\rho\mu t}$, and upon substituting $\rho = \lambda/\mu$, we obtain

$$F(T > t) = e^{-\mu t} e^{\rho\mu t} = e^{-(\mu - \lambda)t}$$

To find the density for time in the system, we take the derivative of the cumulative complement:

$$f(t) = \frac{d(1 - e^{-(\mu - \lambda)t})}{dt} = (\mu - \lambda)e^{-(\mu - \lambda)t}$$

These results could be obtained more directly but less informatively by working with the transform of $g_{n+1}(T)$:

$$L\{F(T)\} = (1-\rho)\sum_{n=0}^{\infty} \rho^n[\mu/(\mu+S)]^{n+1} = \frac{(1-\rho)\mu}{\mu+S}\sum_{n=0}^{\infty}\left(\frac{\rho\mu}{\mu+S}\right)^n$$

$$= \frac{(\mu-\lambda)}{\mu+S}\Delta^{-1}\left(\frac{\rho\mu}{\mu+S}\right)^n\Bigg]_0^{\infty} = \frac{(\mu-\lambda)}{\mu+S}\frac{(\mu+S)}{(\mu-\lambda+S)} = \frac{\mu-\lambda}{\mu-\lambda+S}$$

$$f(t) = L^{-1}\{(\mu-\lambda)/(\mu-\lambda+S)\} = (\mu-\lambda)e^{-(\mu-\lambda)t}$$

The expected time in the system is

$$E(t) = \int_0^{\infty} t(\mu-\lambda)e^{-(\mu-\lambda)t}\,dt = 1/(\mu-\lambda), \quad \text{as before}$$

Multichannel Systems

The probability distributions for multichannel systems are determined in identical ways except that the rate of arrivals differs, being an individual rate in the case of the finite population and a collective (entire population) rate in the case of the infinite population. We shall focus on the finite system for illustrative purposes.

The initial problem facing the analyst in a multichannel finite system (that is, one serving M customers) is to develop a probability distribution for the number of units in the system in the steady state (the steady state is the equilibrium condition of the system that is reached after traffic has settled down). The mathematical approach to obtaining this distribution is through the use of differential equations, and this can become cumbersome. A more humane treatment for developing these equations involves the use of a Markov chain matrix as a bookkeeping device, as it were.

The transition matrix assumes steady state, so Δt does not appear in its elements, nor do terms that involve $(\Delta t)^2$. Assume, for concreteness, that the limited population, M, is machines that need the maintenance of mechanics, k, as in the second illustration in the chapter. The elements of the matrix reflect the number of mutually exclusive ways an arrival or a service could occur. For instance, if three machines were down, there would be $M - 3$ ways an arrival could occur, and if there were two mechanics busy, there would be two chances for a service completion. It is assumed that multiple arrivals or services during the split second of time represented by the matrix have such a small probability that they can be ignored. Both λ and μ are scaled down to correspond to this split second (thus if $\lambda = 60$ per minute and if the matrix were in tenths of a second, $\lambda = .1$ in the matrix). The matrix for two servers is shown below.

		To:				
	0	1	2	3	$\cdots$	M
From: 0	$1 - M\lambda$	$M\lambda$	0	0	$\cdots$	0
1	μ	$1 - \mu - (M-1)\lambda$	$(M-1)\lambda$	0	$\cdots$	0
2	0	2μ	$1 - 2\mu - (M-2)\lambda$	$(M-2)\lambda$	$\cdots$	0
3	0	0	2μ	$1 - 2\mu - (M-3)\lambda$	$\cdots$	0
.	.	.	.	.	$\cdots$	.
.	.	.	.	.	$\cdots$	.
.	.	.	.	.	$\cdots$	.
M	0	0	0	0	$\cdots$	$1 - 2\mu$

The probability distribution for n units needing service is developed recursively by reading down the matrix and introducing the probabilities of the appropriate rows and column.

Using column 0 yields

$$P_0 = (1 - M\lambda)P_0 + \mu P_1$$

$$0 = M\lambda P_0 + \mu P_1; \quad \therefore, \quad P_1 = M\frac{\lambda}{\mu}P_0$$

Using column 1 yields

$$P_1 = M\lambda P_0 + (1 - \mu - (M-1)\lambda)P_1 + 2\mu P_2$$

$$0 = M\lambda P_0 - \left(\mu + \frac{((M-1)\lambda)M\lambda}{\mu}\right)P_0 + 2\mu P_2$$

$$0 = \frac{-M(M-1)\lambda^2}{\mu}P_0 + 2\mu P_2; \quad \therefore, \quad P_2 = \frac{M(M-1)}{2}\left(\frac{\lambda}{\mu}\right)^2 P_0$$

Using column 2 yields

$$P_2 = (M-1)\lambda P_1 + (1 - 2\mu - (M-2)\lambda)P_2 + 2\mu P_3$$

$$0 = \frac{(M-1)\lambda M\lambda}{\mu}P_0 - \frac{(2\mu + (M-2)\lambda)M(M-1)\lambda^2}{2\mu^2}P_0 + 2\mu P_3$$

$$0 = \frac{-M(M-1)(M-2)\lambda^3}{2\mu^2}P_0 + 2\mu P_3; \quad \therefore, \quad P_3 = \frac{M(M-1)(M-2)}{2(2)}\left(\frac{\lambda}{\mu}\right)^3 P_0$$

Using column 3 yields

$$P_3 = (M-2)\lambda P_2 + (1 - 2\mu - (M-3)\lambda)P_3 + 2\mu P_4$$

$$0 = \frac{(M-2)\lambda M(M-1)\lambda^2}{2\mu^2}P_0 - \frac{(2\mu + (M-3)\lambda)M(M-1)(M-2)\lambda^3}{4\mu^3}P_0 + 2\mu P_4$$

$$0 = \frac{-M(M-1)(M-2)(M-3)\lambda^4}{4\mu^3}P_0 + 2\mu P_4;$$

$$\therefore, \quad P_4 = \frac{M(M-1)(M-2)(M-3)}{2(2)^2}\left(\frac{\lambda}{\mu}\right)^4 P_0$$

"Upper" or factorial notation may be introduced to restate this last probability:

$$P_4 = \frac{M^{(4)}}{2(2)^2}\left(\frac{\lambda}{\mu}\right)^4 P_0$$

Assuming that $P_k = \dfrac{M^{(k)}}{2(2)^{k-2}}\left(\dfrac{\lambda}{\mu}\right)^k P_0$, the kth column of the matrix leads to

$$P_k = (M-(k-1))\lambda P_{k-1} + (1 - 2\mu - (M-k)\lambda)P_k + 2\mu P_{k+1}$$

$$0 = \frac{-(M-k)\lambda M^{(k)}\lambda^k P_0}{2(2)^{k-2}\mu^k} + 2\mu P_{k+1}; \quad \therefore, \quad P_{k+1} = \frac{M^{(k+1)}}{2(2)^{k+1-2}}\left(\frac{\lambda}{\mu}\right)^{k+1} P_0$$

P_{k+1} is the same as P_k with k replaced throughout by $k+1$. Hence,

$$P_n = \frac{M^{(n)}}{2!2^{n-2}}\left(\frac{\lambda}{\mu}\right)^n P_0, \quad \text{for } n > 2$$

More generally, if there were k servers,

$$P_n \begin{cases} \dfrac{M^{(n)}}{n!}\left(\dfrac{\lambda}{\mu}\right)^n P_0, & \text{for } n = 0, 1, \ldots, k \\ \dfrac{M^{(n)}}{k!k^{n-k}}\left(\dfrac{\lambda}{\mu}\right)^n P_0, & \text{for } n > k \end{cases} \tag{1}$$

One of these states (that is' 0, 1, 2 . . . ,M) must describe the system at any given time; therefore the probabilities must sum to unity.

$$1 = \sum_{n=0}^{M} P_n = \sum_{n=0}^{k} \frac{M^{(n)}}{n}\left(\frac{\lambda}{\mu}\right)^n P_0 + \sum_{n=k+1}^{M} \frac{M^{(n)}}{k!k^{n-k}}\left(\frac{\lambda}{\mu}\right)^n P_0$$

Equation (2) may then be used to define P_0 as shown earlier. Equation (9) in the text should be compared to the single-channel formula:

Single channel	Multichannel
$E(w) = E(Q) \div \mu$	$E(w) = E(Q) \div \{\mu E(s)\}$

The multichannel denominator would have immediate intuitive appeal if it were $k\mu$; however, a moment's reflection reveals that idle time prevents all k channels from being fully occupied. Therefore, the effective combined service rate is $\mu E(s)$.

Selected References

P. M. Morse, *Queues, Inventories, and Maintenance* (New York: John Wiley & Sons, 1958).

T. L. Saaty, *Elements of Queueing Theory* (New York: McGraw-Hill Book Co., 1961).

D. R. Cos and W. L. Smith, *Queues* (London: Chapman and Hall, 1968).

A. M. Lee, *Applied Queueing Theory* (London: Macmillan and Company Limited, 1968).
R. B. Cooper, *Introduction to Queueing Theory* (New York: The Macmillan Company, 1972).
J. A. Panico, *Queueing Theory* (Englewood Cliffs, N.J.: Prentice-Hall, Inc. 1969)

Problems

1. *Stockbroker.* A stockbroker serves his clientele exponentially at the rate of three per hour. Find the probability that the first client to arrive will spend at least 30 minutes with the stockbroker.

2. *Service level.* Arrivals in a particular system with an unlimited population are Poisson distributed with a mean rate of .2 unit per minute. Management wishes to know the service rate capability necessary to assure implementation of the policy "No customer should expect to spend more than eight minutes in the system." Assume service time is exponentially distributed.

3. *Forgetfulness and the exponential distribution.* The exponential distribution has the fascinating property of forgetfulness (also referred to as "lack of memory"). This means that the probability that it will take t units of time or more to complete a service does not depend on how much time the unit has already spent in service. Prove this property by considering that α units of time have already been spent in the system, letting $f(T) = (\mu - \lambda)e^{-(\mu-\lambda)T}$, and using integration and the definition of conditional probability to show that the following relationship holds:

$$F(T > t) = F(T > (t + \alpha) | T > \alpha)$$

   Hint:

   Saying that T is greater than $t + \alpha$ *and* that T is greater than α reduces to saying that T is greater than $t + \alpha$.

4. *Optimal service rate.* The number of arrivals per period from an infinite calling population follows the Poisson distribution with a mean of 50 units per period. The cost of waiting per unit per period is \$20, while the cost for the service facility is \$36 per service per period. What expected service rate should be established—based on dollar costs—if the service duration is assumed to be distributed exponentially? Determine the total cost of the system given the optimal expected service rate.

5. *Rate of arrivals and investment.* A machine can process a unit of product in 20 minutes. Assuming that arrivals are Poisson distributed, that service time is distributed exponentially, and that management will acquire an additional machine once arrivals can expect to wait in queue at least one hour for service to begin, determine that rate of arrivals which will prompt the securing of a second machine.

6. *Proofs.* Following equation (7) in Appendix B to this chapter are the system expectations for a single-channel, infinite-population system with Poisson arrivals and exponential services. Derive all formulas.

7. *Bookstore and service policy.* Assuming she works exponentially, at what average rate must a cashier at a college bookstore work to insure a probability of .9 that once a customer lines up to pay, he will not have to wait more that 12 minutes? During the hour in question there is only one cashier in attendance and customers arrive for payment *in* Poisson fashion at an average rate of 15 per hour.

8. *A saga of the Golden East.* It is 1872. Jesse James, having travelled to the distant land of Massachusetts and finding himself alone and without funds, has decided to make a nonnegotiable demand on the Amherst Savings Bank. The Amherst of 1872 is a charming rural town, and its savings bank has a single teller (whose name, unfortunately, has never been recorded in the annals of history). Jesse, who has a daring nature, nonetheless feels that he should plan his visit carefully, since he has none of his gang to back his play.

Accordingly, in preparation for the event, Jesse records the arrival and departure times of bank customers for many days. He finds that customers arrive in a Poisson fashion at an average rate of 10 per hour, and that the teller serves customers exponentially, taking four minutes per customer, on average.

His plan is to appear as just another customer, to point his trusty Colt .45—somewhat hidden from view under a copy of the *Springfield Daily News*—at the teller, and to quietly but firmly acquaint the latter with his needs. He then intends to exit unobtrusively, to mount his trusty steed, and to depart with appropriate dispatch.

Jesse wants to estimate how much time he can anticipate spending in the bank. His horse will stay ground-tied and well behaved for as long as 8 to 10 minutes, but after that he tends to wander off. If the horse should wander, Jesse will have had it. Jesse, of course, is a risk seeker and is not unwilling to take a chance provided that odds are no worse than 3 to 1 against him—and assuming the safer estimate of horse reliability.

Can Jesse reasonably expect to continue his winning ways? What costs inspire his desire for analysis?

9. *Derivation of probability distribution for time in queue.* Use transform theory to derive the density function for time spent waiting for service to begin—given a single-channel, unlimited population, Poisson-exponential system. (Keep in mind that we are dealing here with the queue and not the total system, although to have a queue, there must be at least one unit already in the system when the present unit arrives.)

10. *The classical airplane stacking problem.* Since watches are not perfectly synchronized and many things—late starts, head winds, storms, and passenger problems—disrupt their schedules, planes arrive at a small airport in Poisson fashion at an average rate of 14 per hour. Once a plane is given the signal to leave the stack and land, it takes exactly four minutes to complete the landing process. How large is the expected stack and how much time must a plane spend circling the field waiting for permission to land? What costs are involved?

11. *Derivation of multichannel, infinite-population probability distribution.* In Appendix B to this chapter, a Markov chain was used to derive the probability distribution for a multichannel, finite-population system. Use the same approach to derive the multichannel, infinite-population probability distribution.

12. *Multichannel, finite population, fleet service.* Each truck in a fleet of 10 delivery trucks will return to a warehouse for reloading at an average interval of 90 minutes. An average of 10 minutes is required by the driver and one warehouseman to load the next shipment. If the warehouse personnel are busy loading previous arrivals, the driver and his truck must wait in queue. Both the time between arrivals and the loading time are distributed exponentially. The cost of waiting in the system is $18 per hour per truck, and a warehouseman costs $8 per hour.

Required:

Set up—but do not solve—the model to optimize the number of warehousemen and discuss the information you would obtain from the solution.

13. *Multichannel, finite population.* Three turbines are serviced by two electricians. Individual turbine breakdown is Poisson distributed and occurs at the rate of .4 per day. On average, it takes an electrician about one day, exponentially distributed, to repair a turbine. If downtime costs $400 per day in lost revenues, what is the expected lost revenue?

14. *Finite population, multichannel.* Four faculty members share the services of two full-time graduate assistants. On average, each faculty member calls for service in a Poisson fashion at the rate of .33 per day. Also on average, each assistant requires .3 days to complete an assignment. What is the expected time a professor must wait for completed work? What has this to do with costs?

15. *Tennis courts.* A splendid university that is rurally located is planning to install tennis courts in a particular area of its campus. The president of the university has hired you to determine the best number of courts to construct. He specifies that the figure of merit consists not only of the facility costs, but also of the cost of players waiting to play, which he feels would average $50 per hour per group. He also wishes to know (a) how many players can be expected to be seen at the courts at any given time; (b) how long players can expect to be at the courts; and (c) how much time players can expect to spend waiting for a court to become vacant.

Your research shows that player groups (singles or doubles) are likely to arrive in a Poisson fashion at a mean rate of two groups per hour, and that the length of time they will probably play obeys an exponential distribution with a mean of $1\frac{1}{2}$ hours. You also determine that the normalized cost of constructing and maintaining a court comes to $10 an hour.

Required:

(a) Prepare a report to the president supported by proofs of all equations. (If you wish to compute costs for only two possible values for the number of courts, you may do so in lieu of determining the optimal number. Of course, a computer solution is acceptable.)

(b) Explain how you came up with the parameter data for the model and how you think the estimate of waiting cost might be obtained.

(c) Discuss how this problem might be refined. (That is, how would you improve on this problem?)

16. *Computer program and another measure of system running performance.* One often hears that a plant is "running at $x\%$ of capacity." This is at once a measure of system performance—of its productivity—and an indication of unused facilities. It is a simple ratio to calculate. Divide the expected number in service, $E(n) - E(q) = E(s)$, by the number of servers, k. Add this feature to the program presented in Exhibit 1 and then obtain a solution to the following queue problem:

Finite population size:	100 machines
Arrival rate per day (Poisson) per machine:	.1 or .2
Service rate per day (Poisson):	16
Cost per day for a technician:	\$64
Cost for his equipment: (five year life, use a 360-day year, no salvage and 20% yearly discount rate)	\$75,000
Revenues lost per day for a machine needing repair:	\$286

Notes:

(a) If a rate is Poisson distributed, then the time between events is exponentially distributed.

(b) The arrival rate will be .1 now when the machines are new, but is expected to double as they get older.

(c) No more than two pieces of equipment will be acquired because of space restrictions.

17. *Service level discussion.* Assume you are planning to deliver a paper intitled "Service Level: A Practical Means for Implementing Utility Theory." Outline the paper. (Professor: If the time is available, have some student present his or her paper in class. It will be good practice for the student not only to develop speaking ability, but also to formulate a means for approaching management should he or she engage in a consulting career. The rest of the class should be prepared to destroy the presented paper by listing oversights, disadvantages, impracticalities—any objection that management could possibly raise.)

18. *Truncation and lost business.* The chapter ignored a very important fact when it assumed that the number in a single-channel system with an unlimited calling population could approach infinity. In practice there is often some number, say M (for maximum), beyond which the number in the system cannot grow. In other words, the *queue* is truncated at $M - 1$ because when new arrivals appear and see M units in the system, they decide not to stay. M is therefore a balking or reneging limit. The units that renege constitute an approximate measure of lost business for the time period under study. It is also interesting to note that once reneging is considered permissible, we no longer need require $\mu > \lambda$.

Fortunately, adjusting the probability distribution for number in the system is easily accomplished by using the scaling approach for truncation that was presented in Chapter 12 (simply divide the *PMF* by its cumulative probability). The lower the value of λ and the larger the value of M, the better.

Required:

(a) Develop a formula for the expected number in a truncated system.

(b) What is the meaning behind the words "constitute an approximate measure," as used above?

(c) How would you employ truncated queue formulas?

19. *Non-Poisson-exponential system.* The chapter paid little attention to the short-run or transient analysis of queues. While many interesting questions focus on behavior after the system has had time to settle down, nonetheless, predicting either what state the system will be in x periods from now or how many periods must pass before the system effectively reaches equilibrium is also quite important.

Transform theory offers an excellent way of isolating both a steady-state matrix and "transient component" matrices. To illustrate, suppose the transition matrix of a queue with a reneging limit of 2 is

$$P = \text{From:}\ \begin{matrix} 0 \\ 1 \\ 2 \end{matrix} \overset{\begin{matrix} & \text{To:} & \\ 0 & 1 & 2 \end{matrix}}{\begin{bmatrix} .6 & .4 & 0 \\ .42 & .46 & .12 \\ 0 & .7 & .3 \end{bmatrix}}$$

Notes:

(a) Assume arrivals average 24 per hour, that a period takes one minute, and that the server can deal with an average of 42 units in an hour. We may relax the assumption of Poisson arrivals and exponential service and merely assume fixed independent probabilities of arrivals and service each period.

(b) This transition matrix differs from the Markovian matrix used earlier. Heretofore probabilities were obtained by writing equations, using the transition probabilities in the matrix and the state probabilities shown as row and column headings. Reading down the P_0 column, for example, has previously yielded

$P_0 = (1 - \lambda)P_0 + \mu P_1$. Now the completed probabilities are in the transition matrix itself. Here the probability of an arrival is $24/60 = .4$ while the probability of a service is $42/60 = .7$. Consequently, if the beginning state is 0, there is a probability of .6 that the state won't change during this period. If there were one in the system in the beginning, it would require a service and no arrival (that is, $.7(.6) = .42$) to change the system to the zero state. There would be two mutually exclusive ways for the system to start and end in state 1: there could be a service and an arrival ($.7(.4) = .28$) or no service and no arrival ($.3(.6) = .18$). If the system starts in state 2, there will be no chance for an arrival because the reneging limit is then operative; hence the probability of changing to state 1 is the probability of a service or .7.

Required:

(a) Split the transition matrix, P, into steady-state and transient component matrices by following these procedures:

(1) Multiply P by the transforming scalar Z (the Z transform).

(2) Find $(I - ZP)^{-1}$, being sure to factor the determinant. For checking purposes, the determinant is $(1 - Z)(1 - .40446Z)(1 + .04446Z)$.

(3) Obtain three separate matrices by algebra of partial fractions (discussed on p. 000 in Appendix C) applied to each element of the adjoint matrix. (Recall that the inverse is the adjoint divided by the determinant.) Thus, the setup for the 1, 1 element is

$$\frac{1 - .76Z + .054Z^2}{(1 - Z)(1 - .40446Z)(1 + .04446Z)} = \frac{A}{1 - Z} + \frac{B}{1 - .40446Z} + \frac{C}{1 + .04446Z}$$

Solve for A, B, and C and put each in a separate matrix with its respective denominator as shown above.

(4) Obtain the inverse transform of each matrix by looking for its denominator in Table 11 of Appendix A. The matrix with the A values is the steady-state matrix. The combination of the matrix with the B values and the matrix with the C values yields the transient component.

(b) Comment on the result, and be sure to decide how many periods would have to go by before the steady state was achieved and the transient component essentially disappeared.

20. *Tandem queues, convolutions, inventory flows and process costing.* (Challenging!) The manufacture of a product usually takes place in a series of sequential stages; therefore, the output of one stage becomes the input of the next. The key to making such systems work smoothly lies not so much in synchronizing the rates of service as in providing sufficient "bunker" (or storage) space between stages. Without adequate bunkers, a slowdown in a later stage would lead to work stoppage in earlier stages; conversely, a slowdown or downtime in an earlier stage would result in idle time in ensuing stages as they ran out of products to work on.

In the simplest case, the single-server, Poisson exponential, infinite-population model is employed—buttressed with the assumption of bunkers of unlimited size between stages.Since idle time cannot be stored, the effective service rate is $\mu E(s) = \mu(\lambda/\mu) = \lambda$. This means that the input to ensuing stages arrives in Poisson fashion at the same rate, λ, that arrivals appeared to the first stage.

If service rates are synchronized at M for each stage, the basic probablity aistribution, $P_n = (1 - \rho)\rho^n$, applies for each stage, and its convolution for k stages provides the distribution for units in the entire system. Given $P^{\{k\}}(n)$, the ordinary system expectations may be calculated.

Required:

(a) Find $P^{\{k\}}(n)$ and use it to calculate $E(n)$ in closed form.

(b) Assume that there are two stages, each with a different service rate, μ_i, where $\mu_i > \lambda$. Find $E(n)$, $E(Q)$, and $E(s)$ for the total system.

(c) Relate tandem queues to process costing.

Comments:

If time does not permit calculating a general form for the answer in (a), do it for two stages only.

The classical article on this subject is Gordon C. Hunt, "Sequential Arrays of Waiting Lines," *Operations Research*, 4 (1956): 674–83.

21. *Bulk arrivals.* Arrivals often come in groups, not individually. A simple example would be the manufacture of trays containing n of an item—when a tray arrived, n items would arrive. The n items might thereafter be processed on an individual basis. As another example, the number of doubles matches played at a tennis club during, say, a day would result in multiples of four players. If something had to be done for each player individually (register, provide equipment, serve a meal), the queue statistics could indicate level of service and need for facilities. In either of these cases, arrivals could follow the Poisson curve.

Use the Markov chain approach to develop a Z transformed probability distribution and use the resultant $P(Z)$ and the formulas below to develop the equations for $E(n)$, the expected number in the system, and $V(n)$, the variance of the number.

$$E(n) = D_Z P(Z)|_{Z=1} = \sum_{n=0}^{\infty} D_Z(P_n Z^n)|_{Z=1} = \sum_{n=0}^{\infty} nP_n Z^{n-1}|_{Z=1}$$

$$V(n) = D_Z{}^2 P(Z)|_{Z=1} + E(n) - [E(n)]^2$$

Hint:

(a) Develop a transition matrix for two units per arrival and then extend the approach to m units per arrival.

(b) Do not use recursion to develop the probability distribution. Instead, amass several equations (in the reading-down-the-column manner), multiply the equation obtained from the ith column by Z^i, and then sum the respective terms to form geometric series in Z^i and P_i. You may have to use a transformation of variable to bring the summed terms into definitional form (that is, $P(Z) = \sum_{n=0}^{\infty} P_n Z^n$). Gather terms in (Z) and then solve for $P(Z)$. It will simplify notation to let $\rho = \dfrac{m\lambda}{\mu}$

(c) To solve for P_0, use the fact that $P(Z)|_{Z=1} = 1$

(d) *Answers:*

$$P(Z) = \frac{m(1 - Z)(1 - \rho)}{\rho Z^{m+1} - (\rho + m)Z + m} = \frac{-m(1 - \rho)}{?}$$

$$E(n) = \rho(m + 1)/[2(1 - \rho)]$$

$$V(n) = [\rho(m + 1)(-\rho m + \rho + 4m + 2)]/[12(1 - \rho)^2]$$

22. *Golf foursomes.* During weekend busy hours, a golf club allows only foursomes to tee off. A refreshment house is accessible from several places on the course; some foursomes stop in for a snack before commencing play, some stop at various stages during play, and some stop at the end of the round. If foursomes arrive in Poisson fashion at a mean rate of 18 per hour, and if service per individual is exponentially distributed at a rate of .5 minutes per customer, calculate the expected number in the refreshment house during any given minute.

Linear Programming

16

Developing Intuitions for Linear Programming

We come now to a very exciting technique—one that is widely used in business and that holds great promise for accounting. Mathematical programming is the process of optimizing a function subject to restrictions or constraints. In linear programming, the function to be optimized and its constraints are stated in linear form, for example, $a_1x_1 + a_2x_2 + \cdots + a_nx_n$.

The appeal of linear programming (LP for short) lies in the satisfaction of doing the best with what you have. "Doing your best" is the idea behind optimizing the objective function, while "with what you have" refers to the constraints within which the solution must be found.

A partial list of possible constraints that might enter a management decision problem would include

(1) capacity of machines,
(2) number of men available,
(3) quantity of output demanded,
(4) quantity of output that may be supplied,
(5) time,
(6) space restrictions,
(7) capital, and
(8) various managerial policies, such as
  (a) making at least a given quantity of an item,
  (b) using certain types of labor or equipment, and
  (c) making at least a given quantity of every item in the product line.

The ultimate source of most constraints is managerial policy. For example, management determines the budgetary allotment for investing in current inventories and, at some earlier date, dictated capacity restrictions when constructing the storage facilities. And if present warehouse facilities were inadequate, management would be responsible for deciding whether additional facilities should be acquired either by leasing or by building. Hence constraints may be either created or eased by managerial edict.

To identify the factors that restrict a given problem requires skill and lies at the heart of linear programming. Specifying restrictions that are not really relevant (these are known as redundant constraints) merely wastes time, but overlooking pertinent constraints invalidates the solution obtained. In any case, no additional constraint can ever improve the dependent variable being optimized. To further complicate matters, a constraint that is redundant today may become pertinent tomorrow. For this reason one occasionally hears redundant constraints referred to as dormant or inactive constraints.

To illustrate some of these notions, consider the man who struggles to maximize his happiness subject to limitations of time and money. Suppose he decides to rob a bank to eliminate his money constraint. Having succeeded in depleting the cash inventory of his friendly neighborhood bank, our man has thereby solved his money problem (that is, the monetary constraint is no longer binding—it has become redundant). However, although money is no longer an issue, he finds that he is now bothered by pangs of conscience and fear of detection. Of course, if our friend then got married, he would probably find that money once again impinged on his happiness. Changeability characterizes many business problems, and if one restriction is eased another often takes its place. Fortunately, by exercising diligence, an analyst can generally reflect the pertinent constraints for a given planning horizon—but the shorter the horizon, the better.

The LP Problem at a Glance

An understanding of what goes on in linear programming can be obtained graphically. We shall diagram a problem that offers interesting practice in constructing constraints.

Problem: A shoe manufacturer produces both tennis sneakers and golf shoes during a particular portion of the year. The basic quantity measurement for each is a dozen. The company wishes to know how many dozen to make of each given the following considerations:

1. The profit on each dozen tennis sneakers sold will be $50, while each dozen golf shoes sold will net $80.
2. During the ordinary working time available, either 25,000 dozen sneakers or 20,000 dozen shoes or any linear combination of shoes and sneakers implied by these limits may be produced.
3. Demand for sneakers and shoes will not exceed 18,000 and 15,000 dozen respectively.

4. The company wishes to make at least 5,000 dozen of each item.
5. Management feels that the proper balance of production will require that at least two dozen golf shoes be made for each dozen tennis sneakers.

Analysis: Let T stand for a dozen tennis sneakers and G stand for a dozen golf shoes. Then the objective is to maximize $Z = \$50T + \$80G$, which in LP is known as the "objective function."

The first constraint (see consideration 2 above) is that for ordinary working time. Writing $T \leq 25{,}000$ and $G \leq 20{,}000$ is not satisfactory because the permissible linear combinations of T and G are not reflected in these inequalities. What we know is that 25,000 T can be made if no G is made, and that 20,000 G can be made if no T is made. These are the intercepts of the straight line shown below.

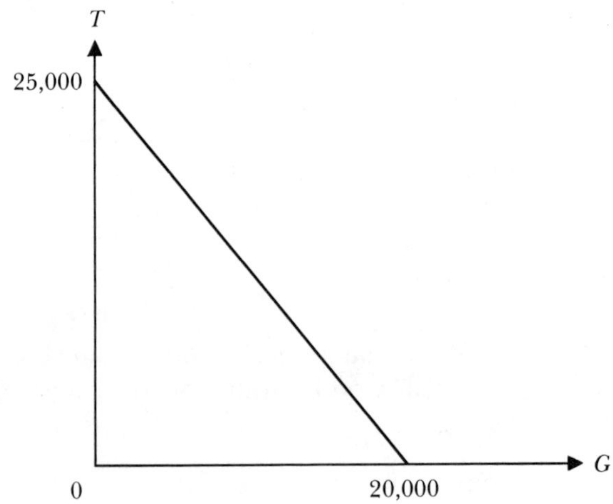

The equation of the line is $T = 25{,}000 - \dfrac{25{,}000}{20{,}000}G$, where slope = fall ÷ run = 25,000 ÷ 20,000. Since T can be less than 25,000, the equation becomes the following inequality: $T + 1.25G \leq 25{,}000$

We next need to reflect the minimum and maximum quantities. The allowable quantity ranges may be expressed as follows:

$$5{,}000 \leq T \leq 18{,}000$$

$$5{,}000 \leq G \leq 15{,}000$$

These relationships are treated in an LP problem as four separate inequalities:

$$T \geq 5{,}000$$
$$T \leq 18{,}000$$
$$G \geq 5{,}000$$
$$G \leq 15{,}000$$

The "balance" constraint calls for the production of at least two dozen G for each dozen T or

$$G \geq 2T$$

That is, $$2T - G \leq 0$$

Note that there are two further restrictions that have not been stated. It would be meaningless in this problem to consider producing negative quantities of G and T; consequently, there are two so-called "nonnegativity restrictions": G, $T \geq 0$. Geometrically, these nonnegativity restrictions place the solution in the first quadrant.

Figure 1 is a graph of these constraints. The shaded area, which is a convex polyhedral set of points formed by hyperplanes, is the "feasible region" in which acceptable solutions must fall. The dashed parallel lines are known as "iso-profit" lines; all combinations of T and G falling on any one line yield the same profit, and the farther the profit line is from the origin, the greater is the profit. The greatest profit occurs at the point in the feasible region that lies on the iso-profit line most removed from the origin. A numerical solution may be obtained by solving for the intersection of the two constraints, $T + 1.25G \leq 25{,}000$ and $G \leq 15{,}000$. We have

$$T + 1.25(15{,}000) = 25{,}000$$
$$T = 6{,}250$$

The maximum constrained profit is therefore

$$Z = \$50(6{,}250) + \$80(15{,}000) = \$1{,}512{,}500$$

Graphing Comment

The iso-profit lines are obtained from $Z = 50T + 80G$ by declaring a profit, say $Z =$ 400,000, and then solving for the intercepts (by alternately setting $T = 0$ to get $G = 5{,}000$ and $G = 0$ to get $T = 8{,}000$). The other lines are then drawn parallel to this one.

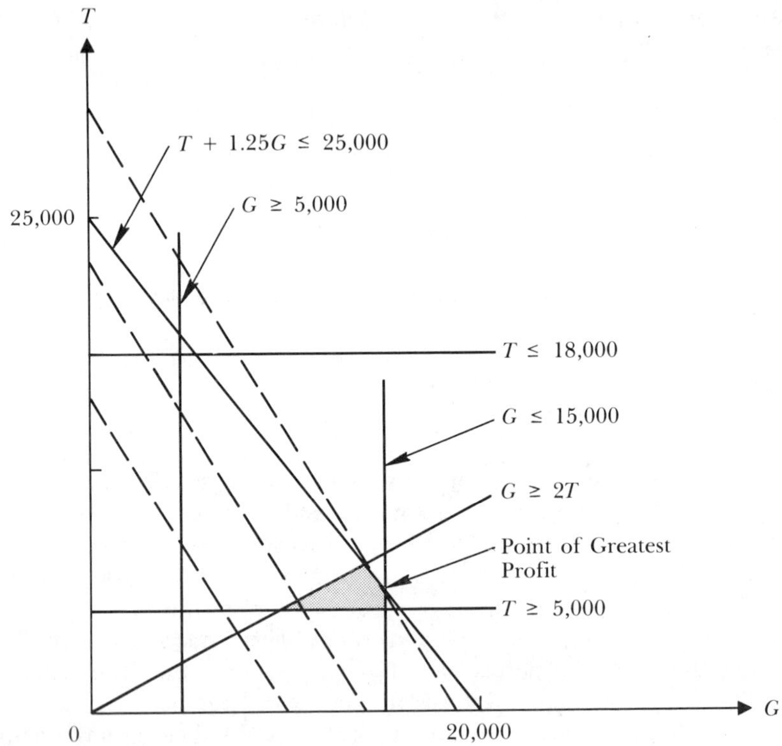

Figure 1

The Simplex Algorithm

The Matrix Theoretic Approach

While a graphic solution could be obtained for any LP problem that had only two or three decision variables, it would be a nuisance to attack each problem this way. And of course many more variables might be involved.[1] Fortunately, there is available a well-developed set of procedures (algorithm)

[1] It is not at all uncommon to encounter LP problems having 50 or 100 variables and as many constraints. Indeed, one occasionally hears about problems that have thousands of variables and constraints.

for solving LP problems. This is the simplex algorithm. Although its name suggests simplicity, the algorithm is really quite ingenious and elaborate.[2]

Since almost every computer center in the United States has a linear programming library routine, you might legitimately raise the question "Why bother discussing the simplex algorithm when I can use any nearby computer?" We shall study simplex because it is important that you understand what the computer is doing. If some problem ever arises with the computer output, knowledge of the simplex algorithm will be most helpful in locating the difficulty. And if you study mathematical programming beyond the present text, you will find an understanding of simplex almost essential.

The usual start of a simplex solution places all decision variables at the zero level—which is equivalent to the origin of the feasible region. Then, through successive applications of the algorithm, other corners of the feasible region are studied until the best corner is eventually reached. The simplex procedures guarantee that each new corner tested will be at least as good as and usually better than the corner just considered. Thus if the problem involves maximizing profit, each iteration will generate a profit at least as great as the profit generated at the preceding iteration. Profits will increase monotonically—but not strictly monotonically. Interestingly, the procedures do not necessarily select the most promising corner for the next iteration, since there are two criteria at work and only one combination of these is considered in selecting the next corner. (This will become clearer when we get to an illustration.)

In Appendix C, I discuss the concept of forming linear combinations of basis vectors as a means of substituting for any given vector. I hope you have instant recall of these manipulations, but to be sure, let us refresh comprehension with an example.

Example: Given the matrix A shown below, and assuming x_1 and x_2 are basis vectors, form the basis matrix B and determine the linear combination scalars necessary to express x_3 in terms of the basis vectors.

$$\begin{array}{c} \\ x_0 \\ \left[\begin{array}{c} 2{,}000 \\ 3{,}000 \end{array}\right.\end{array} \begin{array}{c} A \\ \begin{array}{cccccc} x_1 & x_2 & x_3 & x_4 & x_5 & x_6 \end{array} \\ \left.\begin{array}{cccccc} 1 & 3 & 5 & 4 & 1 & 0 \\ 2 & 4 & 2 & 3 & 0 & 1 \end{array}\right] \end{array}$$

[2] G. B. Dantzig developed the simplex algorithm in 1947. For his description of it, see his "Maximization of a Linear Function of Variables Subject to Linear Inequalities," in *Activity Analysis of Production and Allocation*, ed. T. C. Koopmans, Cowles Commission Monograph no. 13 (New York: John Wiley & Sons, 1951), Ch. 21.

Solution: The basis vectors x_1 and x_2 together form the basis matrix B:

$$B = \begin{bmatrix} 1 & 3 \\ 2 & 4 \end{bmatrix}$$

The problem is to determine the elements (scalars) of vector λ_3 such that:

$$B\lambda_3 = x_3$$

$$\lambda_3 = B^{-1} x_3$$

$$\lambda_3 = \frac{\begin{bmatrix} 4 & -3 \\ -2 & 1 \end{bmatrix}}{-2} \begin{bmatrix} 5 \\ 2 \end{bmatrix} = \begin{bmatrix} -7 \\ 4 \end{bmatrix}$$

Check: $\begin{bmatrix} 5 \\ 2 \end{bmatrix} = -7\begin{bmatrix} 1 \\ 2 \end{bmatrix} + 4\begin{bmatrix} 3 \\ 4 \end{bmatrix}$

Comments:

1. What does this say? It says that one unit of x_3 uses up the same resources as four units of x_2—as reduced by seven units of x_1. In other words, having a unit of x_3 is not quite as demanding on resources as having four units of x_2. Or in still other words, you can have seven units of x_1 and one unit of x_3 in exchange for four units of x_2.
2. Why bother, since $[\begin{smallmatrix}5\\2\end{smallmatrix}]$ is a lot easier to write than the linear combination? $[\begin{smallmatrix}5\\2\end{smallmatrix}]$ may be easier to write, but $-7[\begin{smallmatrix}1\\2\end{smallmatrix}] + 4[\begin{smallmatrix}3\\4\end{smallmatrix}]$ expresses x_3 in terms of x_1 and x_2, thereby facilitating comparisons. If the earnings per unit of x_1, x_2, and x_3 are \$6, \$8, and \$12 respectively, and if x_1 and x_2 are being manufactured but x_3 is not, then the company can achieve a net gain of \$22 by switching over to x_1 and x_3. Why?

Gain from: 7 units of x_1 @ \$6 =	\$42
1 unit of x_3 @ \$12 =	12
Loss from discontinuing	
4 units of x_2 @ \$8 =	(32)
Net Gain	\$22 (See $z_3 - c_3$ on page 575)

Let us continue the example and find $B^{-1} A$.

$B^{-1}A$

	x_0	x_1	x_2	x_3	x_4	x_5	x_6
x_1	500	1	0	−7	−3.5	−2	1.5
x_2	500	0	1	4	2.5	1	−.5

Notice that the column labels have not changed. $B^{-1}A$ merely states the vectors x_i in terms of the linear combination scalars necessary to restate the original vectors in terms of the present basis vectors, x_1 and x_2. Since x_1 and x_2 are in the basis, they have been placed as row labels to the left of the matrix opposite the unit elements in the respective column unit vectors. These unit vectors merely reflect the fact that it takes $1(x_1) + 0(x_2)$ to obtain x_1 and similarly for x_2.

If we introduced some measure of the importance of each variable, we could convert this example into an LP problem. Let us say that the x_j, for $j = 1, 2, 3, 4$, are products that yield profits of \$6, \$8, \$12, \$9. We shall eventually call these profits "contribution margins" and label them c_j, so we might as well begin using the appropriate terminology and notation right away. The vectors in the basis are a subset of the j vectors and will be designated both by the subscript i and the more suggestive symbology $i \in B$, that is, i a member of the basis. x_0 is the vector that originally specifies the total scarce resource limitations, say available machine capacities (expressed in hours) in two departments. Consequently, the numbers appearing under each variable (vector) in matrix A are "technological coefficients" that measure the hours needed in each department to make one unit of that variable. Once B^{-1} multiplies A, the solution will be found in the x_0 elements, as we shall see. Variables x_5 and x_6 are known as "slack variables" and usually, though not necessarily, are assigned zero contribution margins. Temporarily ignoring the bottom row, study the positioning of the labels and contribution margins as shown below in the completed simplex "tableau."

"Stub"		$c_j \to 0$	6	8	12	9	0	0
c_i $(i \in B)$ ↓		x_0	x_1	x_2	x_3	x_4	x_5	x_6
6	x_1	500	1	0	−7	−3.5	−2	1.5
8	x_2	500	0	1	4	2.5	1	−.5
$z_j - c_j$		7,000	0	0	−22	−10	−4	5

The first column in this tableau is the solution at this stage; accordingly, 500 units each of x_1 and x_2 are made for a total profit, Z, of \$7,000 which appears in the lower left-hand corner of the tableau. Only one question seems pertinent now: Is this the best profit that could be obtained in these circumstances? The answer to the question is found in the last or $z_j - c_j$ row. If there are any negative values in this row, the solution can be improved. Before considering how this is done, note that for each column vector j,

$$z_j - c_j = \sum_{i \in B} c_i \lambda_{ij} - c_j \tag{1}$$

Comments:

1. The c_i in the summand appear in the "stub" in the leftmost column while the λ_{ij} are the elements in the body of the matrix itself. The c_j appear above each column heading. For example,

$$\begin{aligned} z_3 - c_3 &= \sum c_i \lambda_{i3} - c_3 \\ &= 6(-7) + 8(4) - 12 = -22, \end{aligned}$$

as we computed earlier.

2. A simplification has been utilized here. Actually total profit is $Z = \sum c_i \lambda_{i0}$ (which is also written $\sum c_i x_i$); however, by writing $c_0 = 0$, equation (1) can be used to obtain both Z and $z_j - c_j$. Consequently, $Z \equiv z_0 - c_0$.

Thus far two vectors were chosen to form a basis, B, and the inverse of this basis matrix was used to multiply the original matrix (tableau) of variables to arrive at a new tableau. $z_j - c_j$ values were determined for the new tableau and three of these values were found to be negative. This indicates that the present is not the optimal corner of the feasible region. We must proceed to some other corner that is more promising. This other corner will constitute a different basis, and to arrive at this new basis, we will need to remove one variable from the present basis and enter a substitute variable. Once the new basis is determined, the inverse of this basis matrix may be used to multiply the original tableau to obtain a new tableau. The $z_j - c_j$ row of this tableau could then be computed. *If* there were *no negative values* in this row, and if all $x \geq 0$, we would have arrived at *the optimal corner*. If there were at least one negative value, we would repeat the iterative process, trying corner after corner of the feasible region until there were no negative $z_j - c_j$ values left and all $x_i \geq 0$.

Undoubtedly the criticality of the $z_j - c_j$ values has become evident to you. These values are really opportunity costs that reflect the gains per unit to be enjoyed at the next iteration by inserting units of each variable into the solution. Since Z is the variable we are trying to maximize, we can let Z_n stand for the value of Z at the nth tableau. How the opportunity costs achieve their significance is brought out in equation (2), which computes the value of Z at the next iteration:

$$Z_{n+1} = Z_n - \frac{\lambda_{p0}}{\lambda_{pk}}(z_k - c_k) \tag{2}$$

Comments:

1. p designates the variable chosen to leave the present basis.

2. k designates the variable chosen to enter the basis at the next iteration.

3. λ_{p0} is in the pth row, 0th column in $B^{-1}A$.

4. λ_{pk} is in the pth row, kth column in $B^{-1}A$.

Study equation (2) for a moment. Assuming that $\lambda_{p0}/\lambda_{pk}$ is positive—which will shortly be shown—what value of $z_k - c_k$ would you choose to increase Z_{n+1} the most? Do you see that it would be convenient to require $z_k - c_k$ not only to be negative, but also to be the most negative of all the $z_k - c_k$? Hence, we have

The Entering Vector Criterion
Choose the most negative $z_j - c_j$

Next consider $\lambda_{p0}/\lambda_{pk}$ in (2). To maintain consistency with our choice of $z_k - c_k$, $\lambda_{p0}/\lambda_{pk}$ must be positive and, you might think, the most positive of the i values. However, you would be algebraically correct but mathematically wrong to choose anything but the *smallest* $\lambda_{i0}/\lambda_{ik}$ value. The mathematical issue here requires recognition of the nonnegativity restrictions (that is, making negative units of a product is not only meaningless but also forbidden by the restriction, $x_i \geq 0$). To guarantee obedience to the nonnegativity restrictions of an LP problem without the bother of including them explicitly in a tableau, the simplex algorithm has

The Exiting Vector Criterion
Choose the minimum $\lambda_{i0} \div \lambda_{ik}$, such that $\lambda_{ik} > 0$

The exiting criterion has the effect of keeping $\lambda_{i0} \geq 0$. By prohibiting the use of ratio values where $\lambda_{ik} = 0$, the minimum idea is adhered to (this would otherwise yield a ratio of ∞). By prohibiting the use of ratio values where $\lambda_{ik} < 0$, the simplex algorithm guarantees that λ_{i0} won't become negative at the next iteration. Once positive, λ_{i0} stays positive!

If you will reflect further on equation (2), you will understand why the simplex criteria only guarantee that an equally good or better corner of the feasible region—but not necessarily the best corner—will be selected in the next tableau. The entering criterion has designated the most negative $z_j - c_j$ as $z_k - c_k$. It is entirely conceivable that the minimum $\lambda_{i0}/\lambda_{ik}$ that multiplies $z_k - c_k$ in (2) does not yield the greatest increase in z_n. Some other less negative $z_j - c_j$ may have a greater minimum $\lambda_{i0}/\lambda_{ij}$ such that this new combination exceeds the increase in z_n that is associated with the variable chosen by applying the entering criterion. (This point is merely interesting; it is not crucial to understanding simplex.)

So where are we? We have completed the matrix approach to obtaining an LP solution! First we choose a basis set of vectors, obtain the inverse of the basis matrix, and multiply the inverse by the original matrix of vectors. The first column vector in the product (that is, x_0) then gives us the readings of the basis variables comprising the present corner of the feasible region. *Any variable not in the basis is automatically assigned a reading of zero.* We have now set up this corner as the focal point and have expressed all vectors (variables) consistently in terms of the basis variables. We next calculate the $z_j - c_j$ row. If there are any negative values, we choose the entering vector, x_k, as the one having the most negative $z_j - c_j$ value (this is the entering criterion). We then apply the exiting criterion to determine which vector p (that vector i having the smallest $\lambda_{i0}/\lambda_{ik}$ ratio) to remove from the basis. The constituency of the new basis matrix is thus established. We repeat the process (algorithm) to determine a new corner (coordinates for which are in the vector x_0 in the product $B^{-1}A$; again, if a variable is not in the basis, its coordinate value is zero). If this corner has a negative $z_j - c_j$, we iterate again; if it does not and if all $x_i \geq 0$, we know that we have finally reached the best corner of the feasible region. A computer program for carrying out these solution processes along with the solution to the problem we have been discussing appear in Exhibit 1.[3]

The Elementary Row Operations Approach

The matrix approach has been presented to help you appreciate the nature of the simplex algorithm. It is an iterative process that uses special criteria and the concept of linear combination to move around in the feasible region space in search of a best corner. But no one solves problems manually in this way; it would simply be too much work to compute a new inverse completely and do the multiplication for each iteration. What is done instead is much easier. The most popular manual approach to the simplex mechanics rests on elementary row operations as embodied in the Gauss-Jordan method of matrix inversion. Simply put, the pivot row (the exiting vector row) is divided by the pivot element, while any other row becomes its old elements (in the last tableau) minus a scalar multiple (the element in the other row

[3] This program is notable for its brevity. Because it is brief, it sacrifices some desirable features. There is no provision for doing sensitivity analysis via parametric programming, and if the nonnegativity restrictions are violated because of an unfortunate choice of a starting basis, the program may not be able to correct the condition. Hence, it may be wise to begin with the slack vectors as the initial basis. That way, the nonnegativity restrictions are sure to be observed. Cautions: 1. If the determinant value is very near zero, the basis matrix may be singular and therefore noninvertible. Owing to roundings, however, the program may be able to invert, thereby giving nonsense results. If you suspect this has happened, try a different initial basis. 2. If you use the program on other problems, you may have to change the number of columns in the output by appropriately restating lines 477, 493, and 511.

Exhibit 1

```
005 DIM A(15,25),Z(25,1),B(15,15),D(15,15),X(25),V(25),E(15,25)
006 DIM C(25)
010 PRINT "NO. OF CONSTRAINTS AND NO. OF VARIABLES"
020 INPUT M,N
030 N = N + I
040 MAT READ A(M,N)
050 MAT READ Z(N,1)
060 PRINT "VARIABLES IN THE BASIS?"
065 PRINT "DO NOT USE VARIABLE #1 AS THIS IS THE REQUIREMENTS COLUMN"
070 MAT INPUT C
080 MAT B = ZER(M,M)
090 FOR J = 1 TO M
100 FOR I = 1 TO M
105 B(I,J) = A(I,C(J))
110 NEXT I
120 NEXT J
130 MAT D = INV(B)
140 MAT E = D*A
150 FOR J = 1 TO N
160 X(J) = 0
165 REM COMPUTE Z - C
170 FOR I = 1 TO M
180 X(J) = Z(C(I),1) * E(I,J) + X(J)
190 NEXT I
200 X(J) = X(J) - Z(J,1)
210 NEXT J
220 K1 = 2
230 L1 = X(2)
235 REM SELECT ENTERING VECTOR
240 FOR J = 2 TO N
250 IF X(J) > L1 THEN 280
260 L1 = X(J)
270 K1 = J
280 NEXT J
285 REM ARE ALL Z - C POSITIVE?
290 IF X(K1) + .01 > = 0 THEN 475
295 REM SELECT EXITING VECTOR
297 LET T2 = 1000000
300 FOR I = 1 TO M
302 IF E(I,1) > = 0 THEN 305
303 IF E(I,K1) > = 0 THEN 330
304 GO TO 310
305 IF E(I,K1) < = 0 THEN 330
310 LET V(I) = E(I,1)/E(I,K1)
315 IF V(I) > T2 THEN 330
320 LET T2 = V(I)
325 LET T1 = I
330 NEXT I
350 IF T2 < > 1000000 THEN 460
440 PRINT "ALL LAMDAS LESS THAN ZERO"
450 STOP
460 C(T1) = K1
470 GO TO 090
475 LET M1 = 1
```

Exhibit 1 (*cont.*)

```
477 LET  M2 = 7
480 PRINT "FINAL TABLEAU"
485 FOR K = 1 TO 1
487 FOR I  = 1 TO M
489 FOR J  = M1 TO M2
491 PRINT USING 493, E(I,J)
493 FIELD ("-",7F9.2)
495 NEXT J
497 PRINT
499 NEXT I
505 PRINT
507 NEXT K
509 LET  M1 = 1
511 LET  M2 = 7
513 FOR I = 1 TO 1
515 FOR J = M1 TO M2
517 PRINT USING 493, X(J)
519 NEXT J
521 PRINT
527 PRINT
529 NEXT I
530 PRINT "VARIABLES IN THE BASIS"
531 FOR K = 1 TO M
533 LET  C(K) = C(K) - 1
535 PRINT C(K)
537 NEXT K
539 PRINT "DETERMINANT = "; DET
550 DATA 2000,1,3,5,4,1,0
551 DATA 3000,2,4,2,3,0,1
552 DATA 0,6,8.12,9,0,0
600 END

RUN

NO. OF CONSTRAINTS AND NO. OF VARIABLES

2,6
VARIABLES IN THE BASIS?
DO NOT USE VARIABLE #1 AS THIS IS THE REQUIREMENTS COLUMN
?
6,7

FINAL TABLEAU
   125.00     -.00      .25     1.00      .62      .25     -.13
  1375.00     1.00     1.75        0      .88     -.25      .63

  9750.00        0     5.50     -.00     3.75     1.50     2.25

VARIABLES IN THE BASIS
 3
 1
DETERMINANT = 8
```

in the pivot column divided by the pivot element) times the corresponding pivot row elements. Notationally, we have

Key:

n and $n+1$ in a pre-script position = the iteration
k = entering vector column (i.e., pivot column)
j = any column, $j = 0, 1, 2, \ldots$
p = pivot row index
o = other row index
λ_{ij} = an element in the i, j position in a tableau

$$ {}_{n+1}\lambda_{ij} = \begin{cases} {}_n\lambda_{pj} \div {}_n\lambda_{pk} & \text{(Pivot row)} \\ {}_n\lambda_{oj} - ({}_n\lambda_{ok} \div {}_n\lambda_{pk})({}_n\lambda_{pj}) & \text{(Other rows)} \end{cases} $$

Exhibit 2 contains an annotated illustration of these techniques applied to the problem we have been using. One important observation must now be made: the slack variables x_5 and x_6 have been introduced to provide an identity matrix as the original basis matrix. Since the original basis is an identity matrix which is its own inverse, the linear combination scalars for each vector (variable) are, conveniently, the original elements of the individual vectors themselves. For instance,

$$ \overset{x_3}{\begin{bmatrix} 5 \\ 2 \end{bmatrix}} = 5 \overset{x_5}{\begin{bmatrix} 1 \\ 0 \end{bmatrix}} + 2 \overset{x_6}{\begin{bmatrix} 0 \\ 1 \end{bmatrix}} $$

Another advantage of adding the identity matrix is that the computations will generate the inverse of the basis matrix as a reading under the slack variable columns. We start with the partitioned matrix $(A \vdots I)$ and through elementary row operations achieve $(\lambda \vdots B^{-1})$, which actually equals $B^{-1}(A \vdots I)$. Knowing B^{-1} is useful, as we shall see. The economic interpretation of the slack variables is that if there is idle time—time not needed for production—at any iteration, it will show up as a reading of the slack variables x_5 or x_6 or both. With slack variables introduced, the problem in Exhibit 2 may be formally restated as follows:

Objective function: Maximize $Z = \$6x_1 + \$8x_2 + \$12x_3 + \$9x_4 + \$0x_5 + \$0x_6$

Constraints:

$$ \begin{aligned} x_1 + 3x_2 + 5x_3 + 4x_4 + x_5 + 0x_6 &= 2{,}000 \\ 2x_1 + 4x_2 + 2x_3 + 3x_4 + 0x_5 + x_6 &= 3{,}000 \end{aligned} $$

Nonnegativity restrictions: $x_i \geq 0$

Be sure to read the observations accompanying Exhibit 2 and to study the tableaus themselves. You are ready to continue with this chapter only when you are certain that you could generate the solution to the problem

Exhibit 2 Observations

Maximize profit: $Z = \$6x_1 + \$8x_2 + \$12x_3 + \$9x_4$

Constraints:

$$x_1 + 3x_2 + 5x_3 + 4x_4 \leq 2{,}000$$

$$2x_1 + 4x_2 + 2x_3 + 3x_4 \leq 3{,}000$$

Nonnegativity Restrictions: $x_i \geq 0$

1. Trace the figures from the statement of the problem to the first tableau.
2. The most negative $z_j - c_j$ is $z_3 - c_3$ or -12 in tableau 1; hence, x_3 enters the basis at the next stage. Then, since the minimum $\lambda_{i0} \div \lambda_{i3}$ is $2{,}000 \div 5 = 400$, the vector that leaves the basis at the next stage is x_5. The next basis, therefore, will consist of x_3 and x_6.
3. Since x_3 is substituted for x_5 in going from tableau 1 to tableau 2, we find c_3 (that is, 12) and x_3 placed in the stub of tableau 2 in the position formerly occupied by c_5 (that is, 0) and x_5 in the stub of tableau 1.
4. For the first row of tableau 2, we apply the pivot row formula to row one of tableau 1: ${}_2\lambda_{1j} = {}_1\lambda_{1j} \div {}_1\lambda_{13}$, for $j = 0, 1, \ldots, 6$.

$$\left(400, \frac{1}{5}, \frac{3}{5}, 1, \frac{4}{5}, \frac{1}{5}, 0\right) = (2{,}000, 1, 3, 5, 4, 1, 0) \div 5$$

   For the second row of tableau 2, we apply the other row formula to row two of tableau 1: ${}_2\lambda_{2j} = {}_1\lambda_{2j} - ({}_1\lambda_{23} \div {}_1\lambda_{13})\,{}_1\lambda_{1j}$, for $j = 0, 1, \ldots, 6$.

$$\begin{array}{r} (3{,}000,\ \ 2,\ \ 4,\ 2,\ 3,\ \ \ 0,\ 1) \\ -(2/5)\,(2{,}000,\ \ 1,\ \ 3,\ 5,\ 4,\ \ \ 1,\ 0) \\ \hline \left(2{,}200, \frac{8}{15}, \frac{14}{5}, 0, \frac{7}{5}, \frac{-2}{5}, 1\right) \end{array}$$

5. If desired, instead of computing $z_j - c_j$ by equation (1), the other row formula could be used as follows:

$$\begin{array}{r} (\ \ 0,\ -6,\ -8,\ -12,\ -9,\ 0,\ 0) \\ -(-12/5)\,(2{,}000,\ \ 1,\ \ 3,\ \ 5,\ \ 4,\ 1,\ 0) \\ \hline \left(4{,}800, \frac{-18}{5}, \frac{-4}{5}, 0, \frac{3}{5}, \frac{12}{5}, 0\right) \end{array}$$

6. If a vector is in the basis, a unit vector appears in its column and its $z_j - c_j$ value is 0.
7. The profit for the next stage may be computed by $Z_{n+1} = Z_n - \frac{\lambda_{p0}}{\lambda_{pk}}(z_k - c_k)$

   For example, $$Z_2 = Z_1 - \frac{\lambda_{10}}{\lambda_{13}}(z_3 - c_3) = 0 - \frac{2{,}000}{5}(-12) = 4{,}800$$

8. Note that only two products are made in the optimal program. There can never be more decision variables in the optimal solution than there are constraints in the problem. If there are fewer decision variables in the basis than there are constraints, the difference in number will equal the number of slack variables in the basis. If a slack variable is in the basis, the constraint associated with it is redundant.
9. The shadow prices shown in tableau 3 indicate what an hour of additional capacity is worth in each of the respective departments. These prices may be used to generate the maximum profits. Since all the available hours were used, we have

$$Z = 2{,}000(\$12/8) + 3{,}000(\$18/8) = \$9{,}750$$

10. Although there is no such column in the example, had there been a column vector that had a negative $z_j - c_j$ value and whose linear combination scalars, λ_{ij}, were all either zero or negative, the profit would be infinite and the problem would be said to be unbounded. The original constraints would then be checked for error or omission.

Exhibit 2 (*cont.*)

Tableau 1

		$c_j \to 0$	6	8	12	9	0	0	
$c_i \downarrow$	$(i \in B)$	x_0	x_1	x_2	x_3	x_4	x_5	x_6	$\lambda_{i0} \div \lambda_{ik}$
0	x_5	2,000	1	3	(5)	4	1	0	$2{,}000 \div 5 = 400 \to$ exiting vector
0	x_6	3,000	2	4	2	3	0	1	$3{,}000 \div 5 = 1{,}500$
	$z_j - c_j$	0	-6	-8	-12 ↑ entering vector	-9	0	0	$Z_2 = 0 - \frac{2{,}000}{5}(-12) = 4800$

Tableau 2

12	x_3	400	$\frac{1}{5}$	$\frac{3}{5}$	1	$\frac{4}{5}$	$\frac{1}{5}$	0	$400 \div \frac{1}{5} = 2{,}000$
0	x_6	2,200	$\left(\frac{8}{5}\right)$	$\frac{14}{5}$	0	$\frac{7}{5}$	$-\frac{2}{5}$	1	$2{,}200 \div \frac{8}{5} = 1{,}375 \to$ exiting vector
	$z_j - c_j$	4,800	$-\frac{18}{5}$ ↑ entering vector	$-\frac{4}{5}$	0	$\frac{3}{5}$	$\frac{12}{5}$	0	$Z_3 = 4{,}800 - \frac{11{,}000}{8}\left(-\frac{18}{5}\right) = 9{,}750$

Tableau 3

12	x_3	125	0	$\frac{1}{4}$	1	$\frac{5}{8}$	$\frac{2}{8}$	$-\frac{1}{8}$	$\to B^{-1}$
6	x_1	1,375	1	$\frac{14}{8}$	0	$\frac{7}{8}$	$-\frac{2}{8}$	$\frac{5}{8}$	
	$z_j - c_j$	9,750	0	$\frac{44}{8}$	0	$\frac{30}{8}$	$\frac{12}{8}$	$\frac{18}{8}$	$\to$ Shadow prices

Comments:

1. Optimal profits are \$9,750 and come from making 1,375 units of x_1 and $125x_3$.
2. B^{-1} $\quad (A \vdots I) \quad (\lambda : B^{-1})$ Tableau 3

$$\begin{bmatrix} \frac{2}{8} & \frac{1}{8} \\ -\frac{2}{8} & \frac{5}{8} \end{bmatrix} \begin{bmatrix} 2{,}000 & 1 & 3 & 5 & 4 & 1 & 0 \\ 3{,}000 & 2 & 4 & 2 & 3 & 0 & 1 \end{bmatrix} = \begin{bmatrix} 125 & 0 & \frac{1}{4} & 1 & \frac{5}{8} & \frac{2}{8} & -\frac{1}{8} \\ 1{,}375 & 1 & \frac{14}{8} & 0 & \frac{7}{8} & -\frac{2}{8} & \frac{5}{8} \end{bmatrix}$$

3. The shadow prices are really Lagrangean multipliers and the objective function could be rewritten as follows:

$$Z = 6x_1 + 8x_2 + 12x_3 + 9x_4 - \frac{12}{8}(x_1 + 3x_2 + 5x_3 + 4x_4 + x_5 - 2{,}000)$$

$$- \frac{18}{8}(2x_1 + 4x_2 + 2x_3 + 3x_4 + x_6 - 3{,}000)$$

$$Z = -5.5x_2 - 3.75x_4 - 1.5x_5 - 2.25x_6 + 9{,}750$$

Then, since any variable not in the basis has a value of zero, $Z = 9{,}750$.

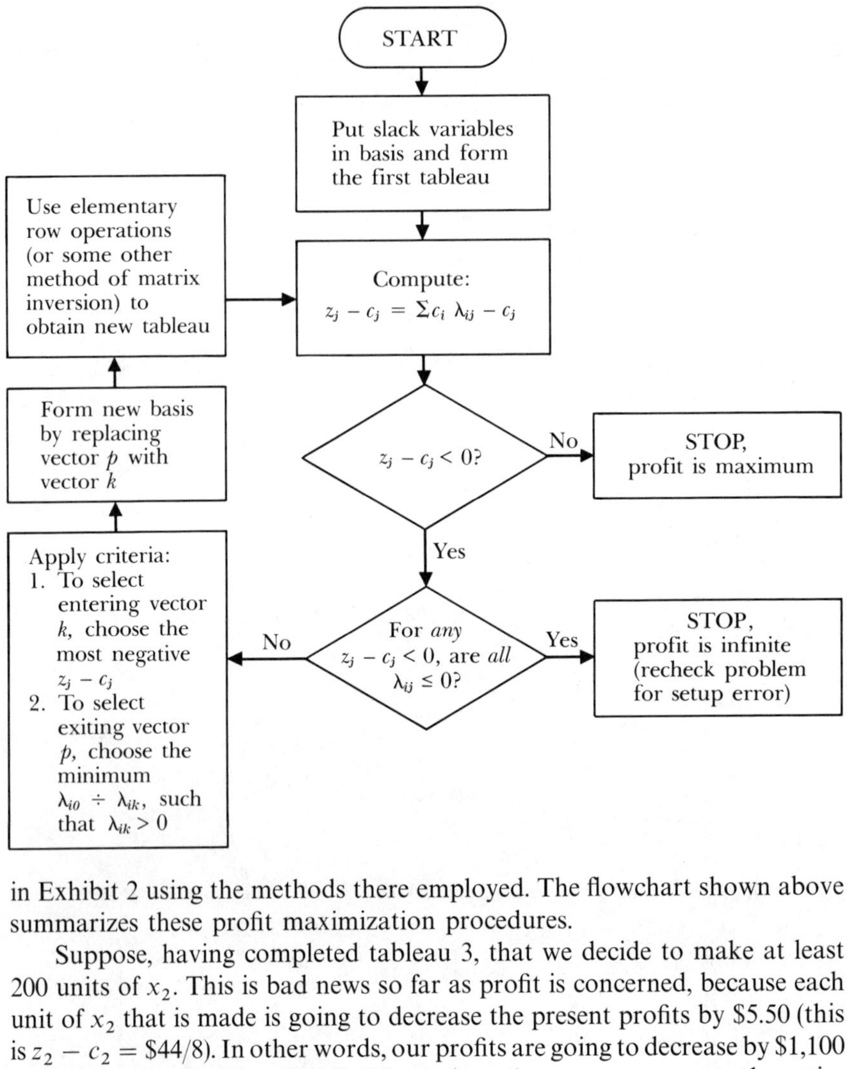

in Exhibit 2 using the methods there employed. The flowchart shown above summarizes these profit maximization procedures.

Suppose, having completed tableau 3, that we decide to make at least 200 units of x_2. This is bad news so far as profit is concerned, because each unit of x_2 that is made is going to decrease the present profits by \$5.50 (this is $z_2 - c_2 = \$44/8$). In other words, our profits are going to decrease by \$1,100 (which is 200 × \$5.50) to \$8,650. We need not, however, recompute the entire problem to determine this result. Multiply each of the λ_{i2} values by 200 to get 50 ($= 200(\frac{1}{4})$) and 350 ($= 200(\frac{14}{8})$), and then substract these results from the λ_{i0} values to get the reduced quantities of x_3 and x_1 that will be produced. The new optimal program will be

$$
\begin{aligned}
\$12x_3 &= \$12(125 - 50) &&= \$\ 900 \\
\$\ 6x_1 &= \$\ 6(1{,}375 - 350) &&= \ 6{,}150 \\
\$\ 8x_2 &= \$\ 8(200) &&= \ 1{,}600 \\
& && \underline{\underline{\$8{,}650}}\text{, as predicted}
\end{aligned}
$$

Further assume that we decide to make $80x_4$. Can you see that this will lead to a new program of

$$\begin{aligned} \$12x_3 &= \$12(25) &= \$\ \ 300 \\ \$\ 6x_1 &= \$\ 6(955) &= 5{,}730 \\ \$\ 8x_2 &= \$\ 8(200) &= 1{,}600 \\ \$\ 9x_4 &= \$\ 9(80) &= 720 \\ & & \overline{\$8{,}350} \end{aligned}$$

We will shortly verify these results by redoing the whole problem.

Sensitivity

I would next like to concentrate on two critical situations that limit the extent of the kind of experimentation that we have just been doing. It is worthwhile knowing how long a particular set of decision variables will remain in the optimal basis even though their solution magnitudes vary. A basis set of vectors will remain optimal as long as (1) nonnegativity restrictions are not violated, and (2) contribution margins of either existing variables or proposed variables do not generate a negative value of $z_j - c_j$.

We can readily make use of the nonnegativity requirements by addressing the following question. "Given that tableau 3 pertained, and that it had also been decided to manufacture 80 units of x_4, how many units of x_2 could be made without requiring us to rework the problem?"

Answer: When 80 units of x_4 are made, λ_{i0} in tableau 3 becomes $(75; 1{,}305)^T$, that is, 75 units of x_3 and 1,305 units of x_1 would be produced. By dividing 75 and 1,305 by 1/4 and 14/8 respectively, we obtain 300 and $745\frac{5}{7}$. This means that the greatest quantity of x_2 that can be made without changing the constituency of the basis is 300 units. If we make more than 300, x_3 will become negative; however, at exactly 300 units x_3 still remains in the basis, although at a zero level (this is known as a "degenerate" solution). (Incidentally, if degeneracy ever appears while you are performing tableau operations, you will find that at least two values of $\lambda_{i0}/\lambda_{ik}$ were tied for designation as minimums when applying the exiting criterion at the previous iteration. Select any of the tied values as your exiting vector and simply continue the ordinary procedures; nothing special need be done to treat degeneracy in the simplex algorithm.)

To illustrate how a changing profit margin would cause an alteration in the constituency of a presently optimal basis, look at, say, vector x_2 in tableau 3 and try to decide what new contribution margin would just render you *indifferent* about making x_2. If the new margin became \$8 + (\$44/8) = \$13.50, $z_2 - c_2$ would equal zero and the condition of "alternative optima" would exist. Geometrically this means that the graph of the objective function coincides with the pertinent constraint farthest out in the feasible region, and hence that there is an infinite number of solutions all having the same finite profit. In our present example, there would be an infinite number of ways to obtain the profit of \$9,750. The analyst would determine these equally attractive programs by entering x_2 into the basis with its new contribution margin of \$13.50 and obtaining a new optimal tableau. Then by taking $a\%$ of the tableau 3 solution and $(1 - a)\%$ of the tableau 4 solution, where $0 \leq a \leq 1$, and adding the results, an infinite number of programs yielding a profit of \$9,750 could be generated. You would cease being indifferent and insist on making x_2 once its contribution margin exceeded \$13.50.

In a similar way we can use tableau 3 to determine the desirability of producing a new product, x_7. Assume this candidate product requires six hours in the first department and eight hours in second department, and that it has a contribution margin of \$30. Should x_7 be manufactured? We use B^{-1} to find the appropriate linear combination scalars, then multiply these scalars by the respective c_i, and finally calculate $z_7 - c_7$:

$$\underset{B^{-1}}{\begin{bmatrix} \frac{2}{8} & -\frac{1}{8} \\ -\frac{2}{8} & \frac{5}{8} \end{bmatrix}} \underset{x_7}{\begin{bmatrix} 6 \\ 8 \end{bmatrix}} = \underset{\lambda_7}{\begin{bmatrix} \frac{1}{2} \\ \frac{7}{4} \end{bmatrix}}$$

$$z_7 - c_7 = 12(1/2) + 6(7/4) - 30 = -54/4$$

Since $z_7 - c_7$ is negative, we would enter x_7 in the basis and continue the algorithm until the new optimal program was obtained.

Parametric Programming and Postoptimality Analysis

The kind of sensitivity study that we have been doing for the last few pages is referred to as postoptimality analysis. In its simplest form, one c_j or one x_{i0} value is altered at a time to see how great a change it can withstand without changing the constituency of the basis. When the linear programmer really gets serious about postoptimality analysis, however, he studies simultaneous changes in these parameters with the help of parametric programming. Studying changes in the a_{ij} is so messy, unfortunately, that although it can be done otherwise, most analysts simply rework the problem with the new a_{ij} values. Let us forget about changes in a_{ij} and instead concentrate on c_j and x_{i0}.

To distinguish between the sensitivity approach we have been employing and the parametric programming approach, we shall use tableau 3 in Exhibit 2, which is reproduced below.

		0	6	8	12	9	0	0
		x_0	x_1	x_2	x_3	x_4	x_5	x_6
12	x_3	125	0	1/4	1	5/8	2/8	−1/8
6	x_1	1,375	1	14/8	0	7/8	−2/8	5/8
$z_j - c_j$		9,750	0	44/8	0	30/8	12/8	18/8

First we shall consider the sensitivity approach.

Suppose you do not know $c_3 = 12$. All you are sure of is that you want to keep x_1 and x_3 in the basis and that $c_1 = 6$. Form the $z_j = c_j$ equations for columns, 1, 2, 4, 5, and 6:

$$0c_3 + 1(6) = 6; \quad \therefore, \quad c_3 = 0$$

$$\frac{1}{4}c_3 + \frac{14}{8}(6) = 8; \quad \therefore, \quad c_3 = -10$$

$$\frac{5}{8}c_3 + \frac{7}{8}(6) = 9; \quad \therefore, \quad c_3 = 6$$

$$\frac{2}{8}c_3 - \frac{2}{8}(6) = 0; \quad \therefore, \quad c_3 = 6$$

$$-\frac{1}{8}c_3 + \frac{5}{8}(6) = 0; \quad \therefore, \quad c_3 = 30$$

If c_3 drops below 6, the left-hand side of either the third or fourth equations above will be less than the right-hand side. This will lead to negative $z_j - c_j$ values and will force x_3 from the basis—via the workings of the simplex exiting criterion. And if c_3 exceeds 30, the fifth equation will run into similar difficulties. In summary, no change in basis constituency occurs if $6 \leq c_3 \leq 30$. The ranges for all the c_j can be found in this manner. So much for the sensitivity approach; next we see how parametric programming would obtain these same ranges.

When studying changes in c_j, parametric programming focuses on the new objective function, $Z = \sum(c_j + \varnothing r_j)x_j$. To understand this function, it is crucial to recognize that r_j is a relative rate of change. Thus we could speak about controlling contribution margins in such a way, for instance, that every dollar of increase in c_1 could be brought about only by a two-dollar decrease in c_2. Then if you consider that both r_1 and r_2 are to be multiplied by a single scalar, $\varnothing$, it becomes plausible that if $\varnothing$ exceeded a certain value, the constituency of the basis would change. If we wished, we could next analyze the new basis to see for what new values of $\varnothing$ it remained intact. In this way we could show how the original relative values, when multiplied by various $\varnothing$ values, caused successive changes in the basis matrix as $\varnothing$ ranged over positive values (i.e., over $\varnothing \geq 0$).

If the new objective function were expressed in vectors, we could have $Z = c^{*T}x = (c + \varnothing r)^T x$; therefore, $c^* = c + \varnothing r$. Allow me to use B as a subscript to designate the basis variables and $z_j^* - c_j^*$ to designate the new opportunity costs (that is, the $z_j - c_j$ values) corresponding to the new c_j values. Then the basis will change when $z_j^* - c_j^*$ *just* becomes negative (this is the entering criterion at work). We have

$$z_j^* - c_j^* = (c_B + \varnothing r_B)\lambda_j - (c_j + \varnothing r_j) = 0$$

$$(c_B\lambda_j - c_j) + \varnothing(r_B\lambda_j - r_j) = 0$$

$$(z_j - c_j) + \varnothing(r_B\lambda_j - r_j) = 0$$

From this last equation we see three things:

1. The smallest value of $\varnothing$ that causes a single vector j to satisfy this equation is the critical value of $\varnothing$ (hereafter designated $\varnothing_c$).
2. If $r_B\lambda_j - r_j \geq 0$, the equation does not hold for all j, because $\varnothing \geq 0$.
3. If $r_B\lambda_j - r_j < 0$, the equation holds, because $\varnothing(r_B\lambda_j - r_j)$ could then become $-(z_j - c_j)$ with suitable choice of $\varnothing$.

If we solve for $\varnothing$, we can state the guiding rule:

$$\varnothing_c = \min \begin{cases} -(z_j - c_j) \div (r_B\lambda_j - r_j), & \text{for } r_B\lambda_j - r_j < 0 \\ \infty \quad , & \text{for } r_B\lambda_j - r_j \geq 0 \end{cases}$$

There is only one nicety to observe in applying this rule: r_B is formed from r by reflecting the row sequence in which the corresponding c_B appear in the optimal tableau. Thus if $c = (c_1, c_2, \ldots, c_6) = (6, 8, 12, 9, 0, 0)$ and $r = (r_1, r_2, \ldots, r_6) = (2, -1, 0, 0, 0, 0)$, and if the row sequence in tableau 3 in Exhibit 2 were represented by $c_B = (c_3, c_1)$, then $r_B = (0, 2)$.

To illustrate the application of this rule, let us initially ignore simultaneous c_j changes and see how high each c_j value could range while still keeping x_1 and x_3 in the basis (tableau 3 in Exhibit 2).

For c_1:

$$r = (1, 0, 0, 0, 0, 0) \text{ and } r_B = (r_3, r_1) = (0, 1)$$

$$r_B\lambda_1 - r_1 = (0, 1)(0, 1)^T - 1 = 0$$
$$r_B\lambda_2 - r_2 = (0, 1)(1/4, 14/8)^T - 0 = 14/8$$
$$r_B\lambda_3 - r_3 = (0, 1)(1, 0)^T - 0 = 0$$
$$r_B\lambda_4 - r_4 = (0, 1)(5/8, 7/8)^T - 0 = 7/8$$
$$r_B\lambda_5 - r_5 = (0, 1)(2/8, -2/8)^T - 0 = -2/8$$
$$r_B\lambda_6 - r_6 = (0, 1)(-1/8, 5/8)^T - 0 = 5/8$$
$$\therefore, \quad \varnothing_c = -(12/8) \div (-2/8) = 6 \text{ and } c_1^* = 6 + 6(1) = 12$$

For c_2:

$r = (0, 1, 0, 0, 0, 0)$ and $r_B = (r_3, r_1) = (0, 0)$; hence, $r_B\lambda_j = 0$ and the only nonzero result is $r_B\lambda_2 - r_2 = (0, 0)(1/4, 14/8)^T - 1 = -1$.

$\therefore,\ \varnothing_c = -(44/8) \div (-1) = 5.5$ and $c_2^* = 8 + 5.5(1) = 13.5$

For c_3:

$$
\begin{aligned}
r &= (0, 0, 1, 0, 0, 0) \text{ and } r_B = (r_3, r_1) = (1, 0)\\
r_B\lambda_1 - r_1 &= (1, 0)(0, 1)^T - 0 = 0\\
r_B\lambda_2 - r_2 &= (1, 0)(1/4, 14/8)^T - 0 = 1/4\\
r_B\lambda_3 - r_3 &= (1, 0)(1, 0)^T - 1 = 0\\
r_B\lambda_4 - r_4 &= (1, 0)(5/8, 7/8)^T - 0 = 5/8\\
r_B\lambda_5 - r_5 &= (1, 0)(2/8, -2/8)^T - 0 = 2/8\\
r_B\lambda_6 - r_6 &= (1, 0)(-1/8, 5/8)^T - 0 = -1/8\\
\therefore,\ \varnothing_c &= -(18/8) \div (-1/8) = 18 \text{ and } c_3^* = 12 + 18(1) = 30
\end{aligned}
$$

For c_4:

$r = (0, 0, 0, 1, 0, 0)$ and $r_B = (0, 0)$; otherwise developed like c_2

$\therefore,\ \varnothing_c = -(30/8) \div (-1) = 3.75$ and $c_4^* = 9 + 3.75(1) = 12.75$

For c_5:

$r = (0, 0, 0, 0, 1, 0)$ and $r_B = (0, 0)$; otherwise developed like c_2

$\therefore,\ \varnothing_c = -(12/8) \div (-1) = 1.5$ and $c_5^* = 0 + 1.5(1) = 1.5$

For c_6:

$r = (0, 0, 0, 0, 0, 1)$ and $r_B = (0, 0)$; otherwise developed like c_2

$\therefore,\ \varnothing_c = -(18/8) \div (-1) = 2.25$ and $c_6^* = 0 + 2.25(1) = 2.25$

For lower bound changes on the individual c_j, we proceed similarly with negative r_j; for example,

For c_1:

$$
\begin{aligned}
r &= (-1, 0, 0, 0, 0, 0) \text{ and } r_B = (0, -1)\\
r_B\lambda_1 - r_1 &= (0, -1)(0, 1)^T - (-1) = 0\\
r_B\lambda_2 - r_2 &= (0, -1)(1/4, 14/8)^T - 0 = -14/8\\
r_B\lambda_3 - r_3 &= (0, -1)(1, 0)^T - 0 = 0\\
r_B\lambda_4 - r_4 &= (0, -1)(5/8, 7/8)^T - 0 = -7/8\\
r_B\lambda_5 - r_5 &= (0, -1)(2/8, -2/8)^T - 0 = 2/8\\
r_B\lambda_6 - r_6 &= (0, -1)(-1/8, 5/8)^T - 0 = -5/8
\end{aligned}
$$

$$
\therefore,\ \varnothing_c = \min\begin{Bmatrix} -(44/8) \div (-14/8) = 44/14 \\ -(30/8) \div (-7/8) \ = 30/7 \\ -(18/8) \div (-5/8) \ = 18/5 \end{Bmatrix} = \frac{44}{14} \text{ and } c_1^* = 6 + \frac{44}{14}(-1) = \frac{20}{7}
$$

For c_2:

$r = (0, -1, 0, 0, 0, 0)$ and $r_B = (0, 0)$; hence $r_B\lambda_j = 0$ and the only nonzero result is $r_B\lambda_2 - r_2 = (0, 0)(1/4, 14/8)^T - (-1) = 1$. Therefore every $r_B\lambda_j - r_j \geq 0$ and $c_2^* = 8 + \infty(-1) = -\infty$

Calculations would continue in this way with the following results:

$$(20/7) \leq c_1 \leq 12$$
$$-\infty < c_2 \leq 13.5$$
$$6 \leq c_3 \leq 30$$
$$-\infty < c_4 \leq 12.75$$
$$-\infty < c_5 \leq 1.5$$
$$-\infty < c_6 \leq 2.25$$

Profits would change if c_1 or c_3 varied within their ranges, but x_1 and x_3 would remain in the basis as long as the c_j stayed in the ranges shown above and assuming change in only one c_j.

Thus far we have seen how parametric programming deals with individual contribution margin changes. Now let us consider a simultaneous change whereby x_1 and x_2 are substitute products for one another and their contribution margins are such that if c_2 is decreased by \$1, c_1 may be increased by \$2. We again start with tableau 3 in Exhibit 2.

Analysis:

$$r = (2, -1, 0, 0, 0, 0) \text{ and } r_B = (0, 2)$$
$$r_B\lambda_1 - r_1 = (0, 2)(0, 1)^T - 2 = 0$$
$$r_B\lambda_2 - r_2 = (0, 2)(1/4, 14/8)^T - (-1) = 9/2$$
$$r_B\lambda_3 - r_3 = (0, 2)(1, 0)^T - 0 = 0$$
$$r_B\lambda_4 - r_4 = (0, 2)(5/8, 7/8)^T - 0 = 7/4$$
$$r_B\lambda_5 - r_5 = (0, 2)(2/8, -2/8)^T - 0 = -1/2$$
$$r_B\lambda_6 - r_6 = (0, 2)(-1/8, 5/8)^T - 0 = 5/4$$
$$\therefore \quad \varnothing_c = -(12/8) \div (-1/2) = 3$$
$$c^* = c + \varnothing r = (6, 8, 12, 9, 0, 0) + 3(2, -1, 0, 0, 0, 0) = (12, 5, 12, 9, 0, 0)$$

We introduce c^* to Tableau 3:

	0	12	5	12	9	0	0
	x_0	x_1	x_2	x_3	x_4	x_5	x_6
$12x_3$	125	0	1/4	1	5/8	2/8	−1/8
$12x_1$	1,375	1	14/8	0	7/8	−2/8	5/8
	18,000	0	19	0	9	0	6

We see that as $\varnothing$ gets slightly greater than 3, c_1 will get slightly greater than 12, causing x_5 to enter the basis and x_3 to leave. Let us continue the analysis to follow what happens as $\varnothing$ is increased. (In the next tableau + designates a slight increase and − a slight decrease.)

		0	12^+	5^-	12	9	0	0
		x_0	x_1	x_2	x_3	x_4	x_5	x_6
0	x_5	500	0	1	4	5/2	1	−1/2
12^+	x_1	1,500	1	2	1	3/2	0	1/2
		$18{,}000^+$	0	19^+	+	9^+	0	6^+

Noting that r and r_B are unchanged, we determine $\varnothing_c$:

$$r_B\lambda_1 - r_1 = 0 \qquad r_B\lambda_4 - r_4 = 3$$
$$r_B\lambda_2 - r_2 = 5 \qquad r_B\lambda_5 - r_5 = 0$$
$$r_B\lambda_3 - r_3 = 2 \qquad r_B\lambda_6 - r_6 = 1$$

Every $r_B\lambda_i - r_i \geq 0$; therefore, $\varnothing_c \to \infty$

Summary of findings: $0 \leq \varnothing \leq 3, \quad \{x_1, x_3\} \in B$

$3 < \varnothing < \infty, \quad \{x_1, x_5\} \in B$

Would you care to see how parametric programming deals with changes in the scarce resources, x_{i0}? The new quantities would be $x_B^* = B^{-1}(x_0 + \varnothing f) = x_B + \varnothing B^{-1}f$. Note that all vectors are column vectors in this equation. Suppose in table 3 in Exhibit 2 we wished to know how many additional hours of capacity might be added to the second department and still retain the existing basis.

$$\begin{matrix} B^{-1} & (x_0 + \varnothing f) & = & x_B & + \varnothing \; B^{-1}f \end{matrix}$$
$$\begin{bmatrix} 2/8 & -1/8 \\ -2/8 & 5/8 \end{bmatrix}\left(\begin{bmatrix} 2{,}000 \\ 3{,}000 \end{bmatrix} + \varnothing\begin{bmatrix} 0 \\ 1 \end{bmatrix}\right) = \begin{bmatrix} 125 \\ 1{,}375 \end{bmatrix} + \varnothing\begin{bmatrix} -1/8 \\ 5/8 \end{bmatrix}$$

The limitation on the increase in x_{20} occurs when the first row equals zero, that is, when $0 = 125 + \varnothing(-1/8)$; therefore $\varnothing_c = 1{,}000$. Had there been more than one negative element in $B^{-1}f$, the minimum value of $\varnothing$ would be chosen as $\varnothing_c$. If all $B^{-1}f$ elements are positive, $\varnothing_c$ and Z both become infinite.

$$\text{Check:} \quad \begin{bmatrix} 2/8 & -1/8 \\ -2/8 & 5/8 \end{bmatrix}\left(\begin{bmatrix} 2{,}000 \\ 3{,}000 \end{bmatrix} + 1{,}000\begin{bmatrix} 0 \\ 1 \end{bmatrix}\right) = \begin{bmatrix} 0 \\ 2{,}000 \end{bmatrix}$$

How much can capacities be simultaneously raised without changing the present basis?

$$\begin{bmatrix} 2/8 & -1/8 \\ -2/8 & 5/8 \end{bmatrix}\left(\begin{bmatrix} 2{,}000 \\ 3{,}000 \end{bmatrix} + \varnothing\begin{bmatrix} 1 \\ 1 \end{bmatrix}\right) = \begin{bmatrix} 125 \\ 1{,}375 \end{bmatrix} + \varnothing\begin{bmatrix} 1/8 \\ 3/8 \end{bmatrix}$$

This says that as long as both capacities are simultaneously increased by the quantity $\varnothing$, the present output will be increased by $\frac{1}{8}\varnothing$ and $\frac{3}{8}\varnothing$ respectively. When $\varnothing \to \infty$, x_B and $Z \to \infty$.

Check: (Say $\varnothing = 800$)

$$\begin{bmatrix} 2/8 & -1/8 \\ -2/8 & 5/8 \end{bmatrix}\left(\begin{bmatrix} 2{,}000 \\ 3{,}000 \end{bmatrix} + 800\begin{bmatrix} 1 \\ 1 \end{bmatrix}\right) = \begin{bmatrix} 225 \\ 1{,}675 \end{bmatrix}$$

$$= \begin{bmatrix} 125 \\ 1{,}375 \end{bmatrix} + 800\begin{bmatrix} 1/8 \\ 3/8 \end{bmatrix}$$

How far can we go with swapping one hour of x_{20} for two hours of x_{10}?

$$\begin{bmatrix} 2/8 & -1/8 \\ -2/8 & 5/8 \end{bmatrix}\left(\begin{bmatrix} 2{,}000 \\ 3{,}000 \end{bmatrix} + \varnothing\begin{bmatrix} 2 \\ -1 \end{bmatrix}\right) = \begin{bmatrix} 125 \\ 1{,}375 \end{bmatrix} + \varnothing\begin{bmatrix} 5/8 \\ -9/8 \end{bmatrix}$$

Hence $\varnothing_c = 1375 \div (9/8) = 122.\bar{2}$

Check:

$$\begin{bmatrix} 2/8 & -1/8 \\ -2/8 & 5/8 \end{bmatrix}\left(\begin{bmatrix} 2{,}000 \\ 3{,}000 \end{bmatrix} + 122.\bar{2}\begin{bmatrix} 2 \\ -1 \end{bmatrix}\right) = \begin{bmatrix} 888.\bar{8} \\ 0 \end{bmatrix}$$

Important Odds and Ends

Minimization

Not all linear programming problems call for maximizing profits. When the objective is to minimize costs, the analyst has the choice of either (1) multiplying all individual costs, c_j, by -1 and thereafter treating the problem as if it required maximization; or (2) changing the entering criterion to "choose the most positive $z_j - c_j$." Probably the first alternative is the more popular, but either approach works equally well.

Contribution Margins

Umpteen pages have been written using the term "contribution margins" and the symbol c_j and not a word has been said about how an analyst would calculate one of these values! We must remedy this oversight. Only those costs and revenues which vary with the program variables should be included in measuring c_j values. Usually the analyst includes only those actual cash outlays which accountants refer to as "variable" costs (that is, raw material, labor costs directly identified with producing each product, and administrative and factory costs that are directly affected by unit changes in quantity produced). However, since imputed interest charges also vary with the investment in a product, these may likewise be included. Thus if the analyst wishes to be very precise, he may multiply the firm's cost of capital times the cash investment in each unit of product (and multiply the result, I suppose, by the fraction of a year that any given unit is expected to be held in order to adjust the yearly cost-of-capital figure) and consider the result as an additional variable cost. (Usually imputed interest is ignored on the grounds that it is probably insignificant.) Since alternatives are reflected as variables, it would be inappropriate to incorporate costs of the opportunity type (i.e., the cost of x_1 is forgoing x_2 while the cost of x_2 is forgoing x_1).

Alternate Ways of Manufacturing a Product

Often LP problems address situations in which a given product can be made either on a fast but expensive machine or on a slower but relatively inexpensive machine. This leads to the creation of new variables, one for each of the various ways in which the product can be processed. Each variable generally has its distinct contribution margin, even though the product is the same and the selling price does not change; the important consideration is that with different processes, different costs are usually incurred.

A variation of the different machine-same product situation occurs when the problem involves different labor inputs to obtain the same product. For instance, if some units of a product may be manufactured during overtime hours, new variables must be introduced to reflect the different contribution margins.

Surplus and Artificial Variables

We have seen how slack variables are introduced in the simplex algorithm to change a "less than" inequality to an equation and to form an identity matrix as the original basis. When the analyst confronts "greater than" inequalities, he subtracts what are known as "surplus" variables to change the inequalities to equations. Then if any of the surplus variables appear in the optimal solution, he knows by how much the minimum stipulated requirements have been exceeded.

Unfortunately, since a surplus variable is subtracted, its nonzero coefficient is -1; hence it cannot yield the unit vector necessary to complete an identity matrix as a basis. The surplus variable has just made an inequality into an equation. We are in much the same position as if the constraint had been stated originally as an equation. To complete the identity matrix, the analyst now introduces what are known as "artificial" variables. An artificial has $+1$ for its nonzero coefficient and its vector representation is a unit vector. Such a variable has no meaning as far as the original problem is concerned; it is just a device for obtaining an identity matrix.

Examples:	$3x_1 + 2x_2 \geq 17$ becomes $3x_2 + 2x_2 - x_3 + a_1 + 0a_2 = 17$
	$x_1 + \ \ x_2 = 10$ becomes $x_1 + x_2 + 0a_1 + a_2 = 10$

Since artificials have no meaning, it is essential that they disappear (that is, be in the basis at a zero level or leave the basis entirely) to have an optimal feasible solution. If an artificial is in the basis of the final tableau at a zero level, *and* if the equation of that constraint has zero coefficients for every decision, slack, and surplus variable (but not necessarily for artificial variables), then the constraint associated with the artificial variable is redundant; the problem could have been solved without that constraint. If an artificial is in the basis of the final tableau at a zero level, any nonartificial variable with *positive* $z_j - c_j$ could be entered in a new basis at a zero level. It would be at a zero level because $\lambda_{p0} = 0$ in the exiting criterion. Furthermore, this new solution would have the same optimal profits because the "other row" elementary row operations would involve addition of a scalar multiple of $\lambda_{p0} = 0$. The resulting solution would merely be degenerate.

If, on the other hand, an artificial vector is in the optimal basis at a positive level, the original problem has no feasible solution. Usually this means that the constraints are inconsistent (for example, $x_3 < 2{,}000$ and $x_3 > 2{,}000$ are inconsistent constraints).

It remains now for us to drive the artificial vectors out of the basis. The favorite method to use when manually solving a linear programming problem involves assigning an extremely large and unfavorable price, M, to the artificial variables.[4] Thus if the problem calls for maximizing profits, the price of each of the artificial variables is $-M$, while if the problem requires minimizing costs, the price of each artificial is M. The idea is that M is so large (say, \$10,000,000,000), and so opposite to what is needed in an optimal solution, that the simplex algorithm acts to remove artificials from the basis—before any other variables are removed, if possible. Once removed from a basis, the undesirable M price prevents the associated artificial vector from ever entering another basis. If we were to solve the latest modification

$$\left(\begin{array}{ll} \text{that is,} & \max Z = 6x_1 + 8x_2 + 12x_3 + 9x_4 \\ \text{subject to:} & \begin{array}{r} x_1 + 3x_2 + 5x_3 + 4x_4 \leq 2{,}000 \\ 2x_1 + 4x_2 + 2x_3 + 3x_4 \leq 3{,}000 \\ x_2 \qquad\qquad\quad \geq \ \ 200 \\ x_4 = \quad 80 \end{array} \end{array}\right)$$

[4] This device was originally suggested by Abraham Charnes. Incidentally, in my experience the best reference book available on linear programming is coauthored by Charnes: A. Charnes and W. W. Cooper, *Management Models and Industrial Applications of Linear Programming* (New York: John Wiley & Sons, 1961), 1, 2.

of the problem we have been working on by this method, the first tableau would appear as follows:

	$c_j \rightarrow$	0	6	8	12	9	0	0	0	$-M$	$-M$	
c_i $\downarrow$	$(i \in B)$	x_0	x_1	x_2	x_3	x_4	x_5	x_6	x_7	a_1	a_2	
0	x_5	2,000	1	3	5	4	1	0	0	0	0	
0	x_6	3,000	2	4	2	3	0	1	0	0	0	
$-M$	a_1	200	0	1	0	0	0	0	-1	1	0	
$-M$	a_1	80	0	0	0	(1)	0	0	0	0	1	$\rightarrow$
$z_j - c_j$		$-280M$		$-M$		$-M$			M			
			-6	-8	-12	-9	0	0		0	0	
						$\uparrow$						

The entering and exiting vectors are chosen in the usual way, and all subsequent tableaus are derived using the customary procedures. If you wish, you may delete (just cross out) columns a_1 or a_2 as soon as either vector exits from solution. This may be done because once out of a basis, an artifical can never return.

The Dual Problem

We have been discussing the "primal" or "direct" problem. For every primal problem, there is an associated "dual" problem and vice versa; both problems yield the same optimal solution and hence constitute alternative ways of addressing a given linear programming problem. It is easier to solve the dual problem if the dual has fewer constraints than the primal. (Rough rule of thumb: the number of tableaus will be approximately one and one-half times the number of constraints.)

When the primal problem calls for maximizing $Z = \sum c_i x_i$, the corresponding dual problem requires minimizing $G = \sum b_j w_j$, where the b_j are the scarce resource limitations previously discussed as x_0 elements, and the w_j are the shadow prices mentioned in Exhibit 2. As shown there,

$$Z = \sum c_i x_i = \$6(1{,}375) + \$12(125) = \$9{,}750 = 2{,}000(\$1.50) + 3{,}000(\$2.25) = \sum b_j w_j = W$$

Charnes and Cooper have introduced the mnemonic diagram shown below for relating the primal and dual problems:

Primal / Dual	Maximize x_j	Resource Limitations
Minimize w_i	a_{ij}	$\leq b_i$
Criteria \$	$\geq c_j$	Solution

The diagram is employed as follows to obtain the statements of both LP problems:

Primal	Dual
Max $Z = \sum c_i x_i$	Min $G = \sum b_j w_j$
$\sum a_{ij} x_j \leq b_i$	$\sum a_{ji} w_i \geq c_j$

In matrices, we have

Max $Z = c^T x$	Min $G = b^T w$
$Ax \leq b$	$A^T w \geq c$

Note how the objective function in each case is formed from the variables on the side or top and their associated parameters directly opposite. The constraints, on the other hand, are formed as "right-angle" readings of the diagram (⌊ for the primal, ⌉ for the dual).

Exhibit 3 solves the dual formulation of the golf shoes-tennis sneakers problem. It has been formulated from the diagram shown below.

	I	G	b_i
w_1	-1	0	$\leq -5{,}000$
w_2	1	0	$\leq 18{,}000$
w_3	0	-1	$\leq -5{,}000$
w_4	0	1	$\leq 15{,}000$
w_5	2	-1	≤ 0
w_6	1	1.25	$\leq 25{,}000$
c_j	≥ 50	≥ 80	MAX Z = MIN G

Observe that the diagram reflects a preliminary multiplication of the $\geq$ constraints (in the primal problem) by -1 to convert them to $\leq$ form.

Comments:

1. The profit is \$1,512,500. It is secured from earning \$50 for each dozen tennis sneakers that can be made during ordinary working time and \$17.50 for each dozen golf shoes permitted to be made under the maximum-demand constraint.

2. The readings of the decision variables in the optimal solution appear as the negative of the $g_i - b_i$ readings for their associated surplus variables. Multiplying these units by their contribution margins yields $Z = 6{,}250(\$50) + 15{,}000(\$80) = \$1{,}512{,}500$, the maximum profit.

Exhibit 3

$b_j \downarrow (j \in B)$		$b_i \rightarrow$ 0	−5,000	18,000	−5,000	15,000	0	25,000	0	M	0	M	
		w_0	w_1	w_2	w_3	w_4	w_5	w_6	w_7	a_1	w_8	a_2	
M	a_1	50	−1	1	0	0	2	(1)	−1	1	0	0	→
M	a_2	80	0	0	−1	1	−1	2.25	0	0	−1	1	
$g_i - b_i$		$130M$	$-M$ +5,000	M −18,000	$-M$ +5,000	M −15,000	M	$2.25M$ −25,000 ↑	$-M$	0	$-M$	0	
25,000	w_6	50	−1	1	0	0	2	1	−1	1	0	0	
M	a_2	17.5	(1.25)	−1.25	−1	1	−3.5	0	1.25	−1.25	−1	1	→
$g_i - b_i$		$17.5M$ +1,250,000	$1.25M$ −20,000 ↑	$-1.25M$ +7,000	$-M$ +5,000	M −15,000	$-3.5M$ +50,000	0	$1.25M$ −25,000	$-2.25M$ +25,000	$-M$	0	
25,000	w_6	64	0	0	−.8	.8	−.8	1	0	0	−.8	.8	
−5,000	w_1	14	1	−1	−.8	(.8)	−2.8	0	1	−1	−.8	.8	→
$g_i - b_i$		1,530,000	0	−13,000	−11,000	1,000 ↑	−6,000	0	−5,000	$-M$ +5,000	−16,000	$-M$ +16,000	
25,000	w_6	50	−1	1	0	0	2	1	−1	1	0	0	
15,000	w_4	17.5	1.25	−1.25	−1	1	−3.5	0	1.25	−1.25	−1	1	
$g_i - b_i$		1,512,500	−1,250	−11,750	−10,000	0	−2,500	0	[−6,250]	$-M$ +6,250	[−15,000]	$-M$ +15,000	

decision variables (w_7 through w_8)

Having seen that max Z equals min G, let us see why it must be so. Shown below is the matrix theoretic development in which a vector will be considered a column.

Primal	*Dual*
Max $Z = c^T x$	Min $G = b^T w$
Introduce slacks to the constraints:	Introduce surplus variables to the constraints:
$Ax + Ix_s = b$	$A^T w - Iw_x = c$
Transpose both sides:	Multiply through by x^T:
$x^T A^T + x_s{}^T I = b^T$	$x^T A^T w - x^T I w_x = x^T c$
$x^T A^T = b^T - x_s{}^T$	Substitute the results to the left (←) for $x^T A^T$:
	$(b^T - x_s{}^T)w - x^T w_x = x^T c = c^T x$
	$b^T w - x_s{}^T w - x^T w_x = c^T x$
	$G - 0 - 0 = Z$
	The products $x_s{}^T w$ and $x^T w_x$ are referred to as the "complementary slackness" conditions and will equal 0; hence, $Z = G$.

To illustrate the complementary slackness matrices above, return with me to the products-departmental capacity problem that was used earlier to illustrate simplex procedures:

	x_1	x_2	x_3	x_4	b_i
w_1	1	3	5	4	≤2,000
w_2	2	4	2	3	≤3,000
c_j	≥6	≥8	≥12	≥9	9,750

If you appended surplus and artificial variables and solved the dual formulation (care to check this?), you would obtain

		0	2,000	3,000	0	M	0	M	0	M	0	M
		w_0	w_1	w_2	w_{x1}	a_1	w_{x2}	a_2	w_{x3}	a_3	w_{x4}	a_4
0	w_{x2}	22/4	0	0	−7/4	7/4	1	−1	−1/4	1/4	0	0
3,000	w_2	9/4	0	1	−5/8	5/8	0	0	1/8	−1/8	0	0
0	w_{x4}	15/4	0	0	−7/8	7/8	0	0	−5/8	5/8	1	−1
2,000	w_1	3/2	1	0	1/4	−1/4	0	0	−1/4	1/4	0	0
	$g_i - b_i$	9,750	0	0	−1,375	1,375 − M	0	−M	−125	125 − M	0	−M

Using these results and the corresponding results of tableau 3 in Exhibit 2, one obtains

$$\begin{array}{ccccccc} b^T w & - & x_s{}^T w & - & x^T w_x & = & c^T x \end{array}$$

$$(b_1, b_2)\begin{bmatrix} w_1 \\ w_2 \end{bmatrix} - (x_5, x_6)\begin{bmatrix} w_1 \\ w_2 \end{bmatrix} - (x_1, x_2, x_3, x_4)\begin{bmatrix} w_{x1} \\ w_{x2} \\ w_{x3} \\ w_{x4} \end{bmatrix} = (c_1, c_2, c_3, c_4)\begin{bmatrix} x_1 \\ x_2 \\ x_3 \\ x_4 \end{bmatrix}$$

$$(2{,}000, 3{,}000)\begin{bmatrix} 3/2 \\ 9/4 \end{bmatrix} - (0, 0)\begin{bmatrix} 3/2 \\ 9/4 \end{bmatrix} - (1{,}375, 0, 125, 0)\begin{bmatrix} 0 \\ 22/4 \\ 0 \\ 15/4 \end{bmatrix} = (6, 8, 12, 9)\begin{bmatrix} 1{,}375 \\ 0 \\ 125 \\ 0 \end{bmatrix}$$

$$\begin{array}{ccccccc} 9{,}750 & - & 0 & - & 0 & = & 9{,}750 \end{array}$$

Primal: If a variable is in the basis, its opportunity cost is zero; if an opportunity cost is positive, the corresponding variable is not in the basis.

Dual: If an opportunity cost is in the basis, its variable is zero; if a variable is positive, its opportunity cost is not in the basis.

Accounting Applications

Adding or Dropping a Product from the Line

Return with me to the intrigues of Catherine de Medici and Edmund Dantes as revealed in the Caribou Snow Equipment Company case in Chapter 10. There we left Dantes pondering how Caribou might most efficiently employ its resources in its existing or in an altered product line. Space does not permit resuming that tale, but let us see what Dantes was concerned about.

Should a product that shows a loss be continued or should it be dropped from the product line? The accountant, according to the traditional viewpoint, first removes both fixed costs and allocated costs that would continue even if the product were dropped and then calculates differential costs and revenues to arrive at the net differential income of the product. Up to this point, the approach is correct. Where error slips in is that traditionally the accountant bases his decision on whether the product differential flow is positive or negative. If it is positive, he rules that the product should be continued; otherwise, not. The existence of a positive flow, however nice, is nevertheless far from compelling. "Is the product an efficient utilizer of scarce resources?" thereafter becomes the crucial issue.

Example: Shown below is a product line operating profit statement.

	x_1	x_2	x_3
Selling Price	$25	$60	$40
Variable Costs	8	27	15
Net	$17	$33	$25
Weekly Quantities sold	150	50	150
Sales	$3,750	$3,000	$6,000
Variable Costs	$1,200	$1,350	$2,250
Fixed Costs	2,625	1,050	3,675
Total Costs	$3,825	$2,400	$5,925
Weekly Net Profit	($ 75)	$ 600	$ 75

Fixed costs are allocated according to labor hours. The labor hours required for each unit as well as the time available in each of the two production departments are as follows:

x_1	x_2	x_3	Capacity
2	5	3	1,000
3	1	4	1,360

Idle time is charged to overhead.

Solution: The traditional answer restores fixed costs:

	x_1	x_2	x_3
Weekly Net Profit	($ 75)	$ 600	$ 75
Fixed Costs	2,625	1,050	3,675
Contribution Margins	$2,550	$1,650	$3,750

Then, since all contribution margins are positive, it would formerly be recommended that all three products be continued. The proper formulation of the problem recognizes the unit contribution margins for each product (for example, $C_2 = \$1,650 \div 50 = \$33$) as well as the labor hour requirements and the departmental capacities. The objective becomes maximizing the overall contribution margin subject to the labor constraints:

Maximize $Z = \$17x_1 + \$33x_2 + \$25x_3$

Subject to:

$$\begin{aligned} 2x_1 + 5x_2 + 3x_3 + 1x_4 + 0x_5 &= 1{,}000 \\ 3x_1 + 1x_2 + 4x_3 + 0x_4 + 1x_5 &= 1{,}360 \\ x_i \geq 0 & \end{aligned}$$

The optimal tableau was obtained by using the computer program in Exhibit 1 and is reproduced below with appropriate labels.

Solution		Variables				
	MAKE:	x_1	x_2	x_3	x_4	x_5
x_3	280 units	0	13	1	3	−2
x_1	80 units	1	−17	0	−4	3
	$8,360	$0	$3	$0	$7	$1
	Total Contribution	Opportunity Costs			Shadow Prices	

Observations:

1. 80 units of x_1 and 280 units of x_3 should be manufactured for a total contribution of $8,360.
2. No x_2 will be made, even though it enjoyed the greatest weekly profit according to ordinary accounting procedures.
3. Total profit has increased from $600 to $1,010 ($8,360 − $7,350 fixed costs), an increase of $410 or 68%.
4. The shadow prices show how much an additional hour of capacity is worth[5] and could be used along with the original capacities to determine the total contribution:

   $$\$7(1{,}000) + \$1(1{,}360) = \$8{,}360$$

   The shadow prices could also be used to determine the viability of investing in additional capacity by contrasting the shadow prices with the normalized discounted cost of securing the additional capacity.
5. The opportunity cost and the numbers in the x_2 column can be used in a sensitivity analysis to determine what the effect would be of making,

[5] The shadow prices or "dual evaluators," as they are also called, only pertain for specified ranges of parameters ("parameters" include the contribution margins, production times, and capacities). To determine these ranges, a more elaborate computer program incorporating parametric programming would ordinarily be employed.

say, 1 unit of x_2. The total contribution would reduce by \$3 to \$8,357—that is, \$8,360 − 1(\$3). Thirteen fewer units of x_3 and 17 more units of x_1 would be made. The program would become

97 units of x_1 at \$17 each	=	\$1,649
1 unit of x_2 at \$33	=	33
267 units of x_3 at \$25 each	=	6,675
TOTAL CONTRIBUTION		\$8,357

The most units of x_2 that could be made without setting up a new problem would be 280/13, but of course each additional unit of x_2 manufactured would reduce total contribution by \$3.

6. If a full product line were considered necessary, or if the products had to be made in certain proportions, or if market limitations needed to be reflected, new constraints would have to be formulated and added as data to the computer program.

Integer Programming and Capital Budgeting

There is a famous problem, introduced into the finance literature by J. H. Lorie and L. J. Savage, in which the decision amounts to choosing from among many proposals that subset which has the greatest net present value while simultaneously honoring constraints on cash outlays in two or more periods. This is the basic Lorie and Savage problem and it could be extended, although we shall not do so, to include a variety of constraints on other resources considered scarce over the planning horizon.

Example: Assume that there are many candidate projects that are individually acceptable and it is necessary at this point to determine which combination of projects should be accepted given that the amount of available capital is limited in this and subsequent periods.[6] We shall keep things simple by assuming only four projects and only two periods in which investment is required by the projects. In practice, of course,

[6] For those who are bothered by the notion that an adopted project generates funds that could be earmarked to eliminate the capital limitations, thereby making a project "self-supporting": to hold such a position is to disregard the "pooling concept of funds," which says that all moneys generated through operations and financing activities go into a common treasury (pool), which is available to support daily transactions as well as to make investments. Any money withdrawn from this common treasury for a given purpose should first have successfully competed with all other demands made on the treasury. According to this concept, earmarking of funds favors one kind of activity (say, daily operations or investments) over another, thereby obviating screening (or control) measures and probably leading to suboptimal employment of funds.

there might well be dozens or hundreds of projects and perhaps ten or twenty periods in the planning horizon (observe that it is not necessary, however, that each project require funds in every period).

Our problem is as follows:

Maximize $\quad Z = \sum c_j x_j = 15x_1 + 12x_2 + 20x_3 + 30x_4$

Constraints, $\quad \sum a_{ij} x_j \leq b_i$:

$$10x_1 + 8x_2 + 6x_3 + 15x_4 \leq 30$$
$$8x_1 + 5x_2 + 10x_3 + 12x_4 \leq 20$$
$$x_i \leq 1$$

Nonnegativity restrictions: $x_i \geq 0$

Key:

c_j = the *net* present value of project j
a_{ij} = the present value of the investment in the ith period for project j
b_i = the present value of the available capital in the ith period

Notice that a project must either be accepted ($x_i = 1$) or rejected ($x_i = 0$); no fractional projects are permitted. The $x_i \leq 1$ constraints together with the nonnegativity restrictions and the fact that we will work for integer solutions will guarantee this "go-no go" (either-or) result.

Since the number of projects and the number of periods are both small, we can determine the optimal combination and optimal profits by listing permissible combinations and their associated total net present values. We note that in either period more than one project, but not all, can be accepted. We can also limit the number of permissible combinations by considering investment requirements for each combination for both periods. We have

Permissible Combinations	Total Net Present Value
(1, 2)	\$27
(1, 3)	\$35
(1, 4)	\$45
(2, 3)	\$32
(2, 4)	\$42

Therefore, the combination that our integer programming procedures must select as optimal is (1, 4). There are many ways to do integer programming, but the most popular seems to be "branch and bound," which is a simple extension of LP.

The branch and bound technique involves introducing new constraints like $x_i \leq a$ and $x_i \geq a + 1$ (where a is an integer) and solving a *series* of straightforward linear programming problems. Since x_i cannot be both less than a and greater than $a + 1$, two alternate new linear programming problems are created each time a particular variable is chosen for treatment.

These alternate problems become the "branches" in the branch and bound technique. The "bound" part has to do with recognizing that the introduction of a new constraint can never improve the value of an objective function; hence the value of the objective function at any stage prior to branching serves as a bound on the value of the objective function at any stage after branching.

When applying branch and bound to an integer programming problem, the first step is to solve the ordinary linear programming problem while disregarding the integer restrictions. If the optimal solution is in integers, no further work need be done. However, if the optimal solution is not in integers, one (any one) of the noninteger variables (say, x_2) is chosen, and from its value (say, 4.3) in the optimal solution, two new linear programming problems are formulated. The first has the setup of the immediately preceding problem except that the constraint $x_2 \leq 4$ is appended, while the second has the setup of the immediately preceding problem with the additional constraint $x_2 \geq 5$. Optimal solutions to these two new problems are obtained. For the sake of argument, let us say that one solution is in integers while the other is not. If the integer solution has a better value of its objective function, this is the optimal solution, because further branching on the noninteger solution could not improve its objective function value. On the other hand, if the noninteger objective function value exceeds the integer objective value, branching (on the noninteger solution) would continue either until an integer solution is obtained or until the objective value of a new noninteger solution becomes worse than the integer objective value first obtained. If calculations produce two integer solutions, the one with the better objective value is the optimal solution.

The creation of the new constraints ($x_2 \leq 4$ and $x_2 \geq 5$ above) bothers some people because one variable is arbitrarily chosen for branching while the others are not—at least not at this original decision level. The other variables need not be given branching treatment at this original level because none of their "important" values has been dismissed from further consideration. Just because x_2 is precluded from taking fractional values between 4 and 5 does not mean that x_1, for instance, will not be allowed to take on any of its important former values. Indeed, x_1 will take on these values, but now over the course of two separate LP problems. The only x_1 values that may possibly be excluded (because of the reduced feasible regions) would be those which would not have corresponding integer values for x_2. Hence if there are any excluded integer values for x_1, they would not be important.

Shown below is the solution to the original LP problem.

$$\text{Solution: } \{x_1, x_2, x_3, x_4\} = \{0, 1, .3, 1\}, Z = 48$$

Since x_3 is fractional, we use it for branching and form two new problems, one with $x_3 \leq 0$ and the other with $x_3 \geq 1$. However, since nonnegativity must be observed, the first of the new constraints becomes $x_3 = 0$, while the second of the new constraints becomes $x_3 = 1$ when considered with the original constraint (that is $x_3 \leq 1$ and $x_3 \geq 1$ simultaneously allow only the value $x_3 = 1$). When $x_3 = 0$, we obtain

Problem 2: $\text{Max } Z = 15x_1 + 12x_2 + 30x_4$

$$\begin{aligned} \text{Constraints: } 10x_1 + 8x_2 + 15x_4 &\leq 30 \\ 8x_1 + 5x_2 + 12x_4 &\leq 20 \\ 0 \leq x_i \leq 1, \text{ where } i &= 1, 2, 4 \end{aligned}$$

Solution: $\{x_1, x_2, x_3, x_4\} = \{.38, 1, 0, 1\}, Z = 47.62$

When $x_3 = 1$, we have

Problem 3: $\text{Max } Z = 15x_1 + 12x_2 + 30x_4$

$$\begin{aligned} \text{Constraints: } 10x_1 + 8x_2 + 15x_4 &\leq 24 \\ 8x_1 + 5x_2 + 12x_4 &\leq 10 \\ 0 \leq x_i \leq 1, \text{ where } i &= 1, 2, 4 \end{aligned}$$

Solution: $\{x_1, x_2, x_3, x_4\} = \{0, 0, 1, .83\}, Z = 45$

Since no integer solutions have been achieved, we continue branching. Let us pursue the problem 2 solution and branch on x_1. Again—as always in a 0, 1 problem—we can simplify calculations by letting $x_1 = 0$ on one branch and $x_1 = 1$ on the other branch.

If $x_1 = 0$ (and $x_3 = 0$), we have

Problem 4: $\text{Max } Z = 12x_2 + 30x_4$

$$\begin{aligned} \text{Constraints: } 8x_2 + 15x_4 &\leq 30 \\ 5x_2 + 12x_4 &\leq 20 \\ 0 \leq x_i \leq 1, \text{ where } i &= 2, 4 \end{aligned}$$

Solution: $\{x_1, x_2, x_3, x_4\} = \{0, 1, 0, 1\}, Z = 42$

If $x_1 = 1$ (and $x_3 = 0$), we obtain

Problem 5: $\text{Max } Z = 12x_2 + 30x_4$

$$\begin{aligned} \text{Constraints: } 8x_2 + 15x_4 &\leq 20 \\ 5x_2 + 12x_4 &\leq 12 \\ 0 \leq x_i \leq 1, \text{ where } i &= 2, 4 \end{aligned}$$

Solution: $\{x_1, x_2, x_3, x_4\} = \{1, 0, 0, 1\}, Z = 45$

There is no point in branching further—on problem 3. No new constraint could raise $Z = 45$ and we already have an integer solution on another branch (problem 5) where $Z = 45$.

When branch and bound is applied to problems not having the 0, 1 structure, each branching usually increases both the number of constraints and therefore the number of variables.

The Minimization of Costs via the Transportation Algorithm

We come now to a problem that calls for the simultaneous recognition of demand and supply constraints. Because of this "out-in" structure, it is possible, though not necessary, to employ a simplification of the simplex known as the transportation algorithm. In the classical transportation the goal is to minimize the cost of shipping units from factories to customers. The general statement of the problem is shown below.

Key:

c_{ij} = the cost (e.g., dollars or distance) to ship from i to j
x_{ij} = the variable designating the route i to j
s_i = the units that can be supplied by factory i
d_j = the units demanded by customer j

$$\text{Objective: Minimize } \underset{i,\,j\in B}{Z} = \sum c_{ij}x_{ij}$$

$$\text{Constraints: (Supply) } \sum_j x_{ij} = s_i$$

$$\text{(Demand) } \sum_i x_{ij} = d_j$$

$$\text{Nonnegativity: } x_{ij} \geq 0$$

There is another constraint, $\sum s_i = \sum d_j$ (that is, total supply must equal total demand), that must be reflected if the transportation modification of the simplex algorithm is to be employed. Since the transportation tableau is a manual delight to use, most analysts simply add "dummy" factories or customers—with M (unfavorably large) for their c_{ij} values—to effect the needed equality.

In the tableaus shortly to be presented, each cell has separately assigned positions for three important pieces of data.

c_{ij}
x_{ij}
$R_i+K_j-c_{ij}$

c_{ij} = the cost to ship from i to j
x_{ij} = the quantity shipped from i to j
$R_i + K_j - c_{ij}$ = the opportunity cost for route i, j (This is the former $z_j - c_j$, as we shall see.)

If a cell has no value showing in its center (x_{ij}) position, this means the cell is an unused route—it is not in the basis.

There is an easily mastered trick for proceeding from tableau to tableau; it is called "looping." Looping is, in reality, the transportation equivalent of the simplex exiting criterion; the objective is to decide how many units to ship from the entering cell (route) at the next stage while selecting an exiting cell and honoring the nonnegativity restrictions. Call this entering amount x and, looking only at presently used cells (routes), determine its value by finding that filled cell with the smallest removable quantity *while* obeying the row supply, s_i, and the column demand, d_j, requirements. Viewed differently, each tableau is a rectangle bordered by the supply and demand requirements (hereafter called "rim" requirements). The rectangle is broken up into cells and *only* used cells can be considered. If it is decided to enter x units in some unused cell, to honor the row-rim requirement requires both that a$(-x)$ appear in one of the *used* cells in that *row* and also that a$(-x)$ appear in one of the *used* cells in that *column*. Since there is then a$(+x)$ and a$(-x)$ in the selected row and the selected column, these rim requirements are maintained. However, by placing a$(-x)$ in another row and in another column, we have created the problem of honoring their rim requirements. In summary, every row and every column that is changed must have both a$(+x)$ and a$(-x)$ in it to observe the rim requirements. Sometimes the completed loop of $+x$'s and $-x$'s is a simple rectangle; at other times, the completed loop is a "dirty" loop.

"Simple" Loop:

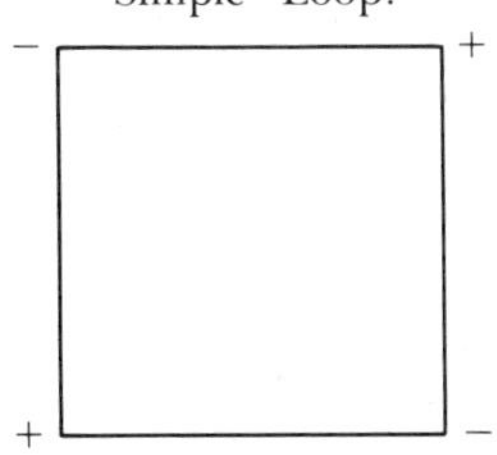

					S_i
	6	14			20
		6	$6-x$	x	12
			$4+x$	$14-x$	18
D_j →	6	20	10	14	50

Decision: $x = 6$, because if $x > 6$, the second cell in the third column would become negative in the next stage and thereby violate the nonnegativity restrictions. The next tableau in this problem reflects the $x = 6$ change and follows directly.

"Dirty" Loop:

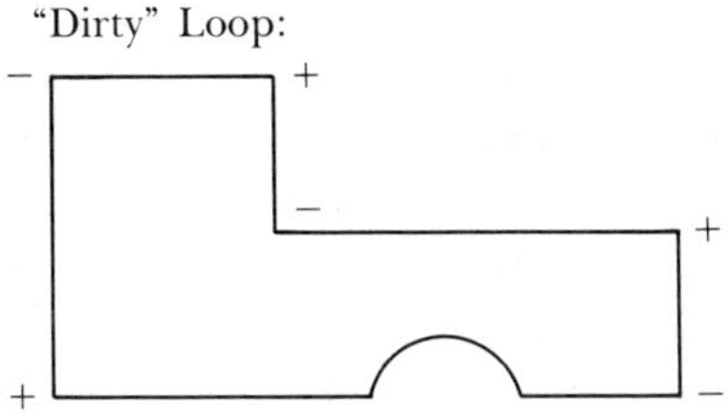

					S_i
	$6-x$	$14+x$			20
		$6-x$		$6+x$	12
	x		10	$8-x$	18
D_j →	6	20	10	14	50

Decision: $x = 6$ again, by coincidence.

So much for looping; now we must consider costs. Although there are other approaches, we shall use the device referred to as row and column "keys." The keys are determined according to

$$R_i + K_j - c_{ij} = 0 \quad \text{for cells in the basis}$$

$$R_i + K_j - c_{ij} = ? \quad \text{for cells not in the basis}$$

One key is assigned an arbitrary value (usually zero, but anything will do) to start things off. If, for instance, R_1 is set equal to zero, and if cell (R_1, K_1) is in the basis, then $K_1 = c_{11} - R_1 = c_{11}$. With R_1 and K_1 known, it is usually possible to use one of the values and some other c_{ij} for a cell in the basis to determine a new row or column key. The process is repeated until all the keys are determined, if possible.

When it is not possible to determine all the keys in the manner just described, the problem is said to be degenerate. This means either that there are fewer than $m + n - 1$ (where m is the number of rows and n is the number of columns) cells in use, or that there are $m + n - 1$ cells in use but not properly situated. To complete the keys, the technique of "ε perturbation" is used whereby a very small and nonexistent amount ε is placed in a strategic unused cell thereby changing its status to that of a used cell. With luck, the analyst will find a$(+x)$ next to the ε when he forms a loop, and this will cause two cells to enter the basis in the next tableau while only one cell exits. Without such good luck, the analyst will find a$(-x)$ next to the ε when he forms a loop. Then, since ε will be the smallest amount opposite a$(-x)$, $x = \varepsilon$. In the next tableau the ε will usually be placed in the cell where the lone x is presently while setting $x = \varepsilon = 0$ for all other cells in the present loop. Nothing will have been accomplished. A different location for ε is then chosen and the process is repeated until there are $m + n - 1$ strategically located cells in the basis.

Once the keys are completed, the opportunity costs for the unused cells are computed according to $R_i + K_j - c_{ij} = ?$ As in the simplex minimization criterion, the greatest positive $R_i + K_j - c_{ij}$ opportunity cost is chosen as the entering cell.

Exhibit 4 illustrates all of the points that have been mentioned. To make $\sum S_i = \sum D_j$, a fictitious customer, D_5, has been introduced. To discourage D_5 from being considered in the real part of the program, $C_{i5} = M$, an incredibly expensive way to ship. The total cost of any program ignores the "inventory" assignment or assignments represented under the D_5 column.

Tableau I Exhibit 4 starts off with the "northwest corner" method of assigning cells. This method has two virtues:

1. It provides a feasible, nondegenerate assignment for the first tableau.
2. It ensures that the student will bump into every little quirk the teacher has designed into the problem.

According to the northwest corner method, the analyst first uses up all the supply of factory S_1 by shipping as much as possible of each customer's demands—in sequence $(D_1, D_2, \dots)$—from this source. Next the analyst

Exhibit 4 The Transportation Problem

I

		$K_1 = 5$	$K_2 = -5$	$K_3 = 3$	$K_4 = 6$	$K_5 = M - 5$	
		D_1	D_2	D_3	D_4	D_5	$S_i\downarrow$
$R_1 = 0$	S_1	5 2,000 − x	9 −14	4 −1	2 x 4	M −5	2,000
$R_2 = 7$	S_2	12 700 + x	2 500	10 2,500 − x	10 3	M 2	3,700
$R_3 = 5$	S_3	8 2	3 −3	8 700 + x	11 1,300 − x	M 1,200	3,200
	$D_j\rightarrow$	2,700	500	3,200	1,300	1,200	8,900

Comments on Tableau I:

1. R_1 was set equal to 0 arbitrarily.

2. Referring only to used cells:

$R_1 + K_1 - c_{11} = 0 + K_1 - 5 = 0; K_1 = 5$
$R_2 + K_1 - c_{21} = R_2 + 5 - 12 = 0; R_2 = 7$
$R_2 + K_2 - c_{22} = 7 + K_2 - 2 = 0; K_2 = -5$

3. Once the keys, R_i and K_j are determined, the opportunity costs for cells not in the basis are gotten by

$R_i + K_j - c_{ij} = ?$:
$R_1 + K_2 - c_{12} = 0 - 5 - 9 = -14$
$R_2 + K_4 - c_{24} = 7 + 6 - 10 = 3$

Exhibit 4 (*cont.*)

II

		$K_1 = 5$	$K_2 = -5$	$K_3 = 3$	$K_4 = 2$	$K_5 = M - 5$	
		D_1	D_2	D_3	D_4	D_5	$S_i\downarrow$
$R_1 = 0$	S_1	5 / 700	9 / −14	4 / −1	2 / 1,300	M / −5	2,000
$R_2 = 7$	S_2	12 / 2,000 − x	2 / 500	10 / 1,200 + x	10 / −1	M / 2	3,700
$R_3 = 5$	S_3	8 / x / 2	3 / −3	8 / 2,000 − x	11 / −4	M / 1,200	3,200
	$D_j\rightarrow$	2,700	500	3,200	1,300	1,200	8,900

Comments on tableau II:

1. Since the most positive $R_i + K_j - c_{ij}$ is 2 and appears in two places, there are two choices for the entering cell. The analyst would choose the one that did not create degeneracy at the next stage; however, in this case both choices lead to degeneracy.

2. Degeneracy is signalled by the appearance in a loop of two cells that are to be reduced by x and that have the same lowest x_{ij} value for that loop.

III

		$K_1 = 5$	$K_2 = -6$	$K_3 = 2$	$K_4 = 2$	$K_5 = M - 3$	
		D_1	D_2	D_3	D_4	D_5	$S_i\downarrow$
$R_1 = 0$	S_1	5 $700 - x$	9 -15	4 -2	2 $1{,}300 + x$	M -3	2,000
$R_2 = 8$	S_2	12 1	2 500	10 3,200	10 $\varepsilon - x$	M x 5	3,700
$R_3 = 3$	S_3	8 $2{,}000 + x$	3 -6	8 -3	11 -6	M $1{,}200 - x$	3,200
	$D_j\rightarrow$	2,700	500	3,200	1,300	1,200	8,900

Comment on tableau III:

Trying to determine the cell in which to place an ε to complete the keys and to wind up with an $\varepsilon + x$ in the loop takes more time than it is worth. Choose a cell and go on.

Exhibit 4 (*cont.*)

IV

		$K_1 = 5$	$K_2 = -1$	$K_3 = 7$	$K_4 = 2$	$K_5 = M - 3$	
		D_1	D_2	D_3	D_4	D_5	$S_i\downarrow$
$R_1 = 0$	S_1	5 $700 - x$	9 -10	4 x 3	2 1,300	M -3	2,000
$R_2 = 3$	S_2	12 -4	2 500	10 $3{,}200 - x$	10 -5	M $\varepsilon + x$	3,700
$R_3 = 3$	S_3	8 $2{,}000 + x$	3 -1	8 2	11 -6	M $1{,}200 - x$	3,200
	$D_j\rightarrow$	2,700	500	3,200	1,300	1,200	8,900

Comments on tableau IV:

1. We now have $\varepsilon + x$, and two cells will enter the basis next time at a positive level, thereby curing the degeneracy.

2. Cost at this point is $700(5) + 1{,}300(2) + \ldots + 2{,}000(8) = 55{,}100$.

3. Since $x = 700$, the improvement in cost equals the product of the opportunity cost, \$3, and the entering quantity or \$2,100, just as in the simplex algorithm. The details of this improvement can be observed by tracing the real part of the loop: $700(4 - 5 + 8 - 10) = -2{,}100$.

V

		$K_1 = 2$	$K_2 = -4$	$K_3 = 4$	$K_4 = 2$	$K_5 = M - 6$	
		D_1	D_2	D_3	D_4	D_5	$S_i\downarrow$
$R_1 = 0$	S_1	5 -3	9 -13	4 700	2 1,300	M -6	2,000
$R_2 = 6$	S_2	12 -4	2 500	10 $2{,}500 - x$	10 -2	M $700 + x$	3,700
$R_3 = 6$	S_3	8 2,700	3 -1	8 x 2	11 -3	M $500 - x$	3,200
	$D_j\rightarrow$	2,700	500	3,200	1,300	1,200	8,900

Comment on tableau V:

Cost at this point is $55{,}100 - 2{,}100 = 53{,}000 = 700(4) + 1{,}300(2) + \dots + 2{,}700(8)$, as predicted in comment 3 on tableau IV.

Exhibit 4 (*cont.*)

VI

		$K_1 = 4$	$K_2 = -4$	$K_3 = 4$	$K_4 = 2$	$K_5 = M - 6$	
		D_1	D_2	D_3	D_4	D_5	$S_i\downarrow$
$R_1 = 0$	S_1	5 / −1	9 / −13	4 / 700	2 / 1,300	M / −6	2,000
$R_2 = 6$	S_2	12 / −2	2 / 500	10 / 2,000	10 / −2	M / 1,200	3,700
$R_3 = 4$	S_3	8 / 2,700	3 / −3	8 / 500	11 / −5	M / −2	3,200
	$D_j\rightarrow$	2,700	500	3,200	1,300	1,200	8,900

Comments on tableau VI:

1. This tableau is optimal because there is no positive $R_i + K_j - c_{ij}$ value.

2. The optimal program and its cost is:

$700S_1 \rightarrow D_3$ @ \$4 =	\$2,800
$1{,}300S_1 \rightarrow D_4$ @ \$2 =	2,600
$500S_2 \rightarrow D_2$ @ \$2 =	1,000
$2{,}000S_2 \rightarrow D_3$ @ \$10 =	20,000
$2{,}700S_3 \rightarrow D_1$ @ \$8 =	21,600
$500S_3 \rightarrow D_3$ @ \$8 =	4,000
Total cost	\$52,000
Inventory at R_2 =	1,200

assigns the supply of factory S_2, commencing with the first customer in sequence who has unfilled demand after S_1 has been distributed. The same is then done for S_3.

People who wish to save work usually do not employ the northwest corner method. Instead they select cells on the basis of row and column minima (that is, the smallest costs are picked first). Teachers sometimes frown on this approach because the student may guess his way past all the hidden traps.

Read the comments in Exhibit 4 carefully, for they contain several observations that have not been brought up elsewhere in this section.

If the optimal tableau of a transportation problem has one or more zeroes for opportunity cost values of unused cells, the condition of alternative optima exists. By putting one of these cells into the basis, an alternative program that costs exactly the same as the previous optimal program will result. Then, if desired, the solution routes of the first optimal program may be multiplied by a number a, where $0 \leq a \leq 1$ and those of the second optimal program may be multiplied by the complementary number $1 - a$. By adding the two results, another way of shipping that has the same optimal cost may be derived. And by varying the value of a, an infinite number of such optimal programs may be generated.

There is a striking phenomenon that the analyst may discover by way of sensitivity analysis. If $R_i + K_j$ is negative for any cell in the optimal tableau, and if the supply in row i and the demand in column j can be increased by a corresponding amount, then additional units can be shipped with a lower overall program cost![7] Note in tableau VI that $R_1 + K_2 = -4$. Assume, for purposes of illustration, that D_2 can be induced to demand 600 units (instead of the present 500), and that in view of this the company is willing to have S_1 increase its supply to 2,100 (instead of the present 2,000). Now place a $(-x)$ in cell (1,2) (that is, $S_1 \to D_2$) and form a loop:

$-x$	$700 + x$
$500 + x$	$2{,}000 - x$

Ignore the $-x$ in cell (1,2) but otherwise use $x = 100$ to obtain the new program. Result:

$$\begin{aligned}
800 S_1 \to D_3 \text{ @ } \$4 &= \$\ 3{,}200 \\
1{,}300 S_1 \to D_4 \text{ @ } \$2 &= \ \ 2{,}600 \\
600 S_2 \to D_2 \text{ @ } \$2 &= \ \ 1{,}200 \\
1{,}900 S_2 \to D_3 \text{ @ } \$10 &= \ 19{,}000 \\
2{,}700 S_3 \to D_1 \text{ @ } \$8 &= \ 21{,}600 \\
500 S_3 \to D_3 \text{ @ } \$8 &= \ \ 4{,}000 \\
& \ \ \ \underline{\underline{\$51{,}600}}
\end{aligned}$$

7 This is referred to as the "more for less paradox" in the literature.

This program has shipped 100 more units at a cost savings of $400. The smallest amount opposite a$(-x)$ in the rest of the loop determines the limit of such activity. Interestingly, S_1 does not benefit from this cost reduction (S_1 total cost was $5,400 and is now $5,800, while S_2 total cost was $21,000 and is now $20,200). The overall company has gained, but the division that made it possible faces rising costs. Undoubtedly the S_1 manager would be irate if standard accounting procedures for measuring divisional performance were used.

The transportation algorithm has many uses. One of its more fascinating applications is in locating plants so as to minimize shipping costs. If one location enjoys a lower minimum shipping cost than another—as determined by solving separate transportation problems—then the first is the preferable site.

Problems

1. *Linear combinations.*

(a) Given the vectors

$$\overset{x_1}{\begin{bmatrix} 3 \\ 2 \end{bmatrix}}, \overset{x_2}{\begin{bmatrix} 5 \\ 1 \end{bmatrix}}, \overset{x_3}{\begin{bmatrix} 2 \\ 4 \end{bmatrix}}$$

and the fact that x_1 and x_2 are in the basis, express x_3 as a linear combination of the basic vectors. Why is the linear combination concept important? If the contribution margins of x_1, x_2, and x_3 are $9, $7, and $12, show how you would determine whether x_3 would enter the basis of the next linear programming tableau.

(b)

$$B^{-1} = \begin{bmatrix} -.2 & .3 \\ .4 & -.1 \end{bmatrix}$$

Required:

(1) Determine the original basis vectors shown in **B**.

(2) Given that a new product requires three and eight units of the respective scarce resources, and that the vectors in the basis have contribution margins of $10 and $15 respectively, what contribution margin for the new product will make the analyst indifferent about producing it?

2. *Tennis rackets.* A company produces three kinds of tennis rackets, A, B, and C, which have $10, $20, and $40 contribution margins respectively. The times to produce each racket in two departments, which have available capacities of 1,000 and 500, are respectively

$$\begin{matrix} A & B & C \\ \begin{bmatrix} 4 \\ 1 \end{bmatrix}, & \begin{bmatrix} 2 \\ 3 \end{bmatrix}, & \begin{bmatrix} 3 \\ 5 \end{bmatrix} \end{matrix}$$

(a) What is the program that maximizes profit?

(b) If five rackets of whatever kind is not called for in (a) must be made, what will the new program be?

3. The statement of a linear programming problem having to do with the optimal selection of products in two departments follows.

Maximize Profits $\quad Z = \$10x_1 + \$21x_2 + \$26x_3$

Constraints:

$$3x_1 + 2x_2 + 6x_3 \leq 105$$
$$5x_1 + x_2 + 2x_3 \leq 70$$

Nonnegativity: $\quad x_i \geq 0$

Use vectors x_1 and x_2 as the first basis.

(a) Use B^{-1} to generate the optimal tableau.

(b) Determine whether product x_4 should be manufactured given that its contribution margin is \$44 and that it makes four units of time in department 1 and three units of time in department 2.

(c) If x_4 is to be manufactured, compute the new program.

4. The statement of a linear programming problem having to do with the optimal selection of products for production in two departments follows.

Maximize $\quad Z = \$15x_1 + \$18x_2 + \$24x_3$

Constraints:

$$2x_1 + 3x_2 + 2x_3 \leq 120$$
$$3x_1 + x_2 + 4x_3 \leq 180$$

Nonnegativity: $\quad x_i \geq 0$

The inverse matrix for the vectors in the basis in the optimal tableau is

$$B^{-1}$$
$$\begin{bmatrix} 2/5 & -1/5 \\ -1/10 & 3/10 \end{bmatrix}$$

Required:

(a) Use B^{-1} to generate the optimal tableau (this is the fast way—but you can start from scratch if you wish) and determine the optimal program and its profits.

(b) Determine whether product x_4 should be manufactured given that its contribution margin, c_4, is \$30, and that it takes two units of time in department 1, and five units of time in department 2.

(c) If x_4 is to be produced, compute the new program (show work neatly).

(d) What are the shadow prices (dual evaluators)?

5. The statement of an LP problem is shown below.

Maximize $$Z = 6x_1 + 7x_2 + 8x_3$$

Constraints:
$$\begin{aligned} x_1 + 2x_2 + x_3 &\le 1{,}000{,}000 \\ 3x_1 + 4x_2 + 2x_3 &\ge 120{,}000 \\ 2x_1 + 6x_2 + 4x_3 &= 200{,}000 \end{aligned}$$

Nonnegativity: $$x_i \ge 0$$

The inverse matrix at one stage is

$$B^{-1}$$
$$\begin{bmatrix} 1 & -1/4 & -1/8 \\ 0 & 1/2 & -1/4 \\ 0 & -1/4 & 3/8 \end{bmatrix}$$

(a) Use B^{-1} to generate the tableau at that stage and insert appropriate simplex column and row labels.

(b) Determine whether x_4 should be manufactured given that $c_4 = \$25$ and that it takes (3, 3, 7) units of time in the respective departments to make a single unit of x_4.

(c) Determine the optimal program using the ordinary simplex procedures.

6. Max $$Z = 8x_1 + 9x_2 + 10x_3 + 11x_4$$

Constraints:
$$\begin{aligned} x_1 + 5x_2 + 7x_3 + x_4 &\le 200 \\ 3x_1 + 2x_2 + 2x_3 + 4x_4 &\le 300 \end{aligned}$$

Nonnegativity restrictions: $$x_i \ge 0$$

Required:

(a)

$$B^{-1} = \frac{1}{18}\begin{bmatrix} 4 & -1 \\ -2 & 5 \end{bmatrix}$$

for the optimal tableau. Use B^{-1} to generate the optimal tableau. Label it.

(b) Use the optimal tableau to determine the new solution if 20 units of x_1 must be made.

(c) Determine the upper and lower limits for c_j (that is, the range over which c_j may change without disturbing the constituency of the basis).

(d) Determine the upper and lower limits for b_i, the capacity limitations.

(e) Use the shadow prices to generate the optimal profits.

(f) State the dual problem.

(g) If product x_5 requires three hours in each department and promises a contribution margin of \$12, use the results of the optimal tableau to determine whether x_5 should be made.

(h) If x_5 is made, determine the new optimal solution using ordinary simplex procedures.

7. If the contribution margin of a product is positive (\$70), should the product be produced?

8. A company has four product lines and suspects that it should drop the one that is losing money based on the unitized profit report shown below.

	x_1	x_2	x_3	x_4
Selling price	\$35	\$50	\$22	\$18
Variable costs	\$27	\$41	\$12	\$ 7
Fixed costs	10	4	6	3
	\$37	\$45	\$18	\$10
Profit (loss)	\$(2)	\$ 5	\$ 4	\$ 8

The fixed costs include depreciation, supervisory and administrative salaries, property taxes, and insurance. They have been allocated to the product lines on the basis of cubic footage, time estimates, and so forth.

Although the company must operate within the confines of many restrictions, nevertheless, nothing is really confining except the production time available in two bottleneck departments. The product production times and the time available are:

	Departments	
	A	B
x_1	1	3
x_2	5	2
x_3	7	2
x_4	1	4
Totals	200	300

Should x_1 be made? Why? If not, what should be made? If a proposed new product that takes three hours to manufacture in department A and four hours in department B offers \$19 contribution margin, should it be made? Why?

9. Shown below is a product line operating profit statement.

Unit Data:	x_1	x_2	x_3
Selling price	\$78	\$44	\$44
Variable costs	60	30	20
Contribution margin	\$18	\$14	\$24

Weekly Net Profit:

Sales	\$11,700	\$4,400	\$13,200
Variable costs	(9,000)	(3,000)	(6,000)
Fixed costs*	(2,550)	(1,500)	(6,000)
Weekly net profit	\$ 150	\$ (100)	\$ 1,200
Quantity sold	150	100	300

* Fixed costs are allocated according to the rates of \$4 and \$3 per direct-labor hour, respectively, in departments 1 and 2. The labor hours required for each unit and the time available in each of the departments follow:

x_1	x_2	x_3	Capacity
2	3	2	1,200
3	1	4	1,800

Unlimited quantities may be sold.

Required:

(a) Should the company, in view of its net loss, drop x_2?

(1) Use the traditional accounting approach.

(2) Use the linear programming approach.

(3) Determine the improvement in profits assuming the optimal program is substituted for the present one.

(b) What total contribution margin would result if a minimum of 10 units of each product must be made?

(c) Assuming the optimal answer to (a)(3), if another product could be made that has a contribution margin of \$30 and that takes three units of time in department 1 and five units of time in department 2, would it be advisable to produce it? Support your answer.

10. *Warehouse model.* Tennis professional Pancho Corcoran acts as a middleman for the sale of fine tennis rackets. He keeps a few rackets on display in his shop and an inventory of rackets in his home. Retailers view the equipment in his shop and place their orders with him. He then either fills the order immediately at the current price or postpones the order to the following month at the price that will then prevail. In this way he is able to control his sales volume—subject to the limitation that all sales must be made from the inventory available at the start of the given month.

Pancho has received the word from his wife that she could get tired of seeing tennis rackets all over the house; therefore, he carefully restricts racket storage to a small room in the cellar that holds 300 rackets. Also by agreement with his wife, Pancho must not invest more than \$1,000 of the family savings in this sideline. His customers pay cash, just as he does at the end of each month when he goes to pick up his purchases.

Pancho has 20 rackets remaining from the previous season and costs and prices are as follows:

Month	Cost	Selling Price
1	\$12	\$20
2	15	28
3	14	25

How should Pancho proceed for the coming three months?

Hint:

Keep a running balance of inventory like this: *beginning balance* + *purchases* − *sales* = *ending inventory* (this is the basic flow relationship that one sees when keeping T accounts while doing bookkeeping).

11. *Gasoline blending.* A refinery markets two gasolines—one for airplanes and one for cars. Two crude oils are used for these gasolines. In a given day up to 10,000 gallons of crude 1 can be obtained at a cost of \$.20 per gallon, while up to 15,000 gallons of crude 2 can be acquired at a cost of \$.16 per gallon. The crudes have different compositions as far as ingredients A, B, and C are concerned; the ratings are

	A	B	C
Crude 1	.6	.3	.1
Crude 2	.5	.2	.3

Airplane gas must have at least a .5 rating in A and at least a .25 rating in B. Car gas can have no more than a .52 rating in A and no more than a .2 rating in C.

Demand for airplane gas never exceeds 8,000 gallons per day. Demand for car gas is at least 10,000 gallons per day.

Airplane gas sells for \$.50 per gallon and car gas sells for \$.40 per gallon. How should crudes be apportioned to maximize profit?

Required:

Set up problem in a tableau. Do one iteration.

Hints:

(a) Double subscript variables to indicate input going to output.

(b) Then total output of gasoline j is $\sum_i x_{ij}$

(c) Assume linear blending of ingredients. Thus for ingredient A and airplane gas:

$$6x_{11} + .5x_{21} \geq .5 \sum x_{i1}$$

12. *Blending, SPAS, SCP, H & H.* When your engine is sluggish, begins to wheeze, and develops that persistent knocking sound, a certain television commercial assures you that you have tired blood and need______. When these things happen to your car's engine, however, you may need a different gasoline. Gasolines are prepared from crude oils that have varying ingredients that affect vapor pressure, octane number, and quality in general.

Old Explodable, Incorporated, the nation's oldest and smallest oil refinery, uses four grades of crude oil to produce three gasolines: (a) Spastic, which is sold as SPAS, occasionally ignites, and has a noticeable aroma of sea water; (b) Snap-Crackle-Pop, which is marketed as SCP and is known not only to give all racers an edge but also to cause engines to snort furiously; and (c) Heroes and Hustlers, which is retailed as H & H and is guaranteed to make any car go from 0 to 80 in five seconds in any weather and under all circumstances. The wholesale prices per gallon for these gasolines are \$.20, \$.25, and \$.30 respectively.

Analysis of the crudes in terms of their principle components, W, X, and Y, as well as data about costs and gallons available each day follow.

Crude	W	X	Y	Cost/Gallon	Available
1	.1	.6	.3	\$.15	10,000
2	.3	.5	.2	.14	15,000
3	.7	.2	.1	.08	80,000
4	.5	.2	.3	.10	40,000

H & H must contain at least 50% of X and not more than 20% of W; SCP must contain at least 40% of X and not more than 40% of W; and SPAS cannot have more than 60% of W or it just won't ignite.

Because only city cab drivers and very young drivers purchase H & H, daily demand is limited to 5,000 gallons. Some older drivers appreciate the uncertainties of SPAS; they collectively demand at least 2,000 gallons per day. SPC, on the other hand, is widely acclaimed by young and old alike in spite of the unsettling noises it causes in engines; daily demand runs between 5,000 and 25,000 gallons.

What is the optimal daily production program for Old Explodable, Incorporated? (If you do not have a computer available, merely set up the first tableau.)

13. Modify the LP computer program in the chapter to include a parametric programming feature.

14. *Integer programming.* Obatin an integer solution to the following problem:

Maximize $\quad 4x + y$

Subject to:

$$x + 2y \leq 5$$
$$3x + y \leq 4$$

15. *Capital budgeting and integer programming.* A choice must be made among three mutually exclusive, acceptable projects. The net present values of these projects are \$10, \$20, and \$22. The present values of the estimated investments required are \$20, \$30, and \$40 respectively for the first year and \$10, \$20, and \$20 respectively

for the second year. The available capital in the first year is \$60 and in the second year is \$40. (All data omit 0000). Use integer programming to make the selection and then check your answer by enumeration of results of investment combinations.

16. *Capital budgeting and integer programming.* Set up the following capital budgeting problem as a linear programming model and then briefly discuss the advantages and disadvantages of the approach.

	Projects						
	A	B	C	D	E	F	G
Immediate investment	\$100,000	\$80,000	\$150,000	\$200,000	\$300,000	\$160,000	\$75,000
TAR	15%	22%	16%	20%	30%	18%	14%
First-year cash flow	\$ 12,000	\$30,000	\$ 30,000	\$ 40,000	\$ 5,000	\$ 20,000	\$40,000

The required rate of return is 15%
The company needs \$150,000 cash flow to satisfy budgetary requirements in first year.
It has \$500,000 available for immediate investment.

17. *Trucking.* A trucking company has three terminals, any of which can serve any of four cities. Terminal 1 has 20 trucks, terminal 2 has 9, and terminal 3 has 14. City 1 requires 7 truckloads, city 2 requires 15, city 3 requires 10, and city 4 requires 11. The distances in miles from each terminal to each city are as follows:

Terminal	City 1	City 2	City 3	City 4
1	200	100	200	400
2	100	300	400	300
3	100	300	200	500

Assuming costs to be proportional to mileage, how should the company program its service to minimize cost?

18. *Transportation problem.* Thompson Enterprises manufactures a vital commodity in each of three plants, which it then markets to four customers, A, B, C, and D. Thompson, a strong proponent of optimization, wishes to minimize the shipping costs given the following data:

Supply: $\sum_{j=A}^{D} x_{ij} = 25; \quad \sum_{j=A}^{D} x_{2j} = 12; \quad \sum_{j=A}^{D} x_{3j} = 18$

Demand: $\sum_{i=1}^{3} x_{iA} = 11; \quad \sum_{i=1}^{3} x_{iB} = 20; \quad \sum_{i=1}^{3} x_{iC} = 10; \quad \sum_{i=1}^{3} x_{iD} = 14$

Shipping Costs per Unit:

From:	A	B	C	D
1	3	1	3	5
2	2	3	4	3
3	1	4	2	6

Required:

Determine the cost of the best shipping program.

19. *Transportation problem.* Shown below is the first tableau for a transportation problem. Determine the optimal solution and scrutinize it to see if any unusual opportunities are present.

	D_1	D_2	D_3	D_4	Total
S_1	25	10	2	30	10
Supply: S_2	5	15	20	10	15
S_3	100	65	0	2	20
Total	5	12	13	15	45

20. A demands 20 units
B demands 30 units
S_1 has 40 units to ship
S_2 has 25 units to ship
Cost per unit to ship from S_1 to A is \$7
S_1 to B is \$4
S_2 to A is \$2
S_2 to B is \$4
Determine the optimal shipping program and its cost. Use the northwest corner method.

21. *Site location and degeneracy.* A bakery has two plants, which also serve as distribution centers to several market areas. Everything seems to indicate that expansion of operations would be desirable. Accordingly, management is trying to decide between two locations. The decision will be based entirely on minimizing distribution costs. This, in turn, reduces to minimizing truckload miles, since the mix of products is essentially the same in any given truck, all of which start out filled and are of the same size. Bakeries A and B are those presently in existence and the choice is between locations C and D. Supply and demand data for each day are as shown below. Which location should be chosen? Unit data in truckloads:

Bakery	Supply	Market	Demand
A	30	1	40
B	50	2	40
C	40	3	10
D	40	4	20

What do you think about the measure of cost used here?

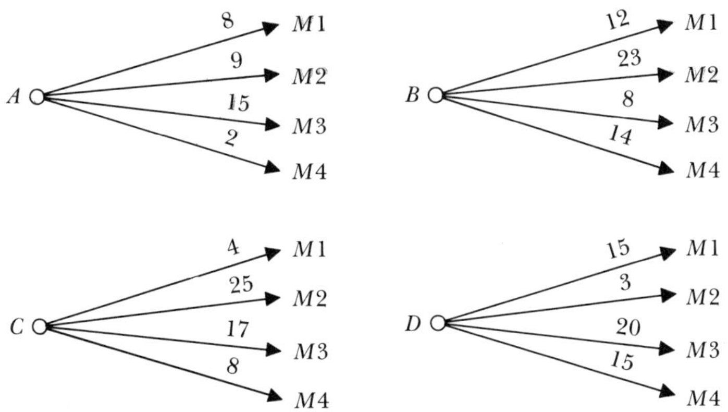

22. *Pollution and profits.* Below is a table that shows the unwanted pollutants emitted to the atmosphere as a result of producing a ton of each of two products.

Pollutant	# Per Ton Product 1	# Per Ton Product 2
Particulates	25	20
Gas 1	6	8
Gas 2	2	4

Management has installed stack controls on two of its three chimneys so that product 1 emissions can be reduced by 80%, 60%, and 50% for particulates, gas 1, and gas 2 respectively, and product 2 emissions can drop to 30%, 50%, and 25% respectively. The operations of the stack controls cost \$12 and \$15 per ton for products 1 and 2 respectively. The local environmental control agency has authority to shut the factory if tests show that daily emissions exceed 500, 200, and 50 pounds for the respective pollutants. Profits per ton of products 1 and 2, exclusive of stack costs, are \$100 and \$125 respectively. Demand targets call for 20 tons of product 1 and 25 tons of product 2 daily.

There are two bottleneck machines (A and B) in the production process that are available eight hours each day. Product 1 takes 25 minutes per ton on A and 12 minutes per ton on B, while product 2 requires 20 minutes on A and 30 minutes on B. The stack controls further slow production by 5 minutes a ton. Product 1 uses chimney 1, and product 2 uses chimney 2.

Management has specified that the minimum satisfactory daily profit performance is $2,000.

Formulate and solve this problem from (a) the financial perspective of maximizing daily profits and (b) the societal viewpoint of minimizing pollution. Discuss interesting prospects. Which is the correct formulation?

23. *Haberdashery and the warehouse model.* A clothing store sells suits only and is presently confronted with planning its spring season. Spring weight suits are sold over a three-month period. Costs and prices peak in the middle month and are as follows:

Month	G_i	P_i
1	$50	$75
2	55	80
3	40	60

It is anticipated that there will be a $12,000 cash balance at the beginning of the three-month period. The store has a minimum cash balance requirement of $5,000. The store has room for 1,000 suits and 50 suits are left over from last year. Assume that sales may be made only from inventory available at the beginning of a month, and that all sales are on a charge basis with a one-month lag in receipts.

(a) Set up the model for this decision in general notation.

(b) Set up the initial tableau and perform one iteration.

(c) Comment on the shadow prices of this problem. What might they be used for?

24. *Dual program.* Use dual simplex procedures to solve the problem given below.

Maximize $30(tips) + $45(flaps) – $150,000

Constraints:

(a) Maximum demand for tips = 6,000 units

(b) Maximum demand for flaps = 4,000 units

(c) Minimum flap production = 1,000 units

(d) Maximum production = 12,000 flaps or 9,600 tips or a linear combination of the two

(e) Minimum production = 5,000 flaps or 4,000 tips or a linear combination of the two

(f) Production mix must consist of at least one tip for every three flaps.

25. *Critical-path analysis and LP (prepared by Professor Bharath Ramachandran, Northern Michigan University).* Any project can be viewed as a set of tasks, all of which have to be completed to fulfill the project.

Suppose enough resources are available for allotment to each of the tasks to complete it in the technologically minimum feasible time.

Now if it were possible to start all the tasks and execute them concurrently, clearly the *minimum* time required to complete the project is the time taken by the task with the longest duration, since meanwhile all the other tasks with lesser duration would have been completed.

However, there is a dependence effect among tasks. Certain tasks can be started only if one or more tasks have been completed (e.g., in building a house, certain activities can be started only after the foundation has been laid). Because of this, the minimum time required to complete a project is not just the time of the *task* with the longest duration, but of the sequence or *chain* of tasks with the longest duration. Each task may be part of one or more chains of tasks, and can be started only if its "immediate predecessors" have been completed.

(a) Study carefully the relationship between the diagram given below and the list of dependence relationships alongside the diagram.

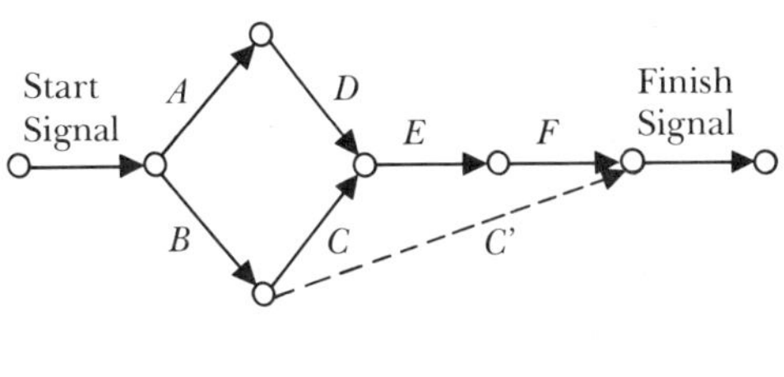

Activity or Task	Immediate Predecessors
A	Start Signal
B	Start Signal
C	B
D	A
E	C,D
F	E
Finish Signal	F

(b) (1) Identify the various chains of activities or tasks involved in this project.

(2) What change in the dependence relationships of the tasks would be implied in changing the position of C to C'?

(c) Given a diagram with dependence relationships and durations as shown below, find the shortest time for completion of the project by identifying the various chains of activities.

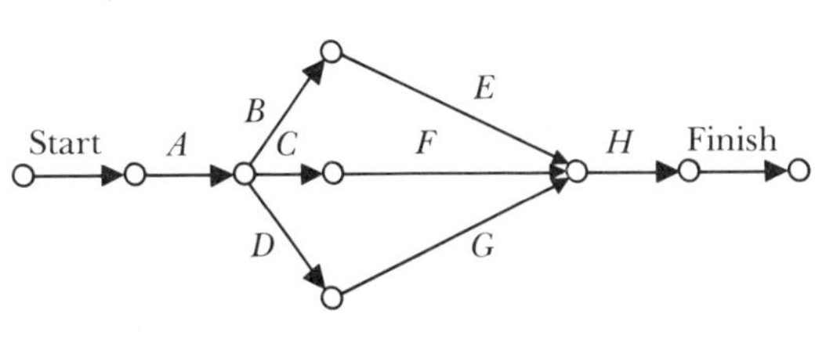

START	0	E	1
A	3	F	6
B	1	G	5
C	3	H	5
D	2	FINISH	0

(d) Let t_x be defined as the earliest possible time at which activity X can be started. Then, if activity X has a set of immediate predecessors P_1, P_2, P_3 . . . , we can say that

$$t_x = \underset{(P_1, P_2, P_3 \ldots)}{\overset{}{\text{MAX over}}} \{t_{P_i} + d_{P_i}\}$$

where d_{P_i} = duration of predecessor activity P_i. So we can express in the case of the diagram shown above:

$$t_{\text{FINISH}} = \underset{H}{\text{MAX over}} \{t_{P_i} + d_{P_i}\}$$

$$= \underset{H}{\text{MAX over}} \{t_H + d_H\}$$

$$= t_H + d_H.$$

and similarly:

$$t_H = \underset{E, F, G}{\text{MAX}} \{t_{P_i} + d_{P_i}\}$$

$$= \text{MAX} \{(t_E + d_E), (t_F + d_F), (t_G + d_G)\} \qquad \text{(A)}$$

—and so on, back to the start of the project. Since "start signal" has no predecessors and no duration, we can take $t_{\text{START}} = 0$.

(e) Equation A above does not seem to be of the form of linear constraints. Show that it can be replaced by three linear constraints without altering the conditions of the problem.

(f) What objective function in terms of t_{FINISH} would be suitable for finding out the least time required to complete the project?

(g) Write out the full LP formulation of this problem by proceeding on the lines of (d) above.

26. *The assignment problem (prepared by Professors A. Wayne Corcoran and Bharath Ramachandran).* The assignment problem is a degenerate form of the transportation problem in which the *number* of suppliers equals the *number* of customers and the decision variable $x_{ij} = \{0, 1\}$. Shown below is an illustration together with a description of a solution procedure that is commonly followed.

Jobs:

Men:		W	X	Y	Z
	A	7	2	1	4
	B	4	3	4	6
	C	8	4	3	9
	D	2	4	5	3

Steps

1. Subtract the minimum column elements from every element in the respective columns. If the smallest number of lines necessary to cross out the zero elements equals the dimension, here 4, of the matrix, an optimal solution can be chosen from among the crossed out zeroes. If not, . . .

2. Subtract the minimum row elements in the new matrix from every element in the respective rows. Then test for zeroes and lines as in (1). Here three lines can still cross out all zeroes, so. . .

After Step 1

	W	*X*	*Y*	*Z*
A	5	0	0	1
B	2	1	3	3
C	6	2	2	6
D	0	2	4	0

3. Find the smallest uncrossed element, subtract it from all uncrossed elements, and add it to the intersections of lines. Test for lines and zeroes.

4. Repeat step (3) as often as necessary until the minimum number of lines needed to cross out the zeroes equals the dimension of the matrix.

5. The solution is obtained by selecting a zero from each row but in a previously unused column. The cost or time associated with this schedule is determined from the original matrix. Alternative optima schedules often exist.

After Step 2

	W	*X*	*Y*	*Z*
A	5	0	0	1
B	1	0	2	2
C	4	0	0	4
D	0	2	4	0

After Step 3

	W	*X*	*Y*	*Z*
A	4	0	0	0
B	0	0	2	1
C	3	0	0	3
D	0	3	5	0

Optimal Schedule

	W	*X*	*Y*	*Z*
A		2		
B	4			
C			3	
D				3

Optimal Time = 12

Required:

(a) Why would this problem necessarily have a degenerate (fewer than $m + n - 1$ variables in the basis) solution?

(b) Why is the optimal solution not affected by subtracting minimal column and row elements from all other elements? (Hint: How many elements are chosen from any row or column?)

(c) Two applications of the assignment algorithm are

(1) A situation in which four contractors make bids of differing amounts for each of four building construction jobs, and the awards authority wishes to give one job to each of them; and

(2) A situation in which a fire department has four trucks to be dispatched one each to four places, and because of the differing capacities, the costs for each truck being allotted the various jobs varies with the job, and similarly the cost for each job varies with the truck. Suggest some other realizations of this model.

(d) Given the cost matrix shown below, what is the best assignment?

		Jobs			
		1	2	3	4
Machines	*A*	48	48	50	44
	B	56	60	60	68
	C	96	94	90	85
	D	42	44	54	46

27. *Fast service restaurant (prepared by Professor Mawsen Liao, University of Houston).* A fast service restaurant is planning to extend its business hours from 16 hours to 24 hours a day. The manager desires to determine the minimum number of employees for each of the six four-hour shifts. The minimum number of employees needed on each shift with the hourly wage rate are given in the following table:

Shift	Minimum Number of Employees Needed	Wage Rate Per Hour
Midnight–4:00 AM	4	$4.80
4:00 AM–8:00 AM	6	4.80
8:00 AM–Noon	16	3.60
Noon–4:00 PM	10	3.60
4:00 PM–8:00 PM	16	3.60
8:00 PM–Midnight	8	4.80

Each employee is hired to work eight consecutive hours per day.

Required:

(1) Formulate the problem as an integer programming problem.

(2) Apply the branch-and-bound algorithm to solve the problem.

28. *Lunch anyone? (prepared by Professor Prabhakant Sinha, University of Georgia.)* A diner is faced with choosing a sumptuous luncheon, complete in three courses. Being of a scientific mind, he has analyzed the cost, caloric, and acceptability data below for a unit serving of each item. Set up and solve the mathematical programming problem to select one entree, one beverage, and one dessert for a meal that maximizes acceptability. He wants to consume no more than 800 calories and to spend, at most, $.75. Comment on the measures of cost in this problem.

	Item	Portion Weight	Acceptability	Cost (cents)	Calories
Entree	Hamburger on a bun	5 oz.	8.0	40	295
	Sausage Pizza	6 oz.	7.5	55	410
	Fruit Plate	11 oz.	6.2	48	410
Beverage	Coca Cola	12 oz.	3.5	27	142
	Whole Milk	8 oz.	2.0	11	150
	Coffee	6 oz.	1.5	5	40
Dessert	Cherry Pie	4 oz.	6.0	25	410
	Apple	5 oz.	5.0	12	70
	Tapioca Pudding	5 oz.	4.5	12	180

29. Integer programming: auditor scheduling. Please see page 659.

Input-Output, Return on Investment, and Transfer Prices

17

Overview

What problems arise when a business deals with itself? We encountered one such situation earlier when discussing secondary allocation en route to developing overhead rates. There—if difficulties with measuring and using effort-expended as a basis for allocation were put aside—things went smoothly from the standpoint of income determination. From a behavioral standpoint, two problems emerged: budgetary gamesmanship and reaction to overlapping responsibilities.

The present chapter expands on the service provider-service consumer concept by considering departments or divisions that are organized as separate profit centers to supply other departments or divisions with services (usually, but not necessarily, in the form of products). It is this status as separate profit centers that is the major cause of difficulty. Each division is cast in a role that emphasizes its own profit achievement to the virtual exclusion of corporate profits and of all other measures of success. Furthermore, profit is related to investment, which results in a particular measure known as return on investment (ROI). ROI is a form of institutionalized myopia that is heralded by an army of theorists as the most practical way to effect decentralization in business.

Input-output (I-O) analysis will be offered as a means for studying the provider-consumer relationship. Here the assumption will initially be made that price is set in the marketplace; consequently sister divisions are treated as if they were unrelated, undeserving of special favors. Next the assumption of market price is set aside, raising the issue of which division should be granted concessions so that its performance (ROI) will improve.

ROI will next be examined for salient features. Then the subject of transfer prices—the prices set on the services (products) produced by one division for another—will be scrutinized with emphasis on the use of linear programming. The chapter will conclude with personal observations about the control issues involved.

Input-Output Analysis

Many years ago, Wasily W. Leontieff developed an input-output (I-O) model that described the interrelationships of industries in the United States.[1] The I-O approach, however, may be used to describe many other, smaller-scale, phenomena. It was first applied to individual businesses by accounting theorists in 1960, and this application has gained momentum steadily ever since.*

At the heart of I-O analysis lies the equation

$$x_i = \sum_j P_{ij} x_j + e_i$$

This says that the output of section i (that is, x_i) equals the amount consumed *internally* by other producing sections (that is, $\sum P_{ij} x_j$) plus the amount consumed *externally* by outside customers (that is, e_i). P_{ij} has been used to restate the amount of *i's output* consumed by j as a percentage of *j's output*.

Example: Two processes, x_1 and x_2, each produce a single product. x_1's product is measured in tons and x_2's in gallons. x_1 transfers 25 tons to x_2 and sells 75 tons to outside customers, while x_2 transfers 50 gallons to x_1 and sells 100 gallons to outside customers. Given that these technological relationships can be expected to persist, determine the total amounts x_1 and x_2 should produce if outside sales next year are forecasted as 275 and 100 respectively.

Solution: The table shown below summarizes the physical flows.

		To: x_1	x_2	e	Σ
From:	x_1	0	25	75	100
	x_2	50	0	100	150

[1] W. W. Leontieff, *The Structure of the American Economy*, 1919–1939 (London: Oxford University Press, 1951).

* Some of the early I-O articles are Allen B. Richards, "Input-Output Accounting for Business," *The Accounting Review*, July 1960, pp. 429–37. Shawki M. Farag, "A Planning Model for the Divisionalized Enterprise," *The Accounting Review*, April 1968, pp. 312–20; Yuji Ijiri, "An Application of Input-Output Analysis to Some Problems in Cost Accounting," *Management Accounting*, April 1968, pp. 49–61; John L. Livingstone, "Input-Output Analysis for Cost Accounting, Planning and Control," *The Accounting Review*, January 1969, pp. 48–64; Trevor E. Gambling and Ahmed Nour, "A Note on Input-Output Analysis: Its Uses in Macro-Economics and Micro-Economics," *The Accounting Review*, January 1970, pp. 98–102.

The percentages or technological coefficients are obtained somewhat indirectly. They are perhaps best explained by the following line of argument:

Total readings for x_i will result from the model. Percentages of each total may be used to obtain the amounts of the physical flows.

$$x_1 = (25/150)x_2 + 75$$

$$x_2 = (50/100)x_1 + 100$$

In matrices, $x = Px + e$

$$x = (I - P)^{-1}e$$

Here, $P = \begin{bmatrix} 0 & 1/6 \\ 1/2 & 0 \end{bmatrix}$ and $I - P = \begin{bmatrix} 1 & -1/6 \\ -1/2 & 1 \end{bmatrix}$

A check of this year's total production:

$$\begin{matrix} & (I-P)^{-1} & e & \\ x = & \dfrac{\begin{bmatrix} 1 & 1/6 \\ 1/2 & 1 \end{bmatrix}}{1 - (1/12)} & \begin{bmatrix} 75 \\ 100 \end{bmatrix} & = \begin{bmatrix} 100 \\ 150 \end{bmatrix} \end{matrix}$$

Next year's total production:

$$x = \dfrac{\begin{bmatrix} 1 & 1/6 \\ 1/2 & 1 \end{bmatrix}}{11/12} \begin{bmatrix} 275 \\ 100 \end{bmatrix} = \begin{bmatrix} 318 \\ 259 \end{bmatrix}$$

Next year's I-O table:

	x_1	x_2	e	$\sum$
x_1	0	43	275	318
x_2	159	0	100	259

Comments

1. Next year's I-O table can be calculated by entering known amounts shown under e and $\sum$, 0 for x_{ii}, and setting $x_{ij} = \sum_i - e_i$. Alternatively, matrix P and vector $\sum$ may be partitioned and multiplied as follows:

$$\begin{matrix} P & \sum & \\ \left[\begin{array}{c|c} 0 & 1/6 \\ 1/2 & 0 \end{array}\right] & \left[\begin{array}{c} 318 \\ \hline 259 \end{array}\right] & \left[\begin{bmatrix} 0 \\ 159 \end{bmatrix} + \begin{bmatrix} 43 \\ 0 \end{bmatrix}\right] \end{matrix}$$

Either way the percentages remain constant.

2. $(I - P)^{-1}$ may be used to perform marginal analysis. Suppose, for instance, that one more unit of outside output is needed for, say, x_1. This

produces a change in total output (designated by Δx_1) of

$$\Delta x_1 = (I - P)^{-1}\begin{bmatrix} 1 \\ 0 \end{bmatrix} = \begin{bmatrix} 12/11 \\ 6/11 \end{bmatrix}$$

3. One feature of working with physical units is that the P matrix has relative stability as contrasted with a matrix that is derived from dollar amounts—which reflects fluctuations in the value of money.

4. Leontieff assumed that an industry produced a single product. A company, however, is often in several industries and almost always makes several products. This suggests modification of our present approach. One such modification—if the several products were not always produced in the same proportion so that they could be treated as one product—would be to develop separate I-O matrices for each product. An easier approach might be to prepare a single I-O matrix in terms of dollars that reflect aggregated transactions, and to introduce exponential smoothing to update the I-O matrix in time. These modifications are discussed below.

5. Money may be introduced by multiplying prices times the corresponding units in each row of the physical units table. If one market price were used for each row, the transfer prices between processes would be at market. If some figure other than market price as reduced by avoided costs (for example, one process need not advertise to the other) were used for internal output, one process would tend to be favored at the expense of the other. External output could simultaneously be priced at market, so that different prices would be used for different elements in each row. If products transferred had no immediate marketplace, an intermediate market price could be set that was equal to end product market price minus identifiable process distribution and production costs—much as when relative market prices are developed when allocating joint production costs.

6. If the percentage matrix changed from year to year, exponential smoothing could be used in the manner illustrated in Chapter 4, when Markov chains were used to forecast cash collections from accounts receivable. This would be desirable if P could not be specified with relative certainty from detailed knowledge of coming year activity.

Let us see how I-O analysis works with dollar amounts. At the same time, let us introduce other inputs—such as materials, labor, and overhead—and gross profit (which is also referred to as value added).

Example: Shown below is an I-O table for 1970. Given that the sales forecast for 1971 is \$195 for A and \$292.5 for B, prepare the I-O table for 1971. All amounts omit 000.

	Departments A	B	External Sales	Σ
A	$ 0	$ 30	$170	$200
B	50	0	250	300
Other Production Costs	120	210		
Profits	30	60		
Σ	$200	$300		$500

Note: The "Profits" row is inserted as a balancing set of figures that results in corresponding rim totals being equal.

Solution:
$$P = \begin{bmatrix} 0 & 30/300 \\ 50/200 & 0 \end{bmatrix}; \quad (I - P)^{-1} = \begin{bmatrix} 1 & .1 \\ .25 & 1 \end{bmatrix} \Big/ .975$$

Production costs and profits may be expressed in a partitioned matrix:

$$B = \left[\begin{array}{c|c} 120/200 & 210/300 \\ 30/200 & 60/300 \end{array}\right]$$

Total production for 1971:

$$x = (I - P)^{-1} \begin{bmatrix} 195 \\ 292.5 \end{bmatrix} = \begin{bmatrix} 230 \\ 350 \end{bmatrix}$$

By partitioning P and x, forming the products Px and Bx and filling in sales forcasts, the 1971 I-O table becomes

	A	B	Sales	Σ
A	$ 0	$ 35	$195.0	$230
B	57.5	0	292.5	350
Other Costs	138.0	245		
Profit	34.5	70		
Σ	$230.0	$350		$580

Comments:

1. If ending inventories were to be changed next year, say increased, the increases could be added to external sales or placed in a separate

column. The system, however, would automatically reflect these inventory increments at retail value, which violates the realization principle of financial accounting.[2]

2. The profit may be allocated to internal and external sales and inventory by placing these quantities in a matrix and premultiplying it by the profit row in B. To illustrate, say the sales figures for 1971 consist of both sales and inventory increases: sales = (170;250), inventory = (25;42.5), intracompany transfers = (35;57.5).

$$(30/200;\ 60/300)\begin{bmatrix} 170 & 25 & 35 \\ 250 & 42.5 & 57.5 \end{bmatrix} = (75.5;\ 12.25;\ 16.75)$$

This says that profits on external sales, inventory additions, and transfers are 75.5, 12.25, and 16.75 respectively (which sums to 104.5 as in the 1971 I-O table). By partitioning, these profits could be segregated by department.

3. Input-output analysis is related to linear programming.[3]
In LP we have: Max $Z = cx$
Subject to: $Ax \leq b$
Solution: $Z = cA^{-1}b$
In I-O we have: $x = (I - P)^{-1}e$.
If market prices form vector c, then the value of total output in I-O is $cx = c(I - P)^{-1}e$.

4. I-O can be extended by LP by reflecting contribution margins and introducing constraints that use $(I - P)^{-1}$ elements as coefficients and recognize departmental output capacity limitations.[4]

Return on Investment (ROI)

Consider a decentralized company. How does corporate headquarters control the performance of the various divisions? We dealt with the behavioral

[2] This refinement is introduced and dealt with (in the manner next described) in Farag, "A Planning Model," pp. 315–17.

[3] More extensive developments of this relationship may be found in G. Hadley, *Linear Programming* (Reading, Massachusetts: Addison-Wesley Publishing Co., 1962), p. 491.

[4] Suggested in Gambling and Nour, "Input-Output Analysis," p. 102.

problems in earlier human behavior and responsibility accounting discussions; now let us focus on the technical side of the question. In most decentralized companies, the major means of motivating divisional managers is through use of return on investment (ROI). According to ROI, that division does best which experiences the greatest return on its invested assets. Raises, promotions, and bonuses all await the manager who repeatedly demonstrates high ROI performance.

ROI consists of two components:

$$\text{ROI} = \text{Asset turnover} \times \text{Profit margin}$$

$$\text{ROI} = \frac{\text{Sales}}{\text{Investment}} \times \frac{\text{Net profit}}{\text{Sales}} = \frac{\text{Net profit}}{\text{Investment}}$$

Both components are barometers of vitality that may be compared with prior performances of both the division and its industry as well as with performances of other divisions. Thus if asset turnover declines, investigation is indicated (and similarly with profit margin). Either there has been a decrease in sales or an increase in investment or both. Why? Can remedial action be taken? If turnover increases, this too should be studied.

Unfortunately, businesses do not agree on how ROI should be calculated. Some businesses use original investment amounts as a base, others include current assets plus fixed assets valued at net book value (original investment as reduced by depreciation), while still others employ current replacement values for inventory and fixed assets. Current replacement value has great appeal theoretically because it is a measure of value of capital tied up in the assets. How to include corporate assets shared by more than one division (that is, common assets) is also a problem—one that can only be settled arbitrarily.

Some businesses do not include recently acquired assets in the investment base. They reason that such assets experience a leadtime or gestation period during which little, if any, profits are generated. Once this leadtime has passed, profits are earned and the asset is added to the investment base. Where this practice is not followed, the manager has strong incentive not to acquire new assets, because if he does so, his ROI will temporarily decline. The new assets may be needed, but their adverse effect on ROI often causes postponement of their purchase.

Where net book value is used for fixed assets, depreciation reduces investment as well as net profit. In such situations, the only things that may be changing are the numbers; performance could remain the same or even deteriorate, but ROI could increase because of a relatively decreasing investment value. By using an annuity method of depreciation, this particular irregularity may be remedied.

Example: Cost $(C) = \$100{,}000$
Life = 4 years
Salvage value $(S) = \$10{,}000$
Discount rate = 10%
Earnings $(E) = ?$

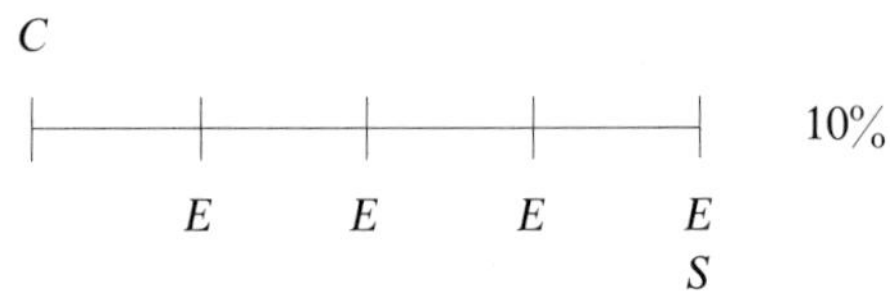

$$100{,}000 = EB(4, 10) + 10{,}000b(4, 10)$$

$$E = 29{,}392$$

Balance (*B*)	10% Interest	Earnings (*E*)	Depreciation (*D*)	Rate = $(E - D)/B$
100,000	10,000	29,392	19,392	.10
80,608	8,061	29,392	21,331	.10
59,277	5,928	29,392	23,464	.10
35,813	3,581	29,392	25,811	.10
10,002				

Here "Rate" is really ROI since it divides net profit by investment. Ignoring the $2 rounding error, we see that the ending balance equals the salvage value. Since the earnings are reduced by the depreciation charge, as is investment ("balance"), the ROI is a constant 10% each year. Of course, if earnings vary from $29,392, the constant 10% would not result, although the levelling tendency of annuity depreciation would still remain.

Further problems arise if ending inventories are evaluated on a LIFO basis. This leads to low-valued investment figures in periods of inflation.

Net profit and Sales amounts also lead to difficulties in ROI. Some companies exclude extraordinary items from net profit and other companies do not recognize revenue until a contract is complete (this is as opposed to the percentage of completion concept of revenues). Purchasing power of money may exert significant unwanted influence on the ROI computation because the profits and sales are essentially in dollars of current purchasing power (with the exception of depreciation expense), while the fixed-asset portion of the investment is expressed in dollars of varied purchasing powers.

So it can be said, charitably, that ROI is a very individualized measure. It is not unlike measuring length with yardsticks that vary from, say, 24″ to 42″. Naturally this diversity of approaches makes it very difficult to compare the ROI of one company with that of another.

Transfer Prices

Earlier it was suggested that transfers between divisions of a company be priced at market-price-minus-avoided-costs if one division was not to be favored at the expense of another. Attractive as this seems, it is nevertheless an oversimplification. One immediate exception to such a rule would occur if the consuming division has an opportunity to buy the product from an outside supplier at a price lower than market-price-minus-avoided-costs. Strictly speaking, this lower price constitutes a new market price; however, if the lower price is a momentary thing quick to disappear, its transitory nature precludes its having a noticeable effect on set market price. In such a circumstance, the consuming division feels wronged when compelled to buy from the supplying division. The consuming division wishes to improve its profit performance (probably measured in terms of ROI) by accepting the lowest price immediately available. It fails to consider that the supplying division might be steadier and more reliable over the long run; to the consuming division, it is current profit that matters.[5]

The company has ambivalent feelings in such a case. On the one hand, it would like to see the supplying division obtain the order to receive the benefits from experience and to keep all money within the company. On the other hand, if the outside supplier gets the contract, it encourages the supplying division to become more efficient; furthermore, good relations with outside suppliers may later prove useful. Making a decision based on the immediate situation without regard to long-run implications is less than wise.

There is the additional problem that insisting on the use of sister divisions interferes with the practice of decentralization. Precise interpretation of decentralization leaves decisions in the hands of the divisions. Given great responsibility, a division may strive to be worthy of it and so become more efficient. Thus decentralization favors open negotiation.

Another drawback inherent in market-price-minus-avoided-costs (MPMAC) is revealed when a supplying division becomes more efficient. If the improvement amounts to $1 per unit, should MPMAC be lowered? If MPMAC is lowered, it will no longer pay the supplying division to strive for progress—all the benefits are passed on to the consuming division, which, incidentally, does nothing directly to merit them. On the other hand, if MPMAC is not lowered, there is no incentive to the consuming division to use more of this input and less of some other—which is what the overall company wants.

[5] Perhaps calculating net profit as the discounted net receipts of the future would alleviate the "temporary disadvantage" problem.

It would appear a simple solution to set transfer prices at marginal cost (which may approximately equal variable costs). After all, the company profits should be maximized, and no transfer between divisions adds anything directly to overall profits. So why not keep transfer prices at cost, thereby building cost as a product passes through successive divisions? There is inherent sense in this scheme, but unfortunately it disregards the profit center organizations by treating them as cost centers.

There is also sense in using transfer prices to regulate demand, that is, (1) to discourage interdivisional demand when a supplying division is inundated with work, and (2) to encourage interdivisional demand when times are slow. Thus the idea of adjusting transfer prices by subsidies and penalties to achieve appropriate motivation has appeal.

The use of opportunity costs is also attractive. Assume (1) that a division has an LP model that recognizes a trade-off between x_1 and x_2 (that is, one is made at the expense of the other); (2) that x_2 is in the optimal basis while x_1 is not; and (3) that x_1 is needed by a consuming division. Then the opportunity cost of each unit x_1 is $z_1 - c_1$ provided basis does not change. In other words, the opportunity cost of x_1 is the profit forgone on x_2 (and any other variables that are in the basis). However, price per unit to the consuming division would equal $z_1 - c_1$ increased by the variable cost of x_1.

In recent years, theorists have turned to the decomposition principle of linear programming to study transfer prices while recognizing profit centers and decentralization.[6] To understand decomposition, it would be helpful to have the revised simplex procedure and the "product form of the inverse" at hand. When introducing LP, the inverse matrix was used to obtain a tableau of linear combination scalars. A new basis was then determined and the process was repeated until all $z_j - c_j$ were positive (assuming a maximization objective). This is essentially the revised simplex method except that revised simplex ignores columns for vectors in the basis (which will obviously be unit vectors) and obtains the inverse in a recursive manner:

$$B_{i+1}^{-1} = EB_i^{-1}$$

where E is an identity matrix with one column replaced by a column derived

[6] Although the decomposition principle itself was developed a few years earlier, the original research on its application to transfer prices appears in W. J. Baumol and T. Fabian, "Decomposition Pricing for Decentralization and External Economics," *Management Science*, September 1964, pp. 1–32.

A related piece written about this same time was A. Whinston, "Pricing Guides in Decentralized Organization," in *New Perspective in Organizational Research*, ed. W. W. Cooper, *et. al.* (New York: John Wiley & Sons, 1964), pp. 405–48.

Many other stimulating papers followed; a representative few are J. E. Hass, "Transfer Pricing in a Decentralized Firm," *Management Science*, February 1968, pp. 310–31; C. S. Colantoni, R. P. Manes, and A. Whinston, "Programming, Profit Rates and Pricing Decisions," *The Accounting Review*, July 1969, pp. 467–81; M. Onsi, "A Transfer Pricing System Based on Opportunity cost," *The Accounting Review*, July 1970, pp. 535–43.

from $B_i^{-1}x_k$, and x_k is the entering vector. This is easier to do than to describe; please study Exhibit 1. The product form of the inverse has computational advantages over other methods of inverting a matrix in that it dispenses with minors and elementary row operations and relies on simple recursion and multiplication.

Let us return to the decomposition principle and transfer pricing. A linear programming problem that has a constraint structure in which there is a group of one or more constraints that relates all decision variables and separate groups of other constraints that pertain only to variables that are in the group and to no other is said to be decomposable. Such a problem has the appearance illustrated below:

Objective function:	$Z = cx$				
Master (global) constraints:	Ax				$\leq b$
Group (strata) constraints:	A_1x_1				$\leq b_1$
		A_2x_2			$\leq b_2$
			$\vdots$		$\vdots$
				A_nx_n	$\leq b_n$

As you can see, the total constraint matrix would consist mostly of zeroes.

Because of its structure, it is possible to work with the strata problems separately and transmit tentatively optimal subproblem solutions to the overall problem via the linkage of the global constraints. The global problem then studies how efficiently these collective tentative solutions utilize global resources. If utilization is not optimal, a stratum is given a set of figures to replace in its objective function that represents original contribution margins as adjusted by subsidies or penalties or both.[7] The stratum then re-solves its subproblem with its new objective function and communicates the results to the global problem. Thus the algorithm continues until an optimum is reached. The optimal solution has each stratum taking a weighted average of one or more of its tentative solutions. It is possible in this way to solve very large problems consisting of thousands of variables and constraints—all with an ease that is deceptive when scope is considered. The trick is simply "divide and conquer"; the subproblems are smaller and tractable, and through a substitution of variables the overall problem assumes a greatly reduced dimension, which makes it tractable as well.

[7] These subsidies and penalties are in fact dual prices of global resources. For a theoretical discussion of these prices, read Baumol and Fabian, "Decomposition Pricing." Essentially these penalties and subsidies reflect the value to the overall objective of the strata employment of global resources. At times a subsidy is granted to encourage strata use of master resources; at other times a penalty is levied to discourage strata use of these resources.

Exhibit 1 Product Form of the Inverse (Inversion by Recursion)

Given:

$$\begin{matrix} x_1 & x_2 & x_3 \\ \begin{bmatrix} 2 \\ 3 \end{bmatrix}; & \begin{bmatrix} 5 \\ 1 \end{bmatrix}; & \begin{bmatrix} 1 \\ 4 \end{bmatrix} \end{matrix}$$

Required: Form a basis, B_i, from x_1 and x_2; invert B_i; obtain a new basis, B_{i+1}, from x_1 and x_3; and compute B_{i+1}^{-1} in terms of B_i^{-1}.

Solution: $B_i = \begin{bmatrix} 2 & 5 \\ 3 & 1 \end{bmatrix}$; $B_i^{-1} = \begin{bmatrix} 1 & -5 \\ -3 & -5 \end{bmatrix} \Big/ (-13)$; $B_i^{-1} x_3 = \begin{bmatrix} 19/13 \\ -5/13 \end{bmatrix} = \begin{bmatrix} \lambda_{13} \\ \lambda_{23} \end{bmatrix}$

Since x_3 is going in for x_2, take an identity matrix and replace its second column (x_2 was the second column in B_i), e_2, as follows:

1. $e_{ii} = e_{22}$ becomes the reciprocal of the pivot element (this is $-5/13$ in $B_i^{-1}x_3$).
2. All other elements, e_{ij}, (where $i \neq j$) become the negative of the element in $B_i^{-1}x_3$ divided by the pivot element; here, $e_{i2} = -\lambda_{i3}/\lambda_{23}$.

$$E = \begin{matrix} e_1 & e_2 & \\ \begin{bmatrix} 1 & -(19/13)/(-5/13) \\ 0 & 1/(-5/13) \end{bmatrix} \end{matrix} = \begin{bmatrix} 1 & 19/5 \\ 0 & -13/5 \end{bmatrix}$$

$$B_{i+1}^{-1} = EB_i^{-1} = \begin{bmatrix} 1 & 19/5 \\ 0 & -13/5 \end{bmatrix} \begin{bmatrix} -1/13 & 5/13 \\ 3/13 & -2/13 \end{bmatrix} = \begin{bmatrix} 4 & -1 \\ -3 & 2 \end{bmatrix} \Big/ 5$$

Check: $B_{i+1} = \begin{bmatrix} 2 & 1 \\ 3 & 4 \end{bmatrix}$; $B_{i+1}^{-1} = \begin{bmatrix} 4 & -1 \\ -3 & 2 \end{bmatrix} \Big/ 5$, as above.

In transfer pricing, the overall problem becomes known as the corporate problem, while the strata problems become known as the divisional problems. Assuming that this area interests you, I shall borrow a problem from Professor Mohamed Onsi so that you may have a familiar vehicle should you care to extend your studies.[8] This article does not go into the decomposition algorithm but rather uses its results and relates them soundly to economic theory.

Example: Max $\quad Z = 0x_1 + 8x_2 + 7x_3 + 5x_4$

Subject to:

$$\begin{aligned} -x_1 \qquad\quad + x_3 \qquad\quad &\leq 0 \\ 3x_1 + 6x_2 \qquad\qquad\qquad &\leq 60 \\ 2x_1 + 4x_2 \qquad\qquad\qquad &\leq 40 \\ 4x_3 + 5x_4 &\leq 28 \\ 3x_3 + 2x_4 &\leq 14 \\ x_i \geq 0 \qquad\qquad\qquad\qquad & \end{aligned}$$

Here division 1 makes products x_1 and x_2, while division 2 makes products x_3 and x_4.

[8] Onsi, "A Transfer Pricing System," p. 540.

In symbols, the problem is set up as follows:

$$\text{Max } Z = cX = (C_1 | C_2)\begin{bmatrix} X_1 \\ \hline X_2 \end{bmatrix} = [(0, 8) | (7, 5)]\begin{bmatrix} \begin{bmatrix} x_1 \\ x_2 \end{bmatrix} \\ \hline \begin{bmatrix} x_3 \\ x_4 \end{bmatrix} \end{bmatrix}$$

$$\text{Subject to: } \begin{bmatrix} A_1 & A_2 \\ A_3 & \varnothing \\ \varnothing & A_4 \end{bmatrix}\begin{bmatrix} X_1 \\ \hline X_2 \end{bmatrix} = \begin{bmatrix} -1 & 0 & 1 & 0 \\ \hline 3 & 6 & & \\ 2 & 4 & & \varnothing \\ \hline & & 4 & 5 \\ & \varnothing & 3 & 2 \end{bmatrix}\begin{bmatrix} \begin{bmatrix} x_1 \\ x_2 \end{bmatrix} \\ \hline \begin{bmatrix} x_3 \\ x_4 \end{bmatrix} \end{bmatrix} \leq \begin{bmatrix} b_0 \\ b_1 \\ b_2 \end{bmatrix} = \begin{bmatrix} [\ 0] \\ \begin{bmatrix} 60 \\ 40 \end{bmatrix} \\ \begin{bmatrix} 28 \\ 14 \end{bmatrix} \end{bmatrix}$$

Solution: By studying the divisional constraints, the possible integer solutions, x_{jk}, may be easily identified. (It would not be necessary to seek integer solutions—they are merely assumed for illustration.)

$$\begin{bmatrix} x_1 \\ x_2 \end{bmatrix} = \left\{ \overset{x_{11}}{\begin{bmatrix} 0 \\ 0 \end{bmatrix}}, \overset{x_{12}}{\begin{bmatrix} 20 \\ 0 \end{bmatrix}}, \overset{x_{13}}{\begin{bmatrix} 0 \\ 10 \end{bmatrix}} \right\}; \begin{bmatrix} x_3 \\ x_4 \end{bmatrix} = \left\{ \overset{x_{21}}{\begin{bmatrix} 0 \\ 0 \end{bmatrix}}, \overset{x_{22}}{\begin{bmatrix} 4 \\ 0 \end{bmatrix}}, \overset{x_{23}}{\begin{bmatrix} 0 \\ 5 \end{bmatrix}}, \overset{x_{24}}{\begin{bmatrix} 2 \\ 4 \end{bmatrix}} \right\}$$

Each solution will be weighted by P_{jk} in the ultimate program; therefore, the optimal outputs will look like this:

$$x_j = \sum_{k=1}^{n_j} x_{jk} P_{jk}$$

where n_j is the number of solutions for division j. The objective becomes

$$Z = (C_1\ C_2)\begin{bmatrix} \sum_{k=1}^{3} x_{1k} P_{1k} \\ \hline \sum_{k=1}^{4} x_{2k} P_{2k} \end{bmatrix}$$

$$= (0, 8)\left[\begin{bmatrix} 0 \\ 0 \end{bmatrix} P_{11} + \cdots + \begin{bmatrix} 0 \\ 10 \end{bmatrix} P_{13}\right] + (7, 5)\left[\begin{bmatrix} 0 \\ 0 \end{bmatrix} P_{21} + \cdots + \begin{bmatrix} 2 \\ 4 \end{bmatrix} P_{24}\right]$$

$$= 0P_{11} + 0P_{12} + 80P_{13} + 0P_{21} + 28P_{22} + 25P_{23} + 34P_{24}$$

The corporate constraint becomes

$$(A_1 | A_2)\begin{bmatrix} \sum x_{1k} P_{1k} \\ \hline \sum x_{2k} P_{2k} \end{bmatrix} \leq [b_0]$$

$$(-1, 0)\left[\begin{bmatrix} 0 \\ 0 \end{bmatrix} P_{11} + \cdots + \begin{bmatrix} 0 \\ 10 \end{bmatrix} P_{13}\right] + (1, 0)\left[\begin{bmatrix} 0 \\ 0 \end{bmatrix} P_{21} + \cdots + \begin{bmatrix} 2 \\ 4 \end{bmatrix} P_{24}\right] \leq [0]$$

$$0P_{11} - 20P_{12} + 0P_{13} + 0P_{21} + 4P_{22} + 0P_{23} + 2P_{24} \leq 0$$

Additionally, the weights for each division must sum to 1; therefore, $\sum_{k=1}^{n_j} P_{jk} = 1$.

Putting all parts together, the overall (corporate) problem is

$$\text{Max} \quad Z = 0P_{11} + 0P_{12} + 80P_{13} + 0P_{21} + 28P_{22} + 25P_{23} + 34P_{24}$$

$$\begin{aligned}\text{Constraints: } 0P_{11} - 20P_{12} + 0P_{13} + 0P_{21} + 4P_{22} + 0P_{23} + 2P_{24} + S &= 0\\ P_{11} + P_{12} + P_{13} &= 1\\ P_{21} + P_{22} + P_{23} + P_{24} &= 1\end{aligned}$$

The usual start of a solution would be to form $B = I = B^{-1}$ by setting $X_B = (S, P_{11}, P_{21})^T$. This would not be particularly illuminating, so let us start with $X_B = (P_{24}, P_{13}, P_{21})^T$.

$$B = \begin{bmatrix} 2 & 0 & 0 \\ 0 & 1 & 0 \\ 1 & 0 & 1 \end{bmatrix}; \quad B^{-1} = \begin{bmatrix} .5 & 0 & 0 \\ 0 & 1 & 0 \\ -.5 & 0 & 1 \end{bmatrix}; \quad \text{and} \quad C_B = (34, 80, 0)$$

Then

We continue the solution in Exhibit 2.

Exhibit 2 Decomposition Algorithm

Picking up from the text, we begin with $X_B = (P_{24}, P_{13}, P_{21})^T$.

$$\overset{B^{-1}}{\begin{bmatrix} .5 & 0 & 0 \\ 0 & 1 & 0 \\ -.5 & 0 & 1 \end{bmatrix}} \left[\begin{array}{c|cccccccc} 0 & 0 & -20 & 0 & 0 & 4 & 0 & 2 & 1 \\ 1 & 1 & 1 & 1 & 0 & 0 & 0 & 0 & 0 \\ 1 & 0 & 0 & 0 & 1 & 1 & 1 & 1 & 0 \end{array}\right]$$

	0	0	0	80	0	28	25	34	0
	Z	P_{11}	P_{12}	P_{13}	P_{21}	P_{22}	P_{23}	P_{24}	S
= $34P_{24}$	0	0	−10	0	0	2	0	1	.5
$80P_{13}$	1	1	1	1	0	0	0	0	0
$0P_{21}$	1	0	10	0	1	−1	1	0	−.5
$W_j = z_j - c_j$	80	80	−260	0	0	40	−25	0	17

Let us analyze $W_{P_{12}}$:

$$W_{P_{12}} = (34, 80, 0)\begin{bmatrix} -10 \\ 1 \\ 10 \end{bmatrix} - 0$$

But $\begin{bmatrix} -10 \\ 1 \\ 10 \end{bmatrix} = B^{-1}P_{12}$ and $c_{P_{12}} = 0 = C_1 x_{12}$; therefore,

$$W_{P_{12}} = (34, 80, 0)\begin{bmatrix} .5 & 0 & 0 \\ 0 & 1 & 0 \\ -.5 & 0 & 1 \end{bmatrix}\begin{bmatrix} -20 \\ 1 \\ 0 \end{bmatrix} - (0, 8)\begin{bmatrix} 20 \\ 0 \end{bmatrix}$$

Exhibit 2 (*cont.*)

However, P_{12} can be partitioned into vectors showing separate effects on corporate and divisional programs:

$$W_{P_{12}} = (34, 80, 0)\begin{bmatrix} .5 & 0 & 0 \\ 0 & 1 & 0 \\ -.5 & 0 & 1 \end{bmatrix}\left[\begin{bmatrix} -20 \\ 0 \\ 0 \end{bmatrix} + \begin{bmatrix} 0 \\ 1 \\ 0 \end{bmatrix}\right] - (0, 8)\begin{bmatrix} 20 \\ 0 \end{bmatrix}$$

$$= (34, 80, 0)\begin{bmatrix} .5 & 0 & 0 \\ 0 & 1 & 0 \\ -.5 & 0 & 1 \end{bmatrix}\begin{bmatrix} -20 \\ 0 \\ 0 \end{bmatrix} + (34, 80, 0)\begin{bmatrix} .5 & 0 & 0 \\ 0 & 1 & 0 \\ -.5 & 0 & 1 \end{bmatrix}\begin{bmatrix} 0 \\ 1 \\ 0 \end{bmatrix} - (0, 8)\begin{bmatrix} 20 \\ 0 \end{bmatrix}$$

But certain efficiencies are possible because of structure; furthermore,

$$-20 = A_1 x_{12} = (-1, 0)\begin{bmatrix} 20 \\ 0 \end{bmatrix}.$$

Therefore,

$$W_{P_{12}} = (34, 80, 0)\begin{bmatrix} .5 \\ 0 \\ -.5 \end{bmatrix}(-1, 0)\begin{bmatrix} 20 \\ 0 \end{bmatrix} + (34, 80, 0)\begin{bmatrix} 0 \\ 1 \\ 0 \end{bmatrix} - (0, 8)\begin{bmatrix} 20 \\ 0 \end{bmatrix}$$

Here the second two columns of B^{-1} will always multiply zeroes in $\begin{bmatrix} -20 \\ 0 \\ 0 \end{bmatrix}$ and will have been dropped; additionally, the first and third columns of B^{-1} will multiply zeroes in $\begin{bmatrix} 0 \\ 1 \\ 0 \end{bmatrix}$ (which will always be a unit vector because of the $\sum P_{jk} = 1$ constraints) and will likewise have been dropped. The final streamlined equation is

$$W_{P_{12}} = \left[(34, 80, 0)\begin{bmatrix} .5 \\ 0 \\ -.5 \end{bmatrix}(-1, 0) - (0, 8)\right]\begin{bmatrix} 20 \\ 0 \end{bmatrix} + (34, 80, 0)\begin{bmatrix} 0 \\ 1 \\ 0 \end{bmatrix} = -260$$

In symbols,

$$W_j = [C_B(B_{(m)}^{-1})A_j - C_j]x_{jk} + C_B(B_{m+j}^{-1}),$$

where (m) designates the first m columns of B^{-1} corresponding to all m corporate constraints and j designates the division; hence the subscript $m + j$ selects that column from B^{-1}.

Next let us revise both corporate and divisional programs using W_j and the product form.

$$W_1 = \left[(34, 80, 0)\begin{bmatrix} .5 \\ 0 \\ -.5 \end{bmatrix}(-1, 0) - (0, 8)\right]\begin{bmatrix} x_1 \\ x_2 \end{bmatrix} + (34, 80, 0)\begin{bmatrix} 0 \\ 1 \\ 0 \end{bmatrix} = -17x_1 - 8x_2 + 80$$

Only P_{11} and P_{12} are not in X_B and P_{12} leads to the minimum $W_1\!: -17(20) - 8(0) + 80 = -260$

$$W_2 = \left[(34, 80, 0)\begin{bmatrix} .5 \\ 0 \\ -.5 \end{bmatrix}(1, 0) - (7, 5)\right]\begin{bmatrix} x_3 \\ x_4 \end{bmatrix} + (34, 80, 0)\begin{bmatrix} 0 \\ 0 \\ 1 \end{bmatrix} = 10x_3 - 5x_4 + 0$$

Only P_{22} and P_{23} are not in X_B, and P_{23} leads to the minimum $W_2\!: 10(0) - 5(5) + 0 = -25$. $W_1 < W_2 < 0$ so P_{12} enters the basis at the next iteration.

Exhibit 2 (*cont.*)

Division 1 is asked to re-solve its problem using \$17 and \$8 (determined in W_1 above) as contribution margins:

Max $\quad Z = 17x_1 + 8x_2$

$$\text{Constraints: } 3x_1 + 6x_2 \leq 60$$
$$2x_1 + 4x_2 \leq 40$$

Solution: $\begin{bmatrix} x_1 \\ x_2 \end{bmatrix} = x_{12} = \begin{bmatrix} 20 \\ 0 \end{bmatrix}$, as anticipated by the corporate problem

The corporate problem continues (using the product form of the inverse and the revised simplex) by determining the exiting vector *in the usual manner*:

$X_B = B_i^{-1}b = B_i^{-1}\begin{bmatrix} 0 \\ 1 \\ 1 \end{bmatrix} = \begin{bmatrix} .5 & 0 & 0 \\ 0 & 1 & 0 \\ -.5 & 0 & 1 \end{bmatrix}\begin{bmatrix} 0 \\ 1 \\ 1 \end{bmatrix} = \begin{bmatrix} 0 \\ 1 \\ 1 \end{bmatrix}$, the present solution vector

$B_i^{-1}P_{12} = B_i^{-1}\begin{bmatrix} -20 \\ 1 \\ 0 \end{bmatrix} = \begin{bmatrix} -10 \\ 1 \\ 10 \end{bmatrix}$, the present linear combination scalars for the entering vector. Since -10 is <0 and is therefore not a candidate, and since 1/1 is greater than 1/10, the pivot element is 10 and the exiting vector is P_{21}.

Hence,

$$X_B = (P_{24}, P_{13}, P_{12})^T, C_B = (34, 80, 0)$$

$$B^{-1} = B_{i+1}^{-1} = EB_i^{-1} = \begin{bmatrix} 1 & 0 & 1 \\ 0 & 1 & -.1 \\ 0 & 0 & .1 \end{bmatrix} B_i^{-1} = \begin{bmatrix} 0 & 0 & 1 \\ .05 & 1 & -.1 \\ -.05 & 0 & .1 \end{bmatrix}$$

$$W_1 = \left[(34, 80, 0)\begin{bmatrix} 0 \\ .05 \\ -.05 \end{bmatrix}(-1, 0) - (0, 8)\right]\begin{bmatrix} x_1 \\ x_2 \end{bmatrix} + (34, 80, 0)\begin{bmatrix} 0 \\ 1 \\ 0 \end{bmatrix} = -4x_1 - 8x_2 + 80$$

Only P_{11} is not presently in the basis and this leads to $W_1 = 80$

$$W_2 = \left[(34, 80, 0)\begin{bmatrix} 0 \\ .05 \\ -.05 \end{bmatrix}(1, 0) - (7, 5)\right]\begin{bmatrix} x_3 \\ x_4 \end{bmatrix} + (34, 80, 0)\begin{bmatrix} 1 \\ -.1 \\ .1 \end{bmatrix} = -3x_3 - 5x_4 + 26$$

P_{21}, P_{22}, and P_{23} are not in the basis but even the best, P_{23}, leads to $W_2 = 1$

We see that $C_B(B_{(m)}^{-1})$, W_1, and W_2 are all positive. The optimal program has been reached. It is

$$X_B = \begin{bmatrix} P_{24} \\ P_{13} \\ P_{12} \end{bmatrix} = B^{-1}\begin{bmatrix} 0 \\ 1 \\ 1 \end{bmatrix} = \begin{bmatrix} 1 \\ .9 \\ .1 \end{bmatrix}$$

$$\begin{bmatrix} x_1 \\ x_2 \end{bmatrix} = \Sigma x_{1k}P_{1k} = 0\begin{bmatrix} 0 \\ 0 \end{bmatrix} + .1\begin{bmatrix} 20 \\ 0 \end{bmatrix} + .9\begin{bmatrix} 0 \\ 10 \end{bmatrix} = \begin{bmatrix} 2 \\ 9 \end{bmatrix}$$

$$\begin{bmatrix} x_3 \\ x_4 \end{bmatrix} = \Sigma x_{2k}P_{2k} = 0\begin{bmatrix} 0 \\ 0 \end{bmatrix} + 0\begin{bmatrix} 4 \\ 0 \end{bmatrix} + 0\begin{bmatrix} 0 \\ 5 \end{bmatrix} + 1\begin{bmatrix} 2 \\ 4 \end{bmatrix} = \begin{bmatrix} 2 \\ 4 \end{bmatrix}$$

$$Z = 2(\$0) + 9(\$8) + 2(\$7) + 4(\$5) = \$106$$

Comments:

1. By jumping into the middle of the solution, Exhibit 2 eliminated several iterations in which divisions were given new penalty/subsidy prices with which to solve their divisional LP programs. The solutions obtained would be anticipated by the corporate program which, in effect, leads the divisions iteratively to the optimum—an optimum it can obtain without any help from the divisions.

2. Central headquarters does not need to know the setups of the divisional problems; it only needs to know contribution margins and feasible solutions.

3. The decomposition principle per se does not bother with sending penalty/subsidy prices to the strata; this is the distinctive characteristic of the transfer pricing problem.

Professor Onsi makes several observations:

1. The best subprogram for division 1 is $(x_1, x_2) = (0, 10)$ for a profit of 80; then, since $x_1 = x_3$, the global constraint calls for $(x_3, x_4) = (0, 5)$ for a total corporate profit of \$105.

2. The best subprogram for division 2 agrees with the end results of Exhibit 2. $(x_1, x_2, x_3, x_4) = (2, 9, 2, 4)$ for a total corporate profit of \$106.

3. Division 1 has been forced to transfer x_1 to division 2 at marginal cost; hence, $c_1 = 0$. This gives division 2 all the profit and is unfair to division 1. An equitable remedy would be to increase the operating budget of division 1 by the \$8 it has forgone by abandoning its best subprogram (profit to division 1 = \$80) and agreeing to the overall optimal program (profit to division 1 = \$72). This \$8 increment in budget is a "motivation" cost. The \$1 increase between present corporate profit (\$106) and the corporate profit resulting if division 1's best program were implemented (\$105) is division 2's additional contribution from further processing x_1. In summary,

	"Old"	"New"	Δ	
Division 1	\$ 80	\$ 72	\$−8	
Division 2	25	34	+9	(8 to division 1, 1 to division 2)
	\$105	\$106	\$+1	

If it happened that a consuming division did not generate an additional contribution, this would indicate that resources should be redirected to other products if possible.

Personal Observations

You may wish to skip the remainder of this section, for I am going to depart from the theories of others and briefly expound my personal views, however heretical they may be.

In this whole area of divisional control, heroic—even herculean—effort has been exerted to make traditional accounting methodology accomplish tasks for which it is unsuited. The traditional model is simply inadequately robust to deal with behavior. In other words, accounting causes more problems than it solves. In part, the present state of affairs exists because of a tradition established in days when knowledge of human behavior was rudimentary and of little concern. In part, the accounting model is used by default—people recognized its limitations but either were unable to come up with something better or could not muster support for a proposed improvement. In part, the model is employed because of the advocacy of certain business schools.

What is going on? Many games are being played, including the budgetary game, the transfer price guessing game (made more obvious by the decomposition procedure), the ROI performance game, and the game of subsidies and penalties (which might be termed the political game). This last is an integral part of all other games. Of course, he who makes the rules has no excuse for losing; so the accountant stands a good chance of coming out ahead.

"Profit" is indeterminate; there are so many ways of arriving at a figure called profit that the term is merely a label for a vague perception. I wince whenever I hear someone say, "The bottom line is what counts." I form a mental image of a gorilla beating its chest, hoping to create the impression of a clear-thinking, tough-minded businessman. It is just so much machismo to sprinkle conversation liberally with words like profit, ROI, and bottom line. To me, all this is the defense mechanism of a person who has succumbed to complexity and has mentally bitten the dust.

Decentralization is illusory. It seems to me that too often divisions are guided through decisions and are apt to have little input when either pursuing a wrong tack or involved with very significant issues. Central headquarters may create the impression that division management has great influence, but this is simply tact. To be in charge only for routine matters is akin to not being in charge at all.

If accounting has caused the transfer pricing problem, perhaps accounting can solve it. Awarding increases in operating budgets as a means of motivation is one example of the variety of bookkeeping adjustments that might be made.

People-created evaluation problems make decentralized profit centers unacceptable to me. As a guiding rule, I would set aside the arbitrary divisions and treat the corporation as a whole. This would bring things back to the primary-secondary overhead allocation level where costs were merely transferred. This amounts to dispensing with profit centers, although I would still provide all centers with revenue data. Thus capital budgeting, "make or buy," production volume, inventory, and similar decisions could be expedited on a departmental basis.

And I would find other measures of performance than ROI—measures that might or might not be in dollar terms. Certainly a manager who has succeeded in smoothing a previously feast-or-famine production schedule has succeeded in stabilizing work force and capital requirements, for instance, and probably deserves praise. The manager who has improved the level of quality—where "improved" may mean lowering actual quality to suit customer demand, as well as "adding to," its usual meaning—has succeeded. The manager who has enhanced service level with no increase in dollar cost also deserves commendation. Along these lines, General Electric Company recognizes these goals:

Profitability	Personnel development
Market position	Employee attitudes
Productivity	Public responsibility
Product leadership	Balance between long- and short-range goals

Some of these goals may conflict, as for instance if profitability and productivity were to increase at the expense of employee morale. (Of course increased profitability and productivity might also increase morale.) But the multiplicity of goals should not prove frustrating—confusing, perhaps, but not frustrating. It would be frustrating to have only a single measure, such as ROI or profit, and to make it do the work where several measures are needed.

I do not think it would be fair to you to leave you with my biases. Therefore, I have asked a good friend, Professor Gerald Zeisel of Boston University, to read this chapter and write an end piece both to fill in missing theory and to present the majority perspective on these matters. Professor Zeisel:

Decentralization and Transfer Prices
by Gerald Zeisel

Those who know Professor Corcoran will not be too surprised by his concluding comments. His dictatorial approach to organizations (I may be as harsh in my criticism of him as he is in his criticism of ROI and transfer pricing) is consistent with his conclusion that all profit centers should be converted into cost centers.

True, ROI is not an unimpeachable measure of performance and transfer prices usually cannot be determined with perfection; but the available evidence does not

continued to page 650

continued from page 649

support the conclusion that these accounting imperfections should result in the elimination of organizational decentralization based on profit centers. There are many reasons for profit center decentralization, including improved motivation, training ground for managers as entrepreneurs, need to make rapid decisions in certain environments, and a decrease in required information flows within the organization. Professor Corcoran's drastic recommendation should only be followed if the costs associated with the dysfunctional aspects of profitability measures and transfer prices exceed the benefits that result from profit center decentralization. In certain organizations this condition probably exists, but the available evidence does not indicate its existence in most settings. Hence, transfer prices are likely to continue to be required, and a student needs to understand transfer pricing theory.

When interrelated organizational subunits operate as profit centers, transfer prices are needed to achieve two primary purposes: (1) to motivate subunit managers to make decisions that are in the best interest of the overall organization (goal congruent behavior), and (2) to evaluate the performance of subunit managers as entrepreneurs. Both of these purposes usually cannot be accomplished by one transfer price. Opportunity costs are relevant transfer prices to achieve the first purpose, whereas market prices are relevant for the second. Market prices are needed so subunit performance can be compared to the performance of other entities operating in similar environments. Only when the market price is the opportunity cost (which it is under conditions of perfect competition, as we shall see) can both purposes be accomplished by one measure. Otherwise, there is a conflict.

In our consideration of the theory of transfer prices we will only examine a few, significant cases—those which will assist the reader to understand the general theory.[9] First we will consider the situation where no outside market exists for the intermediate (transferred) product. Then we will go to the other extreme, where the intermediate product is sold under conditions of perfect competition. Finally we will examine the more realistic case where an outside market exists, but where certain costs are avoided by profit centers that deal with each other. In each of these instances we will determine the best transfer price for purposes of goal congruency, and will then consider the implications of this price on the "net income" performance measure of the profit center.

Exhibit 3 depicts a situation where division P (producing division) transfers an intermediate product (X) to division U (consuming division). MCp represents the marginal cost curve to product X in division P. $NMRPu$ represents the net marginal revenue product in division U from using X. That is, each unit of X when used by U results in a quantity of U's output. The marginal revenue derived from that output less its marginal costs (exclusive of the cost in P) is $NMRPu$ for the unit of X.

In this situation it is advantageous to the overall firm to produce beyond the region where

$$NMRPu > MCp.$$

continued to page 651

[9] These and other situations and an overview are presented by A. R. Abdel-Khalik and E. J. Lusk. "Transfer Pricing—A Synthesis," *The Accounting Review*, January 1974, pp. 8–23.

continued from page 650

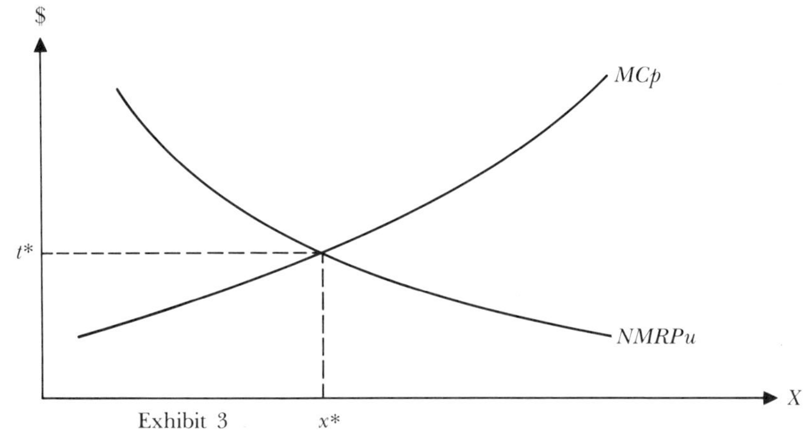

Exhibit 3

but not into the region where

$$NMRPu < MCp,$$

Hence we see that the optimal production is x^*. A transfer price of t^* motivates the profit-maximizing managers of *P* and *U* to produce and demand this amount.

If one wishes to evaluate the performance of the two subunit managers as entrepreneurs, t^* is probably not a satisfactory price. Since there is no outside market for *X*, no market price exists, so we cannot appraise the appropriateness of the profit apportionment that results from the use of t^*.

Further, this situation requires significant intervention on the part of upper-level managers. They must get cost and revenue information from the two divisions and then set a price that, in reality, dictates the production decisions of both subunits. This condition, when combined with the inability to determine a transfer price that can confidently be used to evaluate entrepreneurial performance, significantly detracts from the advantages of profit center decentralization in this situation.

Now let us consider the situation where X is sold in a perfectly competitive market. This is represented in Exhibit 4, with *m* being the market price.

It is advantageous from the viewpoint of the overall firm for *P* to produce *Xp* and for *U* to use *Xu*. Since both subunits can deal in the market at the same price, *m*, any differences between *Xp* and *Xu* can be accounted for by purchases or sales in the market. Hence we see that, in this situation, the market price is not only a good transfer price for performance evaluation but also leads to goal congruent behavior. Further, all of this is achieved without any intervention on the part of upper-level managers.

While the situation just discussed produces a neat solution to the transfer pricing problem, one must be aware that it is not too common. Usually there are costs to buying and selling in a market, so the effective price faced by both subunits is not *m*; instead, the buyer is confronted by a higher price (*m* plus purchasing costs, freight in, etc.), while the seller will realize a lower price (*m* less selling costs). This situation is depicted in

continued to page 652

continued from page 651

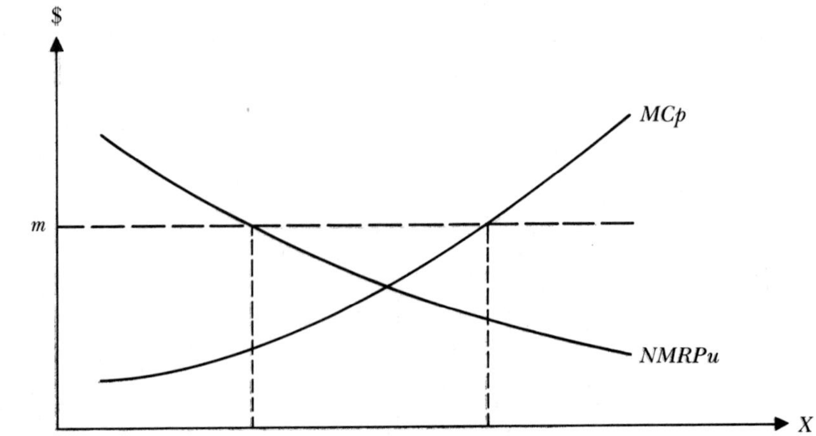

Exhibit 4

A Perfectly Competitive Market

Exhibit 5. $m + b$ represents the gross cost to the buyer, while $m - s$ is the net proceeds realized by the seller.

We see that it is to the overall firm's advantage for P to produce Xp and for U to use Xu. Xu is preferable to any point to its left because if X were sold outside, $m - s$ would be realized, whereas if it were used by U, the benefit to the firm would be $NMRPu$. To achieve this goal congruent behavior, the transfer price should be set at $m - s$.

With this price we have no difficulty in evaluating the performance of P, since $m - s$ is what P would realize if it were in business for itself and everything was sold in the market. However, we have some problem in evaluating U's performance. If U did

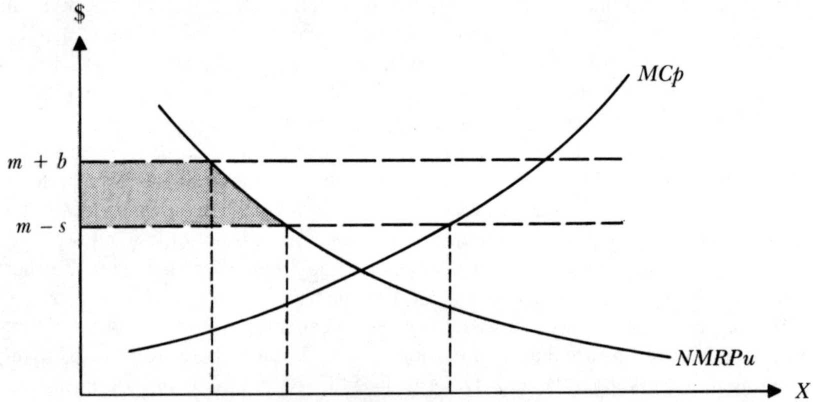

Exhibit 5

Buying and Selling Costs Included

continued to page 653

continued from page 652

not have a relationship with P, U would have to buy at $m + b$ and would only use Xa. Hence we see that the transfer price $m - s$ results in U's profits being greater than they would be if U did not have its relationship with P. The excess profits are represented by the shaded area and make it difficult to use U's profits to evaluate its performance.

It should be pointed out that if the crossing point of MCp and $NMRPu$ was greater than $m + b$, analysis similar to that outlined above would show the goal congruent transfer price to be $m + b$. With this transfer price we would see P usurping all of the excess profits that result from its relationship with U.

We have just examined a few cases in order to convey an understanding of the theory of transfer pricing. Numerous additional works are available to assist the reader in obtaining deeper grasp of the material.[10]

Summary and Concluding Comments

Input-output analysis is an interesting method of forecasting and can be used to study systemwide effects of proposed changes in operating levels. Where the technological coefficients are subject to variation, exponential smoothing may be introduced in the manner illustrated when using Markov chains to predict cash flows from accounts receivable.

ROI, although it is measured in a multitude of different ways from one organization to the next, offers a single measure of overall divisional success.[11] It is subject to manipulation, however, and may motivate inappropriate behavior. Some theorists suggest residual income as a substitute:

Divisional income	\$1,000,000
Cost of capital return on investment (say, 15% × \$4,000,000)	600,000
Residual income	\$ 400,000

Residual income therefore has an imputed interest charge reflected in it. However, it is no panacea. Residual income is subject to quarrels over what should be included in income and investment as well as to shortcomings inherent in calculating the cost of capital. It has the debatable advantage of focusing on amount of income, as opposed to ROI, which focuses on a rate.

[10] In addition to the references previously cited in the chapter, the interested reader should consider J. Hirschleifer, "On the Economics of Transfer Pricing," *Journal of Business*, July 1956, pp. 72–84; J. Ronen and G. McKinney, III, "Transfer Pricing for Divisional Autonomy," *Journal of Accounting Research*, Spring 1970, pp. 99–112; and D. J. H. Watson and J. V. Baumler, "Transfer Pricing: A Behavioral Context," *The Accounting Review*, July 1975, pp. 466–74.

[11] The leading study on ROI and transfer prices is D. Solomons, *Divisional Performance: Measurement and Control* (New York: Financial Executives Research Foundation, 1965).

Transfer pricing is that area in which interdivisional transfers of services are evaluated. A variety of prices are used including market price, adjusted market price, marginal costs, full costs, variable (as a proxy for marginal) costs, executive fiat, negotiated price, and cost plus a percentage return. Transfer pricing raises many complex issues, not all of which are caused by the desire to preserve decentralization and ROI, although most are. For measuring performance, market price (or negotiated price where market is unavailable) is generally preferred. Motivationally, market price or even MPMAC may not be good, and marginal ($\approx$ variable) cost is almost certain to be bad. Here bookkeeping adjustments may be advisable (assuming profit center organization must be retained). For decisionmaking—such as whether to make or buy, or whether to construct a fixed asset for another division—marginal or differential costs are preferable. Again these transfer prices would probably need to be buttressed by bookkeeping adjustments to improve motivation. For financial statements, full cost is advisable so that inventories and fixed assets do not include intracompany profits in their values. Fewer difficulties are encountered if "should be" costs rather than actual costs are always used. In this way the inefficiencies of the supplying division do not become an issue.

There are legal restrictions on transfer pricing. For example, local taxing authorities often insist on full recognition of divisional profit so that local taxes may be as high as possible. Transfer cost is often manipulated to reduce profit in localities with high tax rates.[12]

My own personal preferences are to dispense with ROI and profit center organization, and to develop many measures of performance while retaining a cost center organization. Focus should be on corporate performance and revenue data should be made available to all cost centers. Cost control can be achieved through budgets. This scheme would operate to reduce the number of games in progress and, with luck, the confusion.

Problems

1. *Input-output basics.* The input-output matrix for two industries is

	A	*B*	Outside Sales	Σ
A	100	500	1,400	
B	400	1,000	3,600	

[12] For a discussion of such legal problems, see W. E. Stone, "Legal Implications of Intracompany Transfers," *The Accounting Review*, January 1964, pp. 38–42.

If outside sales for next year are 1,470 and 4,410 respectively, and the technological matrix percentages are thought stable, prepare next year's input-output matrix.

2. *The Farag I-O example.* The actual example in the article by Shawki M. Farag that was summarized in this chapter appears below.

Inputs \ Outputs	Production Departments I	II	III	Sales and Inventory	Output Totals
I	0	30	60	110	200
II	10	0	90	150	250
III	25	25	0	250	300
Raw materials	70	50	30		
Labor	50	55	60		
Overhead	20	40	15		
Profit	25	50	45		
Input Totals	200	250	300		750

If the forecasts for next year are

Department	Sales	Inventory
I	200	100
II	170	30
III	300	100

prepare an I-O table for next year.

3. *ROI.* Discuss return on investment as a divisional manager control technique. Be sure to indicate the advantages and disadvantages of ROI. Suggest ways of remedying shortcomings.

4. *Annuity method of depreciation.* Calculate depreciation using the annuity method and the data given below.

Cost: $320,000 Salvage: $20,000
Life: 6 years Earnings E
Time adjusted return: 20%

Write journal entries to record the first year's transactions.

5. *Transfer prices.* Discuss transfer prices. Set out the problem you intend to solve, comment on the motivational implications of any policy you mention, and suggest means of improving traditional approaches to the problem.

6. *Transfer pricing (prepared by Professor Gerald Zeisel, Boston University).* The XYZ Corporation is made up of two divisions, A and B. A's output is used as an input in B's production. One unit of A is needed to make one unit of B. The total cost function for division A is

$$TC_A(x) = .001x^2 + 1.25x - 100$$

The total cost function for division B, exclusive of the input produced by A, is

$$TC_B(y) = .0005y^2 + 100$$

The output of B is sold in an imperfect market. Its total revenue function is estimated as

$$TR_B(y) = 10y - .005y^2$$

(a) If there is no outside market for the output of A, what transfer price would result in the maximization of firm profits? Show your work.

(b) If the output of A could be sold outside for \$2 per unit, but it would cost B \$2.30 per unit to buy it outside, what transfer price should be set for the output of A to maximize firm profits? Justify your answer.

(c) Same question as (b), only use \$2.40 and \$2.70 as the outside selling and buying prices.

7. *Transfer pricing (prepared by Professor Gerald Zeisel, Boston University).* The Kold-Kare Corporation is a large divisionalized organization. Two of the divisions, P and B, are highly interrelated. Division P produces a product which has no outside market. All of its output is transferred to division B, which uses it as a raw material in the division B production process. The price at which the good is transferred from P is determined (by the controller for Kold-Kare) in order to assure decisions on the part of both division managers that will result in the optimization of overall corporate profits.

At the monthly meeting of all division and corporate managers, the manager of division B announces excitedly: "Due to a development by our division's engineering department, we have been able to make an improvement in our production procedure which will result in the lowering of our division's variable processing costs by 10%." The announcement is very favorably received by other managers. Then the Kold-Kare controller says that he is very happy to hear the news, and that after he gets more specific information about the cost savings he will inform the managers of divisions P and B what the new transfer price will be.

(a) Determine analytically if the new transfer price will be higher or lower than the old one.

(b) How do you think the managers of divisions P and B will react when they are informed of the new transfer price? What are the implications of this case with respect to responsibility accounting and performance evaluation?

(c) Suggest an alternative transfer pricing approach that would avoid the problems created by the one used in this case. Explain how it would avoid the problems.

8. *Decomposition.* The classic illustration of decomposition programming is contained in W. J. Baumol and T. Fabian, "Decomposition, Pricing for Decentralization and External Economies," *Management Science*, September 1964, pp. 1–32. It is presented below. Use the decomposition algorithm to obtain the optimal program.

Maximize $$P = x_1 + x_2 + 2y_1 + y_2$$

Subject to:

$$\begin{aligned} x_1 + 2x_2 + 2y_1 + y_2 &\le 40 \\ x_1 + 3x_2 &\le 30 \\ 2x_1 + x_2 &\le 20 \\ y_1 &\le 10 \\ y_2 &\le 10 \\ y_1 + y_2 &\le 15 \end{aligned}$$

9. *An LP Production Scheduling Problem Involving Interactive Production Processes (prepared by Professor Roland A. Minch, SUNY at Albany).* A chemical manufacturing company makes products 1, 2 and 3 for sale. In making product 1, not only raw materials but also certain amounts of products 2 and 3 are used. Similar statements are true for products 2 and 3. The following data (in physical units) were collected for the last production period:

Production Data

Product Outputs	Product Outputs Used Internally 1	2	3	Net Production	Gross Production
1	0	0	1,250	550	1,800
2	180	0	750	670	1,600
3	360	960	0	1,180	2,500

Cost Data*

Product Outputs	Raw Materials	Labor	Overhead	Total
1	\$32,400	\$21,600	\$18,000	\$72,000
2	19,200	11,200	4,800	35,200
3	7,500	5,000	2,500	15,000

*Standard costs, which comprise only variable expense.

It is assumed that the amount of product i used to make product j is proportional to the gross production level of product j. Raw materials and labor are in abundant supply.

The unit selling price for product 1 is \$70; for product 2, \$50; and for product 3, \$45. For the next production period the capacity for product 1 is 2,000 units; for product 2, 2,000 units; and for product 3, 3,000 units.

The company wishes to use linear programming to develop a production schedule for the next period in order to maximize profit.

(a) Let the decision variable x_j be the *net* production level of product j for the next period. Set up and solve an appropriate linear programming model that will maximize profit (selling price less variable standard cost). (Hint: Let a_{ij} be the amount of product i needed to make one unit of product j; let A be a matrix of the a_{ij}; and let I be an identity matrix. Then the element in the ith row and the jth column of the matrix $(I - A)^{-1}$ gives the number of units of product i that are needed to make one unit of *net* output of product j. Observe that unit profit is the unit selling price less the variable standard cost per unit of *net* output.)

(b) Prepare a production data table similar to the one given that corresponds to the production schedule determined in part (a). Also prepare a table that will show how much money should be budgeted to cover the standard variable costs for each product for the next production period.

(c) Give specific economic interpretations to each of the optimal values of the dual variables associated with the problem in part (a).

(d) Now suppose that the labor supply is limited to 1,000 hours for the next production period. Each unit of *gross* output of product 1 requires 0.2 labor hours; of product 2, 0.3 labor hours; and of product 3, 0.1 labor hours. Answer questions (a), (b), and (c) again taking into account this new restriction.

10. *The managerial ladder (prepared by Mr. Glenn Stowell).* Managers are usually encouraged to run their departments efficiently. If they succeed, they are advanced to higher positions with increased responsibility, status, and pay. One problem associated with this famous managerial ladder is that those ascending it often focus on short-run efficiency in their departments and ignore longer-run consequences. One instance of such behavior would be a manager's purchasing of cheaper equipment that would show markedly improved performance in earlier years of use, but thereafter would become a burden because of increased maintenance, repairs, and downtime. If the manager knew he would be responsible for his department for a prolonged period, he would undoubtedly have acquired more reliable equipment. Because of his apparent high efficiency, he hopes to be promoted, leaving the faltering equipment behind to become his successor's problem. What would you suggest (a) to mitigate this emphasis on efficiency at the expense of effectiveness, and (b) to resolve the conflict between the manager's and the organization's objectives?

11. *Social costs and attitudes (prepared by Mr. Richard Housman).* Since its incorporation a business has been passing the social costs of air, water, and noise pollution onto society. Suppose the SEC announces that all corporations must account for their social costs. Suggest some of the new liabilities that the corporation would have to recognize. How might it change these liabilities to income? Finally, what impact might the inclusion of such costs have on the attitudes of management?

12. *Goal congruence and ROI (Certificate in Management Accounting Examination, December 1973).* A common measure of a management's performance is "return on net worth." This is a particularly important measure from the shareholder's point of view. This ratio can be expressed as the product of three other ratios as shown below:

$$\text{Return on net worth} = \frac{\text{Net income}}{\text{Net worth}} = \overbrace{\frac{\text{Net income}}{\text{Sales}}}^{\text{I}} \times \overbrace{\frac{\text{Sales}}{\text{Assets}}}^{\text{II}} \times \overbrace{\frac{\text{Assets}}{\text{Net worth}}}^{\text{III}}$$

Required:

(a) Discuss the return on net worth as a management goal and as a measurement of management performance.

(b) What management activities are measured by each of the ratios I, II, III?

(c) Would separation of the return on net worth into the three ratios, and use of these ratios for planning targets and performance measures, result in goal congruence (or improvement toward goal congruence) among the responsible managers? Explain your answer.

FROM CHAPTER 16

29. *Integer programming: auditor scheduling (prepared by Professor Andris Zoltners, Northwestern University).* An audit scheduler is faced with the problem of assigning four auditors to twelve engagement tasks over a one month period. The scheduler has compiled the following information (Table 1):

(1) The estimated time required for each auditor to perform each task. An asterisk indicates that the auditor should not be assigned the corresponding task.

(2) A coefficient of difficulty for each task on a scale of 1 to 20.

(3) A competency coefficient for each auditor on a scale of 1 to 20.

If each auditor has 160 hours available over the planning period and each task can be completed by only one auditor, set up (only) a model for assigning the auditors to the tasks so as to match auditor competency and task difficulty. How can the scheduler insure that an auditor is assigned to at most one task per engagement? How can the scheduler insure that two auditors are not assigned to the same engagement? How can the scheduler insure that two concurrent tasks are not performed by the same auditor? How can the scheduler insure that if auditor A performs engagement I, task 1, then he/she will also perform engagement II, task 1?

Table 1

Engagement	Task	Task Difficulty Coefficient	Audit Task Completion Times *A*	*B*	*C*	*D*
I	1	7	32	28	*	45
	2	13	53	50	62	52
	3	13	40	60	44	*
	4	20	*	32	40	*
II	1	5	17	24	12	17
	2	10	62	51	70	55
	3	12	47	52	42	58
III	1	17	60	72	70	57
	2	15	47	47	*	60
⋮	3	18	50	62	60	45
	4	14	41	36	52	*
	5	20	85	97	72	88
Auditor Competency Coefficient			17	14	12	8

LP Applications: Period Budgeting and Package Standards

18

Overview

Our previous discussions of period budgeting and standard costing were necessarily incomplete because we had not yet studied linear programming. Of course, LP will not finish off these subjects for all time, but it will enable us to incorporate combinatorial analysis and thereby reach a higher plane that is at once better theoretically and practically.

In period budgeting, LP will help formulate an overall plan of activities for an entire business and will enable us to study the effects of changing parameters and restrictions. In the process, we shall seize the opportunity to analyze a shadow price in detail.

In standard costing, LP will help the accountant to develop standards for joint products. This has extremely important consequences both for the theory of standard costing and for the practices followed by cost accountants in industry. Companies do not manufacture single products; rather, they make many products that share common corporate facilities. Because this is so, a standard for an individual product is at best an approximation. What is needed is a standard for a package of products, and this standard is apt to change frequently over time. Nevertheless, package standards should be developed—probably using linear programming—and accounting systems should be changed to adopt the optimal results for decisionmaking and control purposes.

LP and Period Budgeting

Many chapters ago we discussed period budgeting and studied how a Markov chain and exponential smoothing might be used to forecast cash flows for budgetary purposes. Let us extend that earlier discussion and introduce an LP perspective. First we must be clear about the distinctions between the approaches.

If you wanted to estimate the cash that customers were going to remit, the Markovian model would hold promise. If, instead, you wished to establish a basic plan that honored all constraints placed upon business transactions, the LP model would be indicated. To formulate a *constraint* on cash collections, you would be wise to forecast cash flow using the Markovian approach. Indeed, without such a restriction, the LP model would allow accounts receivable collections to be whatever was dictated *mutatis mutandis* by all other transactions. This, of course, would be less than useful—except coincidentally—since customers remit according to *their* habits unless the company actively interferes.

Having expressed this caveat, let us proceed to develop the LP model.[1] The objective could be different, but the one that has greatest appeal is to maximize the increase in owners' equity. The constraints will be a mixture of ordinary bookkeeping transactions, marketing, and production limitations. One of the most attractive features of this approach is the relative ease with which the model is formulated—at least, it is easy for the person trained in bookkeeping.

The variables, X_{ij}, in the model will be the amounts of separate bookkeeping transactions, with the first subscript designating the account to be debited and the second the account to be credited. Thus $X_{CA} = 500{,}000$ would be equivalent to writing the entry

Cash	500,000	
Accounts receivable		500,000

To record cash collections.

One other simplification will be used solely to reduce the total number of accounts (variables): temporary accounts will not be recognized. Instead, all revenue and expense transactions will be run through the Owners' Equity account directly rather than through the customary sales and expenses accounts, which must later be closed to Owners' Equity. B_k will designate the balance of account k.

Example:

Beginning Balance Sheet

B_C	Cash	$ 1,000,000	B_L	Liabilities	$ 3,000,000
B_B	Bonds	2,500,000	B_D	Dividends & taxes payable	1,000,000
B_A	Accounts receivable	4,000,000	B_O	Owners'equity	10,000,000
B_I	Inventory	2,100,000			
B_F	Fixed assets	4,400,000			
		$14,000,000			$14,000,000

[1] The following discussion is based on a work that has achieved the status of a classic in accounting literature: Yuji Ijiri, F. K. Levy, and R. C. Lyon, "A Linear Programming Model for Budgeting and Financial Planning," *Journal of Accounting Research*, Autumn 1963, pp. 198–212.

Exhibit 1

		X_{AO}	X_{OI}	X_{CB}	X_{CO}	X_{CA}	X_{BC}	X_{IL}	X_{LC}	X_{OL}	X_{DC}	X_{OF}	X_{OD}														
Constraints	0	1	−1	0	1	0	0	0	0	−1	0	−1	−1	0	−10	0	−10	0	0	0	−10	−10	−10	−10	0	0	−10
	X_0	X_1	X_2	X_3	X_4	X_5	X_6	X_7	X_8	X_9	X_{10}	X_{11}	X_{12}	S_1	A_1	S_2	A_2	S_3	S_4	S_5	A_3	A_4	A_5	A_6	S_6	S_7	A_7
Sales	3,150,000	1												1													
Cost of Sales	0	−2/3	1												1												
Bond Sales	2,500,000			1												1											
Interest Income	12,500			.005	1		−.005										1										
Collections	2,000,000					1												1									
Bond Purchases	1,000,000						1												1								
Merchandise Purchases	1,500,000							1												1							
Payments—Liab.	3,000,000								1	−1											1						
—Div. & Taxes	1,000,000										1		−1									1					
Depreciation	44,000											1											1				
A & G Expenses	400,000							−.1		1														1			
Ending Inventory	300,000		1					−1																	1		
Cash Balance	250,000			−1	−1	−1	1		1		1															1	
Taxes & Dividends	0	−.6	.6		−.6					.6		.6	1														1

Exhibit 2

		X_{AO}	X_{OI}	X_{CB}	X_{CO}	X_{CA}	X_{BC}	X_{IL}	X_{LC}	X_{OL}	X_{DC}	X_{OF}	X_{OD}														
	0	1	−1	0	1	0	0	0	0	−1	0	−1	−1	0	−10	0	−10	0	0	0	−10	−10	−10	−10	0	0	−10
	X_0	X_1	X_2	X_3	X_4	X_5	X_6	X_7	X_8	X_9	X_{10}	X_{11}	X_{12}	S_1	A_1	S_2	A_2	S_3	S_4	S_5	A_3	A_4	A_5	A_6	S_6	S_7	A_7
0 S_1	450,000.00	0	0	0	0	0	0	0	0	0	0	0	0	1	1.5	0	0	0	0	−1.50000000	0	0	0	0	−1.5	0	0
−1 X_2	1,800,000.00	0	1	0	0	0	0	0	0	0	0	0	0	0	0	0	0	0	0	1.00000000	0	0	0	0	1	0	0
0 S_2	16,432.87	0	0	0	0	0	1	0	0	0	0	0	0	0	.902	1	.401	1.002	0	−.34068136	−1.002	−1.002	.601	−.401	−.301	1.002	−1.002
1 X_4	82.17	0	0	0	1	0	0	0	0	0	0	0	0	0	.005	0	1.002	.005	0	−.00170341	−.005	−.005	.003	−.002	−.002	.005	−.005
0 X_8	3,550,000.00	0	0	0	0	0	0	0	1	0	0	0	0	0	0	0	0	0	0	.10000000	1	0	0	1	0	0	0
0 S_4	1,000,000.00	0	0	0	0	0	1	0	0	0	0	0	0	0	0	0	0	1	1	0	0	0	0	0	0	0	0
−1 X_{12}	183,649.30	0	0	0	0	0	0	0	0	0	0	0	1	0	−.897	0	.601	.003	0	.23897796	−.003	−.003	−.598	−.601	.299	.003	.997
0 X_3	2,483,567.13	0	0	1	0	0	−1	0	0	0	0	0	0	0	−.902	0	−.401	−1.002	0	.34068136	1.002	1.002	−.601	.401	.301	−1.002	1.002
0 X_5	2,000,000.00	0	0	0	0	1	0	0	0	0	0	0	0	0	0	0	0	1	0	0	0	0	0	0	0	0	0
1 X_1	2,700,000.00	1	0	0	0	0	0	0	0	0	0	0	0	0	−1.5	0	0	0	0	1.50000000	0	0	0	0	1.5	0	0
0 X_7	1,500,000.00	0	0	0	0	0	0	1	0	0	0	0	0	0	0	0	0	0	0	1.00000000	0	0	0	0	0	0	0
−1 X_9	550,000.00	0	0	0	0	0	0	0	0	1	0	0	0	0	0	0	0	0	0	.10000000	0	0	0	1	0	0	0
0 X_{10}	1,183,649.30	0	0	0	0	0	0	0	0	0	1	0	0	0	−.897	0	.601	.003	0	.23897796	−.003	.997	−.598	−.601	.299	.003	.997
−1 X_{11}	44,000.00	0	0	0	0	0	0	0	0	0	0	1	0	0	0	0	0	0	0	0	0	0	1	0	0	0	0
$z_j - c_j$	122,432.87	0	0	0	0	0	0	0	0	0	0	0	0	0	9.402	0	10.401	.002	0	.15931863	9.998	9.998	9.601	9.599	.199	.002	8.998

Summary of transactions:

X_{CI} = Cost of sales	=	$1,800,000.00
X_{CO} = Interest income	=	82.17
X_{LC} = Payment of liabilities	=	3,550,000.00
X_{OD} = Dividends & taxes	=	183,649.30
X_{CB} = Sale of bonds	=	2,483,567.13
X_{CA} = Collections	=	2,000,000.00
X_{AO} = Sales	=	2,700,000.00
X_{IL} = Purchasing costs	=	1,500,000.00
X_{OL} = A & G expenses	=	550,000.00
X_{DC} = Payment of div. & taxes	=	1,183,649.30
X_{OF} = Depreciation	=	44,000.00

Retained Earnings Increase Statement

Sales		$2,700,000.00
Cost of Sales		1,800,000.00
GROSS PROFIT		$ 900,000.00
Expenses:		
A & G	$550,000.00	
Depreciation	44,000.00	594,000.00
NET OPERATING PROFIT		$ 306,000.00
Interest income		82.17
NET PROFIT BEFORE D&T		$ 306.082.17
Dividends & taxes		183,649.30
NET INCREASE		$ 122,432.87

Balance Sheet

Cash	$ 750,000.00
Bonds	16,432.87
Accounts receivable	4,700,000.00
Inventory	1,800,000.00
Fixed assets	4,356,000.00
TOTAL	$11,622,432.87
Accounts payable	$ 1,500,000.00
Owners'equity	10,122,432.87
TOTAL	$11,622,432.87

Constraints	Transactions and Limitations
$X_{AO} \leq \frac{3}{2}B_I$ $X_{OI} = \frac{2}{3}X_{AO}$	Sales must be less than or equal to beginning inventory balance because of delivery time. Markup is 50% of cost.
$X_{CB} \leq B_B$	Sales of bonds must not exceed beginning balance.
$X_{CO} = .005B'_B$	Interest income equals .5% of ending balance of bonds, where $B'_B = B_B + X_{BC} - X_{CB}$, and is to be received in cash.
$X_{CA} \leq .5B_A$	Collections are from beginning receivables and are not expected to exceed 50% thereof.
$X_{BC} \leq B_C$	By policy, security purchases cannot exceed beginning cash.
$X_{IL} \leq 1{,}500{,}000$	Purchasing (merchandise) budgetary limit is $1,500,000.
$X_{LC} \leq B_L + X_{OL}$	Liability repayment is to improve current ratio; hence repayment is to equal beginning balance plus administrative and general expenses that arise this month.
$X_{DC} = B_D + X_{OD}$	Taxes and dividends accrued both from last month and this must be paid.
$X_{OF} = .01B_F$	Depreciation equals 1% of beginning fixed assets.
$X_{OL} = 400{,}000 + 1X_{IL}$	Administrative and general expenses (other than depreciation) obey the regression formula. Expenses = fixed + variable (as related to purchasing costs).
$B_I + X_{IL} - X_{OI} \geq 1{,}800{,}000$	Purchasing should be such that at least $1,800,000 of inventory is on hand at the end of the month.
$B_C + X_{CA} - X_{LC} - X_{BC} + X_{CB} - X_{DC} + X_{CO} \geq 750{,}000$	A minimum cash balance of $750,000 must be maintained.
$X_{OD} = .6(X_{AO} + X_{CO} - X_{OL} - X_{OI} - X_{OF})$	Taxes and dividends are to be estimated at 60% of net profit.

The objective function is to maximize the increase in Owners' Equity; therefore,

$$\text{Max } Z = X_{AO} - X_{OI} + X_{CO} - X_{OL} - X_{OF} - X_{OD}$$

When the constraints are put in their simplest form (by multiplying by -1 to reverse $\geq$), the beginning tableau is as shown in Exhibit 1. The transaction variables have been renumbered in the appropriate column headings.

The optimal solution appears in Exhibit 2 along with a summary of transactions and forecasted financial statements. All amounts in the body of the tableau have been rounded to three decimal places, except for column S_5, which will receive further attention shortly. All transactions honor the constraints in *mutatis mutandis* fashion. Thus while there was sufficient inventory on hand at the beginning of the month to permit sales of $3,150,000, the budgetary limitation on purchases and the need to have $1,800,000 of inventory available at the end of the month together served to restrict sales to $2,700,000. Also, as desired, the current ratio (current assets/current liabilities) has improved from 9,600,000/4,000,000 to 7,266,432.87/1,500,000. Furthermore, the basis for planning the coming month's activities is available; for example, the Purchasing Department may be told how much to acquire ($1,500,000).

From a theoretical perspective, however, the most intriguing results appear trivial. Planning can be done using the shadow prices. In particular, Exhibit 3 goes into the development of the purchasing shadow price and what it would mean if the Purchasing Department were allowed to spend $1 more (that is, $1,500,001). For this dollar, the increase in retained earnings would be .16 (that is, $.15931863), which seems to be a very respectable return for one month. When you have perused Exhibit 3, you will realize that the most interesting number on the financial statements is also the smallest: Interest income = $82.17.

Why should such an insignificant amount even be worthy of comment? When money is needed to satisfy the minimum cash balance requirement, it is raised by cashing bonds. This, in turn, reduces interest income, which violates the minimum balance, which requires that additional money be raised by cashing more bonds. The process repeats itself ad infinitum. Thus

Exhibit 3 Analysis of Purchasing Budget Shadow Price (S_5)

First approach (based on optimal tableau).

Consult the S_5 column in Exhibit 2. Using only the nonzero c_i, rearranging sequence, and labelling yields

	c_i	λ_{iS_5}		
Sales	1	(1.5)	=	$ 1.50000000
Cost of sales	−1	(1)	=	−1.00000000
GROSS PROFIT				$ .50000000
A & G expenses	−1	(.1)	=	−.10000000
NET OPERATING PROFIT				$ .40000000
Interest income	1	(−.00170341)	=	−.00170341
				$ .39829659
Dividends and taxes	−1	(.23897796)	=	−.23897796 (= .6 × .39829659)
PURCHASING BUDGET SHADOW PRICE				$ .15931863

Where does the .00170341 interest income figure come from? It is the opportunity cost of interest earnings forgone because cash must both be expended and raised to meet the minimum balance requirement. Just as no cash is provided by period sales, so no cash is needed for merchandise costs, since $2,100,000 − $1,800,000 remains from opening inventory.

Feedback loop: When money is needed, it is raised by selling bonds, which causes the interest income to decline and violates the minimum cash balance requirement. Say [\$$a$] are needed. This reduces interest by [a(.005)] leaving cash short by that amount; consequently, [a(.005)] of bonds must be sold. This reduces interest income by [a(.005)].005, which depletes the required cash balance. The series continues ad infinitum and equals

$$a(.005) + a(.005)^2 + \cdots = a \sum_{i=1}^{\infty} .005^i$$

$$= a\Delta^{-1}.005^i]_1^{\infty}$$

$$= a\left[\frac{.005^i}{.005 - 1}\right]_1^{\infty} = a\left(\frac{-.005}{-.995}\right)$$

$$= a(.0050251256).$$

Analysis:		
Cash outlays—A & G		\$ .10000000
—Dividends & taxes		.23897796
		\$ .33897796
Interest forgone in perpetuity		× .0050251256
Interest income forgone		\$ .00170341 (to 8 places)

Second approach (ignoring λ_{is_5} in optimal tableau).

NET OPERATING PROFIT (as before)		\$ .40000000
Dividends and taxes (60%)		−.24000000
		\$ .16000000
Opportunity cost of interest forgone on cash outlays:		
A & G	\$ .10000000	
Dividends & taxes	.24000000	
	\$ .34000000	
Perpetuity rate*	× .002004008	
OPPORTUNITY COST		−.00068136 (to 8 places)
PURCHASING BUDGET SHADOW PRICE		\$ .15931864

* The perpetuity rate here is *net after dividends and taxes*:

$$\sum_{i=1}^{\infty} [.4(.005)]^i$$

a very innocuous figure arises from a feedback loop and acquires a certain dignity theoretically.

Exhibit 3 has been prepared from two viewpoints purely to satisfy the reader who wants a justification of shadow prices that relies on reasoning external to all linear programming considerations—in other words, for the Doubting Thomas who lacks faith. I hope that if you are such a reader, you are now a believer.

Summary and Conclusions—LP and Period Budgeting

Coordinating all policies, goals, and limitations while preparing a company's budget would be a most challenging task without mathematical programming—if, indeed, it could be accomplished at all. Where variables are random, preliminary analysis should be conducted to develop meaningful range constraints for an LP formulation. But all sorts of relationships may be reflected in keeping with the dictates of production, marketing, and financial theories. Thus minimal turnovers, current ratios, and debt-equity ratios may be specified, for example, and the program will honor them, provided greed is not so excessive as to eliminate feasibility.

The shadow prices may be very useful in deciding which constraint or constraints to relax. In view of the comments on Exhibit 3, one might think that lowering the minimum cash balance would be the most desirable action. Exhibit 2 shows, however, that "easing" cash balance ($z_{S_7} - c_{S_7} = .002$) is not nearly as promising as "easing" ending inventory ($z_{S_6} - c_{S_6} = .199$) or purchasing budget ($z_{S_5} - c_{S_5} = .159$). Parametric programming analysis of the capacities shows that if ending inventory is reduced to $1,745,333.31, profit can be increased by about $10,900 (that is, $54,666.69 × .19937879). This is the best that can be done, and it amounts to an 8.9% increase in profit for reducing ending inventory by about $55,000. Care to use parametric programming to see what would happen if two or more constraints were relaxed simultaneously?

Extending Standard Costing by LP

Chapter 8 concluded with (1) an observation that, where joint products are manufactured, individual product standards are theoretically impossible; and (2) a promise to show how to set package standards using linear programming. Let us return to the sawmill and use its joint products to illustrate. Figure 1 may help you to visualize some of these products. In addition to the products depicted there, the sawmill would also produce chips and sawdust.

Situation (Simplified): A sawmill has five main pieces of equipment: debarker, headrig, edger, trimmer, and chipper. Four patterns—like that shown in Figure 1—may be cut to produce two dimension grades (1 and 2), boards, chips, bark, and sawdust. Logs come in 12-inch and 14-inch diameters.

Debarking the log is essential to its full utilization because bark cannot be used for papermaking, and therefore any piece dropped in the chipper has to be free of bark. But the bark can be used for fuel and soil mulch.

The rounded sides of the log, called "slabs," are the first pieces sent to the chipper as the log goes through the sawmill. This idealized picture shows the entire log being used for lumber, except for the slabs. Actually, as cutting continues, other pieces go to the chipper, including edgings, trim ends, and other parts of the log not usable as lumber.

The outer portions of the log have the fewest knots. This "clear" lumber is usually made into boards or planks of varying thickness.

Toward the center of the log, knots increase and the wood is less suitable for boards. Heavier planks, and square or rectangular beams are normally sawed from this section. The center of the log is used primarily for structural beams strong enough so that they are not weakened by knots. Knots are most frequent here because this is the oldest section of the tree. Branches that were removed during the early years of the tree's life left knots that were covered over as the tree grew outward.

Plywood is, in effect, a sandwich of thin wooden veneers. Veneer is made by "peeling," that is, holding a long blade against a rotating log. The wood is continuously peeled off, down to an eight-inch core. The core is then treated as though it were a small log. It can be made into lumber and, of course, the rounded portions go to the chipper.

Figure 1 How the log is used

Scheme: The sawmill has cut the various patterns many times in the past; regression was used to obtain their production times and yields. (Note that it takes longer to cut 1,000 board feet of 12″ logs than it does to cut 1,000 board feet of 14″ logs; the bigger the dimension and the longer the log, the less work is needed to obtain a given amount of output.)

The yields for each pattern are expressed as decimals below; rows sum to 1.

	Diameter	Grades 1	Grades 2	Boards	Chips	Bark	Sawdust
Pattern 1	14″	.10	.30	.15	.30	.10	.05
Pattern 2	12″	.08	.25	.22	.29	.10	.06
Pattern 3	14″	.20	.30	0	.32	.10	.08
Pattern 4	12″	.15	.14	.20	.30	.10	.11

Time (minutes) requirements per MBF (1,000 board feet) are

	Debarker	Headrig	Edger	Trimmer	Chipper
Pattern 1	1.6	8.4	5.0	3.0	6.2
Pattern 2	3.2	12.7	8.3	4.8	5.4
Pattern 3	1.6	8.0	4.2	3.2	6.5
Pattern 4	3.2	12.5	8.7	5.0	5.4

Each machine has 57 minutes available per hour.

Desired market proportions for output:

Grade 1 $\geq$ 10% of total output
Grade 2 $\geq$ 20% of total output
Boards $\geq$ 16% of total output
Chips $\geq$ 30% of total output
Grade 1 $\leq$ 15% of total output

Revenues (net of log costs):

Patterns 1, 2, 3, 4 = \$74, \$80, \$70, and \$73 respectively per MBF

Solution: x_i = pattern i, in MBF

S_i = slack i

$$\text{Total output} = \sum_{i=1}^{4} x_i$$

The yield and market constraints can be combined; for example, grade 1 lower limit:

$$.10x_1 + .08x_2 + .20x_3 + .15x_4 \geq .10\sum x_i$$

So $$0x_1 - .02x_2 + .10x_3 + .05x_4 \geq 0$$

Or $$0x_1 + .02x_2 - .10x_3 - .05x_4 \leq 0$$

The initial tableau with constraints reflected is shown in Exhibit 4.

Exhibit 4 Tableau 1

	0	\$74	\$80	\$70	\$73	0	0	0	0	0	0	0	0	0	0
	x_0	x_1	x_2	x_3	x_4	S_1	S_2	S_3	S_4	S_5	S_6	S_7	S_8	S_9	S_{10}
Time—debarker	57	1.6	3.2	1.6	3.2	1									
—headrig	57	8.4	12.7	8.0	12.5		1								
—edger	57	5.0	8.3	4.2	8.7			1							
—trimmer	57	3.0	4.8	3.2	5.0				1						
—chipper	57	6.2	5.4	6.5	5.4					1					
Grade 1	0	0	.02	−.10	−.05						1				
Grade 1	0	−.05	−.07	.05	0							1			
Grade 2	0	−.10	−.05	−.10	.06								1		
Boards	0	.01	−.06	.16	−.04									1	
Chips	0	0	.01	−.02	0										1

The optimal solution is shown in Exhibit 5. Since $x_1 = 4.95$ MBF, $x_2 =$ 0 MBF, $x_3 = 0\ MBF$, and $x_4 = 1.24$ MBF, we know that 4.95 MBF $(x_1 + x_3)$ of 14″ logs and 1.24 MBF $(x_2 + x_4)$ of 12″ logs are needed each hour. The inventory yields—based on the yield data—per hour in board feet of each product are

Pattern	Grade 1	Grade 2	Boards	Chips	Bark	Sawdust
x_1	495	1,485	743	1,485	495	247
x_2	-0-	-0-	-0-	-0-	-0-	-0-
x_3	-0-	-0-	-0-	-0-	-0-	-0-
x_4	186	174	248	372	124	136
Totals	681	1,659	991	1,857	619	383

Hourly profit with these yields in \$456.25. The slack times (unused capacity) out of every 57 minutes are 45, 22, 36, and 20 minutes for the debarker, edger, trimmer, and chipper respectively. Another minute of time on the headrig would be worth \$8.00 according to the S_2 shadow price.

Exhibit 5 Optimal Tableau

c_j		0	\$74	\$80	\$70	\$73	0	0	0	0	0	0	0	0	0	0
c_i		x_0	x_1	x_2	x_3	x_4	S_1	S_2	S_3	S_4	S_5	S_6	S_7	S_8	S_9	S_{10}
0	S_1	45.13	0	0	1.64	0	1	−.21	0	0	0	0	0	0	14.92	34.01
73	x_4	1.24	0	0	0	1	0	.02	0	0	0	0	0	0	−18.22	−136.88
0	S_3	21.51	0	0	.92	0	0	−.62	1	0	0	0	0	0	22.95	98.35
0	S_4	35.98	0	0	.87	0	0	−.37	0	1	0	0	0	0	9.76	46.90
0	S_5	19.66	0	0	−7.37	0	0	−.66	0	0	1	0	0	0	−69.72	−126.33
0	S_6	.06	0	0	− .06	0	0	0	0	0	0	1	0	0	− .91	− 8.84
0	S_7	.25	0	0	.11	0	0	0	0	0	0	0	1	0	1.36	9.62
0	S_8	.42	0	0	.20	0	0	.01	0	0	0	0	0	1	3.80	18.46
74	x_1	4.95	1	0	3.98	0	0	.09	0	0	0	0	0	0	27.11	52.49
80	x_2	0	0	1	−2.00	0	0	0	0	0	0	0	0	0	0	100.00
$z_j - c_j$		456.25	0	0	64.40	0	0	8.00	0	0	0	0	0	0	676.36	1,892.62

What has been accomplished from the standpoint of managerial accounting?

1. The best program for all the possible combinations of joint products has been determined—assuming all promising patterns were originally identified for analysis.
2. The best use of available equipment has been determined from among all possible combinations.
3. The package standard is at hand that gives not only target equivalent production but *target equivalent production by products.* Under traditional standard costing, the assumption might unthinkingly be made that the most praiseworthy thing to do is to consider market value only, and to make the most of the highest-priced product.
4. All constraints on yield, time, and market have been honored.
5. The bottleneck and slack equipment have been identified to facilitate control. Efficiency on bottleneck equipment is important, while efficiency on slack equipment is of little concern—except possibly from the standpoint of morale.
6. The undesirable patterns have been segregated, and their potential effect on program and profit—as reflected in their shadow prices and linear combination scalars—has been calculated. Someone who favors one of these patterns can be informed of its potential consequences.
7. The potential gain from easing bottlenecks is known—again as reflected in the shadow prices. If less than the full 57 minutes is worked each hour,

variance analysis can be carried out using these shadow prices to measure forgone profits—this is far more appealing than traditional variance analysis, which merely reflects excess labor costs and unabsorbed overhead costs.[2]

What steps should the accountant take at this point?

1. If the outputs were not achieved as called for by the program, reasons for significant differences should be sought. Thus variance analysis and control can be done in terms of equivalent units rather than dollars.

   The prospects for eliminating the headrig bottleneck should be investigated. If the headrig can be used 60 minutes an hour, this would be worth an additional $8 per extra minute or $24 for three extra minutes each hour. If a constraint can be relaxed—for instance, by reducing market proportion for boards from 16% to 15%, profit per hour increases to $502.14, which still leaves the headrig as a bottleneck but now with an increased shadow price of $8.81 per minute. If a second headrig is added, 114 minutes become available for an hourly profit of $716.38 and 21 idle minutes (out of 114 minutes) on the pair of headrigs. With a second headrig, the edger and chipper become bottleneck equipment with shadow prices of $3.27 and $9.30 respectively. Can a second headrig be installed at a normalized cost of less than $214.24 (that is, $716.38 – $502.14)? Could the increased output be marketed? Could the mill acquire some piece of equipment like the headrig but with less capacity (say, some sort of linebar saw) that obtains the added profit without creating idle time and the new bottlenecks? Without new equipment, would it be possible to have workers on idle equipment switch to expediting headrig activity—as time permitted—thereby reducing sawing time? (Some of these questions have been answered by experimenting with a computer program.)

3. To prepare financial statements, market values could be employed in the usual manner to determine unit costs—as described in the discussion of joint costing in Chapter 7.

The package standards would change in time as constraints, costs, prices, and sawing times changed. The resulting dynamic standards, however, would be in the best tradition of accounting theory—the best would be done with the resources available.

Note that other formulations of this problem are possible, and that LP computer programs usually also provide information on how much each

[2] This use of LP was first suggested by J. M. Samuels, "Opportunity Costing: An Application of Mathematical Programming," *Journal of Accounting Research*, Autumn 1965, p. 185.

pattern's net revenue can change before the present production program ($x_1 = 4.95$ MBF, $x_2 = x_3 = 0$ MBF, and $x_4 = 1.24$ MBF) should be set aside.

Summary and Conclusions—Package Standards

Package standards should supplant the ordinary conceptions of individual product standards in *all* factories, although they need not be developed by *linear* programming. Why so? The company that makes only one product is a rarity, if it exists at all. Consequently, several products are made in any given factory, and they share facilities, company image, and time.

Even if products were made separately at different times, when one product was manufactured, others would be delayed; collectively, products share time when time is viewed as a span instead of a long series of instants. And products are also interrelated from the standpoints of complementarity and substitutability. When one is sold, the company's reputation is enhanced or diminished—be it ever so little—and this affects the sales of the others. Factories cannot avoid jointness no matter how they strive for an illusion of separateness.

Combinations are a fact of life. What products should be made on which machines? When? How much?

What is the best we can do with the facilities available? This is what a standard is (or should be) in keeping with the best traditions of accounting. And once this is accepted, the messages for accounting are clear:

1. Discard individual standards.
2. Develop package standards.

Developing package standards calls for regression analysis and probably for linear programming. Dynamic programming and nonlinear programming may supplant linear programming, although the latter seems to be the more practical formulation. Some form of mathematical programming is dictated by the immense number of combinations; furthermore, the frequent changing of constraints compels the resulting package standards to be dynamic.

Individual standards? Ridiculous!

Problems

1. *LP and budgeting in a manufacturing concern.* Shown below are a balance sheet dated July 31 and a statement of transactions and restrictions for the month of August. Prepare pro forma statements for August that reflect optimal budgetary allocations.

Balance Sheet
July 31, 1978

Cash	$ 470,000	Accounts Payable	$ 1,660,000
Securities	2,720,000	Accrued Expenses	480,000
Accounts Receivable	2,875,000	Dividends Payable	360,000
Inventories: Raw Materials	415,000	Owner's Equity	7,500,000
Work in Process	500,000		
Finished Goods	1,520,000		
Prepaid Expenses	120,000		
Fixed Assets (net)	1,380,000		
	$10,000,000		$10,000,000

Transactions and Limitations:

(a) Sales (all on credit) cannot exceed beginning inventory plus one-half of August's completed production. Markup is 100% of cost.

(b) Security sales may not exceed beginning balance of securities.

(c) Security income equals .7% of ending balance of securities and is received in cash.

(d) Collections may be as high as 60% of beginning receivables and are certainly at least 50%.

(e) Security purchases may not exceed beginning cash.

(f) Beginning liabilities—other than dividends—are to be paid.

(g) Raw material purchases (on account) may be no greater than $1,000,000.

(h) The value of raw materials inventory must be at least $200,000 to satisfy demand during leadtime and thereby avoid shutdown.

(i) Raw material requisitions equal 30% of production costs where "production costs" are defined to be costs incurred during month and overhead is included on an absorbed rather than as actual basis.

(j) Direct labor equals 40% of production costs; 90% will be paid (net of 15% payroll taxes), while the balance will be accrued.

(k) Overhead will be absorbed at 75% of direct labor. Underabsorbed or overabsorbed overhead may be treated as an adjustment to income.

(l) Depreciation equals $58,000, of which $8,000 is selling and administrative and the balance is factory related.

(m) Production should be such that at least $1,500,000 of finished goods is on hand at the end of August.

(n) Insurance and property taxes, which have been prepaid, amount to $30,000 for August (75% factory, 25% selling and administrative).

(o) It is expected that 10% of total production costs will be associated with units still in process at the month's end; furthermore, no more production than is represented by $3,200,000 of *total* production costs can be *completed* in August with existing facilities.

(p) Other administrative and general expenses, which must be paid in cash, amount to 10% of sales, while other expected actual overhead costs—which must also be paid in cash—equal 60% of direct labor.

(q) A minimum cash balance of $400,000 must be maintained with any cash in excess of $500,000 being used to acquire securities.

(r) Taxes are to be accrued at 60% of net income.

(s) The ratio of liabilities to owners' equity is not to increase.

(t) The increase in owners' equity is to be maximized.

2. *Refer to Problem* 1. Given the columns below from the optimal solution, analyze the shadow price for the minimum inventory constraint.

Key:

C(cash); A(accounts receivable); S(securities); R(raw materials); W(work in process); G(finished goods); PP(prepaid expenses); F(fixed assets); P(accounts payable); AC(accrued expenses); O(owners' equity).

Solution Stub			Minimum Inventory Constraint Variable
0	X_{RP}	= 671,840.7070	− .4897
−1	X_{OG}	= 3,075,261.0581	.7654
0	S_2	= 146,926.1868	−1.0894
−1	$X_{O,PP}$	= 30,000.0000	0
0	S_4	= 287,500.0000	0
0	X_{PC}	= 1,660,000.0000	0
0	S_5	= 470,000.0000	0
0	X_{CS}	= 2,573,073.8132	1.0894
0	X_{CA}	= 1,725,000.0000	0
0	S_6	= 328,159.2930	.4897
0	S_7	= .0016	0
0	X_{WC}	= 904,577.5211	.5205
0	$X_{W,AC}$	= 277,876.7519	.1599
1	X_{WO}	= 886,840.7048	.5103
−1	X_{OF}	= 58,000.0000	0
−1	$X_{O,AC}$	= 1,530,363.2825	.4241
0	S_9	= 89,477.8837	−1.5309
1	X_{AO}	= 6,150,522.1163	1.5309
1	X_{CO}	= 1,028.4833	−.0076
0	$X_{AC,C}$	= 480,000.0000	0
−1	X_{OC}	= 1,324,524.7754	.5613
0	S_8	= 55,261.0581	.7654
0	X_{WR}	= 886,840.7070	.5103
0	X_{GW}	= 3,110,522.1163	1.5309
	$z_j - c_j$	= 1,020,242.1883	.2827

3. *Regression and LP Constraints.*

(a) When a log is sawed on a headrig, the time required is determined by the thickness and length of the log, the grade of the log, its position in the tree, the density of its growth rings, its irregularities, the number of times the log must be turned in the carriage to position it for sawing, and the number and depth of cuts. Time study data could include observations on all these variables; however, it seems that the percentage of boards cut would have high correlation with many of these variables, including number and depth of cuts and log grade and position. Consequently, the data given below show $(L, B, W, T) =$ (length, percentage of boards, diameter, sawing time in minutes). Fit a curve of the form $T = \alpha + \beta(LBW)$ to these data.

(14′, .6, 18″, 1.49)	(14′, .2, 20″, 1.51)
(18′, .7, 18″, 1.91)	(16′, .5, 18″, 1.69)
(16′, .5, 15″, 2.00)	(16′, .4, 14″, 1.58)
(20′, .8, 20″, 2.25)	(20′, .7, 20″, 1.96)
(18′, .4, 15″, 1.62)	(18′, .6, 18″, 1.79)
(14′, .3, 12″, 1.50)	(18′, .3, 21″, 1.63)

(b) If trees were uniform cylinders free of defects, sawmill operators would become euphoric, for among other things, this would simplify the calculation of the board feet (12″ × 12″ × 1″ = 144 in.^{3}) in a log. In reality, trees taper, and this complicates calculations. A formula for estimating board footage may be obtained by (1) considering a tree as the addition of the areas of an infinite number of infinitesimally thin wafers having varying diameters; (2) reflecting all parameters in inches: and (3) dividing by 144:

$$\text{Board footage} = \frac{1}{144}\int_0^L \int_0^{R-\alpha l} 2\pi r \, dr \, dl$$

where $L =$ log length; $l =$ length variable
$R =$ greatest radius; $r =$ radius variable
$\alpha =$ taper coefficient; $\pi = 22/7$

If an *average* log is 16′ long and 15″ in diameter, and consists of 30% boards, use the results of (a) and $\alpha = .00625$ in the board footage formula to estimate the time needed to saw 1,000 board feet.

4. *LP and a lumber mill: alternate formulation.** Instead of choosing among sawing patterns, it is possible to focus on the different input logs that are available. There are four attributes other than tree specie that serve to distinguish logs: position in tree (butt or upper), diameter, grain (dense or open, depending on the number of annual growth rings per inch), and grade. A lumber company would know the percentage of logs in its inventory that possessed the varying attributes. To keep

* This problem is a simplification of C. Row, C. Fasick, and S. Guttenberg, *Improving Sawmill Profits Through Operations Research* (U.S. Forest Service Research Paper SO-20, 1965).

the size of this problem reasonable, it will be assumed that all logs are butt logs either 15″ or 18″ in diameter, and that there are only two grades: premium and other. The log input distribution is then

	Grades				
	Premium		Other		
Log Size	Dense	Open	Dense	Open	Σ
18″ Butt	.07	.02	.01	.10	.20
15″ Butt	—	—	.35	.45	.80
					1.00

As much as 20 MBF (MBF = 1,000 board feet) are available each hour at a log cost of $50 per MBF. Here board feet are measured in log scale. Lumber scale is an output measure and is invariably greater than the associated log scale estimate (because International scale is not employed).

It would be possible to perform regression analysis (as in problem 3) on each type of log input, but this would require a large number of logs of each type and extensive study time. Moreover, management believes that the diameter attribute has by far the most influence on sawing time, because the vast majority of logs of a given diameter are "bucked" (sawed) for standard length in the forest. Then, assuming any given log follows one of two paths (processes) through the mill, the sawing times per MBF are

	18″ Logs		15″ Logs	
	Process 1	Process 2	Process 1	Process 2
Debarker	1.0	1.0	2.0	2.0
Headsaw	3.4	3.4	5.3	5.3
Linebar	5.8	4.8	7.8	6.2
Resaw	2.6	2.8	4.0	4.1
Edger	3.5	3.5	5.4	5.4
Trimmer	2.3	2.1	3.2	2.9

Note: Fifty-five minutes are available each hour and process 1 has a different type of linebar saw than process 2.

All other machines are common to both processes. The yield from the milling processes would include several grades of dimension, boards, timbers, bark, chips, and sawdust. To keep the present problem tractable, only board and dimension will be recognized. Assume the prices for board and dimension are $160 and $110 per MBF respectively. Such prices, of course, do not recognize differences in widths and lengths—1,000 board feet of 2″ × 6″ that are 12′ long are taken to have the same value as 1,000 board feet of 2″ × 8″ that are 16′ long. If a product is longer and wider, it enjoys a greater market price. (Even though logs are bucked to standard lengths, the existence of defects determines to what length each finished product will be trimmed.) To adjust for this economic fact, a "width-length premium" for each input log type will be introduced. The lumber outputs (yields) expressed as percentages of log inputs—and the width-length premiums are

	Log Size	Log Grade	Log Density	% Board	% Dimension	Width-Length Premium
Process 1:	18″	Premium	Open	.80	.40	$11
	18″	Other	Open	.85	.40	9
	15″	Other	Open	.70	.60	5
Process 2:	18″	Premium	Dense	.60	.60	14
	18″	Premium	Open	.60	.70	10
	18″	Other	Dense	.65	.65	12
	18″	Other	Open	.70	.55	9
	15″	Other	Dense	.65	.75	7
	15″	Other	Open	.80	.70	5

A lumber company would know to exactly what extent its stocks of each product were depleted or excessive relative to anticipated demand. Consequently, market constraints would be formulated for each product and adjusted (perhaps hourly) as new sales data became available. For present purposes, assume dimension must be at least 40% of output.

Required:

Set up (and solve if a computer is at your disposal) the LP problem that maximizes profit. If you have solved the problem, interpret your results.

Dynamic Programming and Job Order Costing

19

Overview

Discussions in cost accounting texts are apt to ignore entirely the vexing problem of how many units to start in production to wind up with a batch of n good units in a job order system. Now this is an interesting question, and someone who replies, "Why all the fuss? Start 10% more than is needed" is responding cavalierly. Extra units are not free and a customer who receives less than he ordered is apt to be displeased. This problem is known variously in the literature as the "production overrun problem" or the "reject allowance problem," the former label being more popular currently.

We will gain several insights in the course of solving the production overrun problem. One will be an understanding of the need to supply cost centers with revenue information. Another will be an appreciation of how elaborate mathematics can serve to disguise a bad solution that arises from a false assumption. In addition we shall see (1) how physical production standards might be set if one product could be isolated from all others, and (2) one method for incorporating random variables and their probability distributions into constrained optimization solutions.

Introduction

The production overrun problem requires an inventory model that at once focuses on safety stock and proper balance of demand and supply, as well as on costs and revenues. In its basic format, the overrun problem deals with determining the best number of units to put into production to obtain some desired or target output. Given some probability of rendering each unit defective, it might be decided, for example, to start 250 units in the hope of obtaining 200 good units. The 50 units would be *safety* units and, again utilizing the probability distribution, the expected production (expected good production) might be 210 units, thereby leading to an expected 10 *extra* units.

Two approaches seem to be recommended for constructing the inventory model. The first will hereafter be called the "ordinary" approach for lack of a better name; and the second is a dynamic programming approach, hereafter simply called "dynamic". The implications for management of the production overrun problem have not apparently received appropriate attention. Nor has there been adequate contrasting of the merits of both approaches. The discussion that follows will be constructed around a numerical example. Manipulations of data are carried out by computer programs rather than needlessly burdening the discussion with mathematical argument, although appendices are provided for those who wish to pursue mathematical detail.

The Ordinary Formulation

An Example. To keep calculations relatively simple, it will be assumed that a contract has been signed that makes the following provisions:

1. Two units will be purchased at $6,000 each.
2. Extra units will be worth $0.
3. Any unit not delivered is subject to a penalty of $3,000.

It has further been determined that

1. The probability of spoiling any unit is .5.
2. The setup cost every time a run is started is $4,000.
3. The production cost is $1,000 per unit.
4. A maximum of two runs will be allowed.
5. Two more units than those needed to satisfy the contract will be started on the second run, should a second run be necessary.

Solution. Exhibit 1 contains an annotated computer program, written in the BASIC language, that performs all calculations. Those interested in the details of the calculations should consult Appendix A to this chapter.

What can be learned from the output of Exhibit 1? Look at the far right-hand column of figures, the first of which in each set of two is expected cost, the second, expected profit.

Exhibit 1

```
100  REM PRODUCTION OVERRUN CALCULATIONS
105  REM R(U)    = PROBABILITY OF U GOOD UNITS ON SECOND RUN
110  REM Z       = THE TARGET
115  REM P(G)    = PROBABILITY OF G GOOD UNITS
120  REM K(G,N) = THE COST WHEN G GOOD ARE PRODUCED GIVEN N AND Z
125  REM W(G,N) = THE PROBABLE COST
130  REM F       = THE PROBABLE FORFEIT (PENALTY)
135  REM B(S)    = THE SUMMED JOINT PROBABILITY OF SHORTAGE
140  REM A(S)    = THE JOINT PROBABILITY OF SHORTAGE
145  REM F,T2,T5,Y, AND E ARE SUMMING VARIABLES
200  DIM  P(25),R(25),K(25,25),W(25,25),B(25),A(25)
201  DIM  G(50),H(50)
205  READ Z,P
210  FOR  N = Z TO 6
250  FOR  Q = 0 TO N
255  LET  A(Q) = 0
260  LET  B(Q) = 0
265  LET  H(Q) = 0
280  NEXT Q
285  LET  F,T2,T5,Y,E = 0
400  REM RECURSIVE PROBABILITY GENERATION ROUTINE
405  LET  V = N
410  LET  P(0) = (1 - P)↑V
430  FOR  X = 1 TO V
435  LET  P(X) = ((V-X+1)/X) * (P/(1-P)) * P(X-1)
440  NEXT X
500  REM COST COMPUTATION ROUTINE
540  FOR  G = 0 TO N
550  LET  H = Z-G
555  IF H > 0 THEN 600
560  LET  K(G,N) = 4000 + (1000 * N)
565  LET  W(G,N) = K(G,N) * P(G)
570  GO TO 644
600  LET  K(G,N) = 8000 + (1000 * (N+2+Z-G))
605  LET  W(G,N) = K(G,N) * P(G)
608  REM RECURSIVE PROBABILITY ROUTINE FOR THE SECOND RUN
610  LET  V = 2+Z-G
615  LET  R(0) = (1 - P)↑V
620  FOR  U = 1 TO V
625  LET  R(U) = ((V-U+1)/U) * (P/(1-P)) * R(U-1)
628  NEXT U
630  REM JOINT PROBABILITY OF GOOD UNITS ROUTINE
632  FOR  U = 0 TO V
638  LET  T4 = G + U
639  LET  G(T4) = P(G) * R(U)
640  LET  H(T4) = G(T4) + H(T4)
642  NEXT U
643  GO TO 650
644  LET  T4 = G
645  LET  H(T4) = P(T4) + H(T4)
649  REM JOINT PROBABILITY OF SHORTAGE
650  FOR  Q = 1 TO Z - G
655  LET  A(Q) = P(G) * P(Z-G-Q)
```

Exhibit 1 (*cont.*)

```
660 LET  B(Q) = B(Q) + A(Q)
670 LET  F = 3000 * Q * (A(Q)) + F
675 LET  T2 = A(Q) + T2
680 NEXT Q
700 LET  Y = Y + W(G,N)
705 NEXT G
710 PRINT "EXPECTED COSTS EXCLUDING PENALTY  =";Y
715 PRINT "EXPECTED PENALTY COST             =";F
720 LET  T1 = Y + F
725 PRINT "EXPECTED COST OF STARTING";N;"UNITS =",T1
730 LET  B(0) = 1 - T2
750 FOR  D = 0 TO Z
755 LET  E = 6000 * (Z-D) * (B(D)) + E
765 NEXT D
770 PRINT "EXPECTED REVENUE                  =";E
775 LET  T3 = E - T1
780 PRINT "EXPECTED PROFIT OF STARTING";N;"UNITS =",T3
781 IF N > = Z + 2 THEN 784
782 LET  T3 = Z + 2
783 GO TO 785
784 LET  T3 = N
785 FOR  G = 0 TO T3
786 PRINT USING 787, G,H(G)
787 FIELD ("P(",F3.0,") = ", F12.8)
788 LET  T5 = T5 + (G * H(G))
791 LET  H(G) = 0
795 NEXT G
800 PRINT "EXPECTED PRODUCTION = ";T5;"UNITS"
815 PRINT
825 NEXT N
850 DATA 2, .5
900 END
```

```
RUN

EXPECTED COSTS EXCLUDING PENALTY = 11500
EXPECTED PENALTY COST            = 468.75
EXPECTED COST OF STARTING 2 UNITS  =           11968.75
EXPECTED REVENUE                 = 11062.5
EXPECTED PROFIT OF STARTING 2 UNITS =          -906.25
P(   0) =        .01562500
P(   1) =        .12500000
P(   2) =        .53125000
P(   3) =        .25000000
P(   4) =        .07812500
EXPECTED PRODUCTION = 2.25 UNITS

EXPECTED COSTS EXCLUDING PENALTY = 10625
EXPECTED PENALTY COST            = 281.25
EXPECTED COST OF STARTING 3 UNITS  =           10906.25
EXPECTED REVENUE                 = 11437.5
EXPECTED PROFIT OF STARTING 3 UNITS =          531.25
P(   0) =        .00781250
P(   1) =        .07812500
```

Exhibit 1 (*cont.*)

```
P(  2) =        .56250000
P(  3) =        .29687500
P(  4) =        .05468750
EXPECTED PRODUCTION = 2.3125 UNITS

EXPECTED COSTS EXCLUDING PENALTY = 10250
EXPECTED PENALTY COST            = 164.0625
EXPECTED COST OF STARTING 4 UNITS  =          10414.0625
EXPECTED REVENUE                 = 11671.875
EXPECTED PROFIT OF STARTING 4 UNITS =         1257.8125
P(  0) =        .00390625
P(  1) =        .04687500
P(  2) =        .49218750
P(  3) =        .35937500
P(  4) =        .09765625
EXPECTED PRODUCTION = 2.5 UNITS

EXPECTED COSTS EXCLUDING PENALTY = 10343.75
EXPECTED PENALTY COST            = 93.75
EXPECTED COST OF STARTING 5 UNITS  =          10437.5
EXPECTED REVENUE                 = 11812.5
EXPECTED PROFIT OF STARTING 5 UNITS =         1375
P(  0) =        .00195313
P(  1) =        .02734375
P(  2) =        .38281250
P(  3) =        .37890625
P(  4) =        .17773438
P(  5) =        .03125000
EXPECTED PRODUCTION = 2.796875 UNITS

EXPECTED COSTS EXCLUDING PENALTY = 10781.25
EXPECTED PENALTY COST            = 52.734375
EXPECTED COST OF STARTING 6 UNITS  =          10833.9844
EXPECTED REVENUE                 = 11894.5313
EXPECTED PROFIT OF STARTING 6 UNITS =         1060.54687
P(  0) =        .00097656
P(  1) =        .01562500
P(  2) =        .27539063
P(  3) =        .35156250
P(  4) =        .24707031
P(  5) =        .09375000
P(  6) =        .01562500
EXPECTED PRODUCTION = 3.171875 UNITS
```

1. If the selection of the number of units to start in run 1 were to be based on the minimum sum of production and penalty costs, four units would be chosen at an expected cost of \$10,414.06. (Note: the unrestricted minimum-cost policy would be to pay the \$6,000 penalty cost and not produce at all; however, it is assumed that meeting the contract is thought desirable, and hence that this is an unacceptable alternative.)

2. If the selection were based on maximum profits, five units would be started in run 1. The expected profit that results, $1,375, is $117 greater than the profit associated with the minimizing cost decision of starting four units. Put another way, if production did not have revenue data to use in making its decision, that is, if production were strictly constructed as a cost center, 9.3% of possible profits would be forgone simply for the pleasure of having the strictly constructed organization. Minimizing costs does not always yield the same results as maximizing profits.

3. If the maximize-profit decision were made, the expected production would be 2.8 units. (Here the small numbers chosen for ease of illustration yield ludicrous results, but if 200 or 2,000 units had been the target originally, this would not be the case.) This expectation provides a benchmark for later comparison; if only 2 units were eventually produced, an investigation should undoubtedly be conducted to find out why. Setting tolerance limits is discussed in Appendix A to this chapter.

4. If the decisionmaker feels that service to customers should be stressed, and that the probability of failing to meet the contract is too high with the maximize-profit decision (that is, that the probability of producing less than two units is .00195 + .02734 or about .029), he might elect to start six units in run 1 to reduce the probability of failure to about .016. (Note: to see the results of starting seven or more units, it would be necessary to change line 210 in the computer program.

Comments: The illustration has a number of shortcomings, although it is adequate for making the following points:

1. The manager is concerned in a job order system with how the "pinch-of-salt" safety margins are chosen.
2. The manager could use expected production as a standard to judge performance.
3. The manager might wish to "push" service level measures such as probability-of-failure in lieu of maximizing dollar profits as a basis for making decisions.
4. Finally, the manager needs to provide production with revenue data regardless of whether production is organized as a cost center or as a profit center or as some other kind of center.

Perhaps the major shortcoming of the model presented is its arbitrary policy for the second run of starting 2 more units than are then needed to complete the contract. If the original target has been 200 units, then "2 more" would not be convincing as providing adequate safety. More attractive would be some policy such as "Add 20% to what is needed." Still more appealing might be a policy that reflected service level, such as "Start enough in run 2 to reduce the probability of failure to 1%."

Another shortcoming, one that is more apparent than real, is the fact that many contracts do not contain penalty clauses. A few moments of thought, however, make it obvious that not filling a contract carries the penalties of causing customer irritation and possible loss of goodwill as well as future profits. An estimate of these costs could be used as a substitute for specified penalty costs (or as an addition to them where it was felt that such costs would exist even after the penalty was paid). The decisionmaker harbors notions of these consequences, at any rate, when he makes his choices. Getting him to quantify what he feels intuitively may be difficult because of the newness of the idea, but with experience, this difficulty should be overcome.

Finally, think about using the service level decision criterion as a practical means for implementing the economist's utility theory. Using dollars as a sole criterion often seems to overlook matters that are difficult to quantify but which are very important nonetheless. Customer irritation when units are not delivered, maintenance of reputation, courtesy, future trade opportunities with the present customer are all examples of considerations that are difficult, but important, to measure. Anybody who is involved with obtaining customers knows many other such examples.

Service level also implicitly recognizes dollars—insofar as the decision maker has subjective feelings for the costs and revenues involved. However, it is possible to supplement the decisionmaker's subjective feelings with a sensitivity analysis of whatever costs have been objectively determined. For instance, to reduce the probability of failure from .029 when five units are input to .016 when six units are input leads to a concomitant loss of profits of \$314.45 (that is, \$1,375.00 – \$1,060.55). The service level decision might now be rephrased as, "Is it worth an opportunity cost of \$314.45 to cut the probability of failure in half?"

Dynamic Programming Formulation

The analyst who uses dynamic programming attempts to examine a problem in a series of sequential stages. He must do the best possible at earlier stages, maximizing profit or minimizing cost, as the case may be. At the same time he must keep in mind that ensuing stages may occur that pick up (resume solving) where each preceding stage leaves off with whatever resources then remain.

An Example. The data from the previous example will be used to illustrate the dynamic programming approach. The one exception is that the arbitrary "add two units" policy for the second run will be discarded, since the dynamic approach sticks with dollars throughout.

The model is described below.

Model	Description
Maximize $f(S, n) = E[F(S_2, n_2)] + E[F(S_1, n_1)]$	$E[F(S_i, n_i)]$ is the expected profit at stage (run) i, while $S = S_1 + S_2$ (S represents the output needed) and n_i is the number of units input at stage i.
$= \Big[6{,}000 \sum_{G_2=0}^{S'_2} G_2 P(G_2)$	= the expected revenue at stage 2. G_2 is the good units obtained in 2; $P(S'_2)$ is $P(S_2$ or more)
$- (4{,}000 + 1{,}000n_2)$	= the setup and production costs
$- 3{,}000 \sum_{G_2=0}^{S_2} (S_2 - G_2)P(G_2) \Big]$	= the expected penalty cost
$+$	
$\Big[6{,}000 \sum_{G_1=0}^{S'_2} G_1 P(G_1)$	= the expected revenue at stage 1; $S_1 = 2$ and $P(S'_1)$ is $P(S_1$ or more)
$+ \sum_{G_1=0}^{S_1} E[F(S - G_1), \hat{n}_2] P(G_1)$	= the expected profit of stage 2 that is anticipated by stage 1; the optimal input, $\hat{n}_2$, will be chosen to obtain S_2 output, where $S_2 = S - G_1$
$- (4{,}000 + 1{,}000n_1) \Big]$	= the setup and production costs

Exhibit 2 contains an annotated computer program, written in the BASIC language, that solves this problem. One table has been prepared for

Exhibit 2

```
005 DIM P(9,9),R(9,9),T(9,9),F(9,9),Z(9,9),Y(9),H(9,9),M(9,9)
006 DIM J(9,9),K(9,9),X(9)
010 REM MATRIX P CONTAINS PROBABILITY DISTRIBUTION
015 REM MATRICES M AND Z CONTAIN PAYOFF TABLES
020 REM MATRICES R, T, F, AND H CONTAIN PROBABLE COSTS AND REVENUES
025 REM VECTOR Y CONTAINS THE MAXIMUM PROFITS OF THE FINAL RUN
030 REM C1 = SETUP (ORDER) COST
035 REM C2 = COST TO MANUFACTURE A UNIT
040 REM C3 = PENALTY COST PER UNIT NOT DELIVERED
045 REM C4 = SELLING PRICE PER UNIT
050 REM  F = PROBABILITY OF ANY UNIT BEING INCURABLY DEFECTIVE
055 REM  S = THE NEED (UNITS REMAINING TO BE MADE) AT ANY STAGE
060 REM  N = THE UNITS INPUT AT A GIVEN STAGE
065 REM  G = GOOD UNITS MADE IN A GIVEN STAGE
070 REM X IS A VECTOR WITH BEST VALUE OF N ASSOCIATED WITH BEST Z(S,N)
075 REM J IS A JOINT PROBABILITIES MATRIX
080 REM K IS A MATRIX WITH SUMS OF MUTUALLY-EXCLUSIVE PROBABILITIES
085 REM T3 IS THE MAXIMUM POSSIBLE OUTPUT RESULTING AFTER BOTH RUNS
100 LET T,T1 = 0
105 LET C1 = 4000
110 LET C2 = 1000
115 LET C3 = 3000
120 LET C4 = 6000
125 LET F = .5
130 LET Q = 1 - F
```

Exhibit 2 (*cont.*)

```
135  PRINT "                                STAGE 2 (FINAL RUN)        "
140  PRINT " NEED,                                 INPUT "
145  FOR N = 0 TO 6
150  PRINT USING 155, N
155  FIELD ("-",2X,7F7.0)
160  NEXT N
165  PRINT
170  REM RECURSIVE PROBABILITY GENERATION ROUTINE
180  FOR N = 1 TO 6
185  LET P(N,0) = Q↑N
190  NEXT N
200  FOR N = 1 TO 6
205  FOR G = 1 TO N
210  LET P(N,G) = ((N - G + 1)/G) * (F/Q) * P(N,G - 1)
215  NEXT G
220  NEXT N
290  LET Z(1,0) = -C3
295  LET Z(2,0) = -C4
300  FOR S = 1 TO 2
305  LET Y(S) = -200000
310  FOR N = 1 TO 6
315  LET S1 = S - 1
320  FOR G = 1 TO N
322  REM REVENUE CALCULATION FOR STAGE 2
325  IF G > S1 THEN 340
330  LET R(S,N) = (C4 * G * P(N,G)) + R(S,N)
335  GO TO 345
340  LET R(S,N) = (C4 * S * P(N,G)) + R(S,N)
345  NEXT G
348  REM COST CALCULATIONS FOR STAGE 2
350  LET T(S,N) = C1 + (C2 * N)
370  FOR G = 0 TO S
375  LET F(S,N) = (C3 * (S - G) * P(N,G)) + F(S,N)
377  NEXT G
380  LET Z(S,N) = R(S,N) - (T(S,N) + F(S,N))
398  REM MAXIMUM PROFIT SELECTION FOR STAGE 2
400  IF Z(S,N) <= Y(S) THEN 410
405  LET Y(S) = Z(S,N)
408  LET X(S) = N
410  NEXT N
430  PRINT USING 435,S
435  FIELD ("-",F4.0)
450  FOR N = 0 TO 6
455  PRINT USING 460,Z(S,N)
460  FIELD ("-",F9.0)
465  NEXT N
466  PRINT
470  NEXT S
475  PRINT
480  PRINT
481  PRINT "                                STAGE 1 (INITIAL RUN)        "
482  PRINT " NEED,                                 INPUT "
485  LET M(1,0) = Y(1)
490  LET M(2,0) = Y(2)
491  FOR N = 0 TO 6
```

Exhibit 2 (*cont.*)

```
492  PRINT USING 493,N
493  FIELD ("-",2X,7F7.0)
494  NEXT N
495  PRINT
505  FOR S = 1 TO 2
508  REM COST AND REVENUE CALCULATIONS FOR STAGE 1
510  FOR  N = 1 TO 6
515  FOR  G = 0 TO S - 1
520  LET  W = S - G
525  LET  H(S,N) = (Y(W) * P(N,G)) + H(S,N)
530  NEXT G
540  LET  M(S,N) = R(S,N) - T(S,N) + H(S,N)
545  NEXT N
550  PRINT USING 555,S
555  FIELD ("-",F4.0)
570  FOR  N = 0 TO 6
575  PRINT USING 580,M(S,N)
580  FIELD ("-",F9.0)
585  NEXT N
590  PRINT
595  NEXT S
695  REM EXPECTED PRODUCTION CALCULATION
700  FOR  N = 2 TO 6
710  PRINT "N = ";N
750  FOR  G = 0 TO N
760  IF G > = 2 THEN 850
780  FOR  U = 0 TO X(2-G)
785  LET  T2 = G + U
790  LET  J(N,T2) = P(N,G) * P(X(2-G),U)
795  LET  K(N,T2) = K(N,T2) + J(N,T2)
800  NEXT U
810  GO TO 870
850  LET  T2 = G
860  LET  K(N,T2) = K(N,T2) + P(N,T2)
870  NEXT G
871  REM SELECTING T3, THE MAXIMUM POSSIBLE OUTPUT
872  IF X(1) > = X(2) THEN 882
876  IF X(2) > = N THEN 888
878  LET  T3 = N
880  GO TO 900
882  IF X(1) > = N THEN 892
884  LET  T3 = N
886  GO TO 900
888  LET  T3 = X(2)
890  GO TO 900
892  LET  T3 = X(1) + 1
900  FOR  G = 0 TO T3
905  LET  T1 = (G * K(N,G)) + T1
920  PRINT USING 930,G,K(N,G)
930  FIELD ("P(",F3.0,") = ",F12.8)
940  NEXT G
950  PRINT "EXPECTED PRODUCTION IS";T1;"UNITS"
960  LET  T1 = 0
980  NEXT N
999  END
```

Exhibit 2 (*cont.*)

STAGE 2 (FINAL RUN)

NEED,	INPUT						
	0	1	2	3	4	5	6
1	−3000	−3500	−2250	−2125	−2562.	−3281.	−4141.
2	−6000	−6500	−3000	−625	625	1031.	875.

STAGE 1 (INITIAL RUN)

NEED,	INPUT						
	0	1	2	3	4	5	6
1	−2125	−3063.	−2031.	−2016.	−2508.	−3254.	−4127.
2	1031.	−2547.	−805.	582.	1283.	1388.	1067.

N = 2
P(0) = .00781250
P(1) = .10156250
P(2) = .51562500
P(3) = .26562500
P(4) = .10156250
P(5) = .00781250
EXPECTED PRODUCTION IS 2.375 UNITS
N = 3
P(0) = .00390625
P(1) = .06640625
P(2) = .55468750
P(3) = .30468750
P(4) = .06640625
P(5) = .00390625
EXPECTED PRODUCTION IS 2.375 UNITS
N = 4
P(0) = .00195313
P(1) = .04101563
P(2) = .48828125
P(3) = .36328125
P(4) = .10351563
P(5) = .00195313
EXPECTED PRODUCTION IS 2.53125 UNITS
N = 5
P(0) = .00097656
P(1) = .02441406
P(2) = .38085938
P(3) = .38085938
P(4) = .18066406
P(5) = .03222656
EXPECTED PRODUCTION IS 2.8125 UNITS
N = 6
P(0) = .00048828
P(1) = .01416016
P(2) = .27441406
P(3) = .35253906
P(4) = .24853516
P(5) = .09423828
P(6) = .01562500
EXPECTED PRODUCTION IS 3.1796875 UNITS

each run with units needed as the row labels and units put into process as the column headings. In addition, the convoluted probability distributions for each input action in the initial run—as folded with the best input action in the second run—are detailed beneath the tables. As shown in the output, the optimal program has five units started in run 1, with another five being started in run 2 if two units are still needed and three units being started in run 2 if one unit is then needed. If, for some reason, it was possible to reduce the target from two units to one (in both stages), Exhibit 2 shows that starting three units would be the least costly (−$2,016) way to do it.[1] Appendix B to this chapter provides a tree diagram of the process, as well as the basic calculations—including expected production—for the optimal action.

Contrasting the Approaches

How do the two approaches, "ordinary" and "dynamic," differ? Which is better? The answers to both questions are interrelated; both approaches provide a sequential program—try run 1 and then have a go at run 2, if necessary, to finish things up. According to customary definitions, this makes both models dynamic. Where they differ is on the arbitrary policy of inputting two safety units on the second run (this is the stipulated "ordinary" approach); the "dynamic" approach sticks to dollars without overt concern for service level. Once the optimal "dynamic" program has been determined, Exhibit 2 then goes on to calculate the convoluted probability distribution and expected production for each starting action in the initial run (designated by N in Exhibit 2 output section). These distributions and expectations may be used, as described in the "ordinary" section, to decide on service level, to perform sensitivity analysis, and to establish production standards. There would seem to be little distinction between the models on first examination—"ordinary" provides for safety units as a matter of policy; "dynamic" provides for safety units by selecting the inputs that maximize profits. Both models then rely on the decisionmaker to review overall service level before choosing a program. There are definite differences, however.

The maximum possible output differs between the two approaches. In the "ordinary" model, the maximum output is either the N units input to run 1 or, because of the "start two safety units" policy, four units, whichever is greater. (Example: If $N = 3$ in run 1 and zero good units result, four units are input in run 2. If $N = 5$ in run 1 and zero good units result, four units are input in run 2.) In the "dynamic" model the best inputs to meet the needs

---

[1] The target might be reduced because the customer changed his mind, or because one unit was already available, or because one unit is to be subcontracted.

in run 2[2] must be compared with N, the units input in run 1, to determine the maximum output. For example,

$x(1)$	$x(2)$	N	Maximum Output (T_3)
4	5	4	$5 = x(2)$
4	4	6	$6 = N$
4	4	4	$5 = x(1) + 1$

(Comment on last row: If one good unit results in run 1 and four are started in run 2, then five units are possible.) It must be remembered that the facts $x(1) = 3$ and $x(2) = 5$ are unknown prior to running the model; hence all possibilities must be provided for in the program. Exhibit 2 does this sorting (searching) in lines 871 through 892, which follow the flow the flowchart shown below.

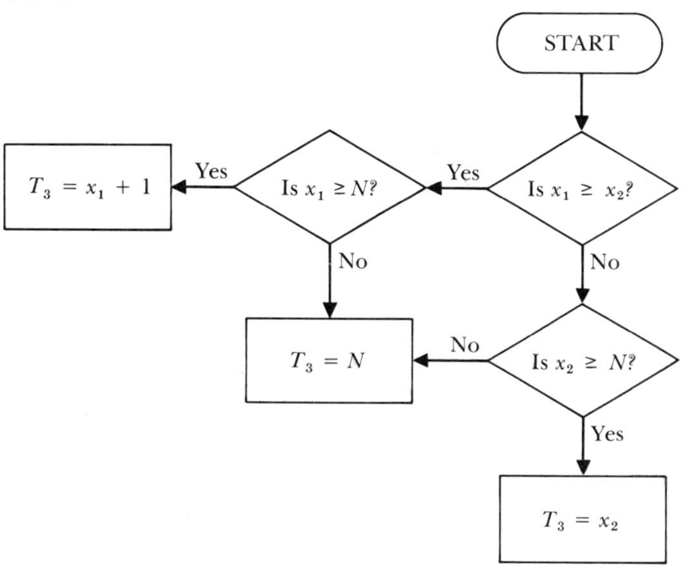

Observe that this neat sorting format applies only for a target of 2 units. When a real problem with, say, 200 or more target units is encountered, the searching problem becomes considerably more complex. It may even become more practical just to print out the first dozen probabilities—$P(0)$, $P(1)$, . . . , $P(11)$—to expedite sensitivity analysis and service level selection.

You will further appreciate how the two models differ if you suppose that "ordinary"—abandoning the "start two safety units" policy—adopts

[2] See lines 398 through 410 in Exhibit 2; $x(1)$ indicates the optimal input if one unit is needed, while $x(2)$ designates the best input if two units are needed.

a service level policy that specifies, "Start V units in the final run such that the joint probability of generating zero units is .002." Suppose three units had been input in run 1; consequently, $P(G_1 = 0) = \binom{3}{0}.5^0.5^3 = .125$. The probability of producing zero units in run 2 is $R(G_2 = 0) = \binom{V}{0}.5^0.5^V \equiv .5^V$. Hence, to determine V,

$$P(0)R(0) = .002$$

$$.125(.5^V) = .002$$

$$.5^V = .016$$

$$V = \frac{\log .016}{\log .5} = \frac{-1.7959}{-.301} \approx 6$$

One thing happens to make coincident model expectations highly unlikely. "Ordinary" inputs 6 on run 2, while "dynamic" inputs 5, the most profitable input quantity.

As far as service level considerations are concerned, in the planning stage—before any actual production takes place—it seems to make no real difference whether choice is made prior to the final run, as in "ordinary," or after both runs are over, as in "dynamic." The optimal programs, however, may have different profits, and in this case "dynamic" will have at least as much profit as "ordinary." Even with the rough "start two safety units" service level policy, it is evident from Exhibits 1 and 2 that the "dynamic" program yields slightly better profit expectations. (Discarding the two safety units worsens the "ordinary" profit expectations—with zero safety units, the best action in run 1 is again to input five units, which in turn leads to reduced expected profits of $671.88.)

Is there any reason to prefer "ordinary"? Yes. In fact, two reasons come to mind, although neither is compelling:

1. "Ordinary" facilitates separation of costs and revenues. "Dynamic," however, could be made to yield cost and revenue data by some adroit changes in the computer program. Expected profit would still govern the optimal program, but the profit at each stage would have to be split into its revenue and cost components. Having cost data available is often helpful for control and price setting purposes; hence splitting expected profit into its components might make sense.

2. "Dynamic," while attractive and straightforward in conception, is nevertheless difficult to describe and almost always looks ominous when expressed symbolically. "Ordinary" has a much simpler structure. Where explanation of the model is not a problem, "dynamic" would be superior.

A third reason that could have been advanced fifteen years ago is that "ordinary" is computationally easier. Now, with ubiquitous computers and software programs like Exhibits 1 and 2, computation is no longer an issue.

The weight of argument favors the dynamic programming approach.

Reflecting Learning

To reflect learning in the overrun problem it would suffice to estimate a decrease in the rate of defective units on subsequent runs. In the previous example defective units had a probability of .5 in run 1. Using the experience gained from this run, production employees can perhaps reduce the rate of defectives to, say, .3 in run 2. In this way the control of costs can be improved by (1) selecting better safety quantities, and (2) setting tighter standards for performance as measured by expected good production.

Conclusions

The weight of evidence favors the adoption of dynamic programming in solving the production overrun problem.

It has been shown that the factory needs revenue data to arrive at optimal decisions. Unfortunately, ignoring revenue and concentrating on costs seems to be the pattern in factories. This position is defended on the seductive grounds that the same revenue will be generated, and therefore that control rests in minimizing production costs. What is overlooked, as Exhibit 1 demonstrates, is that revenue information may alter decisions. Given these improved decisions, it would then be appropriate to minimize production costs by focusing on efficiency.

Undoubtedly the controller would be anxious to supply production with revenue data. He too wants (1) to determine optimal input in a job order costing system, (2) to set meaningful standards for performance, (3) to organize responsibility centers, (4) to control the disposition of extras, and (5) to see that hard to measure but significant variables are reflected in decisions.

"Start 10% safety units" can be either a well-conceived policy that addresses an overrun situation or the uncaring mandate of a manager who has abdicated control even though he must retain responsibility.

Appendix A

Illustrative Production Overrun Calculations

Action: Start four in run 1 in the hope of obtaining two good units.

Probability of G_1 good units in run $1 = P_1(G_1) = \binom{4}{G_1} .5^{G_1} .5^{4-G_1} = \binom{4}{G_1} .5^4$

$$\begin{aligned}
P_1(0) &= \tbinom{4}{0}\ .5^4 = .0625\ \tbinom{4}{0} = .0625\ (1) = .0625 \\
P_1(1) &= \tbinom{4}{1}\ .5^4 = .0625\ \tbinom{4}{1} = .0625\ (4) = .2500 \\
P_1(2) &= \tbinom{4}{2}\ .5^4 = .0625\ \tbinom{4}{2} = .0625\ (6) = .3750 \\
P_1(3) &= \tbinom{4}{3}\ .5^4 = .0625\ \tbinom{4}{3} = .0625\ (4) = .2500 \\
P_1(4) &= \tbinom{4}{4}\ .5^4 = .0625\ \tbinom{4}{4} = .0625\ (1) = .0625 \\
& \qquad\qquad\qquad\qquad\qquad\qquad\qquad\quad 1.0000
\end{aligned}$$

If a second run is undertaken, a second setup cost will be incurred and two more units than necessary will be placed into production. Let $K(G_1) =$ the cost of producing exactly G_1 good units in the first run = setup cost/s + unit production costs.

$$\begin{aligned}
K(4) &= \$4{,}000 + 4\ (\$1{,}000) = \$8{,}000 \\
K(3) &= \$4{,}000 + 4\ (\$1{,}000) = \$8{,}000 \\
K(2) &= \$4{,}000 + 4\ (\$1{,}000) = \$8{,}000 \\
K(1) &= 2\ (\$4{,}000) + 7\ (\$1{,}000) = \$15{,}000 \\
K(0) &= 2\ (\$4{,}000) + 8\ (\$1{,}000) = \$16{,}000
\end{aligned}$$

Hence, if $G_1 \geq 2$, the cost will be only \$8,000.

G_1	$P_1(G_1)$	Cost $[K(G_1)]$	Extension
≥2	.6875	\$ 8,000	\$ 5,500
1	.2500	15,000	3,750
0	.0625	16,000	1,000
EXPECTED PRODUCTION COST			\$10,250

The probability distribution for G good units, where $G = G_1 + G_2$, after both runs are over, is

$$P(G) = \sum_{G_1=0}^{G} P_1(G_1) P_2(G - G_1),$$

where

$$P_2(G_2) = \begin{cases} \dbinom{T - G_1 + 2}{G_2} .5^{G_2} .5^{T+2-G_1-G_2}, & \text{if } G_1 < T \\ 1, & \text{if } G_1 \geq T \end{cases}$$

and $\quad T =$ target (2, in this case)

A probability tree helps us to follow these calculations:

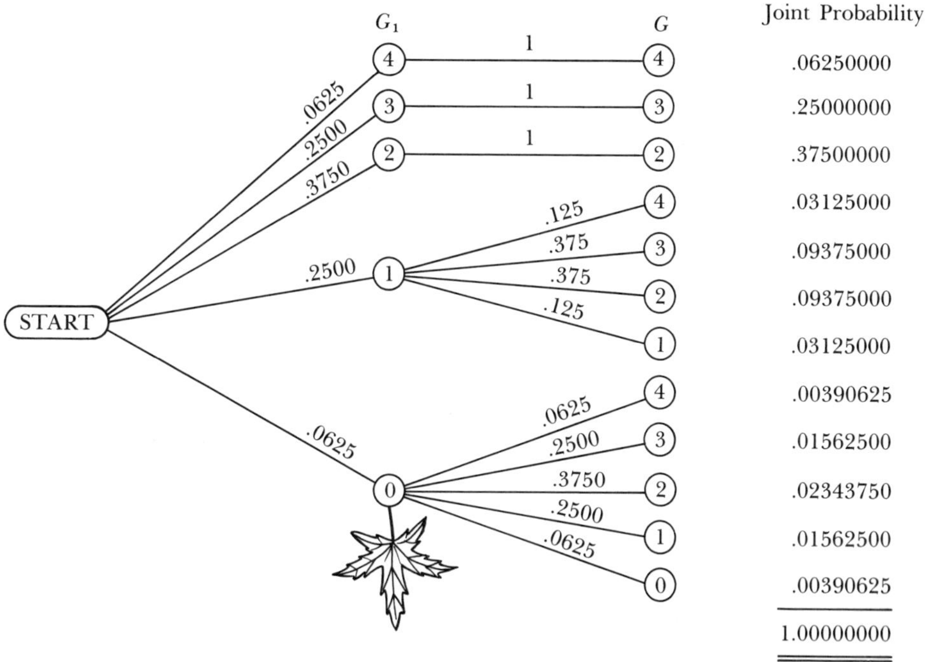

Notes: 1. If $G_1 = 1$, then $P_2(G_2) = \binom{3}{G_2} .5^{G_2} .5^{3-G_2}$ because of the policy to place two more units than necessary into production.

2. The mutually exclusive probabilities for obtaining a given value of G must be added, for example:

$$P(G = 4) = .06250000 + .031250000 + .00390625 = .09765625$$

A penalty cost will be incurred if G is less than two units.

G	$P(G)$	Penalty	Extension
0	.00390625	\$6,000	\$ 23.44
1	.04687500	3,000	140.62
≥ 2	.94921875	0	0
EXPECTED PENALTY COST			\$164.06

The expected revenue may be obtained in a similar way:

G	$P(G)$	Revenue	Extension
0	.00390625	$ 0	$ 0
1	.04687500	6,000	281.25
2	.49218750	12,000	5,906.25
3	.35937500	12,000	4,312.50
4	.09765625	12,000	1,171.88
	EXPECTED REVENUE		$11,671.88

Summary: Expected revenue	$11,671.88
Expected production cost	$10,250.00
Expected penalty cost	164.06
Expected total cost	$10,414.06
Expected profit	$ 1,257.82

$$\text{Expected production} = E(G) = \sum_{G=0}^{4} GP(G) = 2.5 \text{ units}$$

$$\text{Standard deviation} = \sigma = \left(\sum_{G=0}^{4} (G - 2.5)^2 P(G) \right)^{1/2} = \sqrt{.5625} = .75 \text{ units}$$

Although it would be easy to work directly with this distribution, nevertheless it might be instructive to establish control limits in the way ordinarily followed when a normal probability distribution is at work. If tolerance limits were set at $E(G) \pm \frac{2}{3}\sigma = 2.5 \pm .5$, the probability of exceeding 3 would be .10 (rounding .09765625), and of going lower than 2 would be .05 (rounding .00390625 + .04687500); hence the probability of accepting as standard two or three units would .85. Performance outside these limits should be investigated.

Appendix B

The dynamic programming calculations for the decision to input five units in each stage follow:

Stage 2:

$$E[F(S_2 = 1, n_2 = 5)] = \$6{,}000(.968750) - [\$4{,}000 + \$5{,}000 + \$3{,}000(.03125)] = -\$3{,}281$$

$$E[F(S_2 = 2, n_2 = 5)] = \$6{,}000(.156250) + \$12{,}000(.81250) - [\$4{,}000 + \$5{,}000 + \$3{,}000(.156250) + \$6{,}000(.031250)] = \$1{,}031$$

Stage 1:

$$E[F(S_1 = 2, n_1 = 5)] = \$6{,}000(.156250) + \$12{,}000(.81250) + [-\$2{,}125(.156250) + \$1{,}031(.03125)] - (\$4{,}000 + \$5{,}000) = \$1{,}388$$

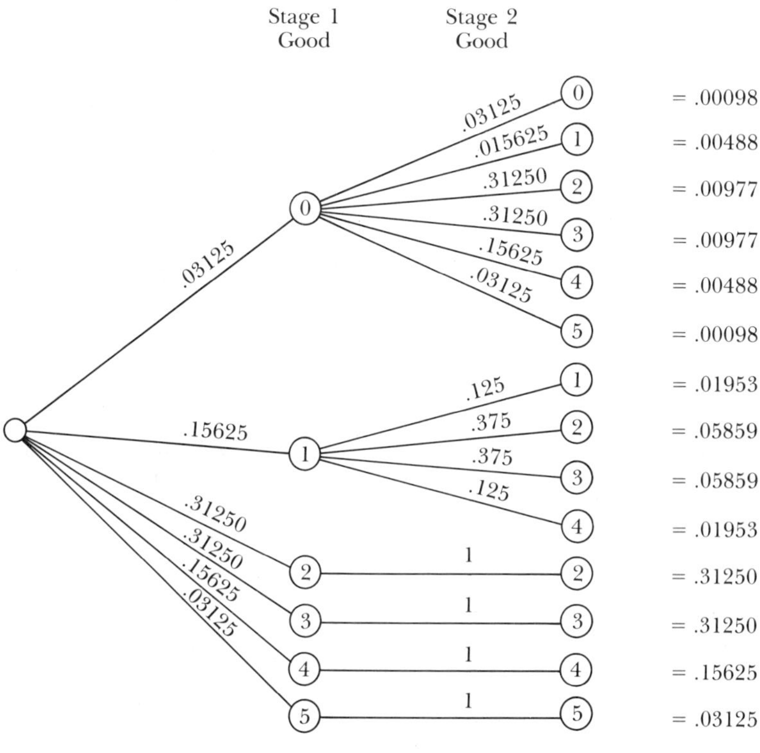

The probabilities shown above were obtained from the binomial distribution

$$P(G) = \binom{5}{G}.5^{G}.5^{5-G} = \binom{5}{G}.03125$$

A probability tree for the good units obtained in both runs is shown on page 697.

Adding mutually exclusive ways to obtain a given output permits us to calculate the probability distribution for good units eventually obtained and the expected production:

G	$P(G)$	$GP(G)$
0	.00098	.00000
1	.02441	.02441
2	.38086	.76172
3	.38086	1.14258
4	.18066	.72264
5	.03223	.16115
	1.00000	$\sum GP(G) = 2.81250$ Expected good units

Problems

1. *Production overrun.* A manufacturer has received an order for four units, each of which must be made to exacting tolerances. These tolerances are so tight that each unit has a one-in-three chance of being incurably defective and worthless. Unit selling price is $12,000. The cost of setting up each run is $2,000, and the manufactured cost of each unit put into process is $3,000. Time available will permit three runs at most. Any unit not completed is subject to a penalty payment to the customer of $5,000. What would the optimal production program be?

2. *The Mao-Haessler cash management model.** Over a given period of time, T, a firm will need a definite amount of cash money, M. However, cash is consumed at a rate of q dollars per day, and consequently not all the cash is needed at once at the start of the period. Thus it would be possible to invest a portion of the cash in short-term securities (so that the cash would not be idle) and then to cash in the securities as needed. Provided (a) that the cost of buying and selling securities, F (taken for convenience as a constant every time there is a security transaction regardless of size of the transaction), is less than the interest earnings, and (b) that risk of adverse market fluctuations can be ignored, the scheme makes sense. The problems are to determine (a) the best amount of securities to purchase at the start

* This model is regarded as a classic. It appeared in article form in J. Mao and R. Haessler, "A Dynamic Programming Approach to Cash Management," *Production and Inventory Management*, 3rd quarter 1968, pp. 75–87.

of the period, (b) the best number of security sales during the period, and (c) the best times to make these security sales (market conditions aside).

The notion of an average cash consumption, q, should be considered in the light of a cash reduction that is in excess of receipts. (This circumstance often prevails for many days each month and is interrupted only by bulk receipts on at most a few days that can be predicted almost to the day of occurrence.) A deterministic rate, q, is, of course, more palatable if the coefficient of variation $(\sigma_q/\overline{q})$ is close to 0. The use of F merely enables transaction cost to be separately recognized in the discussions. It would be a simple matter to express transaction cost as a rate (to set against the security interest rate) to permit recognizing fees based on magnitude of investment. The dynamic formulation of this problem may be grasped by studying the diagrams shown below.

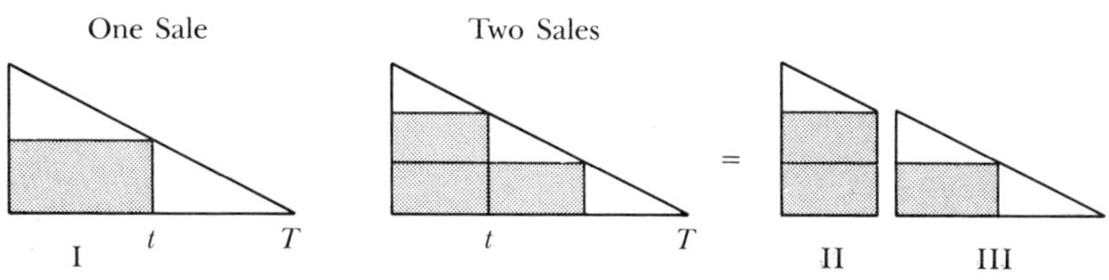

Observations

(a) The shaded areas represent the interest earnings.

(b) Situation III is similar to situation I; the key difference is that I has T units of time to work with while III has only $T - t$ units of time.

(c) The gain from the one-sale case should be developed, then the gain from the two-sale case, then that from the three-sale case, and so forth until it is possible to formulate generally the gain from n sales. In each case i, the gain equals the sum of the gain for a section like II plus the gain (optimized on the time variable t) for case $i - 1$ (with time reduced to $T - t$).

(d) Parameter values should then be inserted in the formula for n sales and an optimum value of n should be calculated.

Suggested Symbols:

r = rate of interest per dollar per day

$q(T - t)$ = dollars originally invested in securities but needed for the last $T - t$ days

t = number of days securities were held prior to first sale

Data:

$M = \$60{,}000$ $\quad r = 5.4\%$ per year $\quad F = \$21.60$

$T = 30$ days $\quad q = \$60{,}000/30 = \$2{,}000$

Recognition and Measurement

20

Overview

The thrust of this concluding chapter, which you will note is blessedly brief, is that even if he cannot *objectively* measure them, the cost analyst must recognize detriments and sacrifices and bring them explicitly to the attention of his decisionmaker.

Delicate Situations

"Stay off shop, politics, and religion; stick with weather, apple pie, and motherhood!"—such was the stern dictate of many a wife to her baffled husband prior to setting out for an evening many years ago. Motherhood, once a respected calling, is, of course, now to be avoided as a topic for polite conversation—along with weather which is almost certain to offend someone in any group because it is bound to be too something (sunny, rainy, snowy, cold, hot. . .). Which leaves us with apple pie.

There simply are not very many innocuous topics left. Therefore, we shall have to look at activities that are favored by some, opposed by others. Indeed, some readers may feel that controversy is being stirred up needlessly; you may regard some of the activities in Exhibit 1 as being so beneficial that even mentioning their cost seems entirely out of place. Nonetheless, try to read Exhibit 1 in the spirit in which it was compiled—it is merely a listing of selected activities and *some* of their perceived nondollar benefits and costs.

What is to be learned from Exhibit 1? Probably it reminded you of the old saying "All that glitters is not gold." The cost analyst, however, would undoubtedly paraphrase this to: "If something glitters, it probably is not gold!" *Every* benefit has its costs, some of which may even be measurable in dollars.

Exhibit 1 is intended to suggest that the cost analyst should study every proposed activity to *recognize* its inconveniences, its sacrifies, and its detriments, even if he cannot *objectively* measure them. Since he can measure

Exhibit 1 (*cont.*)

Activity	Benefits	Costs
A. College class visitation to elderly and retarded children's homes	1. College enhances its humanitarian image. 2. Patients receive attention. 3. Students receive experience.	1. Time is diverted from textbooks and classroom. 2. The patients may feel deprived when courses end and visits cease.
B. Offering new courses and majors in universities	1. Provide students with greater choice. 2. Develop new fields of knowledge. 3. Act as a laboratory for society.	1. Increased confusion and bureaucracy. 2. Spread limited resources thinner, thereby endangering basic programs. 3. Create impression of expertise and viability where none exist.
C. University Without Walls	1. Make college training available in areas far removed from campus. 2. Enhance public image of the university. 3. Obtain greater appropriations from legislature.	1. Diluted courses may have to be offered if the off-campus student is ill prepared. 2. Reputation of both the disciplines taught and the university may suffer if "soft" courses are offered. 3. Public may be deceived by the quality of the program. 4. There may be better uses for state funds.
D. Day-care centers	1. Enable mothers to obtain employment or pursue a career. 2. Facilitate the survival of children and family. 3. Permit family to establish roots in the geographic area. 4. Substitute (possibly) better care than mothers could provide.	1. Mother may be trapped in the job in the geographic area (i.e., reduction of mobility). 2. Possible adverse effects on child of being separated from mother. 3. Possible spoiling of child by better day-care facilities than those available at home.
E. Insurance	1. Spread the risk of loss among many. 2. Satisfy legal requirements.	1. Encourage carelessness. 2. Increase the incidence of the disasters insured against (e.g., "going out of business" fires). 3. Increase bureaucracy.
F. Advertising	1. Acquaint public with advances in technology. 2. Increase sales, and perhaps dollar profits.	1. Make people dissatisfied with what they have. 2. Increase dependence on technology. 3. Foster "keep up with Joneses" attitude. 4. Divert people from activities that might be better for them (e.g., owning a second car leads to less walking).

Exhibit 1 (*cont.*)

Activity	Benefits	Costs
G. Open-heart surgery program	1. Save lives. 2. Offer a full range of hospital services. 3. Obtain practice for doctors.	1. Too many such programs may already exist in the area. 2. Too little demand may deceive patients into believing that they are being serviced by experts. 3. The expert who does not practice sufficiently regains his amateur status. 4. Amateurs may take lives.
H. Promotion from technician to manager	1. Receive greater compensation. 2. Increase responsibilities. 3. Deal with more people. 4. Enhance personal power. 5. Enjoy (possibly) a new circle of friends.	1. Abandon (probably) personal expertise as a technician. 2. Take up a new career—one for which the person may have little prior training or aptitude. 3. Deal with more people. 4. Accomplish through the work of others rather than directly through one's own efforts. 5. Alienate (probably) some of former friends; new circle of friends is apt to include some sycophants.
I. Creating a performing arts group.	1. Enjoyment for performers. 2. Experience for performers. 3. Enjoyment for audience. 4. Create beauty. 5. Spread interest in the art form. 6. Employment for performers. 7. Increased spending in the local economy by both performers and audience.	1. Unfavorable experience for audience may create distaste for art form. 2. If group is successful, the wrong type of people may be attracted to the community, leading to all sorts of undesirable consequences.
J. Growth	1. More of everything. 2. Intensified competition may lead to better quality and lower dollar costs.	1. More is not necessarily better. 2. Growth is often followed by retrenchment with the problems attendant on layoffs, idle facilities, shattered dreams. 3. Growth often means loss of control. 4. If there is a winner, there are usually one or more losers. Who are the losers and what will they lose?

Exhibit 1 (*cont.*)

Activity	Benefits	Costs
K. College attendance	1. Enhance skills and earning power. 2. Satisfy curiosity. 3. Obtain credentials.	1. Time might be better spent for many people. 2. New skills may mean separation from family's business (e.g., the son of a farming family may pursue a career in, say, mathematics). 3. Student in search of credentials only may be deluded about their value.
L. Lowering standards	1. Increase quantity. 2. Decrease dollar costs.	1. Decrease in quality that results may be excessive and prove costly in the long run because of loss of market. 2. People may be deceived. 3. Competitive position may be sacrificed.

how he *feels* about them *subjectively*—arbitrarily selecting a number from 1 to 10 suffices to measure anything subjectively—he should consider incorporating his measure into the analysis. However, since his measure may be relevant only to him, it may lack the objectivity necessary to make it useful to the decisionmaker. That being the case, the best the analyst can do is to specify the nondollar costs associated with the activity.

Relevance in measurement is often a luxury. The only attribute one can be sure of when measurements are taken is convenience. Put another way, man invariably measures that which is convenient; relevance may or may not be present. It almost goes without saying that subjective measurement of the relevant is vastly preferable to objective measurement of the irrelevant.

Exhibit 1 is not intended to betray how I feel about the activities. In that sense, Exhibit 1 is meant to be objective; any cost analyst should be able to come up with the present or some more insightful list of benefits and costs.

Other Considerations

You may have wondered why the previous section advocated—to the point of insistence—that decisionmakers be advised of nondollar costs that are so difficult to measure. Partly, the insistence is to counter the position put forth so frequently by most proponents of activities who so strenuously assert their benefits while so blithely minimizing their costs.

More importantly, the analyst should specify the nondollar costs as a matter of thoroughness. How would you, as a decisionmaker, feel about receiving a report that recognized only some of the costs of a proposal? How would you, as a scholar, feel about being told to ignore certain relevant costs when analyzing a proposal? Possibly you would not object to ignoring relevant costs if you were sure that these costs would be recognized some time prior to the final decision. But even such an assurance is not entirely satisfying.

When a decisionmaker is presented with a detailed analysis carefully supported by numbers and formulas *and* tradition, he is coerced to a great extent into accepting its implicit (or explicit) recommendation. In fact, he would need a lot of courage to elect some contrary course of action. It is indeed possible that numbers, formulas, and tradition coalesce to do a disservice. This being so, the analyst is providing real help to the decisionmaker when he says in effect that consideration of this or that nondollar cost, which is difficult to measure objectively and is not recognized in the formal analysis, might lead to a different conclusion.

Conclusion

And that is what accounting is all about: it is gathering and analyzing data and communicating the results thereof to help people make decisions.

And so we have come full circle, for we have returned to the philosophical definition with which we began the text. I hope you have gained some insights along the way.

Mathematical Tables

Appendix **A**

Table 1 Future Amount of a Single Sum*

$$f(n, r) = (1 + r)^n$$

N\R	.5%	1.0%	2.0%	3.0%	4.0%	5.0%	6.0%	7.0%	8.0%	9.0%
1	1.0050	1.0100	1.0200	1.0300	1.0400	1.0500	1.0600	1.0700	1.0800	1.0900
2	1.0100	1.0201	1.0404	1.0609	1.0816	1.1025	1.1236	1.1449	1.1664	1.1881
3	1.0151	1.0303	1.0612	1.0927	1.1249	1.1576	1.1910	1.2250	1.2597	1.2950
4	1.0202	1.0406	1.0824	1.1255	1.1699	1.2155	1.2625	1.3108	1.3605	1.4116
5	1.0253	1.0510	1.1041	1.1593	1.2167	1.2763	1.3382	1.4026	1.4693	1.5386
6	1.0304	1.0615	1.1262	1.1941	1.2653	1.3401	1.4185	1.5007	1.5869	1.6771
7	1.0355	1.0721	1.1487	1.2299	1.3159	1.4071	1.5036	1.6058	1.7138	1.8280
8	1.0407	1.0829	1.1717	1.2668	1.3686	1.4775	1.5938	1.7182	1.8509	1.9926
9	1.0459	1.0937	1.1951	1.3048	1.4233	1.5513	1.6895	1.8385	1.9990	2.1719
10	1.0511	1.1046	1.2190	1.3439	1.4802	1.6289	1.7908	1.9672	2.1589	2.3674
11	1.0564	1.1157	1.2434	1.3842	1.5395	1.7103	1.8983	2.1049	2.3316	2.5804
12	1.0617	1.1268	1.2682	1.4258	1.6010	1.7959	2.0122	2.2522	2.5182	2.8127
13	1.0670	1.1381	1.2936	1.4685	1.6651	1.8856	2.1329	2.4098	2.7196	3.0658
14	1.0723	1.1495	1.3195	1.5126	1.7317	1.9799	2.2609	2.5785	2.9372	3.3417
15	1.0777	1.1610	1.3459	1.5580	1.8009	2.0789	2.3966	2.7590	3.1722	3.6425
16	1.0831	1.1726	1.3728	1.6047	1.8730	2.1829	2.5404	2.9522	3.4259	3.9703
17	1.0885	1.1843	1.4002	1.6528	1.9479	2.2920	2.6928	3.1588	3.7000	4.3276
18	1.0939	1.1961	1.4282	1.7024	2.0258	2.4066	2.8543	3.3799	3.9960	4.7171
19	1.0994	1.2081	1.4568	1.7535	2.1068	2.5270	3.0256	3.6165	4.3157	5.1417
20	1.1049	1.2202	1.4859	1.8061	2.1911	2.6533	3.2071	3.8697	4.6610	5.6044
21	1.1104	1.2324	1.5157	1.8603	2.2788	2.7860	3.3996	4.1406	5.0338	6.1088
22	1.1160	1.2447	1.5460	1.9161	2.3699	2.9253	3.6035	4.4304	5.4365	6.6586
23	1.1216	1.2572	1.5769	1.9736	2.4647	3.0715	3.8197	4.7405	5.8715	7.2579
24	1.1272	1.2697	1.6084	2.0328	2.5633	3.2251	4.0489	5.0724	6.3412	7.9111
25	1.1328	1.2824	1.6406	2.0938	2.6658	3.3864	4.2919	5.4274	6.8485	8.6231
26	1.1385	1.2953	1.6734	2.1566	2.7725	3.5557	4.5494	5.8074	7.3964	9.3992
27	1.1442	1.3082	1.7069	2.2213	2.8834	3.7335	4.8223	6.2139	7.9881	10.2451
28	1.1499	1.3213	1.7410	2.2879	2.9987	3.9201	5.1117	6.6488	8.6271	11.1671
29	1.1556	1.3345	1.7758	2.3566	3.1187	4.1161	5.4184	7.1143	9.3173	12.1722
30	1.1614	1.3478	1.8114	2.4273	3.2434	4.3219	5.7435	7.6123	10.0627	13.2677

* Table prepared by William Burnham

Table 1 Future Amount of a Single Sum

N\R	10.0%	12.0%	14.0%	15.0%	16.0%	18.0%	20.0%	25.0%	30.0%	35.0%
1	1.1000	1.1200	1.1400	1.1500	1.1600	1.1800	1.2000	1.2500	1.3000	1.3500
2	1.2100	1.2544	1.2996	1.3225	1.3456	1.3924	1.4400	1.5625	1.6900	1.8225
3	1.3310	1.4049	1.4815	1.5209	1.5609	1.6430	1.7280	1.9531	2.1970	2.4604
4	1.4641	1.5735	1.6890	1.7490	1.8106	1.9388	2.0736	2.4414	2.8561	3.3215
5	1.6105	1.7623	1.9254	2.0114	2.1003	2.2878	2.4883	3.0518	3.7129	4.4840
6	1.7716	1.9738	2.1950	2.3131	2.4364	2.6996	2.9860	3.8147	4.8268	6.0534
7	1.9487	2.2107	2.5023	2.6600	2.8262	3.1855	3.5832	4.7684	6.2749	8.1722
8	2.1436	2.4760	2.8526	3.0590	3.2784	3.7589	4.2998	5.9605	8.1573	11.0324
9	2.3579	2.7731	3.2519	3.5179	3.8030	4.4355	5.1598	7.4506	10.6045	14.8937
10	2.5937	3.1058	3.7072	4.0456	4.4114	5.2338	6.1917	9.3132	13.7858	20.1066
11	2.8531	3.4785	4.2262	4.6524	5.1173	6.1759	7.4301	11.6415	17.9216	27.1439
12	3.1384	3.8960	4.8179	5.3503	5.9360	7.2876	8.9161	14.5519	23.2981	36.6442
13	3.4523	4.3635	5.4924	6.1528	6.8858	8.5994	10.6993	18.1899	30.2875	49.4697
14	3.7975	4.8871	6.2613	7.0757	7.9875	10.1472	12.8392	22.7374	39.3738	66.7841
15	4.1772	5.4736	7.1379	8.1371	9.2655	11.9737	15.4070	28.4217	51.1859	90.1585
16	4.5950	6.1304	8.1372	9.3576	10.7480	14.1290	18.4884	35.5271	66.5417	121.7139
17	5.0545	6.8660	9.2765	10.7613	12.4677	16.6722	22.1861	44.4089	86.5042	164.3138
18	5.5599	7.6900	10.5752	12.3755	14.4625	19.6733	26.6233	55.5112	112.4554	221.8236
19	6.1159	8.6128	12.0557	14.2318	16.7765	23.2144	31.9480	69.3889	146.1920	299.4619
20	6.7275	9.6463	13.7435	16.3665	19.4608	27.3930	38.3376	86.7362	190.0496	404.2736
21	7.4002	10.8038	15.6676	18.8215	22.5745	32.3238	46.0051	108.4202	247.0645	545.7693
22	8.1403	12.1003	17.8610	21.6447	26.1864	38.1421	55.2061	135.5253	321.1839	736.7886
23	8.9543	13.5523	20.3616	24.8915	30.3762	45.0076	66.2474	169.4066	417.5391	994.6646
24	9.8497	15.1786	23.2122	28.6252	35.2364	53.1090	79.4968	211.7582	542.8008	1342.7973
25	10.8347	17.0001	26.4619	32.9190	40.8742	62.6686	95.3962	264.6978	705.6410	1812.7763
26	11.9182	19.0401	30.1666	37.8568	47.4141	73.9490	114.4755	330.8722	917.3333	2447.2480
27	13.1100	21.3249	34.3899	43.5353	55.0004	87.2598	137.3706	413.5903	1192.5333	3303.7848
28	14.4210	23.8839	39.2045	50.0656	63.8004	102.9666	164.8447	516.9879	1550.2933	4460.1095
29	15.8631	26.7499	44.6931	57.5755	74.0085	121.5005	197.8136	646.2349	2015.3813	6021.1478
30	17.4494	29.9599	50.9502	66.2118	85.8499	143.3706	237.3763	807.7936	2619.9956	8128.5495

Table 2 Present Value of a Single Sum*

$$b(n, r) = [1/(1 + r)]^n$$

N\R	.5%	1.0%	2.0%	3.0%	4.0%	5.0%	6.0%	7.0%	8.0%	9.0%
1	.9950	.9901	.9804	.9709	.9615	.9524	.9434	.9346	.9259	.9174
2	.9901	.9803	.9612	.9426	.9246	.9070	.8900	.8734	.8573	.8417
3	.9851	.9706	.9423	.9151	.8890	.8638	.8396	.8163	.7938	.7722
4	.9802	.9610	.9238	.8885	.8548	.8227	.7921	.7629	.7350	.7084
5	.9754	.9515	.9057	.8626	.8219	.7835	.7473	.7130	.6806	.6499
6	.9705	.9420	.8880	.8375	.7903	.7462	.7050	.6663	.6302	.5963
7	.9657	.9327	.8706	.8131	.7599	.7107	.6651	.6227	.5835	.5470
8	.9609	.9235	.8535	.7894	.7307	.6768	.6274	.5820	.5403	.5019
9	.9561	.9143	.8368	.7664	.7026	.6446	.5919	.5439	.5002	.4604
10	.9513	.9053	.8203	.7441	.6756	.6139	.5584	.5083	.4632	.4224
11	.9466	.8963	.8043	.7224	.6496	.5847	.5268	.4751	.4289	.3875
12	.9419	.8874	.7885	.7014	.6246	.5568	.4970	.4440	.3971	.3555
13	.9372	.8787	.7730	.6810	.6006	.5303	.4688	.4150	.3677	.3262
14	.9326	.8700	.7579	.6611	.5775	.5051	.4423	.3878	.3405	.2992
15	.9279	.8613	.7430	.6419	.5553	.4810	.4173	.3624	.3152	.2745
16	.9233	.8528	.7284	.6232	.5339	.4581	.3936	.3387	.2919	.2519
17	.9187	.8444	.7142	.6050	.5134	.4363	.3714	.3166	.2703	.2311
18	.9141	.8360	.7002	.5874	.4936	.4155	.3503	.2959	.2502	.2120
19	.9096	.8277	.6864	.5703	.4746	.3957	.3305	.2765	.2317	.1945
20	.9051	.8195	.6730	.5537	.4564	.3769	.3118	.2584	.2145	.1784
21	.9006	.8114	.6598	.5375	.4388	.3589	.2942	.2415	.1987	.1637
22	.8961	.8034	.6468	.5219	.4220	.3418	.2775	.2257	.1839	.1502
23	.8916	.7954	.6342	.5067	.4057	.3256	.2618	.2109	.1703	.1378
24	.8872	.7876	.6217	.4919	.3901	.3101	.2470	.1971	.1577	.1264
25	.8828	.7798	.6095	.4776	.3751	.2953	.2330	.1842	.1460	.1160
26	.8784	.7720	.5976	.4637	.3607	.2812	.2198	.1722	.1352	.1064
27	.8740	.7644	.5859	.4502	.3468	.2678	.2074	.1609	.1252	.0976
28	.8697	.7568	.5744	.4371	.3335	.2551	.1956	.1504	.1159	.0895
29	.8653	.7493	.5631	.4243	.3207	.2429	.1846	.1406	.1073	.0822
30	.8610	.7419	.5521	.4120	.3083	.2314	.1741	.1314	.0994	.0754

* Table prepared by William Burnham

Table 2 Present Value of a Single Sum*

N\R	10.0%	12.0%	14.0%	15.0%	16.0%	18.0%	20.0%	25.0%	30.0%	35.0%
1	.9091	.8929	.8772	.8696	.8621	.8475	.8333	.8000	.7692	.7407
2	.8264	.7972	.7695	.7561	.7432	.7182	.6944	.6400	.5917	.5487
3	.7513	.7118	.6750	.6575	.6407	.6086	.5787	.5120	.4552	.4064
4	.6830	.6355	.5921	.5718	.5523	.5158	.4823	.4096	.3501	.3011
5	.6209	.5674	.5194	.4972	.4761	.4371	.4019	.3277	.2693	.2230
6	.5645	.5066	.4556	.4323	.4104	.3704	.3349	.2621	.2072	.1652
7	.5132	.4523	.3996	.3759	.3538	.3139	.2791	.2097	.1594	.1224
8	.4665	.4039	.3506	.3269	.3050	.2660	.2326	.1678	.1226	.0906
9	.4241	.3606	.3075	.2843	.2630	.2255	.1938	.1342	.0943	.0671
10	.3855	.3220	.2697	.2472	.2267	.1911	.1615	.1074	.0725	.0497
11	.3505	.2875	.2366	.2149	.1954	.1619	.1346	.0859	.0558	.0368
12	.3186	.2567	.2076	.1869	.1685	.1372	.1122	.0687	.0429	.0273
13	.2897	.2292	.1821	.1625	.1452	.1163	.0935	.0550	.0330	.0202
14	.2633	.2046	.1597	.1413	.1252	.0985	.0779	.0440	.0254	.0150
15	.2394	.1827	.1401	.1229	.1079	.0835	.0649	.0352	.0195	.0111
16	.2176	.1631	.1229	.1069	.0930	.0708	.0541	.0281	.0150	.0082
17	.1978	.1456	.1078	.0929	.0802	.0600	.0451	.0225	.0116	.0061
18	.1799	.1300	.0946	.0808	.0691	.0508	.0376	.0180	.0089	.0045
19	.1635	.1161	.0829	.0703	.0596	.0431	.0313	.0144	.0068	.0033
20	.1486	.1037	.0728	.0611	.0514	.0365	.0261	.0115	.0053	.0025
21	.1351	.0926	.0638	.0531	.0443	.0309	.0217	.0092	.0040	.0018
22	.1228	.0826	.0560	.0462	.0382	.0262	.0181	.0074	.0031	.0014
23	.1117	.0738	.0491	.0402	.0329	.0222	.0151	.0059	.0024	.0010
24	.1015	.0659	.0431	.0349	.0284	.0188	.0126	.0047	.0018	.0007
25	.0923	.0588	.0378	.0304	.0245	.0160	.0105	.0038	.0014	.0006
26	.0839	.0525	.0331	.0264	.0211	.0135	.0087	.0030	.0011	.0004
27	.0763	.0469	.0291	.0230	.0182	.0115	.0073	.0024	.0008	.0003
28	.0693	.0419	.0255	.0200	.0157	.0097	.0061	.0019	.0006	.0002
29	.0630	.0374	.0224	.0174	.0135	.0082	.0051	.0015	.0005	.0002
30	.0573	.0334	.0196	.0151	.0116	.0070	.0042	.0012	.0004	.0001

* Table prepared by William Burnham

Table 3 Future Value of an Annuity*

$$F(n, r) = \sum_{i=1}^{n} (1 + r)^i = \sum_{i=1}^{n} f(i, r)$$

N\R	.5%	1.0%	2.0%	3.0%	4.0%	5.0%	6.0%	7.0%	8.0%	9.0%
1	1.0050	1.0100	1.0200	1.0300	1.0400	1.0500	1.0600	1.0700	1.0800	1.0900
2	2.0150	2.0301	2.0604	2.0909	2.1216	2.1525	2.1836	2.2149	2.2464	2.2781
3	3.0301	3.0604	3.1216	3.1836	3.2465	3.3101	3.3746	3.4399	3.5061	3.5731
4	4.0503	4.1010	4.2040	4.3091	4.4163	4.5256	4.6371	4.7507	4.8666	4.9847
5	5.0755	5.1520	5.3081	5.4684	5.6330	5.8019	5.9753	6.1533	6.3359	6.5233
6	6.1059	6.2135	6.4343	6.6625	6.8983	7.1420	7.3938	7.6540	7.9228	8.2004
7	7.1414	7.2857	7.5830	7.8923	8.2142	8.5491	8.8975	9.2598	9.6366	10.0285
8	8.1821	8.3685	8.7546	9.1591	9.5828	10.0266	10.4913	10.9780	11.4876	12.0210
9	9.2280	9.4622	9.9497	10.4639	11.0061	11.5779	12.1808	12.8164	13.4866	14.1929
10	10.2792	10.5668	11.1687	11.8078	12.4864	13.2068	13.9716	14.7836	15.6455	16.5603
11	11.3356	11.6825	12.4121	13.1920	14.0258	14.9171	15.8699	16.8885	17.9771	19.1407
12	12.3972	12.8093	13.6803	14.6178	15.6268	16.7130	17.8821	19.1406	20.4953	21.9534
13	13.4642	13.9474	14.9739	16.0863	17.2919	18.5986	20.0151	21.5505	23.2149	25.0192
14	14.5365	15.0969	16.2934	17.5989	19.0236	20.5786	22.2760	24.1290	26.1521	28.3609
15	15.6142	16.2579	17.6393	19.1569	20.8245	22.6575	24.6725	26.8881	29.3243	32.0034
16	16.6973	17.4304	19.0121	20.7616	22.6975	24.8404	27.2129	29.8402	32.7502	35.9737
17	17.7858	18.6147	20.4123	22.4144	24.6454	27.1324	29.9057	32.9990	36.4502	40.3013
18	18.8797	19.8109	21.8406	24.1169	26.6712	29.5390	32.7600	36.3790	40.4463	45.0185
19	19.9791	21.0190	23.2974	25.8704	28.7781	32.0660	35.7856	39.9955	44.7620	50.1601
20	21.0840	22.2392	24.7833	27.6765	30.9692	34.7193	38.9927	43.8652	49.4229	55.7645
21	22.1944	23.4716	26.2990	29.5368	33.2480	37.5052	42.3923	48.0057	54.4568	61.8733
22	23.3104	24.7163	27.8450	31.4529	35.6179	40.4305	45.9958	52.4361	59.8933	68.5319
23	24.4320	25.9735	29.4219	33.4265	38.0826	43.5020	49.8156	57.1767	65.7648	75.7898
24	25.5591	27.2432	31.0303	35.4593	40.6459	46.7271	53.8645	62.2490	72.1059	83.7009
25	26.6919	28.5256	32.6709	37.5530	43.3117	50.1135	58.1564	67.6765	78.9544	92.3240
26	27.8304	29.8209	34.3443	39.7096	46.0842	53.6691	62.7058	73.4838	86.3508	101.7231
27	28.9745	31.1291	36.0512	41.9309	48.9676	57.4026	67.5281	79.6977	94.3388	111.9682
28	30.1244	32.4504	37.7922	44.2189	51.9663	61.3227	72.6398	86.3465	102.9659	123.1354
29	31.2800	33.7849	39.5681	46.5754	55.0849	65.4388	78.0582	93.4608	112.2832	135.3075
30	32.4414	35.1327	41.3794	49.0027	58.3283	69.7608	83.8017	101.0730	122.3459	148.5752

* Table prepared by William Burnham

Table 3 Future Value of an Annuity

N\R	10.0%	12.0%	14.0%	15.0%	16.0%	18.0%	20.0%	25.0%	30.0%	35.0%
1	1.1000	1.1200	1.1400	1.1500	1.1600	1.1800	1.2000	1.2500	1.3000	1.3500
2	2.3100	2.3744	2.4396	2.4725	2.5056	2.5724	2.6400	2.8125	2.9900	3.1725
3	3.6410	3.7793	3.9211	3.9934	4.0665	4.2154	4.3680	4.7656	5.1870	5.6329
4	5.1051	5.3528	5.6101	5.7424	5.8771	6.1542	6.4416	7.2070	8.0431	8.9544
5	6.7156	7.1152	7.5355	7.7537	7.9775	8.4420	8.9299	10.2588	11.7560	13.4384
6	8.4872	9.0890	9.7305	10.0668	10.4139	11.1415	11.9159	14.0735	16.5828	19.4919
7	10.4359	11.2997	12.2328	12.7268	13.2401	14.3270	15.4991	18.8419	22.8577	27.6640
8	12.5795	13.7757	15.0853	15.7858	16.5185	18.0859	19.7989	24.8023	31.0150	38.6964
9	14.9374	16.5487	18.3373	19.3037	20.3215	22.5213	24.9587	32.2529	41.6195	53.5902
10	17.5312	19.6546	22.0445	23.3493	24.7329	27.7551	31.1504	41.5661	55.4053	73.6967
11	20.3843	23.1331	26.2707	28.0017	29.8502	33.9311	38.5805	53.2077	73.3270	100.8406
12	23.5227	27.0291	31.0887	33.3519	35.7862	41.2187	47.4966	67.7596	96.6250	137.4848
13	26.9750	31.3926	36.5811	39.5047	42.6720	49.8180	58.1959	85.9495	126.9125	186.9544
14	30.7725	36.2797	42.8424	46.5804	50.6595	59.9653	71.0351	108.6868	166.2863	253.7385
15	34.9497	41.7533	49.9804	54.7175	59.9250	71.9390	86.4421	137.1085	217.4722	343.8970
16	39.5447	47.8837	58.1176	64.0751	70.6730	86.0680	104.9306	172.6357	284.0139	465.6109
17	44.5992	54.7497	67.3941	74.8364	83.1407	102.7403	127.1167	217.0446	370.5180	629.9247
18	50.1591	62.4397	77.9692	87.2118	97.6032	122.4135	153.7400	272.5558	482.9734	851.7483
19	56.2750	71.0524	90.0249	101.4436	114.3797	145.6280	185.6880	341.9447	629.1655	1151.2103
20	63.0025	80.6987	103.7684	117.8101	133.8405	173.0210	224.0256	428.6809	819.2151	1555.4838
21	70.4027	91.5026	119.4360	136.6316	156.4150	205.3448	270.0307	537.1011	1066.2796	2101.2532
22	78.5430	103.6029	137.2970	158.2764	182.6014	243.4868	325.2369	672.6264	1387.4635	2838.0418
23	87.4973	117.1552	157.6586	183.1678	212.9776	288.4945	391.4842	842.0329	1805.0026	3832.7064
24	97.3471	132.3339	180.8708	211.7930	248.2140	341.6035	470.9811	1053.7912	2347.8033	5175.5037
25	108.1818	149.3339	207.3327	244.7120	289.0883	404.2721	566.3773	1318.4890	3053.4443	6988.2800
26	120.0999	168.3740	237.4993	282.5688	336.5024	478.2211	680.8528	1649.3612	3970.7776	9435.5280
27	133.2099	189.6989	271.8892	326.1041	391.5028	565.4809	818.2233	2062.9515	5163.3109	12739.3128
28	147.6309	213.5828	311.0937	376.1697	455.3032	668.4475	983.0680	2579.9394	6713.6042	17199.4222
29	163.4940	240.3327	355.7868	433.7451	529.3117	789.9480	1180.8816	3226.1743	8728.9855	23220.5700
30	180.9434	270.2926	406.7370	499.9569	615.1616	933.3186	1418.2579	4033.9678	11348.9811	31349.1195

Table 4 Present Value of an Annuity*

$$B(n, r) = \sum_{i=1}^{n} [1/(1 + r)]^i = \sum_{i=1}^{n} b(i, r)$$

N\R	.5%	1.0%	2.0%	3.0%	4.0%	5.0%	6.0%	7.0%	8.0%	9.0%
1	.9950	.9901	.9804	.9709	.9615	.9524	.9434	.9346	.9259	.9174
2	1.9851	1.9704	1.9416	1.9135	1.8861	1.8594	1.8334	1.8080	1.7833	1.7591
3	2.9702	2.9410	2.8839	2.8286	2.7751	2.7232	2.6730	2.6243	2.5771	2.5313
4	3.9505	3.9020	3.8077	3.7171	3.6299	3.5460	3.4651	3.3872	3.3121	3.2397
5	4.9259	4.8534	4.7135	4.5797	4.4518	4.3295	4.2124	4.1002	3.9927	3.8897
6	5.8964	5.7955	5.6014	5.4172	5.2421	5.0757	4.9173	4.7665	4.6229	4.4859
7	6.8621	6.7282	6.4720	6.2303	6.0021	5.7864	5.5824	5.3893	5.2064	5.0330
8	7.8230	7.6517	7.3255	7.0197	6.7327	6.4632	6.2098	5.9713	5.7466	5.5348
9	8.7791	8.5660	8.1622	7.7861	7.4353	7.1078	6.8017	6.5152	6.2469	5.9952
10	9.7304	9.4713	8.9826	8.5302	8.1109	7.7217	7.3601	7.0236	6.7101	6.4177
11	10.6770	10.3676	9.7868	9.2526	8.7605	8.3064	7.8869	7.4987	7.1390	6.8052
12	11.6189	11.2551	10.5753	9.9540	9.3851	8.8633	8.3838	7.9427	7.5361	7.1607
13	12.5562	12.1337	11.3484	10.6350	9.9856	9.3936	8.8527	8.3577	7.9038	7.4869
14	13.4887	13.0037	12.1062	11.2961	10.5631	9.8986	9.2950	8.7455	8.2442	7.7862
15	14.4166	13.8651	12.8493	11.9379	11.1184	10.3797	9.7122	9.1079	8.5595	8.0607
16	15.3399	14.7179	13.5777	12.5611	11.6523	10.8378	10.1059	9.4466	8.8514	8.3126
17	16.2586	15.5623	14.2919	13.1661	12.1657	11.2741	10.4773	9.7632	9.1216	8.5436
18	17.1728	16.3983	14.9920	13.7535	12.6593	11.6896	10.8276	10.0591	9.3719	8.7556
19	18.0824	17.2260	15.6785	14.3238	13.1339	12.0853	11.1581	10.3356	9.6036	8.9501
20	18.9874	18.0456	16.3514	14.8775	13.5903	12.4622	11.4699	10.5940	9.8181	9.1285
21	19.8880	18.8570	17.0112	15.4150	14.0292	12.8212	11.7641	10.8355	10.0168	9.2922
22	20.7841	19.6604	17.6580	15.9369	14.4511	13.1630	12.0416	11.0612	10.2007	9.4424
23	21.6757	20.4558	18.2922	16.4436	14.8568	13.4886	12.3034	11.2722	10.3711	9.5802
24	22.5629	21.2434	18.9139	16.9355	15.2470	13.7986	12.5504	11.4693	10.5288	9.7066
25	23.4456	22.0232	19.5235	17.4131	15.6221	14.0939	12.7834	11.6536	10.6748	9.8226
26	24.3240	22.7952	20.1210	17.8768	15.9828	14.3752	13.0032	11.8258	10.8100	9.9290
27	25.1980	23.5596	20.7069	18.3270	16.3296	14.6430	13.2105	11.9867	10.9352	10.0266
28	26.0677	24.3164	21.2813	18.7641	16.6631	14.8981	13.4062	12.1371	11.0511	10.1161
29	26.9330	25.0658	21.8444	19.1885	16.9837	15.1411	13.5907	12.2777	11.1584	10.1983
30	27.7941	25.8077	22.3965	19.6004	17.2920	15.3725	13.7648	12.4090	11.2578	10.2737

* Table prepared by William Burnham

Table 4 Present Value of an Annuity

N\R	10.0%	12.0%	14.0%	15.0%	16.0%	18.0%	20.0%	25.0%	30.0%	35.0%
1	.9091	.8929	.8772	.8696	.8621	.8475	.8333	.8000	.7692	.7407
2	1.7355	1.6901	1.6467	1.6257	1.6052	1.5656	1.5278	1.4400	1.3609	1.2894
3	2.4869	2.4018	2.3216	2.2832	2.2459	2.1743	2.1065	1.9520	1.8161	1.6959
4	3.1699	3.0373	2.9137	2.8550	2.7982	2.6901	2.5887	2.3616	2.1662	1.9969
5	3.7908	3.6048	3.4331	3.3522	3.2743	3.1272	2.9906	2.6893	2.4356	2.2200
6	4.3553	4.1114	3.8887	3.7845	3.6847	3.4976	3.3255	2.9514	2.6427	2.3852
7	4.8684	4.5638	4.2883	4.1604	4.0386	3.8115	3.6046	3.1611	2.8021	2.5075
8	5.3349	4.9676	4.6389	4.4873	4.3436	4.0776	3.8372	3.3289	2.9247	2.5982
9	5.7590	5.3282	4.9464	4.7716	4.6065	4.3030	4.0310	3.4631	3.0190	2.6653
10	6.1446	5.6502	5.2161	5.0188	4.8332	4.4941	4.1925	3.5705	3.0915	2.7150
11	6.4951	5.9377	5.4527	5.2337	5.0286	4.6560	4.3271	3.6564	3.1473	2.7519
12	6.8137	6.1944	5.6603	5.4206	5.1971	4.7932	4.4392	3.7251	3.1903	2.7792
13	7.1034	6.4235	5.8424	5.5831	5.3423	4.9095	4.5327	3.7801	3.2233	2.7994
14	7.3667	6.6282	6.0021	5.7245	5.4675	5.0081	4.6106	3.8241	3.2487	2.8144
15	7.6061	6.8109	6.1422	5.8474	5.5755	5.0916	4.6755	3.8593	3.2682	2.8255
16	7.8237	6.9740	6.2651	5.9542	5.6685	5.1624	4.7296	3.8874	3.2832	2.8337
17	8.0216	7.1196	6.3729	6.0472	5.7487	5.2223	4.7746	3.9099	3.2948	2.8398
18	8.2014	7.2497	6.4674	6.1280	5.8178	5.2732	4.8122	3.9279	3.3037	2.8443
19	8.3649	7.3658	6.5504	6.1982	5.8775	5.3162	4.8435	3.9424	3.3105	2.8476
20	8.5136	7.4694	6.6231	6.2593	5.9288	5.3527	4.8696	3.9539	3.3158	2.8501
21	8.6487	7.5620	6.6870	6.3125	5.9731	5.3837	4.8913	3.9631	3.3198	2.8519
22	8.7715	7.6446	6.7429	6.3587	6.0113	5.4099	4.9094	3.9705	3.3230	2.8533
23	8.8832	7.7184	6.7921	6.3988	6.0442	5.4321	4.9245	3.9764	3.3254	2.8543
24	8.9847	7.7843	6.8351	6.4338	6.0726	5.4509	4.9371	3.9811	3.3272	2.8550
25	9.0770	7.8431	6.8729	6.4641	6.0971	5.4669	4.9476	3.9849	3.3286	2.8556
26	9.1609	7.8957	6.9061	6.4906	6.1182	5.4804	4.9563	3.9879	3.3297	2.8560
27	9.2372	7.9426	6.9352	6.5135	6.1364	5.4919	4.9636	3.9903	3.3305	2.8563
28	9.3066	7.9844	6.9607	6.5335	6.1520	5.5016	4.9697	3.9923	3.3312	2.8565
29	9.3696	8.0218	6.9830	6.5509	6.1656	5.5098	4.9747	3.9938	3.3317	2.8567
30	9.4269	8.0552	7.0027	6.5660	6.1772	5.5168	4.9789	3.9950	3.3321	2.8568

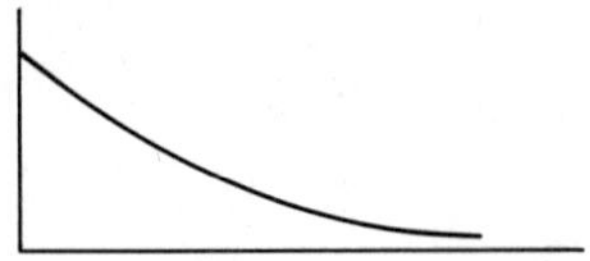

Table 5 Values of e^{-x}

x	0	1	2	3	4	5	6	7	8	9
0.0	1.0000	.9900	.9802	.9704	.9608	.9512	.9418	.9324	.9231	.9139
0.1	.9048	.8958	.8869	.8781	.8694	.8607	.8521	.8437	.8353	.8270
0.2	.8187	.8106	.8025	.7945	.7866	.7788	.7711	.7634	.7558	.7483
0.3	.7408	.7334	.7261	.7189	.7118	.7047	.6977	.6907	.6839	.6771
0.4	.6703	.6636	.6570	.6505	.6440	.6376	.6313	.6250	.6188	.6126
0.5	.6065	.6005	.5945	.5886	.5827	.5770	.5712	.5655	.5599	.5543
0.6	.5488	.5434	.5379	.5326	.5273	.5220	.5169	.5117	.5066	.5016
0.7	.4966	.4916	.4868	.4819	.4771	.4724	.4677	.4630	.4584	.4538
0.8	.4493	.4449	.4404	.4360	.4317	.4274	.4232	.4190	.4148	.4107
0.9	.4066	.4025	.3985	.3946	.3906	.3867	.3829	.3791	.3753	.3716

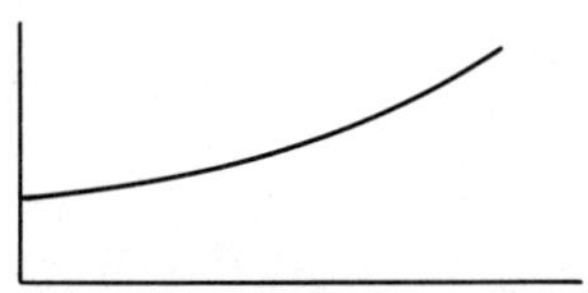

Values of e^{x}

x	0	1	2	3	4	5	6	7	8	9
0.0	1.0000	1.0101	1.0202	1.0305	1.0408	1.0513	1.0618	1.0725	1.0833	1.0942
0.1	1.1052	1.1163	1.1275	1.1388	1.1503	1.1618	1.1735	1.1853	1.1972	1.2092
0.2	1.2214	1.2337	1.2461	1.2586	1.2712	1.2840	1.2969	1.3100	1.3231	1.3364
0.3	1.3499	1.3634	1.3771	1.3910	1.4049	1.4191	1.4333	1.4477	1.4623	1.4770
0.4	1.4918	1.5068	1.5220	1.5373	1.5527	1.5683	1.5841	1.6000	1.6161	1.6323
0.5	1.6487	1.6653	1.6820	1.6989	1.7160	1.7333	1.7507	1.7683	1.7860	1.8040
0.6	1.8221	1.8404	1.8589	1.8776	1.8965	1.9155	1.9348	1.9542	1.9739	1.9937
0.7	2.0138	2.0340	2.0544	2.0751	2.0959	2.1170	2.1383	2.1598	2.1815	2.2034
0.8	2.2255	2.2479	2.2705	2.2933	2.3164	2.3396	2.3632	2.3869	2.4109	2.4351
0.9	2.4596	2.4843	2.5093	2.5345	2.5600	2.5857	2.6117	2.6379	2.6645	2.6912

x	1	2	3	4	5	6	7	8	9	10
e^{-x}	.36788	.13534	.04979	.01832	.006738	.002479	.000912	.000335	.000123	.000045
e^{x}	2.7183	7.3891	20.086	54.598	148.41	403.43	1096.6	2981.0	8103.1	22026

Note: To obtain values of e^{-x} for values of x other than those listed, use the laws of exponents.

Example: $e^{-6.24} = e^{-6.00}(e^{-.24}) = .002479(.7866) = .00195$

Table 6 Four-Place Logarithms

											Proportional Parts								
N	0	1	2	3	4	5	6	7	8	9	1	2	3	4	5	6	7	8	9
10	0000	0043	0086	0128	0170	0212	0253	0294	0334	0374	*4	8	12	17	21	25	29	33	37
11	0414	0453	0492	0531	0569	0607	0645	0682	0719	0755	4	8	11	15	19	23	26	30	34
12	0792	0828	0864	0899	0934	0969	1004	1038	1072	1106	3	7	10	14	17	21	24	28	31
13	1139	1173	1206	1239	1271	1303	1335	1367	1399	1430	3	6	10	13	16	19	23	26	29
14	1461	1492	1523	1553	1584	1614	1644	1673	1703	1732	3	6	9	12	15	18	21	24	27
15	1761	1790	1818	1847	1875	1903	1931	1959	1987	2014	*3	6	8	11	14	17	20	22	25
16	2041	2068	2095	2122	2148	2175	2201	2227	2253	2279	3	5	8	11	13	16	18	21	24
17	2304	2330	2355	2380	2405	2430	2455	2480	2504	2529	2	5	7	10	12	15	17	20	22
18	2553	2577	2601	2625	2648	2672	2695	2718	2742	2765	2	5	7	9	12	14	16	19	21
19	2788	2810	2833	2856	2878	2900	2923	2945	2967	2989	2	4	7	9	11	13	16	18	20
20	3010	3032	3054	3075	3096	3118	3139	3160	3181	3201	2	4	6	8	11	13	15	17	19
21	3222	3243	3263	3284	3304	3324	3345	3365	3385	3404	2	4	6	8	10	12	14	16	18
22	3424	3444	3464	3483	3502	3522	3541	3560	3579	3598	2	4	6	8	10	12	14	15	17
23	3617	3636	3655	3674	3692	3711	3729	3747	3766	3784	2	4	6	7	9	11	13	15	17
24	3802	3820	3838	3856	3874	3892	3909	3927	3945	3962	2	4	5	7	9	11	12	14	16
25	3979	3997	4014	4031	4048	4065	4082	4099	4116	4133	2	3	5	7	9	10	12	14	15
26	4150	4166	4183	4200	4216	4232	4249	4265	4281	4298	2	3	5	7	8	10	11	13	15
27	4314	4330	4346	4362	4378	4393	4409	4425	4440	4456	2	3	5	6	8	9	11	13	14
28	4472	4487	4502	4518	4533	4548	4564	4579	4594	4609	2	3	5	6	8	9	11	12	14
29	4624	4639	4654	4669	4683	4698	4713	4728	4742	4757	1	3	4	6	7	9	10	12	13
30	4771	4786	4800	4814	4829	4843	4857	4871	4886	4900	1	3	4	6	7	9	10	11	13
31	4914	4928	4942	4955	4969	4983	4997	5011	5024	5038	1	3	4	6	7	8	10	11	12
32	5051	5065	5079	5092	5105	5119	5132	5145	5159	5172	1	3	4	5	7	8	9	11	12
33	5185	5198	5211	5224	5237	5250	5263	5276	5289	5302	1	3	4	5	6	8	9	10	12
34	5315	5328	5340	5353	5366	5378	5391	5403	5416	5428	1	3	4	5	6	8	9	10	11
35	5441	5453	5465	5478	5490	5502	5514	5527	5539	5551	1	2	4	5	6	7	9	10	11
36	5563	5575	5587	5599	5611	5623	5635	5647	5658	5670	1	2	4	5	6	7	8	10	11
37	5682	5694	5705	5717	5729	5740	5752	5763	5775	5786	1	2	3	5	6	7	8	9	10
38	5798	5809	5821	5832	5843	5855	5866	5877	5888	5899	1	2	3	5	6	7	8	9	10
39	5911	5922	5933	5944	5955	5966	5977	5988	5999	6010	1	2	3	4	5	7	8	9	10
40	6021	6031	6042	6053	6064	6075	6085	6096	6107	6117	1	2	3	4	5	6	8	9	10
41	6128	6138	6149	6160	6170	6180	6191	6201	6212	6222	1	2	3	4	5	6	7	8	9
42	6232	6243	6253	6263	6274	6284	6294	6304	6314	6325	1	2	3	4	5	6	7	8	9
43	6335	6345	6355	6365	6375	6385	6395	6405	6415	6425	1	2	3	4	5	6	7	8	9
44	6435	6444	6454	6464	6474	6484	6493	6503	6513	6522	1	2	3	4	5	6	7	8	9
45	6532	6542	6551	6561	6571	6580	6590	6599	6609	6618	1	2	3	4	5	6	7	8	9
46	6628	6637	6646	6656	6665	6675	6684	6693	6702	6712	1	2	3	4	5	6	7	7	8
47	6721	6730	6739	6749	6758	6767	6776	6785	6794	6803	1	2	3	4	5	5	6	7	8
48	6812	6821	6830	6839	6848	6857	6866	6875	6884	6893	1	2	3	4	5	5	6	7	8
49	6902	6911	6920	6928	6937	6946	6955	6964	6972	6981	1	2	3	4	4	5	6	7	8
50	6990	6998	7007	7016	7024	7033	7042	7050	7059	7067	1	2	3	3	4	5	6	7	8
51	7076	7084	7093	7101	7110	7118	7126	7135	7143	7152	1	2	3	3	4	5	6	7	8
52	7160	7168	7177	7185	7193	7202	7210	7218	7226	7235	1	2	2	3	4	5	6	7	7
53	7243	7251	7259	7267	7275	7284	7292	7300	7308	7316	1	2	2	3	4	5	6	6	7
54	7324	7332	7340	7348	7356	7364	7372	7380	7388	7396	1	2	2	3	4	5	6	6	7
N	0	1	2	3	4	5	6	7	8	9	1	2	3	4	5	6	7	8	9

* Interpolation in this section of the table is inaccurate.

Table 6 (*cont.*)

N	0	1	2	3	4	5	6	7	8	9	Proportional Parts								
											1	2	3	4	5	6	7	8	9
55	7404	7412	7419	7427	7435	7443	7451	7459	7466	7474	1	2	2	3	4	5	5	6	7
56	7482	7490	7497	7505	7513	7520	7528	7536	7543	7551	1	2	2	3	4	5	5	6	7
57	7559	7566	7574	7582	7589	7597	7604	7612	7619	7627	1	2	2	3	4	5	5	6	7
58	7634	7642	7649	7657	7664	7672	7679	7686	7694	7701	1	1	2	3	4	4	5	6	7
59	7709	7716	7723	7731	7738	7745	7752	7760	7767	7774	1	1	2	3	4	4	5	6	7
60	7782	7789	7796	7803	7810	7818	7825	7832	7839	7846	1	1	2	3	4	4	5	6	6
61	7853	7860	7868	7875	7882	7889	7896	7903	7910	7917	1	1	2	3	4	4	5	6	6
62	7924	7931	7938	7945	7952	7959	7966	7973	7980	7987	1	1	2	3	3	4	5	6	6
63	7993	8000	8007	8014	8021	8028	8035	8041	8048	8055	1	1	2	3	3	4	5	5	6
64	8062	8069	8075	8082	8089	8096	8102	8109	8116	8122	1	1	2	3	3	4	5	5	6
65	8129	8136	8142	8149	8156	8162	8169	8176	8182	8189	1	1	2	3	3	4	5	5	6
66	8195	8202	8209	8215	8222	8228	8235	8241	8248	8254	1	1	2	3	3	4	5	5	6
67	8261	8267	8274	8280	8287	8293	8299	8306	8312	8319	1	1	2	3	3	4	5	5	6
68	8325	8331	8338	8344	8351	8357	8363	8370	8376	8382	1	1	2	3	3	4	4	5	6
69	8388	8395	8401	8407	8414	8420	8426	8432	8439	8445	1	1	2	2	3	4	4	5	6
70	8451	8457	8463	8470	8476	8482	8488	8494	8500	8506	1	1	2	2	3	4	4	5	6
71	8513	8519	8525	8531	8537	8543	8549	8555	8561	8567	1	1	2	2	3	4	4	5	5
72	8573	8579	8585	8591	8597	8603	8609	8615	8621	8627	1	1	2	2	3	4	4	5	6
73	8633	8639	8645	8651	8657	8663	8669	8675	8681	8686	1	1	2	2	3	4	4	5	5
74	8692	8698	8704	8710	8716	8722	8727	8733	8739	8745	1	1	2	2	3	4	4	5	5
75	8751	8756	8762	8768	8774	8779	8785	8791	8797	8802	1	1	2	2	3	3	4	5	5
76	8808	8814	8820	8825	8831	8837	8842	8848	8854	8859	1	1	2	2	3	3	4	5	5
77	8865	8871	8876	8882	8887	8893	8899	8904	8910	8915	1	1	2	2	3	3	4	4	5
78	8921	8927	8932	8938	8943	8949	8954	8960	8965	8971	1	1	2	2	3	3	4	4	5
79	8976	8982	8987	8993	8998	9004	9009	9015	9020	9025	1	1	2	2	3	3	4	4	5
80	9031	9036	9042	9047	9053	9058	9063	9069	9074	9079	1	1	2	2	3	3	4	4	5
81	9085	9090	9096	9101	9106	9112	9117	9122	9128	9133	1	1	2	2	3	3	4	4	5
82	9138	9143	9149	9154	9159	9165	9170	9175	9180	9186	1	1	2	2	3	3	4	4	5
83	9191	9196	9201	9206	9212	9217	9222	9227	9232	9238	1	1	2	2	3	3	4	4	5
84	9243	9248	9253	9258	9263	9269	9274	9279	9284	9289	1	1	2	2	3	3	4	4	5
85	9294	9299	9304	9309	9315	9320	9325	9330	9335	9340	1	1	2	2	3	3	4	4	5
86	9345	9350	9355	9360	9365	9370	9375	9380	9385	9390	1	1	2	2	3	3	4	4	5
87	9395	9400	9405	9410	9415	9420	9425	9430	9435	9440	0	1	1	2	2	3	3	4	4
88	9445	9450	9455	9460	9465	9469	9474	9479	9484	9489	0	1	1	2	2	3	3	4	4
89	9494	9499	9504	9509	9513	9518	9523	9528	9533	9538	0	1	1	2	2	3	3	4	4
90	9542	9547	9552	9557	9562	9566	9571	9576	9581	9586	0	1	1	2	2	3	3	4	4
91	9590	9595	9600	9605	9609	9614	9619	9624	9628	9633	0	1	1	2	2	3	3	4	4
92	9638	9643	9647	9652	9657	9661	9666	9671	9675	9680	0	1	1	2	2	3	3	4	4
93	9685	9689	9694	9699	9703	9708	9713	9717	9722	9727	0	1	1	2	2	3	3	4	4
94	9731	9736	9741	9745	9750	9754	9759	9763	9768	9773	0	1	1	2	2	3	3	4	4
95	9777	9782	9786	9791	9795	9800	9805	9809	9814	9818	0	1	1	2	2	3	3	4	4
96	9823	9827	9832	9836	9841	9845	9850	9854	9859	9863	0	1	1	2	2	3	3	4	4
97	9868	9872	9877	9881	9886	9890	9894	9899	9903	9908	0	1	1	2	2	3	3	4	4
98	9912	9917	9921	9926	9930	9934	9939	9943	9948	9952	0	1	1	2	2	3	3	4	4
99	9956	9961	9965	9969	9974	9978	9983	9987	9991	9996	0	1	1	2	2	3	3	3	4
N	0	1	2	3	4	5	6	7	8	9	1	2	3	4	5	6	7	8	9

Table 7 The Chi-Square Distribution

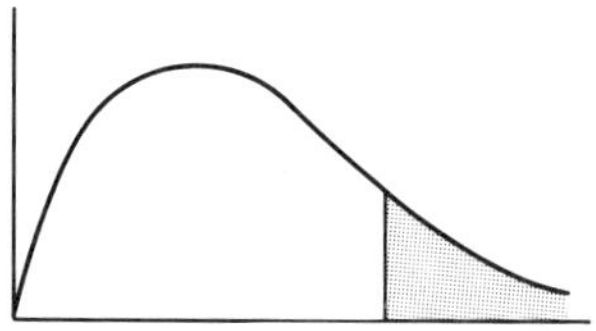

$\chi^2_{v,a}$

$$\alpha = \int_{\chi^2_{v,\alpha}}^{\infty} \frac{(\chi^2)^{\frac{v-2}{2}} e^{-\chi^2/2}}{2^{v/2}\Gamma(v/2)}\, d\chi^2$$

v \ α	.95	.90	.75	.50	.25	.10	.05	.025	.01	.005
1	.00393	.0158	.102	.455	1.323	2.706	3.841	5.024	6.635	7.879
2	.103	.211	.575	1.386	2.773	4.605	5.991	7.378	9.210	10.597
3	.352	.584	1.213	2.366	4.108	6.251	7.815	9.348	11.345	12.838
4	.711	1.064	1.923	3.357	5.385	7.779	9.488	11.143	13.277	14.860
5	1.145	1.610	2.675	4.351	6.626	9.236	11.070	12.832	15.086	16.750
6	1.635	2.204	3.455	5.348	7.841	10.645	12.592	14.449	16.812	18.548
7	2.167	2.833	4.255	6.346	9.037	12.017	14.067	16.013	18.475	20.278
8	2.733	3.490	5.071	7.344	10.219	13.362	15.507	17.535	20.090	21.955
9	3.325	4.168	5.899	8.343	11.389	14.684	16.919	19.023	21.666	23.589
10	3.940	4.865	6.737	9.342	12.549	15.987	18.307	20.483	23.209	25.188
11	4.575	5.578	7.584	10.341	13.701	17.275	19.675	21.920	24.725	26.757
12	5.226	6.304	8.438	11.340	14.845	18.549	21.026	23.337	26.217	28.300
13	5.892	7.042	9.299	12.340	15.984	19.812	22.362	24.736	27.688	29.819
14	6.571	7.790	10.165	13.339	17.117	21.064	23.685	26.119	29.141	31.319
15	7.261	8.547	11.036	14.339	18.245	22.307	24.996	27.488	30.578	32.801
16	7.962	9.312	11.912	15.338	19.369	23.542	26.296	28.845	32.000	34.267
17	8.672	10.085	12.792	16.338	20.489	24.769	27.587	30.101	33.409	35.718
18	9.390	10.865	13.675	17.338	21.605	25.989	28.869	31.526	34.805	37.156
19	10.117	11.651	14.562	18.338	22.718	27.204	30.144	32.852	36.191	38.582
20	10.851	12.443	15.452	19.337	23.828	28.412	31.410	34.170	37.566	39.997
21	11.591	13.240	16.344	20.337	24.935	29.615	32.671	35.479	38.932	41.401
22	12.338	14.041	17.240	21.337	26.039	30.813	33.924	36.781	40.289	42.796
23	13.091	14.848	18.137	22.337	27.141	32.007	35.172	38.076	41.638	44.181
24	13.848	15.659	19.037	23.337	28.241	33.196	36.415	39.364	42.980	45.558
25	14.611	16.473	19.939	24.337	29.339	34.382	37.652	40.646	44.314	46.928
26	15.379	17.292	20.843	25.336	30.434	35.563	38.885	41.923	45.642	48.290
27	16.151	18.114	21.749	26.336	31.528	36.741	40.113	43.194	46.963	49.645
28	16.928	18.939	22.657	27.336	32.620	37.916	41.337	44.461	48.278	50.993
29	17.708	19.768	23.567	28.336	33.711	39.087	42.557	45.722	49.588	52.336
30	18.493	20.599	24.478	29.336	34.800	40.256	43.773	46.979	50.892	53.672

Table 8 Areas Under the Standard Normal Curve from 0 to z

Areas under the Standard Normal Curve from 0 to z

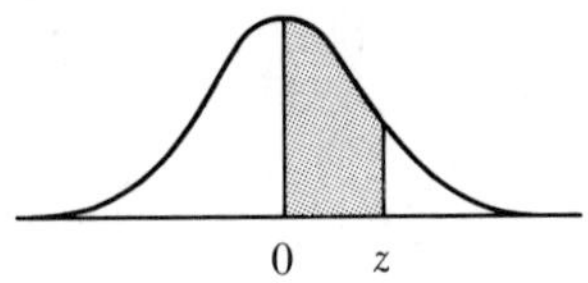

$$P(Z \le z) = \int_0^z \frac{e^{-Z^2/2}\, dZ}{\sqrt{2\pi}}$$

z	0	1	2	3	4	5	6	7	8	9
0.0	.0000	.0040	.0080	.0120	.0160	.0199	.0239	.0279	.0319	.0359
0.1	.0398	.0438	.0478	.0517	.0557	.0596	.0636	.0675	.0714	.0754
0.2	.0793	.0832	.0871	.0910	.0948	.0987	.1026	.1064	.1103	.1141
0.3	.1179	.1217	.1255	.1293	.1331	.1368	.1406	.1443	.1480	.1517
0.4	.1554	.1591	.1628	.1664	.1700	.1736	.1772	.1808	.1844	.1879
0.5	.1915	.1950	.1985	.2019	.2054	.2088	.2123	.2157	.2190	.2224
0.6	.2258	.2291	.2324	.2357	.2389	.2422	.2454	.2486	.2518	.2549
0.7	.2580	.2612	.2642	.2673	.2704	.2734	.2764	.2794	.2823	.2852
0.8	.2881	.2910	.2939	.2967	.2996	.3023	.3051	.3078	.3106	.3133
0.9	.3159	.3186	.3212	.3238	.3264	.3289	.3315	.3340	.3365	.3389
1.0	.3413	.3438	.3461	.3485	.3508	.3531	.3554	.3577	.3599	.3621
1.1	.3643	.3665	.3686	.3708	.3729	.3749	.3770	.3790	.3810	.3830
1.2	.3849	.3869	.3888	.3907	.3925	.3944	.3962	.3980	.3997	.4015
1.3	.4032	.4049	.4066	.4082	.4099	.4115	.4131	.4147	.4162	.4177
1.4	.4192	.4207	.4222	.4236	.4251	.4265	.4279	.4292	.4306	.4319
1.5	.4332	.4345	.4357	.4370	.4382	.4394	.4406	.4418	.4429	.4441
1.6	.4452	.4463	.4474	.4484	.4495	.4505	.4515	.4525	.4535	.4545
1.7	.4554	.4564	.4573	.4582	.4591	.4599	.4608	.4616	.4625	.4633
1.8	.4641	.4649	.4656	.4664	.4671	.4678	.4686	.4693	.4699	.4706
1.9	.4713	.4719	.4726	.4732	.4738	.4744	.4750	.4756	.4761	.4767
2.0	.4772	.4778	.4783	.4788	.4793	.4798	.4803	.4808	.4812	.4817
2.1	.4821	.4826	.4830	.4834	.4838	.4842	.4846	.4850	.4854	.4857
2.2	.4861	.4864	.4868	.4871	.4875	.4878	.4881	.4884	.4887	.4890
2.3	.4893	.4896	.4898	.4901	.4904	.4906	.4909	.4911	.4913	.4916
2.4	.4918	.4920	.4922	.4925	.4927	.4929	.4931	.4932	.4934	.4936
2.5	.4938	.4940	.4941	.4943	.4945	.4946	.4948	.4949	.4951	.4952
2.6	.4953	.4955	.4956	.4957	.4959	.4960	.4961	.4962	.4963	.4964
2.7	.4965	.4966	.4967	.4968	.4969	.4970	.4971	.4972	.4973	.4974
2.8	.4974	.4975	.4976	.4977	.4977	.4978	.4979	.4979	.4980	.4981
2.9	.4981	.4982	.4982	.4983	.4984	.4984	.4985	.4985	.4986	.4986
3.0	.4987	.4987	.4987	.4988	.4988	.4989	.4989	.4989	.4990	.4990
3.1	.4990	.4991	.4991	.4991	.4992	.4992	.4992	.4992	.4993	.4993
3.2	.4993	.4993	.4994	.4994	.4994	.4994	.4994	.4995	.4995	.4995
3.3	.4995	.4995	.4995	.4996	.4996	.4996	.4996	.4996	.4996	.4997
3.4	.4997	.4997	.4997	.4997	.4997	.4997	.4997	.4997	.4997	.4998
3.5	.4998	.4998	.4998	.4998	.4998	.4998	.4998	.4998	.4998	.4998
3.6	.4998	.4998	.4999	.4999	.4999	.4999	.4999	.4999	.4999	4999
3.7	.4999	.4999	.4999	.4999	.4999	.4999	.4999	.4999	.4999	.4999
3.8	.4999	.4999	.4999	.4999	.4999	.4999	.4999	.4999	.4999	.4999
3.9	.5000	.5000	.5000	.5000	.5000	.5000	.5000	.5000	.5000	.5000

Table 9 Poisson Table*

$$P(x) = e^{-M}M^x/x!$$

X/M	.1	.2	.3	.4	.5	.6	.7	.8	.9	1.0	1.1	1.2	1.3	1.4	1.5	1.6	1.7	1.8	1.9	2.0
0	.9048	.8187	.7408	.6703	.6065	.5488	.4966	.4493	.4066	.3679	.3329	.3012	.2725	.2466	.2231	.2019	.1827	.1653	.1496	.1353
1	.0905	.1637	.2222	.2681	.3033	.3293	.3476	.3595	.3659	.3679	.3662	.3614	.3543	.3452	.3347	.3230	.3106	.2975	.2842	.2707
2	.0045	.0164	.0333	.0536	.0758	.0988	.1217	.1438	.1647	.1839	.2014	.2169	.2303	.2417	.2510	.2584	.2640	.2678	.2700	.2707
3	.0002	.0011	.0033	.0072	.0126	.0198	.0284	.0383	.0494	.0613	.0738	.0867	.0998	.1128	.1255	.1378	.1496	.1607	.1710	.1804
4	.0000	.0001	.0003	.0007	.0016	.0030	.0050	.0077	.0111	.0153	.0203	.0260	.0324	.0395	.0471	.0551	.0636	.0723	.0812	.0902
5	.0000	.0000	.0000	.0001	.0002	.0004	.0007	.0012	.0020	.0031	.0045	.0062	.0084	.0111	.0141	.0176	.0216	.0260	.0309	.0361
6	.0000	.0000	.0000	.0000	.0000	.0000	.0001	.0002	.0003	.0005	.0008	.0012	.0018	.0026	.0035	.0047	.0061	.0078	.0098	.0120
7	.0000	.0000	.0000	.0000	.0000	.0000	.0000	.0000	.0000	.0001	.0001	.0002	.0003	.0005	.0008	.0011	.0015	.0020	.0027	.0034
8	.0000	.0000	.0000	.0000	.0000	.0000	.0000	.0000	.0000	.0000	.0000	.0000	.0001	.0001	.0001	.0002	.0003	.0005	.0006	.0009
9	.0000	.0000	.0000	.0000	.0000	.0000	.0000	.0000	.0000	.0000	.0000	.0000	.0000	.0000	.0000	.0000	.0001	.0001	.0001	.0002

X/M	2.1	2.2	2.3	2.4	2.5	2.6	2.7	2.8	2.9	3.0	3.1	3.2	3.3	3.4	3.5	3.6	3.7	3.8	3.9	4.0
0	.1225	.1108	.1003	.0907	.0821	.0743	.0672	.0608	.0550	.0498	.0450	.0408	.0369	.0334	.0302	.0273	.0247	.0224	.0202	.0183
1	.2572	.2438	.2306	.2177	.2052	.1931	.1815	.1703	.1596	.1494	.1397	.1304	.1217	.1135	.1057	.0984	.0915	.0850	.0789	.0733
2	.2700	.2681	.2652	.2613	.2565	.2510	.2450	.2384	.2314	.2240	.2165	.2087	.2008	.1929	.1850	.1771	.1692	.1615	.1539	.1465
3	.1890	.1966	.2033	.2090	.2138	.2176	.2205	.2225	.2237	.2240	.2237	.2226	.2209	.2186	.2158	.2125	.2087	.2046	.2001	.1954
4	.0992	.1082	.1169	.1254	.1336	.1414	.1488	.1557	.1622	.1680	.1733	.1781	.1823	.1858	.1888	.1912	.1931	.1944	.1951	.1954
5	.0417	.0476	.0538	.0602	.0668	.0735	.0804	.0872	.0940	.1008	.1075	.1140	.1203	.1264	.1322	.1377	.1429	.1477	.1522	.1563
6	.0146	.0174	.0206	.0241	.0278	.0319	.0362	.0407	.0455	.0504	.0555	.0608	.0662	.0716	.0771	.0826	.0881	.0936	.0989	.1042
7	.0044	.0055	.0068	.0083	.0099	.0118	.0139	.0163	.0188	.0216	.0246	.0278	.0312	.0348	.0385	.0425	.0466	.0508	.0551	.0595
8	.0011	.0015	.0019	.0025	.0031	.0038	.0047	.0057	.0068	.0081	.0095	.0111	.0129	.0148	.0169	.0191	.0215	.0241	.0269	.0298
9	.0003	.0004	.0005	.0007	.0009	.0011	.0014	.0018	.0022	.0027	.0033	.0040	.0047	.0056	.0066	.0076	.0089	.0102	.0116	.0132
10	.0001	.0001	.0001	.0002	.0002	.0003	.0004	.0005	.0006	.0008	.0010	.0013	.0016	.0019	.0023	.0028	.0033	.0039	.0045	.0053
11	.0000	.0000	.0000	.0000	.0000	.0001	.0001	.0001	.0002	.0002	.0003	.0004	.0005	.0006	.0007	.0009	.0011	.0013	.0016	.0019
12	.0000	.0000	.0000	.0000	.0000	.0000	.0000	.0000	.0000	.0001	.0001	.0001	.0001	.0002	.0002	.0003	.0003	.0004	.0005	.0006
13	.0000	.0000	.0000	.0000	.0000	.0000	.0000	.0000	.0000	.0000	.0000	.0000	.0000	.0000	.0001	.0001	.0001	.0001	.0002	.0002
14	.0000	.0000	.0000	.0000	.0000	.0000	.0000	.0000	.0000	.0000	.0000	.0000	.0000	.0000	.0000	.0000	.0000	.0000	.0000	.0001

* Table prepared by William Burnham

Table 9 (*cont.*)

X/M	4.1	4.2	4.3	4.4	4.5	4.6	4.7	4.8	4.9	5.0	5.1	5.2	5.3	5.4	5.5	5.6	5.7	5.8	5.9	6.0
0	.0166	.0150	.0136	.0123	.0111	.0101	.0091	.0082	.0074	.0067	.0061	.0055	.0050	.0045	.0041	.0037	.0033	.0030	.0027	.0025
1	.0679	.0630	.0583	.0540	.0500	.0462	.0427	.0395	.0365	.0337	.0311	.0287	.0265	.0244	.0225	.0207	.0191	.0176	.0162	.0149
2	.1393	.1323	.1254	.1188	.1125	.1063	.1005	.0948	.0894	.0842	.0793	.0746	.0701	.0659	.0618	.0580	.0544	.0509	.0477	.0446
3	.1904	.1852	.1798	.1743	.1687	.1631	.1574	.1517	.1460	.1404	.1348	.1293	.1239	.1185	.1133	.1082	.1033	.0985	.0938	.0892
4	.1951	.1944	.1933	.1917	.1898	.1875	.1849	.1820	.1789	.1755	.1719	.1681	.1641	.1600	.1558	.1515	.1472	.1428	.1383	.1339
5	.1600	.1633	.1662	.1687	.1708	.1725	.1738	.1747	.1753	.1755	.1753	.1748	.1740	.1728	.1714	.1697	.1678	.1656	.1632	.1606
6	.1093	.1143	.1191	.1237	.1281	.1323	.1362	.1398	.1432	.1462	.1490	.1515	.1537	.1555	.1571	.1584	.1594	.1601	.1605	.1606
7	.0640	.0686	.0732	.0778	.0824	.0869	.0914	.0959	.1002	.1044	.1086	.1125	.1163	.1200	.1234	.1267	.1298	.1326	.1353	.1377
8	.0328	.0360	.0393	.0428	.0463	.0500	.0537	.0575	.0614	.0653	.0692	.0731	.0771	.0810	.0849	.0887	.0925	.0962	.0998	.1033
9	.0150	.0168	.0188	.0209	.0232	.0255	.0281	.0307	.0334	.0363	.0392	.0423	.0454	.0486	.0519	.0552	.0586	.0620	.0654	.0688
10	.0061	.0071	.0081	.0092	.0104	.0118	.0132	.0147	.0164	.0181	.0200	.0220	.0241	.0262	.0285	.0309	.0334	.0359	.0386	.0413
11	.0023	.0027	.0032	.0037	.0043	.0049	.0056	.0064	.0073	.0082	.0093	.0104	.0116	.0129	.0143	.0157	.0173	.0190	.0207	.0225
12	.0008	.0009	.0011	.0013	.0016	.0019	.0022	.0026	.0030	.0034	.0039	.0045	.0051	.0058	.0065	.0073	.0082	.0092	.0102	.0113
13	.0002	.0003	.0004	.0005	.0006	.0007	.0008	.0009	.0011	.0013	.0015	.0018	.0021	.0024	.0028	.0032	.0036	.0041	.0046	.0052
14	.0001	.0001	.0001	.0001	.0002	.0002	.0003	.0003	.0004	.0005	.0006	.0007	.0008	.0009	.0011	.0013	.0015	.0017	.0019	.0022
15	.0000	.0000	.0000	.0000	.0001	.0001	.0001	.0001	.0001	.0002	.0002	.0002	.0003	.0003	.0004	.0005	.0006	.0007	.0008	.0009
16	.0000	.0000	.0000	.0000	.0000	.0000	.0000	.0000	.0000	.0000	.0001	.0001	.0001	.0001	.0001	.0002	.0002	.0002	.0003	.0003
17	.0000	.0000	.0000	.0000	.0000	.0000	.0000	.0000	.0000	.0000	.0000	.0000	.0000	.0000	.0000	.0001	.0001	.0001	.0001	.0001

X/M	6.1	6.2	6.3	6.4	6.5	6.6	6.7	6.8	6.9	7.0	7.1	7.2	7.3	7.4	7.5	7.6	7.7	7.8	7.9	8.0
0	.0022	.0020	.0018	.0017	.0015	.0014	.0012	.0011	.0010	.0009	.0008	.0007	.0007	.0006	.0006	.0005	.0005	.0004	.0004	.0003
1	.0137	.0126	.0116	.0106	.0098	.0090	.0082	.0076	.0070	.0064	.0059	.0054	.0049	.0045	.0041	.0038	.0035	.0032	.0029	.0027
2	.0417	.0390	.0364	.0340	.0318	.0296	.0276	.0258	.0240	.0223	.0208	.0194	.0180	.0167	.0156	.0145	.0134	.0125	.0116	.0107
3	.0848	.0806	.0765	.0726	.0688	.0652	.0617	.0584	.0552	.0521	.0492	.0464	.0438	.0413	.0389	.0366	.0345	.0324	.0305	.0286
4	.1294	.1249	.1205	.1162	.1118	.1076	.1034	.0992	.0952	.0912	.0874	.0836	.0799	.0764	.0729	.0696	.0663	.0632	.0602	.0573
5	.1579	.1549	.1519	.1487	.1454	.1420	.1385	.1349	.1314	.1277	.1241	.1204	.1167	.1130	.1094	.1057	.1021	.0986	.0951	.0916
6	.1605	.1601	.1595	.1586	.1575	.1562	.1546	.1529	.1511	.1490	.1468	.1445	.1420	.1394	.1367	.1339	.1311	.1282	.1252	.1221
7	.1399	.1418	.1435	.1450	.1462	.1472	.1480	.1486	.1489	.1490	.1489	.1486	.1481	.1474	.1465	.1454	.1442	.1428	.1413	.1396
8	.1066	.1099	.1130	.1160	.1188	.1215	.1240	.1263	.1284	.1304	.1321	.1337	.1351	.1363	.1373	.1381	.1388	.1392	.1395	.1396
9	.0723	.0757	.0791	.0825	.0858	.0891	.0923	.0954	.0985	.1014	.1042	.1070	.1096	.1121	.1144	.1167	.1187	.1207	.1224	.1241
10	.0441	.0469	.0498	.0528	.0558	.0588	.0618	.0649	.0679	.0710	.0740	.0770	.0800	.0829	.0858	.0887	.0914	.0941	.0967	.0993
11	.0244	.0265	.0285	.0307	.0330	.0353	.0377	.0401	.0426	.0452	.0478	.0504	.0531	.0558	.0585	.0613	.0640	.0667	.0695	.0722
12	.0124	.0137	.0150	.0164	.0179	.0194	.0210	.0227	.0245	.0263	.0283	.0303	.0323	.0344	.0366	.0388	.0411	.0434	.0457	.0481
13	.0058	.0065	.0073	.0081	.0089	.0099	.0108	.0119	.0130	.0142	.0154	.0168	.0181	.0196	.0211	.0227	.0243	.0260	.0278	.0296
14	.0025	.0029	.0033	.0037	.0041	.0046	.0052	.0058	.0064	.0071	.0078	.0086	.0095	.0104	.0113	.0123	.0134	.0145	.0157	.0169

15	.0010	.0012	.0014	.0016	.0018	.0020	.0023	.0026	.0029	.0033	.0037	.0041	.0046	.0051	.0057	.0062	.0069	.0075	.0083	.0090
16	.0004	.0005	.0005	.0006	.0007	.0008	.0010	.0011	.0013	.0014	.0016	.0019	.0021	.0024	.0026	.0030	.0033	.0037	.0041	.0045
17	.0001	.0002	.0002	.0002	.0003	.0003	.0004	.0004	.0005	.0006	.0007	.0008	.0009	.0010	.0012	.0013	.0015	.0017	.0019	.0021
18	.0000	.0001	.0001	.0001	.0001	.0001	.0001	.0002	.0002	.0002	.0003	.0003	.0004	.0004	.0005	.0006	.0006	.0007	.0008	.0009
19	.0000	.0000	.0000	.0000	.0000	.0000	.0001	.0001	.0001	.0001	.0001	.0001	.0001	.0002	.0002	.0002	.0003	.0003	.0003	.0004
20	.0000	.0000	.0000	.0000	.0000	.0000	.0000	.0000	.0000	.0000	.0000	.0000	.0001	.0001	.0001	.0001	.0001	.0001	.0001	.0002
21	.0000	.0000	.0000	.0000	.0000	.0000	.0000	.0000	.0000	.0000	.0000	.0000	.0000	.0000	.0000	.0000	.0000	.0000	.0001	.0001

X/M	8.1	8.2	8.3	8.4	8.5	8.6	8.7	8.8	8.9	9.0	9.1	9.2	9.3	9.4	9.5	9.6	9.7	9.8	9.9	10.0
0	.0003	.0003	.0002	.0002	.0002	.0002	.0002	.0002	.0001	.0001	.0001	.0001	.0001	.0001	.0001	.0001	.0001	.0001	.0001	.0000
1	.0025	.0023	.0021	.0019	.0017	.0016	.0014	.0013	.0012	.0011	.0010	.0009	.0009	.0008	.0007	.0007	.0006	.0005	.0005	.0005
2	.0100	.0092	.0086	.0079	.0074	.0068	.0063	.0058	.0054	.0050	.0046	.0043	.0040	.0037	.0034	.0031	.0029	.0027	.0025	.0023
3	.0269	.0252	.0237	.0222	.0208	.0195	.0183	.0171	.0160	.0150	.0140	.0131	.0123	.0115	.0107	.0100	.0093	.0087	.0081	.0076
4	.0544	.0517	.0491	.0466	.0443	.0420	.0398	.0377	.0357	.0337	.0319	.0302	.0285	.0269	.0254	.0240	.0226	.0213	.0201	.0189
5	.0882	.0849	.0816	.0784	.0752	.0722	.0692	.0663	.0635	.0607	.0581	.0555	.0530	.0506	.0483	.0460	.0439	.0418	.0398	.0378
6	.1191	.1160	.1128	.1097	.1066	.1034	.1003	.0972	.0941	.0911	.0881	.0851	.0822	.0793	.0764	.0736	.0709	.0682	.0656	.0631
7	.1378	.1358	.1338	.1317	.1294	.1271	.1247	.1222	.1197	.1171	.1145	.1118	.1091	.1064	.1037	.1010	.0982	.0955	.0928	.0901
8	.1395	.1392	.1388	.1382	.1375	.1366	.1356	.1344	.1332	.1318	.1302	.1286	.1269	.1251	.1232	.1212	.1191	.1170	.1148	.1126
9	.1256	.1269	.1280	.1290	.1299	.1306	.1311	.1315	.1317	.1318	.1317	.1315	.1311	.1306	.1300	.1293	.1284	.1274	.1263	.1251
10	.1017	.1040	.1063	.1084	.1104	.1123	.1140	.1157	.1172	.1186	.1198	.1210	.1219	.1228	.1235	.1241	.1245	.1249	.1250	.1251
11	.0749	.0776	.0802	.0828	.0853	.0878	.0902	.0925	.0948	.0970	.0991	.1012	.1031	.1049	.1067	.1083	.1098	.1112	.1125	.1137
12	.0505	.0530	.0555	.0579	.0604	.0629	.0654	.0679	.0703	.0728	.0752	.0776	.0799	.0822	.0844	.0866	.0888	.0908	.0928	.0948
13	.0315	.0334	.0354	.0374	.0395	.0416	.0438	.0459	.0481	.0504	.0526	.0549	.0572	.0594	.0617	.0640	.0662	.0685	.0707	.0729
14	.0182	.0196	.0210	.0225	.0240	.0256	.0272	.0289	.0306	.0324	.0342	.0361	.0380	.0399	.0419	.0439	.0459	.0479	.0500	.0521
15	.0098	.0107	.0116	.0126	.0136	.0147	.0158	.0169	.0182	.0194	.0208	.0221	.0235	.0250	.0265	.0281	.0297	.0313	.0330	.0347
16	.0050	.0055	.0060	.0066	.0072	.0079	.0086	.0093	.0101	.0109	.0118	.0127	.0137	.0147	.0157	.0168	.0180	.0192	.0204	.0217
17	.0024	.0026	.0029	.0033	.0036	.0040	.0044	.0048	.0053	.0058	.0063	.0069	.0075	.0081	.0088	.0095	.0103	.0111	.0119	.0128
18	.0011	.0012	.0014	.0015	.0017	.0019	.0021	.0024	.0026	.0029	.0032	.0035	.0039	.0042	.0046	.0051	.0055	.0060	.0065	.0071
19	.0005	.0005	.0006	.0007	.0008	.0009	.0010	.0011	.0012	.0014	.0015	.0017	.0019	.0021	.0023	.0026	.0028	.0031	.0034	.0037
20	.0002	.0002	.0002	.0003	.0003	.0004	.0004	.0005	.0005	.0006	.0007	.0008	.0009	.0010	.0011	.0012	.0014	.0015	.0017	.0019
21	.0001	.0001	.0001	.0001	.0001	.0002	.0002	.0002	.0002	.0003	.0003	.0003	.0004	.0004	.0005	.0006	.0006	.0007	.0008	.0009
22	.0000	.0000	.0000	.0000	.0001	.0001	.0001	.0001	.0001	.0001	.0001	.0001	.0002	.0002	.0002	.0002	.0003	.0003	.0004	.0004
23	.0000	.0000	.0000	.0000	.0000	.0000	.0000	.0000	.0000	.0000	.0000	.0001	.0001	.0001	.0001	.0001	.0001	.0001	.0002	.0002
24	.0000	.0000	.0000	.0000	.0000	.0000	.0000	.0000	.0000	.0000	.0000	.0000	.0000	.0000	.0000	.0000	.0000	.0001	.0001	.0001

Table 9 (*cont.*)

X/M	10.1	10.2	10.3	10.4	10.5	10.6	10.7	10.8	10.9	11.0	11.1	11.2	11.3	11.4	11.5	11.6	11.7	11.8	11.9	12.0
0	.0000	.0000	.0000	.0000	.0000	.0000	.0000	.0000	.0000	.0000	.0000	.0000	.0000	.0000	.0000	.0000	.0000	.0000	.0000	.0000
1	.0004	.0004	.0003	.0003	.0003	.0003	.0002	.0002	.0002	.0002	.0002	.0002	.0001	.0001	.0001	.0001	.0001	.0001	.0001	.0001
2	.0021	.0019	.0018	.0016	.0015	.0014	.0013	.0012	.0011	.0010	.0009	.0009	.0008	.0007	.0007	.0006	.0006	.0005	.0005	.0004
3	.0071	.0066	.0061	.0057	.0053	.0049	.0046	.0043	.0040	.0037	.0034	.0032	.0030	.0028	.0026	.0024	.0022	.0021	.0019	.0018
4	.0178	.0168	.0158	.0148	.0139	.0131	.0123	.0116	.0109	.0102	.0096	.0090	.0084	.0079	.0074	.0069	.0065	.0061	.0057	.0053
5	.0360	.0342	.0325	.0309	.0293	.0278	.0264	.0250	.0237	.0224	.0212	.0201	.0190	.0180	.0170	.0160	.0152	.0143	.0135	.0127
6	.0606	.0581	.0558	.0535	.0513	.0491	.0470	.0450	.0430	.0411	.0393	.0375	.0358	.0341	.0325	.0310	.0295	.0281	.0268	.0255
7	.0874	.0847	.0821	.0795	.0769	.0743	.0718	.0694	.0669	.0646	.0623	.0600	.0578	.0556	.0535	.0514	.0494	.0474	.0455	.0437
8	.1103	.1080	.1057	.1033	.1009	.0985	.0961	.0936	.0912	.0888	.0864	.0840	.0816	.0792	.0769	.0745	.0722	.0700	.0677	.0655
9	.1238	.1224	.1209	.1194	.1177	.1160	.1142	.1124	.1105	.1085	.1065	.1045	.1024	.1003	.0982	.0961	.0939	.0917	.0895	.0874
10	.1250	.1249	.1246	.1241	.1236	.1230	.1222	.1214	.1204	.1194	.1182	.1170	.1157	.1144	.1129	.1114	.1099	.1082	.1066	.1048
11	.1148	.1158	.1166	.1174	.1180	.1185	.1189	.1192	.1193	.1194	.1193	.1192	.1189	.1185	.1181	.1175	.1169	.1161	.1153	.1144
12	.0966	.0984	.1001	.1017	.1032	.1047	.1060	.1072	.1084	.1094	.1104	.1112	.1120	.1126	.1131	.1136	.1139	.1142	.1143	.1144
13	.0751	.0772	.0793	.0814	.0834	.0853	.0872	.0891	.0909	.0926	.0942	.0958	.0973	.0987	.1001	.1014	.1025	.1036	.1046	.1056
14	.0542	.0563	.0584	.0604	.0625	.0646	.0667	.0687	.0708	.0728	.0747	.0767	.0786	.0804	.0822	.0840	.0857	.0874	.0889	.0905
15	.0365	.0383	.0401	.0419	.0438	.0457	.0476	.0495	.0514	.0534	.0553	.0572	.0592	.0611	.0630	.0649	.0668	.0687	.0706	.0724
16	.0230	.0244	.0258	.0272	.0287	.0303	.0318	.0334	.0350	.0367	.0384	.0401	.0418	.0435	.0453	.0471	.0489	.0507	.0525	.0543
17	.0137	.0146	.0156	.0167	.0177	.0189	.0200	.0212	.0225	.0237	.0250	.0264	.0278	.0292	.0306	.0321	.0336	.0352	.0367	.0383
18	.0077	.0083	.0089	.0096	.0104	.0111	.0119	.0127	.0136	.0145	.0154	.0164	.0174	.0185	.0196	.0207	.0219	.0231	.0243	.0255
19	.0041	.0045	.0048	.0053	.0057	.0062	.0067	.0072	.0078	.0084	.0090	.0097	.0104	.0111	.0119	.0126	.0135	.0143	.0152	.0161
20	.0021	.0023	.0025	.0027	.0030	.0033	.0036	.0039	.0043	.0046	.0050	.0054	.0059	.0063	.0068	.0073	.0079	.0084	.0091	.0097
21	.0010	.0011	.0012	.0014	.0015	.0017	.0018	.0020	.0022	.0024	.0026	.0029	.0032	.0034	.0037	.0041	.0044	.0047	.0051	.0055
22	.0005	.0005	.0006	.0006	.0007	.0008	.0009	.0010	.0011	.0012	.0013	.0015	.0016	.0018	.0020	.0021	.0023	.0025	.0028	.0030
23	.0002	.0002	.0003	.0003	.0003	.0004	.0004	.0005	.0005	.0006	.0006	.0007	.0008	.0009	.0010	.0011	.0012	.0013	.0014	.0016
24	.0001	.0001	.0001	.0001	.0001	.0002	.0002	.0002	.0002	.0003	.0003	.0003	.0004	.0004	.0005	.0005	.0006	.0006	.0007	.0008
25	.0000	.0000	.0000	.0001	.0001	.0001	.0001	.0001	.0001	.0001	.0001	.0001	.0002	.0002	.0002	.0002	.0003	.0003	.0003	.0004
26	.0000	.0000	.0000	.0000	.0000	.0000	.0000	.0000	.0000	.0000	.0001	.0001	.0001	.0001	.0001	.0001	.0001	.0001	.0002	.0002
27	.0000	.0000	.0000	.0000	.0000	.0000	.0000	.0000	.0000	.0000	.0000	.0000	.0000	.0000	.0000	.0000	.0001	.0001	.0001	.0001

X/M	12.1	12.2	12.3	12.4	12.5	12.6	12.7	12.8	12.9	13.0	13.1	13.2	13.3	13.4	13.5	13.6	13.7	13.8	13.9	14.0
0	.0000	.0000	.0000	.0000	.0000	.0000	.0000	.0000	.0000	.0000	.0000	.0000	.0000	.0000	.0000	.0000	.0000	.0000	.0000	.0000
1	.0001	.0001	.0001	.0001	.0000	.0000	.0000	.0000	.0000	.0000	.0000	.0000	.0000	.0000	.0000	.0000	.0000	.0000	.0000	.0000
2	.0004	.0004	.0003	.0003	.0003	.0003	.0002	.0002	.0002	.0002	.0002	.0002	.0001	.0001	.0001	.0001	.0001	.0001	.0001	.0001
3	.0016	.0015	.0014	.0013	.0012	.0011	.0010	.0010	.0009	.0008	.0008	.0007	.0007	.0006	.0006	.0005	.0005	.0004	.0004	.0004
4	.0050	.0046	.0043	.0041	.0038	.0035	.0033	.0031	.0029	.0027	.0025	.0023	.0022	.0020	.0019	.0018	.0016	.0015	.0014	.0013
5	.0120	.0113	.0107	.0101	.0095	.0089	.0084	.0079	.0074	.0070	.0066	.0062	.0058	.0055	.0051	.0048	.0045	.0042	.0040	.0037
6	.0242	.0230	.0219	.0208	.0197	.0187	.0178	.0169	.0160	.0152	.0144	.0136	.0129	.0122	.0115	.0109	.0103	.0097	.0092	.0087
7	.0419	.0402	.0385	.0368	.0353	.0337	.0323	.0308	.0295	.0281	.0269	.0256	.0245	.0233	.0222	.0212	.0202	.0192	.0183	.0174
8	.0634	.0612	.0591	.0571	.0551	.0531	.0512	.0493	.0475	.0457	.0440	.0423	.0407	.0391	.0375	.0360	.0345	.0331	.0318	.0304
9	.0852	.0830	.0808	.0787	.0765	.0744	.0723	.0702	.0681	.0661	.0640	.0620	.0601	.0582	.0563	.0544	.0526	.0508	.0491	.0473
10	.1031	.1013	.0994	.0975	.0956	.0937	.0918	.0898	.0878	.0859	.0839	.0819	.0799	.0779	.0760	.0740	.0720	.0701	.0682	.0663
11	.1134	.1123	.1112	.1100	.1087	.1074	.1060	.1045	.1030	.1015	.0999	.0983	.0966	.0949	.0932	.0915	.0897	.0880	.0862	.0844
12	.1143	.1142	.1139	.1136	.1132	.1127	.1121	.1115	.1107	.1099	.1091	.1081	.1071	.1060	.1049	.1037	.1024	.1011	.0998	.0984
13	.1064	.1072	.1078	.1084	.1089	.1093	.1096	.1098	.1099	.1099	.1099	.1098	.1096	.1093	.1089	.1085	.1080	.1074	.1067	.1060
14	.0920	.0934	.0947	.0960	.0972	.0983	.0994	.1004	.1013	.1021	.1028	.1035	.1041	.1046	.1050	.1054	.1056	.1058	.1060	.1060
15	.0742	.0759	.0777	.0794	.0810	.0826	.0841	.0856	.0871	.0885	.0898	.0911	.0923	.0934	.0945	.0955	.0965	.0974	.0982	.0989
16	.0561	.0579	.0597	.0615	.0633	.0650	.0668	.0685	.0702	.0719	.0735	.0751	.0767	.0783	.0798	.0812	.0826	.0840	.0853	.0866
17	.0399	.0416	.0432	.0449	.0465	.0482	.0499	.0516	.0533	.0550	.0567	.0583	.0600	.0617	.0633	.0650	.0666	.0682	.0697	.0713
18	.0268	.0282	.0295	.0309	.0323	.0337	.0352	.0367	.0382	.0397	.0412	.0428	.0443	.0459	.0475	.0491	.0507	.0523	.0539	.0554
19	.0171	.0181	.0191	.0202	.0213	.0224	.0235	.0247	.0259	.0272	.0284	.0297	.0310	.0324	.0337	.0351	.0365	.0380	.0394	.0409
20	.0103	.0110	.0118	.0125	.0133	.0141	.0149	.0158	.0167	.0177	.0186	.0196	.0206	.0217	.0228	.0239	.0250	.0262	.0274	.0286
21	.0060	.0064	.0069	.0074	.0079	.0085	.0090	.0096	.0103	.0109	.0116	.0123	.0131	.0138	.0146	.0155	.0163	.0172	.0181	.0191
22	.0033	.0036	.0038	.0042	.0045	.0048	.0052	.0056	.0060	.0065	.0069	.0074	.0079	.0084	.0090	.0096	.0102	.0108	.0115	.0121
23	.0017	.0019	.0021	.0022	.0024	.0027	.0029	.0031	.0034	.0037	.0039	.0042	.0046	.0049	.0053	.0057	.0061	.0065	.0069	.0074
24	.0009	.0010	.0011	.0012	.0013	.0014	.0015	.0017	.0018	.0020	.0022	.0023	.0025	.0027	.0030	.0032	.0035	.0037	.0040	.0043
25	.0004	.0005	.0005	.0006	.0006	.0007	.0008	.0009	.0009	.0010	.0011	.0012	.0013	.0015	.0016	.0017	.0019	.0021	.0022	.0024
26	.0002	.0002	.0002	.0003	.0003	.0003	.0004	.0004	.0005	.0005	.0006	.0006	.0007	.0008	.0008	.0009	.0010	.0011	.0012	.0013
27	.0001	.0001	.0001	.0001	.0001	.0002	.0002	.0002	.0002	.0002	.0003	.0003	.0003	.0004	.0004	.0005	.0005	.0006	.0006	.0007
28	.0000	.0000	.0000	.0001	.0001	.0001	.0001	.0001	.0001	.0001	.0001	.0001	.0002	.0002	.0002	.0002	.0002	.0003	.0003	.0003
29	.0000	.0000	.0000	.0000	.0000	.0000	.0000	.0000	.0000	.0001	.0001	.0001	.0001	.0001	.0001	.0001	.0001	.0001	.0001	.0002
30	.0000	.0000	.0000	.0000	.0000	.0000	.0000	.0000	.0000	.0000	.0000	.0000	.0000	.0000	.0000	.0000	.0001	.0001	.0001	.0001

Table 9 (*cont.*)

X/M	14.1	14.2	14.3	14.4	14.5	14.6	14.7	14.8	14.9	15.0	15.1	15.2	15.3	15.4	15.5	15.6	15.7	15.8	15.9	16.0
0	.0000	.0000	.0000	.0000	.0000	.0000	.0000	.0000	.0000	.0000	.0000	.0000	.0000	.0000	.0000	.0000	.0000	.0000	.0000	.0000
1	.0000	.0000	.0000	.0000	.0000	.0000	.0000	.0000	.0000	.0000	.0000	.0000	.0000	.0000	.0000	.0000	.0000	.0000	.0000	.0000
2	.0001	.0001	.0001	.0001	.0001	.0000	.0000	.0000	.0000	.0000	.0000	.0000	.0000	.0000	.0000	.0000	.0000	.0000	.0000	.0000
3	.0004	.0003	.0003	.0003	.0003	.0002	.0002	.0002	.0002	.0002	.0002	.0001	.0001	.0001	.0001	.0001	.0001	.0001	.0001	.0001
4	.0012	.0012	.0011	.0010	.0009	.0009	.0008	.0007	.0007	.0006	.0006	.0006	.0005	.0005	.0004	.0004	.0004	.0004	.0003	.0003
5	.0035	.0033	.0031	.0029	.0027	.0025	.0024	.0022	.0021	.0019	.0018	.0017	.0016	.0015	.0014	.0013	.0012	.0011	.0011	.0010
6	.0082	.0078	.0073	.0069	.0065	.0061	.0058	.0055	.0051	.0048	.0046	.0043	.0040	.0038	.0036	.0034	.0032	.0030	.0028	.0026
7	.0165	.0157	.0149	.0142	.0135	.0128	.0122	.0115	.0109	.0104	.0098	.0093	.0088	.0084	.0079	.0075	.0071	.0067	.0063	.0060
8	.0292	.0279	.0267	.0256	.0244	.0234	.0223	.0213	.0204	.0194	.0186	.0177	.0169	.0161	.0153	.0146	.0139	.0132	.0126	.0120
9	.0457	.0440	.0424	.0409	.0394	.0379	.0365	.0351	.0337	.0324	.0311	.0299	.0287	.0275	.0264	.0253	.0243	.0232	.0223	.0213
10	.0644	.0625	.0607	.0589	.0571	.0553	.0536	.0519	.0502	.0486	.0470	.0454	.0439	.0424	.0409	.0395	.0381	.0367	.0354	.0341
11	.0825	.0807	.0789	.0771	.0753	.0735	.0716	.0698	.0681	.0663	.0645	.0628	.0611	.0594	.0577	.0560	.0544	.0527	.0512	.0496
12	.0970	.0955	.0940	.0925	.0910	.0894	.0878	.0861	.0845	.0829	.0812	.0795	.0778	.0762	.0745	.0728	.0711	.0695	.0678	.0661
13	.1052	.1043	.1034	.1025	.1014	.1004	.0992	.0981	.0969	.0956	.0943	.0930	.0916	.0902	.0888	.0874	.0859	.0844	.0829	.0814
14	.1060	.1058	.1057	.1054	.1051	.1047	.1042	.1037	.1031	.1024	.1017	.1010	.1001	.0993	.0983	.0974	.0963	.0953	.0942	.0930
15	.0996	.1002	.1007	.1012	.1016	.1019	.1021	.1023	.1024	.1024	.1024	.1023	.1021	.1019	.1016	.1012	.1008	.1003	.0998	.0992
16	.0878	.0889	.0900	.0911	.0920	.0930	.0938	.0946	.0954	.0960	.0966	.0972	.0977	.0981	.0984	.0987	.0989	.0991	.0992	.0992
17	.0728	.0743	.0757	.0771	.0785	.0798	.0811	.0824	.0836	.0847	.0858	.0869	.0879	.0888	.0897	.0906	.0914	.0921	.0928	.0934
18	.0570	.0586	.0602	.0617	.0632	.0648	.0663	.0677	.0692	.0706	.0720	.0734	.0747	.0760	.0773	.0785	.0797	.0808	.0819	.0830
19	.0423	.0438	.0453	.0468	.0483	.0498	.0513	.0528	.0543	.0557	.0572	.0587	.0602	.0616	.0630	.0645	.0659	.0672	.0686	.0699
20	.0298	.0311	.0324	.0337	.0350	.0363	.0377	.0390	.0404	.0418	.0432	.0446	.0460	.0474	.0489	.0503	.0517	.0531	.0545	0559
21	.0200	.0210	.0220	.0231	.0242	.0253	.0264	.0275	.0287	.0299	.0311	.0323	.0335	.0348	.0361	.0373	.0386	.0400	.0413	.0426
22	.0128	.0136	.0143	.0151	.0159	.0168	.0176	.0185	.0194	.0204	.0213	.0223	.0233	.0244	.0254	.0265	.0276	.0287	.0298	.0310
23	.0079	.0084	.0089	.0095	.0100	.0106	.0113	.0119	.0126	.0133	.0140	.0147	.0155	.0163	.0171	.0180	.0188	.0197	.0206	.0216
24	.0046	.0050	.0053	.0057	.0061	.0065	.0069	.0073	.0078	.0083	.0088	.0093	.0099	.0105	.0111	.0117	.0123	.0130	.0137	.0144
25	.0026	.0028	.0030	.0033	.0035	.0038	.0041	.0043	.0047	.0050	.0053	.0057	.0061	.0064	.0069	.0073	.0077	.0082	.0087	.0092
26	.0014	.0015	.0017	.0018	.0020	.0021	.0023	.0025	.0027	.0029	.0031	.0033	.0036	.0038	.0041	.0044	.0047	.0050	.0053	.0057
27	.0007	.0008	.0009	.0010	.0011	.0011	.0012	.0014	.0015	.0016	.0017	.0019	.0020	.0022	.0023	.0025	.0027	.0029	.0031	.0034
28	.0004	.0004	.0005	.0005	.0005	.0006	.0007	.0007	.0008	.0009	.0009	.0010	.0011	.0012	.0013	.0014	.0015	.0016	.0018	.0019
29	.0002	.0002	.0002	.0002	.0003	.0003	.0003	.0004	.0004	.0004	.0005	.0005	.0006	.0006	.0007	.0008	.0008	.0009	.0010	.0011
30	.0001	.0001	.0001	.0001	.0001	.0001	.0002	.0002	.0002	.0002	.0002	.0003	.0003	.0003	.0004	.0004	.0004	.0005	.0005	.0006
31	.0000	.0000	.0000	.0001	.0001	.0001	.0001	.0001	.0001	.0001	.0001	.0001	.0001	.0002	.0002	.0002	.0002	.0002	.0003	.0003
32	.0000	.0000	.0000	.0000	.0000	.0000	.0000	.0000	.0000	.0001	.0001	.0001	.0001	.0001	.0001	.0001	.0001	.0001	.0001	.0001
33	.0000	.0000	.0000	.0000	.0000	.0000	.0000	.0000	.0000	.0000	.0000	.0000	.0000	.0000	.0000	.0000	.0001	.0001	.0001	.0001

Table 10 Laplace Transforms

	Function of t		Laplace Transform
(1)	$f(t)$	(definition of Laplace transform)	$F(S) = \int_0^\infty f(t)e^{-St}\,dt$
(2)	$af(t) + bg(t)$		$aF(S) + bG(S)$
(3)	$f'(t)$	(derivative)	$SF(S) - f(0)$
(4)	$\int_0^t f(u)\,du$		$F(S)/S$
(5)	$\int_0^\infty \delta(t)\,dt$	(unit impulse)*	1
(6)	1	(unit step)	$1/S$
(7)	t	(unit ramp)	$1/S^2$
(8)	e^{-at}		$1/(S + a)$
(9)	$e^{-at}f(t)$	(shifting)	$F(S + a)$
(10)	$t^{n-1}/(n-1)!$, for $n = 1, 2, 3, \ldots$ $t^{n-1}/\Gamma(n)$, for $n > 0$		$1/S^n$
(11)	$\dfrac{t^{n-1}e^{at}}{(n-1)!}$, for $n = 1, 2, 3, \ldots$ $\dfrac{t^{n-1}e^{at}}{\Gamma(n)}$, for $n > 0$		$1/(S - a)^n$
(12)	$\sin at$		$a/(S^2 + a^2)$
(13)	$\cos at$		$S/(S^2 + a^2)$
(14)	$f(at)$	(scaling)	$F(S/a)/a$
(15)	$\begin{cases} f(t-a), & \text{for } t > a \\ 0, & \text{for } t < a \end{cases}$	(shifting)	$e^{-aS}F(S)$
(16)	$\int_0^t f(t-u)g(u)\,du$	(convolution)	$F(S) \cdot G(S)$

* $\delta(t)$ is a special function known as the Dirac delta function.

Table 11 *Z* Transforms

	Function of t		Z Transform
(1)	$f(t)$	(definition of Z transform)	$F(Z) = \sum_{t=0}^{\infty} f(t)Z^t$
(2)	$af(t) + bg(t)$		$aF(Z) + bG(Z)$
(3)	$f(t-1)$		$ZF(Z)$
(4)	$f(t+1)$		$\frac{1}{Z}[F(Z) - f(0)]$
(5)	$\left.\begin{array}{ll} 1, & \text{for } t = 0 \\ 0, & \text{otherwise} \end{array}\right\}$	(unit impulse)	1
(6)	1, for $t \geq 0$	(unit step)	$1/(1 - Z)$
(7)	t	(unit ramp)	$Z/(1 - Z)^2$
(8)	a^t	(geometric sequence)	$1/(1 - aZ)$
(9)	$a^t f(t)$		$F(aZ)$
(10)	ta^t		$aZ/(1 - aZ)^2$
(11)	$\sum_{i=0}^{t} f(i)$		$F(Z)/(1 - Z)$
(12)	$\Delta f(t) = f(t+1) - f(t)$		$\frac{1}{Z}[(1 - Z)F(Z) - f(0)]$
(13)	$\sum_{i=0}^{t} f(i)g(t-i)$ (convolution)		$F(Z)G(Z)$

(14) Initial value theorem: $f(0) = \lim_{Z \to 0} F(Z) = \lim_{Z \to 0} \sum_{t=0}^{\infty} f(t)Z^t$

(15) Final value theorem: $\lim_{t \to \infty} f(t) = \lim_{Z \to 1} (1 - Z)F(Z) = \lim_{Z \to 1} (1 - Z) \sum_{t=0}^{\infty} f(t)Z^t$

Table 12 Student's t Distribution with ν Degrees of Freedom

Shaded area $= p$

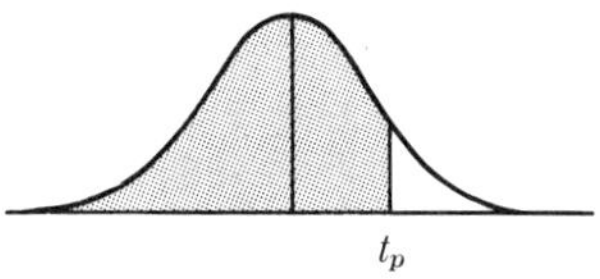

$$f(t) = \frac{1}{\sqrt{\nu\pi}} \frac{\Gamma\left(\frac{\nu+1}{2}\right)}{\Gamma\left(\frac{\nu}{2}\right)} \left(1 + \frac{t^2}{\nu}\right)^{-\frac{\nu+1}{2}} \quad \text{for } -\infty < t < \infty$$

ν	$t_{.995}$	$t_{.99}$	$t_{.975}$	$t_{.95}$	$t_{.90}$	$t_{.80}$	$t_{.75}$	$t_{.70}$	$t_{.60}$	$t_{.55}$
1	63.66	31.82	12.71	6.31	3.08	1.376	1.000	.727	.325	.158
2	9.92	6.96	4.30	2.92	1.89	1.061	.816	.617	.289	.142
3	5.84	4.54	3.18	2.35	1.64	.978	,765	.584	.277	.137
4	4.60	3.75	2.78	2.13	1.53	.941	.741	.569	.271	.134
5	4.03	3.36	2.57	2.02	1.48	.920	.727	.559	.267	.132
6	3.71	3.14	2.45	1.94	1.44	.906	.718	.553	.265	.131
7	3.50	3.00	2.36	1.90	1.42	.896	.711	.549	.263	.130
8	3.36	2.90	2.31	1.86	1.40	.889	.706	.576	.262	.130
9	3.25	2.82	2.26	1.83	1.38	.883	.703	.543	.261	.129
10	3.17	2.76	2.23	1.81	1.37	.879	.700	.542	.260	.129
11	3.11	2.72	2.20	1.80	1.36	.876	.697	.540	.260	.129
12	3.06	2.68	2.18	1.78	1.36	.873	.695	.539	.259	.128
13	3.01	2.65	2.16	1.77	1.35	.870	.694	.538	.259	.128
14	2.98	2.62	2.14	1.76	1.34	.868	.692	.537	.258	.128
15	2.95	2.60	2.13	1.75	1.34	.866	.691	.536	.258	.128
16	2.92	2.58	2.12	1.75	1.34	.865	.690	.535	.258	.128
17	2.90	2.57	2.11	1.74	1.33	.863	.689	.534	.357	.128
18	2.88	2.55	2.10	1.73	1.33	.862	.688	.534	.257	.127
19	2.86	2.54	2.09	1.73	1.33	.861	.688	.533	.257	.127
20	2.84	2.53	2.09	1.72	1.32	.860	.687	.533	.257	.127
21	2.83	2.52	2.08	1.72	1.32	.859	.686	.532	.257	.127
22	2.82	2.51	2.07	1.72	1.32	.858	.686	.532	.256	.127
23	2.81	2.50	2.07	1.71	1.32	.858	.685	.532	.256	.127
24	2.80	2.49	2.06	1.71	1.32	.857	.685	.531	.256	.127
25	2.79	2.48	2.06	1.71	1.32	.856	.684	.531	.256	.127
26	2.78	2.48	2.06	1.71	1.32	.856	.684	.531	.256	.127
27	2.77	2.47	2.05	1.70	1.31	.855	.684	.531	.256	.127
28	2.76	2.47	2.05	1.70	1.31	.855	.683	.530	.256	.127
29	2.76	2.46	2.04	1.70	1.31	.854	.683	.530	.256	.127
30	2.75	2.46	2.04	1.70	1.31	.854	.683	.530	.256	.127
40	2.70	2.42	2.02	1.68	1.30	.851	.681	.529	.255	.126
60	2.66	2.39	2.00	1.67	1.30	.848	.679	.527	.254	.126
120	2.62	2.36	1.98	1.66	1.29	.845	.677	.526	.254	.126
∞	2.58	2.33	1.96	1.645	1.28	.842	.674	.524	.253	.126

Source: R. A. Fisher and F. Yates, *Statistical Tables for Biological, Agricultural and Medical Research* (5th edition). Table III, Oliver and Boyd Ltd., Edinburgh, by permission of the authors and publishers.

Bookkeeping Fundamentals

Appendix B

Preliminaries: Bookkeeping

For some reason one frequently hears accountants criticize bookkeeping, and yet one never hears an engineer apologize for electricity. Bookkeeping is a clever method for recording financial transactions that rests on a simple equation: $A = L + O$ (key: A = assets, L = liabilities and O = owners' equity). Often the system of accounts is very elaborate and the scope of the business served very complex. Regardless of the demands made upon it, the science of bookkeeping always proves adaptable and equal to the task.

This text does not engage in a great deal of bookkeeping; nevertheless, you will understand the manipulation of costing systems better if you can trace the effects of transactions via journal entries. Consequently, a brief review of bookkeeping will be the focus of the next few pages.

The main points to remember when constructing a journal entry are:

(1) the types of accounts and examples of each,
(2) whether an increase in an account requires a debit or a credit, and
(3) the fact that each transaction has at least two parts.

It will help if we expand the balance sheet equation, $A = L + O$, to reveal where the revenue and expense accounts fit in this equation.

Key:

A = assets
L = liabilities
O = owners' equity
O_{BB} = beginning balance of owners' equity
O_{EB} = ending balance of owners' equity
R = revenues
E = expenses
D = dividends paid

To obtain some detail in income statements, accountants temporarily isolate separate revenue and expense accounts from the owners' equity set of accounts. This is merely a convenience, for the revenue and expense accounts remain at all times subsets of (that is, part of) owners' equity. The equation becomes

$$A = \underbrace{L + O} = L + \{O_{BB} + R - E - D = O_{EB}\}$$

A	$L + O$
Increases require debits	Increases require credits

By observing this equation and using the listing shown below, it would be possible to construct any journal entry.

Types of Accounts	Examples	← Effect of → Debit	Credit
Assets	cash, accounts receivable, inventory, marketable securities, prepaid expenses, equipment, buildings, patents	↑	↓
Liabilities	accounts payable, accrued expenses, mortgage payable, bonds payable	↓	↑
Owners' Equity	capital stock, retained earnings, J. Doe owner	↓	↑
Revenues	sales, interest received, dividends received, proceeds from sale of property	↓	↑
Expenses	cost of sales, advertising, repairs and maintenance, depreciation, bad debts, payroll taxes, property taxes, insurance, miscellaneous	↑	↓

How to Use the Listing?

1. Decide on the type of account you are dealing with by looking over the examples.
2. Decide what you wish to do to the account—increase it or decrease it.
3. Remember that at least two things happen with every transaction. For example, if machinery is purchased for \$10,000 cash, two assets are involved—machinery and cash—and machinery is increasing while cash is decreasing; result:

	Debit	Credit
Machinery	10,000	
Cash		10,000

Some typical entries are written and described in Exhibit 1 to help clarify how journal entries are prepared. With these and the foregoing journal entry rules as guides, you should have no trouble understanding the entries presented in the main text.

Exhibit 1 Prototype Entries

Account Type	Increase (+) Decrease (−)		Debit	Credit
A	+	Cash	10,000	
O	+	J. Doe Owner		10,000
		To start business		
A	+	Inventory	20,000	
L	+	Accounts Payable		20,000
		To buy merchandise on account		
A	+	Cash	40,000	
A	+	Accounts Receivable	30,000	
R	+	Sales		70,000
		To record cash and charge sales		
E	+	Telephone (expense)	2,000	
A	−	Cash		2,000
		To pay this month's telephone bill		
A	+	{Prepaid Insurance / Unexpired Insurance / Prepaid Expenses}	12,000	
A	−	Cash		12,000
		To record a four-year insurance policy paid for in advance; any one of the three accounts in the bracket could be debited.		
E	+	Insurance (expense)	250	
A	−	{Prepaid Insurance / Unexpired Insurance / Prepaid Expenses}		250
		To record one month's expense ($12,000 ÷ 48 = $250)		
E	+	Depreciation (expense)	22,500	
A_C	+	Accumulated Depreciation		
A	−	Property, Plant & Equipment		22,500
		To record one year's expense given cost = $100,000, salvage value = $10,000, life = 4 years, and straight-line depreciation method is used. By convention accountants introduce "contra-asset (A_c)" or "evaluation" accounts to permit keeping the amount spent on long-lived assets (buildings, machines, etc.) intact for statement preparation purposes; hence Accumulated Depreciation is used. This refinement, however, is wholly unnecessary, and the estimated decrease in value of assets (that is, the provision for depreciation) could be deducted directly from the asset account, Property, Plant, and Equipment.		
E	+	Salaries and Wages (expense)	4,000	
L	+	{Accrued Salaries and Wages / Accrued Expenses}		4,000
		To accrue four days' payroll given that the six-day payroll usually amounts to $6,000		
E	+	Cost of Goods Sold	80,000	
A	−	Inventory		80,000
		To record the cost of merchandise sold		

Mathematics: Matrix Algebra, Probability, and Calculus

Appendix C

Matrix Algebra

One can stumble his way through cost accounting or, with the aid of a modicum of matrix algebra, he can travel in style. This is partly because many accounting problems require the allocation of data inputs to data outputs—allocation is very pervasive in accounting—and partly because such practical management science techniques as linear programming, regression, and Markov chains make extensive use of the basics of matrix algebra. Furthermore, learning the basics is virtually painless—which makes matrix algebra the bargain of all mathematics.

Ordinary algebra deals with, among other things, equations like $bx = z$. This has the solution of

$$x = \frac{z}{b} \quad \text{or} \quad \left(\frac{1}{b}\right) z.$$

For example, $5x = 10$

$$x = \frac{10}{5} \quad \text{or} \quad .2(10)$$

where .2 is the reciprocal of 5.

Matrix algebra solves similar equations, several equations at a time ("simultaneous equations"), by using an inverse matrix, which in concept is quite like the reciprocal shown above. Let us see what a matrix and its inverse are.

A matrix is a collection of rows and columns of numbers. A single row of numbers is called a row vector, while a single column of numbers is called a column vector. Hence a matrix is a collection of one or more vectors. An example is shown below.

matrix B

$$\text{columns}\downarrow \quad \text{rows}\rightarrow \quad \begin{bmatrix} 3 & 5 \\ 7 & 2 \end{bmatrix} = \begin{bmatrix} b_{11} & b_{12} \\ b_{21} & b_{22} \end{bmatrix}$$

b_{ij} is the element in the ith row and jth column. Think of i and j as an address, row first then column.

To obtain B^{-1} (the inverse of matrix B), look at B and follow the steps described below.

Step 1: Interchange main diagonal $\begin{bmatrix} \surd & \\ & \surd \end{bmatrix}$ elements.

Step 2: Multiply cross-diagonal $\begin{bmatrix} & \surd \\ \surd & \end{bmatrix}$ elements by -1.

Step 3: Divide by the determinant of B (multiply B's main diagonal elements and subtract the product of its cross-diagonal elements).

$$B^{-1} = \frac{\begin{bmatrix} 2 & -5 \\ -7 & 3 \end{bmatrix}}{2(3) - (7)(5) = -29}$$

Matrix multiplication involves multiplying in step 1 the top-row elements of B times the first-column elements of A and summing the results to get the first-row-first-column element of C. Thus $3(3) + 5(1) = 14$. These are the shaded elements in the step 1 diagram. By continuing the indicated steps in the diagrams, one arrives at

$$\overset{B}{\begin{bmatrix} 3 & 5 \\ 7 & 2 \end{bmatrix}} \overset{A}{\begin{bmatrix} 3 & 2 & 0 \\ 1 & -1 & 5 \end{bmatrix}} = C$$

Step 1: $\begin{bmatrix} 3 & 5 \\ & \end{bmatrix} \begin{bmatrix} 3 & & \\ 1 & & \end{bmatrix} = \begin{bmatrix} 14 & & \\ & & \end{bmatrix}$

Step 2: $\begin{bmatrix} 3 & 5 \\ & \end{bmatrix} \begin{bmatrix} & 2 & \\ & -1 & \end{bmatrix} = \begin{bmatrix} & 1 & \\ & & \end{bmatrix}$

Step 3: $\begin{bmatrix} 3 & 5 \\ & \end{bmatrix} \begin{bmatrix} & & 0 \\ & & 5 \end{bmatrix} = \begin{bmatrix} & & 25 \\ & & \end{bmatrix}$

Step 4: $\begin{bmatrix} & \\ 7 & 2 \end{bmatrix} \begin{bmatrix} 3 & & \\ 1 & & \end{bmatrix} = \begin{bmatrix} & & \\ 23 & & \end{bmatrix}$

Step 5: $\begin{bmatrix} & \\ 7 & 2 \end{bmatrix} \begin{bmatrix} & 2 & \\ & -1 & \end{bmatrix} = \begin{bmatrix} & & \\ & 12 & \end{bmatrix}$

Step 6: $\begin{bmatrix} & \\ 7 & 2 \end{bmatrix} \begin{bmatrix} & & 0 \\ & & 5 \end{bmatrix} = \begin{bmatrix} & & \\ & & 10 \end{bmatrix}$

$$\overset{C}{\begin{bmatrix} 14 & 1 & 25 \\ 23 & 12 & 10 \end{bmatrix}}$$

It will help in ensuing work to understand the mathematics of matrix multiplication, which rest on the use of subscripts (addresses) and the summation sign, $\sum$. The summation sign is a way of writing a long string of variables in a compact way, for example;

$$\sum_{i=1}^{500} x_i = x_1 + x_2 + x_3 + x_4 + x_5 + x_6 + \cdots + x_{500}$$

Matrix multiplication is accomplished by

$$c_{ik} = \sum_{i=1}^{n} b_{ij} a_{jk}$$

Pay attention to the relationship among the subscripts as indicated by the connected arrows

For example, if you wished to calculate the c_{13} element, that forces i to equal 1 and k to equal 3 in the equation

$$c_{13} = \sum_{j=1}^{2} b_{1j} a_{j3} = b_{11}a_{13} + b_{12}a_{23} = 3(0) + 5(5) = 25$$

Note that the shape (or dimensions) of C (that is, C is a 2×3 matrix having two rows and three columns) results from the shape of B (which is a 2×2) and that of A (which is a 2×3):

$$\underset{(2 \times 2)}{B} \quad \underset{(2 \times 3)}{A} = \underset{(2 \times 3)}{C}$$

The inverse matrix is used to do substitution in matrix algebra. Suppose that our matrix B consists of the column vectors $\begin{bmatrix} 3 \\ 7 \end{bmatrix}$ and $\begin{bmatrix} 5 \\ 2 \end{bmatrix}$, and that we wish to substitute for the vector $\begin{bmatrix} 4 \\ 5 \end{bmatrix}$, or in other words, to express $\begin{bmatrix} 4 \\ 5 \end{bmatrix}$ as a combination of $\begin{bmatrix} 3 \\ 7 \end{bmatrix}$ and $\begin{bmatrix} 5 \\ 2 \end{bmatrix}$. If we call $\begin{bmatrix} 4 \\ 5 \end{bmatrix}$ "vector z" and the unknown numbers that will bring about the desired combination "vector x," we want to solve

$$Bx = z$$

Step 1: $\underbrace{B^{-1}B}x = B^{-1}z$

Step 2: $I \ x = B^{-1}z$

Step 3: $x = B^{-1}z$

Step 1: Multiply both sides by B^{-1}.

Step 2: Recognize that $B^{-1}B$ yields I.

Step 3: Observe that I is called the "identity" matrix and acts like the number 1 when multiplying. Take the time to multiply B and B^{-1} to see that I results (that is, $BB^{-1} = I = \begin{bmatrix} 1 & 0 \\ 0 & 1 \end{bmatrix}$) and then multiply I and something to see that the something results.

$$\overset{x}{\begin{bmatrix}x_1\\x_2\end{bmatrix}} = \overset{B^{-1}}{\frac{\begin{bmatrix}2&-5\\-7&3\end{bmatrix}}{-29}}\overset{z}{\begin{bmatrix}4\\5\end{bmatrix}} = \overset{x}{\begin{bmatrix}17/29\\13/29\end{bmatrix}}$$ Multiply B^{-1} and z to get x.

Note: $$\frac{17}{29}\begin{bmatrix}3\\7\end{bmatrix} + \frac{13}{29}\begin{bmatrix}5\\2\end{bmatrix} = \begin{bmatrix}\dfrac{51+65}{29}\\[2ex]\dfrac{119+26}{29}\end{bmatrix} = \begin{bmatrix}4\\5\end{bmatrix}$$

Conclusion: The scalars $\frac{17}{29}$ and $\frac{13}{29}$ may be used to multiply the other vectors instead of using $\left[\begin{smallmatrix}4\\5\end{smallmatrix}\right]$. This has the decided advantage of expressing everything in terms of the other (called basis) vectors.

Perhaps we should formally recognize the process illustrated in the note above. It is known as vector addition, and it simply requires that the vectors have the same shape; thereafter elements are added to corresponding elements:

$$(2, 3, -1) + (7, 4, 5) = (9, 7, 4)$$

$$\begin{bmatrix}3\\4\end{bmatrix} - \begin{bmatrix}7\\1\end{bmatrix} = \begin{bmatrix}-4\\3\end{bmatrix}$$

We have restricted ourselves to inversion of a 2×2 matrix, and we have used a technique called the adjoint-determinant method to do the inverting. There are a great many methods for inverting matrices, each having some advantage over the others. However, the adjoint-determinant method is the simplest for inverting a 2×2. Throughout most of the book, illustrations have been done with 2×2 matrices; we will shortly discuss a means for inverting 3×3 and larger matrices. The only civilized way to invert a 5×5 or larger matrix, however, is to use a computer.

There is, of course, an immense number of other concepts and techniques that comprise matrix algebra; nevertheless, the vector addition, matrix multiplication, and matrix inversion techniques that have been presented will go a very long way. Some further comfort can be experienced when multiplying if one of the matrices is a diagonal matrix like matrix A below:

$$\underset{(3\times 3)}{\overset{A}{\begin{bmatrix}2&0&0\\0&3&0\\0&0&4\end{bmatrix}}}\underset{(3\times 4)}{\overset{B}{\begin{bmatrix}4&3&2&5\\-2&1&1&6\\7&5&0&2\end{bmatrix}}} = \underset{(3\times 4)}{\overset{C}{\begin{bmatrix}8&6&4&10\\-6&3&3&18\\28&20&0&8\end{bmatrix}}}$$

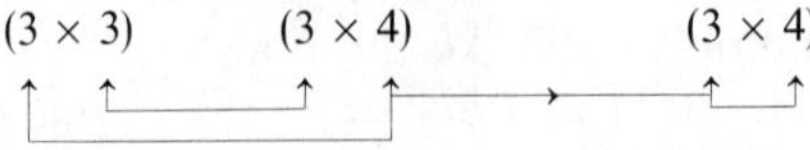

With a diagonal matrix you could multiply in the manner previously discussed, or you could simply multiply each row of B by the corresponding diagonal element of A. Thus (8, 6, 4, 10) is simply 2(4, 3, 2, 5).

One other nicety—partitioned multiplication—has much to offer accounting because it makes possible the isolation of details. The trick here is simply to stop adding products of elements whenever a partition (dashed line) is reached, and to put the result in separate vectors, which are later added to obtain the results of ordinary matrix multiplication. This is easier to do than to describe. Observe:

$$\underset{(3\times 4)}{\overset{A}{\left[\begin{array}{c|c|cc} 1 & 1 & 1 & 1 \\ 2 & -1 & 0 & -5 \\ 3 & 5 & 4 & 0 \end{array}\right]}}\ \underset{(4\times 2)}{\overset{B}{\left[\begin{array}{cc} 3 & 1 \\ \hline 4 & 2 \\ \hline 5 & 3 \\ 6 & 4 \end{array}\right]}} = [A_1 \mid A_2 \mid A_3]\left[\begin{array}{c} B_1 \\ \hline B_2 \\ \hline B_3 \end{array}\right]$$

$$= \underset{(3\times 2)}{\big[[A_1B_1] + [A_2B_2] + [A_3B_3]\big]}$$

$$= \left[\begin{bmatrix} 3 & 1 \\ 6 & 2 \\ 9 & 3 \end{bmatrix} + \begin{bmatrix} 4 & 2 \\ -4 & -2 \\ 20 & 10 \end{bmatrix} + \begin{bmatrix} 11 & 7 \\ -30 & -20 \\ 20 & 12 \end{bmatrix}\right]$$

$$\overset{C}{= \begin{bmatrix} 18 & 10 \\ -28 & -20 \\ 49 & 25 \end{bmatrix}}$$

Comments:

1. Each of the component matrices A_iB_i could provide needed detail in a particular problem.

2. Check the resulting C matrix by ignoring the partitions and multiplying A and B.

Unfortunately, not all matrices requiring inversion have a 2 × 2 shape; hence knowledge of more elaborate inversion methods is desirable. There are many methods; two are presented below. A third, the product form of the inverse, is presented in Chapter 17, where the decomposition algorithm of linear programming is discussed.

GAUSSIAN METHOD

$$A = \begin{bmatrix} 2 & 1 & 3 \\ 3 & 1 & -2 \\ 5 & 1 & 4 \end{bmatrix}$$

Step 1: Augment A by the identity matrix.

$$[A \vdots I] = \left[\begin{array}{ccc|ccc} \textcircled{2} & 1 & 3 & 1 & 0 & 0 \\ 3 & 1 & -2 & 0 & 1 & 0 \\ 5 & 1 & 4 & 0 & 0 & 1 \end{array}\right]$$

Step 2: Select one row as the pivot row and divide the pivot row by the pivot element (this is the element in the pivot row and pivot column—the a_{pp} element). The formula is $a'_{pj} = a_{pj}/a_{pp}$, for $j = 1, 2, \ldots$; $p =$ "pivot." The usual start is row 1.

$$(2 \;\; 1 \;\; 3 \;\; 1 \;\; 0 \;\; 0)/2 = (1 \;\; 1/2 \;\; 3/2 \;\; 1/2 \;\; 0 \;\; 0)$$

Step 3: From each nonpivot row ("other" row) subtract a scalar multiple of the pivot row where the scalar is -1 times the element in the other row—pivot column divided by the pivot element. Through this choice of scalar multipliers, a unit vector will result in the pivot column. The formula is

$$a'_{oj} = a_{oj} - (a_{op}/a_{pp})a_{pj}, \quad \text{for } j = 1, 2, \ldots; o = \text{"other."}$$

$$\begin{array}{rcccccc} (3 & 1 & -2 & 0 & 1 & 0) \\ -(3/2)(2 & 1 & 3 & 1 & 0 & 0) \\ \hline \left(0\right. & -\frac{1}{2} & -\frac{13}{2} & -\frac{3}{2} & 1 & \left.0\right) \end{array} \quad \begin{array}{c} \leftarrow\text{"other" row}\rightarrow \\ \leftarrow\text{"pivot" row}\rightarrow \end{array} \quad \begin{array}{rcccccc} (5 & 1 & 4 & 0 & 0 & 1) \\ -(5/2)(2 & 1 & 3 & 1 & 0 & 0) \\ \hline \left(0\right. & \frac{-3}{2} & \frac{-7}{2} & \frac{-5}{2} & 0 & \left.1\right) \end{array}$$

Step 4: Put the new matrix together.

$$\begin{bmatrix} 1 & 1/2 & 3/2 & 1/2 & 0 & 0 \\ 0 & \textcircled{-1/2} & -13/2 & -3/2 & 1 & 0 \\ 0 & -3/2 & -7/2 & -5/2 & 0 & 1 \end{bmatrix}$$

Step 5: Repeat the process, using the second row if the pivot element is not equal to zero; if it is, skip to the third row and later return and do the second row that then exists.

Pivot row:

$$(0 \;\; -1/2 \;\; -13/2 \;\; -3/2 \;\; 1 \;\; 0)/(-1/2) = (0 \;\; 1 \;\; 13 \;\; 3 \;\; -2 \;\; 0)$$

Other rows:

$$\begin{array}{rcccccc} (1 & 1/2 & 3/2 & 1/2 & 0 & 0) \\ -\tfrac{1}{2}/-\tfrac{1}{2}\;(0 & -1/2 & -13/2 & -3/2 & 1 & 0) \\ \hline (1 & 0 & -5 & -1 & 1 & 0) \end{array} \quad \begin{array}{rcccccc} (0 & -3/2 & -7/2 & -5/2 & 0 & 1) \\ -(-\tfrac{3}{2})/-\tfrac{1}{2}\;(0 & -1/2 & -13/2 & -3/2 & 1 & 0) \\ \hline (0 & 0 & 16 & 2 & -3 & 1) \end{array}$$

New matrix:

$$\begin{bmatrix} 1 & 0 & -5 & -1 & 1 & 0 \\ 0 & 1 & 13 & 3 & -2 & 0 \\ 0 & 0 & \textcircled{16} & 2 & -3 & 1 \end{bmatrix}$$

Step 6: Repeat the process using the third row.

Pivot row:

$$(0 \quad 0 \quad 16 \quad 2 \quad -3 \quad 1)/16 = (0 \quad 0 \quad 1 \quad 2/16 \quad -3/16 \quad 1/16)$$

Other rows:

$$\begin{array}{r} (1 \quad 0 \quad -5 \quad -1 \quad 1 \quad 0) \\ -(-5)/16 \; (0 \quad 0 \quad 16 \quad 2 \quad -3 \quad 1) \\ \hline \left(1 \quad 0 \quad 0 \quad \frac{-6}{16} \quad \frac{1}{16} \quad \frac{5}{16}\right) \end{array} \qquad \begin{array}{r} (0 \quad 1 \quad 13 \quad 3 \quad -2 \quad 0) \\ -13/16 \; (0 \quad 0 \quad 16 \quad 2 \quad -3 \quad 1) \\ \hline \left(0 \quad 1 \quad 0 \quad \frac{22}{16} \quad \frac{7}{16} \quad \frac{-13}{16}\right) \end{array}$$

New matrix:

$$[I \vdots A^{-1}] = \left[\begin{array}{ccc|ccc} 1 & 0 & 0 & -6/16 & 1/16 & 5/16 \\ 0 & 1 & 0 & 22/16 & 7/16 & -13/16 \\ 0 & 0 & 1 & 2/16 & -3/16 & 1/16 \end{array}\right]$$

Comment: Note how the inverse matrix now appears in the position of the original identity matrix, and the identity matrix now shows up where the former A matrix was. This may help you to follow the tableaus of linear programming.

ADJOINT DETERMINANT METHOD

$$A = \begin{bmatrix} 2 & 1 & 3 \\ 3 & 1 & -2 \\ 5 & 1 & 4 \end{bmatrix}$$

Step 1: Obtain the minors of each element by forming the determinants that remain when the ith row and jth column are crossed out for each element a_{ij}.

$$\begin{bmatrix} \begin{vmatrix} 1 & -2 \\ 1 & 4 \end{vmatrix} & \begin{vmatrix} 3 & -2 \\ 5 & 4 \end{vmatrix} & \begin{vmatrix} 3 & 1 \\ 5 & 1 \end{vmatrix} \\ \begin{vmatrix} 1 & 3 \\ 1 & 4 \end{vmatrix} & \begin{vmatrix} 2 & 3 \\ 5 & 4 \end{vmatrix} & \begin{vmatrix} 2 & 1 \\ 5 & 1 \end{vmatrix} \\ \begin{vmatrix} 1 & 3 \\ 1 & -2 \end{vmatrix} & \begin{vmatrix} 2 & 3 \\ 3 & -2 \end{vmatrix} & \begin{vmatrix} 2 & 1 \\ 3 & 1 \end{vmatrix} \end{bmatrix} = \begin{bmatrix} 6 & 22 & -2 \\ 1 & -7 & -3 \\ -5 & -13 & -1 \end{bmatrix}$$

Step 2: Convert the minors into cofactors by multiplying each element by $(-1)^{i+j}$, where i and j are the subscripts of each element.

$$\begin{bmatrix} 6 & -22 & -2 \\ -1 & -7 & 3 \\ -5 & 13 & -1 \end{bmatrix}$$

Step 3: Calculate the determinant of A (that is, $|A|$) by multiplying the elements in any row (or any column) of A by their corresponding cofactors and summing the products.

$$\text{Row 1: } 2(6) + 1(-22) + 3(-2) = -16$$
$$\text{Column 2: } 1(-22) + 1(-7) + 1(13) = -16$$

(Any column or row and its cofactors would yield the same result.)

Step 4: Transpose the cofactor matrix (that is, make its rows into columns) to obtain the adjoint matrix, and then divide by the determinant to obtain the inverse matrix.

$$\frac{\text{Adjoint}}{\text{Determinant}} = \frac{\begin{bmatrix} 6 & -1 & -5 \\ -22 & -7 & 13 \\ -2 & 3 & -1 \end{bmatrix}}{-16} = \begin{bmatrix} -6/16 & 1/16 & 5/16 \\ 22/16 & 7/16 & -13/16 \\ 2/16 & -3/16 & 1/16 \end{bmatrix}, \text{ as above}$$

Probability

The forthcoming outcomes of many events cannot be known with certainty. To deal with chance (random) outcomes, probability theory is most attractive especially because it enables an analyst to consider simultaneously results that are otherwise inconsistent—as, for instance, when profit and loss are considered by weighting each by its probability of occurrence. Thus probability measures are weights given to events.

Throughout the latter half of the text probability theory has been presented and applied to managerial problems. The present discussion will therefore be limited to fundamental concepts necessary to understand the work done in the chapters.

The basic ideas of probability theory are listed below.

1. There is a sample space, S, consisting of mutually exclusive and collectively exhaustive events, E_i. In other words some one E_i must occur, and if E_i occurs, E_j cannot occur (where $E_j \neq E_i$). In set terminology, $S = \{E_1, E_2, \ldots, E_n\}$.

2. The probability that an event will occur is $P(E_i) = P_i$, where P_i is such that $0 \leq P_i \leq 1$.

3. The probability of an event that is certain to occur is 1.
4. The probability of an event that cannot possibly occur is 0.
5. The sum of all probabilities is 1 because one of the events E_i must occur. In other words, S is the union of all events and its probability is 1. In symbols,

$$S = \bigcup_k E_k = E_1 \cup E_2 \cup \cdots \cup E_n \quad \text{and} \quad P(S) = 1 = \sum_{i=1}^{n} P_i.$$

6. $P(E_i \cup E_j) = P(E_i) + P(E_j) - P(E_i \cap E_j),\ i \neq j$
7. $P(E_i \cap E_j) = P(E_i|E_j)P(E_j) = P(E_j|E_i)P(E_i),\ i \neq j$ and $P(E_i),\ P(E_j) \neq 0$

Numbers 2, 6, and 7 are considered the basic axioms of probability theory. The symbol $\cup$ indicates "either and/or both" and refers to summed events. The symbol $\cap$ indicates "both" ($E_i \cap E_j$ is *both* events occur) and therefore refers to joint events. The symbol $|$ designates "given" and refers to "conditional" events (effectively, a portion of the sample space is selected—the given—and the probability of an event within that selected portion is then calculated). Thus $P(A|B)$ means that we seek the probability of A given that event B has occurred, and this probability equals the joint probability that both events occur—$P(A \cap B)$, or more simply $P(AB)$—divided by the marginal probability that B has occurred—$P(B)$. If the two events are *independent*, the fact that B has occurred in no way influences the occurrence of A; then $P(A|B) = P(AB)/P(B) = P(A)P(B)/P(B) = P(A)$. The Venn diagrams shown below clarify these relationships.

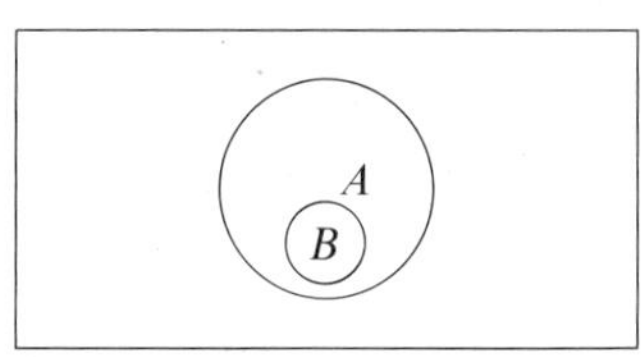

$$P(B|A) = \frac{P(AB)}{P(A)} = \frac{P(B)}{P(A)}$$

Conditional, dependent: If A occurs, B occurs; if B occurs, A occurs.

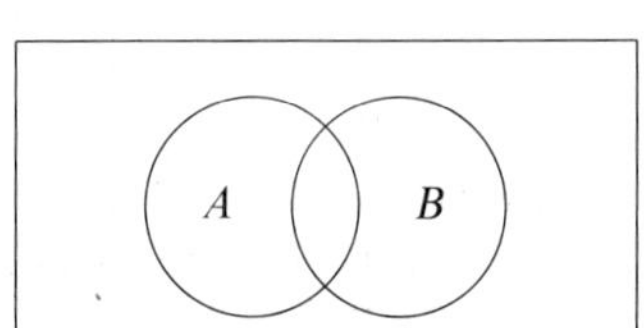

$$P(B|A) = \frac{P(AB)}{P(A)} = \frac{P(A)P(B)}{P(A)} = P(B)$$

Conditional, independent: If A occurs, B *may or may not* occur.

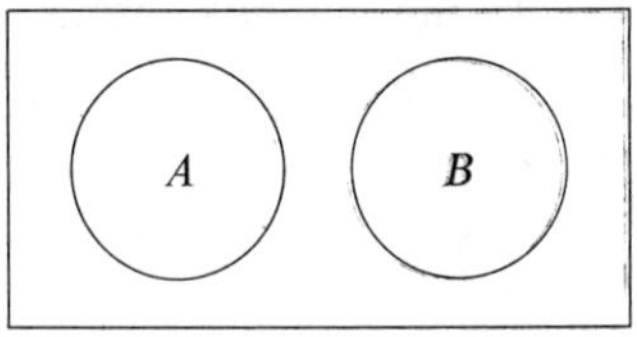

$$P(B|A) = \frac{P(AB)}{P(A)} = \frac{0}{P(A)} = 0$$

Mutually exclusive; therefore, A and B are *not* independent—if we know A has occurred, we know B has not occurred.

$$\begin{aligned} P(A \cup B) &= P(A) + P(B) - P(A \cap B) \\ &= P(A) + P(B) \end{aligned}$$

There are three types of probability: subjective, empirical, and axiomatic. Subjective probabilities reflect someone's best guess; empirical probabilities reflect the frequency with which an event has occurred in the past; and axiomatic probabilities arise from study of theoretical sample spaces like the tossing of a coin.

Examples of Axiomatic Probability: Two six-sided dice are rolled. What is the probability of obtaining any given outcome on one die? What is the probability of obtaining any given sum of the dice?

1. The sample space for the outcomes of one die is

$$S = \{1, 2, 3, 4, 5, 6\}$$

   If the die is fair, the probability of outcome x is

$$P(x) = 1/6$$

   When all outcomes are equally likely, the "uniform probability distribution" is present.

2. The sample space for the sum of the dice is

$$S = \{2, 3, 4, \ldots, 12\}$$

   These outcomes are not equally likely; the most likely outcome is 7, which can occur in 6 out of a possible 36 ways (any outcome of die 1 can occur jointly with any of the 6 outcomes of die 2 and there are 6 possible outcomes of die 1). The outcome 2 can occur in 1 out of 36 ways. The formula for outcome (sum) x is

$$P(x) = (6 - |7 - x|)/36$$

Example of Empirical Probability:

Outcome (x)	Historical Frequency of Outcome		Probability $P(x)$
10	100	$\div$ 400 =	.25
20	120	$\div$ 400 =	.30
30	180	$\div$ 400 =	.45
	400	$\div$ 400 =	1.00

Example of Subjective Probability: "I think the probability of success is .8; hence the probability of failure is .2 since these are the only possible outcomes in this situation."

Probability deals with both discrete and continuous events. The probabilities just illustrated were discrete. Had time been the event, or more generally if an event could be measured in infinitesimal quantities, continuous probabilities would be involved. Discrete probability distributions are known as "probability mass functions"; continuous probability distributions are known as "probability density functions." A probability density function does not exist at a point but rather in an area under a curve.

Often an analyst is concerned with the probability that an outcome is less than or equal to some value. When this happens, he effectively splits his probability distribution into two portions; in symbols;

$$1 = \sum_{x=0}^{\infty} P(x) = \sum_{x=0}^{W} P(x) + \sum_{x=W+1}^{\infty} P(x)$$

Here the *cumulative* probability of W or less is

$$P(x \leq W) = \sum_{x=0}^{W} P(x),$$

and it equals the *cumulative complement*,

$$P(x \leq W) = 1 - \sum_{x=W+1}^{\infty} P(x).$$

Examples: Refer to the empirical example given above. What is the probability that the outcome will be 20 or less?

$$P(x \leq 20) = P(x = 10) + P(x = 20) = \sum_{x=10}^{20} P(x) = .25 + .30 = .55$$

What is the probability that the outcome will be at least 20?

$$P(x \geq 20) = P(x = 20) + P(x = 30) = \sum_{x=20}^{30} P(x) = .30 + .45 = .75$$

In applied mathematics, it is important to have a measure of central tendency and a measure of dispersion. The most popular measure of central tendency is the mean or expected value, $E(x)$, while dispersion is measured by the variance of x, $V(x)$, and its square root, which is known as the standard deviation, $\sigma = \sqrt{V(x)}$. The expected value is defined below.

Discrete	Continuous
$E(x) = \sum_{x=-\infty}^{\infty} xP(x)$	$E(x) = \int_{-\infty}^{\infty} xf(x)\,dx$

In words, each outcome x is multiplied by the probability of its happening, and the products are added over all possible outcomes to obtain an expected value. Many outcomes are restricted to be positive values within a given range. In such cases, it is wise to remember that the probability of impossible events is zero; therefore, if $10 \leq x \leq 100$, $p(-\infty) = \cdots = P(0) = P(1) = \cdots = P(9) = P(101) = P(102) = \cdots = P(\infty) = 0$, because these outcomes are impossible.

The variance of x is defined $V(x) = E(x^2) - [E(x)]^2$, where the expected value of x^2—that is, $E(x^2)$—is determined as follows:

Discrete	Continuous
$E(x^2) = \sum_{x=-\infty}^{\infty} x^2P(x)$	$E(x^2) = \int_{-\infty}^{\infty} x^2f(x)\,dx$

The less the variance and its square root (the standard deviation), the more certain is the expected value.

Example of Empirical Probability: Assume the previous empirical example data.

$$E(x) = \sum xP(x) = 10(.25) + 20(.30) + 30(.45) = 22$$

$$E(x^2) = \sum x^2P(x) = 10^2(.25) + 20^2(.30) + 30^2(.45) = 550$$

$$V(x) = E(x^2) - [E(x)]^2 = 550 - (22)^2 = 66$$

$$\sigma = \sqrt{V(x)} = \sqrt{66} = 8.1$$

Expected values and variances for continuous distributions are illustrated in the calculus section of this appendix.

Calculus

Overview

Calculus is a branch of mathematics devoted to analyzing changes in functions. The most important equation in all of calculus is the difference equation:

$$\Delta_i f(x_1, x_2, \ldots, x_i, \ldots, x_n) = f(x_1, x_2, \ldots, x_i + h, \ldots, x_n) - f(x_1, x_2, \ldots, x_n)$$

In words, the difference with respect to x_i (that is, Δ_i) equals the function evaulated at $x_i + h$, with all other variables held constant, minus the original function. Here h has been used to designate the amount of increase in the x_i reading that is appropriate in the situation being studied. h is often referred to as the "gap," and it takes the analysis from one reading of x to an adjacent reading. It must have some positive value, or else there would be only one reading that could be studied (since no change from the selected x would be possible if h equalled zero).

Calculus will be called "finite" calculus in this text whenever the function being studied exists only for discrete readings of x, and "infinitesimal" calculus whenever the function being studied is continuous (that is, defined for any reading of x). Infinitesimal calculus is the better known, although it is but a special case of finite calculus in which the gap is *almost* zero (that is, "the gap that is no gap").

Calculus uses differences and derivatives to locate optimal points in functions and antidifferences and antiderivatives (also referred to as "integrals") to obtain the sums of functions. Locating optimal points and obtaining sums are the reasons why calculus is useful in applied mathematics.

Finite Calculus

Let us restrict our study of finite calculus to one independent variable x and to the gap $h = 1$. With this value of h, the positive integers become the domain and the difference formula reduces to

$$\Delta f(x) = f(x + 1) - f(x)$$

Observe that the top of a hill or the bottom of a valley—where "hill" and "valley" refer to the bumps in the function—occurs when the sign of $\Delta f(x)$ changes. This fact enables the analyst to locate the peaks and floors in a discrete model; the top of a hill will be a point of local profit maximization, while the bottom of a valley will be a point of local cost minimization. When all such local points are compared along with the end points of the function, the overall ("global") maximum and minimum may be determined. The fewer the bumps, the quicker the procedure.

How can the difference process be reversed? By taking the antidifference (Δ^{-1}) of the difference, the original function is restored, except for a constant:

$$\Delta^{-1}\,\Delta f(x) = \tilde{f}(x) + c = f(x)$$

The mystery here has to do with the possibility (not the certainty) that $\Delta f(x)$ causes the disappearance of a constant term (if one exists) that the analyst has no knowledge of; therefore, when he antidifferences the function in front of him, that is, $\Delta f(x)$, he adds a constant, c (which may even have the value 0), to his results, $\tilde{f}(x)$. From a practical standpoint, c can be ignored whenever there are given limits of summation, because c will be added when evaluating at the upper limit and then subtracted when evaluating at the lower limit.

This brings us to the matter of summation. Antidifferences are most helpful in summing a function to obtain a "closed form" (that is, a form in which no operators—like $\sum$—are present). Here is what happens:

		Comment
Given:	$\Delta f(x) = f(x+1) - f(x) = g(x)$	Set $\Delta f(x) = g(x)$.
	$\Delta^{-1}\,\Delta f(x) = f(x) = \Delta^{-1} g(x)$	Antidifference both sides.
Problem:	$\sum_{x=1}^{n} g(x) = ?$	
Solution:	$\sum_{x=1}^{n} g(x) = g(1) + g(2) + \cdots + g(n)$	
	$= [f(2) - f(1)] + [f(3) - f(2)] + \cdots + [f(n+1) - f(n)]$	See "given."
	$= -f(1) + f(n+1)$	Cancel like terms of opposite sign.
	$= f(n+1) - f(1)$	Commute terms.
	$= f(x)]_1^{n+1}$	Introduce evaluation symbol.
	$= \Delta^{-1} g(x)]_1^{n+1}$	See "given."

In words, the sum of a series (function) from 1 to n equals the antidifference of the series evaluated at $n + 1$ and 1. The trick is to find what $\Delta^{-1}g(x)$ is (in other words, to clear the operator, Δ^{-1}).

Example: Suppose $f(x) = a^x$, a geometric (or exponential) term; then $\sum_{x=1}^{n} a^x$ would be a geometric series.

By definition, $\Delta f(x) = f(x+1) - f(x) = a^{x+1} - a^x = a^x(a - 1)$

Let $a^x = \left(\frac{1}{1.1}\right)^5 = b(5, .10)$ as in Table 2, Appendix A; then

$$\Delta\left(\frac{1}{1.1}\right)^5 = \left(\frac{1}{1.1}\right)^5\left(\frac{1}{1.1} - 1\right) = .6209(.9091 - 1) = -.0564$$

This is $b(6, .10) - b(5, .10) = .5645 - .6209 = -.0564$

Example: $\sum_{x=1}^{n} a^x = \Delta^{-1}a^x]_1^{n+1}$

$$\Delta a^x = a^x(a - 1)$$
$$\Delta^{-1}\,\Delta a^x = a^x = \Delta^{-1}a^x(a - 1)\; a^x/(a - 1) = \Delta^{-1}a^x$$
$$\therefore, \Delta^{-1}a^x = a^x/(a - 1)$$

$$= \frac{a^x}{a - 1}\Big]_1^{n+1} = \frac{a^{n+1}}{a - 1} - \frac{a^1}{a - 1} = \frac{a(a^n - 1)}{a - 1} = \frac{a(1 - a^n)}{1 - a}$$

Let $a^x = \frac{1}{1.1}$ and $n = 5$, then

$$\sum_{x=1}^{5}\left(\frac{1}{1.1}\right)^x = \frac{\left(\frac{1}{1.1}\right)\left[1 - \left(\frac{1}{1.1}\right)^5\right]}{1 - \frac{1}{1.1}} = 10[1 - .6209] = 3.791$$

This is $B(5, .10) = 3.7908$ in Table 4, Appendix A.

These same procedures may be applied to polynomials with very useful results. Here, however, there is a preliminary complication preparatory to summing that involves restatement of the polynomial in upper (or factorial) notation via synthetic division.

Example:

$$f(x) = x^3$$

$$\Delta f(x) = (x + 1)^3 - x^3 = 3x^2 + 3x + 1$$ (In differencing, restatement is not absolutely necessary.)

If $f(4) = 4^3$, then $\Delta f(4) = 5^3 - 4^3 = 3(4^2) + 3(4) + 1 = 61$

Let us restate $f(x) = x^3$ in factorial notation via synthetic division. Our goal is to obtain factorial notation, according to which,

$x^{(n)} = (x - 0)(x - 1)\ldots(x - (n - 1)) = x(x - 1)(x - 2)\ldots(x - n + 1)$
A special case of factorial notation is $x^{(x)} = x! = x(x - 1)\ldots 1$ (so $4^{(4)} = 4{\cdot}3{\cdot}2{\cdot}1 = 4! = 24$, for example), but this is of no concern at present.
Note that $x^{(0)} = x^0 = 1$.

Synthetic Division:

$$f(x) = x^3 = 1x^3 + 0x^2 + 0x^1 + 0x^0$$

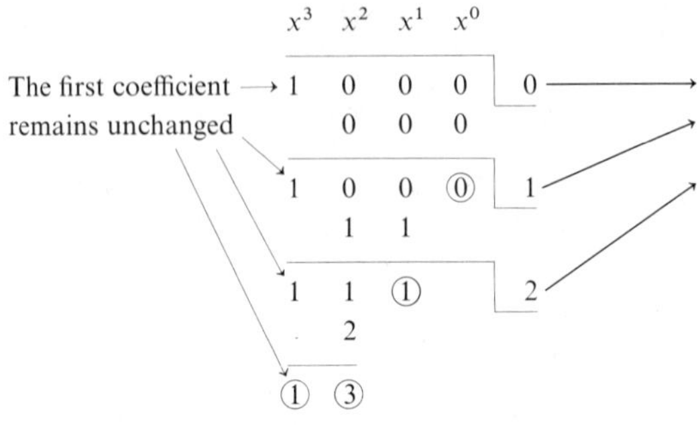

Divisors correspond to the sequence needed in factorial notation (i.e., $x - 0$, $x - 1$, $x - 2, \ldots$).

Process:

1. Multiply first coefficient times the divisor and add result to the adjacent column (x^2) to obtain coefficient of reduced polynomial.
2. Multiply this last mentioned coefficient by the divisor and add result to adjacent (x^1) column to obtain next coefficient of the reduced polynomial.
3. Repeat until rightmost column is done; drop this column from further calculations.
4. Circle the last coefficient of the reduced polynomial; select next divisor.
5. Repeat the process until all columns have been "dropped" and rewrite the circled numbers as coefficients of the column headings with the variables in factorial notation.

RESULT: $x^3 = 1x^{(3)} + 3x^{(2)} + 1x^{(1)} + 0x^{(0)}$

Check:

$$\begin{aligned}
1x^{(3)} &= x(x-1)(x-2) = x^3 - 3x^2 + 2x \\
3x^{(2)} &= 3x(x-1) \qquad\quad = 3x^2 - 3x \\
1x^{(1)} &= x \qquad\qquad\qquad\;\; = x \\
& f(x) = x^3 + 0x^2 + 0x = x^3
\end{aligned}$$

Formula for obtaining new reduced polynomial at any stage:

	x^n	x^{n-1}	$\cdots$	x^i	
"old" reduced	a_n	a_{n-1}	$\cdots$	a_i	$D =$ divisor
		$+Da'_n$	$\cdots +$	Da'_{i+1}	
"new" reduced	a'_n	$Da'_n + a_{n-1}$	$\cdots$	$Da'_{i+1} + a_i$	

Note that $a_n = a'_n$ and $a'_j = Da'_{j+1} + a_j$, for $j = n-1, n-2, \ldots$.

There are two theorems that are especially helpful when working with polynomials; they are derived below.

Prove: $\Delta ax^{(b)} = abx^{(b-1)}$

Proof: $\Delta ax^{(b)} = a(x+1)^{(b)} - ax^{(b)}$ Definition of $\Delta f(x)$

$$= a\begin{bmatrix} (x+1-0)(x+1-1)(x+1-2)\ldots(x+1-(b-1)) \\ -x \qquad (x-1) \quad \ldots(x-(b-2))(x-(b-1)) \end{bmatrix}$$

$$= a\begin{bmatrix} (x+1)x(x-1)\ldots(x-b+2) \\ -x(x-1)\ldots(x-b+2)(x-b+1) \end{bmatrix}$$

$$= ax(x-1)\ldots(x-b+2)[x+1-(x-b+1)]$$

$$\Delta ax^{(b)} = abx^{(b-1)}$$

The trick here is to observe that b factors are called for, and that the count is started at 0 (hence, going to $b - 1$).

$$\Delta^{-1}\,\Delta ax^{(b)} = ax^{(b)} = \Delta^{-1}abx^{(b-1)}$$

$$\frac{ax^{(b)}}{b} = \Delta^{-1}ax^{(b-1)}$$

Replace b by $b + 1$ throughout and rearrange sides to obtain

$$\Delta^{-1}ax^{(b)} = ax^{(b+1)}/(b+1)$$

Example of $\Delta ax^{(b)}$:

$$\begin{aligned}\Delta f(x) = \Delta x^3 = \Delta[x^{(3)} + 3x^{(2)} + x^{(1)}] &= \Delta x^{(3)} + \Delta 3x^{(2)} + \Delta x^{(1)}\\ &= 3x^{(2)} + 3(2)x^{(1)} + 1x^{(0)}\\ &= 3x(x-1) + 6x + 1\\ &= 3x^2 + 3x + 1, \quad \text{as before}\end{aligned}$$

Example of $\Delta^{-1}ax^{(b)}$:

$$\begin{aligned}\sum_{x=1}^{n} x^3 = \Delta^{-1}[x^{(3)} + 3x^{(2)} + x^{(1)}]_1^{n+1} &= \Delta^{-1}x^{(3)} + \Delta^{-1}3x^{(2)} + \Delta^{-1}x^{(1)}]_1^{n+1}\\ &= \left.\frac{x^{(4)}}{4} + \frac{3x^{(3)}}{3} + \frac{x^{(2)}}{2}\right]_1^{n+1}\\ &= \left.\frac{x(x-1)(x-2)(x-3)}{4} + \frac{3x(x-1)(x-2)}{3} + \frac{x(x-1)}{2}\right]_1^{n+1}\\ &= \frac{x(x-1)}{4}[(x^2 - 5x + 6) + (4x - 8) + 2]_1^{n+1}\\ &= \left[\frac{x(x-1)}{2}\right]^2\Bigg|_1^{n+1} = \left[\frac{n(n+1)}{2}\right]^2\end{aligned}$$

Check: Say $n = 4$,

$$\sum_{x=1}^{4} x^3 = 1 + 8 + 27 + 64 = 100 = \left[\frac{4(4+1)}{2}\right]^2$$

Note: In this manner one may determine, for instance, that

$$\sum_{x=1}^{n} x = n(n+1)/2 \quad\text{and}\quad \sum_{x=1}^{n} x^2 = n(n+1)(2n+1)/6$$

Summary of selected useful finite formulas with their infinitesimal counterparts:

Finite	Infinitesimal
1. $\Delta a^x = a^x(a-1)$	$Da^x = a^x \ln a$
2. $\Delta^{-1}a^x = a^x/(a-1)$	$\int a^x\,dx = a^x/\ln a$
3. $\Delta ax^{(b)} = abx^{(b-1)}$	$Dax^b = abx^{b-1}$
4. $\Delta^{-1}ax^{(b)} = ax^{(b+1)}/(b+1)$	$\int ax^b\,dx = ax^{b+1}/(b+1)$
5. $\Delta f(x)g(x) = f(x)\,\Delta g(x) + g(x+1)\,\Delta f(x)$	$Df(x)g(x) = f(x)Dg(x) + g(x)Df(x)$
6. $\Delta^{-1}(f(x)\,\Delta g(x)) = f(x)g(x) - \Delta^{-1}(g(x+1)\,\Delta f(x))$	$\int f(x)Dg(x) = f(x)g(x) - \int g(x)Df(x)$

Example: In queuing theory, the clearing ratio is $\rho = \lambda/\mu$ (ρ is < 1), and the probability of n units in the system is $P(n) = \rho^n(1 - \rho)$. Find the expected number in the system.

$$E(n) = \sum_{n=0}^{\infty} nP(n) = \sum n\rho^n(1-\rho) = (1-\rho)\sum n\rho^n$$

$$= (1-\rho)\,\Delta^{-1} n\rho^n\Big]_0^\infty$$

We use finite formula (6), which can be obtained from formula (5) by antidifferencing both sides and rearranging terms:

Let $f(n) = n$ $\qquad\qquad \Delta g(n) = \rho^n$

$\Delta f(n) = n + 1 - n = 1 \qquad \Delta^{-1}\,\Delta g(n) = g(n) = \rho^n/(\rho - 1)$

$g(n+1) = \rho^{n+1}/(\rho - 1)$

$$= (1-\rho)\left[\frac{n\rho^n}{\rho - 1} - \Delta^{-1}\left(\frac{\rho^{n+1}}{\rho - 1}(1)\right)\right]_0^\infty$$

$$= (1-\rho)\left[\frac{n\rho^n}{\rho - 1} - \frac{\rho}{\rho - 1}\Delta^{-1}\rho^n\right]_0^\infty$$

$$= (1-\rho)\left[\frac{n\rho^n}{\rho - 1} - \frac{\rho^{n+1}}{(\rho - 1)^2}\right]_0^\infty = \frac{(1-\rho)\rho}{(1-\rho)^2} = \frac{\rho}{1-\rho} = \frac{\lambda}{\mu - \lambda}$$

When evaluating the first term at the upper limit—keeping in mind that $\rho < 1$—an indeterminate form ($\infty \cdot 0$) results. By rewriting $n\rho^n$ as $n/(1/\rho)^n$, L'Hôpital's rule may be applied (that is, by taking separate derivatives of numerator and denominator and evaluating each at the limit: $\lim_{n\to\infty} Dn/D(1/\rho)^n = \lim_{n\to\infty} 1/[(1/\rho)^n ln(1/\rho)] = 0$) to arrive at a value of 0. (Observe that $1/\rho = \mu/\lambda > 1$.)

Infinitesimal Calculus

In finite calculus we obtained changes or differences. In infinitesimal calculus we shall take derivatives (designated in the earlier summary by the operator D) that divide the previous change in the function by the change (the gap) in the independent variable to obtain a rate of change. The derivative is therefore the rate of change of a function, or in other terms, the ratio of the rise divided by the run. In symbols:

$$D = \frac{\text{Rise}}{\text{Run}} = \frac{\text{Opposite}}{\text{Adjacent}} = \text{Tangent} = \text{Slope} = f'(x) = y' = \frac{dy}{dx} = \lim_{h\to 0}\frac{\Delta f(x)}{h}$$

Note that $D = f'(x) = y' = dy/dx$ are all equivalent notations for the derivative.

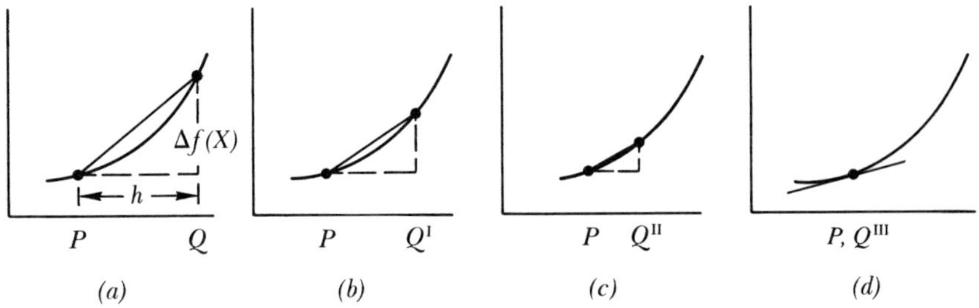

Figure 1

Figure 1 is a pictorial representation of the derivative. In diagram (a), P and Q are joined by a line segment (secant) that has the slope $\Delta f(x)/h$, which is the rise divided by the run (or opposite/adjacent). In diagram (b), Q moves to Q' and both the rise and run diminish. This decreasing of run and rise continues in diagram (c) as Q moves to Q''. Finally, in diagram (d), P and Q''' are almost coincident, as are the line segment connecting them and the line tangent to the curve at point P. The gap between P and Q''' is imperceptible—almost zero—but it is there. If there were no gap, there would be no line segment and hence no rise divided by run. Let us develop some differentiation theorems.

Proof: $f(x) = ax^b$

$$\frac{dy}{dx} = \lim_{h\to 0} \frac{\Delta f(x)}{h} = \lim_{h\to 0} \frac{a(x+h)^b - ax^b}{h}$$

$$= \lim_{h\to 0} \frac{a}{h}\left[\sum_{i=0}^{b} \binom{b}{i} x^i h^{b-i} - x^b\right] \qquad \text{(Substitute binomial expansion.)}$$

$$= \lim_{h\to 0} \frac{ah}{h} \sum_{i=0}^{b-1} \binom{b}{i} x^i h^{b-i-1}$$

$$= \lim_{h\to 0} a\left[\sum_{i=0}^{b-2} \binom{b}{i} x^i h^{b-i-1} + bx^{b-1}\right]$$

$$= abx^{b-1}$$

Proof:

$$y = e^{f(x)}$$

$$lny = f(x)lne = f(x)$$

$$Dlny = f'(x)$$

$$\frac{1}{y}\frac{dy}{dx} = f'(x)$$

$$\frac{dy}{dx} = yf'(x) = f'(x)e^{f(x)}$$

Comments: Obtaining dy/dx by the limit approach is tedious; therefore the log of the original equation is taken, and use is made of a theorem, $D \ln(f(x)) = f'(x)/f(x)$. Recall that $\ln e = \log 10 = \log_a a = 1$.

Example of Dax^b: $f(x) = 6x^3 - 5x^4 + 2 - 6x^{-2}$

$$f(x) = 6(3)x^{3-1} - 5(4)x^{4-1} + 2(0)x^{0-1} - 6(-2)x^{-2-1}$$
$$= 18x^2 - 20x^3 + 12x^{-3}$$

Example of $De^{f(x)}$: $y = e^{3x^2+1}$ or $y = ee^{3x^2}$

$$y' = 6xe^{3x^2+1} \quad \text{or} \quad y' = e6xe^{3x^2} = 6xe^{3x^2+1}$$

There are, of course, many other theorems for derivatives that are useful to the applied mathematician. Only the most widely used theorems in managerial applications can be presented in this appendix.

Proof: $y = f(x)g(x)$

Let us begin with the finite derivation, the results of which appear in our previous summary as formula 5.

$$\begin{aligned}\Delta y &= f(x+1)g(x+1) - f(x)g(x) \pm f(x)g(x+1) \qquad \text{(Add zero in a convenient form.)}\\ &= [f(x)g(x+1) - f(x)g(x)] + [f(x+1)g(x+1) - f(x)g(x+1)]\\ &= f(x)\,[g(x+1) - g(x)] + g(x+1)\,[f(x+1) - f(x)]\\ &= f(x)\,\Delta g(x) + g(x+1)\,\Delta f(x) \qquad \text{(Finite formula 5)}\end{aligned}$$

Now let the gap be h and we shall obtain the derivative.

$$\begin{aligned}\frac{dy}{dx} &= \lim_{h\to 0}\frac{\Delta y}{h} = \lim_{h\to 0}\frac{[f(x)\,\Delta g(x) + g(x+h)\,\Delta f(x)]}{h}\\ &= \lim_{h\to 0} f(x)\left[\frac{\Delta g(x)}{h}\right] + \lim_{h\to 0} g(x+h)\left[\frac{\Delta f(x)}{h}\right]\\ &= \left[\lim_{h\to 0} f(x)\right]\left[\lim_{h\to 0}\frac{\Delta g(x)}{h}\right] + \left[\lim_{h\to 0} g(x+h)\right]\left[\lim_{h\to 0}\frac{\Delta f(x)}{h}\right]\\ &= f(x)Dg(x) + g(x)Df(x) \qquad \text{(Infinitesimal formula 5)}\end{aligned}$$

This is known as the "product rule" of differentiation.

Comments: In a similar way, the "quotient rule" of differentiation can be shown to be

$$D\left(\frac{f(x)}{g(x)}\right) = \frac{g(x)Df(x) - f(x)Dg(x)}{[g(x)]^2}$$

Example of $Df(x)g(x)$: $y = (6x+3)(4x^5)$

$$y' = (6x+3)20x^4 + 4x^5(6)$$

Example of $D[f(x)/g(x)]$: $y = (6x+3)/4x^5$

$$y' = [4x^5(6) - (6x+3)20x^4]/(4x^5)^2$$

Another theorem regularly needed is the chain rule:

$$\frac{dy}{dx} = \frac{dy}{dZ} \cdot \frac{dZ}{dx}$$

Example:

$$y = (6x^3 - 4x + 2)^4$$

$$\text{Let } Z = 6x^3 - 4x + 2, \quad \text{then } \frac{dZ}{dx} = 18x^2 - 4$$

Restating original function:

$$y = Z^4, \quad \text{then } \frac{dy}{dZ} = 4Z^3$$

$$\frac{dy}{dx} = \frac{dy}{dZ} \cdot \frac{dZ}{dx} = 4Z^3(18x^2 - 4) = 4(6x^3 - 4x + 2)^3(18x^2 - 4)$$

All these formulas apply equally well when there are several independent variables present and "partial" derivatives must be taken instead of the single-variable derivatives shown above. A partial derivative simply amounts to treating all other variables as constants while allowing one variable to change. The symbol $\partial f/\partial x$ will designate the partial of a function with respect to the variable x.

By definition,

$$\frac{\partial f(\cdot)}{\partial x_i} = \lim_{h \to 0} \frac{f(x_1, x_2, \ldots, x_i + h, x_{i+1}, \ldots, x_n) - f(x_1, x_2, \ldots, x_i, x_{i+1}, \ldots, x_n)}{h}$$

Example:

$$Z = 3x^3 - 6xy^2 + y^{-3}$$

$$\frac{\partial Z}{\partial x} = 9x^2 - 6y^2; \quad \frac{\partial Z}{\partial y} = -12xy - 3y^{-4}$$

Derivatives of derivatives (second-order derivatives) are usually taken when determining whether an *optimal* point is a maximum or a minimum as well as for other purposes. These introduce nothing new to the process of single-variable differentiation, but they make possible "cross" partial derivatives in the multivariable function, which can be designated $\partial^2 f/\partial x_i \partial x_j$ or $f_{x_i x_j}$. More will be said about this shortly.

One use of derivatives is especially prominent in applied mathematics. This is the Taylor series and its modification, the Maclaurin series. Both series relate to Isaac Newton's series, which was developed originally in terms of finite differences.

The idea behind the Taylor series is to substitute some polynomial series for some function that is not a polynomial and that may even be too complicated to work with in its native form. Here is how the substitution is developed:

$$f(x) = \sum_{i=0}^{\infty} b_i(x-a)^i,$$ where b_i is some unknown coefficient of the polynomial term $(x-a)^i$

$$f(x) = b_0 + b_1(x-a) + b_2(x-a)^2 + b_3(x-a)^3 + b_4(x-a)^4 + \cdots.$$

First derivative $= f^{I}(x) = b_1 + 2b_2(x-a) + 3b_3(x-a)^2 + 4b_4(x-a)^3 + \cdots$

Second derivative $= f^{II}(x) = 2b_2 + 6b_3(x-a) + 12b_4(x-a)^2 + \cdots$

Third derivative $= f^{III}(x) = 6b_3 + 24b_4(x-a) + \cdots$

Fourth derivative $= f^{IV}(x) = 24b_4 + \cdots$

ith derivative $= f^{i}(x) = i!b_i +$ terms in $(x-a)$

$$f^{i}(a) = i!b_i + 0$$

$$\therefore, b_i = f^{i}(a)/i!$$

> Note: $i! = i(i-1)(i-2)\ldots1$
>
> $0! = 1$
>
> $f^{0}(x) = f(x)$, the 0th derivative is the original function.

Substituting for b_i in the original series yields

Taylor Series:
$$f(x) = \sum_{i=0}^{\infty} f^{i}(a)(x-a)^i/i!$$

Maclaurin Series: $f(x) = \sum_{i=0}^{\infty} f^{i}(0)x^i/i!$ Note: Here $a = 0$ in the Taylor series.

Example:

$$f(x) = e^{ax}$$

$$f'(x) = ae^{ax}$$

$$f''(x) = a^2e^{ax}$$

$$f^{i}(x) = a^ie^{ax}$$

$$f^{i}(0) = a^i$$

Therefore, the Maclaurin expansion is

$$f(x) = e^{ax} = \sum_{i=0}^{\infty} \frac{a^ix^i}{i!} = \sum_{i=0}^{\infty} \frac{(ax)^i}{i!}$$

This is a most useful result and is worth committing to memory.

Next let us turn our attention to antiderivatives (integrals). Figure 2 shows a curve with several rectangles inscribed beneath it. One approximation of the total area under the curve would be obtained by setting the base, h, of each rectangle equal to 1, reading its height from the curve, calculating each separate area, and summing the results. This would lead to the errors appearing at the top of each rectangle and beneath the curve. By decreasing the base in width, fortunately, these errors can be reduced. In the limit, error virtually disappears and the definition of an integral is obtained:

$$A = \int_{x_0}^{x_n} f(x)\,dx = \lim_{\substack{h\to 0\\ n\to\infty}} \sum_{i=0}^{n-1} \overset{\text{height}}{f(x_i)}\ \overset{\text{base}}{h}$$

= area under the curve. Here dx is the "differential of x" essentially obtained by treating the symbol dy/dx as a fraction. h equals dx in the limit.

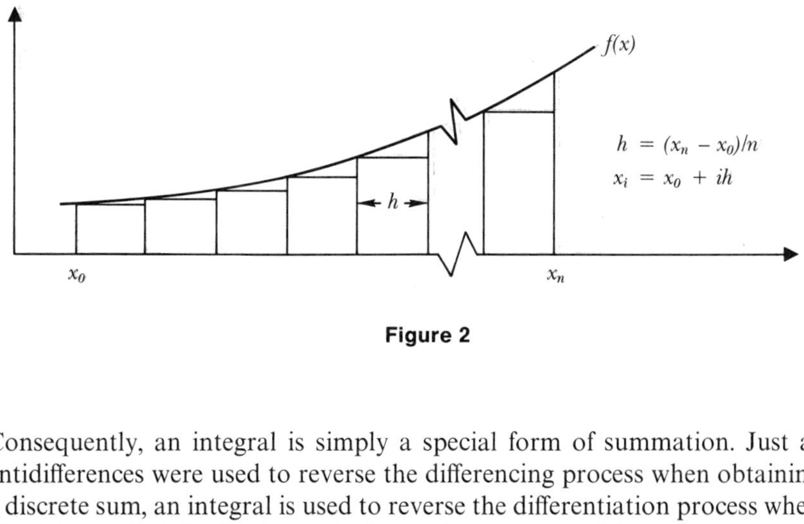

Figure 2

Consequently, an integral is simply a special form of summation. Just as antidifferences were used to reverse the differencing process when obtaining a discrete sum, an integral is used to reverse the differentiation process when obtaining an infinitesimal sum. Refer to the summary of formulas presented earlier and consider the examples given below.

Example of $\int ax^b dx$: $\displaystyle\int_1^2 (6x^3 + 5x + 2)\,dx = \left.\frac{6x^4}{4} + \frac{5x^2}{2} + 2x\right]_1^2$

$$= \frac{6}{4}(16) + \frac{5}{2}(4) + 2(2) - \left[\frac{6}{4}(1) + \frac{5}{2}(1) + 2(1)\right] = 32$$

Example of $\int a^x dx$: $\displaystyle\int_0^1 e^x\,dx = \left.\frac{e^x}{\ln e}\right]_0^1 = \left.\frac{e^x}{1}\right]_0^1 = e^1 - 1 = 1.7183$

Usually it is not possible to integrate an exponential function without making some preliminary modifications. Keep in mind that the integral is an antiderivative and that $De^{f(x)} = f'(x)e^{f(x)}$; hence, $\int f'(x)e^{f(x)} = e^{f(x)}$. The mathematician often supplies $f'(x)$ by multiplying by 1 in a/a form, where a is some constant.

$e^{f(t)}$	$f'(t)e^{f(t)}$

Example: $$\int_0^\infty \mu e^{-\mu t}\,dt = \int_0^\infty \left(\frac{-1}{-1}\right)\mu e^{-\mu t}\,dt = \frac{1}{-1}\int_0^\infty (-\mu)e^{-\mu t}\,dt$$
$$= -1e^{-\mu t}\Big]_0^\infty = -e^{-\mu(\infty)} + e^{-\mu(0)} = 0 + 1 = 1$$

The integration-by-parts theorem in the previous summary (formula 6) may be obtained from integrating both sides of formula 5 and rearranging terms. This is applicable to finding expected values of probability density functions, among other things.

Example: Find the expected value of the exponential distribution.

$$E(t) = \int_0^\infty t(\mu e^{-\mu t})\,dt = \mu\int_0^\infty te^{-\mu t}\,dt$$

$$\begin{array}{ll} \text{Let } f(t) = t & Dg(t) = e^{-\mu t}\,dt \\ \dfrac{df(t)}{dt} = 1 & \int Dg(t) = \int e^{-\mu t}\,dt \\ df(t) = 1dt & g(t) = -\dfrac{e^{-\mu t}}{\mu} \end{array}$$

$$= \mu\left[t\left(\frac{-e^{-\mu t}}{\mu}\right)\Bigg|_0^\infty - \int_0^\infty\left(\frac{-e^{-\mu t}}{\mu}\right)(1dt)\right]$$
$$= -te^{-\mu t}\Big]_0^\infty + \int_0^\infty e^{-\mu t}\,dt$$
$$= -te^{-\mu t} + \left(\frac{-e^{-\mu t}}{\mu}\right)\Bigg]_0^\infty$$
$$= -0 - 0 - \left(-0 - \frac{1}{\mu}\right) = \frac{1}{\mu}$$ (Use L'Hôpital's rule to evaluate $te^{-\mu t}$ at $t \to \infty$.)

Ordinary integration by parts proves cumbersome whenever $f(x)$ has a nonlinear form. This is because it takes several iterations of the theorem to reduce $f(x)$ to a constant (observe that $D^n x^n = n!$, where D^n designates the *n*th derivative). There is a modified form, which I call "deluxe integration by parts," that expedites the process:

Key:

$$f^i(x) = i\text{th derivative} \qquad (f^0(x) \equiv f(x))$$

$$g^{-[i+1]}(x) = (i+1)\text{th integral} \qquad \left(g^{-[1]}(x) = \int g(x)\,dx\right)$$

$$\int_a^b f(x)Dg(x) = \sum_{i=0}^{\infty} (-1)^i f^i(x) g^{-[i+1]}(x) \Big]_a^b$$

This looks rougher than it is. Choose $f(x)$ so that it disappears with successive derivatives, take one more integral of $g(x)$ than you have derivatives of $f(x)$, and alternate the signs.

Example: $\int_0^\infty x^3 e^{-2x}\,dx = \int_0^\infty f(x)Dg(x)$

$$= \frac{x^3 e^{-2x}}{-2} - \frac{3x^2 e^{-2x}}{(-2)^2} + \frac{6xe^{-2x}}{(-2)^3} - \frac{6e^{-2x}}{(-2)^4}\Big]_0^\infty$$

$$= -e^{-2x}\left[\frac{x^3}{2} + \frac{3x^2}{4} + \frac{6x}{8} + \frac{6}{16}\right]_0^\infty = 0 + \frac{6}{16} = \frac{3}{8}$$

Suggestion: Rework this problem using repeated ordinary integration by parts to appreciate the effort and time saved by using the deluxe formula.

We have discussed derivatives. And we have discussed integrals. Now let us put the two together via Leibnitz's rule and see what is involved in taking the derivative of an integral. The Leibnitz formula follows.

Given: $g(x) = \int_{h(x)}^{k(x)} f(x, y)\,dy$

$$\frac{dg(x)}{dx} = \int_{h(x)}^{k(x)} \frac{\partial f(x, y)}{\partial x}\,dy + \underbrace{f[x, k(x)]\frac{dk(x)}{dx} - f[x, h(x)]\frac{dh(x)}{dx}}_{\text{"appendages"}}$$

Key:

$g(x)$, $k(x)$, $h(x)$ are all functions of x, while $f(x, y)$ represents a multivariable function. $f[x, k(x)]$ is the original function $f(x, y)$ with $k(x)$ substituted for y wherever y appears.

This appears formidable, but it is very welcome in applied mathematics. Sometimes $h(x)$ and $k(x)$ are constants, and the fact that their derivatives are then zero causes the "appendages" to equal zero. At other times, an appendage disappears because $f[x, k(x)]$ or $f[x, h(x)]$ equals zero. So the process is not as bad as it may seem.

Example: In inventory theory, if demand is a continuous variable or large enough to be so considered, the expected cost of stocking S units given that demand takes place gradually over time is

$$E[K(S)] = C_o + C_h \int_0^S \left(S - \frac{D}{2}\right) f(D)\, dD + \int_S^\infty \left[C_h \frac{S^2}{2D} + C_s \frac{(D - S)^2}{2D}\right] f(D)\, dD$$

Key:

$EK(S)$ = expected cost of stocking S units
C_o = ordering cost per order
C_h = cost of holding per unit per time period
C_s = cost of shortage per unit per time period
S = supply
D = demand
$f(D)$ = probability density function for demand

$$\frac{dE[K(S)]}{dS} =$$

$$C_h \begin{bmatrix} \int_0^S f(D)\, dD \\ + \left(S - \frac{S}{2}\right) f(S)(1) \\ - 0 \end{bmatrix} + C_h \begin{bmatrix} \int_S^\infty \frac{2S}{2D} f(D)\, dD \\ + 0 \\ - \frac{S^2}{2S} f(S)(1) \end{bmatrix} + C_s \begin{bmatrix} \int_S^\infty - 2\frac{(D - S)}{2D} f(D)\, dD \\ + 0 \\ - 0 \end{bmatrix}$$

Most of the zeroes for the values of individual appendages result from recognizing that ∞ is a constant, albeit an unusual one. The last zero arises from $(S - S)^2 = 0$. If optimization procedures were continued and a fair amount of algebra were employed, during which a cumulative complement was substituted for a cumulative distribution, the end result would be

$$\int_0^S f(D)\, dD + \int_S^\infty \frac{S}{D} f(D)\, dD = \frac{C_s}{C_s + C_h}$$

The amount to stock would be that value of S which honored this equation.

Optimization

We have already discussed how optimal points are located in finite calculus by determining when the sign of $\Delta f(x)$ changes. But obtaining optimal points and deciding whether they are maximums or minimums is a very complex subject—one that can scarcely be done justice in the few pages of an appendix. Accordingly, finite calculus optimums are discussed in Chapter 14, as are infinitesimal calculus optimums. This section focuses mainly on theory and rules.

Infinitesimal calculus optimization may be studied using the taxonomy shown below.

	Single Variable	Multivariable
Unconstrained objective	I	II
Constrained objective	III	IV

The easiest of these is category I, while the most difficult is category IV.

Category I involves optimizing a single variable function where there are no restrictions on the outcome. The process is easily understood, since the first derivative yields the slope of the function, and when the slope has a zero value and changes from rising to falling or vice versa, a peak or floor occurs at that critical point. If the slope has a zero value but continues to rise or fall, the critical point is merely a point of inflection. Viewed another way, the value of the slope increases steadily through a minimum point, decreases steadily through a maximum point, and alternates without, however, changing sign as the curve passes through an inflection point. Figure 3

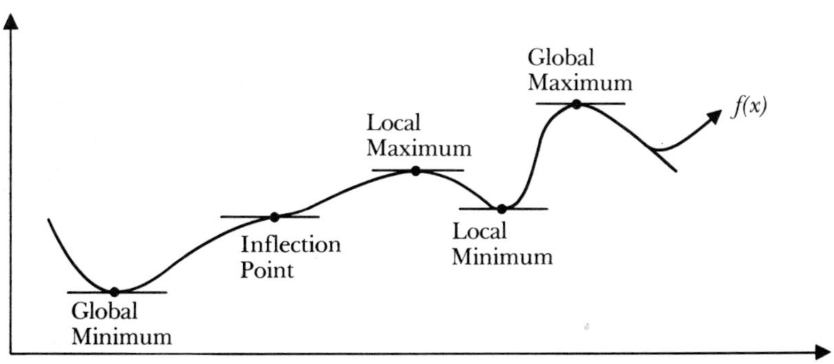

Figure 3

illustrates these distinctions. The derivative function, when set equal to zero to locate roots (critical points), identifies all critical points *interior* to the curve; it does not, unfortunately, locate global optima that occur at endpoints. Therefore, in deciding on global optima, the values of the original function at its endpoints must be contrasted with its values at all other critical points.

Consider a peak. The value of the slope is there zero because, since it is a peak, there is no additional rise in the immediate area. The slope is positive (as you go from left to right) until the peak and negative thereafter. For a floor, the slope is again zero at the critical point, but the curve's slope is negative to the left and positive to the right of the floor. The inflection point in Figure 3 has a positive slope to its left that decreases to zero at the inflection point; the slope to its right is again positive. When drawing tangent lines and approaching this inflection point, the lines are on one side of the curve to the left of the point and then cross over to the other side to the right of the point.

Optimization Procedures:

1. Set $f'(x) = 0$.
2. Determine the roots, $\hat{x}_i$.
3. Obtain $f''(x)$.
4. Evaluate $f(\hat{x}_i)$:

   (a) If $f''(\hat{x}_i) > 0$, the curve is convex, and $\hat{x}_i$ is a minimum.

   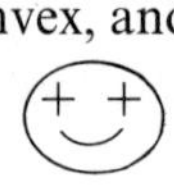

   (b) If $f''(\hat{x}_i) < 0$, the curve is concave, and $\hat{x}_i$ is a maximum.

   (c) If $f''(\hat{x}_i) = 0$, $\hat{x}_i$ *may* be an inflection point; if $f'(\hat{x}_i \pm \alpha)$ has the same sign, an inflection point occurs at $\hat{x}_i$. Here α is any amount such that $\hat{x}_i \pm \alpha$ does not reach the next critical point.

The words "convex" and "concave" were introduced above; they are defined as follows: A function is strictly concave if a line connecting any two points on its graph falls entirely below the graph. If the line lies entirely above the graph, the function is strictly convex. The formula that is used to determine convexity if a graph is not drawn is

$$f((1-t)x_1 + tx_2) \le (1-t)f(x_1) + tf(x_2), \quad \text{for } 0 < t < 1.$$

If $\le$ can be replaced by $<$, the function is strictly convex; if the inequality is reversed, the function is concave ($\ge$) or strictly concave ($>$).

Example: $f(x) = x^2$, which has a U-shaped graph; $t = .2$

$$f((1-.2)x_1 + .2x_2) \overset{?}{\le} .8f(x_1) + .2f(x_2)$$

$$f(.8x_1 + .2x_2) \overset{?}{\le} .8f(x_1) + .2f(x_2)$$

$$(.8x_1 + .2x_2)^2 \overset{?}{\le} .8x_1{}^2 + .2x_2{}^2$$

$$0 \overset{?}{\le} x_1{}^2 - 2x_1x_2 + x_2{}^2, \quad \text{which is true for all } x_i$$

$$0 \overset{?}{\le} (x_1 - x_2)^2$$

Conclusion: $f(x)$ is strictly convex and the right side is >0 because x_1 cannot equal x_2.

Example: Find the global optima for

$$f(x) = \frac{x^3}{3} - x^2 - 15x, \quad \text{for } -5 \le x \le 10$$

$$f'(x) = x^2 - 2x - 15 = 0 = (x+3)(x-5)$$

$$\hat{x} = \{-3, 5\}$$

$$f''(x) = 2x - 2$$

$f''(-3) = -8$, 

, local maximum

$f''(5) = 8$, 

, local minimum

endpoint $f(-5) = 25/3$

$f(-3) = 27$

$f(5) = -175/3$ global minimum

endpoint $f(10) = 250/3$ global maximum

Category III merely introduces constraints to the foregoing analysis, which amounts to creating new critical points. For example, if x in this example were constrained to be a *positive integer* less than 5, since we know there are no humps or inflection points between $-3 \le x \le 5$ (had there been, they would have been identified by $f'(x) = 0$, we need only examine the new endpoints, 1 and 4. $f(1) = -47/3$ and $f(4) = -164/3$; hence, 1 is the new global maximum while 4 is the new global minimum.

What happens if more than one independent variable is involved? This brings us to Category II, and all first derivatives must simultaneously equal zero as in single variable optimization. Determining maximums and minimums, however, becomes more involved; the major complication lies in the increased number of second-order derivatives that make their appearance. Fortunately, the complication poses no severe difficulty, for determinants may be used as a structural device to preserve some semblance of order. If there are three independent variables,

$$\Delta_3 = \begin{vmatrix} f_{x_1x_1} & f_{x_1x_2} & f_{x_1x_3} \\ f_{x_2x_1} & f_{x_2x_2} & f_{x_2x_3} \\ f_{x_3x_1} & f_{x_3x_2} & f_{x_3x_3} \end{vmatrix}$$

The procedure generalizes to

$$\Delta_n = \begin{vmatrix} f_{x_1x_1} & f_{x_1x_2} & \cdots & f_{x_1x_n} \\ \vdots & & & \vdots \\ f_{x_nx_1} & f_{x_nx_2} & \cdots & f_{x_nx_n} \end{vmatrix}$$

Note: Δ_n is the determinant of what is known as the Hessian matrix.

The second-order conditions for maxima and minima in terms of Δ_k become[1]:
A critical point $(x_1, x_2, \ldots, x_n)$ is
(1) a local minimum if $\Delta_i > 0$, for all i; and
(2) a local maximum if $\Delta_{2i-1} < 0$ and $\Delta_{2i} > 0$, for all i.
To be certain that this is clear, let me restate these conditions:

LOCAL MINIMUM: $\Delta_1 > 0, \Delta_2 > 0, \Delta_3 > 0, \Delta_4 > 0, \ldots$

LOCAL MAXIMUM: $\Delta_1 < 0, \Delta_2 > 0, \Delta_3 < 0, \Delta_4 > 0, \ldots$

If the conditions do not hold, further investigation in the region of the critical point must be undertaken.

When the solution to an optimization probelm is constrained (Category IV)—as, for instance, when limited amounts of resources are available—the constraints effect a number of changes in the second-order conditions. The introduction of m constraining equations or inequalities simultaneously introduces m constraining variables, which together with the original n decision variables augment Δ_n to Δ_{m+n} (which is the determinant of the

[1] These Δ_k are known as "principal minors," which are determinants formed from the first k rows and k columns of Δ_n—hence there are n principal minors (Δ_1, $\Delta_2, \ldots, \Delta_n$.).

"bordered" Hessian). The analyst concerns himself, however, with *only* the *last* $n - m$ (this determinantal approach requires $m < n$) principal minors, because the first $2m$ principal minors of the bordered Hessian either are zero or reflect only the constraints, as we shall see. If these last principal minors are of the same sign (they will be negative if m is odd and positive if m is even), a local minimum is present; conversely, if the principal minors alternate in sign, a local maximum is present.

Before illustrating these rules, we need first to consider the subject of Lagrangean optimization. In Lagrangean optimization the analyst optimizes a multivariable objective function subject to constraints; the method rests on the Kuhn-Tucker (K-T) conditions:

Given:

$$f(\cdot) = f(x_1, x_2, \ldots, x_n)$$

$$g(\cdot) = g(x_1, x_2, \ldots, x_n)$$

$$\text{Maximize } L(\cdot) = f(\cdot) - \sum_{j=1}^{m} \lambda_j (g_j(\cdot) - b_j)$$

Conditions:

$$(1)\quad \frac{\partial L(\cdot)}{\partial x_i} = \frac{\partial f(\cdot)}{\partial x_i} - \sum_{j=1}^{m} \lambda_j \frac{\partial g_j(\cdot)}{\partial x_i} = 0$$

$$(2)\quad \frac{\partial L(\cdot)}{\partial \lambda_j} = g_j(\cdot) - b_j = 0$$

$$(3)\quad \lambda_j (g_j(\cdot) - b_j) = 0$$

$$(4)\quad g_j(\cdot) - b_j \leq 0$$

These conditions hold for maximizing $L(\cdot)$ given (1) that $f(\cdot)$ and $g(\cdot)$ are both concave (or for minimizing $L(\cdot)$ if $f(\cdot)$ and $g(\cdot)$ are both convex), and (2) that both $f(\cdot)$ and $g(\cdot)$ have their separate maximum and minimum points in the first orthant. If $f(\cdot)$ and $g(\cdot)$ are not both of the same curvature, the Lagrange technique is not guaranteed to locate the global optimum. In such a situation, the endpoints allowed by $g(\cdot)$ must also be inserted in $f(\cdot)$ to select the global optimum.

The above objective function, $L(\cdot)$, is the Lagrangean formulation and the λ_j are the Lagrange multipliers. To obtain some notion of what is going on, assume there is a function $Z = f(x, y)$ that must satisfy a constraint $g(x, y) = 0$. The function may be graphed as a contour map that also reflects the constraint:

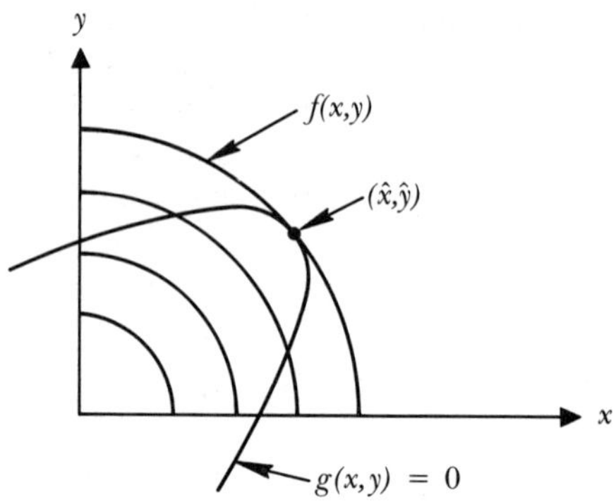

At the point $(\hat{x}, \hat{y})$ where the curves meet, there is the single line that is tangent to both curves. Since there is but a single tangent, the slopes of the curves are equal at this point. Now consider $Z = f(x, y) = C$, a particular contour value. The slope of Z may be determined from its total derivative as follows:

$$\frac{dZ}{dx} = \frac{d(C)}{dx} = 0 = \frac{\partial f}{\partial x}\frac{dx}{dx} + \frac{\partial f}{\partial y}\frac{dy}{dx}$$

$$\therefore, \frac{dy}{dx} = -\frac{\partial f/\partial x}{\partial f/\partial y}$$

We could similarly find the slope of $g(x, y) = 0$. Then, writing the slope of the common tangent line as the ratio of the respective partial derivatives, we have

$$-\frac{\partial f/\partial x}{\partial f/\partial y} = -\frac{\partial g/\partial x}{\partial g/\partial y},$$

or in simpler notation,

$$\frac{f_x}{f_y} = \frac{g_x}{g_y} = \lambda, \quad \text{the slope value that is here known as the Lagrange multiplier}$$

$$\frac{f_x}{g_x} = \frac{f_y}{g^y} = \lambda$$

and consequently,

$$f_x = \lambda g_x$$

$$f_y = \lambda g_y$$

We therefore know that $f_x - \lambda g_x = 0$ and $f_y - \lambda g_y = 0$ are simultaneously solved at the point of tangency $(\hat{x}, \hat{y})$.

Example: Max $f(x, y) = 5x + 60y - 3x^2 + 3xy - 2y^2$

Constraint: $x + 2y = 50$

Unconstrained solution

$$\partial f(\cdot)/\partial x = 5 - 6x + 3y = 0$$

$$\partial f(\cdot)/\partial y = 60 + 3x - 4y = 0$$

$$\begin{bmatrix} -6 & 3 \\ 3 & -4 \end{bmatrix}\begin{bmatrix} x \\ y \end{bmatrix} = \begin{bmatrix} -5 \\ -60 \end{bmatrix}$$

$$\begin{bmatrix} x \\ y \end{bmatrix} = \frac{\begin{bmatrix} -4 & -3 \\ -3 & -6 \end{bmatrix}}{15}\begin{bmatrix} -5 \\ -60 \end{bmatrix} = \begin{bmatrix} 40/3 \\ 25 \end{bmatrix}$$

$$f(40/3, 25) = 2{,}350/3 = 783.\bar{3}$$

Lagrangean solution

$$L = 5x + 60y - 3x^2 + 3xy - 2y^2 - \lambda(x + 2y - 50)$$

$$\partial L/\partial x = 5 - 6x + 3y - \lambda = 0$$

$$\partial L/\partial y = 60 + 3x - 4y - 2\lambda = 0$$

$$\partial L/\partial \lambda = -(x + 2y - 50) = 0$$

$$\begin{bmatrix} 0 & -1 & -2 \\ -1 & -6 & 3 \\ -2 & 3 & -4 \end{bmatrix}\begin{bmatrix} \lambda \\ x \\ y \end{bmatrix} = \begin{bmatrix} -50 \\ -5 \\ -60 \end{bmatrix}$$

$$\begin{bmatrix} \lambda \\ x \\ y \end{bmatrix} = \frac{\begin{bmatrix} 15 & -10 & -15 \\ -10 & -4 & 2 \\ -15 & 2 & -1 \end{bmatrix}}{40}\begin{bmatrix} -50 \\ -5 \\ -60 \end{bmatrix} = \begin{bmatrix} 5 \\ 10 \\ 20 \end{bmatrix}$$

$$L(5, 10, 20) = f(10, 20) = 750$$

Comments:

1. The constraint reduced the unconstrained maximum.
2. The constrained values for x and y are less than the unconstrained values.

3. The Lagrange multiplier is > 0.

4. Endpoints may be ignored because $f(\cdot)$ is concave, and $g(\cdot)$, being a straight line, is both concave and convex.

If you concocted many problems like this example and compared the unconstrained results to the Lagrangean results, you would find that the value of λ is useful in deciding when to keep and when to drop (if possible) its associated constraint. It would be embarassing, for instance, if an analyst implemented a constrained solution only to learn later that he could have done better by using fewer resources. The summary below lists the messages of the λ values.

Action Indicated by Value of Multiplier

	Constraint Type	"Optimal"	Decision
A.	Equality	$\lambda > 0$	Constraint restricts necessarily.
		$\lambda < 0$	Constraint restricts wastefully; relax constraint if possible.
		$\lambda = 0$	Constraint has no effect.
B.	Inequality ($\leq$ and $\geq$ made into $\leq$ by multiplying by -1	$\lambda > 0$	Constraint restricts necessarily and is treated as an equation.
		$\lambda < 0$	Constraint restricts unnecessarily; redo the problem without the constraint.
		$\lambda = 0$	Constraint has no effect.

A great deal of confusion is caused by the latitude permissible when setting up the Lagrangean function. Let me designate the original $f(x_1, x_2, \ldots, x_n)$ and $g(x_1, x_2, \ldots, x_n)$ by $f(\cdot)$ and $g(\cdot)$ respectively. Then consider the possibilities:

$$L = f(\cdot) - \lambda(g(\cdot) - b)$$

$$L = f(\cdot) + \lambda(g(\cdot) - b)$$

$$L = f(\cdot) - \lambda(b - g(\cdot))$$

$$L = f(\cdot) + \lambda(b - g(\cdot))$$

Is L to be maximized or minimized?

How the problem is set up determines the signs of the λ values, among other things. Consequently, in the interest of consistency, desire to preserve the summary just presented, and the urge to obtain optimal answers, I urge you to adopt the following setup rules:

Summary of Setup Rules	
Original $g(\cdot)$ or $f(\cdot)$	Alteration
1. $g(\cdot) \leq b$	$g(\cdot) - b \leq 0$
2. $g(\cdot) = b$	$g(\cdot) - b = 0$
3. $g(\cdot) \geq b$	$-g(\cdot) + b \leq 0$
4. $\min f(\cdot)$	$\left\{\begin{array}{l} \left.\begin{array}{l} g(\cdot) \leq b \\ g(\cdot) = b \end{array}\right\} \; L = f(\cdot) - \lambda(b - g(\cdot)) \\ g(\cdot) \geq b \rightarrow L = f(\cdot) - \lambda(-b + g(\cdot)) \end{array}\right.$
5. $\max f(\cdot)$	$\left\{\begin{array}{l} \left.\begin{array}{l} g(\cdot) \leq b \\ g(\cdot) = b \end{array}\right\} \; L = f(\cdot) - \lambda(g(\cdot) - b) \\ g(\cdot) \geq b \rightarrow L = f(\cdot) - \lambda(-g(\cdot) + b) \end{array}\right.$

Now let us return to the matter of illustrating the use of principal minors In the process we shall learn how roots to functions may be found and more about how Hessians and principal minors are related.

To locate roots for functions, the Newton (also known as the Newton-Raphson) formula may be employed. The Newton formula weights the gradient vector by the inverse of the Hessian matrix of the system. We have

Key:

x_j = the vector of roots at stage j
H = the Hessian matrix containing the second order partial derivatives of $f(\cdot)$
$f(\cdot)$ = the objective function
∇ = the gradient vector containing the first order partial derivatives of $f(\cdot)$

$$\text{Formula: } x_{j+1} = x_j - H^{-1}\,\nabla$$

Source of the Newton formula:
Given the Taylor formula:

$$f(x) = \frac{\sum f^i(a)(x-a)^i}{i!}$$

If the first two terms were sufficient to generate a root of $f(x)$,

$$f(x) = 0 = f(a) + f'(a)(x - a)$$
$$x = a - [f(a)/f'(a)]$$

This is the familiar formula used to locate roots by iteration. The usual form is stated $x_{i+1} = x_i - [f(x_i)/f'(x_i)]$. If the analyst sought roots not for $f(x)$ but for $f'(x)$, which

continued to page 766

continued fron page 765

would often occur when the first derivative was used to locate optima, the Taylor formula would be adjusted throughout, and the root iteration formula would become

$$x_{i+1} = x_i - [f'(x_i)/f''(x_i)]$$

When several variables and equations are involved, vectors and matrices are invoked, leading to

$$x_{i+1} = x_i - H^{-1}\nabla$$

Sometimes the Newton method takes many iterations to find roots, and at other times the roots located may not be of acceptable magnitudes. (Simply trying a new range of values in the program may locate other roots that are acceptable.) Searching is a complex mathematical problem, and every search technique suffers from some imperfection. The Newton method, however, has much to recommend it.

In the unconstrained solution in the last example, we could have iterated our way to the solution via the Newton formula. While doing so, we could have developed principal minors and determined convexity. Let us continue that example.

$$f(x, y) = 5x + 60y - 3x^2 + 3xy - 2y^2$$

$$f_x = 5 - 6x + 3y \qquad f_y = 60 + 3x - 4y$$

$$f_{xx} = -6 \qquad f_{yy} = -4$$

$$f_{xy} = 3$$

$$H = \begin{matrix} & x & y \\ x & -6 & 3 \\ y & 3 & -4 \end{matrix}; \quad \nabla = \begin{bmatrix} 5 - 6x + 3y \\ 60 + 3x - 4y \end{bmatrix}$$

Let us guess $x_i = \begin{bmatrix} 30 \\ 20 \end{bmatrix}$ as an initial solution.

$$x_{i+1} = \begin{bmatrix} 30 \\ 20 \end{bmatrix} - \frac{\begin{bmatrix} -4 & -3 \\ -3 & -6 \end{bmatrix}}{15} \begin{bmatrix} 5 - 6(30) + 3(20) \\ 60 + 3(30) + 4(20) \end{bmatrix} = \begin{bmatrix} 40/3 \\ 25 \end{bmatrix}$$

$$x_{i+2} = \begin{bmatrix} 40/3 \\ 25 \end{bmatrix} - H^{-1} \begin{bmatrix} 5 - 6(40/3) + 3(25) \\ 60 + 3(40/3) - 4(25) \end{bmatrix} = \begin{bmatrix} 40/3 \\ 25 \end{bmatrix} + 0 = \begin{bmatrix} 40/3 \\ 25 \end{bmatrix}$$

This is our previous result; usually several iterations would be necessary.

Let us next employ the principal minors of H to determine convexity.

$$\Delta_1 = -6$$

$$\Delta_2 = |H| = \begin{vmatrix} -6 & 3 \\ 3 & -4 \end{vmatrix} = 15,$$ where $|H|$ designates the determinant of the Hessian

The signs are alternating; therefore, the point obtained as an optimum is a maximum; the function $f(\cdot)$ *is concave.*

One promise remains unfulfilled: the use of principal minors of a bordered Hessian to determine convexity has not been illustrated. Return to the preceding Lagrangean solution and take the second partials:

$$\partial^2 L/\partial\lambda^2 = 0 \qquad \partial^2 L/\partial\lambda\,\partial x = \partial(-(x+2y-50))/\partial x = -1$$

$$\partial^2 L/\partial x^2 = -6 \qquad \partial^2 L/\partial x\,\partial y = \partial(5-6x+3y-\lambda)/\partial y = 3$$

$$\partial^2 L/\partial y^2 = -4 \qquad \partial^2 L/\partial y\,\partial\lambda = \partial(60+3x-4y-2\lambda)/\partial\lambda = -2$$

The order in which cross partials are taken doesn't usually matter, so

$$\partial^2 L/\partial x\,\partial\lambda = -1, \quad \partial^2 L/\partial y\,\partial x = 3, \quad \text{and} \quad \partial^2 L/\partial\lambda\,\partial y = -2$$

$$H = \begin{matrix} \lambda \\ x \\ y \end{matrix} \overset{\begin{matrix} \lambda & \ \ x & \ \ y \end{matrix}}{\begin{bmatrix} 0 & -1 & -2 \\ -1 & -6 & 3 \\ -2 & 3 & -4 \end{bmatrix}} \qquad \begin{aligned} \Delta_1 &= 0 \\ \Delta_2 &= \begin{vmatrix} 0 & -1 \\ -1 & -6 \end{vmatrix} = -1 \\ \Delta_3 &= |H| = +40 \end{aligned}$$

Here $n = 2$ and $m = 1$. The last $n - m = 1$ principal minor, Δ_3, is positive; then since m is odd and a minimum would expect Δ_3 to be negative, we conclude that the point is a global maximum.

Transform Theory

Complicated manipulations in mathematics may often be simplified by use of transform theory. In applying the theory, an analyst first transforms real-world functions, then manipulates and simplifies the transformed functions, then manipulates and simplifies the transformed functions, and finally returns to the real world by taking inverse transforms. The process is much like that of logarithms.

The Z transform is used for discrete variables (either singly or in matrix form), while either the Laplace or the S transform is used for continuous variables.

The Z Transform

Consider a function $f(t)$. By definition, its Z transform is $F(z) = \sum_{t=0}^{\infty} f(t)Z^t$. Think of Z as, say, .7. Then, provided that (1) $f(t)$ is defined for only non-negative integer values, and (2) $f(t)$ cannot increase faster than a geometric sequence, $F(Z)$ will converge to a closed-form expression. Let us develop a few of the basic transforms that appear in Table 11 in Appendix A. $T\{f(t)\}$ will designate the Z transform of a function, while $T^{-1}\{F(Z)\}$ will designate the inverse transform.

We see that transform 1 defines $Tf(t) = F(Z) = \sum_{t=0}^{\infty} f(t)Z^t$, where $0 < Z \leq 1$. Since a is a constant, transform 2 merely observes that it may be factored outside the summation sign, that is, $\sum af(t)Z^t = a\sum f(t)Z^t = aF(Z)$. Transform 5: This is the unit impulse, which is graphed as shown below.

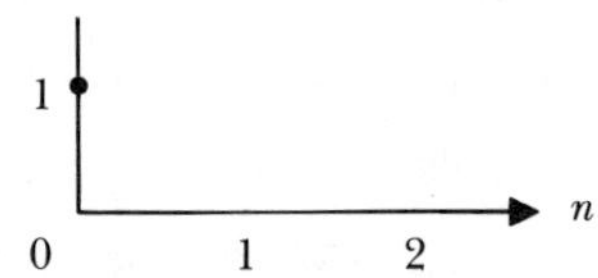

$$F(Z) = 1Z^0 + \sum_{t=1}^{\infty} 0Z^t = 1$$

Transform 6: This is the unit step, which is graphed as shown below.

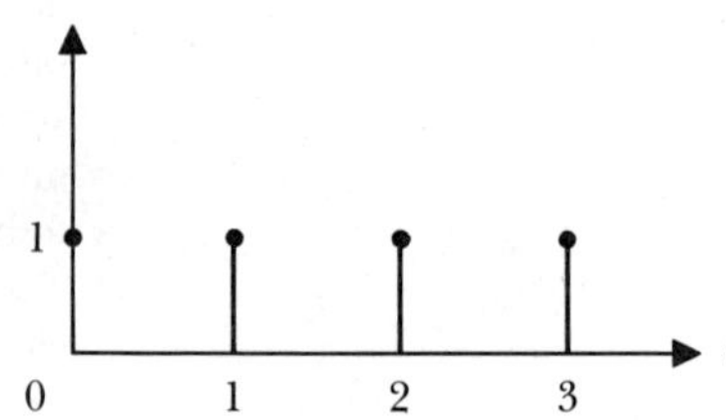

$$F(Z) = \sum_{t=0}^{\infty} 1Z^t = \Delta^{-1}Z^t\Big]_0^{\infty} = \frac{Z^t}{Z-1}\Big]_0^{\infty} = -\frac{1}{Z-1} = \frac{1}{1-Z}$$

Transform 7: This is the unit ramp, which is graphed as shown below.

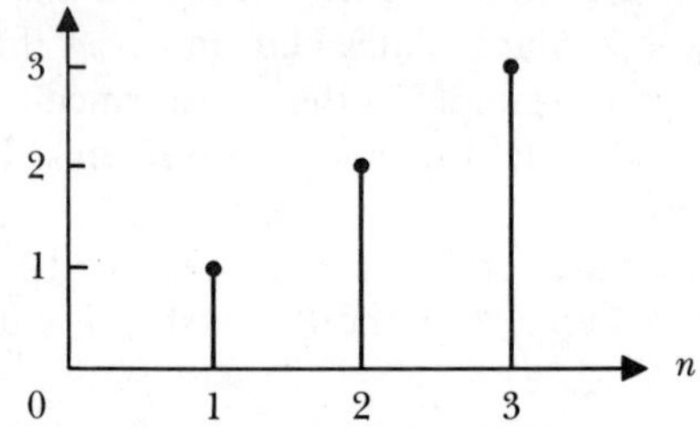

$$F(Z) = \sum_{t=0}^{\infty} tZ^t = \Delta^{-1}t^{(1)}Z^t\Big]_0^{\infty}$$

$$= \frac{tZ^t}{Z-1} - \frac{Z^{t+1}}{(Z-1)^2}\Big]_0^{\infty} = \frac{Z}{(1-Z)^2}$$

Here L'Hôpital's rule has been used to evaluate $t\,Z^t$ as $t \to \infty$

Transform 8: This is a geometric sequence, which is graphed as shown below.

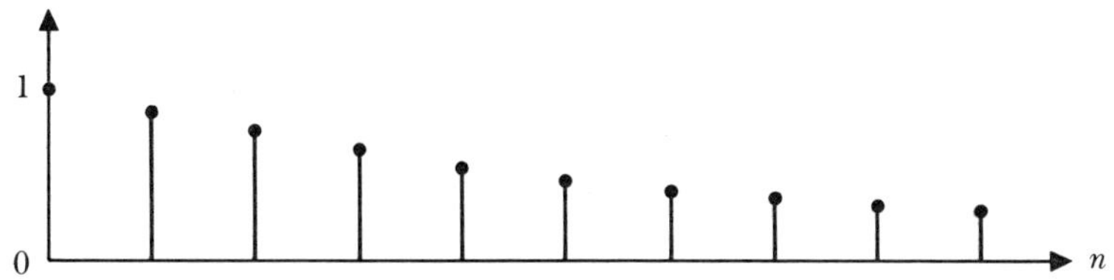

$$F(Z) = \sum_{t=0}^{\infty} a^t Z^t = \Delta^{-1}(aZ)^t \Big]_0^{\infty} = \frac{1}{1 - aZ}$$

Transform 9:

$$T\{a^t f(t)\} = \sum_{t=0}^{\infty} a^t f(t) Z^t = \sum_{t=0}^{\infty} f(t)(aZ)^t = F(aZ)$$

This, in effect, says that $a^t f(t)$ yields the transform of $f(t)$ with Z replaced wherever it appears by aZ. Transform 10, which combines transforms 7 and 8, demonstrates the validity of transform 9.

Transform 10:

$$T\{ta^t\} = \sum_{t=0}^{\infty} ta^t Z^t = \sum_{t=0}^{\infty} t(aZ)^t = \Delta^{-1} t^{(1)}(aZ)^t \Big]_0^{\infty} = \frac{t(aZ)^t}{aZ - 1} - \frac{(aZ)^{t+1}}{(aZ - 1)^2}\Big]_0^{\infty}$$

$$= \frac{aZ}{(1 - aZ)^2}$$

Now let us consider transform 3, which delays input one period (that is, shifts t to the left one unit to $t - 1$).

Example: If $f(t) = t$, then $f(t-1) = \begin{cases} t - 1, & \text{for } t = 1, 2, 3, \ldots \\ 0, & \text{otherwise} \end{cases}$

$$T\{t - 1\} = 0Z^0 + \sum_{t=1}^{\infty} (t - 1)Z^t$$

$$= \sum_{t=1}^{\infty} tZ^t - \sum_{t=1}^{\infty} Z^t$$

$$= \frac{tZ^t}{Z - 1} - \frac{Z^{t+1}}{(Z - 1)^2} - \frac{Z^t}{Z - 1}\Big]_1^{\infty} = -\frac{Z}{Z - 1} + \frac{Z^2}{(Z - 1)^2} + \frac{Z}{Z - 1}$$

$$= \frac{Z^2}{(1 - Z)^2} = Z\left(\frac{Z}{(1 - Z)^2}\right),$$ which is Z multiplied by $T\{t\}$. To check results we may take the inverse transform:

$$T^{-1}\left\{\frac{Z^2}{(1 - Z)^2}\right\} = t - 1$$

Let us see how transforms are applied in analysis to study the inputs and outputs of a system. Suppose we have statistically determined that output in period t—that is, $y(t)$—is related to input—that is, $x(t)$—by the difference equation $y(t) = .6x(t) + 1.2y(t-1) - .36y(t-2)$. Further suppose that we want to know how the system would respond to a unit step increase in input. We transform this equation using transforms 1, 2, 3:

$$Y(Z) = .6X(Z) + 1.2ZY(Z) - .36Z^2Y(Z)$$

Gather terms in $Y(Z)$

$$Y(Z)(1 - 1.2Z + .36Z^2) = .6X(Z)$$

$$\frac{Y(Z)}{X(Z)} = \frac{.6}{(1-.6Z)^2}$$

Note: $\frac{Y(Z)}{X(Z)}$ is known in systems analysis as the *transfer function.* It is the ratio of the output to input transforms.

If $x(t)$ (known as the *driving function*) is a unit step, then

$$X(Z) = \frac{1}{1-Z},$$

according to transform 6 and

$$Y(Z) = \frac{1}{1-Z}\frac{.6}{(1-.6Z)^2} = \frac{A}{1-Z} + \frac{B}{(1-.6Z)^2} + \frac{C}{1-.6Z},$$

where we have adopted the algebra of partial fractions.

Algebra of Partial Fractions

A complete review of partial fractions would require too much space; however, the technique can be generally reviewed in terms of the equation shown above.

1. Note that the left-hand side (LHS) consists of two multiplied fractions—one with a linear denominator and one with a linear denominator raised to a power.
2. Note that the right-hand side (RHS) has three fractions added.
3. The RHS fractions have constants in their numerators because their denominators are linear functions or "repeated linear functions" (i.e., $(1 - .6Z)^2$ is a repeated linear function). The rules are (a) to have a polynomial of one degree less in the numerator than exists in the denominator, and (b) to write separate denominators for "repeated functions," reducing their power until the function is raised to the first power. Since the denominators are linear above, the numerators are constants because a constant is a polynomial of one degree less than a linear function.
4. A common denominator will be found for the RHS.
5. The LHS and RHS will have the same denominators, so the latter are cancelled.
6. The coefficients of like powers of Z will be equated, and the resulting system of equations will be solved to determine A, B, and C.

$$.6 = A(1 - .6Z)^2 + B(1 - Z) + C(1 - Z)(1 - .6Z)$$

$$= A(1 - 1.2Z + .36Z^2) + B(1 - Z) + C(1 - 1.6Z + .6Z^2)$$

$$.6 = A + B + C$$

$$0Z = (-1.2A - B - 1.6C)Z$$

$$0Z^2 = (.36A + 0B + .6C)Z^2$$

$$\begin{bmatrix} .6 \\ 0 \\ 0 \end{bmatrix} = \begin{bmatrix} 1 & 1 & 1 \\ 1.2 & 1 & 1.6 \\ .36 & 0 & .6 \end{bmatrix} \begin{bmatrix} A \\ B \\ C \end{bmatrix}; \begin{bmatrix} A \\ B \\ C \end{bmatrix} = \frac{\begin{bmatrix} .6 & -.6 & .6 \\ -.144 & .24 & -.4 \\ -.36 & .36 & -.2 \end{bmatrix}}{.096} \begin{bmatrix} .6 \\ 0 \\ 0 \end{bmatrix} = \begin{bmatrix} 3.75 \\ .9 \\ -2.25 \end{bmatrix}$$

Therefore, $$Y(Z) = \frac{3.75}{1 - Z} - \frac{.9}{(1 - .6Z)^2} - \frac{2.25}{1 - .6Z}$$

$$= 3.75\left(\frac{1}{1 - Z}\right) - \frac{-3}{2Z}\left(\frac{.6Z}{(1 - .6Z)^2}\right) - 2.25\left(\frac{1}{1 - 6Z}\right)$$

Taking the inverse transforms (transforms 2, 4, 6, and 10), we obtain

$$T^{-1}\{Y(Z)\} = y(t) = 3.75 - \frac{3}{2}(t + 1)(.6)^{t+1} - 2.25(.6)^t$$

Let us see how $\frac{3}{2}(t + 1)(.6)^{t+1}$ was derived from $\frac{3}{2Z}\left(\frac{.6Z}{(1 - .6Z)^2}\right)$. First, transform 2 tells us that we may factor out constants like 3/2 that multiply a transform. Next consider the term $[.6Z/(1 - .6Z)^2]$ in light of transform 10. Ask yourself what the boundary condition $f(t = 0)$ would do to $f(t) = ta^t$. We would have $f(0) = 0$—correct? Consequently, $F(Z) - f(0) = F(Z)$ and transform 4 tells us that division by Z advances the inverse transform to $t + 1$. We may simplify our results somewhat:

$$y(t) = 3.75 - (.6)^{t+1}\left(\frac{3t + 3}{2} + 3.75\right)$$

$$y(t) = 3.75 - (.6)^{t+1}\left(\frac{3t + 10.5}{2}\right) = \frac{15 - (6t + 21)(.6)^{t+1}}{4}$$

By rewriting the exponential factor as $1/(10/6)^{t+1}$, the RHS can be brought into indeterminate form—essentially, $(6t + 21)/(10/6)^{t+1}$, where it may be evaluated by L'Hôpital's rule (separate derivatives of top and bottom yield $\lim_{t\to\infty} 6/[(10/6)^{t+1} \ln(10/6)] = 0$) and seen to converge to 0. Therefore, given a unit step input, in time the system output settles down to 3.75.

Comments: The unit step makes the table general. Thus if sales increased \$5,000, the \$5,000 would multiply the unit step. In other words, \$5,000 would become the size of the step.

The Laplace Transform

The transforms for treating continuous variables are called either S transforms, where the range of transformation is from $-\infty$ to ∞, or Laplace transforms, where the range is from 0 to ∞. We are mainly interested in Laplace transforms.

The definition of a Laplace transform is

$$F(S) = \int_0^\infty f(t)e^{-St}\,dt$$

In its simplest formulation, S is a positive constant, and $f(t)$ can be transformed as long as it does not grow faster than exponentially (this is simply a requirement for convergence to 0 when $f(t)e^{-St}$ is evaluated—perhaps by L'Hôpital's rule applied to an indeterminate form). Let us develop a few of the transforms in Table 10 in Appendix A.

Transform 6: This is the unit step, which is graphed as shown below.

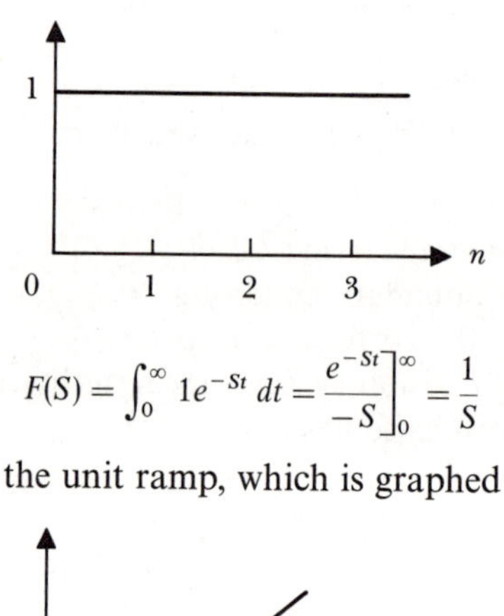

$$F(S) = \int_0^\infty 1e^{-St}\,dt = \left.\frac{e^{-St}}{-S}\right]_0^\infty = \frac{1}{S}$$

Transform 7: This is the unit ramp, which is graphed as shown below.

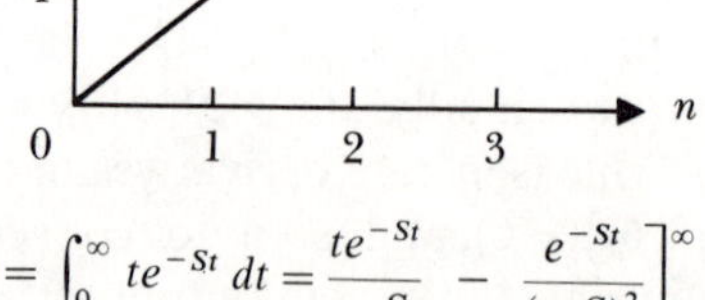

$$F(S) = \int_0^\infty te^{-St}\,dt = \frac{te^{-St}}{-S} - \left.\frac{e^{-St}}{(-S)^2}\right]_0^\infty = \frac{1}{S^2}$$

Transform 8: This is an exponential function.

$$F(S) = \int_0^\infty e^{-at}e^{-St}\,dt = \int_0^\infty e^{-(S+a)t}\,dt = \left.\frac{e^{-(S+a)t}}{-(S+a)}\right]_0^\infty = \frac{1}{S+a}$$

Transform 11: This is a gamma function, and deluxe integration by parts is extremely helpful in finding the closed form.

$$F(S) = \int_0^\infty \left(\frac{t^{n-1}e^{at}}{(n-1)!}\right) e^{-St}\,dt$$

$$= \frac{1}{(n-1)!}\left[\frac{t^{n-1}e^{-(S-a)t}}{-(S-a)} - \frac{(n-1)t^{n-2}e^{-(S-a)t}}{[-(S-a)]^2} + \cdots + \frac{(-1)^{n-1}(n-1)!e^{-(S-a)t}}{[-(S-a)]^n}\right]_0^\infty$$

$$= \frac{1}{(S-a)^n},$$ after applying L'Hôpital's rule and assuming $S > a$ to obtain convergence

The Laplace transform of a function is commonly designated $L\{f(t)\}$, and its inverse transform becomes $L^{-1}\{F(S)\}$. Let us conclude by seeing how Laplace transforms may be generally applied.

Example 1: Find the inverse transform.

$$L^{-1}\left\{\frac{2}{(S-3)(S-1)^3}\right\} = 2L^{-1}\{F(S)\cdot G(S)\}$$

$$= 2\int_0^t f(t-u)g(u)\,du,$$

according to transform 16. But if $F(S) = \frac{1}{S-3}$, $f(t) = e^{3t}$ according to transform 8. Similarly, if $G(S) = \frac{1}{(S-1)^3}$, $g(t) = t^2e^t/2!$, according to transform 11. Consequently, $f(t-u) = e^{3(t-u)}$ and $g(u) = u^2e^u/2!$. Our integral becomes

$$= 2\int_0^t \frac{e^{3(t-u)}u^2e^u}{2!}\,du$$

$$= e^{3t}\int_0^t u^2e^{-2u}\,du$$

$$= e^{3t}\left[\frac{u^2e^{-2u}}{-2} - \frac{2ue^{-2u}}{(-2)^2} + \frac{2e^{-2u}}{(-2)^3}\right]_0^t$$

$$= -e^{3t}e^{-2u}\left(\frac{u^2}{2} + \frac{2u}{4} + \frac{2}{8}\right)_0^t$$

$$= -e^t\left(\frac{t^2}{2} + \frac{t}{2} + \frac{1}{4}\right) + \frac{e^{3t}}{4}$$

Example 2: Same as example 1 except that we shall use partial fractions rather than convolutions in the solution.

$$L^{-1}\left\{\frac{2}{(S-3)(S-1)^3}\right\} = L^{-1}\left\{\frac{A}{(S-3)} + \frac{B}{(S-1)^3} + \frac{C}{(S-1)^2} + \frac{D}{S-1}\right\}$$

$$2 = A(S-1)^3 + B(S-3) + C(S-3)(S-1) + D(S-3)(S-1)^2$$

If $\quad S = 3, \quad 2 = A(3-1)^3 \quad \text{and} \quad A = \frac{1}{4}$

If $\quad S = 1, \quad 2 = B(1-3) \quad \text{and} \quad B = -1$

Therefore, $2 = \frac{1}{4}(S-1)^3 - 1(S-3) + CS^2 - 4CS + 3C + DS^3 - 5DS^2 + 7DS - 3D$

Expanding:

$$2 = \frac{S^3 - 3S^2 + 3S - 1}{4} - S + 3 + CS^2 - 4CS + 3C + DS^3 - 5DS^2 + 7DS - 3D$$

Equating coefficients of like powers of S:

$$0 = \frac{1}{4} + D$$

$$0 = -\frac{3}{4} + C - 5D$$

$$0 = \frac{3}{4} - 1 - 4C + 7D$$

$$2 = -\frac{1}{4} + 3 + 3C - 3D$$

Solving these simultaneous equations yields

$$C = -\frac{1}{2}; \quad D = -\frac{1}{4}$$

We seek inverse transforms for

$$L^{-1}\left\{\frac{1/4}{S-3} - \frac{1}{(S-1)^3} - \frac{1/2}{(S-1)^2} - \frac{1/4}{S-1}\right\}$$

and all four inverses may be obtained from applying transforms 2 and 11:

$$= \frac{e^{3t}}{4} - \frac{t^2e^t}{2!} - \frac{te^t}{2} - \frac{e^t}{4} = \frac{e^{3t}}{4} - e^t\left(\frac{t^2}{2} + \frac{t}{2} + \frac{1}{4}\right)$$

This, of course, is the same answer as was previously obtained; however, the partial fractions approach does not seem as efficient as the convolution approach.

Example 3: Given $L\{f'(t)\} = 1/(S-2)$ and $f(0) = 3$, find $f(t)$. We apply transforms 2, 3, 6, and 8:

$$SF(S) - f(0) = SF(S) - 3 = 1/(S-2)$$

$$F(S) = \frac{3}{S} + \frac{1}{(S(S-2)} = \frac{3}{S} + \frac{A}{S} + \frac{B}{S-2}$$

$$\boxed{1 = A(S-2) + B(S) \quad \text{and} \quad A = -\frac{1}{2} \quad \text{while } B = \frac{1}{2}}$$

$$f(t) = L^{-1}\{F(S)\} = L^{-1}\left\{\frac{3}{S} - \frac{1/2}{S} + \frac{1/2}{S-2}\right\} = \frac{5}{2} + \frac{e^{2t}}{2}$$

Example 4: Given $f'(t) + f(t) = e^t$ and $f(0) = 3$, find $f(t)$.

$$SF(S) - f(0) + F(S) = 1/(S-1) \qquad \text{(see transforms 1, 3, and 8)}$$

$$SF(S) - 3 + F(S) = 1/(S-1)$$

$$F(S) = \frac{1}{(S+1)} + \frac{1}{(S+1)(S-1)} = \frac{3}{S+1} + \frac{A}{S+1} + \frac{B}{S-1}$$

$$\boxed{1 = A(S-1) + B(S+1) \quad \text{and} \quad A = -\frac{1}{2} \quad \text{while } B = \frac{1}{2}}$$

$$f(t) = L^{-1}\{F(S)\} = L^{-1}\left\{\frac{3}{S+1} - \frac{1/2}{S+1} + \frac{1/2}{S-1}\right\} = \frac{5e^{-t}}{2} + \frac{e^t}{2}$$

Example 5: Given $f''(t) + f'(t) = 2e^t$ and $f(0) = 5$ and $f'(0) = -1$, find $f(t)$.

$$(S^2F(S) - Sf(0) - f'(0)) + (SF(S) - f(0)) = 2/(S-1)$$

$$S^2F(S) - 5S + 1 + SF(S) - 5 = 2/(S-1)$$

$$F(S)(S^2 + S) = \frac{2}{S-1} + 5S + 4$$

$$F(S) = \frac{2}{S(S+1)(S-1)} + \frac{5}{S+1} + \frac{4}{S(S+1)}$$

$$\boxed{\begin{gathered} 2 = A(S+1)(S-1) + BS(S-1) + CS(S+1); \quad \therefore, (A, B, C) = (-2, 1, 1) \\ \text{and} \\ 4 = A(S+1) + BS; \quad \therefore, (A, B) = (4, -4) \end{gathered}}$$

$$f(t) = L^{-1}\{F(S)\} = L^{-1}\left\{\frac{-2}{S} + \frac{1}{S+1} + \frac{1}{S-1} + \frac{5}{S+1} + \frac{4}{S} - \frac{4}{S+1}\right\}$$

Therefore, $$f(t) = 2 + 2e^{-t} + e^t$$

Example 6: Given $f'(t) + \int_0^t f(u)\, du = 1$ and $f(0) = 2$, find $f(t)$.

This is an "integrodifferential" equation, and we employ transforms 3, 4, and 6 in setting it up:

$$(SF(S) - f(0)) + \frac{F(S)}{S} = \frac{1}{S}$$

Substituting the given boundary condition, we obtain

$$SF(S) = 2 + \frac{F(S)}{S} = \frac{1}{S}$$

$$F(S)\left(S + \frac{1}{S}\right) = 2 + \frac{1}{S}$$

$$F(S) = \frac{2S}{S^2 + 1} + \frac{1}{S^2 + 1}$$

We now call on transforms 12 and 13 to obtain

$$f(t) = L^{-1}\{F(S)\} = L^{-1}\left\{\frac{2S}{S^2 + 1} + \frac{1}{S^2 + 1}\right\}$$

$$f(t) = 2 \cos t + \sin t$$

INDEX

A

B

C

D

E

F

G

H

I

J

K

L

M

N

O

P

Q

R

S

T

U

V

W

X

Y

Z